The 1973 Compton Yearbook

A summary and interpretation of the events of 1972 to supplement Compton's Encyclopedia

F. E. Compton Company

William Benton, Publisher

CHICAGO · LONDON · TORONTO · GENEVA
SYDNEY · TOKYO · MANILA

The 1973 Compton Yearbook

Editor in Chief Richard L. Pope
Editor Patricia Dragisic
Assistant Editor Emily A. Friedman
Feature Editor Edith Wasserman
Staff Editors Dave Etter, Linda Tomchuck
Contributing Editors Samuel Allen, Judy Booth, Herbert Glaettli, Mary Alice Molloy, Joseph Zullo

Editorial Production Manager Jane Samuelson
Production Supervisors Constance Hall, Robin O'Connor
Production Editor Susan A. Bush
Proof Supervisor Lynn K. McEwan
Proofreaders Marleda CarlLa Horton, Cathleen Ann McCoy, Madonna Niles, Mary Lee Sandholm
Production Clerk/Typist Yvette Wesley

Editorial Coordinator Barbara J. Gardetto
Production Coordinators Kenneth B. Alwood, Janina Nalis

Editorial Research Manager Louise R. Miller
Research Staff Mary S. Walker, supervisor; Deborah D. Bennett, Bruce M. Ezerski, Catherine E. Kinsock, James Lange, Loretta Smith, Karen Ruse Strueh, Deborah R. Szajnberg, Liesel E. Wildhagen
Research Clerk/Typist Diane Truvillion

Acting Art Director Bette Schon
Art Production Manager Howard L. Baumann
Senior Picture Editor Florence Scala
Picture Editor Adelle Weiner
Assistant Picture Editor Kathleen Picken
Senior Artist George Sebok
Designer David Alexander
Layout Artist Ozzie Hawkins

Librarian Janet L. Warner
Assistant Librarian Hari Sharma
Library Assistants Judy Childs, Barbara Fagan

Index Maybelle Taylor, editor; Laura Birg, associate editor; Juanita Bartholomew, Norma B. Ebright, Patricia E. Thomas, Frank Young, Margaret Ziemer

Manuscript Typists Eunice Mitchell, Linda Ulrich

Secretary Marie Lawrence

Compton's Encyclopedia
Donald E. Lawson, Editor in Chief
Leon Bram, Executive Editor

Catherine McKenzie, Senior Vice-President and Director of Editorial, F. E. Compton Company

Library of Congress Catalog Card Number: 58-26525
International Standard Book Number: 0-85229-285-6

Printed in U.S.A.

Contents

© KARSH, OTTAWA

Publisher's Message

by Senator William Benton

For me, as a reader of *The Compton Yearbook,* it is not just the reminder of the known that gives substance to it; it is also the impact of the unknown—it is the sense of discovery of the new that gives a heightened interest. "The mind adventures," said poet Mark Van Doren, "and the mind stays home." If these yearbooks are a success, it is because in these pages we find the mind of our time alternating, in the tradition of intellect at its best, between exploring the unknown and reminding us of the known.

I confess to my pleasure at such random discoveries as finding, in Professor Curtis MacDougall's piece, that *muckraker* has a classical etiology: that it is from *Pilgrim's Progress,* in which a character uses a "muck rake" to gather "straws, small sticks and dust of the floor" while disregarding the offer of a celestial crown called truth. Or to find in the article on Hsing-hsing and Ling-ling that the giant pandas—so lovable and engaging—have complex behavior patterns worthy of close study. Or to find in Irna Phillips' article on soap operas that the dedication of Scheherazade was as much to the saving of life—principally her own!—as to the telling of tales. For, in an analogy that Miss Phillips clearly wants to draw to modern-day TV, if Scheherazade failed to fascinate her master in any of the 1,001 nights of storytelling, she would immediately share the fate of her predecessors: death by beheading.

But it is not simply the quantity of discovery that deepens this yearbook; it is also the quality. The editors of *The Compton Yearbook* are ever aware that these are times when it appears that man is so preoccupied with the world he is creating that he has already lost a sense for what may be missing. We seek to discuss that element. For instance, we do not confine ourselves to the horrors of the Vietnam war; rather we offer a three-part article on the difficulty that the Vietnam veteran encounters in readjusting to peacetime America and suggest ways of reducing that difficulty. We do not talk simply of the friendly initiatives taken by President Nixon toward Peking and Moscow; we've included an article on whether a similar move might be made toward Cuba. And we do not simply mark the give-and-take over the environment; we include a thoughtful article, "Enriching the Quality of Life," by Hugh Downs, the TV personality turned ecologist.

To illuminate the continuity of man's hopes is both ambitious and difficult. There has long been the feeling that the precise bonds and sequences between the years must await the clarity of history. But we at Compton's believe that the creative thrust in any era can be seen as well as felt. In all our publications, we cannot help but feel that without an understanding of man's aesthetic insight and spiritual fiber we cannot comprehend man's continuing experience. It was Jacques Barzun who reminded us that the humanities are a mirror in which we can continue to view the more or less meaningful disorder of man's desires.

Our task in the yearbook is to delineate the subtle powers of aesthetic desires as well as the naked power of science and technology. This necessarily involves emotions as well as thought. "Opinion is ultimately determined," wrote Herbert Spencer, "by the feelings and not by the intellect." So you will see herein some of the turbulence of man's passions; you will experience it not only in the bloody episodes of history but also in the subtleties of the three-part article "Arts of Black America." You will see something of the hope and faith that has long animated the mind of man, not only in the continued exploration of the moon and deep space, but in the quieter though no less venturesome excursion into an innovative education described in "The Unfinished Curriculum."

In all of this there is, I think, an almost tactile sense to the march of years, a permanence that binds this one year to history, and there is insight into the mind and spirit of man. *The Compton Yearbook* has always tried to reflect and exalt the dual impulse of man: to go forth and to return. To be locked in the enduring values of man and to be exhilarated by what might yet be. It is what inspires us to look back at what we've already seen and known, and then to turn the next page of history—in joy and in anticipation.

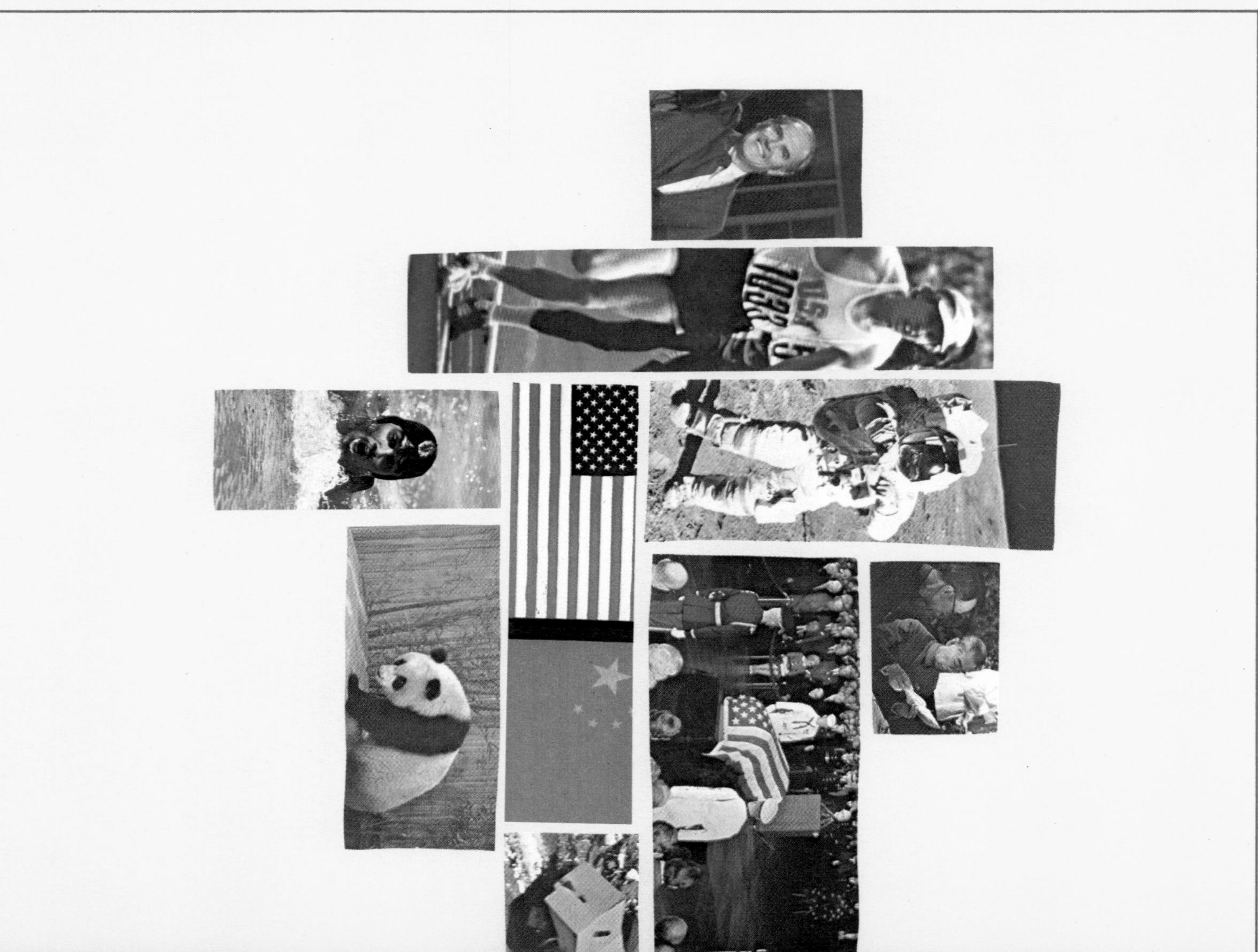

Compton's Pictured Highlights and Chronology of 1972

Sheikh Mujibur Rahman (on truck, waving), leader of the Bengali people, returned in triumph to Bangladesh in January. The new nation had won independence from Pakistan in 1971.

JASON LAURE FROM RAPHO GUILLUMETTE

JANUARY

1 An agreement providing for free travel between West Germany and West Berlin over East German territory goes into effect.

2 South Vietnamese military sources reveal that intensive U.S. air raids over North Vietnam on Dec. 26–30, 1971, were not as effective as had been hoped because of bad weather.

3 William R. Tolbert, Jr., is formally inaugurated as president of Liberia.

5 U.S. President Richard M. Nixon orders the National Aeronautics and Space Administration (NASA) to begin work on a manned space shuttle.

7 President Nixon and Japan's Prime Minister Eisaku Sato announce final terms for the return of Okinawa to Japan on May 15, following two days of talks.

8 Sheikh Mujibur Rahman, president of Bangladesh, is freed from detention in Pakistan; Pakistan's former President Agha Mohammed Yahya Khan is reported to be under house arrest.

9 The ocean liner *Queen Elizabeth* is destroyed by fire in Hong Kong harbor.

10 A U.S. federal judge orders the predominantly black schools of Richmond, Va., to merge with predominantly white schools of two suburban counties.

12 Sheikh Mujib resigns as president of Bangladesh and assumes the post of prime minister; Abu Sayeed Choudhury is sworn in as president under a provisional constitution.

13 Ghana's Prime Minister Kofi A. Busia, in London for medical treatment, is deposed in a military coup led by Col. Ignatius Kutu Acheampong.

14 The formation of a new government in the Yugoslav republic of Croatia is announced in a continuing purge of nationalists begun late in 1971.

Queen Margrethe II of Denmark (below), shown with her husband, Prince Henrik, began her reign in January. President and Mrs. Richard M. Nixon (right) were hosted by China's Premier Chou En-lai in Shanghai in February.

BELOW: NORDICK PRESSEFOTO FROM PICTORIAL PARADE
RIGHT: UPI COMPIX

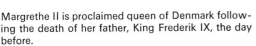

15 Margrethe II is proclaimed queen of Denmark following the death of her father, King Frederik IX, the day before.

16 Two opposition candidates win congressional seats in Chilean by-elections widely regarded as tests of strength for President Salvador Allende Gossens.

The Dallas Cowboys win the National Football League championship by defeating the Miami Dolphins 24–3 in the Super Bowl.

18 The second session of the 92d U.S. Congress convenes in Washington, D.C.

19 A North Vietnamese MiG-21 is shot down over North Vietnam by a U.S. plane for the first time since March 29, 1970, as the air war over Indochina intensifies.

22 A treaty providing terms for the entry of Great Britain, Denmark, Ireland, and Norway into the European Economic Community (EEC) is signed in Brussels, Belgium.

24 Three officers of the Soviet fishing fleet are charged in an Anchorage, Alaska, court with violating U.S. fishing regulations.

25 President Nixon, in a television address, reveals that he submitted an eight-point plan to end the Vietnam war to the Paris peace talks and that secret negotiations over the plan have gone on for some months without results.

27 Soviet Foreign Minister Andrei A. Gromyko, visiting in Japan, joins Premier Sato in announcing an agreement to begin within the year negotiations toward a peace treaty.

30 U.S. Secretary of Defense Melvin R. Laird announces that no men will be drafted before April 1972.

British troops kill 13 civilians as violence erupts during an illegal protest march by Roman Catholics in Londonderry, Northern Ireland.

FEBRUARY

2 The British Embassy in Dublin, Ireland, is burned by a crowd protesting the killing of 13 civilians in Londonderry on January 30.

4 Great Britain recognizes Bangladesh; Bangladesh announces it will seek membership in the Commonwealth of Nations.

The United Nations (UN) Security Council, meeting in Addis Ababa, Ethiopia, ends a special session, the first held outside New York City since 1952; Great Britain vetoes a resolution condemning the terms of a Great Britain–Rhodesia settlement.

7 John R. Marshall succeeds Sir Keith Holyoake as prime minister of New Zealand.

8 A U.S. appeals court grants a stay in the consolidation of the Richmond public schools with two suburban systems.

11 The U.S. and the Soviet Union sign an agreement establishing a committee of cooperation in matters of public health and medical science.

13 The XI Winter Olympic Games close in Sapporo, Japan; the Soviet Union leads the 35 competing nations with 16 medals.

14 President Nixon liberalizes restrictions on U.S. trade with the People's Republic of China to achieve the same status given trade with the U.S.S.R.

Twelve European nations sign an agreement in Oslo, Norway, to cut down the dumping of industrial wastes in the Atlantic Ocean.

15 President Nixon names U.S. Deputy Attorney General Richard G. Kleindienst to succeed John N. Mitchell as attorney general; Mitchell resigned to head the president's reelection campaign.

16 Ecuador's President José María Velasco Ibarra is deposed in a bloodless coup.

17 The British House of Commons passes, by an eight-vote margin, a bill adapting British law to EEC regulations.

The U.S. ends 29 hours of intensive bombing raids against artillery positions in southern North Vietnam and the demilitarized zone (DMZ).

19 The Chilean congress votes overwhelmingly in favor of a series of constitutional amendments that would block government efforts to expropriate private property to achieve economic reforms.

21 President Nixon arrives in Peking, China, to begin his week-long visit to that country, meeting later in the day with Communist Party Chairman Mao Tse-tung.

Longshoremen return to work on the U.S. West coast, ending a strike that had tied up Pacific ports for 134 days.

22 An explosion at an army base in Aldershot, England, kills seven persons; the official branch of the Irish Republican Army (IRA) in Dublin claims responsibility.

23 Eight IRA leaders are arrested in Dublin at the order of Ireland's Prime Minister John Lynch.

24 The British Parliament passes a bill legalizing Northern Ireland's emergency measures, which had been declared unconstitutional by the High Court of Northern Ireland the preceding day.

26 An agreement ending 16 years of civil war in Sudan is reached in Addis Ababa.

27 A communiqué issued in Shanghai, China, by President Nixon and China's Premier Chou En-lai at the end of Nixon's visit to China indicates agreement on general principles of international relations despite "essential differences."

28 Israeli troops withdraw from southern Lebanon at the end of four days of heavy action against Palestinian commandos.

29 The People's National party headed by Michael Manley defeats the ruling Labour party of Prime Minister Hugh L. Shearer in Jamaica's general elections.

MARCH

1 Morocco's voters overwhelmingly approve a new constitution proposed by King Hassan II.

Customs agents in Marseilles, France, seize 937 pounds of pure heroin in what is said to be the biggest drug seizure ever made.

2 Pioneer 10, an unmanned U.S. interplanetary probe, is launched from John F. Kennedy Space Center in Florida.

6 Laotian troops call off their month-old offensive in the vicinity of the Plain of Jars.

7 U.S. Senator Edmund S. Muskie (D, Me.) wins the Democratic presidential primary in New Hampshire, gaining 46.4% of the vote.

9 President Nixon orders the immediate enforcement of tighter security measures for U.S. airlines following an extortion plot directed against Trans World Airlines.

10 Cambodia's Prime Minister Lon Nol seizes power as head of state following the resignation of Chief of State Cheng Heng; he dissolves the National Assembly, nullifies the nearly completed republican constitution, and dismisses the cabinet.

Pioneer 10, an unmanned space vehicle, began its 21-month journey to Jupiter in March. The spacecraft was expected to reach the planet in December 1973.

NASA

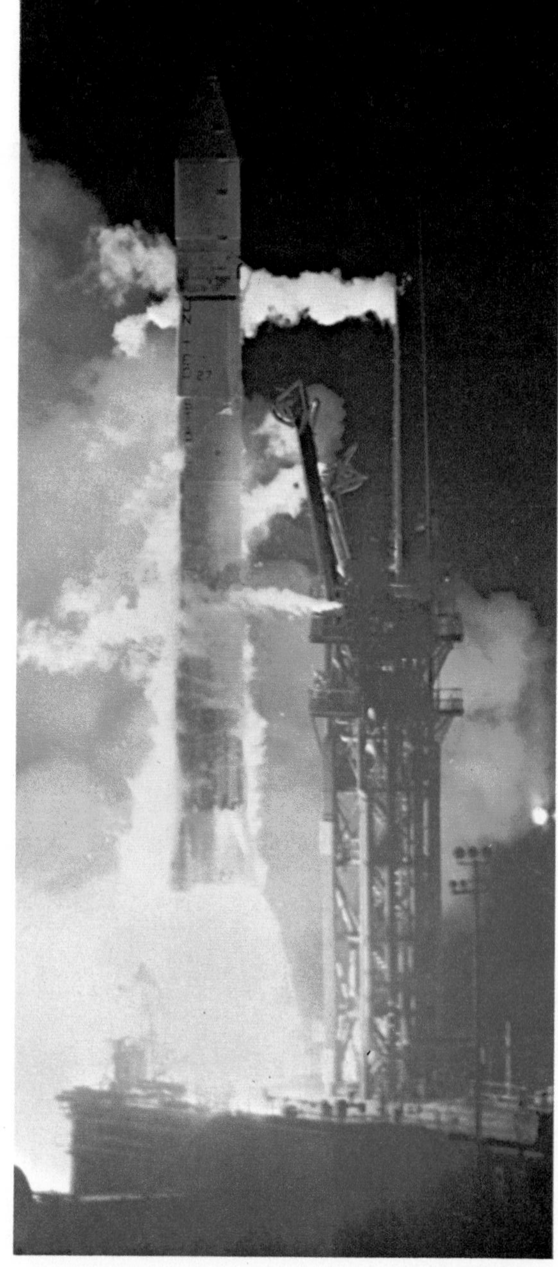

The remains of what was the small coal-mining town of Saunders, W.Va., lie in receding floodwaters following a disastrous dam collapse in the state's Buffalo Creek valley in February. The flooding left 125 people dead.

CHARLES MOORE FROM BLACK STAR

12 Regional elections in India end in victory for Prime Minister Indira Gandhi's Ruling Congress party, which wins absolute majorities in the legislatures of 14 of 16 states and one of two union territories.

13 Great Britain and China establish diplomatic relations at the ambassadorial level after Britain agrees to recognize the government of the People's Republic as the sole legal government of China, with Taiwan as a province of China.

14 Alabama Gov. George C. Wallace, with 41.5% of the vote, wins the Democratic presidential primary in Florida.

15 The U.S. Congress approves a temporary $20-billion increase in the national debt ceiling, extending it to $450 billion through June 30, 1972.

17 President Nixon asks Congress for legislation forbidding courts to order busing of elementary school children to achieve racial integration.

19 India and Bangladesh sign a 25-year treaty of friendship and mutual defense in Dacca, Bangladesh.

21 Chiang Kai-shek is elected by the National Assembly to his fifth term as president of Taiwan.

22 The U.S. National Commission on Marijuana and Drug Abuse urges the elimination of all criminal penalties for the use and possession of marijuana in the home.

23 A U.S. delegate to the Paris peace talks, William J. Porter, announces that the U.S. is suspending the talks indefinitely.

24 Great Britain's Prime Minister Edward Heath announces his intention to impose direct rule on Northern Ireland and suspend its Parliament; William Whitelaw, leader of the British House of Commons, is named secretary of state for Northern Ireland.

26 Great Britain and Malta sign a seven-year defense agreement, ending six months of negotiations on the continued use of the island's military bases.

27 Northern Ireland's Protestants begin a two-day general strike to protest the imposition of direct rule by Great Britain.

29 Bolivia orders the expulsion of 49 Soviet nationals attached to the embassy staff in La Paz.

30 Uganda's President Idi Amin orders the Israeli embassy in Kampala closed, charging that Israelis living in Uganda are engaged in antigovernment activities.

APRIL

2 South Vietnamese forces abandon the northern half of Quang Tri province.

3 A clash occurs in Belfast, Northern Ireland, between Catholic women opposing the IRA and women supporting it, following the funeral of a woman killed by a stray IRA bullet in a skirmish with British troops.

4 U.S. Secretary of State William P. Rogers announces formal U.S. recognition of Bangladesh.

U.S. Senator George S. McGovern (D, S.D.) wins the Wisconsin Democratic presidential primary with 30% of the vote.

5 The "Harrisburg Seven" jury fails to reach a verdict after hearing evidence on charges that the defendants conspired to kidnap U.S. president's security adviser Henry A. Kissinger and blow up heating ducts of federal buildings; the Rev. Philip F. Berrigan and Sister Elizabeth McAlister are convicted of smuggling letters out of a federal prison.

6 U.S. planes and naval artillery begin heavy, sustained strikes on North Vietnamese targets.

Chile's President Allende vetoes a constitutional amendment that would have required congressional approval of expropriations; the left-wing Radical party withdraws from the government in protest.

7 Reputed Mafia leader Joseph (Crazy Joe) Gallo is slain in New York City in what authorities fear is an escalation of a crime syndicate war.

8 The Soviet novelist Aleksandr I. Solzhenitsyn's hopes of receiving his 1970 Nobel prize for literature suffer another setback; a private ceremony is canceled after Soviet officials reject the visa application of the Swedish Academy officer who was to present the award.

10 U.S. B-52's begin deep penetration raids into North Vietnam for the first time since November 1967.

13 The first players' strike in the history of organized baseball ends in its 13th day; the delayed opening of the regular season is scheduled for April 15.

14 The U.S. Department of Justice files an antitrust suit against three commercial television networks charging that they monopolize entertainment programming.

A South African appeals court overturns the 1971 conviction of the Very Rev. Gonville A. ffrench-Beytagh for plotting to overthrow the government.

15 President Nixon ends a two-day visit to Canada by signing, with Prime Minister Pierre Elliott Trudeau, an agreement on joint U.S.-Canadian efforts to combat pollution of the Great Lakes.

16 U.S. B-52's and Navy fighter-bombers attack the Hanoi-Haiphong area of North Vietnam.

18 A North Vietnamese tank assault is repulsed in continued fierce fighting around An Loc, South Vietnam.

21 Zulfikar Ali Bhutto is sworn in as president of Pakistan under the new constitution he signed the preceding day; martial law is lifted.

23 The Christian Democratic Union (CDU) of West Germany wins 53% of the vote in the Baden-Württemberg state elections, regarded as a referendum on the *Ostpolitik* of West Germany's Chancellor Willy Brandt.

25 Senator McGovern wins the Massachusetts Democratic presidential primary with 52% of the vote.

26 East and West Germany's state secretaries reach an agreement on a treaty regulating traffic between the two states.

27 The Apollo 16 spacecraft splashes down in the Pacific after a successful mission during which U.S. astronauts Capt. John W. Young and Lieut. Comdr. Charles M. Duke, Jr., spent over 71 hours on the moon.

29 Former King Ntare V of Burundi is killed in fighting as supporters attempt to free him from house arrest.

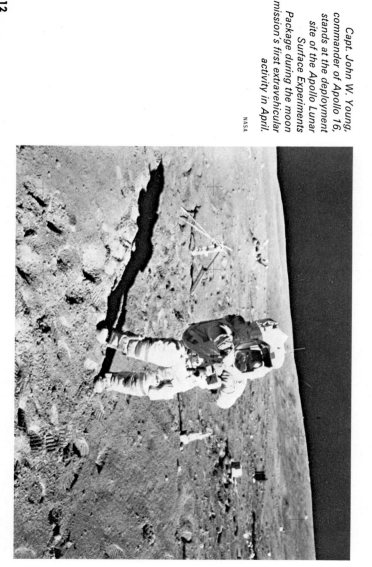

Capt. John W. Young, commander of Apollo 16, stands at the deployment site of the Apollo Lunar Surface Experiments Package during the moon mission's first extravehicular activity in April.

NASA

Ling-ling, one of the young giant pandas presented to the U.S. by the People's Republic of China (left), explores her new quarters at the National Zoological Park in Washington, D.C., in April. The U.S. gave China two musk-oxen, one of whom, Milton (below), developed a bad cold. He soon recovered and became a star attraction at the Peking Zoo, along with his partner Matilda.

LEFT: DON CARL STEFFEN, "SMITHSONIAN," © SMITHSONIAN NATIONAL ASSOC.: 1972
BELOW: GEORGE KNIGHT

MAY

2 Anastasio Somoza Debayle resigns as president of Nicaragua in accordance with an agreement by which a triumvirate will govern until the presidential elections in 1974.

3 President Nixon names Assistant Attorney General L. Patrick Gray III acting director of the Federal Bureau of Investigation (FBI); he succeeds J. Edgar Hoover, who died on May 2.

4 The U.S. and South Vietnam call another indefinite suspension of the Paris peace talks.

6 The White House announces that Japanese and major European steel producers have agreed to limit exports to the U.S. for three years.

8 President Nixon announces in a television speech that he has ordered the mining of North Vietnamese ports and the intensified bombing of supply routes; he says that these moves will end if North Vietnam releases U.S. prisoners of war and agrees to an internationally supervised cease-fire throughout Indochina.

9 U.S. and Brazil sign a treaty regulating the operation of U.S. shrimp boats within the 200-mile offshore territorial limit claimed by Brazil.

10 South Vietnam's President Nguyen Van Thieu declares martial law and replaces the military commander in the Central Highlands.

11 U.S. Secretary of the Interior Rogers C. B. Morton announces that he will grant a permit for the oil pipeline across Alaska.

12 The U.S. Environmental Protection Agency refuses to delay from 1975 to 1976 the effective date for emission controls on automobiles.

13 South Vietnamese forces begin a series of counterattacks in Quang Tri province and the Central Highlands.

15 Alabama Governor Wallace is seriously wounded in an

The U.S. Supreme Court ruled in May that Amish schoolchildren (right) who have completed their primary education cannot be forced to attend public high schools; the Amish had protested that continued schooling threatened their way of life. Alabama Gov. George C. Wallace lies seriously wounded (below) after a would-be assassin shot him while he was campaigning for the Democratic primary election in Maryland in May.

JOHN LAUNOIS FROM BLACK STAR

UPI COMPIX

assassination attempt while campaigning at a shopping center in Laurel, Md.

16 U.S. Secretary of the Treasury John B. Connally, Jr., resigns; George P. Shultz is named to succeed him.

Governor Wallace easily wins the Michigan and Maryland Democratic presidential primaries.

17 The West German Bundestag (lower house) ratifies, with most CDU members abstaining, nonaggression treaties with the Soviet Union and Poland.

20 Soviet secret police and paratroop units are reported to have quelled rioting in Kaunas, Lithuania, that followed the funeral of a Catholic youth who had burned himself to death "for political reasons."

21 Michelangelo's 'Pieta', in St. Peter's Basilica in Rome, is damaged when Laszlo Toth, a Hungarian-born émigré to Australia, attacks it with a sledgehammer while shouting, "I am Jesus Christ."

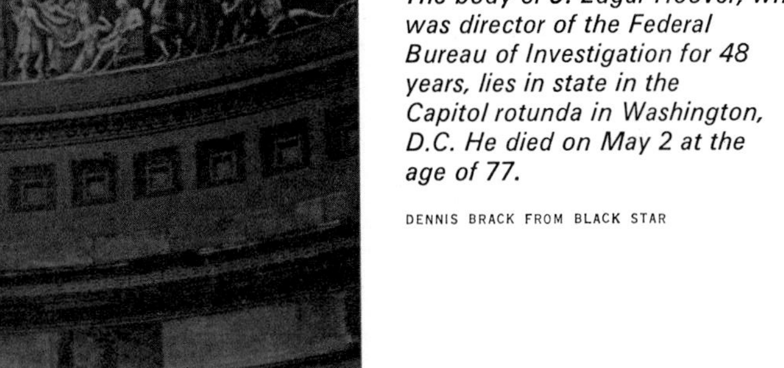

22 President Nixon arrives in Moscow to begin the first official visit of a U.S. president to the U.S.S.R.

Ceylon becomes the Republic of Sri Lanka.

23 Great Britain's Foreign Secretary Sir Alec Douglas-Home tells the House of Commons that the Pearce commission has found that the Rhodesian people do not favor the November 1971 agreement on Rhodesian independence; the settlement is being dropped and sanctions against Rhodesia are to remain in effect.

26 President Nixon and Soviet Communist Party General Secretary Leonid I. Brezhnev sign agreements limiting the U.S. and Soviet antiballistic-missile systems and offensive-missile launchers.

28 President Nixon expresses his desire for peace in an unprecedented television address to the Soviet people.

30 Three Japanese gunmen involved in the Palestine liberation movement kill 25 persons and wound 75 at Lod International Airport, Tel Aviv, Israel.

The body of J. Edgar Hoover, who was director of the Federal Bureau of Investigation for 48 years, lies in state in the Capitol rotunda in Washington, D.C. He died on May 2 at the age of 77.

DENNIS BRACK FROM BLACK STAR

JUNE

1 President Nixon, returning to Washington, D.C., from the U.S.S.R. (after stops in Iran and Poland), reports to Congress that the trip has laid the basis for a "new relationship" between the U.S. and the Soviet Union.

3 The "big four" foreign ministers sign a comprehensive agreement on relations between the divided portions of West Berlin, Germany.

4 Black militant Angela Davis is acquitted of charges of murder, kidnapping, and conspiracy in a San Jose, Calif., court.

6 A U.S. appeals court reverses a lower court order that would have merged the school systems of Richmond and two suburban counties.

Senator McGovern wins the California, New Jersey, New Mexico, and South Dakota Democratic presidential primaries, giving him 930 delegate votes.

8 The U.S. Senate approves the nomination of Kleindienst as U.S. attorney general.

10 A flash flood in Rapid City, S.D., kills more than 200 persons and causes $120 million in property damage.

12 A former commander of the U.S. Air Force, Gen. John D. Lavelle, Ret., admits before a House Armed Services investigating subcommittee that he ordered about 20 air strikes in violation of regulations barring all but protective reaction strikes over North Vietnam.

14 A U.S. district court judge orders a massive busing program to integrate schools in Detroit, Mich., and 53 suburban districts.

15 Nikolai V. Podgorny, Soviet chief of state, arrives in Hanoi; the U.S. Air Force announces that bombing raids in the Hanoi area are suspended for the duration of his visit.

17 Five men are seized while apparently trying to bug the Democratic National Committee headquarters at the Watergate complex in Washington, D.C.

19 The International Federation of Air Line Pilots' Associations declares a 24-hour strike to dramatize its demands for more protection against hijacking; most U.S. pilots obey court orders forbidding the strike.

The U.S. command in Saigon, South Vietnam, reveals that more than 2,000 U.S. pilots and 150 planes have been transferred from South Vietnam to Thailand.

20 Senator McGovern wins 230 of 248 delegates from New York in the last of the major Democratic presidential primaries.

22 President Nixon, at his first press conference in three months, criticizes the court-ordered busing of schoolchildren in the Detroit area.

23 President Nixon designates five eastern states as a federal disaster area as Hurricane Agnes begins to dissipate after causing record flooding.

26 The White House announces the lifting of quota restrictions on meat imports in an effort to curb rising food prices.

28 India and Pakistan begin talks in Simla, India, aimed at settling their common frontier, the future of Kashmir, and the disposition of Pakistanis captured in the December 1971 war.

The White House names Gen. Frederick C. Weyand commander of U.S. forces in Vietnam, succeeding Gen. Creighton W. Abrams—who is to become U.S. Army chief of staff.

29 The U.S. Supreme Court rules that the death penalty as usually enforced in the U.S. constitutes "cruel and unusual punishment" as described in the 8th Amendment to the Constitution.

U.S. President Richard M. Nixon (above) delivered a television address to the people of the Soviet Union from the Grand Kremlin Palace during his visit there in May. The city of Wilkes-Barre, Pa. (right), was inundated by torrential rains and subsequent flooding when a severe storm lashed much of the eastern U.S. in June, causing extensive damage.

ABOVE AND RIGHT: UPI COMPIX

JULY

1 John N. Mitchell resigns as President Nixon's campaign manager after his wife, Martha, announces she will leave him unless he quits politics; he is replaced by Clark MacGregor.

3 India's Prime Minister Gandhi and Pakistan's President Bhutto end six days of summit talks in Simla by signing an agreement to renounce force in settling their differences, to improve economic and cultural relations, and to hold further negotiations.

4 North and South Korea, in a joint communiqué, announce that they have agreed to hold negotiations on reunification.

6 Pierre Messmer is appointed to form a new government following the resignation the preceding day of Jacques Chaban-Delmas as premier of France.

Kakuei Tanaka takes office as prime minister of Japan at a special session of the Diet, succeeding Eisaku Sato, who announced his retirement June 17.

7 The Canadian Parliament passes emergency legislation ending a seven-week longshoremen's strike in Quebec.

8 President Nixon announces an agreement under which the Soviet Union will purchase at least $750 million worth of U.S. grain over a three-year period.

9 The provisional wing of the IRA is ordered to resume its terrorist activities, ending a 13-day truce in Northern Ireland.

12 Senator McGovern wins the Democratic presidential nomination on the first ballot; earlier in the day the Democratic National Convention had adopted the party platform following an 11-hour session.

14 U.S. Senator Thomas F. Eagleton of Missouri wins the Democratic vice-presidential nomination following a prolonged first-ballot roll call; later in the day Jean M. Westwood is elected chairman of the Democratic National Committee—the first woman to hold the post.

20 U.S. railroads and the United Transportation Union announce a complex new contract that ends a 35-year dispute over featherbedding.

21 In less than two hours 20 bombs explode in Belfast, killing at least 13 persons and wounding 130; the provisional wing of the IRA claims responsibility.

25 Senators McGovern and Eagleton reveal that Eagleton had been hospitalized for nervous exhaustion and that McGovern had not known this when Eagleton became his running mate; McGovern insists that Eagleton will remain on the ticket.

26 Terrorist incidents occur throughout Argentina on the 20th anniversary of the death of Eva Perón.

27 President Nixon says at an impromptu press conference that UN Secretary-General Kurt Waldheim had been "taken in" by North Vietnamese propaganda when he charged the U.S. with deliberately bombing North Vietnamese dikes.

28 A Chinese government spokesman confirms that former Defense Minister Lin Piao had died in a plane crash in 1971 after attempting to overthrow Chairman Mao.

31 British troops dismantle barricades barring entry to Catholic and Protestant areas of Belfast and Londonderry and make "selective" searches for suspects and arms in a three-hour, predawn military drive, the biggest ever mounted in Northern Ireland.

Senators McGovern and Eagleton announce that Eagleton is withdrawing as the Democratic vice-presidential candidate because of public debate over his having been hospitalized for psychiatric care.

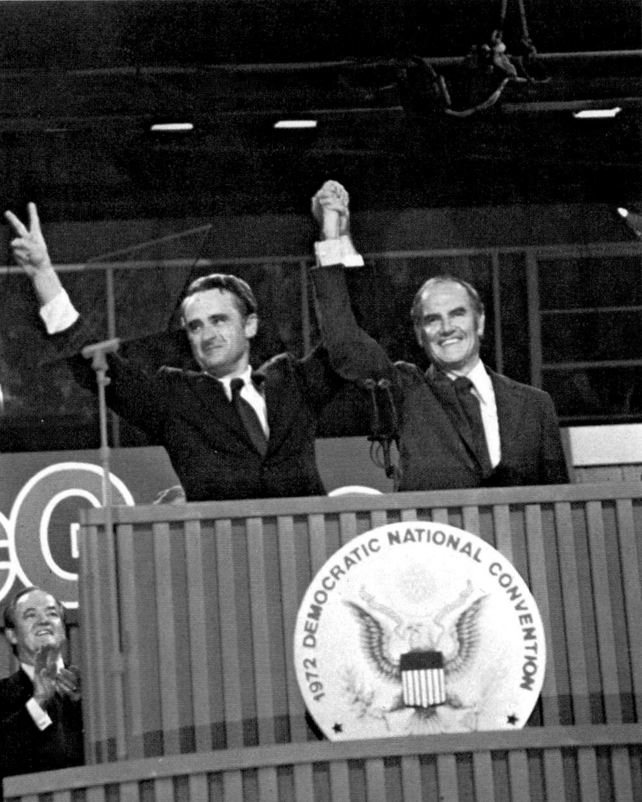

Senators George S. McGovern of South Dakota (right) and Thomas F. Eagleton of Missouri became the Democratic party's nominees for president and vice-president at the party's convention in Miami Beach, Fla., in July. They are applauded by Senator Hubert H. Humphrey of Minnesota (at left of podium). Eagleton later withdrew from contention because of a controversy surrounding his medical history; he was replaced on the ticket by R. Sargent Shriver.

FREDERIC OHRINGER FROM NANCY PALMER AGENCY

AUGUST

2 Libya's leader, Col. Muammar el-Qaddafi, and Egypt's President Anwar el-Sadat agree to establish a "unified political leadership" for their two countries by Sept. 1, 1973.

3 The U.S. Senate overwhelmingly approves the U.S.-Soviet treaty limiting antiballistic missile sites.

4 Arthur H. Bremer is found guilty of having shot Governor Wallace and three other persons on May 15 and is sentenced to 63 years in prison.

5 Explosions shatter oil storage tanks at the terminal of the transalpine pipeline near Trieste, Italy; Palestinian commandos claim responsibility for the incident.

R. Sargent Shriver is named by Senator McGovern as his choice for vice-presidential candidate after Senator Muskie, Senator Edward M. Kennedy (D, Mass.), and several others decline the post.

6 In a recorded interview broadcast over Hanoi radio, former U.S. Attorney General Ramsey Clark describes bomb damage to dikes and other civilian installations he saw while visiting North Vietnam.

7 A Protestant militiaman, the 500th victim in three years of sectarian violence in Northern Ireland, is shot down outside his home in Armagh.

The U.S. Council on Environmental Quality states in its third annual report that the nation's air is becoming cleaner but its water more polluted.

10 The U.S. House of Representatives rejects a Senate-approved amendment to a foreign-aid bill mandating an end to the Vietnam war by October 1.

Eight Czechoslovaks are sentenced to prison for subversion in the latest of a series of trials that have resulted in prison terms for at least 46 persons.

12 The last U.S. combat troops leave South Vietnam; the U.S. Air Force announces its planes have made, during the preceding 24 hours, "probably their heaviest raids ever" over North Vietnam.

15 A U.S. district court lifts an injunction issued in 1970 against the construction of the oil pipeline across Alaska.

16 Morocco's King Hassan II narrowly escapes assassination when air force jets strafe the plane in which he was returning to Rabat, Morocco, from France.

President Nixon vetoes as inflationary a bill appropriating $30.5 billion for the Department of Health, Education, and Welfare (HEW) in fiscal 1973.

17 The International Court of Justice, in an interim decision, rules that Iceland cannot enforce its newly proclaimed 50-mile territorial fishing limit.

21 Chile's President Allende declares a state of emergency in the province of Santiago following a 24-hour strike by retailers that resulted in violence.

22 The Republican National Convention renominates President Nixon as its presidential candidate.

The International Olympic Committee, in a move to head off a boycott by African and black athletes, bars Rhodesia from participating in the forthcoming games.

23 Vice-President Spiro T. Agnew is renominated as the Republican vice-presidential candidate by the party's national convention.

24 A U.S. court of appeals panel issues an indefinite stay of the massive busing program ordered for the schools in the Detroit area.

26 The XX Olympiad is declared open at ceremonies in Munich, West Germany.

29 The U.S. Price Commission refuses requests by Ford Motor Co. and General Motors Corp. (GM) for price increases on 1973 model cars.

GERRY CRANHAM FROM RAPHO GUILLUMETTE

Among the outstanding competitors at the summer Olympic Games, which began in August in Munich, were: Nikolai Avilov of the Soviet Union (left), who set a new world record for the decathlon; U.S. swimmer Mark Spitz (below), who won seven gold medals; and Dave Wottle of the U.S. (bottom, in golf cap), who won the 800-meter sprint event, barely defeating Evgeni Arzhanov of the Soviet Union, who fell crossing the finish line.

RICH CLARKSON FROM TIME © TIME INC.

UPI COMPIX

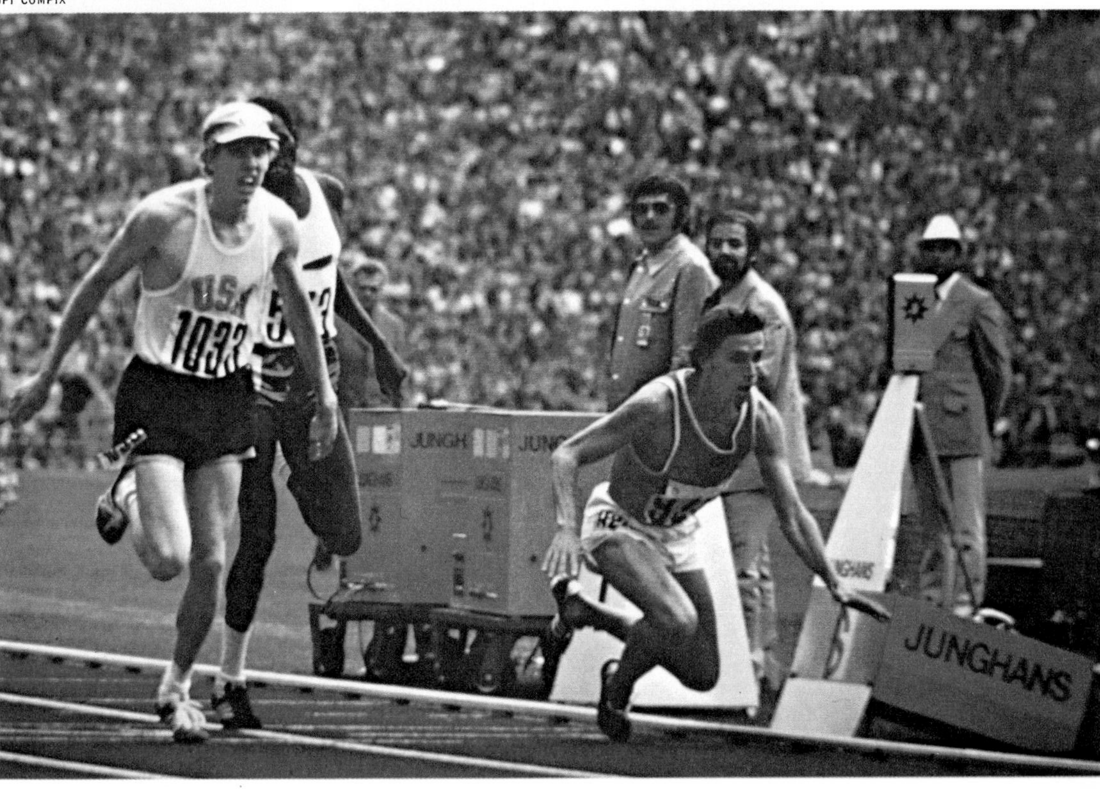

Mourners grieve at the coffins of the Israeli Olympic athletes and coaches slain by Arab terrorists (right). Three U.S. prisoners of war who had been released by North Vietnam returned to the U.S. in September (far right), accompanied by a delegation of peace activists to whom they had been released.

RIGHT: MICHA BAR-AM FROM MAGNUM

FAR RIGHT: STEVE ROSE FROM NANCY PALMER AGENCY

SEPTEMBER

1 President Nixon and Japan's Prime Minister Tanaka end two days of talks in Hawaii with an agreement designed to reduce the U.S. trade deficit with Japan.

Robert J. (Bobby) Fischer wins the 21st game of his championship match with Boris Spassky of the Soviet Union, thus becoming the first U.S. world chess champion.

Iceland extends its territorial fishing limit to 50 nautical miles despite an interim judgment to the contrary by the International Court of Justice.

2 The North Vietnamese announce that they plan to release three U.S. prisoners of war, the first to be freed since 1969.

5 Black September Palestinian terrorists force their way into the Israeli dormitory in the Olympic Village at Munich, shoot two Israelis, and hold nine other athletes and coaches hostage for several hours before being transported to a Munich airport where all the hostages, five terrorists, and one West German policeman die during a shoot-out; the games are postponed for 24 hours.

7 South Korea announces that its 37,000 troops remaining in South Vietnam will be withdrawn beginning in December.

8 Cambodian troops and civilians loot food stores as food riots in Phnom Penh, brought on by a severe rice shortage, enter their second day.

Israeli planes attack 10 Arab guerrilla bases in Lebanon and Syria in retaliation for the deaths of the 11 Israelis at Munich.

11 U.S. planes destroy the Long Bien Bridge over the Red River in downtown Hanoi.

14 West Germany and Poland agree to establish diplomatic relations immediately.

15 South Vietnamese troops recapture the devastated provincial capital of Quang Tri.

16 The Spanish police take into custody 9 Croatians, 3 of whom had hijacked an airliner to obtain the release from Sweden of the other 6; in Sydney, Australia, Croatian terrorists bomb two Yugoslav businesses, injuring 16 persons.

19 The UN General Assembly opens its 27th annual session in New York City; Stanislaw Trepczynski of Poland is elected president.

An Israeli diplomat in the embassy in London is killed by a bomb mailed in a letter; a number of other bombs mailed to Israeli officials in various countries are intercepted before delivery.

22 The U.S. Food and Drug Administration (FDA) issues stringent rules on the use of hexachlorophene; 39 babies had died in France in August following treatment with talcum powder containing excessive amounts of the germicide.

23 Ferdinand E. Marcos, president of the Philippines, declares a state of martial law to combat a "Communist rebellion"; the action follows several bombing incidents in Manila and an attempt to assassinate the secretary of defense.

26 Australia's Prime Minister William McMahon announces new measures aimed at curbing foreign takeovers of Australian companies.

28 Team Canada wins, 6–5, the eighth and decisive game of its ice hockey championship series with the Soviet Union's national team.

29 China and Japan, in a joint communiqué signed at the end of Japan's Prime Minister Tanaka's official visit to Peking, agree to end the legal state of war existing between the two countries since 1937 and to establish diplomatic relations; Taiwan breaks relations with Japan.

As part of a U.S.-Soviet grain deal, this wheat (left) was loaded onto a freighter at Houston, Tex., for shipment to the Soviet Union.
In Chicago, 45 people died in a commuter train crash (below) on October 30.

LEFT: JOHN OLSON FROM LIFE MAGAZINE © TIME INC. BELOW: EARL HOKENS FROM KEYSTONE

OCTOBER

1 India and Pakistan agree to a cease-fire following troop clashes on the Kashmir border the day before.

3 Denmark's Prime Minister Jens Otto Krag resigns in a surprise announcement made the day following victory in a referendum on Danish entry into the EEC; he is succeeded by Anker Jorgensen, leader of the General Worker's Union.

President Nixon and Soviet Foreign Minister Gromyko sign, in Washington, D.C., documents putting into effect the two arms limitation agreements reached in Moscow in May.

5 The foreign ministers of Uganda and Tanzania announce in Mogadishu, Somalia, that they have signed an agreement ending hostilities between their countries.

10 The U.S. Supreme Court upholds a ruling by a lower court that an Ohio plan to reimburse parents for their children's tuition in private or parochial schools is unconstitutional.

11 Headquarters of the French diplomatic mission in Hanoi is severely damaged in a U.S. bombing raid and the delegate general is seriously injured.

12 Chile's President Allende extends martial law to 13 provinces in an effort to cope with an emergency brought on by a trucking strike begun October 10.

16 Grand jury subpoenas are served on more than 600 persons throughout the New York City area in a massive probe of organized crime.

17 South Korea's President Park Chung Hee declares martial law, dissolving the National Assembly and suspending all political activities.

The Philippine government announces the arrest of at least four persons suspected of taking part in an alleged plot to assassinate President Marcos.

18 The U.S. Congress adjourns after refusing to give President Nixon authority to set a ceiling on spending and overriding his veto of a water pollution bill.

20 President Nixon signs the compromise revenue-sharing bill passed by Congress on October 13 in ceremonies at Independence Hall in Philadelphia, Pa.

21 A summit conference of present and prospective EEC members in Paris ends with a joint communiqué approving the principle of economic, monetary, and limited political union by 1980.

22 The Oakland Athletics defeat the Cincinnati Reds, 3–2, in the seventh and deciding game of the World Series.

23 U.S. president's security adviser Kissinger leaves Saigon following five days of secret talks held amid persistent rumors of an imminent in-place cease-fire in Vietnam.

24 South Vietnam's President Thieu says in a nationwide broadcast that peace terms reportedly worked out between the U.S. and the North Vietnamese and Viet Cong are unacceptable.

Peter J. Bridge, the first newsman jailed after the U.S. Supreme Court ruled in June that journalists could be compelled to answer grand jury questions on criminal matters, is freed from a Newark, N.J., jail after being held 21 days for contempt of court.

26 Dahomey's President Justin T. Ahomadégbé and other members of the ruling Presidential Council are deposed in a military coup.

29 West Germany releases three Arab guerrillas arrested in connection with the Olympic Games massacre of Israeli athletes and coaches as ransom for a hijacked airliner.

30 The Liberal party of Canada's Prime Minister Trudeau loses its substantial majority in Canadian Parliamentary elections.

U.S. President Nixon and Vice-President Agnew were reelected in a landslide victory in November.

FRED WARD FROM BLACK STAR

NOVEMBER

1 South Vietnam's President Thieu, in a National Day speech, denounces the draft cease-fire agreement as a "surrender of the South Vietnamese people to the Communists."

2 President Nixon, in a nationally televised political address, says a Vietnamese cease-fire will be signed only "when the agreement is right."

Canada's Prime Minister Trudeau announces his intention to remain in power and let the newly elected Parliament determine the fate of his government.

3 U.S. military sources disclose that additional North Vietnamese reinforcements are moving into South Vietnam; a U.S. Department of Defense spokesman confirms that the U.S. is increasing shipments of military supplies to South Vietnam.

4 North and South Korea agree on terms of political and economic cooperation as a step toward reunification.

6 Great Britain's Prime Minister Heath announces a 90-day freeze on wages, prices, rents, and dividends in an effort to curb inflation.

7 President Nixon wins reelection in a sweep of 49 states, losing only Massachusetts and the District of Columbia to Senator McGovern; a massive ticket splitting enables the Democrats to retain control of Congress and to take 11 of 18 state governorships.

8 Militant American Indians end their week-long occupation of the Bureau of Indian Affairs headquarters in Washington, D.C., after reaching agreement on their demands for reforms.

9 The "big four" powers announce that they will support East and West German applications for UN membership and will continue to maintain their rights and responsibilities on Berlin.

12 A Southern Airways jetliner, its tires shot out by FBI

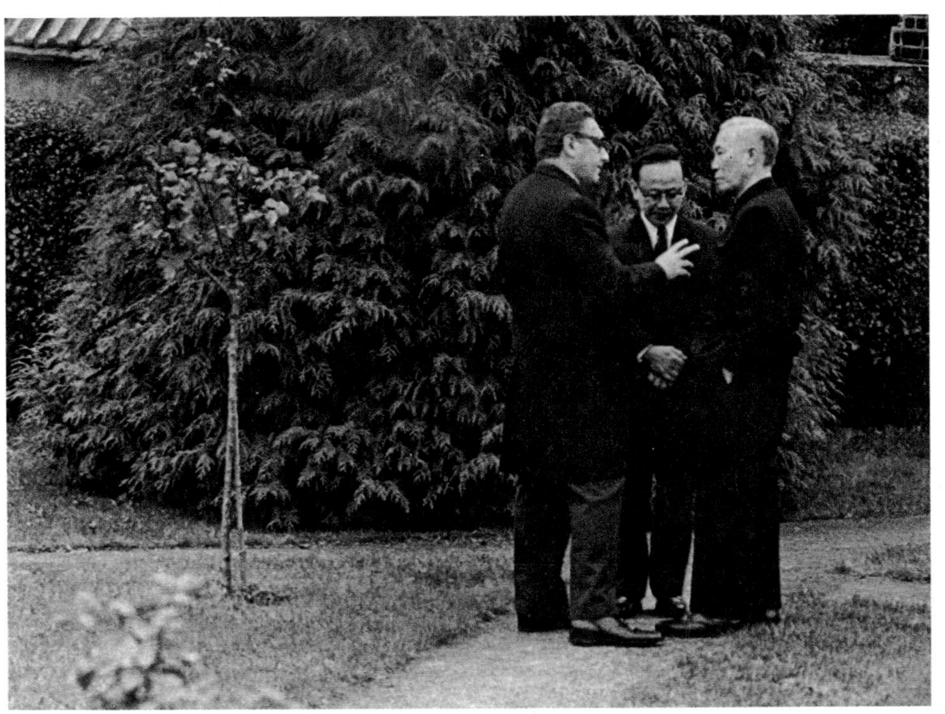

Peace in Vietnam, which had seemed imminent earlier, eluded the U.S. and North Vietnam in late 1972. Secret negotiations continued between U.S. president's security adviser Henry A. Kissinger (left) and North Vietnam's Le Duc Tho (right) at a villa near Paris.

GAMMA

agents, lands in Cuba 29 hours after it was hijacked by three gunmen who ordered it flown 4,000 miles, with multiple stops, and who received $2 million in ransom.

16 Two students are killed on the Baton Rouge, La., campus of Southern University as police attempt to end a student occupation of the administration building.

19 The coalition government of West Germany's Chancellor Brandt receives a resounding vote of confidence in federal elections, obtaining a 48-seat majority in the Bundestag.

21 Syrian and Israeli forces fight air, artillery, and tank battles for eight hours on the Israeli-occupied Golan Heights in their most serious clash in two years.

South Korean voters ratify constitutional revisions giving President Park complete power and unlimited tenure in office.

22 The Belgian coalition government headed by Prime Minister Gaston Eyskens resigns after ten months in office over its inability to resolve language problems.

23 Bolivia's president, Col. Hugo Banzer Suárez, imposes a nationwide state of siege as factory, commercial, and bank workers begin an antigovernment strike.

24 Finland becomes the first Western nation to formally recognize East Germany and the first to establish ties with both Germanys.

26 An unidentified submarine is reported to have escaped to open sea two weeks after having first been sighted in Sogne Fjord in Norwegian territorial waters.

29 President Nixon nominates construction union leader Peter J. Brennan to succeed Secretary of Labor James D. Hodgson.

30 India's Foreign Minister Swaran Singh announces in Parliament that India is ready to normalize relations with the U.S. and China.

Former president of Argentina Juan D. Perón returned there in November, ending a 17-year exile. He waves to his supporters from a window; they were prevented by the government from greeting him when he first arrived. He left the country again in December.

BILL RAY FROM LIFE MAGAZINE © TIME INC.

DECEMBER

1 India and Pakistan exchange prisoners captured on the western front in the 1971 Indo-Pakistani war.

2 The Australian Labor party, headed by Gough Whitlam, receives a comfortable majority in national elections, ousting the Liberal-Country party government after 23 years in power.

4 Private peace talks resume in Paris between U.S. president's security adviser Kissinger and North Vietnam's adviser Le Duc Tho.

5 The White House announces that Undersecretary of Commerce James T. Lynn will be nominated secretary of housing and urban development and that Rogers Morton will continue as secretary of the interior.

6 President Nixon announces that Secretary of Agriculture Earl L. Butz will continue in office and that textile manufacturer Frederick B. Dent will replace Secretary of Commerce Peter G. Peterson.

7 India and Pakistan announce agreement on the delineation of a Kashmir truce line.

8 The U.S. unemployment rate is reported to have dropped from the 5.5% plateau set in June to 5.2% in response to a strong expansion of the economy.

9 Robert Strauss is elected chairman of the Democratic National Committee after Mrs. Westwood resigns.

11 U.S. Senator Robert J. Dole of Kansas announces his resignation as Republican national chairman and the choice of George H. Bush, U.S. representative to the UN, as his successor.

12 South Vietnam's President Thieu proposes that a truce between North and South Vietnam be declared before Christmas and maintained during peace talks.

13 Over Soviet and Cuban objections, the UN General Assembly approves a reduction in the U.S. share of the UN budget from 31.5% to 25.0% following vigorous U.S. campaigning.

15 U.S. B-52 bombers conclude the heaviest raid of the war to date, a record 16-mission attack on supply bases in southern North Vietnam.

18 The White House announces that President Nixon personally ordered the resumption of full-scale bombing and mining of North Vietnam "until such time as a settlement is arrived at."

The Soviet Union's economic plan for 1973, calling for sharp cutbacks in production of consumer goods, is presented to the Supreme Soviet.

20 Terrorist gunmen kill at least 8 persons in Belfast and Londonderry in the bloodiest day of violence in Northern Ireland in several months; the death toll for 3 years of sectarian violence reaches at least 675.

23 Earthquakes destroy more than half of Managua, Nicaragua, killing what is estimated to be more than 10,000 persons.

26 The U.S. command in Saigon announces the resumption of bombing of North Vietnam after a 36-hour Christmas pause; a U.S. Department of Defense spokesman in Washington, D.C., says the U.S. has been losing 2%–3% of its attacking planes.

Harry S. Truman, 33d president of the U.S., dies in Kansas City, Mo.

27 Lester B. Pearson, 1957 Nobel peace prize winner and Canada's prime minister from 1963 to 1968, dies in Rockcliffe, Ont.

29 Soviet Communist Party General Secretary Brezhnev puts off his scheduled visit to the U.S. until the autumn of 1973 "because the political climate is not right."

30 The White House announces that President Nixon has ordered a halt in the bombing of North Vietnam above the 20th parallel.

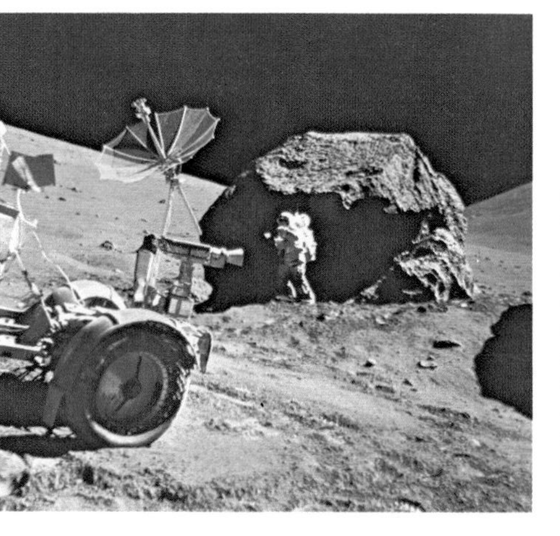

Apollo 17 astronaut Harrison H. Schmitt (left) works next to a large boulder on the surface of the moon during the final mission of the Apollo series in December. Much of the city of Managua, the capital of Nicaragua, lies in ruins (below) after a series of devastating earthquakes on December 23.

LEFT: NASA. BELOW: UPI COMPIX

WELCOME
HOME

OUR BOYS
IN THE ARMED FORCES

today's veterans

I. The High Cost of Low Benefits
by Senator Vance Hartke

II. The Urgent Need for New Policies
by Peter N. Gillingham

III. The Question of Amnesty
by Senator Hubert H. Humphrey

part I

THE HIGH COST OF LOW BENEFITS

by Senator Vance Hartke

Chairman, Senate Veterans' Affairs Committee

Vance Hartke

A veteran of the U.S. Navy and Coast Guard, Senator Hartke served in World War II. He was born at Stendal, Ind., on May 31, 1919, and was educated at Evansville College and at Indiana University, where he received a doctorate in law. He was mayor of Evansville from 1956 to 1958 before his election to the U.S. Senate. His books include 'The American Crisis in Vietnam'.

During the 1960's, the people of the U.S. were drawn, almost imperceptibly, into a major war. A commitment to South Vietnam that began with "advisers" and Green Berets, the Army Special Forces troops, had by mid-decade evolved into all-out warfare waged by a large draftee army on the mainland of Asia. The case for U.S. involvement in Vietnam is challenged bitterly today, from the college campus to the U.S. Congress. Arguments pro and con comprise a major part of any national political discourse. Whatever the conclusion that history will provide, Vietnam is certain to be recorded as an agonizing epoch in the U.S. experience. But we are living with the present, and the purpose of this article is not to pass judgment on our national intentions in Southeast Asia, or on the manner of their pursuit. Rather, it is to point out an ultimate wrong resulting from the war, the treatment accorded the Vietnam veteran. We have fought unpopular wars before, from Mexico to Korea, but seldom was the opprobrium of a conflict applied to the serviceman engaged in it. Today, any blanket condemnation of the Vietnam war would appear to encompass the veteran himself. The number of veterans so regarded is not a small one. Since 1964, more than 6 million U.S. servicemen who have been discharged from the armed forces have tried to resume normal lives in what we are told is an affluent society. It has been a bleak reception for all too many of these young people; national indifference seems to begin with the very nature of their return. Once, men came home by thousands, lining the rails of troopships and cheering as they passed through the Golden Gate. From Vietnam they have come back to the U.S. individually, in twos and threes, hurled by jet plane through nine or ten time zones and abruptly deposited in a separation center with scant time for readjustment. As one veteran said, "You come back anonymously."

Fresh out of uniform, the first thing the returnee encounters is a public attitude ranging from apathy to hostility. Recently Dr. Jonathan F. Borus, a psychiatrist formerly with Walter Reed Army

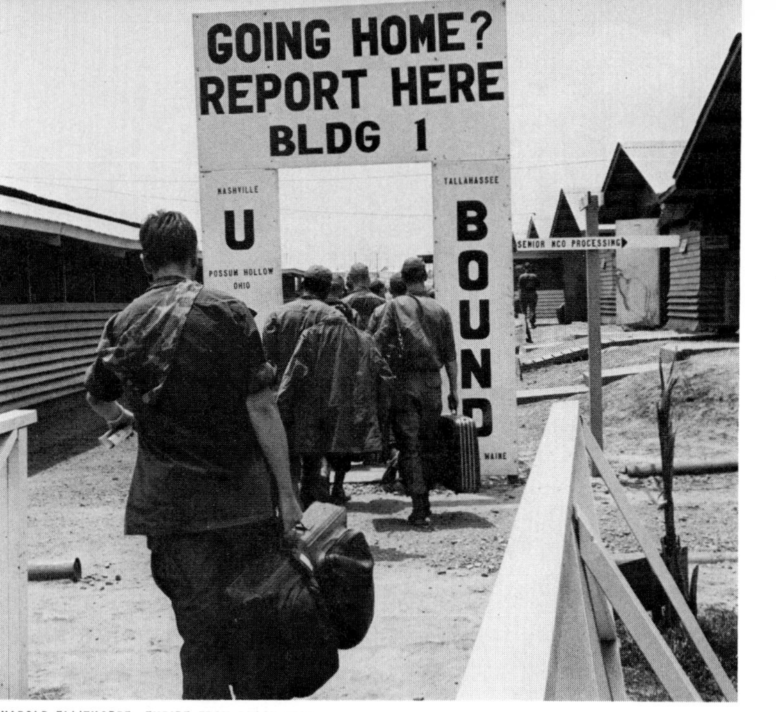

HAROLD ELLITHORPE—EMPIRE FROM BLACK STAR

At Bien Hoa air base, Long Binh, South Vietnam, GI's walk out to jetliners for the long trip back to the States.

Hospital in Washington, D.C., observed that the veteran "has had to deal with his feelings about the war and his participation in it in the context of the antiwar, antimilitary atmosphere prevailing in our society." A 1971 Harris poll commissioned by the Veterans Administration (VA) indicated that the enmity experienced by the Vietnam veteran is most pronounced in the ranks of his contemporaries. Hatred of the war among young people apparently transmits itself to those young men who were forced to fight for their lives in that remote, cruel land. The unwitting young of the U.S. would make of the Vietnam soldier a symbolic legatee of My Lai (where Vietnamese civilians were massacred by U.S. troops in 1968) and the indiscriminate use of napalm over Vietnamese villages. Some older people, including veterans of other wars, see in the Vietnam GI an exacerbation of the social problems of a generation. Many Vietnam veterans sense a veiled public curiosity that seems to ask, "Who did you kill? What drug are you on?" This produces a natural reaction in the veteran of Vietnam; he is often silent about his service and defensive in his conduct.

The Hurdles in Seeking a Job

Social attitudes may be overcome in time. Of more pressing concern is the basic necessity of making a living, and here the Vietnam veteran comes up against the major obstacle in his civilian adjustment. Unemployment in the nation is bad; it is worse for the veteran and significantly higher for those who entered the service after August 1964. In mid-1972 the jobless rate continued to hover at about 6% for the overall labor force on a seasonally adjusted basis. The rate for Vietnam veterans—who totaled under 5% of the civilian work force—ranged up to 10% and as high as 20% if the returnee was black. *The New York Times* stated early in 1972 that more than 4 million veterans between the ages of 20 and 29 were in the civilian labor market and that their unemployment rate meant that up to 345,000 men were out of work.

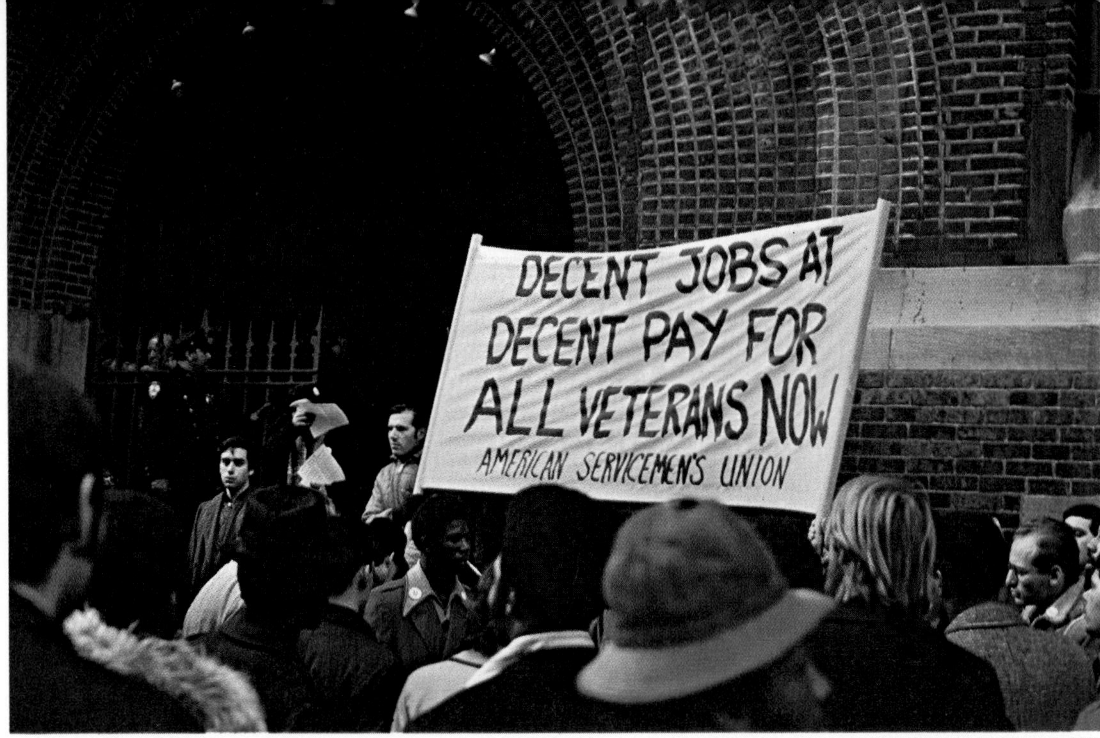

LEONARD FREED FROM MAGNUM

Vocal veterans rally for jobs in New York City. Even educated vets are finding it hard to get employment.

For a large proportion of GI's who served in Vietnam, nothing at home has changed much. Youths inducted from the big city ghettos return to the ghetto. The rural poor find themselves back where they started. A rifleman or helicopter door gunner has not learned a marketable trade, and even a college graduate finds a labor market saturated with academic degrees. With exceptions, many veterans say they have found no special sympathy, no preferential treatment among potential employers. These young veterans are quite vocal about their problems, if they can find anyone who will listen. In May the American Veterans Committee sponsored a seminar in Washington, D.C., on problems of the Vietnam era. Government officials, university personnel, and veterans' organizations took part. Pointing out that in World War II "everybody went," one veteran asked the panel, "Who went to Vietnam?" He answered his own question: "The sort of people who were already losers." These were individuals, the veteran said, who were not students, who did not have a doctor to exempt them, or who just did not know the loopholes that would keep them out of service. Another Vietnam GI warned the conference, "You are losing a whole generation of people by not dealing with the problems of vets. These people, they're falling away." Further testimony dealt with ill-educated, ill-prepared veterans who cannot even make their needs known. After the conference, a spokesman asserted that government and industry must take the initiative to help ex-servicemen and not just wait for veterans to ask for help.

There is widespread opinion, moreover, that existing government programs for the readjustment of Vietnam-era veterans are not working. A 1971 Harris poll reported that a plurality of veterans (36%) who had heard of the U.S. Labor Department's Jobs for Veterans project rated it "not so effective," while a plurality of employers (39%) said they were "not sure." The Harris report said that only 14% of the Vietnam returnees were familiar with VA

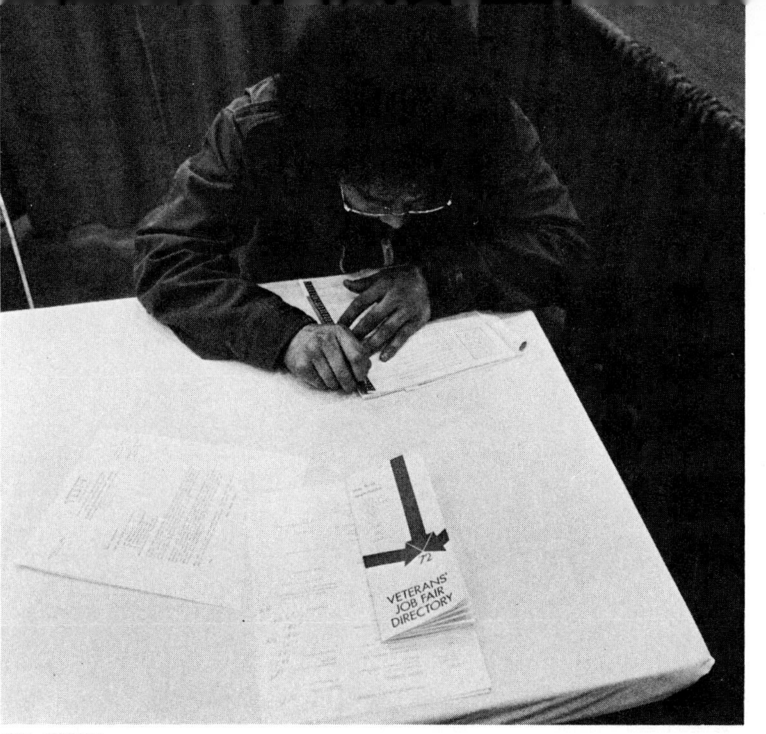

PAUL SEQUEIRA

VA job fairs attempt to help vets find employment. The fairs are often ineffective because vets either are not aware of them or are suspicious of their positive value.

job marts and job fairs and that "there is suspicion voiced that Jobs for Veterans is all talk and no action." The report concluded that less than 1% of those employed obtained their jobs through job marts or job fairs.

Besides those discouraging findings, there is evidence that some veterans not only failed to receive preferential treatment in employment offices but also received *less* counseling and job training than was given to nonveterans. Legislation passed late in 1972 required employment offices to have staff members who dealt exclusively with veterans. Project Transition, the Department of Defense plan that trains a soldier for civilian employment during the last six months of his service time, has had success. In this program, the soldier learns a skill off base at the behest of local businessmen. Project Transition should be expanded and advanced under the premise that any man who has been subjected to the discipline and training of the military is employable.

Shortchanging in Educational Benefits

The Vietnam serviceman comes home not only to a tight labor market but also to a period of serious penury in U.S. higher education. Even more than the limited employment opportunities, today's GI education bill will have a damaging long-term effect on the Vietnam generation. Simply put, the Vietnam-era GI bill is not adequate. In trying to assess a better future for today's veteran, it is revealing to look back over 25 years to the educational benefits following World War II. The ex-GI then returned to a heartfelt welcome and a VA that was funding a booming business in higher education. The GI Bill of Rights offered him up to $500 a year for all of his tuition, books, supplies, and fees plus $75 a month to live on while he finished high school or went to college. A married veteran with one child could receive $310 a month in living expenses alone. Colleges and universities did their utmost to accommodate the

COURTESY, VETERANS ADMINISTRATION

COURTESY, VETERANS ADMINISTRATION

Some veterans take advantage of the education provisions of the GI bill. A veteran (above) uses the counseling service at Bellevue Community College in Washington. GI bill students (above, right) are studying at the Washington College of Law.

GI and his small family. Some lived in Quonset huts and other improvised housing on campus. It was certainly not luxury, but it afforded the World War II veteran a priceless education at a total cost of almost $15 billion in federal benefits. That money has been returned, three to six dollars for each dollar expended, in additional tax revenues from the educated veteran. The GI bill was not a case of federal altruism but a sound investment by the government.

As 1972 opened the student veteran faced a cool welcome from the VA, which offered only the bare essentials in benefits. The unmarried Vietnam veteran found that the most he could get was $175 a month for everything. A married man received $205 a month, which was below the national poverty level of $2,500 annual income. If he had a child, the student got $230 a month and each additional child boosted the benefits by $13. It was a stipend at best; it did not even take into account the soaring cost of college tuitions. The price tag in some of the nation's better private universities has more than tripled since the late 1940's, necessitating attendance at the already crowded public colleges. Expensive tuition, skimpy VA benefits, and the high cost of living have combined to produce a prevailing reaction among potential student veterans: they don't bother. The Harris poll found that returning veterans of the Vietnam war rate educational assistance as the most important benefit, yet 59% of those returnees have never even applied for the GI bill benefit. The poll also showed that 53% of those who have never applied would do so if the benefits were raised to a realistic level.

In many cases, the Vietnam GI's who do undertake to further their education are angered by delays in receiving their benefit payments. A sympathetic view of their special problems was recently presented by Joseph Mulholland, assistant dean of Fordham University. In a letter to *The New York Times,* Mulholland wrote, "We have sent members of the poor and lower middle class to fight this war. These men, most of whom, by definition, attended inferior schools, need extra help if they are to do college-level work. . . . Yet the bureau-

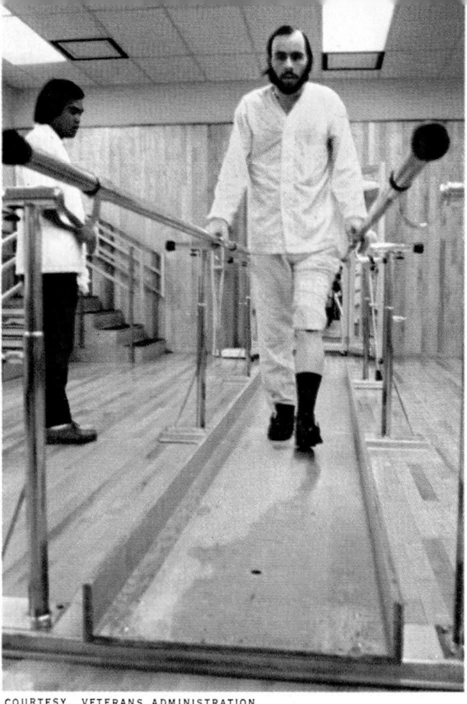

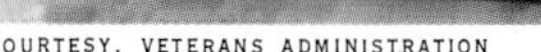
COURTESY, VETERANS ADMINISTRATION

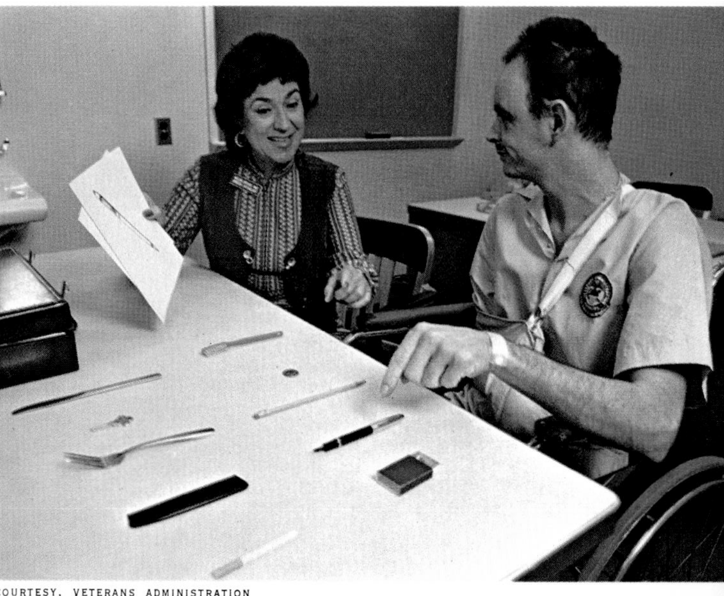
COURTESY, VETERANS ADMINISTRATION

A Vietnam veteran receives speech therapy (above) at the VA hospital in San Diego, Calif. Another veteran (above, left) learns to use a prosthetic device.

cratic maze through which they, and college administrators like myself, must travel in order to obtain funds for tutoring is all but impenetrable." In 1972 some notice of the student veteran's plight had begun to appear in the national press. The headline of a Scripps-Howard article put it quite succinctly: "Viet Vets Getting Shaft."

Early in fiscal 1972, Congress and the Administration of U.S. President Richard M. Nixon agreed that an increase in the GI allowance was needed. The somewhat meager Administration proposal called for an 8.6% raise in benefits. In March the House approved a measure that would hike benefits by 14%. The Senate Committee on Veterans' Affairs went much farther. It proposed legislation that would elevate GI educational benefits more than 43% over the present VA rates, to achieve parity with World War II entitlement levels. Specifically, under the Senate bill, the present $175 monthly allowance would be raised to $250. Married students would receive $297 instead of the current $205 a month. With the addition of a child, the benefits would be boosted from $230 a month to $339. In addition, the bill demanded a new advance payment system that would ensure the student veteran a check at the beginning of the school term, wiping out the onerous delays that have raised a chorus of veterans' protests. Another provision of the measure asked for an innovative work-study program that would encourage use of the GI bill by veterans. In late 1972 monthly educational benefits were increased by a compromise rate. Payments to unmarried veterans rose from $175 to $220 and to married veterans from $205 to $261, and payments for veterans with one child rose from $230 to $298. Allotments for each additional child were boosted by $5 from $13 to $18. Payments were to be made in advance.

Substantial Aid to the Handicapped

Congress acted in 1972 to aid the men who paid a special price in Vietnam. The extensive use of mines and booby traps and other

EB INC.

Draft resistance was a big problem in the U.S. during World War I. In one day police, soldiers, and sailors questioned 20,000 men to find those who had escaped registering for the draft.

antipersonnel weapons by the enemy has left a poignant residue of crippled men, young men badly handicapped early in life. Of the 2 million U.S. veterans on the disabled list, 287,000 served during the Vietnam era. By the end of June 1972, Congress had produced two meaningful laws affecting the disabled—the Disability Compensation Act and the Disabled Housing Grants Act, both unanimously approved by the Senate Veterans' Affairs Committee. The Disability Compensation Act provides for a 10% increase in compensation rates and a corresponding raise for dependent allowances of veterans who are rated 50% or more disabled. An important feature of the act is the creation of a new clothing allowance of up to $150 a year for those who must wear prosthetic devices, such as braces and artificial limbs, that tend to wear away clothing.

The Disabled Housing Grants Act increases the maximum payment for specially adapted housing to $17,500. These so-called wheelchair homes are necessary for the continued care of paralytics and other severely disabled veterans.

The national malaise of drug addiction extends to the armed forces, as the national media has been quick to emphasize. Following the press accounts of widespread use of marijuana and heroin in Vietnam, the Department of Defense, the VA, and Congress have taken a number of remedial steps. In Vietnam itself, under Defense Department orders, military personnel are carefully screened before they return to the U.S. An addict is sent to a treatment center before he is allowed to return home. In the U.S. up until 1972, there were 32 drug treatment facilities working under the VA. In June, the VA announced that 6 of the existing centers would be expanded and 12 new facilities would be opened by the end of summer. About 20,000 veteran addicts were treated in VA hospitals during fiscal 1972, compared with 5,000 the previous year. The new capability in VA in-house treatment would be some 40% over the old, but this is still a small percentage for an estimated 100,000 vet addicts.

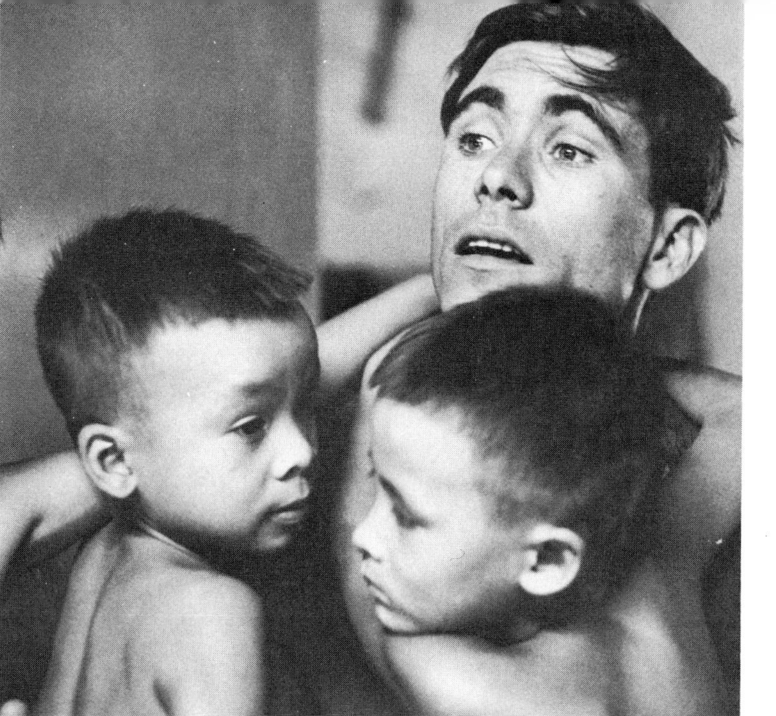

ABOVE AND RIGHT: MARK GODFREY FROM LIFE MAGAZINE © TIME INC.

Dick Hughes, a conscientious objector, went to Vietnam as a reporter and ended up opening his house to the homeless boys of Saigon. There they can find food, shelter, and love.

In the fall of 1972, action was pending on S. 2108, the Veterans' Drug and Alcohol Treatment and Rehabilitation Act of 1972. This measure, sponsored by Senator Alan Cranston (D, Calif.), chairman of the Health and Hospitals Subcommittee, on his behalf and mine, would provide comprehensive drug and alcohol treatment to addicted veterans regardless of the nature of their discharge. The Senate bill is based on the premise that a broken man who may have developed his addiction while in the service of his country is owed every chance for recovery. Improved and expanded treatment of veteran addicts is a matter of the utmost urgency.

Fair Treatment to Those Who Serve

Most people in the U.S. would agree that the decade of the 1960's was one of the most tumultuous in the nation's history and that its scars will long be borne. If, indeed, U.S. foreign policy was steered into an era of great blundering, and if domestic injustice demanded drastic correction, then it is hoped the nation will learn from its mistakes to the ultimate benefit of the future. In the meantime, an apathetic public and its national leadership must not make of the Vietnam veteran a final victim of the war. The limitation on benefits and services for these young men and women can seriously impede their return to a useful and happy civilian life.

One former GI said recently, "We are getting 61% of the benefits others got after World War II. But we didn't serve only 61% as effectively or suffer 61% as much. We want equality and nothing less." As the veteran stated at the Washington conference, "You are losing a whole generation of people." For these young people, the war was painful enough. We must not compound the experience by alienating them in their own country. Until the rights and benefits of those who served in Vietnam compare favorably with those who served under a unified nation's blessing, we have the makings of a national disgrace.

Patients in a methadone maintenance program discuss methadone in preparation for a life that will always involve a daily ration of the drug. Critics of methadone maintenance dislike the idea of continuing drug addiction, even though a "safer" drug is used.

WIDE WORLD

part II

THE URGENT NEED FOR NEW POLICIES

by
Peter N. Gillingham

Director, Illinois Veterans Working Group, Southern Illinois University at Edwardsville

Peter N. Gillingham

While he was doing research for a book on U.S. involvement in Indochina, Mr. Gillingham's talks with Vietnam veterans led to the Veterans World Project. He was born in San Francisco, Calif., on Nov. 12, 1930. After service in the Korean War, he finished his law studies at Yale. He has worked for many years in the field of international development.

Hundreds of thousands of Vietnam war veterans are experiencing a persistent sense of isolation, confusion, and rejection on returning to their native land. Psychiatrists refer to a post-Vietnam syndrome that frequently appears months or even years after military duty. When the frustration of a tight job market is heightened by indifference or hostility, sometimes even from family and friends, many veterans react to what they see as deliberate rejection by returning it with interest.

Vietnam veterans have almost always been regarded and discussed in the framework of pathology—what is or might be wrong with them in terms of violence, drugs, mental illness, antisocial attitudes, unemployability, and reluctance to utilize the GI Bill of Rights, the major instrument of U.S. policy concerning veterans. This attitude and its reflection in national policies denies the positive potential of valuable human beings.

Very few of the Vietnam-era veterans want to go on thinking of themselves as veterans; they want to move into constructive roles. A generation ago the whole society challenged itself to bend every rule in helping the returned veteran explore and use his own undetermined potential; we can and must do the same again.

THE ROOTS OF THE PROBLEM

The nature of the war in Vietnam has been unique in U.S. history, and the experiences of the men fighting that war have differed profoundly from those of the men in earlier wars. For contrast, we need to look back only one generation to World War II—a popular war whose GI's were welcomed home as heroes. World War II was a declared war with front lines. Vietnam, an undeclared war, had no front lines. In World War II men went to war in units with a sense of unit identity. They knew they were in service for the duration

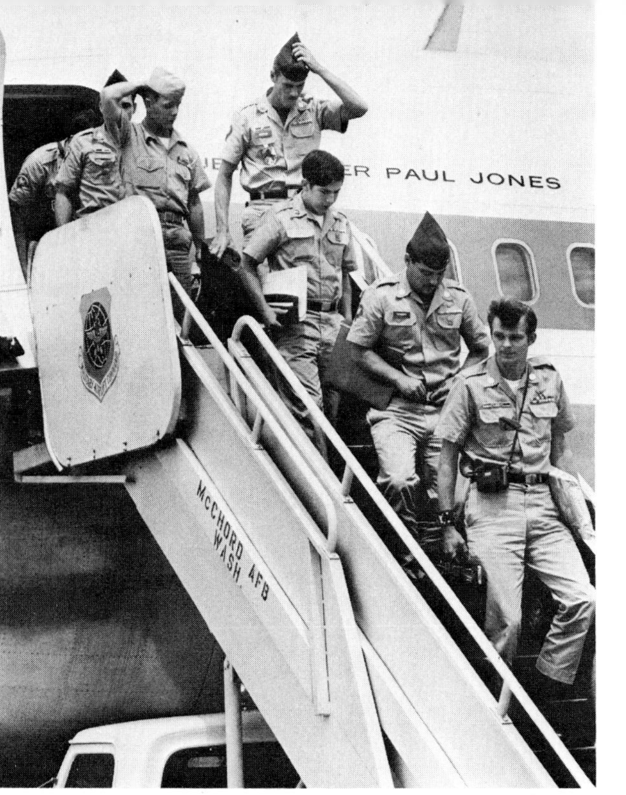

TED SPIEGEL FROM BLACK STAR

"THE NEW YORK TIMES"

These GI's returning from Vietnam do not receive an enthusiastic welcome from a grateful country. Returning to civilian life demands adjustment anyway, without the added difficulty of facing hostility or suspicion.

of the war. Every man who went to Vietnam knew that he was going for one year, and each man kept track of his year on his own calendar. There was a sense of isolation even in the time dimension of the experience.

Vietnam presented nearly insurmountable problems to the traditionally trained soldier. The lack of territorial objectives denied units a sense of involvement with their missions. The enemy in World War II, generally identifiable, was considered a clear aggressor against the U.S. and its Allies. In Vietnam the enemy was visually unidentifiable. In World War II the Allied troops generally felt a common bond. In Vietnam the Army of the Republic of Vietnam (ARVN) was widely distrusted by U.S. troops, many of whom felt that the Saigon government was "ripping off" the U.S. In World War II the armed forces knew it when the war was drawing to an end. In Vietnam many men lost the sense of relationship to a purpose. The World War II GI felt that he had made a personal contribution, but it is a rare Vietnam veteran who feels that he personally helped win the war.

Anonymous Destruction

There has been a quantum leap in destructive power since World War II. In general, the World War II GI was trained to fire at an individual enemy; the Vietnam combat man, carrying automatic weapons, was trained to spray the landscape with rounds of ammunition. Military ground units in Vietnam sought out the enemy; but once contact was made, a radiotelephone was used to call in the anonymous and indiscriminate destructive power of gunships, long-range artillery, rocket rounds, napalm, and B-52 bombers. In World War II the artillery was targeted on a specific installation. In Vietnam artillery often was used to bombard quadrants on a map

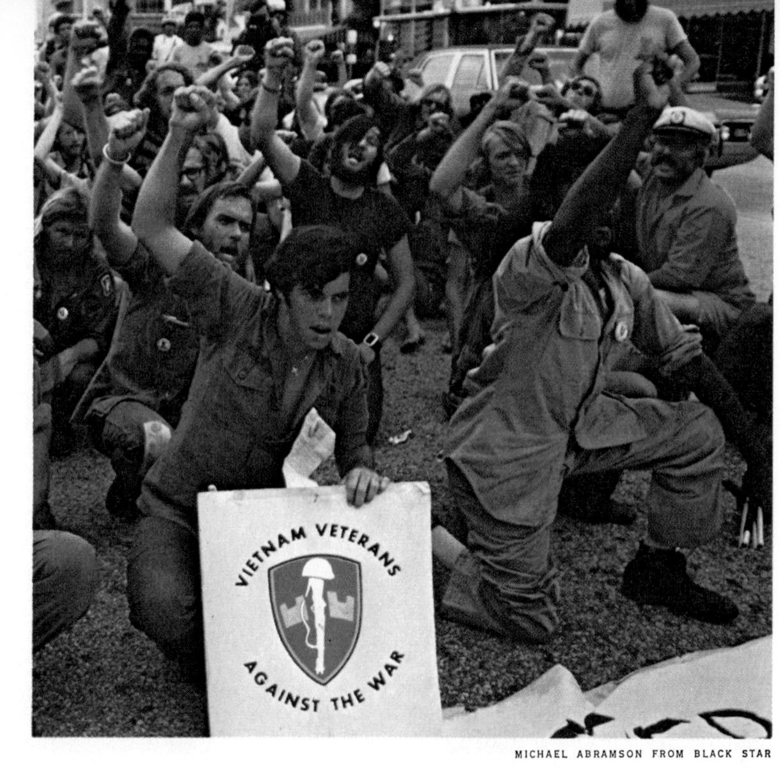

MICHAEL ABRAMSON FROM BLACK STAR

In July 1972 a group of Vietnam Veterans Against the War staged a peace demonstration in Miami Beach, Fla., as the Democratic National Convention was in progress.

without concern for whether people were there—or if they were, who they were.

Many former combat soldiers feel uneasy, if not guilty, about their part in loosing tremendous and often disproportionate power—a guilt that might be lessened considerably if there were a balancing sense of putting one's own life on the line. The high percentage of wounds and deaths of U.S. soldiers in Vietnam caused by booby traps and land mines is the other side of the coin. The Vietnam ground troops endured the sustained tension of awaiting unpredictable violence. They never knew when death might come.

Stateside Influences

The U.S. serviceman in Vietnam remained an absentee member of both his overall society and his peer group. In the face of widespread public opposition to the Vietnam war, the soldier could feel tainted by his own involvement, and the highly volatile antiwar sentiments of his own generation increased his guilt feelings. The contemptuous attitude of some of the fighting man's contemporaries contrasted sharply with that of their counterparts in World War II, when practically every man of military age who was not at war was involved in civilian support functions. Veterans of earlier wars also upset the new veterans with remarks such as "You kids should have fought a real war" or "How many gooks did you kill?"

Most World War II combat soldiers came home on troopships, and that experience provided a beneficial transition period. A Vietnam veteran can, within 72 hours, go from combat environment to his own front door. After a brief "outprocessing," the veteran threads his way home through indifferent strangers.

Many of the people at home do not want to think or talk about the war and what it has meant for the veteran, except in the most superficial way. Moreover, many civilians feel that because Vietnam was

TED SPIEGEL FROM BLACK STAR

On one leg of their return trip home from Vietnam, these veterans travel through Fort Lewis Army Base, Washington. Two flash the "peace" sign.

a "bad" war, its veterans could have gained from it nothing of value. As one veteran put it: "I know that in primitive tribes they used to put to death the guy who brought bad news, but you'd think we've progressed beyond that in the United States."

Besides feeling bitter because they are discussed in terms of pathology, many veterans resent the widespread assumption in the U.S. that this war has been fought by dropouts and losers. The educational background of the draftees and one-term enlistees in Vietnam is relatively higher than that of the veterans of Korea and World War II.

Failure of "the System"

Consistent evidence indicates many veterans believe that what they call "the system" is not operating as well or as fairly on behalf of Vietnam veterans as it did for earlier generations. One reason is that government programs concerned with veterans are designed and run by veterans of earlier wars. Some Vietnam veterans return from the Vietnam war with suspicions about U.S. leadership triggered by their own view of the war and a feeling of having been used. Their first contact with the government then is through the agencies charged with veterans' welfare; and the treatment they receive there has tended to harden their most negative stereotypes about the government's good intentions—whether the issue is civilian employment, GI bill educational benefits, hospitalization and medical service, or other matters.

A number of programs that fitted the needs and interests of the veterans of earlier wars are inadequate for the Vietnam veterans. An example is the GI bill program of educational benefits, which was used by more than 50% of the World War II veterans and about 45% of the Korean War veterans. In late 1970, about 20% of the Vietnam-era veterans were taking advantage of GI bill education

PAUL SEQUEIRA

This job fair had to close early. Dozens of men wrecked booths and displays at a job fair in Chicago. The veterans felt that the fair involved only a token effort; applications were being taken for jobs that did not exist.

and training benefits. The tight job market for veterans seems to be the sole reason that they have more recently been using the GI bill in rising numbers—more than 30% in 1972.

The problem is not merely that the GI bill provides less real dollar help today. Besides that, Vietnam veterans are showing less interest in higher education than the World War II veterans, despite, or maybe because of, the substantially higher average level of pre-service education among the younger group. There are ways in which Vietnam veterans want to try to prepare themselves for their future work that are outside the present framework of academic institutions and job training or apprenticeship. Here the fault lies less with the executive agencies dealing with veterans than with the U.S. Congress and the general public.

SPECIFIC ASPECTS OF THE PROBLEM

Employment is the largest single problem by far for veterans returning to civilian society. Vietnam veterans have been going home in a time of economic recession. At least a third of them have no civilian job experience—only their military training for a combat job with few or no corresponding civilian occupations. Even the veterans who have marketable skills in electronics, machinery repair, or medicine often discover that these fields are restricted by union quotas, low rates of employment, and requirements for academic degrees. Many employers, in fact, are doubtful about the motivation and qualifications of veterans.

The federal government's Jobs for Veterans program has been carried on throughout the U.S. primarily through the vehicle of job fairs. At these fairs, dozens or even hundreds of employers man booths in large arenas while thousands of veterans attempt to match up their skills and interests with what is usually an inadequate or almost nonexistent supply of jobs above entry level.

COURTESY, VETERANS ADMINISTRATION

Operating and servicing duplicating machines, this man is enrolled in a VA vocational rehabilitation program. More such programs are urgently needed.

Significant work roles for returning veterans constitute a paramount national priority. For those veterans who want to continue their education, the concept of "job splitting," in which two veterans are hired to assume responsibility for one significant full-time job, is particularly appropriate. The employer and society get better value for the money spent, and the veterans can resume work in "the world" while they earn money to supplement the GI bill stipend.

Veterans and Education

In general, veterans appear to be lukewarm toward higher education. Blacks and other minority group veterans are skeptical of the idea that higher education paves the way to social and economic benefits. This cynicism stems both from the conviction that discrimination restricts employment opportunities and from an acute awareness (often acquired or intensified in service) of the handicap presented by inferior early schooling.

To make the situation worse, colleges and universities are not welcoming veterans as they did after World War II, when it was the rule to give generous academic credit for training, experience, and maturity garnered in the service. College administrations competed to enroll veterans, to ensure that their stipend checks arrived on time, and to design academic programs to fit their needs. The Veterans Administration (VA) kept representatives on most campuses. Almost none of those conditions prevail now. In addition, some veterans hesitate to enroll or to re-enroll in college for fear of rejection by antiwar faculty or students.

At least 17% of those leaving military service have not completed a high school education or its equivalent. In view of that fact, a continuing estrangement between veterans and the educational community would damage not only the individuals involved but also society as a whole.

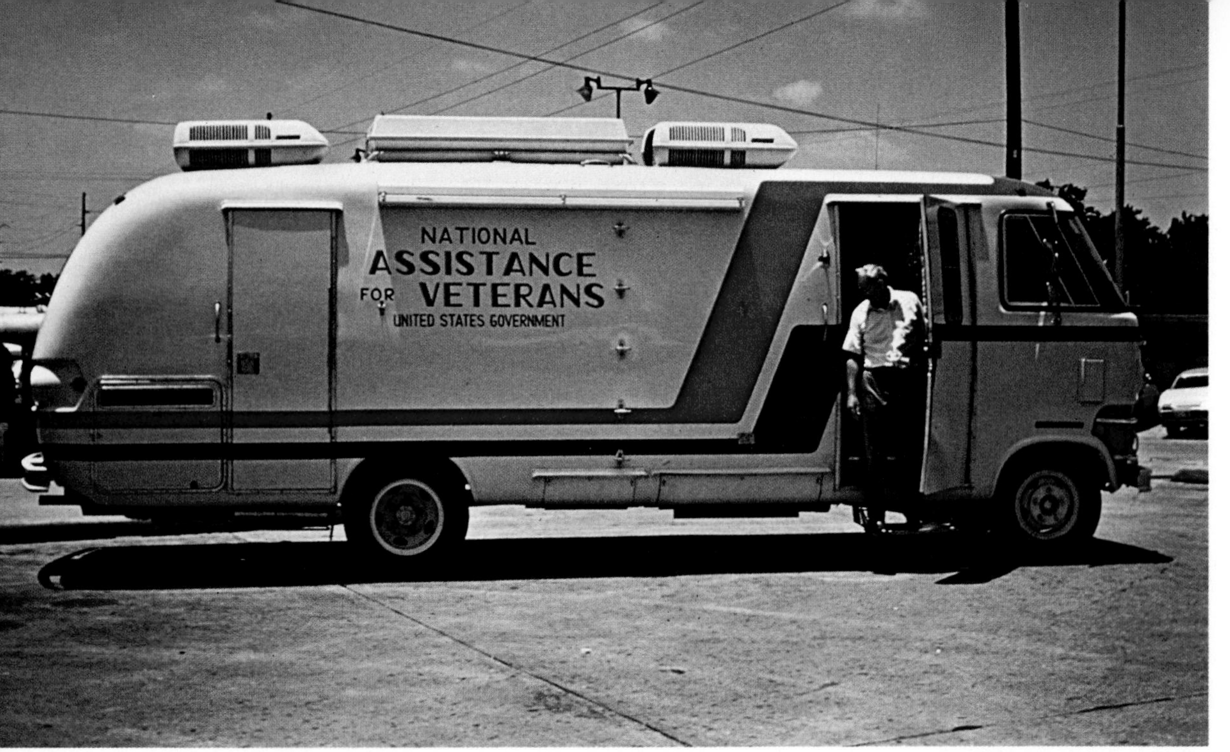

COURTESY, VETERANS ADMINISTRATION

In 1972 the VA inaugurated a system utilizing vans that move from town to town to reach veterans who find it difficult to travel to the 72 U.S. Veterans Assistance Centers scattered throughout the country.

If the Vietnam war has drawn disproportionately from the poor and minority groups, it has also been a "latebloomers'" war. A substantial percentage of returning veterans chose to interrupt their normal educational pattern in order to gain additional maturity and direction. Unless it reaches these individuals, higher education runs a risk of cutting itself off from a group that has uncommon personal resources. Like their nonveteran contemporaries, many veterans are not finding what they want and need either in higher education or in vocational education and training. Emphasis should be put on changing education to fit the veteran, not the other way around. Some veterans, for example, might want to spend two years preparing for a rewarding and dignified skilled or paraprofessional job, or for self-employment, and then return afterwards to a college or university for liberal or professional education.

A valuable U.S. investment might begin with recognition that the dissatisfaction of veterans with jobs as they are and with education and vocational training as they are represents an asset. We should remodel our programs relating to veterans and encourage their experimentation with patterns of work and education that might be of benefit to them now and to others in the future.

Drugs and Alcohol

Since the early 1960's, U.S. military personnel in Indochina have been heavy users of marijuana, or "grass," and alcohol. Generally there has been a split along generation lines, with the younger men—draftees, one-term enlistees, and junior officers—using marijuana and hashish, and the older commissioned and noncommissioned officers using alcohol. Among the Vietnamese there was traditionally almost no use of drugs except for a limited use of opium by the elderly. But Vietnamese marijuana came into relatively wide use by U.S. servicemen and to some degree by ARVN troops.

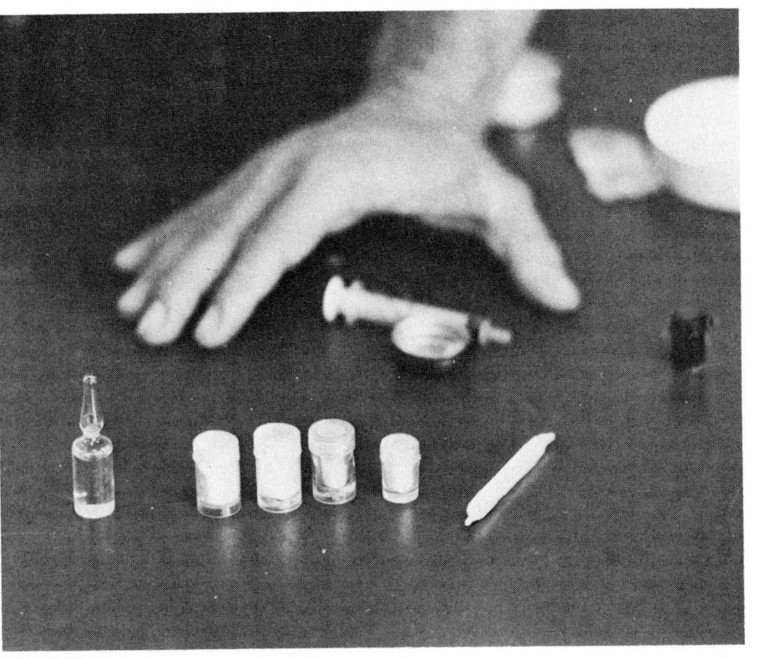

WIDE WORLD

Drug problems among GI's in Vietnam are grave. These drugs were photographed in Saigon; containers of heroin are in the foreground, next to a marijuana cigarette. A syringe to inject the heroin lies in the background.

A new factor was introduced in the late 1960's when undiluted heroin became widely available to U.S. personnel throughout Vietnam. Many Vietnam veterans are convinced that such heroin, generally refined from opium grown by hill tribes in Laos and Thailand, could not have been manufactured, distributed, and sold without the connivance of high ranking military and civilian officials, both South Vietnamese and to some extent U.S. The surge of heroin addiction among young U.S. military personnel in 1970–72 set off expressions of grave concern by governmental spokesmen and the media. Estimates were made that heroin addiction among returning veterans might run as high as 25%, but continued experience resulted in lowering the figure to about 5%.

If significant research were done on Vietnam veterans who became addicted overseas compared with the general addict population in the U.S., the study almost certainly would show a remarkably high motivation and ability on the part of the veterans to rid themselves of the habit. Toward the end of 1972, as the number of U.S. servicemen and the proportion of draftees among them dwindled sharply, use of hard drugs appeared to be dropping quickly as well. But alcoholism was becoming more prevalent among the young veterans.

The Black Veteran

When the national furor arose over drug addiction among the GI's in Vietnam, black veterans reacted with bitter amusement; they saw what had been a serious problem in their communities for two or three decades begin to get high-level attention only when a concentrated population of middle-class whites became addicted by the thousands. Many of these blacks had come from ghetto communities where drugs were a rampant plague. Some of the men had enlisted to get away from the drug-saturated environment.

COURTESY, VETERANS ADMINISTRATION

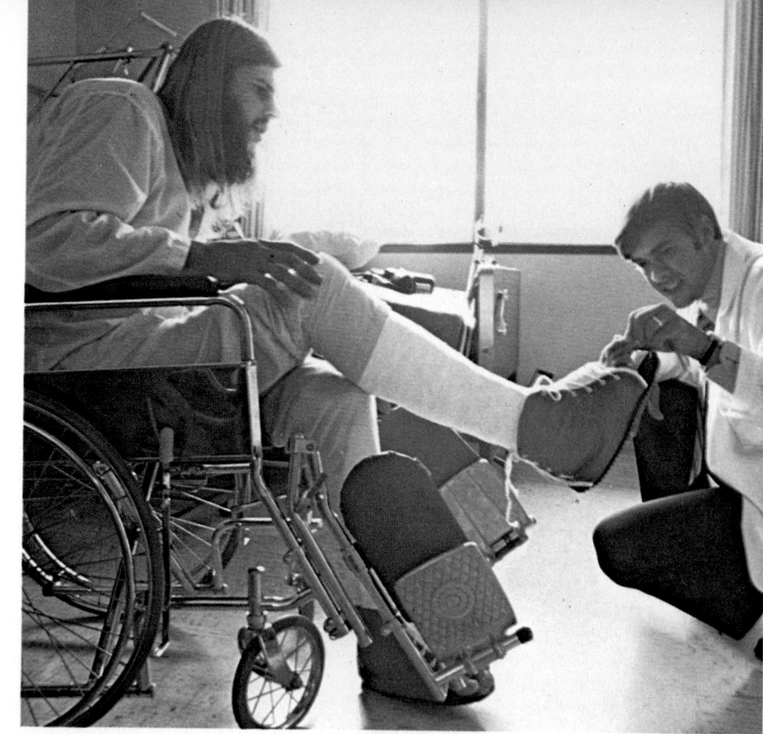

COURTESY, VETERANS ADMINISTRATION

Thousands upon thousands of young Americans were wounded, and many maimed, during the Vietnam war. A veteran who lost his hands (above) learns to use prosthetic devices. Another veteran (above, right) has his cast examined by an orthopedic surgeon.

Blacks and other nonwhites are represented in the U.S. armed forces out of proportion to their numbers in the national population. An obvious reason is the lack of money or quality education that would enable them to go to college and get student deferments. Another reason is the high unemployment rate among young men in black ghettos, which forces them to join the services or be drafted out of economic necessity. To some degree, another reason is the legacy of the 10 or 15 years after World War II when the military services, more effectively desegregated than civilian society, were viewed by many young blacks as the best way out of the conditions in which they grew up.

The black veterans returning now from the Vietnam war find conditions even worse than those met by veterans as a group. Having served their country under conditions of great hardship, they react to continuing discrimination with rage and resentment.

The Disabled Veteran

A higher percentage of veterans have been left with serious physical disabilities from combat wounds in the Vietnam war than in any earlier war. More GI's survived in Vietnam because fewer men are killed outright by an enemy who generally uses small-arms fire, grenades, and booby traps and because men were evacuated swiftly by helicopter to nearby field hospitals.

The mental health picture is in some respects even more disturbing. The rate of hospitalization for mental disorders while in active service is lower than in any war from World War I through Korea—partly because of combat psychiatry designed to speed a man's return to duty and partly because of the one-year limit on time served in Vietnam, coupled with rest and recreation trips away from Vietnam during the year. But the rate of hospitalization for mental illness after the veterans are back in civilian life is the highest in his-

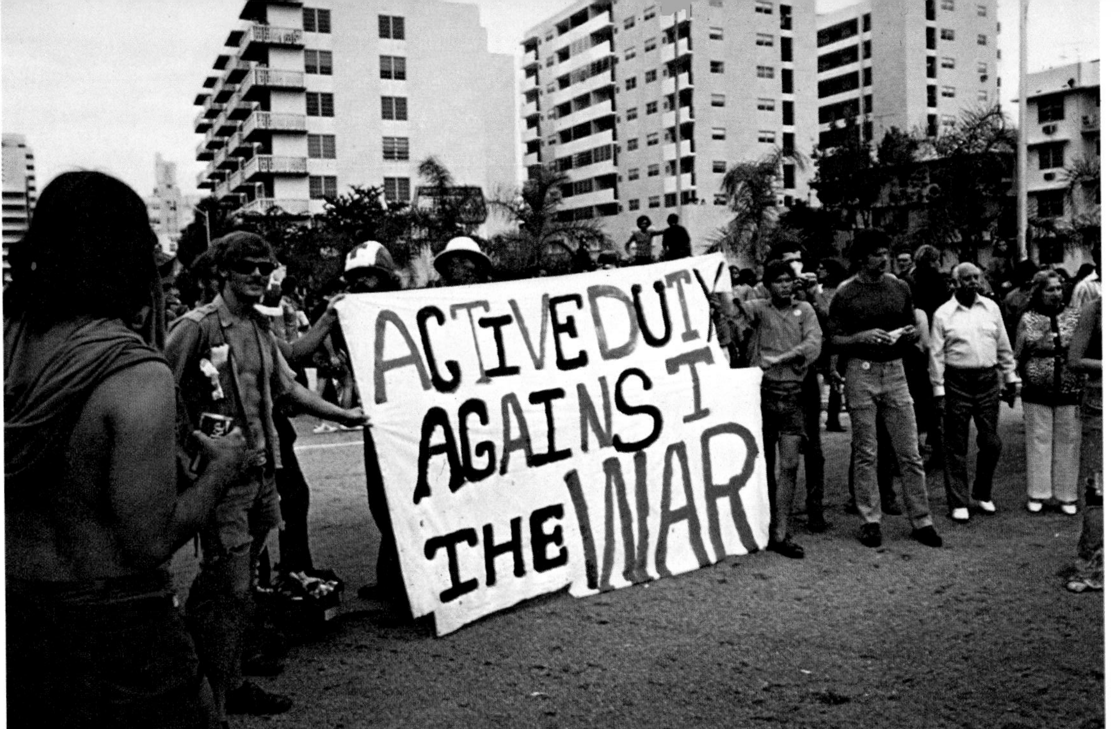

FIGARO

Holding a peace sign, active-duty soldiers demonstrate against the Indochina war at the Republican National Convention in Miami Beach, Fla., in August.

tory. To darken the picture even more, VA facilities have denied many veterans psychiatric help because they sought it too late for their illness to be classified as service-connected. The concept of service-connected disability should be greatly broadened.

Bad Paper

Another kind of disability under which tens of thousands of Vietnam veterans are laboring in civilian life is so-called bad paper, some form of less than honorable discharge meted out as punishment for a violation of regulations while in the service. A veteran with a less than honorable discharge is in a nearly hopeless position in a competitive job market. He is denied the right to GI bill educational and training benefits that could give him the chance to improve his earning capability and position in life.

There is increasing evidence that during the Vietnam war the military services used other than honorable discharges as a simple administrative method to handle offenses normally dealt with on the basis of summary punishment or courts-martial. A number of the offenses for which servicemen received bad paper discharges were the type widespread among GI's of the Vietnam era—using marijuana or engaging in antiwar or black power activities. In some cases, the serviceman's superior officers urged him to accept bad paper, claiming that once he was back in civilian life he could easily have his discharge converted to an honorable one. In fact, the process of appealing through the military review process in the Department of Defense is complex and time-consuming. In mid-1972 the rate of conversion of discharges to honorable was less than 3%.

PROPOSALS AND RECOMMENDATIONS

If Vietnam veterans are to make positive contributions to their society, that society must display compassion, wisdom, and imagina-

EB INC.

Antiwar marchers assemble for a May Day parade in New York City in 1935. The demand for "the bonus" on their banner refers to a pay bonus promised to World War I veterans by Congress, to be paid in 1945. A veterans' movement began in 1932, demanding immediate payment of the bonus. Thousands of veterans had marched on Washington, D.C., in 1932, but Congress had refused the early payment.

tion. In every community, discussion groups can examine civilian attitudes toward the war and how these may have colored the reactions to its veterans. Groups and organizations at a local level can help veterans work with each other in research and action programs in order to integrate into community life on their own terms and on their own timetables.

Several programs around the country provide possible models. One of these is based at Southern Illinois University at Edwardsville. In its first phase, known as the Veterans World Project, during 1971 and 1972, a group of about 60 Vietnam veterans designed and carried out a program of research, information gathering, and analysis that resulted in 'Wasted Men: The Reality of the Vietnam Veteran', a report that drew national attention for its unique contribution to understanding the current generation of veterans. More recently a group of veterans organized the Illinois Veterans Working Group to carry some of the insights and proposals of the Wasted Men report into action programs at the local and state levels.

At the national level, attention and action are needed in the Executive branch and in the Congress. Major executive agencies such as the VA, the Department of Defense, and the Department of Labor need substantial overhaul in the way they deal with veterans or with short-time servicemen soon to become veterans. They also need to increase radically the percentage of Vietnam veterans on their staffs and in their planning. To simplify the tangle of laws, legal authorizations, and restrictions under which the agencies now operate, action is required of the Congress.

The GI bill of World War II and afterwards was a tremendous success (though it is now almost irrelevant to the needs and aspirations of Vietnam veterans); but when it was being proposed and passed into law, the bill was regarded as a tremendous gamble. We have not gambled since, and the result is stagnation.

RICHARD BALAGUR FROM NANCY PALMER AGENCY

Military medals and decorations were thrown away by veterans in a war protest in front of the Capitol in Washington, D.C., on April 24, 1972.

The period from 1918 to 1945 added up to 27 years, a full chronological generation and more; and the U.S. moved a light-year to the GI bill of World War II from the veteran's bonus of World War I (paid in three or more installments, as Congressmen advocated in public debate, so that veterans could not "drink it up all at once"). The time from 1945 to 1972 was another period of 27 years—a time of more profound changes than ever there were in any comparable period of U.S. history. Is it not possible that we need to stretch our imagination beyond the GI bill of World War II in order to perceive what *this* generation of veterans really needs?

The 52–20 program of unemployment benefits for veterans after World War II ($20 weekly for 52 weeks) barely survived an acrimonious national debate in which major leaders charged that the plan would turn the GI's into a generation of loafers. More than 9 million veterans used the benefits to carry out their readjustment, and less than 10% used the entire 52 weeks of benefits. Today we need to make an equally venturesome investment in helping veterans carry out the more difficult readjustment to a fast-changing society that is unsure of its own directions and values. If this is not done, it is probable that thousands of men who might have become self-directing and productive will fill the nation's mental hospitals, drug abuse centers, and prisons for decades. The human tragedy and social damage will be intolerable.

A second-generation GI bill must be developed with the participation of the Vietnam veterans themselves at the policy and operating levels. The focus should not be on expanding the service agencies and bureaucracies that now exist. They should be transformed into channels for helping veterans operate in ways that they themselves find most effective, with the greatest possible flexibility and initiative at local levels. This course will result in sound and imaginative new policies and programs in record time.

A member of Vietnam Veterans Against the War works for the war's end.

MICHAEL ABRAMSON FROM BLACK STAR

part III

THE QUESTION OF AMNESTY

by Senator Hubert H. Humphrey

Former Vice-President of the United States

Hubert H. Humphrey

A long career in public service reached its apogee for Senator Humphrey when he was U.S. vice-president, 1965–69, and Democratic presidential candidate in 1968. He was born in Wallace, S.D., on May 27, 1911. After teaching political science, he was mayor of Minneapolis, Minn., 1945–49, and senator from Minnesota, 1949–64 and 1971–.

Amnesty is the act of pardoning individuals for their violation of the law. Governments have most often used amnesty declarations to forgive individuals who rebelled against the law because of internal conflicts or foreign wars. Amnesty has also been used to restore order, compliance with the law, and national unity. It can be an act of compassion toward the young, or a mistreated segment of society.

Thomas Jefferson called amnesty an act of "restoring to social intercourse that affection without which liberty and even life itself are but dreary things." This attitude reflects the strong theme in Western civilization that administering the law with compassion and mercy maintains strength and a sense of renewal.

The use of amnesty is as old as the use of law. One of the earliest recorded declarations of amnesty came in the 5th century B.C. and, thereafter, became an accepted principle in Roman law. Thrasybulus, an Athenian general, in 403 B.C. forbade punishment of Athenian citizens for their past political acts.

In 1598, Henry IV of France issued the famous Edict of Nantes, which "forgave" the French Protestants (Huguenots) for their heresy and brought an end to the government's policy of encouraging persecution of them. Just as there have been numerous examples of amnesty declared by a government, so have there been an equally significant number of cases where amnesty has been regulated by treaty among several nations. For example, the Congress of Vienna at its closing session in 1815 extended amnesty to Poles and Swedes.

In U.S. history amnesty in one form or another has been granted after a number of major conflicts in which the U.S. has been engaged. George Washington declared the first presidential amnesty, in pardoning participants in the 1794 Whisky Rebellion.

At the outbreak of the American Civil War, President Abraham Lincoln extended pardons to many political prisoners and others held in military custody. In 1862 Congress passed the Confiscation Law authorizing the president to extend pardon and amnesty to persons who had joined the Confederacy. Lincoln's amnesty proclamation of Dec. 8, 1863, insisted political criminals were expected to "resume their allegiance to the United States. . . ."

Amnesty proclamations made in the U.S. in the 20th century have been relatively insignificant because they are so few in number, far fewer than during and just after the Civil War. Even so, a variety of pardons were granted up through the Administrations of Presidents Franklin D. Roosevelt and Harry S. Truman.

On Dec. 23, 1946, President Truman established by executive order an Amnesty Board to review a total of 15,805 cases of those persons who had evaded or otherwise violated the Selective Service Acts during World War II. The following year President Truman, on the recommendations of the board, pardoned 1,523 persons out of the total.

Historical parallels have been drawn between the current debate under way in the U.S. and the kind of divisiveness that characterized the period of the Civil War. But if history is to be our guide, the Vietnam war could be more accurately compared to the Korean War and to the two world wars than to the Civil War. Vietnam, however, is different from these earlier wars. Vietnam has been an undeclared war, which over time has lost the support of the majority of people in the U.S.

The U.S. Supreme Court loosened the definition of a conscientious objector during the Vietnam war. Conscientious objectors, as a result of the U.S. Supreme Court decisions in Seeger *vs.* U.S. and Welsh *vs.* U.S., can reject the draft and accept alternative service on the grounds of a sincere nonreligious belief, whereas earlier decisions required proof of religious belief in opposition to war in general. The U.S. Congress has repealed the 1964 Gulf of Tonkin Resolution, which was Congress' official approval of large-scale U.S. involvement in the war. Since that time, Congress has passed a resolution making it clear that U.S. policy should be aimed at ending military involvement in Vietnam.

PHOTOREPORTERS

A U.S. deserter speaks at a rally in Stockholm, Sweden. A number of deserters were known to be in Sweden.

Against this backdrop of changing attitudes and laws, U.S. policy makers must face the issue of amnesty squarely. The country is worthy of a fully reasoned national debate on this important question. A considerable number of youths will be affected by any decision. It is estimated that the number of deserters and draft evaders may be 70,000.

We must balance our compassion for the expatriate with our concern for the hundreds of thousands who obeyed the law at great personal sacrifice to themselves and their families. Nearly 50,000 U.S. servicemen have been killed and more than 303,000 wounded in that war from 1954 to 1972. More than 500 gave up years of their lives as prisoners of war, and more than 1,150 were missing and unaccounted for as of November 1972. Amnesty must be considered within the context of reunifying the U.S. and bringing families together again.

I favor an amnesty program with the requirement of civilian service along the lines of the obligations of those who have the status of conscientious objector.

I favor the immediate creation of a National Commission on Repatriation to present the Congress and the president with recommendations for planning and implementing an amnesty program.

Who should serve on this commission? Students, professors, legislators, judges, veterans, and working men and women—all are vitally concerned with the fate of those abroad, and all should be represented on the commission by presidential nomination and Congressional approval. Perhaps the most crucial assignment for the National Commission will be to determine who shall be eligible for the program.

What should a program of repatriation and civilian service include? The men who want to return to U.S. society under such a program should demonstrate a willingness to serve their country. This service should include provisions for alternate service for those returning: a two-year commitment equivalent to the draft. I would envisage many possibilities: work in mental hospitals, paramedical assistantships and other vocations in the health field, inner-city and rural area service projects, and conservation work are just a few possibilities.

In this manner, the repatriated men can both contribute to the welfare of the country and demonstrate their seriousness about returning. These are not just menial tasks. They are jobs and work that need to be done.

Repatriation and conditional amnesty should not be viewed as a policy of weakness or as an attempt to undermine the law or patriotism within a country. On the contrary, they should be viewed as means of strengthening the law and instilling a new sense of patriotism in the country. A comprehensive, qualified program of repatriation and service can help recreate a national spirit of cooperation.

Enriching the Quality of Life

BY HUGH DOWNS

Television Personality and Cochairman of the Citizens' Committee on Population and the American Future

Hugh Downs

After a long career as announcer and host of radio and television programs, Mr. Downs left broadcasting in 1971 and turned his attention to the environment. He was born on Feb. 14, 1921, at Akron, Ohio. He attended Bluffton College in Ohio, Wayne State University in Detroit, Mich., and Columbia University. He lives in Carefree, Ariz., with his wife, Ruth.

Future civilizations—and despite the doomsayers there is a chance that there will be future civilizations—surely will have come to believe that *human* resources deserve consideration beyond all other concepts of resource. That consideration will mean guarantees for individuals in heritage, health, justice, and education. It will mean forging, through cooperation and hard work, the tools to realize what has been all along the dream of civilized men.

If poison ivy were growing all around us, we would have a problem; but I don't think any of us would believe we could solve the problem by passing laws against scratching. Yet much of our effort to deal with our deepest problems today is almost as pathetically short-range.

We have been talking a lot lately about quality of life. This means that in some sense we have formed a concept of quality of life. The concept may be as hazy as a concept of love. Love is notoriously difficult to define with the kind of accuracy demanded by those who seek to pin it down and to quantify something that is itself a quality. Experts in any scientific discipline tend to panic when asked to investigate or deal with love. But almost everyone knows that love is a reality—more of a reality than some scientific propositions that have been accepted and "proved," and then disproved, such as a flat world.

In the same way, quality of life is difficult to deal with; but we know there is something under that name that we can believe in. We further know that there are conditions, methods, and circumstances that can affect quality of life—things we can deal with in logical ways to effect changes in that quality.

Happiness is a root concept that helps define quality of life, and happiness requires a mixture of hope, fulfillment, growth, and joyousness in an individual's existence. We can take as axiomatic that the opposites of these elements—despair, frustration, stunting, and misery—are sure to prevent any meaningful quality of life in a given individual. We further believe that individuals and organiza-

MARVIN KONER FROM PHOTO RESEARCHERS

RAIMONDO BOREO FROM PHOTO RESEARCHERS

A fast-paced society can generate tensions and feelings of inadequacy in many people. The idea of quality of life encompasses emotional, as well as physical, well-being for everyone.

tions can take certain actions and follow certain methods that will improve the quality of life for someone or everyone, particularly those yet to be born. Intelligent approaches will guide us to those actions and methods. The quality of life simply cannot be left to chance.

How do we quantify happiness? I have seen cheerful hospital patients, convalescent and full of hope, regarding themselves as happy (and there is no other criterion); and I have seen affluent hypochondriacs, bitter and complaining. The sources of this happiness or unhappiness reach far back into the early lives and backgrounds of these individuals. Over the years philosophers, sociologists, religious leaders, anthropologists, and psychiatrists have wrestled with the problem, and they can be certain only that it is very complex. Lately with the aid of computers we have been able to glimpse how much more complex the problems of humanity are than we had ever imagined.

Computers have thus far shown us how much we need extension of human thought processes—the very kind of extension the computers themselves provide. The question arises: is this self-serving on the part of the computers? Will they generate more problems than they solve?

A more hopeful view is justified if we base it on history; life is tenacious and it moves upward. In early times, biological specialization evolved, and life struggled to higher levels of consciousness. Since man appeared on the scene, whenever deep needs and problems have arisen, the means to fill them and cope with them have somehow arisen simultaneously, or at least in time to prevent complete unraveling. The appearance of the computer and technology in general is an answer to a need.

The world seems to increase in complexity. This is because our knowledge about it and ourselves as part of it becomes increasingly complicated. Our attempts to pick out general truths and rules are outstripped by accelerating change and the fast breeding of speciali-

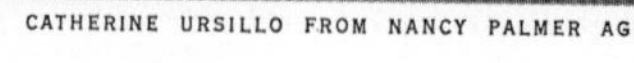

CATHERINE URSILLO FROM NANCY PALMER AGENCY

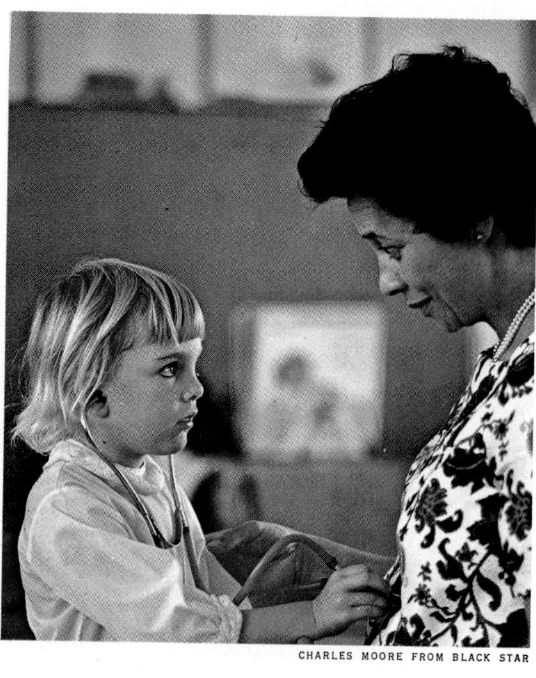

CHARLES MOORE FROM BLACK STAR

Quality of life must begin with the health of the mother, whose body nourishes the unborn child. A little girl listens in awe (above, right) to the heartbeat of a fetus. Parental love is of course crucial for every child, as is a life free from poverty or discrimination. One mother provides a secure home for her family (above) despite poverty.

zations. And so words such as *interdisciplinary* and *synergistic* come into more frequent use because we are realizing that there is an interdependence of human issues, a sort of ecology of human problems. They are so intricately interwoven and symbiotic that it is impossible to work on each problem in total isolation from the others, just as it would be impossible to remove a man's damaged liver and take it to a hospital for repair while the man stayed in a bar drinking.

Part of the ineffectiveness of a piecemeal approach to a large and intricate problem lies in the sense of futility that almost invariably accompanies partial remedy. One's work may be a small part of a large project, but morale requires an understanding of the way that the work fits into ongoing work from other directions to advance a larger goal.

Medical people know that even if they could give perfect health to everyone on earth right now, conditions of injustice, ignorance, and degraded environment would quickly erode that health. Similarly, environmentalists are coming to realize that if they could by magic clean the world's air and water this instant it would not stay that way without political, social, and cultural changes in man.

Requisites for Quality in Living

There are no piecemeal solutions to any of these problems. There are, in fact, no piecemeal problems. There is one overall problem: how to ensure the survival of man through stabilization (of his numbers and ecological life-support systems) and enhance the quality of his life. That quality of life cannot be conferred on some and withheld from others or it will not have the vitality to survive.

So the concept of quality of life is more like an organism than a machine. The parts of a machine can be isolated and tested, repaired, and perfected, but the components of a quality of human

ARNOLD HINTON FROM NANCY PALMER AGENCY

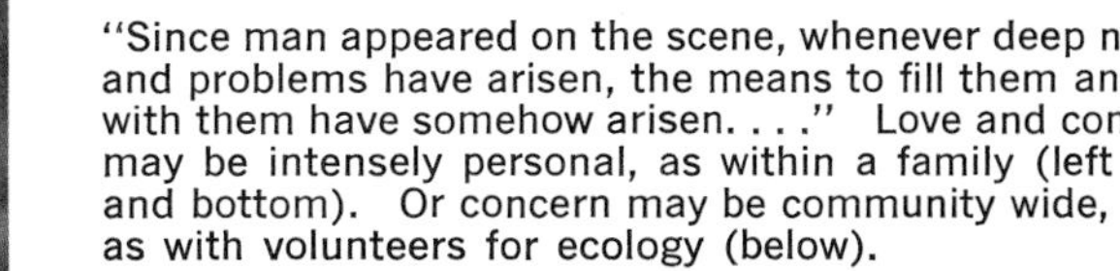

"Since man appeared on the scene, whenever deep needs and problems have arisen, the means to fill them and cope with them have somehow arisen. . . ." Love and concern may be intensely personal, as within a family (left and bottom). Or concern may be community wide, as with volunteers for ecology (below).

TOM MC HUGH FROM PHOTO RESEARCHERS

life can function only within the framework of the total concept.

For quality in living one needs:

1. A degree of comfort with his physiological machinery and in his relations with other people, institutions, and general surroundings.

2. Belief that one is loved and to a certain extent respected. Self-respect is necessary first, as a foundation.

3. Challenges that produce reasonable goals, faith in one's ability to reach them, and an abiding hope of accomplishing those goals.

4. Enough material possessions or income to provide all necessities, among which is a modicum of luxury. Let's be careful how we define necessities. Oxygen is a necessity. Fresh water is a necessity. Some kind of adequate balanced food supply, clothing for warmth, and shelter space are necessities. Parental love and a place in a community are necessities. Luxuries are relative—an ice-cream cone or a book of poetry is a luxury, the same as a stable of thoroughbreds or a yacht; but some feeling of luxury, or a feeling of the right to it, is essential to a life that is to have quality. There have been lives of quality that had and needed no luxury, but a degree of maturity was entailed that cannot be achieved universally by any method yet developed in human society; so we have to provide as a guarantee a feeling of the right to some degree of luxury.

5. A sense of freedom from dependency. One may depend on others—in a complex society we must depend on others—but the sense of freedom from dependency we speak of here involves participating in the decision-making apparatus of social interdependence. And this must be present for a good life.

6. Ability to conform selectively—a sense of making our own decisions about when to conform and when to exert strength to change a situation.

DOUGLAS KIRKLAND

"Civilization doesn't need to find new goals." Man has built communities that enhance the quality of life for some; needed are commitment and effort to provide humane surroundings for everyone. A tenement (right) and a hotel specializing in welfare recipients (bottom) stand in sad contrast to a planned "new town" (below).

LYN K. DANIELS FROM PHOTO RESEARCHERS

VICTOR ENGLEBERT FROM PHOTO RESEARCHERS

GERVAL FROM NANCY PALMER AGENCY

To the Roots of the Problem

A belief that blighting of human lives can be prevented is reasonable. An approach emphasizing the foundation years is indicated. Efforts to remedy, to alleviate suffering, to provide custodial care for the heavily blighted should continue, of course. Such efforts deserve our praise and support, but we will never overtake the real problem of blight by any amount of remedial activity. Only by identifying conditions and events that affect life, by inaugurating actions far enough in advance of the advent of individual life, and by securing the broadest possible cooperation among sectors and groups will we begin to push back the tide of suffering and waste. And a considerable by-product of success in this effort is the enormous amount of money to be saved in corrective health care, institutional care, compensatory training, special rehabilitative services, and crime control.

Quality of life must begin with health; and this involves the health of one's parents, particularly the mother, whose body provides the building materials for the first three quarters of a year after conception. If the mother is too young, or malnourished, or infected with transmissible disease, or drug addicted, the risks are high that prematurity, retardation, congenital infection, or other damage will cut down drastically the quality of one's life—no matter what subsequent opportunities of education and environment present themselves.

Quality of the homelife in early years is next. There is risk again if one arrives in this world undamaged and healthy but lacks the supportive surroundings of parental love and guidance and the opportunity to grow and develop autonomy, or if one suffers the bitterness of racial discrimination or grinding poverty (or both), or if the physical surroundings are dirty and dangerous.

COURTESY, COMMUNITY RESOURCES INSTITUTE, CITY UNIVERSITY OF NEW YORK

BURK UZZLE FROM MAGNUM

"The school environment is the one in which we can forge our first formal habits of thought and our first techniques for educating ourselves. . . ."

If the quality of education available is poor—if one is made to feel alien and inferior because of poor teachers and outmoded concepts of schooling and irrelevant classroom material—life will likely always be a little uphill, no matter how fortunate circumstances might be otherwise.

If all these hurdles are cleared and adolescence is reached without too many scars, but peer-group goals are bad and natural feelings of rebellion do not have constructive outlets, there is still risk—risk that any real quality living will always remain just out of reach.

Environments of the Human Condition

So we see that there are a number of environments through and into which a human passes in the process of becoming an adult, and each of these must meet certain standards to maximize the chances for quality of life. Some of them overlap, but in sequence they are the intrauterine environment, the home environment, the school environment, the social and political environment, and the physical environment.

Our bodily health and mental efficiency are highly dependent on the intrauterine environment, the first one we exist in. Is the mother's body balanced, mature, healthy, sufficient in the chemicals of which we are to be built and free of chemicals and diseases that will harm us?

In the home environment we will acquire the emotional balance and nutriments of love and support that foster the growth of a sense of security and the capacity to love—ourselves and others. Does the home have a father? Does the mother have the maturity to know what to do and how to care, the economic security to spend time with the child? Is a sense of identity available to the child through the model of a happy home?

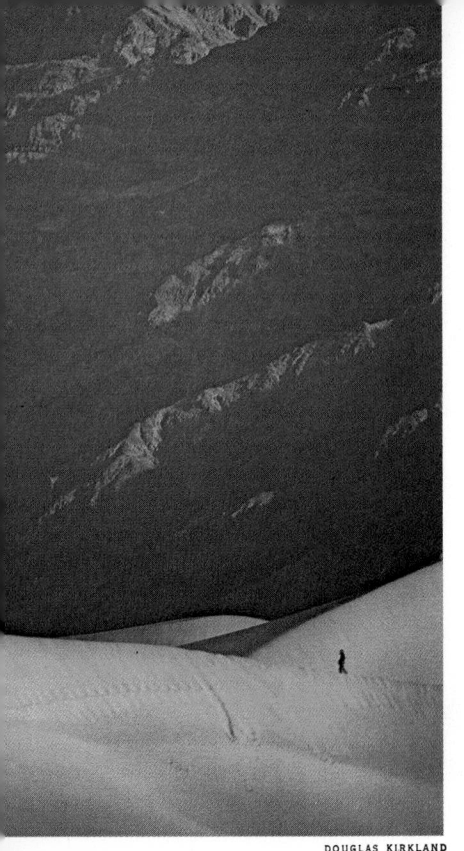

DOUGLAS KIRKLAND

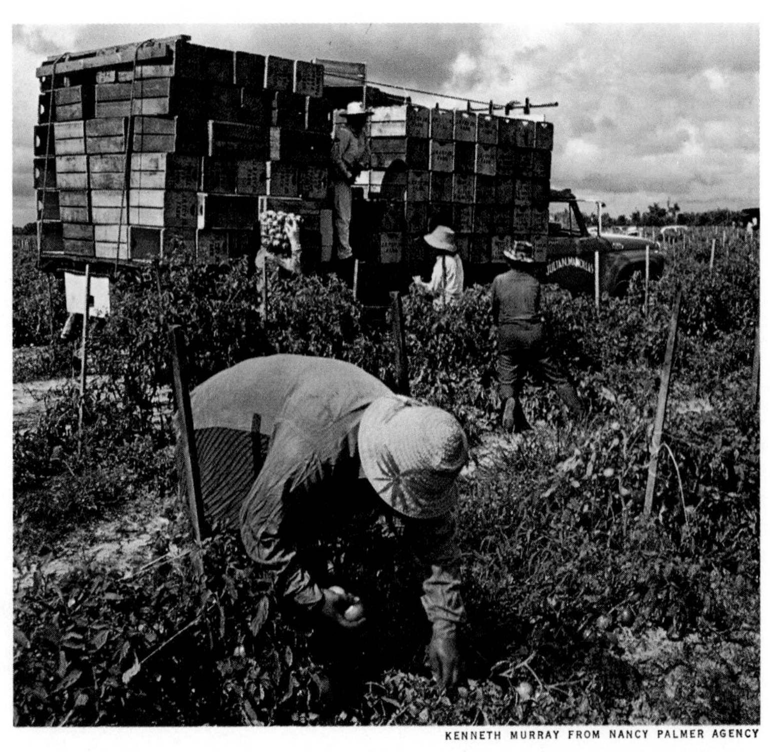

KENNETH MURRAY FROM NANCY PALMER AGENCY

The school environment is the one in which we can forge our first formal habits of thought and our first techniques for educating ourselves through reading and learning the thoughts of others besides our parents and friends. Is the curriculum relevant? Does the school fit our background? We cannot be expected to fit the school's background. The school must be the flexible party, but often it is completely rigid.

Meanwhile we have also been immersed unavoidably in the sociopolitical and physical environments, and we will remain in these. In the first of these we are to experience and form our attitudes toward justice, freedom, and personal safety. If our larger society is oppressive, we will feel oppressed, both through sensing our parents' feelings on the matter and through direct, personal experience. If our government fails to deliver on guarantees of freedom and a single standard of justice for the rich and the poor, we will come to believe that as citizens we do not count. We will understandably feel bitter at being deprived of something basic to a good life, and we will understandably feel insecure.

The physical environment—the air we breathe, the water we drink, the food we ingest, and the temperatures we change or endure—is certainly a factor in the quality of our living. And in this environment there is a little less injustice than in some of the others. For example, DDT accumulates in the livers of rich and poor alike, and an increase in the background count of radiation will not single out one race to harm. As important as this environment is, I list it last because how we deal with it collectively will be determined largely by how safely we have come through the hazards of the other environments—particularly the earliest. As adults we can do something about our own air and food sources and our own

DENNIS BRACK FROM BLACK STAR

WOLF VON DEM BUSSCHE FROM PHOTO RESEARCHERS

government. As embryos, we can do nothing about our mothers' eating or drug habits; but we can do something about the fate of oncoming generations in these early environments—by enhancing conditions of nutrition, education, and justice for their parents.

"Meaningful, interesting jobs and possible nonmaterial rewards are a must for any community that pretends to support individual happiness."

The Need for Commitment

All of these requisites merely describe a frame of conditions within which some quality of life is possible. They deliver no guarantee of quality. Some sort of extra ingredient would seem to be necessary for such a guarantee. It may be that no assurance is possible. Attempts to "guarantee" or "deliver" may in themselves be inimical to such an elusive thing as quality of living. They may be self-defeating because of the very nature of that quality. So when a mass technological-industrial-business complex powered by merchandising-promotion provides what it says we ought to have for a quality of life, it may be doomed to fail in that goal—even if a compassionate society and its conscientious government take steps to smooth out uneven distribution of the goods.

When we consider carefully what we really want in life, we begin to realize that motivation, commitment, effort, and attainment are involved. None of these can be handed to us. If we need exercise for muscle tone, it does no good to have our limbs moved about through some therapeutic technique passively accepted. If we need to climb a hill, the need is in the climbing, not in the arriving at the top; so to ride in the ski lift would be worse than useless. It would also show that we had not understood the real nature of the need.

Here one aspect of the discredited Protestant ethic appears to be of value. It deserves to be scorned to the extent that the ethic has eroded empathy and has led to such cruel cultural values as the idea

EARL HOKENS FROM VJK

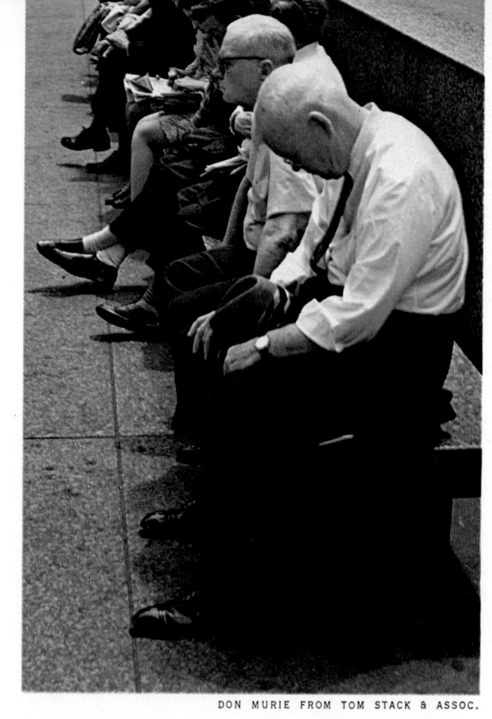

DON MURIE FROM TOM STACK & ASSOC.

"The community must contrive to provide social security for its members." Loneliness and poverty are persistent problems for many older people.

that poverty is a crime. The foundation on which it rested, however, remains a proper site for building useful cultural attitudes: *no lasting happiness is accessible to humans without commitment and effort.* Where this concept went astray was in exaggerating the idea of deferred reward to the point that work became drudgery and earthly life a kind of purgatory through which we were to slog unhappily, in order to enjoy a vaguely defined eternity in another world. Reaction to this idea tends to result in the creation of life-styles that deny the importance of commitment and effort. But commitment and effort will not be denied.

The real nature of our desire is worth examining. When we prescribe the specifics that we think will fulfill that desire, we may be wrong. Our efforts may lead us away from what we want instead of toward it.

Working Toward the Ideal

We reacted strongly to the fierce Puritan idea that in order to enjoy an eternity following life on earth, we dare not enjoy anything now. Our reaction led us to the opposite conclusion that we should avoid any and all work that is not immediately gratifying—that we should "have fun." Fun and pleasure are, however, only by-products of effort and commitment; when conceived as ends in themselves, they are *not* themselves. Pleasure pursued is pleasure destroyed. Fun is no fun by itself. Idle play as a goal unmasks itself as boredom.

Education, the media, government—each has a proper role in shaping cultural set. "Find pleasure in your work, or you will not find pleasure," someone said. Meaningful, interesting jobs with proper material compensation and possible nonmaterial rewards are a must for any community that pretends to support individual happiness. Such a community must contrive to provide some social security for its members while minimizing any flavor of make-work. This security can encourage self-motivation by being built around community or national goals that we already have. Civilization

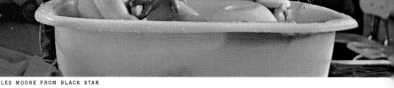

DOUGLAS KIRKLAND

CHARLES MOORE FROM BLACK STAR

Positive steps must be taken to enrich the quality of life for *all* children everywhere.

doesn't need to find new goals. It needs only to transfer from the realm of lip service to reality its already sublime ideals: equality of opportunity, genuine justice, and clear concepts of human rights and responsibilities. Bringing these about requires hard work.

A regime or administration that understands and encourages the realization of these ideals is helping civilization to grow. A regime or administration that fails to understand or serves interests too narrow or special (for purposes of self-perpetuation) undermines civilization. Through education and the increased public awareness resulting from media expansion, we find more and more people able to dedicate themselves to these established ideals, promoting them within the systems that encourage them and working to change the systems that ignore them. There is no lack of challenge or opportunity here, but the foundations must be solid and extended under every human being. A blighted life cannot divert enough energy from coping to work for any aspect of a common good and find the quality of life such work provides.

A Reasonable Petition

So we must start at the beginning, and this is before a human is born. We must be guided by what an unborn human might reasonably ask for himself and his future if he could:

"Whoever my mother is, I want her body to be a fit factory for the building of my own. I want her mind to be free of oppression and able to want me and to care for me, and to love me as I will one day come to love her.

"Whatever race I am born to, for the sake of all races, I want my home to be secure enough that no feeling of hopelessness or myth of inferiority will be passed on to me.

"Whatever schooling is available to me, I want the chance to learn what I will need to learn in order to grow.

"Under whatever kind of government I am born, I want equal justice under which I will forge my own freedom."

Arts of Black America

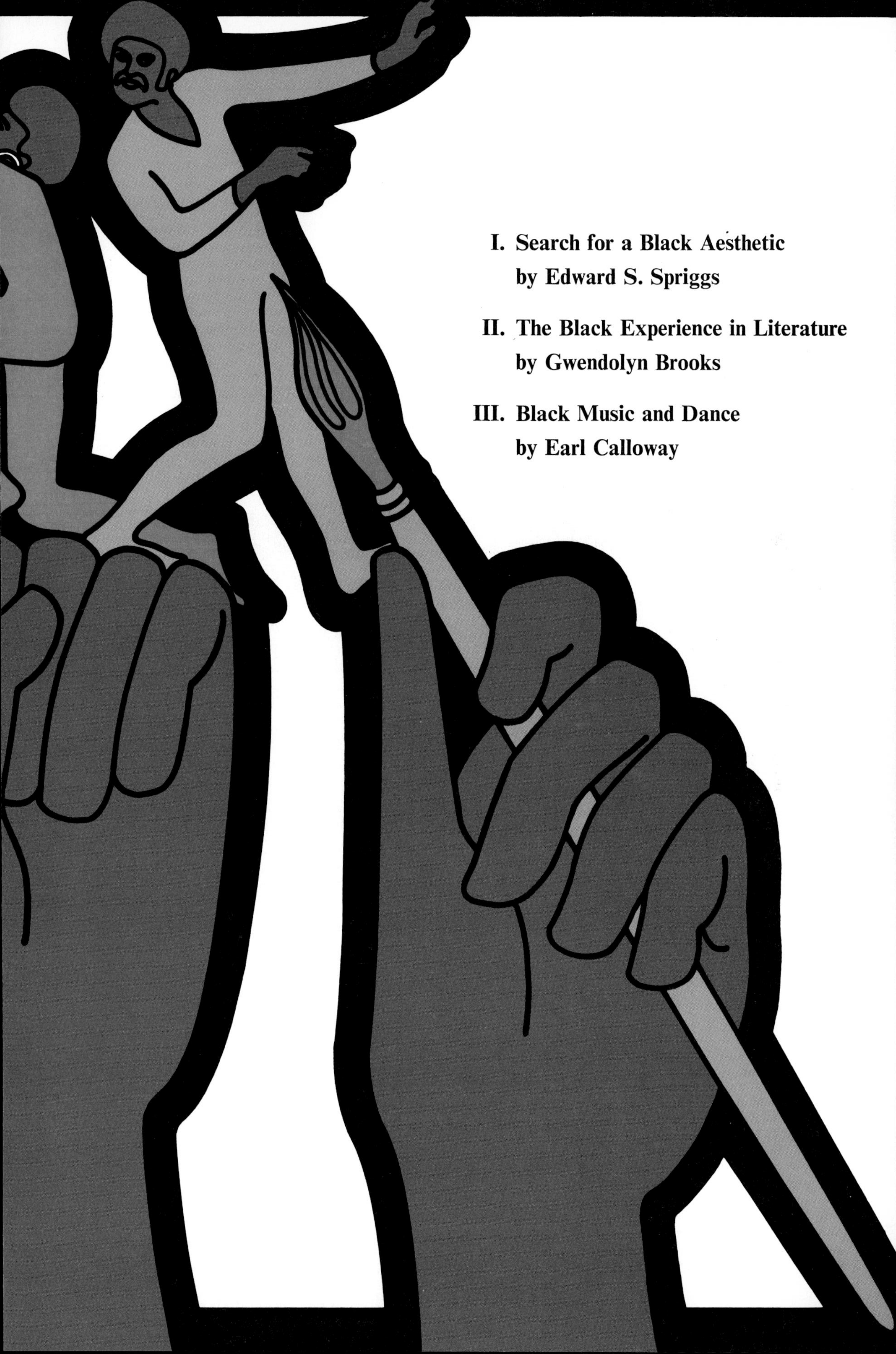

part I

SEARCH FOR A BLACK AESTHETIC

by
Edward S. Spriggs

Executive Director,
The Studio
Museum in Harlem

Edward S. Spriggs

The Studio Museum in Harlem, where Edward S. Spriggs serves as executive director, is a vital center of New York City's black artistic community. Mr. Spriggs is deeply committed to the black arts movement and to the concept of a "black aesthetic." In this very personal essay, he shares some of his feelings about what it means to be black and an artist in today's society.

> After achieving what is today recognized as great art and a tradition of great art in Africa, the Negro artist in America had to make another start from scratch, and has not yet completely recaptured his ancestral gifts or recovered his ancient skills.
>
> Alain Locke, 1936

Some black artists in the 1970's are stepping out from the shadow of the slave ships, out from the shadow of the plantations, out from the shadow of the cultural imperialism of the international art marketplaces. As the sun sets on these social and political chapters of the history of the African in the Americas, some Afro-American artists are marching out of those shadows to control the moon of their life. Since 1619 this movement, this progression toward self-determination, has been both an internal and an external one. It has been both political and cultural. The black experience on these shores encompasses both positive and negative experiences. It has been a historically tragic saga that includes the physical and psychical abuses suffered here. It is also a saga that includes the strengths, renewals, celebrations that have evolved from the struggle and pain of past and present.

The fact of this reality, this black experience, is central to all honest discussions about any aspect of black life and culture in the Americas. As much as it disturbs many Americans, white and black, no sincere observations or projections about our affairs can be broached without acknowledging the fact of the slave and postslave life of the black man under European domination.

The subject of this article is neither the question of the European's guilt nor the protest that characterizes much of what we call black art. My theme is the emerging concept of black creations and values that motivate the black artists of the 1970's. However,

COMMUNITY MURAL PROJECT, PHOTO BY JOHN WEBER

'Wall of Truth' (detail), William Walker (1969)

in order to fully appreciate how the seemingly new attitudes have evolved, one must (and I emphasize it again) keep in mind both the social and the political relationships that blacks have had here in the West. For it is these relationships that have in part shaped the ideas and motivations of the contemporary black artist.

The Artist as Activist

Because so much is going on by way of the creative outpouring from black communities all over the United States, there is considerable confusion concerning what it is all about, how to talk about it, and what it means. The visual arts in black communities are taking on meanings and functions other than those that normally obtain in other communities. Furthermore, many young black artists are projecting their art in a fundamentally different way even from that of black artists of earlier periods.

The black artists who have come to maturity during the 1950's and 1960's are social activists, community-oriented people. They are political. They are committed to putting their talents and energies to the service of the black community. Witness the large outdoor murals that are being created in metropolitan areas such as Boston, Mass.; Chicago; St. Louis, Mo.; San Francisco; New York City; and elsewhere. Many of these projects were initiated by the artists themselves. The paintings just appeared suddenly, without sanction from landlords or any kind of outside-the-community approval. (Some of them, of course, have been commissioned and approved.) Witness too the storefront galleries, community or neighborhood museums, artists' cooperatives and workshops that are springing up in most large ghetto areas. Even the artist himself has taken to the streets to disseminate his creations at prices that attract community residents. For some of these artists the streets have become both studio and gallery.

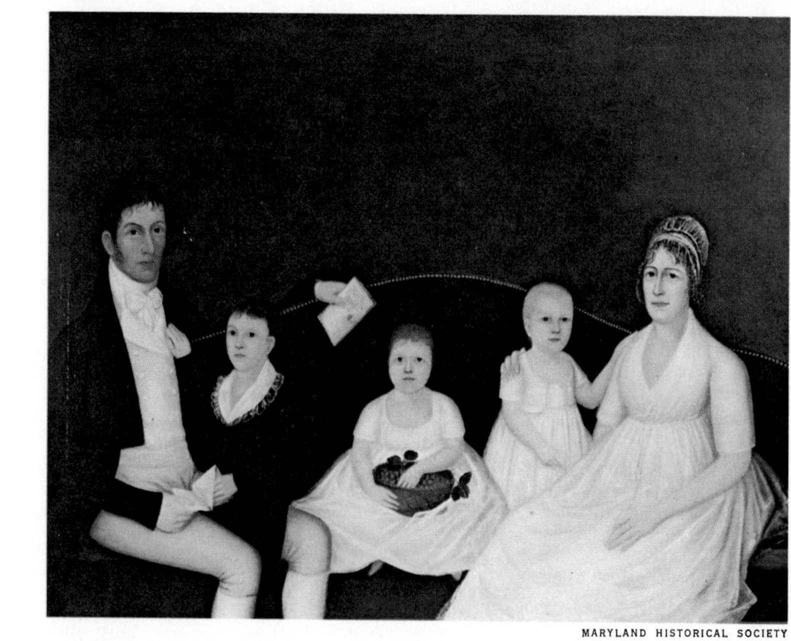

'James McCormick Family', Joshua Johnston (1805)

MARYLAND HISTORICAL SOCIETY

Black artists hold frequent local and national meetings in order to share ideas and information. While this activity has not produced a local, regional, or national style of art, there has developed a unifying sense of dedication and common purpose among many artists of African descent. A definite supportive atmosphere has developed as well. It is an atmosphere that holds great promise for contemporary black artists.

Being Black Is First

How then does the contemporary activist-artist define himself, and what does he see as his role? The general attitude of the black activist-artist is that he is black—of African descent—first and an artist second. By that he means that he accepts his "Africanness" as a gift of birth, and this fact is more important to him than his talent in art. He is not concerned about whether his consciousness of being of African descent came before or after his conscious choice to be an artist. He sees his talent as a gift of personality to be used in the celebration of black life.

Two important things are implicit in this attitude. The first is of cultural importance. It is the conscious act of defining oneself, in no uncertain terms, as a person with specific spiritual and cultural links that connect him with black people wherever they are in the world. It further recognizes that what motivates and informs his creations is a history that embraces specific impulses and a specific heritage. The second thing of importance in this attitude is political. It involves the coming to terms with the sociopolitical reality that surrounds black people daily, rather than adopting the Western posture of alienation from self and environment. The contemporary activist-artist assumes the role of a liberator. He sees it as his duty to establish a synergetic relationship between himself and his environment, believing that each gives shape and form to the other. Of course, an art for art's sake is not possible with such an orientation.

PHILADELPHIA MUSEUM OF ART, W. P. WILSTACH COLLECTION, PHOTO BY ALFRED J. WYATT

'The Annunciation',
Henry Ossawa Tanner (1898)

Let me here offer the reader some background to the ideas and attitudes that motivate a great number of black artists and thinkers today. Above all, one should keep in mind that the cultural explosion occurring in black America is the result of ideas that have been fermenting for several decades in the black world.

Negritude and Soul

The social and political background for the term "black art" can be found, just as can that for the term "black power," in the synthesis of ideas and efforts of such men as Edward W. Blyden, Marcus Garvey, W. E. B. Du Bois, George Padmore, Kwame Nkrumah, Nnamdi Azikiwe, Julius Nyerere, and a host of other figures in recent African and Afro-American history. These men were the architects of such ideological views as "African personality," "African socialism," "Pan-Africanism," and "negritude." Alexander Okanlawon, in an article titled "Africanism—A Synthesis of the African World-View," (*Black World,* July 1972) combines these views in what he projects as a more comprehensive ideology—"Africanism." He says:

> In other words, each represents a certain aspect of the doctrine of Africanism: Négritude, the cultural-literary; Pan-Africanism, the political; African Socialism, the socio-economic; African Personality, the humanistic.

The more specifically literary antecedent to black art is the concept of *negritude.* This concept was initiated primarily by French-speaking African colonials who were concerned about the situation of the Negro in a culturally alien world. They saw the position of any one group of blacks as being common to that of the vast majority of blacks wherever they were in the world. This philosophy gave rise to an interest in the characteristic impulses, traits, and habits that may be considered more markedly Negro or African than white or European.

DALE LEHMAN

'Untitled',
Dalton Brown (1972)

A similar cultural concept paralleling the French-speaking African one of negritude is the English-speaking Afro-American concept of *soul*. The term "soul" did not gain widespread use until the 1950's, when black jazz musicians began to use it. In the early '60's black intellectuals adopted the term to refer to the black way of doing certain things as opposed to the white or nonblack way. More importantly, they used the concept of soul in discussing negritude and its expression in the United States. To date, Lerone Bennett has provided the most celebrated definition of soul, in 'The Negro Mood' (1965). For him:

> *Soul* is a metaphorical evocation of Negro being as expressed in the Negro tradition. It is the feeling with which an artist invests his creation, the style with which a man lives his life. It is, above all, of the spirit rather than the letter: a certain way of feeling, a certain way of expressing oneself, a certain way of being.

Bennett's definition of soul is also a definition of negritude. Although the two concepts are not at all dissimilar, of the two soul has been less debated. Afro-Americans from all walks of life understand and use the term "soul." It is at once a household word and a philosophical concept.

'Be Worthy of
Your Brother's Trust',
Carolyn Mims Lawrence,
AFRICOBRA II

THE STUDIO MUSEUM IN HARLEM,
PHOTO BY DOUG HARRIS

The Function of Art: Celebration and Liberation

This, then, is the background of the political and cultural ideas that have informed present-day black artists in their search for a black aesthetic. It is this background that determines their approach to art and life. They take the position that black art is first of all a subjective art; it is subjective because it affirms that there is a collective, though not entirely identical, experience that blacks the world over share. It affirms and objectifies the way of life and dignity of black people.

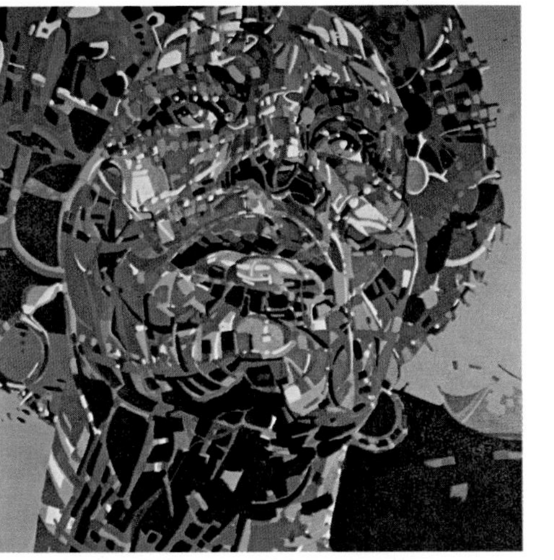

THE STUDIO MUSEUM IN HARLEM, PHOTO BY DOUG HARRIS

SHOREWOOD REPRODUCTIONS, INC.—COURTESY, ROMARE BEARDEN

THE STUDIO MUSEUM IN HARLEM, PHOTO BY DOUG HARRIS

THE MUSEUM OF MODERN ART, GIFT OF MRS. DAVID LEVY—PHOTO BY MALCOLM VARON

'In the North the Negro had better educational facilities' (above), Jacob Lawrence; 'Summertime' (top right), Romare Bearden; 'Spirit Sister' (top left), Nelson Stevens, AFRICOBRA II; 'Wives of Shango' (above left), Arnicia R. Donaldson, AFRICOBRA II

The black artist takes the position that his is a functional art, in that it serves to revive self-pride and confidence and recognizes no dichotomy between art and life. It celebrates life and provides at the same time a unifying sense of significance in the world. Through his art he liberates the African personality from cultural servitude.

The influence of these political and cultural doctrines on black artists who matured during the 1950's and 1960's can best be appreciated by examining the recent manifesto of a group called 'AFRICOBRA: Ten in Search of a Nation', by Arnicia R. Donaldson, published in 1970. AFRICOBRA (The African Commune of Bad Relevant Artists) is a Chicago-based cooperative that was founded in 1968. Its members are Donaldson, Napoleon Henderson, Jae Jarrell, Wadsworth Jarrell, Barbara J. Jones, Carolyn Mims Lawrence, Howard Mallory, Jr., Frank Smith,

Nelson Stevens, and Gerald Williams. This group of talented and committed artists is in the fore of black artists who are developing a body of creations that incorporate the common characteristics of what is generally conceded to be "black art." AFRICOBRA's collective ideas are projected quite clearly, yet poetically, in a statement by Donaldson, one of the founding members:

> We strive for images inspired by African people/experience and images which African people can relate to directly without formal art training and/or experience. Art for people and not for critics whose peopleness is questionable. We try to create images that appeal to the senses—not to the intellect. . . . images which deal with concepts that offer positive and feasible solutions to our individual, local, national, international, and cosmic problems. The images are designed with the idea of mass production. An image that is valuable because it is an original or unique is not art—it is economics, and we are not economists. We want everybody to have some.

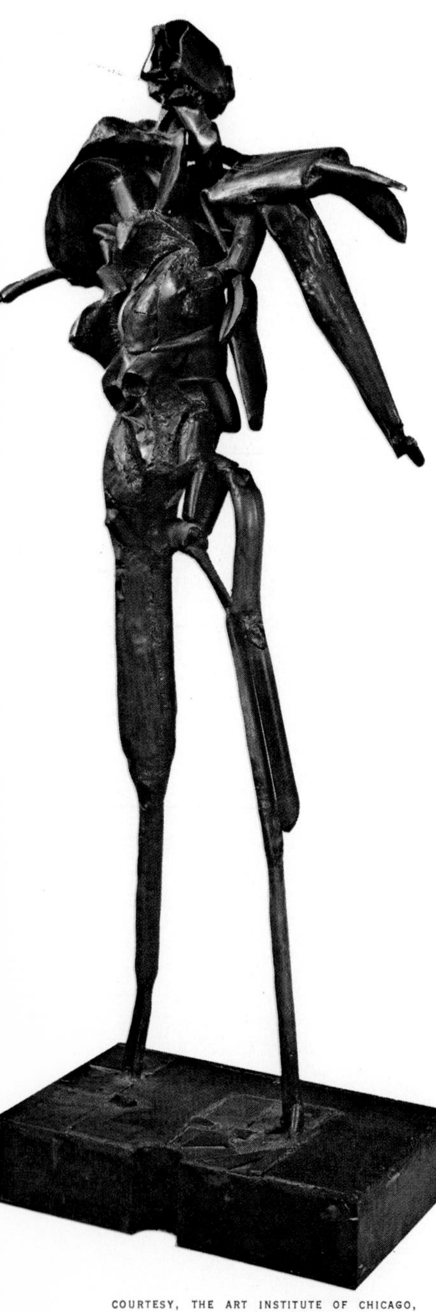

COURTESY, THE ART INSTITUTE OF CHICAGO, GIFT FROM MR. AND MRS. ARNOLD H. MAREMONT

'Hero Construction', Richard Hunt (1958)

Toward a True "Black Art"

With AFRICOBRA we are witnessing a group of artists, in this the era of "the black aesthetic," who from their perspective as Afro-Americans are attempting to identify style and rhythm qualities that are expressive of black people everywhere. Theirs is a Pan-African perspective. AFRICOBRA should be looked at more closely as an indication of the direction of black artists in the 1970's.

The new black artists are not motivated in the direction of establishing cultural parity between white (European) art and their own. Convinced of the depth and richness of their own creative heritage, they strive to validate that heritage in the eyes of other blacks while simultaneously carving out a supportive and humanistic environment for its survival.

The black artist of the '70's will move beyond the protest art of the '60's and renew the celebration and pageantry of our collective ethos. He will no longer need to avenge personal and collective suffering through art but will direct his energies to articulating the needs, spirituality, direction, and values that will liberate or reorient his own and the colonial mind.

This is indeed a new epoch for black Americans. For many black artists it signals a time for reviving those "ancestral gifts" and "ancient skills" that Alain Locke referred to more than three decades ago. It is an age for moving beyond mere rage—it's Nation Time and black artists are searching. Black artists are immigrating into self, family, and nationhood—and celebrating the process.

Bibliography

Baraka, Imamu Amiri. 'A Black Value System'. Newark: Jihad Productions, 1970.

Césaire, Aimé. 'Return to My Native Land'. Baltimore: Penguin Books, 1969.

Okanlawon, Alexander. "Africanism—A Synthesis of the African World-View," *Black World,* July 1972, pages 40–44 and 92–97.

Shapiro, Normand R., ed. 'Negritude: Black Poetry from Africa and the Caribbean'. New York: October House, 1970.

part II
THE BLACK EXPERIENCE IN LITERATURE

by
Gwendolyn Brooks

Pulitzer Prizewinning Poet

Gwendolyn Brooks

When she was awarded the Pulitzer prize for poetry in 1950, Gwendolyn Brooks was the first Negro to be so honored. She had already received an award from the American Academy of Arts and Letters and two Guggenheim fellowships. Now an established figure in American literature, she works to encourage aspiring young black writers.

> This turning away from white models and returning to their roots has freed black poets to create a new poetry. . . . They no longer imitate white models, strain toward white magazines, defer to white critics, or court white readers. They are in the process of creating a new literature. Whatever the outcome, they are taking care of business.
>
> Dudley Randall, 1971

The prologue of black literature in the U.S. includes the cautious imitations of Phillis Wheatley, the burning braveries of George Moses Horton, the wide vision of Benjamin Banneker, the anti-slavery intonings of Frances E. W. Harper, the grand and clarifying dramatics of Frederick Douglass, the engaging prose reaches of William Wells Brown (first black novelist herein), the adroit opposites of fictionist Charles W. Chesnutt, the striding teachings of Booker T. Washington, the severe philosophical triumphs of world-mind W. E. B. Du Bois, the spicy spun sugar of Jean Toomer, the clean sight and insight of Marcus Garvey (black blueprinter for a new age), the family ingatherings of Paul Laurence Dunbar (to whom young poets of this day are more indebted than they at first realized), the substantial sparkle of folklorist Zora Neale Hurston, the stately scholarship and limber poetics of James Weldon Johnson, the transforming culturalism of Alain Locke, the "lyre"-mastery of Countee Cullen, the heady incense of Claude McKay, the pioneering geniality and blackness-warmth of Langston Hughes.

And more. In general, the cry of these earlier generations was "We are equal! We are like you." But the new black ideal italicizes black identity, black solidarity, and black self-address. And the new black literature subscribes to these. Furthermore, the *essential* black ideal vitally acknowledges African roots. To those roots the new black literature cooperatively subscribes.

PILES & FILES OF PHOTOS

Phillis Wheatley (1753–1784), a poet in Boston, Mass., wrote 'To the University of Cambridge in New England' (1766) and 'To the King's Most Excellent Majesty' (1768).

Black Life Is Different

There is frequent impatience with the phrase "black literature." Can literature be black or white? Is not literature just literature?

The prevailing understanding today: black literature is literature by blacks, about blacks, directed *to* blacks. Black literature is the distillation of black life. Black life is different from white life. Different in nuance, different in nitty-gritty. Different *from* birth, different *at* death.

1966. 1967. 1968. Years of explosion. In those years a young black with pen in hand responded not to pretty sunsets and the lapping of lake water but to the speech of physical riot and spiritual rebellion. Young blacks went to see 'The Battle of Algiers' rather than the latest Paul Newman movie. Young blacks stopped saluting William Shakespeare, A. E. Housman, T. S. Eliot. They began to shake hands with Frantz Fanon and Malcolm X—gulping down Fanon's now classic 'The Wretched of the Earth' and Malcolm's 'Autobiography'. And after such seeing, after such gulping, there *had* to be a difference. There had to be an understanding that now the address must be to blacks; that shrieking into the steady and organized deafness of the white ear was frivolous.

There were things to be said to black brothers and sisters, and these things—annunciatory, curative, inspiriting—were to be said forthwith, without frill and without fear of the white presence. There was impatience with idle embroidery, with what was considered avoidance—avoidance of the gut issue, the blood fact. Literary rhythms altered! Sometimes the literature seemed to issue from pens dipped in, *stabbed* in, writhing blood. Music was very important. It influenced the new pens. There were veerings from Benny Goodman to John Coltrane and Charlie Mingus—from 'I'll Be Seeing You' to 'Soulful Strut'.

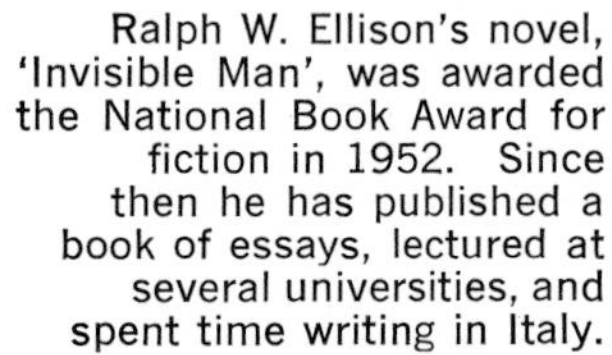

Ralph W. Ellison's novel, 'Invisible Man', was awarded the National Book Award for fiction in 1952. Since then he has published a book of essays, lectured at several universities, and spent time writing in Italy.

EBONY MAGAZINE

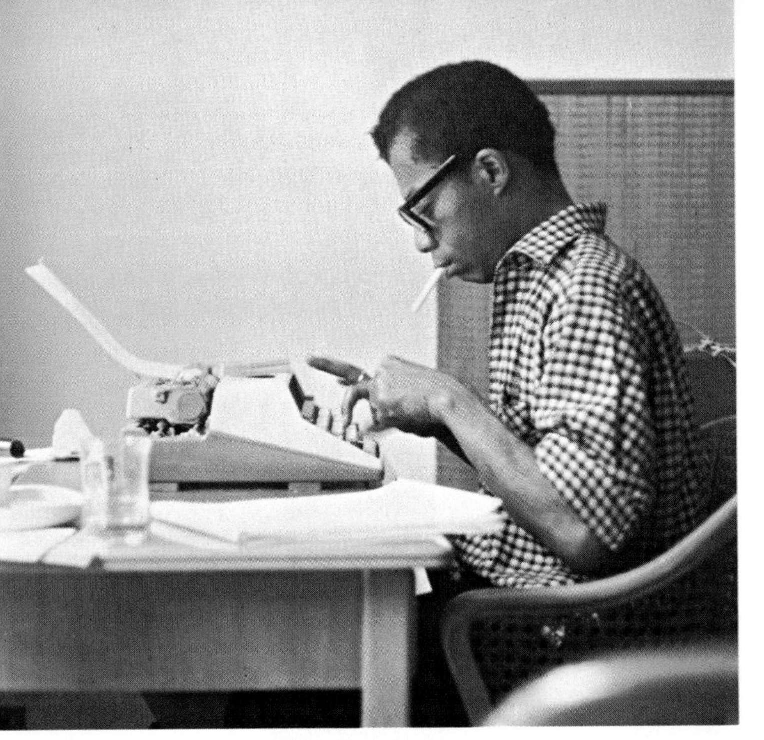
EBONY MAGAZINE

James Baldwin's many novels, essays, and plays have won him critical acclaim and popular success. Among these are 'Go Tell It on the Mountain', 'Nobody Knows My Name', 'Another Country', and 'The Fire Next Time'.

Literary Revolution: The Destruction of Dead Ideas

'Black Fire', a fat anthology of "the new writing," was issued by Larry Neal and Imamu Amiri Baraka (then LeRoi Jones) in 1968. Pandemonium. 'Black Fire' was an electric springboard. Flaming poetry, fiction, drama, and essays. Especially did the essays "make a difference." They were listened to, loved, quoted. "The West is dying, as it must, as it should," shouted Neal. "The black artist must link his work to the struggle for his liberation and the liberation of his brothers and sisters." Neal wanted black literature to aim at collective ritual, "directed at the destruction of useless, dead ideas. . . . black literature must become an integral part of the community's life style. . . . We can learn more about what [black] poetry is by listening to the cadences in Malcolm's speeches than from most of Western poetics."

James T. Stewart—essayist, painter, and singer—opened 'Black Fire' with his essay "The Development of the Black Revolutionary Artist": "We must . . . be estranged from the dominant culture. This estrangement must be nurtured in order to generate and energize our black artists." Stewart is disdainful of the concept of fixity. He advises disregard for the "perpetuation of the product—the picture, the statue, the temple." (And most certainly the piece of "literature!")

The new feeling, among the *earnest* young black creators, was that concern for long-lastingness was Western and was wrong. One created a piece of art for the enrichment, the instruction, the extension of one's people. Its usefulness may or may not be exhausted in a day, a week, a month, a year. There was no prayerful compulsion—among the earnest—for its idle survival into the centuries. The word went down: we must chase out Western measures, rules, and models.

Frederick Douglass (1817–1895) is famous for his writings against slavery, especially his autobiography, 'Life and Times of Frederick Douglass'.

SOPHIA SMITH COLLECTION, SMITH COLLEGE

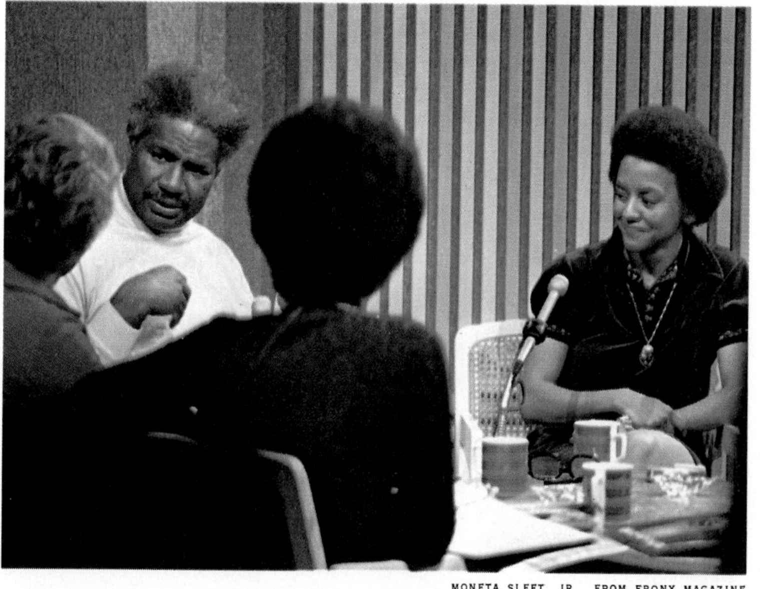

MONETA SLEET, JR., FROM EBONY MAGAZINE

Ossie Davis (left), author of 'Purlie Victorious', and poet Nikki Giovanni participate in a discussion.

The Literature of Integration

Much of the work that preceded the days of considerable black fire belongs in a category I call "condition literature." You remember, in 'Song of Myself', Walt Whitman loves animals because they do not tirelessly "whine about their condition." A good many of us who preceded the pioneering influence of Baraka did a lot of poetic, dramatic, and fictional whining. And a lot of that was addressed to white people. We sensed ourselves crying "up" to them. "Help us," we seemed to cry. We were fascinated by the sickness of the black condition. One of my own 20-year-old poems semi-begs: "Grant me that I am human, that I hurt, that I can cry."

The Harlem Renaissance writers and the post-Harlem Renaissance writers created, and felt, in terms of integration. The great "Negro" dream was "Hand in hand toge-ether!" Langston Hughes, who identified himself as the "darker brother," looked ahead to equality and acceptance:

Tomorrow,
I'll be at the table
When company comes.
Nobody'll dare
Say to me,
"Eat in the kitchen,"
Then.

Besides,
They'll see how beautiful I am
And be ashamed—

I, too, am America.

Richard Wright (1908–1960) and his work have greatly influenced black writers, including Ralph Ellison and James Baldwin. His books such as 'Uncle Tom's Children', 'Native Son', and 'Black Boy' have won numerous awards.

PILES & FILES OF PHOTOS

In 'Tired', the poet Fenton Johnson decided that it is "better to die, than to grow up and find that you are colored," but this was *because* he, as "darker brother," could not get a grip on the great

EBONY MAGAZINE

Poet and lyricist James Weldon Johnson (1871–1938) was also a major figure in the early civil rights movement. His first book of poetry, 'Fifty Years and Other Poems', was published in 1917. His autobiography was finished in 1933, five years before his death.

American goodies. Claude McKay's 'If We Must Die' was remarkably in the spirit of the late 1960's, but midfury he weakened, evincing a regrettable concern for and interest in "the monsters we defy":

If we must die—oh, let us nobly die,
So that our precious blood may not be shed
In vain; then even the monsters we defy
Shall be constrained to honor us though dead!

Hughes, however, in many of his poems was able to put his keen ear to the later black ground and to interpret the "militant" rumblings therein:

I could tell you
If I want to
What makes me
What I am.

But I don't
Really want to—
And you don't
Give a damn.

Baraka, feeling much the same, could "bring it all on down" into the succinct, no-nonsense incandescence of 'SOS':

Calling black people
Calling all black people, man woman child
Wherever you are, calling you, urgent, come in
Black People, come in, wherever you are, urgent, calling
you, calling all black people
calling all black people, come in, black people, come
on in.

Alain Locke (1886–1954) edited an anthology, 'The New Negro', which presented work by young black writers to show the general public the worth and achievements of black people.

EBONY MAGAZINE

FRIEDMAN-ABELES

In a scene from the musical 'Purlie', taken from a play by Ossie Davis, are: (from left) Navello Nelson as Missy, Melba Moore as Lutiebell, Sherman Hemsley as Getlow, and Cleavon Little as Purlie.

Richard Wright made us look at helpless black men whose histories were fear-flight-fate, in varying proportions. But even though he could speak meaningfully to blacks about what blacks know and instantly recognize, he hoped to attract, stun, charm, and enlist white sympathy, to stimulate white empathy.

Ralph Ellison. The critic George Kent says of him, "Permeating all his statements is the emphasis which he gives to the Americanness of all positions and his engagement with all strands of the American cultural fabric."

James Baldwin was finally driven to a dire promise, "The *fire* next time!" It was a launch. But it hurt him. There was pain. He had made such a heavy investment in integration.

The New Mood: Poems Are Teeth

Then came Baraka, rejecting all lovely little villanelles and sonnets—to Orpheus or anything else. Prettiness was out. Fight-fact was in. Baraka demanded black poems. Poems must be teeth, fists, daggers, guns, cop wrestlers. Why? These would be cleansers! "Clean out the world for virtue and love," Baraka ordered.

Came Don L. Lee, a further pioneer, born in 1942, on February 23, the birthday of Du Bois. Lee told us, "The black artist by defining and legitimizing his own reality becomes a positive force in the black community." He told us, "Black poetry is like a razor; it's sharp and will cut deep." He believed in speaking directly to his people. He addressed them in shrewd, tough words whose meaning they could not mistake. They could not mistake, either, the attendant affection—affection for all blackness. Long ago I saw him as a screamer in the sun. And David Llorens accurately wrote of him, "At one he will be hailed and damned for the same reason: because he refuses to write a single line in forgetfulness of his blackness."

Lee was the stimulus and star for an entire new renaissance of fire-filled young black poets, many of whom were given a platform by older poet Dudley Randall (of the Broadside Press, Detroit):

Novelist John A. Williams achieved recognition with such works as: 'Night Song', 'This Is My Country Too', and 'The Man Who Cried I Am'.

PICTORIAL PARADE

NORMAN L. HUNTER FROM EBONY MAGAZINE

Historian Lerone Bennett, contemporary author of 'Before the Mayflower: A History of the Negro in America', is considered one of the foremost authorities on black history.

Etheridge Knight. John Raven. Sonia Sanchez. Nikki Giovanni. Everett Hoagland. James Emanuel. Doughtry Long. Carolyn Rodgers. Johari Amini. Sterling Plumpp. Hoyt Fuller. George Kent. Keorapetse Kgositsile. . . .

A rich prose-poetry piece in the new mood is the slain George Jackson's 'Soledad Brother', jagged-poignant and merciless. Contemporary stars in the field of fiction include the novelist John O. Killens, who wrote 'And Then We Heard the Thunder', 'Youngblood', and 'The Cotillion' and who is also an essayist and scriptwriter; Julian Mayfield, 'The Long Night' and 'Nowhere Street' (originally called 'The Grand Parade'); Ishmael Reed, celebrated especially for his tour de force 'Yellow Back Radio Broke-Down'; Sam Greenlee, 'The Spook Who Sat By the Door'; Ann Petry, 'The Street'.

In the field of drama, eminent, of course, is Baraka, whose 'Dutchman', 'The Toilet', and 'The Slave' were style setters; but we have also the impact of such innovators as the penetrating Ed Bullins, 'A Son, Come Home', 'Goin' a Buffalo', and 'In the Wine Time'; Douglas Turner Ward, 'Day of Absence' and 'Happy Ending'; Lonne Elder, 'Ceremonies in Dark Old Men'; Ron Milner, 'Who's Got His Own'; Charles Gordone, the recent Pulitzer prizewinner, 'No Place to Be Somebody'.

Author Paul Laurence Dunbar (1872–1906) is well known for his verse written in Negro dialect. Two of his celebrated works are 'Oak and Ivy' and 'Lyrics of Lowly Life'.

EBONY MAGAZINE

Judging by Black Standards

Further, there are black critics for the curative assessment of black literature. Thoughtful blacks understand that white critics, even those with the best will in the world and the strictest "objectivity," even the most brilliant and widely read, cannot judge black works with the intuition and empathy of blacks intimate with both substance and essence of the life involved. In addition to longtime-valued J. Saunders Redding, some of the strongest of these contemporary black literary critics are: George Kent, 'Blackness and the Adventure of Western Culture'; Addison Gayle, author of

MONETA SLEET, JR., FROM EBONY MAGAZINE

Writer Charles Gordone won a Pulitzer prize for his play 'No Place to Be Somebody'.

'The Black Situation' and the article "Claude McKay" and editor of such anthologies as 'The Black Aesthetic'; Hoyt Fuller, editor of *Black World* and author of 'Journey to Africa'; Don Lee, 'Dynamite Voices'; Stanley Crouch and Ron Welburn, poet-essayists; Clayton Riley; Joe Goncalves; Paula Giddings; Francis Ward; Lisbeth Gant; Houston Baker; Eugenia Collier; Carolyn Gerald. These people are welcome in the pages of such new-purpose magazines as *Journal of Black Poetry* (edited by Goncalves), *Black World, Black Dialogue, The Black Scholar, Black Theatre, Essence, Freedomways, Liberator, Nommo, Free Lance.* A serious magazine of an older stamp is *Phylon,* in which the respected critic Arthur P. Davis has written since the 1940's.

There are additional black publishing companies, too. Drum and Spear Press of Washington, D. C., Chicago's Johnson Publishing Co. (which publishes the works of the historian Lerone Bennett), Chicago's Free Black Press, New York City's Emerson Hall Publishers and The Third Press; and Jihad Productions of Newark, N.J. (directed by Baraka). These companies work sympathetically with the new writers, knowing when to allow extravagantly and when to pull in the reins. They are not concerned if white critics, referring inevitably to European "standards," spit on the fledglings.

Poet Don L. Lee, advising his fellow artists to "live their poems," fills his works with provocative social content.

EBONY MAGAZINE

Toward Future Strength

The understood black station now is an organic *enough!*—a creative rebellion that often yearns toward revolution. There is certainly no going back to puny imploring, to integration worship, to labeled slavery. Black literature: a reflection of the black mood, intuition, fury, and resolve. Where is it going?

There may be more of the oblique subtleties of Ishmael Reed—with extensions, and departures. There may be further Larry Neal blendings of music, ritual, and black homily—with extensions, and departures. There may be more of the seasoned folk delineations of

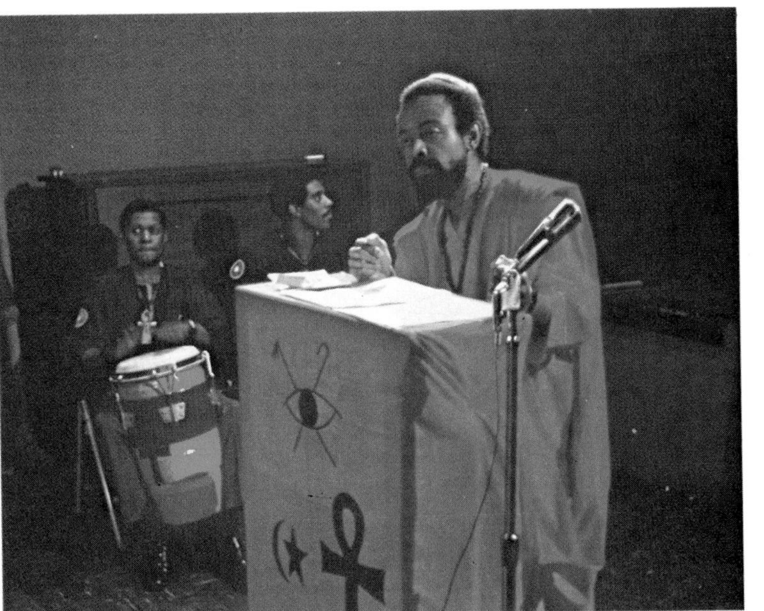

MONETA SLEET, JR., FROM EBONY MAGAZINE

Poet and playwright Imamu Amiri Baraka, coeditor of the anthology 'Black Fire', is noted for his shockingly honest treatment of racial conflict.

Lucille Clifton. There will be black lyrics, reliant on the specifics of black daily life for their inspiration. Here is Cheryl Davis' bittersweet and educated comprehension of special rejection; rejection of blacks by blacks—because of blackness:

Like most children
I was born
on the day
my mother
couldn't stand it
any longer.

And from all over
people came to see
what she had had;
not knowing of course
that she had had *me*.

When they found
that she had had *me*
they all left,
wondering
how she could ever
have done
such a thing.

There will be differences. Differences only the new developers—or the advanced old—can apprehend. But the differences will be in form and approach. For certainly a present basic that I recently observed will continue: an agreeable invasion of the folk element, an appropriation of "supplies," wonderful supplies, to shape, to fill, to enhance with substantial embroidery a fundamental strength, which is being returned with proud respect.

A major American writer of the 20th century, poet and critic Langston Hughes is often called the Negro poet laureate. He died in 1967, famous for such works as 'The Weary Blues' and 'The Panther and the Lash'.

PICTORIAL PARADE

part III BLACK MUSIC AND DANCE

by
Earl Calloway

Music Critic,
Chicago Daily Defender

Earl Calloway

In the course of his career, Earl Calloway has been a concert singer, a choral director, and a music columnist. A graduate of the Chicago Musical College of Roosevelt University, he sang in recitals in cities across the U.S., as well as in Korea and Japan. Since 1964 he has been the music critic of the *Chicago Daily Defender,* the daily newspaper of the city's black community.

> . . . negroes should write negro music. We have our own racial feeling and if we try to copy whites we will make bad copies.
>
> James Reese Europe, 1919

The expressions of frustration and hostility so prominent in the statements of young black American artists and writers seem strangely lacking among black musicians, composers, singers, and dancers. If black people do not appear to be alienated from the mainstream of American music, it is probably because they have been the ones, from colonial times to the present, who have shaped and directed its development. In fact, nearly all the forms of music that can be considered uniquely American—spirituals, blues, jazz, ragtime, gospel, and rock, as well as the popular dances of stage and ballroom—have been contributions of the American Negro.

African Roots

Kidnapped from the shores and jungles of western Africa, the first black slaves brought no luggage, no clothing, no cooking utensils; they came only with their languages, their tribal memories, and—above all—their music and dance. The musical tradition was highly developed in the kingdoms of western Africa. Within the tribes, professional musicians and composers were organized into guilds; they were supported by the community out of respect for their great talents. Their music was very different from European music. The African sense of melody and harmony was totally subordinate to the sense of rhythm. And it was rhythm—subtle, complex, and sophisticated—that dominated the music.

ABBY ALDRICH ROCKEFELLER FOLK ART COLLECTION

An unknown artist of the 1790's painted this watercolor 'The Old Plantation' somewhere in South Carolina. It is a rare record of the stick dance done to the music of a drum and a stringed instrument.

Transplanted Traditions

Even on the decks of crowded slave ships, at periods of compulsory recreation and exercise, black Africans expressed themselves in music and dance. Early slave celebrations and holidays were also observed with music. There were musicians among the slaves on nearly every plantation, and often they were called to entertain at the dances of their white owners. Some slaves even studied musical instruments alongside the master's children. For the most part, however, black musicians created their own kind of music, using a variety of homemade instruments. The banjo was actually an adaptation, using native American materials, of an African stringed instrument. Other makeshift instruments gave off sounds appropriate to the African musical tradition—sounds of scraping, clicking, clanging, and rattling.

In the northern cities during colonial times African music and dances were performed at special slave festivals. To the white colonists these spectacles were exceedingly strange and exotic. Homemade drums beat out African rhythms, and the dancers leaped and twirled in frenzied exercises. In New Orleans, La., as late as the early 19th century, it was customary for slaves to gather on Sundays at the Place Congo (now Beauregard Square). Many tribes were present, each assembled on a different part of the square. The dancers formed rings, moved to the sound of drums, and chanted.

The tradition of black participation in ballet was pioneered in the 1940's by Pearl Primus and Katherine Dunham, two dancers who—somewhat in the manner of the nationalist composers—incorporated black African motifs into the contemporary dance style. Today the

Duke Ellington, a tremendously influential musician, is known for his accomplishments as a jazz orchestra leader, pianist, and composer.

PETER C. BORSARI FROM CAMERA 5

CBS RECORDS

CULVER PICTURES

Gospel singing was exemplified in its highest form by the beloved Mahalia Jackson. The opening of the musical 'In Dahomey' in 1902 established the team of Bert Williams and George Walker as the top Negro stars in both the U.S. and England.

two outstanding leaders of black ballet are Alvin Ailey of the Alvin Ailey City Center Dance Theater and Arthur Mitchell, founder of the Dance Theater of Harlem. Their examples have awakened tremendous interest in ballet among black youngsters.

Spirituals and Secular Songs

Brought into sudden contact with the white man's culture, language, and religion, black forms of expression were gradually affected. During the religious revival of the mid-18th century, black converts to Christianity were zealously proselytized. Historical accounts tell us that the Negroes received the Christian religion and its traditions with wholehearted emotion. The hymns and spoken prayers, with their obvious resemblance to African ritual, delighted the black converts.

At the camp meetings a new kind of religious song came into being—the spiritual. While the words of these songs were inspired by the Bible, the musical structure was derived from African musical patterns. Early accounts of Negro religious gatherings mention that stomping of feet and slapping of thighs sometimes reinforced the rhythm of the music.

Black slaves made up other songs besides spirituals—work songs, sorrow songs, narratives or "ballets," and field hollers. Much of this music was performed at plantation festivals called Jubilees. The music and dances of the Jubilees impressed white performers. With blackened faces, their voices imitating Negro speech, these performers staged a new kind of entertainment called the minstrel show. Although the show was essentially a white invention, black minstrel companies were soon touring North America and Europe in productions of their own. Among the great black musicians to begin their careers as minstrels were composers James Bland and W. C. Handy

MARBETH

Arthur Mitchell's Dance Theater of Harlem was the first black classical ballet group to perform on an international scale. Lydia Abaca (left), William Scott, and Virginia Johnston are shown in 'Fete Noire', choreographed by Arthur Mitchell.

and comic Bert Williams. Although the minstrel show ended about 1870, it had a permanent effect on American musical traditions.

Everywhere that black people settled in America, their native musical expressions were exposed to local, regional, and ethnic influences. Black music did not develop as a monolithic, cohesive entity, but rather as many different kinds and styles of music. In Virginia and the upper South, for example, black music was strongly melodic and was influenced by Irish and English folk ballads. In New York and the Northeast, black musicians played in the sophisticated bands and large dance halls; there the instrumental idiom, later influential in jazz, developed. The mountain music of the highlands of Kentucky, Tennessee, and West Virginia was still another influence. French, Spanish, and Caribbean traditions came together in New Orleans, a city that was a gathering place for black musicians of all kinds.

Blues

Nobody knows where the blues began, or when. Like other kinds of black music, it just seemed to grow and evolve out of existing folk songs. Certainly spirituals were an important influence in the development of the mournful blues sound. The music derived from the earthy music of the Mississippi Delta area. Blues lyrics reflected the misery of black life—hard work and low pay—and the despair of love gone wrong.

When questioned about the origin of the blues, some black musicians claimed that the tradition went back at least to the 1880's. "Ma" Rainey, a nightclub singer of the early 1900's, was the first professional blues performer. It was not until 1912, however, when W. C. Handy published his 'Memphis Blues', that the new musical style became popular. Probably the most famous blues singer of

Bessie Smith (1898–1937) is still considered the "Empress of the Blues." Her recordings continue to express the hopes and frustrations of black Americans.

COURTESY, PETE WELDING FROM CBS RECORDS

RICHARD BALAGUR FROM NANCY PALMER AGENCY

Before his death in 1970, Jimi Hendrix was acclaimed one of the most electrifying performers in the field of hard rock. His records remained popular in 1972.

all time was Bessie Smith, the "Empress of the Blues." Other great performers included Mamie Smith, Blind Lemon Jefferson, Huddie (Leadbelly) Ledbetter, Sonny Terry, and B. B. King.

Ragtime

Ragtime music, another development of the postemancipation era, swept America and Europe in the early 1900's. The first rag players were itinerant black pianists who entertained in cafés and saloons. Improvising freely (most of them had no formal musical training) and using one hand to pound out the beat, they developed the syncopated music that became known as ragtime. Black composer Scott Joplin, author of the famous 'Maple Leaf Rag', earned the title "King of Ragtime." Other famous rag musicians were James Sylvester Scott, Joe Jordan, and Eubie Blake.

William Grant Still's 'Afro-American Symphony', ballet 'Sahdji', and opera 'Troubled Island' reflect his concern with blacks in American society. He was the first Negro to conduct a professional symphony in the U.S.

COURTESY, VERNA ARVEY STILL

Jazz

The city of New Orleans is popularly thought of as the birthplace of jazz. After the Civil War that city became a gathering place for emancipated black musicians. The New Orleans style of jazz grew out of the inventive, highly unorthodox music of black marching bands and of the players who entertained in the Basin Street nightclubs. The music was an incredible mixture of elements from blues, spirituals, ballads, French and Spanish dances, and all kinds of popular songs. One of the key figures in the development of New Orleans jazz was cornet player Charles (Buddy) Bolden. Bolden was an important influence on a whole generation of young jazz musicians.

The instrumental music of northern Negro bands was another element in the development of jazz. The tradition of black musicians playing for white dancers, which began during colonial times, continued long after emancipation. During the late 19th century, black dance bands flourished in all the large cities of the U.S.

COURTESY, CBS RECORDS

Miles Davis helped make famous the so-called cool style of jazz through his recording beginning in the late 1940's.

In New York City in 1910, Negro dance-band leader James Reese Europe organized a black "symphony orchestra." Two years later at a concert in Carnegie Hall, Europe's Clef Club Orchestra introduced the public to the kind of syncopated popular music that was later called jazz. Criticized for not including traditional symphonic music in the program, Europe defended his feeling that "negroes should write negro music. We have our own racial feeling and if we try to copy whites we will make bad copies. . . ." Before long, in fact, many white composers of classical music were to be profoundly influenced by jazz and blues. And by the mid-20th century, black composers such as Edward Kennedy (Duke) Ellington were creating jazz music in the classical symphonic idiom.

Stage Shows

As the minstrel show died, the Negro stage musical was born. Some were revues, featuring cakewalkers and singing acts, while others were actual musical comedies. 'The Creole Show', an early all-Negro production, played a full season at the 1893 Chicago World's Columbian Exposition; in 1896 'Oriental America' became the first all-Negro musical to play on Broadway. 'In Dahomey' and 'Bandana Land' were other turn-of-the-century successes. These provided a showcase for the talents of trained black composers and musicians. J. Rosamond Johnson and his brother, poet James Weldon Johnson, wrote many hit tunes. Will Marion Cook wrote scores for several shows, including the Broadway sensation 'Clorindy—The Origin of the Cake Walk', with lyrics by Paul L. Dunbar.

Black stage shows hit a new high in the 1920's. 'Shuffle Along', with songs by the team of Sissle and Blake (Noble Sissle and Eubie Blake), was a smash hit in New York City, establishing such performers as Florence Mills and Josephine Baker and introducing the song hit 'I'm Just Wild About Harry'. Among the players in the

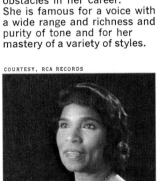

Contralto Marian Anderson achieved fame despite major obstacles in her career. She is famous for a voice with a wide range and richness and purity of tone and for her mastery of a variety of styles.

COURTESY, RCA RECORDS

RICHARD BALAGUR FROM NANCY PALMER AGENCY

B. B. King is considered one of the greatest blues performers ever.

theater orchestra were two black musicians, Hall Johnson and William Grant Still, who later made their reputations as composers.

Following 'Shuffle Along' was a string of successful black productions, including 'The Chocolate Dandies', 'Blackbirds', and 'Hot Chocolates'. Although the Depression seemed to put an end to black stage musicals, the form seems to be undergoing a revival. Recent black shows have included 'Purlie' (a musical adaptation of Ossie Davis' 'Purlie Victorious') and Melvin Van Peebles' 'Don't Play Us Cheap'.

Gospel

Contemporary jazz artist Aretha Franklin originally achieved fame with her "soul music."

COURTESY, ATLANTIC RECORDS CORP.

In the early 19th century, rural Negroes invented the spiritual as an expression of their religious fervor. Gospel developed later, becoming the religious music of urban black congregations. The first gospel singers were vocalists in city churches. They borrowed elements from spirituals, blues, and popular songs. They improvised freely, giving new interpretations to old music. Credit for writing the first gospel songs, as well as for popularizing gospel music, is given to Thomas Dorsey, a black jazz musician and composer. The music of the great gospel performers, such as Mahalia Jackson and the Clara Ward Singers, spread its popularity throughout the black community and beyond. The style and sound of gospel have been influential in popular music, as heard in the songs of Ray Charles, James Brown, and Aretha Franklin.

The Black Classicists

Before the 20th century most black composers did not have the opportunity to learn by experience the qualities of orchestral instruments. Perhaps this limitation was the reason for the vast store-

CENTRAL PRESS FROM PICTORIAL PARADE

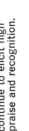

The great actor and singer Paul Robeson is shown in the title role of 'Othello', which set an all-time record run in the U.S. in 1943.

house of vocal concert music composed and arranged by such black composers as John Wesley Work, Sr., Hall Johnson, Edward Boatner, and Will Marion Cook. The performance of Negro spirituals on the concert stage owes much to the talents of composer-arranger Harry T. Burleigh.

Perhaps the first notable exception to this choral tradition was black composer William Grant Still, known as the dean of Afro-American composers. Still began his career playing in dance bands and working in the music publishing business of W. C. Handy. After two years of study in New York City with the French composer Edgar Varèse, Still began to write orchestral music. His 'Afro-American Symphony', premiered in 1931 by the Rochester Philharmonic Orchestra under the direction of Howard Hanson, brought Still his first professional recognition.

Still is the most famous of the black nationalist composers, those who drew upon traditional Negro music as a source of thematic inspiration. Other nationalists include Clarence Cameron White, R. Nathaniel Dett, Harry Lawrence Freeman, William Levi Dawson, and Florence B. Price. In developing their concept of Negro symphonic music, these composers were greatly influenced by the ideas of Czech composer Antonín Dvorák. Although committed to traditional musical forms, they were also devoted to the folk idiom.

The succeeding generations of black composers, those born in the 20th century, are perhaps better identified as experimentalists. Educated at the best U.S. music schools, their outlooks broadened by study in Europe, these composers cannot be classified by race. From the serial techniques of Hale Smith's 'Contours for Orchestra' to the electronic music of Olly Wilson, their compositions represent most of the trends in current musical thought.

Billie Holiday, the great jazz singer of the 1930's and 40's, and her music continue to elicit high praise and recognition.

MY THOUSAND AND ONE DAYS

by Irna Phillips

Creator and Writer of As the World Turns

Scheherazade, they say, spun out her tales for a thousand and one nights, to entertain and distract her lord, the king, so that he would spare her from the fate of her predecessors—death by beheading. Each new dawn she contrived a new crisis in her story, and the king, anxious to hear its outcome, permitted her another day of life. In the end she proved such an accomplished storyteller that the king spared her and made her his wife. And so ended the terror against the maidens of his realm.

Irna Phillips

A writer of radio and television serials, Miss Phillips has been creating daytime drama for 40 years. She lives and works in Chicago, where she was born on July 1, 1901. Miss Phillips was educated at Northwestern University and the University of Illinois. She took graduate work at the University of Wisconsin. Miss Phillips has an adopted son and daughter.

In the field of daytime drama, the writers are modern Scheherazades. They must never stop their storytelling—not after a thousand and one chapters, nor ten thousand and one. It is their job to contrive new situations each day to please our monarchs—the sponsors, producers, and audiences of American television. The curtain must never come down on one of these dramas, and woe unto one whose tale cannot bring the listener back another day. For such a one the punishment is not beheading but a dropped option. It amounts to the same thing.

Someone has suggested that the daytime serial, the so-called soap opera, is the one truly American art form. If so, it owes its uniqueness to the invention of radio. Before radio, there was no medium that could accommodate the day-to-day development of a character extending over a period of months and years. The serialized story in literature (several of Dickens' works first appeared in episodic form) and motion pictures preceded soap opera, of course, but neither involved situations that went beyond perhaps 20 chapters. Most important, each drove toward a narrative conclusion. But in the soap opera the whole point is to depict human lives as they unfold in real life: without cataclysmic denouements, but rather in small, overlapping doses of drama, each dose dealt with as it arises.

With the development of radio it became possible for the first time to perform these dramas before millions of people simultaneously in a context that presented no logistic difficulties to the listener. (Scheherazade at her liege lord's side.) The listener was not required to move to a theater. He did not have to dress up, make reservations, or travel long distances. It became easy to pick up the thread of the narrative each day at a certain time. The variety of the human condition took care of the rest. The element that makes the serial what it is—the conclusion that lures the listener (or reader or viewer) back for the following episode—was well established. For the long haul, it became vital to pay close attention to the basic honesty of situations and the responses of the characters.

CULVER PICTURES

Young Dr. Malone was a daytime serial about metropolitan doctor Jerry Malone, played by Alan Bunce (center), and his nurse wife Ann, played by Elizabeth Reller (right). Richard Coogan (left) played the role of Robert Hughes. Originating on NBC Blue network in 1939, the program moved to CBS in April 1940.

Does this mean that the troubles depicted in a month or so of soap opera are realistic? Probably not, in the sense that most human lives are not so vexed in such a short time span; but none of these problems is unknown to the human condition. Each is based on fact. A certain amount of compression becomes necessary, to keep the drama from dragging or toppling of its own weight, but nothing beyond the realm of possibility should ever inject itself. The average life is neither so glamorous nor so tragic as the lives we see in *any* dramatic form—from 'King Lear' to 'Death of a Salesman'. What the serial writer must ask himself is: are my situations honest? Are my characters honest? Would a human being act this way?

The Guise of Reality

The modern soap opera is a living thing. It has pace and pulse and, it sometimes seems, a will of its own. In As the World Turns, for example, the Hughes family is so well established in my mind and the minds of its audience that the family's behavior and responses are largely dictated by what has gone before. The Hughes family believes in certain values, and it would be uncharacteristic—that is, dishonest—to tamper with those beliefs in the story. Contrary to popular opinion, the writer of a daytime serial cannot play God, manipulating characters as if they were puppets. The writer who hopes to have a successful series must think of characters as flesh-and-blood entities.

Part of my particular approach to my characters and my program results from my way of working. I never type my stories, nor will I dictate into a tape recorder. Like Scheherazade, I work best before a live audience; and so I dictate to a secretary who takes down what I say, and this gives me the sense of a responding entity out there. Beyond that, I try to put myself into each role. From the time I was a little girl I wanted to be an actress. So when I dictate a script I become all the people. I find great emotional release in this process. I never think of a vast, faceless audience somewhere out there in

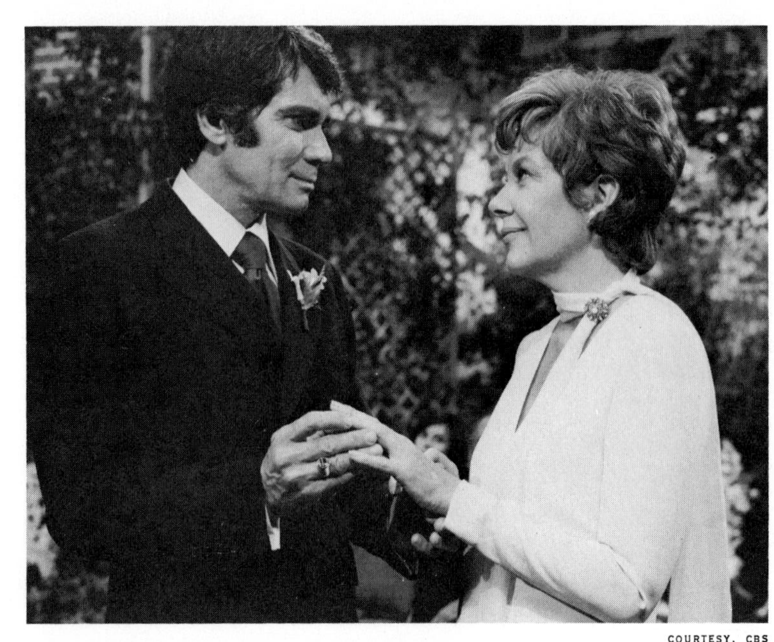
COURTESY, CBS

Search for Tomorrow had its premiere on Sept. 3, 1951, and was the oldest soap opera on TV in 1972. In a recent episode Joanne Tate (played by Mary Stuart, an original cast member) married Dr. Tony Vincent, played by Anthony George.

Televisionland. Rather, I think of myself as my audience and of myself as performer. In the end, I must interest and entertain *me* or I am unsatisfied. I cannot write about what does not engage my imagination or curiosity.

Where does the serial writer get inspiration? The answer is, from many sources—newspapers, radio (I turn mine on in the early morning), and, of course, from other people. By and large, people are the best source of information about themselves, and I will talk, literally, with everyone. My circle of acquaintances is wide—doctors, lawyers, workingmen, and TV moguls—and I gain something from each of them. I enjoy phoning people who write in to the show. It surprises and pleases them to hear from a live body at the other end of the mails. One correspondent, a music professor in California, wrote to complain that she felt I had hurt the cause of women's liberation in a script that urged one of my characters, a girl named Susan, to remain at home with her child instead of going out to work. The letter writer was astonished to get my call, and we found we were not so far apart as her letter implied.

Keeping the Troubles Timely

I have been told that my programs reflect traditional American values—by which I suppose are meant a belief in God, patriotism, and the virtues of a cohesive family unit. I suppose that is right, but it is an oversimplification. I also believe in, and try to reflect, some of today's problems and aspirations. I think my young people are "with it," in the sense that they are concerned about things most young people worry about. One of my characters recently graduated from law school. He did not choose to go into a lucrative private practice; he went into neighborhood law—not quite a storefront lawyer, but almost. He is also very much "into" organic foods and the practical, manual skills to which so many of today's young people are turning. Or returning.

CULVER PICTURES

The radio comedy serial Vic and Sade originated in Chicago in 1932. This married couple who lived in "the little house halfway up the next block" was portrayed by Art Van Harvey (left) and Bernardine Flynn (center). The series was broadcast on the NBC Blue network. At one time NBC had two networks, called Red and Blue, which carried different programs to different affiliate stations in a number of cities.

What I try hard to avoid are fads. Programs that try to stay on top of every turn in the public fancy are doomed to a kind of restless wandering. The writer cannot properly maintain his characterizations by this kind of device. Among the daytime dramas now on the networks, it is possible to find several that are engaged in such a hopeless pursuit. One network had murder trials going on in four of its daytime programs at once.

I often listen to other soap operas, not to imitate but to avoid imitation. In many cases, I have shuffled entire synopses because another program anticipated a plot line that I was considering. But basically I write in a way to please myself. I think the 40 years I have spent writing serials make me a fairly good judge of what plays and what does not.

Early Bubbles in the Air

The mechanics of the soap opera have become enormously more complex since the days of radio when I began to write (and act in) my first original, Painted Dreams. I got that assignment when a programming man called and asked if I could write a family situation show. I had never written one, but I replied, "Of course I can." I never said no to anything. In those days we did everything. We wrote the scripts, directed the shows, played the roles, and did the sound effects. It was a wondrously free and creative time. We didn't worry about things like ratings or censorship. If we felt like laughing at a joke we had made, or at a slip of the tongue, we laughed. (The station manager might tell us, as he did from time to time, "You girls are the only ones who thought that was funny," but we didn't care—or stop.) We merchandised like crazy. I would mention a recipe, and then we would tell people to write in if they wanted a copy. It was our own rating sampling of sorts.

Time, of course, brought complications. Painted Dreams went out on only one station—WGN in Chicago. Later on, the networks

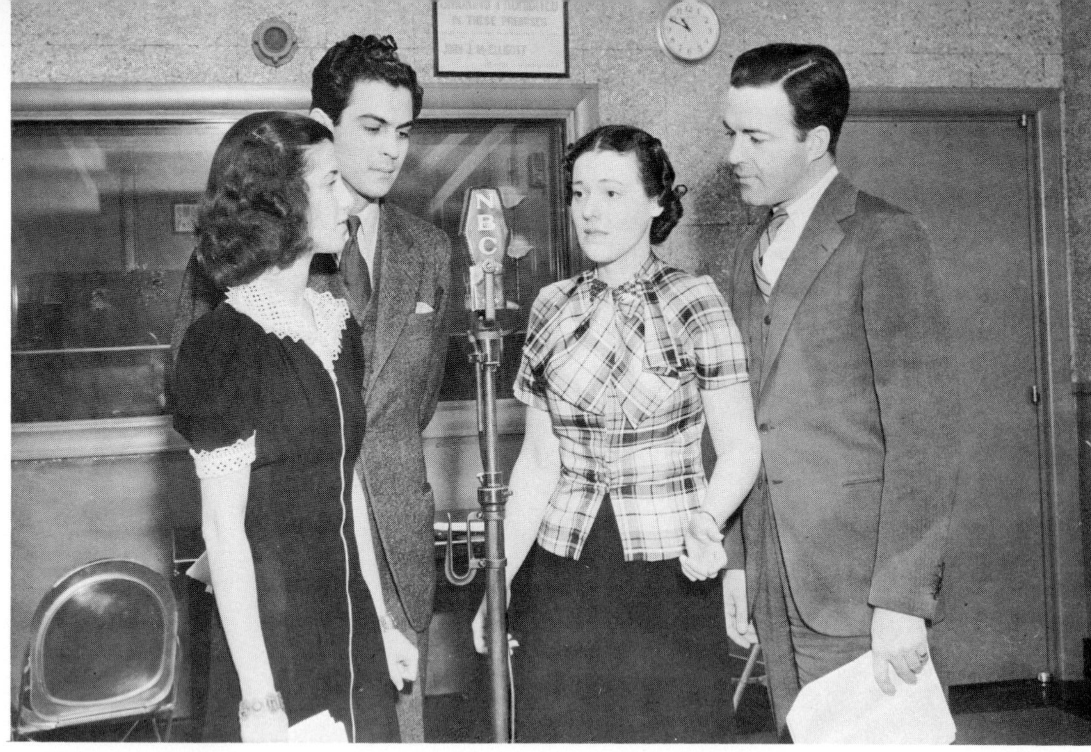

CULVER PICTURES

Beginning on NBC Red on Sept. 14, 1936, John's Other Wife ran as a daytime serial until 1942. John Perry owned a store and his "other wife" referred to his secretary.

came along, and suddenly we found our stories being heard by a million, then by several million, people. (Imagine the effect on Scheherazade!) The early sponsors were mostly soap companies, although food manufacturers soon came in. The expression "soap opera" came along, probably in the 1930's, as a result of a critic's inspiration—following the lead of "horse operas," I suppose. In the early 1940's a *Liberty* magazine writer named J. P. McEvoy came to interview me. His wife came up with a variation on soap opera. She called the programs "washboard weepers." When McEvoy's interview came out, he dubbed me the Scheherazade of Daytime Drama.

As now, sponsors of the radio serials were interested primarily in selling their products. There are a couple of differences today, however. In the early days, what counted was whether the product moved off the grocers' shelves. It was fairly easy to gauge the popularity of your program through the simple measurement of sales. There were relatively unsophisticated ratings systems—the Hooper and the Crossley, to name two—but they were never relied upon to the extent of today's Nielsen television measurements.

The Price of Progress

In a sense, the Nielsen—which, after all, is based on samplings taken in only a limited number of homes in the country—has become a kind of tyrant of the industry. It not only guides the thinking of sponsors and agencies about whether to cancel this program or that, but in the case of daytime drama it may even dictate what the writer must do with story lines. There is no arguing with the ratings; they stand unassailable in the minds of the network executives and many advertising agencies, who decide how the sponsors' dollars are spent. (I should hasten to add that my own association with my sponsors over the years has been gratifyingly open, honest, and straightforward.) Scheherazade would never have made it through her thousand and one nights if Nielsen had been around.

COURTESY, ABC

CULVER PICTURES

Emily McLaughlin and John Beradino star in the ABC television series General Hospital (above, left), an audience favorite in 1972. Medical problems were also a subject of high interest to the 1940's listeners of Joyce Jordan, Girl Interne, starring Ann Shepherd and Paul Henreid (above).

With these complications have come the added ones of producing a program on television, as opposed to radio. Radio was a perfect medium for presenting drama. It was possible to paint almost any scene, construct any set, arrange any situation simply by leaving things to the imagination of the listener. A train whistle, the hiss of steam, the voice of a train caller and—presto!—you had created Grand Central Station. You might as easily whisk your audience to a city sidewalk (sounds of auto horns, streetcar bells) or a hospital corridor (chimes, loudspeaker: "Doctor Brent, call surgery . . ."), with a few instructions to the special-effects department. To perform the same tricks in television requires the expenditure of thousands of dollars in sets or the movement of your entire crew and cast to a location somewhere. In the end, the result is still not as good as the mental pictures the audience builds for itself from the radio.

Still, soap opera is trying to break the bonds that have held it to a studio for all these years. On As the World Turns, for example, we have begun to experiment with location tapings for special events—including the wedding of two main characters in a recent episode. This took place in a small church in New York City, with results that delighted everyone. These location trips are expensive and time-consuming, however—probably three times as costly as a similar setup in the studio, where lighting and sound can be carefully controlled. Yet, if the daytime serial is to grow, I believe it must begin to flex its imagination in this direction.

Getting It All Together

The evolution of a daytime drama from concept to broadcast follows lines more or less the same as those in other television programming, except that ours is a daily, not a weekly or monthly, process. In the case of As the World Turns, it starts with a long-range outline, which I compose. This describes in very broad strokes—and is subject to change at any time—the general direction in which

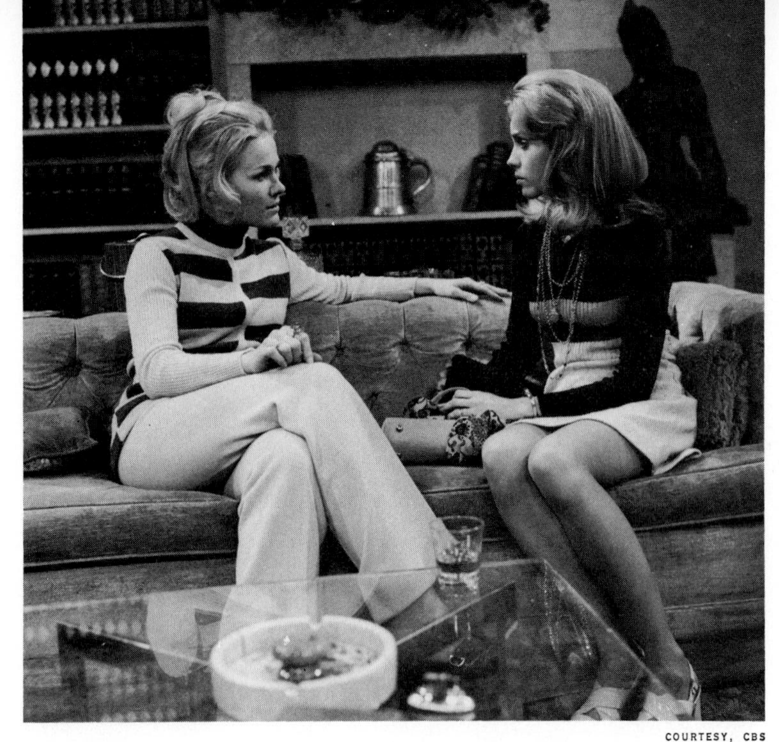

COURTESY, CBS

Love Is a Many Splendored Thing regularly features Bibi Besch (left), who plays Iris Garrison. Barbara Stanger plays her sister Laura Elliott. The series began in 1967.

I expect to take the characters and situations. I go over the outline with representatives of the sponsor and agency. Changes are discussed, sometimes incorporated, sometimes not. Once the long-range projection is established, I settle down to work on daily outlines. I leave the creation of daily finished scripts to a pair of creative associates who work out specific dialogue and stage directions. Their script comes back to me for changes, if necessary, and final OK.

At the end of each day's production, the producer, director, and cast sit down with the next day's script for a preliminary reading. By the following morning, the players have memorized most of their lines, and they go through three walk-throughs, or dress rehearsals, before air time. Each of these rehearsals gives the director a chance to make adjustments in the show and get it timed for the allotted 30-minute period.

To stay current with the story lines, it is necessary for the writer to turn out a day's worth of program every 24 hours—or five shows a week. I dictate my outline to a secretary, who transcribes it and sends it along to the scriptwriters. Occasionally, when I wish to get a few weeks ahead to take a vacation, I will write scripts myself so that within a couple of weeks I am ahead of production by five weeks.

How close do I stay to the original long-range projection? Put it this way: as close as possible without unduly restricting myself. In other words, if a situation develops in the news that makes a certain plot development impractical (let's say a character comes down with an ailment for which a cure is suddenly found) I need to have enough flexibility to be able to drop it. Conflicting situations on other serials also cause me to shift gears on As the World Turns. Occasionally an actor will request some time off (actors are frequently asked to perform in stage productions, and we feel it is important for their professional well-being to have this freedom); so I will write him out of several weeks' episodes.

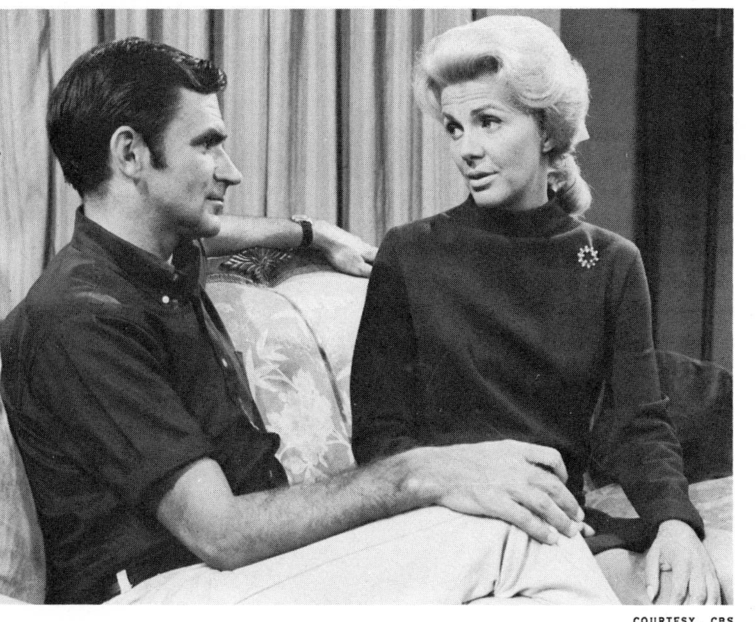

COURTESY, CBS

Audrey Peters and Ronald Tomme star as Vanessa and Bruce Sterling in the CBS Television Network soap opera Love of Life, which premiered on Sept. 24, 1951.

Memories and Medicine

People too young to remember radio serials probably think the half-hour format of daytime television drama has always been the standard. Actually, as most people over 40 years of age will recall, the radio drama came in 15-minute segments. The names of those programs still evoke memories: Lorenzo Jones, Ma Perkins, Our Gal Sunday, Today's Children, The Guiding Light. Yes, The Guiding Light. I originated this program on radio in 1937, and we recently celebrated its 35th birthday. It is the longest-running serial program in the history of broadcasting. Many of the characters in those programs were as memorable as the titles. As far as my own characters are concerned, I find myself most intrigued by the ones with the most complex personalities, such as Lisa on As the World Turns. Some people might call her immoral; I would call her amoral. In any case, she is fascinating. Some others I have enjoyed were Bert (Bertha) Bauer of The Guiding Light, a too-ambitious wife who put her husband through many trying times (she eventually drove him to drink, fostering radio's first dipsomaniac); Doctor Rutledge, from the radio days of The Guiding Light; and Rose Kransky, from that show, probably radio's first unwed mother.

Among my favorite programs from radio days, Road of Life is high on the list because of its attention to the progress of medicine. This interests me to this day, and I think most listeners feel the same way. Soap opera is, in a way, a popularized history of modern medicine. If a real-life medical breakthrough takes place, it is usually dramatized on one or more daytime serials. We have passed from the era of sulfa drugs to open-heart surgery, with every incision and suture played out on the stage of daytime drama.

Doctor Brent was another favorite character of mine. The Woman in White came out of a two-month stay I made in the hospital back in the 1920's. I always have felt that the women involved—the

As the World Turns, written by the author, is the ongoing story of the Hughes family. In a scene from this CBS television program are Don MacLaughlin, who plays Chris Hughes, with Eileen Fulton, who is Lisa Shea. As the World Turns had its television premiere on April 2, 1956.

nurses—really saved my life. They were with me day and night, working 12-hour shifts. Some of their lectures were precious and also memorable. That's why I decided to write The Woman in White.

Answering Human Needs

What has kept the audiences involved in daytime drama for all these years? Two great human events were largely responsible for the success of the early years. During the Great Depression and World War II, people had a tremendous need for human contact. Families were drawn closer, even while being rent by the tragedy of privation and war. Communication was important, identification imperative. Daytime drama answered much of the longing these people felt for meaningful and accessible escape and identification. Today, I credit these two elements, plus a third, for the continuing popularity of the daytime serial format. The third factor is a sense of conviction. Taken in order:

1. Escapism. While I reject the theory that the U.S. housewife is a downtrodden and unchallenged slave to her kitchen, I do recognize that her life, as all of ours, contains a degree of tedium and monotony. I think the soap opera listener, therefore, ought to be given some insights into other lives and life-styles. She (or he) should be offered the chance to participate vicariously in problem solving, from minor matters such as how to settle a family quarrel to weightier issues such as crime, punishment, and retribution. The listener should be asked to think a little. With it all, there should be some means to achieve the second element:

2. Identification. It is a perilous practice among dramatic writers to allow their situations or characters to become too remote from the average listener. On As the World Turns, for example, I have tried to keep my characters on a life-size scale. They are well off, but not wealthy. They are average in intelligence. My villains (though I reject the concept of the totally irretrievable character)

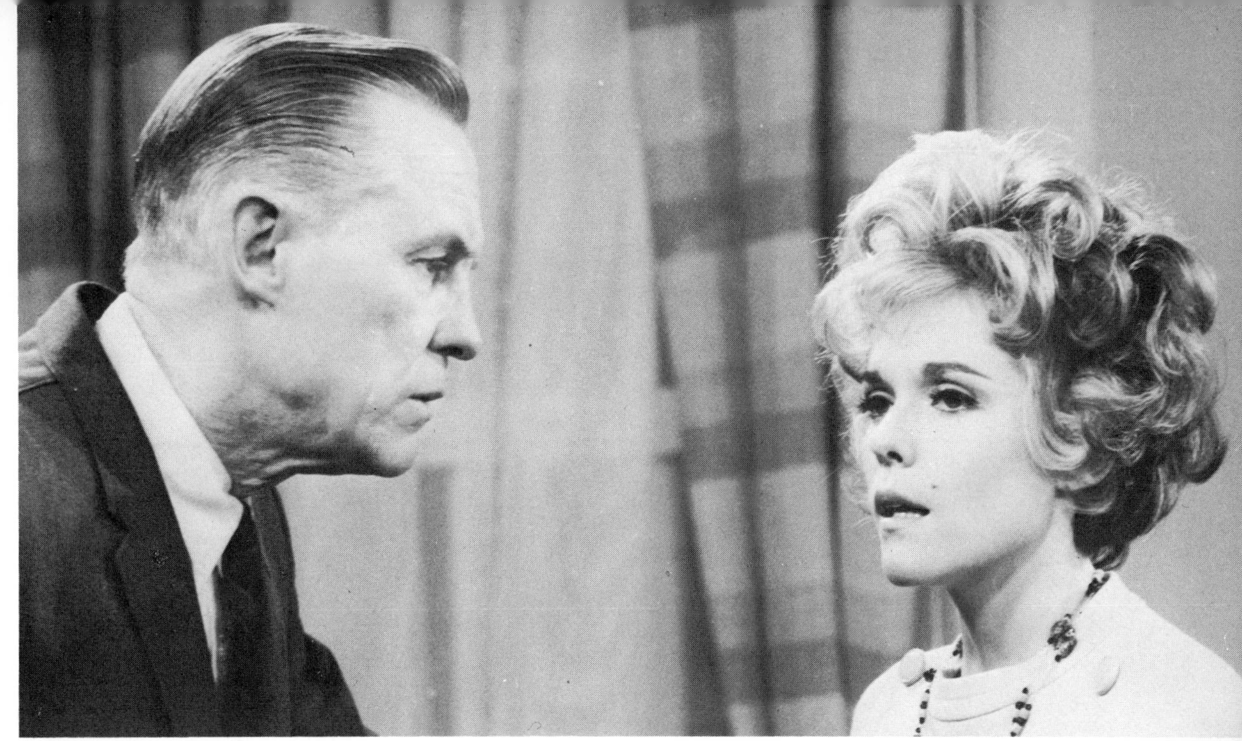

COURTESY, CBS

are never so villainous that the listener turns away in disgust. There must be that element of universality in everything—that something that causes the listener to say, "Yes, I have felt that way," or "I have known someone very much like that."

3. Conviction. I suppose there is a little of the evangelist in all of us, and I am no exception. I have always tried to impart a point of view to my stories, to carry a message, if you will, that I believe is important for the viewer to hear. He or she may not agree with it; that is obviously one's privilege. It is not a heavy-handed message, I hope, but one that comes across only from prolonged exposure to a program like The Guiding Light or As the World Turns.

What is the message? Nothing earthshaking. I have tried to let my programs convey my own faith in the family unit—not necessarily the unit of yesterday, but also the possible unit of today and tomorrow. I believe in a stable home, in healthy mental attitudes, in discipline, and in cooperation. The critics say, "But why then do soap operas convey such a sense of overwhelming tragedy, of lives gone wrong?" First of all, I don't believe they do; but as for the tragedy that is seen, I can only point out that unrelenting bliss can be (in dramatic terms) as tedious as unrelenting misery. It is true, however, that there is a school of serial writing that might be characterized as "never a dull moment." I try to leaven my story lines with problems of the sort anyone may encounter from time to time—some of us, to be sure, more often than others. These troubles, or tragedies, are a kind of crucible in which I try to expose the inner strengths or weaknesses of my characters. I ask myself what forms escapism should take—on television or in real life. Many people today simply do not want to face reality, and they look to television to escape it. I believe that answering their need is part of my mission as a writer.

Even Scheherazade must have felt that her storytelling was more than an exercise in lifesaving.

Confrontation: Dialogue with Youth

A Compton Forum

Is there a generation gap?

What is the biggest problem that high school students face today?

What kind of hard information does youth want about education, government, jobs, drugs, health?

These as well as numerous other "no holds barred" queries were posed to two youth panels by the editors of Compton's during the past year. The responses were illuminating and beneficial for future editorial planning.

The first of these conferences, held in April, consisted of delegates from a cross section of city schools in Chicago. Fourteen students representing the Crane, Farragut, Metropolitan, Schurz, Taft, and Tuley schools participated. The second, held in July, was made up of delegates from a selection of schools across the country. Fourteen students from Arkansas, California, Florida, Illinois, Maine, Michigan, Minnesota, New York, and Pennsylvania met and voiced their opinions. Both conferences were moderated by Dr. Frank S. Endicott of Northwestern University. His summary of the first session included these observations:

All students but one stated that they planned to go to college. Almost all had some idea concerning what vocation they were most interested in—medicine, journalism, conservation, art, psychology.

Is there a generation gap? *Yes.* It was agreed that they found it difficult to communicate with adults but, as they put it, "Adults have had more experience" and "Parents worry about us."

What is the biggest problem that high school students face today? Jobs and career choice; how to get needed guidance; lack of understanding by older people; how to achieve personal identity; uncertainty about what role to play; bewilderment about matters such as the draft, birth control, abortion; how to get a good education; getting grades that are good enough to get into a university; how to bring about change; staying in school; getting along with teachers; racial relations; and being accepted.

What concerns youth most when thinking of the more distant future? Ecology; growth and control of population; peace; boredom; use of leisure and recreational activities; jobs and effects of automation; politics and government—how to bring about change; disease and treatment; cost of living and inflation; dependency on government; and the relationship between the individual and society. What kind of help does youth need regarding these problems: causes; specific information; facts, with statistics? What can *we* do about it?

In discussing drugs, the students agreed that they were constantly confronted by the problem, often invited to take them, and sometimes given them free for a first trial. They wanted real facts and information about drugs and their effects.

In discussing venereal disease, they indicated that they were concerned about the problem and that they wanted to know "real facts"—such as causes, cures, and what to do. Not "scare statistics with pictures of people with sores all over them."

On the whole, most of them were critical of their schools. To improve them, one even suggested "fire the board of education." They respect teachers who treat them as adults, show real interest in them, give help when they need it, are friendly and approachable, and are fair in evaluations. They do not respect teachers who do not know their subjects or have no control over their classes.

Final comments by the students were responses to a request for their suggestions for adults, including parents and teachers, who would like to deal helpfully with them. "Trust us; listen to us; think first and make no snap decisions; don't just say 'don't do it' but give reasons; try to understand us; remember that things are different for us."

The following are thought-provoking, verbatim excerpts from the second session:

Moderator: How much faith do you have in the political leadership of our nation?

D: I think the democratic process is fine in theory, but I wish there were more safeguards against dirty politics, and it's unfortunate that they exist because people do lose faith.

A: I think a lot of what's wrong with the government is that it's a great big bureaucracy. The priorities are kind of screwed up. Our nation is botched up with certain matters, and important things are put aside.

E: You see slums and people starving and living in deplorable conditions, and it's sickening when the government's spending all kinds of money on the war in Vietnam and landing a man on the moon.

N: There's so much unemployment that it's not funny. People can't find jobs and have to support a family and they're forced to go on welfare, which keeps going up and up in cost.

F: Sometimes it seems that our president overlooks a lot of the problems that really are important to us. He should take these things more seriously and weigh them carefully.

E: I feel that a lot of people think that youth should be seen and not heard. I think that we have knowledge and a lot of interesting ideas, and we live here, too. Ideas should be contributed for whatever purposes they might serve. Everyone should have an equal right, and we should be allowed to voice opinions.

C: Right on. I think a major problem is that no one ever does anything until a crisis happens. Like, for instance, Attica, the prison riot that took place there. Prison problems have been prevalent for a long time, but no one does anything about it until it's too late, until people, innocent or otherwise, are killed.

K: Now, I could understand if I was making $3,000 a year and had seven children to support and I didn't have a job why people have to rob to support their families and live in slum areas because they can't help themselves.

C: That is exactly what the problem is today, and nobody seems to care a damn about it or, at least, try to help these poor people out in any way.

H: I hear this all the time—"America may not be perfect, but it's still better than any other country." Well, the fact remains that with the potential, wealth, and resources we possess we should be able to raise the standard of living for millions of poor people. These things are changing, but not rapidly enough.

Moderator: Do you have a suggestion as to how we might bring about these changes more swiftly?

H: I think it's got to be partially through education, but then, of course, you are never going to succeed in educating a person without first feeding him. He has to eat, you know.

D: I agree with that, but to get a bit more optimistic about it, it seems to me that the United States makes out better with our diverse peoples and citizenry than a lot of countries.

H: I don't think you could compare the United States to any other country in the world, and I don't think you should compare it. We have to look at ourselves and reorder our priorities. We have to reform it so that it can be meaningful.

I: I really can't appreciate the politicians who have shoe boxes; but I still think that there are some politicians who are dedicated to their work and to their government, and thank goodness we still do have some of them.

Moderator: Do you think that change can be brought about within the system?

F: I certainly do, if it's done right.

N: You would need organization and togetherness.

K: I think revising the system itself would have to be done first. I don't like the term "changing the system" because it's a euphemism. I think they say that so people don't get scared. It's whenever people face change that they get flustered, but it does need revision.

N: I think there is one part of our system that I don't think should be kept and that is patronage. It just leads from one person who has the same ideas to another. That stops change.

M: It seemed for a while we were making progress, like people were beginning to give up their prejudices a little bit, but I think there is regression because people are starting flag-waving. People are more proud of their prejudice.

Confrontation:

A Compton Forum

I: I think we should revise our ways of choosing political candidates. I don't particularly like the convention method or the electoral college. I would prefer an open primary. At the quadrennial conventions they are not going to necessarily choose who the people have selected.

H: We have all grown up in a generation where there has been more violence in the political world, and I am sure I don't have to start by relating each occurrence—but you had John F. Kennedy, Martin Luther King, Jr., Robert Kennedy, Malcolm X, and on and on, ending most recently with George Wallace. I think that we must change the way the people campaign and more of the laws. Even though it's nice for the candidates to get out in front of the people, we should take more advantage of the media.

E: I really think that we have been misled. In school we hear about democracy and about the government, but now we are being hit with the fact that this really isn't happening like it is supposed to, that this beautiful America isn't so beautiful after all. I feel sorry for immigrants who come to this country wanting to live in better conditions and are hit in the face with the same things here again.

B: I think a direct election is needed. If the people banded together and used their entire weight and authority, instead of letting the rich push them around, to support a candidate who they think should be nominated, this to me would be the right way of getting someone elected for the highest office of the land.

Moderator: How many of you, if you had the opportunity, would consider a political career?

L: No way.

K: I guess if it were possible to make changes, I would try, but I am on a local level. I know of a couple of politicians in my community and they were really nice guys, and if they could do something for you, they would try, but as it is, the back scratching of politics is ridiculous. You can't do anything because of all the material interest that is around. You can't do one thing because another group will get offended or because the politician is over you. I would like to work with poor people, and I might want to be a teacher and just try with my students to build individuality, to help them to be able to think for themselves and not follow along with the sheep.

L: I agree. You have to do your own thing.

F: All the money that was raised for the campaigns could have been spent for things of more importance, and there could be so many other people who would be really good to run for office but can't because of money.

C: I would like to try, but I know I'm the type of person that if I see something that is going wrong and I can't do anything about it, I'm totally helpless, and useless, and frustrated.

F: I know so many people who have seen things wrong and tried to change them, but they are kicked out because there are so many people above them making demands.

N: The waste that goes on is horrendous. Politicians should be required to let the people know just what they're doing, where their money is going, and account for all the funds that are handled by them.

G: Whatever the newspapers print is the only way some people have of finding out about their government, but the newspapers are biased because they print their versions of what they think of the government.

J: I want the government to tell the truth, and that way, everybody will be able to mutually trust one another. Every reference work that I have picked up talks about the government being judicious, righteous, and good, that it's truly the best system known. But it's not so according to what you hear and see happening. I'm up to my ears with that, and I want to know how our government really is, how it should be, and if it's being run right.

B: I think one thing which might be included in such books is a section on third parties that has some honest revelations about what these parties stand for.

H: Reference books should be something like—well, something you always wanted to know about but were afraid to ask. Writers shouldn't be afraid to put in what the real truth actually is.

Moderator: How many of you think that schools by and large are doing a good job?

E: I would say some are.

A: Oh, that is impossible.

H: They may be doing a good job, but for wrong things. They may be doing a good job in teaching people to copy, but I don't think they are doing it in teaching people to learn.

J: I don't think that when a person gets into the 12th grade that he should have to read 3d-grade books, which is what many do in my school. I just don't think it's right, and I think it stems from poor elementary schools.

K: In the American high school, the student is really oppressed, and there are creativities that should be explored but aren't. I feel that you are taught to remember facts and that

that is the extent of it. The teachers are only a source of knowledge, and you are not asked to inquire and you don't have a say in what you learn. There are stupid rules like hall passes, and it's like a prison. You have to abide by those rules. You can't even go to the washroom without having to ask for permission. It's childish.

N: The priorities of school are wrong. What a school should be doing is teaching you how to learn for yourself, but you can come out of high school having no idea of how you could find out about a subject or, once you are interested in something, how you could learn it. You need a teacher that knows what the hell he's teaching because you are brought up depending on that teacher as your source of information.

D: I think there ought to be more emphasis in schools on self-help, such as instruction as to where you go to get information from sources. And then whatever you learn, you do it at your own pace. You do it as fast as you want.

F: It really pisses me off because they say that everyone must go to school. Well, school is not for everybody, you know. My school is a college preparatory school, and everything revolves around college, and it's sickening. They have got to start changing it because otherwise it's going to go down the drain.

G: I agree that there should be some kind of basic education that every student should receive. Up to the tenth grade there should be requirements for every individual. I think the school classroom should be more relaxed than when you are lined up in rows, and I think teachers ought to get rid of some of their prehistoric methods. A teacher should go among groups to discuss each idea.

M: They tell you, "Oh, you have to learn all of this stuff so you will have a good job. If you go to college and graduate, you'll really advance and get somewhere in life." They don't care about fulfillment. You don't get to learn because you want to; it's all external. Adults are dissatisfied with their jobs because they are always after money. They have never learned to do things just because it makes them happy or offers fulfillment.

H: I think what this all goes to prove is just no sense of direction, which is mindless. We fail to see a purpose.

Moderator: Do you think that some of the procedures that you have proposed will work with the lower percentage of the high school students who are less able and less self-directive than you are?

K: Well, it's worked in a couple of progressive schools. It's been proven that individualized instruction programs have worked on the lower-level kids because individualized instruction lets you work at your own level.

B: Well, in our school, they teach alternative subjects for high school. And by individualizing education for each student, it works.

M: We had a series of lectures, and dropouts were invited, and they really loved it. They could learn what they wanted and on their own because they like it. It works for them.

N: The whole thing is that you have to start it with the younger students.

E: I really had a bad time in my first school. You really have to want to learn in order to progress in a school like that. Then I had to want to progress in the school that I'm in. It's a free school, but you still have to have that will to learn and a desire to better yourself. I nearly flunked out when I transferred because I was nervous. It wasn't that I didn't want to learn, but I was scared. When you put a person into something that is totally new to them, they will withdraw sometimes. They get shook up or frightened.

N: I agree. I have seen it happen when a new student comes in and becomes uncertain.

Moderator: Are you concerned with anything in particular as you think about college?

E: Well, I hate the idea of thinking that maybe I would be accepted just because I was black and would be used to meet a quota. I really hope to attend college and make a career for myself, but when those people sit down and think, "Oh, we have got to have a certain amount of blacks, chicanos, Puerto Ricans, Chinese, and so on," that's what really gets me. I want to be accepted as a person.

K: I think the admission procedures for college are poor. The college tests, the requirements, for example; four years of English to get into college, two years of this, three years of that. I feel that you should be judged by your personality and your character and just what you have achieved, not because you took two years of a foreign language. It's how well you did in all subjects, not just what you took.

H: I think you've got a good point because it prevents us from going to a school of our choice if we don't take their requirements.

J: The usual university has a four-year course, but perhaps in certain subject areas or depending on the curriculum perhaps it should be a two- or three-year course.

D: Costs bother me, also. I think it's the colleges' fault, too. They scream about the cost of education. They are going way up, you know, and we can't do a thing about it. Yet I walk down the halls and see some professor's office and it shows all the courses that he teaches which amounts to one or two. Now, if that guy taught more courses, the cost would go down.

G: I don't see how a group of people can sit down and write one test and give it to students all over the country to try and pass and say, "You are going to take this test, and if you do bad on this, you can't go to college." I think there should be a verbal kind of thing given.

J: They make up a test in the East, okay? So I'm living in the West, and others live elsewhere. We are not going to do as good as the student who lives in the East, not because he is smarter, but because it's a cultural test. I don't know where they dig them up, but I've never heard of those words they give you.

L: I don't think I agree with that because I know a lot of students in the East who have taken those tests and get nowhere with them, and even though the tests are made right there, they still give it out all at the same time.

E: I want to be able to meet people in school, and I feel that when you get into college, people are apt to go to class, come back, and that's it. I feel that a person who succeeds intellectually and doesn't succeed socially is just plain stupid. Education is fine, but there are other things to consider. I think it's all part of gaining an education.

K: If you're well-adjusted socially, you are able to handle a lot more than factual answers.

Moderator: What would you like to say to teachers that would help them most?

G: I would suggest that they shouldn't teach for the money. In other words, don't look at it just as a job and you want to earn as much as you can and just ignore what you're doing. You should show some enthusiasm, some spirit in what you're doing. Be dedicated. Be conscientious.

J: Don't be afraid to let the students teach you something. I think teachers are afraid to teach, afraid to correspond and relate with students.

K: Be humane. Teachers should show more human decency, more interest in each student.

L: Learn to relate with your students.

M: Don't teach. I mean, let the kids learn, but don't stand up there and feed it to them.

H: I'll say it in one word—love. I think that's the simplest and easiest way to put it. Love has to be shown. There has to be feeling.

F: Well, I would say just to stop lying. A student should try to be honest with a teacher, and the same goes for the teacher. She should try to be honest with her students and not say, for example, that Johnny is doing well when he isn't. They should tell it like it is, you know? If you don't know it, admit it.

B: You should recognize that each student is different and create individualized education.

D: I would give the teacher advice to continue being a student himself and don't take the attitude that he knows everything. Have an open mind and be willing to learn from others. Quit going for advanced degrees; learn on your own.

Moderator: Are any of you concerned about vocations?

C: I don't see why people have to pick a certain profession that they want to do for the rest of their lives. I mean, I don't see why we have to pick it now. I just want to live and learn and decide later on what I'd like to do. We are compelled to follow a course too soon.

F: With living and earning money, too. It seems like people are forcing you to do this.

C: Yes, you have to go to school so you can reach some sort of a goal so that you can earn a living. Nothing's wrong with this, but we shouldn't be compelled to do that right now.

F: It's constantly going on since you are in kindergarten. It's always harped on, "Well, I think what you want to do is to become a doctor or a lawyer," and here you're only in grade school. Parents always ask you, "What do you want to be when you grow up?" Or else they will tell you what they would like you to be without your deciding. I think this is something that you should decide for yourself and that it should come much later on in life. They always seem to stress making more money and having a profession. Not everyone can become a doctor, a lawyer, an engineer, or a teacher. We all have our limits.

C: Right, they tell you about thinking of making money all the time, and "Forget about being a ceramics person because you can't make any money doing that"; or if you want to be a cook, "You can't make a living doing that."

L: You have to think of the future. Like there is an abundance of psychologists now. In five years what kind of job would you have then? How many more psychologists will we need?

K: I feel like you have been prompted since you're knee-high to a grasshopper.

H: There's always been a difference in the way that we have treated little girls and little boys in choosing jobs. That pressure has always been greater for boys, and now recently, girls have been feeling that more so.

I: Especially with women's lib.

K: I will wager that the jobs that two thirds of the people in this room will be doing when they are middle-aged aren't even in existence yet, and I see no reason to hassle about what you are going to do. The better thing is to prepare the student, give him a diverse education with a lot of choices, prepare him for the future. When the year 2000 rolls around, there are going to be so many different kinds of things that people will be suffering from shock if they are not educated right. You have to bring this into the proper perspective.

L: I think that you should get your education, but not choose a certain field because you can make more money and live out in the suburbs when you're more interested in doing something that you would really enjoy, that's all.

D: I'm not going to let oversupply or overabundance determine what I do. I'm going to pursue my vocation for my own self. I'm going to learn many skills that can be used in what I'm attempting to do. I would like to go into mechanical engineering probably the most, but I'm still going to pursue other fields. When in college, I intend to take flight training and learn about aviation, so I will have something to fall back on. I think it's good to have more than one skill. I would like to try many options and exercise them as best as I can. And maybe in my lifetime, I'll get to try them all.

Moderator: What help do you get from counselors?

M: None.

Moderator: What kind of help would you like?

M: Well, if you have an idea what you want to do, they should tell you what you have to learn; sometimes you don't realize how much time is involved and you have to find out where you can learn about it. Let's say I want to take Spanish, and he says, "You should take calculus because you will derive a greater benefit from it." Well, damn it, I don't want to take calculus. I want to learn Spanish. I want to take a course that I don't feel will benefit me in the greatest way but that which I would enjoy. I realize it may benefit me too, but let me do the choosing.

J: When I come in and say to my counselor, "I think I would like to be a teacher," I'd like to know the facts and figures and what kind of colleges that I may attend in getting the best education. All I ask is that they don't put me in a room and say, "Here, look," and then when I come out, "Did you find anything else that you like?" and, "Okay, I'll try to see you later." I don't get anything out of that.

K: I think they should get rid of the job of guidance counselor. I think it's the biggest farce the public school system has ever had. All they do is sit in their offices and tell high-level kids to go to Yale and Harvard and the lower-level kids, "It's not for you, so why don't you get a nice job as an auto mechanic?"

F: I agree with what you're saying because the whole thing winds up with nothing. It's useless because chances are you're not going to follow what they originally tell you to do.

K: If they had teachers who were really competent and cared for every student, then they would have no need for guidance counseling.

J: If you have to have guidance counselors, maybe the answer would be to train someone to be a guidance counselor before they start to advise you on what you should do. The fact is, they're not competent.

E: He's usually a coach that has to have a job, you know; so give him a guidance counselor's job. That's what their attitude is. That's what it amounts to, and it's a waste of time.

B: I learn more from the people who go to college than from talking to either guidance counselors or parents. You're able to find out from them just what's going on.

K: I think a guidance counselor should be experienced in sociology. Each school should have a social worker for troubled kids, like schizophrenics, paranoids, and what have you.

J: I feel the parents play a role in your choosing your profession and your way of life. Maybe it's an unconscious role; maybe it's imitative. If a parent discourages you to do this or that is why a lot of girls do get married at the age of 18 because they don't want to fulfill parents' dreams.

H: In a lot of ways, there could be problems with parents in the area of does everyone have to go to college? Certainly not as far as I can see, because some students just don't have the ability to make it in college. But so many parents want something better for their children and insist on their going to college.

B: I think it's important to not only say what's good about a profession, but what's wrong with it, not giving it a one-sided viewpoint, but to reason the good points and the bad. You have to weigh things carefully. What you want to do now might be boring, you know, after you discover it too late. Tell it like it is, in other words.

FROM LEFT: CAMERA PRESS; UPI COMPIX; PICTORIAL PARADE; UPI COMPIX; WIDE WORLD; PICTORIAL PARADE; A.F.P. FROM PICTORIAL PARADE; FREDERIC OHRINGER FROM NANCY PALMER AGENCY; A.F.P. FROM PICTORIAL PARADE

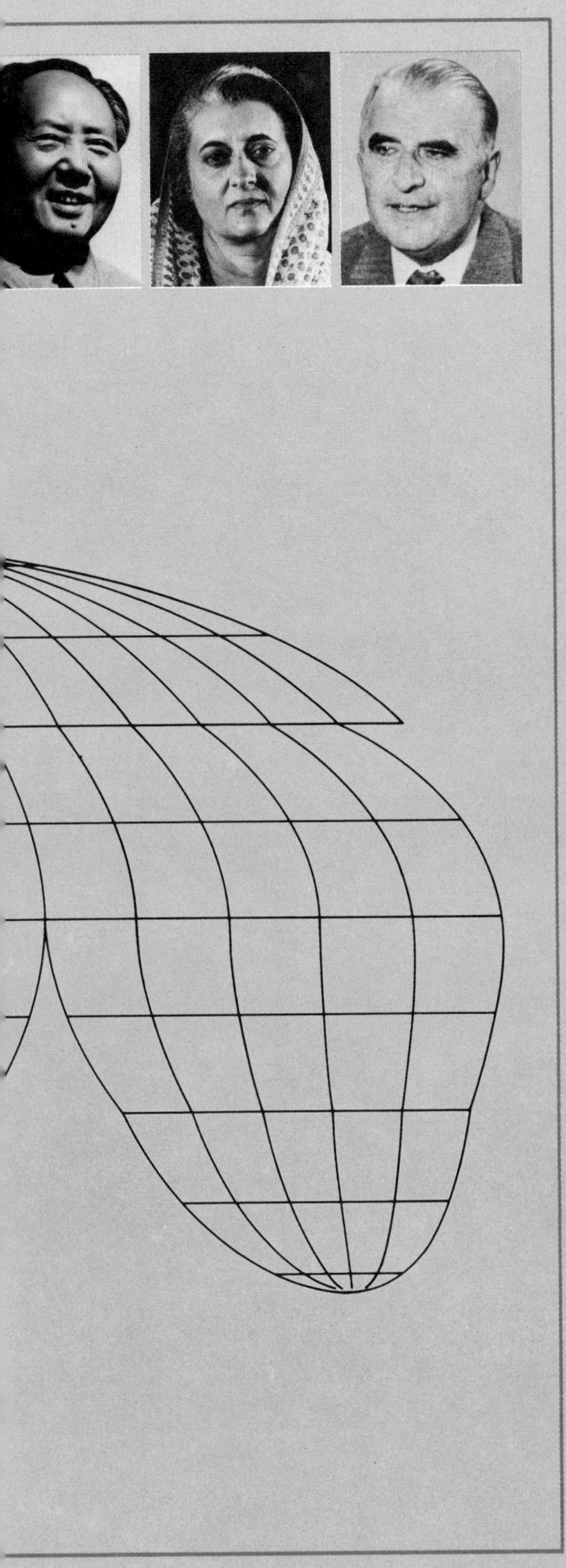

Events of the Year 1972

ADVERTISING. The estimated advertising expenditures in the U.S. for 1972, prepared by a recognized authority, the McCann-Erickson Inc. media research department, New York City, came to $22.5 billion. This represented a gain of 9.3% over 1971. McCann-Erickson reported in August 1972 that all indications pointed to a boom in advertising spending and that a high growth rate could be expected for the following five years. The U.S. Department of Commerce was more optimistic about the 1972 total than McCann-Erickson was, putting it at $22.8 billion. This figure would include $5.4 billion in newspapers, $3 billion in television advertising, $2.8 billion in direct mail, $1.3 billion in radio, and $1 billion in consumer magazines.

More than 600 advertising agencies billed a combined $10.5 billion in 1971, according to the annual report published by *Advertising Age*. This was a record figure, representing a gain of $377 million over the 1970 total.

In June 1972 Theodore L. Bates, 70, died. He was the founder of Ted Bates & Co., the agency that introduced hard-sell advertising in the 1940's and used it to become one of the largest agencies in the world. In September Bernard C. Duffy, 70, died. He had been president of Batten, Barton, Durstine & Osborn from 1946 to 1956 and had been largely responsible for the agency's growth. John K. Herbert, former executive publisher of the old *New York Journal-American* and onetime president of the Magazine Publishers Association, died in September at 69.

The Federal Communications Commission (FCC) looked into the subject of counteradvertising, after being urged by the Federal Trade Commission (FTC) to consider such a measure for television. The FCC was advised by a number of experts that many broadcast advertisers would quit the medium rather than face the possibility that their commercials would bring counterclaims onto the air from consumerists. The FCC started an inquiry into the situation, in response to a petition calling for a ban on advertising during children's programs on television. (*See* Consumer Protection.) The Food and Drug Administration proposed to stop the sale of antiperspirants containing hexachlorophene.

Peter W. Allport, president of the Association of National Advertisers, assailed the Federal Trade Commission (FTC) as a quasi-judicial body acting as judge, prosecutor, and jury. Early in 1972 the FTC singled out breakfast cereals—admittedly a concentrated industry with four companies controlling 91% of sales—for a major test of advertising and marketing as antitrust factors. The federal agency instituted a "shared monopoly" case against Kellogg Co., General Food Corp., General

As part of a new ad campaign for the Brooklyn Museum School of Art, this striking ad by Dick Levy not only brought in its share of new students but won four national awards as well.

ARNOLD BECKERMAN FOR BROOKLYN MUSEUM SCHOOL OF ART FROM KEYSTONE

Television commercials aimed at children were criticized at a Congressional hearing by Dawn Ann Kurth, 11, of Melbourne, Fla. She went before a Senate consumer subcommittee to expose "worthless junk" offered as prizes in advertised products. She displayed a board showing prizes that did not work or that were disappointing.
UPI COMPIX

Mills, Inc., and Quaker Oats Co. The FTC alleged that some of the companies had falsely advertised that their cereals could be effective in controlling weight, and that some of them had featured athletes in their advertising in such a way as to misrepresent the effect of cereals on the athletes' performance. The FTC's allegations contained no claim that the cereal companies had conspired in the traditional sense, with the result that this seemed to be a pioneering effort to determine whether "market structure," in itself, was evidence of illegal monopoly. The FTC charged that the four cereal-industry leaders had attained the status of a shared monopoly by means of such devices as artificial product differentiation, intensive trademark promotions, brand proliferation, restrictive trade and consumer promotions, and restrictive allocation of shelf space in retail outlets, as well as by using advertising that misled children and adults as to the merits of the companies' products. (*See also* Food.)

A little later in the year, the FTC issued one of the most extensive orders in its advertising substantiation program. This order sought proof for the advertising claims made by 16 marketers of cough and cold remedies, including Whitehall Laboratories (for Dristan), Miles Laboratories (Alka-Seltzer Plus), and Father John's Medicine Co. (Father John's Medicine). (For example, the agency demanded "documentation and other substantiation" for the television-commercial claim: "Dristan, the remarkable cold medication, works in your sinuses, the critical area of cold's infection, and helps drain and dry all eight sinuses.") The FTC also demanded specific support for advertising claims advanced by marketers of airconditioners and electric shavers.

The federal agency decided that Ocean Spray Cranberries, Inc., had to run corrective advertising (one of every four advertisements, or 25% of its media expenditures for a year) and no longer talk about "food energy" in its Cranberry Juice Cocktail unless it disclosed that it was referring to calories, but not to vitamins or minerals. The FTC charged that the Coca-Cola Co. had misrepresented the nutritional merits of its Hi-C drink product and said that the company should be required to run corrective advertising. However, an FTC administrative judge later praised Hi-C as a "sensible" and "excellent" source of Vitamin C for children and said that FTC attorneys had failed to establish that Hi-C advertisements misled or deceived people about the product's nutritional values. The FTC ruled that the Firestone Tire & Rubber Co. had falsely advertised that its Wide Oval tires stopped "25% quicker" and that the use of the words "the safe tire" falsely implied that Firestone tires were "safe under all conditions of use." Firestone disputed the FTC ruling and filed an appeal with the U.S. Circuit Court of Appeals.

In another action, the FTC and E. I. du Pont de Nemours & Co. settled the Zerex case, in which the commission had charged that a "can-stabbing" commercial misrepresented the ability of Zerex to seal automobile radiator leaks. The FTC had been widely criticized for publicizing its complaint and then later discovering that its charges were groundless. After two years, the FTC dropped a case of false and unfair advertising against Un-Burn (made by Pfizer Inc.) after failing to prove that advertising claims for Un-Burn were conclusively wrong.

The Colgate-Palmolive Co. became the first advertiser to agree to change an advertisement, after a complaint was made to the National Advertising Review Board (NARB), which had been set up by the industry for self-regulatory purposes. The charge involved Bright Side shampoo's use of the word "organic." The complaint charged that the word took advantage of the public's understanding that it meant something made from naturally grown plants. The NARB also upheld a complaint against the American Dairy Association's television cartoon ads for milk because the ads erroneously implied there was instant energy benefit from drinking milk.

For daily newspapers, the companies with the greatest 1971 advertising revenues were the publishers of the *Los Angeles Times,* $566,085,000; the *Chicago Tribune,* $478,900,000; and *The New York Times,* $290,922,000. The U.S. business press reported advertising revenues of $813.8 million in 1971, a decline of 2.7%. (*See also* Magazines; Newspapers. *See in* CE: Advertising.)

AEROSPACE. Aeronautical technology, for years advanced by military aviation, was beginning to get innovations from civil aviation in 1972. At least this was the general feeling voiced by John H. Shaffer, head of the Federal Aviation Administration (FAA), in a speech at Dayton, Ohio, in August. Shaffer also pointed out that the U.S. aircraft industry built 80% of the transport planes used by the Western nations. As a result, the U.S. economy relied to some extent on export sales of civil aircraft to offset balance-of-payments deficits incurred from the importation of other items. Shaffer thus urged the aircraft industry to seek the technological breakthroughs needed to keep its marked competitive edge in the world market.

SST Thoughts Surface Again

The program for a supersonic transport (SST) was scrapped by the U.S. Congress in 1971 after opponents argued successfully against the plane's high costs, sonic booms, and pollution effects. But FAA administrator Shaffer predicted that the program would be reinstated at a future date. When finally developed, he said, the U.S. SST would operate within the same environmental limits imposed upon the huge jetliners in current operation.

The Boeing Co., which was to have built the SST, and the National Aeronautics and Space Administration (NASA) joined in the study of a unique SST design that embodied an antisymmetric wing system. The tips of the wing would move in opposite directions as the wing pivoted on a central point in the fuselage. Anyone viewing the plane in flight would confront a strange sight. One half of the wing would be angled 45° forward and the other half 45° backward. But the oblique wing design would reduce greatly the drag caused by shock waves generated when identical structures, such as wings and engines, are arranged symmetrically on both sides of an aircraft. The bold new design would enable the SST to cruise at Mach 1.2 speeds (800 mph) over land without producing the annoying sonic booms. The design, however, would provide only a maximum cruising speed of Mach 1.5 (1,000 mph) instead of the Mach 2.7 (1,800 mph) envisioned in the original U.S. SST.

While the SST was only a wistful dream for some U.S. engineers, the British-French offering, the Concorde, continued to log air miles and flight time. By year's end the Concorde had amassed more than 580 flights and surpassed 1,200 hours in the air. The Concorde test program experienced no major problems, but marketing plans for the aircraft were not as fruitful as hoped. The high cost of the plane, more than $50 million each with spare parts, was a factor. However, it fared much better in the marketplace than the Tu-144, its Soviet counterpart. For example, five Concordes were ordered by British Overseas Airways Corp. early in 1972. Later in the year, the People's Republic of China signed a preliminary order for two Concordes, for 1977 delivery. The Tu-144, the first civil aircraft to fly faster than sound, approached its anticipated 1974 operational date without arousing much interest from the world's airlines. Meanwhile, the British government sent Michael Heseltine, minister for aerospace, on a ten-nation promotional tour aboard a Concorde.

A New Jumbo Jet in Service

The L-1011 TriStar from Lockheed Aircraft Corp. was added to the inventory of operating super

The F-15 jet fighter, built by the McDonnell Douglas Corp., is unveiled in St. Louis, Mo., in June. Assistant Secretary of the Air Force Grant Hansen praised the new plane for its maneuverability and powers of acceleration. Target cost of the F-15 was put at $10.5 million apiece.

UPI COMPIX

jetliners in 1972. The L-1011 joined the Boeing 747 and the McDonnell Douglas DC-10 to form the "big three" of U.S. airline jets. Lockheed had more than its share of normal problems in meeting delivery deadlines for the L-1011, however. It was plagued by money problems stemming from cost overruns of its C-5A military transport, plus doubts about engine deliveries when its British engine supplier for the TriStar, Rolls Royce Ltd., became bankrupt and then went into receivership. Nonetheless, the problems were worked out, and by the summer of 1972 the L-1011 was in commercial service with Trans World Airlines and Eastern Air Lines.

Transair of Canada, a regional carrier, introduced a smaller jetliner, the F-28, to North American service in September. Developed mainly by Fokker-VFW of the Netherlands, the F-28 is a 65-passenger twin-turbofan jetliner. When introduced into North American service, it was the only jetliner of its class to have complied with stringent FAA low-noise requirements.

In 1972 Canada and the U.S. began a cooperative effort to increase short-haul air carrier service. The Canadian Ministry of Transport loaned a De Havilland Twin Otter short-takeoff-and-landing (STOL) aircraft to the FAA for analysis and flight testing to gather data on STOL aircraft behavior and STOL airport needs for use by both the U.S. and Canada.

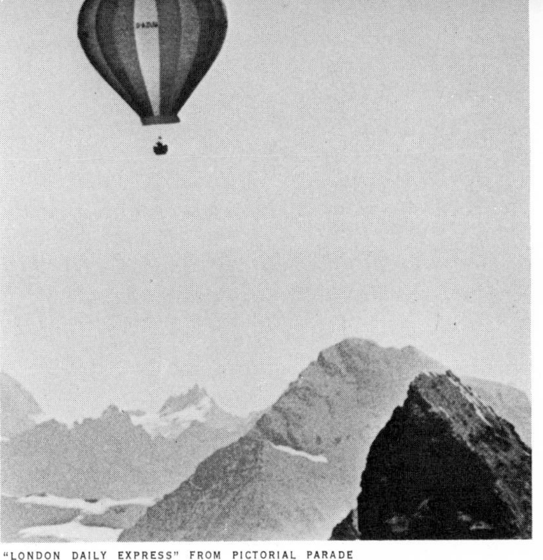

"LONDON DAILY EXPRESS" FROM PICTORIAL PARADE

In August 1972 Don Cameron and Mark Yarry became the first adventurers to cross the Alps in a hot-air balloon.

Military Aviation

The U.S. Air Force (USAF) hoped to replace its aging Boeing B-52 bomber with an advanced manned strategic bomber, the B-1. Flight trials for the new bomber were scheduled for 1974, but acceptance of the new aircraft was far from unanimous. It was under constant cost scrutiny, especially in view of the excessive costs of some recent military planes, such as the C-5A and the Grumman F-14 fighter. Also, the B-1's detractors argued that sophisticated advances in long-range missiles made the manned bomber a relic in the space age. Senator George S. McGovern (D, S.D.) during his presidential campaign charged that the costly bomber would add little to national defense.

Fairchild Industries and Northrop Corp. both continued to vie for the USAF's A-X contract. The A-X, a new attack fighter for close support of ground troops, would have a top speed of more than 400 knots (460 mph), a high-velocity 30-mm. gun, and a mixed bomb load. The Fairchild A-10A and the Northrop A-9A, the two top contenders for the A-X contract, were each test-flown in May. The Air Force, however, would not announce which jet won the competition until early 1973.

Firemen of the Royal Air Force Fire Service demonstrate a foam for extinguishing aircraft fires. The protein foam, also known as light water, is fluorinated. The foam is being sprayed on a burning cylinder representing a plane.

"THE TIMES," LONDON, FROM PICTORIAL PARADE

Northrop's new F-5E Tiger II made its maiden flight at Edwards Air Force Base in August. The F-5E was developed to provide U.S. allies with a versatile tactical jet fighter capable of supersonic flight.

The ill-fated F-111A, built by General Dynamics Corp., was ordered back to combat in Vietnam in 1972 after an absence of more than four years. Although the F-111A was plagued by a number of crashes, many of its pilots had great confidence in it. But just days after its reintroduction to battle on September 28, the plane was temporarily withdrawn from action after one mysteriously disappeared during a mission. The plane was returned to combat a few days later, but at least two more crashed before the end of the year.

The McDonnell Douglas F-15 was slightly ahead of its initial test flight schedule when it took to the air in late July. The F-15 was touted by its promoters as the best fighter plane in the world, mainly because it had unprecedented maneuverability afforded by its lightweight, powerful twin engines and revolutionary wing design. The company's F-4 Phantom design, nearly 20 years old in 1972, was expected to be replaced by the F-15 sometime in the mid-1970's.

Helicopters

When Hurricane Agnes ravaged the East coast of the U.S. in the summer of 1972, the rescue worth of the helicopter was again emphasized. An estimated 3,000 or more persons stranded by the storm were rescued from precarious places by military helicopters. The rescues came off without incident because many of the copter pilots were Vietnam veterans who were thoroughly versed in helicopter hover operations.

Funding for the Lockheed AH-56A Cheyenne, unveiled in 1967 and sent to Vietnam, was cut off in 1972. However, the U.S. Army authorized Lockheed to develop an advanced rigid rotor control system based on its pioneering work in the area.

In 1972, as in recent years, the helicopter gained considerable attention as a law enforcement tool. For example, during the year Los Angeles boasted a fleet of three Bell 206A Jet-Ranger turbine-powered helicopters and seven Bell 47G piston-engine craft. The helicopters performed patrol work, aerial surveillance, and transport duties for the city. (*See in* CE: Aerospace articles.)

AFGHANISTAN. The second year of the worst drought in the nation's history produced suffering and economic chaos that overshadowed all other events in Afghanistan in 1972. The country lost a huge portion of its livestock, especially sheep, causing widespread protein deficiencies in the heavily meat-based diet of the people. Food crops suffered as well. Reports of lack of food and starvation in some areas continued throughout the year, and by fall the situation was termed desperate. Statistics were impossible to obtain in the isolated and mountainous nation, but it was estimated that thousands of people had died and some 50,000 more were starving. Wheat was sent by Pakistan, Iran, the U.S., and to a smaller degree the Soviet Union, but the lack of roads and vehicles prevented prompt distribution. The United Nations Children's Fund rushed food, medicine, and clothing to the most distressed areas, especially the hard-hit province of Ghor. The crisis had not abated at the end of the year.

The only bright spot in this dismal picture was Afghanistan's tourist industry. Travelers on the roads to India and Nepal provided much-needed foreign exchange, and the government continued to improve tourist facilities.

Prime Minister Abdul Zahir resigned on September 24. He was succeeded by Mohammad Moussa Shafiq, the minister of foreign affairs, on December 8. (*See in* CE: Afghanistan.)

AFRICA. The major events in Africa in 1972 included the ending of the 17-year civil war in Sudan; the killing of tens of thousands of people in Burundi; the expulsion of thousands of Asians from Uganda; the withdrawal by the British of their plan for reconciliation with Rhodesia following African opposition; and the overthrow in Ghana of the only democratically elected African government that had come into being *after* a coup d'etat. In 1972 also occurred the death of perhaps the most important African of the 20th century, Kwame Nkrumah.

The death on April 27 of Nkrumah, former president of Ghana, at age 62, brought an era to an end. Having led the first country south of the Sahara to independence from colonial rule in 1957, Nkrumah continually exhorted Africans to forge a Pan-African union. Energetically, articulately, and inspiringly, he preached that Africans could avoid the reimposition of economic, political, and cultural neocolonialism only by joining closely together to work for common goals. (*See also* Ghana; Guinea.)

The Civil War in Sudan

The 17-year civil war in Sudan came to an end with the signing of a pact in Addis Ababa, Ethiopia, on March 27. For his efforts in persuading the southern peoples to agree to the accord, Ethiopia's Emperor Haile Selassie I received Sudanese diplomatic support in his own efforts against Eritrean secessionists in his country. Since 1955, and more especially since 1962, the 12 million Muslim northerners were opposed by the 4 million largely pagan blacks.

Half a million may have died in the war. Villages were burned, and tens of thousands of refugees were in neighboring lands. Much of the south lay desolate. The accord provided for a southern people's council to deal with regional matters.

CAMERAPIX FROM KEYSTONE

Emperor Haile Selassie I of Ethiopia (in uniform) and President Jomo Kenyatta of Kenya talk with Masai tribal dancers at the opening of the first All Africa Trade Fair in Nairobi, Kenya.

Burundi and Uganda

Long-standing tribal animosity came to a climax in Burundi during the year. President Michel Micombero, who had overthrown King Ntare V in 1966 and had ruled as president since then, permitted the former ruler to return from exile in March with assurance of his safety. Arrested shortly thereafter on the charge of involvement in a plot to regain power, Ntare was killed when a group of pro-royalists and disaffected Hutus (comprising the majority of the population) attacked the government on April 29.

Twenty thousand Tutsis were reported slain. The government put down the uprising with the aid of troops sent by neighboring Zaire. In the following weeks the ruling Tutsis (thousands of whom had been ousted and massacred in neighboring Rwanda a decade earlier) killed tens of thousands of Hutus in revenge.

In Uganda on August 5, Maj. Gen. Idi Amin, who had come to power in a coup in January 1971, ordered the expulsion within 90 days of Asians with British passports. Their numbers, originally reported to be about 50,000, were calculated as about 25,000 in October. Later, those holding Pakistani, Indian, and Bangladesh passports were also ordered to leave. Uganda criticized the Asians for controlling much of the economy and not merging with African society.

Coups d'Etat

Army officers in Ghana, led by Col. I. K. Acheampong, seized power on January 13 from the democratically elected government of Prime Minister Kofi A. Busia. Seven months after the coup, an attempt to restore Busia was aborted. Tunisian police dispersed 7,000 striking university students with tear gas on February 5 in the first major protest against President Habib Bourguiba's rule in 15 years.

In Dahomey, which had undergone four coups since 1963, an agreement to rotate the presidency among three men on a two-year basis had been arranged. The transfer of power was peacefully brought about on May 7. On October 26, however, a junta of army officers, led by Maj. Mathieu Kerekou, seized power.

Organization of African Unity (OAU)

On June 15, after 11 days of meetings involving representatives of 40 nations, including 23 heads of state, the Organization of African Unity (OAU) concluded its 19th meeting of the council of ministers and its 9th annual meeting at Rabat, Morocco. General accord prevailed. A new secretary-general, 38-year-old Nzo Ekangaki of Cameroon, succeeded Diallo Telli of Guinea, who had held the post for eight years.

Criticism of the Western powers was expressed because they had not done more to oust the white regimes of southern Africa. The financial commitment to the guerrillas fighting in southern Africa was raised from $2.6 million to $3.9 million. Spain was urged to conduct a referendum on self-government among the 40,000 nomads of Spanish Sahara. Israel was criticized for not returning lands taken in the six-day war in 1967. As an expression of harmony, Morocco and Algeria signed documents formally ending their frontier dispute. The two nations planned to establish cooperative development of iron mines in southwestern Algeria.

Southern Africa

The most notable development during the year was the negating of an accord of November 1971 between Great Britain and Rhodesia. Negotiations between the two countries had gone on intermittently since the European-dominated regime of Rhodesia's Prime Minister Ian D. Smith declared its independence in November 1965. The 1971 agreement angered the African majority. In mid-January, in violent demonstrations in the industrial city of Gwelo, Rhodesia, the Africans indicated to the visiting British commission headed by Lord Pearce that they did not approve the reconciliation. In a month 1,505 people were arrested and 14 killed. The recently formed African National Congress voiced its emphatic opposition before the Pearce commission, and Great Britain formally rejected the 1971 agreement on May 23. While this constituted an important political victory for the Africans, economic sanctions against Rhodesia seemed largely to have failed.

Upon his return from a visit to the U.S., Chief Kaiser Matanzima of the Transkei, one of South Africa's four self-governing homelands, said that he was inspired with a feeling of nationalism and would refuse second-class citizenship. United Nations Secretary-General Kurt Waldheim visited South-West Africa (Namibia) in March and was greeted by black demands for self-government for the territory. On March 8 Waldheim said he believed that the government of South Africa intended to grant self-determination to South-West Africa. (*See also* individual countries by name; International Relations. *See in* CE: Africa.)

These Africans were being smuggled into France, via Italy, when the truck carrying them was intercepted by French police. The men were then sent back to Italy. The United Nations called for an investigation of such human traffic, which a Kenyan official termed a new form of the slave trade. Many Africans have been brought to France illegally to work in very low-paying jobs.

SIPAHIOGLU FROM JOCELYNE BENZAKIN

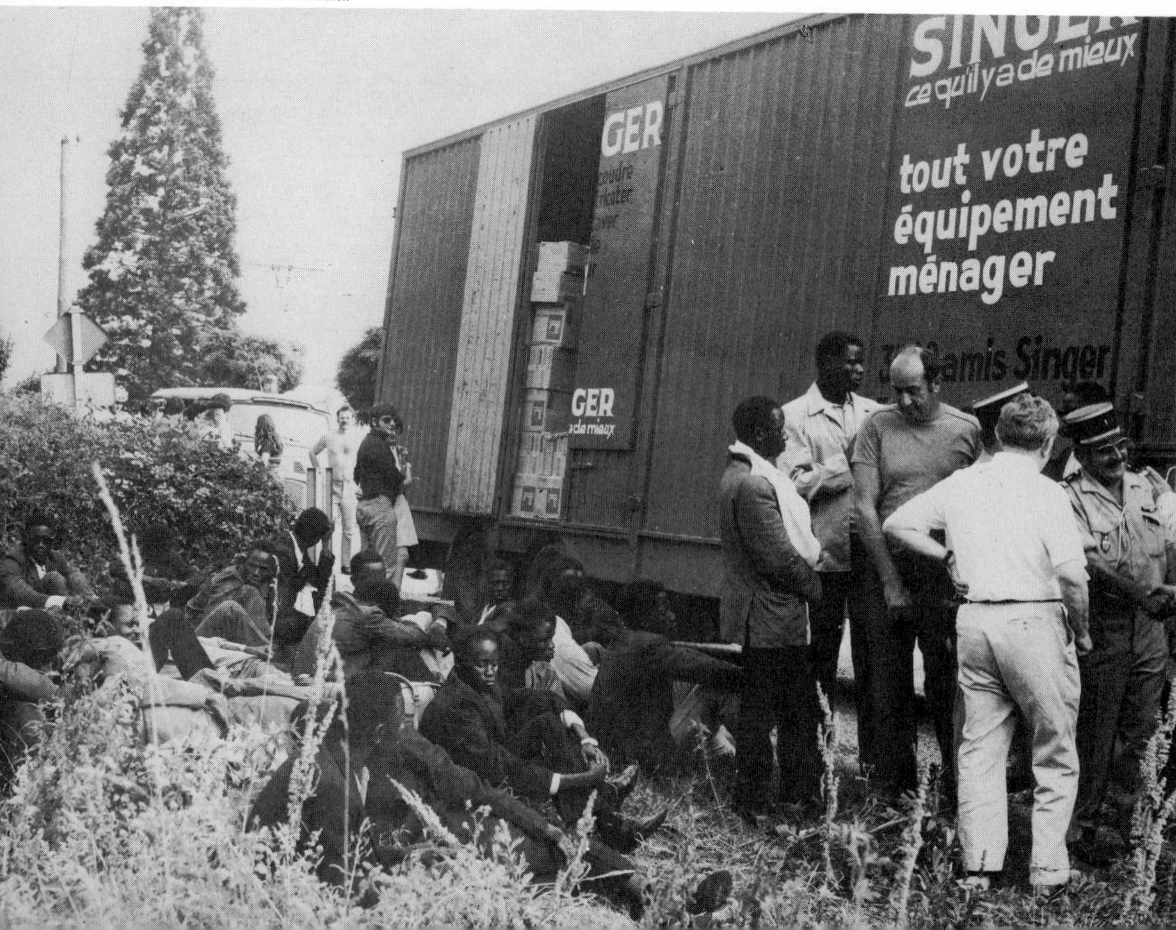

AGNEW, SPIRO T. With the landslide victory of U.S. President Richard M. Nixon in 1972, Spiro T. Agnew retained the vice-presidency and, at the same time, became the first unannounced presidential candidate for 1976. Although he talked little and guardedly about his future during the presidential campaign, Agnew pointed out earlier in the year that he would have little reason to run for reelection if he had no thoughts of at least keeping his options open to seek the presidency. Every U.S. vice-president after 1940 ran for president, with the exception of Alben W. Barkley, whose advanced age made him objectionable in some quarters.

During the 1972 campaign, Agnew was extremely active as Nixon's principal "surrogate," advancing the Nixon Administration's program while the president seldom left the White House. In the course of his travels, Agnew made friends and cemented relations with many Republican politicians. At the Republican National Convention, political allies obviously were looking out for Agnew's interests. They won their fight for a delegate structure at the next convention that would favor rural and conservative states. Clarke Reed, the Mississippi state chairman, was assembling a Southern bloc in the fall of 1972 and planning to deliver it, he said, "to the conservative who can win the election in 1976." If Agnew still looked strong then, Reed said, the Southern unit would back him.

Amid speculation about whether he would ask Agnew to be his running mate again, President Nixon said in January 1972 that he saw no reason to break up 1968's "winning combination." He made the choice official in July. Agnew's popularity with the conservative wing of the Republican party was seen to carry weight in Nixon's decision, as some Republicans were angered by the president's visits to the People's Republic of China and to the Soviet Union.

When the Republican campaign began, the vice-president indicated that he wanted to change the image he reaped in 1970 of being an aggressively irate campaigner. He said that he had not enjoyed being "the cutting edge" for the party and that he welcomed the chance to be able to campaign on the issues. (In criticizing the policies of the Democratic candidates for president and vice-president, Agnew stayed within the generally acknowledged limits of conventional political discourse.) He stressed, however, that regardless of a change in his rhetorical style, his views on various issues remained about the same.

In April Agnew said that U.S. history books and reference books were beginning to show the same New Left bias that, in his opinion, had permeated much of the daily press. In a speech to the Texas Bar Association in July, he renewed his criticism of the federal legal services program. He charged that its lawyers found time to engage in "practically every cause célèbre that comes along" while disregarding individual poor clients.

Toward the end of his campaign, Agnew made news with his responses to hecklers. When a small group began to heckle him at a rally in southern Idaho, he pulled out a whistle and blew on it; he then grinned at the startled audience. From then on, the Agnew antagonists showed up at rallies with their own whistles.

Confronted in San Diego, Calif., on November 1 with the most effective heckling that had yet been organized against him, Agnew declared, "We will have free speech in this country." He called the hecklers the spiritual descendants of Nazi Germany. (*See also* Elections; Nixon.)

In 1972 Spiro T. Agnew was reelected vice-president of the U.S., as the running mate of President Nixon. In the campaign Vice-President Agnew projected a new image, generally low-key.

WIDE WORLD

AGRICULTURE. Farm production throughout the world was generally abundant in 1972. Grains in the U.S. and wheat in Canada, however, were at levels somewhat lower than the 1971 yield. Because of active domestic and foreign demand for U.S. farm products, prices for many of them rose during the year. As a result, farmers' income showed an increase. Anti-inflationary price controls set by the Administration of U.S. President Richard M. Nixon did not directly affect most farm sales. High food prices—of meat in particular—caused by rising middleman profits and expenses, tended to mar the farmer's image in the minds of consumers. Price controls on foods were limited to transactions following initial sale by the farmer.

Family Farms Still on the Wane

There were fewer family-operated farms in 1972 than ever before. They were being preempted by "agribusiness," the large-scale operation of farms as a corporate enterprise of major businesses, many of which held no traditional ties with farming. Those who remained in family farming showed some success during the year. The revised parity ratio, an overall measure of the purchasing power of the farmer, stood at 101, a seven-point increase from the year earlier. The sale of farm products was forecast at $57 billion in 1972. This gave the nation's farmers a total net income of about $18.5 billion, nearly $2.5 million more than they received in 1971. For the average family farmer, this meant an income of about $6,000 a year for his work in the fields. To supplement this, many farmers and

George Wells Beadle, Nobel prizewinning scientist, is doing research on corn. He wants to trace the evolution of corn and its origins.
WIDE WORLD

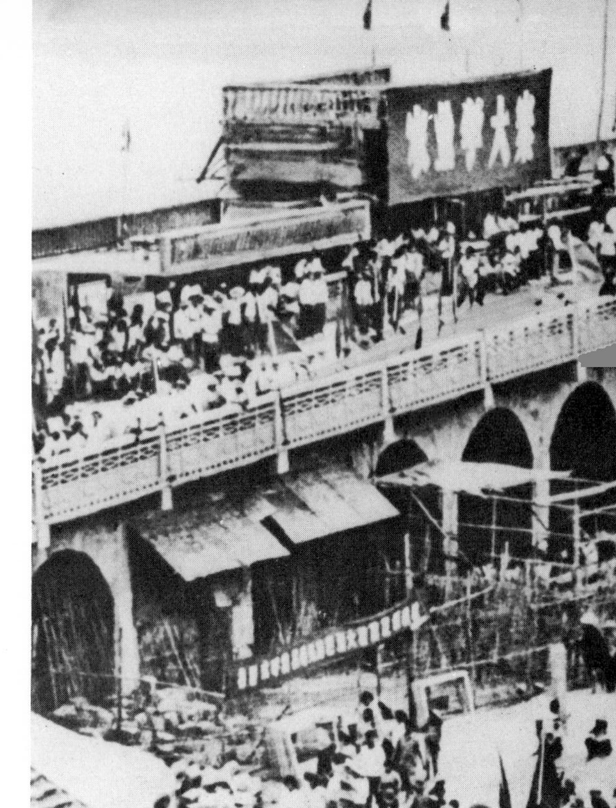

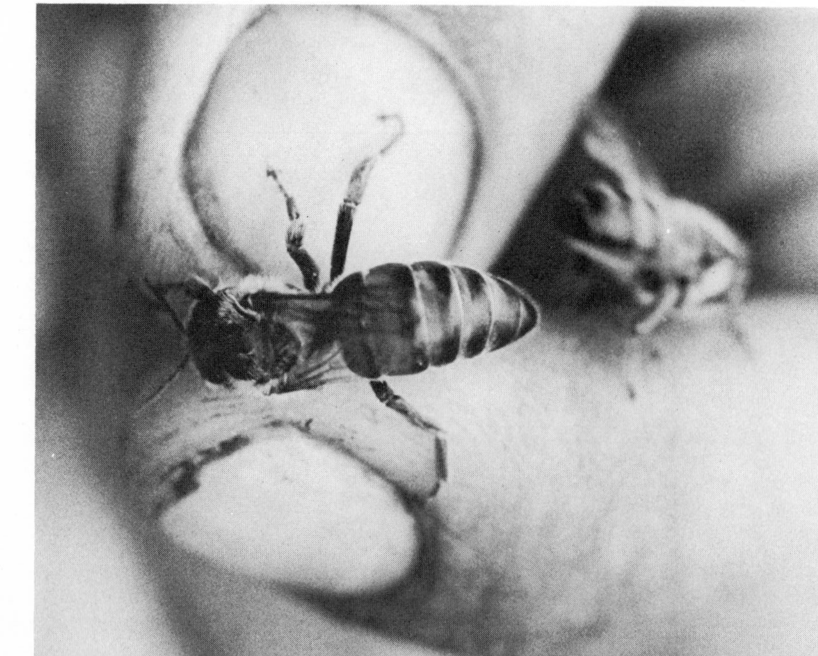

The Brazilian honeybee is dangerous to animals and man, and its sting has been blamed for ten deaths in Brazil. The bees are the offspring of swarms of African bees brought to Brazil in an attempt to develop the perfect honeybee.
AGÊNCIA-JB

KEYSTONE

The newly finished sluice gates in Chaoyang county in the People's Republic of China were designed to irrigate a large rice-growing area. A record rice harvest was expected in 1972.

their families held jobs in town. It was believed that average off-farm wages in 1972 would be more than farm income. Advocacy by U.S. Secretary of Agriculture Earl L. Butz of higher farm income even at the expense of higher consumer prices was hailed by farmers but criticized by consumer interests and the Price Commission. Nevertheless, the farm community argued that it had subsidized the U.S. food buyer for years, and now it wanted its share of the general prosperity.

Farm unions grew and wages rose in 1972, while the supply of farmhands tightened. Farmhands received $1.84 an hour in the early part of the year, excluding room and board. This represented a 4.5% wage increase over the same period of 1971. Thus, when housing and other allowances were considered, farm laborers were receiving $351 a month, $20 a month more than in 1971. Even so, it was hoped that legislative programs would be devised to provide more rural jobs and encourage the growth of farms and towns. A domestic "Marshall Plan," blueprinted on the U.S. effort to rebuild Europe after World War II, was under consideration for the economic expansion of rural areas.

Less than Record Crops

Some 21 million acres of crops were expected to be harvested in 1972. This was considered a remarkable achievement in view of the ravages of Hurricane Agnes and the harsh effects of late spring frosts, drought in the Southwest, and a cool, wet summer, particularly in the Midwest. Estimated total crop production was at an index of 111 (1967 = 100), just under the 1971 record index of 112.

Corn, sorghum, barley, and oats—the feed grains basic to a healthy livestock industry—yielded about 189 million tons, about 8% less than in 1971. The preliminary estimate of the corn crop was for more than 5.12 billion bushels, about 400 million bushels less than the 1971 record yield. However, the corn yield per acre rose to 89.7 bushels. Since there was considerable carry-over of corn from 1971, farmers were not encouraged to plant as much of it in 1972. Iowa was the leading corn state with a harvest of 1.12 billion bushels, followed by Illinois with 915.8 million bushels.

Production of the food grains wheat, rye, and rice dropped slightly, to about 52 million tons in 1972. The wheat crop totaled nearly 1.6 billion bushels. Because of sharp cutbacks in rye acreage, the rye crop was only 31.3 million bushels, nearly 40% less than the 1971 yield. The rice harvest set a new record yield of 4,649 pounds per acre.

Production of winter and spring vegetables increased somewhat in 1972, but summer vegetable production dropped below the 1971 mark. Yields of deciduous fruit, as a whole, were not as high as in 1971, either. Apples, cranberries, and nectarines were the exceptions. The forecast was for

6.26 billion pounds of apples. California produced about half of the 1972 peach crop of 2.52 billion pounds. California grapes also constituted about 85% of the entire U.S. grape crop. Many of the California grapes, some 1.45 million tons, were raisin varieties. The rest were slated for wine or table use.

Air pollution had begun to show an effect on agriculture. Fragile crops in smoggy areas such as the Los Angeles basin were jeopardized. Particularly hard-hit were leafy vegetables. Estimates of the severity of annual crop losses caused by air pollution varied from $130 million (excluding growth suppression and farmer relocation costs) to some $500 million.

Livestock Production

Output of livestock and livestock products edged up to an index of 109 (1967 = 100) during the year. At the beginning of 1972 there were 117.9 million head of cattle on U.S. farms and ranches, a new record. The value per head averaged $209, almost $25 more than in 1971. Texas was the top cattle-producing state with 12.83 million head, followed by Iowa and Nebraska. Demand for beef was heavy in 1972 in spite of the vocal public complaint against high retail prices. In June U.S. President Nixon removed all restraints against the importation of foreign beef in face of the demand.

The long decline in the number of dairy cows seemed at last to be at an end. At the start of 1972 there were 12.28 million dairy cows in the U.S., about 1% fewer than the 1971 inventory. However, replacement heifers were expected to hold this figure at an even level. Wisconsin had the most dairy cows, followed by New York. Total milk production in the first three quarters of 1972 was 82.97 billion pounds, 2% more than in the same period of 1971.

As of June 1 there were some 61.6 million hogs and pigs on U.S. farms. Although pork prices ranged high while feed costs were lower than before, hog breeders unexpectedly failed to increase their stock. As a consequence, a period of reduced hog slaughter was predicted to extend well into the first half of 1973.

The sheep and lamb inventory at the start of 1972 totaled some 18.5 million head, 6% fewer than at the start of 1971. This was a continuation of the downward trend, beginning in 1961, in the number of sheep. However, there were slightly more lambs available for slaughter in 1972 than there had been a year earlier.

Poultry Production and Problems

By mid-1972 there were about 308 million hens in the U.S. Although there were fewer hens, they were laying more eggs than in the same period in 1971. Egg prices dropped in 1972 due to an oversupply; also, people were eating fewer eggs.

More broiler-type chicks were hatched in 1972, and the total number of broiler chickens was expected to surpass the 3.17 billion broilers produced in 1971. Egg-type chicks totaled about 527.5 billion at the end of 1971, but it was forecast that only about 475 billion egg-layers would be producing in 1972. The cutback was in response to the lessened national demand for eggs.

An extremely virulent chicken disease called exotic Newcastle disease raged in several regions during the year. In California and Arizona, for example, health officials destroyed some 4 million birds and immunized a considerable number of others.

Trade in Farm Products

Despite dock strikes and international trade problems, exports of U.S. farm items in the 1971–72 year rose to an all-time high of $8 billion. These exports were the output of 65 million crop acres, 20% of the total land harvested.

Trading in wheat futures was active early in the year in anticipation of sales to the Soviet Union, which wanted to make up for its wheat losses caused by frost. About 75% of the total Soviet grain output was believed to be ruined, including about half of the Soviet winter wheat crop. After Secretary Butz's return from Moscow in April, when the groundwork for a major purchase of U.S. grain was set, he predicted that the Soviet Union would be buying U.S. corn and soybeans, some $200 million worth each year, for quite a while. In July President Nixon announced that the Soviet Union had bought $750 million worth of wheat, corn, and other grain from the U.S. over a three-year period in the largest grain deal ever transacted between the two nations.

Canadian Agriculture

The 1972 Canadian wheat harvest was larger than anticipated, totaling 525 million bushels. The lively world demand for wheat—Canada's major farm crop—plus a flourishing livestock industry ensured Canada a net farm income that would hit the $1.5-billion point in 1972.

Some 21.3 million acres were planted in wheat. Canadian wheat exports for 1971–72 were large, mostly as a result of massive exports to the Soviet Union and the People's Republic of China. However, the dock strikes that affected shipping on the U.S. West coast did play a part in increasing the volume of farm goods moving from Canadian ports. In November the Canadian Wheat Board announced that 62.7 million bushels of Canadian wheat had been purchased by China. The sale amounted to some $50 million.

By mid-1972 cattle numbers were at record levels but hog numbers had declined. Pork production dropped prices to their lowest levels since 1960.

Milk production started to rise in 1972. In May Canadian agriculture officials announced that 20¢ would be added to the base support level per hundredweight of manufactured milk for the 1972–73 year. (*See also* Food. *See in* CE: Agriculture.)

ALBANIA. Early in 1972 Albania, the only faithful European ally of the People's Republic of China, continued its strong criticism of the Soviet Union and the U.S. Its vituperation was muffled suddenly, however, following U.S. President Richard M. Nixon's visit to Peking, China, in the spring. Soviet propaganda did not omit Albania's embarrassment, and Albanian-language broadcasts from Moscow argued that Communist Party First Secretary Enver Hoxha could not greatly decrease his criticism of the U.S. because this would reduce, if not destroy, his prestige at home.

Chinese economic aid to Albania since the Soviet-Albanian rupture in 1961 was estimated at more than $125 million. On Dec. 5, 1971, a protocol on the use of unspecified Chinese credit to Albania for 1972 was signed in Tirana, the capital, by Fang Yi, China's minister of economic relations with foreign countries, and Kico Ngjela, Albanian minister of trade.

Replying in the British House of Commons on April 24, 1972, to the question of whether the British government would consider restoring diplomatic relations with Albania, Anthony Royle, parliamentary undersecretary at the Foreign and Commonwealth Office, said that the matter was being considered, and the government would be happy if it were possible to find a way around the obstacles. The chief obstacle was the question of compensation arising from the blowing up of two British destroyers in the straits between Corfu and the Albanian coast in October 1946; 46 officers and men were killed, and many were wounded. The International Court of Justice at The Hague, Netherlands, awarded damages of $2,154,296 to Great Britain but the Albanian government refused payment. (*See in* CE: Albania.)

ALGERIA. As Algeria celebrated in July 1972 the tenth anniversary of its independence, President Houari Boumédienne predicted that by 1980 his country would have a place among the developed nations of the world. Judging by the progress made in the first three years of the four-year development plan for 1970–73, this was no idle boast. Industrialized countries continued to execute loans and contracts that furthered Algeria's program, and the U.S. approved substantial imports of Algerian natural gas over a 25-year period.

Sonatrach, the Algerian state oil corporation, expected revenues of $1 billion in 1972. Heavy demand from Western Europe was supplemented by long-term supply arrangements with two U.S. companies.

Gas pipelines were laid, the Hadjar steelworks was opened, and a tractor production plant at Constantine became operative in 1972; but much of Algeria still depended on agriculture. As many as half the potential work force of 4.5 million were unemployed or partly employed in Algeria. Many jobs created under the four-year plan were by their nature temporary. As a palliative to the rural unemployed, the government tried to push the agricultural revolution (inaugurated in 1971), under which the larger private landholdings were to be nationalized and distributed to landless peasants organized into cooperatives. Progress was slowed by failure to complete the land census and by the traditional conservatism existent among Algerian peasants.

Following Boumédienne's two visits to Morocco in June 1972, Algeria's border dispute with that neighbor was finally buried. The two countries planned joint exploration of the Tindouf mineral deposits in the border area.

West Germany and Canada became political and economic partners of Algeria in 1972. Boumédienne remained hesitant to reestablish full diplomatic relations with the U.S., but there were signs of a thaw when Algeria handed back to U.S. airlines the ransom money taken to Algiers by hijackers in June and August. On both occasions, the hijackers claimed connections with the Black Panther party. While that organization was still accorded refuge in Algiers, a dispute that arose over return of the airlines' money further taxed the already strained relations between the Panthers and their host. (*See in* CE: Algeria.)

Algeria's President Houari Boumédienne (right) and Cuba's Premier Fidel Castro clasp hands in solidarity during Castro's visit to Algiers, Algeria, in May.

KEYSTONE

ANIMALS AND WILDLIFE. Ling-ling and Hsing-hsing, two young giant pandas, arrived at the Smithsonian Institution's National Zoological Park in Washington, D.C., in April 1972. They were gifts from the people of China, made in exchange for two musk-oxen presented to China by U.S. President Richard M. Nixon during his February visit to China. (*See* Animals and Wildlife Special Report.) The musk-oxen, a 9-month-old male named Milton and a 21-month-old female named Matilda, fell ill with a skin ailment almost as soon as they arrived in Peking; Milton also developed a cough. Zoo officials felt that the oxen were simply not used to the warm Chinese climate after living in the much colder Alaskan tundra. Milton and Matilda soon recovered and by summer were drawing the largest crowds in the zoo—even outdrawing the ever-popular giant pandas.

Milton is one of two musk-oxen presented to China by U.S. President Richard M. Nixon. Milton and Matilda got a big welcome in Peking.

GEORGE KNIGHT

A hopeful sign for rare species was the breeding of several animals in captivity in 1972. The birth of a bald eagle at the Patuxent Wildlife Research Center in Maryland encouraged hopes for the breeding of endangered birds. A biologist at the State University of New York also bred three peregrine falcons in captivity. Because the mating behavior of falcons includes a soaring flight, biologists had previously doubted the possibility of breeding falcons in captivity.

At Cornell University in May, three golden eagles, probably the first ever produced by artificial insemination, were hatched in a poultry incubator. Biologists hoped to transfer two of them to their natural habitats by placing them in the nests of wild eagles in one of the western states. A red-tailed hawk and four goshawks were also successfully bred in captivity in 1972 at Cornell.

In its latest Red Data Book, the International Union for the Conservation of Nature and Natural Resources listed over 600 varieties of birds and mammals considered endangered. The most rapid rates of decline occurred among the larger species—storks, eagles, cranes, and condors among the birds, and tigers, leopards, rhinos, bears, giant otters, and the great apes among the mammals.

Eight wild cats were added to the official U.S. Endangered Species list in 1972—cheetah, leopard, tiger, snow leopard, jaguar, ocelot, margay, and tiger cat. This action put into effect a ban on further importation of any parts or products from these animals. The lion was the only big cat left unprotected.

Also still unprotected by U.S. action was the polar bear. Scientists from the five countries where polar bears were found met in Geneva, Switzerland, and recommended a ban on further hunting of the animals. The Soviet Union, Canada, and Norway all had partial or total bans on polar bear hunting. Estimates of the polar bear population varied from 6,000 to 20,000.

U.S. Fish and Wildlife investigators uncovered records of the illegal slaughter of more than 127,000 alligators by poachers operating in the southeastern states. Discovery of a shipment of alligator hides bound for Japan on the docks at Savannah, Ga., led to charges against about 40 poachers for violation of state game laws. In Louisiana, one alligator poacher was sentenced to five years in jail, the most severe sentence ever imposed for violation of that state's game laws.

On the Red Rock reserve north of Lordsburg, N.M., five rare desert bighorn sheep were released in an effort to reestablish them in their former habitat. A similar restoration effort with desert tortoises was made in the Vallecito Mountains of the Anza-Borrego desert park in California.

Both India and Pakistan took action during the year to protect endangered animals. The Indian Board of Wildlife estimated that there were fewer than 2,000 tigers and fewer than 500 rhinos left in that country and began tighter enforcement of game laws to protect them. Most of India's rhinos were in the Kaziranga Wildlife Sanctuary, but even there several were killed by poachers. Pakistan banned hunting or exportation of 40 species.

At a meeting of the International Whaling Commission in London, the U.S. government was asked to halt the "strangulation and drowning of porpoises in tuna nets." For many years U.S. fishermen have been catching tuna by setting their nets on schools of porpoises or dolphins. The fishermen use high-powered skiffs to round up the porpoises in a tight circle, then set their nets over both porpoises and tuna. The process of drawing the net together often prevents porpoises from surfacing for air, thereby drowning them. Although tuna nets have been modified to prevent porpoise snouts and flippers from becoming entangled in them, some marine biologists believe that the number of porpoises killed by tuna nets may exceed the capacity of the species to reproduce itself.

The commission also set tighter quotas on whale catches. These quotas were expected to reduce the 1973 catch from about 40,000 to 34,000 whales. Included in the quotas were finback, sei, and sperm whales. The commission refused, however, to support U.S. demands for a ten-year moratorium on whaling.

The U.S. Navy announced that, because of the extremely high intelligence of porpoises and dolphins, they were being trained to serve as body-

Furious, a 13-year-old golden eagle, is the first to have produced offspring by artificial insemination.
UPI COMPIX

guards for divers working in shark-infested waters. Although porpoises are normally peaceful, they can usually overcome sharks in combat. The Navy had previously used porpoises experimentally for carrying tools and messages, turning valves, and locating lost equipment and divers.

In March the U.S. Forest Service set aside 11,000 acres of the Tongass National Forest in Alaska as a sanctuary for American bald eagles. The location was chosen because southeastern Alaska contained North America's largest remaining concentration of bald eagles and thus would offer biologists an opportunity to study the birds' feeding habits and routes of migration. The U.S. also banned the use of predator poisons on federal lands or by federal officials assisting private landowners. Predator poisons were aimed at coyotes but often killed eagles and other wildlife. The National Wildlife Federation also offered a standing bounty of $500 for information leading to the conviction of anyone who was known to have killed a bald eagle anywhere in the U.S.

New regulations for protection of circus and exhibition animals were announced by the U.S. Department of Agriculture. All animal exhibitors were required to register with the agency and to conform with animal care regulations and standards of the Animal Welfare Act of 1970.

According to a survey made in 1972, pets outnumbered people in the U.S. by three to one. About half of all households owned a dog, a cat, or both. Another marketing survey estimated the U.S. dog population at about 33 million and the cat population at about 22 million. The most popular pets, however, were fish, with dogs, cats, and birds following in that order. (*See also* Zoos. *See in* CE: Animals and related articles.)

In 1972 the U.S. failed to take steps to protect the polar bear, an endangered species.
KAREN TWEEDY-HOLMES FROM ANIMALS ANIMALS

Animals and Wildlife

Special Report: PANDAS

by Larry Collins and James K. Page, Jr.

Collins is a zoologist and chief of the Panda Unit at the Smithsonian Institution's National Zoological Park in Washington, D.C. Page is a member of the Board of Editors of Smithsonian *magazine.*

"They give you an extra dimension of joy. I think everyone would like to cuddle them." Mrs. Richard M. Nixon's words as she welcomed the young giant pandas from the People's Republic of China, Ling-ling and Hsing-hsing, were an accurate description of the feelings that the pandas had evoked since their arrival. A gift from the people of China to the people of the U.S., Ling-ling and Hsing-hsing charmed Mrs. Nixon, zoo officials, and everyone else from the moment they arrived at the Smithsonian Institution's National Zoological Park in Washington, D.C., on April 16, 1972.

One of the first things that Ling-ling, the female, did was to knock her water pan skittering across the cement floor of her enclosure, much to the delight of the small group of U.S. and Chinese dignitaries watching through the panda-proof glass. On the other hand, Hsing-hsing, the male, hid in his green lacquer shipping crate for five minutes before venturing out into his new quarters.

Thus their personalities were apparent from the outset. Ling-ling, 136 pounds and 18 months old upon arrival, was a bold extrovert, curious, playful, and sometimes aggressive. Hsing-hsing, 74 pounds and only a year old when he came, was comparatively shy and much less adventurous, taking to new experiences with caution.

This was not surprising. Male pandas are by nature less outgoing than the females, and Hsing-hsing, being younger, also had less time than Ling-ling to adjust to captivity in the Peking Zoo. Both had been captured wild in the southwestern mountains of China, high in the cold bamboo forests that are the only place in the world where giant pandas occur naturally. (According to the Chinese, only two pandas have been successfully raised from birth in captivity in Chinese zoos.)

During their first days in Washington, D.C., the pandas spent most of their time sleeping, particularly the male—so much time, in fact, that Yang Chung, the Chinese zoo keeper who accompanied them, feared that Hsing-hsing would not adjust to his new environment. But we had arranged for 24-hour watches to be kept during the first few days and found that the problem lay in the change of time zone. Both pandas were active at night, playing in the potted bamboo and on the log chaise longues in their enclosures. The keepers noticed, soon after his arrival, that Hsing-hsing scent-marked his enclosure in a peculiar way. He would back up to a wall and, standing on his forelegs, walk his hind feet up the wall. Then in this supported handstand, he would press the scent glands of his hindquarters against the wall. Scent-marking is not unusual among pandas; it is a sign of territorial behavior (which we took as another indication that Hsing-hsing was indeed taking to his new home), but this posture had never been reported for any other panda.

What Is a Panda?

Not a great deal was known zoologically about pandas at this time. There were only seven in captivity outside China at the time Ling-ling and Hsing-hsing arrived in the U.S.: An-an in Moscow, Chi-chi in London, three in the North Korean Zoo at Pyongyang, and the two U.S. arrivals. (Chi-chi died in her sleep at age 15 on July 22, 1972; An-an

Hsing-hsing, the shy male panda, clung to the door of his den when he first arrived at the zoo in Washington, D.C.

DON CARL STEFFEN, "SMITHSONIAN," © SMITHSONIAN NATIONAL ASSOC.: 1972

died three months later on October 15. He was also 15. On September 29 China presented two pandas to Japan, so that at the end of 1972 there were still seven pandas in captivity outside China.)

The four keepers assigned to our panda unit, Tex Rowe, Curley Harper, David Bryan, and Mike Johnson, were all armed with pencil and paper and were keeping detailed notes in the hope of building up a complete record of panda behavior, including such activities as Hsing-hsing's unusual marking posture. This information would perhaps help shed light on a number of panda mysteries, including the still unsettled question: what is a panda?

In terms of its anatomy, the giant panda (whose scientific name is *Ailuropoda melanoleuca*) is a "highly specialized bear," and there are, furthermore, great similarities between panda blood and that of bears. But there are several ways in which pandas are closer to raccoons. Actually, the giant panda is most closely related to a reddish, raccoon-like animal from the Himalayan mountains, the lesser panda (*Ailurus fulgens*); and lesser pandas were long thought to be part of the group of animals that includes raccoons, coatis, and kinkajous.

Assessing this and other evidence, John Eisenberg, resident scientist at the National Zoological Park, and Henry Setzer, curator of mammals at the Smithsonian Institution's Museum of Natural History, suggested that the two kinds of pandas be considered a separate family, between the bear family and the raccoon family. We were told that Chinese zoologists had reached the same conclusion, giving the name *Ailuropodidae* to the family.

Throughout their first three months at the National Zoo, the pandas proved to be eager eaters. They were fed rice gruel, bamboo, apples, bananas, carrots, kale, sweet potatoes, and milkbone. Keeping the pandas supplied with bamboo was a considerable task. Bamboo was planted throughout the zoo and, in addition, local citizens of Washington, D.C., were encouraged to contribute their bamboo stands. The pandas not only ate bamboo, they played with it. Ling-ling was often brown and black from doing headstands in her bamboo pots, and both inside enclosures were strewn with bamboo tatters from their playful attacks on the pots.

Separate Quarters—For a While

As of June 1, both animals were permitted to go into their outdoor enclosures (temporary areas which were expected to be replaced in 1973 with landscaped half-acre playgrounds). There the pandas found both more bamboo and plots of grass; on her first trip outdoors Ling-ling proceeded to dig up pieces of turf the size of welcome mats. Hsing-hsing, characteristically, took longer to feel at home outside, and it was not until 16 days after the outside enclosures were opened to them that the pandas saw each other for the first time through a double thickness of wire mesh fence.

Chi-chi, the beloved panda of the London Zoo, died in 1972. She lived to be 15 years old, an exceptional age for pandas.

"LONDON DAILY EXPRESS" FROM PICTORIAL PARADE

An-an of the Moscow Zoo is shown while on a visit to London to mate with Chi-chi in 1968. The attempt to mate them was a failure.

"THE TIMES," LONDON, FROM PICTORIAL PARADE

On that day Hsing-hsing approached the fence and, spying Ling-ling standing on the other side, slapped at the wire mesh. She somersaulted and performed cartwheels, and before long they were nose to nose against the fence, bleating at one another. On several occasions after that, Ling-ling tried unsuccessfully to climb the fence.

It seemed highly likely that the pandas would enjoy being together, but our policy was to keep them separate—for a particular reason. Ling-ling was by far the most dominant of the two personalities; she was also larger, though by midsummer Hsing-hsing was beginning to gain on her in weight. If the pandas were placed together at this stage, the male would almost certainly assume a subservient role and this would very likely prevent him from being able to breed with Ling-ling when the time came for that. (The Chinese told us that females come into heat for the first time when they are between five and six years of age; the London Zoo's Chi-chi, however, apparently came into heat at age three and a half.)

Breeding pandas in captivity is a very tricky business. Not only must the male be dominant, but neither of the animals can be too dependent on people. Chi-chi had apparently become imprinted by her keeper, thus losing her interest in pandas and dooming the attempts made to breed her with Russia's An-an. For that reason, our keepers were spending the smallest possible amount of time in contact with the pandas.

There was another reason for the keepers' standoffishness. As one of them said, he would rather handle a bull crocodile or wrestle a bear (both of which he had done) than play with Ling-ling. She was big, fast, agile—and very clever. She seemed consistently able to figure out what the keepers had in mind and could thus thwart their plans. She prevented them from closing her den door by deliberately keeping her foot against the door or her head in the door's track. On several occasions she charged the keepers, chasing one around a bamboo pot several times and catching another briefly in a corner. Hsing-hsing was less likely to charge an intruder but had a reputation among the Chinese of biting the hand that fed him. Whether this was aggression or playfulness was open to question; it was probably a bit of both.

However wary their keepers may have been at times, the pandas captivated their visitors. During the summer they rapidly became the biggest tourist attraction in Washington, D.C., outdrawing such time-honored landmarks as the Washington Monument and the White House. The musk-oxen that the U.S. gave to the Peking Zoo were the biggest attraction there, but U.S. officials felt that it was more than a fair exchange. As Theodore Reed, director of the National Zoological Park, said, "Frankly, I don't think musk-oxen have the sex appeal pandas do. You like musk-oxen, but pandas can steal your heart away." The Chinese could not have given the U.S. a more appealing present.

Ling-ling made herself at home almost immediately when she was released into her new home at the Washington zoo. She is playing with her water dish in the main room of her den.

WIDE WORLD

ANTARCTICA. Four major international research programs involving Antarctica were conducted in 1972. Japan, New Zealand, and the U.S. joined together in the Dry Valley Drilling Project, with the aim of studying the physical, chemical, and biological regimen of the unique dry valleys in Victoria Land, 60 miles west of McMurdo Sound. The International Antarctic Glaciological Project—undertaken jointly by Australia, France, the U.S.S.R., and the U.S.—is a continuing ten-year glaciological research program on the vast ice sheet of eastern Antarctica. Six countries continued to develop plans for the Ross Ice Shelf Project, including the drilling of holes through the 1,500-foot-thick floating shelf to study the ice, underlying waters, and ocean floor. Argentina, Chile, Great Britain, the U.S.S.R., and the U.S. combined scientific and logistic resources in assessing results of the three violent volcanic eruptions that had rocked and reshaped Deception Island since 1967.

The Convention for the Conservation of Antarctic Seals met in London in February, and the International Whaling Commission held its 24th meeting there in June. The 12th plenary session of the Scientific Committee on Antarctic Research of the International Council of Scientific Unions was held in Canberra, Australia, in August, and the 7th Consultative Meeting of Antarctic Treaty Nations was held in Wellington, New Zealand, in November. Brazil launched a scientific expedition to Antarctica, and Italy announced plans to send a small group of scientists to participate in New Zealand's 1973 research program. Some of the worst winter weather in years was experienced; storms and winds damaged pier facilities and power distribution and utility systems. Byrd Station was closed after 15 years as a year-round base, but the new Amundsen-Scott South Pole station was nearly completed. (*See in* CE: Antarctica.)

ANTHROPOLOGY. The discovery in 1972 that the members of the primitive Tasaday tribe of the Philippines were living in caves provided modern anthropologists with their first opportunity to study a cave-dwelling people totally untouched by outside influences. The Tasadays, first discovered in 1971, were contacted in March by an expedition of anthropologists and journalists, who were invited to the tribe's cave homes on a mountainside in a Mindanao rain forest. According to tribesmen, it was the first time outsiders had ever seen the caves, where ancestors of the tribe had always lived. To protect the tribe, the Philippine government designated some 50,000 acres of the forest as a preserve.

Several important discoveries were reported by anthropologists during the year. These included a *Homo erectus* fossil, found in the French Pyrenees by Henry and Marie-Antoinette Be-Lumley, which might yield information on the development of European man before the Neanderthals. The largest fossil of *Australopithecus* found to date was discovered by Richard E. Leakey near Lake Rudolf in Kenya; it is probably more than 2.5 million years old. In November Leakey announced that he had found a skull in the same area that was probably 2.6 million years old; he considered the skull to be a new link in human evolution, more modern than but contemporary with *Australopithecus*. The find could extend the origins of modern man back more than a million years. Also reported was the discovery by Mary N. Leakey of a human footprint at least half a million years old. The oldest ever found, the print was excavated in the Olduvai Gorge in Tanzania. Mrs. Leakey's husband, the noted anthropologist Louis S. B. Leakey, died in London on October 1. (*See* Obituaries.)

Among the issues concerning anthropologists during 1972 was their responsibility to protect the people they study from exploitation and from harmful consequences of research. A developing trend in anthropology was the study of urban populations—often called urban anthropology—which embraces a wide range of research. There was increasing work in the study of language in its social contexts, particularly among poor urban blacks and whites. (*See in* CE: Anthropology.)

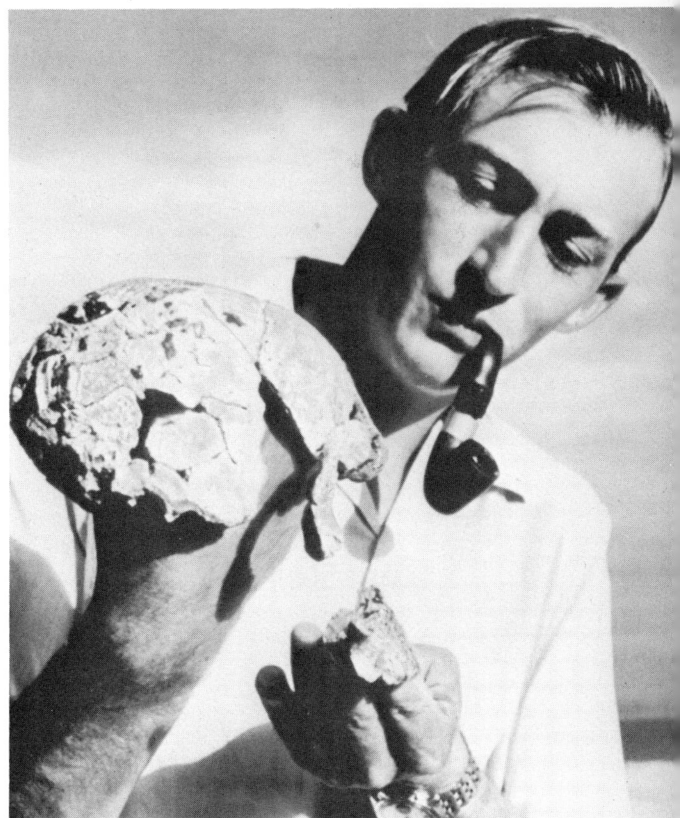

NATIONAL GEOGRAPHIC VIA UPI COMPIX

Anthropologist Richard Leakey discovered a skull in East Africa that he believed was the oldest complete skull of early man ever found.

WIDE WORLD

These camel riders are Trucial Oman Scouts on a routine patrol near the Buraimi Oasis. The Scouts were organized by the British 20 years ago to protect oil crews and to stop slave trains. Today their role in the Gulf area is one of peace-keeping among villages.

Sheikh Khalid bin Mohammed al Qásími of Sharjah, on the Persian Gulf, was murdered in January in a coup led by his cousin. Sharjah is part of the United Arab Emirates.

KEYSTONE

ARAB EMIRATES, UNITED. In 1972 the United Arab Emirates (UAE), formed late in 1971 from the Persian Gulf sheikhdoms of Abu Dhabi, Dubai, Sharjah, Ajman, Fujairah, and Umm al-Qaiwan, experienced its first year as an independent nation. In February Ras al-Khaimah also joined the UAE after being assured that it could maintain relations with Iran. At the opening of the National Consultative Assembly at Abu Dhabi on February 13, UAE President Zaid bin Sultan al-Nahayan declared that foreign policy would be based on support of Arab and Islamic causes. The government was to provide free, compulsory education as well as medical and social services.

In April the government announced that a standard currency, the UAE dirham divided into 100 fils, would be issued by the year's end. Sharjah expected to benefit from an oil strike off Abu Musa Island, and Abu Dhabi was among the Arab states to win concessions from Western oil firms. In September plans were announced for a large dry dock at Dubai. (*See* Iraq; Saudi Arabia.)

During the year the UAE established diplomatic relations with all Arab states and most leading Western nations. Although the UAE and the Soviet Union held talks on establishing relations, the UAE abandoned the plan, apparently due to Saudi Arabian anti-Communist pressure.

In January the ruler of Sharjah was killed during an attempted coup; he was replaced by his youngest brother. After fighting over land erupted between Fujairah and Sharjah tribesmen in June, a cease-fire was imposed by UAE defense forces and the dispute settled by mediation.

ARCHAEOLOGY. Looters continued in 1972 to upset the attempts of archaeologists to conduct methodical excavations at some sites by leaving the sites in disarray in their scramble to steal marketable antiquities. In at least one case, vandals even murdered a person who happened upon them at a Mayan site. Incensed over the illegal trade in antiquities, professional archaeologists took a strong stand against the practice. A growing number of institutions adopted a policy of refusing to buy or accept as gifts specimens thought to be wrongfully acquired.

New dating techniques and sophisticated means of detecting archaeological forgeries made news during the year. A new method of assaying the age of ancient bones by analyzing the structure of their amino acids was reported in August. Developed by a team of University of California scientists, the method was based on a switch in the geometry of the amino acids over a period of time, which causes a reversal in the direction that they rotate light waves. This new archaeological clock gave scientists hope that they could now span the time gap between the latest date that carbon-14 methods can place on a specimen—to about 40,000 years ago—and the earliest that potassium-argon methods can—no more recently than some 250,000 years

RON JENKINS

The Koster site in the lower Illinois River Valley reveals 12 different periods of Indian habitation dating back to 6000 B.C. Student diggers working on the site have the aid of a conveyer belt down the middle of the excavation. This conveyer belt removes the back dirt after it has been screened through mesh, to catch the large artifacts such as bone, shells, or flint chips.

ago. Forgeries of ancient Greek statues were expected to be more difficult to pass off because of a new method that analyzed the abundance of two isotopes in the marble—carbon-13 and oxygen-18. Each of the various quarries in the Mediterranean area that furnished marble to ancient sculptors had a distinctive "fingerprint"; its marble had a measurable variation in isotope content. By analyzing the variation in a particular piece of statuary, scientists could determine whether or not its marble came from an ancient quarry or from a recent one—say, from Vermont.

Museums and private collectors were forced to increase their vigilance against being duped by forgers of antiquities. But subtle laboratory methods in addition to the one already discussed were handy to thwart the attempts. For instance, as a result of tests, 48 of 66 pieces of pottery and figurines reputedly from a Turkish site proved to be forgeries. Also, several U.S. museums were said to have paid some $25,000 each for fake Etruscan tomb paintings. However, these woes were received with little sympathy from archaeologists who disdained the idea of buying antiquities because it only encouraged destructive diggers.

Archaeology in the Eastern Hemisphere

One of the most spectacular finds reported in 1972 was a pair of lavish tombs dating from the Han Dynasty, found in a cliff in the central part of the People's Republic of China. Described as the Chinese equivalent of the rich Tutankhamen find in Egypt during the 1920's, the two tombs contained the remains of a Han Dynasty prince who died in 113 B.C. and his wife. The bodies were shrouded in suits of jade pieces wired together with gold. The tombs also contained a rich horde of metal, glass, lacquer, and silk items. Chinese archaeologists also briefly described a pair of T'ang Dynasty tombs, large and princely too, that dated from about A.D. 700. They reportedly contained a hundred well-preserved wall paintings.

Another spectacular find was announced by Soviet archaeologists who unearthed a Scythian royal tomb in the Ukraine. It housed the remains of a princely couple and an infant. Many of the fine gold items buried there bore the evidence of Greek craftsmanship. The artisans responsible for the work probably lived in the ancient Greek settlements known to have existed along the northern

In the summer of 1972 archaeologists from the University of Pennsylvania discovered this village temple (center) in the Phoenician village of Sarepta, Lebanon. The dig had been in progress for two years before the temple was found. The temple may be the first ever discovered in Phoenicia.

WIDE WORLD

coast of the Black Sea. Soviet workers in Armenia also uncovered a fortress and a cemetery dating from the 14th century B.C. The site contained remains of war chariots and skeletons. All but one of the skeletons had snapped neck vertebrae, leading archaeologists to surmise that a dead chief had been buried with some of his sacrificed warriors.

Excavations at two village sites in Yugoslavia were carried on with blocked funds during the year. Such funds consist of money owed to the U.S. but usable only within the debtor nations. Both sites yielded evidence of a succession of early agricultural occupation, beginning earlier than 5000 B.C.

Two classical Greek painted statues, probably of a brother and sister, were located in a shallow pit 25 miles southeast of Athens, Greece, in August. The life-size marble statues were credited to the sculptor Aristion of the 6th century B.C., because the bottom of the girl's statue fit a base signed by Aristion that was already in the National Archaeological Museum in Athens. Also in 1972 a series of 3,500-year-old frescoes was unearthed on the Greek island of Thíra. They were expected to answer many long-standing questions about everyday Greek life around 1500 B.C.

Archaeology in the Western Hemisphere

Many areas of archaeological interest in the Western Hemisphere were being bulldozed or flooded to satisfy the needs of a growing population. In a move to reduce site losses, the California legislature set up an archaeological task force to evaluate all causes of site destruction in the state. Protective legislation could then be drawn up.

Computer technology was edging into archaeology in 1972. An Arizona State University team made imaginative use of a computer by calling data into it by telephone from the field, receiving immediate evaluation of the data, and then proceeding with or modifying their research plans on the basis of the computer information. Likewise, the Florida Bureau of Historic Sites and Properties implemented a computer program for the storage and retrieval of archaeological data so that it could tie in with similar systems in other states.

A New York archaeologist came up with a new idea while studying how the means of food acquisition by prehistoric people along the Maine coast began to shift from that of hunting and fishing to that of shellfish collecting sometime around the start of the Christian era. In conflict with the traditional view that one population was replaced by another, he believed that the same population could have changed its way of life after becoming affected by an interplay of factors arising from changes following the last glaciation.

Work at the Little Salt Springs site in Florida uncovered a human bone dating from about 6000 B.C. It was deposited at a time when the water level at the site was 35 feet lower than at present. The site might have been used by prehistoric people as a water hole at a time when the climate was drier and the sea level lower.

Archaeologists in Mexico and South America worked feverishly at times to amass as much data as they could from potentially rich sites before the waters of hydroelectric dams inundated the sites. For example, workers at a Mexican site near Guatemala feared that the waters of the Angostura Dam, slated for completion in 1973, would drown a thousand-year-old pyramid and other cultural treasures. (*See in* CE: Archaeology.)

ARCHITECTURE. Deeper involvement with the pervasive concerns of the public was a growing trend among architects in 1972. Environmental impact, urban crisis, and crime prevention were major considerations.

The prestigious American Institute of Architects (AIA) proposed plans meant to improve the quality of community life. The AIA's multibillion-dollar program for planned "growth units" called for the U.S. government to buy one million acres of urban land in 58 areas, to be used as sites for communities of 500 to 3,000 units and "utility corridors" providing services for the communities. The recommendations were part of a report, "A Strategy for Building a Better America," which stated that the alternative would be to "continue to build the world's first throwaway civilization."

Security consultants urged architects in 1972 to incorporate crime-reducing features in their plans. Buildings could be made less vulnerable, they said, if architects gave more thought to such points as the location of doors and windows.

Environmental aspects of high-rise buildings were emphasized at the first international conference on the planning and design of tall buildings, which took place at Lehigh University in Bethlehem, Pa. Designers were challenged to minimize the adverse effects of the concentration of people—effects, for example, on transportation and utilities—and to maximize the building's aesthetic impact on the total urban environment. A Japanese delegate to the conference said that Tokyo designers must provide enough sunlight for people adjacent to high-rises in order to comply with a court ruling that stated everyone was entitled to sunlight. (*See also* Feature Article: "Enriching the Quality of Life.")

High-Rise Buildings

As the building-height marathon proceeded in 1972 and the twin towers of New York City's World Trade Center took second place to Chicago's Sears Tower, climbing to 1,450 feet, a voice was heard from the mighty Empire State Building. Owners of the 102-story skyscraper explored ways

The 1972 Olympic Games were held in part in this 740-acre Olympic Park in Munich, West Germany. The huge complex, which was covered by a sculptured roof made of acrylic glass and steel cables, housed a swimming hall (foreground), a sports hall (right), and a vast stadium that could seat 80,000 people.

of adding 11 stories to make it the world's tallest building again. It would thus achieve a height of 1,494 feet—144 feet higher than the 110-story World Trade Center towers and 44 feet higher than the 110-story Sears Tower.

The marble-sheathed Standard Oil Building, which at 1,136 feet would be the second highest in Chicago, was topped out in October 1972. Associated architects for the 80-story building were Edward Durell Stone & Associates and Perkins & Will.

In Atlanta, Ga., construction was scheduled to start on the Peachtree Plaza, a 70-story glass-plated tower that would be the world's tallest hotel. John Portman, its architect, said the 1,200-room hotel would exceed by 50 feet the one currently tallest, Moscow's Ukraine Hotel.

The new Transamerica Pyramid in San Francisco, Calif., became the tallest building in the West. At 853 feet, it towered over the financial district.

In Paris new zoning regulations limited high-rise buildings in order to save what remained of the city's harmonious skyline. In a central zone, rich in the city's history, building heights were limited to 82 feet. Just outside this zone, the new 680-foot Maine-Montparnasse Tower became the tallest office building in Europe.

Civic and Cultural Buildings

Alvar Aalto's Finlandia concert hall in Helsinki, Finland, set a handsome example for cultural buildings of the 1970's. The structure of reinforced concrete clad in white marble and gray granite was the first stage of a new civic center.

The Smithsonian Institution's new Renwick Gallery in Washington, D.C., was a fine example of the growing trend toward recycling landmarks. Before it was restored, the 19th-century building had been slated for demolition. It became the country's showcase for design, crafts, and decorative arts. The gallery was named for the original architect, James Renwick, Jr., who also designed the first Smithsonian building.

The Siqueiros Cultural Polyforum at Mexico City, Mexico, was a 12-sided concrete structure housing a museum, an auditorium, a theater, and offices. Murals by David Alfaro Siqueiros depicted the history of humanity on the inside and outside of the concrete building.

The increasing use of fabric in building was represented by the Olympic Stadium at Munich, West Germany. A translucent acrylic roof—the largest pivoted suspension roof ever built—was wrapped around the stadium to cover both a sports hall for 12,000 spectators and a swimming stadium. The Stuttgart, West Germany, firm of Gunther Behnisch won a competition with the design.

School and University Architecture

A group of new dormitories for Bradford College in Massachusetts were conceived by architects Campbell, Aldrich & Nulty as domestically scaled residences, each housing ten students. The houses were grouped around a landscaped quadrangle.

Paul Rudolph was the architect for the new five-story Sid W. Richardson Physical Sciences Building of Texas Christian University, at Fort Worth. Broad overhangs throw dramatic shadow patterns in the strong Texas sunlight.

Northwestern University at Evanston, Ill., announced plans in 1972 for a $20-million center for the fine arts and performing arts on its 74-acre lakefill campus. A new library is the key structure in a broad improvement program there.

A milestone in the development of "membrane architecture" was the skin of weatherproofed fiberglass cloth used to enclose a student center at La Verne College near Los Angeles. John Shaver of Salina, Kan., designed the lightweight tensile structure, which covers an area of approximately 68,000 square feet.

Other Events

R. Buckminster Fuller, unorthodox thinker in architecture and other fields, announced in 1972 that he would turn over his lifework of "reforming the environment of man" to a new nonprofit corporation, the Design Science Institute in Washington, D.C. The institute, headed by Glenn A. Olds, president of Kent State University, made plans to perpetuate and promote Fuller's ideas and designs, such as the geodesic dome.

The American Institute of Architects awarded a Gold Medal for 1972 to Pietro Belluschi, who achieved fame for his imaginative use of wood in buildings of the Pacific Northwest. The Royal Institute of British Architects gave a Gold Medal for 1972 to the U.S. architect Louis I. Kahn. (*See also* Construction; Landmarks and Monuments. *See in* CE: Architecture.)

The Transamerica Pyramid in San Francisco, Calif., was completed in 1972.

AUTHENTICATED NEWS INTERNATIONAL

WIDE WORLD

The research ship *Knorr* made a voyage into Arctic waters in 1972. The ship, shown here in port at Reykjavik, Iceland, was designed to hold its position in a 40-knot wind, thus allowing easier deployment and recovery of equipment.

ARCTIC. After more than two years of delay, formal approval was given in 1972 for the proposed Alaskan oil pipeline, thus opening the way for oil production and transportation in the Arctic. Environmentalists had waged a futile battle to block the pipeline through lobbying and court actions. Despite their efforts, U.S. Secretary of the Interior Rogers C. B. Morton gave the project his approval on the grounds that the pipeline was in the interests of both the U.S. as a whole and the state of Alaska. He also felt that planned environmental protection measures were adequate. Conservationists then went to court again and obtained injunctions, but the U.S. Court of Appeals was expected to rule in favor of the pipeline.

The hard-fought environmental campaign had its effects, however. The pipeline's threats to land and wildlife were carefully studied, and legislation was passed to protect the areas involved as much as was feasible. The Alaskan legislature passed several laws protecting against exploitation of the state's resources; several oil companies then challenged the constitutionality of the statutes. Some 80 million acres of land in Alaska were set aside for inclusion in the national park system.

The Canadian government response to the imminent construction of the pipeline was a proposal for a transarctic railroad; plans for roads and other transportation systems were also studied. The Canadian government also relaxed regulations dealing with oil pollution in Arctic waters.

The Arctic Ice Dynamics Joint Experiment (AIDJEX) continued during the year with its studies of ice movements in the Arctic Ocean. Another project studied large areas in northern Baffin Bay. (*See in* CE: Arctic Regions.)

ARGENTINA. Violence and uncertainty plagued Argentina in 1972. With the world's highest inflation rate—running 60% at midyear—demonstrations, strikes, and riots flared over economic and political issues. Meanwhile, Lieut. Gen. Alejandro Agustín Lanusse, president of the ruling junta, tried to lead the country toward free elections in March 1973. The credibility of his plan was strengthened when he stayed in office after August 25, the resignation deadline for officials who wished to become candidates.

Supporters of former President Juan D. Perón, who was living in Spain, sought to have him run for election. He failed to meet the government's requirement that presidential candidates be resident in Argentina by August 25. However, in October he announced plans to return and also sent a program for national reconstruction that Lanusse called a "positive contribution."

Perón, who was dictator of Argentina from 1946 to 1955, still commanded the loyalty of labor and of others ranging from the nationalist right to the underground left. His following was believed to represent as much as 60% of the vote.

Perón returned to Argentina on November 17. Thousands of his supporters were prevented by police from greeting him at the airport, but public reaction to his return was generally peaceful. He stated his desire to unify the country, but the question of his being allowed to seek election as president remained unsettled.

For political reasons, the government avoided imposing an austerity program, which might have slowed the inflation. Some efforts in that direction sparked strikes and rioting.

Argentina sought $1 billion in foreign credits to help strengthen the economy and to pay more than $300 million in public foreign debts due to mature in 1972. Some improvements were registered in the country's growth rate—largely because of increased manufacturing output. An import ban was expected to improve the balance of trade, which showed a deficit of more than $200 million early in 1972.

In April political extremists killed a senior general and shot to death a Fiat industries executive kidnapped in March. In August police killed 16 guerrilla prisoners at the remote Trelew naval base. (*See in* CE: Argentina.)

ARMED FORCES, UNITED STATES. In 1972 the changing nature of the war in Indochina led to a much larger role for the U.S. Air Force and the Navy while reductions of troops decreased Army participation. The U.S. armed forces were concerned during the year with cutting troop strengths and with the development of new procedures and technology.

AIR FORCE

U.S. President Richard M. Nixon's decision to bomb military targets in North Vietnam without the provocation of enemy ground fire gave the role of the Air Force new importance in 1972. Air Force bombers attacked military installations, factories, and transportation routes for most of the year with the intention of slowing the flow of troops and supplies into South Vietnam. Capt. Richard S. Ritchie and Capt. Charles B. DeBellevue became the first two aces of the war by downing five enemy aircraft each.

The Air Force celebrated its 25th year of service as a separate military department in 1972, concentrating on the development of new planes and systems and on the recruitment and retention of quality personnel.

In the area of hardware, development continued on the B-1 bomber, considered the most powerful manned bomber system ever designed. The first test flight for the B-1 was scheduled for April 1974. The first prototype for the F-15 fighter was completed on June 26, 1972, and the first test flight took place the following month. Two prototypes of the A-X close-support aircraft flew test flights in May 1972. The A-X program followed the "fly-before-buy" procurement approach, which replaced the "paper-study" concept with flyable hardware prior to any production decision. In February the first aircraft of the Airborne Warning and Control System (AWACS) began test flights.

Reflecting a commitment to equal opportunity within the Air Force, the service's second woman general, Brig. Gen. Ann Hoefly, was promoted during the year. Col. Norma Brown set a military precedent by assuming command of the 6970th Air Base Group at Fort Meade, Md.—the first time a woman officer had headed a major unit composed of both men and women. Col. Lucius Theus was promoted to brigadier general and became the Air Force's second black general on active duty.

The functioning of the Air Force chain of command came under intense scrutiny in 1972 following disclosures that Gen. John D. Lavelle, former commander of the Seventh Air Force and commanding officer of all Air Force units in Vietnam from August 1971 to March 1972, had ordered bombing of military targets in Vietnam whether ground fire had hit the bombers or not. This was a violation of President Nixon's directive that bombings take place only in retaliation for enemy ground fire. Lavelle had apparently ordered sorties over North Vietnam to prevent troop and supply buildups near the demilitarized zone and then had ordered all raids reported as "protective reaction strikes"—meaning that the bombers had been fired upon from the ground.

Lavelle was relieved of command in March by Gen. John D. Ryan, Air Force chief of staff, after an investigation showed that at least 20 unauthorized raids had taken place. Lavelle retired with a demotion of one rank on April 7. The House Armed Services Committee, however, pursued an investigation and held hearings on the Lavelle case in June to determine if any officer higher up in the

A group of three U.S. prisoners of war was released by North Vietnam in September. The men arrived in New York City accompanied by a delegation of U.S. peace activists to whom the POW's had been released. Navy Lieut. (jg) Norris Charles (left), Air Force Maj. Edward Elias (center), and Navy Lieut. (jg) Markham Gartley refused offers of U.S. military transportation to the U.S.

UPI COMPIX

WIDE WORLD

Gen. Creighton Abrams was sworn in as U.S. Army chief of staff in October. In an outdoor ceremony that included members of the 3d Infantry Old Guard Fife & Drum Corps, U.S. Secretary of Defense Melvin R. Laird (left) administered the oath while Mrs. Abrams held the Bible. Abrams previously had served as commander of all U.S. forces in South Vietnam. He succeeded retiring Chief of Staff Gen. William C. Westmoreland.

chain of command—particularly General Ryan or Gen. Creighton Abrams, commander of all forces in Vietnam at the time—had known of the illegal raids. Lavelle testified that Abrams had known of the raids, which Abrams vigorously denied. In September the Senate Armed Services Committee also began hearings on the question and on October 6 voted to demote Lavelle one additional rank to major general. The major issue was whether the traditional concept of civilian control over military authorities was true in practice.

The Air Force also faced problems with two of its aircraft. The F-111A fighter-bomber, which had been reintroduced in 1972 after being grounded in 1968 for mechanical defects, was involved in several crashes during the year and was grounded again but was restored to flying status after investigations found no mechanical defects. At least two more subsequently crashed. A defect discovered in the B-52 bomber indicated that as many as 40% of the planes might be unsafe. (*See also* Aerospace. *See in* CE: Air Force, U.S.)

ARMY

In Vietnam U.S. Army strength declined from 119,700 at the beginning of 1972 to about 14,000 by December 1. The year marked the end of the U.S. ground combat role in Vietnam with the departure from the combat zone of the 3d Battalion, 21st Infantry, in August. Overall Army strength declined as well; during the first five months of the year active Army strength dropped from 966,000 to just over 800,000.

On June 28, 1972, President Nixon announced an end to the assignment of draftees to Vietnam unless they volunteered for duty there. Shortly thereafter President Nixon announced a probable formal end to the draft by July 1973. (*See* Selective Service.) Phasing out the draft reduced voluntary enlistments for active Army and severely cut enlistments in the National Guard and Army Reserve forces. Special offers of bonuses for combat arms enlistees and other measures to make service life more attractive helped overcome some enlistment difficulties.

Women gained an increased role in the Army during 1972. In August a plan to double the strength of the Women's Army Corps (WAC) over the next several years was announced. Women were admitted for the first time to Reserve Officers Training Corps (ROTC) programs.

In a continuing effort to make service life more attractive, the Army improved soldier housing, attempted to reduce compulsory weekend duty, and

UPI COMPIX

Air Force Lieut. Delbert Terrill, Jr., filed charges against Air Force Gen. John D. Lavelle after Lavelle admitted ordering illegal bombing raids. The charges were later dismissed.

adopted numerous other personnel policies to appeal to potential recruits.

General Abrams, former U.S. commander in Vietnam, was selected by President Nixon to become the new Army chief of staff to replace Gen. William C. Westmoreland. General Abrams' confirmation was delayed by Senate investigations into allegations that he had approved Air Force General Lavelle's illegal bombing raids over North Vietnam. (*See* section on Air Force in this article.) Abrams' nomination was finally confirmed on October 12.

In 1972 the Army increased and broadened its program against drug abuse, adding a number of innovative programs stressing rehabilitation and treatment. There were also continuing efforts to combat traffic in drugs.

Army efforts were redoubled in the area of race relations and equal opportunity. Five black colonels were selected for promotion to brigadier general, and the Army's first black division commander, Maj. Gen. Frederic E. Davison, assumed command of the 8th Infantry Division in May. A second black division commander, Maj. Gen. James F. Hamlet, assumed command of the 4th Infantry Division in August. Other efforts included sanctions against military suppliers who were guilty of discrimination. Both at home and overseas, landlords refusing to rent to blacks had their establishments placed off limits to soldiers.

In August the Army announced cancellation of its Cheyenne helicopter program after nearly $400 million had been spent. This was followed by the awarding of helicopter research and development contracts to Boeing and Sikorsky amounting to $150 million. The new helicopter to be developed would be called the Utility Tactical Transport Aircraft System (UTTAS). A new system of contracting called for a competitive fly-off between the two companies to see which would win an eventual production contract. In January the Army abruptly canceled development of the MBT-70 main battle tank after having spent nearly $100 million on the project.

In September Pvt. Billy D. Smith became the first Army enlisted man to be court-martialed in the U.S. for "fragging," or murder of another soldier or officer by use of a fragmentation grenade. Smith was charged with murdering two Army officers in Vietnam. After a long and highly publicized trial, he was acquitted of murder and convicted of assault from another incident. (*See in* CE: Army, U.S.)

COAST GUARD

Budget cuts forced the Coast Guard to reduce ship and shore units as well as personnel strength in 1972. Ten ships were decommissioned and forces were reduced by some 1,700 men. Two cutters were recommissioned later in the year for fisheries law enforcement. In January the Coast Guard seized two ships from the Soviet Union that were operating within the U.S. 12-mile offshore limit. The Coast Guard also began a pilot security program to reduce cargo thefts in ports.

The Coast Guard operation International Ice Patrol began on February 29 and ended September 4, the longest season on record. The operation recorded almost 1,600 icebergs that had slipped into major North Atlantic shipping lanes, forcing many ships into more southerly routes. Coast Guard icebreakers aided Navy supply ships in the Arctic and Antarctica while performing oceanographic and scientific studies.

The Ports and Waterways Safety Act of 1972 gave the Coast Guard broad authority to protect the marine environment; the act also authorized mandatory vessel traffic systems on ships to avoid collisions. Strict new safety standards for pleasure boats were instituted, and the Coast Guard also moved to require licensed personnel on U.S. towboats. Rescue work continued to be a major area of operation. (*See in* CE: Coast Guard, U.S.)

MARINE CORPS

Under its new commandant, Gen. Robert E. Cushman, Jr., the Marine Corps was able to maintain satisfactory troop levels under congressional limitations while participating in a variety of missions—including increased involvement in Vietnam. At the beginning of 1972, fewer than 500 Marines remained in Vietnam as advisers and security guards and in Air and Naval Gunfire Liaison teams.

Following the April invasion of South Vietnam by North Vietnam, however, Marine Aircraft Groups 12 and 15 were quickly recommitted to the combat zone. They flew close air support missions for South Vietnamese forces and strike missions against the logistical support system within North Vietnam. During the same period, elements of the 9th Marine Amphibious Brigade, operating from amphibious ships of the U.S. Seventh Fleet, provided support for South Vietnamese marines.

In August General Cushman ordered an end to "voluntary segregation" within the Marine Corps. Marines had traditionally been allowed to bunk with their friends, thus creating de facto–segregated living areas. Cushman banned this and other practices that violated the concept of equal treatment of all Marines.

The Marine Corps acquired two new items of equipment in 1972. The AV-8A attack jet demonstrated its capacity for vertical or short takeoff and landing (V/STOL), while the LVTP-7, the new family of assault amphibian personnel carriers, proved to be lighter, safer, and more reliable than the carriers they replaced.

During the disastrous floods in the Philippines in July and August, Marines worked with the Philippine government in providing civil relief and rescue services for flood victims. Marine helicopters lifted more than 1½ million pounds of food and medicine and moved 2,096 passengers in 670 flying hours. (*See in* CE: Marine Corps, U.S.)

NAVY

Following President Nixon's decision in May 1972 to mine the Haiphong harbor in North Vietnam (which was accomplished by Navy planes operating from aircraft carriers off the Vietnamese coast), carrier-based Navy aircraft participated in bombing raids and air support activities for the remainder of the year.

Adm. Elmo R. Zumwalt, Jr., chief of naval operations, continued to make news with his innovative policies in 1972, many of them announced by directives known as Z-grams. One of the most important of these was Z-gram 116, issued in August 1972, which announced plans to eliminate discrimination against Navy women. Zumwalt's program included the opening of all job categories to women and the assignment of women, for the first time in history, to ship duty. In a related action, Adm. Alene Duerk became the Navy's first woman officer of flag rank. Environmental protection and human relations were important areas of study.

A series of racial incidents rocked the Navy in the fall. On the carrier *Constellation,* 130 sailors, most of them black, refused to work in protest of alleged racist treatment by the ship's captain. The dissidents were eventually reassigned on shore; most of them received punishment. This and several other black protests led Zumwalt to angrily criticize Navy officers for lax enforcement of equal opportunity directives, and to take steps to remedy the situation as racial outbreaks continued.

Secretary of the Navy John H. Chafee resigned on April 3. He was succeeded by John W. Warner, whose nomination was confirmed by the Senate on April 25. (*See in* CE: Navy, U.S.)

The new LVTP-7 amphibian tractor replaced the LVTP-5 at Camp Pendleton, Calif. On land the tractor can speed along at 40 mph; its water jets give it an 8-mph capability in the water.

COURTESY, U.S. MARINE CORPS

ARMS CONTROL AND DISARMAMENT.

After two and one half years of negotiations between U.S. and Soviet representatives, the Strategic Arms Limitation Talks (SALT) resulted in two historic major accords during 1972. These were a Treaty on the Limitation of Anti-Ballistic Missile Systems, known as the ABM Treaty, and an Interim Agreement on the limitation of strategic offensive arms. The negotiations were carried out at alternating sessions in Helsinki, Finland, and Vienna, Austria; final compromises were reached by U.S. President Richard M. Nixon and Soviet Communist party leader Leonid I. Brezhnev at a summit meeting in Moscow in May 1972. Nixon and Brezhnev signed the agreements on May 26.

The ABM Treaty limited the U.S. and the U.S.S.R. to two ABM sites each, one site for the defense of the national capital and the other for the defense of one field of intercontinental ballistic missiles (ICBM's); as many as 100 ABM's were permitted at each site. Both nations were prohibited from deploying nationwide ABM defense systems or the bases for such systems and from upgrading air defense systems for ABM capability. The treaty was of unlimited duration.

Under the Interim Agreement the U.S. and the U.S.S.R. pledged to freeze the number of land- and submarine-based intercontinental missiles in their arsenals while further negotiations on offensive weapons were pursued; the freeze applied to operational missiles and to those under construction. The agreement was to hold for five years. During that time both nations could make qualitative improvements in their weapons systems and replace older missiles with newer ones.

Neither agreement called for on-site inspection to investigate violations; each nation was to use national methods of verification and agreed not to interfere with the other's methods of verification. Either nation could withdraw from the agreements on six months' notice if national security were jeopardized. The accords did not place limits on the number of strategic bombers and offensive nuclear warheads that each nation might maintain.

On August 3 the U.S. Senate gave the approval required before ratification of the ABM Treaty. The Interim Agreement was approved by both houses of Congress in September after an amendment was added stipulating that future treaties controlling intercontinental arms should aim at equality in the number of weapons possessed by the signatories. The agreements went into effect on October 3 after U.S.–Soviet signing ceremonies in Washington, D.C., at the White House. The next phase of the SALT negotiations, dealing with the control of offensive weapons, began on November 21 in Geneva, Switzerland.

In April more than 70 nations, including the U.S., signed an international convention banning the development, production, and stockpiling of biological weapons and requiring the destruction of existing stockpiles. The agreement was to go into effect when it had been ratified by 22 nations.

On May 18 the U.S., the U.S.S.R., and Great Britain signed an international treaty prohibiting the placing of nuclear and other weapons of mass destruction on the seabed. This ratification by the three major powers brought to 87 the number of countries signing the treaty since February 1971.

During the year the United Nations Conference of the Committee on Disarmament, meeting in Geneva, conducted negotiations for a treaty banning chemical weapons and for a ban on all nuclear arms testing. U.S.–Soviet differences over verification procedures remained the principal obstacle to progress when the talks ended in September.

A South Vietnamese soldier prays in the ruins of the La Vang Cathedral in South Vietnam.

WIDE WORLD

ARTS. While the safety of works of art in museums and other public places was a matter of concern during 1972, there was also increased attention to the grave threats posed by pollution, weather, and time. In Italy, where national treasures were deteriorating at a frightening rate, a top government official urged the immediate appropriation of funds for restoration and preservation of the country's buildings and monuments. A $480-million appropriation had been recommended by the government in the fall of 1972, but the measure was never passed into law.

In October the Roman Colosseum, one of Rome's main tourist sights, was closed indefinitely because of danger from falling masonry. The cost of restoration was estimated at $430,000. Serious weakening of the supporting structure of the beautiful cathedral in Milan, Italy, prompted the mayor of the city to ban motor traffic around the building. The Roman Forum, the bronze doors of the Baptistery in Florence, and St. Mark's Cathedral in Venice were also included on the list of endangered monuments.

Private foundations in the U.S. continued to be an important source of funds for artistic and cultural programs. A grant of $200,000 to underwrite a three-year assistance program for playwrights in residence was announced by the Rockefeller Foundation. The John Simon Guggenheim Memorial Foundation awarded fellowships totaling more than $3 million to scholars, scientists, and artists.

Corporate support of the arts increased during 1972, amid predictions that the year's total corporate donations would reach nearly $75 million. Among the companies supporting major dramatic and musical programs on educational television were Mobil Oil Corp., General Telephone & Electronics Corp., and Standard Oil Co. (New Jersey) and its affiliate Humble Oil & Refining Co. In Chicago five banks announced gifts totaling $450,000 to the rehabilitation fund of the city's Field Museum of Natural History.

Funds from the federal government were also on the increase. A record appropriation of more than $76 million for fiscal 1973 was voted by the U.S. Congress for the arts and humanities. The National Endowment for the Arts received $38.2 million of the total appropriation. Among its 1972 programs was a grant of more than $500,000 to finance 47 projects in film, television, and radio. Its sister agency, the National Endowment for the Humanities, embarked on a new program to make the humanities more accessible to the public. One of the first projects announced was a television series on the period of William Shakespeare.

In 1972—for the first time in the history of the U.S.—the election platforms of both major political parties called for strong financial support of the arts. Both parties recognized a responsibility of government to preserve the vitality of the nation's cultural life. The Democratic platform specifically noted the importance of supporting public broadcasting, while at the same time keeping it "insulated from political pressures." (*See also* Architecture; Dance; Museums; Music; Painting and Sculpture; Theater. *See in* CE: Arts, The.)

ASIA. Perhaps the most influential event of 1972 in Asia was U.S. President Richard M. Nixon's visit to the People's Republic of China in February. Nixon's new China policy had been announced in 1971, and it unsettled many Southeast Asian governments that had hitched their wagons to the star

Laszlo Toth (lower right) is dragged away from the famous Pietà sculpture in St. Peter's Cathedral in Rome after he attacked the statue with a hammer. The Michelangelo masterpiece was damaged, but Vatican officials believed that it could be restored. The incident was a sad illustration of the vulnerability of many great art works to vandalism.

UPI COMPIX

UPI COMPIX

Japan's Prime Minister Kakuei Tanaka (right) and China's Premier Chou En-lai drink a toast during Tanaka's visit to China in September. During their historic meeting, an agreement was signed ending the technical state of war that had existed between the two countries. The agreement also established diplomatic relations between China and Japan.

of the U.S. and adopted a hostile attitude toward the government in Peking, China. When Nixon followed up his China initiative with a visit to Moscow—and when neither China nor the Soviet Union did anything to stop the U.S. from bombing in North Vietnam or from mining the country's harbors—the impression grew in Southeast Asia that small nations must be increasingly self-reliant.

At various panel discussions, seminars, and conferences, Asian leaders began advising one another and the peoples in their general region on how to meet the developing challenge. Malaysia's Prime Minister Tun Abdul Razak bin Hussein said Southeast Asia would have to defend its sovereignty and integrity if it wanted the respect of the big powers. Indonesia's Foreign Minister Adam Malik asked Asian nations to avoid developing a ghetto mentality but to guard against manipulations by the richer nations to use them as tools to wage other people's wars. Singapore's Foreign Minister Sinathamby Rajaratnam wanted Southeast Asian nations collectively to create a situation in which big powers would find their assistance essential to ensure world peace and stability.

The groping for effective policies assumed another dimension of urgency in September with the visit to Peking by Japan's new prime minister, Kakuei Tanaka. The resultant establishment of diplomatic relations between Japan and China struck Asians as an event of even greater significance than the détente between China and the U.S. The U.S. was thought to be in a mood to disengage itself from Asia, while Japan was seen as further entrenching itself in the region.

The question being asked in Asian capitals in the wake of the Tanaka visit to Peking was how the reconciliation of the traditional enemies would affect the region. The joint statement issued at the end of Tanaka's visit specifically mentioned that neither Japan nor China would aim at gaining a hegemony in the Asia-Pacific region. Nevertheless, it was recognized by Southeast Asian governments that both countries were already too involved in the region to leave it alone.

A short-term fear that seemed to grow out of the China-Japan détente was based on strictly economic concerns. Many Southeast Asian countries had been supplying vast quantities of raw materials to Japan and receiving substantial capital investments from Japanese sources. These countries began worrying that Japan would, on the one hand, turn to China for some of the raw materials, depriving the traditional Southeast Asian sources of significant revenue, and, on the other, divert its investment capital also to China. This could leave Southeast Asia as merely a market for Japanese goods, further tilting the balance of payments against the countries of the region.

At the political and military levels, as well, an air of uncertainty held sway. Most countries made friendly overtures to China and tried to maintain friendly relations with all big powers. However, there were significant differences of opinion among the governments on basic policies.

Malaysia steadfastly campaigned for the objective of a neutral Southeast Asia, arguing that it would not only safeguard the interests of Southeast Asian countries but would also help the big powers disengage themselves from the Indochina conflict without loss of prestige. However, Malaysia's Prime Minister Tun Abdul Razak, during his official visit to Moscow in October, found little encouragement from the Soviet Union, one of the countries that were asked to guarantee neutralization. The joint communiqué issued at the end of the prime minister's visit made no mention of the neutralization proposal.

On the other hand, the neutralization plan appeared to have a direct impact on the five-power defense arrangement between Malaysia, Singapore, Great Britain, Australia, and New Zealand. Singapore was vehemently in favor of continuing the arrangement on the grounds that it guaranteed the security essential for the maintenance of international business confidence in the stability of the region. But Malaysia made it clear that it was against all defense pacts and that the five-power arrangement ran counter to the spirit of neutralization. Australia's growing coolness for the arrangement cast a shadow that could not be ignored. There was controversy inside Australia over the efficacy of the arrangement and, during a visit to Indonesia, Australia's Prime Minister William McMahon went so far as to say there was no real need for the arrangement. This was later explained as a slip of the tongue. (*See also* Australia; Commonwealth of Nations; Singapore.)

Meanwhile, the nonalignment lobby in Southeast Asia received a jolt at the conference of foreign ministers of nonaligned nations at Georgetown, Guyana, in August. The conference voted to seat the Viet Cong delegation from South Vietnam and the delegation representing the Cambodian exile government. Charging that the vote violated the principle of consensus, the delegations of Indonesia, Malaysia, and Laos walked out of the conference but explained they were not abandoning the nonaligned movement altogether.

ASEAN

The air of uncertainty that surrounded the five-power defense arrangement extended to other regional organizations as well. For the most significant of these, the Association of South-East Asian Nations (ASEAN), it was another year of much talk with little action. The ASEAN summit idea, vigorously pushed by the Philippines in 1971, was indefinitely put off when senior ministers of the five member countries (Thailand, Malaysia, Singapore, Indonesia, and the Philippines) met in Manila, Philippines, in July and failed to reach an agreement. In April the foreign ministers of the five ASEAN countries met in Singapore. At the end of the two-day conference they proposed that new guidelines and criteria of priorities be formulated to make the association a more effective instrument for cooperation.

One idea that gained ground during the year was that ASEAN should coordinate discussions between member countries and the European Economic Community (EEC). A special coordination committee was set up for the purpose. The basic issues were European tariff discrimination against products from ASEAN countries and eventual associate membership status for ASEAN countries in the EEC.

With a view to strengthening the collective bargaining position of ASEAN countries, chambers of commerce executives from member countries met in Djakarta, Indonesia, in April to set up an ASEAN Chamber of Commerce and Industry. Elimination of unhealthy economic competition among member countries was stated as one of the objectives of the conference.

Professedly an economic association, ASEAN continued to chase political shadows. Although Thailand's former Foreign Minister Thanat Khoman had said that the member countries were slowly developing a common foreign policy, evidence pointed to the contrary. The most serious potential source of friction arose over the Strait of Malacca early in the year when the Indonesian and Malaysian governments claimed it as their joint property. The U.S., Great Britain, Japan, and the Soviet Union asserted that the strait was an international passageway. The one country conspicuously silent was Singapore, the principal port commanding the strait.

ASEAN attempted to play the role of an honest broker in Vietnam, as it had tried the previous year in Cambodia. But its efforts fared no better in 1972, and North Vietnam refused to take the initiative seriously. In October Japan was reported to have suggested to Thailand that ASEAN membership be extended to countries willing to join. There was no official response, although Indonesia's President Suharto had made a similar proposal earlier in the year.

SEATO and ECAFE

In the wake of U.S. and Japanese détente with the Peking government there was some discussion on the irrelevance of the Southeast Asia Treaty Organization (SEATO), formed primarily for the containment of Communism based in China. In July Pakistan announced its withdrawal from the organization. In November the prime minister–elect of New Zealand, Norman Eric Kirk, announced that his country would soon begin to phase out of SEATO.

A two-day conference of military advisers in July resolved that the military effectiveness of SEATO should be strengthened in the face of continuing Communist subversion in the treaty area. However, there was no evidence during the year that SEATO was making its presence felt in any area. A two-day military exercise in Thailand in June left the insurgency problem in northern and northeastern Thailand as vexatious for Thailand as ever.

Criticism of the organization by member countries continued. At the annual meeting of the SEATO Council of Ministers, held in Canberra, Australia, U.S. Secretary of State William P. Rogers publicly warned Australian government leaders that criticism of SEATO could lead to a U.S. withdrawal from the organization. He was referring primarily to a statement by Australia's opposition leader, Gough Whitlam, that SEATO had become moribund.

Having achieved little more than the accumulation of a vast collection of paper plans over the years, the United Nations Economic Commission for Asia and the Far East (ECAFE) received a slight boost during 1972 with the prospect that China would become an active member. By year's end China had not participated in any ECAFE meeting, but Executive Secretary U Nyun was invited to visit Peking in November.

In September, on the occasion of its 25th anniversary, ECAFE had only an increase in membership from the original 10 to 30 to report. However, with the prospects of peace in Indochina improving, there were fresh hopes that one of ECAFE's many pending projects—the Mekong River development—might receive a shot in the arm. An expert group met in Bangkok, Thailand, in September and suggested the formation of a new permanent forum to promote economic cooperation in the Mekong area. It was announced that China had expressed interest in cooperating with the countries in that area. (*See also* individual countries by name. *See in* CE: Asia.)

This large luxury apartment building in Hong Kong was hit by a rain-triggered mud slide in June that extensively damaged the structure. Three days of torrential rains, the heaviest in 83 years in the British colony, caused flooding and touched off mud slides that left thousands of people dead or homeless.

UPI COMPIX

ASTRONOMY. A total eclipse of the sun—perhaps the most awesome of nature's displays that can be predicted—took place on July 10, 1972. It cast its first 110-mile-wide shadow over an area north of Japan. Then the path of totality swept eastward over portions of Alaska and Canada, veered southward over the Canadian maritime provinces, and ended over the Atlantic Ocean. Worth the watch just for its beauty (though not without eye protection), a total solar eclipse also affords scientists a unique look at the sun's corona, or atmosphere. Viewing time was restricted to about two minutes only, but the eclipse featured one of the most finely structured coronas ever seen. Huge pearly streamers shot outward several solar diameters from the center of the sun.

Thousands of persons traveled to points along the path of totality for a firsthand look at the spectacle. The largest and most unusual expedition consisted of more than 800 enthusiasts who sailed to cloudless waters 900 miles off the Atlantic coast for a clear view of the event.

Some scientists were particularly anxious to check out their equipment during the 1972 eclipse in anticipation of the longer solar eclipse, more than seven minutes long, scheduled over Africa on June 30, 1973. Another one over North America will not occur until 1979.

Stormy Weather

If your homing pigeons were late returning to their roosts in 1972, blame it on the severe geomagnetic storms caused by solar flares during the year. These flares result when regions of the sun become extremely hot and produce a burst of high-energy particles that can affect conditions on Earth.

In addition to possibly affecting bird navigation, the geomagnetic storms caused communications fade-outs, commercial power failures, and, on the aesthetic side, such auroral displays as the northern lights. Large solar flares were unusual for 1972 because the 11-year solar-activity cycle was on the wane and would reach a low by 1975.

Another Planet in the Solar System?

Every science textbook discussing the solar system would have to be changed if Joseph L. Brady of the University of California and others are correct on one point. According to them, the sun might have another planet in orbit around it. Puzzled by irregularities during the 76-year-long journey of Halley's comet around the sun, Brady deduced that the gravitational pull of another planet beyond Pluto might account for the four-day deviations in the predicted time of the comet's arrival into view. Not only would the purported

Brilliant streamers in the sun's atmosphere fringe the black shadow of the moon during a total solar eclipse photographed in northern Canada on July 10.
WAMBOLDT-WATERFIELD

planet be farther from the sun than any other—6 billion miles away—but it also would revolve in a direction opposite to that of the other nine.

Although computer studies gave some credence to the possibility of planet X, Brady conceded that only visual confirmation would validate the find. But scientists who discounted the hypothesis said that the comet's strange behavior could be due to other forces, including a change of the ice of which comets are believed to consist into gases that would act in the same way as rocket thrusters.

A Fresh Look at Mars

Astronomers have long been uncertain exactly how to depict our planetary neighbor Mars. Through earlier Mariner space probe observations, they saw Mars as devoid of geophysical activity, a dead planet. However, data sent from Mariner 9 during 1971 and 1972 suggested quite another picture, one in which such dynamic processes as volcanism and even water erosion might have taken place on Mars within recent geologic time. Mars emerged as a planet with a look distinctly its own, neither a carbon copy of our own nor of our moon.

A planet-wide dust storm originated on Mars in September 1971 and threatened to thwart whatever photographic data Mariner 9 could amass after its arrival in November. But the storm eventually subsided and the spacecraft began a surveillance that resulted in a global map of the red planet, pieced together from photographs taken at various times. The map boasted surface features a hundred times smaller than those delineated with equipment here on Earth. As a consequence, scientists could begin to analyze the true geological surface of Mars. They found, for example, a field of huge volcanoes. They also discovered an astonishing chain of canyons 2,500 miles long, 75 miles wide, and at points nearly 20,000 feet deep.

A photograph of Mars taken by Mariner 9 shows a vast chasm with branching canyons. The formation is apparently unique to the planet.

UPI COMPIX

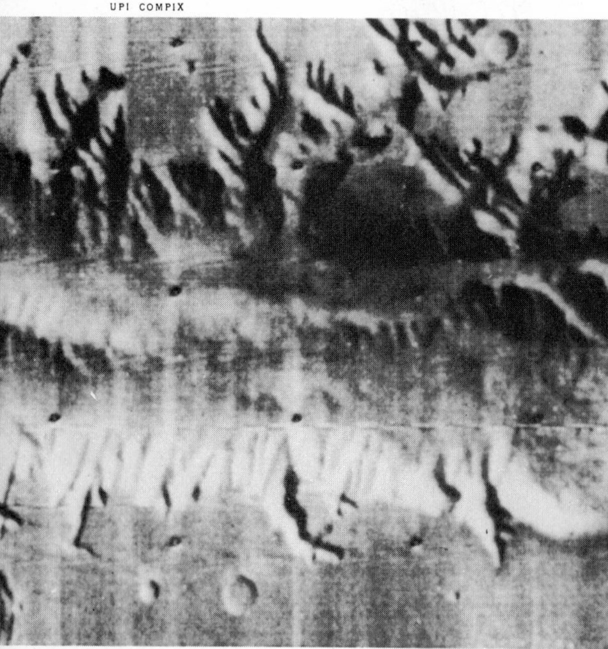

Mars's two tiny moons, Phobos and Deimos, were photographed by Mariner 9, too. This gave scientists their first close-up look at natural satellites other than our own moon. The photographs showed that both Martian moons are irregularly shaped and have heavily cratered surfaces that imply great age and considerable structural strength.

Telescopic studies here augmented much of the Mariner 9 data. Also, scientists at the Lunar and Planetary Laboratory in Arizona proved conclusively that the south polar cap of Mars is composed of frosty carbon dioxide, although the compound could exist in frozen form, too. Although no detectable water ice was present, its existence was not ruled out. Meanwhile, scientists at McDonald Observatory in Texas and at Mount Hopkins in Arizona successfully ended a 70-year search for molecular oxygen in the Martian atmosphere. Even though the oxygen in the atmosphere of Mars is less than 1% of the amount in ours, it still is more than can be accounted for by the breakdown of Mars's known carbon dioxide content. Scientists speculated that the extra molecular oxygen might be derived from the breakdown of water. Although no trace of life had yet been found on Mars, water is one of the prerequisites for any of the known forms of life.

Venus Findings; New Telescopes

The Soviet space probe Venus 8 soft-landed on the bright side of the planet on July 22. Faring better than a 1970 probe, Venus 8 withstood the hostile conditions of the planet to transmit 50 minutes of data. Scientists thus learned that the surface temperature of Venus was confirmed to be about 880° F, its atmospheric pressure was 90 times greater than that at Earth's surface, and its wind blew up to 110 mph. It was also learned that sunlight penetrates the dense atmosphere of Venus to strike its granitelike surface.

Before long, the 200-inch optical telescope at Palomar Observatory in California, presently the world's largest, was to be superseded by a 236-inch Soviet reflecting instrument that was in the final stages of construction in 1972, some 800 miles south of Moscow. And in August the U.S. launched the last in its series of orbiting astronomical observatories. Called Copernicus, the 4,900-pound unit featured a 32-inch reflecting telescope to pick up ultraviolet light that cannot penetrate Earth's atmosphere. It also had three smaller X-ray telescopes. The purpose of Copernicus was to observe distant stars, study the interstellar gases that give rise to them, and locate some of the universe's baffling X-ray sources. (*See also* Space Exploration. *See* Astronomy reprint, page 499.)

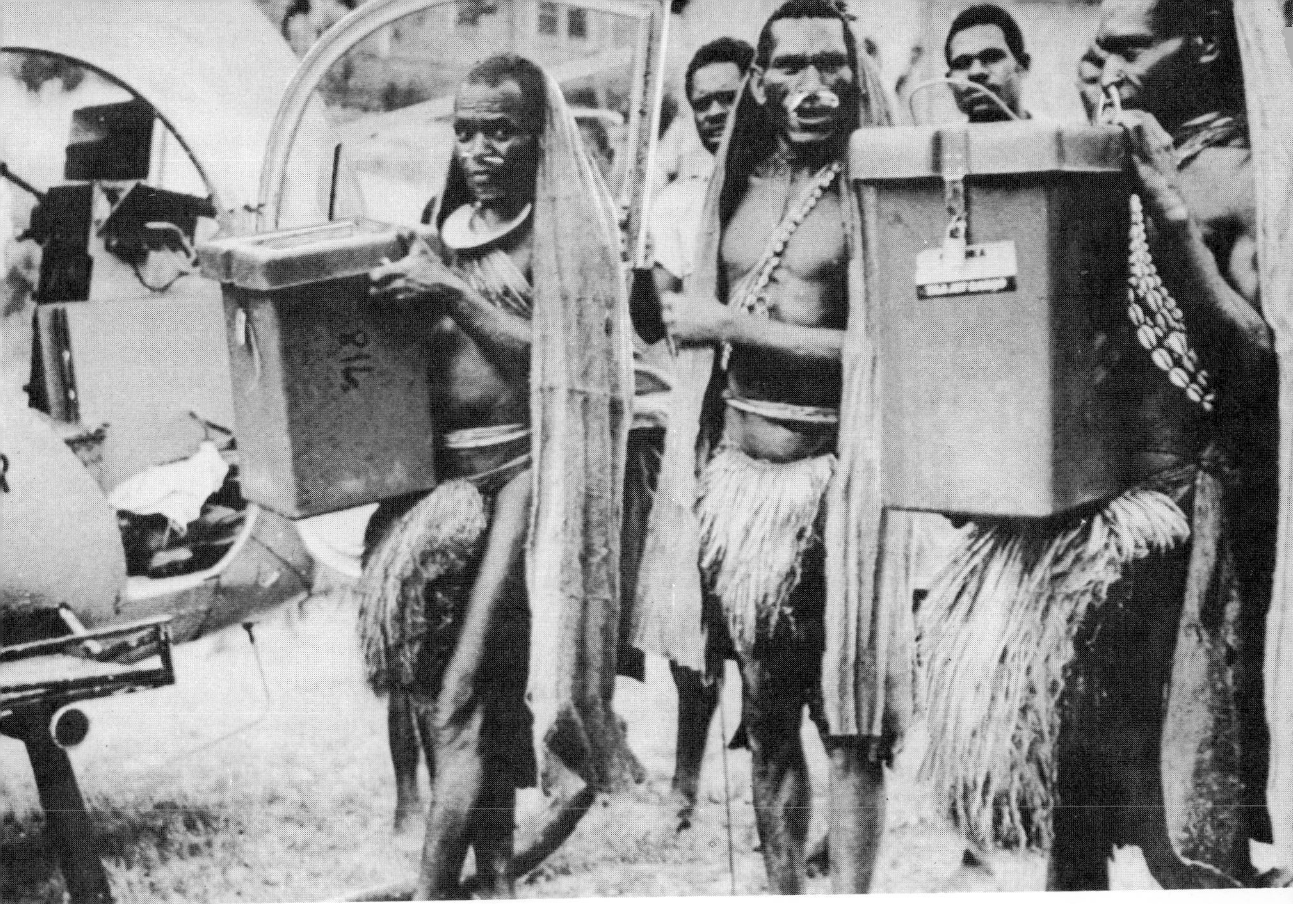

UPI COMPIX

The United Nations trust territory of Papua New Guinea, which is currently administered by Australia, held elections in 1972 for a House of Assembly that will eventually be an independent governing body. These villagers are loading ballot boxes onto a helicopter. Lack of roads and modern transportation made the balloting a difficult process.

AUSTRALIA. In 1972 the Liberal-Country party (LCP) coalition government of Australia was voted out of power for the first time in 23 years. The Labor party, led by 56-year-old Gough Whitlam, was given a comfortable majority after an election that focused more on personalities than on sharply delineated issues. The LCP defeat was laid to a general feeling among Australians that a change in government was overdue. Whitlam, who succeeded Prime Minister William McMahon, had campaigned on a program of social betterment, reductions in the armed forces, and establishment of diplomatic relations with the People's Republic of China. The election results were ironic in that 1972 was a relatively stable year for the usually factionalized LCP.

The government's handling of aborigines received considerable criticism. In January aborigines camped in tents outside Parliament House in Canberra, the capital, to draw attention to their claims for land rights. In Perth an aboriginal "consulate" was set up outside the state parliament to draw attention to the aborigines' housing problem, and a similar camp was set up in Adelaide. The federal government subsequently passed an ordinance under which the aborigines were forcibly removed from their camp in Canberra. Challenges by aborigines to the legality of the ordinance were successful, the court finding that the ordinance had not been properly announced. Immediately the aborigines recamped outside Parliament House, but the government remedied the legislative defect and again ejected the campers. On the brighter side, the government decided to increase expenditure on advancement for aborigines to $68.4 million in 1972–73, 70% more than in 1971–72. Federal grants to the states for expenditure by them on housing, health, and education for aborigines increased by 58% to $18 million. Of this amount, $6 million was made available in 1972–73 for the acquisition of property.

Economic Affairs

The LCP gained prestige following its success in selling $60 million worth of wheat to the Soviet Union and $72 million worth to the People's Republic of China. Another bright spot was the strength of wool sales. There was a 100% clearance, with prices for merino fleece wool 10% to 20% above the closing rates of the preceding season. By October wool prices had reached their highest level in 20 years.

The government was not successful during the year in its attempt to reduce unemployment. By September 1972 Australia had 2.14% of its work force unemployed, the highest unemployment level since October 1961. The growth rate of the economy in 1971–72 was only 3%, as the year was a difficult one from both domestic and international standpoints.

Foreign Affairs

International terrorism affected Australia during the year. Letter bombs were sent from overseas to the Israeli Embassy in Australia, and Croatian extremists were held responsible for explosions in Sydney which destroyed two Yugoslav businesses.

In 1972 Australia began to examine more closely its use of the Indian Ocean after the Soviet Union and the U.S. showed an increasing interest in the area. A foreign affairs committee of the federal Parliament pointed out that the Indian Ocean was of great strategic significance to Australia; more than 60% of Australia's total exports and imports passed through the Indian Ocean. Prime Minister McMahon discussed the security of the Indian Ocean during visits overseas with U.S. and British government officials.

The Australian combat role in Vietnam ended in December 1971. By March 1972 the army and air force rear parties that remained in South Vietnam to complete withdrawal arrangements had finished their tasks and returned to Australia.

The Australian government opposed French nuclear tests in the Pacific in June. In a note to the French government, the Australian foreign minister recalled Australia's past opposition to the tests.

President Suharto of Indonesia visited Australia in 1972. He had meetings with Foreign Office officials and with members of the Department of Trade and Industry, and he spoke to businessmen in both Melbourne and Sydney. The visit was followed by an agreement, signed on October 9, that finally settled the boundary between Australia and Indonesia in the Timor and Arafura Sea area. (*See also* Commonwealth of Nations. *See in* CE: Australia.)

Slogans condemning U.S. President Richard M. Nixon were painted on several shop windows in Salzburg, Austria, shortly before he was scheduled to arrive there in May.

UPI COMPIX

AUSTRIA. The most important act for making Austria's economy "ready for Europe," to use the words of Chancellor Bruno Kreisky, was achieved by means of a special relations agreement with the European Economic Community (EEC), signed on July 22, 1972, after nearly ten years of discussion and delay. The complexity of Austria's relations with the EEC derived largely from the need to combine economic advantages with the preservation of Austrian neutrality and with other obligations under international law. The kernel of the agreement was a mutual concession of free trade in industrial products, to be phased in gradually over a period of years. The first tariff cut came into force on October 1.

Developments during the year in the welfare state included a 42-hour workweek for all employees, flexible working hours in the public service, free schoolbooks, the extension of free travel for schoolchildren, and income tax reform. After heated debates and much initial opposition, legislation was passed to introduce taxation of the salaries of members of parliament and state officials.

From November 1971 to February 1972 the sixth session of Strategic Arms Limitation Talks (SALT) took place in Vienna, the capital. In November 1971 President Franz Jonas made a state visit to Italy, the first republican head of state of Austria to do so, marking the end of the long dispute over the South Tyrol. U.S. President Richard M. Nixon's stopover in Salzburg on his way to Moscow in May 1972 was the occasion of serious clashes between police and demonstrators. As a result of incidents on the Czechoslovak border, Austria lodged a complaint with the Council of Europe in May, and a resolution was passed condemning Czechoslovakia. In August Yugoslavia accused Austria of assisting Croatian terrorists and aiding their entry into Yugoslavia. Austria denied the charges.

Increases in the gross national product of 7.1% in 1970 and 5.2% in 1971 put Austria at the forefront of the world's industrial states in growth of the gross national product. The economic boom, favored by capital investment, full employment, increased production and private consumption, and new record earnings from tourism, together with domestic peace and stability, continued unabated in 1972. At the same time, however, the rate of inflation reached 6%, forcing the government to decide upon a drastic new economic policy of price control.

On March 10 two former Nazi SS (Elite Guard) officers, Walter Dejaco and Fritz Karl Ertl, were acquitted of criminal charges, including murder, by a court in Vienna. The two men, who designed and built the gas chambers and cremation furnaces at Auschwitz and Birkenau, both in Poland, claimed that they were merely following orders and did not know at first that the facilities were to be used for exterminating Jews during World War II. (*See in* CE: Austria.)

AUTOMOBILES. Boosted into a position of price advantage by the devaluation of the dollar abroad and by the repeal of the excise tax at home, the U.S. automobile industry set a new record for sales during 1972. Domestic car sales for the 1972 model year were 10.7 million, more than a million above the record set in 1969. Truck sales also reached a new high for the model year—2.5 million, compared with just over 1.9 million in the record year of 1969.

Prices

U.S. President Richard M. Nixon's price freeze, instituted in mid-1971, was carried over into the 1973 model year and spurred the record sales. In late 1972 the auto companies were denied price increases that they said were needed to cover the cost of new safety and antipollution equipment. Later, however, the four largest U.S. auto makers were granted price hikes; all except the General Motors (GM) increase were smaller than requested.

Because of the devaluation of the dollar, the list price advantage of the imports shrank dramatically during 1972, and in some cases the little foreign cars ended up costing hundreds of dollars more than their domestic counterparts—which they had historically underpriced. Foreign car sales, therefore, took a smaller share of the U.S. market for the first time in more than a decade.

Bumpers

Bumpers that would protect safety-related parts from damage in 5-mph front and 2½-mph rear collisions were the most obvious changes in the 1973 models. They were heavier as well as stronger, adding as much as 80 pounds to the weight of the car. Smaller cars required less complex systems that weighed little more than 1972 bumpers.

Each of the car companies had its own special design. Ford used a shock-absorbing unit made up of two rubber blocks, about the size of hockey pucks, that bonded the bumper support to the frame. On impact the rubber blocks stretched,

ULUSCHAK—"EDMONTON JOURNAL," CANADA, FROM BEN ROTH AGENCY

"That reminds me—we received a recall letter a while back . . . something about a minor defect in the steering wheel and door latch!"

permitting the front bumper to move rearward as much as three inches, then snapped back into their original position.

The GM hydraulic system, used on the full-size and intermediate 1973 models, worked in a similar manner. The GM units looked much like the telescoping shock absorbers used in the suspension system.

New Models

Some name changes took place at the 1973 model introductions, and one new line was introduced by Oldsmobile. Buick dropped the Skylark name for its intermediate series and adopted the name Century instead. Oldsmobile introduced its Omega for the first time, a compact-size car that was a thinly disguised Chevrolet Nova with special front-end and interior styling. Omega came in three body styles—two-door, four-door, and hatchback. Hatchback models were also added to the Nova, Ventura, and Hornet lines for the first time.

The 1973 Oldsmobile Cutlass 'S' Colonnade hardtop coupe had a new bumper that was designed to lessen collision damage. The bumper tilts back, absorbing the force of the collision. At the same time the grille is hinged to swing away after the impact.

COURTESY, OLDSMOBILE

The Ford Motor Company's entire emissions testing program on its 1973 model engines was invalidated because of unscheduled and unauthorized maintenance of the test cars. The company then withdrew its application for engine approval from the Environmental Protection Agency.

COURTESY, FORD MOTOR CO.

A slight increase, from 297 to 301, was noted in the number of models offered by the domestic auto makers for 1973. GM added high-price coupes to its intermediate lines, while the rest of the industry produced three fewer coupes. Most of the model emphasis was placed on expanding the smaller car offerings and cutting back on the full-size models, in a continuation of the trend toward smaller cars. Only nine convertible models were offered in the 1973 lineup from the four domestic auto makers, six from GM and three from Ford. Chrysler and American Motors had dropped their convertibles two years before. The industry was expected to phase out the present softtops in keeping with the government's expected requirement for rollover protection on all cars.

Recalls

The industry was plagued by recall campaigns again during 1972. Chevrolet's Vega experienced three major recalls that affected the buyers of virtually every Vega produced since the car was brought to market in 1970. Three problems forced the Vega recalls: a small part in the carburetor had a tendency to drop down into the throttle linkage, thus jamming it open; the muffler had a tendency to rip open after repeated backfires; and the rear axle on some models was prone to falling off. In mid-1972 Ford recalled 900,000 late-model full-size Fords and Torinos for power steering failures. The entire production run of 1972 Torinos was also recalled to make repairs that would prevent the rear wheels from falling off.

Even Cadillac was not immune. The luxury-car maker campaigned to bring in 3,878 sedans to replace rear axles that were made too short, causing rear wheels to come off. At Chrysler 37,000 Dodge trucks were called in for repairs to brake pedal hinges. In all, the number of recalled cars approached the number of cars produced in a year.

The Wankel

One of the biggest stories of 1972 concerned plans by the U.S. auto industry for producing the Wankel rotary engine. Speculation was rampant that GM would announce plans to build the revolutionary power plant and install it in a 1974-model Vega. In late August GM confirmed that such a plan was in effect. The exact wording of the momentous announcement was typically obtuse, but there was no mistaking its message. GM Chairman Richard C. Gerstenberg said: "Engine development and manufacturing processing work will continue and if this progresses as anticipated public introduction of the engine as an option in the Vega line may be made in about two years." GM's Wankel had been developed in single- and twin-rotor versions for installation in compact or smaller cars. By mid-1972 at least 100 experimental engines had been built, and 20 were installed in GM cars of sizes ranging from Pontiac Bonnevilles to the tiniest Opels. Meanwhile, the Japanese-made Mazda, the first rotary-engine car available in the U.S., was selling well considering the fact that it was almost unknown in many parts of the country.

Two of the major problems in Wankel engine development had been poor fuel economy and short-lived apex seals. But both GM and Mazda reported progress in those areas.

Emissions

The battle over emission standards continued during 1972, with the industry losing more than winning in its skirmishes with government rule-makers. Ford, near the deadline of its 1973 model development program, discovered that its emission tests for 1973 model engines were not following the legally prescribed procedure, and the company was ordered to begin the 50,000-mile tests all over again. Eventually, all Ford engines were certified except the 200-cubic-inch six that was standard equipment in the Maverick and Comet models, and most 1973 model lines went on sale as scheduled.

To combat oxides of nitrogen emissions in the exhaust, all the auto makers installed an exhaust gas recirculation (EGR) system. This had a serious effect on the fuel economy of the 1973 cars, cutting mileage by an average 5% to 6% from the levels in 1972 models. The effect of the EGR system was to lower the temperature of combustion in the engine—just the opposite of what the designer wants for top efficiency. Engineers pointed out that more systems like EGR would be added to cars in the future, and buyers could expect even more erosion of operating economy. (*See also* Safety. *See in* CE: Automobile articles.)

AUTO RACING. In Grand Prix (Formula One) auto racing, Emerson Fittipaldi of Brazil won the 1972 world championship with a convincing series of victories in the Spanish, Belgian, British (John Player), Austrian, and Italian races. Jackie Stewart of Scotland captured the Argentinian Republic, French, U.S., and Canadian events; Denis Hulme of New Zealand took the South African race; Jean-Pierre Beltoise of France won the Monaco event; and Jackie Ickx of Belgium captured the German Grand Prix.

The 24-hour sports-car race at Le Mans, France, was won by Graham Hill of Great Britain and Henri Pescarolo of France. They drove a French Matra-Simca MS670. It was the first victory for France since 1950.

There were few surprises in U.S. auto racing in 1972. The year's champions were well-known names. Joe Leonard repeated as U.S. Auto Club (USAC) Championship Trail king; Richard Petty became the first driver to win four National Association for Stock-Car Auto Racing (NASCAR) Winston Cup crowns; and George Follmer captured the Canadian-American (Can-Am) Challenge Cup, the premier series of the Sports Car Club of America (SCCA). Bobby Allison was voted driver of the year.

Mark Donohue won the Indianapolis 500, and Allison won the largest number of NASCAR 500-mile races. It was as a substitute for Donohue in the Roger Penske turbocharged Porsche that Follmer amassed his enviable Can-Am record. At Daytona Beach, Fla., veteran A. J. Foyt won the Daytona 500 classic and $44,600 by leading 167 of 200 laps in his Wood Brothers Mercury. His 161.5 mph set a record speed for the race.

Once again the most important auto race in the world, the Indianapolis 500, was mired in controversy—a double one this time. Foyt led the critics of the 1972 race's surprise start that occurred when chief steward Harlan Fengler ordered the green flag to be waved after the pace car and the drivers had been signaled that one more pace lap would be run. This move left Foyt, whose engine started slowly, sitting in the pits, a nonstarter. As Foyt pointed out, the race was begun two minutes early with an absolute minimum of pace laps.

Donohue's new race record of 162.962 mph, in his Sunoco Penske McLaren-Offenhauser, was overshadowed when USAC officials took second place away from Jerry Grant for having his gas tank filled from the fuel supply of teammate Bobby Unser. Grant had pitted 12 laps from the end to change a tire as a precaution, and only a check of television film footage revealed the pit crew's error. For that incident he was penalized 12 laps, thereby losing more than $70,000 in prize money and ten places in the finishing order. Donohue's Indianapolis winnings were $218,768.

The second jewel of the USAC 500-mile triple crown had its own controversy because of Hurricane Agnes, which flooded Pocono International Raceway in northeastern Pennsylvania. The race was postponed at the behest of the governor after the drivers had taken time trials. A month later, Joe Leonard was declared the winner of $84,080 after teammate Al Unser, who finished first, was penalized a lap for passing on a caution light. Vet-

George Follmer of Arcadia, Calif., won a Canadian-American Challenge Cup series race, Road America, by five miles. Driving a Roger Penske turbocharged Porsche, Follmer set a course record of 110.426 mph. The victory was his third in the Can-Am series; he went on to win two more races and capture the championship.

WIDE WORLD

Driver Mike Mosley sits on the track while his car burns after a mishap during the Indianapolis 500 race in May. He had been leading the race until the accident, in which he suffered burns.

WIDE WORLD

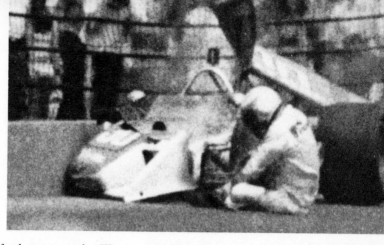

eran driver Johnny Rutherford was second. The Pocono win was a key victory, helping Leonard to his second national championship.

Bobby Unser, who had set pole-winning and single-lap records at Indianapolis (195.94, 196.6 mph), won the pole at almost every USAC stop; teammate Jerry Grant won it at Ontario. Bobby Unser also won the opening Phoenix 150 and the closing Phoenix 200 in Arizona, the Rex Mays (Milwaukee) 150, and the Trenton 300 in New Jersey. Gary Bettenhausen won the first Trenton race. Al Unser won two dirt races—Springfield, Ill., and the Hoosier 100. Foyt, injured soon after the Indianapolis 500 in a freak fire at Du Quoin, Ill., returned to clinch the USAC dirt championship. Butch Hartman repeated as USAC stock-car champion.

Richard Petty won the Winston Western 500 at Riverside, Calif., over Bobby Allison in Junior Johnson's Coca-Cola Chevrolet. In moving toward his fourth NASCAR crown and the Winston Cup money, Petty won eight races, mostly on shorter tracks, and campaigned over the entire circuit. Even so, Petty did not clinch the crown until the Texas 500, the final race of the season (won by his former teammate, Buddy Baker). Allison won ten races and the most prize money—$271,395—but by finishing fourth to Petty's third in the Texas race, he missed the championship.

David Pearson won the Rebel 400 at Darlington, S.C., the Daytona Beach Firecracker 400 in Florida, the first Winston 500 series race at Talladega, Ala., two events at Michigan International Speedway at Cambridge Junction, and one at Dover Downs International Speedway, in Delaware. Allison beat Foyt by 0.16 second at Atlanta, Ga. Allison won twice at Bristol, Tenn., and at Trenton, Atlanta, and Dover. He also took the Southern 500 and the National 500 at Charlotte, N.C.

The SCCA's premier series, the Can-Am, was interesting because the domination by Denis Hulme and the McLaren Chevrolets was shattered, and there was a clear changing of the guard—from the big inch nonturbocharged Chevrolet to the 900-horsepower turbocharged Porsche. George Follmer won the Road Atlanta, Mid-Ohio, and Road America races. He should also have won the Donnybrooke, at Brainerd, Minn., but he ran out of gas with a lap to go. Frenchman François Cevert, in an independent McLaren, inherited the victory. Donohue then won at Edmonton, Alta., assuring his teammate the Can-Am title. Follmer wrapped matters up by winning in California at Laguna Seca in Monterey and in the Los Angeles Times Grand Prix at Riverside. (*See in* CE: Automobile Racing and Rallies.)

AWARDS AND PRIZES. In November 1972, Nobel prizes were awarded in five categories—physiology or medicine, literature, chemistry, physics, and economics. There was no peace prize given in 1972; it was the 19th time that the prize had been omitted since the awards began in 1901. The Nobel prize for literature went to Heinrich Böll, a West German author and playwright. Böll, one of the few West Germans published in East Germany, wrote about the German experience during World War II and in the postwar period. The award recognized his contribution to "a renewal of German literature in the postwar era."

The Nobel prize for physiology or medicine was awarded to two scientists—Gerald M. Edelman of the U.S. and Robert R. Porter of Great Britain—for independent research on the chemical structure of antibodies. The prize for economics was shared by Kenneth J. Arrow of Harvard University and Sir John R. Hicks of Oxford University.

Six U.S. scientists won the chemistry and physics prizes. Christian B. Anfinsen, Stanford Moore, and William H. Stein shared the chemistry prize for their "pioneering studies" in enzymes. In physics, for their jointly developed theory of superconductivity, the winners were John Bardeen, Leon N. Cooper, and John Robert Schrieffer. Bardeen, who had shared the physics prize in 1956, became the first Nobel laureate to have won twice in the same category.

In a historical footnote to the 1970 Nobel prizes, it was announced in January 1972 that a representative of the Swedish Academy would travel to Moscow to present the Nobel medallion and diploma to Soviet writer Aleksandr I. Solzhenitsyn, winner of the 1970 prize for literature. In April, however, the Soviet embassy in Stockholm, Sweden, refused to issue a visa to Karl Ragnar Gierow, the secretary of the Swedish Academy, who was scheduled to meet privately with Solzhenitsyn and present his award. Originally Solzhenitsyn had planned to attend the official awards ceremony in Stockholm; he later changed his mind because he feared he would not be allowed to return to the U.S.S.R., where his works were banned and he was officially in disgrace.

Pulitzer Prizes

An atmosphere of controversy surrounded the awarding of the Pulitzer prizes in 1972. The debate centered around the prize for meritorious service, which went to *The New York Times* for publication of the Pentagon papers, and the award for national reporting, which was given to columnist Jack Anderson for his disclosures about U.S. policy making during the 1971 India-Pakistan war. In an unprecedented action, the Columbia University Board of Trustees, who officially present the awards, issued a statement expressing reservations about the "timeliness and suitability of certain of the journalism awards." U.S. Vice-President Spiro T. Agnew was highly critical of the proceedings; he decried presentation of an award for "the theft of government documents."

In the field of special local reporting the winners were four reporters on the *Boston Globe,* cited for their exposure of political corruption in Somerville, Mass. The reporters were Timothy Leland, Gerard M. O'Neill, Stephen A. Kurkjian, and Ann DeSantis. Peter R. Kann of the *Wall Street Journal* received the award for international reporting for his coverage of the India-Pakistan war. For general local reporting, the winners were Richard I. Cooper and John W. Machacek of the *Rochester Times-Union* for their coverage of the riots in September 1971 at the state prison at Attica in upstate New York. Both of the photography awards in 1972 went for pictorial documentation of war. Dave Kennerly of United Press International won the feature photography prize for his portfolio of pictures on the desolation caused by the war in Vietnam. "Death in Dacca," a picture series showing Bengali vengeance against Pakistanis, was cited in the category of spot news photography. The Dacca photographs were taken by Horst Faas and Michel Laurent. It was the second Pulitzer prize for Faas. The criticism award went to music critic Frank L. Peters, Jr., of the *St. Louis Post-Dispatch.* Columnist Mike Royko of the *Chicago Daily News* won the prize for commentary. In the category of editorial writing, the award went to John Strohmeyer of the *Bethlehem Globe-Times* for his editorial campaign to reduce racial tensions. The prize for editorial cartooning was won by Jeffrey K. MacNelly of the *Richmond News Leader.*

In the category of arts and letters the winners were: Wallace E. Stegner for 'Angle of Repose' (fiction); Barbara W. Tuchman for 'Stilwell and the American Experience in China, 1911–1945' (general nonfiction); James Wright for his 'Collected Poems' (poetry); Carl N. Degler for 'Neither Black nor White' (history); and Joseph P. Lash for 'Eleanor and Franklin: The Story of Their Relationship, Based on Eleanor Roosevelt's Private Papers' (biography). The music award went to Jacob Druckman of New York City's Juilliard School of Music for 'Windows', an orchestral piece. No award for drama was made in 1972.

Awards in Literature

The 1972 National Book Awards—prizes of $1,000 for "distinguished books" by Americans, published in the U.S.—were announced in April. As usual, the awards were accompanied by notable disagreement among the jurors. The subject of the most heated dispute was 'The Last Whole Earth Catalog: Access to Tools', which won the prize in the new category of contemporary affairs. There were some objections to the book on the grounds that it was an edited compilation by several authors, rather than an original effort by a single writer.

Other National Book Awards went to the late Flannery O'Connor (fiction) for 'Flannery O'Connor: The Complete Stories', the first complete edition of her stories to be published, and to

Gerald M. Edelman shared the 1972 Nobel prize for physiology or medicine. He was honored for his work with antibodies.

WIDE WORLD

Allan Nevins (history) for 'The War for the Union', an eight-volume history of the U.S. Civil War (also honored posthumously). Lash received the biography award for 'Eleanor and Franklin', which also won a Pulitzer prize; Charles Rosen (arts and letters) for 'The Classical Style: Haydn, Mozart, Beethoven'; Donald Barthelme (children's literature) for 'The Slightly Irregular Fire Engine or The Hithering Thithering Djinn', with illustrations by the author; Martin E. Marty (philosophy and religion) for 'Righteous Empire: The Protestant Experience in America'; and George L. Small (science) for 'The Blue Whale'. The poetry prize was divided between the late Frank O'Hara, for his collected poems, and Howard Moss, for a volume entitled 'Selected Poems'. Austryn Wainhouse received the translation award for a translation from the French of Jacques Lucien Monod's 'Chance and Necessity: An Essay on the Natural Philosophy of Modern Biology'.

Lewis Mumford, whose works include 'The City in History' and 'The Myth of the Machine', received the 1972 National Medal for Literature from the National Book Committee. The award is made to a living U.S. writer in recognition of the "excellence of his or her total contribution to the world of letters." Mumford had received the National Book Award in 1962. (*See also* Literature.)

Other Awards

The Atomic Energy Commission's annual Enrico Fermi award was given to two of the world's leading experts on radiation—Stafford L. Warren of the University of California at Los Angeles, and Shields Warren of the Harvard Medical School. They were cited for helping make possible "the early development of atomic energy so as to assure the protection of man and the environment."

John Bardeen won his second Nobel prize for physics in 1972. He shared the award with John R. Schrieffer and Leon Cooper for the theory of superconductivity that they had developed.

WIDE WORLD

The Browning Achievement awards for distinguished international achievement in the areas of religious, moral, social, economic, and intellectual endeavors were presented in October. The recipients were: Paul Bigelow Sears, an early conservationist; Orville Alvin Vogel, producer of the Gaines wheat strain that made possible the so-called Green Revolution in food production; E. Cuyler Hammond, for his work in epidemiology and statistics on the dangers of cigarette smoking; Nathan Browne Eddy, for more than 40 years' research on drug abuse; and the Rev. Manoel de Mello of Brazil, for his work in spreading the Gospel.

UPI COMPIX

"...AND FOR OUR PEACE PRIZE THIS YEAR...."
NOBEL JURY

BAHRAIN. In 1972 Bahrain established diplomatic relations with most Arab states and the principal non-Communist countries. In January it was announced that part of the naval base formerly used by Great Britain would be leased to the U.S. Middle East fleet. In March there was serious rioting by workers demonstrating sympathy with striking Manama Airport employees. An agreement on May 1 settled a number of workers' grievances. In June Sheikh Isa bin Salman Al Khalifah, ruler of Bahrain, announced the pending formation of a constituent council as a first step toward democracy.

In March the Organization of Arab Petroleum Exporting Countries chose Bahrain as the site for its dry dock, to be completed by 1975 at an estimated first-stage cost of $60 million and to be capable initially of handling 400,000-ton tankers. The contract, originally awarded to the British firm Vickers, was transferred to the Portuguese firm Lisnave when it was revealed that Vickers was supplying three submarines to Israel.

BANGLADESH. The new nation of Bangladesh faced a multitude of problems in 1972. The nine-month civil war that ended with Bangladesh's independence from Pakistan in December 1971 had crippled the economy, created millions of refugees, and led many observers to question whether the new Bengali state could survive.

Under the leadership of Sheikh Mujibur Rahman, acknowledged leader of the Bengalis who was released from a Pakistani jail in December 1971 and returned to Bangladesh in January, the country began work on some of its most immediate problems. Sheikh Mujib became prime minister and organized a new cabinet with Abu Sayeed Choudhury as president.

In March Sheikh Mujib announced the nationalization of the country's major industries—jute, textile, and sugar mills and a major portion of inland and coastal shipping. Many industries had previously been owned by non-Bengalis. The war had severely affected production of jute and tea, the main products earning foreign exchange; jute production for 1971–72 was estimated to be 30% lower than normal, and tea production 60% lower than normal. Inflation also continued at an alarming rate.

The return of some 10 million Bengali refugees from India accelerated during the year, creating critical shortages of food, housing, and medical supplies. These shortages became a political issue when it was revealed that many government and Awami League (Sheikh Mujib's ruling party) officials were profiteering in relief goods and that only a small percentage of supplies were reaching the refugees. Sheikh Mujib promised to punish those responsible.

The Awami League was challenged during the year by the National Awami opposition party, which was strengthened by student defectors from the Awami League. An opposition demand for a new general election led to the setting of March 1973 as an election date. A government-appointed committee drafted a new constitution, which was approved by the National Assembly on November 4 and took effect on December 16.

Relations with Pakistan remained tense during the year but were eased somewhat by the signing in July of a pact between the two countries to work for a durable peace. Bangladesh joined the Commonwealth of Nations in April and was officially recognized by 86 countries shortly thereafter. A veto by the People's Republic of China, however, frustrated Bangladesh's efforts to join the United Nations (UN). Bangladesh was awarded UN observer status in October. Massive foreign aid from the U.S., the Soviet Union, India, Canada, Great Britain, and West Germany helped the economy.

The generally sympathetic attitude of other nations toward Bangladesh was tempered after repeated reports of mass killings of members of the Bihari minority who were suspected of having collaborated with the Pakistani army. Sheikh Mujib also remained determined to bring some Pakistani prisoners of war to trial on charges of genocide against the Bengalis.

A cookware vendor walks on railroad tracks near Jessore, Bangladesh. The return of thousands of Bengali refugees from India in 1972 worsened Bangladesh's already-strained economy.

JASON LAURE FROM RAPHO GUILLUMETTE

BANKS. Despite international monetary uncertainty, 1972 was a year of tremendous growth for U.S. banks. The number of branch banks continued to increase, largely because of the demand for financial services in the nation's suburbs, with the 1970 branch total of 21,424 rising to a Jan. 1, 1972, total of 22,955. Total deposits held by the nation's commercial banks also continued their rapid growth. The 1972 increase saw commercial bank deposit holdings climb by almost $66.5 billion, from 1971's $489.96 billion to a Sept. 6, 1972, tally of $556.44 billion. Perhaps because of lower interest rates than in the two preceding years, loans outstanding rose to $355.9 billion, from the $305.7-billion total recorded in September 1971.

Interest rates remained relatively low for most of 1972, with the prime rate—the rate that banks use to determine the interest charged their most credit-worthy corporate customers—hovering around 5% during the first half of the year. Toward the end of 1972, however, the rate began to climb slowly toward the 6% that had been in effect when U.S. President Richard M. Nixon announced the wage-price freeze in August 1971.

Of increasing concern to bankers across the nation, as well as to the Board of Governors of the Federal Reserve System, was the apparently limitless increase in the number of checks being written and cleared. Some industry spokesmen feared that the volume of paper checks would soon be too great to be processed; they anticipated that the 24 billion checks written annually in the U.S. would double by 1980. As a result, banks had begun to consider seriously the possibilities of checkless electronic banking.

In the meantime, in an attempt to cope with the growing volume of checks, the Federal Reserve Board announced plans for new, highly automated regional check-processing centers to be established around the country. The board also announced plans to compel banks to process checks faster, allowing reduced reserve requirements for banks that are members of the Federal Reserve System. The revised check-clearing rules did not go into effect, however, because of legal action taken by a group of small nonmember banks.

An important controversy arose from the publication late in December 1971 of the report of the President's Commission on Financial Structure and Regulation. Better known as the Hunt Report, the brief summary of the commission's work suggested sweeping changes in the nation's financial structure. Representatives of almost all types of financial institutions had some criticism of the proposals, but the harshest comments came from spokesmen for savings and loan institutions, who claimed that certain proposals would weaken their institutions while strengthening their major competition, the commercial banks.

The controversy came at a time when savings and loan associations—and mutual savings banks, in the states where they operated—were enjoying a period of increasing prosperity. Perhaps because of uncertainty over the future of the economy, coupled with increased personal income, people put more money than ever before into savings accounts. Savings and loan assets soared from $197.47 billion in August 1971 to $231.37 billion at the beginning of September 1972. (*See also* Economy. *See in* CE: Bank.)

UPI COMPIX

A new unit of a savings and loan institution is dropped into place in a Woodbridge, N.J., shopping center. The "space-bank" was transported by the extremely powerful Sikorsky Skycrane helicopter.

BARBADOS. An intensification in economic nationalism in Barbados was foreshadowed in 1972 when Minister of Home Affairs Rameses Caddle tightened controls over work permits for expatriates. There were also reports of increased bias against the island's small white elite and of increased militancy at the local campus of the University of the West Indies.

Sugar production from the 1971 crop totaled 130,343 tons, and the figure for 1972 was 113,855 tons. Both figures reflected a decline in production caused primarily by drought and indiscriminate burning of sugarcane. The minister of agriculture subsequently decided to reduce from 12% to 5% the compulsory percentage of arable land to be planted in vegetable and food crops, with a view toward fulfilling Commonwealth Sugar Agreement quotas for 1973 and 1974. In July Barbados, along with the other three independent countries, six associated states, and two colonies comprising the Caribbean Free Trade Association, agreed to seek a group relationship with the enlarged European Economic Community and to try to make arrangements for safeguarding essential exports.

Tourism figures for 1971 were up nearly 20% over the preceding year. Early reports for 1972 were encouraging, with a high ratio (35%) of repeat visitors. (*See in* CE: Barbados.)

BASEBALL. The first general player strike in organized baseball's 102-year history delayed opening day in the major leagues and shook the sport to its very moorings in 1972. But the season ended on its usual suspenseful note when the underdog Oakland Athletics beat the Cincinnati Reds 3–2 in game seven of the World Series to win the series.

The Strike

The Major League Baseball Players Association, headed by Marvin Miller, executive director, sought higher pension benefits to offset a 17% boost in the cost of living since adoption of the last schedule of pension payments in 1969. Miller and John Gaherin, the owners' chief negotiator, were key figures in the negotiations that followed. The strike began on April 1 and lasted until April 13. The opening games were postponed until April 15. The players asked for $1,072,000 to accommodate the pension hike. This request involved the transfer of $817,000 on reserve in the pension fund plus an additional $255,000 from the clubs. They settled for $500,000 in transferred funds. The agreement stipulated that all games delayed as a result of the strike would be canceled, with the players forfeiting their pay for that period. The number of games canceled ranged from six to nine per team, depending on the schedule. A number of spring-training games also were canceled prior to the scheduled start of the regular season on April 5. While estimates varied, the strike possibly cost the club owners $5 million in revenue and the players $1 million in pay.

Final attendance figures for 1972 reflected the loss due to canceled games. The National League total attendance was 15,529,395, a decline of 1,795,462, and the American League total was 11,445,318, a decline of 423,242.

Prominent Newsmakers

Death claimed two of the all-time greats of the old Brooklyn Dodgers during the year. Popular Gil Hodges, 47-year-old manager of the New York Mets, died of a heart attack on April 2. He was succeeded by Yogi Berra. A heart attack was also responsible for the death on October 24 of Jackie Robinson, 53, the major leagues' first black player. Robinson became one of the greatest performers in baseball history and was elected to the National Baseball Hall of Fame in 1962.

WIDE WORLD

Former Brooklyn Dodger star Jackie Robinson was honored at a World Series game in a ceremony marking the 25th anniversary of his becoming major league baseball's first black player. He died a few days after the ceremony.

Another of the game's immortals, Willie Mays, was traded by the San Francisco Giants to the New York Mets late in May. The Giants received pitcher Charlie Williams in exchange and a reported $100,000.

The Hall of Fame, at Cooperstown, N.Y., boosted its membership by eight in 1972. The new members were: Sanford (Sandy) Koufax, Lawrence P. (Yogi) Berra, Early Wynn, Joshua (Josh) Gibson, Walter F. (Buck) Leonard, Vernon L.

WIDE WORLD

Outfielder Joe Rudi of the Oakland Athletics made one of the most spectacular catches of the 1972 World Series when he jumped high against the left-field wall to grab a fly ball hit by Cincinnati's Denis Menke. His ninth-inning catch in the second game of the series assured Oakland of a 2–1 victory.

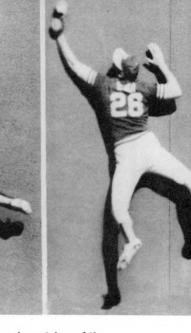

(Lefty) Gomez, Ross M. (Pep) Youngs, and William (Will) Harridge.

The U.S. Supreme Court, by a 5–3 vote, decided to extend baseball's exemption from antitrust laws in an opinion handed down on June 19. The decision was an outgrowth of a suit filed by St. Louis outfielder Curt Flood, who in 1970 challenged baseball's reserve clause binding a player to the team with which he originally signs unless that team elects to sell his contract or trade him.

Bernice Gera, a Jackson Heights, N.Y., housewife, became the first woman umpire in professional baseball in 1972 following a long legal fight. She then decided to quit baseball after umpiring one game in the New York–Pennsylvania League.

Pennant Races and World Series

Detroit won the American League's East Division by half a game over Boston in the most dramatic of the four divisional races in 1972. The two teams were matched in the final three games of the regular season, and the Tigers captured the first two to clinch Eastern honors. Baltimore and New York also had seriously threatened to win the title until faltering in the last week. Oakland survived the American League West by putting down the heroic bid of the Chicago White Sox, who lost out by 5½ games after a frantic neck-and-neck struggle with the A's almost to the end. Pittsburgh and Cincinnati grabbed division championships with ease in the National League. The Pirates took the East by 11 games over the Chicago Cubs. Cincinnati prevailed by 10½ over Houston and Los Angeles in the West. In the divisional play-offs, Cincinnati defeated Pittsburgh, and Oakland downed Detroit. Both series went the five-game limit.

The World Series opened on October 14 in Cincinnati. A Riverfront Stadium crowd of 52,918 was on hand to see Oakland catcher Gene Tenace become the first player in history to hit home runs in each of his first two times at bat in series competition. The blasts by Tenace propelled the A's to victory, 3–2. The starting and winning pitcher for the A's was Kenny Holtzman; the Reds' loser, Gary Nolan. Holtzman got airtight relief help from Rollie Fingers and Vida Blue in the last four innings.

Oakland won game two, 2–1, when left fielder Joe Rudi made a spectacular ninth-inning defensive play after his third-inning homer developed into the winning run. The winning pitcher was Jim (Catfish) Hunter, and the losing pitcher was Ross Grimsley.

The series switched to Oakland for game three. Rain forced a 24-hour postponement before Cincinnati registered its first win, 1–0. Tony Perez, who had singled and had moved to second on a sacrifice hit, scored the lone run in the seventh on Cesar Geronimo's single. A crowd of 49,410 witnessed a stirring pitching duel between winner Jack Billingham and loser John (Blue Moon) Odom. Billingham surrendered only three hits before giving way to Clay Carroll in the ninth.

Oakland erased a 2–1 deficit with two runs in the bottom of the ninth to bail out game four, 3–2, and take a commanding lead of three games to one. The winning pitcher in relief was Fingers; the loser, Carroll.

The Reds kept their hopes alive by capturing game five, 5–4. The contest ended on a spectacular double play when Joe Morgan caught a pop-up foul behind first base, then threw home to get pinch runner Odom, who was attempting to score from third with the tying run. The first pitch of the game resulted in a home run by Pete Rose off Hunter, and it was Rose who also singled home Cin-

Detroit's Gates Brown (in batting helmet), trying to prevent a double play, trips Oakland second baseman Gene Tenace in the tenth inning of the fourth American League play-off game. Tenace dropped the ball, a run was scored, and Detroit went on to win, 4–3. Oakland won the play-offs in five games.
WIDE WORLD

cinnati's winning run in the ninth. Grimsley was the winner in relief; Fingers, the loser.

The teams returned to Cincinnati for game six and the Reds evened things at three games apiece with an 8–1 rout. A five-run outburst in the seventh, keyed by two-run singles by Bobby Tolan and Geronimo, climaxed the Reds' offensive. Grimsley earned his second straight win in relief.

Oakland then took game seven, 3–2. Tenace singled home Oakland's first run following a three-base error by center fielder Tolan in the first inning. The Reds tied it at 1–1 in the fifth on Hal McRae's sacrifice fly. Run-scoring doubles by Tenace and Sal Bando sent across two runs for the A's in the sixth, and Oakland was ahead to stay. Victim of this rally was the loser, Pedro Borbon. Hunter secured the victory in relief.

Individual Stars

The Cy Young awards for best pitchers went to Steve Carlton of Philadelphia in the National League and Gaylord Perry of Cleveland in the American. George (Sparky) Anderson of Cincinnati and Chuck Tanner of the Chicago White Sox won the honors for best managers of the year. The Most Valuable Player awards were presented to Johnny Bench in the National League and to Dick Allen in the American. Rookie-of-the-year honors were given to the Mets' Jon Matlack in the National and Boston's Carlton Fisk in the American.

On September 30 Pittsburgh's Roberto Clemente collected his 3,000th hit, becoming the 11th player ever to reach that plateau. Hank Aaron of Atlanta

Umpire Bob Engel (center) calls Oakland's John (Blue Moon) Odom (right) out at home plate, ending the fifth World Series game. Cincinnati catcher Johnny Bench helps out with the call. The Reds won the game, 5–4, but lost the series to Oakland.
WIDE WORLD

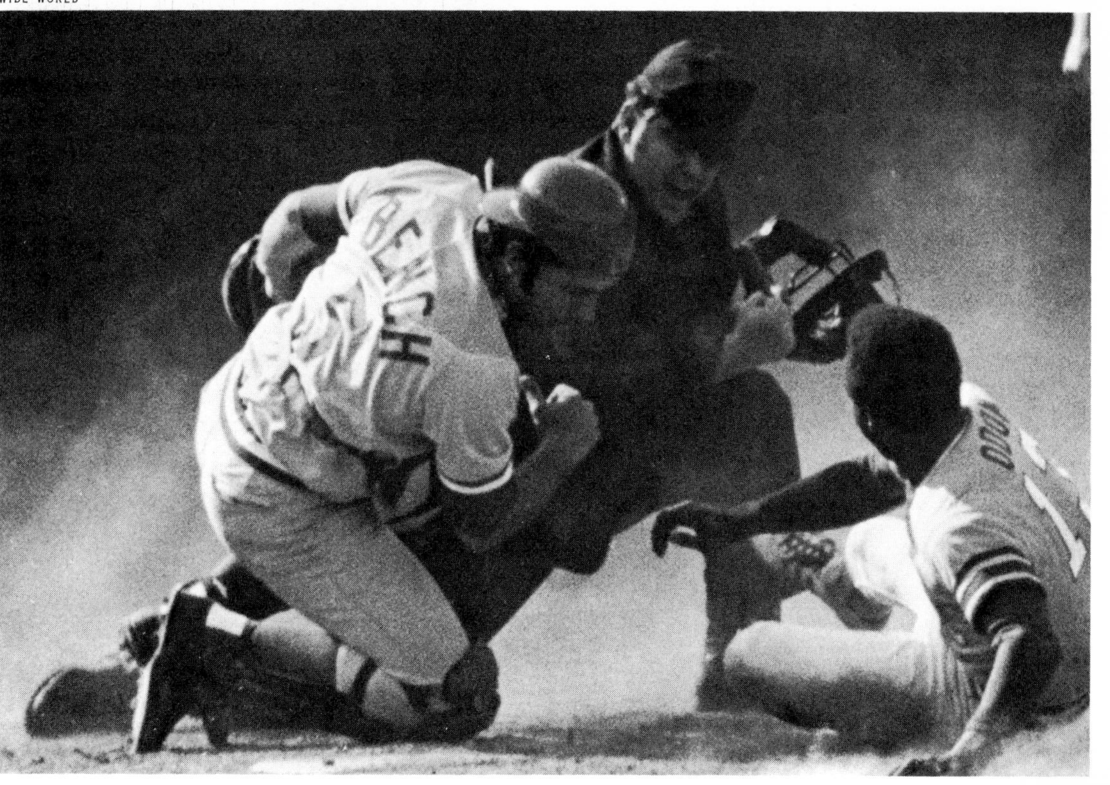

smashed 34 home runs, bringing his career total to 673 and moving him within striking distance of Babe Ruth's all-time record of 714. Carlton turned in a sensational season, winning 27 games for a last-place team which won only 59 in all. He was the top winner in the majors.

Three National League pitchers accounted for no-hit, no-run games: Burt Hooton and Milt Pappas of the Chicago Cubs and Bill Stoneman of Montreal. Pappas came within one pitch of a perfect game. He walked Larry Stahl of San Diego on a 3–2 pitch with two out in the ninth. Pappas later posted his 200th major-league win.

For the eighth straight season, Lou Brock of St. Louis surpassed the 50 mark in stolen bases, matching the record of Ty Cobb. Brock stole 63 in 1972. San Diego's Nate Colbert broke three National League records and tied another on August 1 when he hit five home runs and drove in 13 runs during a doubleheader against Atlanta.

Billy Williams of the Cubs won the National League batting title with .333, finished second to Cincinnati's Bench in runs batted in, and ranked third to Bench and Colbert in home runs. Bench drove in 125 runs to 122 for Williams. Bench hit 40 homers, Colbert 38, and Williams 37. The *Sporting News* named Williams as Player of the Year in the major leagues.

In addition to Carlton, the National League's 20-game winners included Tom Seaver of the New York Mets with 21 and the Cubs' Ferguson Jenkins and the Los Angeles Dodgers' Claude Osteen with 20 each. It was the sixth successive 20-game season for Jenkins.

Allen, the prime force behind the rejuvenated White Sox in 1972, dominated American League batting figures. Allen slugged 37 home runs and drove in 113 runs for leadership in both categories. But the batting title was won by Minnesota's Rod Carew, who hit .318.

The American League produced six 20-game winners. Wilbur Wood of the White Sox and Perry of Cleveland posted 24 wins apiece, and Detroit's Mickey Lolich won 22. Oakland's Hunter, Baltimore's Jim Palmer, and Chicago's Stan Bahnsen each registered 21.

Atlanta Stadium was the site of the 1972 All-Star Game, won by the National League 4–3 in ten innings. It was the seventh extra-inning All-Star Game, the Nationals prevailing in all seven. Joe Morgan singled home the winning run in the bottom of the tenth to clinch the pitching verdict for the Mets' Tug McGraw. The loser was Dave McNally of Baltimore. Hank Aaron of the Nationals and Cookie Rojas of the Americans hit home runs. The National League thus gained its 24th All-Star triumph against 18 losses; one game ended in a tie.

Amateur Baseball

The University of Southern California edged Arizona State 1–0 to win its third straight National Collegiate Athletic Association championship tournament at Omaha, Neb. The Trojans tallied their lone run in the third on a wild pitch.

The Far East kept a firm hold on the Little League world championship in 1972, as the Nationalist Chinese team from Taipei, Taiwan, blanked the U.S. North team from Hammond, Ind., 6–0 in the finals at Williamsport, Pa. The 26th playing of the World Series saw Taiwan garner its second straight series win, the third in the four years in which a Nationalist Chinese team had competed. In the final game, the Taiwan nine collected ten hits, including a home run and three doubles. The Taiwan pitcher Chih-shun gave up one double and three singles, struck out 12, and allowed no bases on balls. Both teams entered the series with 12–0 records in pre-series tournament play. Taiwan opened its series play with a 9–0 victory over New City, N.Y., and then defeated Pearl City, Hawaii, 9–1. Hammond turned back San Juan, Puerto Rico, 10–7 in the semifinals. (*See in* CE: Baseball.)

Pittsburgh first baseman Willie Stargell eyes a dog that wandered onto the field during the playing of the national anthem before a game.

WIDE WORLD

UPI COMPIX

Wilt Chamberlain (right) of the Los Angeles Lakers takes control of the ball with a smile during the fifth NBA championship game in Los Angeles on May 7. Jerry Lucas of the New York Knickerbockers responds with a pained expression as he catches Chamberlain's elbow in his chest. Los Angeles won the game and the championship, their first since leaving Minneapolis many years before.

BASKETBALL. The unprecedented collegiate basketball dynasty at the University of California at Los Angeles (UCLA) remained unsullied in 1972. Three sophomores, most notably 18-year-old Bill Walton, named player of the year by U.S. coaches, led the Bruins to a 30–0 record and their sixth consecutive National Collegiate Athletic Association (NCAA) championship. By accomplishing this, UCLA, coached by Johnny Wooden, bettered its own record of five straight NCAA titles, ran its postseason tournament winning streak to 32 games, won its eighth title in nine years, and boosted its record for that period to 251–15.

Marquette University, the University of Pennsylvania, and the University of North Carolina were considered prime threats to UCLA. In the NCAA's Mideast Regional, Marquette fell to the University of Kentucky 85–69. North Carolina, champion of the 1971 National Invitational Tournament (NIT), destroyed any hopes Penn's Quakers had, 73–59, in the Eastern Regional; but they went on to get bumped, 79–75, in the semifinals by the surprising Florida State University.

Meanwhile, the Bruins were mowing down every tournament team that crossed their path. Weber State College was first, losing 90–58. California State University, Long Beach, was next, falling 73–57. The Bruins then defeated the University of Louisville in the semifinals, 96–77. In the final game UCLA beat Florida State, 81–76, in a contest that grew close in its last minutes. Although Walton was far from at his best in the championship game, he was named the tournament's most valuable player. Roanoke College won the championship in the NCAA's college division, which is limited to smaller schools, by defeating University of Akron, 84–72. Maryland won the 1972 NIT tournament in New York City. The Terrapins humbled Niagara 100–69 in the final game.

Adolph F. Rupp, possessor of more victories than any other collegiate coach in history, was retired by the University of Kentucky at the end of the season. At 70, the school's mandatory retirement age, Rupp had just finished leading the Wildcats to the NCAA tournament for a record 20th time. In his 42 years at Kentucky, Rupp compiled a record of 879 wins against 120 losses. His teams won four NCAA championships and one NIT title.

Violence flared up for a brief period during the 1971–72 season. The University of Minnesota and Ohio State University, the leading contenders for the Big Ten Conference championship, ended their January 25 game in Minneapolis, Minn., with a brawl involving players, coaches, police, and fans. Two Minnesota players, Ron Behagen and Corky Taylor, were suspended for the season for their part in the fracas.

College Standouts

Dwight Lamar, a junior guard from the University of Southwestern Louisiana, led the U.S. in scoring by averaging 36.3 points a game and producing a total of 1,054 points. For the second straight year Greg Starrick of Southern Illinois University won the free-throw percentage title, converting 148 of 160 penalty shots for a .925 average. The best percentage shooter from the field was Kent Martens of Abilene Christian College, who sank 136 of 204 shots for a .667 mark. Kermit Washington, a 6-foot, 8-inch center for American University, averaged 19.8 rebounds per game to lead in that department.

Two UCLA players, Henry Bibby and Walton, were elected to the All-American team of the National Association of Basketball Coaches. They were joined by Ed Ratleff of Long Beach State, Tom Riker of the University of South Carolina, and Jim Price of Louisville.

Karen Wise became the first woman player on the Windham College varsity basketball team, despite objections from other colleges.

UPI COMPIX

Professional Basketball

The Los Angeles Lakers, frustrated in seven attempts to win a National Basketball Association (NBA) championship since their 1960 move to the West coast, finally succeeded in 1972. After establishing a spate of regular-season records, the Lakers, coached by ex-Boston Celtics star Bill Sharman, beat the Chicago Bulls four straight games; the Milwaukee Bucks, four games to two; and the New York Knickerbockers, four games to one, to win the play-offs and the championship. New York, which finished second to Boston in the Atlantic Division, advanced to the finals by defeating Baltimore and the Celtics.

While running away with the Pacific Division title, the Lakers set league records for the highest winning percentage (.841) and the most victories in a season (69). Of these victories, 33 came in a row, breaking the professional sports record of 26 set in 1916 by the New York baseball Giants. The Lakers also established NBA records for the widest victory margin in a game (63 points) and the highest number of games over 100 points (81), wins on the road (31), and wins at home (38). Center Wilt Chamberlain, maligned for having been on only one championship team in his 12 years in the NBA, was named the most valuable player in the play-offs.

Milwaukee's Kareem Abdul-Jabbar won the Podolof Cup, symbolic of the league's most valuable player during the regular season, for the second straight year. He finished ahead of Chamberlain and Jerry West of the Lakers, who was second for the third straight season. Sidney Wicks was named the NBA's rookie of the year for his play with the Portland Trail Blazers.

Abdul-Jabbar and West headed the NBA all-star team selected by the players. They were joined by guard Walt Frazier of New York and forwards Bob Love of Chicago and Spencer Haywood of the Seattle Super Sonics. Abdul-Jabbar led NBA scorers with a 34.8 average. Chamberlain was the leading rebounder, grabbing 19.2 rebounds per game. He also shot .649 from the field to be the top man in field-goal percentage. Other chief statistical performances came from West, who averaged 9.7 assists a game, and Jack Marin of Baltimore, who shot .894 from the free-throw line.

A less pleasing statistic to the owners was the NBA's total attendance of 5,896,052, a drop of 298,554 from 1971. The Cincinnati franchise, which had the league's lowest attendance (147,514), was shifted to Kansas City, Mo.–Omaha, Neb., at the end of the season.

In the American Basketball Association (ABA), the Indiana Pacers proved to be the best team in 1971–72. The Pacers defeated the New York Nets, four games to two, for their second championship in three years. Indiana also had to defeat the champion Utah Stars in the semifinals. (*See in* CE: Basketball.)

AUTHENTICATED NEWS INTERNATIONAL

Delegates from Great Britain, Ireland, Denmark, and Norway met in Brussels, Belgium, in January to sign a treaty paving the way for their nations' entry into the European Economic Community. The citizens of Norway voted later in the year to reject EEC membership.

BELGIUM. Seventy-five days after a general election, a new Belgian government was sworn in on Jan. 21, 1972, again presided over by Premier Gaston Eyskens. The new cabinet reflected a coalition of Social Christians and Socialists reelected the preceding November. For the first time the cabinet included ten secretaries of state, as stipulated by constitutional reforms approved in 1971. The government announced intentions to implement other constitutional revisions affecting cultural autonomy, economic planning, and decentralization, and measures were initiated to stimulate a slightly stagnating economy.

A try for decentralization failed to pass in parliament. The constitutional reforms recognized three national regions: Brussels, Flanders, and Wallonia, and provided for delegating certain powers to a representative body. Advocates of federalism wanted a regional executive and an elected assembly separate from the parliament.

Friction between Dutch-speaking Flemish and French-speaking Walloons developed over the size of the Brussels region. Although requested by Walloon politicians, the introduction of bilingualism in the small Voer region in eastern Belgium caused further discord. Walloon politicians also criticized the government and major oil companies following a unilateral decision by Minister of Economic Affairs Henri Simonet to cut the profit margin on gasoline and increase excise duties.

After ten embattled months, Eyskens resigned on November 22 when Social Christian coalition members refused to accept his compromise plan for implementing decentralization. King Baudouin accepted Eyskens' resignation in December and asked Edmond Leburton, French-speaking copresident of the Socialist party, to form a new coalition government. (*See in* CE: Belgium.)

BHUTAN. On July 21, 1972, King Jigme Dorji Wangchuk of Bhutan died in a Nairobi, Kenya, hospital where he had been receiving treatment for a heart ailment. He was succeeded by the 17-year-old crown prince, Jigme Singye Wangchuk, who was enthroned on July 24. Also in July a ministry of foreign affairs was established with Dawa Tsering as foreign minister.

A trade agreement was signed with India on January 19, and Bhutan was one of 12 developing nations to which generalized trading preferences were extended by the European Economic Community on June 27. On March 1 the Bank of Bhutan was reorganized under royal charter as a step in the kingdom's decade-long effort to change from a barter to a money economy. The State Bank of India was to hold 40% of the shares and nominate three of the bank's seven directors. The 300-kilowatt Wangdü Phodrang hydroelectric project was inaugurated on April 26.

Jigme Singye Wangchuk, 17-year-old crown prince of Bhutan, became king in July after the death of his father, King Jigme Dorji Wangchuk. The young king was the fourth member of the Wangchuk dynasty to rule Bhutan.

WIDE WORLD

BIOLOGY. Not since Charles Darwin introduced the world to the theory of evolution had biological matters been the object of so much public attention as they were in 1972. "Ecology" continued to be important in popular vocabulary, but often with little understanding of its meaning. The proceedings of the United Nations Conference on Human Environment, held in Stockholm, Sweden, in the summer, while producing few concrete plans to protect the environment, were followed with an interest unusual for a scientific meeting. People were more aware that the survival of any community depends on the interdependence of the life-forms it contains and that if man disturbs these complex relationships he threatens his survival as much as that of plants and animals.

The complexity of life also manifests itself in the day-to-day work of biologists. The worldwide economic situation in 1972 meant that they had to make stricter accountings of their expenditures and emphasize "useful" rather than basic research. In addition, efforts to divide the life sciences into disciplines crumbled. Each announcement of a breakthrough in one field filled in a piece in a puzzle being posed in another. For example, a plant pathologist studying diseases in potato plants found the smallest viroid yet isolated. It was 80 times smaller than any other known viroid but was still capable of damaging up to 3% of the Maine potato crop each year. The viroid lacked the coat of protein that usually surrounds the genetic material of a virus. This led to speculation that what had been found was a missing link in the chain of life, falling between viruses and genes.

In another example, scientists at Harvard and Columbia universities announced isolation of the first protein repressor for an enzyme that builds up substances. Their work added to the evidence being used to prove the theory that the differences between cells in various parts of the body are caused by a class of genes that make repressors. When a repressor is attached to a gene, that gene is prevented from making its particular product. Repressors controlling enzymes that break down substances had been isolated before, but this was the first isolation of a repressor for an enzyme that builds a substance. The amino acid that this repressor controls is tryptophan, a substance that was also being studied in many parts of the world by psychiatrists who believed that too much of it in brain cells may be the cause of the psychotic disorder schizophrenia.

Several developments made use of the revolutionary discovery in 1970 that an enzyme, reverse transcriptase, can make DNA from RNA. Three independent research groups accomplished the first partial synthesis of a human gene, and the first synthesis of any gene without first knowing its complete DNA sequence, by using reverse transcriptase to make synthetic deoxynucleotides, the building blocks of a DNA molecule. In other work reverse transcriptase, first found in tumor viruses and later in animal and human cancer cells, was also isolated in animal embryo cells. One theory of cancer holds that since the wild growth of cancer cells resembles the rapid development of an embryo, something causes the cancer cell to act like a cell of an unborn baby. Perhaps that something is the removal of the repressor for reverse transcriptase.

One of the most fascinating questions continually being raised was whether life exists elsewhere in the universe. Scientists were hoping that better knowledge about how life began on earth would give clues of what to look for in space exploration. One popular notion was that ultraviolet radiation and lightning caused simple molecules to become rearranged into chains that could reproduce themselves. Biologists were looking for these simple chains, or precursor molecules, and trying to decide whether they would be precursors of protein or nucleic acid. Two reports released in 1972 differed: one said proteins came first, and the other said neither did—that the precursor was a polynucleotide enzyme. Later research tended to discount the protein theory. Two substances known to be necessary for life, amino acids and formaldehyde, had been found in meteorites coming to earth from outer space. (*See in* CE: Biology).

The Cooperative Forest Fire Prevention Campaign continued its work of informing the public that the need for care in prevention of forest fires has never been greater. Part of the effort was a poster of a wounded Smokey the Bear praying for more consideration: ". . . and PLEASE make people more careful."

COURTESY, U.S. FOREST SERVICE

BIRTHS. Among the births that drew public attention in 1972 were:

To Muhammad Ali, former world heavyweight boxing champion, and his wife, Belinda, on May 14, a son.

To Anne Bancroft, actress ('The Miracle Worker'; 'The Graduate'), and Mel Brooks, comedian and screenwriter ('The Producers'), on May 22, a son.

To Peter J. Bridge, New Jersey newspaper reporter who went to jail in 1972 rather than reveal the names of his sources, and his wife, Anne, on October 30, a daughter.

To Petula Clark, British singer, and Claude Wolff, French businessman, on September 7, a son.

To Sue Lyon, film actress ('Lolita'), and Roland Harrison, photographer, on May 22, a daughter.

To Juliet Prowse, actress and dancer, and John McCook, actor, on August 2, a son.

To U.S. Senator Strom Thurmond (R, S.C.), and his wife, Nancy, former beauty queen, on October 18, a son.

To Susannah York, British film actress ('The Killing of Sister George'), and Michael Wells, actor, on May 9, a daughter.

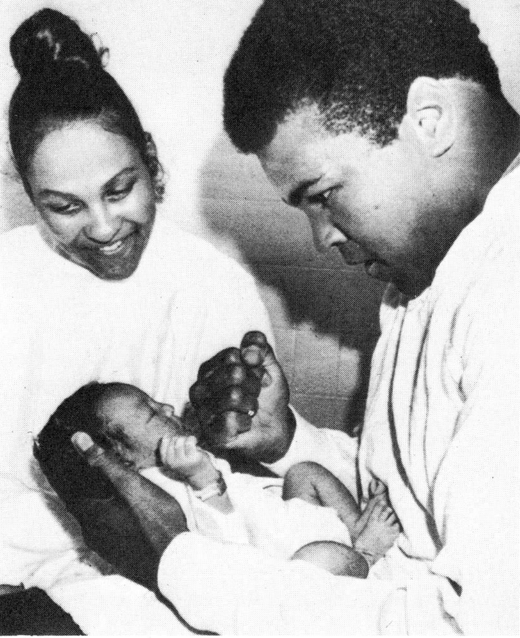

UPI COMPIX

Heavyweight boxer and former world champion Muhammad Ali visits his wife, Belinda, and their first-born son in a hospital in Philadelphia, Pa. The child, born May 14, was named Muhammad Eban Ali.

UPI COMPIX

In their Hollywood, Calif., home, actress-dancer Juliet Prowse and actor John McCook pose for a picture with their newborn son, Seth.

BOATS AND BOATING. It was an off year for America's Cup action, but in the 1972 Olympic Games, the city of Kiel, West Germany, played host to six classes of small sailboats in a seven-race series in which 42 nations participated. In the past the competition had often been dominated by the Scandinavians, but the winner in 1972 was clearly Australia with gold medals in the Star and Dragon classes. The U.S. accounted for one gold and two bronze medals. Buddy Melges of the U.S. had poor luck at the Olympic trials on San Francisco Bay, in California, but nevertheless won the right to represent the U.S. in the Soling class. Accomplishing a complete turnabout, Melges so dominated the races in Kiel that it was not necessary for him to sail in the seventh and final contest, but he did and won again. Not since 1960 when Denmark's Paul Elvström won the gold medal in the Finn class had a skipper so completely dominated his competition. The result was even more remarkable in 1972 because the skillful Elvström sailed against Melges in the Soling event.

In other sailing events, the important race from Newport, R.I., to Bermuda was won by Ted Hicks of Great Britain in the 48-foot sloop *Noryema.* Approximately 178 boats competed in the event that was one of the roughest of all Bermuda races, principally because of Hurricane Agnes, which crossed in the path of the boats. Ron Amey, also of Great Britain and the owner of *Noryema,* was scheduled as skipper, but Hicks took over when Amey was called home on business. The 635-mile race was so well planned that Hicks used only two helmsmen. The 2,700-mile transatlantic race to Bayona, Spain, was won by Richard S. Nye of New York City in his 48-foot sloop *Carina.*

A stiff test of man's endurance, skill, and ability to fight loneliness, the Observer Singlehanded Transatlantic race had attracted a great deal of attention in recent years. The 1972 event was won by Alain Colas in his 67-foot aluminum trimaran *Pen Duick IV,* designed by Eric Taberly of France. In 20 days, 13 hours, and 15 minutes, he sailed—completely alone—from Plymouth, England, to Newport. Sir Francis Chichester, always a favorite, was forced to withdraw during the race; he died shortly thereafter.

In powerboat contests, the Offshore class, in which wealthy men match speed and navigating skills over ocean courses at least 150 miles long, continued to be very popular. Quick to catch the public's fancy in 1972 was Sandy Satullo, a Cleveland, Ohio, restaurant owner, who won the first four offshore races he had ever entered in his *Copper Kettle,* a 36-foot Cigarette hull, powered with twin MerCruiser engines. Bobby Rautborg, a Miami, Fla., boat company executive, was busy all over the world winning enough points to claim the Union of International Motorboating (UIM) world championship. Rautborg's boat, *Fino,* was identical to that of Satullo.

The Gold Cup, long considered the highest prize in hydroplane racing, went to veteran Bill Muncy in *Atlas Van Lines.* Muncy won all four heats of the annual running of the event on the Detroit River on June 25, making him the first man to match Gar Wood's string of five wins in the 1920's. Tragedy struck during the year when Jerry Waldman, who had won more racing-outboard events than any other man, was killed in a class D Outboard Hydroplane race in Hot Springs, Ark., on June 3. Waldman's racing career spanned 25 years. The Russians became members of the UIM in 1969 and in 1972 sent their first representative beyond the Iron Curtain for the world championships for OB class outboards (350-cc piston displacement), held at Auronzo, a lake in the Italian Alps. The Soviet pilot, Eugene Radko, won the event using a two-year-old German motor. (*See in* CE: Boats and Boating.)

The *Noryema,* skippered by Ted Hicks, was the overall fleet champion and Class C winner of the 635-mile Newport-to-Bermuda race. She also won the performance prize for the largest margin of victory within a class.

STANLEY ROSENFELD FROM MORRIS ROSENFELD & SONS

UPI COMPIX

Bolivian troops armed with automatic weapons blocked the roads leading to the University of La Paz in November after President Banzer declared a state of siege. The state of siege began shortly after industrial workers in the capital went on a 24-hour strike.

BOLIVIA. Col. Hugo Banzer Suárez, the president of Bolivia, survived several crises in 1972 without appreciably loosening his grip on the government. The most serious incident followed a 66.7% devaluation of the peso on October 27. Prices began to soar and trade-union leaders criticized the move. The government retaliated by denouncing "left-wing infiltration" of the unions. A 24-hour general strike was called for November 23 by the union leaders; Banzer almost immediately imposed a state of siege. The strike ended the next day, but some strikers continued to defy the government and the state of siege remained in effect.

Banzer reshuffled his cabinet earlier in the year and removed Interior Minister Col. Andres Selich, who had played an important role in Banzer's ouster of leftist Gen. Juan José Torres in a bloody coup in 1971. Selich was then made ambassador to Paraguay but was later recalled and retired from the army amid charges that he had plotted against Banzer. Col. Mario Adett Zamora became the new interior minister.

Foreign Minister Mario Gutiérrez Gutiérrez announced on March 29 that 119 staff members of the Soviet embassy in La Paz, the capital, had been asked to leave the country within seven days. While Bolivia did not sever diplomatic relations with the Soviet Union, the government charged that Igor Sholokov, the embassy's first secretary, had been in contact with left-wing antigovernment elements. Eventually only 49 Soviet citizens were expelled. Banzer's government had started a drive a few weeks earlier to eradicate the National Liberation Army (ELN), a guerrilla organization, and had arrested 150 suspected guerrillas and killed at least two alleged ELN members. The government claimed that by the end of March more than 80% of the ELN members in Cochabamba and La Paz had been killed or arrested, but authorities still feared an invasion by Bolivian exiles living in Chile.

Divisions appeared within the National Revolutionary Movement (MNR), one of the two parties that supported the government, but the coalition of the MNR and the Bolivian Socialist Falange continued to support Banzer. (*See in* CE: Bolivia.)

BOTSWANA. With its remarkable economic development reflected in a budget balanced (at $31 million) for the first time without British aid for 1972–73, Botswana's political importance in southern Africa grew proportionately during 1972. President Sir Seretse Khama made major changes in the government in 1972. Under an agreement with Nigeria, T. A. Aguda was sworn in as chief justice in February.

On the economic front, more than 40 separate agreements were completed with West German, U.S., and other interests—some involving the Shashe copper-nickel mining project. Economic cooperation with South Africa continued. But the devaluation of the rand led to an escalation in development costs, particularly because of the gathering momentum of the Shashe project. About 400 workers on the project went on strike, protesting South African job preference.

Sir Seretse officially opened the Orapa diamond mining operation on May 26; it was estimated that production would represent one third of the diamond output of all southern Africa and would provide Botswana with a revenue exceeding $10.6 million per year. Although heavy rains brought widespread flooding and damage during January, major road construction continued, supported by British, Swedish, and International Development Association funds. A $12-million U.S. loan was secured for the projected Botswana–Zambia highway link. (*See in* CE: Botswana, Republic of.)

BOWLING. The increasing popularity of bowling was reflected on all levels in 1972. Approximately 52 million people in the U.S. bowled at least once in 1971, according to data collected in two national surveys commissioned by the National Bowling Council.

Long Beach, Calif., hosted the 69th annual American Bowling Congress (ABC) tournament, which attracted 4,732 teams. The Classic (professional) championship was won by Basch Advertising, of New York City, which totaled 3,099 in the six-team roll-off. In other Classic competition, Carmen Salvino, Chicago, and Barry Asher, Costa Mesa, Calif., topped the doubles with 1,366; Teata Semiz, River Edge, N.J., led the singles and all-events with 754 and 1,994, respectively. The ABC's regular division champions were: team, Hamm's Beer, Minneapolis, Minn., 3,101; doubles, Jerry Nutt and Bill Stanfield, Grand Rapids, Mich., 1,350; singles, Bill Pointer, Pontiac, Mich., 739; and all-events, Mac Lowry, Seattle, Wash., 2,026. Bill Beach of Sharon, Pa., won the 22d annual ABC Masters in spectacular fashion, coming out of the losers' bracket to dethrone defending champion Jim Godman of Lorain, Ohio.

The 53d annual Woman's International Bowling Congress (WIBC) tournament, held in Kansas City, Mo., was the richest ever ($351,305 prize fund) and the second largest (5,898 teams). Champions included D. D. Jacobson, Playa Del Rey, Calif., who won the singles with a record 737; Judy Roberts and Betty Remmick, Denver, Colo., doubles, 1,247; Mildred Martorella, Rochester, N.Y., all-events, 1,877; and Angeltown Creations, Placentia, Calif., team, 2,838. Left-handed Dotty Fothergill of North Attleboro, Mass., captured the 12th annual WIBC Queens tournament title, defeating Maureen Harris of Madison, Wis., in the finals, 890–841.

More than 350 bowlers from 32 states, competing individually or representing clubs, showed up in 1972 for the 16th annual National Wheelchair Games in Woodside, Queens, N.Y.

WIDE WORLD

In the year's top professional events, Don Johnson of Akron, Ohio, won the U.S. Open. Mike Durbin of Chagrin Falls, Ohio, triumphed in the Tournament of Champions.

In collegiate ranks, Harding College of Searcy, Ark., won the 11th annual National Association of Intercollegiate Athletics team championship for the third year in a row. George Yadrich of Rockhurst College, Kansas City, won individual honors.

Named to the ABC Hall of Fame were Bill Lillard, Houston, Tex.; Marty Cassio, Rahway, N.J.; Milton Raymer, St. Petersburg, Fla.; and the late LeRoy Chase, Peoria, Ill.

Elected to the WIBC Hall of Fame were Stella Hartrick, Detroit, Mich.; Gertrude Rishling, Omaha, Neb.; and Beverly Ortner, Tucson, Ariz. (*See in* CE: Bowling.)

BOXING. Joe Frazier of the U.S. remained world heavyweight boxing champion in 1972, but the long-awaited return fight against Muhammad Ali (Cassius Clay) for the championship did not materialize. Frazier twice defended the title, stopping U.S. challengers Terry Daniels and Ron Stander each in four rounds. Ali was more active, scoring point victories over Mac Foster of the U.S. in Tokyo and George Chuvalo of Canada in Vancouver, B.C. He knocked out other U.S. opponents including Jerry Quarry at Las Vegas, Nev.; Al (Blue) Lewis at Dublin, Ireland; and Bob Foster, the world light-heavyweight champion, at Stateline, Nev.; and he stopped an old rival, Floyd Patterson, at New York City. George Foreman, another U.S. heavyweight world contender and a former Olympic champion, retained his undefeated professional record in 1972 and brought his total of victories to 38, 35 of them inside the distance. His five victims in 1972—each knocked out in two rounds—were Clarence Boone, Murphy Goodwin, Ted Gullick, Miguel Angel Paez, and Terry Sorrells.

Despite his defeat by Ali, Bob Foster remained supreme in the light-heavyweight division, successfully defending the World Boxing Council (WBC) championship four times. He beat Brian Burden of the U.S. in three rounds, Vicente Rondon of Venezuela in two, Mike Quarry of the U.S. in four, and Chris Finnegan of England in 14.

Carlos Monzon of Argentina continued to dominate the world middleweights and traveled to Europe three times to defend his title successfully,

UPI COMPIX

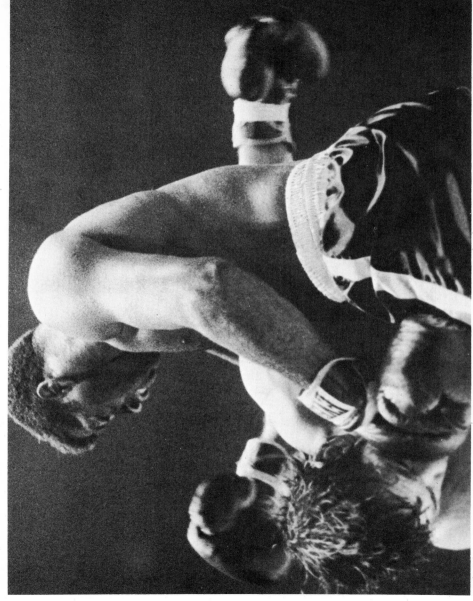

The 37-year-old former world heavyweight champion Floyd Patterson (right) scored a unanimous decision over his Argentine opponent Oscar Bonavena in their ten-round bout that took place on February 11 in New York City.

beating Denny Moyer of the U.S. in 5 rounds in Rome, Jean-Claude Bouttier of France in 12 in Paris, and Tom Bogs of Denmark in 5 in Copenhagen, Denmark. Koichi Wajima of Japan retained the junior middleweight championship, beating Domenico Tiberia of Italy in one round and Matt Donovan of Trinidad in three.

José Napoles of Mexico remained welterweight champion with knockout wins against England's Ralph Charles in London and Adolph Pruitt of the U.S. at Monterrey, Mexico. The junior welterweight crown continued to be shared: Bruno Arcari of Italy successfully defended the WBC version against Juan Henrique of Brazil with a 12th-round knockout and against Everaldo Costa Azeredo of Argentina with a win on points. The World Boxing Association (WBA) junior welter-

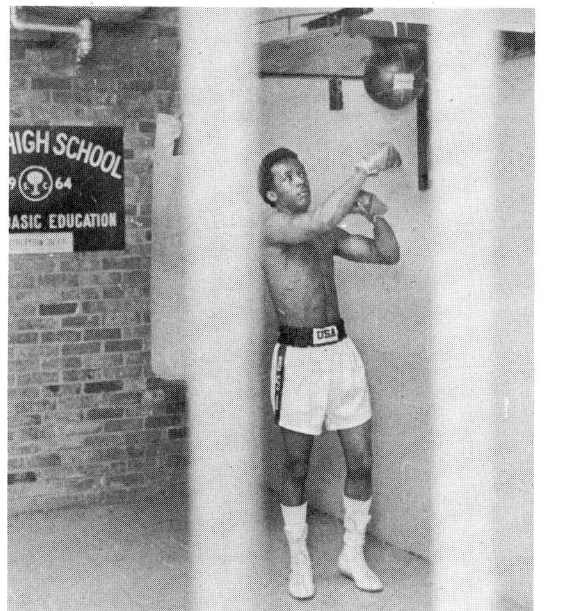

Boxer Bobby Lee Hunter, serving a prison term in South Carolina for manslaughter, is allowed to take leaves from prison for boxing matches.

WIDE WORLD

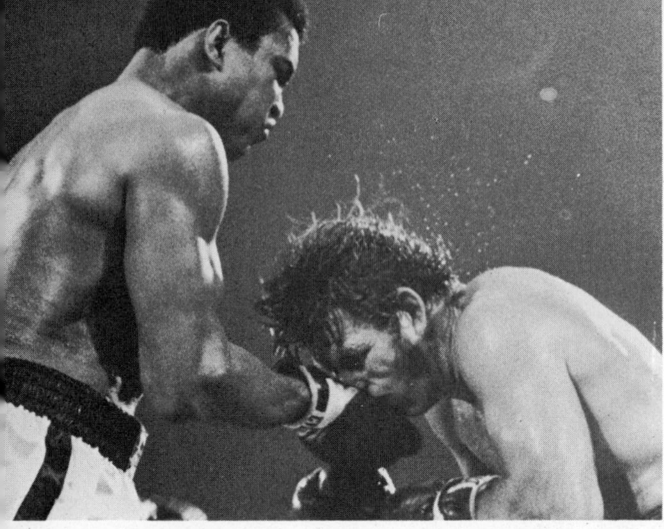

WIDE WORLD

Muhammad Ali (left) flattens the nose of Jerry Quarry during their heavyweight fight in Las Vegas, Nev., in June. Ali won by a technical knockout in the seventh round.

weight championship, however, changed hands twice. Alfonso Frazer of Panama took the title from Nicolino Loche of Argentina with a win on points in Panama City, Panama, but later dropped it to Antonio Cervantes of Colombia when he was knocked out in ten rounds, also in Panama City.

Panama's Roberto Duran took the WBA lightweight title from Ken Buchanan of Scotland in 13 rounds in New York City. There was considerable argument and confusion after Mando Ramos of the U.S. received a disputed decision over Spain's Pedro Carrasco in a contest in Madrid, Spain, for the vacant WBC version of the title. Later, Chango Carmona of Mexico stopped Ramos in 8 rounds in Los Angeles. The WBC title was settled when Rodolfo Gonzalez of the U.S. was accepted as champion.

Ricardo Arredondo of Mexico retained the WBC junior lightweight championship with knockout wins against William Martinez of Nigeria in 5 rounds in Mexico City, Mexico, and Susumu Okabe of Japan in 12 rounds in Tokyo. Ben Villaflor of the Philippines captured the WBA junior lightweight title with a decision over titleholder Alfredo Marcano of Venezuela in Honolulu, Hawaii. Villaflor later retained the title when held to a draw by Victor Echegaray of Argentina.

Two new featherweight champions were crowned. After retaining the WBA title with a seventh-round knockout against Raul Martinez Mora of Mexico, Antonio Gomez of Venezuela lost it on points to Panama's Ernesto Marcel. The WBC championship was taken by Clemente Sanchez of Mexico with a third-round knockout win against Kuniaki Shibata of Japan in Tokyo.

The world bantamweight championship changed hands twice. After successfully defending his title by stopping Jesus Pimental of Mexico in 11 rounds in Los Angeles, Ruben Olivares of Mexico was knocked out in 8 rounds by Rafael Herrera of Mexico in Mexico City. Herrera later lost the title to Enrique Pinder of Panama.

Masao Ohba of Japan retained the WBA flyweight championship, defeating Susumu Hanagata of Japan on points and stopping Orlando Amores of Panama in five rounds. The WBC flyweight title changed hands when Venice Borkorso of Thailand stopped Betulio Gonzalez of Venezuela in ten rounds. (*See in* CE: Boxing.)

WORLD BOXING CHAMPIONS

As of Dec. 31, 1972

Division	Boxer
Heavyweight	Joe Frazier, U.S.
Light Heavyweight	Bob Foster, U.S.
Middleweight	Carlos Monzon, Argentina
Junior Middleweight	Koichi Wajima, Japan
Welterweight	José Napoles, Mexico
Junior Welterweight	Bruno Arcari, Italy Antonio Cervantes, Colombia *
Lightweight	Rodolfo Gonzalez, U.S. Roberto Duran, Panama *
Junior Lightweight	Ricardo Arredondo, Mexico Ben Villaflor, Philippines *
Featherweight	Clemente Sanchez, Mexico Ernesto Marcel, Panama *
Bantamweight	Enrique Pinder, Panama
Flyweight	Venice Borkorso, Thailand Masao Ohba, Japan *

* Recognized as champion by the World Boxing Association.

BRAZIL. Despite rumors of sporadic unrest, Brazil remained relatively calm during 1972. The strong executive regime established after the 1964 revolution—under the provisions of the 1967 constitution as amended in 1969 and the special emergency laws known as Institutional Acts—appeared consolidated. The national congress continued to go about its business of discussing and approving the legislative measures either proposed or backed by the administration. In May 1972 it passed constitutional amendment number one, proposed by President Emílio Garrastazú Médici. This amendment provided for the indirect election of state governors and vice-governors. The constitution already had provided for the indirect election of the nation's president and vice-president. In nationwide municipal elections held in November, the government swamped the official opposition party, but an estimated 25% to 30% of the voters abstained or nullified their ballots.

There were reports that many opposition political leaders were harassed or were under police surveillance and that the authorities continued their censorship of news by indirect pressure or outright prohibition. Despite popular pressure favoring immediate reintegration into the country's political life of many citizens who had been deprived of their political rights under Institutional Act number five, the government continued to refuse to take action. It declared that this act (signed in December 1968) would continue in force as long as the

UPI COMPIX

Law enforcement officers from Brazil, the U.S., and Interpol inspect 132 pounds of heroin confiscated on board the ship *Mormac Altair* while in port in Rio de Janeiro. One officer holds an automatic weapon at the ready in case of intruders.

special powers granted under it to the executive were necessary to control terrorism and subversion.

Certain influential newspapers were allowed to freely criticize the authorities for the arbitrary arrest of citizens, who were jailed even though terrorism was said to have virtually disappeared. The military courts continued to try cases of subversive activity as defined under the national security laws. Nowhere, however, was arrest generally accompanied by torture, as allegedly had happened in preceding years.

In mid-1972 it was announced that 779.2 miles of the Trans-Amazon Highway had been finished and would be inaugurated by President Médici as part of the 150th independence anniversary. Paving of the road connecting Brasília, the capital, with Belém was completed during the year.

Brazil commemorated the 150th anniversary of its independence with an elaborate program that included a huge industrial exposition (Brazil-Export '72) staged in the city of São Paulo September 4–15. In April, as part of the commemoration, the body of the first emperor, Dom Pedro I—who headed the independence movement and first declared the nation's independence from Portugal on Sept. 7, 1822—was removed to Brazil from Lisbon, Portugal, where it had reposed in the pantheon of his ancestors since 1834. The body was interred in a monument at Ipiranga, near the city of São Paulo, where independence was first declared.

The largest increase in the economy was reported to have been in industrial production. Exports in 1972 included automobiles (total production was 516,000 units in 1971), sugar (200,000 metric tons sold to the Soviet Union in 1972), meats ($100 million sold to the U.S.), and fresh fruit and concentrated frozen citrus juices (total production of fruit was estimated at 58.3 million boxes, of which 35 million were processed for juice, mostly for export). Also exported were a variety of other products including steel, shoes, rubber products, and, of course, the old standby items of coffee and cotton. Iron ore exports increased during the year. New mineral deposits estimated at ten basic metric tons were discovered in the northern state of Pará.

Agricultural production increased at the slow rate of 2.6% in 1971. It was expected to be much higher in 1972. Production of coffee, still the largest item among Brazil's exports ($900 million in 1971), was expected to be lower in 1972 because of heavy frosts in July. (*See in* CE: Brazil.)

BULGARIA. Despite the fact that 75% of its trade was with East European countries (more than half with the U.S.S.R. alone), Bulgaria continued to progress in 1972. Industrial production increased, but agriculture, which employed 40% of the work force, was responsible for 55% of exports.

In February Todor Zhivkov began his 19th year as head of the Bulgarian Communist party. He was 60 years old, and 5 of the 11 members of the Politburo were over 70. The age factor was partly responsible for friction between official ideology and Bulgaria's younger populace.

In April Vladimir Boneve replaced Georgi Traikov as chairman of the presidium of the National Assembly. Peter Mladenov succeeded as minister of foreign affairs Ivan Bashev.

The management of Bulgaria's national economy changed little; it was still centrally planned and directed. The seventh congress of Bulgarian Trade Unions, held in March in Sofia, the capital, criticized this centralization and insisted that unions start defending working-class interests.

Cuba's Premier Fidel Castro visited Bulgaria for ten days in May, the first and longest stop on his tour of Eastern Europe. Michael Ramsey, archbishop of Canterbury and primate of England, paid a five-day visit in June and was cordially received by Maksim (Minkov), patriarch of the Eastern Orthodox church in Bulgaria, who had been named head of the church in July 1971.

Bulgarian and Romanian leaders met in September in Varna and decided to jointly build a new hydroelectric complex on the lower Danube River. (*See in* CE: Bulgaria.)

BURMA. During 1972 the Burmese government took two major political steps toward the realization of a socialist state. In March Gen. Ne Win and the other members of the ruling Revolutionary Council dropped their military ranks and became civilians, thus ending ten years of continuous military rule. In May the first draft of a socialist constitution was announced. A trained cadre of the Burmese Socialist Program party (BSPP) was to carry the constitution to the people before its official proclamation as law in 1974. The document provided for a socialist democratic republic with a unicameral People's Congress, to which only BSPP members would be elected. To placate rebellious minorities such as the Mons, Arakanese, and Chins, Ne Win accepted the formation of separate minority states within the Socialist Union of Burma. More than 150 political detainees were released during the year to demonstrate Ne Win's confidence despite the presence of insurgents, who still seemed to pose a threat to the government.

Economic problems were a continuing area of concern. A National Economic Committee was set up to study plans and problems, and Revolutionary Council members toured the countryside to urge farmers to produce more. A land reform bill limiting land holdings to 50 acres per family was put into effect. Several development projects were commissioned, and Japan, West Germany, the Soviet Union, and Canada provided some economic aid. (*See in* CE: Burma.)

BURUNDI. Tribal massacres and a refugee exodus to neighboring countries decimated Burundi's population in 1972. Somber developments began when the exiled King Ntare V traveled from West Germany to Uganda on March 21. In the presence of Uganda's president, Gen. Idi Amin, he was promised safe conduct and amnesty by the Burundian government. On arrival in Burundi on March 30, he was taken by the army to an undisclosed destination, and on March 31 an official broadcast announced his arrest for trying to invade the country with mercenaries. On April 29 the Burundian government was dismissed by presidential decree. On the following day an official broadcast stated that an attempted coup on April 29 had been averted, but that the king had been killed while his supporters were attempting to rescue him from the palace at Gitega. President Michel Micombero disclosed later that Ntare had been tried and executed the night of the attack.

A new military government under presidential control was established and public assembly prohibited. At first, confusion reigned over whether the uprising was monarchist or Maoist; it was later officially accepted as far-leftist because Burundi had long been a center of Chinese infiltration. But it seemed obvious that the uprising was the result of the repression of the Hutu people by the dominant Tutsis. According to plan, the uprising started with simultaneous slaughter of Tutsis in Bujumbura, the capital; the Bururi region in the south; and Gitega in the middle of the country. With aid from Zaire the rebellion was largely crushed within two weeks, but harsh reprisals by the Tutsis continued throughout May, and the toll of the double genocide was estimated at anything from 50,000 to 200,000 victims. At least 500,000 people were rendered homeless, and thousands of refugees entered Tanzania, Rwanda, and Zaire. On May 28 President Micombero broadcast that "calm reigned" following the execution of the original rebel leaders. On May 30 an official announcement stated that the 31 days' tragedy, allegedly an attempt to exterminate the Tutsis by "criminal men aided by foreign mercenaries," was over. According to reports, however, the execution of Hutus continued throughout June and July. (*See in* CE: Burundi.)

BUSINESS AND INDUSTRY. Recovery, expansion, and record corporate profits were good news for U.S. business and industry in 1972. Increased outlay for new plants and equipment, record spending by consumers, and the tantalizing prospect of greatly increased trade with the Soviet Union and the People's Republic of China all contributed to the resurgence. Optimism reigned, despite the involvement of several well-known firms in scandals and labor disputes during the year.

Beneath the surface ebullience, however, lay an undercurrent of deep concern for the direction business would take in 1973. The possibilities of greater inflation, narrower profit margins, rising interest rates, and labor strife all qualified the generally positive outlook. This mood was reflected in the stock market, which drifted along in uncertainty for most of the year before rising to record levels in November.

U.S. President Richard M. Nixon's new economic policy, launched in 1971, was generally considered to be a success. Unemployment persisted, however, particularly among professionals in engineering, science, and education; and new college graduates found a tight job market awaiting them. Both business and labor bristled under the restraints of wage and price controls, and consumers grumbled at rising food and rent costs. While consumer price increases were smaller than in previous years, they still were present, and wholesale prices, fueled by extraordinary farm price rises, increased faster in the 12 months following the controls than in the previous 12 months.

The thaw in East-West relations following President Nixon's trips to China and the Soviet Union carried broad implications for U.S. business. The promise of increased trade in those areas spurred hopes that the U.S. could reduce its massive trade deficit, which was expected to run close to $6 billion in 1972. The trade imbalance between the U.S. and Japan accounted for about two thirds of the deficit. Early hopes for increased trade were fulfilled by a $1-billion purchase of grain from the

U.S. by the Soviet Union. Besides yielding large profits for grain exporters, the pact was expected to aid U.S. cargo shippers. A sorry note was introduced, however, when the U.S. Department of Agriculture was accused of "tipping off" large grain exporters on the expected deal, thus allowing them to purchase grain before news of the pact caused price rises. (*See* World Trade.) Other large international trade agreements included a proposed $3-billion, 20-year pact between Occidental Petroleum Corp. and the Soviet Union and the sale by Boeing Co. of $150 million worth of model 707 jet airplanes to China. Tenneco Inc. was discussing an agreement with the Soviets for $55 billion worth of liquefied natural gas, and Occidental Petroleum, Pullman Inc., Pepsico Inc., and the Chase Manhattan Bank were allowed to open Moscow offices.

Grain exporters were not the only U.S. business concerns involved in controversy during the year. The giant International Telephone & Telegraph Corp. (ITT) endured a political nightmare for its efforts to lure the Republican National Convention to San Diego, Calif., where the firm owned a major hotel. Evidence was unearthed that indicated ITT had guaranteed the Republicans several hundred thousand dollars if the party's convention were held in San Diego. The offer apparently coincided with a tempering by the U.S. Department of Justice of its earlier ruling that ITT would have to divest itself of several holdings if it wished to retain the newly acquired Hartford Fire Insurance Co. A compromise settlement worked out between the Justice Department and ITT on the Hartford question came uncomfortably close on the heels of the ITT convention offer. Fueled by election-year claims from the Democratic party that favoritism was being shown, the dispute became a national issue involving a number of high government officials, newspaper columnist Jack Anderson, and acting Attorney General Richard G. Kleindienst, whose permanent appointment was held up for weeks while a Senate committee investigated the charges. Kleindienst had been implicated in the controversy, but his appointment was eventually confirmed. (*See* Newspapers Special Report.)

ITT's troubles continued throughout the year. When extensive ITT holdings in Chile were nationalized by the Marxist government of President Salvador Allende Gossens in September 1971, ITT wrote a long memo to the White House outlining an 18-point plan for forcing Allende out of office. Although the government apparently did not follow ITT's suggestions, exposure of the memo in July did not help ITT's sagging reputation. Perhaps the most threatening action was the filing of a civil complaint by the Securities and Exchange Commission (SEC) against ITT for a long series of violations of securities laws. Among the SEC charges were allegations that ITT officials had sold unregistered stock and had taken advantage of inside knowledge to dump shares of Hartford stock.

In January the Federal Trade Commission accused the four largest producers of ready-to-eat cereal of price-fixing and unfair advertising practices. (*See* Food.) In October the huge International Business Machines Corp. (IBM) was charged by the U.S. Department of Justice with monopolizing the computer industry. A suit filed

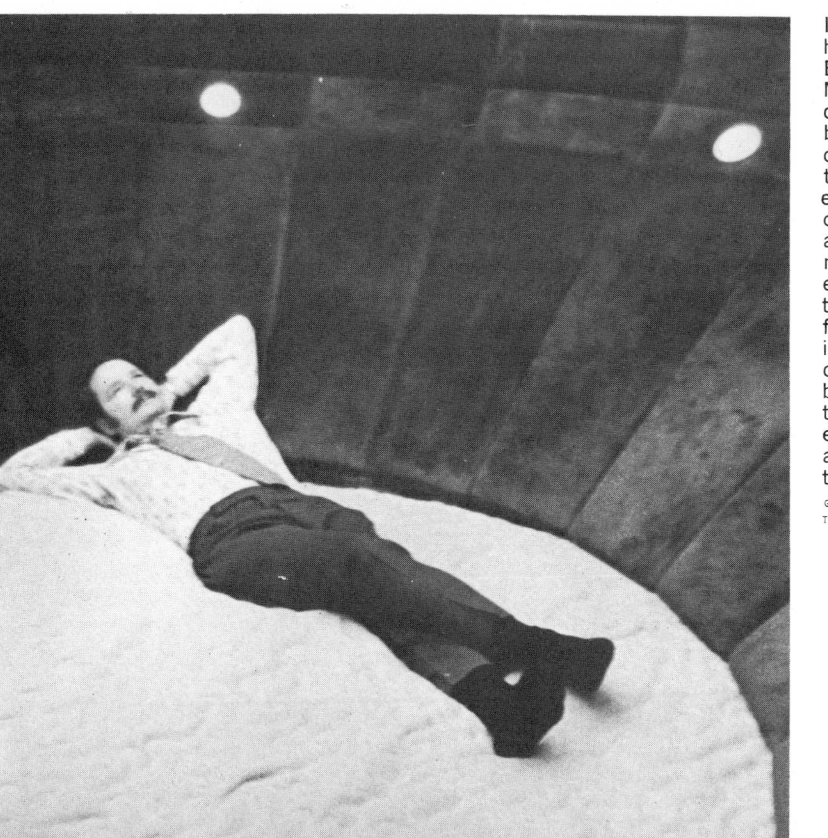

In its new corporate headquarters in Oak Brook, Ill., the McDonald's hamburger chain installed a water bed to foster relaxed, creative thinking among the company's executives. The unusual office interior also uses a "task response module" for each employee, instead of traditional office furniture. The module is one movable unit containing desk, files, bulletin boards, telephones, and other equipment. Few walls are needed in the office.

GARY SETTLE FROM "THE NEW YORK TIMES"

by the department three years before was described as demanding the breakup of the firm into separate, competitive companies. (*See* Computers.)

The automobile industry fared well in 1972; auto sales rose to a new record despite a series of strikes against the industry's largest producer, General Motors Corp. (*See* Labor Unions.) Facilities were strained by attempts to meet unprecedented demand for new cars. The upsurge was marked by the comeback of American Motors Corp., which registered a 230% increase in profits (to $27.2 million) and sales of $1.04 billion in the nine months ending June 30. The prosperity was shadowed by several problems, however. The industry was straining to produce a pollution-free engine and install adequate safety features that would meet new federal standards due to become effective in 1975; attempts failed to have the federal deadlines postponed. In addition, gasoline distributors were hit by a sudden shortage of the fuel during the summer. (*See* Automobiles.)

The gasoline shortage was indicative of a growing fuel crisis in the U.S. Gasoline consumption was running more than 5% higher than in 1971, and new cars using low-lead gasoline were found to be burning 8% more fuel than conventional cars. Although the federal government increased oil import quotas in September, shortages in all fuel areas were becoming acute. Price increases for gasoline and fuel oil were expected in 1973. A shortage of heating oil threatened homeowners in the East, and electric power crises in cities were becoming commonplace. (*See* Fuel and Power.)

Despite this and other grave problems, business was cheered by several new products that made impressive debuts in 1972. These included minicalculators, the Wankel rotary automobile engine, and the electronic watch. Checkless banking became available to most California residents, with most commercial banks using electronic systems to transfer funds. Video cassettes gained greater commercial use, although they were not yet within reach of the home market. An independent postal delivery service showed a profit in delivering second-, third-, and fourth-class mail, which the U.S. Postal Service had insisted was responsible for huge deficits.

Companies continued to feel the wrath of the growing consumer movement, and many of them reorganized public relations efforts toward a positive rather than defensive posture, offering advertisements of programs for pollution control and minority hiring. Corporate annual meetings sometimes became battlegrounds as antiwar groups and environmentalists disrupted stockholders' meetings or used their positions as stockholders to make their views known. Women's liberation groups and churches were especially active in stockholders' protests; the World Council of Churches voted in 1972 to divest itself of holdings in any firm doing business with South Africa.

Third-quarter figures showed a rise in U.S. corporate profits of $4.2 billion to an annual rate of $95.8 billion. The real-growth rate for the gross national product was 6.3%. (*See in* CE: Industry, American.)

". . . and so it is with some degree of pride that I say there is no fat in this budget."

WIDE WORLD

Policemen in Phnom Penh extinguish a blaze in the car regularly used by the U.S. ambassador to Cambodia, Emory C. Swank. One embassy official barely escaped from the booby-trapped auto while two other persons were killed. Swank was away on leave at the time of the incident in September.

CAMBODIA. Sudden changes in leadership at the top and a string of highly controversial elections held the spotlight in Cambodia (officially the Khmer Republic) for most of 1972, but it was the Indochina war that dominated everything for the third year in succession. So hopeless was the military situation and so flimsy the country's internal cohesion that the real achievement of the year appeared to be the survival of the government of Lon Nol.

The year dawned with rumors that Lon Nol would order a drastic reshuffle of his cabinet; these had replaced earlier rumors that the government faced imminent collapse. A movement erupted among students in Phnom Penh, the capital, for the removal of Sisowath Sirik Matak, the delegate prime minister who had been in virtual control since Lon Nol's paralytic stroke the previous year.

On March 10 Cheng Heng, chief of state, announced that he was stepping down and handing over his post to Lon Nol. The announcement coincided with Lon Nol's return to Phnom Penh from a five-week rest cure in the city of Kompong Som (formerly Sihanoukville). Two days later Sirik Matak announced the dissolution of the whole government.

A period of confusion followed. Three days after he became chief of state, Lon Nol declared himself president. Simultaneously he said he would also be prime minister. All this was in addition to his position as commander in chief. It appeared that Lon Nol was making desperate efforts to contain student opposition to his trusted aide. But widespread feeling that Sirik Matak would find a key position in the new system kept the agitation going, with some military and Buddhist circles joining the students.

On March 16 Sirik Matak publicly announced his withdrawal from political life, and Lon Nol found himself president of a country without a government. After six days of governmental vacuum, the political chaos ended on March 21 with the announcement that a 17-man cabinet had been formed. Lon Nol retained the title of prime minister, but the effective prime minister was Son Ngoc Thanh, officially called prime minister and minister of foreign affairs. Son Ngoc Thanh, 64, was a veteran nationalist leader with a militant following, but he was suspected by students and intellectuals of being too close to the U.S. undercover establishment.

Lon Nol's attempts to legitimize the political organization of his country continued. On April 30 a referendum was held to approve a newly drafted republican constitution. Official spokesmen said 97.45% of the voters had voted in favor and that the new constitution would come into force on May 12. This was followed by another election on June 4 to choose the country's president. Opposing Lon Nol were In Tam, a former minister

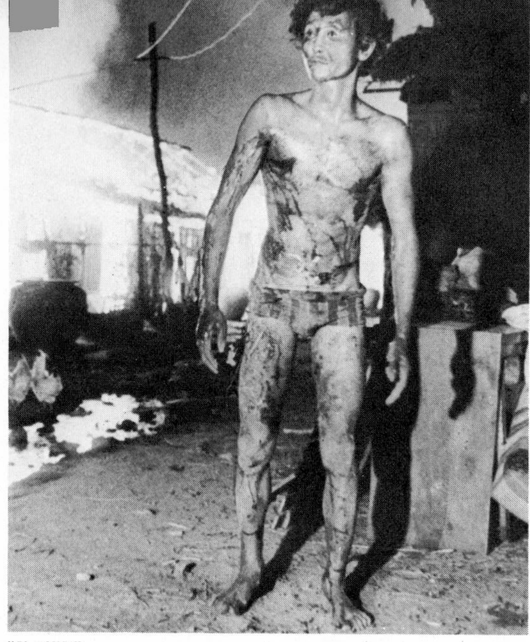

UPI COMPIX

A dazed Cambodian civilian walks from the burning ruins of his home during an enemy assault on Phnom Penh.

and popular leader, and Keo An, dean of the law faculty of Phnom Penh University. Lon Nol obtained 55% of the votes, In Tam 26%, and Keo An 19%. Both the losing candidates alleged "gross irregularities" in the election. Lon Nol was officially sworn in on July 3. Elections for the lower house of the National Assembly took place on September 3 and for the Senate on September 17. A month before the elections for the lower house, In Tam's Democratic party and Sirik Matak's Republican party withdrew from the race, alleging that unconstitutional ground rules and gerrymandering had all but guaranteed a government victory. This left only the progovernment Socio-Republican party and a dummy organization called the People's party, both organized by Lon Nol's influential younger brother Col. Lon Non. The Socio-Republican party won all 26 seats. All 40 Senate seats also went to government candidates. Popular apathy toward the elections and alienation from the government was obvious.

The elections focused attention on the disunity among Cambodia's top leaders. An unsuccessful assassination attempt in August on Prime Minister Son Ngoc Thanh was also attributed to internal disunity rather than to Communist terrorism. He resigned on October 14 and was replaced the following day by Hang Thun Hak.

Communists in Cambodia were holding their own on the military front. As government troops were locked in what one army spokesman called "a battle in which the Khmer Republic has all to lose and nothing to win," Communist forces held effective control of much of the countryside. Six of the seven highways linking Phnom Penh with the provinces remained cut off for most of the year. These included the "rice road" from Battambang in the northeast; at one point in September, rice was selling in the capital at prices 500% higher than they had been at the beginning of the war. Revealing light was thrown on the scarcity of essential items, as well as on the caliber and morale of government troops, when bands of uniformed soldiers early in September ransacked the central market in Phnom Penh and took everything they could carry. The looting lasted a whole day but the government did not intervene.

The Communists seemed able to mount major offensives at will, including rocket attacks on Phnom Penh. Repeated attempts by the Cambodian army to launch counteroffensives and eject the guerrillas from their strongholds either were stalled or ended in routs of the army. In August government spokesmen said that the guerrillas were using tanks for the first time in Cambodia. In September the government announced that one whole battalion of up to 400 men was missing after the abandonment of rear garrisons along the main highway from Phnom Penh to Saigon, South Vietnam.

There was apparently no lack of military aid from outside. The U.S. was reportedly sending in supplies—half of them ammunition—at the rate of 5,000 tons a month. Also, some 50,000 Cambodian troops were said to have received training in South Vietnam, Thailand, the U.S., Indonesia, Malaysia, and elsewhere by mid-1972. The total strength of the Cambodian armed forces was placed officially at 200,000, while government sources reported the presence in Cambodia of 50,000 North Vietnamese troops and 15,000–20,000 Khmer Rouge (Cambodian Communist) fighters. The Khmer Rouge had been estimated to number barely 2,000 during the administration of Prince Sihanouk. (*See also* Asia; Vietnam. *See in* CE: Cambodia.)

CAMEROON. On May 6, 1972, President Ahmadou Ahidjo announced that the people of Cameroon would be consulted by means of a referendum on the immediate establishment of a unitary state, to be called the United Republic of Cameroon, with a single national assembly. Under the new government the rights of the country's two official languages—French in the east and English in the west—were to be formally guaranteed. In the referendum, which was held on May 21, an overwhelming majority of the electorate voted in favor of the unitary state. The first cabinet of the newly constituted United Republic of Cameroon was announced on July 3. Major ministries went to Charles Onana Awana (finance) and Vincent Efon (foreign affairs).

Cameroonian foreign policy in 1972 was marked by coolness toward the French-speaking African bloc, together with a marked rapprochement with the countries of eastern Africa. In September Cameroon and North Vietnam agreed to establish diplomatic relations at the embassy level. (*See in* CE: Cameroon.)

WIDE WORLD

A concentration of tents blocks the view for campers in the Yosemite Valley. The National Park Service began setting quotas for campers in heavily used sites within its jurisdiction. Congress and ecologists weighed human recreational needs against the ideals of preservation.

CAMPING. The boom in family camping continued unabated in 1972. During the year 549,400 recreational vehicles were sold in the U.S., including trailers, pickup coaches, and motor homes. This was an increase of 16% over 1971 sales. Despite this large upswing in purchases of camping vehicles, tenting remained popular and the Family Camping Federation claimed that tents were the best-selling camping cover. A 1971 survey had revealed that there were over 6 million tent owners in the U.S. Many private campground owners who traditionally had catered to recreational vehicles were paying more attention to tent campers and planning separate tents-only areas in their campgrounds. The lower cost of tents and the growing trend toward more primitive camping styles indicated that tents could become even more popular.

In response to the growing popularity of European camping vacations, a nationwide camping magazine in the U.S. began to offer camping tours of Europe, Africa, and Australia in 1972. Airlines and travel agencies featured more "fly-camp" vacation plans in which campers could fly into and out of camping areas.

During 1972 the U.S. government reaffirmed its policy of noncompetition with private campgrounds by encouraging them to locate near state and national parks, thus taking some of the pressure off public facilities. A federally sponsored report released in September recommended a ban on the use of national parks by vehicle campers. This idea aroused strong opposition in Congress, where a bitter fight loomed over the report's recommendations. (*See* National Park Service.)

Organized camping seemed to be recovering from the moderate slump of 1970 and 1971. More children were attending camp in 1972, but for shorter periods of time. Many camps utilized federal funding programs to help low-income inner-city children attend camp. (*See in* CE: Camping.)

CANADA. In October 1972, Canadians went to the polls in a test of confidence in Pierre Elliott Trudeau's Liberal government, which was installed four years earlier with a strong mandate. The result was a substantial withdrawal of support for the Liberal party. The Liberals and the Progressive Conservative party emerged from the election with almost the same number of seats in the House of Commons—109–107. Some observers interpreted the fall in Liberal strength as a reaction against the Trudeau government's efforts to extend French language rights across Canada. Most Canadians, however, put the blame on the government's failure to deal effectively with the twin problems of unemployment and inflation.

The Liberal party showed a solid base in Quebec and lighter representation in Ontario and the Maritime provinces. The Conservatives held most of the Maritime seats and made gains in Ontario and in the West. Thus, party strength reflected the persistent regional divisions of Canada, challenging the goal of national unity. In addition, the deadlock indicated that Canada was reentering a time of minority governments that had been the pattern from 1962 to 1968, when Trudeau won.

Prime Minister Trudeau called the election on September 1 at the dissolution of the fourth ses-

WIDE WORLD

Prime Minister Pierre Elliott Trudeau and his wife, Margaret, go to vote in the Canadian federal election in late October. Trudeau continued as prime minister, though his Liberal party won only 109 of the 264 seats in the House of Commons.

sion of the 28th Parliament. He did not dwell on major issues in his campaign. "Trudeaumania," the personal appeal that had been so characteristic of Trudeau's 1968 campaign, was noticeably absent in 1972. Instead, Trudeau campaigned on the record of his government, seeking to make the election "a conversation time with Canadians." In a series of speeches, he dwelt on his government's efforts to satisfy linguistic and regional aspirations through a flexible federal system. The Conservatives concentrated on what they called the government's deplorable record in meeting economic problems. The party's leader, Robert Lorne Stanfield, of Nova Scotia, urged immediate cuts in personal income tax to stimulate the economy, and he stated his readiness to impose wage and price controls to cope with inflation. David Lewis, leader of the New Democratic party, seized on an effective issue early in the campaign when he criticized large corporations for not paying their fair share of taxes. He called for a sweeping reform of the taxation structure and the policy of incentive grants to industry to eliminate what he called "the corporate welfare bums." The Social Credit party, led by its longtime mainstay, Réal Caouette, attempted to reach the mass of voters by emphasizing improved welfare benefits and income and job security.

About 20% of the 12.9 million eligible voters were young people between the ages of 18 and 21 who were voting for the first time following changes in the franchise. In the polling 74% of the eligible voters cast ballots, almost 1.5 million more than voted in 1968.

The New Democratic party made inroads in urban areas of Ontario and British Columbia but failed to win a seat in the Maritime provinces or Quebec. Its popular vote came to 18%, a slight gain over 1968. The Social Credit party's share of the popular vote was only 7% across Canada, but it rose to 24% in Quebec. Two independents—one of them Lucien Lamoureux, the speaker of the previous House of Commons—were elected to the new Parliament. Five women were elected, a gain of four from the previous House. Sean O'Sullivan, 20, of Ontario, became the youngest member of Parliament in Canada's history.

The election results did not indicate a repudiation by English-speaking Canadians of a French Canadian prime minister. Almost half of the seats in predominantly English-speaking Toronto, Ont., went to Liberals, and other Ontario centers regarded as bulwarks of the English Canadian point of view also supported Liberal candidates. The Conservatives, and especially their leader, played down racial and linguistic issues in the campaign.

Following the election, Trudeau indicated that he and his ministers would remain in office to meet the new Parliament and test its sentiments. In taking this stand, he was following constitutional practice that makes the will of Parliament, and not popular support, the ultimate arbiter of a government's fate. Although no clear choice was made by the electorate, it was necessary for the existing government to submit itself to the new Parliament for confirmation or rejection. In the new Parliament, with the two major parties evenly balanced, voting power would rest with the 31 members of the New Democrats.

While minority government posed many problems, it also had the advantage that a minority administration would be more responsive to currents of opinion in Parliament and in the country. Trudeau had been severely criticized for depreciating the role of Parliament in the governing of Canada and moving the country toward a presidential system in which wide powers rested with appointed advisers of the prime minister. A major consequence of the 1972 election was expected to be a stronger role for Parliament.

Parliament

The third session of Canada's 28th Parliament was formally ended on February 16, though the effective end of the session came on New Year's Eve 1971. Parliament sat for 242 days, making the session the third longest in Canadian history and the first in 30 years to extend over three calendar years. The latter part of the session was occupied with consideration of a 743-page tax reform measure that gained 150 amendments as it made its way through the Commons and the Senate. The legislation, which took effect at the beginning of 1972, provided tax cuts of 7% for corporations and 3% for individuals. More important, it introduced the principle of taxes on capital gains into the Canadian tax structure and made many changes in allowances and exemptions in the tax schedule. As a result of its adoption, about one million Canadians were removed from the tax rolls, and another 4.3 million were paying less in taxes. A farm products marketing bill, which also issued from the last days of the session, created a Canada-wide farm marketing council with national agencies that could set marketing and production regulations.

The fourth session opened on Feb. 17, 1972, with the expectation that it would be the last before the general election. The Speech from the Throne listed 29 items on the government's legislative program, but fewer than 10 had been approved when the session ended on September 1. Some major measures left pending were: an election expenses act, a bill to set up a screening agency to review foreign take-overs of Canadian business, a new competition policy for business, legislation regarding wiretapping, and an amendment to the labor code permitting the process of technological change to be a subject for negotiation between management and labor. Through a technicality in procedure, the family income security plan was not approved and could not be reintroduced before the end of the session, though the government was committed to its principle. The measure would abolish universal family allowances and replace them with higher payments for children of needy parents.

During the summer Parliament had to take up the problem of two dock strikes. One involved three ports on the St. Lawrence River where 3,200 longshoremen refused to carry out new working arrangements made the previous year. The strike, which lasted eight weeks, was brought to an end on July 7, when Parliament ordered the men back to work and outlawed strikes, slowdowns, or lockouts by unions or management. In new disputes, the federal minister of labor would be empowered to order compulsory arbitration. The other strike was at six British Columbia ports where 3,300 longshoremen and grain handlers were on strike most of August. Called into session for two days (August 31 and September 1), Parliament passed the West Coast Ports Operations Act, which sent longshoremen and their employers back to the bargaining table. At the same time, it called for the immediate resumption of port activity.

Foreign Affairs

Visits were exchanged by Prime Minister Trudeau and U.S. President Richard M. Nixon following trade difficulties that arose between Canada and the U.S. after Nixon imposed import surcharges in August 1971. When Trudeau visited Washington, D.C., on Dec. 6, 1971, the president assured him that the U.S. did not desire a continuing surplus in its overall trade statistics with Canada. (The surcharge was lifted at the end of 1971.) In April 1972, President and Mrs. Nixon paid a two-day visit to Ottawa, Ont., the capital of Canada.

Shortly before he left Ottawa, Nixon signed the Great Lakes Water Quality Agreement, designed to achieve an improvement in the quality of water by 1975, particularly in Lakes Erie and Ontario. The agreement provided for the construction and upgrading of municipal sewage treatment facilities in all communities bordering on the Great Lakes. Canadian expenditures under the agreement were expected to reach $400 million to $500 million and U.S. expenditures $2 billion to $3 billion.

Oil pipeline construction and oil transportation on the Pacific coast of Canada created problems with the U.S. in 1972. Canada expressed serious reservations about the environmental effects of the planned pipeline across Alaska. The tanker route through the closed waters of Puget Sound to Cherry Point, Wash., was seen as a hazardous part of the oil transport from Alaska; a spill at Cherry Point on June 4 added to Canada's apprehensions, as did a U.S. Coast Guard report indicating that an annual spillage of 140,000 barrels was possible. Canada urged the study of an alternate route for Alaskan oil down the Mackenzie Valley to the east of Alaska, but an official U.S. report early in May rejected that route and recommended that the project proceed.

There was considerable activity in Canadian-Chinese relations during 1972. Mitchell Sharp,

Bryce S. Mackasey, then Canada's immigration minister, offered an enthusiastic welcome to the first group of Asians to arrive in Canada after being evicted from Uganda.

UPI COMPIX

the secretary of state for external affairs, led a delegation of 600 Canadians to the People's Republic of China in August to take part in events connected with a Canadian trade fair in Peking. Besides officials and businessmen, the party included skaters and basketball players who competed with Chinese athletes. The fair, first of its kind in the relationship between the two countries, earned Canada $25 million in sales of nickel, potash, aluminum, electrical machinery, and animal breeding stock.

For the year, it was expected that Canadian sales to China would total more than $250 million, with most of it represented by wheat. China's Premier Chou En-lai confirmed the rumor that his country would continue to buy wheat from Canada as long as the price was competitive. The premier also thanked Canada for giving impetus to the movement for recognition of mainland China. In October it was announced that a direct air link between Canada and China would be set up in 1973.

Defense

At the end of March, 56 Bomarc B nuclear missiles at the Canadian North American Air Defense Command bases at North Bay, Ont., and La Macaza, Que., became nonoperational. The missiles had been in Canada since 1961; but with the reduced threat of bomber attack on North America, the government decided to phase them out.

The North Bay missile base closed in September, but the adjoining Royal Canadian Air Force establishment remained active. (*See also* Commonwealth of Nations; Trudeau. *See in* CE: Canada.)

CABINET

The 30-member Canadian Cabinet was overhauled substantially at the end of November 1972 in the wake of serious losses by the Liberal government during the general election a month earlier. Controversial ministers were shifted out of a number of sensitive posts as Trudeau hoped to hold onto power in the new Parliament. Only 12 of the 30 Cabinet positions were left unchanged.

In an attempt to improve public understanding of the government's commitment to industrial development in slow-growth areas, Donald C. Jamieson, a former broadcaster, was made minister of regional economic expansion. The regional programs had been attacked as unfair and wasteful.

Embarrassing incidents in the Canadian penitentiary system, including escapes and major parole violations, had damaged the credibility of Solicitor General Jean-Pierre Goyer. He was replaced by Warren Allmand, a lawyer from Montreal, Que.

Canada's unemployment insurance system, described as one of the most generous in the world, was attacked during the election campaign. Trudeau accepted the postelection resignation of Bryce S. Mackasey, the minister responsible for liberalizing the system, and replaced him with Robert K. Andras.

Four Cabinet members were defeated in the election. Only 7 Liberals were returned from the 68 constituencies west of Ontario, and Trudeau kept 4 of the 7 as Cabinet ministers. He promoted James A. Richardson, minister of supply and services, to the defense post.

Trudeau named a woman, Jeanne Sauvé, to the Cabinet. The former writer and broadcaster was made minister of state for science and technology.

THE CANADIAN CABINET

Members of the Canadian Cabinet at the close of 1972, listed in order of precedence, were:

Prime Minister . . Rt. Hon. Pierre Elliott Trudeau
Leader of the Government in the Senate . . . . Hon. Paul Joseph James Martin
Secretary of State for External Affairs . . . . Hon. Mitchell Sharp
President of the Queen's Privy Council for Canada . . . . Hon. Allan Joseph MacEachen
President of the Treasury Board . . . . Hon. Charles Mills Drury
Minister of Transport . . . . . Hon. Jean Marchand
Minister of Finance . . . Hon. John Napier Turner
Minister of Indian Affairs and Northern Development . . . . Hon. Jean Chrétien
Minister of Energy, Mines, and Resources . . . . Hon. Donald Stovel MacDonald
Minister of Labor . . . . . . Hon. John Carr Munro
Minister of Communications . . . . Hon. Gérard Pelletier
Minister of the Environment . . . . Hon. Jack Davis
Minister of Public Works . . . . Hon. Jean-Eudes Dubé
Minister of State for Urban Affairs . . . Hon. Stanley Ronald Basford
Minister of Regional Economic Expansion. . . Hon. Donald Campbell Jamieson
Minister of Manpower and Immigration . . . . . Hon. Robert Knight Andras
Minister of National Defense . . . Hon. James Armstrong Richardson
Minister of Justice and Attorney General of Canada . . . . Hon. Otto Emil Lang
Minister of Consumer and Corporate Affairs . . . . Hon. Herbert Eser Gray
Minister of National Revenue . . . . Hon. Robert Stanbury
Minister of Supply and Services . . . . Hon. Jean-Pierre Goyer
Minister of Industry, Trade, and Commerce . . . Hon. Alastair William Gillespie
Minister of State . . . . Hon. Stanley Haidasz
Minister of Agriculture . . . . . Hon. Eugene Francis Whelan
Solicitor General of Canada . . . . Hon. Warren Allmand
Secretary of State of Canada . . . . Hon. James Hugh Faulkner
Postmaster General . . . . Hon. André Ouellet
Minister of Veterans Affairs . . . . Hon. Daniel MacDonald
Minister of National Health and Welfare . . . . Hon. Marc Lalonde
Minister of State for Science and Technology . . . . Hon. Jeanne Sauvé

PROVINCES

The trend toward electing younger leaders in the Canadian provinces carried into 1972, when the last two aging regimes in Canada were unseated. In both instances, men in their 70's who had governed for more than 20 years were replaced by men of a different generation.

Newfoundland

An indecisive election in Newfoundland late in 1971 left the Progressive Conservatives under Frank Moores, 39, with a one-seat advantage over the Liberals' 71-year-old Premier Joseph Smallwood. He was the only premier in the history of the province, which entered the confederation in 1949. A judicial inquiry led to the award of a disputed seat to the Progressive Conservatives, and Smallwood and his cabinet resigned on Jan. 18, 1972. Moores was sworn in as premier on the same day. He named 15 persons to his cabinet; their average age was 40.

After grappling with urgent government business, Moores called an election for March 24, asking for the support that would give him a working majority in the legislature. He achieved his goal when the voters elected 33 Progressive Conservatives in the 42-seat house. On February 4 and 5 the Liberals held a party convention at which they selected a new leader. He was Edward Roberts, 31, who had served in the Smallwood cabinet.

British Columbia

Another long-term government was turned out of office in British Columbia, where W. A. C. Bennett, who had presided over a Social Credit administration for more than 20 years, was defeated in a provincial election on August 30. The Bennett government, though successful in developing the economy of the Pacific province, had made many enemies during the course of its long career; and at 71 years of age, Bennett was beginning to lose his appeal for the voters. Thus, a startling upset resulted when the New Democratic party, which he had kept at bay, gained enough popular support to unseat him in 1972.

The New Democratic party increased its standing from 12 to 38 seats in the 55-seat legislature, the Social Creditors dropped to 10 seats, the Liberals held 5 seats, and the Conservatives took 2. In the popular vote, the Social Credit share dropped from 46% to 31%, while the New Democratic party share rose from 33% to 40%. Bennett held onto his own seat, but 13 of the 17 members of his cabinet were defeated. The new premier of British Columbia, who took office Sept. 15, 1972, was David Barrett, 41, who had led his party for only three years.

Federal-Provincial Relations

The equalization payments program was extended for another five years. This program, which allows the federal government to transfer funds to the less prosperous provinces to bring their public services to a standard roughly comparable with that of other provinces, was due to expire on March 31.

WIDE WORLD

The good showing of the Progressive Conservative party in the federal elections placed the party leader, Robert Lorne Stanfield, in a position to succeed Prime Minister Trudeau —should the coalition created by Trudeau's government fail.

The program could represent a transfer of funds of more than $1billion annually. This would be about 20% of the conditional and unconditional grants made by the federal government to the provinces.

Leaders' Meeting

A conference of provincial premiers took place at Halifax, N.S., on August 3 and 4. There, Quebec's desire for more fiscal independence in the federation had a large measure of support. The provinces emphasized their constitutional right to control municipal affairs.

At a special meeting before the main sessions, the premiers of the five Atlantic Provinces (including Quebec on this occasion) took up the critical question of the sharing of revenues from offshore oil and gas royalties. The Ottawa government's claim to exclusive jurisdiction in this area was rejected, and so was the federal proposal to share revenues from offshore resources on an equal basis with all ten provinces. Federal jurisdiction, at least in respect to Pacific resources, was upheld by the Supreme Court of Canada in 1967 in an ownership dispute with British Columbia. The eastern provinces made it clear that they did not want to refer the Atlantic resources matter to the Supreme Court but preferred to negotiate directly with the government. Although the Halifax meeting was supposed to produce an agreement on a counterproposal to Ottawa's offer to share the resource revenues, it failed to reach accord on a specific stand. This failure probably reflected the differences of opinion between Nova Scotia and Newfoundland on the one hand, with strong legal and historical claims to jurisdiction on the continental shelf, and Quebec, New Brunswick, and Prince Edward Island on the other, with less claim to ownership.

Quebec

The long-term future of Quebec within the Canadian confederation remained in as much doubt as ever in 1972. One political party, the Parti Quebecois, continued to try to persuade French-speaking residents of Quebec that the province should separate from the rest of Canada. Premier Robert Bourassa's Liberal provincial government was beset with cabinet squabbles about demands for more control over critical services where jurisdiction was shared with the federal government. One of the main issues in that area was the control of family allowances—the amounts paid by the federal government to mothers of school-age children. Another was a federal-provincial dispute over control of cable television. Neither was completely resolved in 1972. Public servants across the province launched a bitter and costly strike for higher wages.

Young protesters sit on railway tracks to block a Burlington Northern freight train in the city of White Rock, about 30 miles southeast of Vancouver, B.C. The protesters wanted a ban on coke trains and wanted the U.S.-owned Burlington Northern to relocate tracks away from the city's waterfront.

ROSS KENWARD FROM "VANCOUVER SUN"

The government of Quebec made a strong legislative move during the year to deal with organized crime. According to a 1971 study, organized crime had established a grip on gambling, loan sharking, narcotics trafficking, prostitution, and the fraud and bankruptcy rackets in Quebec. The new legislation permitted the province's police commission to assume broad new powers of investigation, search, and seizure.

Saskatchewan

At the annual meeting of the Saskatchewan Liberal party at Regina in December 1972, officials from the Prairie Provinces joined with Prime Minister Trudeau to examine the Liberal party's fortunes in the West. David Steuart, the Saskatchewan Liberal leader, stressed that there should be more federal presence in the western provinces.

Steuart criticized Jean Marchand for not making more appearances in the area when he was minister of regional economic expansion. Marchand was replaced in that post in November and moved to the ministry of transport in a major reorganization of the Canadian Cabinet.

CANADIAN ECONOMY. High unemployment was a major exception to a banner year for the Canadian economy in 1972. The growth in total output of goods and services appeared certain to exceed 10%, with the real, or noninflationary, growth making up more than 6% of the increase. National output exceeded $100 billion during the year, which meant that the economy had doubled in size by this statistical measure in just eight years. During the same period, the labor force increased in size by more than one quarter. As usual, however, many Canadians regarded their prosperity as precarious. They examined more seriously than ever Canada's ability to sustain its standard of living in competition with the giant economic units of the U.S., Europe, and Japan.

Economic planners have contended that, in the long run, Canada's economic health depends on development of much stronger secondary industry, competing successfully in export markets. In 1972 industry was regarded as a threatened sector of the economy. In response to this situation, the Canadian government in May announced a program of corporate tax cuts and investment incentives through increased depreciation rates. It was hoped that this action would improve the competitive position of Canadian manufacturing and processing industries.

Concern about the fundamental ability of the Canadian economy to stand up to the giants of international trade was reflected in the continuing national debate on the limitation of foreign investment. A strongly nationalistic element centered in Ontario had been in favor of tough legislation limiting or controlling all new foreign investments. In May, when the government finally revealed its long-awaited program, the nationalists were severely disappointed. Although tighter strictures were imposed on the take-over of Canadian businesses by foreign interests, the new legislation did not apply to fresh foreign investment. Under the new system, a prospective buyer of a Canadian company would have to show that his ownership would be of significant benefit to Canada. Critics of the new policy dismissed it as a feeble gesture. In the Atlantic Provinces, Quebec, and western Canada, however, where foreign investment was crucial to the economy, there was no significant opposition.

The biggest and most immediate economic question of 1972 was how to explain and correct high unemployment. Unemployed persons made up an average of more than 6% of the labor force at almost all times in 1972. The problem persisted despite a tremendously high rate of overall economic growth. The economy was creating new jobs rapidly, but Canada's labor force continued to grow rapidly. As a result, little dent was made in the numbers of unemployed.

Inflation was also reemerging as a serious problem in the public consciousness. Anti-inflationary measures in 1969 and 1970 had originated much of the unemployment still lingering in the economy. In June a report was issued by the Canadian Prices and Incomes Commission recommending that the country adopt some form of temporary controls over wages and prices. The government was urged to rely less in the future on reduced public spending, high interest rates, or similar restrictive measures. (*See also* Canada.)

CENTRAL AFRICAN REPUBLIC. In February 1972 at a congress of the country's sole political party—the Movement for Social Evolution in Black Africa (MESAN)—Gen. Jean-Bedel Bokassa was proclaimed president for life. Known for his erratic behavior, President Bokassa remained unpredictable in 1972. During the summer he decided to conduct an all-out crusade against crime, particularly theft, and personally supervised the beating of convicted thieves in the prison at Bangui, the

President Jean-Bedel Bokassa at the prison in Bangui, Central African Republic, announced, "Thieves must all die. There will be no more theft in the Central African Republic."

HUGUES VASSAL FROM GAMMA

HENRI BUREAU FROM GAMMA

President Bokassa ordered his soldiers to club men imprisoned for theft. Of the 46 men beaten, at least 3 died.

capital. The survivors were then exhibited to the population, along with the mangled bodies of those who had died. The prison beatings provoked strong criticism, including a reported protest from United Nations Secretary-General Kurt Waldheim. In response President Bokassa rejected the criticism and openly insulted Waldheim.

After a period of tense relations during the winter of 1971–72, Bokassa pursued a policy of rapprochement with France. During May and June he visited in Paris with France's President Georges Pompidou. (*See in* CE: Central African Republic.)

CHAD. On Sept. 1, 1972, French military intervention in Chad officially ended when Gen. Édouard Cortadellas, military representative of France and commander in chief of the Franco-Chadian forces, left the country and was not replaced. Col. Félix Malloum, chief of staff of the Chad national army, took command of the security forces and the army. In theory the 15,000-strong Chadian army stood alone against an internal rebellion that it had managed to contain but not entirely to quell. In practice, however, about 2,500 French personnel remained in Chad.

Government forces were least in control of the situation in the north, near the Libyan border, where dissident Toubou factions received diplomatic and military aid from Libya through the Chad National Liberation Front (Frolinat). Elsewhere, the deployment of government troops deterred further rebel attacks. (*See in* CE: Chad.)

CHEMISTRY. Analysis of data gathered during moon exploration missions provided important information for chemistry in 1972. Ultraviolet spectroscopy carried out during the Apollo 16 moon voyage indicated that the source of much of the earth's oxygen is water, rather than plant photosynthesis as had long been believed. Films taken during the mission showed a massive cloud of atomic hydrogen enveloping the earth. Chemists believed that the hydrogen was a product of dissociation of water vapor by solar radiation. Analytical chemists who had been examining lunar rock samples at the Argonne National Laboratory in Illinois announced that neptunium-237, a transuranic element, had been detected in rock samples. Traces of uranium-236 had also been found, in greater concentration than it is found on earth. So far, lunar rocks had been found with maximum ages ranging from 3.1 to 4.2 billion years.

Another Argonne research project produced a startling new theory of the origin of most of the carbon monoxide (CO) found in the earth's atmosphere. Chemists had long believed that industrial and automotive sources were responsible for most CO production. Scientists at Argonne, however, theorized that natural processes such as the decay of methane produced up to 3.5 billion tons of CO,

This sequence of photographs shows the progressive decomposition of a plastic cup lid made with new biodegradable plastic. Decomposition occurs because of a predictable photochemical reaction. The first two photos (top) show a litter-free environment and then introduction of the lid as litter. Decomposition takes place gradually over a period of 6 to 12 months.

BIO-DEGRADABLE PLASTICS, INC.

or 90% of the earth's atmospheric CO, every year. The research showed that only about 7% of the CO in the atmosphere was produced by man-made sources; the rest came from the decay and growth of chlorophyll, production in oceans, and oxidation of naturally occurring methane.

Hydrogen in the atmosphere was looked to in 1972 as a possible solution to the world fuel crisis. Many scientists felt that hydrogen would become the fuel of the future, with the bulk of it being supplied by the decomposition of water and not from hydrocarbons as was currently the case. Hydrogen could provide effective chemical fuels for all applications employing fossil fuels, as well as for some that are beyond the capacity of fossil fuels, such as the powering of airplanes whose speeds exceed six times the speed of sound. The most important aspect of hydrogen power, however, is that when hydrogen burns it produces nothing except water vapor. Thus pollution from fossil fuel combustion, a major problem, could be radically decreased. The ultimate source for production of hydrogen would probably be nuclear or fusion reactors.

Several promising materials were discovered or produced in 1972, among them a new radioactive isotope, silicon-33. The isotope, developed at the Brookhaven National Laboratory in New York, has a half-life of 6.3 seconds. Chemists at Biodegradable Plastics, Inc., of Boise, Idaho, claimed to have developed a plastic that would begin to degrade in sunlight in 30 to 90 days through absorption of ultraviolet light.

Organic chemists were researching new applications for familiar organic substances. Prostaglandins, a family of chemicals derived from fatty acids, were being researched as therapeutic agents with a wide variety of applications. Prostaglandins are found in almost every part of the human body and are linked to the actions of many drugs, including aspirin. It has been found that aspirin inhibits prostaglandin synthesis. Scientists also studied enzymes, already used in laundry detergents, to find ways to reuse them after they have participated in chemical reactions. Enzymes usually work by becoming thoroughly mixed into a reaction, and they must be filtered out and discarded afterwards. If a way were found to keep them separated from the reaction, but still effective as catalysts, they could be used repeatedly. Work was also continuing on the use of insect hormones as a possible replacement for insecticides. (*See in* CE: Chemistry.)

CHESS. In what was billed as the match of the century, challenger Robert J. (Bobby) Fischer, 29, in 1972 became the first person from the U.S. ever to win the world chess championship. He defeated titleholder Boris Spassky, 35, of the Soviet Union in summer competition at Reykjavik, Iceland. The match, which began July 11 and ended September 1, was a defeat not only for Spassky but also for

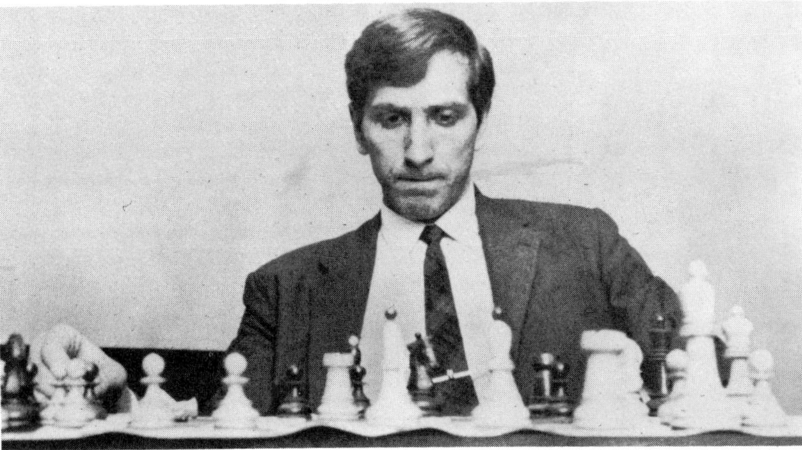

Robert J. (Bobby) Fischer brought the U.S. its first world chess title. "Chess is like war on a board. The object is to crush the other man's mind," he believes.

WIDE WORLD

the U.S.S.R., which had dominated international chess for a generation, holding the championship since 1948.

Fischer, whose temperament and demands at times threatened to ruin the match, lost the first game and defaulted the second, but thereafter outplayed his opponent to such an extent that he was leading by three points when only half the match had been played. Spassky resisted bravely in the second half but could not keep Fischer from a decisive victory of 12½–8½. Until the match, Fischer had never beaten Spassky in the five times they had met across the chessboard. Spassky said after his defeat that Fischer was "chessman number one," but added that he did not consider Fischer "a power that cannot be conquered," indicating the strong probability of a rematch. (The next world title match was set for 1975.) Along with the victory for Fischer came prize money of $156,000, the winner's share of the $250,000 purse, the largest ever offered in international competition.

In October Fischer was sued for $3.25 million in the New York State Supreme Court for refusing to permit the filming and televising of the match. Chester Fox & Co. Inc. of New York City claimed that Fischer had accepted and then rejected an agreement under which Fox would have exclusive rights to produce films, videotapes, and documentaries of the match.

Fischer for years had been considered one of the world's great chess players. He played the game at the Manhattan Chess Club when he was under 10, and at 13 he became the youngest player ever to win the U.S. Junior Open Championship (open to players under 20). At 14 he was the youngest ever to win the U.S. championship and at 15 the youngest to win the title of an international grand master. He had long been considered a major problem at any tournament in which he played. Described as both genius and brat, Fischer often refused to play, frequently was late for games, walked out of events, and was generally moody, demanding, and difficult. For the preceding decade Fischer had claimed he was the unofficial world champion and charged that a Communist plot kept him from the title. In fact, he refused to enter the two world championships before 1971–72, saying the agonizing play-off rounds favored the "Russian cheaters."

HARRY BENSON FROM LIFE MAGAZINE © TIME INC.

Russian Boris Spassky, former world champion of chess, and his wife, Larissa, consider a play. Spassky lost his title to Bobby Fischer in a 21-game match in Reykjavik, Iceland, in 1972.

Despite Fischer's renown in chess circles, his fame was generally limited until the 1972 championship match. The match itself almost did not take place because of Fischer's behavior. For example, just before the tournament was to begin, he demanded more money and went into hiding in New York City, until a British millionaire doubled the $125,000 purse. Even then he did not attend the opening ceremony, and he appeared at Reykjavik only at the last minute. Then he complained about discomfort at the chessboard and had his favorite chair flown in from New York. Spassky was declared winner of the second game on a forfeit after Fischer did not show up, and Fischer claimed there was a conspiracy against him and threatened to leave. At the last minute he agreed to play the third game in seclusion. After winning this game, Fischer made a list of 14 demands that included a new hotel room and car and the exclusive use of a swimming pool and tennis court. All this only helped bring more excitement to the match and more international attention to Fischer. When the young champion returned to New York City, he was greeted by a crowd of 1,000 and was honored at a reception. Mayor John V. Lindsay saluted him as "the grandest master of them all," and Brooklyn Borough President Sebastian Leone praised him as "the new world champion of a truly Brooklyn sport—the sport of intellectuals."

The 21st annual national championship was held in New York City in May. Bobby Fischer did not enter. The tournament ended in a triple tie between Robert Byrne of Ossining, N.Y., Lubomir Kavalek of Washington, D.C., and Sammy Reshevsky of Spring Valley, N.Y. The Annual American Open held at Santa Monica, Calif., in November was won by Larry Remlinger. Walter Browne, an Australian grand master, won the 73d annual U.S. Open Chess Championship held in Atlantic City, N.J., in August.

International chess master George Kuprejanov of Toronto, Ont., ponders a move against an eight-year-old opponent at the start of a seven-day chess festival in Toronto where masters took on all comers. Kuprejanov played 47 games in seven hours.

"TORONTO STAR"

A record field of 61 countries entered the 20th Chess Olympiad held in Skopje, Yugoslavia, in September. The men from the U.S.S.R. retained the world's team championship, as did the Soviet women's team. (*See in* CE: Chess.)

CHILE. President Salvador Allende Gossens of Chile learned the hard way in 1972 that a Marxist president does not mix well with a parliamentary system based on private property. Racked by repeated crises, Allende could look forward to the March 1973 congressional elections with a justifiable sense of impending doom.

Demonstrators march through Santiago streets protesting against the high cost of living. Inflation had been bad; prices increased 5% per month in 1972. The cost of a dollar on the black market had risen from 80 escudos in January to 175 escudos in July.

"THE NEW YORK TIMES"

Economic problems and the government's nationalization of private property were the key to most of the problems. Inflation soared; the unofficial parity value of the escudo to the U.S. dollar dropped more than 50%. Chronic food shortages and import restrictions also caused discontent, as did runaway prices for the food that was available. The government had used up its money reserves and was facing a huge deficit; it increased the money supply by 115%, but this only fueled inflation. Production at the five huge copper mines that had been expropriated from U.S. firms in 1971 fell sharply. In addition, one of the U.S. companies, Kennecott Copper Corp., initiated an embargo on copper sold to France and Sweden by Chile after Allende refused to fully reimburse Kennecott for its losses. The resulting drastic reduction in copper profits strained the economy.

Although Allende was still supported by Chile's poorer classes, bitter opposition to his government existed in the congress and among middle- and upper-class Chileans. In by-elections held in January, two antigovernment candidates won handily. The cabinet resigned to allow Allende to restructure it after the unexpected defeats. Congress added to Allende's troubles by censuring (and thus removing from office) Minister of the Interior José Toha Gonzalez, the number-two man in the government, and by passing retroactive antiexpropriation legislation. Allende vetoed the legislation and then suspended the congress to negotiate with the opposition. The new cabinet was reshuffled in June, and a state of emergency was declared in August after anti-Allende groups rioted.

In October the trucking industry, fearing a nationalization move, called for a strike. Shortly thereafter strikes were called by doctors, nurses, civil engineers, bank employees, shopkeepers, and

UPI COMPIX

Antigovernment protest in Chile turned to violence in October. Demonstrators hurled rocks at police in Santiago, the capital, and were turned back by tear gas. President Allende made cabinet changes in the fall and finally settled the strikes that had drastically affected the nation's economy.

other professional groups; and the nation ground to a halt. Allende again declared a state of emergency on October 12 in an attempt to force the truck drivers back to work. The strikers' demands included both economic and political changes that Allende was unwilling to allow. Consumer protests and a national "Day of Silence" stay-at-home strike on October 24 led to yet another cabinet change. Three military officers were appointed, including army commander in chief Gen. Carlos Prats Gonzalez as interior minister. The move, generally interpreted as a slight swing to the right by Allende, ended the strikes on November 5.

Allende was still supported by the army—the key to political power in Chile—which was sworn to uphold the constitution and thus support the elected head of state. The disclosure early in 1972 of an attempt by the U.S. International Telephone & Telegraph Corp. (ITT) to overthrow Allende by subversion strengthened the Chilean leader's claims that the U.S. was trying to promote a coup. Allende had nationalized ITT's extensive Chilean holdings in 1971. Finally, the opposition in Chile remained divided and polls showed that Allende could still draw 36% of a presidential vote—enough to retain power if he ran against more than one candidate. In November Allende went on a journey to Algeria, Mexico, Cuba, the Soviet Union, and the United Nations (UN). At the UN he bitterly denounced what he called U.S. interference in Chilean affairs. (*See in* CE: Chile.)

CHINA, PEOPLE'S REPUBLIC OF. Historic visits by the political leaders of the U.S. and Japan and major internal political upheavals marked 1972 as a year of great change in the People's Republic of China. U.S. President Richard M. Nixon's trip to China in February and the visit by Japan's Prime Minister Kakuei Tanaka in September were the most widely publicized results of a new trend in Chinese foreign policy. Pragmatism in dealing with major powers—inspired to a large extent by continuing fears of the Soviet Union's nearby presence—was coupled with a restructuring of the government, many new internal political policies, and an increasing withdrawal from the militancy born in the "cultural revolution." The overall effect was that China turned in 1972 from a quiet role in world affairs to a highly visible one.

New Friends and Old Enemies

Since the admission of China to the United Nations (UN) in October 1971, many nations had

GIHAUSEN FROM BLACK STAR

Improved relations between the governments of China and the U.S. and other Western countries make the people of these nations more aware of one another. A man in the People's Republic studies a chart displaying Latin letters, which are foreign to him.

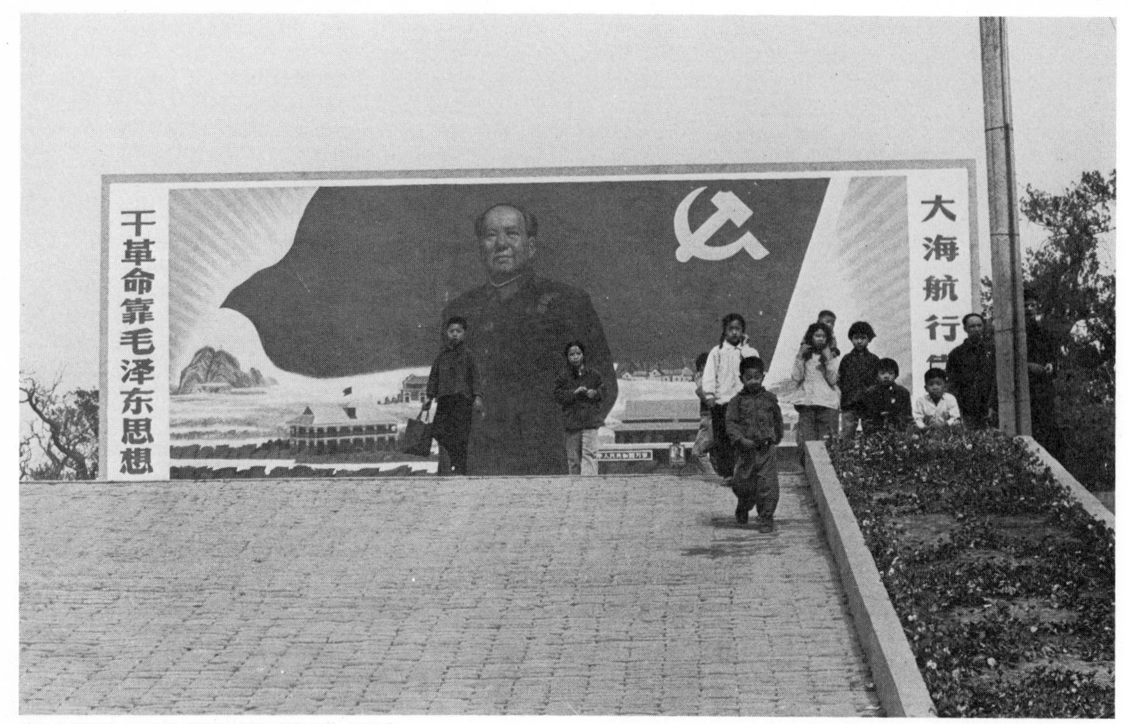

MAX HASTINGS—CAMERA PRESS FROM PICTORIAL PARADE

Chinese children on their way home from school pass a gigantic poster of Chairman Mao Tse-tung. Images of Mao seemed to be everywhere in 1972, continuing the trend of recent years.

established diplomatic relations with the government in Peking, the capital. The Chinese government generally asked that any nation seeking to form diplomatic ties agree to at least two points: the sole legitimacy of the Communist government as the rightful government of China (as opposed to the Nationalist Chinese government on Taiwan) and the right of the Peking government to claim Taiwan as Chinese property. In addition, though it was not explicitly stated, China obviously sought in 1972, through its new role in the UN, to establish itself as the champion and protector of small, unaligned nations in Asia, Africa, and Latin America. It was in this latter role that China continued to supply matériel to North Vietnam even as new ties were sought with the U.S.

Undoubtedly the most important diplomatic event of the year was the visit by President Nixon in February. The summit meeting had been preceded by several other actions on the part of the U.S. to indicate warming relations with China. On February 9, in his foreign-policy report to Congress, Nixon had stressed that better relations with China were essential for the good of both nations. On February 14, trade restrictions on China were further relaxed (the original ban on importation of Chinese goods had been lifted in 1971), to place U.S.–China trade on an equal footing with trade between the U.S. and the Soviet Union. Finally, on February 21, Nixon, Mrs. Nixon, the president's security adviser Henry Kissinger, Secretary of State William P. Rogers, and a large U.S. party stepped off a plane in Peking and were met by Premier Chou En-lai. The welcome at the airport was rather subdued, without large crowds, and a huge U.S. television audience was left wondering about a possible snub. The Chinese people, who had not known as much about the visit, were probably not as interested. However, shortly after his arrival and before the official banquet, Nixon was escorted by Chou to a meeting with Communist Party Chairman Mao Tse-tung. The meeting between the two leaders—a summit that would have been considered at best unlikely a few years before—apparently was taken as a sign of Mao's approval; the Nixon visit became a much more newsworthy topic in China as a result.

Nixon stayed in Peking for five days, engaging in long discussions with Chou on a variety of topics. The talks continued as the visitors traveled to Hangchow and Shanghai. On February 27, the day before Nixon left, a joint communiqué was released. It was obvious from the communiqué that many issues had been discussed, among them the war in Vietnam, the Taiwan question, tensions in Asia, and future U.S.–China relations. On the question of Taiwan, the U.S. no longer challenged China's claims of sovereignty; however, the U.S. was firm in asking for a peaceful settlement of the question. (*See* Taiwan.) Overall, it was clear that while groundwork had been laid for possible future agreements, the major ideological and political divisions between the two nations would not be easily resolved. Plans that were agreed upon included the maintenance of official contacts through periodic meetings at the ambassadorial level, development of bilateral trade, and development of scientific, cultural, journalistic, and sports exchanges. The maintenance of U.S. ties with Taiwan barred establishment of official diplomatic recognition for the foreseeable future.

The Nixon visit was not totally consumed by diplomatic discussions; a high-spirited banquet in Peking saw Nixon and Chou in an undeclared contest of toasts and graciousness. Chiang Ching, Mao's wife and the most powerful woman in China, accompanied the Nixons to a performance of a ballet, 'The Red Detachment of Women', which depicted the liberation of a peasant woman. The most famous source of entertainment from China, however, was undoubtedly the two young giant pandas presented to the people of the U.S. (*See* Animals and Wildlife Special Report.)

Following the Nixon visit, Senators Mike Mansfield (D, Mont.) and Hugh Scott (R, Pa.), the Democratic and Republican Senate leaders, toured China at Chou's invitation from April 18 to May 7. Representatives Hale Boggs (D, La.) and Gerald R. Ford (R, Mich.) traveled to China in June.

In the area of cultural exchanges, a long series of visits to China by U.S. professors, scientists, and journalists continued throughout the year. A Chinese Ping-Pong team toured the U.S. in April, as did a team of Chinese doctors in the fall. For the first time U.S. businessmen attended the trade fair in Canton, China, in April. The Boeing Co. contracted to sell jet planes to China, and the U.S. also sold large amounts of wheat and corn to China during the year.

Another historic meeting occurred in China on September 25, when Japan's Prime Minister Tanaka met with Chou to establish diplomatic relations between the two countries. Once the bitterest of enemies, the Chinese and Japanese agreed on most conditions, and on September 29 diplomatic relations were formally established. China abandoned its right to demand war reparations and did not press Japan to abrogate its 1952 treaty with Taiwan. (The Japanese later invalidated the treaty themselves.) Plans were also made to conclude a series of treaties on trade, navigation, and other areas. (*See* Japan.)

Westerners had new opportunities in 1972 to gain insights into daily life in China. The Shuangchio China-Cuba Friendship People's Commune contains schools, stores, farms, and factories. A woman shops in the commune store (top), while children study in a commune school. Shanghai (right) continued to be China's chief port, as the People's Republic stepped up its trade with other nations. Chinese harvests were plentiful for the ninth straight year; bananas grown in Kwangtung province are shipped to market.

FROM TOP: WIDE WORLD; WIDE WORLD; KEYSTONE; AUDREY TOPPING FROM RAPHO GUILLUMETTE

KEYSTONE

U.S. President Nixon reviews an honor guard with Premier Chou En-lai during departure ceremonies at Peking Airport, at the end of the Nixons' five-day stay in the Chinese capital in February.

By the end of the year, heads of state of most of the major non-Communist nations had visited or been in contact with China. Chinese political and cultural delegations had visited more than 50 countries. By the end of October, some 80 nations had extended diplomatic recognition to China; many of them had terminated relations with Taiwan at the same time. At year's end, all East European nations, all West European nations except Spain, and a host of small nations recognized China.

Successful as the new diplomacy was, the Soviet Union continued as a major threat to Chinese security. The breach between the two Communist powers continued unhealed, and many observers saw the Chinese diplomatic offensive as a scheme to cultivate enemies of the Soviet Union. The Soviet press condemned China's détente with the U.S. as plotting with imperialists, despite the fact that Nixon visited the Soviet Union as well in 1972. The hostilities spilled into the UN. China cast its first veto to deny membership to Bangladesh, which had been heavily supported by the Soviet Union during the war on the Indian subcontinent in 1971. Talks between Chinese and Soviet representatives over the disputed Sino-Soviet border were resumed in Peking in March, and after a trade agreement was signed in June, tensions seemed to ease. However, a new Chinese atlas that claimed 600,000 square miles of Soviet territory as Chinese was bitterly attacked by the Soviet press in August, and in December a border skirmish was reported. However, China denied the reports. No border fighting had occurred since 1969.

Both China and the Soviet Union continued their support of North Vietnam during the year; it was perhaps the only area in which the two Communist giants could agree. While Senators Mansfield and Scott were touring China, the Chinese government announced the signing of a supplementary military and economic aid agreement with North Vietnam. China expressed grave concern over the U.S. mining of North Vietnamese ports and the bombing of North Vietnam's highways and railroads. After the mining took place, China allowed the Soviet Union to transport supplies to Vietnam across Chinese territory. While China did not wish a military confrontation with the U.S. over Vietnam, it was obvious that Chinese support for the North Vietnamese would continue.

Fall of the Heir Apparent; Other Changes

On October 1 the People's Republic celebrated its 23d anniversary amid speculation about the ultimate direction the nation would take. Shock waves emanated from disclosures that army head Lin Piao, Mao's former comrade-in-arms and the heir apparent to the aging Communist party chairman, was dead. Rumors had been circulating about Lin's fate ever since he disappeared in September 1971. Stories that he was involved in a plot against Mao circulated throughout the world. After several implications by government officials that the stories were true, Mao confirmed them by telling Prime Minister Sirimavo Bandaranaike of Sri Lanka that Lin had been killed in a plane crash in Mongolia while fleeing the country. Evidently Lin; his wife; Huang Yung-shen, army chief of staff; Wu Fa-hsien, deputy chief and commander of the air force; Li Tso-peng, deputy chief and political commissioner of the navy; and Chiu Hui-tso, deputy chief and head of the logistics department, died while flying out of China after their coup attempt failed. Their plans were said to have involved the assassination of Mao. As head of the People's Liberation Red Army, Lin had been the designated successor to Mao; but apparently his emphasis on military leadership and heavy military participation in the government was not in keeping with Mao's plans. The coup attempt was said to have followed a decision by Mao and Chou to cut back military influence in China.

Lin's fall was the most spectacular indication of a new and somewhat antimilitary feeling. The army had reached its highest level of influence during and after the cultural revolution, when ultraleft military leaders had directed sweeping internal policy changes. Nearly half of the Central Committee of the Chinese Communist party was made up of military officers, as was the Standing Committee of the Politburo. Revolutionary committees (the supervisory and administrative organs of the provinces) had come to be dominated by military leaders. By 1971 the Red Army was the most dominant political force in China. Mao and Chou apparently saw the army's political strength as a threat to development of the Chinese revolution along the lines they had chosen. Sometime late in 1971 or early in 1972, a purge was ordered to replace many military leaders with civilians, including the reinstatement of many civilians who had lost their offices during the cultural revolution. The relative roles of Mao and Chou in the struggle were unclear, but observers felt that Chou had been much more opposed to the ultraradical tendencies in the army than had Mao. The success of the antimilitary policy was seen as an indication of growing power for Chou.

The purge and subsequent confusion left the party hierarchy somewhat weakened. Lin was dead and during the year Chen Yi, minister of foreign affairs, also died. Chi Peng-fei became the new foreign minister, and Yeh Chien-ying became the new minister of defense in Lin's place. Yeh was a close associate of Chou and vice-chairman of the military affairs commission of the party. Li Hsien-nien continued as first deputy premier. As a result of the purge and of natural deaths, however, more than half the Politburo's members disappeared from the scene, and the Standing Committee was left with an active membership of two—Mao and Chou. This was not considered a disastrous state of affairs, but the rebuilding of the party after the cultural revolution was obviously far from complete.

Some political reforms were enacted during the year. The unwieldy State Council's 40 ministries, 11 commissions, and 21 special agencies were reduced to 17 ministries, 3 commissions, and 15 special agencies. This streamlining, like many political moves during the year, was conceived by Chou. At the county level, restructuring of party committees numbering more than 2,000 continued, if very slowly. The slow pace of reconstruction forced the postponement of the long-overdue Fourth People's Congress, which was to adopt a new constitution and elect a new head of state.

The new softer line in foreign policy extended to a number of internal areas. Many books that had been banned during the cultural revolution, including some classical novels, reappeared, as did the teaching of foreign languages, notably English. Examinations were restored in the educational system, and some material incentive programs such as higher pay for greater productivity were reintroduced into agricultural work. Economic reports were not available, but 1972 was thought to have been a good year for agricultural production. (*See also* Asia; Vietnam. *See in* CE: China, People's Republic of.)

During their China visit, the Nixons saw this "modern revolutionary ballet" entitled 'The Red Detachment of Women' at a cultural show in the Great Hall of the People.

UPI COMPIX

CITIES AND URBAN AFFAIRS. During 1972 the Commission on Population Growth and the American Future issued its report, "Population and the American Future," containing sections on trends and problems of metropolitan growth. The report noted that during the decade of the 1960's the metropolitan population in the U.S. increased by 26 million; one third of the increase was due to territorial expansion of urban areas and two thirds due to population increases within the metropolitan areas defined by the 1960 U.S. census. Of the total increase, one fourth was due to migration to the cities and the remainder to the excess of births over deaths (natural increase). The commission estimated that in 1970 some 71% of the nation's people lived in metropolitan areas.

Looking to the future, the report indicated that by the year 2000 about 85% of the population would be living in metropolitan areas and that natural increase would be the main source of this growth. In 1970 more than 40% of the population lived in urban areas of one million or more people, and there were 29 such areas. By 2000, about 60% were expected to be living in large urban concentrations, and the number of urban areas of one million people would be between 44 and 50.

The report also noted the continuing development of "urban regions"—continuous zones of urban areas interspersed with counties within which one is never far from a city. In 1920 there were 10 such areas containing over a third of the population; in 1970 about three fourths of the population lived in some 19 urban regions; and by 2000, the report estimated, urban areas would comprise one sixth of the continental U.S. and contain five sixths of the population. (*See* Feature Article: "Enriching the Quality of Life.")

Finances and Revenue Sharing

In the U.S. 1972 was another year of crises in urban affairs, with finances constituting the major critical problem in spite of substantially increased federal contributions to city governments. The passage of U.S. President Richard M. Nixon's revenue-sharing legislation in Congress in October promised further financial aid to the nation's cities. Under the revenue-sharing system, the federal government turns over tax revenues to state and local governments, to use the money as they wish.

During the first year, states were to receive one third and local governments two thirds of $5.3 billion, retroactive to Jan. 1, 1972; amounts were to be somewhat increased over the following four years. The legislation also imposed a $2.5-billion limit on federal reimbursement for social service programs with amounts allocated on a per capita basis. This limitation threatened to reduce funding for some states and cities having substantial social service programs; New York State, New York City, and Illinois would be particularly affected.

Although the aim of revenue sharing was to help state and local governments finance public services with federal funds, many city administrations indicated that they would use the money to cut taxes—particularly property taxes. In some cities battles loomed over whether the money should be earmarked for capital improvements or public needs. Many cities planned such capital improvements as new water and sewer facilities and new city halls. Subsidies for public transportation and new recreational facilities were also planned. Under formulas devised by Congress, the distribution of federal money generally favored low-income areas over high-income areas.

U.S. Bureau of the Census reports indicated that in fiscal 1971 the cities spent $39.1 billion, an excess of $1.7 billion over their revenues of $37.4 billion. This represented a 14% spending increase over 1970, while revenues also increased by 14%.

Regional Management Problems

Also continued during 1972 was a trend toward the creation of means of dealing with metropolitan and regional problems. A number of legislatures authorized the establishment of planning districts, clearinghouses for federal aid, water districts, rapid transit systems, and regional airports. With the increasing need to coordinate public services and to deal with problems arising from conflicting and

Children play near abandoned buildings in the Woodlawn area of Chicago. Abandonment of dilapidated old buildings was a serious problem in many inner-city areas across the U.S. in 1972.

DICK SRODA FROM "THE NEW YORK TIMES"

ELAINE HANDLER

The city of Rio de Janeiro, Brazil, inaugurated a new service to protect Copacabana beach from dog litter. Litter stands were installed along the beach for the area's 25,000 dogs.

overlapping jurisdictions, cooperation between local governments continued to expand. Growing public pressure for the elimination of environmental pollution, which most seriously affects dense urban populations, led to legislative action in several states.

The Nixon Administration endeavored to ease the critical problem of public transportation in urban areas by asking Congress to allow cities to spend part of their federal highway funds for mass transit systems. This legislation was defeated, however, in the House of Representatives.

Other City Issues

Housing shortages, substandard housing, and segregation remained serious aspects of the urban crisis. Of potential significance was a federal district court order in 1971 aimed at breaking up patterns of segregated public housing in Chicago's black areas. An ominous development was the growing ownership by the federal government of abandoned and decaying inner-city housing, resulting from massive defaults in mortgage payments on federally subsidized homes. Faulty construction, increasing taxes and management costs, high crime rates, and avaricious speculators were among the factors leading to housing abandonment and defaults on mortgage payments. Chicago; Philadelphia, Pa.; Detroit, Mich.; and Boston, Mass., were among the cities where the federal government was becoming a major landlord.

The use of abandoned housing for criminal activities and by narcotics addicts further contributed to city problems. According to Federal Bureau of Investigation (FBI) figures, the total incidence of crime in 1971 rose by 7.4%, crimes of violence increased by 10.5%, and crimes against property rose by 6.9%. During 1971, 126 law officers were killed by criminal action—a 25% increase over the figure for 1970.

Although the number and severity of civil and race-related disorders continued to decrease, the frustration, alienation, and hostility of underprivileged minority groups remained serious aspects of the urban crisis. High unemployment among minority groups, segregation, decaying neighborhoods and housing, poverty, and the poor quality of public education in the inner city were all components of urban friction, which made the continuation of violence seem likely to persist. (*See also* Crime; Population; Race Relations. *See in* CE: City.)

The walls of New York City subway cars are favorite locations for grafitti "artists." The city spends millions of dollars each year to repaint such walls.

WIDE WORLD

COURTESY, SCHULMAN COIN & MINT, INC.

This gold medal was struck in A.D. 242–243 for presentation to a winner at the Olympic Games held to honor Alexander the Great.

COIN COLLECTING. The U.S. Mint did not issue any new designs of coins in 1972, but it did make coin collectors happy by producing the first in a series of five dollar-size bronze medals observing the bicentennial of the American Revolution. The 1972 medals, plus four annual ones to follow, were being planned and issued by the American Revolution Bicentennial Commission, established by Congress to coordinate the observance of the 200th anniversary of the U.S.

At the annual convention of the American Numismatic Association (ANA), held in New Orleans, La., in August, Mint Director Mary Brooks announced that the cupronickel Eisenhower dollar would be included in the 1973 proof sets. Limited numbers of these specially struck sets were to be available from the U.S. Assay Office, Numismatic Services, in San Francisco, Calif. The 40% silver-clad proof dollars, along with the uncirculated ones, were to be struck again in 1973.

As usual, many nations struck coins in new designs or values during the year. This was particularly true of the many new and small countries established in recent years, some of which issue coins primarily for collectors, and at premium prices. Somewhat surprisingly, there was an increase in the number of silver coins being issued, especially those intended to appeal to collectors, such as a set of five coins of Iran containing a total of nearly five ounces of commercially pure silver.

This silver medal honors the Sioux of the Rosebud reservation in South Dakota. The medal is one of a series honoring Indians.

COURTESY, INDIAN TRIBAL SERIES

Numismatists interested in history and art continued to have the opportunity to collect a wide variety of medals, mostly from private firms. Included in the hundreds of such issued in 1972 were medals honoring Moses and the Ten Commandments, Sir Walter Raleigh, Walt Whitman, James Fenimore Cooper, the Baha'i House of Worship, the Apollo 16 moon flight, the 75th anniversary of Lincoln Memorial University, and a series relating to physicians. The ANA selected Elizabeth Jones of Rome as the recipient of its annual award for Sculptor of the Year and presented the gold award medal to her at its New Orleans convention.

Interest in coin collecting continued to grow in 1972. The ANA showed a net increase in membership of more than 1,000 for the third consecutive year. Most dealers reported good business and advancing prices. A 1794 U.S. cent piece reportedly brought a new record price of $15,000 for a copper coin in an auction sale. New records were set also in the reported sale of an 1894-S dime for $50,000, an 1804 silver dollar for $80,000, and a 1913 liberty head nickel for $100,000. Pennies dated 1972 and struck from dies that had a double outline of the lettering and date sold for approximately $100 each.

In spite of efforts by the ANA and other organizations, counterfeit, altered, and other types of specious coins were still being offered to collectors. Modern manufacturing techniques had permitted the production of such coins, and they were very difficult to detect. The ANA had established a certification service which enabled collectors to have their coins checked (at a modest fee) for authenticity. This service was expected to slow somewhat the sale of false coins. (*See also* Hobbies; Postal Service; Stamps. *See in* CE: **Mint, U.S.**; Money.)

COLLEGES AND UNIVERSITIES. The financial crisis continued at many U.S. colleges and universities during 1972, affecting even some state-supported institutions. For the latter the problem was mainly one of a leveling of appropriations by state legislatures as costs rose. The difficulty was compounded for large numbers of private colleges, where the gap between income and costs widened because of decreased enrollment. A total of 300,000 places went unfilled in the fall. Yet enrollment was up in most state institutions, particularly community colleges. It was the private sector that bore the brunt of the registration decline.

Two large institutions, New York University and Northeastern University, Boston, Mass., admitted publicly their dire financial straits stemming from decreased enrollments. They charged that the situation resulted from increasing competition from community colleges and state university systems, in which costs were lower because of tax subsidies. The lower cost of education at a state college or university had been drawing students away from private campuses. In the 1950's about half the college students in the U.S. attended private institutions; in 1972 some 70% enrolled in public institutions. Most administrators at private colleges favored some sort of adjustment—either through the raising of state tuition to the level of costs or through a voucher system that would allow any state resident to enter the college of his choice, public or private, with the state covering the basic cost of his education.

A handful of private colleges pulled themselves out of the deficit pattern, starting the 1972–73 year with balanced budgets. Tighter management procedures and the elimination of some courses and staff members accounted for much of the financial improvement on those campuses. Elsewhere a variety of steps were taken to bring costs into line.

Much of this anticipated a midyear report of the Carnegie Commission on Higher Education, 'The More Effective Use of Resources: An Imperative for Higher Education'. In it the commission called for a slackening in the rate of increase of campus expenditures. A desirable goal, the report said, would be a 20% reduction in costs by the end of the decade; that is, colleges and universities as a group should plan on 1980 budgets that would total about $41.5 billion instead of the $51 billion (1970 dollars) that could be expected if the spending trend of the 1960's continued. The commission expressed the opinion that half the saving could be effected by shortening the time a student spends in college, the other half in a variety of ways such as larger teaching loads, more off-campus study, higher student-faculty ratio, minimum effective size for campuses and departments, management training for personnel, and consortiums.

Experiments aimed at cutting the time required for a degree took different forms across the U.S. The State University of New York set up a three-year program for high school graduates as well as a four-year program for high school juniors. Several private colleges, including Dartmouth and Colgate, began three-year degree programs.

Meanwhile, the University Without Walls (UWW), which had initiated experimental efforts in 20 institutions the preceding year, issued its first annual report. After one year of operation, 3,000 students were enrolled in UWW programs that were designed as "a distinct alternative" to customary undergraduate programs. Most of these enrollees, ranging in age from 16 to 73 and including many members of minority groups, probably would not have continued their education except for the opportunity offered by UWW.

Most campuses were notably free of violence or protest in 1972, with the tragic exception of Southern University in Baton Rouge, La., the nation's largest black university. Protests by students demanding a larger voice in university operations and improved food and housing included the occupation of Southern's administration building in November. Law enforcement officers moved in to evict the protesters; a smoke bomb was thrown, the police fired tear gas, and when the smoke cleared, two students, Denver A. Smith and Leonard D. Brown, lay dead from gunshot wounds. Each side accused the other of the killings, and the university was closed until Jan. 3, 1973. One investigating commission later indicated that a sheriff's deputy apparently fired the fatal shots.

Other campuses were relatively quiet. Antiwar demonstrations fell off sharply as U.S. troops were pulled out of Vietnam, though the renewal of bombing in the North and the mining of Haiphong harbor sparked rallies, sit-ins, and teach-ins on a number of campuses in April. Some campuses were affected, too, by the "corporate responsibility" movement. Concerned about the social effect of policies pursued by certain corporations, some students pressed university trustees to cast proxies against the management of those corporations or to shift to other securities. Efforts focused on Polaroid Corp. for operating in South Africa and Gulf Oil Corp. for operating in Angola, because these activities supported "oppressive" govern-

This statue of John Harvard in Harvard Yard is covered with sheets, Ku Klux Klan style, to protest the university's refusal to sell its stock in Gulf Oil, which is active in Angola.

UPI COMPIX

LEIGH BRINTNELL

Three graduates received their degrees from Brock University in St. Catharines, Ont., in the first Canadian convocation north of the Arctic Circle.

ments; some students wanted pressure put on General Motors Corp. to make its activities and policies more open and democratic and to move ahead more quickly with car safety and antipollution devices. Preferring to base investment decisions on financial return, trustees and administrators typically heard students out but refused to follow their advice.

There was greater response to women's demands for recognition and status on campus. In some places the focus was on admitting more women and on adding courses relating to women. More commonly the aim was to obtain more women faculty members, opportunity for promotion for qualified women, and salaries equal to those of men in similar positions. Dartmouth College opened its doors to women in the fall, and two women were nominated for the first time for admission to the U.S. Naval Academy. Congress supported the feminist movement by prohibiting sex discrimination in all schools and educational programs receiving federal funds, through the Education Amendments of 1972.

Faculty unionization took on new dimensions as the American Association of University Professors (AAUP), the long-established professional organization, in convention voted overwhelmingly to pursue aggressively the right of collective bargaining. The AAUP had felt competition from the American Federation of Teachers (AFT) and the National Education Association (NEA), which had begun to recruit college campus members.

As Ph.D.'s continued to experience difficulty in finding employment commensurate with their training, some graduate schools scaled down their doctoral programs. The popularity of medical and law programs increased, however, as a record number of about 120,000 students took the Law School Admissions Test in 1971–72, and an estimated 35,000 competed for 13,000 places in medical schools.

An omnibus higher-education bill, authorizing an estimated $18.5 billion over three years, became law after a lengthy struggle between two factions, those favoring grants directly to colleges and those supporting direct aid to students. Provisions for both were included in the complicated law. The formula for student aid introduced a new concept. Designed to assist low- and middle-income students, it established a level of aid according to family income, then tied grants, loans, and work-study earnings together to make up an aid package for each qualifying student.

New rules governing the guaranteed loan program soon produced complications. Problems of interpretation left large numbers of students without funds needed for the fall term. As a result, U.S. President Richard M. Nixon gained Congressional approval to postpone implementing the new guidelines until March 1973. (*See also* Education. *See in* CE: Universities and Colleges.)

BILL RAY FROM LIFE MAGAZINE © TIME INC.

Gail Thain Parker is the new president of Bennington College in Vermont. She and her husband, Thomas, the new vice-president, are working as a team to administer the college. The couple were at Harvard previously: she as an assistant professor and he as a senior tutor. She holds their six-year-old daughter, Julia.

"THE NEW YORK TIMES"

Eight Colombians stood trial for luring 16 Indians to a ranch and killing them for fun. "From childhood, I have been told that everyone kills Indians," said one defendant.

COLOMBIA. The municipal and provincial elections held in April 1972 were the most important political event of the year in Colombia. In a decisive victory, the traditional Liberal and Conservative parties not only regained control of all the provincial assemblies—many of which had been in the hands of the National Popular Alliance, the party of ex-President Gustavo Rojas Pinilla—but also won majorities on a large number of municipal councils. Despite this setback, Rojas Pinilla announced in July that he would accept his party's nomination for the 1974 presidential election.

In February strikes by teachers in technical and intermediate schools brought education in Colombia to a virtual standstill. Shortly afterward, high school teachers joined in the walkout. In April thousands of university students boycotted classes in support of the striking teachers, and there were several violent clashes between strikers and police. The teachers' strike was finally settled on April 17 when the government agreed to raise salaries and repeal the unpopular Teaching Statute, which regulated salaries and promotions.

In mid-1972 the minister of finance, in a review of the economy, stated that there were signs of recovery in all sectors and that the prevailing confidence of investors and business would be an important factor in sustaining progress. Significant loans from the World Bank and the U.S. Agency for International Development were announced during the summer. (*See in* CE: Colombia.)

COMMONWEALTH OF NATIONS. During 1972 a shadow of uncertainty hung over economic relations among members of the Commonwealth of Nations following Great Britain's moves to enter the European Economic Community (EEC). On January 22 Great Britain signed the Treaty of Accession providing for entry into the EEC on Jan. 1, 1973, pending ratification by Parliament. Approval by the House of Commons was completed in July and by the House of Lords in September. At a meeting of Commonwealth finance ministers in London in September, several nations criticized a joint British-EEC proposal to phase out the reserve role of sterling as part of a monetary reform.

Far East

The consequences of the December 1971 war between India and Pakistan, which resulted in the establishment of East Pakistan as the independent nation of Bangladesh, continued to be felt in the Commonwealth in 1972. Pakistan withdrew from the Commonwealth on January 30, after Great Britain, Australia, and New Zealand announced their intentions of recognizing the Bangladesh government. Pakistan's President Zulfikar Ali Bhutto declared, however, that his nation would expand bilateral relations with Commonwealth countries. Through its withdrawal Pakistan stood to lose the benefits of Commonwealth educational and technical aid. Bangladesh applied for Commonwealth membership in February and was formally admitted on April 18, thereby restoring the number of member nations to 31.

Elsewhere in the Far East, Ceylon adopted a new constitution under which it became the independent Republic of Sri Lanka on May 22. Ceylon had held dominion status in the Commonwealth since 1948; Sri Lanka retained its membership.

In February and March Great Britain's Queen Elizabeth II and Prince Philip undertook a 46-day Far Eastern tour that included the Commonwealth nations of Singapore and Malaysia, as well as Thailand. The integrated Air Defense System of Great Britain, Australia, New Zealand, Malaysia, and Singapore, created in 1971, held its first combined exercises early in 1972. The South Pacific Forum held meetings in February and September and established a permanent bureau in Fiji. British entry into the EEC led New Zealand to seek new trade links in the Pacific and in South America. New Zealand also played a central role in a dispute over possession of the Minerva Reefs, claimed by both the U.S. and Tonga.

Africa

The Commonwealth faced serious problems in Africa in 1972, largely as a result of actions by Uganda's dictator, Gen. Idi Amin. Threatened by

The Commonwealth was unable to come to terms with the recalcitrant government of Rhodesia's Prime Minister Ian D. Smith.

WIDE WORLD

PICTORIAL PARADE

The people of Antigua celebrated May 27 as African Liberation Day in solidarity with the Organization of African Unity of Ethiopia and the Liberation Committee in the U.S. They expressed their support for the struggle of their brothers and sisters in South Africa.

severe economic crises and political unrest, Amin chose to vent his wrath on foreign residents. He ordered the closing of the Israeli Embassy in March. In August he ordered the expulsion of some 25,000–55,000 Asians holding British passports, and later he expelled Asians with Ugandan citizenship as well. His accusations of economic sabotage were directed toward Uganda's Asian population, which controlled local commerce, business, and the professions; his aim was to give African Ugandans control in these fields, but the effect was a threat of further economic disruption. England set up an emergency program to handle the influx of expelled Asians who began arriving by airlift in September.

In September Uganda was invaded by a small Ugandan force operating from Tanzania, which General Amin claimed was an attempt to restore former President Milton Obote to power. The invasion was repulsed, and a peace settlement worked out by Somalia was announced.

At the annual meeting of the Organization of African Unity, held in Morocco in June, Commonwealth nations of Africa supported moves to strengthen guerrilla actions against South Africa but refused to set up official armies in their territories. During the year Zambia, torn by economic deterioration and tribal dissent, became a one-party state and a virtual dictatorship. In Ghana Col. Ignatius Acheampong established a military dictatorship after ousting Prime Minister Kofi A. Busia in January. Zanzibar's Communist dictator was assassinated in April and was replaced by a cabinet minister loyal to the ruling Revolutionary Council.

The Caribbean and the Mediterranean

Governments in the West Indies continued to be provoked by militant black power movements in 1972. Racial and industrial strife in Trinidad resulted in another state of emergency. In August Guyana was host to the fourth conference of nonaligned nations, which came out in support of guerrilla movements against South Africa. Canada, preoccupied with Northern Territory developments and its relations with the U.S., maintained ties with the Commonwealth Caribbean through member nations of the Caribbean Free Trade Association (CARIFTA).

In Malta, Prime Minister Dominic Mintoff in 1971 had unilaterally abrogated the 1964 defense agreement. He demanded and eventually obtained in March 1972 a promise of increased aid from England and the North Atlantic Treaty Organization (NATO) powers. (*See also* individual countries by name. *See in* CE: British Empire and the Commonwealth of Nations.)

COMMUNICATIONS. Open competition in U.S. domestic satellite communications was decreed in 1972, following landmark events of the period immediately before. Such events included open entry into data and other specialized transmission services and the development of rules under which cable television systems would become cable telecommunications networks. The first specialized common carrier to take the field with actual commercial service was Microwave Communications, Inc. (MCI), between Chicago and St. Louis, Mo., in January. MCI reported doing a modest volume of private-line business, in which a customer leases one or more links of varying bandwidth between locations on his own premises.

As the year progressed, MCI's lawyers and economists were even busier than its technicians. MCI repeatedly voiced its fear that the established common carriers' version of the "full and fair competition" decreed by the Federal Communications Commission (FCC) would engulf it. It became involved in a whole series of proceedings on rate and tariff regulations.

A direct confrontation came first, not from the Bell system as originally expected, but from the other, much smaller, established nationwide carrier, Western Union Telegraph Co. Western Union, which obtained appreciably less than half its revenues from the familiar message telegram, filed reduced private-line rates with the FCC just for the Chicago–St. Louis route to "match" the lower charges of MCI. The FCC planned to investigate Western Union's private-line rates.

Domestic Communications Satellites

The FCC's June 1972 announcement in favor of a "multiple" domestic satellite system was the longest awaited of the verdicts on telecommunications entry policy of recent years, but in some respects it was the least decisive in terms of launching that portion of a new industry. Most of the areas in conflict in the decision, adopted by only four of the seven FCC members, related to American Telephone & Telegraph Co. (AT&T) in one way or another. This was becoming traditional, no doubt because of the huge size and far-reaching services of the Bell system. But, in the words of FCC Chairman Dean Burch in a strongly worded dissenting statement, joined by the other two dissenting commissioners: "The big loser seems to be the one applicant with genuine experience in space-segment management—namely, the Communications Satellite Corp." (Comsat).

Comsat attacked the majority decision requiring it to make a choice between being a "carrier's carrier," serving all comers including AT&T, and becoming a "retail end-to-end" communications service company. The FCC, in the process, had rejected an agreement between Comsat and AT&T under which the former would have provided the domestic satellite system for the telephone companies.

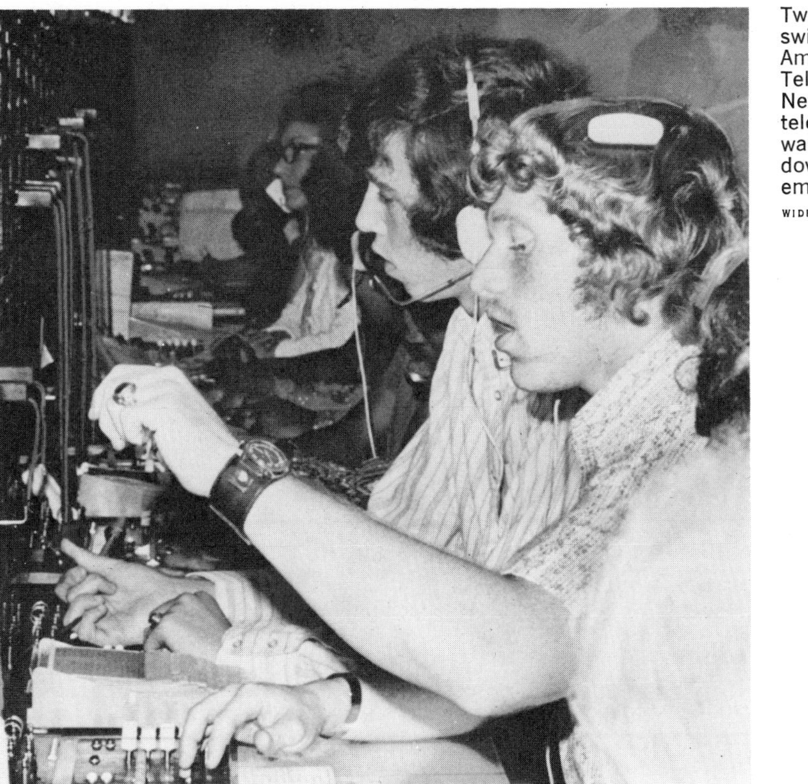

Two men operate a switchboard for the American Telephone & Telegraph Co. in New York City. The telephone industry was a leader in breaking down sex barriers to employment.
WIDE WORLD

AUTHENTICATED NEWS INTERNATIONAL

A telephone cable was laid in 1972 to connect the 200 isolated inhabitants of Sandy Island with the mainland of South Carolina.

AT&T took particular umbrage at restrictions stating that it could not use satellite facilities for the private-line and other services for which it competed with others. It could use them, however, for regular long-distance telephone and wide-area telephone services.

In the words of Chairman Burch, the FCC majority attempted to "structure" the marketplace, "rather than permit full and fair competition between new and existing carriers." The domestic satellite applicants joined in various prospective partnerships, and the second half of 1972 was occupied with legal wrangling.

Cable Television

Evolution, and not revolution, continued to be the word during the year for cable television systems. Growth of new systems, held up for more than two years while basic rules for operation were considered by the federal government, began to move again after the FCC issued a whole new set of rules for cable television. Basically, the FCC said, it was striving toward cable television systems in local communities that would be "something more than an antenna service." FCC Chairman Burch took a dim view of solely "hustling master antenna television signals from one community to another." He said, "We're trying to open up cable to find out if other services are really required by the public."

The FCC sought to find acceptable answers by setting up advisory committees, composed of both industry and public representatives. In general, in its rules, the FCC tightened federal control over cable television, but the future role of the systems remained largely to be determined by the marketplace. (*See also* Television and Radio. *See in* CE: Communication.)

COMMUNIST MOVEMENT.

The continuing conflict between Chinese and Soviet Communism became an even more important factor in the Communist movement in 1972. This conflict was complicated by U.S. President Richard M. Nixon's visit to the People's Republic of China in February and his decision to mine North Vietnamese harbors two weeks before his visit to the Soviet Union in May. It was increasingly evident that the rift between the two largest Communist powers was affecting Communist parties adversely throughout the world.

Competition in the World Arena

The Soviets had consistently maintained that each Communist party or state must work with and have influence on others. The Chinese had maintained support of the principles of noninterference and "peaceful coexistence." In March Soviet Communist Party General Secretary Leonid I. Brezhnev stated that he was willing to make an exception to the Soviet position in the case of China and accept "peaceful coexistence" if the two states could not work out their differences in any other way. A skirmish on the Sino-Soviet border was reported in December, however. Brezhnev's new position was undoubtedly a recognition of China's increased involvement in world affairs. The Soviet Union was faced with President Nixon's visit to China in February, followed later by the Chinese-Japanese decision to renew diplomatic relations.

Europe and the Indian subcontinent were two areas where Sino-Soviet competition was most intense. After the India-Pakistan war late in 1971, in which the Soviet Union had aided India and China had supported Pakistan, the Chinese commitment to Pakistan was reaffirmed with new military and economic assistance in 1972. The Soviet Union and its East European allies provided aid to Bangladesh, the new state created by the war, while China cast its first veto in the United Nations to deny membership to Bangladesh. Meanwhile, pro-Chinese Communists in Bangladesh and India had been virtually eliminated. Pro-Soviet Communists in Bangladesh gained some support. However, the Communist party of India lost electoral support as Prime Minister Indira Gandhi gained in popularity as a result of the Indian victory—a victory that ironically had been won with Soviet aid.

The Chinese seemed particularly concerned that the Soviet Union and the U.S. would reach agreement on the stabilization of Europe, thus allowing Soviet leaders to concentrate more of their attention on dealing with China. The Chinese had been encouraging the independence of Eastern Europe from Soviet hegemony. China had attempted to cultivate relationships with Yugoslavia and Romania, in addition to its traditionally close relationship with Albania, but met with several defeats during the year. At a January meeting of leaders of the Warsaw Treaty Organization countries, the implementation of the Polish and Soviet nonaggression treaties with West Germany, the four-power

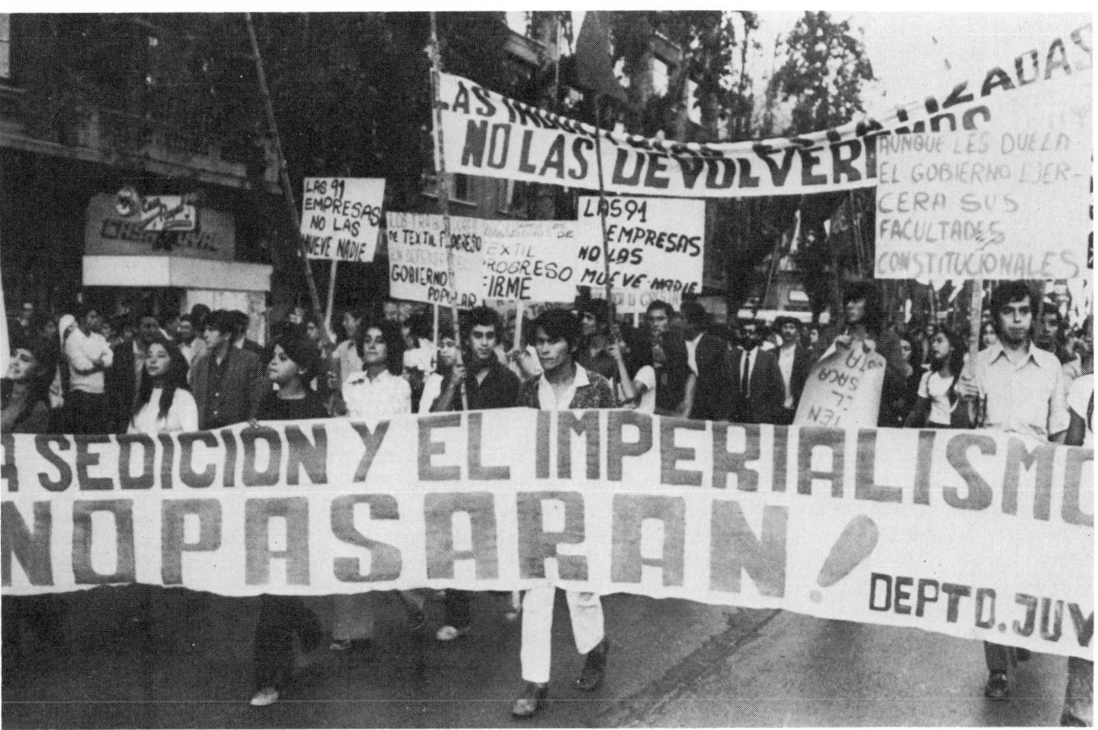

KEYSTONE

Young supporters of President Salvador Allende Gossens' government march in the streets of Santiago, Chile, carrying a sign that reads: "Sedition and Imperialism Will Not Pass."

agreements on Berlin, and measures taken during the year for regularization of relations between the two Germanys were all hailed by the Soviet Union as preliminary steps toward agreement on larger issues at the European security conference planned for 1973. At other meetings of European Communist leaders during the year, both Romania and Yugoslavia displayed increased friendliness to the Soviet Union, while Albania denounced the enlargement of the European Economic Community (EEC); China had supported the EEC move.

To complicate matters further, there was increased Soviet fear of Chinese influence on West European powers as the foreign ministers of France, West Germany, and Great Britain visited Peking for talks during the year. There was also speculation that the Chinese might be obtaining new economic and technical assistance from the West.

Cooperation and Conflict over Vietnam

In May the Soviets were presented with another dilemma when, two weeks before President Nixon was due to arrive in Moscow for summit talks, he decided to mine the harbors of North Vietnam, thereby denying Soviet ships access to ports of their ally. The Soviet Union had to decide whether to cancel the Nixon visit or put their desire for top-level discussions ahead of national pride and obligations to North Vietnam. The visit was not canceled, but there were indications that Soviet leadership had been divided on the question, and one Politburo member was demoted from his post, presumably for opposing the Nixon visit.

The entire situation tended to give validity to Chinese claims that the Soviet Union was more interested in its role as a superpower than in its revolutionary obligations. Despite this wrangling, the Chinese responded to the mining by allowing Soviet supplies to be transported across China into North Vietnam, and both countries increased their aid to the North Vietnamese. The Chinese were still unwilling, however, to allow Soviet ships into their southern ports.

Internal Problems

The Soviet Communist party had a difficult year. Economically it was a disastrous year for agriculture, particularly grain crops, and large amounts of grain had to be purchased on foreign markets, thus damaging the party's plans for improving the standard of living. Several steps were taken toward ideological consolidation, including preparations for a general party purge and several cultural-educational decrees aimed at less party-minded individuals in the literary and motion-picture fields. However, there were still a number of manifestations of ideological dissent and of anti-Russian nationalism, notably in Lithuania.

During the year official Chinese sources confirmed rumors that Politburo Chairman Mao Tse-tung's former heir apparent, Lin Piao, had been killed in a plane crash in September 1971 while attempting to flee to the Soviet Union. Lin was said to have been involved in a plot to take over the government, which included plans to assassinate Mao. It was also asserted that Chen Po-ta, Mao's former personal secretary and a leader in the "cultural revolution" prior to his demotion in 1970, was implicated in the plot. Overall, the Chinese seemed to be moving away from the orientation of the cultural revolution and more toward increased economic production (particularly of consumer goods) and restriction of Red Guard activity. The decision to meet with President Nixon provoked some strong criticism from other Asian Communist parties, particularly the North Vietnamese, who viewed the U.S.-China thaw as a betrayal of the Vietnamese revolutionary struggle.

Communist parties in other areas continued to work for party unity with varying success. Nationalist Croatian dissidents troubled the Yugoslav government, while the Czechoslovak party held a series of trials of liberal reformists. Perhaps the most severe setbacks occurred in Latin America, where the Marxist government of Chile's President Salvador Allende Gossens was faltering after a crippling series of strikes led by shopkeepers and professional workers. Latin American Communist guerrilla organizations met with severe repression, especially in Bolivia, where the government undertook a campaign to eradicate revolutionary forces. (*See in* CE: Communism.)

COMPUTERS.

Many facets of life—including the earliest—were involved with computers in 1972. A group of physicians at the University of Alabama developed a fetal-monitoring system for use in hospital obstetrical wards. The system prints out a warning within ten seconds after detecting an abnormality in critical functions such as fetal heart-beat or uterine activity. The printer need not be placed in the labor room.

This tiny electronic chip can store 960 bits of computer information. The chip is shown greatly magnified against a window screen.
AUTHENTICATED NEWS INTERNATIONAL

The U.S. Department of Health, Education, and Welfare planned to place computer terminals in drugstores, linking them to doctors' offices and data banks containing prescriptions and health information on the entire U.S. population. The terminals would link more than 50,000 pharmacies that were expected to be dispensing 2 billion prescriptions a year by 1975.

Airlines and airfreight companies began to use computers extensively to automate the documentation and routing of airborne cargo. One of the most sophisticated installations began operation at the Air France terminal at Orly International Airport in Paris. Using two computers, the System 360 model 40 from International Business Machines Corp. (IBM), it could handle up to 250,000 long tons of freight in a year.

Volkswagenwerk, West Germany's largest automobile manufacturer, introduced a computerized system to help pinpoint problems in cars. The system carries out as many as 88 tests and prints out the results.

Fairchild Camera & Instrument Corp. introduced a 1,024-bit bipolar random-access memory in a single integrated circuit roughly 0.150 inch square. In February IBM unveiled an experimental operating semiconductor memory system using charge-coupled devices. These devices store data at densities about ten times as great as those of conventional semiconductor arrays. IBM also produced a storage cathode-ray tube for display systems. It can project its image on a screen and requires no power to store the image.

The Univac division of Sperry Rand Corp. acquired 500 new customers who had installed about 1,000 computers from the Radio Corp. of America (RCA) worth perhaps $1 billion and then were stranded when RCA dropped out of computer manufacturing in 1971. To serve these customers, Univac hired 2,500 former RCA employees. Digital Equipment Corp. bought RCA's former ferrite-core memory system manufacturing operation and began to make memories for its computers. Univac announced its new model 9700 in 1972.

The Arpanet, an experimental coast-to-coast network of computers put together by the Advanced Research Projects Agency of the U.S. Department of Defense, became largely operational in 1972. It linked about two dozen government and university computer centers with high-speed telephone lines. (*See in* CE: Computers.)

CONGO, PEOPLE'S REPUBLIC OF THE.

In February 1972 the People's Republic of the Congo announced the failure of an attempted coup, and a large number of public figures were arrested. The detainees included former Prime Minister Ambroise Noumazalay and former head of state Alfred Raoul, who had been dismissed as vice-president in the purge of December 1971. (Raoul's

KEYSTONE

Marien Ngouabi, president of the People's Republic of the Congo, paid a goodwill visit to France in March. The Congo is a former French colony.

release in April seemed as inexplicable as his arrest.) Also arrested was the former first secretary of the Congolese Workers' party political bureau, Claude-Ernest Ndalla.

Opponents of President Marien Ngouabi accused him of having set a trap for them, engineering a plan whereby they would be provoked into an attempted coup that he could crush in his own good time. On March 25 death sentences were passed on 13 of the defendants, including Noumazalay. Later, all 13 sentences were commuted to life imprisonment by presidential decree. (*See in* CE: Congo, People's Republic of the.)

CONGRESS, UNITED STATES. The 92d Congress adjourned on Oct. 18, 1972, completing a performance that alternated between meek cooperation with U.S. President Richard M. Nixon and stiff defiance of his wishes. The 93d Congress, scheduled to open in January 1973, faced the prospect of sharp clashes over spending. The White House had insisted that a tax increase could be avoided only by a $250-billion limit on federal spending. The dispute extended to the record of the 92d Congress, with the Nixon Administration asserting that federal spending was $9.5 billion over the president's budget and some Congressional leaders insisting that presidential requests had been cut by more than $5 billion.

In the closing days of the 92d Congress, there was sharp controversy over President Nixon's request for authority to cut appropriations as he saw fit in order to stay within the $250-billion limit. The request was refused.

Coupled with this refusal was the Congressional action to override a veto of the most costly and far-reaching environmental protection in the history of the U.S. The bill authorized $24.7 billion to make all waters in the U.S. safe for fish, shellfish, and people by mid-1983 and to eliminate the discharge of all pollutants by 1985.

Of the $24.7 billion, $18 billion was earmarked for waste-treatment grants covering 75% of the cost of new plants to localities and states. A strict permit program for pollutant discharges was established. Industries would be required to use the "best practicable" technology for pollution control by mid-1977. By mid-1983 they would be required to use the best available equipment. Suits by interested citizens or the federal government were authorized. A citizen's interest could be either economic or recreational. Grants were authorized for planning agencies, manpower training, research, and demonstration projects.

In separate legislation, the Environmental Protection Agency was given power to regulate pesticides and pesticide factories, but it was also required to compensate manufacturers for losses if a product was taken off the market. An independent agency was created to set safety standards for consumer products and collect data on injuries or illnesses related to product use.

The secretary of transportation was authorized to set automobile-bumper standards to reduce damage in low-speed collisions, effective no earlier than July 1, 1973. A consumer information agency was authorized to compare different models of automobiles for susceptibility to damage and cost of repairs. Five to ten demonstration diagnostic centers were authorized to check for compliance with auto safety and emission standards.

A constitutional amendment guaranteeing equal rights to women was passed during the year. It was first considered in 1923. To become part of the U.S. Constitution, it must be ratified by 38 states within seven years. It would take effect two years after ratification.

Twelve states split by time-zone boundaries were authorized by Congress to exempt their sections of one time zone from daylight saving time. Previously, states had to choose daylight time on an all-or-none basis. States affected were Alaska, Indiana, Florida, Tennessee, Kentucky, Texas, Kansas, Nebraska, North Dakota, South Dakota, Oregon, and Montana.

A major Congressional achievement in 1972 was the passage of a system of general revenue sharing, providing for the distribution of more than $30.2 billion to state and local governments. The system constituted a sharp change in policy. In the past, federal grants were made to state and local gov-

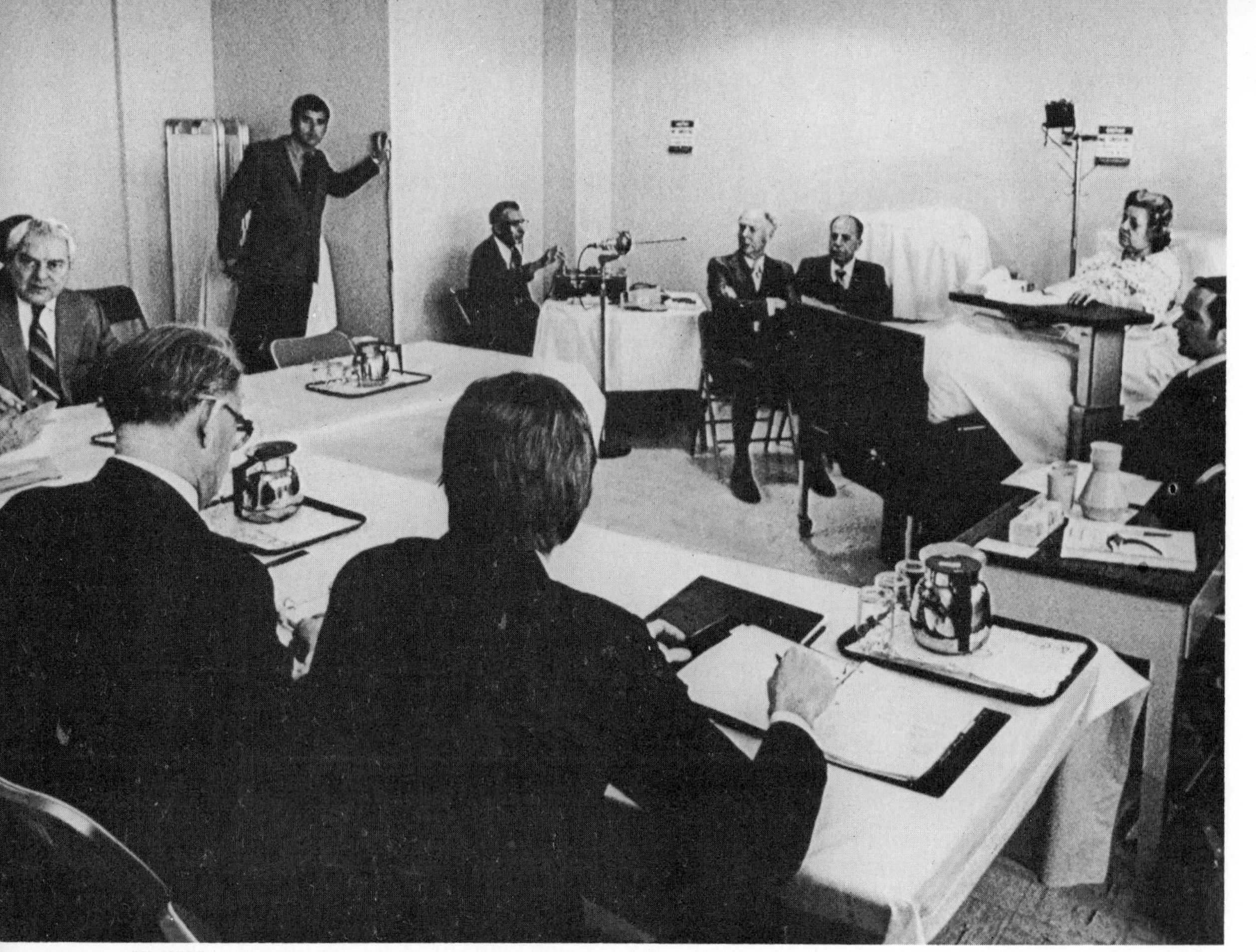

UPI COMPIX

In March the Senate Judicial Subcommittee held a hearing with Dita Beard in her hospital room. She is a lobbyist for the International Telephone and Telegraph (ITT) Corp., accused of making a deal with the Nixon Administration to settle an antitrust suit.

ernments for clearly defined purposes. Spending was strictly controlled. The general revenue-sharing law had few restrictions, although it set up priority items for which grant money should be used. These included capital expenditures authorized by state law and the ordinary cost of essential government services. These were defined as public safety, environmental quality, public transport, health, recreation, libraries, social services for the poor and aged, and financial administration.

The House of Representatives, whose members are elected on the basis of population, passed a bill favoring the large industrial areas. The Senate, with two members from each state, passed a bill that gave relatively larger amounts of capital to the less populous states. The final measure allowed each state to choose the most suitable formula.

A landmark bill for aid to colleges and college students was passed during the year, but only after a fight on school busing that threatened the entire measure. The question of busing to achieve racial balance in schools caused controversy throughout the 1972 session of Congress.

In March the president asked Congress to block new busing orders by federal courts until July 1, 1973, or until Congress passed legislation to equalize educational opportunities in all schools. He requested $2.5 billion to help schools in which 30% or more of the students came from poor families. He asked also that Congress forbid busing for desegregation except as a last resort.

An antibusing amendment was tacked to the more or less unrelated higher education bill. Considered somewhat milder than the president's proposal, it postponed busing ordered by federal district courts until all appeals were exhausted, but no later than Jan. 1, 1974. It also barred the use of federal funds for busing to achieve racial balance except on request of local school boards. It barred use of federal funds for busing if time or distance was so great that it would adversely affect pupils, or if busing moved them to inferior schools. Parents were given the right to take busing disputes to court. The question of constitutionality of the delay in enforcing federal court orders appeared almost certain to be tested in the courts. Congress appropriated $2 billion to help school districts desegregating in the following two years.

The busing dispute overshadowed major changes in federal education policy. One change was the establishment of the principle of making some federal money available to every student who could not afford a college education. A second was the authorization of some federal money for virtually every college to use as it saw fit. In the past, grants were normally for sharply defined purposes.

The higher-education bill would deny federal aid to any graduate school or public undergraduate college that discriminated against women. The ban would not apply to private colleges. The provision on student aid stated that any college student in good standing would be entitled to $1,400 each year, minus the amount his family could reasonably be expected to contribute toward his educational expense. However, if appropriations were not sufficient in any year, grants could be reduced or new grants blocked. A student loan marketing association was set up to free funds that private lenders advanced in student loans, provided the released money was invested in more student loans. GI student allowances were increased and payment in advance was authorized, thus helping veterans pay tuition when it was due. A military medical school was authorized in the Washington, D.C., area.

The new social security law passed by Congress in October increased benefits to about $6 billion a year; it also increased payroll taxes. In 1972 the tax was 5.2% on the first $9,000 of earnings for each employee and an equal amount for each employer, with a maximum of $468 each. It was to be 5.85% of the first $10,800 (a maximum of $632 each) in 1973 and 5.85% of $12,000 (a maximum of $702) in 1974.

Under the new law, retired persons would be allowed to earn $2,100 a year without loss of benefits. Above that, they would lose $1 in benefits for each $2 earned. The maximum earning without loss of benefit in 1972 was $1,680. Persons who worked and did not draw benefits beyond age 65 would have their benefits increased 1% a year when they retired, up to age 72. Low-wage workers covered by social security for 30 years would get a special minimum benefit of $170 a month, or $255 for a maimed couple. This would be decreased by $8.50 for every year less than the 30 years worked, until the amount reached the regular minimum of $84.50 a month.

Medicare coverage was extended to an additional 1.7 million persons already on social security and railroad retirement pensions. Almost all persons needing treatment were guaranteed the cost of dialysis with kidney machines or the cost of kidney transplants under Medicare.

The federal government took over federal and state programs for assistance to the aged, blind, or disabled, guaranteeing them an income of $130 a month, or $195 for a maimed couple. States that had paid more would be allowed to make supplemental payments to continue benefits at past levels.

Widows and widowers were guaranteed 100% of the amount received under social security by a deceased spouse, instead of the previous 82.5%.

WIDE WORLD

Elizabeth Holtzman defeated U.S. Rep. Emanuel Celler (D, N.Y.) in the primary and went on to win his seat in Congress.

Men were allowed the same retirement formula available to women, which would mean higher benefits in some cases.

Congress appropriated an additional $1.38 billion to combat heart and lung diseases, extended programs for control of communicable diseases through 1975, and appropriated $115 million for diagnosis, prevention, and control of sickle-cell anemia. It also broadened the definition of total disability to help miners with black-lung disease establish claims for benefits. A presidential veto was overriden to increase pension benefits by 20% for approximately 900,000 retired railroad workers. Drug education, treatment, and rehabilitation programs were allotted $800 million.

Two agreements announced at the end of President Nixon's summit visit to Moscow in May were approved. Both houses of Congress approved a five-year interim agreement limiting deployment of all offensive nuclear weapons. The Senate, which has sole constitutional authority to approve treaties, ratified an antiballistic missile pact.

The agreement on offensive nuclear weapons allowed the Soviet Union 1,618 land-based intercontinental ballistic missiles and the U.S. 1,054. It would also allow both powers to convert missile-launching submarines to newer types. By taking

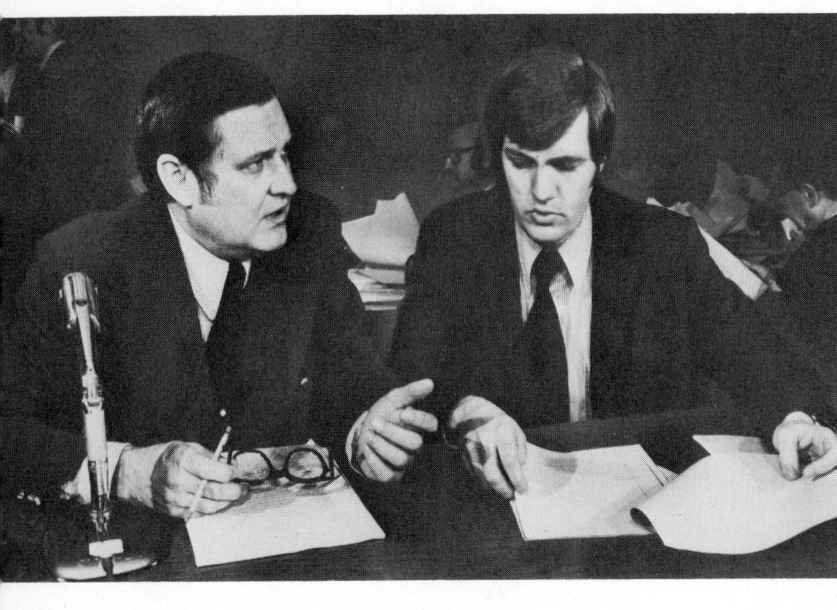

Jack Anderson (left), syndicated newspaper columnist, testified at a Congressional hearing on the ITT case. With him is his assistant Brit Hume. Anderson's muckraking column concentrates on government affairs and practices.

WALTER BENNETT

full advantage of this clause, the allowable strength for the Soviet Union would be 950 missiles on 62 submarines, and the U.S. would be allowed 710 missiles on 44 submarines. The agreement did not cover medium-range missiles capable of spanning the distance between Western Europe and the Soviet Union. The Senate added to its approval a provision that any future treaty on strategic nuclear arms allow countries rough numerical equality.

The 1972 defense bill was the largest single appropriation in the history of the U.S., totaling \$74.4 billion. Spending in 1944, during World War II, was \$86.4 billion for the armed services, but it was split into two appropriations, one for the Army and Army Air Forces and one for the Navy.

Foreign economic and military aid programs were left at their current spending rate of \$3.65 billion until Feb. 28, 1973. The Senate and House were unable to agree on a new foreign-aid bill because of a deadlock over a Senate amendment designed to force an end to the Vietnam war.

A new law required the Administration to submit to both houses of Congress texts of all international executive agreements. It was one of the few successful attempts of Congress to impose its authority on the president in foreign affairs.

The Senate also approved an 87-nation treaty forbidding the deployment of nuclear weapons on the ocean floor. (*See in* CE: Congress of the United States.)

This is the earliest known photographic image of the U.S. Capitol—believed to be the work of John Plumbe, Jr., in 1846. The daguerreotype was one of six found in a flea market in San Francisco, Calif., and acquired by the Library of Congress in 1972.

LIBRARY OF CONGRESS

Members of the Congress of the United States

1st session, 93d congress*

THE SENATE

President of the Senate: Spiro T. Agnew

State	Senator	Current Service Began	Current Term Expires
Ala.	John Sparkman (D)	1947	1979
	James B. Allen (D)	1969	1975
Alaska	Theodore F. Stevens (R)	1969	1977
	Mike Gravel (D)	1969	1975
Ariz.	Paul J. Fannin (R)	1965	1977
	Barry M. Goldwater (R)	1969	1975
Ark.	John L. McClellan (D)	1943	1979
	J. W. Fulbright (D)	1945	1975
Calif.	Alan Cranston (D)	1969	1975
	John V. Tunney (D)	1971	1977
Colo.	Peter H. Dominick (R)	1963	1975
	Floyd K. Haskell (D)	1973	1979
Conn.	Abraham Ribicoff (D)	1963	1975
	Lowell P. Weicker, Jr. (R)	1971	1977
Del.	William V. Roth, Jr. (R)	1971	1977
	Joseph R. Biden, Jr. (D)	1973	1979
Fla.	Edward J. Gurney (R)	1969	1975
	Lawton Chiles (D)	1971	1977
Ga.	Herman E. Talmadge (D)	1957	1975
	Sam Nunn (D)	1973	1979
Hawaii	Hiram L. Fong (R)	1959	1977
	Daniel K. Inouye (D)	1963	1975
Idaho	Frank Church (D)	1957	1975
	James A. McClure (R)	1973	1979
Ill.	Charles H. Percy (R)	1967	1979
	Adlai E. Stevenson III (D)	1971	1977
Ind.	Vance Hartke (D)	1959	1977
	Birch E. Bayh (D)	1963	1975
Iowa	Harold E. Hughes (D)	1969	1975
	Dick Clark (D)	1973	1979
Kan.	James B. Pearson (R)	1962	1979
	Robert Dole (R)	1969	1975
Ky.	Marlow W. Cook (R)	1969	1975
	Walter D. Huddleston (D)	1973	1979
La.	Russell B. Long (D)	1948	1975
	J. Bennett Johnston, Jr. (D)	1973	1979
Me.	Edmund S. Muskie (D)	1959	1977
	William D. Hathaway (D)	1973	1979
Md.	Charles McC. Mathias, Jr. (R)	1969	1975
	J. Glenn Beall, Jr. (R)	1971	1977
Mass.	Edward M. Kennedy (D)	1962	1977
	Edward W. Brooke (R)	1967	1979
Mich.	Philip A. Hart (D)	1959	1977
	Robert P. Griffin (R)	1966	1979
Minn.	Walter F. Mondale (D)	1964	1979
	Hubert H. Humphrey (D)	1971	1977
Miss.	James O. Eastland (D)	1943	1979
	John C. Stennis (D)	1947	1977
Mo.	Stuart Symington (D)	1953	1977
	Thomas F. Eagleton (D)	1969	1975

State	Senator	Current Service Began	Current Term Expires
Mont.	Mike Mansfield (D)	1953	1977
	Lee Metcalf (D)	1961	1979
Neb.	Roman L. Hruska (R)	1955	1977
	Carl T. Curtis (R)	1955	1979
Nev.	Alan Bible (D)	1954	1975
	Howard W. Cannon (D)	1959	1977
N.H.	Norris Cotton (R)	1955	1975
	Thomas J. McIntyre (D)	1963	1979
N.J.	Clifford P. Case (R)	1955	1979
	Harrison A. Williams, Jr. (D)	1959	1977
N.M.	Joseph M. Montoya (D)	1965	1977
	Pete V. Domenici (R)	1973	1979
N.Y.	Jacob K. Javits (R)	1957	1975
	James L. Buckley (C)†	1971	1977
N.C.	Sam J. Ervin, Jr. (D)	1954	1975
	Jesse A. Helms (R)	1973	1979
N.D.	Milton R. Young (R)	1945	1975
	Quentin N. Burdick (D)	1960	1977
Ohio	William B. Saxbe (R)	1969	1975
	Robert Taft, Jr. (R)	1971	1977
Okla.	Henry Bellmon (R)	1969	1975
	Dewey F. Bartlett (R)	1973	1979
Ore.	Mark O. Hatfield (R)	1967	1979
	Robert W. Packwood (R)	1969	1975
Pa.	Hugh Scott (R)	1959	1977
	Richard S. Schweiker (R)	1969	1975
R.I.	John O. Pastore (D)	1950	1977
	Claiborne Pell (D)	1961	1979
S.C.	Strom Thurmond (R)	1955	1979
	Ernest F. Hollings (D)	1966	1975
S.D.	George S. McGovern (D)	1963	1975
	James Abourezk (D)	1973	1979
Tenn.	Howard H. Baker, Jr. (R)	1967	1979
	William E. Brock III (R)	1971	1977
Tex.	John G. Tower (R)	1961	1979
	Lloyd M. Bentsen (D)	1971	1977
Utah	Wallace F. Bennett (R)	1951	1975
	Frank E. Moss (D)	1959	1977
Vt.	George D. Aiken (R)	1941	1975
	Robert T. Staffords (R)	1971	1977
Va.	Harry F. Byrd, Jr.‡	1965	1977
	William Lloyd Scott (R)	1973	1979
Wash.	Warren G. Magnuson (D)	1944	1975
	Henry M. Jackson (D)	1953	1977
W.Va.	Jennings Randolph (D)	1959	1979
	Robert C. Byrd (D)	1959	1977
Wis.	William Proxmire (D)	1957	1977
	Gaylord Nelson (D)	1963	1975
Wyo.	Gale W. McGee (D)	1959	1977
	Clifford P. Hansen (R)	1967	1979

*Convened January 1973.

†Party designation: Conservative Party (of New York).
‡No party designation (Independent).

THE HOUSE OF REPRESENTATIVES*

Speaker of the House: Carl Albert

Alabama
Jack Edwards, 1 (R)
William L. Dickinson, 2 (R)
Bill Nichols, 3 (D)
Tom Bevill, 4 (D)
Robert E. Jones, 5 (D)
John Buchanan, 6 (R)
Walter Flowers, 7 (D)

Alaska
Vacancy†

Arizona
John J. Rhodes, 1 (R)
Morris K. Udall, 2 (D)
Sam Steiger, 3 (R)
John B. Conlan, 4‡ (R)

Arkansas
Bill Alexander, 1 (D)
Wilbur D. Mills, 2 (D)
John Paul Hammerschmidt, 3 (R)
Ray Thornton, 4 (D)

California
Don H. Clausen, 1 (R)
Harold T. Johnson, 2 (D)
John E. Moss, 3 (D)
Robert L. Leggett, 4 (D)
Philip Burton, 5 (D)
William S. Mailliard, 6 (R)
Ronald V. Dellums, 7 (D)
Fortney H. Stark, 8 (D)
Don Edwards, 9 (D)
Charles S. Gubser, 10 (R)
Leo J. Ryan, 11 (D)
Burt L. Talcott, 12 (R)
Charles M. Teague, 13 (R)
Jerome R. Waldie, 14 (D)
John J. McFall, 15 (D)
B. F. Sisk, 16 (D)
Paul N. McCloskey, Jr., 17 (R)
Robert B. Mathias, 18 (R)
Chet Holifield, 19 (D)
Carlos J. Moorhead, 20 (R)
Augustus F. Hawkins, 21 (D)
James C. Corman, 22 (D)
Del Clawson, 23 (R)
John H. Rousselot, 24 (R)
Charles E. Wiggins, 25 (R)
Thomas M. Rees, 26 (D)
Barry M. Goldwater, Jr., 27 (R)
Alphonzo Bell, 28 (R)
George E. Danielson, 29 (D)
Edward R. Roybal, 30 (D)
Charles H. Wilson, 31 (D)
Craig Hosmer, 32 (R)
Jerry L. Pettis, 33 (R)
Richard T. Hanna, 34 (D)
Glenn M. Anderson, 35 (D)
William M. Ketchum, 36 (R)
Yvonne B. Burke, 37 (D)
George E. Brown, Jr., 38 (D)
Andrew J. Hinshaw, 39‡ (R)
Bob Wilson, 40‡ (R)
Lionel Van Deerlin, 41‡ (D)
Clair W. Burgener, 42‡ (R)
Victor V. Veysey, 43‡ (R)

Colorado
Patricia Schroeder, 1 (D)
Donald G. Brotzman, 2 (R)
Frank E. Evans, 3 (D)
James T. Johnson, 4 (R)
William L. Armstrong, 5‡ (R)

Connecticut
William R. Cotter, 1 (D)
Robert W. Steele, Jr., 2 (R)
Robert N. Giaimo, 3 (D)
Stewart McKinney, 4 (R)
Ronald A. Sarasin, 5 (R)
Ella T. Grasso, 6 (D)

Delaware
Pierre S. du Pont IV (R)

District of Columbia
Walter E. Fauntroy (D)§

Florida
Robert L. F. Sikes, 1 (D)
Don Fuqua, 2 (D)
Charles E. Bennett, 3 (D)
Bill Chappell, Jr., 4 (D)
William D. Gunter, Jr., 5 (D)
C. W. (Bill) Young, 6 (R)
Sam Gibbons, 7 (D)
James A. Haley, 8 (D)
Louis Frey, Jr., 9 (R)
L. A. Bafalis, 10 (R)
Paul G. Rogers, 11 (D)
J. Herbert Burke, 12 (R)
William Lehman, 13‡ (D)
Claude Pepper, 14‡ (D)
Dante B. Fascell, 15‡ (D)

Georgia
Ronald B. Ginn, 1 (D)
Dawson Mathis, 2 (D)
Jack Brinkley, 3 (D)
Benjamin B. Blackburn, 4 (R)
Andrew Young, 5 (D)
John J. Flynt, Jr., 6 (D)
John W. Davis, 7 (D)
W. S. Stuckey, 8 (D)
Phil M. Landrum, 9 (D)
Robert G. Stephens, Jr., 10 (D)

Hawaii
Spark M. Matsunaga, 1 (D)
Patsy T. Mink, 2 (D)

Idaho
Steven D. Symms, 1 (R)
Orval Hansen, 2 (R)

Illinois
Ralph Metcalfe, 1 (D)
Morgan Murphy, 2 (D)
Robert P. Hanrahan, 3 (R)
Edward J. Derwinski, 4 (R)
John C. Kluczynski, 5 (D)
Harold R. Collier, 6 (R)
Vacancy, 7♦
Dan Rostenkowski, 8 (D)
Sidney R. Yates, 9 (D)
Samuel H. Young, 10 (R)
Frank Annunzio, 11 (D)
Philip M. Crane, 12 (R)
Robert McClory, 13 (R)
John N. Erlenborn, 14 (R)
Leslie C. Arends, 15 (R)
John B. Anderson, 16 (R)
George M. O'Brien, 17 (R)
Robert H. Michel, 18 (R)
Tom Railsback, 19 (R)
Paul Findley, 20 (R)
Edward R. Madigan, 21 (R)
George E. Shipley, 22 (D)
Melvin Price, 23 (D)
Kenneth J. Gray, 24 (D)

Indiana
Ray J. Madden, 1 (D)
Earl F. Landgrebe, 2 (R)
John Brademas, 3 (D)
J. Edward Roush, 4 (D)
Elwood Hillis, 5 (R)
William G. Bray, 6 (R)
John T. Myers, 7 (R)
Roger H. Zion, 8 (R)
Lee H. Hamilton, 9 (D)
David W. Dennis, 10 (R)
William H. Hudnut III, 11 (R)

Iowa
Edward Mezvinsky, 1 (D)
John C. Culver, 2 (D)
H. R. Gross, 3 (R)
Neal Smith, 4 (D)
William J. Scherle, 5 (R)
Wiley Mayne, 6 (R)

Kansas
Keith G. Sebelius, 1 (R)
William Roy, 2 (D)
Larry Winn, Jr., 3 (R)
Garner E. Shriver, 4 (R)
Joe Skubitz, 5 (R)

Kentucky
Frank A. Stubblefield, 1 (D)
William H. Natcher, 2 (D)
Romano Mazzoli, 3 (D)
M. G. (Gene) Snyder, 4 (R)
Tim Lee Carter, 5 (R)
John B. Breckinridge, 6 (D)
Carl D. Perkins, 7 (D)

Louisiana
F. Edward Hebert, 1 (D)
Vacancy, 2†
David C. Treen, 3 (R)
Joe D. Waggonner, Jr., 4 (D)
Otto E. Passman, 5 (D)
John R. Rarick, 6 (D)
John B. Breaux, 7 (D)
Gillis W. Long, 8 (D)

Maine
Peter N. Kyros, 1 (D)
William S. Cohen, 2 (R)

Maryland
William O. Mills, 1 (R)
Clarence D. Long, 2 (D)
Paul Sarbanes, 3 (D)
Marjorie S. Holt, 4 (R)
Lawrence J. Hogan, 5 (R)
Goodloe E. Byron, 6 (D)
Parren Mitchell, 7 (D)
Gilbert Gude, 8 (R)

Massachusetts
Silvio O. Conte, 1 (R)
Edward P. Boland, 2 (D)
Harold D. Donohue, 3 (D)
Robert Drinan, 4 (D)
Paul W. Cronin, 5 (R)
Michael Harrington, 6 (D)
Torbert H. Macdonald, 7 (D)
Thomas P. O'Neill, Jr., 8 (D)
John J. Moakley, 9¶
Margaret M. Heckler, 10 (R)
James A. Burke, 11 (D)
Gerry E. Studds, 12 (D)

Michigan
John Conyers, Jr., 1 (D)
Marvin L. Esch, 2 (R)
Garry Brown, 3 (R)
Edward Hutchinson, 4 (R)
Gerald R. Ford, 5 (R)
Charles E. Chamberlain, 6 (R)
Donald W. Riegle, Jr., 7 (R)
James Harvey, 8 (R)
Guy Vander Jagt, 9 (R)
Elford A. Cederberg, 10 (R)
Philip E. Ruppe, 11 (R)
James G. O'Hara, 12 (D)
Charles C. Diggs, Jr., 13 (D)
Lucien N. Nedzi, 14 (D)
William D. Ford, 15 (D)
John D. Dingell, 16 (D)
Martha W. Griffiths, 17 (D)
Robert J. Huber, 18 (R)
William S. Broomfield, 19 (R)

*Numbers after names indicate Congressional districts; where no number is given, congressman is elected at large.
†Rep. Nick Begich (D, Alaska) and Rep. Hale Boggs (D, La.) disappeared while on a plane flight in Alaska on Oct. 16, 1972.
‡New district.
§Nonvoting elected delegate.
♦Vacancy caused by the death of Rep. George Collins (D) on Dec. 8, 1972.
¶No party designation (Independent).

Minnesota
Albert H. Quie, 1 (R)
Ancher Nelsen, 2 (R)
Bill Frenzel, 3 (R)
Joseph E. Karth, 4 (D)
Donald M. Fraser, 5 (D)
John M. Zwach, 6 (R)
Bob Bergland, 7 (D)
John A. Blatnik, 8 (D)

Mississippi
Jamie L. Whitten, 1 (D)
David R. Bowen, 2 (D)
Gillespie V. (Sonny) Montgomery, 3 (D)
Thad Cochran, 4 (R)
Trent Lott, 5 (R)

Missouri
William Clay, 1 (D)
James W. Symington, 2 (D)
Leonor K. Sullivan, 3 (D)
William J. Randall, 4 (D)
Richard Bolling, 5 (D)
Jerry Litton, 6 (D)
Gene Taylor, 7 (R)
Richard H. Ichord, 8 (D)
William L. Hungate, 9 (D)
Bill D. Burlison, 10 (D)

Montana
Richard G. Shoup, 1 (R)
John Melcher, 2 (D)

Nebraska
Charles Thone, 1 (R)
John Y. McCollister, 2 (R)
Dave Martin, 3 (R)

Nevada
David Towell (R)

New Hampshire
Louis C. Wyman, 1 (R)
James C. Cleveland, 2 (R)

New Jersey
John E. Hunt, 1 (R)
Charles W. Sandman, Jr., 2 (R)
James J. Howard, 3 (D)
Frank Thompson, Jr., 4 (D)
Peter H. B. Frelinghuysen, 5 (R)
Edwin B. Forsythe, 6 (R)
William B. Widnall, 7 (R)
Robert A. Roe, 8 (D)
Henry Helstoski, 9 (D)
Peter W. Rodino, Jr., 10 (D)
Joseph G. Minish, 11 (D)
Matthew J. Rinaldo, 12 (R)
Joseph J. Maraziti, 13 (R)
Dominick V. Daniels, 14 (D)
Edward J. Patten, 15 (D)

New Mexico
Manuel Lujan, Jr., 1 (R)
Harold L. Runnels, 2 (D)

New York
Otis G. Pike, 1 (D)
James R. Grover, Jr., 2 (R)
Angelo D. Roncallo, 3 (R)
Norman F. Lent, 4 (R)
John W. Wydler, 5 (R)
Lester L. Wolff, 6 (D)
Joseph P. Addabbo, 7 (D)
Benjamin S. Rosenthal, 8 (D)
James J. Delaney, 9 (D)
Mario Biaggi, 10 (D)
Frank J. Brasco, 11 (D)
Shirley Chisholm, 12 (D)
Bertram L. Podell, 13 (D)
John J. Rooney, 14 (D)
Hugh L. Carey, 15 (D)
Elizabeth Holtzman, 16 (D)
John M. Murphy, 17 (D)
Edward I. Koch, 18 (D)
Charles B. Rangel, 19 (D)
Bella Abzug, 20 (D)
Herman Badillo, 21 (D)
Jonathan B. Bingham, 22 (D)
Peter A. Peyser, 23 (R)
Ogden R. Reid, 24 (R)
Hamilton Fish, Jr., 25 (R)
Benjamin A. Gilman, 26 (R)
Howard W. Robison, 27 (R)
Samuel S. Stratton, 28 (D)
Carleton J. King, 29 (R)
Robert C. McEwen, 30 (R)
Donald J. Mitchell, 31 (R)
James M. Hanley, 32 (D)
William F. Walsh, 33 (R)
Frank J. Horton, 34 (R)
Barber B. Conable, Jr., 35 (R)
Henry P. Smith III, 36 (R)
Thaddeus J. Dulski, 37 (D)
Jack F. Kemp, 38 (R)
James F. Hastings, 39 (R)

North Carolina
Walter B. Jones, 1 (D)
L. H. Fountain, 2 (D)
David N. Henderson, 3 (D)
Ike F. Andrews, 4 (D)
Wilmer (Vinegar Bend) Mizell, 5 (R)
Richardson Preyer, 6 (D)
Charles G. Rose III, 7 (D)
Earl B. Ruth, 8 (R)
James G. Martin, 9 (R)
James T. Broyhill, 10 (R)
Roy A. Taylor, 11 (D)

North Dakota
Mark Andrews (R)

Ohio
William J. Keating, 1 (R)
Donald D. Clancy, 2 (R)
Charles W. Whalen, Jr., 3 (R)
Tennyson Guyer, 4 (R)
Delbert L. Latta, 5 (R)
William H. Harsha, Jr., 6 (R)
Clarence J. Brown, 7 (R)
Walter E. Powell, 8 (R)
Thomas L. Ashley, 9 (D)
Clarence E. Miller, 10 (R)
J. William Stanton, 11 (R)
Samuel L. Devine, 12 (R)
Charles A. Mosher, 13 (R)
John F. Seiberling, Jr., 14 (D)
Chalmers P. Wylie, 15 (R)
Ralph S. Regula, 16 (R)
John M. Ashbrook, 17 (R)
Wayne L. Hays, 18 (D)
Charles J. Carney, 19 (D)
James V. Stanton, 20 (D)
Louis Stokes, 21 (D)
Charles A. Vanik, 22 (D)
William E. Minshall, 23 (R)

Oklahoma
James R. Jones, 1 (D)
Clem R. McSpadden, 2 (D)
Carl Albert, 3 (D)
Tom Steed, 4 (D)
John Jarman, 5 (D)
John N. Happy Camp, 6 (R)

Oregon
Wendell Wyatt, 1 (R)
Al Ullman, 2 (D)
Edith Green, 3 (D)
John Dellenback, 4 (R)

Pennsylvania
William A. Barrett, 1 (D)
Robert N. C. Nix, 2 (D)
William J. Green, 3 (D)
Joshua Eilberg, 4 (D)
John H. Ware III, 5 (R)
Gus Yatron, 6 (D)
Lawrence G. Williams, 7 (R)
Edward G. Biester, Jr., 8 (R)
E. G. Shuster, 9 (R)
Joseph M. McDade, 10 (R)
Daniel J. Flood, 11 (D)
John P. Saylor, 12 (R)
R. Lawrence Coughlin, 13 (R)
William S. Moorhead, 14 (D)
Fred B. Rooney, 15 (D)
Edwin D. Eshleman, 16 (R)
Herman T. Schneebeli, 17 (R)
H. John Heinz III, 18 (R)
George A. Goodling, 19 (R)
Joseph M. Gaydos, 20 (D)
John H. Dent, 21 (D)
Thomas E. Morgan, 22 (D)
Albert W. Johnson, 23 (R)
Joseph P. Vigorito, 24 (D)
Frank M. Clark, 25 (D)

Rhode Island
Fernand J. St. Germain, 1 (D)
Robert O. Tiernan, 2 (D)

South Carolina
Mendel J. Davis, 1 (D)
Floyd Spence, 2 (R)
Wm. Jennings Bryan Dorn, 3 (D)
James R. Mann, 4 (D)
Tom S. Gettys, 5 (D)
Edward L. Young, 6 (R)

South Dakota
Frank E. Denholm, 1 (D)
James Abdnor, 2 (R)

Tennessee
James H. Quillen, 1 (R)
John J. Duncan, 2 (R)
LaMar Baker, 3 (R)
Joe L. Evins, 4 (D)
Richard Fulton, 5 (D)
Robin L. Beard, Jr., 6 (R)
Ed Jones, 7 (D)
Dan Kuykendall, 8 (R)

Texas
Wright Patman, 1 (D)
Charles Wilson, 2 (D)
James M. Collins, 3 (R)
Ray Roberts, 4 (D)
Alan Steelman, 5 (R)
Olin E. Teague, 6 (D)
W. R. Archer, 7 (R)
Bob Eckhardt, 8 (D)
Jack Brooks, 9 (D)
J. J. Pickle, 10 (D)
W. R. Poage, 11 (D)
Jim Wright, 12 (D)
Robert Price, 13 (R)
John Young, 14 (D)
Eligio de la Garza, 15 (D)
Richard White, 16 (D)
Omar Burleson, 17 (D)
Barbara C. Jordan, 18 (D)
George H. Mahon, 19 (D)
Henry B. Gonzalez, 20 (D)
O. C. Fisher, 21 (D)
Bob Casey, 22 (D)
Abraham Kazen, Jr., 23 (D)
Dale Milford, 24‡ (D)

Utah
K. Gunn McKay, 1 (D)
Wayne Owens, 2 (D)

Vermont
Richard W. Mallary (R)

Virginia
Thomas N. Downing, 1 (D)
G. William Whitehurst, 2 (R)
David E. Satterfield III, 3 (D)
R. W. Daniel, Jr., 4 (R)
W. C. (Dan) Daniel, 5 (D)
M. Caldwell Butler, 6 (R)
J. Kenneth Robinson, 7 (R)
Stanford E. Parris, 8 (R)
William C. Wampler, 9 (R)
Joel T. Broyhill, 10 (R)

Washington
John Hempelmann, 1 (D)
Lloyd Meeds, 2 (D)
Julia Butler Hansen, 3 (D)
C. G. (Mike) McCormack, 4 (D)
Thomas S. Foley, 5 (D)
Floyd V. Hicks, 6 (D)
Brock Adams, 7 (D)

West Virginia
Robert H. Mollohan, 1 (D)
Harley O. Staggers, 2 (D)
John M. Slack, 3 (D)
Ken Hechler, 4 (D)

Wisconsin
Les Aspin, 1 (D)
Robert W. Kastenmeier, 2 (D)
Vernon W. Thomson, 3 (R)
Clement J. Zablocki, 4 (D)
Henry S. Reuss, 5 (D)
William A. Steiger, 6 (R)
David R. Obey, 7 (D)
Harold V. Froelich, 8 (R)
Glenn R. Davis, 9 (R)

Wyoming
Teno Roncalio (D)

‡New district.

UPI COMPIX

In October a section of the Foothill Freeway collapsed and fell to the bottom of the Arroyo Seco Wash in Pasadena, Calif., resulting in the deaths of 6 workmen. At least 21 men were injured; several had been trapped in the debris. The freeway was still under construction.

CONSTRUCTION. Reduced pressure to increase costs and a record number of new housing units were two notable developments in the U.S. construction industry in 1972. Federal programs continued to be aimed at curbing inflation; the combined cost of construction labor and materials had increased at mid-1972 by less than 5% over the figure a year earlier, as measured by the composite index of the U.S. Department of Commerce. This figure was a substantial improvement over the same period in 1971, when a 7.4% increase over the preceding year had underscored the inflationary trend in the construction industry.

Further deceleration in labor costs (which account for about one fourth of the cost of new construction) was expected as a result of labor agreements during the first half of 1972. These called for annual wage and benefit increases of about 7.6% during the life of the union contract, a much lower figure than the 12.1% recorded in 1971. For the first time in several years, wage settlements in 1972 were in line with the national averages for other industries.

Construction also benefited from long-term funds available at the lowest interest rates in several years. Through August, total expenditures for all new construction averaged a seasonally adjusted annual rate of more than $120 billion, about 11% higher than all 1971. This was about one tenth of the nation's total output of goods and services.

One unsettling factor was a sharp increase during the summer in the inventory of new unsold single-family homes. There were 357,000 new unsold homes, up 26% from the inventory of 284,000 for sale at the beginning of 1972.

Approximately one fourth of new construction during the first eight months of 1972 involved facilities of federal, state, and local governments—such as schools, hospitals, sewage and water plants, and highways. A little less than one third involved shopping centers, factories, office buildings, and similar privately owned nonresidential structures. The remainder consisted of privately owned dwellings, ranging from single-family units to high-rise apartments and condominiums. Altogether, new housing starts totaled a seasonally adjusted average annual rate of some 2.3 million units, a record high.

Apartments accounted for about two fifths of all housing starts in 1972. The housing supply in the U.S. was bolstered by record shipments of new mobile homes—more than 580,000 units during the first seven months of 1972, 17% above the total for all 1971. (*See also* Housing Special Report.)

The Naval Civil Engineering Laboratory began work on scale models of offshore concrete structures that would each be as large as 80 football fields. The structures would serve as military facilities, airports, refueling stations, transshipment ports, and similar facilities.

Owners of residential property spent some $6.5 billion for maintenance and repairs and $10.8 billion for construction improvements in 1972, both record highs. A total of about 3.5 million persons were employed directly in construction work. (*See also* Architecture; Engineering Projects. *See in* CE: Building Construction.)

CONSUMER PROTECTION. Hopes that a large amount of consumer protection legislation would be passed by the U.S. Congress were not fulfilled in 1972; nevertheless, it was evident that the consumer movement had become a source of considerable power. During the year U.S. industry, Congress, and the Federal Trade Commission (FTC) all took action to consider demands.

Legislative Efforts

The Consumer Product Safety Act, signed into law by U.S. President Richard M. Nixon on October 28, was described by consumer leaders as landmark legislation comparable to the Motor Vehicle Safety Act of 1968. Produced after a two-year study, the new law created an independent five-member commission that would have authority to set standards to guard against "unreasonable" hazards in many household items. Enforcement of several other consumer laws, including those covering hazardous substances and flammable fabrics, was also assigned to the new agency. Excluded from the commission's domain were automobiles, food, drugs, and cosmetics.

Two other pieces of consumer legislation became law in 1972. The Drug Listing Act of 1972 authorized the Food and Drug Administration (FDA) to secure listings of all drug-producing firms and their products. The Motor Vehicle Information and Cost Savings Act provided for several new standards to be set for domestic and imported cars. Among qualities to be studied were bumper performance, collision worthiness, damage susceptibility, and ease of diagnosis and repair. Two bills that consumer groups considered unwelcome were defeated in 1972: a proposal to reimburse firms that lost money as a result of the banning of cyclamate sweeteners, and a bill that would have exempted soft-drink producers from some antitrust laws.

However, two of the consumer movement's highest-priority bills were defeated in Congress. The proposed Consumer Protection Organization Act of 1972, which would have created a special government agency to represent consumer interests in courts and agency hearings, was strangled by a Senate filibuster and had to be abandoned when three attempts to shut off debate failed. The bill was considered to be consumerism's most important 1972 legislative goal. The proposed Consumer Product Warranties and Federal Trade Commission Improvements Act, providing for greatly increased powers for the FTC, also went down to defeat, as did legislation dealing with credit practices, truth in advertising, "no fault" automobile insurance, and class-action lawsuits.

Safety and Advertising

Among new safety standards enacted during the year were requirements of "childproof" caps for several potentially dangerous products such as aspirin and furniture polish; a ban on explosive fireworks; and intensified regulation of unsafe toys. The number of food plant inspectors and the frequency of their inspections both increased. Use of the antibacterial chemical hexachlorophene was restricted during the year, and flammability regulations for children's sleeping apparel came into effect. (*See* Safety.) Continuing pressure on automobile manufacturers resulted in 240 recalls involving some 7 million cars in the first nine months of 1972. Bulletins warning car owners of potential defects were issued at early stages of investigation.

In June Secretary of Commerce Peter G. Peterson announced new voluntary guidelines for packaging and labeling of products.

WIDE WORLD

Probably the biggest battle of the year was a running contest between the FTC and advertisers over the quality of advertising and the power of the FTC to regulate it. The Federal Communications Commission (FCC) held the opinion that a television commercial could be condemned by the FTC only if it went beyond "an affirmative product claim" used to argue one side of a public controversy. The FCC held, for example, that antipollution claims in a gasoline advertisement were "affirmative" claims and thus exempt from FTC action. The FTC held that its powers included regulation and condemnation of any advertising on television, sparking a heated debate between the two federal agencies.

The controversy focused mainly on the concept of "corrective advertising"—an order from the FTC to an advertiser to run commercials correcting what had been deceptive or unfair claims in prior ads. Government spokesmen argued that the threat of "corrective advertising" would undermine commercial television. The FTC continued to negotiate corrective advertising settlements, and several of these ads appeared during the year, among them one for Ocean Spray Cranberry Juice Cocktail. However, no corrective requirements were passed on an advertiser who resisted negotiation and demanded a full hearing.

Other FTC actions during the year were the adoption of rules requiring the posting of gasoline octane ratings and an elimination of television network policies that prevented an advertiser from naming "Brand X." The FTC was also involved in several cases concerning its ruling that ad claims had to be supported by publicly available data.

On the local level, several states and cities adopted consumer offices; dating of perishables and unit pricing increased. "No fault" insurance, however, encountered difficulties in the states, as it had in Congress. The number of states with "no fault" insurance rose to 12, but 14 rejected it and 7 others delayed consideration in favor of further study. (*See* Insurance.)

Organizations such as the Consumer Federation of America and the Consumers Union took a more active stance during the year, but much of the promotion of consumer issues originated with lawyers and centers operating in the public interest, many of them under the leadership of Ralph Nader. The Nader groups continued to work in the areas of tax reform, health, advertising, and auto safety. (*See also* Automobiles; Drugs; Food.)

In July new flammability standards for children's sleepwear up to size 6X took effect. Fabrics must extinguish flames on contact; also, any charring resulting from such an exposure to flames must be confined to a seven-inch radius around the point of contact. Manufacturers claimed that they would have to find new fabrics to meet these standards, but one large retailer has been offering nightwear meeting these standards for several years.

HELLA HAMMID FROM RAPHO GUILLUMETTE

Many families find the use of food co-ops an inexpensive way to buy fresh produce. This woman sorts vegetables bought cooperatively by a dozen families in New York City.

COOPERATIVES. A number of consumer cooperatives in the U.S., especially those in the supermarket business, had one of their worst years in 1972. Although sales were up, profits were off, and a few cooperatives folded. Major consumer cooperatives, however, continued to do well—including Greenbelt Consumers Cooperative, in Washington, D.C.; Consumers Cooperative of Berkeley, in California; Hyde Park Cooperative Society, Inc., in Chicago; Consumers Cooperative Association of Eau Claire, in Wisconsin; and Mid-Eastern Cooperatives, Palisades, N.J. At year's end there were some 250 major consumer cooperatives in the U.S., with more than 560,000 members. Group health cooperatives, through which medical needs are taken care of at a reduced cost on a prepaid basis, continued to increase in membership in 1972.

Of major interest in the cooperative field was the continued growth during the year of cooperative action by minority groups. Blacks in the South banded together in the Federation of Southern Cooperatives, which included farmer co-ops, credit unions, craft cooperatives, and housing co-ops. Lobbying by cooperative organizations in many states led to legislation favorable to cooperatives and consumers. In Wisconsin, for example, legislation to ban corporate farming was backed—and won—by cooperatives. (*See in* CE: Co-operative Societies.)

COSMETICS. In tune with current ecological preoccupations, fresh air, fresh water, and natural ingredients became constant leitmotifs in cosmetics in 1972, and there was continued emphasis on the quality and safety of beauty products. For consumers the biggest breakthrough came in April when the Cosmetic, Toiletry, and Fragrance Association—whose members produced about 90% of U.S. cosmetics—and the Food and Drug Administration (FDA) agreed upon a plan for voluntary disclosure of product ingredients. Under the new plan, manufacturers would be called upon to justify to the FDA any request that product information be kept confidential. The program, which did not require listing of ingredients on labels, would make the information available to doctors only. However, Avon Products, Inc.—the nation's largest cosmetics manufacturer—announced that it had already initiated a policy of making ingredient lists available to consumers on request.

The use of natural ingredients in cosmetics was a trend that continued from 1971. Estée Lauder produced a range of products utilizing a milk base and Max Factor introduced a new line of skin care products blended with essence of fresh strawberries. Other cosmetics firms advertised new products that incorporated honey, bananas, peaches, cucumber, avocado, lemon, and all kinds of herbal extracts.

With fall fashions more discreet and subdued, wearers relied on makeup to avoid possible drabness and to add sophistication when needed. Dark colors—cranberry, eggplant, plum, dark green—predominated for eyes and nails. The deeper lip colors, reintroduced in 1971, continued to gain popularity.

For hair styles, a natural look prevailed, with shorter-cut, well-brushed, glossy hair being most important. To complement the new tailored look in fashion, straight shiny bangs and the sleekly turned-under pageboy reappeared on the scene after an absence of many years. The shorter, more geometric cuts were parted on the side or just off-center. (*See also* Fashion.)

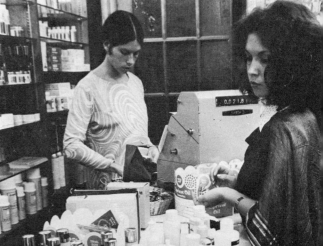

Organic cosmetics are based on natural foods such as lemons, apricots, and cucumbers.

CHIE NISHIO FROM NANCY PALMER AGENCY

COSTA RICA. The first concrete step toward developing Costa Rica's bauxite resources was taken in 1972 with the initiation of feasibility studies on establishing a hydroelectric plant and an aluminum smelter. President José Figueres Ferrer hoped that the Soviet Union would supply capital equipment for the power station in exchange for primary products.

As the advantage of fostering trade relations overrode Costa Rican fears of subversion, Soviet and Czechoslovak embassies were opened in San José, the capital. Commercial agreements were signed in 1972 with the Soviet Union, Bulgaria, and Romania.

The World Bank provided Costa Rica with a $24-million loan, the country's largest in 1972. It was directed toward the electric-power and telecommunications program. A loan from West Germany was granted to develop the Atlantic port of Limón, a link with major export markets.

While teachers and public employees struck for higher wages in 1972, the government attempted to cope with inflation by tightening credit and imposing new taxes. The trade position continued to deteriorate. An agreement scheduled to run until February 1974 was signed by the five Central American Common Market countries, increasing the price of nonessential Central American imports while holding the price of essential imports at the official rate. (*See in* CE: Costa Rica.)

CRIME. During the first six months of 1972, crime in the U.S., as measured by offenses in the Crime Index, increased 1% compared with the same period in 1971. According to the Federal Bureau of Investigation (FBI) Uniform Crime Reports, the percentage increase of 1% for a six-month period was the lowest since the FBI began issuing quarterly releases on crime in 1960. Instances of forcible rape rose 14%, while robberies and auto thefts each declined by 4%. Violent crime—murder, forcible rape, robbery, and aggravated assault—was up 1%. Violent crime rose 11% in suburban areas and 8% in rural areas.

For the calendar year 1971, the estimated number of Crime Index offenses in the U.S. totaled 5,995,200, of which 810,020 were violent crimes and 5,185,200 were property offenses. The rate of Crime Index offenses per 100,000 people was 392.7 for violent crimes and 2,514.0 for property offenses. In cities of more than 250,000, the rate for violent crimes was 1,047.5; in suburban areas it was 205.7 and in rural areas 133.4.

Airline hijackings continued to present a serious crime problem in 1972. Many of them involved demands for huge ransom payments, and some ended in fatal shoot-outs.

In one of the more unusual hijackings, a Hughes Air West Airlines plane en route from Las Vegas, Nev., to Reno, Nev., was hijacked on January 20 by a man demanding $50,000, two parachutes, and a crash helmet. Using the rear emergency door of the plane, he bailed out at 12,000 feet and made a parachute landing about 80 miles northeast of Denver, Colo. Two U.S. Air Force jets had trailed the plane and spotted the hijacker as he landed. Richard Charles LaPoint, 23, a former U.S. Army paratrooper, was arrested with the ransom money.

On November 10 three men commandeered a Southern Airways flight from Birmingham, Ala., to Montgomery, Ala. Armed with guns and grenades, they demanded $10 million in ransom and various supplies and guarantees. They wounded the copilot, demanded to be put in radio contact with U.S. President Richard M. Nixon, and threatened to crash the plane into an atomic plant near Oak Ridge, Tenn. During the 29-hour hijacking the plane either landed at or circled airports in Cleveland, Ohio; Toronto, Ont.; Lexington, Ky.; Chattanooga, Tenn.; and Key West, Fla. The plane also landed in Havana, Cuba, where authorities would not meet the hijackers' demands. In a controversial move, FBI agents shot out the plane's tires when it landed at McCoy Air Force Base in Florida after leaving Cuba. Eventually, an emergency landing was made in Havana when the plane returned there. Cuban authorities arrested and imprisoned the hijackers.

At a political rally in Laurel, Md., May 15, Alabama Gov. George C. Wallace, who was campaigning for the Democratic party's presidential nomination, was shot, seriously wounded, and paralyzed. Also wounded in the shooting were three other persons: Nicholas Zarvos, a U.S. Secret Service man; Dora Thompson, a Wallace campaign worker; and Capt. Eldred Cole Dothard of the Alabama state police, a Wallace bodyguard. Television cameras recorded the shootings. Arthur H. Bremer, 21, a busboy and odd-job worker from Milwaukee, Wis., was promptly arrested. His personal diary, later introduced at his trial, revealed that before he shot Wallace he had been stalking U.S. President Richard M. Nixon. When brought to trial in state court in Upper Marlboro, Md., on July 31, Bremer entered a plea of not guilty by reason of insanity. A jury found him guilty, and he received sentences totaling 63 years.

In a Raleigh, N.C., shopping center on May 29, a gunman fired repeatedly into a crowd with a rifle. Three shoppers were killed and eight others were wounded, including an aide to Senator B. Everett Jordan (D, N.C.) who had accompanied the senator on a noonday handshaking tour. The senator was not injured. The gunman, 22-year-old Harvey McLeod, committed suicide with the .22-caliber semiautomatic rifle he had purchased that day.

In Barrington Hills, Ill., a wealthy Chicago suburb, on August 4, gunmen herded a retired businessman, his wife, and two other members of the family into the kitchen of their home on a large wooded estate and murdered them. The slayings were later connected to other crimes in the Chicago area. The accused were reportedly members of a black separatist group known as De Mau Mau.

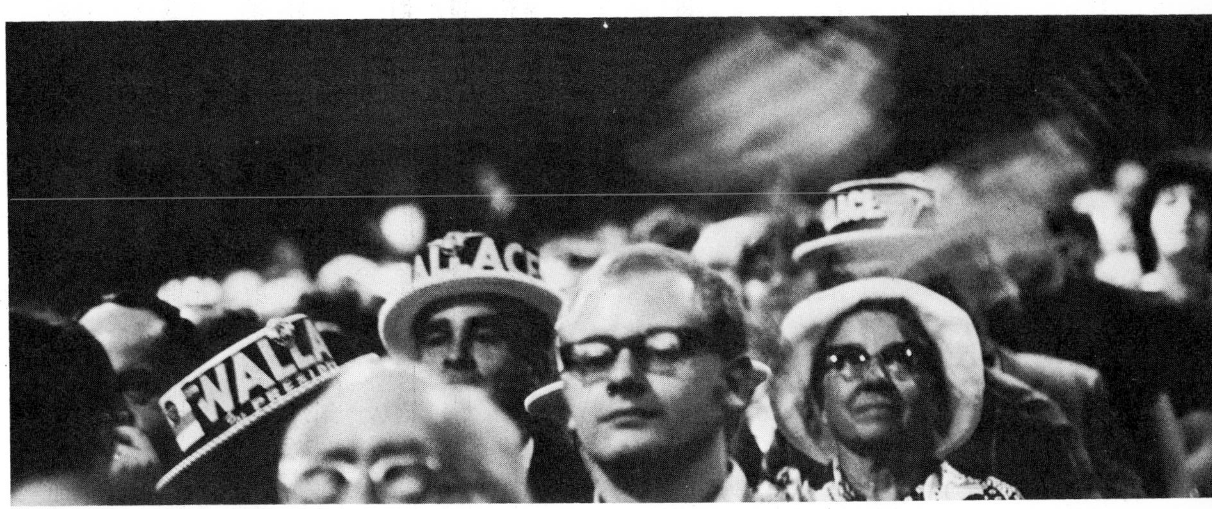

SONIA KATCHIAN FROM NANCY PALMER AGENCY

Arthur H. Bremer (foreground, wearing glasses) is just another face in a crowd at a Michigan rally for Alabama Gov. George C. Wallace. He apparently stalked the governor for some time before the assassination attempt in Maryland in May.

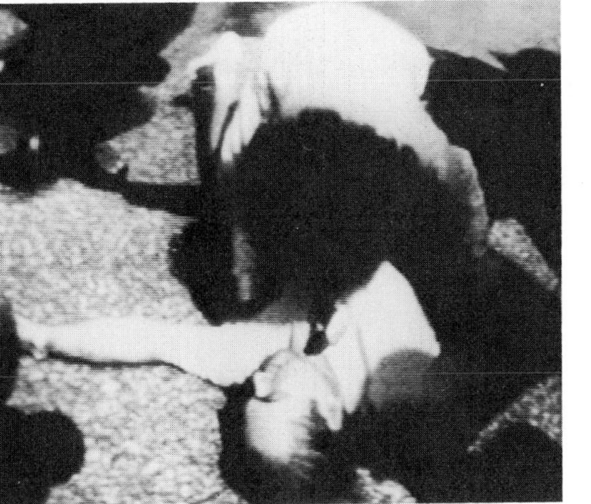

UPI COMPIX

Moments after Gov. Wallace is shot, his wife, Cornelia, kneels down to comfort her fallen husband. Wallace was campaigning for the Democratic presidential nomination.

On May 27 Johnnie Lee Brooks, 30, a twice-convicted robber, was found guilty in St. Louis, Mo., of robbing an apartment the preceding September and stabbing the eyes of a schoolgirl baby-sitter, Wilma Chestnut, to make sure that she could never identify him. Judge P. F. Palumbo of the circuit court sentenced Brooks to 55 years on the assault charge and 15 years for the robbery.

In Washington, Pa., on March 1, a jury of seven men and five women found Paul E. Gilly, 38, a Cleveland, Ohio, house painter, guilty of the murders of Joseph A. Yablonski, United Mine Workers (UMW) insurgent, and his wife and daughter on the morning of Dec. 31, 1969. Three weeks before the slayings, Yablonski was defeated by W. A. (Tony) Boyle in a bitterly fought election for the presidency of the UMW. The election was later voided and a new election ordered for December 1972. On March 2 Gilly was sentenced to death in the electric chair. Several others were later indicted for the murders. Boyle, 67, was convicted on March 31 by a federal jury in Washington, D.C., of conspiracy and of making illegal political contributions with union funds. On June 27 Boyle was sentenced to five years in prison and fined $130,000. He was also ordered to make restitution of the $49,250 he had diverted from the union treasury to various political campaigns. He continued to campaign for reelection while awaiting a court decision on his appeal. However, he was defeated by reform candidate Arnold R. Miller.

On June 4, at the conclusion of a trial that attracted international attention, Angela Davis, 28, black activist and member of the Communist party, was found not guilty of kidnapping, murder, and conspiracy by an all white jury in San Jose, Calif. The trial, which lasted more than 12 weeks, was based on a bloody shoot-out at the Marin County Courthouse in San Rafael, Calif., in 1970.

Warfare among some of New York City's most powerful organized crime groups resulted in numerous gangland-type slayings in 1972. On April 7 Joseph (Crazy Joe) Gallo was killed and his bodyguard injured when four men entered a New York City restaurant and emptied their guns at them. In recent years Gallo had feuded with the underworld family headed by Joseph A. Colombo, who was critically wounded in an assassination attempt on June 28, 1971. Following the Gallo murder, Joseph Luparelli, an associate of the acting head of the Colombo family, turned himself in to the FBI and reportedly admitted that he and four other men were involved in the assassination of Gallo, who had been marked for execution by the Colombo family for several months.

CO RENTMEESTER FROM LIFE MAGAZINE © TIME INC.

A masked Arab commando kept watch from the balcony of the Israeli Olympic team's quarters where two Israelis had already been killed and nine others were being held hostage. Ultimately, in a battle at a Munich air base, the remaining hostages also were murdered.

On July 16, the body of Thomas Eboli, alias Tommy Ryan, 61, one of the top Mafia-type leaders in New York City, was found in a residential section of the Crown Heights district of Brooklyn. The murder of Eboli was the ninth gangland slaying in New York City after Gallo's assassination.

In federal court in New York City on April 25, Louis Cirillo was convicted as a major distributor of heroin smuggled into the U.S. from France. He was one of 23 men indicted by a federal grand jury on January 4 on charges of having smuggled 1,500 pounds of heroin into the U.S. during the preceding two years. The smuggled heroin had an initial import value of $8 million and a street value of more than $200 million. On May 25 Cirillo was sentenced to 25 years in prison.

Author Clifford Irving, 41, and his wife, Edith, 36, pleaded guilty in federal court in New York City on March 13 to charges of conspiracy to swindle the publishing house of McGraw-Hill, Inc., out of more than $750,000 with a bogus autobiography of wealthy industrialist Howard R. Hughes. Irving had convinced McGraw-Hill that he had compiled an autobiography of Hughes on the basis of numerous secret meetings with him. Mrs. Irving had used a doctored passport and the name of H. R. Hughes to open a Swiss bank account for the money intended by McGraw-Hill for Hughes. On June 16 Judge John M. Cannella of federal court sentenced Irving to a prison term of two and one-half years. Edith Irving received a two-year prison term, though all but two months of it was suspended. (*See* Publishing, Book.)

One of the largest art robberies in modern times occurred on May 17 when two thieves wearing ski masks stole four paintings valued at more than $1

New York City police demolition experts examine a letter-bomb. More than 50 such devices were sent to Israelis and to Jews in a number of countries. Arab terrorists were responsible.

JACK SMITH FROM THE "NEW YORK DAILY NEWS"

WIDE WORLD

Wounded hijacking victims are removed by medical personnel from a Southern Airways plane on November 12. The plane and its passengers were returned to Miami, Fla., from Cuba, and the Cuban authorities arrested the hijackers.

million from the Worcester Art Museum in Massachusetts and fled after shooting a guard who tried to question them. One of the paintings, Rembrandt's 'St. Bartholomew', was worth more than $450,000; the others were Paul Gauguin's 'Brooding Woman' and 'Head of a Woman' and Pablo Picasso's 'Mother and Child'. On May 20 William Carlson, 25, and Carol Naster, 28, both from central Massachusetts, were arrested. Carlson was charged with assault and battery with a dangerous weapon and Carol Naster was accused of being an accessory. The art treasures were not found.

On the night of May 30, three Japanese gunmen opened fire with automatic rifles and exploded grenades in the crowded passenger terminal of Lod International Airport near Tel Aviv, Israel. The gunmen had alighted from an Air France plane with their weapons and grenades concealed in their suitcases. They then rode with the passengers and crew on airport buses to the terminal, where they threw the grenades and opened fire with bursts from Soviet-made weapons. Twenty-five air travelers and visitors to the airport were killed and more than 70 were injured. Two of the terrorists were killed, but Kozo Okamoto, 24, was captured. Before a military tribunal at Rishon Le Zion, Israel, in July, he readily admitted his role in the massacre and was sentenced to life imprisonment.

On September 5, in Munich, West Germany, a Palestinian commando squad stormed the quarters of the Israeli Olympic team, shooting and killing two of the Israelis who resisted the forced entry. Following negotiations in which the terrorists demanded the release of 200 Arabs held in Israeli prisons, nine hostages and their captors were flown by helicopters to a nearby air base. German police ambushed the terrorists before they could get their hostages aboard a jetliner. In the ensuing struggle all nine Israeli hostages were killed, as well as five guerrillas and one Munich policeman. The surviving commandos were imprisoned by German authorities. On October 29, however, Palestinian guerrillas hijacked a West German jetliner over Turkey and threatened to blow up the plane, along with its passengers and crew, if three of the Munich terrorists were not released. German authorities acceded to the demands and the plane stopped in Zagreb, Yugoslavia, to pick up the released prisoners, who had been flown there. The plane then flew to Tripoli, Libya, where the prisoners and the hijackers were welcomed by the Libyan government. (*See* Olympic Games. *See also* Law; Police; Prisons.)

CUBA. Stronger ties with other Latin American nations and some improvement in the economy were two encouraging developments in Cuba in 1972. Premier Fidel Castro continued in a stable leadership position that was strengthened during the year by the expansion of several mass organizations that supported the government, notably youth groups and trade unions.

Castro made an extensive tour of several African and East European countries from May to early July, which culminated on June 26 in his first visit to the Soviet Union since 1964. During his visit he requested and obtained increased economic and technical aid in return for greater Soviet influence on Cuban economic policy. In April the two countries had signed a new agreement, to remain in force until 1975, under which the Soviet Union would supply Cuba with essential goods and technical assistance and would purchase at least 80% of the Cuban sugar crop. On July 11 Cuba became a full member of the Council for Mutual Economic Assistance and could therefore expect increased aid from East European countries.

Several Latin American countries showed increasing friendliness toward Cuba during the year. Relations with Chile improved as a result of Castro's state visit there in late 1971, an important trade agreement was signed with Mexico, and it was reported that both Panama and Ecuador were considering resuming diplomatic relations with Cuba. Peru submitted a proposal in April to the Organization of American States (OAS) to readmit Cuba. The proposal was defeated. Peru established diplomatic relations with Cuba on July 8 after the OAS rejected another Peruvian proposal that each OAS member be permitted to decide independently if it wished to establish formal relations with Cuba. Trade relationships with Japan, Great Britain, and Italy improved during the year.

There were faint signs of improvement in Cuba's relationship with the U.S. A limited resumption of official communications was indicated by the attendance of a U.S. delegation at an oceanographic conference in Havana in June. This positive note may have helped mitigate the ill feeling caused by the U.S. refusal in March to allow a Cuban film festival to be held in New York City. Agents of the U.S. Treasury Department had seized one film and blocked the showing of seven others by informing the festival's sponsors that the films had been brought into the country in violation of licensing regulations and the Trading with the Enemy Act. Four Cuban film directors were also refused visas that would have allowed their participation in the festival. The refusal provoked protests from New York City's Mayor John V. Lindsay and others. In November the U.S. proposed talks with Cuba on preventing hijackings. The Cuban government agreed, and on November 25 the talks began with the Swiss ambassador to Cuba representing the U.S.

The Cuban economic picture brightened in 1972; planning was concentrated on diversification of the economy to reduce its dependence on sugar. While the 1972 sugar crop was only 4.1 million tons, a drop from the 1971 crop of 5.9 million tons, improved mechanized harvesting methods were employed with good results. There were significant rises in industrial production, living standards improved somewhat, and the fishing industry expanded. In 1972 Cuba was the fourth largest exporter of fish products in Latin America.

Improvements in education continued, with a record number of schools under construction. A total of 24 million Cubans were enrolled in schools and universities, although there was a decline in the number of children between the ages of 13 and 16 attending school. (*See in* CE: Cuba.)

After her release from prison in June, Angela Davis visited several countries. During her visit to Cuba in October, she spoke at the 12th anniversary of the Committees for Defense of the Revolution.

KEYSTONE

Special Report: A NEW U.S. POLICY?

by Sol M. Linowitz

Following the U.S. presidential visits to the People's Republic of China and to the Soviet Union, U.S. observers have begun wondering about the cold war closest to home—that with Premier Fidel Castro's Cuba. Ironically, the spirit of reconciliation that U.S. and big-power Communist leaders sought to project in the spring of 1972 has not applied where the Latin American revolutionary is concerned. On the other hand, glimmers of interest both in Washington, D.C., and Havana, Cuba, indicated that the hard-line official attitudes in both capitals had softened into a willingness for at least limited negotiations.

Each side has stated publicly that the other must give up certain policies and practices before any change in relations is possible. Premier Castro sees no alteration of Cuba's position as long as U.S. policy seeks to maintain what he calls "an international reactionary police force" directed against Cuba and other Latin American countries. He has characterized U.S. President Richard M. Nixon as "a criminal worse than Adolf Hitler." On the U.S. side, Secretary of State William P. Rogers told the General Assembly of the Organization of American States (OAS) in April 1972 that "Cuba's continued interventionist behavior and its support for revolution . . . still constitute a threat to the peace and security of the [Western] Hemisphere." He also cited Cuba's "close and active military ties with the Soviet Union" as a matter "of obvious concern" to this hemisphere.

Yet, even in such a hostile environment, three U.S. government ocean scientists attended a United Nations–sponsored meeting in Havana in June 1972, the first such official mission of U.S. citizens to Cuba since diplomatic relations were broken in 1961. Does this visit to Cuba bear some resemblance to the famous 1971 visit of a U.S. Ping-Pong team to China?

Where U.S. Policy Stands

The U.S., along with most of the other OAS member countries, took measures in 1962 to ostracize Cuba from all participation in the inter-American system. The wall of isolation around Cuba was completed in 1964 by an OAS resolution under the Rio Pact (1947) that established a full trade and diplomatic quarantine. Since then, the U.S. has adhered firmly to the OAS resolution as a matter of foreign policy.

It is interesting, though, that U.S. policy has shifted to some degree during the last ten years. In 1962 U.S. policy—and OAS policy—held that a Marxist-Leninist government was, by its very nature, incompatible with the inter-American system. But a State Department official said in 1972: "The underpinnings of the U.S. policy . . . do not really pertain to the *internal* situation in Cuba." The U.S. government has indicated on more than one occasion that if those acts that it considers a threat to the hemisphere were to cease, the U.S. would not even object to having a Communist Cuba rejoin the inter-American family.

On the other hand, it is also obvious that the Nixon Administration does not want the Soviet Union to believe that the U.S. is now prepared to tolerate further extensions of Soviet power in this hemisphere in the form of military bases or facilities. A military relationship that has Cuba receiving military aid from the Soviets might be acceptable to the U.S., but the use of Cuban territory as a forward Soviet base is clearly going too far.

Domestic policy is also a factor. Large sectors of the U.S. population have felt outraged at the thought that Castro could, in effect, "kick the U.S. in its teeth and get away with it." But with the passage of time, the climate may be changing. Meanwhile, the anti-Castro militancy of nearly half a million Cuban expatriates in the U.S. helps keep the subject of U.S. relations with Cuba alive as a political issue.

The U.S. has committed itself not to undertake any policy changes toward Cuba without coordinating its actions with the OAS. Accordingly, the U.S. is not entirely free to act on its own if it desires to maintain the close coordination with other OAS members that Presidents John F. Kennedy, Lyndon B. Johnson, and Nixon all advocated at one time or another.

Cuba Policy Criticized

The critics of the present U.S. policy toward Cuba have become numerous. Senator Edward M. Kennedy (D, Mass.) maintains that in view of our new relationship with China, to maintain an attitude of hostility and isolation toward Cuba is a "double standard of diplomacy that leads us nowhere." Senator Harold E. Hughes (D, Iowa) has stated that U.S. policies toward Cuba have accomplished nothing but to drive Cuba into the

CAGNONI FROM MAGNUM

arms of the Soviet Union and to provide an excuse for Cuban economic failures. Cuba is no threat to the U.S., he says, and our attitude is a contradiction of President Nixon's stated foreign policy intention to deal with Latin American governments "as they are."

John N. Plank, professor at the University of Connecticut, a student of Cuba policy, has stated that U.S. policy ignores the fact that the terms of reference of the cold war and the role of the U.S. in the Western Hemisphere have both changed. Other academicians point out that the major effect of the U.S. embargo is to hurt the Cuban people and to entrench Castro's leadership, making him more dependent upon the Soviet Union.

On the other hand, some journalists have reported that the Soviets, having sunk more than $5 billion into Cuba over the years, are now moving strongly to consolidate control over their investment through an increased role in the management of the island's economy. It is doubtful, the implication runs, that Castro now could move to a more independent position even if he so desired.

Cuban Positions

What is the Cuban attitude toward a possible policy shift? Premier Castro, speaking on July 26, 1972, the anniversary of the Cuban revolutionary movement, said that Cuba was fully determined to chart its own course and that the island could remain 5, 10, or 20 years without having any relations with the U.S. Certainly Cuba's ties with the Soviet Union are closer than ever. Cuba recently joined the Council for Mutual Economic Assistance, Eastern Europe's common market. Economic and military assistance from the East was being provided at the rate of almost $2 million a day in mid-1972.

Cuba is also doing a considerable amount of business with the nonsocialist world. In 1970 Europe and Japan exported more than $400 million worth of goods to Cuba.

Latin American Views

Can we perceive a shift in Latin American attitudes toward Castro? In May 1972 the government of Peru formally proposed to the OAS that each member be permitted to decide independently whether or not to "normalize" its relations with Havana. (Mexico, Chile, and Jamaica already maintained diplomatic relations with Cuba.) When the final vote was taken, 13 countries opposed the Peruvian initiative, 7 supported it, and 3 abstained. Peru subsequently renewed diplomatic relations with Cuba on its own, and there were indications that Panama and Ecuador might be giving thought to similar moves.

The sanctions adopted in 1964 under the Rio Pact, therefore, still stand as official OAS policy. In accordance with the terms of the 1964 resolution, two thirds of the OAS members must vote to discontinue the sanctions, and only when they have determined that the government of Cuba "shall have ceased to constitute a danger to the peace and security of the hemisphere." It is notable from a juridical standpoint and significant for the voting that the Peruvian initiative in 1972 did not call upon the OAS to consider the central issue of the 1964 resolution—whether or not Cuba constitutes a threat—and, moreover, it did not specifically call for the repeal of the earlier resolution.

Four countries opposed the imposition of sanctions against Cuba in 1964; and of the seven countries that supported Peru in 1972, two were not members in 1964. There has not been, therefore, a decisive shift within the OAS since the policy was originally adopted.

Looking to the Future

In November 1972 the Cuban government announced its opposition to the hijacking of U.S. planes to Cuba and proposed a "broad agreement" with the U.S. on the issue. The agreement included demands that the U.S. not tolerate actions taken against Cuba by Cuban exiles living in the U.S. In a startling departure from past policy, the U.S. agreed to discuss the proposal—face-to-face if necessary. The Swiss ambassador to Cuba was asked to represent the U.S. in the talks, however, which began on November 25.

It appears that today there is a growing potential for the U.S., in coordination with the OAS, to negotiate with Cuba on broader issues. No longer does U.S. policy call for the rejection of the existence of a Marxist-Leninist state in the Western Hemisphere, and Cuba's economic difficulties have made it relatively unattractive as a model for other countries to follow. Nor has the export of Castro-style guerrilla warfare proved to be much of a threat anywhere in the hemisphere. What must evolve, then, is some sort of understanding between Cuba and the U.S. (involving the Soviet Union) concerning the abstention from use of Cuban territory for Soviet military bases and facilities. In an era when the Strategic Arms Limitation Talks (SALT) have finally begun to produce tangible results, such an understanding may be more than just an impossible dream.

WIDE WORLD

Students eagerly shake hands with Archbishop Makarios, the president of Cyprus, outside the presidential palace in June. They were demonstrating in support of his confrontation with the Greek junta over future relations between Cyprus, Greece, and Turkey.

CYPRUS. In January 1972 a quantity of arms purchased from Czechoslovakia by the government of Archbishop Makarios III was delivered clandestinely to Cyprus. Unhappily, at that time there was a renewal of tension between the Greek and Turkish Cypriot communities—a Greek Cypriot was shot dead in Nicosia, the capital, by a Turkish Cypriot on January 10—and the news that President Makarios had acquired armaments threatened to increase the discord further. Therefore, in February Greece and Turkey, the two foreign powers most interested in a peaceful resolution of the Cyprus problem, insisted that Makarios hand over the arms to the United Nations (UN) peace-keeping force. Since Makarios was unwilling to do this, the Greek and Turkish governments held up the resumption of intercommunal talks that had been suspended since September 1971. The Turks were satisfied when Makarios gave effective custody of the weapons to the UN force late in April, but the president's relations with Greece were not eased until May.

The expanded intercommunal talks, long delayed because of the dispute with the Greek and Turkish governments, were resumed on June 8. The briefing stage was completed in September. Although the atmosphere prevailing at these meetings was described as friendly, the Cyprus government remained opposed in principle to the concession of a wide measure of autonomy to the

EASTFOTO

At the May Day celebration in Prague, Czechoslovakia, in 1972 were (from left) Gustav Husak, Communist party leader; President Ludvik Svoboda; and Premier Lubomir Strougal. Although it had been four years since the Soviet-led invasion, hostility toward the Soviets lingered.

Turkish Cypriots. On July 17 the president declared that a solution based upon a form of cantonization or federation was unacceptable, since this would presage a division of the island between Greece and Turkey. (*See in* CE: Cyprus.)

CZECHOSLOVAKIA. The slow grind of "normalization" continued to claim its victims in Czechoslovakia during 1972. Gustav Husak, the Communist party first secretary, held with some justification that no one was being tried for supporting the deposed Alexander Dubcek in 1968, but only for "acts committed against the state" since the Soviet invasion in the summer of that year. Husak's balancing act was not easy. The Soviet Union was reluctant to jeopardize its plans for a European security conference, but political dissidents in Czechoslovakia had to be curbed if stability in Eastern Europe was to be maintained.

Early in February the journalist Jiri Lederer was sentenced to two years' imprisonment for writing articles critical of the Polish Communist regime. In March it was reported that more than 200 dissidents were in jail, including former members of the party's Central Committee, well-known journalists, and the prominent Marxist ideologist Karel Kosik, as well as former student leaders and representatives of the New Left. In April the Journalists Center of Czechoslovakia announced that 40% of Czechoslovak journalists (more than 1,200 individuals) had been dismissed from the profession since the Soviet invasion because they had rejected "the fundamental postulates of socialism." The Czechoslovak chess master Ludek Pachman, held in jail since January 1972 for protesting the Soviet occupation, was released in May on grounds of poor health. However, in July 46 others went on trial in Prague, the capital, and in Brno.

Intellectual conformity was also enforced by administrative means. For example, the avant-garde "Theater Beyond the Gate" was closed down under safety and fire regulations, and publishing firms were instructed to submit the names of their readers and editors for approval. The congress of the Czech Writers' Union, which took place early in June, confirmed that the regime had no intention of allowing a return to former freedoms.

Unlike most of the other East European countries, Czechoslovakia had not followed a policy of coexistence with the Roman Catholic church. In

June *Obrana Lidu,* the daily newspaper of the ministry of defense, accused the Vatican of maintaining a vast subversive espionage network in the socialist countries. There were no official contacts with the Holy See, and the 10 million Catholics in Czechoslovakia were virtually leaderless as no bishops or apostolic administrators were being appointed. On October 27 a British priest, the Rev. David Hathaway of the Pentecostal church, was sentenced in Tachov to two years' imprisonment for "incitement"; he had been arrested at the Czechoslovak border earlier with contraband Bibles.

The Husak regime tried hard to compensate for the absence of political freedom by offering a greater measure of consumer satisfaction. But the psychological effects of the Soviet invasion persisted, and the regime found it difficult to persuade working people to do more than the absolute minimum. Too many experts had been removed for political reasons. The economy consequently suffered. Many enterprises lagged behind their designated targets, and the return to centralized planning forced the planners back to political slogans as a means of increasing productivity. (*See in* CE: Czechoslovakia.)

DAHOMEY. The fragile stability of the government of Dahomey was shaken and then dissolved entirely in 1972, as an unsuccessful coup in February was followed by a successful military takeover in October. The February attempt was led by a group of army mutineers including Lieut. Col. Maurice Kouandeté, deputy secretary-general for defense and a leader of two previous coups. Seven other military figures were arrested along with Kouandeté. They refused to cooperate with the court, and Dahomean lawyers refused to defend them, so it was not until May that they were tried by a military tribunal. On May 16 Kouandeté and five other defendants were sentenced to death.

Dahomey's President Justin T. Ahomadégbé was installed in office in May and overthrown in a coup in the fall.

MARVINE HOWE FROM "THE NEW YORK TIMES"

On May 7, in accordance with a 1970 agreement providing for a three-man Presidential Council with rotating two-year presidential terms for each member, Justin T. Ahomadégbé took power from Hubert Maga. His term was cut short by an army coup on October 26 led by Maj. Mathieu Kerekou. Troops loyal to Kerekou surrounded the presidential palace; gunfire was reported. The border with Togo was closed and communications with Paris were inoperative. On October 27 Kerekou named an 11-man cabinet composed of military officers. (*See in* CE: Dahomey.)

DANCE. Milestones in dance in 1972 included the death of Ted Shawn, one of the most influential leaders on the U.S. scene, and the deaths of two Russian-born U.S. residents—teacher and choreographer Bronislava Nijinska and Alexandra Fedorova, teacher and former ballerina. José Limón, the Mexican-born dancer and choreographer, died in December. The internationally famous Danish-born dancer Erik Bruhn announced his retirement from the stage at the age of 43.

U.S. Dance Companies

Certainly the most impressive, most highly publicized U.S. dance event of 1972 was the week-long Stravinsky Festival presented by the New York City Ballet (NYCB) at the New York State Theater. Creatively unparalleled in the sheer volume of production, it consisted of some 30 ballets, 20 of them choreographed especially for the occasion and thus classified as world premieres. All the ballets were set to scores by Igor Stravinsky. The festival honoring the great Russian composer, who died in 1971 at the age of 89, was conceived by Lincoln Kirstein, general director of the NYCB, and by George Balanchine, the troupe's artistic director and a lifelong collaborator and friend of Stravinsky.

New Balanchine ballets set to Stravinsky music included 'Violin Concerto' (the most highly praised new work of the entire festival), 'Symphony in Three Movements', 'Duo Concertant', and a short movement from a sonata that Stravinsky had composed 70 years earlier (2 years before Balanchine was born). The Stravinsky-Balanchine collaborations revived for the festival included 'Apollo', 'Orpheus', and 'Agon'. Jerome Robbins, Todd Bolender, John Taras, and John Clifford were among the other choreographers who contributed works for the festival.

The NYCB also presented the world premiere of Robbins' 'Watermill', a rather controversial theater piece, set to music by Teiji Ito, with decor by Robbins and David Reppa. All elements were joined in a total-theater expression, with Edward Villella—acting instead of dancing—as the focal point.

JACK MITCHELL

The New York City Ballet presented Jerome Robbins' 'Watermill'. Edward Villella portrayed a man contemplating his life. In this scene, Villella (center, in brief costume) stands among figures depicting the rituals of life.

Another of the year's highlights for the NYCB was an extensive foreign tour, including performances in the Soviet Union and Poland.

The American Ballet Theatre (ABT), 32 years old in 1972, enjoyed successful national tours during the year. Eliot Feld, who had returned to the ABT following the demise of his own American Ballet Company, not only brought with him some ballets he had originated for that short-lived ensemble but also created two new ballets to Stravinsky music. Carla Fracci and Natalia Makarova continued to head the roster of ABT's most popular ballerinas. Cynthia Gregory received ovations for her new interpretation of 'Giselle', her ever-popular 'Swan Lake', and her performances in modern ballets—all of which earned her crowds of fans rushing toward the stage with flowers and with showers of confetti.

The City Center Joffrey Ballet played a 12-week season at its home theater. New works included 'Double Exposure' (based very loosely on Oscar Wilde's 'The Picture of Dorian Gray'), choreographed by Joe Layton to a score made up of music by Alexander Scriabin and electronic sounds by Henri Pousseur; 'Chabriesque', danced to the music of Emmanuel Chabrier and choreographed by Gerald Arpino, the company's resident choreographer; and Arpino's 'Sacred Grove on Mount Tamalpais'.

During the year the interracial company headed by Alvin Ailey was made a constituent of the New York City Center of Music and Drama as the Alvin Ailey City Center Dance Theater. Among the company's new productions were 'The Lark Ascending'; 'A Song for You', with music and lyrics by rock singer Leon Russell; and 'Mary Lou's Mass', in which the dancers were accompanied by jazz musician Mary Lou Williams.

Among the many U.S. ballet troupes not centered in New York City but producing new works in their home cities and on tour were the Boston Ballet, the Pennsylvania Ballet; the Cincinnati Ballet Company; and the National Ballet, of Washington, D.C. Modern dance, including avant-garde activities, was represented by many troupes, among them Utah's Repertory Company; the Juilliard Dance Company; the Los Angeles–based Inner City Repertory Dance Company, headed by black choreographer Donald McKayle; and the companies of Alwin Nikolais, Murray Louis, Merce Cunningham, Rod Rodgers, the late José Limón, and Erick Hawkins. (*See* Feature Article: "Arts of Black America.")

Dance Companies Abroad

London's Royal Ballet, moving toward a repertoire relating its classical background with more

Jerome Robbins conducts the 'Circus Polka' in the New York City Ballet's homage to Stravinsky.

MARTHA SWOPE

contemporary forms, took Glen Tetley's 'Field Figures' (score by Karlheinz Stockhausen), previously mounted by the touring group, into the Covent Garden repertoire. During the summer Tetley created a work especially for the larger company—'Laborintus', for eight dancers including Lynn Seymour and Rudolf Nureyev. Kenneth MacMillan, the company's new director, also created a new work, 'Triad', which featured Antoinette Sibley, Anthony Dowell, and Wayne Eagling. In May the Royal Ballet made its annual New York City appearance.

On the mainland of Europe the greatest dance activity was in the Netherlands and West Germany. The Netherlands Dance Theatre toured the U.S. and Australia. New works introduced during the year were Louis Falco's 'Huescape' and 'Journal' and Tetley's 'Small Paradise'. The Stuttgart Ballet, of West Germany, had great successes in the U.S. and was well received on a tour of the Soviet Union. (*See in* CE: Ballet; Dance.)

DEFENSE. The signing of two treaties on arms limitation by the U.S. and the Soviet Union in 1972 marked a significant change in the defense strategies of both nations. The treaties, one limiting antiballistic missile systems and the other concerning strategic offensive arms, were the first of an expected series of agreements on limiting defense systems. (*See* Arms Control and Disarmament.) However, massive spending for military forces and weapons continued unabated.

WIDE WORLD

U.S. President Richard M. Nixon signs legislation approving the interim agreement between the U.S. and the Soviet Union reached in the Strategic Arms Limitation Talks (SALT).

U.S. Defense Posture

The last year of U.S. President Richard M. Nixon's first term saw the achievement of a number of basic defense policy objectives he had set. U.S. personnel were largely withdrawn from ground action in Vietnam while air support from U.S. planes in Thailand, in Laos, and from the Seventh Fleet continued. The savings involved ($7.5 billion for fiscal 1972 on paper) were transferred to preserving strategic deterrent forces and moving from a conscript to an all-volunteer army. U.S. capacity to provide military aid to Japan and Western Europe was not decreased.

During the year the number of U.S. forces in Vietnam fell from 151,000 to about 27,000 residual troops. All ground combat units were withdrawn, and the remaining support troops, mostly from the Seventh Air Force, seemed likely to follow. U.S. troop strength in Thailand, however, increased to about 50,000, including seven fighter-bomber squadrons transferred from Da Nang, South Vietnam, to Thailand in June. There were plans for the withdrawal of these troops as well as the 20,000-man infantry division and air support stationed in South Korea.

The probable termination of the draft in June 1973 and Congressionally ordered ceilings on troop strength dropped the number of overall armed forces personnel to 2,391,000 men by July 1972. The planned final strength of 2,336,000 by June 1973 would be the lowest figure since 1950. These cuts meant that the fiscal 1973 obligational authority of $83.4 billion, of which $76.5 billion was likely to be spent, would provide considerably fewer effective army divisions. The nominal division total increased to 13, comprising 3 armored, one air cavalry, one triple-capability (TRICAP), one airmobile, 4 mechanized infantry, and 3 infantry divisions. In addition, there were two independent infantry and one independent airborne brigades and five armored cavalry regiments. The major overseas area of deployment was West Germany, with four divisions, two armored cavalry regiments, and one mechanized brigade. Other large deployments were in South Korea and Vietnam. The goal under the zero-draft program was 11 divisions, with the decrease largely accounted for by withdrawals from Indochina. While the smaller number of divisions caused concern among some military men, the continuing effectiveness of the TRICAP division being tested at Fort Hood, Tex., was a positive note.

The U.S. Navy had increased its share of the defense budget, reflecting the need to replace obsolete World War II vessels and the increased use of naval firepower in the war in Vietnam. The replacement program, due for completion by 1980, envisaged a naval strength of 15 attack carriers, 4 antisubmarine warfare carriers, and 3 nuclear submarines to be built each year and amphibious lift for one and two-thirds marine divisions, plus support vessels. The average annual cost was estimated at $2.3 billion. Construction of a nuclear-powered carrier to replace the two carriers due to retire in 1973 was authorized for fiscal 1974. The core of the fleet remained its 14 attack carriers, including the USS *Nimitz,* which was launched in 1972—the largest, fastest, and most powerful carrier in the fleet. The Navy was plagued, however, by cost overruns and Congressional criticism of some of its contracts.

The U.S. Marine Corps remained at its 1971 level of 199,000 troops in three divisions with air support. Increased use was made of helicopters.

The U.S. Air Force was anxious to preserve the triad of deterrent forces composed of bombers, intercontinental ballistic missiles (ICBM's), and submarine-launched ballistic missiles, since the Air Force controlled two of the three systems. Procurement of the B-1 strategic bomber was accelerated although doubts persisted about its ability to survive an attack. The increased emphasis on air support from secure U.S. land or sea bases in Vietnam was part of a long-term trend. Overall Air Force troop strength stood at 260,000, with 120,000 personnel stationed in the Pacific area.

Western Europe

Continuing talks in preparation for a European security conference to be held in 1973 emphasized the increased role of the Soviet Union in Europe. North Atlantic Treaty Organization (NATO) nations were caught between desires to reduce military spending and fears of unpreparedness. Including French forces, there were 700,000 NATO troops in northern and central Europe in 1972. Two major NATO maneuvers were held during the year, one in May in southern Greece and another in September in Norway. (*See also* Aerospace; Armed Forces, U.S.; Europe.)

The colors of the 3d Battalion, 21st Infantry, the last U.S. combat unit in Vietnam, are rolled up during the unit's deactivation ceremony.

UPI COMPIX

DENMARK. King Frederik IX of Denmark, 72, died in Copenhagen, the capital, on Jan. 14, 1972. He was succeeded by his eldest daughter, Princess Margrethe, 31, who became modern Denmark's first reigning queen.

On January 22 Prime Minister Jens Otto Krag signed a treaty by which Denmark would become a member of the European Economic Community (EEC) as of Jan. 1, 1973. Almost 90% of Denmark's registered voters cast ballots in a later referendum, approving entry two to one. The referendum, held on October 2, was considered a victory for Krag and his Social Democratic government, which had negotiated for entry into the market. The day after the referendum, however, Krag stunned the nation by resigning to return to private life. The Social Democrats quickly chose as his successor Anker Jorgensen, 50, a leader of the General Worker's Union, Denmark's largest trade union. Jorgensen thus took command of the Social Democratic minority government, which could muster a working majority of one in the parliament with the support of the Socialist People's party (the only party in parliament that voted unanimously against entry into the EEC).

HENRI BUREAU FROM GAMMA

Denmark's Queen Margrethe II succeeded her father, King Frederik IX, after his death.

The referendum had been preceded by a stormy campaign with exaggeration on both sides. The People's Movement Against the Common Market predicted a loss of sovereignty and a take-over of the economy by huge multinational corporations. Those favoring EEC entry concentrated on stressing the sad state of the Danish economy.

Danish agriculture was expected to prosper from the entry because of its extensive exports of foodstuffs. There was also optimism that the economy would be strengthened and its deficit balance of payments improved. (*See in* CE: Denmark.)

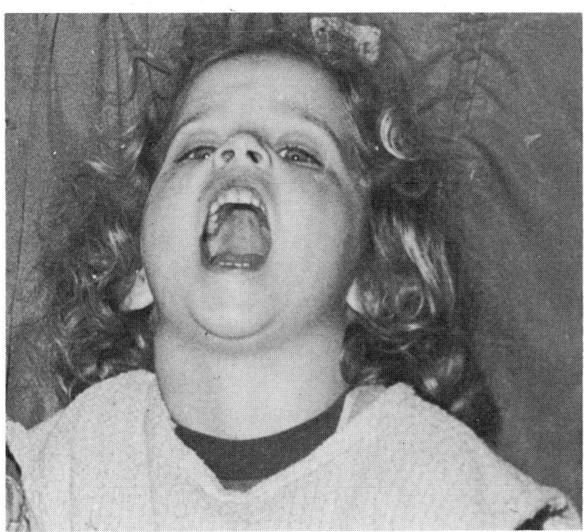

"LONDON DAILY EXPRESS" FROM PICTORIAL PARADE

This child has had her teeth "painted" with a protective plastic solution that prevents decay.

DENTISTRY. Dental researchers were homing in on ways to stop tooth decay and periodontal (gum) disease in 1972. Attempts were being made to single out the specific bacteria which when linked in filmy plaque produced the acids that destroyed tooth enamel. Some workers thought that a class of hormone-like chemicals called prostaglandins might be implicated in gum disease.

Some 95 million people in the U.S. were served by fluoridated water supplies in 1972. But in a survey of eight states, the Environmental Protection Agency found that millions of children might be deprived of full dental health benefits. Only half the water supplies surveyed were fluoridated at recommended levels.

In April the American Dental Association (ADA) provisionally approved a product that claimed to seal the pits and fissures that are particularly likely to harbor decay in children's teeth. Dental researchers also studied a cement exuded by a tiny sea animal that enabled it to stick to underwater objects. Hopes were that once the chemical composition of the cement was found, a similar compound could be made to permit dentists to place crowns, bridges, and inlays in the mouth quickly.

The ADA continued to refuse sanction to any national health insurance program that did not include a comprehensive dental scheme for children. It also recommended that such a dental program should provide care for the aged as well.

In 1972 a number of dental schools coped with demands for more dentists by reducing the curriculum to three years. To encourage dentists to keep abreast of new developments, some state dental societies considered making programs of continuing education a must for annual membership.

Researchers found that women reluctant to stop or reduce smoking stood a risk nine times greater of developing oral cancer than female nonsmokers. (*See also* Medicine. *See in* CE: Dentistry.)

DISASTERS OF 1972. Among the fatal catastrophes occurring in the world in 1972 were:

Air Disasters

Jan. 7 Ibiza, Spain. A passenger jet crashes into a mountain; all 104 persons aboard die.

March 14 Near Kalba, United Arab Emirates. A charter jet crashes in a torrential rainstorm; all 112 persons aboard perish.

May 6 Palermo, Italy. A jetliner slams into a mountain; all 115 persons aboard are killed.

May 18 Khar'kov, U.S.S.R. A turboprop plane falls, killing 108 persons.

June 18 London. A passenger jet stalls and crashes, killing all 118 persons aboard.

Aug. 14 Königs Wusterhausen, East Germany. The crash of a charter jet kills all 156 aboard.

Sept. 24 Sacramento, Calif. A surplus Air Force jet hits an ice-cream parlor; 22 persons, including 12 children, die; the pilot, who had little flight experience, lives.

Oct. 3 Sochi, U.S.S.R. An airliner explodes after takeoff; all 100 aboard perish.

A resident of Rapid City, S.D., checks the lists of several hundred people who were missing or dead in major flooding there in June.

UPI COMPIX

WIDE WORLD

Homes in Wilkes-Barre, Pa., stand askew while debris litters the ground. This picture was taken almost a month after the June floods.

Oct. 13 Krasnaya Polyana, U.S.S.R. In the worst air disaster in history, a passenger jet crashes and explodes; 176 passengers and crewmen die.

Oct. 13 Near San Fernando, Chile. A turboprop crashes in the snowy Andes Mountains; 21 die immediately, and 8 others die later in avalanches; 16 survive, partially through cannibalism of the dead, and are rescued after 70 days.

Dec. 3 Canary Islands. A charter jet falls; all 155 persons aboard are killed.

Dec. 8 Chicago. A passenger jet plows into a row of homes; 45 persons die; 15 passengers survive.

Dec. 29 Florida Everglades. A huge jet slides into a swamp; 99 persons die; 77 survive.

Fires and Explosions

May 13 Osaka, Japan. Patrons of a penthouse cabaret are trapped by a fire; 117 die of asphyxiation or of falls from windows.

Sept. 1 Montreal, Que. Arsonists bomb a nightclub, causing a flash fire; 36 persons die.

Dec. 2 Seoul, South Korea. A theater is gutted by fire; 51 persons die, and 76 are injured.

Marine Disasters

Jan. 3 Persian Gulf. A launch sinks; 80 drown.

May 11 Montevideo, Uruguay. Two ships collide and are covered with flaming oil; 83 persons die.

Mining Disasters

Feb. 26 Buffalo Creek, W.Va. A coal-waste pile used as a dam by a mining company collapses and sends a wall of water into a narrow valley; 125 persons die and 4,000 are left homeless.

May 2 Kellogg, Idaho. Fire sweeps a silver mine; 91 miners die, and 2 are rescued a week later.

June 6 Wankie, Rhodesia. An explosion rips through a mine, killing 427 mine workers.

Natural Disasters

April 2 Mymensingh district, Bangladesh. Tornado kills at least 200 persons; 25,000 are left homeless.

April 10 Southern Iran. A violent earthquake kills an estimated 4,000 persons in some 60 towns.

May 21 Southern Chile. The strongest earthquake ever recorded—9.0 to 9.2 on the Richter scale—kills at least 5,700 persons.

May 23 Northern India. Heat wave with temperatures of up to 138° F. kills at least 500 persons.

June 9–10 Rapid City, S.D. Massive downpour collapses a dam and causes floods; 236 die, and total damage is estimated at $100 million.

June 15–25 Eastern U.S. and Cuba. Hurricane Agnes slams into Cuba and the southeastern U.S., then moves inland with torrential rains, causing widespread flooding and devastation; 134 persons die, 28,000 homes and businesses are destroyed, and total damage is put at more than $60 billion.

June 18 Hong Kong. Heavy rains trigger mud slides that kill about 250 persons; 69 others are missing.

Aug. 6 Philippines. Incessant rains cause month-long floods on Luzon; 427 persons die.

Aug. 19 Bihar, India. A drought causes the deaths by starvation of at least 250 persons.

Aug. 20 South Korea. A 17-inch deluge of rain kills 467 persons; 100 others are missing, some 326,000 are left homeless, and damage is estimated at $17 million.

Dec. 5 Philippines. Tropical Storm Theresa slams into the islands, killing 169 persons.

Dec. 23 Managua, Nicaragua. A series of earthquakes levels the city, killing more than 10,000 persons, injuring some 15,000, and leaving more than 300,000 survivors homeless.

Railroad Disasters

June 4 Jessore, Bangladesh. A passenger train hits a stopped train; 76 are killed and 600 injured.

June 16 Vierzy, France. A railway tunnel partially collapses, derailing one train; a second train plows into the derailed cars; at least 107 die, and 90 are injured.

Oct. 5 Saltillo, Mexico. A speeding train overturns and catches fire; 208 die, and nearly 700 are injured.

Oct. 30 Chicago. A rush-hour commuter train rams another commuter train jammed with passengers; 45 persons die, and at least 320 are hurt.

Miscellaneous

Jan. 23 New Delhi, India. Wood alcohol mixed with varnish is substituted for whiskey at a wedding party; almost 100 people die of poisoning.

Sept. 16 Naga, Philippines. A wooden bridge gives way beneath the weight of hundreds of pilgrims; at least 100 persons are killed.

DOMINICAN REPUBLIC. On Jan. 12, 1972, 12 persons were killed just outside Santo Domingo, the Dominican Republic's capital, as police battled a leftist guerrilla gang wanted for bank robbery. The gang leaders escaped, but four of their band were among those killed in the conflict. Student riots in support of the guerrillas followed and schools were closed.

Political events early in 1972 focused on far-reaching tax and agrarian reform legislation proposed by President Joaquín Balaguer in February and enacted by the government in early March. A package of 14 bills, the reforms involved the prohibition of sharecropping contracts and the transfer to the Agrarian Reform Institute of exhausted land, rice-producing land, and reclaimed state land that had fallen into private hands. By midyear the proposal that caused most concern was the ricelands law. Parcels of less than 80 acres were exempt, so that the measure affected major landowners who had been using public irrigation facilities to maximize their own profits.

Mining operations in 1972 were considerably expanded under a new Dominican law that levied a flat 40% tax on mining projects and an 18% tax on profits. The government encouraged investors by granting exemptions from import duties on mine equipment and freedom to move all clear dividend earnings out of the country. New York and Honduras Rosario Mining, a U.S. company, took up a concession to dig an open-pit gold and silver mine. (*See in* CE: Dominican Republic.)

Friends aid a University of Santo Domingo student after she was shot by police. Some 15 students were injured by police who were allegedly searching for Communists on campus.

WIDE WORLD

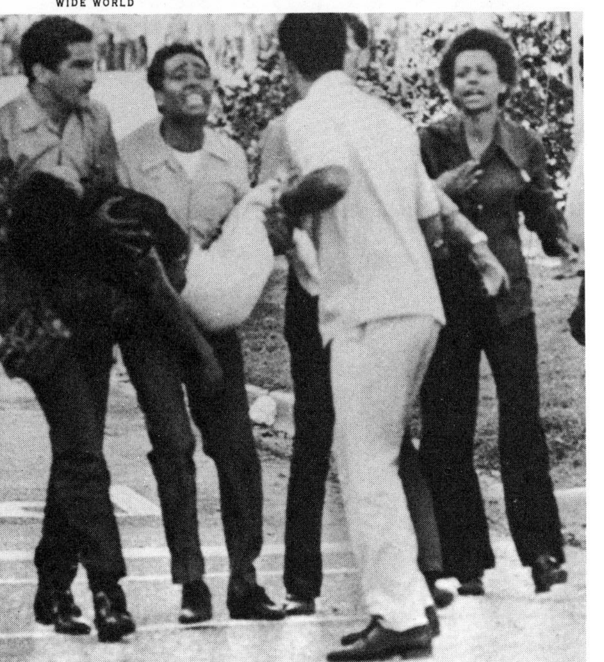

WIDE WORLD

Auguste Joseph Ricord was charged with narcotics conspiracy in a U.S. federal court after being extradited from Paraguay.

DRUGS. The number of narcotics addicts in the U.S. continued to grow in 1972 despite more funding for control of drug abuse, more drug seizures and arrests, and the higher cost of heroin. The estimated addict population was 600,000 or more in 1972 as compared to a population of 315,000 only three years earlier.

In March 1972 U.S. President Richard M. Nixon called for "total war" on drug addiction. He placed high hopes in the approach through law enforcement. Government funding in programs on drug abuse was heavily weighted in 1972 toward solving the problem of heroin addiction, on which the public placed most of the blame for proliferating crimes of violence. This public concern was responsible for a growing trend within the federal government to revert to harsh penalties for the addict.

Typical of the Nixon Administration's thrust was the office for Drug Abuse Law Enforcement, created by executive order in January 1972 as a part of the law enforcement campaign against street peddlers and narcotics distributors. The office put task forces into operation in more than 30 cities and operated a free Heroin Hot Line through which citizens could telephone in strict confidence reports of alleged narcotics violations.

"World Opium Survey 1972," a report issued in August by the Cabinet Committee on International Narcotics Control, included information on legal and illegal markets and illicit trade networks. An assessment by the U.S. and other governments indicated that at least 1,000 tons of illicit opium were

KEYSTONE

The world's largest known shipment of heroin, 937 pounds, was seized on board the *Caprice des Temps* in the port of Marseilles, France.

produced in 1971—mostly in the hills of Burma, Thailand, and Laos.

In a climate that sometimes approached desperation, methadone maintenance programs of treatment for heroin addiction continued to grow in 1972 despite the controversial aspects of treating one addiction with another addictive drug. Methadone itself became an illicit, street-market drug. Some pioneering employers and trade unions were providing jobs for addicts as long as they stayed actively in methadone maintenance programs.

Heroin was by no means the major drug of abuse. The Bureau of Narcotics and Dangerous Drugs seized—in addition to narcotics—more than 210 million units of hallucinogens, depressants, and stimulants in fiscal 1972, more than 30 times the dosage units seized in fiscal 1971.

In 1972 the National Institute of Mental Health launched a project, "Alternative Pursuits for America's Third Century." Its proposed aim was to involve voluntary community groups in a search for ways to capitalize on the creative potential of individuals. It was hoped that substituting creative accomplishment for boredom and frustration would provide a climate in which drugs had no place.

After a year of hearings, surveys, and more than 50 projects, the National Commission on Marihuana and Drug Abuse made its recommendations to the president and the Congress in March 1972. It advocated a policy of de-emphasis on marijuana as a major drug problem. Commission Chairman Raymond P. Shafer asked for uniformity and rationality in marijuana laws. The commission did not advocate legal access to marijuana, but it recommended that possession of marijuana for personal use should no longer be an offense. The commission's recommendations on law enforcement were based on the findings of an American Bar Association committee that would like to rid the courts of victimless crimes so that police could concentrate their efforts on drug traffickers and crimes against persons and property.

A report by the National Institute on Alcohol Abuse and Alcoholism in 1972 cited alcohol abuse as the greatest drug problem in the U.S. The report claimed that drinking is directly or indirectly responsible for almost half of all arrests made in the U.S. and for about 28,000 traffic deaths a year. A drug commonly used for controlling irregular heartbeats showed initial promise in blocking the behavioral effects of drinking alcohol; but the drug, propranolol hydrochloride, failed to block the effects of alcohol at high levels of drinking.

Both the Food and Drug Administration (FDA) and the Federal Trade Commission increased their surveillance of the over-the-counter drug market. A scientific evaluation was initiated on the safety and effectiveness of more than 100,000 nonprescription items. Dr. Charles C. Edwards, commissioner of the FDA, called for strict regulation of the labeling of nonprescription drugs and promotion of sales of these items.

The FDA also moved in 1972 to extend requirements for safe packaging to nonprescription drugs. Until then, it had required that among the nonprescription drugs only aspirin and compounds containing aspirin be subject to the safety requirements of the 1970 Poison Prevention Packaging Act. The FDA asked manufacturers to submit data to help determine which drugs that had been sold without prescription had been a significant cause of accidental injury to children.

A team of physicians at the Mayo Clinic reported some success with medical treatment of gallstones in 1972. The researchers said that for the first time a single drug—chenodeoxycholic acid, or CDC—was used in scientifically controlled human experiments to dissolve gallstones. The still-experimental drug was to be studied for long-term effects.

In Great Britain two separate studies indicated in 1972 that clofibrate, a cholesterol-lowering drug, may prevent cardiac deaths and nonfatal heart attacks in patients suffering from angina pectoris. Clofibrate's effects in both groups of patients were unrelated to its action on cholesterol levels in blood. Further study was recommended to learn how the drug works its benefits and on whom. (*See also* Medicine. *See in* CE: Drugs.)

EARTH SCIENCES. More than 700 scientists gathered in Houston, Tex., in January 1972 for the third Lunar Science Conference to review the findings of the Apollo program. One of the obvious outcomes was the clear demonstration that the methods of geology can be applied to the moon. It was shown that the moon is heterogeneously layered, much the same as Earth. The ages of rocks collected on these missions ranged between 3.2 billion and 4.0 billion years; however, lunar soil presented the enigma of appearing to be about 4.6 billion years old.

In April, during the 71 hours Apollo 16 spent on the moon, the astronauts steered their lunar rover to a variety of lunar features characteristic of the Descartes region. Their rock collection surpassed in size and variety the samples collected previously. Perhaps the most interesting type consisted of white anorthosite (a plagioclase feldspar rock). It appeared to have been formed by the crushing of more primitive crustal rocks. Perhaps the moon at one time melted to great depth, allowing the low-density plagioclase to float to the surface.

Harvard-trained geologist Harrison H. (Jack) Schmitt became the 12th man and the first geologist to set foot on the moon when he landed at the Taurus-Littrow site during the Apollo 17 mission in December. The geology of this area was the most complex of any Apollo landing. During three separate excursions totaling more than 22 hours outside the lunar lander, using the lunar roving vehicle, the astronauts collected even more samples than Apollo 16. The most exciting find was orange-colored soil. All other materials previously seen on the moon had been gray, black, or tan. This orange material appeared to represent the last stages of volcanism, which could have occurred relatively recently in the moon's history. Upon closer examination in laboratories in Houston, Tex., the soil proved to be about 90% glass; this finding made the volcanic-origin theory less likely but did not eliminate it entirely. Seismic studies, aided by the detonation of explosive charges, revised earlier estimates of the thickness of the lunar crust from an apparent thickness of approximately 36 miles to a mere 15 miles.

Remarkable insight into the geology of Mars began when Mariner 9 revealed early in 1972 that the planet has features quite unlike anything seen either on the moon or Earth. Mars is an active planet with fracturing, collapse, huge volcanic cones, and other features of internal origin. For instance, Nix Olympica is at least nine miles high, higher than any comparable volcanic cone on Earth. A branching set of huge chasms several thousand miles long and 40 miles wide dwarfs any such formations on Earth. Although volcanic processes and tensional faulting seem active on the red planet, compressional faulting and fold mountains seem absent, implying that the plate tectonic theory does not apply on Mars. (*See also* Astronomy; Space Exploration.)

Geologists from more than 90 countries participated in the 24th International Geological Congress in Montreal, Que., in August. An increasingly im-

Sculptor-lecturer Ken Gillham works on the world's first earthquake globe. This "terrasphere," six feet three inches in diameter, shows the earthquake belt of the Earth.

KEYSTONE

Scientists searched the Greenland ice cap for mineral resources under the ice. In some places the ice is two miles thick.

WIDE WORLD

portant theme in geology was sounded by the first session, which was devoted to "Earth Sciences and the Quality of Life." Concern was expressed about conflicting needs for vast amounts of nonrenewable mineral and energy resources and for the avoidance of environmental degradation. In the U.S. a similar concern had been expressed in the keynote address to more than 4,000 geologists attending the annual meeting of the American Association of Petroleum Geologists and the Society of Economic Palaeontologists and Mineralogists in Denver, Colo., in April.

The July launching of the first Earth Resources Technology Satellite (ERTS-1) into a near-polar orbit about 560 miles from Earth presented an unparalleled opportunity for geographers to study a variety of regional growth and change characteristics. Almost 2,500 geographers from 74 countries convened at the University of Montreal for the 22d International Geographical Congress in August. The next full meeting of the congress was scheduled to be held in Moscow in 1976.

On December 23 a 2½-hour series of increasingly strong earthquakes destroyed much of Managua, the capital of Nicaragua. The strongest quake, centered in the city, registered 6.25 on the Richter scale. In May the strongest earthquake ever recorded—9.0 to 9.2 on the Richter scale—killed almost 6,000 people in Chile. (*See also* Disasters of 1972. *See in* CE: Earth; Geology; Moon.)

ECONOMY. A marked upswing in the U.S. economy was an acknowledged fact in 1972, but observers were at odds on almost every facet of the recovery. U.S. President Richard M. Nixon's Phase II economic controls were credited by many with responsibility for the awakening, but some economists and the overwhelming majority of U.S. labor unions viewed the controls as a mixed blessing at best. Throughout the year debate raged on the effectiveness of the Pay Board and the Price Commission, on the record profits being reaped by corporations, and on the undeniably high price of food. Election-year politics fueled the discussion, which by the end of the year had produced a grudging admission by Phase II's critics that it had accomplished some good. The controversy also resulted in a spectacular walkout by Labor's representatives on the Pay Board. Though the dust was far from settled, it appeared that inflation and rising prices had been slowed down; but both were still climbing, and it was hoped that the blooming of corporate sales and profits would provide more jobs and economic stability in 1973.

Phase II Boards Under Fire

The three mainstays of the Phase II controls—the Cost of Living Council, the Pay Board, and the Price Commission—entered their second year of operation in 1972 with a confidence inspired by the economic resurgence. None of the panels, however, had an easy year. The Cost of Living Council, under the leadership of Donald Rumsfeld, was not in the public eye as much as the other two boards, but there were many reminders during the year that the council held the real Phase II authority. Rumsfeld's decisions had a marked effect on most Phase II activities, since the council was the umbrella group for most economic control organizations. The council also held the authority to exempt sectors of the economy from wage and price controls and the power to tighten or slacken restrictions as economic conditions warranted. Undoubtedly the most important single action taken by the council in 1972 was the exemption of millions of small businesses from Phase II controls. On May 1 it was announced that businesses with 60 or fewer employees were not liable under wage and price controls. Businesses falling into this category were responsible for 28% of the nation's total sales, amounting to about $500 billion. About 26% of the U.S. work force—some 19 million workers—were involved. The exemption provided that, of those workers, those who were members of large labor unions and who were covered by blanket contracts were still under Phase II restrictions. This provision was viewed by labor union leaders as a direct slap at organized labor. Many Phase II decisions came under fire from labor during the year, including a decision to exempt all workers earning $1.90 or less per hour. Union spokesmen criticized the standard as too low and urged that it be raised to $2.50 per hour.

The quarrels over exemptions, however, were minor brush fires compared to the explosions that

WIDE WORLD

President Nixon talks with Marina Whitman after he appointed her the first woman member of the President's Council of Economic Advisers.

occurred on the Pay Board. Originally formed as a 15-man panel with five representatives apiece from business, labor, and the public sector, the board was criticized for partiality from all sides. Two of its 1971 decisions granted large pay raises to coal miners and railway signalmen—raises that greatly exceeded the board's 5.5% guidelines. Critics accused the board of being lenient toward organized labor. In a decision early in 1972, how-

"... However, while remaining truly thankful, I have been asked to draw your attention to the ridiculous price hereof!"

OLIPHANT—© 1972 THE LOS ANGELES TIMES SYNDICATE, "THE DENVER POST"

JERRY CABLUCK FROM "THE NEW YORK TIMES"

Price Commission Chairman C. Jackson Grayson, Jr., interviews a shopper about price controls.

ever, the board cut a settlement for first-year raises under an aerospace contract from 12.3% to 8.3%. The board's labor members, who had opposed the cutback, responded by accusing the Nixon Administration of favoritism toward business, and the board's nonlabor members of "cynical perversion" of the board's work. The decision, which allowed the 4% increase to be reinstated in second-year raises, was also criticized by some business leaders as inflationary. The main effect of the aerospace dispute, however, was to set the stage for a disastrous confrontation in March.

The labor members became increasingly restive and critical of the Pay Board as they were consistently outvoted by the other members. They also faced criticism from many labor unions. The final break came when the nonlabor majority on the Pay Board ordered a cutback in a recently settled longshoremen's contract. Instead of the original 20.6% raise, the board allowed only 14.9%. The longshoremen had defended the raise on the basis of greatly increased productivity on the docks in recent years. The Pay Board remained firm, however, and four of the labor members resigned amid a chorus of name-calling and accusations. George Meany, president of the American Federation of Labor–Congress of Industrial Organizations; I. W. Abel, president of the United Steelworkers of America; and Floyd R. Smith, president of the International Association of Machinists, quit the board on March 22. They stated that the Pay Board offered labor "no hope for fairness, equity, or justice." President Nixon angrily replied that he would not allow a few labor leaders to "sabotage the fight against inflation." On March 23, Leonard Woodcock, president of the United Automobile Workers, also resigned, leaving only Frank E. Fitzsimmons, president of the International Brotherhood of Teamsters, as a labor member. The Pay Board's chairman, George H. Boldt, declared his willingness to continue the board's work. The Nixon Administration then reconstituted the board as a seven-member panel, with Fitzsimmons, one business member, and the five public members remaining. (*See* Labor Unions.)

The Price Commission had a calm year in comparison to the Pay Board. Faced with mounting inflation and a complex food-price situation, the Price Commission was still able to hold the line on prices in some areas. Since raw agricultural products were exempt from price control, there was little to be done about food prices, which spiraled upward throughout the year. Record farm and wholesale prices were passed along to consumers in virtually every area of retail food. The commission was considering two possible solutions at year's end: placing controls on farm prices and prohibiting retailers from passing price increases on to food buyers. There were problems with both plans, however: the complexities of the U.S. farm economy would tend to make price controls an excessive hardship on farmers. Retailers were also opposed to the proposed price restrictions. As a result of the impasse, food prices, particularly those of meat, became the largest factor in the Consumer Price Index increases each month, as well as a burning political issue. After Meany resigned from the Pay Board, he took a load of groceries to a Price Commission hearing and lectured the members about the widespread practice of charging the same price for a reduced quantity of food as for formerly larger quantities.

The Price Commission was much more successful in other areas. It ordered price rollbacks when a number of large firms were found to have violated the 2.5% annual ceiling. It ruled that when companies wished to use productivity figures as a basis for price increases, industry-wide productivity figures had to be used. The commission's president, C. Jackson Grayson, Jr., attacked Secretary of Agriculture Earl L. Butz for praising large increases in farm prices. Automobile producers' requests for price increases were trimmed considerably. In October the commission exercised its subpoena power for the first time in compelling representatives of two firms to attend hearings.

The complicated rules governing corporate profits led the Price Commission to some seemingly contradictory decisions. When third-quarter economic figures showed extremely high corporate profits, the commission ruled that the profits—some as high as 500%—were within the guidelines. Profits were measured on a relative scale and overseas profits were exempt, thus allowing a large windfall for corporations. The obvious hope was that much of the money would be channeled back into the economy to produce new jobs and industrial expansion.

A Modified Boom

Despite charges and countercharges, the fact remained that the formerly sluggish U.S. economy was in the midst of a tremendous resurgence. On July 21 Herbert Stein, chairman of President Nixon's Council of Economic Advisers, hailed second-quarter figures as "the best combination of economic news to be released on one day in a decade." At that time the gross national product (GNP) had risen 9.4% for the second quarter; the Consumer Price Index had risen only .2% in June; real earnings were 4% higher than a year before; and consumers were spending more of their after-tax earnings than they had since 1969. The median family income rose above $10,000 for the first time in 1971, and that news, also reported in July, produced a rosy economic picture.

The optimism was largely justified; the rosy view, however, had to be modified when seen in the context of inflation and its effects. The new median family income of $10,285, for example, reflected no change in real earnings over 1970. The Consumer Price Index climbed to 126.2 in September (the 1967 base of 100 was used) for a 3% rise for the first nine months of the year. Costs of food and medical care registered gains of 4.3% and 2.8% for the same period. Housing costs rose 3.1%. Wholesale prices, including those of food, had risen at an adjusted annual rate of 5.7% in the ten months since the institution of Phase II. All indications were that the Nixon goal of a 2.5% ceiling on inflation would not be met in 1972.

On the positive side, third-quarter figures showed a real-growth gain in the GNP of 6.3%—less than the second-quarter figure but still encouraging. The GNP gained $24.6 billion to $1.164 trillion. Corporate profits rose by 20% above third-quarter figures for 1971. Total consumer credit at the end of August stood at $145.6 billion, up $2.1 billion from July, and personal income rose $5.7 billion in September to a seasonally adjusted annual rate of $945.7 billion. In November the Dow-Jones industrial average closed above 1,000 for the first time in history.

While inflation continued to cast its shadow, the healthy growth rates indicated a large measure of success for Phase II. While rumors of a lifting of controls were discounted by government spokesmen, there were signs of change. The dollar was officially devalued by about 8%. Several government economists predicted more price exemptions in 1973 and a possible total dismantling of the Price Commission. Tighter wage controls were also being predicted. A rise in the ceiling on the national debt seemed almost inevitable, though it was opposed by Congress, and there were fears of new federal taxes. President Nixon continued to voice strong opposition to new taxation, however. The problems that would be faced in 1973 were both obvious and stubborn: the unemployment rate, food prices, and inflation. (*See also* Business and Industry; Employment; Food; Money and International Finance; Stocks and Bonds; World Trade. *See in* CE: Economics.)

The Internal Revenue Service (IRS) ordered all stores to make price lists "readily accessible" to shoppers. After examining prices and price list displays in stores, Judy Samuels and others of the IRS found that there was only spotty compliance with the law.

BARTON SILVERMAN FROM "THE NEW YORK TIMES"

ECUADOR. José María Velasco Ibarra, five times president of Ecuador, was deposed by the armed forces on Feb. 16, 1972, for the fourth time in his career. A new government, described as nationalist and revolutionary, was proclaimed by the commanders in chief of the army, navy, and air force. Brig. Gen. Guillermo Rodríguez Lara was appointed president. The general elections scheduled for June 4 were canceled. The new cabinet included two civilians, in charge of finance and foreign affairs.

The new government's program aimed at a basic reorganization of economic, social, and administrative structures. President Rodríguez stated that he would revise foreign oil contracts "if necessary," defend Ecuador's claim to a 200-mile territorial waters limit, and permit absolute freedom of expression for news media. On the matter of agrarian reform, he said that the government would guarantee legally acquired property. Plans for reducing the large unfinanced deficit inherited from the previous administration included an austerity program and the channeling of bank loans toward diversification and development in the agricultural sector.

In August 1972 Ecuador became an oil exporter when the Lake Agrio–Esmeraldas pipeline went into operation. The Texaco–Gulf Oil consortium estimated that the daily output of its wells would reach 250,000 barrels a day by 1973 and 325,000 by 1974. The government reserved the right to transport up to 50% of oil exports. Tankers were to be chartered on the international market, pending the acquisition of a tanker fleet. Despite uncertainty as to the government's intentions, most oil companies announced increased investments for 1972. The International Atomic Energy Agency concluded in 1972 that development of uranium deposits near Loja could become as important as that of oil. (*See in* CE: Ecuador.)

Oil pipelines are laid in Ecuador through a basin that extends into Peru and Colombia.

MANUEL GUEVARA FROM "THE NEW YORK TIMES"

EDUCATION. Schools in the U.S. admitted 35.9 million students at the elementary level and 15.5 million at the high school level in the fall of 1972, though the schools opened under a cloud of uncertainty. Just how long the school year would run was in doubt in some financially hard-pressed cities. Detroit, Mich., expected to have enough funds to operate for 117 days, 63 short of the mandated year. Philadelphia, Pa., after conducting a summer school program in students' homes, faced the possibility of a curtailed calendar. Los Angeles contemplated cutting back school days or holding double sessions if additional funds were not found. And Chicago warned of extra-long holiday periods unless more money was forthcoming.

The problem in these cities, as in most districts of varying size across the country, was one of educational budgets caught between rising costs and voter resistance. The electorate continued to turn down about half the proposed tax levies and bond issues while school costs increased. Salaries in particular sent budgets soaring. Over the preceding ten years the average teacher's pay had jumped from $5,500 per year to over $9,000. Other charges had also risen in a period of inflation.

Strikes marred the opening of the new school year in more districts than in 1971. These tended, however, to affect smaller districts. Philadelphia, Washington, D.C., and Providence, R.I., were the only major cities where teachers went on strike.

The trend was away from walkouts. Strikes numbered 89 in the 1971–72 school year, compared with 181 two years earlier. Both the American Federation of Teachers and the National Education Association were turning more toward political action, seeking the election of candidates favorable to teachers and education. Increased federal funding, in the face of local and state fiscal problems, was one of the goals. The target was to get at least one third of school financing from federal aid.

Busing and Desegregation

Public opposition to forced busing reached a new high in 1972. In March a Gallup Poll reported that 69% of people in the U.S. were against compulsory busing to achieve school desegregation, and 20% were in favor. The intensity of feeling became evident in the spring when a group of women from Pontiac, Mich., marched to Washington, D.C., in protest, gathering adherents along the way. A motorcade from Richmond, Va., protesting a court-ordered merger of school districts, snarled traffic as it approached and entered the national capital.

Some politicians were surprised by the antibusing fervor. They had not expected it to be a major campaign issue. Even liberals such as Senator Hubert H. Humphrey (D, Minn.) either took a position against busing or tried to duck the question in the spring presidential primaries. President Richard M. Nixon, already an avowed champion of

UPI COMPIX

Members of a Memphis, Tenn., antibusing group buried an orange school bus in March in a symbolic protest against court-ordered busing.

neighborhood schools, took up the cudgel against large-scale busing more fervently. He decried court decisions that ordered massive transporting of students and urged the U.S. Congress to put a stop to it, by constitutional amendment if necessary.

Congress responded by enacting one of the two restrictions the president wanted passed. This, an amendment to the Higher Education Amendments Act, prohibited implementation of court-ordered busing, pending appeal, until Jan. 1, 1974. The other measure sought by President Nixon would have required judges to consider alternative methods for achieving desegregation before resorting to busing. Such a bill passed the House, but was dropped by the Senate after a filibuster by liberals could not be broken.

Contributing to the fervor were two court decisions in 1971 affecting Detroit and Richmond schools. In these, judges had ruled that black city schools would have to exchange students with white suburban schools to break the segregated pattern. The Richmond verdict was reversed in 1972, but the Detroit ruling stood after an appeal was rejected by the U.S. Circuit Court of Appeals in Cincinnati, Ohio, in December. The antibusing action of Congress was believed by legal experts not to apply to the Detroit decision, handed down prior to enactment of that legislation. Desegregation by busing affected Detroit and 53 suburban communities. Opposition within the state was strong. As a result, in Detroit all school board members supporting the plan were voted out of office.

Meanwhile, a desegregation case involving Denver, Colo., schools moved into the U.S. Supreme Court. This case provided the first test by the high court affecting a city that never had had a dual school system.

On the state level some school districts faced challenges over segregation. The Buffalo, N.Y., school board defied an order from the state education commissioner to submit a busing plan to achieve integration. Illinois districts were chastised by state officials for noncompliance with a desegregation ruling and were ordered to submit desegregation plans within 90 days. Transportation was cited as one means to this end.

The Boston School Committee continued to joust with the Massachusetts State Board of Education over state funds withheld because of the committee's failure to comply with the terms of the state's law on racial imbalance. In 1971–72 Boston lost $14 million in state aid to education on this account; in 1972–73 the schools risked losing $54 million. The law in question—the first state statute of its type, passed in 1965—required that no school enrollment be more than 50% nonwhite, the penalty being the loss of state funds to the district. The school committee tried to compromise with the state board, arguing that no viable method was available for achieving integration. In reply the state board cited a study purporting to show that the redrawing of district lines plus small-scale busing would produce the desired results and satisfy the law. But the committee rejected this approach in the face of community hostility.

This was not the only problem facing Boston on racial imbalance. During the school year the sys-

(*continued on page 237*)

Education

Special Report: THE UNFINISHED CURRICULUM

by Frances R. Link

After more than a decade of unprecedented curriculum development, in 1972 most schools in the U.S. were still teaching obsolete material organized in a single textbook. During the late 1950's and early 1960's, a quest began for the newest theories of learning, the newest ways to improve instruction. After the Soviet Union launched Sputnik I, the first space satellite, in 1957, a fear of losing technological preeminence spurred the U.S. to reexamine the quality of its schools. Interest was stimulated in working out new curriculum models.

In the post-Sputnik years there was an explosion of new information. The latest discoveries by scientists, mathematicians, economists, linguists, and other scholars had to find a way into the schools. These were exciting years for teachers and scholars working together to improve instructional methods. The materials that the teacher and student have as primary sources for learning are powerful in shaping what is taught; yet, in 1972 teachers and students had limited access to multimedia reference materials—still considered supplementary.

In the continuing effort to improve education, some educators are confusing "crisis" social issues with the curriculum. Some are substituting them *for* the curriculum. Some are responding in desperation to the need for curriculum change. When they hear youths in high schools say that they learn more outside school than inside, the signals of curriculum obsolescence are flashing. Most schools, however, have maintained the status quo, and the textbook is still the curriculum.

The movement toward curriculum development in the U.S. was still in its infancy in the early 1970's. The models that emerged through support and funding by government and foundations (such as the Office of Education and the Ford, Carnegie, and National Science foundations) actually gave birth to the movement. Simply stated, sufficient money was made available to bring together scholars in many fields of knowledge to concern themselves with the development of materials for introducing changes in school curricula. A distinguishing characteristic of the changes that took form was the creation of multimedia reference materials and technology to provide access to new information in a variety of formats. Among the distinguished scholars and educators who contributed to the curriculum development movement were: Max Beberman, Jerrold Zacharias, Robert Davis, Robert Wirtz, Jerome Bruner, David Page, and Robert Karplus. A variety of curriculum developments that emerged breathed new life and experimentation into science, mathematics, and social studies curricula. The schools that began to experiment were searching for ways to update information, to foster creativity on the part of students and teachers, and to value individual differences in learning and thinking. These experimental schools enabled teachers and students to highlight the need for variety and flexibility in curriculum materials as a way to humanize the curriculum.

Case Study of an Innovation

It would be impossible to attribute the start of the curriculum reform movement to any one person, for projects in science and mathematics were created simultaneously. To develop a case study of a curriculum development, however, may be a simple way to explain the process and its difference from the traditional methods that institutionalized age- and grade-level expectations.

Although many people contribute to a curriculum development project, it usually becomes known by the name of one person or institution. It seemed appropriate to develop this case study of a curriculum development around the work of Jerome S. Bruner. Until September 1972 Bruner was associated with Harvard University's Center for Cognitive Studies. He then settled into a new position as professor of psychology at Oxford University.

'The Process of Education' (1960), which Bruner wrote, summed up the thoughts of subject-oriented academics and psychologists on what to teach and when and how to teach it. In his book, Bruner asserted that the foundation of any subject could be taught honestly to anybody at any age in *some* form. Immediately after 'The Process of Education' (now translated into more than 20 languages) reached the professional education community, it became the subject of study, discussion, and criticism that persisted into the next decade. Shortly after its publication, Bruner took a year's leave of absence from Harvard. Trading the laboratory for the classroom, he worked with 10-, 11-, and 12-year-olds to test his research and theories. It was at this time that Bruner set an intellectual framework with three powerful questions for the social sciences curriculum, "Man: A Course of Study":

What makes man human?
How did he get that way?
How can he be more so?

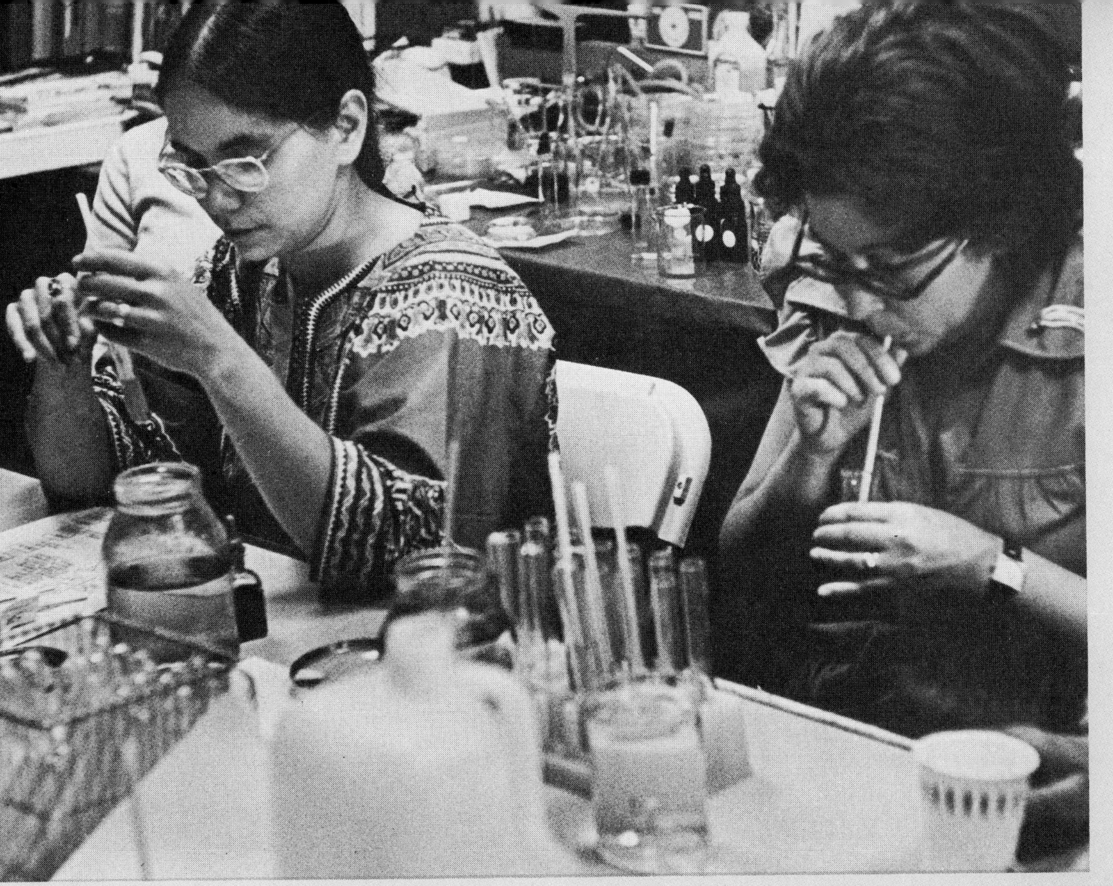

COMMUNITY RESOURCES INSTITUTE OF THE CITY UNIVERSITY OF NEW YORK

The Community Resources Institute of the City University of New York runs special workshops for teachers and paraprofessionals, to equip them for working with children in open classrooms.

The curriculum development stages and the production of materials for "Man: A Course of Study" were made possible under grants from the National Science Foundation to the Education Development Center. The pursuit of a curriculum with anthropology as its core involved the work and talents of numerous professional educators, film makers, artists, and scholars. The student materials were created from ethnographic films and field research previously included in the studies of college and graduate students. Much of the data represented the most recent findings in anthropology. Fundamental questions about the nature of man were introduced by way of animal contrasts. The core of the animal studies in the curriculum was the ethnographic film studies by scientists Konrad Z. Lorenz and Nikolaas Tinbergen on the behavior patterns of herring gulls and the study of free-ranging baboons.

The film studies were based on the field research of Sherwood Washburn and Irven DeVore. Drawing from the writings of the famous explorer Knud Rasmussen and film-based ethnographic studies of the Netsilik Eskimos conducted by Asen Balikci, the curriculum enabled the learners to investigate the concept of culture. By the end of such a study, students and teachers developed a vocabulary for thinking about the distinctiveness of man with increased sensitivity to the common humanity that all cultures share.

"Man: A Course of Study" was being introduced into 4,000 upper elementary, middle, and secondary schools in the early 1970's by Curriculum Development Associates (CDA) of Washington, D.C. The CDA had experimented with a variety of "professional diffusion models" that made teacher education a prerequisite for implementing the new curriculum. Interdisciplinary teams of educators and social science scholars were introducing "Man: A Course of Study" into schools and university curricula and were teaching courses in the U.S., Canada, England, Australia, and New Zealand. As each educator or anthropologist put "Man: A Course of Study" on the professional agenda, each brought to it new ways of developing and enhancing teacher education and the intellectual substance of the course. Thus, a model curriculum development that had a design, a structure, and scholarship behind it became an unfinished curriculum. It enabled other scholars, teachers, parents, and students to spin off ideas from the model, fostering inquiry, interaction, and independence in learning without destroying the integrity of the scholarship or initial curriculum design.

A Challenge to Creativity

A curriculum—if it is in fact a curriculum—must have a *design* that can be described, analyzed, and tested. Although clarity of design is essential, if a curriculum is to contribute to teacher development the design must also be sufficiently open-end so that teachers can adapt the materials to their styles of teaching and to their students' styles of learning. The process of examining and testing a clear and identifiable curriculum design with teachers enables them to understand it well enough to have a sense of control over the materials. It empowers them to adapt, modify, and go beyond the original structure. This is the paradox of the unfinished curriculum: because it has a finite clarity, it creates conditions for infinite modification.

The Need for Continuing Support

The crisis in our schools has little to do with curriculum per se, but the schools have had to become crisis-oriented. The real crisis has been with our value system, urban living, the war in Vietnam, and our coming face-to-face with racial issues. The politics of education is crisis-oriented in our country; this creates confusion in the schools about what should be taught or indeed what the nature of schooling or deschooling should be. (Extreme advocates of deschooling would abolish formal schooling and compulsory education.)

The nature of our culture is crisis-oriented on the one hand; on the other hand it honors great diversity. We need to place greater value on creating diverse models of unfinished curricula that continue to demand scholarship and competence and that cherish uniqueness on the part of the teacher, the learner, and the community. Schools must exist in some form to transmit the culture of our highly technological society; no other institution exists to provide this function. The 1970's must continue to foster curriculum development. Yet, the present danger—noted by many experts—is that curriculum developments will lose large-scale support as government and foundations shift funding to crisis issues instead of supporting both with equal vigor. In fact, it might be predicted that if curriculum developments are not supported, those who have advocated the deschooling movement will find it has happened without the drastic measures they proposed. We should be ushering in more sophisticated ideas and models of preschool curricula, for example, because the need has been established.

The idea of introducing innovative curricula to three school levels simultaneously needs study and new curriculum developments. This effort could overcome a persisting educational problem that has heretofore brought new information to only a small segment of school learners. In the 1960's an entire generation of students might have continued with old or traditional "stuff" in the curriculum if they had advanced beyond the grade where a new course was introduced. Some students waited six years or more before they encountered new material. Grade-level designations and outmoded procedures forced educators to update the curriculum a grade at a time. A new curriculum model could create approaches to presenting recent findings and intellectual advances to a total school community.

Around the world, educators have studied with great admiration the curriculum developments that were created in the U.S. in the 1960's. It is a political reality that federal support to education was responsible in many ways for fostering the inventive developments. Thus, the politics of education may also create a regressive period that could relegate curriculum reform to the historical annals of education. Hope lies in the possibility that the community and educators will join forces to understand what the curriculum has been and what it should become.

Open classrooms are organized into areas, or learning centers. Each area contains special materials, equipment, and books to help children explore their interests.

COMMUNITY RESOURCES INSTITUTE OF THE CITY UNIVERSITY OF NEW YORK

(*continued from page 233*)
tem was charged with violating the 1964 Civil Rights Act. This was the first action taken by the U.S. Department of Health, Education, and Welfare (HEW) against a major school district outside the South and was interpreted as a possible model for similar charges against other cities in the North and West. At issue were federal funds of $12 million to $15 million. Though avoiding charges of deliberate school segregation against the school committee, HEW officials claimed segregation resulted from committee policy, the effects of which the committee should have foreseen and prevented. State officials, however, declared that the Boston School Committee discriminated deliberately.

Forces across the U.S. both for and against busing referred often to "quality education" as the real issue. One side said that it favored busing as an aid to quality education; the other side said that it too wanted quality education but busing would not help achieve it. The antibusing viewpoint was buttressed in mid-1972 by a study of the effects of busing blacks in five Northern cities, conducted by a Harvard University professor. He concluded that busing had not resulted in a raising of the students' academic standing, nor had it improved race relations, the students' self-esteem, or their aspiration level. However, a group of university professors rejected these findings, issuing a detailed report based on the same data that pointed to positive results of the busing.

Financing the Schools

Although no clear solution to school fiscal problems surfaced in 1972, there was a definite turning toward state financing of education as the thrust of the future. Just how states could and should manage this was a matter of major attention from coast to coast. The governor of Michigan proposed a state income tax to produce the necessary revenue. The governor of New Jersey advocated a combination of income tax and statewide property tax. Officials in other states studied a variety of means to replace reliance on the local property tax as the principal source of school funds. There was growing awareness of the burden of the property tax, as well as the unlikelihood of obtaining substantially larger sums from that source.

It was thought that the decisive factor in the search for state revenues for education would prove to be the Serrano decision of the California Supreme Court in 1971. The court had ruled that children in a poor district were entitled to as good an education as children in a more affluent district. Other cases moving through the courts in 1972, including a key one brought against the schools of San Antonio, Tex., appeared certain to strengthen the principle enunciated in the Serrano case.

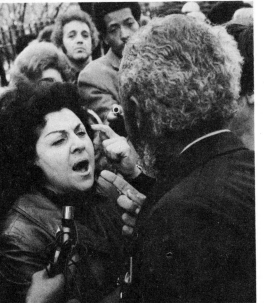

Parents argue outside a Canarsie junior high school, where white parent protest kept minority children from entering the school.

WIDE WORLD

Other Developments

As the role of the states in education grew larger, a desire developed in various parts of the country for measurable results of the effectiveness of schooling. This movement toward accountability was evident in several states, where "models" were being worked out to be applied locally. Statewide tests were fashioned along the lines of those used in the national assessment being conducted over a period of years by the Education Commission of the States, to check pupils' present standings and pinpoint their progress.

Side by side with the effort to cut costs were new programs and other needs that seemed essential to educators. In New York City 450 security guards were assigned to high schools and selected junior high schools. Also in New York, a stepped-up bilingual curriculum was designed to aid the 250,000 Puerto Rican youngsters in the city schools, of whom about 50,000 spoke little or no English. New efforts to deal with the problems of Spanish-speaking children in Massachusetts began in the fall under a state law requiring instruction by a bilingual teacher when a certain number of Spanish-speaking youngsters were enrolled.

On the federal level a Right to Read program was launched with the awarding of $4 million to 68 school districts for developing approaches to reading and serving as demonstration centers. Federal aid was promised to parochial schools by President Nixon to sustain them in a time of financial crisis. The principal avenue for aid appeared to be legislation granting tax credit to parents for a portion of private and church-related school tuition. Several bills were introduced in the U.S. Congress to grant credits up to several hundred dollars per child. (*See also* Colleges and Universities. *See in* CE. Education.)

GAMMA

After expelling Soviet experts from Egypt, President Anwar el-Sadat speaks before his party congress in July explaining his political objectives.

EGYPT. Affairs in Egypt during 1972 were marked by a major change in the country's relations with the Soviet Union, the reordering of domestic priorities, and a policy of "no peace, no war" with Israel. As the year began there was mounting criticism within Egypt of the lack of preparedness for war. Economists and others called for a reduction in consumer spending, which had been rising in recent years, and for a diversion of resources from consumer production to industrial expansion. In a speech on January 13 President Anwar el-Sadat urged the Egyptian people to make sacrifices for war. Also, he disclosed that he had ordered a military attack on Israeli forces in December 1971 but had been forced to cancel it when the Soviet Union, Egypt's ally, became involved in the Indian-Pakistani war.

Sadat's speech touched off a series of demonstrations by university students, who demanded an unequivocal commitment to war with Israel, military training for students, increased taxation of the middle class, and economic reprisals against the U.S. for its support of Israel. These were the first major demonstrations by students against the government in three years.

On January 16 Sadat appointed a new prime minister, Aziz Sidky, who almost immediately submitted to the People's Assembly an austerity program based on economic mobilization for a total confrontation with Israel. The program included a 50% increase in customs duties on imported luxuries, increased property taxes, a ban on the importation of many consumer items, and the restriction of wholesale trade in basic commodities to state-owned companies. The new government also announced a 10% cut in investments for 1971–72, a reduction in expenditures to help the war effort, and an expanded program of military training for students.

The Sidky program fell short of student demands, however. In spite of a ban on demonstrations, students launched sit-ins at Cairo and Ein Shams universities and rioted in downtown Cairo, the capital. Some 1,000 students were arrested. Sadat refused to bow to student pressure and explained that even though war with Israel was inevitable, preparations had to be made first.

Egyptian-Soviet Relations

In February and in April President Sadat visited the Soviet Union, obtaining Soviet pledges for increased military aid and an implied approval of his intention to regain Israeli-occupied lands by force if other means failed. However, during the spring there were indications of growing strains in Egyptian-Soviet relations. Diplomatic efforts to settle Middle East problems appeared to be held in abeyance pending U.S. President Richard M.

Nixon's visit to Moscow in May. There was growing criticism of the Soviet Union within Egypt, including articles in the press pointing out that while the Soviets and others benefited from the "no peace, no war" situation, Egypt did not. In a secret memorandum to Sadat, high-ranking Egyptian military officers complained of dependence on the Soviets and demanded more freedom from Soviet military advisers.

On July 18 Sadat astounded the Egyptians, the Soviets, and the world by announcing that he had ordered the withdrawal of Soviet military advisers and personnel from Egypt. He also declared that all military installations and equipment set up in Egypt after the 1967 Arab-Israeli war would become Egyptian property under Egyptian administration. He emphasized, however, that the Soviet-Egyptian friendship treaty of 1971 was still in effect and asked for a Soviet-Egyptian meeting on future relations. In his speech announcing the withdrawal, and in subsequent statements, Sadat declared that he had repeatedly asked the Soviets to make good on their promise to deliver advanced offensive weapons. It was hoped these weapons would enable Egypt to recover its territory from Israel by force or to negotiate from strength. Failure of the Soviets to honor the commitment led him to review the Egyptian position. Also influencing his decision on the ouster were the Soviet-U.S. summit meetings in May—which Egyptians believed had resulted in a secret agreement to avoid war in the Middle East—and Soviet attempts to impose conditions on the use of Soviet equipment in Egypt. The Soviet Union complied promptly with the withdrawal order; by October some 20,000 Soviet military personnel and their dependents had been evacuated, and only 300 military instructors remained in Egypt. Soviet warships continued to use Egyptian ports on the Mediterranean Sea.

By early September Egyptian-Soviet relations had worsened, with each country carrying on campaigns against the other in the press. To prevent a complete break in relations, mediation efforts were undertaken by President Hafez al-Assad of Syria, who succeeded in arranging for Prime Minister Sidky to visit Moscow in October for the first high-level Soviet-Egyptian talks since the Soviet withdrawal. Sidky returned from the talks with a Soviet pledge to resume deliveries of spare parts and replacements for military equipment left behind in Egypt and with Soviet acceptance in principle of a visit to Cairo by Russian leaders. Subsequently the Soviets agreed to restore to Egypt's air defense system the SAM-6 (surface-to-air) missiles they had removed during the withdrawal. In an unusual action late in October, President Sadat put the future of Soviet-Egyptian cooperation up to a meeting of party and parliamentary representatives, editors, and leading members of the government. He received approval for a policy of guarded cooperation with the U.S.S.R., so long as there would be no reversion to the previous situation of Egyptian dependence upon the Russians.

Relations with Arab States and the West

Egypt's expulsion of the Soviets was favored by Libya's leader, Col. Muammar el-Qaddafi, who had been seeking a union of Egypt and Libya. President Sadat's disillusionment with the Soviets contributed to his willingness to pursue the merger. After a series of meetings between the two leaders it was announced on August 2 that Egypt and Libya would work toward a complete union by September 1973. During further talks Sadat and Qaddafi agreed that the union's capital would be Cairo, that it would have a single president elected by popular vote, and that there would be a single political party. Other Arab nations would be free to join the union.

Relations between Egypt and its other neighbors Jordan and Sudan deteriorated during 1972. Egypt broke diplomatic relations with Jordan in April after King Hussein I of Jordan disclosed a plan for an eventual federation of Jordan's east- and west-bank regions. Sadat was angered because Hussein's plan accepted, by implication, Israeli occupation of the west bank. (*See* Jordan.) This was the first time President Sadat had deviated from his policy of maintaining ties with all other Arab regimes. Egyptians feared that the plan would result in a separate peace between Israel and Jordan and would weaken Egypt's strategic position.

Egyptian-Sudanese relations grew steadily worse following Sudan's renewal of relations with the U.S. In the fall Sudan asked for the recall of some 200 Egyptian teachers at the Khartoum branch of Cairo University. Sudan also closed the Khartoum offices of two major Egyptian trading companies and withdrew some of its forces from the Suez Canal front.

During the year Egyptian criticism of the U.S. continued unabated, and President Sadat rejected once more a U.S. proposal for an interim agree-

E. A. HARRIS—CANADA FROM BEN ROTH AGENCY

UPI COMPIX

Soviet Defense Minister Andrei Grechko (left) is greeted by Gen. Mohammed Sadek upon arriving for a four-day official visit to Egypt in May.

ment on the Suez Canal issue. Following his ouster of the Soviets, Sadat launched a campaign for political, economic, and military support in Western Europe. The campaign received a serious setback in September when Palestinian guerrillas massacred 11 members of the Israeli Olympic team in Munich, West Germany. Egyptian–West German relations, which had been reestablished in June, were particularly affected. In the interests of the campaign, Egypt refrained from responding militarily to Israeli reprisals against the guerrillas. In September Sadat offered to recognize a Palestinian government in exile, to be based in Cairo, but he was turned down by the guerrillas.

Internal Affairs

A major step toward establishing civil liberties in Egypt was taken by the government in October when it abolished the long-standing practice of arbitrarily seizing citizens' property by administrative order. The government also decreed that all cases involving property seizure since 1964 would be reviewed by a 3-man court and a jury of 12 laymen; this would be the first time in Egyptian history that a jury system would be used. Although property seizures made before 1964 were not to be reviewed, since they were considered part of the revolution led by the late President Gamal Abdel Nasser, compensation for such seizures was increased under the new decrees.

Beginning in the summer Egypt experienced several outbreaks of violence between Muslims and members of the Coptic Christian church. Sadat blamed the incidents on provocation by outside influences.

During the year the Sidky government continued to work toward economic development, and considerable progress was made in heavy industry. There was also a marked recovery in Egyptian tourism. (*See in* CE: Egypt.)

In January, for the first time, the red, white, and black flag of the new Federation of Arab Republics was raised in a ceremony outside the Abedeen Republican Palace in Cairo. Similar ceremonies were carried out in Libya and Syria, the two other federation members.

UPI COMPIX

ELECTIONS. U.S. President Richard M. Nixon was reelected on Nov. 7, 1972, by a historic landslide. Its ranking depended on the measure used, but it was clearly among the three greatest in the 20th century. The president received 47,042,923 votes—more than any other candidate in U.S. history. He received 60.7% of the popular vote, approximately the same percentage cast for President Franklin D. Roosevelt in 1936 and slightly under the 61.1% for President Lyndon B. Johnson in 1964. He captured the electoral votes of all the states except Massachusetts. With the additional loss of the electoral votes of the District of Columbia, Nixon won a total of 520 of a possible 538. Johnson won 486 of a possible 538; Roosevelt lost Maine and Vermont but won 523 of a possible 531.

Clearly, President Nixon won a greater electoral victory than any other Republican in history. The only one who approached it was Warren G. Harding in the election of 1920. Harding received 60.3% of the popular vote and 404 of 531 electoral votes. Quite as clearly, Senator George S. McGovern suffered the greatest political defeat of any Democratic candidate for president in U.S. history.

Voter turnout for the 1972 elections—about 55% of those eligible to vote—was the smallest proportion since 1948. In some cases, voters seemed to stay away from the polls to register a "no" vote on both candidates. In other instances, indications of a landslide, especially the results of the public opinion polls, may have convinced citizens that their votes would make no difference.

First-time voters, 18 to 21 years old, appeared to have participated in the balloting to a lesser degree than their elders. About 47% voted, according to one analysis. This followed the pattern of past elections, in which the percentage turnout of younger voters had been significantly lower than the turnout of their elders.

Strategies and Outcomes

During the campaign, the president remained a fairly inactive candidate. Frequently, those campaign trips he did schedule were to normally Republican areas. They seemed designed more to get out the Republican vote than to persuade the doubtful. The bulk of the campaign fell to "surrogates": members of the president's family, the Cabinet, and especially to Vice-President Spiro T. Agnew. The president was in a position to rely on his record and thus avoid concrete pledges, in most cases. Intense diplomatic activity for a truce in Vietnam during the last days of the campaign pointed up his position on foreign affairs; his running feud with the U.S. Congress over government spending symbolized his stance on domestic issues.

McGovern and his vice-presidential nominee, R. Sargent Shriver, crisscrossed the country during the campaign. They hit tirelessly at the issues of the war, taxes, unemployment, inflation, and ethics in government and politics—especially the investigation of spying on Democratic headquarters by persons connected with the Republican campaign organization. The Democratic strategy called for carrying the major industrial states.

GENE FORTE FROM PICTORIAL PARADE

U.S. President Richard M. Nixon (right) and Vice-President Spiro T. Agnew smile after winning a landslide victory in November.

The Democrats hoped to hold blue-collar, ethnic, and black voters and to attract enough new voters, women, and liberal, well-educated suburbanites to form a new majority. The Republicans hoped to form a new coalition of blue-collar workers and ethnic and Jewish voters joined with voters from traditionally Republican areas and the pro-Nixon South.

Surveys showed that about one third of the Democrats who went to the polls voted for President Nixon. Blue-collar workers switched from 5-to-4 Democratic to 5-to-4 Republican in the presidential contest. The president increased his black and Jewish votes over his showing in 1968. Nixon captured more than half the Roman Catholic vote, which overlaps the ethnic vote in many instances.

Democrats Control Congress

Future students of U.S. history may find another facet of the 1972 elections almost as remarkable as President Nixon's landslide victory. Despite the Republican sweep in the presidential contest, Congress remained solidly Democratic. The Republicans suffered a net loss of two seats in the Senate.

PAUL SEQUEIRA

A group of nuns, enthusiastic supporters of Senator George S. McGovern's presidential campaign, join some exuberant young people at a neighborhood rally in Chicago.

In the House, Democrats lost 12 seats to make the new balance 242 Democrats, 192 Republicans, and one independent. The effect of the Republican gain in the House was diluted by the fact that five of the seats they gained were taken from Southern conservative Democrats, who frequently voted with the Nixon Administration.

The Democrats took six Senate seats formerly held by Republicans. Republicans took four from Democrats. Twenty incumbent senators were re-elected, and three new senators were to succeed senators of their own parties.

Joseph R. Biden, Jr., almost a political unknown before the campaign, was elected to the Senate from Delaware two weeks before his 30th birthday. He thus became the youngest person to qualify as a senator at the start of a new Congress. Biden, a lawyer serving his first term as a New Castle County councilman, ran on the Democratic ticket against incumbent **J. Caleb Boggs,** 63, a heavy favorite. Biden asked for a quick end to the war in Vietnam, legislation to protect wetlands, tax reform, morality in government, and consumer protection.

Other Democratic winners in the Senate were:

Rep. William D. Hathaway, 48, scored an upset victory over **Margaret Chase Smith,** 74 (Me.), a senator for 32 years. Candidates' ages clearly mattered. Hathaway, a liberal, avoided direct mention of Mrs. Smith's age but stressed his own.

Dick Clark, a former college professor, national debating champion, and assistant to Rep. John C. Culver (D., Iowa), defeated **Senator Jack Miller.** Clark followed a pattern set by Daniel Walker before the Illinois Democratic primary for governor. He walked the length and breadth of Iowa, talking to people.

Rep. James Abourezk, a Rapid City attorney, was elected to fill the seat of **Senator Karl E. Mundt**

Senator McGovern originally chose Missouri Senator Thomas F. Eagleton as his running mate.

WIDE WORLD

(S.D.), who retired because of ill health. Abourezk, a first-term congressman, stressed his efforts in Congress to protect family farms.

Floyd K. Haskell, a Colorado state senator, defeated incumbent **Senator Gordon Allott,** chairman of the Republican Policy Committee. Haskell was a Republican who changed parties in reaction to Nixon's decision to invade Cambodia in 1970.

Walter D. Huddleston, a radio executive and state senate majority leader, took the Kentucky seat vacated by **Senator John Sherman Cooper** (R). He defeated former **Gov. Louie B. Nunn.**

Sam Nunn, 34, a farmer, lawyer, and state legislator, was elected to succeed **Senator David H. Gambrell** (Ga.). He had defeated Gambrell in the Georgia Democratic primary earlier in 1972.

J. Bennett Johnston, Jr., 40, a Shreveport lawyer and former state senator, won over two major opponents, **Benjamin C. Toledano** and former **Gov. John J. McKeithen,** in Louisiana. Johnston was a candidate in the Democratic primary against **Senator Allen J. Ellender.** Ellender died before the primary balloting.

The following Republican senators were elected:

Dewey F. Bartlett, 53, an oilman and former governor, was elected to succeed **Senator Fred Harris** (Okla.), who did not run for reelection.

Jesse A. Helms, a conservative Republican who in the past had denounced social security and rural electrification, took the seat formerly held by **Senator B. Everett Jordan** (N.C.). Helms's only previous office was as a Raleigh, N.C., city councilman.

Pete V. Domenici, 40, an Albuquerque lawyer, took the seat vacated by **Clinton P. Anderson** (N.M.). Domenici had lost a gubernatorial race.

Rep. William Lloyd Scott, a three-term congressman, defeated **Senator William B. Spong, Jr.** (Va.). Scott, a 57-year-old conservative, made McGovern's presidential candidacy a major issue.

Rep. James A. McClure, 47, a conservative, survived a hard-fought Idaho primary and went on to win the seat of retiring **Senator Len B. Jordan.** Like Scott, McClure stressed unpopular Democratic positions.

The Congressional Black Caucus was strengthened by the election of three more black representatives: the Rev. Andrew Young (D, Ga.), Yvonne Brathwaite Burke (D, Calif.), and Barbara Jordan (D, Tex.). Young was an aide to the late Rev. Martin Luther King, Jr., in the Southern Christian Leadership Conference. His district included much of Atlanta plus several affluent, largely white suburbs. Representative Burke, of Los Angeles, was vice-chairman of the Democratic National Convention. Representative Jordan, of Houston, was president pro tempore of the Texas Senate.

The 13 black incumbents were all reelected. All were Democrats. They included William Clay (Mo)., George Collins (Ill.), John Conyers, Jr. (Mich.), Ronald V. Dellums (Calif.), Charles C. Diggs (Mich.), Shirley Chisholm (N.Y.), Walter E. Fauntroy (D.C.), Augustus F. Hawkins (Calif.), Ralph Metcalfe (Ill.), Parren Mitchell (Md.), Robert N. C. Nix (Pa.), Charles Rangel (N.Y.), and Louis Stokes (Ohio). Collins was later killed in a plane crash.

UPI COMPIX

Democratic vice-presidential candidate R. Sargent Shriver greets University of Houston students during a campaign stop in Texas.

Five women won seats in Congress. Nine others were reelected. Incumbent congresswoman Louise Day Hicks (D, Mass.) was defeated by John J. Moakley, a former Democrat who ran as an independent. Besides Representatives Burke and Jordan, women elected to Congress for the first time were Marjorie Holt (R, Md.), Patricia Schroeder (D, Colo.), and Elizabeth Holtzman (D, N.Y.), who defeated Emanuel Celler in a primary.

The nine congresswomen reelected were Ella T. Grasso (D, Conn.), Patsy T. Mink (D, Hawaii), Bella Abzug (D, N.Y.), Leonor K. Sullivan (D, Mo.), Margaret M. Heckler (R, Mass.), Edith Green (D, Ore.), Julia B. Hansen (D, Wash.), Martha W. Griffiths (D, Mich.), and Mrs. Chisholm.

Two men who were missing and later presumed dead were reelected. House majority leader Hale Boggs (D, La.) and Rep. Nick Begich (D), Alaska's only representative in the House, were lost when their light plane disappeared on a campaign flight from Anchorage to Juneau, Alaska. An intensive air search failed to locate the plane.

State Contests

A series of changes in state houses brought the Democrats a net gain of one more governorship. The new total was 31 Democrats, 19 Republicans.

Daniel Walker, a Chicago lawyer who walked the state and battled Chicago Mayor Richard J. Daley's Democratic organization to win in the primary, went on to defeat Gov. Richard B. Ogilvie (R, Ill.).

UPI COMPIX

Crippled in an attempt on his life, Alabama Gov. George C. Wallace speaks from his wheelchair at the Democratic National Convention.

Ogilvie was hurt by his advocacy of the state income tax passed during his administration.

Thomas P. Salmon, former Democratic leader of the Vermont House, succeeded Republican Gov. Deane C. David, who was not a candidate. Sherman W. Tribbitt, an old-guard Democrat, defeated incumbent Gov. Russell W. Peterson of Delaware, who, like Ogilvie, had pushed through tax increases. In Missouri, state Auditor Christopher S. Bond, 33, ended a long period of Democratic rule. He attacked cronyism and the spoils system.

North Carolina elected its first Republican governor since the beginning of the 20th century, James E. Holshouser, Jr. Lieut. Gov. Thomas L. Judge, a Democrat, won in Montana with a program that advocated expansion of state services. In Washington, Gov. Daniel J. Evans (R), was re-elected on a platform that called for more spending for mass transit and pollution control. In Texas, reform Democrat Dolph Briscoe won on an anti-corruption campaign. In West Virginia, Republican Gov. Arch A. Moore, Jr., defeated Secretary of State John D. Rockefeller IV, who had been considered as a prospect for national Democratic leadership. In Indiana, Dr. Otis R. Bowen, a physician, was elected on the Republican ticket. Gov. Robert D. Ray (R) won a third term in Iowa.

Trends in Referendum Results

In addition to voting for candidates, citizens of some states voted directly on a variety of issues through referenda. Voters rejected property tax freezes that would limit the amount of funds available for education. They approved measures for improvement of the environment but defeated proposals for sharp social change.

Californians defeated a proposal that would have cut property taxes by $3.2 billion and shifted the burden of school support to the state. Michigan rejected a proposal to reduce the reliance of school districts on the property tax. It also voted against a graduated state income tax, as did Massachusetts. Colorado rejected a proposal to allow use of school district property taxes only for retiring bonds, and Oregon voted against a ban on the property tax for school support. California voters endorsed a proposal to curb busing for school desegregation. Maryland defeated a proposal for aid to private and parochial schools through tuition grants to parents.

Colorado voted to ban the use of public funds for the 1976 Winter Olympics. The principal issue was cost; a strong secondary issue was fear that runaway growth would follow. In New Jersey, a $650-million transportation bond was defeated partly through environmentalists' arguments that it favored road building at the expense of mass transit. In New York, voters authorized $1.15 billion for projects for clean air and water. Florida voted $240 million to buy endangered recreation lands. Massachusetts and North Carolina passed measures making environmental protection a state duty.

Californians approved restoration of the death penalty in cases of treason, train wrecking, murdering a prison guard while serving a life sentence, or committing perjury in a case involving the death penalty. The measure was drafted to meet U.S. Supreme Court objections to laws imposing the death penalty. A court test seemed certain.

Liberalized rules on abortion were defeated in Michigan and North Dakota. Also voted down was a proposal in California to legalize the growing, processing, or transport of marijuana for personal use by persons over 18.

California assemblywoman Yvonne Brathwaite Burke became the first black woman elected to the U.S. Congress in the state's history.

WIDE WORLD

ELECTRONICS. The electronics industry continued in 1972 to shift its emphasis away from military systems and toward more commercial and consumer uses. To put the price of the equipment within the budgets of businesses and home users, makers of electronic products reduced their own costs by automating manufacturing processes and by redesigning previously expensive equipment.

One product that showed the effect of increased sales and production was the electronic calculator for home use. Some were selling for less than $75, significantly meeting the 1971 goal of reducing prices to below $100. Calculators also were one area in which U.S. firms were able—because of rapid advances in the development of semiconductor devices—to reestablish themselves in the face of foreign competition.

The inexpensive new minicalculators intended for home use could display only the numerical results, but many business users of slightly higher-priced calculators—those selling in the $200 range—wanted permanent records of the results of the calculations. To meet this need, and still keep the overall calculator price low and the size small, semiconductor firms developed thermal printers that actually burned the image of the numeral into special paper. The advantage of the thermal printer over completely mechanical types was that it was smaller and lighter in weight, while being almost noiseless and more reliable.

Another area that suddenly grew up in 1972 was that of computer input-output terminals for use in department stores and supermarkets. With the terminal, the salesclerk could not only total up a purchase, as with a standard cash register, but also send information to a central computer to keep track of the goods sold and maintain up-to-date inventory records. On charge account purchases, the clerk could find out from records stored in the computer whether the customer's account was in order; the computer then could revise the account to show the new balance.

It was also a big year for electronics in sports. Events at the summer Olympic Games in Munich, West Germany, were timed and distances were measured with electronic equipment. Finishes were recorded with electronically controlled cameras and the familiar tape at the end of the track was replaced with an infrared beam that was interrupted by the winner. Swimmers touched pressure plates at the ends of the lanes to stop the clock and indicate the winning time. The swimmers also were checked for false starts by weight-sensing switches in the takeoff platform.

Four-channel audio units increased their sales during 1972, but the lack of standardization in the recording method continued to be a point of contention among manufacturers. Tape players simply were made with four separate channels, but long-playing discs were made with two methods of carrying four-channel information—the "discrete" method and the "matrix" method. Manufacturers were making amplifiers and tuners that would be able to handle any of the recording methods.

COURTESY, CARTRIDGE TELEVISION INC.

Cartridge television is a system that allows a viewer to tape television broadcasts, view prerecorded cartridges, or just watch TV.

Despite technical and economic barriers, the first video recording system for home use became available in 1972. The system, called Cartrivision, retailed for about $1,600; it included a 25-inch television set and a video tape unit. (*See in* CE: Electrons and Electronics.)

EL SALVADOR. Presidential politics dominated events in El Salvador during 1972. Gen. Fidel Sánchez Hernández, president since 1967, was constitutionally banned from succeeding himself. In the February 20 election, four candidates vied for his office. The winner, Col. Arturo Armando Molina of the incumbent National Conciliation party, defeated his nearest opponent by a slim—and disputed—margin. Because Molina failed to gain a majority of the popular vote, the decision on who was to become the new president rested with the Legislative Assembly. That body met on February 25 and proclaimed Molina the next president.

Amid accusations of election fraud, there were several outbreaks of violence. In March an abortive coup by rebel army troops resulted in more than 100 deaths of military personnel and civilians and left some 200 persons wounded. In the wake of this uprising the assembly imposed a two-month state of siege.

Colonel Molina began his five-year presidential term on July 1. His first major action in office was to order troops to occupy and close the National University, in an attempt to purge left-wing influences. (*See in* CE: Salvador, El.)

EMPLOYMENT. If one economic indicator could be singled out that would spoil the overall economic resurgence of 1972, it would be employment statistics. In a year when the economy generally seemed to be blooming, unemployment never dropped below 5.2% of the work force. The number of people who were employed reached the highest level in history—but so did U.S. population figures. Unemployment stubbornly refused to decrease. U.S. President Richard M. Nixon characterized it in January as "the one great problem remaining" on the road to economic stabilization.

When Nixon presented his $246.3-billion budget for fiscal 1973 in January, he predicated it on what he termed full employment—a maximum unemployment level of 4% or lower. He considered the reduction of unemployment to that level one of his most important goals for 1972; but by the fall it was obvious that the magic number would not be achieved. In March and April unemployment was 5.9%; April figures also showed that 56 U.S. cities had unemployment rates of 6% or more. Seattle, Wash., depressed for several years by severe cutbacks in aerospace contracts, had the highest rate: 13.7%. By September unemployment had dropped to 5.5%; it stood at 5.2% in November. The Nixon Administration took some comfort in the fact that unemployment had been at about 6% for the 18 months before June; but the goal of 4% still seemed hopelessly out of reach.

There were some bright spots, however. The steel industry had suffered massive unemployment in 1971 after customers stockpiled huge inventories in anticipation of a strike that never happened, but it began to recover somewhat in 1972. Gary, Ind., a city that depends on steel for a majority of its population's jobs, was facing a staggering 41% unemployment rate in December 1971; by the spring of 1972 that figure had dropped considerably and the steel mills were hiring again. The auto industry, in the midst of a boom year, had a slight increase in hiring, although many auto workers were unhappy about higher production quotas. In September the number of people employed in the U.S. rose to a record high of 82.2 million. In addition, for the first time in three years, graduating college students found a slightly more receptive job market.

The bleakest situation continued to exist among minority groups and young veterans. Unemployment among veterans aged 20–29 was 6.6% in September; it had been as high as 8.6% earlier. In the cities, the unemployment rate was higher, particularly for black veterans; in New York City during the year it reached a depressing 23%. In an effort to aid the veterans, a number of local governments, in conjunction with businessmen, arranged to hold "job fairs" where prospective employers gathered to discuss jobs with unemployed veterans. At the job fair held in Chicago in May, violence broke out when angry young veterans, claiming the employers were "not serious" about offering jobs, broke up many booths and then

The jobless formed long lines to collect their unemployment checks in Seattle.

DOUG WILSON FROM BLACK STAR

HOWARD SIMMONS FROM THE "CHICAGO SUN-TIMES"

Angry veterans hold a protest march after disrupting a veterans' job fair in Chicago in May. They accused the employers at the fair of not being serious about hiring veterans.

marched away from the fair. The fair closed and reopened the next day, but a number of employers and veterans chose not to return. Secretary of Labor James D. Hodgson announced in May that 25% of the new jobs created in the U.S. in 1971 had gone to Vietnam veterans but recognized that the problem was far from solved. He attributed much of the difficulty to the large numbers of men returning to civilian life—more than 3 million between 1969 and 1971.

Another disturbing problem began to surface in 1972: "underemployment," or the fact that millions of people in the U.S., although working full-time, were still unable to maintain a comfortable living standard. The federal government considered an income of $4,000 a year for a family of four to be the poverty level; however, in many cities a family required more than $7,000 to live on a level higher than poverty. If the $7,000 figure were used, six of every ten workers in the inner city could not maintain a standard of living above the poverty level. (*See also* Economy; Labor Unions.)

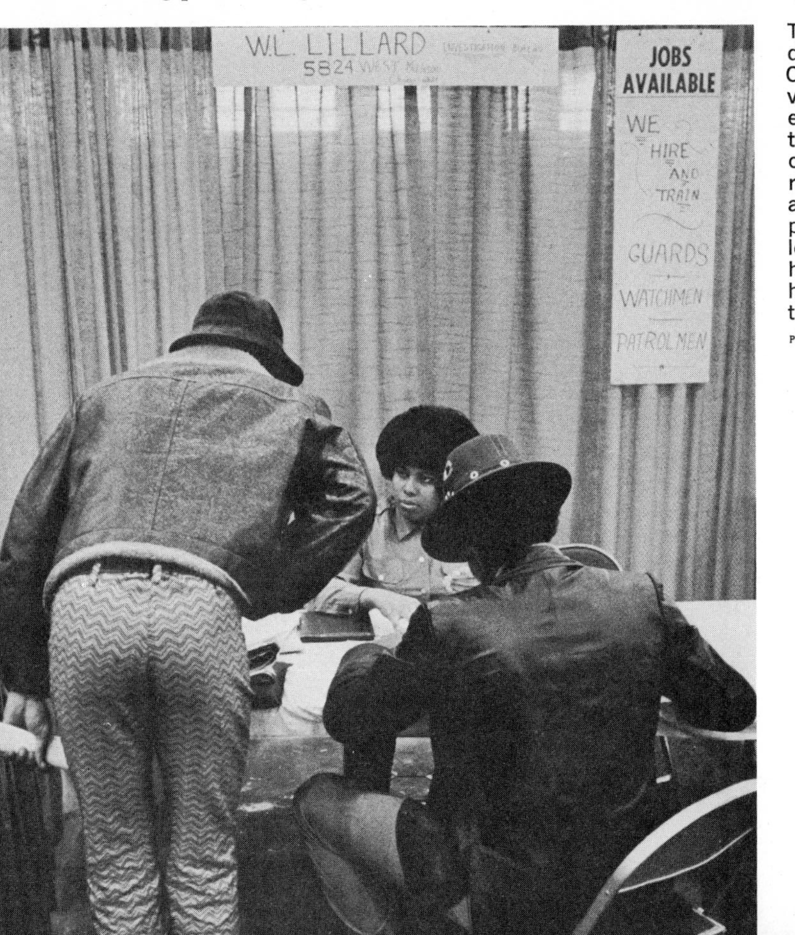

The day after the disruptions at the Chicago job fair, many veterans and some employers returned to discuss job opportunities. The high rate of unemployment among young veterans, particularly blacks, had led businessmen to hold the fair in the hope of alleviating the problem.

PAUL SEQUEIRA

ENGINEERING PROJECTS. The prospect grew in 1972 for shortening distances between population centers and meeting the needs for power and water. Major engineering projects that would serve these purposes were progressing or completed during the year.

BRIDGES

The Federal Highway Administration reported in 1972 that 89,000, or nearly one sixth, of the bridges in the U.S. were critically deficient. However, only certain elements of the bridges were unsafe, not whole structures. The report said that 400,000 of the country's bridges were built before 1935. A bridge replacement program was begun.

The largest suspension bridge in Asia (center span 2,336 feet) was completed in 1972. It spans the Kammon Straits between Honshu and Kyushu, Japan. A smaller suspension bridge came into service in the U.S.—the Dent Bridge over the Clearwater River in Idaho. Like the Japanese bridge, it has prefabricated cables.

Cable-stayed structures made an appearance in the U.S. in 1972. The John O'Connell Memorial Bridge above the port of Sitka, Alaska, was a timid beginning; the main span was only 450 feet long, whereas the main advantage of cable-staying is that it permits extremely long spans.

Erskine Bridge, on the Clyde River west of Glasgow, Scotland, opened to traffic. This bridge, 4,326 feet long, has a 1,000-foot-long cable-stayed main span. In Australia work resumed on the building of West Gage Bridge, on the Lower Yarra River, Melbourne. Work had been stopped after an accident in October 1970 killed 35 workmen. The reinforced concrete floor in the original design was replaced by a lighter orthotropic floor, and the number of provisional piles needed for the work was increased as a safety measure.

Work was held up on the Fremont Bridge in Portland, Ore., when wide gaps were discovered at the deck and arch junctures. With an opening of 1,255 feet between the supports, it was to be the largest metal arch in the world. A three-mile-long bridge across the Mississippi River between Crittenden County, Ark., and Memphis, Tenn., opened to traffic in 1972. Its two bowstrings spanning 900 feet provided nearly 60 feet of clearance

Europe's largest multilevel interchange, near Birmingham, England, was opened in 1972. The $76.6-million project was part of the final link of the London-to-Carlisle expressway system.

FOX PHOTOS FROM PICTORIAL PARADE

above the deepest navigable water. The U.S. continued to build large trellis-girder bridges such as the ones over the Thames River between New London and Groton, Conn. (main span 540 feet), and the Grandad Creek Bridge in Idaho (center span 504 feet).

A 4,500-foot-long prestressed-concrete bridge was under construction in the Netherlands on the Waal River near Tiel. In West Germany on the Main River near Frankfurt, a 4,860-foot-span prestressed bridge was finished in 1972.

During 1972, accidents involving loss of life occurred in the collapse of falsework that was supporting bridges under construction in the U.S., Great Britain, and West Germany. Research was being conducted with a view to establishing standards for falsework design. (*See in* CE: Bridge.)

DAMS

The reservoir of the world's highest dam, the 1,017-foot-high Nurek earth-fill dam in the U.S.S.R. near Afghanistan, was filled in autumn 1972. A total of 8,424,000 acre-feet of water was drained from the Vakhsh River. Also under construction in the Soviet Union was the Andizhan concrete gravity dam on the River Kara Darya in central Asia's earthquake country. The dam (height 328 feet, volume 5 million cubic yards) was designed to withstand earthquakes up to force 9 on the 12-point Mercalli scale. It was to consist of 35 sections joined with seams of rustless steel, rubber, and other materials, with allowance for some vertical movement.

Construction continued in India on the Idikki multiple-arch dam, which would be the highest of its kind in Asia. Work on the earth-core, gravel-shell Beas dam on the River Beas, planned to be built in five stages, ran into difficulty in the first stage. About 150,000 cubic yards of unsound rock had to be removed. Special treatment was necessary to seal plastic seams in the core and trench areas. In Laos the Nam Ngum concrete gravity dam on the Mekong River was inaugurated in January 1972.

In Europe the Odivelas multiple-arch and earth dam (height 361 feet), on the Odivelas River in Portugal, was completed in 1972. Other work was under way in Spain and in Austria. In Yugoslavia, three dams were under construction. They were the Mratinje double-curvature arch dam (height 722 feet) on the Piva River; the Sjenica rock-fill dam (height 361 feet) on the Uvac River; and the Gazivode rock-fill dam (height 354 feet) on the Ibar River.

The Dworshak concrete gravity dam on the Clearwater River in Idaho neared completion in 1972. Construction continued on the Auburn arch dam on the north fork of the American River in California and also on the Lower Teton earth-and-rock-fill dam in eastern Idaho.

The zoned earth- and rock-fill Mica dam on the Columbia River in Canada (height 800 feet) neared completion in 1972. It was scheduled to start impounding water in April 1973. In Peru the Kichuas arch-gravity dam on the Mantaro River, built in a narrow gorge, was finished.

KEYSTONE

The Dworshak Dam on the Clearwater River in the state of Idaho neared completion in 1972. It is 634 feet high.

In Australia construction started in 1972 on the Dartmouth earth- and rock-fill dam on the Mitta River in northeast Victoria. This dam (length 2,300 feet, volume 20.3 million cubic yards) was to be completed in 1978. (*See in* CE: Dam.)

ROADS

The most ambitious and costly road project in U.S. history was 80% complete by the end of 1972. Of the planned 42,500 miles in the interstate highway system, 33,796 were open to traffic by November. Of the remaining miles, a total of 3,742 were under construction.

Several European countries completed important highway projects in 1972. France finished work on 20 miles of the Orange-Perpignan highway, the highway from Aix-en-Provence to Marseilles, and the first section of the St. Nazaire-Nantes highway.

Italy completed the 110-mile road between Genoa and Livorno and opened the first Sicilian freeway, a link between Catania and Messina. In May a 20-mile section was opened to traffic between Foggia and Canosa di Puglia. East Germany opened two sections of the Leipzig-Dresden expressway in 1972. An 11-mile stretch connected Grimma and Leisnig, and a 12-mile section from Döbeln to Deutschborn linked up with the Eisenach-Dresden highway. The construction of new roads slowed in Great Britain, with only 62 miles opened to traffic in 1972. Included, however, were important additions to the network.

In a massive engineering project conducted largely by the army, Brazil continued to build a highway system intended to make it the transportation hub of South America. The most impressive part of the network, the controversial highway along the Amazon River, was opposed by conservationists; they pointed out that the easily navigable Amazon ran in the same direction. The highway was planned to link with Peru and Bolivia, ensuring a direct road from the Atlantic Ocean to the Pacific.

Bolivia completed a 177-mile road complex running to Villa Tunari in the interior. Part of it rose to 12,000 feet above sea level. Venezuela opened the 14-mile-long Valencia Camp de Carabobo freeway to traffic in 1972. Work began on the 9-mile stretch of road from Canitas to the Bayano River in Panama. The road was to be part of the Pan-American Highway.

In Africa, Egypt put the 193-mile-long Pyramids-Bahria Oasis road into use, and Ethiopia completed 80 miles of road between Nazareth and Awash in April. Also engaged in road projects were Angola, Guinea, Nigeria, and Malawi.

A new subway tunnel linking Welfare Island and Manhattan Island in New York City was being built with prefabricated sections laid under the East River.

LEE ROMERO FROM "THE NEW YORK TIMES"

Japan published plans in 1972 for a 4,722-mile network of expressways, of which 1,243 miles were already under construction. The Asian Highway network, a project started in 1960, included by 1972 a total of 40,937 miles; 24,062 were classified as primary routes. When complete, the network would link the capitals and other major towns and cities in South Asian countries. (*See in* CE: Roads and Streets.)

TUNNELS

Engineers at the Los Alamos Scientific Laboratory in New Mexico were experimenting in 1972 with what could be the tunneler of the future. The subterrene, also known as a hot-hole digger, would melt its way through solid rock the way a hot knife cuts through butter. When fully developed, it was expected to penetrate a mountainside and leave a glass-lined tunnel 35 feet wide. Meanwhile, tunneling was progressing the hard way throughout most of the world.

The first section of a subway in Washington, D.C., was under construction in 1972. It was to be part of a subterranean, surface, and elevated rail transit network. Subsidence problems were solved by creating a grout curtain wall around the tunnel. The opening date for the first section, about 12 miles long, was scheduled for late 1974. Work continued on New York City's first new subway tunnel in almost four decades. It was to be made up of a section cut through rock under Welfare Island and two steel tubes under the two channels of the East River.

International tunneling interest centered on the construction of the world's longest railway tunnel in Japan. The Seikan Railway Tunnel (almost 33 miles long) was to link Honshu and Hokkaido.

In Switzerland work progressed on what was to be the world's longest vehicular tunnel (about 11 miles long). This would serve as an alternate route to the St. Gotthard Pass, usually closed about half the year by weather conditions. Because of bad rock, ground pressures, and floods, the job was a year behind schedule by late 1972.

In Great Britain, London's new Fleet Underground Line was expected to open in 1977. An experimental tunnel eventually to be incorporated into the line was driven in water-bearing gravel with a Bentonite shield. This method was expected to reduce dependence upon compressed air for tunneling in noncohesive water-bearing soils.

In Australia cut and cover methods were used for the construction of underpasses prior to the main tunneling on the $54-million subway loop in Melbourne. Boring for the tunnels was planned for 1973. The project was to include four tunnels and three underground stations. A tunneling machine operated by laser control was used to drive the tunnel for the Potts Hill Water Scheme in Sydney. (*See in* CE: Tunnels.)

PER-OLOF ODMAN

Young environmentalists set up a tent city at an abandoned airport near Stockholm, Sweden, during the United Nations Conference on the Human Environment held there in June. The young people protested pollution and environmental problems by giving educational "eco-skits."

ENVIRONMENT. Delegates from 114 countries met June 5–16, 1972, at Stockholm, Sweden, for the first United Nations (UN) Conference on the Human Environment. Observers from independent environmental organizations generally agreed that the conference was important more as a symbol of change in national attitudes than for any concrete actions. Anthropologist Margaret Mead hailed the conference as "a revolution in thought comparable to the Copernican revolution by which, four centuries ago, men were compelled to revise their whole sense of earth's place in the cosmos." The major accomplishment of the conference was a recommendation for the establishment of Earthwatch, a worldwide environmental monitoring system to be supported by the UN. Earthwatch would consist of ten base-line stations operating in remote areas such as jungles, deserts, and tundra. Scientists at these stations would monitor worldwide environmental changes, warning of dangers and recommending solutions. In addition, a large number of substations would monitor air quality and identify pollution sources ranging from local and regional to worldwide. Waterborne stations, including some undersea bases, would monitor changes caused in aquatic and marine ecosystems by oil spills and other damaging activities of man. Included in the Earthwatch system would be a continuous monitoring for possible food contamination from chemicals and pathogens. Eventually research centers were to be established to analyze the effects of man's activities upon soils, water, plants, and animals around the world.

International Agreements; Marine Pollution

Important international agreements made during the year included a pact between the U.S. and Canada to preserve and protect the Great Lakes. The U.S. and the Soviet Union arranged for environmental collaboration in several fields, and a 12-nation agreement was secured to control pollution of the seas in the northeastern Atlantic.

Under the U.S.–Canada agreement, the Great Lakes, which are a repository for one fifth of the world's fresh water, were to be made clean enough by 1976 so that swimming and trout fishing could be restored to all the lakes, including heavily contaminated Lake Erie. Because the U.S. was largely responsible for the lakes' pollution, it would finance most of the estimated cost of $3.5 billion. All municipalities discharging wastes into the Great Lakes were required to begin construction by 1975 of waste treatment plants that must include facilities for removal of phosphorus. Steps would also be taken to restore oxygen to the bottom waters of the central basin of Lake Erie.

At the time of U.S. President Richard M. Nixon's visit to the Soviet Union in May, the two nations signed an agreement to collaborate in several environmental areas, a major goal being the enhancement of urban environments. The agreement was followed in September by a meeting in Moscow of

GARY SETTLE FROM "THE NEW YORK TIMES"

Sludge, the liquid residue of treated sewage, proved to be an effective fertilizer for Illinois land damaged by strip mining. Treated sludge from Chicago was used on this cornfield.

environmental specialists of both countries. Arrangements were made for 30 joint projects involving exchanges of experts and data over the following five years.

An important step in the control of marine pollution was taken when the governments of Great Britain and 11 other European nations established a commission to regulate dumping of harmful substances into the waters of the northeastern Atlantic. The commission was to monitor the marine environment and provide enforcement of the rules.

In November 91 nations, including all major maritime countries, agreed on a convention ending the dumping of harmful materials at sea. The convention prohibited the discharge of high-level radioactive waste, biological and chemical warfare agents, crude oil, and some pesticides and plastics. Less harmful substances, including certain metals, could be dumped only by special permit.

Although massive oil pollution of the seas appeared to be partially checked in 1972, an increase in minispills was reported from around the world. In the Gulf of Mexico, leaks from oil wells followed accidental fires; along the beaches of Long Island Sound in New York, congealed oil washed ashore after spillage of 10,000 gallons of black low-sulfur fuel. West of New London, Conn., a three-mile stretch of beach was polluted by a film of refined oil when a vessel ruptured its tanks on Bartlett Reef; and near Cape Hatteras, off the North Carolina coast, a five-mile slick formed after two tankers collided. Indictments were brought against several oil companies for damage to U.S. beaches and marine life. Fines under laws in force in 1972, however, ranged no higher than $2,500.

Combating Pollution

Air, water, and noise pollution in the U.S. attracted considerable attention from all levels of government during the year. Studies made by the Environmental Protection Agency (EPA) indicated that 170 million people in the U.S. were exposed to levels of air pollution beyond established public health standards. An EPA map showed at least two thirds of U.S. land area was affected.

In cooperation with agencies of several states, the EPA set goals for control of the most dangerous pollutants by 1975, or by 1977 at the latest. The five air pollutants designated for control were carbon monoxide, hydrocarbons, nitrogen oxides, sulfur oxides, and particulates.

In response to a 1970 directive from the U.S. Congress, the EPA completed a lengthy report on the effects of noise upon the nation's population. The data indicated that at least 40 million people in the U.S. were exposed regularly to hazardous noise levels. Other research showed that when levels reached 90 decibels, noises impaired time judgment, caused errors in observation, and made it difficult for the subjects to remain vigilant.

After receiving the EPA report, Congress began processing noise control legislation. During the year, several states and cities either adopted new antinoise laws or tightened enforcement of laws that were already in existence.

The Federal Water Pollution Control Act of 1972 became law in October when Congress overrode a veto by President Nixon, who had condemned the bill as inflationary. It authorized $24.6 billion over three years to clean up U.S. lakes and rivers; $11 billion was to go to the states for waste treatment plants. In November, however, Nixon ordered the EPA to allot only $5 billion to the states and threatened to cut spending on other environmental programs. A bitter and politically tinged battle over pollution control seemed certain in 1973. (*See also* Congress, U.S.)

Reaction to recent environmental legislation in the U.S. arose from representatives of business and manufacturing, who claimed that the public was not being fully informed of the high costs of pollution abatement. They warned that unless compliance deadlines were extended, wholesale layoffs of workers would follow, which would have severe impact upon the nation's economy. Spokesmen stated that the goals for automobile emission control in 1975 and 1976 might add several hundred dollars to the price of an automobile. They also said that restrictions on certain fossil fuels for power plants would deepen the energy crisis and that noise reduction of engines and machinery might create other hazards and would be expensive.

Pollution in Agriculture

Farmers in 1972 were in the unenviable position of being harmed by pollutants while at the same time being accused of creating them. Incidents of serious crop damage from air pollution were reported by truck farmers in New Jersey, Pennsylvania, New York, and Illinois; by tobacco growers in Virginia, potato growers in Michigan, and citrus growers in Florida; and by fruit, vegetable, and grain farmers in California. Peroxyacetyl nitrate and sulfur dioxide carried by warm, moist smogs caused rapid damage to leafy plants, burning or wilting them in a few hours to such a degree that they were unmarketable. Experiments at the University of California at Riverside showed that air pollution reduced yields of fruit by as much as 60%.

Farmers were blamed for contaminating drinking water used by city dwellers through the overuse of nitrogen fertilizer and by the practice of concentrating livestock in feedlots. Nitrate counts in water sources for several cities were found to be near or above the safety limit of 45 parts per million set by the U.S. Public Health Service. The major source of nitrate contamination was found to come from chemical fertilizers used by farmers to guarantee heavy crop yields. Some state pollution control agencies recommended that limits be imposed on applications of nitrogen-based fertilizers. Although most states had recently enacted regulations for control of feedlots, heavy rains during the year created flash floods that swept wastes from these heavy concentrations of animals into nearby streams. Nitrogen compounds in the wastes, combined with runoffs from chemically fertilized fields, killed fish in some areas.

Another problem created by modern agricultural technology was brought to the forefront in meetings of medical scientists and environmentalists. Since the 1950's, when antibiotics were found to promote rapid growth in animals, these drugs had been added to animal feeds in most countries raising livestock. Some scientists were afraid that overuse of antibiotics in meat animals might be creating groups of bacteria resistant to antibiotics. Resistant bacteria might then be transmitted through meats to human consumers and cause diseases that could no longer be controlled by antibiotic therapy. These concerned scientists suggested that advanced techniques in genetics and recent discoveries in nutrition be used instead of antibiotics to speed livestock growth. The U.S. Food and Drug Administration began a study of the problem and was expected to ban use in animal feeds of antibiotics that are of life-and-death importance to human beings.

In June the U.S. government banned virtually all uses of DDT because of its hazards to man and his environment. The effective date of the ban was delayed to Dec. 31, 1972, in order to give farmers time to convert to less persistent pesticides. DDT had often been cited as a killer of marine life, and studies showed that it could produce cancer in animals. It was proved to be the cause of severe population declines among many fish-eating birds such as bald eagles, brown pelicans, and peregrine falcons, and some catches of fish were banned in interstate commerce because of unsafe levels of the pesticide.

Use of DDT had already declined sharply because of federal legal action and the application of substitutes. In areas where it was still effective against mosquitoes, DDT would continue to be used for control of malaria. The only uses of the pesticide permitted for crops would be for protection of green peppers, onions, and sweet potatoes in storage—a requirement of about 1% of the total used in recent years. Methyl parathion, a highly toxic pesticide which does not build up in the environment, was recommended as a possible replacement for DDT.

Experimental Satellite

The first experimental Earth Resources Technology Satellite (ERTS) was launched in July for the purpose of gathering continuous data on the condition of the world's resources and environment. Scientists using ERTS expected the satellite to provide information on outbreaks of plant diseases, the spread of water and air pollution, rainfall and stream flow, crop conditions, buildup of sediment, coastline changes, snow and ice coverage, and countless other conditions.

ERTS carried a one-ton package of scientific equipment, consisting of three television cameras, a multispectral point scanner, and a data collection system that picked up signals from 150 automated ground stations. These stations measured factors such as precipitation, air pollution, and stream flow and every 12 hours transmitted this data to ERTS, which relayed it to scientists at headquarters stations.

Decisions in Alaska

In spite of opposition from leading conservation organizations, U.S. Secretary of the Interior Rogers C. B. Morton decided in favor of construction of a proposed 800-mile-long trans-Alaska pipeline. The decision followed the release in March of a massive nine-volume impact study that still left conservationists dissatisfied with the environmental effects of the pipeline, designed eventually to carry

2 million barrels of oil a day from Alaska's North Slope to the port of Valdez. In addition to damages to the ecology of Alaska, conservationists predicted that oil spills were bound to occur between Valdez and West coast ports, with lethal effects upon marine life in the Pacific Ocean.

The Department of the Interior also came under attack for its transfer of large grants of Alaskan public land from federal to state and local ownership without providing restraints upon commercial exploitation of the land. Although 80 million acres were set aside for possible addition to the national parks, forests, wilderness, and scenic river systems, conservationists opposed the release to the state of Alaska of important land areas near Mount McKinley and the proposed Gates of the Arctic Park in the Brooks Range.

Other Developments

In San Francisco, Calif., a U.S. district judge granted a preliminary injunction banning road building and timber cutting in 34 million acres of national forests in California and other western states until full environmental impact studies had been made. In New Mexico a conservationist group brought suit to halt construction of a 33-mile mountain road inside the Santa Fe National Forest on the basis that construction of the road would be ecologically unsound. Wilderness Watch, an organization of environmentalists, challenged a 20-year-old agreement between the U.S. Forest Service and the Department of Defense that permitted military use of millions of acres of national forests. The forest areas were used for tank maneuvers and guerrilla training, for rifle and artillery ranges, and for bivouacs and mountain warfare training. The environmentalists claimed that under the recent National Environmental Protection Act impact statements should be required in order to assure prevention of ecological damages by such military uses.

On April 28 tree seedlings were planted by 1,000 children on 177 acres in George Washington National Forest in Virginia as the main feature of the dedication of the nation's third Children's Forest, the first to be opened in the eastern states. The area replanted had been destroyed by fire in 1971. Other Children's Forests are in Mark Twain National Forest in Missouri and the San Bernardino National Forest in California.

Bills to control strip mining were introduced in both houses of Congress but failed to pass. Opponents of strip mining feared that thousands more acres would be stripped before a law could be enacted in 1973. Strip mining was continuing to disrupt the land surface of the U.S. in 1972 at a rate of almost 5,000 acres a week, and controversies continued between coal operators and environmentalists over proper reclamation of spoil banks. (*See also* Feature Article: "Enriching the Quality of Life." *See in* CE: Conservation; Pollution, Environmental.)

The use of herbicides by the U.S. military in Vietnam to deprive enemy troops of ground cover has sparked an international debate over the question of "ecocide"—intentional destruction of a life-supporting environment. The long-term effects of U.S. herbicidal sprayings, which were ended in 1970, are evidenced in this destroyed mangrove stand. Half of South Vietnam's mangrove forests have been wiped out and show no signs of regeneration.

ARTHUR H. WESTING

EQUATORIAL GUINEA. At the second national congress of Equatorial Guinea's Party of National Unity, on July 14, 1972, President Francisco Macías Nguema was appointed president for life. On April 11 Interior Minister Angel Masie Natutumde announced that Equatorial Guinea was arranging to recruit 15,000 Nigerians to work on the Fernando Po plantations. A new labor agreement providing better pay and conditions had been signed by Equatorial Guinea and Nigeria in December 1971. Previously, 20,000 Nigerians had returned to Nigeria after completing contracts under the old terms, and it was feared that the cocoa crop might be adversely affected by the loss of these workers. In November a Nigerian newspaper stated that "hundreds" of Nigerian workers had been shot to death while attempting to flee Fernando Po.

In September Gabon occupied the two disputed Atlantic islands of Mbanie and Cocotiers after Gabonese fishermen had allegedly been attacked by an armed force from Equatorial Guinea. President Macías on September 12 demanded United Nations intervention to oust the Gabonese.

ETHIOPIA. The 80th birthday of Ethiopia's Emperor Haile Selassie I was marked by a three-day national celebration in July 1972. During the year he also received the United Nations (UN) Peace Medal. The emperor's active personal diplomacy played an important part in resolving disputes between northern and southern Sudan and between Senegal and Guinea. In July Ethiopia and Sudan reached an agreement on the demarcation of their border and on a peaceful solution to agricultural and population problems arising from the border settlement.

The emperor's diplomacy also resulted in significant economic agreements with the People's Republic of China, Great Britain, Italy, Japan, Canada, and other nations. Plans were announced for the establishment of airline service between Ethiopia and China, Great Britain, Saudi Arabia, and the Central African Republic. Several important discoveries were reported by teams searching for minerals. Investigators from Japan found extensive deposits of high-grade copper, zinc, and other minerals in Ethiopia's Asmara and Adi Nefas regions, and UN research yielded vast sources of potential geothermal power in the Afar plains.

Although in rural Ethiopia some progress was made in building schools and feeder roads and in increasing aid to peasant farmers, the conservative parliament again failed to pass much-needed land reform legislation; consequently Sweden threatened further cuts in its vital agricultural aid. Industrial developments included the opening of tire and steel factories in Addis Ababa, the capital, and the installation of a cotton gin in Gondar.

Seven people tried to hijack an Ethiopian Airways plane on December 8. Six were killed and one wounded by guards. (*See in* CE: Ethiopia.)

EUROPE. Despite various setbacks, 1972 was, on balance, a year of progress toward greater unity in Europe. This was especially true for the European Economic Community (EEC) and the two ancillary groups, the European Coal and Steel Community and the European Atomic Energy Community.

Expansion of the EEC

The year began on a high note, a formal ceremony on January 22 in the Palais d'Egmont in Brussels, Belgium, pledging the accession of four new members—Great Britain, Ireland, Denmark, and Norway—to the EEC. The Treaty of Accession, effective on Jan. 1, 1973, would create a common trading and economic area with more than a quarter billion in population, more than a third of the world's imports and exports, and a gross national product second only to that of the U.S.

Having been formally signed in January, the Treaty of Accession required ratification by the ten nations involved. The process was complicated by the decisions in certain states that ratification must be accomplished by popular referendum rather than by representative parliamentary means—or that a referendum should supplement parliamentary action. Considerable publicity attended the first of these referenda, that held by France's President Georges Pompidou on April 23. Although the treaty was safely ratified, only a little more than half the French voters went to the polls and, of those, two thirds voted for the expansion of the EEC and one third voted against it.

In Great Britain the idea of a referendum was seized upon by the Labourite foes of British membership in the EEC and complicated Prime Minister Edward Heath's effort to ratify the treaty. Since public opinion polls had rejected British participation in the EEC by as much as 70%, a popular vote might well have been in the negative and prevented Britain's accession. Advocacy of a referendum, however, proved to be ill-advised for the Labour party. Ultimately it caused certain leading party members to give up their posts in the shadow government and announce their future adherence to the prime minister's bill. Heath eventually won his victory in Parliament although by a very narrow margin.

Elsewhere among the six original EEC members there appeared to be no doubt of parliamentary ratification; the three other applicant states, however, had provided for referenda. The referendum held in Ireland on May 10 secured a surprising affirmative majority of 83% of those voting. Perhaps equally surprising was the decisive rejection of EEC membership by voters in Norway. The antimarket coalition included conservative nationalists, pan-Scandinavians, farmers, fishermen, environmentalists, and young radicals—all of whom had reasons, although often contradictory, for opposing membership. It was feared that the Norwegian vote would influence Danes to follow suit.

However, in the Danish referendum held the following week, a record voter turnout was nearly two to one in favor of joining the EEC.

Movement Toward Monetary Union

The major element in the year's EEC record was the continuing difficulty besetting moves toward monetary union. The monetary crisis of 1971 largely reduced to naught what seemed to have been promising earlier steps toward such a union. Another beginning was made after the settlement at Washington, D.C., in December 1971, in which subscribing nations agreed that national currency values might fluctuate from established parity no more than 2¼%—a total range of 4½%. In March the six original and four prospective EEC members agreed that currency fluctuations among themselves should not total more than half the allowable maximum range—that is, 2¼%—and that even this discretion should gradually be narrowed until their currencies enjoyed fixed parity.

By June, however, even this modest effort had been seriously undermined by Britain's decision to allow the pound to seek its own level and by the demands of Italy and Denmark for more flexible arrangements. Some EEC states, especially France, continued to insist upon the development of closer monetary ties within the EEC, while others, notably West Germany, were equally insistent that efforts to harmonize monetary policy would not succeed unless EEC states were willing to submit to a more supranational discipline.

Italy's ambivalent attitude and the doubts that it could or would play by the rules were emphasized when the president of the Common Market Commission, Franco Maria Malfatti, resigned to run for a seat in the Italian parliament. Italy's EEC partners, obviously nettled by this apparently cavalier attitude, thereupon rejected the candidacy of an Italian replacement and elected instead Sicco Leendert Mansholt, the Dutch father of EEC's common agricultural policy.

A summit conference had been proposed by President Pompidou in August 1971 as a means of forging a European monetary policy with which to face the U.S. Major trade talks among the nations were scheduled to begin in 1973 under the auspices of the General Agreement on Tariffs and Trade (GATT). That the summit would be held at all was in doubt during most of 1972. It was only after EEC foreign and finance ministers had reached a limited monetary agreement in the September meeting that Pompidou issued invitations to the summit. Held in October and attended by leaders from the nine EEC member nations, the summit talks reaffirmed the goal of monetary, economic, and some degree of political unity by 1980. Another conference was scheduled for 1975.

The EEC and the EFTA

With three of the member states of the European Free Trade Association (EFTA) engaged in seeking entrance to the EEC, the remaining EFTA states (Austria, Switzerland, Portugal, Sweden, Finland, and Iceland) gave serious consideration to their future posture. Treaties were signed in Brussels on July 22 establishing a free-trade area for 15 nations and effectively merging the EEC and EFTA into a single trading bloc to be established with the formal enlargement of the EEC in 1973. (Finland, the 16th nation, was expected to sign the treaty at a later date.) The agreements provided for mutual reductions of tariffs on industrial goods by 20% each year until 1977; longer transition periods were permitted for certain products—notably paper, special steels, and a few local agricultural products—for which free trade would seriously affect local economies.

These arrangements inspired protests on the part of the U.S., which regarded special trade arrangements by GATT members as contrary to GATT policy. It was thought that the anticipated GATT conference of 1973 might, therefore, bring these new agreements up for review and possible modification.

The Council of Europe

One of the oldest European groups (created in 1949) and also the largest (17 members), the Council of Europe continued to provide the machinery for cooperative European action on many fronts. Meeting in May, the council's Committee of Ministers reaffirmed the organization's desire to continue liaison with the EEC after the EEC achieved expanded membership. The Consultative Assembly, or parliament, gave much attention to the economic and political consequences of enlargement of the EEC and to the political situation in Greece, the status of aid programs for less developed countries, and the need for a European monetary system.

East-West Relations

In January leaders of the seven Warsaw Pact powers conferred in Prague, Czechoslovakia, on the question of European security. They issued a joint communiqué calling for mutual East-West troop reductions and urging speedy convocation of a European security conference to be attended by the U.S., Canada, and all European countries. The preliminary discussions began in Helsinki, Finland, in November.

The Helsinki meetings were directed toward the planning of an agenda and other preparations for the full-scale security conference in 1973. It appeared that the conference itself would indeed happen, although its nature was still uncertain when the Helsinki conferees adjourned in December for Christmas. The Eastern bloc seemed to be seeking a formalization of the status quo, while the Western nations pushed for a lowering of political barriers. (*See also* individual countries by name; International Relations; Money and International Finance. *See in* CE: Europe.)

"CHICAGO TRIBUNE PHOTO"

PUSH Expo '72, also called the Black and Minorities Business and Cultural Exposition, opened at the International Amphitheatre in Chicago in September. An opening address was delivered by the Rev. Jesse Jackson of Operation PUSH (People United to Save Humanity).

FAIRS AND SHOWS. The world's public and trade fairs and shows reported record gains for 1972, with revenues rising nearly 22% and attendance up between 8% and 20%. More than 1.1 billion persons attended the world's 14,400 public shows, 2.1 billion more visited amusement centers, and 1.8 billion others were attracted to stadiums, auditoriums, and other facilities. A record 46 million buyers attended 1,000 commercial trade fairs in 78 countries.

Spokane, Wash., received approval from the Bureau of International Expositions in Paris to hold a 1974 world's fair. The city, smallest ever to host a world's fair, planned to stage its Expo 74 on two islands in the Spokane River. Philadelphia, Pa., gave up its plan to hold a Bicentennial Exposition in 1976; instead, regional celebrations were planned throughout the U.S. by federally sponsored bicentennial commissions in each state.

Environmental concern prompted a number of special exhibitions and conferences during the year. Among them were the Pollution Control Exhibition and Congress "Project 2000" in Vienna, Austria, and similar conferences in London; Jerusalem, Israel; and Edinburgh, Scotland.

More than 150 million persons attended 4,000 state, county, provincial, and district fairs in the U.S. and Canada in 1972. The Texas State Fair in Dallas and the Canadian National Exhibition in Toronto, Ont., maintained attendance leads among North American shows with a record of more than 3 million visitors.

Sales of exhibit space at industrial shows open to both the trades and the public in 1972 declined, as many smaller shows canceled or consolidated with larger ones. Prices for exhibit space remained about on a par with 1968 prices, but attendance increased as much as 30% over that year. Since 1968 some $60 billion had been appropriated for new exhibit halls, including New York City's $100-million convention center, started in 1972.

Gross income from "kiddielands," roadside attractions, zoos, and amusement parks around the world was estimated at $4.5 billion for 1972, and an estimated 1,000 new such facilities were created during the year. The 2,100 facilities in North America alone attracted 445 million persons, who spent more than $1 billion. Walt Disney World near Orlando, Fla., in late 1972 announced a $50-million expansion program for the $400-million complex. Attendance during the park's first year topped original estimates and reached 10,720,000. Such other superparks as Hemisfair Plaza in San Antonio, Tex. (1.8 million visitors), and Man and His World, the former Expo 67 park in Montreal, Que. (3 million visitors), still suffered deficits. Accounting was completed during the year for the 1964–65 New York World's Fair, and it was revealed that the fair realized only 62.4¢ on each dollar invested by bondholders. A court ordered that the money be given to the city of New York for educational purposes.

An estimated 1,925 mobile carnivals and 1,200 independent operators appeared at fairs in over 80 countries. The 200-odd carnival units booked at 90% of U.S. and Canadian fairs reported record years with gross revenues of $1 billion.

The International Rodeo Association won a long-fought battle when an Ohio state code prohibiting use of the "flank strap" on rodeo animals was declared unconstitutional. This cleared the way for rodeos in that state after a long absence. Over 2,600 independent rodeos toured 48 states and 5 Canadian provinces with total prize money of more than $5 million, the highest total in rodeo history. Rodeo events remained unpopular in Europe.

Some 665 circuses toured the world in 1972, with indoor shows reporting business up 15% and outdoor tent shows reporting declines. The Moscow State Circus made its first U.S. appearance since 1964, visiting New York City and eight other East coast cities.

A total of 2,400 world livestock shows drew capacity crowds during the year. The International Live Stock Exposition in Chicago observed its 72d anniversary. A total of 17,500 horse shows were held during the year, 4,500 of them in the U.S. and Canada. The crippling Venezuelan equine encephalomyelitis outbreak in Mexico in 1971 limited 1972 participation as stricter health regulations were imposed in some areas of the U.S. The American Horse Shows Association sponsored 90 shows in the U.S. and Canada, offering $2 million in prizes.

Among the major fairs reporting attendance of more than a million were the International Trade Fair in Algiers, Algeria; the Royal Easter Show in Sydney, Australia; the Agricultural Fair in Wels, Austria; the International Motor Exhibition in Paris; the Fair of Rome; the Comptoir-Suisse National Fair in Lausanne, Switzerland; and the Swiss Industries Fair in Basel. More than one million visitors also attended international fairs in Damascus, Syria; Izmir, Turkey; Cairo, Egypt; Thessaloníki, Greece; and Budapest, Hungary. (*See in* CE: Fairs and Expositions.)

FAMILIES. Throughout 1972 family life in the U.S. continued to be buffeted by pressures thrust upon it by fast-changing morals, standards, and attitudes. The problem of just staying together continued to be a very real one for many families. The U.S. Census Bureau reported that one fourth of the 5.7 million U.S. women in their 30's in 1972 were expected to have been divorced by the time they were 50. A sixth of these women had had at least one divorce already. According to the bureau, divorce among U.S. women age 35 and under was 50% more common in 1972 than it was 15 years earlier.

The cherished institution of parenthood came under fire during 1972 from a new group called the National Organization for Non-Parents (NON). NON, whose members include parents and childless couples, doctors, teachers, and psychologists, called for an end to the cultural and economic pressures that push people into having children. The new group's motto: "None is fun."

New View of the Working Mother

The traditional belief that the best mothers are those without careers or high professional accomplishments was sharply challenged during the year. The Soviet Institute of Concrete Research, after an exhaustive study of career women in the U.S.S.R., reported that those with professional skills appear to be the best mothers and the most efficient housewives. The results of the survey contradict the widespread opinion in the U.S. that career women often become so caught up in professional life that they neglect home and children. The Soviet study suggests instead that careers and family life can be harmoniously blended and may perhaps produce greater satisfaction than traditional life-styles.

Custody and Adoptions

The U.S. Supreme Court handed down a 1972 decision that unwed fathers, like unwed mothers, cannot be denied custody of their illegitimate children without first being given a chance to prove themselves fit parents. The case centered around a Chicago man, Peter Stanley, who had fathered three children while living intermittently for 18 years with Joan Stanley. When their mother died the children automatically became wards of the state, because Illinois law did not regard unwed fathers as parents with rights of custody. Stanley sued to gain custody of his children, on the grounds that the Illinois statute violated his 14th Amendment guarantee of equal protection.

The case of "Baby Lenore," a focus of nationwide attention in 1971, was finally settled during 1972. A New York court had previously ordered that the child be returned to her natural mother, but the adoptive parents fled to Florida, where an appeals court ruled in their favor. By refusing to hear an appeal from the natural mother, the Supreme Court ended her chances to regain custody.

The practice of transracial adoption drew sharp criticism from the National Association of Black Social Workers. The association charged that putting black children up for adoption or foster care with white parents posed a growing threat to the preservation of the black family in the U.S. (*See also* Population; Women. *See in* CE: Family.)

Thomas Mallias and his family, who overpowered the crew of an Albanian trawler to escape to Corfu, Greece, arrived in New York City in October.

MEYER LIEBOWITZ FROM "THE NEW YORK TIMES"

KEN REGAN FROM CAMERA 5

High-heeled, and sometimes thick-soled, shoes for men were increasingly popular in 1972.

FASHION. In 1972 fashion did an about-face, ushering in a new era of classicism. The direction was toward a more traditional silhouette with a revived taste for quality and discreetness. The aim was no longer to shock or dazzle, but to charm with a kind of understated elegance discernible only to the knowledgeable eye. The images of three recently departed fashion greats—Gabrielle (Coco) Chanel, Norman Norell, and Cristobal Balenciaga—hovered over the scene. (*See also* Obituaries.)

Hemlines, stabilized at just above knee level, ceased to be in the limelight. As if rescued from the quicksand of indecision, women began to look upon fashion with renewed interest, searching beyond the safe trouser suit for something more feminine. Although still very much a basic, pants were worn with softer tops, blousons, and shirtlike styles, shirred at the waist or loosely belted.

At the beginning of the year a Chinese breeze swept through the New York City shops following news of U.S. President Richard M. Nixon's plans to visit the People's Republic of China. Chinese inspiration was reflected in most of the designer collections. The Oriental influence made itself felt in jewelry design as well. Carved jade and ivory were popular, frequently appearing in reproductions of antique Chinese jewels.

For spring, couture designers softened shoulders and rounded lapels, playing down the aggressiveness of the 1940's as previously revived by Yves St. Laurent. They retained the idea of the separate jacket, pairing it with the long-torso print dress. This twosome gained top marks for the spring look on city streets. The perennial navy and white spring harmony was underscored by the popularity of nautical motifs.

Balancing the casual, tailored daytime looks, clothes for evening took on a definite romantic flavor. Bill Blass and Marc Bohan were among the leading designers to feature ruffles in their evening wear. Flounces appeared at necklines, on sleeves, and at hemlines of silk crepe and organdy dresses; Blass showed two dresses that were covered with ruffles from shoulder to hem. Memories of the 1950's began to stir the fashion world, reintroducing curves and sophistication. There was a gleam of Hollywood and of Rita Hayworth in the plunging necklines, billowing skirts, and bare backs.

In New York City, as in London and Paris, it was in the sweater field that designers really showed imagination during 1972. The persistence of the layered look, the chilly summer, the classic fall styles—all called for an extra sweater to brighten the scene. The close-fitting sweater with a high, ribbed waistband was a natural with the new straight-legged flannel pants. The sweater set, matching cardigan and pullover, reappeared on the fashion scene in a tremendous variety of patterns and colors. After Kenzo Takada launched wide kimono sleeves with square armholes on sweaters, even tank-top models developed small, winged shoulder effects. Necklines were cut in vee, square, or round shapes in order to show the collar of the shirt worn underneath. Mohair, angora, and cashmere enjoyed renewed popularity.

Along with sweaters, fall looks featured flared pants and a variety of "toppers"—cropped jackets just perfect for topping off the new styles. Blanket plaids and camel hair were favorite materials for the wrap coats introduced for winter.

From the St. Laurent offensive of 1972 a few whiffs of the 1940's remained in the development of shoe styles. Soles got thicker and thicker, first in wedge and then in platform shape. Heels became higher—four and a half inches and more—but remained heavy. Cork- and wooden-soled clogs were widely popular with the young crowd.

Men's Wear—The Return to Elegance

The return to gentlemanly elegance was the theme of men's fashion in 1972. Manifestations of the trend included the revival of such classics as the vest, the blazer, the gray flannel suit, and the button-down collar. Certain innovations of the 1960's remained—wider lapels and slightly flared pants—but the emphasis was on subdued fabrics and conservative tailoring. Denim, chino, and seersucker were the favorite fabrics for spring and summer suits; and white and off-white suits were very popular during the summer of 1972.

If men's suits showed a new conservatism, footwear seemed headed in the opposite direction. The new shoes for men featured platform soles, higher heels, and two-tone designs in combinations of suede and shiny patent leather. Even the most conservative manufacturers were predicting a continuation of the trend toward higher heels for men. (*See also* Cosmetics. *See in* CE: Dress; Dress Design; Fashion.)

FIJI. In a quiet general election in 1972, Fiji's prime minister, Ratu Sir Kamisese Mara, and the Alliance party retained office, winning 33 of 52 seats in the new house of representatives. The National Federation party won the remaining 19 seats. The Alliance party claimed that its policy of multiracial harmony had triumphed.

The government agreed to pay the Colonial Sugar Refining Co. $12.5 million for the assets of South Pacific Sugar Mills Ltd., to be taken over in 1973. The sole right to manufacture sugar would then be given to the Fiji Sugar Corp. Ltd., in which the government would have the majority of shares and nominate the board of directors in consultation with the opposition party. The future of this vital industry depended on obtaining associate membership or a trade agreement with the European Economic Community after expiration of the Commonwealth Sugar Agreement in 1974. The government considered opening a mission in Brussels, Belgium, in early 1973.

During the year the South Pacific Forum decided to establish a South Pacific Bureau of Economic Cooperation in Suva, the capital. An increasingly unfavorable balance of trade with Australia and New Zealand pointed to the need for substantial trade concessions. In October Fiji was struck by a hurricane that caused extensive damage and left thousands of people homeless. About 85,000 people needed emergency aid. (*See in* CE: Fiji.)

FINLAND. Premature general elections in Finland on Jan. 2–3, 1972, did not help solve the political difficulties that on Oct. 29, 1971, had led to the resignation of the four-party coalition of Prime Minister Ahti Karjalainen. The non-Socialist majority in parliament was reduced from 112–88 to 108–92, but the slight change did not pave the way for an easy decision on the nation's economic and farming policy. The Social Democratic party confirmed its position as the largest political group, increasing its number of seats in parliament from 52 to 55. General elections had originally been scheduled for 1974, when President Urho K. Kekkonen's third six-year period as head of state was to expire. A caretaker cabinet headed by Teuvo Aura was in power for four months until Feb. 23, 1972, when a Social Democratic minority government took office under the party chairman, Rafael Paasio.

The second new political cabinet of the year, similar to Karjalainen's four-party coalition, was sworn in on September 4. The new prime minister was the Social Democratic party secretary-general, Kalevi Sorsa.

On July 22 at Brussels, Belgium, Finland initialed an agreement with the European Economic Community, and the Finnish cabinet was expected to take the agreement to parliament for ratification at the end of the year. President Kekkonen met twice in 1972 with Soviet leaders. As a result of

On the Day of the Innocent Children, a procession bearing small coffins walked through Helsinki, Finland, demonstrating against Finland's liberal abortion law.

"THE TIMES," LONDON, FROM PICTORIAL PARADE

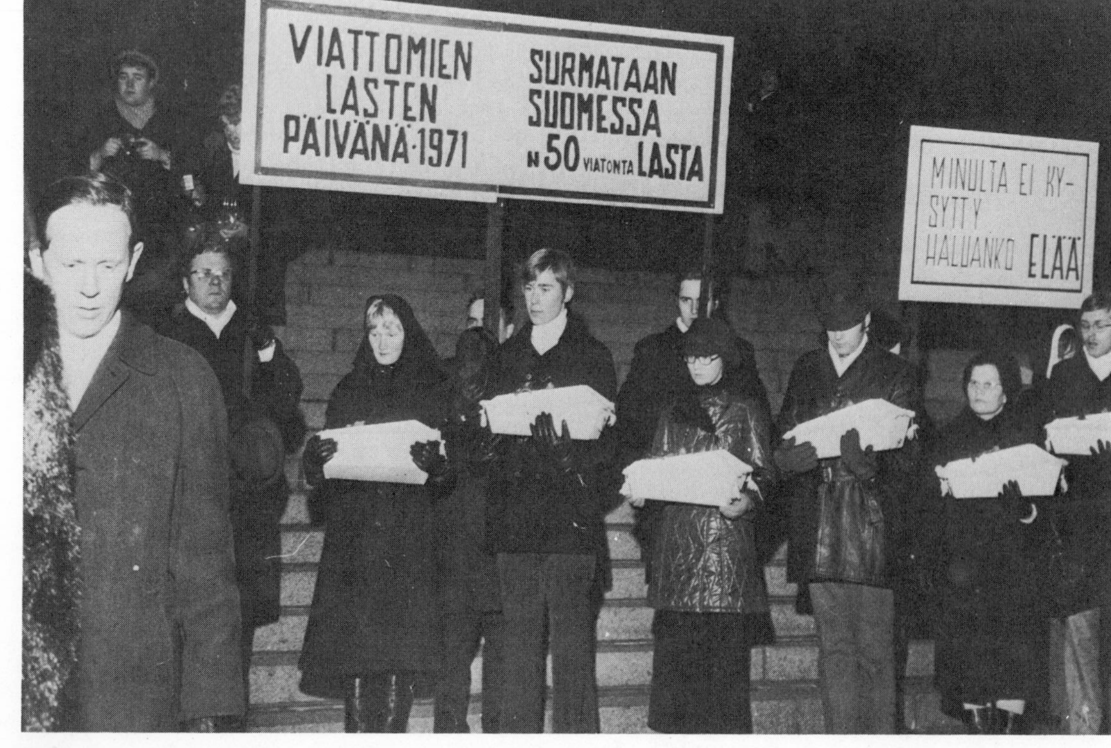

these talks an agreement was signed by which Finland could sell all its surplus grain and butter to the Soviet Union if difficulties arose from placing these products on Western markets. (*See in* CE: Finland.)

FISH AND FISHERIES. In 1972 the problem of sea limits threatened the world of fish and fisheries. For some years South American nations (notably Ecuador) had been claiming exclusive fishing rights up to 200 miles. Although the U.S. shrimp and tuna fleets had been harassed by these limits, which were not accepted by the U.S. government, their effect was relatively limited. But during the year other nations decided to enlarge their own sea limits. Iceland claimed a 50-mile limit that virtually encompassed its continental shelf, and Senegal claimed 110 miles.

In late summer poisonous "red tide" algae spread along the northern New England coast, dealing a severe blow to thousands of persons who depended upon the sea for their livelihood. On September 15, Massachusetts' Gov. Francis W. Sargent forbade the sale of fresh and frozen shellfish, including clams, quahogs, mussels, and cape scallops. The harvesting of almost all varieties of mussels and clams was stopped by Maine and Massachusetts authorities. More than 30 persons became ill from eating contaminated seafood, but there were no fatalities. The "red tide" began to disappear two weeks after first being sighted, and the ban was lifted for most areas by October 25.

In April the scarcity of Maine lobsters sent retail prices to record levels; some restaurants even removed lobster from their menus. Exceptionally bad weather in February and March, which kept lobstermen from going to sea, was blamed. In June prices came down somewhat but lobsters remained relatively scarce.

The watermen of Maryland's eastern shore of Chesapeake Bay were also given a rough time by the weather. The culprit this time was Hurricane Agnes, which hit the Atlantic coast in June. It was reported that the storm was responsible for killing most of the upper bay's oysters and more than 90% of the clams. Torrential rains, a low salinity level, and temperatures far above normal produced the damage. (*See in* CE: Fisheries.)

Maine wardens destroy clams contaminated by poisonous "red tide" algae (above). Mussels were also affected by the red tide. Animals died after eating contaminated shellfish; more than 30 persons were stricken with paralysis after partaking of clams or mussels. In Long Island, N.Y., "aquafarms" (right) were being developed so that oysters, clams, and scallops could be grown in pollution-free nursery beds.

ABOVE: UPI COMPIX.
RIGHT: MEYER LIEBOWITZ FROM "THE NEW YORK TIMES"

BARTON SILVERMAN FROM "THE NEW YORK TIMES"

A new garden for blind people was opened at the Jewish Braille Institute in New York City in 1972. Special features included braille signs. Plants were chosen for fragrance and texture.

FLOWERS AND GARDENS. Mounting concern over quality and purity of prepared foods and the soaring costs of fresh produce combined in 1972 to stimulate a rebirth of interest in home vegetable gardening. Seed companies and nurseries in the U.S. reported that the sale of vegetable seeds had increased as much as 50% over sales in 1971. Tomatoes, peppers, and leaf lettuce were among the most popular home garden crops. Some enthusiasts were even reported to be giving up their flower gardens in favor of vegetables.

A promising new method for treating trees infected with Dutch elm disease was announced during the year. Previously, the only known way to save threatened trees was to destroy the breeding places of the beetles that spread the disease and to spray healthy trees before they could become infected. In 1969 Benomyl, a systemic fungicide, had been found effective in saving diseased young elms. Applied to the soil in its normal form, however, Benomyl was not readily taken up by mature trees. In 1972 plant pathologists Winard K. Hock and Lawrence R. Schreiber and technician Donald E. Wuertz of the U.S. Agricultural Research Service's Shade Tree and Ornamental Plant Laboratory, Delaware, Ohio, found a way to make Benomyl more soluble in water and also developed a pressure technique to inject solutions into trees. The pressure technique was developed in cooperation with plant pathologist Eugene B. Himelick, associated with the Illinois Natural History Survey, at Urbana. It was expected that it would take two to four years to put the new method into general use.

A new type of seed-propagated geranium, the midi-geranium, or semidwarf, was grown by researchers at Pennsylvania State University and by commercial plant breeders. Its development started in 1965 when three dwarf geraniums resulted from a breeding project at the university. These were crossed with tall varieties, and the resulting F_1 hybrids were all intermediate in size. Continued crossing resulted in midi-geraniums, which were believed to combine the best characteristics of the tall and dwarf parents. They were more self-branching than the talls and more vigorous than the dwarfs, and the size of flower clusters was nearly equal to that of the talls.

Air pollution injury to vegetation in the U.S. caused losses of about half a billion dollars in 1972, according to estimates by plant pathologist H. E. Heggestad of the Agricultural Research Service's Plant Air Pollution Laboratory, at Beltsville, Md. However, while some plants had become unable to mature or produce fruit, scientists were identifying others—including cultivars of poinsettia, chrysanthemum, and petunia—that were particularly resistant to air pollution injury.

Three hybrid tea roses won 1973 All-America awards: Electron, bright rose-pink; Gypsy, orange-red; and Medallion, apricot-pink. In honor of the first lady of the U.S., a dark red, velvety floribunda rose was named the Pat Nixon Rose by C. W. Stuart & Co., Newark, N.Y. The rose was created by Mme Louise Meilland, the widow of Francis Meilland, who had hybridized the famous Peace Rose. Plants were expected to be available for purchase in 1973. (*See in* CE: Gardens and Gardening; Flower, Fruit, and Plant articles.)

FOOD. Increases in retail food prices in the U.S. during 1972 fueled a lively debate among consumer and retail spokesmen, politicians, and public officials, all of whom took turns blaming the situation on one another, on farmers, and on an anonymous, all-encompassing "middleman." Figures released by the U.S. Bureau of Labor Statistics indicated that February food prices had risen 1.7% over the preceding month, the largest increase in 14 years. Higher meat prices accounted for a large proportion of the increase. Early in June there were reports that retail food chains were contemplating new price hikes. The Price Commission recommended that the Cost of Living Council extend price controls to raw agricultural products—a move resisted by U.S. President Richard M. Nixon. Later in the month the president did move to stabilize meat prices, ordering the removal of all quota restrictions on meat imports for the balance of the year. The Nixon Administration conceded, however, that this act would not have any immediate effect on U.S. meat prices.

As the summer wore on, there was no discernible slackening in food price increases. Early in September, the director of the Cost of Living Council, Donald R. Rumsfeld, notified the nation's larger food retailers that beef prices were still too high and informed them that he had ordered the Internal Revenue Service to monitor the profit margins of about 100 major chains. A September report by the Department of Agriculture was interpreted to show that food processors and retailers had widened the gap between farmers' and consumers' prices of beef to a record margin in August. The department also reported that shortages of fresh produce, resulting from poor weather on the East and West coasts, had caused sharp increases in the summer farm prices for fruits and vegetables; it was only the second time in 35 years that August produce prices had not fallen below those for June.

Despite the reports of their high profit margins, retail food chains appeared to be in deep financial trouble. Throughout much of 1972, U.S. food retailers were affected by a severe price war that began with a policy of price discounting and moved to the scrapping of retail promotion "frills," such as trading stamps and games. The Great Atlantic and Pacific Tea Company (A&P), the nation's largest retail food chain, began a program of gradual conversion of its more than 4,000 stores from regular A&P stores to WEO (short for "Where Economy Originates") discount stores. A&P management instituted the program in the hope of increasing volume and reversing the course of the chain's plummeting profits. Other large chains followed suit, reducing prices and extending store hours.

Early in the year the Federal Trade Commission (FTC) brought suit against four of the largest manufacturers of ready-to-eat breakfast cereals. The four, which shared 91% of the industry, were charged with restraint of competition. The FTC complained that the trade structure of the industry had created a noncompetitive market in which the four companies had achieved a shared monopoly.

A list made public by the Food and Drug Administration (FDA) in March disclosed that certain maximum limits of food contamination were allowed by FDA inspectors. It revealed that processed food products may contain—in small quantities not considered a health hazard—insect parts, rodent hairs and excreta, bacteria, mold, worms, and other foreign matter. Shortly after the public disclosure, the FDA promised to take "prompt, vigorous action" to promote cleanliness in the food industry. (*See also* Agriculture.)

Robert H. Cagan (left) and James A. Morris check a purified sample of Monellin, a new natural sweetener 3,000 times more intense than sugar.

AUTHENTICATED NEWS INTERNATIONAL

Special Report: FOODS FOR THOUGHT

by Annette Ashlock Stover

Since the late 1960's, a drastic change in eating habits has been made by increasing numbers of people in the U.S. Although no accurate count has been made, perhaps several million people have given up the eating habits of the past and have turned to "natural foods" or "organic foods." What is this movement all about? What caused it? Is it based on fact? And are these recruits to a new eating style headed in the right direction?

Curiously, the movement has not occurred through the urgings of doctors or dietitians. Instead, many followers exhibit a good deal of anti-establishment thinking and often a disrespect for scientists and the medical profession. Some of the followers are older people with an understandable desire for good health. Some are mothers worried about whether their children are eating properly. Some are young people with counterculture leanings. Others are simply people with a newfound interest in healthful eating.

Actually, the movement is somewhat divided into supporters of organic foods, fans of natural foods, and purchasers of "health foods"—a rather nebulous term. These people have turned to their new style of eating for a variety of reasons—most of which can be narrowed to three areas of attack:

1. The claim is made that today's agricultural practices, with the widespread use of chemical fertilizers and pesticides, are dangerous and harmful to our food. Advocates of organic foods say that our soil is becoming impoverished and is producing nutrient-depleted plants. Organically fertilized plants are said to be nutritionally superior.

The concern is ecological as well. Quite a gloomy picture is painted of the future if we do not change our ways. Advocates visualize organic fertilizers and methods of growing, with control of pests through biological methods using natural enemies of insects, as the way to save our world.

Critics of pesticides point to the fact that in the U.S. there are thousands of pesticides, about 200 of which are highly toxic. These have been detected in many foods, in humans, in animals, and in various parts of our natural surroundings. The President's Science Advisory Committee says that the variety, toxicity, and persistence of pesticides affect biological systems in nature and may eventually affect human health. Not all pesticides can accumulate, however, and many are broken down, destroyed, and excreted by the body. "We have no proof that the effects of these chemicals are cumulative—except for DDT," says Dr. Jean Mayer, chairman of the White House Conference on Food, Nutrition and Health, "but we must take it very seriously."

2. The advocates of natural foods claim that modern processing methods rob food of its nutrients and that dangerous chemicals are being added to preserve food or to make inferior food more attractive. White bread, white flour, white rice, and refined sugar are popular targets. In the processing of white flour, the germ and the outer bran layer are removed; these are the parts that contain most of the vitamins. High on the preferred list of foods, therefore, are whole grains, as well as "natural" sweeteners such as honey and blackstrap molasses.

Other items on the shopping list include fresh fruits and vegetables (organic advocates, of course, choose organic varieties), fresh meats and poultry, brown rice, rice polishings, raw milk, natural cheeses, soybeans, lecithin, sunflower seeds, brewers' yeast, rose hips, wheat germ, carob, and sea salt. The natural-food advocates, but not necessarily the health-food advocates, try to eliminate all foods containing chemical additives or synthetic ingredients of any kind. Some have even become like religious zealots in their condemnation of processed foods.

3. The purchasers of health foods claim that an improper diet is the cause of a variety of diseases, from cancer and heart disease to arthritis, baldness, and mental disorders. At the least, eating recommended foods or taking large doses of vitamins is said to make a person feel better and have more energy. Particular vitamins are cited as cures for certain maladies; usually these are taken in large doses without a doctor's supervision. Often these health-food advocates soundly denounce the medical profession for being ignorant of nutrition.

Clarification Through Definition

An organic food is one that has been produced without artificial fertilizers or pesticides and has been grown in soil whose humus content has been increased by the addition of organic matter. The food is free of preservatives or additives of any kind.

A natural food, in the correct sense, is a food as it occurs in nature—fresh, unprocessed, and even uncooked. Some foods, however, such as meat and grains, are not fit to eat without cooking.

The term health food ought to mean any food

containing nutrients needed by the body for good health. In the health-food movement of today, however, the term has come to apply to a small group of foods and products available in special health-food stores. Some are processed, some not. Some are organic, some not. Many items are uncommon, unusual in our diet, and not available in great quantities.

In 1972 there was no legal interpretation of what is, or is not, organic. The term was used loosely in food labeling and advertising. There were no federal regulations or standards for organic foods or checks on the authenticity of label claims. A number of stores have been discovered to be selling foods that were falsely labeled organic.

Production of foods advertised and labeled as organic is limited, and usually the food costs more than its counterpart produced by regular methods. Family economists of the U.S. Department of Agriculture compared a market basket of foods. The organic items at a health-food store cost $21.90. Similar regular foods at a supermarket cost $11.00.

Many experts take issue with the claims of enthusiasts of organic, natural, and health foods. These include almost all doctors, dietitians, and scientific nutritionists. Dr. Frederick Stare, chairman of the Department of Nutrition at Harvard University, says, "All the necessary foods are available in the supermarket, and goodness is still in our foods. The poisons are in the pens and tongues of those who—by peddling misinformation, half-truths, statements out of context, and downright falsehoods—gain some temporary notoriety, inflate their own egos, and hope to make a profit."

Advocates of natural vitamins feel that the cheaper synthetics are not comparable in quality.

CHIE NISHIO FROM NANCY PALMER AGENCY

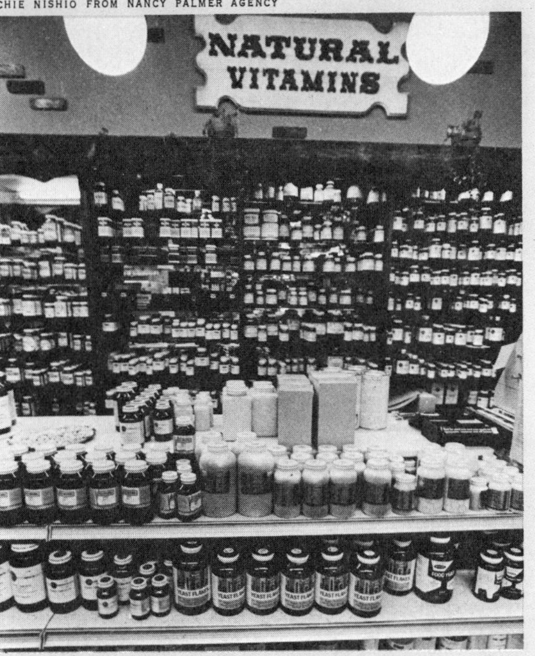

Nutritionists cannot find evidence for the commonplace horror stories of a national food supply that is depleted and debased. In fact, the B-vitamin deficiencies said to be so prevalent by the advocates of whole grains fail to appear. The reason is that meat is a better source of B vitamins than the highly touted whole grains. Good nutrition depends upon securing sufficient amounts of the essential nutrients—amino acids (proteins), vitamins, minerals, fats, and carbohydrates. Nutritionists stress eating a wide variety of foods in order to obtain them all.

Too many health-food advocates insist on strange foods or rely on limited diets. It makes no difference, however, if your vitamin C comes from citrus fruit or areola berries, riboflavin from milk or rice polishings, and protein from beef or fish. Natural-food advocates also insist on vitamin supplements only from natural sources. All scientific studies, however, have shown that the chemical composition of a natural vitamin is identical to the laboratory-made version.

Processed Foods and Additives

What do food scientists say about processed foods? Are they robbed of nutrients? Some are; some are not. Some processed foods, including many cereals, are fortified with more nutrients than the natural product. White bread and white rice do not have the nutrients of the natural products, although white bread is enriched with iron and the three major B vitamins. White bread is the subject of scorn by health-food advocates; they claim the refining is some sort of evil perpetrated on the public. This is hardly the case. Whole-grain breads and brown rice have always been available in stores. It is consumer demand for the white product that makes sales so great.

Some nutrients partially lost in processing are the same nutrients lost when that raw food is cooked. Vitamin C is reduced in the canning of vegetables and fruits, just as it is when you cook them at home; but drinking one glass of frozen orange juice supplies a day's vitamin C, so the loss is not critical. Fortunately, vitamin A, of which fruits and vegetables are an important source, is stable through heat processing. Thus, processed and unprocessed foods both contain and retain vitamin A.

As for organic food production, much as we would like to go back to a simpler time when everyone raised his own food by organic methods, agricultural scientists say this is impossible in feeding our large, primarily urban population. Ecological considerations were too often ignored in the past, but in recent times agricultural scientists have been making efforts to find and promote biodegradable sprays that are ecologically sound. DDT has been banned. The Food and Drug Administration (FDA), the Environmental Protection Agency, and state control agencies set strict rules for the use of pesticides and strict levels, with safety margins, over which pesticide residues are not permitted. Foods may not be marketed if they exceed these levels. Most crops are not sprayed as harvesttime approaches.

Interestingly, in the providing of nutrients for plants, chemical fertilizers function in exactly the same way as organic fertilizers. Chemical fertilizers are more efficient, however, because it takes time for organic matter to be broken down and there is not a large enough supply for crop needs. The nutritive value of a plant is the same, whether the soil was fertilized organically or chemically.

What about the chemical additives in foods? Advocates of natural foods condemn all additives, but food scientists disagree. The laws regulating the use of food additives are quite specific. A new additive may not be used until its safety has been documented. There must be evidence that the additive will perform a useful function; it may not disguise the use of faulty ingredients or manufacturing practices. Forgetting that everything in the universe has a chemical formulation, too many people get needlessly upset by seeing a chemical name on a list of ingredients. The labeling laws are such that a substance added to the food must be named on the label, even though it occurs naturally in other foods.

The more informed criticism of additives is made of some on the GRAS (generally recognized as safe) list. This is a list of commonly used additives that scientists considered safe at the time of passage of the Food Additives Amendment of 1958. Since then, the safety of some additives has become doubtful and they have been taken off the approved list. Through urgings of critics, the FDA has ordered tests and a review of the list.

It is true that some people feel better after beginning a health-food diet. This can be partly psychological and partly because they have eliminated the junk foods from their former diet. Switching to the basic-four eating plan can produce the same results. The health foods recommended are nutritious—but the purchaser pays a high price for his nutrition. A wise selection of economical and nutritious foods from the supermarket is all he needs to keep himself in good nutritional health.

A shopper selects organically grown produce at The Good Earth, one of more than 100 health food stores in New York City. In 1962 there were barely a dozen such stores in the city.

CHIE NISHIO FROM NANCY PALMER AGENCY

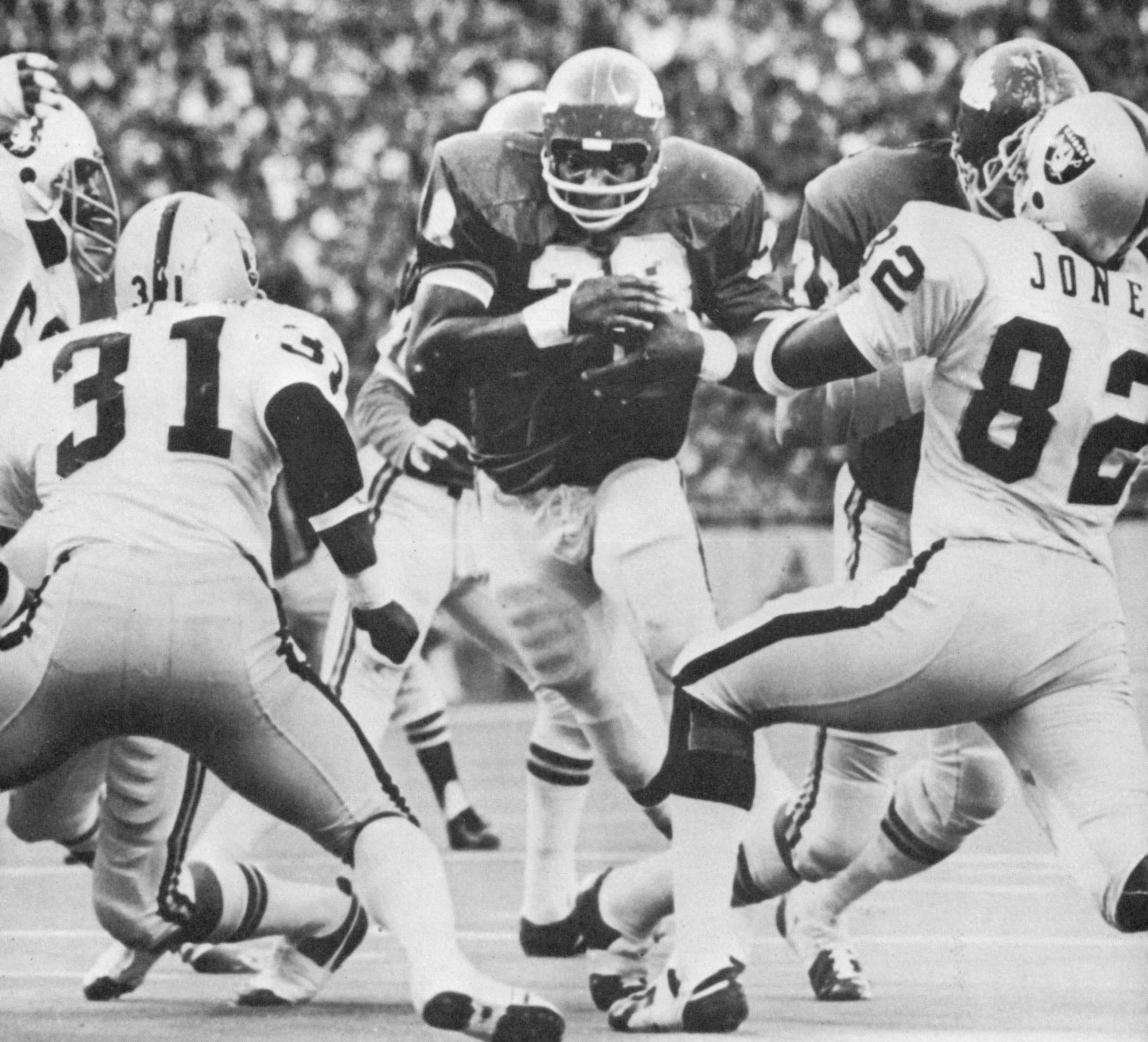

WIDE WORLD

Kansas City Chiefs' Wendell Hayes (center) finds an opening in the Oakland Raiders' line. The Chiefs won the game, 27–14, in November.

FOOTBALL. On Jan. 14, 1973, before a crowd of 90,182 in Los Angeles, the Miami Dolphins of the American Conference defeated the Washington Redskins of the National Conference, 14–7, to win the seventh annual Super Bowl and the National Football League (NFL) title. Miami ran up a 14–0 lead in the first half as quarterback Bob Griese threw a 28-yard touchdown pass to Howard Twilley, and Jim Kiick later scored on a one-yard run. Washington's lone score came in the fourth quarter when Mike Bass ran the ball in for the touchdown.

Regular-Season Games and Play-offs; Canadian Football

Before they ever reached the Super Bowl, the Miami Dolphins assured themselves a place in the NFL record book by romping to 14 regular-season victories without a defeat. The NFL had not had an unbeaten team since 1942, and then the Chicago Bears accomplished the feat in only 11 games. The Bears also went undefeated in 1934 with a 13-game schedule. Although the 1948 Cleveland Browns won 14 straight regular-season games and one play-off game, they did it in the old All-America Football Conference, causing NFL jingoists to look askance at their performance.

No professional team ever displayed as potent a running attack as that of the Dolphins. The Eastern Division champions of the American Conference amassed 2,952 yards rushing for an NFL record, and they were the first team in history to have two running backs, Larry Csonka and Eugene (Mercury) Morris, who gained 1,000 or more yards each. Larry Little, a 6-foot-3-inch, 265-pound guard, cleared the way for them repeatedly and also provided protection for Earl Morrall, Miami's 38-year-old quarterback. Morrall took over the job when Bob Griese, all-NFL at the position in 1971, suffered a broken leg in the fifth game of the season. Frequently forgotten in the clamor over the Miami offense was what came to be known as the Dolphins' "no-name defense"—including linebacker Nick Buoniconti, tackle Manny Fernandez, and safety Dick Anderson. Miami had lost the 1972 Super Bowl to the Dallas Cowboys, 24–3, but coach Don Shula got the Dolphins back for a second try with victories over the Cleveland Browns, 20–14, and the Pittsburgh Steelers, 21–17, in the American Conference play-offs.

By defeating Dallas for the National Conference title, the Washington Redskins became a champion team for the first time in 30 years. Place-kicker Curt Knight put the Redskins in the Super Bowl and—by kicking a record four field goals in the 26–3 victory—made sure the Cowboys, the "wild card" team in the National Conference play-offs, would not get there again. Knight, who endured a mid-season slump, booted three field goals one week earlier when Washington defeated the Green Bay Packers 16–3 in the first play-off round.

Victory justified the means George Allen took to build the Redskins in his two years as head coach. Eschewing rookies (only one made the team in 1972), he sought veterans, and he wheeled and dealed to get them. Allen devoted most of his efforts to building a defense around tackle Diron Talbert, end Ron McDole, linebackers Jack Pardee and Chris Hanburger, cornerback Pat Fischer, and safety Roosevelt Taylor. Washington's offense revolved around Larry Brown, the NFL's premier runner in the year of the running back. Aided by the blocking of Charlie Harraway, his partner in the backfield, Brown gained 1,216 yards in the Redskins' first 12 games and then sat out the last two, which Washington lost. Injuries haunted Redskins quarterback Sonny Jurgensen, so Billy Kilmer once again inherited his job and three sterling receivers, Charley Taylor, Roy Jefferson, and Jerry Smith.

The San Francisco '49ers finally emerged as champions of the National Conference Western Division when veteran quarterback John Brodie came off the bench to throw a touchdown pass that beat the Minnesota Vikings in the regular-season finale. One week later, Roger Staubach of Dallas did the same thing to beat the '49ers 30–28 in a play-off.

The Green Bay Packers, the dominant force in professional football in the mid-1960's, regained some of their past glory by winning the Central Division championship in the National Conference. Victorious in just four games in 1971, they won ten in 1972 while the Vikings, division champions for four straight years, could attain no better than a .500 record. Rookie place-kicker Chester Marcol led the NFL in scoring with 128 points and made the Packers a threat anywhere inside the 50-yard line. Running backs John Brockington and MacArthur Lane frequently put Green Bay there, if not across the goal line.

Unlike Green Bay, Pittsburgh waited 40 years for a championship team. The American Conference Central Division title was the first ever won by the Steelers. Their patient owner, 71-year-old Art Rooney, saw the bad times turn good with the arrival of Franco Harris, a rookie running back from Pennsylvania State. Harris rushed for more than 100 yards in six straight games—coming within one yard of an NFL record. The Steelers' 11–3 finish put them a game ahead of Cleveland, whose second-place record got the team into the play-offs as a "wild card."

Controversy surrounded Pittsburgh's 13–7 play-off victory over the Oakland Raiders, champions of

Washington Redskin defender Mike Bass (41), blocks a pass right out of the hands of Dallas Cowboy Calvin Hill (35) in the first quarter of the National Football Conference championship game in Washington on New Year's Eve. The Redskins defeated the Dallas Cowboys 26–3 but lost to the Miami Dolphins in the 1973 Super Bowl in Los Angeles.

WIDE WORLD

the American Conference's Western Division. Officials ruled that a pass thrown to John Fuqua of Pittsburgh with five seconds left in the game bounced off Fuqua and then was touched by Oakland safety Jack Tatum before Harris plucked it out of the air and ran 42 yards for the winning score. If Tatum had not touched the ball, the play would have been voided, for no two receivers on the same team can touch a pass consecutively. A television instant replay showed the officials' decision to be correct.

Ten ball carriers in 1972 ran for 1,000 yards or more. O. J. Simpson of the Buffalo Bills took advantage of Larry Brown's two-game absence to capture the ground-gaining title with 1,251 yards. Brown finished second. After him, in order, came: Ron Johnson of the New York Giants (1,182); Csonka of Miami (1,117); Maru Hubbard of Oakland (1,100); Harris of Pittsburgh (1,055); Calvin Hill of Dallas (1,036); Mike Garrett of San Diego (1,031); Brockington of Green Bay (1,027); and Morris of Miami (1,000). An 11th man, Dave Hampton of the Atlanta Falcons, reached 1,000 yards in the last game of the season, but he was thrown for a 5-yard loss on a subsequent play and finished with 995 yards.

The Hamilton Tiger-Cats, five times champions between 1953 and 1967, regained possession of the Grey Cup, the Canadian Football League's top prize. Hamilton defeated the Saskatchewan Roughriders, 14–10, for the title.

College Football

The University of Southern California (USC) won the 1972 U.S. collegiate championship. The Trojans, number one in every poll in the country, concluded their season by demolishing third-ranked Ohio State, 42–17, in the Rose Bowl, as Anthony Davis gained 157 yards and fullback Sam Cunningham scored four touchdowns. It was the 12th victory without a defeat for USC, which won the Pacific Eight championship and its 4th national title in 11 years.

The Nebraska Cornhuskers, who were seeking their third consecutive national championship, finished second to Oklahoma in the Big Eight Conference. The Sooners' strength showed in their 14–0 Sugar Bowl victory over Penn State. Nebraska, meanwhile, drubbed Notre Dame, 40–6, in the Orange Bowl. Powerhouse Alabama did not fare as well, being upset 17–13 by Texas in the Cotton Bowl. Auburn defeated Colorado 24–3 in the Gator Bowl.

Johnny Rodgers, Nebraska's 5-foot-9-inch running back, wide receiver, and kick returner, won the Heisman trophy as the outstanding player of the year. Rodgers' nonfootball past, which included a number of scrapes with the law, was overlooked when voters selected him over teammate Rich Glover, who wound up receiving the Outland trophy as the nation's foremost collegiate lineman, and Greg Pruitt, a diminutive running back from Oklahoma. Rodgers established a collegiate record by gaining 5,586 yards on runs, pass receptions, and kick and punt returns. The smallest running back in the U.S., 5-foot-5-inch Howard Stevens of Louisville, led the major colleges in all-purpose running, averaging 213.2 yards a game rushing, receiving, and returning kicks. Pete Van Valkenburg, a senior tailback from Brigham Young, averaged 138.6 yards a game to lead the nation in rushing.

College football's top passer was Don Strock of Virginia Tech, who completed 53% of his passes for 3,243 yards and 16 touchdowns during the season. Although Tony Adams of Utah State had to

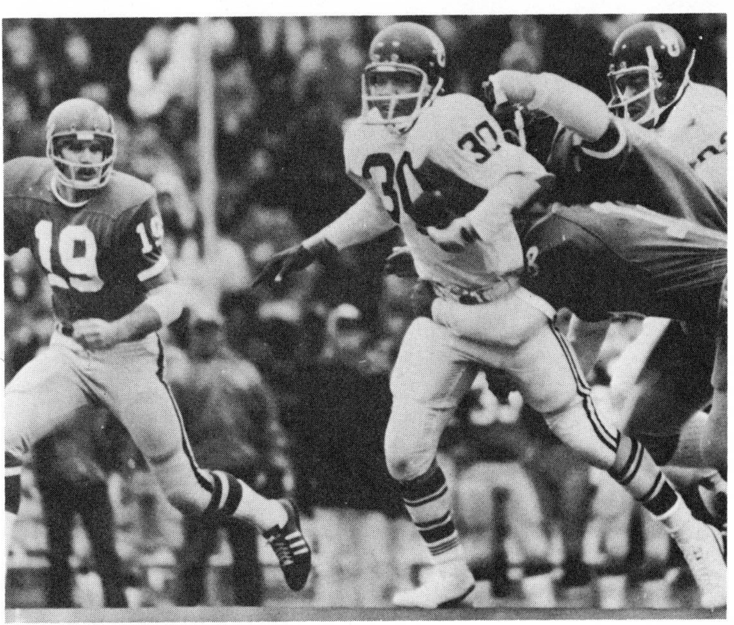

Oklahoma halfback Gregg Pruitt (30) churns away against Kansas. Oklahoma won the game, 31–7, and went on to defeat Nebraska in the Big Eight title game.
WIDE WORLD

content himself with being the third leading passer, he established a National Collegiate Athletic Association record by throwing for 561 yards in a 44–16 rout of Utah.

Oklahoma was the country's best rushing team for the second straight year, averaging 368.8 yards a game, but Arizona State was far and away the best at offense. The Sun Devils amassed an average of 516.5 yards and 46.6 points for their 11-game regular season.

Penn State, an independent power, compiled a 10–1 regular-season record, losing only to Tennessee, to win the Lambert trophy, symbolic of supremacy in the East. Dartmouth won its fourth Ivy League championship in a row to establish a record. Second-place Yale overcame a 17–0 deficit to defeat Harvard 28–17 in the 89th meeting between the two schools. In the East's other major traditional, the 73d Army-Navy game, the Cadets commandeered a 23–15 victory. Massachusetts became the champion of the Yankee Conference for the second consecutive year, winning all five league games.

Alabama was undefeated through its first ten games of the season, hungering all the while to overcome USC in the race for the national championship. But when the Crimson Tide met Auburn, Bill Newton blocked two Alabama punts and teammate David Langner ran both back for touchdowns to give the Tigers a 17–16 victory. The Crimson Tide's consolation prize was the Southeastern Conference championship. Tampa's 9–2 record stamped it as the South's leading independent. Quarterbacks Bert Jones of Louisiana State and Gary Huff of Florida State were the most-heralded players in the South.

In the Atlantic Coast Conference, North Carolina won its second straight title with a 6–0 league record. The Tar Heels were 10–1 overall. East Carolina triumphed in the Southern Conference, finishing one game ahead of Richmond, the 1971 champion. Tennessee Tech prevailed in the Ohio Valley Conference.

Though its national stature had diminished in recent years, the Big Ten produced two teams worthy of national ranking, Michigan and Ohio State. They shared the conference championship with 7–1 records, but Ohio State traveled to the Rose Bowl on the strength of its 14–11 upset of the Wolverines. Kent State won the Mid-American Conference and Drake, Louisville, and West Texas tied for the Missouri Valley Conference title.

Arkansas was supposed to run away with the Southwest Conference, but it was Texas that accomplished that feat. The Longhorns, powered by the running of sophomore Roosevelt Leaks, won their fifth consecutive league title by 3 games, the biggest margin in conference history. Arkansas finished 3–4 in the conference and 6–5 overall. Arizona State, the nation's highest-scoring team, won the Western Athletic Conference, the nation's highest-scoring league. (*See in* CE: Football.)

FOREST PRODUCTS. In 1972 preliminary estimates of U.S. lumber production, measured in board feet, were made available for 1971. Based on information compiled by the National Forest Products Association, the total 1971 output was 36.65 billion board feet, including 30.28 billion board feet of softwood lumber and 6.36 billion board feet of hardwood lumber. The combined output of softwood and hardwood lumber was approximately 2 billion board feet over the 1970 figure but still below the post-World War II high of 38.9 billion board feet reached in 1950. U.S. exports of lumber totaled 1,096,700,000 board feet in 1971. Imports were 7,619,300 board feet. The wholesale price index of lumber in June 1972 was 159.0, up 18.3% from the index in 1971.

In January 1972 the Administration of U.S. President Richard M. Nixon, under pressure from the timber industry, decided against issuing an executive order that would have restricted the practice of "clear-cutting"—felling trees of all ages and kinds, in areas that could range from a few acres to many hundreds of acres. Conservation groups had strongly urged that such an order be made, claiming that clear-cutting practices were wasteful and damaging to the environment.

Because hardrock maple was being sent to Japan to supply a boom in the construction of bowling alleys, supplies of the wood in the U.S. dwindled alarmingly during the year. The price was sent skyward; it was reported that the Japanese were paying $600 or more per thousand board feet for this wood.

Trees in large areas of the northeastern U.S. were plagued by the gypsy moth caterpillar. A quarantine was set up to keep the insect from traveling westward. (*See also* Environment. *See in* CE: Lumber; Wood.)

Logs surrounded by a boom are towed to a mill in the Soviet Union.
TASS FROM SOVFOTO

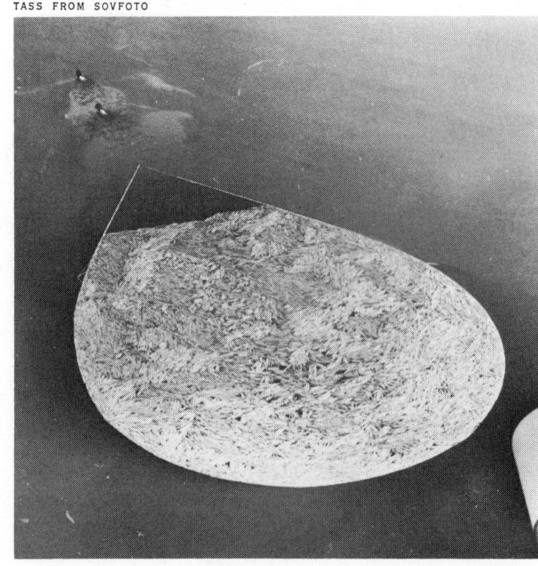

FRANCE. Political activity intensified in 1972 as France prepared for a general election in March 1973, when for the first time the ruling majority would face a united opposition from the left. The French Communist and Socialist parties reached their first agreement on a common policy since 1936. Moreover, the political center regrouped in 1972 as the Reform Movement. The centrists hoped to win a fair number of seats from the Gaullists, whose image was tarnished during the year by a succession of financial scandals. The most unsettling was the revelation of tax avoidance involving Prime Minister Jacques Chaban-Delmas. He was replaced by Pierre Messmer, an orthodox Gaullist, and a major governmental reorganization followed in an effort to improve the majority's chances in the forthcoming election.

Domestic Affairs

Electoral considerations were reflected at a press conference in September, when President Georges Pompidou concentrated on internal problems and scandals, particularly the Aranda affair that flared up earlier in the month. Gabriel Aranda, who had been press adviser to a former minister of equipment and housing, threatened to disclose photocopies of documents that compromised prominent figures in planning and development. The contents were leaked to the press, and the affair took on the proportions of a major political scandal. The documents were finally handed over to a magistrate, who recommended a thorough investigation of several incidents. In his press conference, Pompidou stressed that corruption had to be eliminated wherever it was found.

Pompidou said that he would form a government in the spring of 1973 no matter which side won the elections. Then, he said, if his government were voted down by the National Assembly, he could dissolve parliament and appeal to the country. He made it clear that he did not intend to invite either the Socialist leader Francois Mitterrand nor the Communist leader Georges Marchais to take part in the government.

Pompidou's own image was bruised by the results of a referendum in April 1972. The nominal reason for the popular referendum on April 23 was to determine whether France should ratify the treaty enlarging the European Economic Community (EEC). It was plain, however, that an affirmative response would be a vote of approval for Pompidou. The vote failed to bring him the increased prestige that he expected. The Socialists had advised their supporters to abstain, and the Communists had counseled outright opposition. Fewer than 16 million of the country's 30 million registered voters submitted valid votes, and 5 million of those were against the proposal. A further 2 million submitted blank or spoiled ballots. The massive rate of abstention—twice as high as in any previous referendum—clearly represented a political gesture. Nevertheless, the treaty was ratified.

The resignation of the government and the replacement of Chaban-Delmas in July marked the end of a period in which the prime minister's relations with the ruling majority had become increasingly strained. His personal authority had been shaken by the disclosure that he had contrived, though legally, to pay no tax from 1966 to 1970.

After a long silence and despite a vote of confidence in favor of Chaban-Delmas on May 24, Pompidou finally replaced him on July 5. On the following day, Messmer, who had been minister of national defense under Charles de Gaulle from 1960 to 1969, was appointed prime minister, and the government was reorganized. Olivier Guichard,

French farmers from Larzac drove their sheep onto the Champ de Mars in Paris to protest plans of the Ministry of National Defense to appropriate parts of their farms to expand military training camps.

JAMES ANDANSON FROM GAMMA

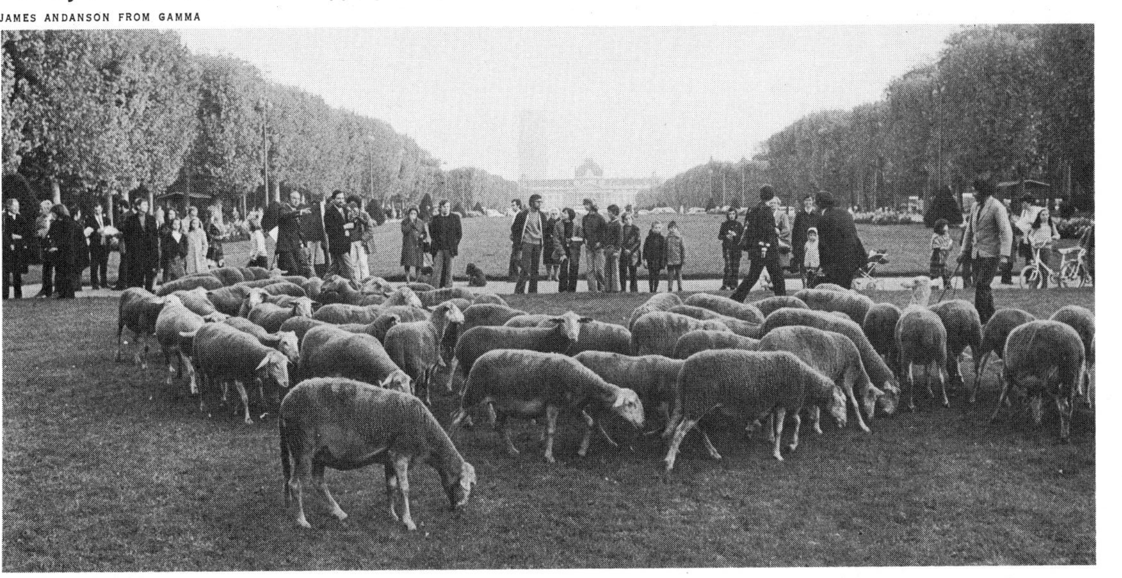

a close confidant of Pompidou, was entrusted with a new superministry that combined supply, housing, and regional planning.

On October 3 the new prime minister made his first statement to the National Assembly. He announced several definite proposals that favored the least privileged sectors in order to create "a just and more humane society."

In 1972 the trade unions in France continued to demand a minimum monthly wage of $200 and retirement at the age of 60. A number of one-day strikes took place during the summer and fall. In August, after talking with union and management leaders, Messmer proposed a system of "economic participation aimed at improving capitalism socially without destroying it." Unimpressed, the labor movement took part in further work stoppages, culminating in an "action week" in October.

Prominent among the social issues in 1972 was the 52-year-old abortion law. Addressing a Gaullist women's rally in November, Messmer hinted that liberalization of the law—which prohibited abortion except when the mother's life was threatened—would be a matter for the next parliament.

For the first time, a woman was elected president of the Council of Paris, the capital's highest office, in 1972. She was Nicole de Hauteclocque, deputy and councillor for the 15th arrondissement.

Foreign Affairs

Pompidou's main concern in the international sphere was the enlargement of the EEC. Toward that end the European summit meeting was held in Paris in October. In preparation for the meeting, Pompidou met in Paris and other European capitals with leaders of member and applicant countries.

In connection with an EEC expansion and the lifting of the French veto on British entry, Queen Elizabeth II and Prince Philip of Great Britain made a state visit to France in May. They were received at the Elysée Palace for the second time since Queen Elizabeth's accession to the British throne (they had been received in 1957), an exception to the British rule that a head of state never makes more than one official visit to a non-Commonwealth country.

While the EEC meeting was taking place in Paris, the initial agreement for construction of the channel railway tunnel was signed simultaneously in London and Paris. Excavation was scheduled to start in the fall of 1973. France and Poland signed a ten-year friendship and cooperation agreement on October 6, climaxing a five-day visit to Paris by Edward Gierek, first secretary of the Polish Communist party. Africa remained a constant preoccupation, and France continued to maintain close ties with its former colonies. Pompidou visited Niger, Chad, Togo, and Upper Volta.

Other visitors to France in 1972 included Queen Juliana of the Netherlands and Emperor Haile Selassie I of Ethiopia. Tunisia's President Habib Bourguiba also visited.

During the summer, French nuclear tests in the Pacific brought strong criticism from several countries, but the series was completed. On July 14, Bastille Day ceremonies included for the first time a ballistic missile that was paraded down the Champs Elysées.

The buildings of the French diplomatic mission to North Vietnam were wrecked in October during a U.S. bombing raid on a nearby rail yard in Hanoi. The head of the mission was fatally wounded, and five employees died in the raid. The French government officially protested, and U.S. President Richard M. Nixon sent a letter of regret to Pompidou. (*See in* CE: France.)

Pierre Messmer was named prime minister by President Georges Pompidou. Messmer succeeded Jacques Chaban-Delmas after a series of scandals rocked Pompidou's Gaullist party.

MARIE-LAURE DE DECKER FROM GAMMA

KEYSTONE

Scientists and engineers at the General Electric Research and Development Center, Schenectady, N.Y., are researching methods for converting coal into clean fuel gas.

FUEL AND POWER. Developments in the field of fuel and power during 1972 made it clear that the U.S. was going through a fundamental change, from a position of abundant, cheap energy to one of more expensive energy associated with supply problems. Imports as a percentage of total oil consumption continued to rise, although Texas allowed oil wells there to produce without limitation for the first time since 1948. The search for new reserves of oil and gas carried drilling of wells to new record depths. In January a well in western Texas was bottomed at 28,500 feet, exceeding by 2,900 feet the previous record depth set in 1970. Only 22 days later a well in western Oklahoma equaled that depth, and in March it bottomed at a new record of more than 30,050 feet. Neither produced from their record depths, but in May a new producing depth record was set by a well, also in western Oklahoma, that yielded commercial quantities of gas from a depth of 24,500 feet.

The electric power supply was again critically short during the periods of peak demand in summer heat waves. In July there were voltage reductions in New York City and Michigan and the situation was precarious in several other localities until cooler weather arrived. In late summer a gasoline supply shortage suddenly developed. It was the result of a surge in demand in the face of a tight supply of crude oil and refinery operations already at the effective limit of 90% of theoretical capacity. An apparent contribution to the high level of demand was the sharply reduced mileage performance of 1972 model automobiles, which were equipped with emission-control devices in compliance with new regulations on air pollution. Although some gasoline marketers were forced to close their pumps, no motorists were deprived of gasoline. It was, however, a new peacetime experience for the U.S., and gasoline prices in most parts of the country rose by several cents a gallon.

The situation in natural gas continued to worsen, as pipelines and distributing companies instituted curtailments that limited or stopped the addition of new customers and reduced deliveries to some large industrial users. In an effort to improve the supply of gas over the longer term, in August the Federal Power Commission (FPC) adopted a new policy that permitted producers to commit new gas reserves to pipelines at any price that could be demonstrated to be in the public interest, subject to certain limitations on future price increases for existing gas commitments. The industry also took steps to obtain supplemental gas supplies. Additional projects were instituted to obtain liquefied natural gas from North Africa and from Australia, and negotiations were begun with the government of the U.S.S.R. to supply liquefied natural gas to the U.S. from the enormous gas fields of western Siberia.

New projects for the production of synthetic gas from coal, in addition to those begun in the preceding year, were also announced.

Exploration of the North Sea continued to make news, with large oil and gas discoveries in almost all the national sectors announced throughout the year. Several large new oil fields were discovered in both the British and Norwegian sectors. Denmark became the second country to produce North Sea oil with the first commercial shipment in the country's history from the Dan field in its sector. One of the oil discoveries in the British sector recorded a potential flow of 28,000 barrels a day, the largest yet reported for the North Sea and large even by Middle East standards.

As a test of public acceptance of natural gas as a smog-abating fuel, the world's first two service stations dispensing natural gas for automotive use were opened in Riverside, Calif. Announcements by the automobile industry in the U.S. indicated that within a few years the revolutionary new Wankel engine would be introduced into U.S. cars. The Wankel, named for its inventor, is a rotary engine with only a few moving parts. The automobile industry hoped that it would be the means of satisfying the standards for exhaust emission that had to be met in 1975. The Wankel was already being used in British motorcycles and German and Japanese automobiles. Plans for its adoption for small-engine applications—as in lawn mowers and boats—were announced by several U.S. companies. (*See also* Automobiles.)

COAL

Demand for bituminous coal in 1972 in the U.S. was expected to exceed the record consumption in 1943 of 593.8 million tons. In 1971, about 553 million tons of bituminous coal and lignite were produced, 8.3% short of the 603 million tons produced in 1970. A fall in noncommercial demand was offset by the growth in consumption by the electric power utilities, which accounted for 64.9% of total national coal consumption. Demand from the electric power sector was expected to increase by more than 6% yearly during the next five years.

U.S. exports in 1971 dropped 20% below the 1970 record. Falling exports to Japan and Europe accounted for most of the decline. Anthracite production, at 8.7 million tons, was down 11% from 1970.

World production of hard coal in 1971, at an estimated 2.536 billion tons, was 7 million tons greater than the 1970 production. A work stoppage in the U.S. had accounted for a loss of more than 66 million tons. Japan's imports from Australia and Canada grew. Increases in production in Western Europe amounted to 0.7%, while Eastern Europe's production (including the Soviet Union) increased 2.66%. The People's Republic of China, with an estimated level of 430 million tons for a gain of 33 million tons, maintained the position of the world's third largest producer.

In Canada, where coal production had doubled since 1969, a total of 19.3 million tons of all types of coal was produced in 1971, an increase of 16.4% over the 1970 figure. This total exceeded the record of 19.1 million tons set in 1951. Canada's exports reached a record of about 7.8 million tons—an impressive increase compared to the 1.4 million tons exported in 1969. By the mid-1970's, exports were expected to reach 14 million tons a year. Contracts to provide 200 million tons of coking coal to Japan during the next 15 years assured a bright future for the industry, with coal production forecast to reach 30 million tons a year by 1975. (*See in* CE: Coal.)

ELECTRICITY

In 1972 the rate of increase in electricity production continued to slow down, a trend already noticeable in 1971, despite the steady growth in consumption of electricity by noncommercial and commercial users. Nuclear power achieved competitiveness with fuel oil, although it was not likely to replace oil for several years. When fast breeder reactors were perfected, one ton of uranium would supply more power than 650,000 tons of oil, and it was not surprising that leading oil companies showed interest in the building of reactors. In May 1972 world production of nuclear electricity passed 500 billion kilowatt-hours, Great Britain leading the field with 43.7% of the total.

At the beginning of 1972, there were 22 nuclear power stations in service in the U.S., with a further 104 stations under construction or on order—about twice the capacity of the rest of the world. For these all to be fully operational by the end of the decade, the U.S. nuclear industry would need to overcome legal, administrative, and juridical chaos,

Power failure caused by burned out feeder cables affected more than 215,000 New York City residents during a summer heat wave in July.

WIDE WORLD

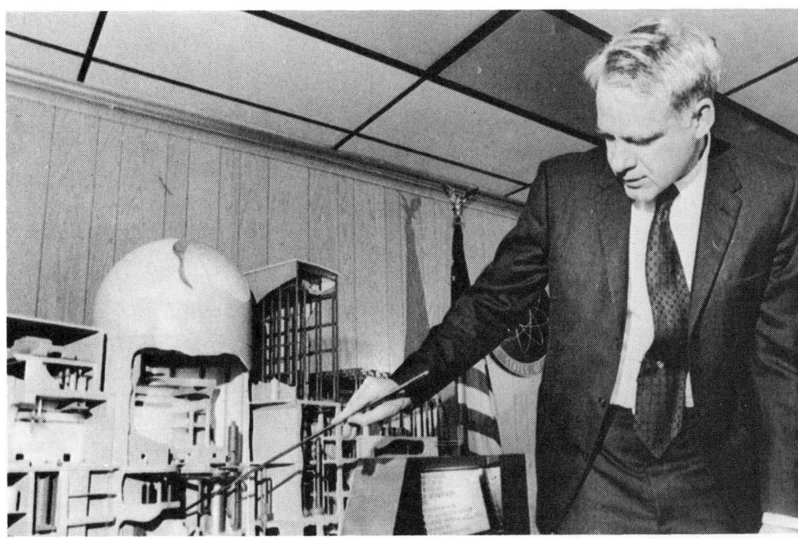

James R. Schlesinger, chairman of the Atomic Energy Commission, discusses a model of the nation's first demonstration Liquid Metal Fast Breeder Reactor plant. The proposed plant would be built at an estimated cost of a half billion dollars and would be located on the TVA system.
UPI COMPIX

as well as attacks from persons and groups opposed to the development of nuclear power stations. In 1971 there were no authorizations for the inauguration of new U.S. nuclear stations. Legislation introduced in 1972, however, allowed the U.S. Atomic Energy Commission to give temporary authorization for putting stations into service where local demands for electricity were urgent; 15 new stations were expected to be covered.

Orders for nuclear reactors for 1972 were expected to reach 35 units as compared with 23 units in 1971. The Commonwealth Edison Co. and the Tennessee Valley Authority (TVA) set up the Breeder Reactor Corp. to build and exploit the first large-scale demonstration breeder reactor in the U.S., with government finance providing $100 million and the rest of the money coming from the electricity companies and the plant manufacturers.

The Gentilly nuclear station in Canada reached maximum capacity, and the third sector of the Pickering station was brought into operation in May. Canada's nuclear program was delayed by the failure of the heavy-water factory at Glace Bay, in Nova Scotia, and it seemed that supplies of heavy water would have to be obtained abroad.

Conventional thermal stations still provided for most of the increased consumption of electricity, with oil continuing to advance at the expense of coal. The TVA's Cumberland power station, largest of its kind in the world, was inaugurated in July.

The developing countries still had natural resources to exploit, while the industrialized countries concentrated on pumped storage equipment. Ten conventional hydroelectric groups and seven reversible generator-motor pumping groups were brought into operation in the U.S. In Canada the Churchill Falls project, in Labrador, started to supply electricity. Bids were invited for the underground station at Mica Dam on the Columbia River. Work started on the James Bay project in Quebec, scheduled for completion in 1981, and on the Nelson River project at Long Spruce, Man. (*See in* CE: Electric Power.)

GAS

Demand for natural gas in the U.S. continued to diminish reserves in 1972. The situation brought more certain movement toward ensuring an adequate future supply. Federal regulators allowed higher returns on newer discoveries but within the nation's cost-of-living controls. Greater incentive toward future gas exploration and production was hoped for. The courts continued to iron out transportation and ecology litigation affecting the supply of natural gas. Users once again tapped one trillion cubic feet (Tcf) more gas yearly. They were expected to require as much additional gas each year for the next two decades. An estimated 278.8 Tcf of proven reserves were set to meet the increasing demand, including 31 Tcf in Alaska, plus whatever could be found in proven reserves opened up by federal government lease sales off Louisiana.

New discoveries off southern Alaska were said to rival earlier untapped deposits on the state's North Slope. Geological surveys and bottom samplings were being made by the federal government along the Atlantic outer continental shelf north of Cape Hatteras, in North Carolina. Public Service Co. of Indiana, Inc., and Westinghouse Electric Corp. began tests of turning high-sulfur coal into nearly pollution-free synthetic gas to fuel a power plant. A group of 11 companies planned to help finance the Continental Oil Co. and the British and Scottish gas councils in testing to raise coal gas to natural-gas standards. Peoples Gas Co. set up a $50-million plant near Chicago to convert petroleum liquids into substitute natural gas.

During the year the Independent Natural Gas Association of America made several recommendations: immediate development of a price structure that would take into account the true value of gas in relation to alternate fuels; sanctity of contract gas

WIDE WORLD

Ignited by an explosion, millions of gallons of gasoline burned in a Tennessee storage tank.

prices within current regulatory jurisdiction; impetus for synthetic gas; accommodation with Canada on gas; resolution of Arctic gas transportation problems; and expediting the importation of liquefied natural gas. The association also recommended a statutory time frame for the conclusion of regulatory processes and procedures; streamlining of price, facilities, and service jurisdiction; orderly, flexible, accelerated, and timely policy for federal leasing of lands; and a practical and timely approach to environmental laws.

Toward similar goals of cutting red tape, the U.S. Price Commission allowed regulatory agencies such as the FPC to set price increases under its watchful eye. The FPC moved to allow higher price ceilings for new gas contracts and was reevaluating its cost classification and allocation regulatory techniques. The U.S. Supreme Court upheld the FPC's right to allocate gas supplies between industrial and home users in time of scarcity. In December the FPC recommended rate increases of up to 18% for natural gas producers in the Permian Basin area of Texas and New Mexico. The action was taken to spur interstate sales of Permian gas.

Canada's proven reserves climbed by 2.1 Tcf in 1971 to 55.5 Tcf. Production was at 2 Tcf. Reserves were estimated at the 50-Tcf mark for the next 25 years—two thirds for domestic use, and one third earmarked for export. Discoveries in the Canadian Arctic were to be added later, with 10 Tcf already earmarked for export to the Wisconsin-Michigan area over two decades, beginning in the mid-1970's. Current exports to the U.S. increased in 1971 for the 12th consecutive year, almost reaching one Tcf. (*See in* CE: Gas, Manufactured; Gas, Natural.)

PETROLEUM

The year was again marked by discussions between members of the national oil industries and those from the Organization of Petroleum Exporting Countries. Initially the discussions centered around the impact of the de facto devaluation of the U.S. dollar upon tax reference prices. The organization claimed an increase in prices of 11.7%, but the principal oil companies contended that the provisions of the Iranian and Libyan five-year agreements covered the situation. A compromise solution of the dispute was reached at Geneva, Switzerland, on Jan. 20, 1972, and an 8.49% increase was granted.

Middle East production continued to be important, providing almost one third of the world's total consumption, with reserves approaching nearly 60%. Outside the Middle East, interest centered on the North Sea. A string of discoveries during 1972 confirmed the area as a major source of recoverable reserves. In the U.S., where import restrictions were further eased, the projected shortage of energy caused considerable concern. On the North Slope of Alaska activity was suspended pending the outcome of appeals by conservationists against proposals to authorize the construction of the planned pipeline. In the U.S.S.R. discussions took place with U.S. and Japanese interests on opening up the oil and gas fields of Siberia for commercial production and constructing the necessary pipelines to the coastal terminals.

The growth rate for petroleum products declined during the first six months of 1972. The earnings

This service capsule was the first used to complete an offshore wellhead, which was 375 feet deep, in the Gulf of Mexico.

WIDE WORLD

and profits of the oil industry fell at the same time, while the need for finance for increased investment rose. At the beginning of 1972 the world's total proven and probable oil reserves were estimated to be enough for 33 years at current rates of consumption and discovery. During 1971 world production of crude oil increased by 5.6%, consumption of petroleum increased 5.4%, and refining capacity increased 9%. Capacity of the world tanker fleet at the beginning of 1972 totaled 175.3 million deadweight tons, a sizable increase of 19.6%. (*See also* Automobiles; Transportation. *See in* CE: Fuel; Petroleum articles.)

GABON. Domestic affairs in Gabon proceeded smoothly in 1972. A major event was the release of the former foreign minister and opposition leader Jean-Hilaire Aubame, imprisoned after the abortive coup put down by the French in 1964. Despite his declared commitment to a liberal economy, President Albert-Bernard Bongo decided in June that all private companies should give 10% of their shares to the government.

Relations with Equatorial Guinea deteriorated steadily. A dispute over a number of offshore islands was exacerbated by Gabon's decision to extend its territorial waters to 170 miles. Serious clashes occurred, and both sides appealed to the United Nations. Ostensibly a purely territorial matter, there were deeper political and economic reasons for the disagreement: the disputed area was particularly rich in petroleum, and it also seemed that territory in Equatorial Guinea was being used for training Gabonese opponents of President Bongo's regime. However, due to the conciliatory efforts of Zaire and the People's Republic of the Congo, the two countries later agreed to seek a peaceful settlement. (*See in* CE: Gabon.)

GAMBIA, THE. A general election was held in The Gambia in March 1972, and President Sir Dauda Jawara and his People's Progressive party (PPP) won a resounding victory. The PPP, which had held 28 out of 32 seats in the House of Representatives prior to the election, retained all the seats and Jawara was reelected president, though the PPP received only 63% of the vote.

Already a member of the Commonwealth of Nations, The Gambia sought a reciprocal trade agreement with the European Economic Community (EEC) during the year. Neighboring Senegal, to which The Gambia was closely tied economically, was already working under such an agreement.

The economy, which was largely dependent on the production of groundnuts, showed signs of improvement as prices for groundnuts continued to rise. Tourism also grew, with 8,000 visitors in 1972 as compared to 2,700 in 1971. Diversification of the economy was also planned, with emphasis on increased production of rice. (*See in* CE: Gambia.)

GERMANY. The year 1972 was a momentous one in the history of the two German states. The status of West Berlin was eased by a four-power agreement, and East and West Germany signed treaties relaxing travel restrictions and opening the way to normal diplomatic relations.

The final protocol of the four-power Berlin accord was signed by the foreign ministers of Great Britain, France, the U.S., and the Soviet Union on June 3. The agreement—while it did not change the status of divided Berlin—recognized the links between West Berlin and West Germany and provided for unimpeded traffic of persons and goods between the two. West Berlin's Mayor Klaus Schütz declared that the accord brought an end to the "era of crisis within and concerning our city."

The first treaty ever to be concluded between the two German states was signed on May 26 in East Berlin, the capital of East Germany. The agreement, which went into force at midnight on October 18, settled technical details of traffic by road, rail, and water but made no mention of air traffic between the two nations. Under the terms of the treaty, citizens of West Germany would be allowed to visit friends and family in the East for a total of 30 days per year; there was also a provision for business and tourist visits above this quota. Under the treaty any East German might visit the West on pressing compassionate grounds; before, only pensioners had been allowed to visit. In addition, East German citizens were to be allowed to make several visits to West Germany each year, instead of only one as before.

Talks aimed at normalizing relations between East and West Germany began on June 15 and were brought to fruition in November, when representatives of the two governments initialed a comprehensive general treaty that prepared the way for normal diplomatic relations between the two

West Germany's Chancellor Willy Brandt spoke at an election rally from within a bulletproof box.

WIDE WORLD

A historic treaty normalizing relations between the two Germanys was initialed in November by Egon Bahr (right) and Michael Kohl, representing West and East respectively. The treaty is expected to open the way for both nations to enter the United Nations.
KEYSTONE

countries and provided for their eventual admission into the United Nations. Although the treaty left open the issue of German reunification—to which West Germany was committed—East Germany's Socialist Unity party leader Erich Honecker expressed the view that history had already decided in favor of two separate German states; Honecker called the Berlin wall and the heavily guarded frontier "existing realities." The general treaty was officially signed in December but at the end of the year still awaited ratification.

West Germany

On November 19 the citizens of West Germany gave Chancellor Willy Brandt and his *Ostpolitik* (Eastern policy) an overwhelming vote of confidence in the federal election. In a record voter turnout of 91.2%, the coalition of the Social Democratic party (SPD) and the Free Democratic party (FDP) gained a majority of 48 seats in the 496-seat Bundestag. The SPD took 45.9% of the vote and 230 seats, and the FDP a remarkable 8.4% and 42 seats; the opposition Christian Democratic Union (CDU) and its Bavarian sister party, the Christian Social Union (CSU), took 44.8% and 224 seats.

For several months prior to the November election there had been considerable doubt as to the future of the Brandt government. A major ground for disagreement was Brandt's policy of rapprochement with the Communist-bloc countries—his so-called *Ostpolitik*—specifically, the nonaggression treaties he had negotiated with the U.S.S.R. and Poland. Opposition party leaders feared that the treaties would legitimize the existence of two Germanys and would extend Soviet power in Western Europe. When the treaties were finally ratified in the Bundestag on May 15, affirmative votes were cast by only 248 members—exactly half the total. The 238 opposition members abstained, thereby allowing the ratification but not endorsing it.

At the end of April Brandt's power had been even more directly challenged. Confidence in the ruling coalition had been shaken by the CDU victory in state elections in Baden-Württemberg, and Brandt's majority in the Bundestag had been reduced by the defection of some FDP and SPD members. On April 27 an attempt was made to oust him and elect opposition leader Rainer C. Barzel of the CDU as chancellor. When the vote was taken, Barzel received 247 votes, 2 fewer than the 249 needed to unseat Brandt. On the next day, however, shifting party loyalties produced a tie vote of 247–247 on a government budget proposal; it was this deadlock that made the November federal election inevitable.

Under the country's 1949 constitution, a midterm federal election was virtually impossible, unless the ruling government had lost a vote of confidence. Thus the only course open to Brandt was to ask the Bundestag for a vote of confidence and, in the event of not achieving it, to dissolve parliament and hold elections within 60 days, as provided for in the constitution. On September 22 the Bundestag rejected Brandt's motion for a vote of confidence by 248 to 233, with members of the government abstaining to ensure failure; Brandt was then able to go ahead with the election.

The Olympic Games held during the summer in Munich were overshadowed by the tragic deaths of 11 Israeli athletes and coaches, most of whom were killed during a gun battle between West German police and Arab guerrillas. Five of the Arabs were killed and three captured. An official inquiry into the tragedy, conducted by the federal government, the Bavarian government, and the Munich police, concluded that it had been unavoidable. The West German decision to open fire on the Arabs was widely criticized, and many persons felt that the West German government was responsible for the Israeli deaths. A report issued by the government of Israel was critical of the security arrangements made by West German and Israeli agencies. (*See also* Crime; Israel.)

On October 29 the West German government released the three captured guerrillas—who were awaiting trial in West Germany—after two Palestinians hijacked a Lufthansa passenger plane and threatened to blow it up with the crew and passengers if their demands were not met. The hijacked plane circled over Zagreb, Yugoslavia, while the prisoners were taken from their separate prisons and flown to the site. In Tripoli, Libya, the passengers and crew were released, and the Arabs were welcomed as "heroes of the Munich operation."

West German Foreign Affairs

Foreign Affairs Minister Walter Scheel visited Peking, People's Republic of China, in October and signed an agreement establishing diplomatic relations between West Germany and China. The Brandt government had hesitated in taking this step, evidently for fear of offending the U.S.S.R.

Diplomatic relations with Lebanon and Egypt were resumed in 1972, after a break of seven years, but a stricter control of Arabs in West Germany following the tragedy at the Olympics caused friction between the government and the Arab world. Many Arabs suspected of having contacts with terrorist organizations were ordered to leave Germany, and hundreds were refused entry. Relations with Israel reached a low ebb following the release of the captured Munich terrorists; unofficial Israeli sources accused the West German government of having planned the release of the Arabs

These three West German officials directed police action against Arab commandos holding Israeli hostages in Munich; the hostages were slain in a battle between police and the Arabs.

WIDE WORLD

to avoid the embarrassment and possible violence resulting from a trial on West German soil.

East Germany

Several non-Communist countries took steps to initiate or fully develop diplomatic relations with East Germany during 1972. Switzerland agreed to exchange trade missions authorized to carry out certain consular functions; these included issuing visas, legalizing documents, and giving legal aid and assistance in safeguarding the interests of citizens. India granted full diplomatic recognition to East Germany, and the two countries agreed to raise their diplomatic representations to embassy level. (India had established a consulate general in 1970.) At the end of the year it was reported that unofficial contacts between the U.S. and East German governments had taken place; U.S. recognition of East Germany was expected to follow. (*See in* CE: Germany.)

GHANA. The two-year-old government of Ghana's Prime Minister Kofi A. Busia was overthrown on Jan. 13, 1972, by a group of disgruntled army officers led by Col. Ignatius K. Acheampong. A deteriorating economy, cuts in the army budget, and compulsory retirement of senior army officers were the main factors that led to the coup.

The new regime established a 12-man National Redemption Council headed by Colonel Acheampong. Political activity was banned and the constitution was suspended. Many supporters of Busia were held in preventive detention, and the assets of the Busia regime were frozen. Trade union activities were suppressed later in the year.

In July an attempted coup by supporters of Busia and his disbanded Progress party was defeated. The coup attempt led to a "subversion decree," which imposed the death penalty for sabotage, sedition, smuggling, and other crimes.

In the area of foreign policy, Acheampong assumed a nonaligned position that included more missions to Communist countries. The new government was opposed to black African dialogue with South Africa. Attempts to reestablish relations with neighboring Guinea, which had been broken off in 1966, were successful.

In an effort to strengthen the economy, the cedi (which had been devalued by 44% in December 1971) was revalued by 42%, many national debts (most notably those owed to British interests) were repudiated, and repayment of other debts was postponed for at least ten years. A crash agricultural program, Operation Feed Yourself, concentrated on the raising of crops and food animals in an attempt to cut Ghana's massive food imports.

Kwame Nkrumah, Ghana's first president, who was deposed by a coup in 1966, died in Romania in April. He was buried in Ghana after lengthy negotiations with Guinea over the disposition of his remains. Nkrumah had lived in Guinea after his regime was overthrown. (*See in* CE: Ghana.)

GOLF. The transcending skill of Jack Nicklaus was the dominant theme of the international golf scene in 1972. His attempt to achieve the grand slam of professional golf was of compelling interest until Lee Trevino broke the spell in the British Open at Muirfield, East Lothian, Scotland. But failure had no adverse effect on Nicklaus. He won seven tournaments and in so doing he set a new record for official prize money won in the U.S. with $320,542, surpassing his total of the preceding year, $244,490. Since he had played in far fewer events than his nearest rivals, headed inevitably by Trevino, the achievement was an extraordinary mark of his supremacy.

Earlier in the year Nicklaus had said he thought that winning the grand slam would be possible, especially as the four championships were on courses that suited his game. When he opened with a 68 in the Masters at Augusta, Ga.—a score that proved to be the lowest of the tournament—he took a grip he did not seem likely to lose. Although he was not at his commanding best, the failure of his competitors to mount an effective challenge suggested that he had cast a jinx on them. For the first time in many years the last round was devoid of drama, and Nicklaus won the tournament by three strokes

Joyous Bobby Mitchell won the Tournament of Champions in a sudden-death play-off in April.
UPI COMPIX

UPI COMPIX
Jack Nicklaus (left) won the 72d U.S. Open against former winner Lee Trevino.

over Bruce Crampton, Bobby Mitchell, and Tom Weiskopf.

The situation was similar at Pebble Beach, Calif., where the U.S. Open was played. After the second round Nicklaus was never out of the lead. The course, with its numerous challenging shots, especially on the ocean holes, and its small, fast greens, took a terrible toll of many distinguished players. Scores rising into the high 70's and beyond were frequent; and on the last day, when a strong wind rose, the only player to equal par was Jim Simons, then an amateur. Trevino, who had been ill only a few days before, made a brave attempt to retain his title; Arnold Palmer, summoning some of his greatest golf, was in the running for the lead until the last few holes; but in the end Crampton's unshakable steadiness enabled him to win second place. Nicklaus, who almost holed a majestic one-iron shot into the teeth of the wind at the 17th, cruised safely home by three strokes.

When the scene shifted to Muirfield for the British Open, the whole golf world became excited. Nicklaus prepared for the tournament with ruthless care, but it was not until the final round, when his cause was almost lost, that he was able to command his finest golf. With one round to go, Nicklaus trailed Trevino by six shots and Tony Jacklin by five, and he knew that only a monumental performance could give him any chance of victory. On the last afternoon Nicklaus came within a fraction of the greatest last round in British Open history. At one point he had regained the six strokes and actually was leading; he completed the day with a 66.

When Nicklaus finished, Trevino and Jacklin each needed two pars to win. The par-five 17th hole produced one of the largest swings of fortune that had occurred in modern golf: Trevino, bunkered from the tee, was through the back of the green in four shots, and Jacklin was 15 feet from the hole in three. Trevino chipped hurriedly, and yet the ball dropped into the hole. Jacklin took three putts on the hole, and a solid par four at the last hole made Trevino one of the luckiest of champions. Nicklaus finished second, and Jacklin third.

The Professional Golfers' Association of America (PGA) championship at the Oakland Hills Country Club in Birmingham, Mich., was won by Gary Player. Later Player won the first prize, amounting to $50,000, in the World Series of Golf at Akron, Ohio. Gay Brewer took the Canadian Open title and the Pacific Masters. Bob Charles captured both the John Player Classic at Turnberry, Ayr, Scotland, and the Dunlop Masters.

Graham Marsh of Australia won the German and Swiss Open tournaments, and Jack Newton, also of Australia, took the Dutch Open in the Netherlands and the Benson and Hedges Festival in England. Peter Thomson won both the Wills tournament in Scotland and the Qantas Australian Open in Adelaide. The World Cup, won by Taiwan, was played at Melbourne, Australia, in November.

In amateur golf, the U.S. players were successful in the three biennial contests that were held during the year. In the world team championships at Buenos Aires, Argentina, strong finishes enabled the men to overtake and beat Australia by five strokes, and retain the Eisenhower Trophy. Meanwhile, the women finished four strokes ahead of France in the contest for the Santo Espirito Trophy.

In the Curtis Cup match at Western Gailes, in Scotland, the U.S. women led 5–3 on the first day and went on to win by a 10–8 score. Michelle Walker of Great Britain was the outstanding player of the match and the only one undefeated. Later she retained her British Women's Amateur Championship title, beating Jane Booth and Laura Baugh in the process. In her first U.S. tournament she defeated Mrs. Booth in the final of the Trans-Mississippi tournament. Susie Maxwell Berning, the champion in 1968, won the U.S. Women's Open, edging out Pam Barnett by only one stroke. (*See in* CE: Golf.)

GREAT BRITAIN AND NORTHERN IRELAND, UNITED KINGDOM OF.

The British Parliament in 1972 approved the legislation necessary for Great Britain's entry into the European Economic Community (EEC), to take effect on Jan. 1, 1973. Worsening strife between the Protestant and Roman Catholic communities in Northern Ireland led to the imposition of direct rule from London, the British capital. Economic difficulties involving inflation, unemployment, and industrial unrest obliged the government to abandon a fixed parity for sterling and to introduce a 90-day freeze on wages and prices.

In June the British public was saddened by the death of the duke of Windsor, who had ruled briefly as King Edward VIII. Thousands of mourners paid tribute to the duke as he lay in state at Windsor Castle. (*See also* Obituaries.)

Domestic Affairs

British Prime Minister Edward Heath, who had made few changes in the structure of his government since his Conservative party was elected in June 1970, was forced by events to reshuffle several of his senior Cabinet posts during 1972. The decision to transfer to London responsibility for the government of Northern Ireland was announced on March 24. It was accompanied by the appointment of William Whitelaw, the leader of the House of Commons, as secretary of state for Northern Ireland—a new office. In July there was a further switch of Cabinet posts when Reginald Maudling resigned as home secretary because of past business involvement with architect John Poulson, whose bankrupt firm was about to become the subject of an official inquiry. Maudling was succeeded by Robert Carr, who had earlier succeeded Whitelaw as leader of the House of Commons.

Disagreements over entry into the EEC resulted in significant changes in the Labour party hierarchy. Roy Jenkins, the strongly pro-European deputy leader of the party, resigned from Harold Wilson's

Dockers staged a march in London to protest the imprisonment of five dockers who were jailed for contempt of the Industrial Relations Court.

CENTRAL PRESS FROM PICTORIAL PARADE

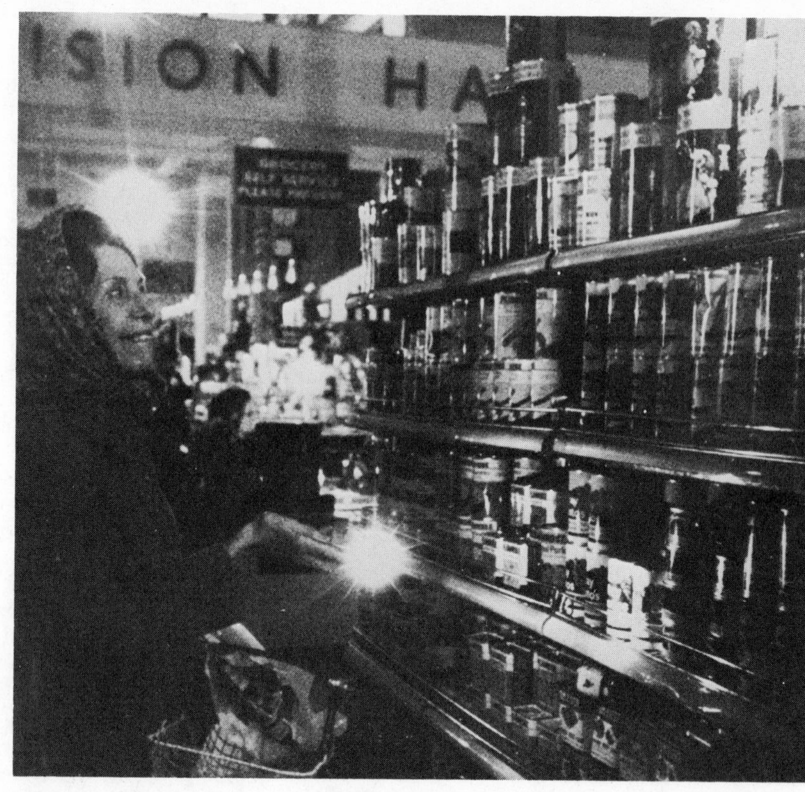

A woman shops by flashlight in a candlelit London store during power cuts in homes and industry. Striking coal miners blockading power stations nearly caused a total industrial shutdown, threatening 20 million jobs.

UPI COMPIX

shadow cabinet in April. Two other shadow cabinet members resigned with Jenkins, saying they could not join in the shadow cabinet's decision to vote with antimarket Conservatives on a proposal to submit entry into the EEC to a national referendum. Several other key Labour spokesmen followed suit. Jenkins' place as deputy leader was taken by Labour's former minister of education, Edward Short, who—although supporting British entry into the EEC—had kept clear of the controversy within the party.

The question of entry into the EEC overshadowed Parliamentary affairs in the opening months of the year. Although in October 1971 the Commons had voted 356–244 to approve British entry on the terms negotiated during 1971, Labour opposition began to harden toward the end of the year. In February, at a second Parliamentary reading of the European Communities Bill, the government's majority declined sharply. Particularly at issue was the key provision, Clause 2, which stated that the rights, liabilities, obligations, and restrictions of the EEC would have precedence over existing British law. Labour party spokesmen complained that this would diminish the power of Parliament, particularly in the area of taxation. The Heath government, however, successfully resisted all attempts by its opponents to change the bill, and it was passed by the House of Commons after a third reading in July.

Soon after the enactment of the bill, Heath took part in a summit meeting of the nine current and future member states of the EEC in Paris. The meeting agreed on steps toward achieving some degree of European union by 1980 and on a regional policy of special importance to Britain. (*See also* Europe.)

Tomatoes that could not be unloaded in England because of a strike are dumped into a quarry.

WIDE WORLD

Labor and the Economy

The year opened with the British economy in seemingly good shape. A substantial balance-of-payments surplus of more than $2.55 billion had been achieved during 1971. The reserves stood at $6.44 billion, more than double what they had been at the beginning of 1971. The parity rate for the British pound had been confirmed at $2.60 in the realignment of currencies set out in the so-called Smithsonian agreement of December 1971. Although unemployment remained obstinately high—topping one million in mid-January—the yearly inflation rate had been brought back to 6%. Britain's overseas loans incurred in coping with the sterling crises of recent years had been completely repaid by the end of April, yet the reserves reached $6.98 billion.

These relatively encouraging trends were offset by a serious worsening of labor relations. A strike by coal miners—the first nationwide coal strike since the general strike of 1926—lasted from January 9 to February 28. It was accompanied by the picketing of coal-fired power stations, which led to extensive power cuts affecting the employment of more than 1.5 million British workers. A state of emergency was declared on February 9, giving the government power to protect vital services and supplies; restrictions on the use of electricity followed. After strikers had rejected pay increases proposed by the National Coal Board, the dispute was finally submitted to a court of inquiry under Lord Wilberforce. The court's conclusion was that public opinion would support the miners' claims for "a general and exceptional increase." It recommended increases averaging about 20%, which the miners accepted.

A trooper of the Household Cavalry guards the catafalque of the duke of Windsor in St. George's Chapel in Windsor Castle.

UPI COMPIX

When Chancellor of the Exchequer Anthony Barber introduced his new budget in March, he was still able to show that the rate of price inflation had been cut in half since the summer of 1971. The visible trade surplus, however, had declined sharply, unemployment remained high, and investment was recovering too slowly. To boost the sluggish economy, Barber announced a program of tax cuts amounting to $3.06 billion, three quarters of it on personal income taxes. He also announced the introduction of a 10% value-added tax (replacing the sales tax and selective employment tax and coming into line with EEC tax policies), scheduled to take effect in April 1973. To stimulate investment (which in Great Britain stood at 15% of the national income, compared with 19% in the EEC), Barber instituted a first-year depreciation allowance of 100% on all investment in capital equipment, plus grants for regional development areas.

Although Barber's cuts were hailed as a sunshine budget, the sunshine did not last long. Three months later, on June 23, the government was forced to float the pound after one third of the reserves had been lost in a speculative run on sterling. The pound fell from its fixed dollar parity of 2.60 to around 2.45 and steadied there, only to be overtaken by another crisis of nerves in October, when it fell below 2.35.

In August a three-week strike by Britain's 42,000 longshoremen forced the government once again to declare a state of emergency. Job security was one of the major issues in the dispute. Even after delegates representing the dock workers had voted to return to work, the strike continued and militant strikers staged violent protests.

In a climate of inflationary trends and industrial unrest, the government began in July to make new approaches to the Confederation of British Industry (CBI) and the Trades Union Congress (TUC) for a voluntary prices and incomes policy. The CBI was persuaded to accept a three-month extension of the price freeze it had agreed to in 1971. In September, after a number of preliminary talks, Heath put forward a package proposal for voluntary limitation of increases in wages and prices. The subsequent rejection by the TUC of voluntary restraints led many observers to predict that the government would respond with a compulsory freeze on wages and prices. These predictions

POPPERFOTO FROM PICTORIAL PARADE

A British paratrooper seizes a suspect at gunpoint during "Bloody Sunday" disturbances in Londonderry, Northern Ireland, in January.

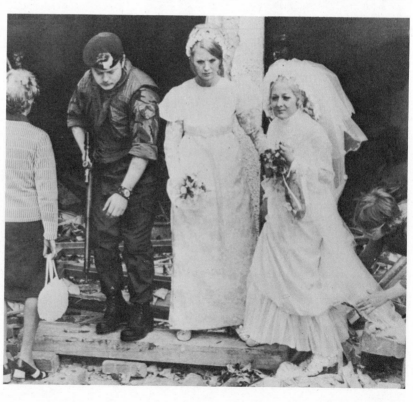

came true on November 6, when Heath announced a 90-day standstill on wages, prices, rents, and dividends. The period was to be used to frame a system of statutory price and wage controls.

Foreign Policy

Diplomatic relations with the People's Republic of China were established during 1972. Britain had voted for China's admission to the United Nations (UN) in October 1971. An exchange of ambassadors was announced in March 1972, and in October Britain's foreign secretary, Sir Alec Douglas-Home, paid an official visit to Peking, China.

A new defense agreement was signed with Malta after more than six months of difficult negotiations that ultimately led to the withdrawal of some British troops. The new agreement, jointly with the North Atlantic Treaty Organization (NATO), was to run for seven years, with Britain paying about 40% of the costs. It excluded the Warsaw Pact nations from being given military facilities in Malta.

The attempt to reach a settlement with Rhodesia failed. The terms agreed to in November 1971 were dependent on their acceptability to the Rhodesian people as a whole. Early in 1972 a commission led by Lord Pearce went to Rhodesia to sound local opinion. In its report published on May 23 the Pearce commission said that while the terms were acceptable to Europeans, they were rejected by a majority of Africans. The British government therefore concluded that there was no basis for independence and determined to maintain the status quo, including the UN sanctions. (*See also* Rhodesia.)

After President Idi Amin of Uganda ordered the expulsion of all Asians from Uganda, the British government accepted the responsibility to admit those who held British passports (estimated at about 50,000). A Uganda Resettlement Board was set up to supervise the settlement of the refu-

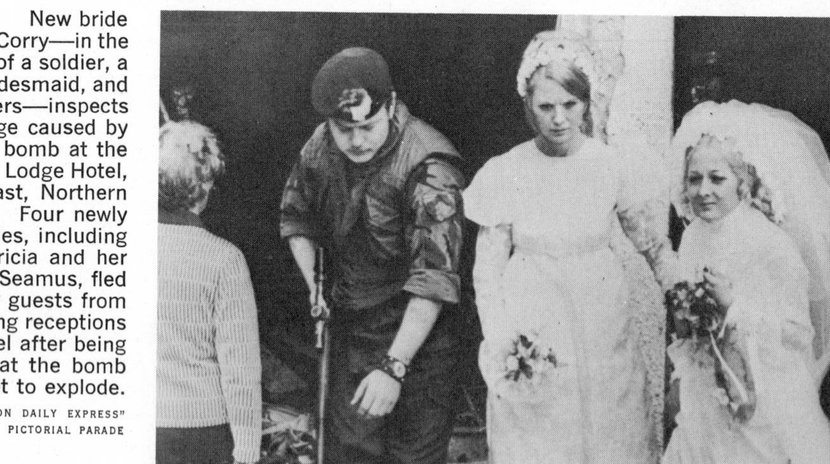

New bride Patricia McCorry—in the company of a soldier, a bridesmaid, and bystanders—inspects the damage caused by a terrorist bomb at the Greenan Lodge Hotel, Belfast, Northern Ireland. Four newly wed couples, including Patricia and her husband, Seamus, fled with their guests from their wedding receptions at the hotel after being warned that the bomb was set to explode.

"LONDON DAILY EXPRESS" FROM PICTORIAL PARADE

POPPERFOTO FROM PICTORIAL PARADE

In 1972 Bernadette Devlin, member of Parliament from Northern Ireland, continued her battles with British authorities.

gees in Britain. The Heath government subsequently froze a $24.5-million loan to Uganda. (*See also* Uganda.)

Northern Ireland

Terrorism in Northern Ireland—marked by indiscriminate bombings and brutal assassinations—intensified in 1972. In Londonderry on January 30—or "Bloody Sunday," as it became known—an illegal civil rights march by Roman Catholics led to a clash with soldiers that resulted in the deaths of 13 civilians. A government inquiry headed by Lord Widgery, the lord chief justice of England, blamed both the marchers and the soldiers for the violence on Bloody Sunday. The failure of the report to condemn the army aroused Roman Catholics, who bitterly declared it "a whitewash."

The situation continued to deteriorate during February and March. John Taylor, Northern Ireland's minister of state for home affairs, was seriously wounded in an unsuccessful attempt to assassinate him on February 25. In March a series of daytime bombings in public places left several persons dead and hundreds wounded. Against a background of escalating violence, talks were held between Prime Minister Heath and Brian Faulkner, the prime minister of Northern Ireland. Heath proposed that the British government assume responsibility for internal security in Northern Ireland, a move strongly opposed by Faulkner. The British government thereupon suspended the constitution and Parliament of Northern Ireland and assumed direct rule of the province; Faulkner resigned his post as prime minister. Britain repeated the assurance that the position of Northern Ireland as part of the United Kingdom would not be changed without the consent of the people of Northern Ireland.

William Whitelaw, the newly appointed administrator of Northern Ireland, said that while there would be no relaxation in the fight against terrorism, he did not think it could be defeated by purely military means. Whitelaw was immediately confronted by the Ulster Vanguard, a militant new Protestant movement that called a two-day general strike protesting direct rule by the government in London. Former Prime Minister Faulkner made a surprise appearance at a Vanguard rally, thus ally-

The royal family is pictured at Balmoral Castle on the occasion of the royal couple's 25th wedding anniversary (from left): Prince Philip, Queen Elizabeth II, Prince Andrew (rear), Prince Edward, Princess Anne, and Prince Charles.

PATRICK LICHFIELD FROM KEYSTONE

ing himself with the movement and with its leader, his former political enemy William Craig. The pro-Irish Social Democratic and Labour party (SDLP), led by Gerry Fitt, and the middle-of-the-road Alliance party welcomed the British take-over.

In his first actions, Whitelaw sought to pacify the militant Catholics by releasing Catholic internees (suspects held without trial) and lifting the ban on marches. To help bridge the gap between the religious communities, an advisory commission was set up with seven Protestant and four Catholic members. Yet the terrorism continued. Bombing incidents intensified during May. The army clashed with militant Protestants of the Ulster Defence Association (UDA). Growing weariness with violence led to a short-lived truce, declared by the Irish Republican Army (IRA) and then broken by the Provisionals—a militant IRA wing led by Sean MacStiofain, based in Dublin, Ireland. The Provisionals resumed an even more violent terrorist campaign. On July 21 Belfast, Northern Ireland, suffered its worst day of bombings—20 bombs were exploded without warning within half an hour, one at a crowded bus station. Thirteen persons died, and more than 100 were wounded.

Having failed to bring about any conciliation, British security forces went on the offensive. Another 4,000 soldiers were sent to Northern Ireland, bringing the total to 21,000. On July 31, troops moved into the "no-go" areas of Londonderry, which had been IRA sanctuaries, and cleared them of barricades. Searches uncovered large stocks of arms, explosives, and ammunition. In the meantime, Whitelaw had been trying to bring about talks on a political settlement among all parties. Discussions were held at Darlington, England, but several of the factions refused to attend. The talks had no concrete results.

After the opening up of the "no-go" areas, violence declined during the autumn. In September, slightly more than a year after it was begun, the controversial policy of internment was terminated by the British government. The security forces began to make more arrests, and by the end of October, 300 persons had been charged with terrorist offenses. On October 30 the government issued a green paper, "The Future for Northern Ireland," as a basis for discussion on the future constitution when direct rule ended.

In November Prime Minister John Lynch of Ireland announced an all-out campaign against the outlawed IRA. Provisional-wing leader MacStiofain was arrested, convicted of membership in an illegal organization, and jailed in Dublin. It was reported that IRA guerrillas threatened to retaliate by launching rocket attacks against the Irish Republic. (*See also* Ireland. *See in* CE: Great Britain and Northern Ireland, United Kingdom of.)

Workers demonstrate in London against the arrival of Asian émigrés from Uganda.

WIDE WORLD

GREECE. In 1972 there were many indications that Premier George Papadopoulos of Greece was preparing to abolish the monarchy of the exiled King Constantine II and declare a presidential republic with himself as chief executive. Implementation of the 1968 constitution, which the government thus far had largely avoided doing, did not seem at all likely. On March 21, Papadopoulos dismissed Gen. Georgios Zoitakis as regent and took over the post himself, while retaining his position as premier and the portfolios for defense, foreign affairs, and government policy and planning. On July 31 the government was reshuffled and posts assigned to the original 12 junta members who, with then-Colonel Papadopoulos, had engineered the 1967 coup. Papadopoulos defended his highly authoritarian actions by stating on April 21: "Greece today is an oasis in a strife-torn, problem-ridden world precisely because she is governed in a manner absolutely geared to her national needs."

The overall peace and order of the regime were being maintained, but arrest, exile, and martial law were commonplace. Martial law was restricted to the areas of Athens-Piraeus and Salonika, but arrest and detention of antigovernment civilians continued on a large scale. Exile was ordered for eight prominent Greeks, among them John Pesmazoglu, economist and former deputy governor of the Bank of Greece. Pesmazoglu had been chairman of the Society for the Study of Greek Problems and an outspoken critic of the government. Two periodicals that opposed the regime were suppressed, and opposition political activity was at a low ebb. A United Nations panel on human rights reportedly concluded, after a study of evidence submitted to the panel, that a "consistent pattern" of violation of human rights existed in Greece.

Increasingly friendly relations between the Papadopoulos regime and the U.S. government were manifested in a visit by U.S. Secretary of State William P. Rogers on July 4 and in a joint agreement that the Athens-Piraeus port would become a "home port" for a U.S. Carrier Task Group. This

"LONDON DAILY EXPRESS" FROM PICTORIAL PARADE

Greece's Premier George Papadopoulos greets members of his government shortly after assuming the post of regent. He was already in charge of foreign affairs, government planning, and defense. Papadopoulos had dismissed Gen. Georgios Zoitakis as regent.

involved the stationing of an aircraft carrier and other vessels, with a complement of 6,600 officers and men, in the Athens area. U.S. Navy families were allowed to settle in the port area and were granted extraterritorial rights. Critics of the U.S. policy of support for the Greek regime were rebuffed by Secretary Rogers, who stated that for the U.S. to put pressure on Greece to initiate more democratic rule would be "the ultimate arrogance of power."

Visits by a number of West European ministers indicated a virtual abandonment of the boycott of Greece imposed after the 1967 coup. Diplomatic relations were established with the People's Republic of China, which led to the severing of relations with Taiwan. Relations with Cyprus, already strained, became even more tenuous when a Greek plan to remove Cyprus' president, Archbishop Makarios III, was uncovered. Greece apparently viewed Makarios as the main obstacle to a settlement with Turkey on the question of Cypriot sovereignty. (*See* Cyprus.)

The Greek economy continued to prosper with a 7.5% growth in the gross national product. A 15-year master plan that promised increased economic growth and a higher standard of living was unveiled in September. (*See in* CE: Greece.)

GUATEMALA. Early in March 1972 the newspaper *El Grafico* reported that the preceding year in Guatemala was characterized by a paroxysm of violence unprecedented in the history of the country. The press officially listed about 1,000 violent deaths (including those of 15 mayors and 3 deputies), 171 kidnappings, and 174 persons missing. In June and July 1972, after a lull, renewed attacks by leftist elements resulted in the deaths of five prominent members of the ruling rightist National Liberation Movement, including Olivero Castañeda Paíz, first vice-president of the Guatemalan Congress. Castañeda was the fourth victim of assassination among the members of the Congress elected in 1970.

For more than ten years, violence from both left and right factions had torn Guatemala. Yet, while the lawlessness went on, Guatemalans were agreeing in mid-1972 that conditions were improving. Nevertheless, wealthy businessmen were varying their routes to work and going at varying times of the day because they feared kidnappers. Soldiers with loaded submachine guns guarded newspaper offices, and armed soldiers patrolled the streets.

The Central American Common Market was thrust to the forefront of Guatemalan politics on June 16 when the Central Bank of Costa Rica ended the preferential treatment of exchange remittances to other Central American countries. Further restrictive measures followed in August, when Costa Rica decided to apply the free market rate of exchange to regional imports. Negotiations resulted in an agreement that introduced certain adjustments in the exchange rate to help rectify Costa Rica's trade deficit.

In the second half of 1972, the exploratory drilling conducted by Resources International struck oil in the Las Tortigas Valley. Subsequently, the area's commercial possibilities were being assessed. (*See in* CE: Guatemala.)

AUTHENTICATED NEWS INTERNATIONAL

A three-member team from the United Nations Special Committee of 24 on decolonization stops at a school during an observational trek through liberated areas of Portuguese Guinea.

GUINEA. Uncertainty continued to plague Guinea in 1972 following two years of attempted invasions and conspiracies against the government. President Sékou Touré continued to denounce alleged threats of invasion and in September accused France of planning an invasion by way of neighboring Portuguese Guinea. In April it was announced that the National Assembly had ratified verdicts passed by local revolutionary courts in the mass trial of "fifth-column agents" that began in July 1971, but sentences were not disclosed. Also in April the post of prime minister was created, and Louis Lansana Beavogui was appointed to fill it.

Guinea achieved a reconciliation with Senegal in 1972 after several years of dispute. Relations with Ghana were strained by Guinea's refusal to return the body of Ghana's former President Kwame Nkrumah, who died in April. Nkrumah had lived in Guinea after being deposed in 1966. After long negotiations the body was returned to Ghana, however, and the two countries later agreed to resume diplomatic relations. (*See in* CE: Guinea.)

GUYANA. In 1972 Guyana concentrated its spending mainly on agriculture, education, and co-operatives, and plans were made to enter the shrimping industry. The state-owned Guyana Bauxite Co. Ltd. (formerly the Canadian-owned Demerara Bauxite Co., nationalized by Guyana in July 1971) reported a profit, after tax, of $38 million in its first year's trading. New customers were found in the People's Republic of China and the Soviet Union, while others in the socialist bloc were being sought.

At the annual convention of the People's National Congress in April, Prime Minister Forbes Burnham told members of plans for localizing vital sectors of the economy, not excluding the remaining U.S.-owned bauxite plant. Timber holdings of the Commonwealth Development Corp., the sole foreign timber holdings in the country, were acquired by the government during the year. Burnham's power in 1972 remained unshaken, despite grave charges of corruption leveled against two ministers. (*See in* CE: Guyana, Republic of.)

HAITI. In 1972 Haiti enjoyed political stability and made some economic progress. President Jean-Claude Duvalier seemed firmly established in office, but many considered him merely a titular head of state with the real power belonging to Simone Duvalier, widow of President François Duvalier.

Plans were announced in March for constitutional reforms, with proposals for a national assembly and a prime minister. Luckner Cambronne, minister of the interior and defense, was the leading contender for this office. His position appeared under threat in September as Mrs. Duvalier gradually transferred support to Haiti's consul general in New York City, Robert Lafontant.

On November 15 Duvalier dismissed Cambronne from office. A series of decrees followed that included the removal of Cambronne supporters in the government, a warning against government corruption, a reorganization of security services, and the pardoning of 60 prisoners. The sentences of 29 other prisoners were cut in half.

The U.S. Department of State announced in January it had licensed Aerotrade, of Miami, Fla., to sell arms to Haiti, and several Haitian air force officers were trained under U.S. auspices. A top-level mission from Haiti visited Washington, D.C., in March to seek economic and military aid but was politely rebuffed. In July an eight-man team of U.S. military experts visited Port-au-Prince, the capital, and discussed the resumption of full military aid (cut off since 1962). A request for $10 million in U.S. military assistance was rejected, and it was made clear that any aid was to be used for legitimate defense purposes only. Private U.S. investors showed renewed interest in Haiti during the year.

A report by the Organization of American States (OAS) said that industrial and agricultural production had increased in 1971 and the tourist boom had continued. The state planning board forecast an annual growth rate of 7.7% between 1972 and 1976, with a yearly increase of 12% in industrial output. A 70% increase in coffee exports and a 60% increase in sugar shipments over the five-year period were also predicted. (*See in* CE: Haiti, Republic of.)

HOBBIES. In 1972 hobbies continued to grow steadily. Retail sales approached the billion-dollar level. The 1970 total was put at $906 million.

Interest in model railroads enjoyed a strong revival. Reasons for this pickup were thought to be associated with the increasing interest in mass transportation and with nostalgia for the good times remembered by those who knew the railroads when they were the chief means of transportation. The boom in model train activity was also perpetuated by specialty swap-and-buy shops that opened in some key marketing areas in the East.

New model racing cars, built to 1/12 scale, were introduced in 1972. They are equipped with wheel and throttle controls, require batteries and fuel, and can be raced on any concrete or asphalt surface. The cars have radio controls with a range of 200 feet. They can reach speeds of 240 scale miles per hour; they have a four-foot turning radius and a .049-cubic-inch engine.

Plastic model kits were very popular again in 1972, with airplanes, cars, and ships leading in sales. Snowmobile kits were popular in some areas, and they were available in four different lines. The Wankel rotary engine kit became very popular in 1972 because of the publicity given it in the automobile industry.

There were several new products for hobbyists in sculpture and carving. Chip-Away is a sculpture set with three blocks, each containing a finished statue. The sculptor chips away the outside marble to reveal the figure within. Sculpt Sure is a clay modeling kit. It comes with a pre-

A participant in the 41st National Model Airplane Championships launches a glider.

GARY SETTLE FROM "THE NEW YORK TIMES"

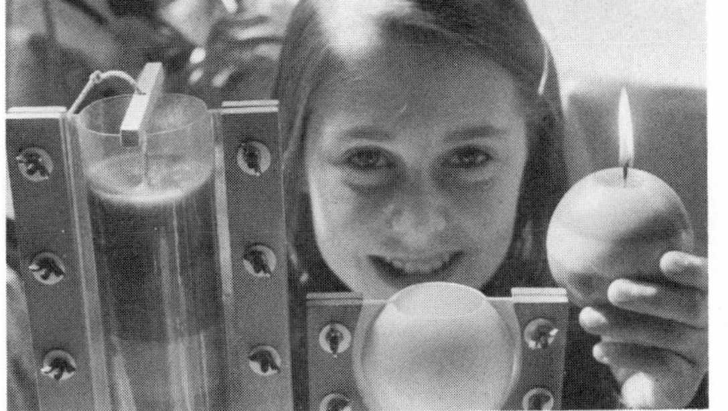

AGIP FROM PICTORIAL PARADE

Candlemaking was popular in 1972. These candles were made from a prizewinning kit.

formed head, armature wire, tools, base, plasteline wood stone, and instructions. Wire Sculpture is a kit to teach the art of wire sculpting.

Candlemaking was reported as the number-one craft activity by some wholesalers. Floating candles were made attractive by a spray high-gloss finish. A new craft was the transformation of bottles and jugs into vases, glassware, and candelabra by the use of a bottle and jug cutter. (*See also* Toys and Games. *See in* CE: Hobbies.)

HONDURAS. The United Fruit Co., a major U.S. business venture and landholder in Honduras since 1899, was in the news in Honduras in 1972 for having finally lived down its "colonialist" past. The company had anticipated the changes that had swept Latin America for 20 years and had been adjusting to them. Better wages, housing, health care, schooling, and paid vacations were all part of the "Honduranization" program under way in the 1970's.

President Ramón Ernesto Cruz of Honduras made intensive efforts to settle border disputes that had caused the bloody battle with El Salvador three years earlier. He hoped to do this before July 1, when El Salvador's new president took office, but he failed. Then in December a bloodless coup, led by Gen. Oswaldo López Arellano, overthrew Cruz after only 18 months in office. Cruz had been the first directly elected president in Honduras since 1932. General López Arellano had ousted President Julio Lozano Diaz in 1956 and Ramón Villeda Morales, constitutional president, in 1963; he was then elected by Congress to a six-year presidential term in 1965. He was appointed commander of the armed forces by the National party three days before Cruz was elected president. Supposedly, the reason for the junta take-over was the failure of a bipartisan agreement announced before the 1971 elections intended to unite the country by sharing power between the two major parties. They had agreed to evenly divide the 64-seat Congress and give the tie-breaking vote to the elected president. Friction broke out, however, and another agreement was formulated, which Cruz later denounced. (*See in* CE: Honduras.)

WIDE WORLD

Riva Ridge (center), ridden by jockey Ron Turcotte, leads No Le Hace (left) by 3¼ lengths and Hold Your Peace (right) by 6¾ lengths to win the 98th Kentucky Derby at Churchill Downs.

HORSE RACING. The highlight of thoroughbred racing in the U.S. in 1972 was the domination of the two-year-old-filly division by La Prevoyante and of the two-year-old-colt division by Secretariat. La Prevoyante, a Canadian horse owned by Jean-Louis Lévesque, was undefeated in 12 starts to equal the record established by J. R. Keene's legendary juvenile colt Colin in 1907. However, Secretariat edged the filly for honors as horse of the year.

Secretariat, owned and bred by the Virginia-based Meadow Stable of Christopher T. Chenery (which provided the 1971 champion two-year-old colt in Riva Ridge), won the Laurel Futurity in Maryland the same day La Prevoyante annexed the Selima at the same track. Secretariat also captured the Sanford, Hopeful, Futurity, and Garden State stakes for an overall record of seven victories and one second in nine starts, earning $456,404.

Dividing competition between Canada and the U.S., La Prevoyante won most races by wide margins, including such U.S. stakes as the Matron, Frizette, and Gardenia, while amassing winnings of $417,109. Other champions in the annual poll by the Thoroughbred Racing Associations, the *Daily Racing Form,* and the National Turf Writers Association were: Key to the Mint, three-year-old colt; Susan's Girl, three-year-old filly; Typecast, older mare; Autobiography, older horse; Cougar II, grass horse; and Chou Croute, sprinter.

Riva Ridge became the early leader of his division by sandwiching easy victories in the Kentucky Derby at Churchill Downs, Louisville, Ky., and the Belmont Stakes, Elmont, N.Y., with a shocking loss to Bee Bee Bee in the Preakness Stakes at Pimlico, Baltimore, Md., raced on a sloppy track. Riva Ridge finished fourth there and later took the Hollywood Derby in California but failed in the final four races of the season.

Jockey Willie Shoemaker broke Eddie Arcaro's career record of 554 stakes victories. He guided Royal Owl home to win the San Jacinto Stakes at Santa Anita, Arcadia, Calif.

Major laurels in harness racing in 1972 belonged to the four-year-old pacer Albatross and the three-year-old trotter Super Bowl, two of the most successful performers in the sport's history. Each was named best of the year at its gait, and Albatross outpolled the young trotting champion in the balloting by U.S. harness writers to become harness horse of the year for the second straight season. Clinching those honors for Albatross were a 1:54.6 mile at Sportsman's Park in Chicago in July, the fastest race mile in 166 years of harness racing history, and another world record effort of 1:55.6—the fastest ever on a half-mile track—at Delaware, Ohio, in September. Trainer Stanley Dancer drove on both occasions.

Before retiring at the end of the year, Super Bowl also wrote new chapters in the record books.

The horse won 18 straight races in 1972, including the $119,000 Hambletonian at Du Quoin, Ill., the $100,000 Colonial, the $93,097 Yonkers Futurity, and the $56,210 Kentucky Futurity. In capturing the Hambletonian, Super Bowl trotted the fastest mile in history by a three-year-old—1:56.4; and the horse's earnings of $441,711 in 1972 represented an all-time record for a single season by a trotter.

As usual, Herve Filion of Quebec was the world's leading driver during the year. In 1972 he became the first driver in history to win more than $2 million in purses in a single season and the first North American to win 4,000 career victories. (*See in* CE: Horse.)

HOSPITALS. Delivery of, and methods of paying for, health care services were the central issues facing hospitals in 1972. The demand for services was reflected by increases in facilities and utilization among the 7,097 hospitals registered with the American Hospital Association (AHA) in 1971. By the beginning of 1971 (the latest year for which figures were available), specialized services, including intensive care units, open-heart surgery, and radioisotope facilities had increased markedly. In community hospitals, emergency visits increased 10.5% and clinic outpatient visits rose 9.3% in 1971—indicating the trend toward substitution of hospital services for those of the private physician.

The shifting emphasis toward outpatient facilities, in part, complemented the decrease in the number of hospitals (down to 7,097 from 7,123) and number of beds (down 60,211 to 1.56 million). More persons were admitted to hospitals (30.1 million to community hospitals) but stayed there shorter lengths of time (average stay, eight days). The average occupancy rate dropped from 78.0% to 76.7%. Another indicator of utilization, the number of hospital bassinets, declined 2.8%. This reflected, in part, a 1.9% decline in the nation's births. Hospital costs continued on an upward trend, but at a slower rate than in preceding years. The cost of caring for a patient in the nation's community hospitals stood at $92.31 per day at the beginning of 1971, representing an annual increase of 13.9%.

Staff members at Harlem Hospital in New York City block streets with hospital beds during a demonstration for better medical care.

"THE NEW YORK TIMES"

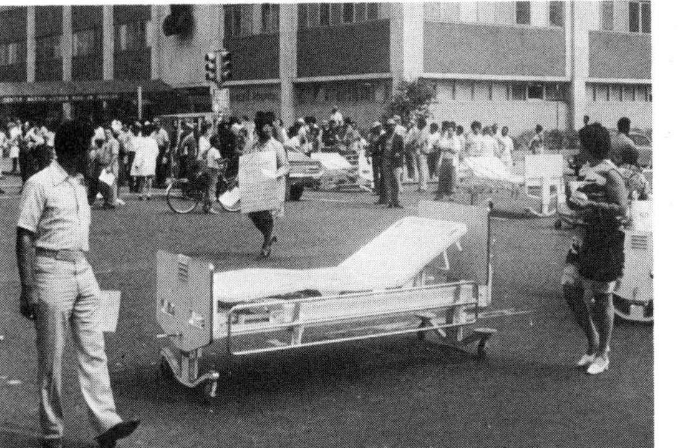

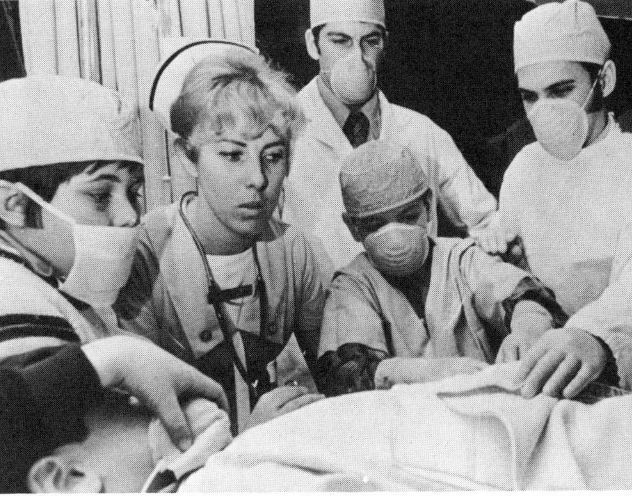

WIDE WORLD

At a special hospital exhibit at Children's Museum in Boston, Mass., children go through the motions of a mock appendectomy.

The AHA's concept of the geographically responsible Health Care Corp. (HCC), an organization of a community's health care providers, was presented as legislation by U.S. Rep. Al Ullman (D, Ore.) in 1972. Under federal and state regulation, the HCC would be responsible for providing a full range of comprehensive health care services to all the people in the U.S. Care would be financed by government, private health insurance, employers, or employees; fees would depend on the ability of the individual to pay. Coverage for catastrophic illness, paid through federal revenues, would provide guarantees against the threat of destitution because of illness. The continuing debate on national health insurance heard renewed support for proposals as sweeping as the Health Security Act sponsored by Senator Edward M. Kennedy (D, Mass.) and as limited as the American Medical Association's tax credit plan.

Working with the U.S. Department of Health, Education, and Welfare, hospitals and the AHA were able to reach a compromise on regulations defining the amount of charity care a hospital must donate to qualify for federal funds. A bill killing the tax exemption of not-for-profit hospitals was opposed because of its inflationary aspects.

In 1972 legislation was the most widely publicized example of increased public involvement in hospital affairs. Of more lasting impact, however, was public involvement at the community level. Representation on hospital governing boards was reordered or extended to reflect, more than ever before, the ethnic and socioeconomic characteristics of the hospital service area. (*See also* Medicine; Nursing; Social Services. *See in* CE: Hospitals.)

HOUSING. Late in 1972 housing construction appeared well on the way to setting a record of 2.3 million conventional starts, topping the previous record of 2.1 million set in 1971. The two-year boom had stimulated so much building activity that in some cities the housing market was flooded; Houston, Tex., for example, ran a 15% vacancy rate in its rental market, despite the fact that Houston was one of the country's fastest-growing urban areas.

It was a lopsided boom: 70% of the new housing starts in the first half of 1972 were in the southern and western U.S. Less than half the nation's population lived in these areas, but 66% of the new jobs were there. An example of the effect of new jobs on housing construction was in Orlando, Fla., where the opening of the Disney World amusement park provided an 11% increase in employment—and a 90% increase in housing permits in the first six months of the year.

Condominium apartments were the biggest growth area of the housing market. Condominium starts in 1972 were expected to triple the 1971 level, which in turn was double the 1970 rate. Experts estimated that by September 1972 about 160,000 units were under construction, 60,000 of them in Florida. (*See* Housing Special Report.)

Factory-built housing continued to share a larger portion of the market, with experts predicting that as much as two thirds to three fourths of the nation's housing would be substantially or completely factory-built by 1975. This bright outlook was darkened, however, by the failure of several industrialized-housing concerns, notably the Stirling Homex Corp., once considered the industry's leading company. Stirling Homex filed for bankruptcy in July. Several other companies dropped manufactured housing voluntarily.

Operation Breakthrough, the U.S. government's effort to stimulate mass production of housing, moved into its major production stage in several areas. In September Secretary of Housing and Urban Development George Romney announced plans for a 1,200-unit housing development in Worcester, Mass., of which 1,000 units would be factory-built. Other federal programs ran into trouble in 1972, however; federally subsidized low- and middle-income housing, especially, was criticized for numerous failures. Builders were accused of producing substandard homes, and speculators of procuring inflated cost estimates from the Federal Housing Administration (FHA); homeowners abandoned deteriorating FHA-subsidized homes in many cities, leaving the government in possession of substandard houses—and of mortgages. In spite of almost continuous scandal, a bill containing some reforms of federal housing practices, which also would have authorized continuation of existing subsidy programs for two years, was killed by the House Rules Committee on Sept. 27, 1972.

Other problems plagued the housing industry in 1972. Spiraling lumber prices, moratoriums on sewer connections, refusals to rezone, and environmental protests blocked home builders' plans in many areas. Consumer protection advocates zeroed in on dubious construction practices, and local building codes placed major obstacles in the path of producers of factory-built housing. The latter problem was gradually being overcome, however; by midsummer some 19 states had state building codes on their books, and 20 states had passed codes for factory-built housing. Such legislation was pending in several other states.

Two promising new areas in housing continued to grow in 1972. Mobile-home shipments pointed to a record 600,000 units for the year, surpassing the previous 1971 record of 497,000 units, while the market in vacation homes also expanded. Second homes accounted for more than 10% of all new housing starts in 1971, and resort-area real estate was seen to be one of the fastest-growing markets of the 1970's. (*See also* Construction. *See in* CE: Housing.)

This home in Arizona was built by its owners from two geodesic domes—structures made by attaching outside panels to rigid framework—connected by a patio.

JOHN DOMINIS FROM LIFE MAGAZINE © TIME INC.

Housing

Special Report: NEW ALTERNATIVES

by Resa W. King

Young couples shopping for their own homes had more to choose from in the early 1970's than did their counterparts of a few years before. The economy-class house was once again on the market, and moderate- to middle-income families were responding to it as enthusiastically as their parents did to the economy-class car in the late 1950's.

A housing breakthrough was inevitable. The cost of land, labor, materials, and financing had risen so rapidly through the 1960's that by 1969 fewer than two in ten U.S. home buyers could afford to buy the single-family homes the industry was building. Home builders, many of whom were unable to obtain or afford financing in that period of tight money, built fewer and higher-priced homes.

Total private and public starts averaged fewer than 1.5 million annually from 1968 through 1970, despite a housing shortage that was becoming acute in many areas. Virtually the only low-cost housing available was the mobile home, and that market, too, was beset with problems. Around the end of the 1960's, however, several forces began to move toward a solution to the nation's housing crisis.

The industry's biggest builders—Levitt & Sons, Kaufman & Broad, the Larwin Group, and others—began to build their version of the compact car: the stripped-down house that eliminated such frills as attached garages, air conditioning, fireplaces, and extra bathrooms. Selling for as little as $22,000, these economy houses were soon in great demand, and other builders jumped on the bandwagon as money markets eased.

The town house emerged as a major force in the housing market. In areas where land and building costs made individual houses unprofitable, builders erected handsomely designed town houses in well-planned communities with many recreational facilities. Consumers who liked renting town houses moved easily into the condominium market, particularly in the area of low-priced town houses that cost as little as $11,000. The condominium concept soon became popular both in new housing and in converted rental housing.

The federal government provided an impetus to housing construction with the launching of Operation Breakthrough, an attempt to enlist the mass-production capabilities of U.S. industry in the production of manufactured housing of all types. Hundreds of major industrial companies responded

This "fourplex"—a cluster of four living units with individual courtyards—was assembled from modules and shipped by truck to a moderate-income housing project in New Haven, Conn.

COURTESY, ARMSTRONG CORK CO.

Mobile homes have become larger and more luxurious over the past few years. Yet they are cheaper than the traditional single-family house. This arrangement of mobile homes in Minnesota is reminiscent of an apartment complex.

to the challenge, and even those that failed to win Breakthrough contracts went on to develop important products and processes to speed the industrialization of home building. Other federal programs financed rentals or housing purchases by low- and moderate-income families, and federal agencies permitted many more liberal lending practices: 5% down payments, lower reserve requirements, and broader lending powers on mobile homes and second homes.

All these factors, combined with a general easing of conditions for borrowing, helped power a housing boom that for the first time in years appealed to those families earning less than $15,000 a year. The median price of a new single-family home declined 8.6% in 1970 to $23,400 from $25,600 the year before, even though the price per square foot continued to increase. The typical house was now smaller and equipped with fewer luxuries.

The U.S. government's role in the boom was like that of a pump primer. In 1970 government-assisted housing accounted for 44.4% of all starts and 57% of all new homes selling for less than $25,000. As the demand for economy-class housing soared, the private market took over from the government. Federally assisted housing dropped to less than 38% of the total in 1971 and to 28% in 1972. Private loans, which did not involve the large amount of paper work and delays necessitated by Federal Housing Administration (FHA) loans, began to edge out federally backed mortgages.

The mobile home, traditionally one of the few single-unit dwellings that low- and moderate-income families could afford, became a runaway best seller as site problems and the myth of cramped inconvenience faded away. Mobile homes became larger at a time when single-family detached homes were shrinking. The old house trailer became a comfortable home with cathedral ceilings, window walls, and many new luxuries. Most importantly, larger mobile homes took on the attractiveness of permanent housing as they were delivered to pads in mobile-home parks where they were likely to remain. Classed as a vehicle under most state laws, the mobile home often escaped property taxes, though many states were beginning to tax them. Even this proved to be a boon, since the promise of new tax revenues made mobile homes welcome in communities that previously were reluctant to admit mobile-home parks. With the median cost of a mobile home in 1971 at $7,130, it was not surprising that one out of two families that bought a single-unit home in 1971 chose a mobile home.

Town house condominiums, too, brought home ownership within reach for millions more families in the early 1970's. These units, which still sold in some areas for as little as $12,000 to $18,000, are a vast improvement over the earlier row house concept. Developers have learned a great deal about land planning, site selection, and attractive use of common open spaces. Relief from maintenance chores is attractive to the elderly as well as to young couples who prefer freedom for other activities. Security-conscious home owners can feel protected from crime without being isolated in suburbs. All these features tend to compensate for the lack of privacy—an area in which detached family homes are still more attractive.

These high-density communities have in some ways created a new life-style for young families. Day-care and early-learning centers free the mothers of preschool children for salaried jobs and other pursuits. Swimming pools, gymnasiums, tennis courts, and in some cases golf courses also have great appeal. When young couples begin to move up the economic scale, they more frequently move to luxurious town house communities than to single-family detached homes that involve more chores and fewer recreational conveniences.

Not all town houses are condominiums—many are part of the rental market. All condominiums are not town houses, either. But there is no denying the growing importance of both in serving the middle- and moderate-income market. A survey of major builders revealed that plans for 1972 called for little more than 70% in detached homes with the balance in town houses and condominiums. A year earlier, 80.3% of home construction was in detached single-family units.

During 1972 one of the most successful applications of the condominium concept was the "fourplex" (also called the quadrominium, quadplex, or mansion house). In its most familiar form the fourplex looks like an oversize single-family home, but it contains four separate living units. The fourplex was designed to accommodate would-be home owners who could not afford single-family detached homes. California designers produced exceedingly attractive fourplex plans, and many of the nation's builders were producing them in attractively landscaped communities with a broad array of recreational facilities. Units could be purchased individually or the entire building could be sold to one individual who then rents the units. Price per unit ran as little as $13,000 or as much as $25,000. Typical prices were $15,000 to $18,000. Thus an entire fourplex could be bought for $60,000 to $80,000. Some developers offered a management and maintenance service to purchasers; other projects were managed and maintained by homeowners' associations. In either case, the purchaser was relieved of maintenance and repair chores, though he still paid for them.

From a strictly sociological viewpoint, the fourplex, more than any other housing design, lends itself to a properly balanced community where young and old, married and single, swinger and porch sitter can live together in relative harmony. It is a marked departure from the rigidly structured housing market of the 1960's that tended to isolate these groups.

Equally important, the fourplex, like the town house and the economy-class house, lends itself to what was probably the most important trend in the housing market of the 1970's: factory-produced housing. Many builders were using totally factory-produced housing, while many others were using factory-built components and housing sections to fight the rising cost of home building.

Like most new industries, manufactured housing has attracted far more entrants than can possibly survive and prosper. Observers estimated that 500–1,000 companies were involved in manufactured housing in 1972. More than 300 companies were building mobile homes. Modular housing, an extension of the mobile-home concept, has attracted hundreds of companies. Concrete wall and panel, as well as modular, systems abound, many of them based on well-tried and successful European systems.

While some companies have failed and others undoubtedly will collapse or withdraw voluntarily from the market, it seems apparent that industrialized housing is here to stay. It appears to be the only way the U.S. will be able to produce housing in the volume and at the price level needed to meet housing needs of the decade. Factory production enables builders to evade two major obstacles of on-site construction: the lack of skilled craftsmen in the building trades, and seasonal shutdowns necessitated by weather conditions. Factory production permits year-round schedules and provides job opportunities for less skilled workers. Accompanied by prudent management of the environment and rapidly diminishing land supply, factory-built housing could, by 1980, place within reach a decent home for every U.S. family.

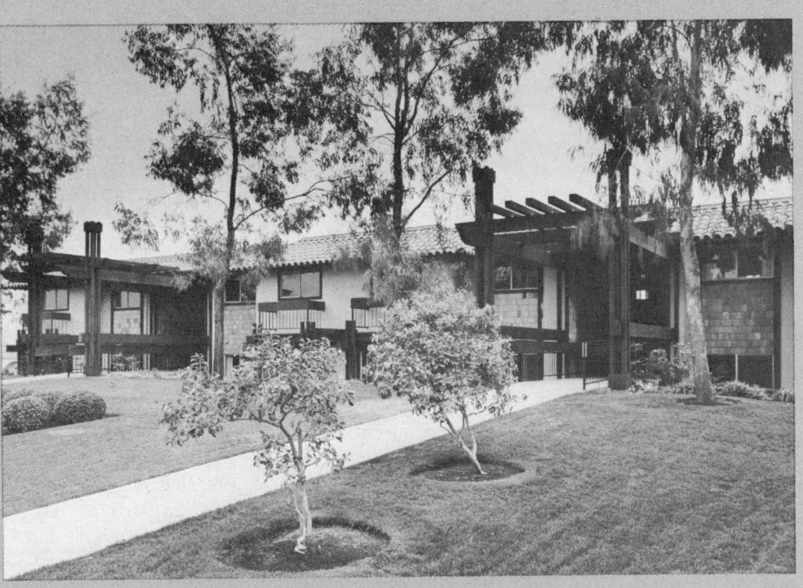

This two-story town house development in California has underground parking. Each unit has two bedrooms, two baths, and a private balcony.
AUTHENTICATED NEWS INTERNATIONAL

HUNGARY. Economic problems, political reforms, and difficulties with the Soviet Union were major areas of concern for Hungary in 1972. Criticism of the four-year-old Hungarian economic reform program, as well as charges of "bourgeois nationalism" in Hungary, appeared in the Soviet press early in the year. In February Hungarian Communist Party First Secretary Janos Kadar went to Moscow to meet with Soviet leaders. He and Communist Party General Secretary Leonid I. Brezhnev held talks on "questions of specialization and cooperation in production between the two countries and joint participation in the carrying out of the comprehensive program of socialist economic integration." On March 27 and 28 Hungary's Premier Jeno Fock and several government officials went to the Soviet Union to discuss economic relations between the two countries. On his return, Fock spoke openly of "major and minor difficulties" that were being encountered under the five-year plan then in effect and stated that he had been unable to get assurances from Soviet leaders about future aid, particularly in the area of much-needed raw materials. Hungary continued to emphasize foreign trade, an important sector of the economy; the foreign-trade balance had dropped for two consecutive years. The U.S. was also paid $20 million for prewar debts in return for granting most-favored-nation status to Hungary.

On April 20 the National Assembly adopted a series of amendments to the 1949 constitution, among which were guarantees of freedom for creative scientific and artistic work. The amendments replaced a plan for a totally new Socialist constitution after Kadar told the assembly that the new constitution would be premature. On March 15, Hungary's national day marking an 1848 uprising, a group of young demonstrators broke away from a commemorative rally and held a protest march—the first known street demonstration in Hungary since the 1956 rebellion. (*See in* CE: Hungary.)

ICE HOCKEY. The normal activity of the National Hockey League (NHL) was transcended in 1972 by two events of overriding consequence. One was an eight-game series by the professional Team Canada against a picked squad from the Soviet Union. The other event was the formation of a rival professional league, the World Hockey Association (WHA).

The eight-game series represented the first time that a team of Canadian professionals had confronted the Soviet national team. The Canadians, composed of players recruited from NHL teams, won four games, lost three, and tied one. They won the last one in Moscow on September 28, when Paul Henderson of the Toronto Maple Leafs scored a goal in the last minute for a 6–5 conquest. The games in Canada were played in Montreal, Que.; Toronto, Ont.; Winnipeg, Man.; and Vancouver, B.C. The games in the Soviet Union were confined to Moscow.

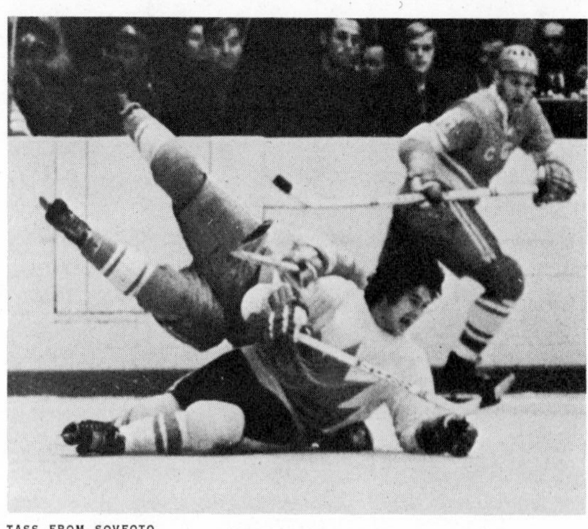

TASS FROM SOVFOTO

Team Canada's Brad Park falls during a game against the U.S.S.R. The Soviets won 5–4.

The challenge of the WHA cost the NHL some outstanding performers like Bobby Hull, who abandoned the Chicago Black Hawks for the Winnipeg Jets, in exchange for a ten-year contract worth about $2.5 million. Hull was followed into the WHA by such stars as Derek Sanderson, who deserted the Boston Bruins for the Philadelphia Blazers; Gerry Cheevers, who left Boston for the Cleveland Crusaders; and goalkeeper Bernie Parent, who quit the Toronto Maple Leafs for the Blazers.

The WHA teams were split into two divisions, Eastern and Western, each with six teams. The Quebec Nordiques, New England Whalers, New York Raiders, Ottawa Nationals, Cleveland, and Philadelphia make up the Eastern section. The Los Angeles Sharks, Alberta Oilers, Houston Aeros, Minnesota Shooting Stars, Chicago Cougars, and Winnipeg are in the West.

National Hockey League Season

In 1972 the Boston Bruins, winners in the Eastern Division of the NHL, won their second Stanley Cup in three years. Boston eliminated Toronto and St. Louis in preliminary series before beating New York four games to two in the final. New York qualified for the final by disposing of Montreal and the Western Division winner, Chicago.

Bobby Orr, the innovative Boston defenseman, continued his dominance of the individual awards. He won the Hart Trophy as the most valuable player in the NHL for the third successive year and the James Norris Trophy for the fifth consecutive time as the league's best defenseman. Phil Esposito, Boston's rangy center, accumulated 133 points and won the Art Ross Trophy for the second straight season as the game's top goal producer. Jean Ratelle, a smooth New York center, received the Lady Byng Trophy as the player best combining proficiency with gentlemanly conduct. Tony Esposito and Gary Smith of Chicago combined to

The Boston Bruins won the Stanley Cup by beating the New York Rangers 3–0. Bruins goalie Gerry Cheevers spreads his arms in joy to his oncoming teammates (from left) Bobby Orr, Dallas Smith, and Wayne Cashman.

WIDE WORLD

win the Vezina Trophy as the goalkeepers whose team allowed the fewest number of goals.

Amateur Ice Hockey

Czechoslovakia won both the Group A amateur world championship and the European title in 1972. Poland won the Group B tournament, and Austria the Group C.

The Soviet Union captured the gold medal at the Winter Olympics. Boston University took the National Collegiate Athletic Association championship. (*See in* CE: Ice Hockey.)

ICELAND. On Sept. 1, 1972, the extension of Iceland's fisheries limit from 12 to 50 miles came into effect, provoking strong protests from other nations, particularly Great Britain and West Germany. Iceland claimed that the extension was needed to combat excessive fishing by other countries and that it needed a larger share of the catches in order to strengthen its economy. (The fisheries industry provided about 80% of Iceland's exports.) The protesting nations, however, claimed that the extension violated the fisheries agreement of 1961. The Icelandic government, which had passed legislation declaring the agreement no longer applicable, refused to recognize the jurisdiction of the International Court of Justice at The Hague, Netherlands, and disregarded an interim ruling favoring the protesters, who, meanwhile, continued to ignore the new limit. In October an Icelandic gunboat cut the trawling wires of a British boat that was fishing within the new limit.

Relations with the U.S. improved, however, during the year. Prime Minister Olafur Johannesson had threatened in 1971 to evict U.S. military forces from his country. In 1972 it was agreed that the U.S. would keep its air base at Keflavík but that U.S. troops would be gradually phased out.

The world chess championship in Reykjavík, the capital, in which Bobby Fischer of the U.S. beat Boris Spassky of the U.S.S.R., attracted worldwide interest on an unprecedented scale. (*See* Chess. *See in* CE: Iceland.)

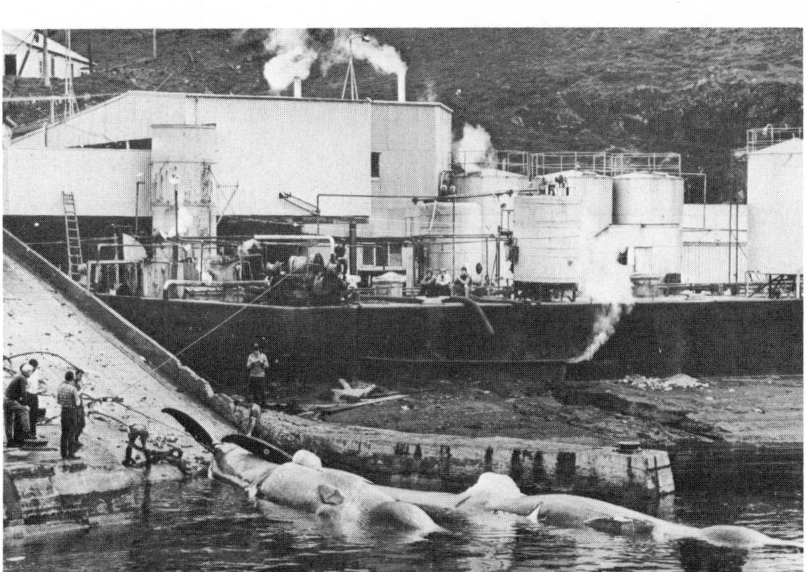

Icelandic whalers take fin whale carcasses to the whaling station of Hvalfjordue. About 400 whales are taken there each year, and the oil and meat from these whales—caught in Greenland seas—are two of Iceland's most valuable products.

WIDE WORLD

ICE SKATING. Only three weeks after the Winter Olympic Games, held in Sapporo, Japan, in February 1972, 103 ice skaters from 18 countries contested the world ice-dance and figure-skating championships at Calgary, Alta., on March 7–11. Ondrej Nepela of Czechoslovakia comfortably retained the men's title with a freestyle performance that was methodically yet undramatically efficient, including cleanly landed triple Salchow and triple loop jumps. Sergei Chetverukhin of the Soviet Union was runner-up. He got two scores of six for artistic impression but was too far behind in figures to catch Nepela. Another Russian, Vladimir Kov-alev, was third.

Beatrix Schuba of Austria retained her women's crown with conservative free-skating, which proved adequate after her 130-point lead in the figures, and she finally beat Karen Magnussen of Canada by a 6–3 judges' decision. The freestyle duel for second place between Miss Magnussen and Janet Lynn of Illinois was a spirited one. Spurred on by her home supporters, Miss Magnussen emerged the better all-arounder, but Miss Lynn, ultimately third, was top freestyle scorer, with two sixes.

Russians Aleksei Ulanov and Irina Rodnina of Moscow became the sixth couple to win the pairs championship for a fourth time. Their freestyle performance was short of their best; but three blatant timing errors were understandable results of reaction from Miss Rodnina's earlier training fall, and just before going on the ice she complained of double vision. Their brilliant double twist and overhead lifts were thus the more creditable, and they again defeated their Leningrad, U.S.S.R., rivals Andrei Suraikin and Ludmila Smirnova. A superbly thrown axel by Ken Shelley and Jo Jo Starbuck (both of California) was probably the factor that decided the judges to award them their third-place finish.

The ice-dance event provided the closest competition of the meet—between the defending husband-and-wife team of Aleksandr Gorshkov and Ludmila Pakhomova of the Soviet Union and West Germany's new European champions, brother and sister Erich and Angelika Buck. Scoring a six, the Russians split the judges 5–4 in their favor. Third place went to the U.S. duo of James Sladky and Judy Schwomeyer.

Dianne Holum of the U.S. won the women's 500-meter Olympic speed-skating event.

UPI COMPIX

Speed Skating

Ard Schenk of the Netherlands achieved the rare distinction of winning all four distance events (500-, 1,500-, 5,000-, and 10,000-meter) to retain the men's world speed-skating title in Oslo, Norway, on February 19–20. Roar Grønvold of Norway, overall runner-up, shared first place with Schenk in the 500-meter. Schenk's Netherlands team colleague, Jan Bols, was third best overall in the four races.

Dutch supremacy was also confirmed in the women's world speed championship, at Heerenveen, Netherlands, on March 4–5. Atje Keulen-Deelstra, first in both the 1,000-meter and the 1,500-meter, narrowly outpointed her compatriot Stien Baas-Kaiser, the 3,000-meter winner. Dianne Holum of Illinois won the 500-meter and finished third overall. Separate world sprint championships for men and women held at Eskilstuna, Sweden, on February 26–27, were won by Leo Linkovesi of Finland and Monika Pflug of West Germany, respectively.

Records Broken

New world records during the year were set over four men's and two women's distances. The time of 38.0 seconds for the 500-meter was clocked three times—by Erhard Keller of West Germany, Linkovesi of Finland, and Hasse Börjes of Sweden. Keller also lowered the 1,000-meter to 1:18.5, and Schenk completed his outstanding season with new marks of 4:8.3 in the 3,000-meter and 7:9.8 in the 5,000-meter. Anne Henning of Illinois lowered the women's 500-meter to 42.5 seconds and the 1,000-meter to 1:27.3. All these records were achieved at Inzell, West Germany, and at Davos, Switzerland, generally considered to be the world's fastest rinks for speed skating. (*See also* Olympic Games. *See in* CE: Skates and Skating.)

On March 19, Prime Minister Sheikh Mujibur Rahman of Bangladesh and Prime Minister Indira Gandhi of India signed the Indo-Bangladesh 25-year Treaty of Friendship and Peace. The signing took place in Dacca, Bangladesh.

FREDERIC OHRINGER FROM NANCY PALMER AGENCY

INDIA. The nation of India completed 25 years of independence from Great Britain in 1972, but because of growing economic difficulties there was little cause for celebration. A 13-day war in December 1971, which split Pakistan and created the new nation of Bangladesh out of the former eastern wing, proved a troubled victory.

All Indian troops stationed in Bangladesh were withdrawn by March 12, and the return was organized of 10 million refugees who had sought shelter in India. India gave Bangladesh $27 million in cash and 900,000 tons of grain and assisted in a rebuilding program. Indira Gandhi, the prime minister of India, visited Dacca, Bangladesh, in March and the two countries signed a 25-year treaty of friendship and cooperation.

Mrs. Gandhi met with Pakistan's President Zulfikar Ali Bhutto June 28–July 3 and signed an agreement pledging peaceful and bilateral solutions to the differences plaguing the new nations. India offered to restore to Pakistan 5,140 square miles of territory won in the December war, in return for 69 square miles to be returned by Pakistan. Both agreed to respect the "line of control" set up on Dec. 17, 1971, in Kashmir when the India-Pakistan cease-fire went into effect. However, a dispute in late August between the two nations concerning the cease-fire threatened the agreement, which was ratified by both countries on August 5. India insisted that the line of control be along the cease-fire line established in December 1971, but Pakistan argued that the delineation should be along an old cease-fire line established in 1949. India said that until the issue was settled there could be no troop withdrawals from the Rajasthan and Punjab borders as scheduled. In October the two nations were deadlocked on the issue and efforts to improve relations received an additional setback when a day of fighting broke out between Indian and Pakistani troops near Srinagar in Kashmir. On December 7, however, there was a breakthrough when Pakistan agreed to use the 1971 cease-fire line as a temporary boundary. Military commanders were instructed to respect the 500-mile line, and troop withdrawals by both sides were ordered.

Tribal women vote in the Bastar district of Madhya Pradesh in India.

PANA FROM KEYSTONE

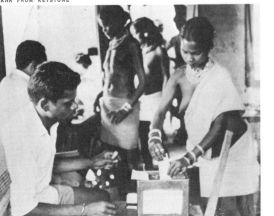

Pakistan's recognition of Bangladesh, which President Bhutto had hinted at, never materialized during the year. India continued to maintain that the prisoners of war (some 92,000) could not be released without agreement with Bangladesh, since they had surrendered in Bangladesh to an Indo-Bangladesh joint command. The deadlock remained, as Pakistan withheld recognition of Bangladesh, and the People's Republic of China vetoed the admission of Bangladesh to the United Nations. In an effort to induce India to release the Pakistani prisoners of war without the approval of Bangladesh, Pakistan released all of the 617 Indian prisoners it had been holding in November.

Relations with the Soviet Union and the U.S.

Relations with the U.S. continued to be strained, despite a July visit to India by former U.S. Secretary of Treasury John B. Connally, Jr. When the

KEYSTONE

Workers on this riverbed were digging in an effort to reactivate the river, which dried up during a severe drought in India.

India-Pakistan war broke out, the U.S. had halted development aid to both nations. In India's case, the aid already agreed to totaled $87.6 million. Aid to India remained suspended, and in February India rejected U.S. President Richard M. Nixon's offer of a "serious dialogue" because the U.S. continued to withhold recognition of Bangladesh and maintained a policy of arming Pakistan as a counterweight to India. U.S. policy on Vietnam was also strongly criticized. In October the U.S. Central Intelligence Agency was accused of stirring up trouble against the Gandhi government throughout India. In the meantime, the U.S. was without an ambassador to India after Kenneth B. Keating resigned in July. The Indian government blocked visas for several hundred U.S. scholars.

In September D. P. Dhar, minister of planning, visited Moscow to finalize arrangements for Indo-Soviet economic cooperation under a 1971 friendship treaty. His visit came shortly after the first series of annual political discussions between the two countries, as laid down in the treaty, was held in Moscow.

Domestic Affairs

Manipur, Meghalaya, and Tripura became full states and Mizoram and the North-Eastern Frontier Agency (renamed Arunachal Pradesh) became union territories in 1972. Elections for state assemblies were held in March throughout the country, except in Kerala, Orissa, Tamil Nadu, Uttar Pradesh, and Nagaland. The Ruling Congress party won a majority in all the states except Manipur and Meghalaya. Damodaram Sanjivayya, 50, president of the party, died on May 7 in New Delhi, the capital, after suffering a heart attack.

Mrs. Gandhi reorganized her cabinet in July. The Ruling Congress party directed its governments to carry out land reforms quickly. Andhra Pradesh, Gujarat, and Jammu and Kashmir led the way in adopting legislation to enforce a ceiling on land holdings and redistribute surplus land among landless laborers. The Supreme Court struck down an order of the government limiting the size of newspapers to ten pages, because the order was a restriction on freedom of speech.

The Economy

Prices spiraled during the year. Among the factors contributing to inflation were lower farm and factory production, a power shortage, and an increase in public expenditures due to refugee relief, military operations, drought relief, and wage hikes to government employees. The late arrival and erratic behavior of the 1972 monsoon affected summer crops and also contributed to inflation. The wholesale price index on September 16 was 8% higher than it had been 12 months earlier. The index for grains was 14.7% higher and for sugar 33.5% higher. Personal money supplies had increased by 12.6% over the same period. In October the government announced a package of measures for distribution of essential supplies through fair price shops, for the take-over of the wholesale grain trade, and for absorption of the money supply.

Earlier in the year Mrs. Gandhi had ordered the finance ministry and planning commission to redirect economic plans on the assumption that no further aid would be sought from the U.S., implying a further decline in India's trade with the U.S. in favor of Eastern bloc countries. In May L. N. Mishra, India's minister of foreign trade, visited Moscow, indicating that the Soviet Union would probably become India's largest single trading partner. India expressed fears that Great Britain's entry into the European Economic Community (EEC) on Jan. 1, 1973, would place severe restrictions on some Indian exports. In May India renewed its application for a trade agreement with the EEC before 1973. India appeared particularly anxious to enter the market as a major seller of military armaments. Such equipment brought in $10 million in 1972 in trade with Nepal, Kenya, Malaysia, and Egypt and other nations in the Middle East.

The country's second nuclear power station opened near Kota during the year, as did the first unit of a Soviet-financed steel plant at Bokaro. The government took over the Indian Iron and Steel Co., British Incorporated Indian Copper, the entire domestic trade in raw jute, and 46 textile mills. Under a formula for progressive nationalization, foreign companies were to be allowed to expand only if they agreed to increase Indian equity participation in proportion to their growth. (*See in* CE: India.)

INDIANS, AMERICAN. The National Tribal Chairmen's Association, one year old in July, 1972, held its first annual convention in Eugene, Ore., in August. From an initial membership of 52 tribes, the organization had expanded during the year to include more than 100 tribes and bands. Elected chiefs from every federally recognized tribe were invited to attend, along with U.S. government officials and members of Congress. Speaking at the convention, U.S. Secretary of the Interior Rogers C. B. Morton applauded the efforts of emerging Indian leaders to stimulate Indian self-determination.

At another important meeting, representatives of 19 western Indian tribes gathered in July in Denver, Colo., to discuss the protection of Indian land and water resources. Many of the tribal leaders expressed dissatisfaction with the present system, under which the federal government is expected to act as trustee for the Indians. Since most of the Indians' legal claims are against the government itself, they feel that the situation creates a clear conflict of interest. Some tribes have hired private lawyers, but for most of them this is simply too expensive. The Native American Rights Fund, an independent organization with a staff of 11 lawyers and an all-Indian board of directors, has taken part in court action on behalf of Indians. During 1972 the fund was given a three-year grant of $1.2 million by the Ford Foundation, to be used in the litigation of major issues concerning American Indians.

The restoration of lost Indian territory and the protection of land and water rights were major focuses of Indian activity during 1972. In May U.S. President Richard M. Nixon signed an executive order restoring 21,000 acres of land in the state of Washington to the Yakima tribe, land from which the Indians had been displaced because of a government error. The restored area included Mount Adams, a sacred mountain of the Yakima people.

A number of court suits during the year involved Indian land and water rights. The most outstanding victory for the Indians was a decision in favor of the Paiute tribe of Nevada's Pyramid Lake reservation. The Paiutes had accused the Department of the Interior of allowing the Truckee River, which feeds the reservation's Pyramid Lake, to be diverted for the benefit of white farmers near Reno, Nev. The court ordered the department to revise its regulations regarding diversion of the Truckee and strongly criticized its handling of trust and treaty obligations with the Paiutes.

In other court action a U.S. district court in Portland, Me., ordered U.S. Attorney General Richard G. Kleindienst to file a protective land claim suit against the state of Maine on behalf of the state's Passamaquoddy Indians. The Oneida tribes of New York and Wisconsin, however, lost an appeal to regain tribal lands in central New York.

Other Indian groups continued to follow a more militant path in the assertion and defense of their rights. In the summer of 1971 a small group of Indians had seized and occupied an abandoned U.S.

At the Rocky Boy Elementary School, conducted by the Crees on their reservation in Montana, children are being educated through a curriculum based on Indian culture.

BARBARA GLUCK TREASTER FROM "THE NEW YORK TIMES"

WIDE WORLD

Indians armed with clubs stood guard in front of the Bureau of Indian Affairs building in Washington, D.C. A group of 400 militant Indians occupied the building for several days.

Coast Guard station at Milwaukee, Wis. They defended their action under an 1868 treaty that allowed nonreservation Indians to file claims on federal land "not used for specific purposes." During 1972 the American Indian Movement pursued the necessary steps toward legal possession of the property, and in August the Indians celebrated the first anniversary of their take-over. They requested a grant from the federal government for an Indian educational and cultural center on the property.

Another militant action—one that drew nationwide attention in November—was the occupation of the Bureau of Indian Affairs (BIA) building in Washington, D.C., by a group of angry Indians seeking revision of treaties and review of land, water, and mineral rights. When some government officials threatened to evict them, the Indians obtained a court injunction allowing them to stay. They left after six days, taking with them thousands of documents and many Indian art pieces and leaving extensive damage behind them. The stolen documents were made available to newspaper columnist Jack Anderson for publication; the Indians claimed that the documents were proof of ill-treatment of Indians over the years. The incident led to a massive shakeup of the BIA, including the dismissal of most of the agency's highest officials, in December. (*See in* CE: Indians, American.)

INDONESIA. In 1972, for the first time since the proclamation of Indonesia's independence in 1945, a People's Consultative Assembly (MPR) was sworn in. Internationally, partly as a reaction to U.S. disengagement from Vietnam and rapprochement with the People's Republic of China, Indonesia moved to strengthen ties with its immediate neighbors and with Japan.

Domestic Affairs

Ironically, for a year that ended on a high note of political stability, 1972 opened harshly with the eruption of what was popularly called the mini-Indonesia affair. The issue developed when Tien Suharto, the wife of Indonesia's President Suharto, launched a plan to build a multimillion-dollar Disneyland-style amusement park—"Indonesia in Miniature"—to attract tourists and to strengthen national unity through a display of the country's richly diverse cultural heritage. Several senior army officers and their wives emerged as the plan's cosponsors, and rumors spread that pressure was being brought to bear on private firms to make "voluntary contributions."

The affair mushroomed into a political crisis as the press, students, and some economic planners denounced the scheme as a wasteful expenditure. President Suharto, visibly upset by the public outcry, rushed to his wife's defense and accused her critics of exploiting the issue to undermine the government. Both the government and the opposition appeared surprised by the tension that the issue generated, and both sides retreated. The project was submitted to parliament for a feasibility study, and, for all practical purposes, the scheme was dropped.

With the collapse of the mini-Indonesia project, a new climate of political stability emerged. The critics appeared satisfied that they had been heard and heeded, and the government was relieved that the criticism was not "opposition for opposition's sake" but rather the work of a "loyal opposition."

In the new atmosphere, political events moved smoothly for the remainder of the year. On October 1, the seventh anniversary of the abortive putsch of the Indonesian Communist party (PKI), the 920-member MPR was convened for the first time. The MPR, scheduled to elect a new president and vice-president in March 1973, is allowed under the constitution to determine the broad lines of national policy.

The Economy

The economy continued to display marked improvement, regaining the momentum lost during the troubled tenure of President Sukarno. Under Suharto's stewardship the rate of inflation decreased from 650% in 1966 to 2.5% in 1972; developmental expenditure rose during 1971–72 by 15%; export earnings rose at an appreciable rate; and the mobilization of domestic funds through savings increased dramatically.

The implementation of the country's first five-year plan (1969–74) continued. Rice production increased annually under the plan, and the fixed targets were surpassed. Suharto expressed concern, however, that the market price of rice would drop if output continued to rise, ultimately causing a drop in income for the greater part of the Indonesian population. Accordingly, the rice

KEYSTONE

At the Grand Trianon in Versailles, President Georges Pompidou of France (left) greets President Suharto of Indonesia, who was in France on a state visit.

target for 1973–74 was cut from 15.4 million to 14.8 million tons. The 1972 rice crop fell short of internal needs, however, and there were reports in December of shortages and starvation in some places.

Indonesian oil production during the year averaged 1.3 million barrels daily, and the oil industry earned almost $1 billion in foreign exchange. In addition, progress was registered in bringing copper, nickel, iron, and sand mines into production. In a surprising development, forestry emerged in 1972 as the country's third largest source of exports after oil and rubber.

Foreign Affairs

During 1972 President Suharto continued to pursue his policy of cultivating Japan as a prime source of massive economic, technical, and military assistance. In the aftermath of U.S. President Richard M. Nixon's journey to Peking, China, and the open invasion of South Vietnam by North Vietnam, Suharto flew to Japan to confer "unofficially" on the shifting situation in Eastern Asia. At the conclusion of the talks, Japan extended a new loan of $200 million to Indonesia in return for guaranteed shipment of 50 million tons of Indonesian oil over a ten-year period. As a result of this new agreement, Japan, already Indonesia's major trading partner, became its principal donor of foreign aid.

Suharto also labored to strengthen ties with Indonesia's immediate neighbors. He paid state visits to Australia, New Zealand, and the Philippines, while the Indonesian armed forces carried out joint military exercises with Australia, Malaysia, and the Philippines. A program of economic and military aid from Australia was announced in July.

Following the visits to Peking by President Nixon and Japan's Prime Minister Kakuei Tanaka, Indonesia made its first moves to improve relations with China. A major condition for the resumption of normal relations was Indonesia's insistence that China abandon its propaganda attacks on the Suharto regime and withdraw its diplomatic, political, and financial support of the remnant PKI faction operating out of Peking. In October Foreign Minister Adam Malik announced that Indonesia was seeking a "normalization" of relations with China. (*See in* CE: Indonesia, Republic of.)

A Clear Case of Whiplash! (New York state's "no fault" insurance bill was not enacted in 1972.)

ROSEN, "ALBANY TIMES-UNION" FROM BEN ROTH AGENCY

INSURANCE. In 1972 the hotly debated "no fault" automobile insurance plan continued to claim much attention. In August the U.S. Senate voted 49–46 to send a bill designed to create a national system of "no fault" insurance to its Judiciary Committee for more study. The proposal was made by Senator Roman L. Hruska (R, Neb.) and was backed by the Administration of President Richard M. Nixon.

The federal government, in June, cut the cost of subsidized flood insurance by 40%. It was hoped that this reduction would encourage widespread buying of this type of protection.

The insurance business in the U.S. employed about 1.49 million people in all its branches in 1971. During 1967, the most recent year for which detailed data were available, some 740,000 persons worked in life insurance.

Life

At the end of 1971, approximately 140 million people in the U.S. owned life insurance policies with legal reserve life insurance companies. This accounted for $1.5 trillion of protection, an increase of $102 billion of coverage over 1970. The average amount of life insurance carried by the insured U.S. family increased to $25,700. Life insurance benefit payments grew to $17.2 billion in 1971. This was an increase of 4.4% over the preceding year. Benefits to living policyholders totaled $9.8 billion of this amount.

A total of $189.2 billion worth of life insurance was bought in 1971. Some type of life insurance protection was carried by 86% of the nation's men. The figure for women was 74%. In 1971 approximately two thirds of new life insurance was purchased on an individual basis rather than as part of a group plan.

In recent years one of the most significant actions in the life insurance business has been preparation by some life insurance companies to issue what has become known as "variable life insurance." This type of policy would pay benefits above a guaranteed minimum that would either rise or fall depending on the result of the investment of its premiums in the stock market. Several major life insurance firms had proposals pending before the Securities and Exchange Commission that would enable them to write those variable life policies.

Health

During 1972 the large majority of health care expenses in the U.S. continued to be financed through private health insurance. Throughout the year, however, national health insurance continued to be a topic that received a great deal of debate.

At the close of 1971 the number of people protected by some form of private health insurance in the U.S. rose to 187 million, up 5.5 million over the preceding year. During 1971, health benefit payments totaled $18.5 billion. Of this amount, insurance companies paid $9.7 billion while the remainder came from Blue Cross, Blue Shield, and other plans.

All types of health insurance showed increases in the number of persons covered during 1971. The new totals were: 187 million covered against hospital expenses, 175 million covered against surgical expenses, 153 million covered against regular medical expenses (doctor visits), 83 million covered against major medical expenses, 60 million covered against loss of income due to short-term disability, and 12 million covered against loss of income due to long-term disability (more than two years). (*See in* CE: Insurance.)

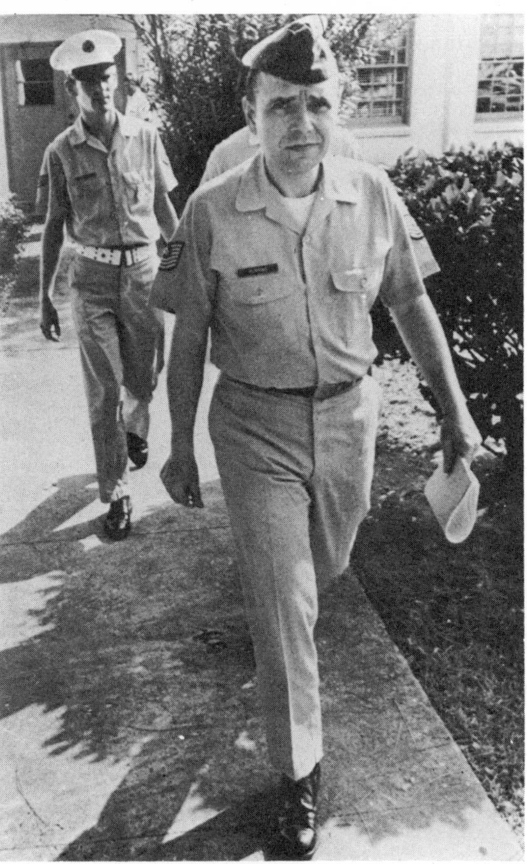

WIDE WORLD

M. Sgt. Walter T. Perkins was convicted of stealing defense secrets and attempting to pass them on to unauthorized persons.

INTELLIGENCE OPERATIONS. Testifying before the U.S. Senate Committee on Foreign Relations in March 1972, Ray S. Cline, the director of the Bureau of Intelligence and Research in the Department of State, stated that the U.S. spent "about $3 billion" per year on the collection of intelligence. The new budget request was estimated at $7.3 billion.

On August 11, at Tyndall Air Force Base in Florida, M. Sgt. Walter T. Perkins of the U.S. Air Force was convicted on a charge of stealing military secrets for the Soviet Union. He was given a dishonorable discharge and sentenced to a three-year prison term.

On February 14 Valeri Ivanovich Markelov, a citizen of the Soviet Union employed as a translator for the United Nations (UN) Secretariat, was charged with espionage for his attempt to obtain secret data on the U.S. Navy's new supersonic fighter plane, the F-14A. He was the fifth Soviet employee at the UN to be arrested on spy charges.

Enrico Berlinguer, new first secretary of the Italian Communist party, declared shortly before Italy's general elections in May 1972 that the activities of foreign secret services in Italy had been intensified. At the same time, foreign correspondents in Rome were supplied with photographic copies of the most recent U.S. Defense Intelligence Agency manual allegedly instructing agents as follows: "The Department of Defense has a manifold interest in acquiring information on both civil and military intelligence, counterintelligence, security, and subversive organizations of foreign nations, to include not only those of an enemy or potential adversary, but also those of allies. . . . "

In Great Britain John Vassall, who had served 10 years of his 18-year sentence for spying for the Soviet Union at the Royal Navy Portland base in Dorset, England, was released on parole on Oct. 24, 1972. Sub-Lieut. David James Bingham, a 31-year-old Royal Navy officer, was sentenced on March 13, at Winchester, England, to 21 years in prison for selling secrets "almost beyond price" to the Soviet Union. Later, his wife, Maureen, was charged with having committed an act preparatory to a spying offense. In April Leonard Michael Hinchliffe, an assistant administrative officer in foreign and Commonwealth affairs for Great Britain, was sent to prison for ten years. He was convicted of passing secret documents on ciphers to a Soviet agent named Andrei while assigned to the British embassy in Khartoum, Sudan, in 1970.

The *London Daily Telegraph* on August 24 expressed the belief that Col. Rudolf Abel, Soviet master spy who died in Moscow in November 1971, was the son of Henry Fisher, a friend of Nikolai Lenin. Fisher had left St. Petersburg (now Leningrad), Russia, in 1891 and had settled in England. Fisher returned to the Soviet Union after the Russian Revolution of 1917, taking back with him his son, who was 17; this would explain Abel's faultless English, a key factor in his successful spying.

President Schneor Zalman Shazar of Israel ordered the release of British photographer Arthur Paterson on April 18 to mark Israel's Independence Day (April 19). In February 1971 Paterson had been convicted in Israel of passing security information and photographs to Egypt and was sentenced to eight years in prison—reduced later on appeal to five years.

INTERIOR DESIGN. The Museum of Modern Art in New York City once again stirred up a good deal of controversy and excitement with its provocative show "Italy: The New Domestic Landscape" that opened May 26, 1972, and remained to September 11. The exhibition, largest in the museum's history, contained 157 individual pieces of successful design from the preceding decade, as well as twelve radical prototype "environments" for prepackaged living units.

The objects displayed included household articles (ceramic and glass vases and stackable dishes), appliances (steamer trunk radios, AM-FM units, and steel, chrome, and plastic lamps), and furniture (modular seating and shelving units, molded plastic chairs and tables, and convertible beds). Most

JIM WOOD FROM LIFE MAGAZINE © TIME INC.

Frank Gehry (right) designs furniture made of glued layers of corrugated fiberboard.

were well-known in the U.S., and many already much-copied.

The environments, or "machines for living," however, were something else. Commissioned by the museum and executed under subsidies from Italian manufacturers, each presented new ideas and solutions to housing problems of the future. The portable architectural units varied from a subterranean living unit for the year 2000, to an expandable metal crate resembling a folding camera, to a shippable mobile home designed to conform to transatlantic container specifications. It was thought these efficient, innovative plug-in cores might well revolutionize the architectural and design thinking throughout the world in the coming decades.

A Touch of Whimsy

Attractive, inexpensive, practical, and fun furniture built of corrugated fiberboard, designed by architect Frank Gehry of Los Angeles, created a sensation when introduced early in the year. The ingenious idea, first developed for scale-model projects, blossomed into a full line of furniture for the entire home—bedroom, living room, study, children's room, dining room, and bar. Knockdown furniture as well as floor and ceiling tiles were also planned.

The 25 or so pieces are compact, forward-looking, sculptural, light, and versatile. With cross-laminated layers of the fiberboard and alternate directions of the corrugations, the design achieves an interesting textural surface, suedelike to the touch, and a surprising strength. The furniture is sound-absorbent and inherently nonflammable, and it can be spray waxed for protection. Liquids can be wiped off with a cloth or sponge, dust and crumbs can be vacuumed away, and stained or charred areas can be removed with a stiff brush. Some of the pieces are easily stackable; others are multifunctional.

The Year's Highlights

At the January International Home Furnishings Market in Chicago it was decided to continue holding the twice-a-year exhibition on its traditional dates in January and June. There had been some efforts to change the dates to March and September.

Early in the year the American Institute of Interior Designers (AIID) and the National Society of Interior Designers (NSID) made a major move in unifying the interior design profession by appointing a National Council for Interior Design Qualification. The new group also represents the Industrial Designers Society of America, Institute of Business Designers, American Institute of Architects, and independent designers. In early July the NSID met in Dallas, Tex., for its ninth national conference, the theme of which was "New Directions." The AIID held a number of regional conferences throughout the country.

The second annual "Come to the Market Place," held primarily for designers, was sponsored in New York City by the Resources Council during the second week of October. Also during the year, the new Pacific Design Center was under construction in Los Angeles. The six-story showroom and exhibit complex—being built exclusively for the interior design, decoration, and furnishings trades—was scheduled to open in the summer of 1974. (*See in* CE: Interior Decoration.)

This Totem hi-fi set with detachable speakers was designed by Mario and Dario Bellini.

AUTHENTICATED NEWS INTERNATIONAL

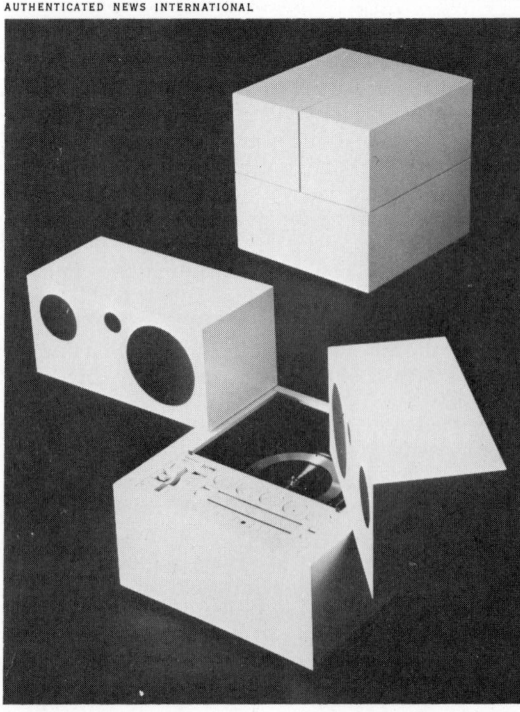

WIDE WORLD

Chairman Mao Tse-tung (second from right) talks with U.S. President Richard M. Nixon (right) in Peking, China, in February. Premier Chou En-lai (left) was also present.

INTERNATIONAL RELATIONS. International attention was focused during 1972 on U.S. diplomatic moves to end the Vietnam war and to strengthen friendly relations with the Soviet Union and the People's Republic of China. The Administration of U.S. President Richard M. Nixon, faced with a presidential election, was under pressure to end the Vietnam war. While fighting continued throughout the year, U.S. forces in Vietnam were reduced from some 180,000 men in November 1971 to 27,000 in November 1972. To exert pressure for a peace settlement, the U.S. carried out intensive bombing raids over North Vietnam and mined North Vietnamese harbors. During the summer Henry Kissinger, the president's security adviser, began a campaign of secret negotiations with North Vietnam to work out a peace agreement. In October a draft agreement between the U.S. and North Vietnam was made public. Its provisions were to take effect upon the signing of the document. (*See* Vietnam.)

Signing of the agreement was delayed by U.S. insistence on clarifying several points. Another delay came when President Nguyen Van Thieu of South Vietnam rejected the agreement. He continued to demand North Vietnam's withdrawal from the South and to refuse Communist political participation in the South. While negotiations between the U.S. and North and South Vietnam continued, the U.S. completed its Vietnamization program with huge arms shipments to South Vietnam.

At the end of the year, however, the agreement had not been signed, and hopes for peace dimmed considerably when, in December, the U.S. hit North Vietnam with the heaviest bombing of the war. It was feared that the new bombing would threaten the improved diplomatic climate that the U.S. had achieved in 1972 with China and the Soviet Union. The shift, begun in 1971, from hostility to coexistence in U.S.-Chinese relations, was affirmed by a week-long visit to China by President Nixon in February. Sino-U.S. talks continued throughout the year, bilateral trade and cultural exchanges developed further, and the U.S. lifted its ban on travel to China by U.S. ships and planes.

In a move to further U.S.-Soviet relations, President Nixon held talks with Soviet leaders in Moscow in May. The most significant result was the signing of the antiballistic missile treaty and interim arms limitation agreement, the culmination of two years of negotiations. In November the two nations began the second phase of the arms control talks, aimed at limiting offensive nuclear weapons. (*See* Arms Control and Disarmament.)

While it was apparent that the U.S., in making its diplomatic moves, was using Sino-Soviet rivalry to strengthen its own position, there were also far-reaching effects on the policies and relations of other nations. In diplomatic strategy aimed at countering improved U.S.-Chinese relations, the Soviets succeeded in becoming a powerful influence on the Indian subcontinent. They also made important inroads in the Arab oil industry in Iraq and promoted an East-West détente in Europe.

Nixon's trip to China stirred resentment and fears of isolation in Japan. It led Japan to move toward a rapprochement with China, to recognize Mongolia, and to set up a diplomatic delegation in North Vietnam. Japan and China normalized relations in September, ending a state of war dating from 1937. As a result, diplomatic relations between Japan and Nationalist China were severed, though trade relations were maintained.

India and Pakistan agreed on peace plans for the Indian subcontinent in July, but a final settlement of the 1971 Indo-Pakistani war was thwarted by a deadlock over the Kashmir cease-fire line and the return of war prisoners. In December India and the U.S. moved toward improved relations, which

UPI COMPIX

On May 23, in Moscow, President Nixon (left) and Soviet President Nikolai V. Podgorny signed several agreements for joint action against cancer, heart disease, and air and water pollution.

had been cool because of U.S. support for Pakistan in the 1971 war.

Indicative of improving relations between Western and Eastern Europe in 1972 was the negotiation of a treaty, signed in December, establishing formal ties between West Germany and East Germany. The treaty, which ended 23 years of hostility, left open the question of German unification and paved the way for the admission of both German states to the United Nations (UN). In a related agreement, the U.S., Great Britain, France, and the Soviet Union reaffirmed their rights and responsibilities in divided Germany, thereby ensuring Western access to Berlin. Other accords provided for an easing of travel restrictions between the two Germanys. An East German amnesty released many West German political prisoners.

Contributing to the détente in Europe were several important conferences. The U.S., Canada, and all European nations except Albania began consultations in November to lay the groundwork for a European security conference in 1973. Preparations were also made for talks between the U.S. and the Soviets and their European allies on a reduction of military forces in central Europe.

During 1972 Great Britain, Denmark, and Ireland signed the treaty of accession to the European Economic Community (EEC), to which they would formally be admitted on Jan. 1, 1973. Norway's rejection of EEC membership was seen as a blow to European unity. At a summit meeting in October the expanded EEC adopted a goal of European unity on the policy level by 1980.

Prospects for a peace settlement in the Middle East were seriously damaged in 1972 by Arab terrorist campaigns against Israel, which became increasingly international in scope and threatened an increasing number of non-Israelis through airline hijackings and letter bombs. The massacre by Arab terrorists of Israeli athletes and coaches at the Olympic Games in West Germany outraged the world and adversely affected Israeli-West German relations. Israel retaliated with massive attacks against guerrilla camps in Syria and Lebanon, and heavy fighting erupted between Israeli and Syrian forces late in the year. (*See* Israel.)

A major event in the Arab world was Egypt's ouster of most Soviet military advisory personnel in July, following Soviet refusal to deliver offensive missiles to Egypt. A proposal by Jordan's King Hussein I to unify his nation was condemned throughout the Arab world and led to a break in Egyptian-Jordanian relations. The long war between Yemen (Sana) and Yemen (Aden) ended in November with an agreement to unify the two nations. (*See* Middle Eastern countries by name.)

Another development during the year was the expulsion from Uganda of some 50,000 Asians who held British passports. Great Britain endeavored to absorb most of the refugees, and others found asylum in Europe, the U.S., and Canada. North Korea and South Korea took steps toward a reunification of their nations, although some observers saw these moves as tactics by each nation to topple the other and to impose its system on the whole of Korea. The U.S. and Cuba, though still hostile and without diplomatic relations, began negotiations in November on measures to curb airline hijackings. The talks, which were handled with Swiss diplomats acting as intermediaries, followed a rash in hijackings of U.S. planes to Cuba. (*See in* CE: International Relations.)

IRAN. The country of Iran entered 1972 in a mood of well-founded confidence. The solid foundation of popular approval on which the monarchy rested had been increasingly demonstrated during the preceding 12 months, not only by the angry reaction of organizations of peasants and workers to student unrest in Teheran (the capital) and elsewhere, but also by the outcome of the general elections. These elections resulted in an overwhelming victory for the New Iran party, on which Prime Minister Amir Abbas Hoveyda's government was based. The party won 229 of the 268 seats in the National Consultative Assembly and 27 of the 30 seats that made up the elected half of the senate.

Secret trials of political opponents of the regime were reported to have been taking place. Early in the year at least ten people accused of guerrilla activities, ranging from the murder of policemen to membership in Communist underground movements, were executed by firing squad. Many others were thought to be held (and some tortured) by the secret police. The procedure of the courts was criticized for the vagueness of charges, the absence of witnesses, the paucity of legal advice available to accused persons, and the methods used by the police to obtain information.

In April Iran was hit by a disastrous earthquake in the southern part of the country. Known casualties were put at more than 10,000, with more than 4,000 dead. Offers of help and medical supplies came from many countries, especially from Iran's partners in the Regional Cooperation for Development project, Turkey and Pakistan.

An earthquake destroyed 45 villages in the Ghir and Karzine areas of Iran in 1972.
HUGUES VASSAL FROM GAMMA

Iran was encouraged in its attitude of pursuing friendly relations and fostering economic progress throughout the Middle East by the détente accomplished between the U.S. and the Soviet Union and between the U.S. and the People's Republic of China. In May U.S. President Richard M. Nixon made a brief visit to Teheran and held frank discussions with Shah Mohammed Reza Pahlavi and his prime minister on the range of common interests in the Middle East, the Persian Gulf, and Southeast Asia. (*See in* CE: Iran.)

IRAQ. External affairs in Iraq in 1972 were marked by closer ties with the Soviet Union, the nationalization of some Western-owned oil facilities, better relations within the Arab world, and border clashes with Iran. Internally, there were threats of economic difficulties and of renewed trouble with the Kurdish minority.

Early in 1972 a high-ranking Iraqi delegation visiting the Soviet Union obtained Soviet agreement to increase economic and military aid, to help in establishing a national Iraqi oil industry, and to foster closer links between Iraq's ruling Ba'ath Socialist party and the Soviet Communist party. When Soviet Premier Aleksei N. Kosygin visited Iraq in April, a 15-year Soviet-Iraqi treaty of friendship and cooperation was signed, providing for mutual consultations in case either nation was threatened. During his stay Kosygin, whose visit was the first by a Soviet premier to Iraq, inaugurated production in Iraq's North Rumaila oil field; the field had been developed with Soviet aid after being nationalized in 1961. This increasing Iraqi-Soviet involvement was viewed as strengthening the roles of both nations in the Persian Gulf region and as furthering Soviet penetration of the international oil trade.

The Iraqi government and the Iraq Petroleum Co. (IPC), owned by U.S. and European interests, began negotiations in February on Iraqi demands for a 10% annual increase in oil production, payment to Iraq of more than $200 million in back royalties, and 20% ownership by Iraq in the company. When the IPC cut production at its Kirkuk oil fields because of increased shipping costs, Iraq suffered a decrease in royalties and was forced to halt some public works programs. Iraq accused the IPC of trying to force compensation for the North Rumaila seizure in 1961. On May 17 Iraq issued an ultimatum to the IPC based on its February demands; the negotiations subsequently broke down, and on June 1 the government nationalized all IPC assets in Iraq and set up a government company to run the IPC facilities. Iraq's move was backed by other Arab nations, which provided Iraq with a loan to offset the serious loss of royalties entailed in the take-over. Although the IPC threatened legal action to block marketing of Kirkuk oil, Iraq was able to secure sales contracts with France (one of the IPC owners) and with other European nations.

Faced with a loss of oil revenues, the government planned cutbacks in imports and development projects, instituted an austerity program, and banned most foreign travel. The economy was aided, however, by a surplus in the cereal harvest. In October Iraq was one of five oil-producing Persian Gulf nations to win from major Western oil companies the right to an eventual 51% participation in company oil concessions.

A new Iraqi cabinet appointed in May included Communists, for the first time since 1963, and pro-Egyptians—evidence of a rapprochement between Iraq and Egypt, even though an Iraqi bid to join a federation with Egypt, Libya, and Sudan was rejected. Iraq's continuing border dispute with Iran erupted into frequent armed clashes along the frontier during 1972. In January fighting also broke out between government forces and the Kurdish minority in northwestern Iraq, in spite of the 1970 truce. Although Kurdish became an official language in the northern provinces in April, Kurdish discontent was evident and the government was blamed for an attempt in July to kill the Kurdish Democratic party leader, Mustafa Barzani. (*See in* CE: Iraq.)

IRELAND. The nation's decision to enter the European Economic Community (EEC) was a highlight of 1972 in the Republic of Ireland. Voters approved entry into the EEC by a five-to-one majority in a national referendum held May 10.

The continuing turmoil in Northern Ireland—a part of the United Kingdom—affected Ireland, too. Strengthened by the vote for the EEC and a landslide victory in the mid-Cork by-election early in August, Prime Minister John Lynch showed an increasingly tough attitude throughout the year toward the Provisional wing of the Irish Republican Army (IRA) and its political branch, Sinn Fein. In May, Sinn Fein leaders were arrested, but efforts to prosecute them failed. In August, special courts were set up to deal with IRA offenses more effectively.

Relations between Ireland and Great Britain had hit their lowest point after 13 people were killed by British soldiers in Londonderry, Northern Ireland, on January 30. Subsequently, the British Embassy in Dublin (the capital) was burned, and Ireland's envoy to Britain was recalled. The introduction of direct British rule in Northern Ireland in March was welcomed by the Irish government, but subsequent meetings between Lynch and Great Britain's Prime Minister Edward Heath achieved little. Britain published its green paper on Northern Ireland in the fall, stating that any new administrative structure in the North should be acceptable to the republic.

The government announced in October a referendum that included the provision for deleting Article 44 of the national constitution, which bestowed a special position on the Roman Catholic church. However, no changes were proposed in other articles dealing with territorial claims to Northern Ireland, the position on the Irish language, or legislation covering divorce and contraception. A Dublin housewife earlier had challenged the constitutionality of legislation under which contraceptive materials belonging to her were seized by Irish customs officials. Her action failed, as did a Senate reform bill, but the council of the Irish Medical Association called for a change in contraception laws.

The Irish economy continued to be seriously threatened by inflation. Food prices increased by 12% and the cost of living was up 10%. Tourism was severely hit both by inflation and by the Northern Ireland situation.

The Irish government pressed for an investigation by the European Human Rights Commission into charges of brutality in Northern Ireland. Five of the seven charges brought against Great Britain were accepted.

Twelve leaders of Irish business and industry were killed in an air crash at London's Heathrow airport on June 18 while they were on their way to EEC talks in Belgium. (*See in* CE: Ireland.)

Irish troops and police hold back supporters of the "People's Democracy" outside the Curragh Military Detention Camp in Dublin. Demonstrators protested the detention of political prisoners in the camp.

UPI COMPIX

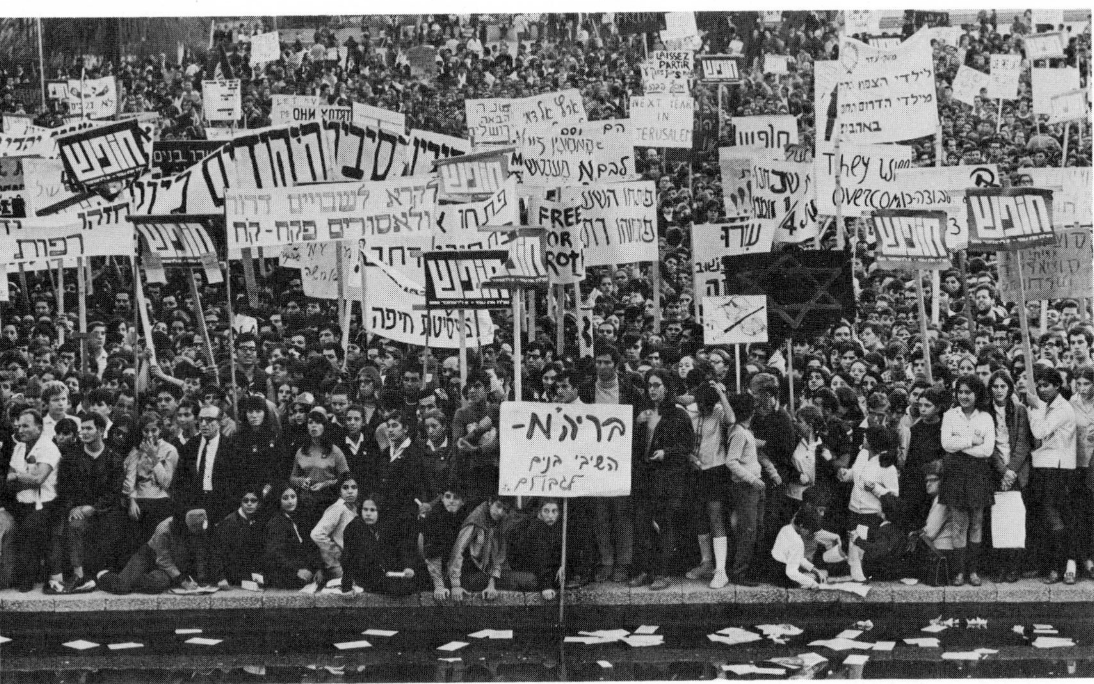

MICHA BAR-AM

Israelis hold a massive demonstration in Tel Aviv to publicize their sympathy for the plight of Jews in the Soviet Union.

ISRAEL. For much of 1972, Israeli concerns were focused on internal affairs, in contrast to other years since the 1967 war when border conflicts and security problems occupied the nation. Under conditions of relative peace, normality, and prosperity, Israelis celebrated in April the 24th anniversary of their country's founding. These conditions brought into prominence long-pent-up dissatisfactions of organized labor and a major controversy over business ethics. In a mood of self-criticism, Israelis questioned the morals, the values, and the direction of their society. These issues became linked with the approaching 1973 general election as political maneuvering got under way.

In the controversy over national policy the voices of Prime Minister Golda Meir and Defense Minister Moshe Dayan were most prominently heard. Mrs. Meir argued that Israel had never been in a better position, that the status quo was Israel's best possible strategic stance, and that there was no reason to seek changes or take initiatives that might alter the balance of forces. Under Mrs. Meir, Israel had established excellent relations with the U.S. and enjoyed considerable U.S. military and diplomatic support.

Defense Minister Dayan, while agreeing to the wisdom of Israel's strategic position, argued that this position could be maintained only by intense policy initiatives at home and abroad. In his view Israel and the Arab states might remain far apart in their terms for peace for many years, requiring Israel to make military and political plans that would be as valid in 1985 as in 1972.

Occupied Lands and Arabs in Israel

The effectiveness of Dayan's policies was demonstrated in Israeli-occupied Arab territories—the Gaza Strip and the west bank of the Jordan River. In 1972 these areas enjoyed an unprecedented economic boom, with thousands of Arabs from the west bank and Gaza traveling daily to jobs in Israel. Guerrilla activities in Israel and in the occupied regions were minimal. Over the summer some 153,000 Arabs from outside Israel visited relatives and friends in the occupied territories.

For most of 1972 relative stability prevailed in the Gaza Strip, as the Israeli military government continued to advance the economic integration of Gaza with Israel. Also under way was a program to resettle Gaza's many Palestinian refugees, most of whom lived in crowded United Nations (UN) camps, in new housing developments in Gaza and in the Sinai Peninsula. Israel disclosed plans to allow Gaza Arabs increased freedom of movement across Israeli lines. In July the mayor of the town of Gaza obtained authorization from Jordan for Gaza residents to use Jordanian passports in traveling to Arab countries where Israeli documents were not accepted.

In October, however, Gaza's atmosphere of coexistence was shattered by minor terrorist activities and by the dismissal of Gaza's mayor and town council by the Israeli authorities. The dismissal followed the town's refusal to supply a nearby refugee camp with water, electricity, and sanitation services, in defiance of an Israeli order that was

KEYSTONE
Israelis return from a search-and-destroy mission against Arab terrorists in Lebanon.

obeyed by other Arab towns. Gaza's mayor claimed that obedience to the order would impair the camp's eligibility for UN aid and accused Israel of planning to annex Gaza. Israel denied intending to annex the strip immediately, but the government often declared that it would not be returned to Egypt. The government's apparent intention of establishing Jewish settlements on former Arab lands in Gaza stirred debate in Israel.

Peaceful coexistence was also the general rule in the occupied west bank and in relations with Jordan. In response to demands by west-bank Palestinian activists for municipal elections, which had not been held since the 1967 war, Israeli authorities scheduled elections in the province of Samaria in March and in Judea in May. Although a number of independents were elected, the results generally favored neither closer cooperation with Israel nor the radical stand of the Palestinian guerrillas. (*See* Jordan.) Jordan's King Hussein I proposed a plan for the creation of a semiautonomous west-bank Palestinian state federated with the monarchy of the east bank. It met with a cool reception from Israel. The future of the west bank became an Israeli election issue.

In August Arabs and Jews in Israel protested the government's refusal to allow Christian Arabs from two villages near the Lebanese border to return to their homes. Expelled from the villages during Israel's war of independence in 1948, the Arabs had since lived elsewhere in Israel. While commending the villagers for their loyalty, the government rejected their demands on grounds of security. Late in the year Israel approved a $100-million plan to pay reparations to dispossessed Arabs.

Labor Unrest and Economic Scandal

Beginning in the spring, relations between the government and Israeli trade unions grew progressively worse. Only the imposition of legal sanctions prevented a wildcat strike of airport maintenance workers from shutting down the nation's airline system in April. By autumn, there was an epidemic of wildcat strikes by customs clerks, doctors, truck drivers, and others, which tied up major ports and affected nearly all sectors of the economy. A strike by aviation workers and communications technicians in December paralyzed Israel's international airline operations and its television, radio, and telephone systems. The unrest resulted from labor's resentment at the growing gap between rich and poor, from a breakdown of Israel's system of industry-wide contracts, and from the pressing of demands by workers who had postponed action during the years when security problems occupied the nation.

Economic scandals involving cabinet ministers and officials contributed to labor's dissatisfaction and aroused controversy over business ethics and profiteering in Israeli society. An investigation into the government's management of the Sinai oil fields uncovered a maze of irregularities and led to the resignation of the oil field's manager. Nonetheless, investigators absolved the manager of criminal wrongdoing and concluded that irregularities could be forgiven if an enterprise was successful. These conclusions left many questions unanswered and failed to satisfy the suspicions of the public.

Guerrilla Tactics and Their Impact

During the year terrorist activities of the Palestinian guerrillas became increasingly international in scope as the guerrillas' ability to strike within Israel remained frustrated. In May the underground Black September organization hijacked a Belgian airliner en route from Europe to Lydda, Israel, and held it at Lydda as ransom for the release of some 300 guerrillas in Israeli prisons; Israeli forces stormed the aircraft, freed the passengers, and killed two of four hijackers. In May three

Kozo Okamoto, the only survivor of the commandos who massacred tourists at the Lod airport, identifies his gun to police.
ROTH FROM GAMMA

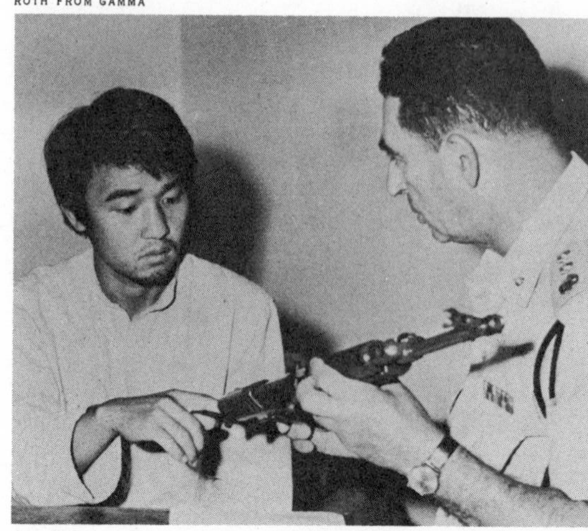

ROTH FROM GAMMA

Mourners in Tel Aviv meet the coffins of 10 of the 11 Olympic athletes and coaches who were murdered by Arab terrorists in Munich, West Germany.

Japanese terrorists, acting for the Palestinian guerrillas, opened fire with machine guns and grenades in Lod International Airport, near Tel Aviv, killing 25 persons; another died later. Two of the terrorists were killed and one was captured.

The most sensational guerrilla attack, however, was a Black September invasion of the Israeli team's quarters at the Olympic Games in Munich, West Germany, on September 5. Two Israelis were killed and nine taken hostage for the release of 200 guerrillas held by Israel. During a gun battle between German authorities and guerrillas, the hostages and five guerrillas were killed, and three guerrillas were captured. These three were freed in October when guerrillas hijacked a West German airliner and held it as ransom against the captives' release. The Munich attack was followed by the killing of an Israeli diplomat in London and the mailing of letter bombs to numerous Jews and Israeli officials in Europe and North America, also attributed to Black Septembrists.

Israel's response was to vow a widespread fight against guerrilla organizations, to call on other nations to curb Palestinian activities, and to unleash massive attacks against guerrilla bases in Lebanon and Syria. The Munich incident shattered Israel's complacent and accommodating mood, dimmed prospects for negotiations with the Arabs, and strengthened the position of Israelis who felt that guerrillas should be crushed before negotiations began. Israeli-West German relations also deteriorated, even though West Germany granted $1 million in compensation to the families of Munich victims. Israel criticized security measures at Munich and assailed the release of the captured assassins to hijackers. Three Israeli security officials, who reportedly had been responsible for making arrangements to protect Israel's Olympic team, were dismissed from their posts in October.

Further Problems at Home and Abroad

Israel's international position weakened considerably during the year. Symptomatic of worsening Israeli-African relations was the expulsion of Israeli diplomats and advisers from Uganda, which Israel attributed to Libyan influence. European nations exhibited a growing tendency not to become involved in Israel's disputes with the Arabs, and the UN General Assembly passed a resolution asking members to bar aid to Israel that might help Israel consolidate its control over occupied lands. The emigration of Soviet Jews to Israel was expected to drop because of a new decree by the Soviet Union requiring Jewish emigrants to repay the Soviet state for the cost of their higher education. This decree was relaxed later in the year. During 1972 more than 25,000 Soviet Jews emigrated to Israel.

In the fall Israel put into effect a new policy of striking at Arab guerrilla camps without warning or provocation; previously, Israeli strikes had been in reprisal for specific guerrilla attacks. Subsequently the most serious fighting between Israeli and Syrian forces since 1970 erupted along the Golan Heights, forcing Israel to seal off the area in November. A month later Israel was shocked by the arrest of four Israeli Jews on charges of spying for Syria.

The conflict between religious and secular authority in Israel was expected to be eased following the election in October of liberal rabbis to head the nation's Western and Oriental Orthodox communities. They replaced conservative incumbents whose rigid interpretations of rabbinical law, particularly on marriage and divorce, had caused political and social friction in Israel. (*See also* Egypt; International Relations; Middle East. *See in* CE: Israel.)

ITALY. Tensions between the many political parties, continuing labor unrest, and attempts by the new president to form a government all contributed to a confused political and economic situation in Italy in 1972. President Giovanni Leone, a former premier who had been elected to the presidency in December 1971, faced the unenviable task of appointing a new premier who could organize a stable coalition government. In a traditional gesture, Premier Emilio Colombo had submitted his resignation when Leone was elected. In January, however, the Republican party (which, with the Christian Democrats, Socialists, and Social Democrats, had originally formed Colombo's coalition government) announced that it would no longer support the existing coalition. Colombo was then forced to resign in earnest. Leone asked him to form a new coalition, but Colombo's inability to induce the coalition parties to agree on certain issues led him to refuse Leone's offer.

On February 5 Leone asked Giulio Andreotti, a Christian Democrat, to attempt to form a new government. Andreotti put together a Christian Democratic cabinet but was refused a vote of confidence by the Senate. Finally, on February 28, Leone dissolved parliament, announced general elections for May 7 and 8—a year ahead of schedule—and asked the Andreotti government to perform caretaker duties until the elections.

Two questions were paramount in the hotly contested campaign. One was whether a successful coalition could indeed be formed; the other was how much strength would be shown by the neo-Fascist Italian Social Movement (MSI), which had aligned itself with monarchist elements. Violence broke out before the elections, particularly between ultra-left and ultra-right factions. The results of the elections were not dramatic; the Christian Democrats suffered a slight loss, while the MSI gained a very few percentage points. On June 4 Leone asked Andreotti to try again, and on June 26 a cabinet was announced that contained Liberal,

Romans demonstrate for new housing after being evicted to make way for a subway extension.

WIDE WORLD

VITTORIANO RASTELLI FOR "THE NEW YORK TIMES"

Protective scaffolding is placed around the deteriorating Colosseum in Rome.

Christian Democratic, and Social Democratic members. It was the first time in 15 years that the Liberals had participated actively in the cabinet. The cabinet announced plans for economic stabilization, greater interest in international relations, and greater respect for law and order. The latter concern had become a major issue after a Milan police official who had been investigating political terrorism was murdered in May. Earlier in the year a millionaire leftist publisher had been killed in a mysterious explosion.

On April 1 a new regional government plan came into effect, giving wide self-government powers to 15 "ordinary" regions. Five other regions already held "special" status for ethnic, economic, or historical reasons.

The economy continued to suffer from inflation and a rash of strikes; Italy continued to have more strikes than any other European nation. An attempt by the government to control food prices resulted in a mass business shutdown by food merchants. Construction, chemical, agricultural, and civil service workers also staged walkouts. The consequent loss of production did not help the situation. Reduced domestic consumption also affected imports, but continued drain of capital abroad worsened the balance of payments, which showed a deficit after a 1971 surplus.

Internationally, Leone engaged in talks with several European leaders during the year and visited both the Vatican and the Soviet Union. World concern for the safety and preservation of Italy's many cultural landmarks was highlighted by attempts to pass "Save Venice" legislation. The program, concerned with flood control on the Venice lagoon, was being held up by clashes between conservationist and industrial interests. (*See also* Europe; Landmarks and Monuments. *See in* CE: Italy.)

AUTHENTICATED NEWS INTERNATIONAL

The Ghana–Ivory Coast Border Demarcation Commission met to iron out differences.

IVORY COAST. A broadly based diplomacy abroad and austerity at home remained salient features of the Ivory Coast's government policy in 1972. President Félix Houphouët-Boigny's spectacular reconciliation with President Léopold S. Senghor of Senegal in December 1971 was an event of major significance for French-speaking Africa in general and for the West Africa Economic Community in particular. It also led to renewed attempts at reconciliation with Guinea, and on July 24 Houphouët-Boigny met with Guinea's President Sékou Touré. The discussions broke down, however, when Touré demanded the immediate return of Guinean political exiles in the Ivory Coast.

While the sharp fall in world cocoa prices was more than sufficient to explain the austerity measures, the measures resulted in exaggerated alarm abroad when a World Bank report seemed to cast doubt upon the Ivory Coast's economic stability. Nevertheless, the Ivory Coast maintained a balanced budget and a continuing surplus in the balance of trade. (*See also* Africa. *See in* CE: Ivory Coast.)

JAMAICA. A general election in Jamaica on Feb. 29, 1972, resulted in a landslide victory for the People's National party (PNP) headed by Michael Manley, son of the party's founder. The PNP had been the opposition party throughout Jamaica's ten years of independence. Two of the major election issues were alleged widespread corruption and the denial of voting rights to people under 21. After taking office the new government attempted to act on both these issues. A commission of enquiry was set up to investigate the awarding of contracts and the expenditure on public projects since 1962. A law was passed lowering the voting age to 18 years, and administrative arrangements were made for establishing permanent facilities for the registration of voters.

Censorship of literature coming into the country was eased, confiscated passports were returned, and freedom of speech was encouraged. It was also announced that a new daily paper was to be published beginning in June 1973. (*See in* CE: Jamaica.)

JAPAN. "The Japanese side is keenly aware of Japan's responsibility for causing enormous damages in the past to the Chinese people through war and deeply reproaches itself." With these words, Japan's Prime Minister Kakuei Tanaka acknowledged the long-standing enmity between Japan and the People's Republic of China. The hostility came to an end in 1972 with the restoration of diplomatic relations between the two countries.

Tanaka had become prime minister earlier in the year and was at 54 one of the youngest men in Japanese history to be elected to the post. While Japan's unprecedented economic growth continued to make the country a major world force, some indications of growing pains appeared in 1972: a recession, frightening environmental problems, and increasing restlessness among the people over a number of issues.

Foreign Relations

The resumption of diplomatic relations with China, continuing close relations with the U.S., and the reversion of Okinawa to Japan highlighted foreign affairs in 1972. Tanaka traveled to China on September 25, following preliminary meetings

Kakuei Tanaka exults after a vote that assured him election as Japan's new prime minister.

UPI COMPIX

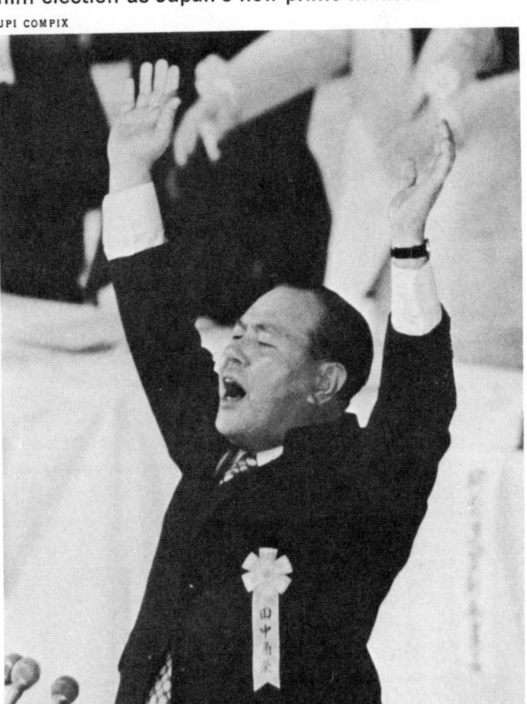

WIDE WORLD

In Japan a U.S. military truck halts as it is approached by a Buddhist priest. The priest was among 6,000 demonstrators protesting against the transportation of combat vehicles from Japan.

between Tanaka and U.S. President Richard M. Nixon and with consensus from Diet members of Tanaka's Liberal-Democratic party (LDP). Within hours of their historic meetings, Japan's prime minister and China's Premier Chou En-lai agreed in principle to establish diplomatic relations after four decades of separation. A joint communiqué was issued, after five days of meetings during which Tanaka expressed regret for past Japanese aggression in China and Chou subsequently renounced any request by China for indemnities "in the interest of the friendship between the peoples of China and Japan." Among the major points in the communiqué were Japan's recognition of the People's Republic "as the sole legal government of China," reaffirmation by China that Taiwan was "an inalienable part" of mainland Chinese territory, restoration of diplomatic relations as of September 29, and a declaration of intention to exchange ambassadors as soon as possible. Thus Tanaka was able to settle the issue he had considered the most important diplomatic question facing Japan. (*See* Tanaka.)

Relations with the U.S. continued on a friendly basis, though undertones of economic competition were present throughout the year. A proposed visit to Japan by Henry Kissinger, the president's security adviser, was canceled twice. Japanese resentment over the two cancellations lessened after Kissinger finally arrived in June with an invitation to Japan's Emperor Hirohito to visit the U.S. Hirohito was expected to make the trip in 1973. Kissinger traveled to Japan again in August and received assurances from Tanaka that the planned Japan-China talks would not affect Japan's relationship with the U.S. Finally, on August 31, Tanaka met with President Nixon in Hawaii, where both expressed hope that Tanaka's visit to China would ease tensions in Asia. On his return to Japan, Tanaka reaffirmed his country's intention to maintain its Asian security commitments.

The U.S. returned Okinawa to Japanese control on May 15, fulfilling an agreement made between then-Prime Minister Eisaku Sato and President Nixon during summit talks in California in January. A joint statement issued after the talks had confirmed U.S. intentions of removing all nuclear weapons from Okinawa. Sato felt the return of a nuclear-free Okinawa was the climax of his long career. Yet it was the reversion agreement that led to Sato's downfall. On March 27, two Socialist Diet members charged that Japan had undertaken the payment of $4 million in damages to Okinawans whose property had been damaged during the U.S. occupation. Originally the U.S. had agreed to pay the damage costs. The disclosures injured Sato's political reputation severely.

Preliminary meetings with representatives of the Soviet Union on the subject of the eventual signing of a peace treaty were held during the year. The meetings were also indicative of Japan's desire to lessen its political dependence on the U.S. A five-year trade agreement with North Korea was signed, and diplomatic relations were established with Bangladesh and the Mongolian People's Republic. The massacre of airline passengers and visitors at Lod International Airport near Tel Aviv, Israel, by young Japanese terrorists led Japan to issue an official apology and to pay compensation to victims and their families. (*See* Crime.)

Internal Affairs

Many of the new directions in Japanese foreign and domestic policy could be traced to the change in leadership of the ruling Liberal-Democrats. Prime Minister Sato was shaken by results of the midyear election and of a private poll that showed a disastrous decline in his party's popularity. Embarrassed also by the disclosures of irregularities in the reversion of Okinawa, Sato announced his resignation in June after a record seven years and eight months in office. Tanaka, minister of international trade and industry, was elected leader of the LDP (and thus prime minister) on July 5 in a runoff with Minister for Foreign Affairs Takeo Fukuda. The new prime minister formed a new cabinet and dedicated himself to improving social conditions and normalizing relations with China.

In September a new poll showed a rise in support for the LDP, with 46% of those polled approving Tanaka; but problems abounded. The expansion of the economy had slowed, causing a severe recession. Housing costs soared and 70% of Japanese workers expressed dissatisfaction with their housing in an urban survey. Aged Japanese struggled to survive on inadequate pensions, and the suicide rate among elderly Japanese women was the highest in the world. Pollution became a matter of deep concern as public health problems increased. In a landmark case decided on July 24, a district court ruled that six industrial firms were responsible for air pollution that had caused cases of serious lung disease. The court ordered the companies to pay damages to victims and their families. Three other court cases dealt with serious cases of cadmium and mercury poisoning caused by industrial pollution. Japan's strong support of environmental improvement at the United Nations Conference on the Human Environment in June was a result of dismal experience. On November 13 Tanaka dissolved the Diet and called for elections on December 10. The election results reflected discontent among voters: the LDP won a majority, but the Communist party doubled its Diet representation and drew a record 10.4% of the vote. The Socialist party also gained.

The government continued to be troubled by ultra-leftist political groups. On February 28, after a bloody 8-hour battle, police finally captured five members of the radical United Red Army, but this and other organizations still posed a threat.

Despite the prosperity indicated by the revaluation of the yen in December 1971 and a continued expansion of the economy, Japan suffered financial problems in 1972. The growth rate slowed to a real gain of only 5.7% in fiscal 1971–72 (as compared to a 9.5% gain in 1970). Inflation continued to spiral upward, causing hardships for consumers. The critical trade imbalance between the U.S. and Japan was a subject of concern for both sides, and a joint meeting of business leaders of both countries promised to "redress the current trade payments imbalance." Observers predicted another revaluation of the yen, probably in 1973, and Japan's surplus in balance of payments continued to increase despite government efforts to curb exports. On August 1, foreign-exchange reserves totaled $15.9 billion. (*See in* CE: Japan.)

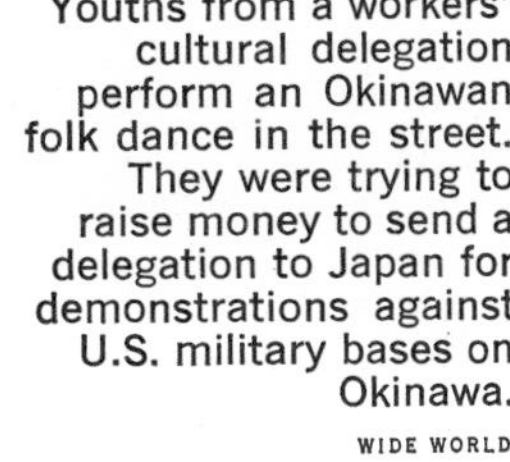

Youths from a workers' cultural delegation perform an Okinawan folk dance in the street. They were trying to raise money to send a delegation to Japan for demonstrations against U.S. military bases on Okinawa.

WIDE WORLD

KEYSTONE

There was a heavy turnout of voters when municipal elections were held in the Israeli-occupied west bank of Jordan. The voters appeared unmoved by Arab threats of retaliation.

JORDAN. Throughout 1972 the regime of Jordan's King Hussein I remained secure in spite of Jordan's extreme isolation in the Arab world, which was largely attributable to his expulsion of Palestinian guerrillas in 1970. Guerrilla leaders refused in 1972 to negotiate further with the regime, and accusations by hostile Arab nations forced the king to deny repeatedly that he was negotiating separately with Israel. Such accusations were voiced particularly after the king disclosed on March 15 his plan for federating Jordan's west-bank region (occupied by Israel) with the east bank.

Under the king's proposal, which was drawn up in consultation with leaders from the east and west banks, Jordan would become the United Arab Kingdom, joining under the authority of the crown two semiautonomous regions: the east bank and a Palestinian region on the west bank. Each region would be led by a governor-general chosen by an elected regional council and would have its own court system and cabinet. Federal power would rest with the king and a national assembly representing each region equally. There would be a single armed force under the king's command and a federal supreme court. Amman would be both the federal and the east-bank capital; Jerusalem would be the Palestinian capital. Other "liberated" Arab areas, such as Gaza, would become part of the Palestinian region if they desired.

Hussein's plan was the first peace proposal by an Arab leader in more than a year. The plan was unanimously approved by both houses of the Jordanian parliament on March 25. On March 29 Hussein made a second proposal, calling for joint Jordanian-Israeli administration of Jerusalem as part of a Middle East peace settlement. While this proposal retained the principle of Arab sovereignty over east Jerusalem, it went far beyond previous Arab stands, which demanded total Israeli withdrawal to the 1967 frontiers.

Although the king emphasized that his federation plan was contingent on a complete Arab-Israeli settlement, the reaction of other Arab nations was almost completely hostile. Egypt broke diplomatic relations with Jordan over the issue, and the Palestinian guerrillas condemned the plan for betraying guerrilla objectives and called for the overthrow of the monarchy. Israel rejected the proposals on Jerusalem but left the door open for negotiations. An Arab delegation from Gaza held talks on the plan with Jordanian officials in August.

In March and in May municipal elections were held in the Israeli-occupied west bank for the first time since 1963. King Hussein abandoned his objections to the Israeli-ordered elections, fearing that antiroyalist candidates would take over the region if unopposed. There was a heavy turnout of Arab voters in spite of terrorist threats, which observers viewed as evidence that Palestinian guerrillas had failed to prevent some peaceful coexistence between Arabs and Israelis. The defeat of many Arab incumbents and the election of young independents was seen as an upset against King Hussein and a rejection of his federation plan.

Elections to the Jordanian National Union (JNU) were held in the fall. The east- and west-bank regions each elected 120 members, and 120 more were appointed by the king.

Although the Jordanian cabinet was reorganized in February and in August, the political character of the administration remained unchanged. The precarious Jordanian economy continued to be heavily dependent on U.S. aid, and the Jordanian dinar was devalued by 8.5% in May following the U.S. devaluation of the dollar. During a visit to Washington, D.C., in the spring, King Hussein obtained U.S. agreement to sell Jordan between 12 and 24 F-5 fighter jets.

Early in 1972 Jordan and Israel agreed to establish radio communications between the Israeli airfield at Elath and a new Jordanian airfield at Aqaba; the aim was to prevent air collisions. King Hussein opened the Aqaba airport in May. Improving Jordanian relations with the Persian Gulf Arab sheikhdoms was indicated by an agreement to establish air service between Jordan and Qatar and by a visit to Jordan by the sultan of Oman during which Jordan offered him aid in his war with left-wing Dhofari rebels. Kuwait undertook diplomatic efforts to restore relations between Jordan and Egypt. Although Iraq resumed trade relations with Jordan, and Syria relaxed border restrictions against some Jordanian exports, Jordan closed down its section of the main road between Syria and Saudi Arabia. In November King Hussein revealed that a plot to assassinate him, allegedly masterminded by Palestinian guerrillas and the Libyan government, had failed. (*See also* Egypt; Israel; Middle East. *See in* CE: Jordan.)

KENYA. In January 1972 a total ban on some imports and further restrictions upon others were put into effect by the government of Kenya. This was accompanied by a plea to local manufacturers to produce more goods, in order to help the country's finances and to provide greater employment opportunities. These developments followed the imposing of credit restrictions toward the end of the preceding year. Also, on Dec. 1, 1971, the minister of finance and economic planning, Mwai Kibaki, announced that foreign exchange would not be made available for the purchase of commodities that could be produced in Kenya. Industrialists were also urged to seek new markets in Ethiopia, Zambia, and Somalia. By the middle of the year concern was developing at the prospect of a serious decline in exports to Uganda and Tanzania because of the exchange controls that had been introduced between the three countries and the consequent reduction in the purchase of Kenya's manufactured goods by its neighbors. Up to this time, sales to neighboring territories had largely offset Kenya's overseas trade deficit.

Early in the year assistance came in the form of a grant of approximately $1,375,000, spread over five years, from the Swedish government and the Swedish International Development Authority to support the special rural development program in southern Nyanza. A United Nations Development Programme mission also visited Kenya to investigate causes of unemployment and to suggest methods of overcoming it. To support rural development, the government was already spending about $50 million on roads each year.

In August, at the Egerton College, 100 miles north of Nairobi, the capital, the brother of a man mistakenly taken for an assassin was beaten to death by a crowd that had come to hear President Jomo Kenyatta speak. Following expulsion of the Asian community from his country by Uganda's President Idi Amin, Kenya increased its border patrols to stop infiltration by Asian refugees. The Kenyan government announced in November that many noncitizens (mostly Asians) would be ordered to sell their businesses to Kenyans. The order was seen as the beginning of a more stringent anti-Asian policy. (*See* Uganda. *See in* CE: Kenya.)

Asians wait in a Kenyan airport on their way to Great Britain. They rushed to get there before new immigration quotas were enforced.

MARION KAPLAN FROM RAPHO GUILLUMETTE

President Park Chung Hee has been taking more and more power into his own hands. His critics accuse him of becoming a life-long dictator and of stifling Korean development. His admirers claim that strong leadership is what South Korea needs at this time in its history.

UPI COMPIX

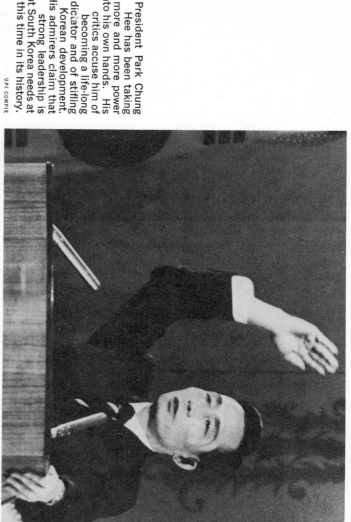

KOREA. It seemed that the impossible was becoming possible in Korea in 1972. On July 4, after more than 20 years of hostile confrontations across the 38th parallel, the North and South Korean governments issued a joint statement revealing that secret talks between them had been going on for several months and that agreement had been reached to begin negotiations for unification. The statement stipulated that unification would come about through peaceful means. It also provided for a North-South coordinating committee to handle the negotiations. The two sides agreed to refrain from armed provocation and to take positive measures to prevent inadvertent military incidents. Both countries also agreed to cooperate positively for the early success of the Red Cross talks aimed at reuniting families separated by the Korean War. A direct telephone line between Seoul and Pyongyang (capitals of the South and the North, respectively) was installed just after the announcement.

The euphoria over the prospect of peace seemed to die down immediately after the dramatic joint declaration. South Korean leaders asked their people to remain vigilant against Communist machinations. They expressed the view that the North was still to be considered a military and political threat. Nevertheless, the historic meetings of the North-South coordinating committee finally began in October at Panmunjom.

The Red Cross talks did take place later in the year but made very limited progress. After initial disagreements about procedural matters, the opening session of the conference began in Pyongyang on August 30. Further talks were held in the following months.

In the South, the state of emergency declared by President Park Chung Hee in December 1971 continued into 1972 despite wide public criticism. The Park government defended its actions, invoking the threat of invasion from the North. Following the July agreement, the opposition New Democratic party asked President Park to "give up the dictatorial system" and show the people that the accord with the North was not intended to prolong his rule.

But, in fact, Park went in the opposite direction. On October 17 he suddenly declared martial law, suspended parts of the constitution, banned all political activity, and dissolved the National Assembly. A short time later, in a national referendum, South Korean voters approved a revised constitution that extended the president's power, placing no limit on the number of terms he could serve. Under its provisions, Park could remain in office indefinitely. On December 27 Park was elected to a six-year term under the new constitution.

North Korea moved actively to build up international support for its policies, especially on the issues of Korean unification and the role of the United Nations (UN) in Korea. A more relaxed, flexible position toward Japan and the U.S. was evident in 1972. Premier Kim Il Sung was elected president in December under a new constitution that reflected the North's softer position on the unity issue. Kim retained the title of premier.

In September the UN was asked to support the goal of Korean unity, and it was requested that the General Assembly hold a debate on the issue. The UN, however, voted to postpone the Korean question until the 1973 assembly session. (*See in* CE: Korea.)

KUWAIT. Oil revenues in Kuwait were expected to rise in fiscal 1973 above the 1972 total of $1.395 billion. However, a U.S. firm of consultants reportedly estimated that oil reserves were much less than had been forecast and that reserves would be exhausted in 12–15 years at the current rate of increase in production. Although a later government report was more optimistic, a decision was made to keep production below 3 million barrels a day.

In 1972 the Kuwait Fund for Arab Economic Development provided loans for Jordan and Sudan. In disapproval of Jordan's treatment of the Palestinian guerrillas, however, the Kuwait government, with support from the national assembly, continued to withhold the aid to Jordan agreed upon after the 1967 Arab-Israeli war. In contrast, Kuwait gave Syria some $30 million following a visit to Kuwait by Syria's president.

In July U.S. Secretary of State William P. Rogers visited Kuwait and spoke warmly of U.S.-Kuwait relations, but the official Kuwaiti reaction was cool. Kuwait rejected a U.S. offer to supply arms and blamed the U.S. for its support of Israel. (*See in* CE: Kuwait.)

LABOR UNIONS. Confrontations with the federal government over pay controls, divisions within individual unions, and several major strikes made 1972 a year of uncertainty and frustration for labor unions. George Meany, the 78-year-old president of the American Federation of Labor–Congress of Industrial Organizations (AFL-CIO), was involved in battles with both the government and some sections of his AFL-CIO constituency. Overall, higher unemployment and pinched finances caused problems for many unions during the year.

Politics and Labor

George Meany remained firmly in control of the AFL-CIO despite open challenges to his leadership from a substantial number of unions. Five union leaders, including Meany, who were labor members of the tripartite Pay Board of U.S. President Richard M. Nixon's economic control system, found themselves under increasingly heavy criticism from union members who considered the wage and price controls unfair. Rising prices and corporate profits, high unemployment, and restriction of pay raises all became major issues of contention. The five labor representatives on the Pay Board found themselves consistently outvoted by the business and public members. The situation became tense when the board majority ordered a cutback in aerospace workers' first-year wage increases; the final break came when the board ordered a similar cutback in a new longshoremen's settlement. All the labor members except International Brotherhood of Teamsters (IBT) President Frank E. Fitzsimmons quit the board, firing angry accusations at the Nixon Administration. Their protest resignations came in March; subsequently the Pay Board served as a seven-member panel.

Meany also came under fire from many labor unions when he succeeded in persuading the AFL-CIO Executive Council to withhold endorsement of any of the U.S. presidential candidates. Many unions, angry at the Nixon Administration's labor policies, bolted Meany's authority and supported Senator George S. McGovern (D, S.D.). In the most serious incident, the Colorado AFL-CIO chapter endorsed McGovern despite Meany's directive. Meany attempted to suspend the Colorado leadership but was prevented from doing so by a federal court injunction.

Labor won at least one victory in its running battle with the Nixon Administration when support for the proposed Transportation Strike Emergency Act—designed to prevent railroad, trucking, airline, and maritime strikes—was withdrawn by the president. All labor groups had voiced strong opposition to the bill.

Dissidents and Boycotts

Several unions made headlines during the year for activities other than strikes. Undoubtedly the

AFL-CIO President George Meany is prepared for a TV interview on Face the Nation; he refused to endorse any of the presidential candidates.

UPI COMPIX

most publicized labor group was the United Mine Workers (UMW), which was racked by scandals and dissidence throughout the year. In March UMW President W. A. (Tony) Boyle was convicted on 13 counts of conspiracy and illegal use of union funds for political contributions. He was sentenced to five years in prison and fined $130,000. Earlier in the year a federal judge had ordered the troubled union leadership to repay $11.5 million to the UMW as a settlement of a case involving misuse of miners' pension funds. In May another federal court voided the 1969 UMW election in which Boyle defeated dissident Joseph A. (Jock) Yablonski, who was subsequently found murdered. A new election was ordered for December 1972. Boyle, free while awaiting the results of an appeal, ran for reelection against Arnold R. Miller, a disabled mine electrician and chairman of the West Virginia Black Lung Association. Miller was supported by Miners for Democracy, the dissident caucus within the UMW that had been formed after Yablonski's murder. After a bitterly contested campaign, the election was held December 1–8 under close federal supervision to prevent any irregularities such as had occurred in the 1969 election. Miller and the dissident slate won, and Boyle promptly resigned. Boyle was voted a $50,000-a-year pension that Miller promised to revoke. Boyle's loss marked the first time that the incumbent president of a major AFL-CIO union had been voted out of office.

Convictions and arrests continued in the Yablonski murder case. The involvement of UMW officials in the case was indicated by the arrest of Albert E. Pass, a member of the union's executive board, in connection with the murder. A number of other UMW officials had already been questioned, indicted, or convicted. (*See* Crime.)

Despite the chaotic state of their union, miners won two victories in 1972. A bill providing cash benefits for victims of black-lung disease was signed by President Nixon after West Virginia miners staged a walkout in protest of a threatened veto. Miners also won the right to strike against unsafe working conditions, which they claimed were prevalent in most of the nation's mines. (*See* Mines and Mining.)

The United Farm Workers (UFW) drew national attention when an intensive lobbying effort at the Democratic National Convention produced widespread—and televised—support for the union's boycott of lettuce harvested by nonunion workers in California. The UFW was gaining public support for its boycott, which was called by UFW leader Cesar Chavez, when California lettuce growers refused to negotiate with the union. UFW efforts were hampered in a number of states by legislation passed or pending that declared secondary boycotts or harvesttime strikes illegal. The UFW did win a victory in Florida when it signed a contract with the Coca-Cola Co. that provided sizable pay increases for farm workers.

A number of unions showed interest in mergers in 1972. The Communications Workers of America made progress toward a merger with postal unions that could produce the AFL-CIO's second largest affiliated union. The American Federation of Teachers held low-level talks with the National Education Association (NEA), a nonunion professional organization, but the NEA's na-

During the West coast dock strike, union presidents Harry Bridges (right) and Edward Flynn (left) appeared under subpoena before a House subcommittee on labor.

UPI COMPIX

tional convention in 1972 refused to consider mergers with any AFL-CIO affiliates.

James R. Hoffa, controversial former IBT president, was freed from prison in 1972 and was said to be interested in rejoining the union as president. IBT President Fitzsimmons was in a strong position, however, and Hoffa's prospects were rated dim.

Strikes and Settlements

The United Auto Workers (UAW) engaged in several strikes in 1972, some of them with a new tactic: the hit-and-run strike, which lasted only a few days. UAW walkouts at two General Motors Corp. (GM) plants in Ohio made the biggest news. Workers struck at GM's plant in Lordstown, Ohio, in March for 22 days. The year's longest auto strike, at the GM plant in Norwood, Ohio, lasted 174 days. Both disputes concerned speedups that demanded greater productivity from fewer personnel.

The Ohio strikes were followed by hit-and-run stoppages at a number of other GM factories, with no walkout lasting more than a week. The tactic was designed to settle disputes over production standards without reducing the union's multimillion-dollar strike reserves, which were possibly going to be needed in 1973. Young workers in particular supported the strikes; they were bored and felt dehumanized by assembly-line repetitiveness. The UAW announced that humanization of assembly-line work would be a major objective in the contract negotiations of 1973.

Major dock strikes by longshoremen hit both the East and West coasts of the U.S., as well as Hawaii, in 1972. The International Longshoremen's & Warehousemen's Union (ILWU) on the West coast resumed a strike on January 17 that had been halted in 1971 by an antistrike court injunction. The dispute was settled a month later with agreement on a 21% first-year pay raise. The Pay Board later cut back the size of the raise; the ILWU threatened to go out again but instead accepted the reduction, calling it "a tragedy for collective bargaining." It was this settlement that led the Pay Board's labor members to resign. East coast longshoremen also saw their settlements reduced by the board.

Strikes also hit communications, airlines, and construction industries during the year. Negotiated settlements were reached in shipping, mining, and lumber, as well as in many other industries. A settlement of the 35-year-old dispute between the United Transportation Union and the railroad industry put an end to new hiring of railroad firemen but guaranteed the jobs of firemen who remained.

Overall, there were fewer strikes in 1972 than in the previous year: 3,745 walkouts had occurred through September 1972, as opposed to 4,900 in all of 1971. There was a possibility that the total number of worker days lost in 1972 would be the lowest since 1965. The wage and price controls were cited as one reason for the lack of strikes. Wage increases in 1972 averaged 6.6% in major collective-bargaining agreements, down from 8.1% in 1971.

Labor statistics released in 1972 reported 19.4 million union members in the U.S. in 1970; the addition of international members pushed the total to nearly 21 million, a new peak. This total, however, reflected a smaller percentage of the work force: 27.4% in 1970, as opposed to a high of 34.7% in 1954. The AFL-CIO reported a membership of 15.9 million in 116 unions, its largest single member being the United Steelworkers with about 1.2 million members. The two largest U.S. unions were the IBT with 1.8 million members and the UAW with 1.5 million members. Most union growth in 1972 was in public employment and in service professions. (*See also* Business and Industry; Economy; Employment. *See in* CE: Labor.)

In 1972 Penn Central railroad announced that it was taking the initiative and reducing the traditional four-man crew to two or three men, for economic reasons.

JOHN MAY FROM "THE NEW YORK TIMES"

NATIONAL PARK SERVICE

The Longfellow National Historic Site in Cambridge, Mass., was the home of poet Henry Wadsworth Longfellow until his death in 1882. George Washington used the house as military quarters.

LANDMARKS AND MONUMENTS. Urban construction and highway development were among the many environmental factors that threatened historic buildings and landmarks in the U.S. in 1972. In Boston, Mass., high-rise construction around Scollay Square and Haymarket Square left buildings from the 17th and 18th centuries surviving as anachronisms. Federal plans for a highway extending into and under the grounds of the Lincoln Memorial and the Washington Monument in the District of Columbia aroused concern.

A number of sites were officially added to the nation's roster of historic sites during the year. The home of poet Edna St. Vincent Millay, near Austerlitz, N.Y.; the Litchfield, Conn., home of Oliver Wolcott; and the 136-year-old Treasury Department building in Washington, D.C., became national historic landmarks. Cliveden, once the home of Chief Justice Benjamin Chew of colonial Pennsylvania and an important strategic site in the battle of Germantown during the American Revolution, was donated to the National Trust for Historic Preservation in the U.S. Federal Hall National Memorial in New York City, on the site where George Washington took his first oath of office, was dedicated on October 20.

As in the U.S., urban construction and highway projects roused concern in Great Britain. Plans to reconstruct London's Piccadilly Circus drew heavy criticism, and the city of Bath's Preservation Trust resolved to fight all developments until plans respecting the city's unique Georgian heritage were submitted. In Kirkwall in the Orkney Islands Britain's most important Viking monument, the 12th-century St. Magnus Cathedral, was saved by repairs funded by an international campaign.

Industrial pollution, automobile traffic and fumes, and rainy weather seriously threatened a number of Italy's most important historic and artistic treasures with decay. In Rome the Colosseum, the Forum, buildings on the Palatine Hill, and the Arch of Titus were closed to visitors when masonry began to crumble. Traffic was banned from the square surrounding the Milan cathedral. Also endangered were the Baths of Caracalla and the Claudian Aqueducts in Rome, Ghiberti's Baptistery doors in Florence, and the bronze horses atop St. Mark's Cathedral in Venice. Although an international "Save Venice" campaign provided funds for flood control to prevent further sinking of the city, the project was stalled by Italian parliamentary disputes over continued industrialization of the region. In the fall protective scaffolding was erected around the Colosseum in Rome, and Pisa's famed Leaning Tower had to be trussed with steel cables to prevent it from falling to the ground. An international competition was started to find a way to save the tower.

As high-rises continued to be built along the Seine and elsewhere in Paris, a Committee to Save Paris was established. France's oldest iron bridge, the Pont des Arts in Paris, was threatened with demolition to make way for an expressway.

Steps were taken in Japan to create protective zones around major temples and the Imperial Palace in Kyoto. Restoration of Angkor Wat in Cambodia was halted by the Indochina war. Studies were carried out on the preservation of the Bronze Age site of Mohenjo Daro in Pakistan and the monument of Borobudur in Indonesia. (*See also* Archaeology; Architecture; Environment; National Park Service.)

Once a Central Intelligence Agency stronghold, Skyline Ridge near Long Tieng, Laos, was under constant mortar attacks in early 1972 as Laotian troops dug in amidst the rubble. The fires in the background were started by Communist shelling.
WIDE WORLD

LAOS. The royalist government in Laos in 1972 came closer than ever to a military defeat, in the context of the U.S. rapprochement with the People's Republic of China and the prospect of an end to the Vietnam war. In July the government began discussions with the Neo Lao Hak Sat (Laotian Patriotic Front, or LPF), the political wing of the pro-Communist Pathet Lao forces. The annual winter offensive of the North Vietnamese and Pathet Lao, which had begun unusually early in December 1971, gave them control by mid-January of both the Plain of Jars in the north and the southern Bolovens Plateau. In similar occupations during 1970 and 1971, the Communists had withdrawn in the summer months, but in 1972 the already decimated government forces failed to launch a successful offensive in either sector. By August it was estimated that only one third of the country remained under government control.

Maj. Gen. Vang Pao's Meo tribesmen—who formed a major part of the U.S. Central Intelligence Agency's operations in Laos—had been reduced from about 38,000 in 1968 to fewer than 3,000 by March 1972, and they were being replaced by a force of Thai "volunteers." The increasingly precarious situation of the Laotian government was referred to in a February report of the U.S. Senate Foreign Relations Committee which stated that Laos was "closer to falling now than at any time in the past nine years." In May it was revealed that the U.S. had undertaken to organize and finance a 25-battalion Thai expeditionary force for Laos at an estimated annual cost of $100 million.

The North Vietnamese, Pathet Lao, and left-wing-neutralist offensive in the northern provinces began on Dec. 18, 1971, and was the biggest and best-equipped offensive to date. It overran the Plain of Jars within four days and caused several Thai battalions to flee back to Thailand. On January 11–13, Communist troops gained control of a range of hills overlooking Long Tieng, which was Gen. Vang Pao's main headquarters and a major base for U.S. military and intelligence operations. The Communists then managed to cut Highway 13, the only road linking Vientiane, the administrative capital, with the royal capital of Luang Prabang. The siege against Long Tieng lasted for nearly three months, but despite heavy damage to the base, Vang Pao's forces remained in control. Government troops failed to regain command of the plain from the Communists.

A simultaneous Pathet Lao offensive in the southern provinces had begun in December 1971 on the Bolovens Plateau. On December 12 the strategic town of Ban Tha Teng fell, followed by Pak Song on January 3. Ban Nhik, the last government outpost on the plateau, was abandoned on January 10; ten days later Communist forces had advanced to within 14 miles of Pakse, the second largest town in Laos. Its surrounding villages had been captured, so the town received supplies only via Highway 10, running west to Thailand.

Prince Souphanouvong, half brother of Premier Souvanna Phouma and leader of the Pathet Lao, requested in July that the two sides resume talks toward achieving a cease-fire. Weekly negotiating sessions began in October, and a five-point peace plan proposed earlier by the Pathet Lao was accepted as a basis for discussion. Progress in the talks was slowed by disputes over minor procedural matters.

Within the government itself Premier Souvanna Phouma had some difficulty retaining control. His authority was challenged by the newly formed right-wing Group for the Protection of the Constitution. The premier's position was strengthened, however, by support from the U.S., the army, and the Union of Laotian Parliamentarians for Peace. (*See also* Vietnam. *See in* CE: Laos.)

LATIN AMERICA. In 1972 it was increasingly felt by many observers that the Administration of U.S. President Richard M. Nixon viewed Latin America as being not very important to the U.S. Indeed, no new initiative was undertaken during the year. Yet President Nixon was unwilling to relinquish the U.S. role as "Colossus of the North," and any threat to this position continued to be dealt with by traditional means.

U.S. relations with Paraguay were impaired when the latter refused to extradite a Frenchman, Auguste Joseph Ricord, whom the U.S. authorities suspected of running a drug smuggling circuit. In response, the U.S. Senate threatened to cut off aid to Paraguay, and a Senate committee revised an earlier recommendation of a House of Representatives committee to give Paraguay a sugar quota. Ricord was finally extradited.

U.S. relations with Chile and Peru did not improve, and no aid was forthcoming to those countries. President Nixon and his former secretary of the treasury, John B. Connally, Jr., visited several Latin American countries in June. Both hinted that any countries that did not pay prompt, adequate, and effective compensation for the nationalization of U.S. property would not receive further aid. John M. Hennessy, the assistant secretary for international affairs at the U.S. Treasury, also emphasized that Latin American countries could not expect Congress to vote for further massive capital injections for the Inter-American Development Bank unless prompt compensation for nationalization of U.S. companies was paid.

In the case of Chile, the nationalized concerns took their own action. In October Kennecott Copper Corp., a U.S. firm, requested a French court to impound a 1,250-ton shipment of copper from Chile, which Kennecott claimed as part compensation for its nationalization in 1971. The copper was to have been sold in France, and the court was deciding on the legality of Kennecott's request for payment to be diverted to the corporation.

Juan D. Perón (arms raised), former president of Argentina, got a big welcome when he returned there after 17 years in exile. His return was certain to affect the scheduled 1973 elections.

ROBERTO BUNGE FROM BLACK STAR

Chile was also in conflict with one of its neighbors, Argentina. In August a group of guerrillas escaped from prison in Argentina, hijacked an airplane, and then flew to Chile, where they asked for political asylum. Initially, Chile's President Salvador Allende Gossens handed the guerrillas over to the courts to decide whether Argentina's demand for extradition should be granted. However, it was later discovered that a group of prisoners in Argentina had been shot after trying to escape. President Allende decided to allow the guerrillas to stay and then gave them safe passage to Cuba—much to the chagrin of the Argentinian government.

With President Nixon's increasing preoccupation with Vietnam, the Middle East, and relations with the Soviet Union and the People's Republic of China, many Latin Americans began to argue if the U.S. could make new approaches to its fellow protagonists in the cold war, why should Latin Americans not do the same with Cuba? Peru established diplomatic relations with Cuba in July. Earlier, in May, Peru had submitted a proposal to the Organization of American States (OAS) to permit individual nations to resume bilateral relations with Cuba at whatever level seemed appropriate. This move was defeated 13–7, with 3 abstentions. The votes in favor of the proposal were cast by Peru, Chile, Mexico, Panama, Ecuador, Jamaica, and Trinidad and Tobago; the abstainers were Argentina, Barbados, and Venezuela. Although few expected Peru to obtain the required two-thirds majority, the margin of the actual majority was a surprise. There was little evidence that Cuba wanted to rejoin the OAS; on July 11 it was admitted into full membership in the socialist countries' Council for Mutual Economic Assistance. This had the effect of spreading the responsibility for aid to Cuba among council members in addition to the Soviet Union. (*See* Cuba Special Report.)

Inter-American Organizations

The most newsworthy of the inter-American organizations in 1972 was the Inter-American Development Bank, which held its 13th annual meeting in Quito, Ecuador, during May. First of all, it was agreed at this meeting that terms for the granting of soft loans from the Fund for Special Operations would be eased, the length of term for each loan would be relaxed, the rate of interest would be 2%, and the period of grace would be extended to between seven and ten years. Second, greater emphasis was to be placed on granting loans involving two or more Latin American countries to spur economic integration. Third, the wealthier countries of Latin America were to take up future bond issues of the bank; Mexico agreed to buy $25 million worth of new bonds.

After heated debate over the admission of Canada and further extensions of membership in the bank, Canada was finally admitted as the 24th member. The Latin American countries insisted on retaining at least 55% of the bank's voting shares.

WIDE WORLD

Managua, capital of Nicaragua, was shattered by earthquakes in December. At least 10,000 people apparently died in the tragedy.

Canada's $300-million entrance contribution entitled it to 6% of the shares; thus the only alternative, which was finally agreed on, was to reduce the U.S. holding from 42% to 36%. The U.S., however, stated that it would not allow its share to be reduced below 35%, the minimum for retaining veto rights.

Regional and Subregional Integration

The nations of Latin America showed little inclination to act in concert in their own organizations. The Special Latin American Coordinating Committee (CECLA) failed to agree on a joint position for the "Group of 77" meeting in Lima, Peru, on whether developing nations should take joint action outside the International Monetary Fund to solve international monetary problems.

There were no signs that the members of the Central American Common Market (CACM)—El Salvador, Honduras, Nicaragua, Guatemala, and Costa Rica—were any nearer reaching agreement on the continuation and future progress of the market, although at the beginning of the year there had seemed to be grounds for cautious optimism. In November 1971 the five ministers of economy of the CACM member countries had met at San José, Costa Rica, and agreed on the immediate initiation of bilateral negotiations between Honduras, Nicaragua, Guatemala, and Costa Rica. (*See also* articles on individual countries. *See in* CE: Articles on individual countries; Latin America.)

PAUL SEQUEIRA

Edward V. Hanrahan, state's attorney of Cook County, Ill., was acquitted of conspiracy charges in connection with the 1969 police slayings of two Black Panther party members. However, he was not reelected in November.

LAW. The "Conspiracy Eight" case returned to national legal prominence in 1972. Eight men, including Yippies Jerry Rubin and Abbie Hoffman, antiwar activist David T. Dellinger, and Black Panther party leader Bobby G. Seale, had been tried in 1969–70 on charges of crossing state lines with the intent to incite riot at the 1968 Democratic National Convention in Chicago. The trial had been marked by constant disruptions and erratic behavior on the part of everyone involved. Seale's case had been separated from the others and all charges against him were ultimately dropped. Of the remaining seven, five were convicted on the riot charges, and all seven—as well as their lawyers—received stiff sentences for contempt of court from U.S. District Court Judge Julius J. Hoffman.

On May 11, 1972, the contempt sentences were overturned by the U.S. court of appeals because of irregular procedures used by Hoffman. On November 21, the U.S. court of appeals voided the riot convictions on the basis of judicial error. In an unprecedented action, the court severely criticized Hoffman for his "antagonistic" behavior during the trial. A new trial on the contempt charges was planned for January 1973.

A mistrial was declared in December in the case of Daniel Ellsberg and Anthony J. Russo, Jr., accused of releasing classified Pentagon papers to the public. After a jury had been impaneled, a complex question concerning wiretapping held up the trial for four months. When it reconvened, Judge William M. Byrne, Jr., dismissed the jury because the long delay had allowed them time to become prejudiced about the case. A new trial was to be held in 1973.

A trial of seven antiwar activists accused of plotting to kidnap Henry A. Kissinger, security adviser to U.S. President Richard M. Nixon, was also declared a mistrial in 1972. The defendants, including the Rev. Philip F. Berrigan and Sister Elizabeth McAlister, both Catholic peace activists, were freed on the conspiracy charges after the jury reported itself deadlocked on April 5. Father Berrigan and Sister McAlister were convicted, however, on several counts of smuggling letters into and out of the prison where Berrigan was serving time for destroying draft records.

Six members of the Vietnam Veterans Against the War (VVAW) were indicted in July on charges of conspiring to launch an armed attack on the Republican National Convention in Miami Beach, Fla., in August. Four VVAW members, including one of the defendants, were jailed for refusing to answer federal grand jury questions on the case. Another VVAW member and a supporter were indicted on the convention charges in October.

On July 31, a U.S. district court voided the 33-year-old Hatch Act, which forbade political activity by government employees. The court found the statute unconstitutionally vague. (*See also* Crime; Families; Newspapers; Prisons; Race Relations; Supreme Court of the U.S.)

WIDE WORLD

The Rev. Philip Berrigan was paroled Dec. 20, 1972. He had served more than four years on a conviction of damaging draft board records.

Law

Special Report: CHILDREN'S RIGHTS

by Lisa Aversa Richette

Only in recent years has the justice system modified its traditional view of children as a special class of citizens with few, if any, constitutional rights. In this stance, U.S. democratic processes have not differed radically from some notions held by ancient and medieval societies, which regarded children as chattels. Until the passage of the juvenile court acts at the beginning of the 20th century, children accused of crimes were subjected to the same procedures and penalties as adults. The paradox of dual treatment—as pawns to be moved at will by the state on the one hand, and as adults with full responsibility for antisocial behavior that threatens the state on the other hand—still persists. There is today a widespread movement for change in the system.

Historical Background

The doctrine used by courts to justify state intervention in the lives of children is summed up in the Latin phrase *parens patriae*, a term that the Illinois Supreme Court used in 1882 upon removal of a child from home to an institution. *Parens patriae*, meaning that the state is the ultimate parent and, hence, can deal with the child at will, "proved to be a great help," as the U.S. Supreme Court stated in 1967, "to those who sought to rationalize the exclusion of juveniles from the constitutional scheme, but its meaning is murky and its historical credentials are of dubious relevance."

During the 18th and 19th centuries, homeless, poor, disturbed, neglected, and orphaned children were committed to workhouses and asylums, where they mingled with other community outcasts. The basic system of herding children into dehumanizing institutions persisted into the latter half of the 20th century. Early in 1972 Massachusetts took the heroic step of abolishing all correctional institutions for children and providing instead group homes and therapeutic communities.

The establishment in 1899 in Cook County, Ill., of the juvenile court system and its rapid spread to many other states in the next decade were heralded as a new era for the child; actually, the juvenile court movement congealed *parens patriae* into a monolithic dogma. In 1905 the Pennsylvania Supreme Court summarized the prevailing attitude in a legal challenge to the juvenile court system: the juvenile court law is not for punishment, but "for the salvation of children. . . ."

The total lack of constitutional procedures coupled with scandalous conditions in children's institutions finally compelled the U.S. Supreme Court to pry open the closed doors of juvenile courts in the historic Gault decision of 1967. This guaranteed juveniles accused of delinquent behavior the right to a day in court with notice of the charges, the right to counsel, the right to confront and cross-examine their accusers, and the right to remain silent. The court's majority opinion in the 8–1 ruling appeared to set aside *parens patriae* as the cornerstone doctrine by stating unequivocally that "the 14th Amendment and the Bill of Rights are not for adults alone."

Legal cases that have surfaced in various courts indicate the low levels of juvenile justice that prevail in many areas and the reluctance of communities, social agencies, and law enforcers to confront what really happens to children caught in administrative, bureaucratic, and legalistic machinery. Many places have no formal system for providing counsel to children, a class that is almost totally indigent.

The Supreme Court has not elaborated on the legal rights of children, except for granting them the 1st Amendment freedom of speech rights in schools as long as the health, safety, and welfare of other pupils are not in jeopardy (1969), and except for establishing the principle that the test of reasonable doubt used in adult courts must be met before a delinquency adjudication. In a 1971 ruling that jury trials for juveniles are not part of their rights to due process, the court expressed faith in the underlying *parens patriae* concepts of the juvenile court.

New Directions

The narrow Gault ruling left unchanged the dreary area of neglected, dependent, and abused children. Because the juvenile court can here cling to the label of a civil proceeding in which its role of child savior seems less vulnerable to attack than in a delinquency case, it probably will continue to dispose of these children in secret and informal proceedings. In a situation of possible need or neglect, the court would likely sanction the policy of imposing purported help against the will of children and parents who are without lawyers or knowledge of court procedures. Thus, emotionally ill and retarded children without family means of securing therapy would continue to be warehoused in facilities that range from mediocre to deplorable. Television viewers were shocked in 1972 by the documentary on Willowbrook, a facility maintained for

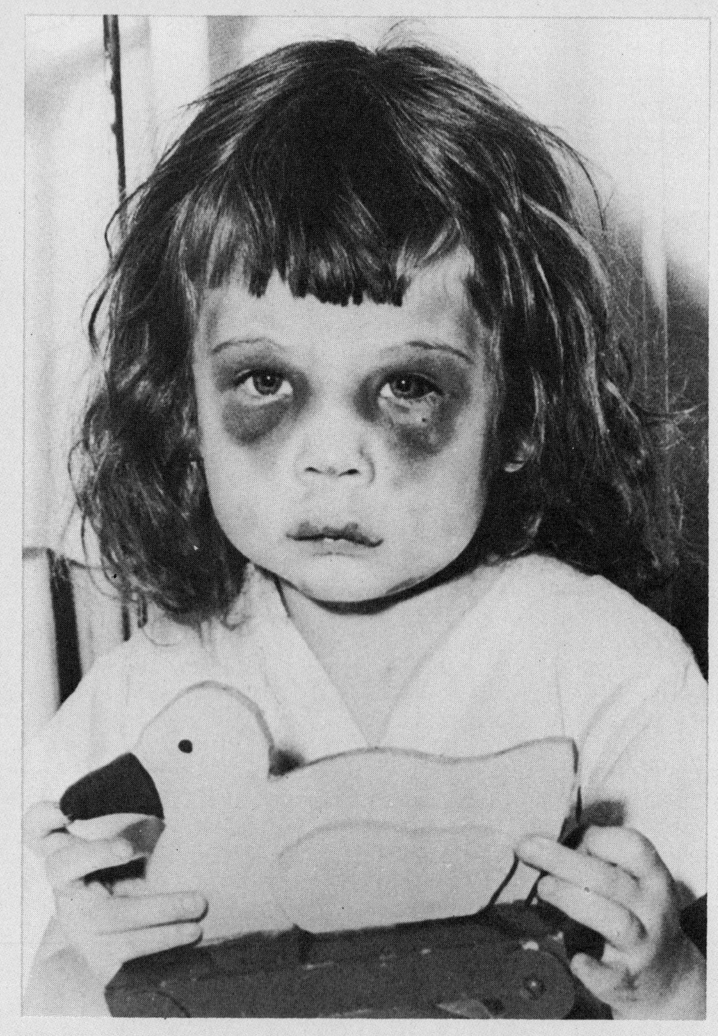

A three-year-old child bears head injuries apparently from a beating in her home. A neighbor heard the child screaming and called police. As public attention is focused on such cases of child abuse, thought is being given to the legal rights of children.

UPI COMPIX

the mentally retarded by the state of New York. Naked and desperate children were penned into filthy premises as a result of judicial indifference and community neglect.

The rights of children involved in private custody disputes between parents are also undefined. In a recent decision, the Court of Appeals for the Third Circuit refused to order a state court to permit a lawyer chosen by three teen-age children to appear on their behalf.

Arrests without warrants remain widespread, and interrogation of children without the counsel of parents or lawyers forms the basis of so-called confessions and statements. Whether or not a child can voluntarily and intelligently waive the right to remain silent or to have counsel present is a perplexing issue not faced up to by our legal system. Considering the fear and anxiety of children detained under custodial interrogation, it seems unlikely that the waiver of constitutional rights is legal under the prevailing law.

The right to bail is an uncertain hope for children detained before a full hearing. In 1972 Arkansas was the only state that guaranteed bail for children. In the absence of a national policy enunciated by the Supreme Court, however, local courts when challenged in an individual case have released a child without bail or—alternatively—have demanded a speedy trial.

The final and perhaps the most important part of a juvenile court proceeding is its disposition. The court often bases its decision on hearsay statements and on psychiatric and social reports that are inaccessible to the child's counsel. The child's right to substantive due process and rehabilitation may be the greatest legal problem of all. Remaining in question is whether the Supreme Court will continue its nonintervention in a state's juvenile court processes (a posture it advocated in the 1971 decision denying jury trials to children) or whether it will assert that the right to diagnosis and treatment is a fundamental guarantee of the juvenile justice system. As long as the civil-criminal label game is played and sanctions are placed against children in the name of rehabilitation, little fundamental change can be expected.

LEBANON. In 1972 Lebanon's economic prosperity was endangered by clashes with Israel that became increasingly severe as the year progressed. Israeli incursions into southern Lebanon in January and February, in retaliation for isolated attacks from Lebanese territory by Palestinian guerrillas, caused right-wing Lebanese politicians to level strong criticism against the 1969 agreement between the guerrillas and the Lebanese army. The Palestine Liberation Organization (PLO) made efforts to conciliate the army, and the government maintained that it stood by the 1969 agreement.

Following the May 30 massacre at Lod International Airport, near Tel Aviv, Israel, an exceptionally heavy Israeli attack on Lebanon caused some 70 deaths among guerrillas and Lebanese civilians. The Israelis claimed that the massacre at the airport had been planned in Lebanon, but Lebanese authorities strongly denied this. The guerrillas evacuated the border areas, and the PLO agreed to suspend its activities and discipline its members; some extremist groups repudiated the agreement, however. After the murder of 11 members of the Israeli Olympic team on September 5, the Israelis launched an even more powerful attack with brigade strength on September 16 and followed it up by bombarding refugee camps that it claimed were sheltering guerrilla bases. On July 8 Ghassan Kanafani, leader of the extremist Popular Front for the Liberation of Palestine, was killed by a bomb planted in his car. Following a series of violent strikes in November, the army was asked to take charge of domestic security. (*See also* Israel. *See in* CE: Lebanon.)

LESOTHO. Following the reconciliation of Lesotho's prime minister, Chief Leabua Jonathan, with King Moshoeshoe II, the April 1972 congress of the Basuto National party (BNP) confirmed the prime minister's leadership and his policy of conciliation with Ntsu Mokhehle's opposition Basutoland Congress party (BCP). Two leading members of the BNP, suspected of subversion, were expelled: Thomas Mofolo, president of the senate, and former Assistant Minister J. Mokotoso.

In June Chief Jonathan set up a nationwide campaign for the establishment of a national government, which would include BCP members. Though its survival continued to depend upon South Africa's goodwill, such a coalition necessarily would stiffen Lesotho's stance. But by September the proposed coalition seemed a dimmer possibility. Talks with South Africa were postponed until a joint Organization of African Unity approach could be worked out. (*See also* Africa. *See in* CE: Lesotho.)

LIBERIA. William R. Tolbert, Jr., was formally inaugurated president of Liberia in 1972, in a ceremony attended by many foreign dignitaries, including Mrs. Richard M. Nixon. The ceremony took place on January 3, although Tolbert had been serving in the office since the death of President William V. S. Tubman in July 1971. One week after his inauguration, Tolbert announced a sweeping reorganization of the Liberian cabinet. New appointees took over the offices of secretary of state, secretary of the treasury, and attorney general. Mai Padmore was appointed minister of health and welfare and became the first woman to hold cabinet rank in Liberia.

BEN MARTIN

Mrs. Richard M. Nixon (center) is dressed in an authentic Liberian costume during the festivities attendant upon her visit to the inauguration of William R. Tolbert, Jr., as president of Liberia.

During the year the government notified foreign corporations with holdings in Liberia that it wished to renegotiate existing long-term leases. The announcement was seen as a response to growing popular resentment of foreign control of Liberia's economy. On June 10 Liberia and the Soviet Union announced a planned exchange of ambassadors. (*See in* CE: Liberia.)

LIBRARIES. The United Nations Educational, Scientific, and Cultural Organization (UNESCO) celebrated its International Book Year (IBY) in 1972. The IBY greatly stimulated the production, use, and appreciation of books and libraries in many countries, and IBY committees were set up in 57 countries with a view toward promoting economic development through reading. A 'Charter of the Book' was published by UNESCO, and special IBY activities were reported from more than 100 member countries. UNESCO's Department of Documentation, Libraries, and Archives promoted the establishment of national information and documentation systems in developing countries, and two pilot projects were already under way for national documentation centers in Morocco and Bulgaria, financed by the UN Development Programme.

The International Standard Book Number (ISBN) was widely adopted for numbering of books by publishers. At a meeting of a technical committee of the International Standards Organization in the Netherlands in September, further progress was made with the introduction of the International Standard Serial Number (ISSN) for the identification of periodical publications and of the International Standard Record Number (ISRN) for products of the music industry (such as records, tapes, and cassettes). Another advance of international importance was the distribution in the fall of the year of the first machine-readable tape records of films by the Library of Congress, in Washington, D.C.

In the U.S. the National Library of Medicine was sued for violation of copyright in connection with photocopying. The American Library Association (ALA) tried to safeguard the right to photocopy for interlibrary loan and the right of "fair use" for library users. A committee of Congress was working on a bill to revise the law of copyright.

The ALA, as active as ever, organized special activities for the International Book Year, including a "Black Caucus" project for cultural exchanges between the U.S. and Africa, notably an exchange between Fisk and Howard universities and libraries in Botswana and Malawi. The ALA's Intellectual Freedom Committee developed a revision of the "freedom to read" statement, including a claim for free access to libraries for minors.

Robert Wedgeworth, Jr., 34, became executive director of the ALA on August 1, succeeding David H. Clift, who had held the post for 20 years. Wedgeworth was the first black to direct the ALA. A doctoral candidate at Rutgers, The State University, he had served in a number of positions at academic and public libraries alike.

The New York Public Library continued to suffer financial difficulties. The science and technology division was temporarily closed to the public because of a shortage of funds. Similarly, the library was forced to cease publication of its *Bulletin,* a periodical esteemed among bibliographers. The National Endowment for the Humanities made a grant of $500,000 to the library, subject to matching gifts from the public. Public gifts surpassed the necessary $500,000, and the endowment made another grant of $750,000 subject to two-for-one matching public gifts.

Many new library buildings were opened during 1972, including the National Library of Macedonia at Skopje, Yugoslavia, rebuilt after destruction by the earthquake of 1963, and an exemplary public library at Miskolc, Hungary, for the county of Borsod. The first phase of the great third building for the Library of Congress was completed, and the building, designed by Ludwig Mies van der Rohe, was scheduled for completion by 1975. (*See in* CE: Libraries.)

"Yes George, it does say, 'No part of this may be reproduced, stored in a retrieval system, or transmitted, in any form or by any means . . . without prior written permission.'"

HERB BRAMMIER FOR AMERICAN LIBRARIES

LIBYA. In July 1972 Libya's 18-man cabinet took a new shape when civilians were appointed to all the key positions except that of minister of the interior, which was filled by a military officer. Col. Muammar el-Qaddafi, head of the military government, again urged union with Egypt, although such a move was by no means universally popular at home. Union was promised within a year by President Anwar el-Sadat of Egypt, after a three-day meeting in the Libyan cities of Tobruk and Benghazi, one of Libya's two capitals, early in August. The combination of Libya's wealth with Egypt's industrial and military strength had much to recommend it, especially in view of Qaddafi's avowed intention of deeper involvement in the Arab struggle against Israel.

Relations with other Arab states were often poor, especially with Jordan and other surviving monarchies. Diplomatic relations with the revolutionary regime in Iraq were strained after Iraq signed a treaty with the Soviet Union in April. On several occasions during the year, Qaddafi made clear his wish to intervene in international and guerrilla conflicts, despite the distance of his country from the trouble centers and Libya's weakened military competence. He claimed to be supporting the black power movement in the U.S. and to be supplying arms to the Irish Republican Army. Later he afforded heroes' burials in Tripoli (the second capital) to the Arabs killed while implementing the kidnappings and murders at the Olympic Games in Munich, West Germany. His response to internal upheavals in Uganda in September was to dispatch a force of 400 troops by air to assist Uganda's President Idi Amin. (*See* Olympic Games; Uganda.)

Libya's relations with Great Britain were poor throughout 1972, following the nationalization of the British Petroleum Co. in December 1971. The Anglo-Libyan defense treaty was broken off on January 26, and an open demonstration of hostility came in August when the British Embassy in Tripoli was attacked. The assault was made in reaction to the reported extradition from Gibraltar of Moroccan air force officers who had fled by helicopter after a second attempted coup. Qaddafi made no secret of his antipathy toward King Hassan II and his regime in Morocco.

In 1971 Libya fell from fifth to seventh place in the world league of oil producers in terms of tonnage. It seemed unlikely that the country's output for 1972 would top the 133 million metric tons produced in 1971. Production had been affected by an increase in royalties and other dues (rather than in output), by Libya's policy of conservation, and by the loss of markets due to nationalization of the British Petroleum Co. (*See also* Egypt; Middle East. *See in* CE: Libya.)

The Libyan government organized an elaborate funeral for the five Arab terrorists who died in the Olympics massacre.

GOKSIN SIPAHIOGLU FROM JOCELYNE BENZAKIN

LITERATURE. The tendency of U.S. publishers to look upon books as an adjunct of the newspaper industry received a setback in 1972 with the public disclosures of plagiarism and fraud attendant to books like 'The Memoirs of Chief Red Fox' and a proposed "authorized" new biography of Howard Hughes by Clifford Irving. The publishers' inclinations to go increasingly to works written by newspapermen and professional journalists and to view the books as perishable, extended, and intensive examinations of topical issues, fostered procedures a few years ago that eliminated the earlier safeguards once used to avoid such occurrences. Large sections of the 'Memoirs' were lifted from James H. McGregor's 'The Wounded Knee Massacre: From the Viewpoint of the Sioux', published in 1940. And, although the disguises were much more elaborate, the Irving manuscript proved similarly to be plagiarized from published and unpublished material. Both books were contracted by McGraw-Hill. The Irving scandal generated two new "documents"—'Hoax', by Stephen Fay, Lewis Chester, and Magnus Linklater, and Irving's own account, 'What *Really* Happened'—and led a second publisher to remove from circulation a prize-winning novel by West African Yambo Ouologuem when it was discovered that it, too, was plagiarized in part from Graham Greene's novel 'It's a Battlefield'. At the same time, several New York City publishing firms filed suits against reprint houses for unauthorized facsimile editions of books still under copyright to those firms. The writers pirated included such well-known authors as T. S. Eliot, F. Scott Fitzgerald, Van Wyck Brooks, and Edmund Wilson.

Still, most of the books published during the year remained journalistic and topical. U.S. President Richard M. Nixon issued his own policy statements in 'A New Road for America', and he was the focus directly or indirectly of such books as Edwin P. Hoyt's 'The Nixons: An American Family', Leonard Lurie's 'The Running of Richard Nixon', Bruce Mazlish's 'In Search of Nixon', John Osborne's 'The Third Year of the Nixon Watch', Henry D. Spalding's 'The Nixon Nobody Knows', and Jerry Voorhis' 'The Strange Case of Richard Milhous Nixon'. Charles P. Henderson, Jr., penned 'The Nixon Theology', and the president's running mate,

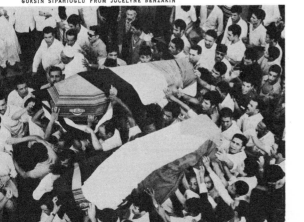

Vice-President Spiro T. Agnew, came in for attention with such works as Joseph Albright's 'What Makes Spiro Run?', Theo Lippman, Jr.'s 'Spiro Agnew's America', and Jules Witcover's 'White Knight'. The various contenders for the Democratic presidential nomination received their due in Robert Sam Anson's 'McGovern: A Biography', David Nevin's 'Muskie of Maine', and William W. Prochnau and Richard W. Larsen's 'A Certain Democrat: Senator Henry M. Jackson'. Senator Edward M. Kennedy (D, Mass.) is the subject of Lester David's 'Ted Kennedy: Triumphs and Tragedies', Burton Hersh's 'The Education of Edward Kennedy', and William H. Honan's 'Ted Kennedy: Profile of a Survivor'. The senator's 'In Critical Condition' presented Kennedy's own views on health care in the U.S.

Foreign policy of the U.S., past and current, is the subject of such works as John Lewis Gaddis' 'The United States and the Origins of the Cold War, 1941–1947', Richard M. Freeland's 'The Truman Doctrine and the Origins of McCarthyism', Joyce and Gabriel Kolko's 'The Limits of Power', Sidney Lens's 'The Forging of the American Empire', Gaddis Smith's 'Dean Acheson', and Richard J. Walton's 'Cold War and Counterrevolution'. Vietnam and the My Lai massacre are issues in Frances FitzGerald's 'Fire in the Lake', Daniel Ellsberg's 'Papers on the War', Seymour M. Hersh's 'Cover-Up', and Mary McCarthy's 'Medina'. Economic issues inform Roger LeRoy Miller and Raburn M. Williams' 'The New Economics of Richard Nixon' and Leonard Silk's 'Nixonomics', and the problems of the republic triggered 'Crises of the Republic', by Hannah Arendt, and 'A Republic, If You Can Keep It', by Earl Warren, former chief justice of the U.S. Law, lawyers, and court procedures come under scrutiny in F. Lee Bailey's 'The Defense Never Rests', Irving Brant's 'Impeachments: Trials and Errors', Joseph C. Goulden's 'The Superlawyers', and Robert Shogan's 'A Question of Judgment'. Bill Lawrence wrote of his experiences as a White House reporter in 'Six Presidents, Too Many Wars', and Vance Packard provided an analysis of the effects of mobility on the character of people in the U.S. in 'A Nation of Strangers'.

The experiences of growing up in the U.S. provided the bases of James Baldwin's 'No Name in the Street', Bruce Catton's 'Waiting for the Morning Train', Dan Greenburg's 'Scoring', Emmett Grogan's "Ringolevio: A Life Played for Keeps', A. E. Hotchner's 'King of the Hill', Norman Mailer's 'Existential Errands', Margaret Mead's 'Blackberry Winter: My Earlier Years', and Barbara Probst Solomon's 'Arriving Where We Started'. Anne Morrow Lindbergh's 'Bring Me a Unicorn', using diaries and letters from 1922–28, details her courtship by Charles Lindbergh, and Alan Watts wrote of his interest in Zen Buddhism in 'In My Own Way: An Autobiography, 1915–1965'.

Igor Stravinsky provided the impetus for Robert Craft's 'Stravinsky' and Paul Horgan's 'Encounters with Stravinsky', and James Thurber is the subject of Charles S. Holmes's 'The Clocks of Columbus'. Sir Rudolf Bing described his 22-year reign at the New York Metropolitan Opera in '5000 Nights at the Opera'. William D. Miller's 'A Harsh and Dreadful Love' focuses on Dorothy Day and the Catholic worker movement, and Budd Schulberg concentrated on boxer Muhammad Ali for his 'Loser and Still Champion'. Christopher Isherwood wrote movingly of his parents in 'Kathleen and Frank'. Poet Wendell Berry continued his interest in ecology with a new collection of essays, 'A Continuous Harmony', and Roger Kahn's 'The Boys of Summer' and Roger Angell's 'The Summer Game' kept baseball green in the minds of readers. Arthur Koestler's 'The Case of the Midwife Toad' supports the theory that some acquired traits may be transmitted genetically. W. A. Swanberg wrote of 'Luce and His Empire', Stephen Birmingham of 'The Late John Marquand', and Howard Teichmann of 'George S. Kaufman'. Abba Eban reviewed the 25-year history of Israel in 'My Country', and Larry Collins and Dominique Lapierre's 'O Jerusalem!' recalls the recent violent history of that city.

COURTESY, MACMILLAN CO.

Richard Bach wrote 'Jonathan Livingston Seagull', an adult fable that surprised critics by becoming a best seller.

New biographies of George Sand by Samuel Edwards, of Samuel Taylor Coleridge by Norman Fruman, and of Anthony Trollope by James Pope Hennessy, along with David Duff's 'Victoria and Albert', Cecil Woodham-Smith's first volume of 'Queen Victoria', and two new novels based on the life of James Whistler, suggested that the 19th century was still topical enough to serve U.S. publishers as a standard against which the present might be measured. An equally discernible tendency to revive decades of history at a 30-year interval was evinced in such works as Walter C. Langer's "official" psychological study, 'The Mind of Adolf Hitler: The Secret Wartime Report', Ladislas Farago's best-selling 'The Game of Foxes', about German wartime espionage in the U.S. and Great Britain, J. C. Masterman's 'The Double-Cross System in the War of 1939 to 1945', and Cecil Beaton's 'Memoirs of the Forties'. Joseph P. Lash followed his prizewinning, earlier biography of 'Eleanor and Franklin' with 'Eleanor: The Years Alone', tracing her life after the death of President Roosevelt in 1945, and Maisie and Richard Conrat's 'Executive Order 9066' follows the harrowing relocations of Japanese Americans during World War II. The perennially reliable audience for mid-19th-century history was treated to Joan Haslip's biography of Maximilian and Carlota, 'The Crown of Mexico', and to Justin G. Turner and Linda Levitt Turner's attempts to rehabilitate Mary Todd Lincoln in 'Mary Todd Lincoln: Her Life and Letters'.

The year's nonfiction output also included Michael Harrington's 'Socialism', two further volumes of Robert Coles's 'Children of Crisis' along with a collection of Coles's essays, 'Farewell to the South', and, after a labor of 17 years, Robert Manson Myers' 'The Children of Pride', the history of a Georgia family from 1854 to 1868 as conveyed by letters written between its various members. The fifth and final volume of Leon Edel's monumental biography 'Henry James: The Master, 1910–1916' appeared, bringing to a close that 20-year-long effort. The letters of F. Scott Fitzgerald to his agent, Harold Ober, and to his editor, Maxwell Perkins, were edited respectively by Matthew J. Bruccoli and Jennifer McCabe Atkinson into 'As Ever, Scott Fitz-' and by John Kuehl and Jackson Bryer into 'Dear Scott/Dear Max'. The American public was prevented by court order from reading President Warren G. Harding's love letters to Mrs. Carrie Phillips until 2014. The letters promised to shed no new light on his character.

Fiction

Rather than monumental works, novellas and short stories seemed to occupy the energies of serious novelists. Eudora Welty's 'The Optimist's Daughter' powerfully evokes moods of subjectivity to reflect a fiction-honored theme that everyone changes differently after what he experiences and that these differences cause the irreconcilable misunderstandings, tensions, and lonelinesses of the present. John Barth, on the other hand, continued his avant-garde battles with self-consciousness in 'Chimera', indicating how the various images of self that man now faces finally create a monster of impotence which must be overcome by action. In this final call for action Barth differs from Vladimir Nabokov, whose 'Transparent Things' again reflects an inner sense of identity, won by a pursuit past the various pitfalls of bad faith that constitute contemporary life, and a final inner calm rather than continued self-dramatization.

WIDE WORLD

Wallace E. Stegner, a retired English professor, won the 1972 Pulitzer prize for fiction with his novel 'Angle of Repose'.

Larry McMurtry offered another look at conflicting sensibilities and naturalistic backgrounds in 'All My Friends Are Going to Be Strangers', while Philip Roth's 'The Breast' goes on with his attempt to liberate the id by making its sexual drives acceptable to the superego by way of Freudian witwork. Ishmael Reed's 'Mumbo Jumbo' presents a mixture of fiction and witchcraft as his view of the black imagination. Joyce Carol Oates's fourth collection of short stories, 'Marriages and Infidelities', deals, like Nabokov's work, mainly with problems of intersubjectivity and bad faith. Donald Barthelme's 'Sadness' continues his surreal glimpses of the U.S., and new, less impressive collections of stories were issued by Joanne Greenberg ('Rites of Passage'), Doris Lessing ('The Temptation of Jack Orkney and Other Stories'), and John Updike ('Museums and Women and Other Stories').

Other fiction offerings were John Gardner's transference of King Arthur's court in 'The Sunlight Dialogues' and George P. Elliott's neorealistic views of love, marriage, and widowhood in 'Muriel'. Alix Kates Schulman received a number of good reviews for 'Memoirs of an Ex-Prom Queen', with the theme of women's liberation. John Le Carré's departure from the realm of espionage in 'The Naive and Sentimental Lover' proved disappointing, as did 'The Scorpion God', an edition of three short novels by William Golding. Jan de Hartog ventured into historical fiction with 'The Peaceable Kingdom', and George MacDonald Fraser added another episode to the Flashman saga with 'Flash for Freedom!' Meyer Levin's 'The Settlers' relates the migration of a family from Russia to Palestine in 1905, while philosophical notions again underlie Iris Murdoch's 14th novel, 'An Accidental Man'.

Best-selling novels included Eric Ambler's 'The Levanter', Louis Auchincloss' 'I Come as a Thief', Pierre Boulle's 'Ears of the Jungle', Taylor Caldwell's 'Captains and the Kings', Michael Crichton's 'The Terminal Man', R. F. Delderfield's 'To Serve Them All My Days', George V. Higgins' 'The Friends of Eddie Coyle', Victoria Holt's 'On the Night of the Seventh Moon', Elia Kazan's 'The Assassins', John Masters' 'The Ravi Lancers', Jane McIlvaine McClary's 'A Portion for Foxes', Chaim Potok's 'My Name Is Asher Lev', Frank G. Slaughter's 'Convention, M.D.', Irving Wallace's 'The Word', and Joseph Wambaugh's 'The Blue Knight'. A novel, 'The Ewings', and a collection of stories, 'The Time Element and Other Stories', by John O'Hara were issued posthumously.

Philip Young edited 'The Nick Adams Stories', adding to the original Hemingway tales eight fragments and stories previously unpublished; and 'John Thomas and Lady Jane', the second version of the D. H. Lawrence classic 'Lady Chatterley's Lover', was published. The year also marked the return to fiction of John Hersey, after 5 years, with 'The Conspiracy', and of Isaac Asimov, after 15 years, with 'The Gods Themselves'. C. P. Snow's first novel since the completion of his 'Strangers and Brothers' series, 'The Malcontents', was published, but the year's biggest surprise was the success of Richard Bach's adult fable about a sea gull, 'Jonathan Livingston Seagull', which zoomed to the top of the best seller lists without benefit of the author's having made TV appearances or of the book's having been a major book club selection.

Novelist V. S. Pritchett concluded his autobiography with 'Midnight Oil', and James Dickey offered 'Sorties'. Works of criticism included John Crowe Ransom's 'Beating the Bushes', Horace Gregory's 'Spirit of Time and Place', William Jay Smith's 'The Streaks of the Tulip', Joyce Carol Oates's 'The Edge of Impossibility: Tragic Forms in Literature', Paul Goodman's 'Speaking and Language', John Ciardi's 'Manner of Speaking', George P. Elliott's 'Conversions: Literature and the Modernist Temptation', Edmund Wilson's 'A Window on Russia', Philip Young's 'Three Bags Full: Essays in American Fiction', Hugh Kenner's 'The Pound Era', and studies of T. S. Eliot by Russell Kirk ('Eliot and His Age'), Roger Kojecky ('T. S. Eliot's Social Criticism'), and John D. Margolis ('T. S. Eliot's Intellectual Development'). A real delight was the publishing of a portion of Theodore Roethke's notebooks, 'Straw for the Fire'.

Poetry

The poetry offerings of the year included E. E. Cummings' 'Complete Poems: 1913–1962', A. R. Ammons' 'Collected Poems, 1951–1971', and Donald Davie's 'Collected Poems 1950–1970'. Archibald MacLeish's 'The Human Season: Selected Poems, 1926–1972', John Woods's 'Turning to Look Back: Poems 1955–1970', and John Weiners' 'Selected Poems' were published as well.

In 1972 there were also new individual volumes by W. H. Auden ('Epistle to a Godson'), John Berryman ('Delusions, Etc.'), David Wagoner ('Riverbed'), Robert Bly ('Sleepers Joining Hands'), Richard Emil Braun ('The Foreclosure'), Michael Casey ('Obscenities'), Robert Creeley ('A Day Book'), Irving Feldman ('Lost Originals'), John Hollander ('Town and Country Matters'), Denise Levertov ('Footprints'), James Merrill ('Braving the Elements'), Sylvia Plath ('Winter Trees'), A. Poulin, Jr. ('In Advent'), Lawrence Raab ('Mysteries of the Horizon'), M. L. Rosenthal ('The View from the Peacock's Tail'), Anne Sexton ('The Book of Folly'), James Tate ('Absences'), and Eleanor Ross Taylor ('Welcome Eumenides'). (*See also* Feature Article: "Arts of Black America.")

Literature Abroad

In France, Claude Levi-Strauss published 'L'Homme nu', the fourth and final volume of his monumental 'Mythologies'. Jean-Paul Sartre issued the third long section of his biography of Flaubert, and, in 'L'Arrière-pays', the French poet Yves Bennefoy related his travels to various places and paintings as an art critic. 'Maltaverne', a 73-page fragment from François Mauriac's final work, was published posthumously. Yasunari Kawabata's novel 'The Master of Go' was also published posthumously. The Japanese author, winner of the 1968 Nobel prize for literature, committed suicide in April.

Efforts to award Aleksandr I. Solzhenitsyn his Nobel prize in private ceremonies in Moscow during the spring went awry. A few days before the ceremony was to have taken place, Solzhenitsyn consented to his first interview in nine years. In that interview he accused the government of trying to drive him out and complained bitterly of attacks on him, his family, and his work. He said that he was prevented from doing research in the state archives and from hiring assistants to do the research for him. The research, he said, was essential for the completion of the trilogy for which 'August 1914' is the first installment. After the interview, Soviet authorities would not permit the Nobel ceremony.

In what appeared to be a continued tightening of control over ideology, Yevgeny F. Markin was expelled from the Writers Union for defending Solzhenitsyn in a poem, as was Aleksandr A. Galich for encouraging Jews to emigrate to Israel. Soviet officials also tried to have a pornographic work, 'Moscow Nights', branded a forgery. The book was published in the West by Olympia Press. Officials claimed it was really written by a West German named Heinz Konsalik. (*See also* Awards and Prizes; Magazines; Newspapers; Publishing, Book. *See in* CE: Literature.)

LITERATURE, CHILDREN'S. Although children's books that reflect new interests are usually slower to appear than are such books for adults, there was evidence in 1972 of a quickening response on the part of publishers in an attempt to narrow the gap. The numbers of books of poetry and books about pollution and ecology were as large as in the preceding year, and there were many books that fulfilled children's and young people's needs for information about world affairs. Many new books also indicated a growing reader interest in the People's Republic of China, a continuing awareness of the plight of minority groups, and an appreciation of the changing role of women.

For Younger Children

A gentle reminder of sex equality was Charlotte Zolotow's 'William's Doll', in which a small boy's yearning for a doll to cuddle is defended by his grandmother, who says that he needs practice in being a father. Two quite different picture books dealt with ecology and pollution: Ib Spang Olsen's 'Smoke' is a fanciful, humorous tale of a family's efforts to cut down pollution, and Alvin Tresselt's 'The Dead Tree' is a very simply written, poetic book about ecology in a forest. 'Franklin Stein', by Ellen Raskin, is an amusing story of creativity, illustrated with flair. In book form for the first time in 1972 was Beatrix Potter's 'The Sly Old Cat', another funny story in which Mr. Rat outwits a greedy feline. 'The Bear Who Had No Place to Go', by James Stevenson, is both touching and hilarious. It is about a lonely bear that looks for a niche, having lost its circus job as a trick bicycle rider.

Janina Domanska illustrated the old rhyme 'I Saw a Ship A-Sailing' with handsome, stylized pictures. The familiar song of 'Waltzing Matilda', illustrated by Desmond Digby with vigorous, softly colored scenes, won the year's picture book award when it was first published in Australia. Jane Yolen's 'The Fireside Song Book of Birds and Beasts', with engaging pictures by Peter Parnall, had a special appeal for young children.

Among the excellent informational books for this age group were Marie Winn's 'The Thief-Catcher', a story that explains taxation very lucidly; Tana Hoban's 'Count and See', a photographically illustrated first counting book; and 'Use Your Brain', by Paul Showers, which gives basic facts about the brain and the nervous system. The sights one sees from the driver's seats of various vehicles and the intriguing intricacy of control panels are pictured in Edward Koren's 'Behind the Wheel'.

A story that is captivating in its portrayal of friendship was written and illustrated by Arnold Lobel: 'Frog and Toad Together', a fine book for the beginning reader because of its distinct episodes. One of the most striking books of the year, with bold colors and African motifs in its design, was Gerald McDermott's 'Anansi the Spider'. The

COURTESY, ATHENEUM PUBLISHERS

'The Malibu and Other Poems', by Myra Cohn Livingston, was illustrated by James J. Spanfeller.

musings of Frances, the irrepressible little badger that has romped through several books by Russell Hoban, are collected in a new volume of poetry, 'Egg Thoughts, and Other Frances Songs'.

A little boy enjoys playing with a doll in Charlotte Zolotow's 'William's Doll'.

COURTESY, HARPER & ROW

The 8-to-12 Group

For the intermediate age group there was a steady flow of fantasy, including tales in the folk genre and contemporary stories. An original fantasy by the British author Philippa Pearce, 'The Squirrel Wife', involves the traditional folk theme of an animal that assumes human form. Familiar fairy tales were selected by Virginia Haviland for 'The Fairy Tale Treasury', illustrated with vital, amusing, and handsome pictures by Raymond Briggs. Two sparkling modern stories were Mary Rodgers' 'Freaky Friday', in which a girl wakes up one morning to find she has temporarily turned into her mother, a situation that affords some very funny incidents, and Felice Holman's 'The Future of Hopper Toote', the story of a boy who is trying to avoid the publicity that would ensue if it became known that he had powers of levitation.

One of the best sports books was Frank Orr's 'The Story of Hockey', a lively history of an increasingly popular sport. A reflection of a development in the arts, Mickey Klar Marks's 'Op-Tricks: Creating Kinetic Art' gave clear instructions for a series of fascinating projects. Another fine informational book was 'Zoo Safari', by Terry Shannon and Charles Payzant, which describes practices and innovations in modern zoos.

'The Malibu and Other Poems', by Myra Cohn Livingston, was one of the outstanding poetry books of the year. The biography of a black doctor, 'Daniel Hale Williams', by Lewis Federson, is notable not only for its description of the famous pioneer in open-heart surgery but also for its picture of the practice of medicine at the turn of the century.

For Adolescents

Much of the good fiction for young people came from abroad: K. M. Peyton's 'The Beethoven Medal', the story of a surly youth who becomes a concert pianist; Hester Burton's 'The Henchmans at Home', a story about a Victorian family; John Christopher's story of the future, 'The Sword of the Spirits'—all from England. From the Netherlands came S. R. Van Iterson's dramatic 'Village of Outcasts', set in a Colombian leper colony. Of the American books, one that is both amusing and trenchant is M. E. Kerr's 'Dinky Hocker Shoots Smack'; Dinky does not use drugs at all, but she does rebel against those who are too busy doing good for others to see their own child's unhappiness. Isabelle Holland's 'The Man Without a Face' is a dignified and poignant picture of the relationship between a boy and an older man.

New U.S. ties with China brought several books, the best of which was 'Modern China', by Orville Schell and Joseph Esherick. Richard Erdoes' 'The Sun Dance People' is a sympathetic overview of the Plains Indians, and Robert Froman's 'Racism' is a broad and objective survey of prejudice in the United States.

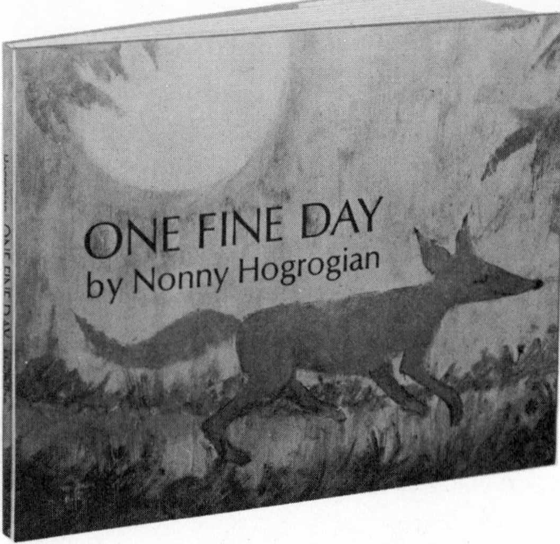

COURTESY, THE MACMILLAN COMPANY © 1971 NONNY HOGROGIAN

The 1972 winner of the Caldecott Medal was 'One Fine Day', by Nonny Hogrogian.

Gary Jennings' 'The Shrinking Outdoors' was one of the best of the many books on pollution, and Janet Stevenson's 'Women's Rights' is a fine history of the struggle of women in the U.S. to gain equality. The fascinating scientific frontier of lasers and holography is explored in Irwin Stambler's 'Revolution in Light'.

Awards

The National Book Award for children's literature was won by Donald Barthelme for 'The Slightly Irregular Fire Engine or the Hithering Thithering Djinn', a sophisticated and whimsical fantasy. The Randolph J. Caldecott Medal, given by the American Library Association, was awarded to Nonny Hogrogian for 'One Fine Day', based on an Armenian folktale. The John Newbery Medal went to Robert C. O'Brien for 'Mrs. Frisby and the Rats of NIMH', in which a mouse in need is helped by the erudite rats that have been trained in a laboratory experiment.

The Canadian Library Association's award for the best children's book of the year went to 'Mary of Mile 18', by Ann Blades, who taught in the remote Mennonite community she described therein; the medal for the best illustrated book was given to Shizuye Takashima for 'A Child in Prison Camp'. The Carnegie Medal of the Library Association of the United Kingdom went to an Australian author for the first time. Ivan Southall, who has won several Australian awards, described a gentle, poetic boy's conflict with small-town bullies in 'Josh'. The Kate Greenaway Medal for illustration was awarded to Jan Pienkowski for his work in 'The Kingdom Under the Sea'.

The Hans Christian Andersen Medals, awarded biennially by an international jury, go to an author and an illustrator for their contributions to children's literature. The 1972 medals were given to Ib Spang Olsen, a Danish artist, and to Scott O'Dell, who was also a past winner of the Newbery Medal.

LUXEMBOURG. On Jan. 13, 1972, the Chamber of Deputies of Luxembourg approved, by a vote of 54–0, a constitutional amendment reducing the age of voting eligibility from 21 to 18 years. The amendment also lowered the qualifying age for election from 25 to 21 years.

Luxembourg's economy, heavily dependent on steel production, continued to prosper. National economic policy still emphasized diversification of industry, however, and steel's contribution to the gross national product (GNP) dropped from 30% in 1971 to 25% in 1972. Overall increase of the GNP was estimated for 1972 at 2%. As part of the general realignment of European currencies approved by the International Monetary Fund, the Luxembourg franc was revalued 11.57% to a parity of $.0223135 with the U.S. dollar. The three Benelux states (Belgium, the Netherlands, and Luxembourg) also adopted a 1.5% permissiveness band on either side of the new parity. (*See in* CE: Luxemburg.)

McGOVERN, GEORGE S. After racing from behind to win the Democratic nomination for U.S. president in 1972, Senator George S. McGovern of South Dakota suffered the greatest political defeat of any Democratic presidential candidate in the country's history. Only Massachusetts and the District of Columbia remained in the Democratic party column after the election. U.S. President Richard M. Nixon was reelected with 60.8% of the popular vote and 520 out of a possible 538 electoral votes. The public opinion polls had predicted the outcome. For that reason, perhaps, and also because many voters did not favor either candidate, only about 55% of the potential electorate turned out to vote.

McGovern was considered too liberal, or even radical, by the conservative wing of the Democratic party and by many of its moderates as well; and when he moderated his stand on certain issues, his move toward center was "flexibility" to some of the people but "indecisiveness" to many more. In addition, McGovern had promised candor in his campaign, but serious mistakes tarnished his credibility shortly after his nomination.

The Democratic National Convention itself drove many voters away. While convention speakers stressed that the 1972 conclave was the first that truly represented Democratic voters, large segments of the Democratic coalition—including white Southerners and various ethnic groups—could not identify with the delegates. After losing the national election in 1968, the Democratic party had established a commission to reform delegate selection. For a time, McGovern himself had headed that commission. The new guidelines opened the party's nominating process to more women and young people and to more blacks and other minorities. While these reforms helped McGovern win the nomination in 1972, they caused resentment among established politicians who were unseated at the convention. Moreover, to many who watched the proceedings on television, the Democratic party seemed to consist of radicals, militants, and eccentrics of assorted stripe.

Senator George S. McGovern of South Dakota was the unsuccessful Democratic party candidate for president of the U.S. in the 1972 election.

FRED WARD FROM BLACK STAR

Delegates wave banners and posters after Senator McGovern is nominated for the presidency at the Democratic National Convention in July.

UPI COMPIX

First and foremost, McGovern was an antiwar candidate. The U.S. citizenry was anxious to end the war in Vietnam, but McGovern's pledge to cease hostilities within a month of inauguration day and to "plead" for the release of U.S. prisoners of war disturbed many voters. McGovern's social and economic proposals—especially a poorly prepared welfare plan—also damaged his chances even though he reconsidered and contradicted his earlier stands in mid-campaign.

A soft-spoken man with a rather professorial manner, McGovern started his campaign with an asset that compensated for his lack of dramatic appeal: his reputation for honesty and moral courage. That advantage was lost in his handling of the Eagleton affair. Twelve days after McGovern chose Senator Thomas F. Eagleton of Missouri to be his running mate, Eagleton admitted that he had been hospitalized three times in the 1960's for nervous exhaustion and that he had undergone electric shock treatments for depression as recently as 1966. A furor arose as to whether Eagleton should remain on the ticket in view of his medical history and his failure to tell McGovern about it when the nomination was offered. McGovern said at first that he was "1,000%" for Eagleton, but soon he asked Eagleton to withdraw because the issue of his fitness threatened to obscure the major campaign issues. Eagleton withdrew reluctantly, and "1,000% in favor of" became a popular term of negation.

McGovern was embarrassed further when several of his choices to replace Eagleton turned him down. Finally he got an acceptance from R. Sargent Shriver of Maryland, who had served the U.S. government in executive and diplomatic posts and who was the brother-in-law of Massachusetts Senator Edward M. Kennedy, McGovern's first choice for vice-president.

Although some bizarre activities involving Republicans associated with the Committee to Re-elect the President cast shadows on the Republican campaign, the Democrats never were able to get President Nixon to comment on their charges of political espionage nor meet their candidate on a debating platform. Nixon campaigned largely by surrogate, depending largely on Vice-President Spiro T. Agnew to do the public speaking.

McGovern was born on July 19, 1922, in his father's parsonage at Avon, S.D. He was graduated from Dakota Wesleyan University in Mitchell and, after World War II, from Northwestern University at Evanston, Ill., where he earned his master's and doctor's degrees. Serving in the war as a B-24 bomber pilot in southern Italy, he won the Distinguished Flying Cross. His wartime experiences led him into the ministry briefly before he took his graduate work.

After teaching history and political science for a time at Dakota Wesleyan, McGovern became executive secretary of the moribund South Dakota Democratic party in 1953. He launched a grass-roots organizing campaign that ultimately gave him his political base. In 1956 he was elected to the U.S. House of Representatives for the first of two terms. In 1961 President John F. Kennedy appointed him director of Food for Peace. McGovern was elected to the Senate in 1962 and was reelected in 1968.

After his friend Senator Robert F. Kennedy (D, N.Y.) was assassinated while campaigning for the presidency in 1968, McGovern became a nominal candidate. He announced his candidacy again in 1971, a full year before any opponent. His strong showing in the New Hampshire primary undermined the favored position of Senator Edmund S. Muskie of Maine, and his victory in Wisconsin effectively put Muskie out of the running. McGovern's nomination was all but assured when he defeated former Vice-President Hubert H. Humphrey in the California primary. (*See also* Elections; Political Parties.)

MAGAZINES. Threatening the life of smaller magazines and the profits of larger magazines, the U.S. Postal Service imposed a gigantic postage increase in 1972. Second-class magazine rates were scheduled to go up an average of 127% over a five-year period. Not surprisingly, scientific, literary, and religious periodicals and magazines of opinion—because of their limited circulation and small advertising revenue—were gravely jeopardized by the increase. Mass circulation magazines also felt threatened. Spokesmen for Time Inc. estimated that the company's postage costs for its four magazines would reach nearly $35 million in five years. In December the company announced that *Life*—for 30 years the world's foremost mass circulation weekly—would suspend publication at the end of the year. Eroding ad revenues and rising postage costs were blamed for the magazine's demise. The end of photojournalism's premier publication was greeted with almost universal dismay.

There was considerable activity in the field of women's magazines. *Ms.*, the first mass publication of the women's liberation movement, began publication with an initial circulation of more than 300,000. Warner Communications, a media conglomerate, expressed confidence in the new venture and put up $1 million. Gloria Steinem and the editorial staff maintained control over what promised to be the most controversial women's magazine in a decade. Established magazines for women, from *McCall's* to *Good Housekeeping,* began to initiate columns, features, and stories reflective of changes in the role of U.S. women.

In keeping with the spirit of the women's liberation movement, *Cosmopolitan* offered its own center fold, a coyly posed nude photograph of actor Burt Reynolds. The issue sold out overnight and became an instant collector's item.

Second to women, the fastest-growing special audience group was blacks. By the close of 1972 there were more than 50 different black-directed periodicals. Among a dozen 1972 entries were: *Relevant,* a news magazine, and *Encore,* a black version of *Time.*

Consumers Union, publishers of *Consumer Reports,* introduced a new magazine in the ever-growing field of consumer publications—*Media & Consumer,* which would discuss press coverage of consumer issues. Time Inc. opened the fall season with *Money,* a magazine focusing on personal and family finance.

A number of other specialized magazines began publication in 1972. Among them were *World,* billed by publisher Norman Cousins as a "review of ideas, the arts and the human condition," and *Oui,* a new contribution from Hugh Hefner, aimed at younger readers who often find *Playboy* more for their fathers than for themselves.

There were also innovations in format and production. *Good Housekeeping* investigated possibilities of a national television series to be based on the magazine's most popular features. *Black Box,*

WIDE WORLD

Robert Clive, art director of *Life* magazine, grimly reflects on the news that *Life* would fold at the end of 1972. The magazine, started in 1936, was known as a pioneer in photojournalism.

a new poetry "magazine," was to be issued exclusively on cassette tape, and *Current Audio* magazine, fittingly enough, was available only on LP record. To help librarians keep up with these developments, the publishers of *Library Journal* began issuing a new magazine, *Previews: News and Reviews of Non-Print Media.*

Pending U.S. Supreme Court rulings on various aspects of present obscenity laws, the year was relatively quiet in censorship cases. Ralph Ginzburg, convicted ten years before for distributing the short-lived quarterly called *Eros,* lost his last appeal in the case and began serving a three-year sentence. In retrospect, many thought the sentence harsh for a work that seemed mild compared to titles found on most current newsstands. But the appeals court was not of this opinion, and Ginzburg was ordered to jail. He served part of his sentence but was paroled in the fall. (*See in* CE: Magazines.)

Riots by striking students in Tananarive, the capital of the Malagasy Republic, left at least 15 wounded in May.

A.F.P. FROM PICTORIAL PARADE

MALAGASY REPUBLIC. While 1972 began auspiciously enough in the Malagasy Republic for President Philibert Tsiranana, reelected in January with more than 99% of votes cast, it was nonetheless to be the year of his political doom. In October he was divested of all power and retired.

The process began in May with disturbances at the University of Madagascar at Tananarive, the capital. The school was promptly closed, provoking a wave of protest that spread to other schools and colleges. The government retaliated by closing the schools and colleges and arresting the students' leaders. Security forces opened fire on crowds of demonstrators, killing large numbers of people. The following day a huge crowd set fire to the city hall, bringing further reprisals and more deaths. In desperation, Tsiranana gave full powers to the army chief of staff, Gen. Gabriel Ramanantsoa, whom he placed in charge of the government. (*See in* CE: Malagasy Republic.)

MALAWI. In mid-March 1972 President J. J. Fouché of South Africa paid the first state visit by a South African president to an independent black African state when he visited Malawi. He appealed for peaceful coexistence and for cooperation among African states to make possible a concerted effort against poverty, ignorance, and disease. On his departure, Malawi's President H. Kamuzu Banda called on African governments not to attack South Africa because to do so might lead to their downfall.

Following President Banda's description of the banned sect of Jehovah's Witnesses (numbering between 20,000 and 30,000) as "devil's witnesses," the youth wing of the ruling Malawi Congress party reportedly mounted an attack on them with axes, clubs, and similar weapons. At least ten members of the sect, and perhaps more, were reported killed. About 17,000 refugees had fled the country by October. (*See in* CE: Malawi.)

MALAYSIA. Prompted by the desire for a peaceful and stable Southeast Asia that would be free from the pressure and manipulation of power politics, Malaysia in 1972 renewed the call for neutralization of the region by the superpowers, including the People's Republic of China. This concept had become one of the main priorities of Malaysia's foreign policy and was endorsed by the foreign ministers of Indonesia, Malaysia, the Philippines, Singapore, and Thailand at a meeting of the Association of Southeast Asian Nations (ASEAN) held in Singapore in April.

In association with neighboring Indonesia, Malaysia rejected the call by the larger powers that

Barbed wire is used to enforce a new curfew for Malaysia's Chinese, "temporarily" moved to fenced-in villages more than 20 years ago.

WIDE WORLD

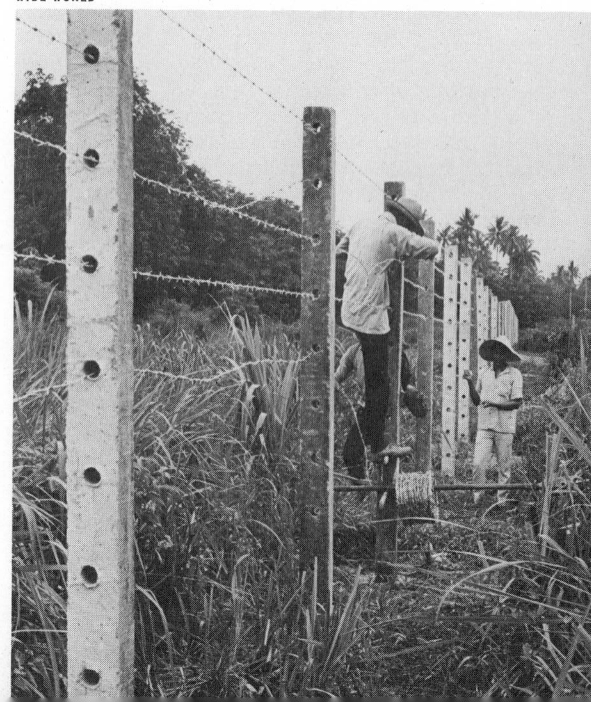

the Strait of Malacca be internationalized. The two countries reiterated their claim that the waterway was their property, although open to all ships for "innocent passage."

Internally, Communism and antigovernment activity, although under control, remained a threat to security. In the state of Sarawak, Communist terrorist activities were more pronounced. In February the government issued a white paper to highlight the growing threat of armed conflict. Later in the year, Malaysia and Indonesia signed a joint agreement for better cooperation and formed a committee to conduct antisubversion operations along their common border in East Malaysia.

In February Queen Elizabeth II of Great Britain paid a three-week state visit to Malaysia and was installed as vice-chancellor of the University of Malaya. Prime Minister Tun Abdul Razak made a very successful tour of Eastern Europe and the Soviet Union in October. The Malaysian Airlines System was launched as the national flag carrier following the split-up of Malaysia-Singapore Airlines. (*See in* CE: Malaysia.)

MALDIVES. The visit of Great Britain's Queen Elizabeth II to Maldives in March 1972, during the royal tour of the Indian Ocean, helped improve Britain's relations with the Maldivian government. The queen's gesture of friendship and gifts to education and medicine helped dispel long-standing tension based on official suspicion of British complicity in local unrest.

The queen's trip also eased the delicate relationship with the staging post leased by the Royal Air Force (RAF) on Gan in Addu atoll. The RAF maintained a force of 800 men on Gan. Except on rare occasions, they were not permitted to visit the neighboring settlements. The queen visited Gan for the first time, officially opening the new radio station and meeting the atoll chief, Ahmed Salih Ali Didi. The RAF staging post continued to demonstrate its value as a link between Great Britain and Hong Kong in the defense of Southeast Asia and as an invaluable source of meteorological information for the whole area. (*See in* CE: Maldives, Republic of.)

MALI. In 1972 Mali's foreign relations were marked by a distinct rapprochement with France and with other states of French-speaking Africa. Development of cooperation with the U.S.S.R. also continued.

In April Col. Moussa Traoré, president of Mali's ruling Military Committee for National Liberation (CMLN), paid an official visit to France. President Georges Pompidou renewed an earlier French promise of increased economic and technical assistance, and the two heads of state discussed the problems caused by the influx of Malian immigrant workers into France. During an exchange of visits between Malian and Soviet government defense officials, plans were made for the supply of Soviet equipment to the Malian army. In August Capt. Yoro Diakité, the former vice-president of the CMLN, was sentenced to life imprisonment for his part in an attempted coup. (*See in* CE: Mali.)

MARVINE HOWE FROM "THE NEW YORK TIMES"

Mali's new Functional Literacy courses may help the people earn a better living.

MALTA. A new relationship was established between Malta and Great Britain in 1972. Protracted negotiations more than once reached a critical stage during the first three months of the year. The archbishop of Malta, Secretary-General Joseph Luns of the North Atlantic Treaty Organization (NATO), and the Italian government all intervened

Demonstrators protest the closing of British bases on Malta. They were not pro-British; they disliked layoffs of Maltese workers.

UPI COMPIX

during the discussion, while the withdrawal of British forces from the island proceeded steadily.

Finally, on March 26, an agreement on defense and financial aid was signed in London, superseding the ten-year agreement entered into by the Nationalist government, which was defeated in elections in 1971. Under the new accord, the Malta base could be used only for British and NATO defense purposes, and it could not be used against any Arab country. Great Britain undertook to pay Malta $36 million annually for the next seven years. The Maltese government would also enter into agreements with the Italian, West German, Canadian, and other governments, leading to a further $18 million, part grant and part loan.

Two weeks later Malta's Prime Minister Dominic (Dom) Mintoff concluded an economic agreement in Peking, People's Republic of China. The Chinese government was to provide an interest-free loan of $43 million repayable up to 1994 with commodities exported to China.

On May 16 decimal currency was adopted. The budget for 1972–73 was planned to tackle the ills affecting the Maltese economy. Underlining this plan was a new policy that would limit borrowing to the barest minimum, and then only for economic projects. (*See in* CE: Malta.)

MARRIAGES.

Famous weddings in 1972 included:

David Brinkley, 51, well-known TV news commentator for the National Broadcasting Co., to Susan Benfer Adolph, 32; June 10, at Carter's Grove Plantation near Williamsburg, Va.

WIDE WORLD

Shoichi Yokoi, a sergeant in the Japanese army, hid in the jungles of Guam for 28 years to evade possible captors; he was unaware of any world events after World War II. He was found in 1972 and returned to Japan. There he married Mihoko Hatashin, in a traditional Japanese ceremony. This was the first marriage for both.

Johnny Carson, 46, popular host of TV's long-running Tonight show, to Joanna Holland, 32, actress; September 30, in Santa Monica, Calif.

Patty Duke, 25, stage and film actress who won an Academy Award for 'The Miracle Worker', to John Astin, 42, television actor (The Addams Family); August 5, in Bethesda, Md.

Arthur Garfunkel, 30, former singer (Simon and Garfunkel) and more recently a film actor ('Carnal Knowledge'), to Linda Marie Grossman, 27; October 12, in Nashville, Tenn.

Abraham Ribicoff, 62, U.S. senator (D, Conn.) and former secretary of health, education, and welfare, to Lois Mell Mathes, 50; August 4, in Washington, D.C.

George C. Scott, 44, controversial Academy Award-winning actor ('Patton'), to Patricia Louise Carroll (Trish) Van Devere, 29, actress; September 14, in Santa Monica.

James Taylor, 24, popular singer and composer ('Fire and Rain'), to Carly Simon, 28, also a singer and composer ('That's the Way I've Always Heard It Should Be'); November 3; in New York City.

Peter Ustinov, 51, actor, raconteur, and playwright ('Romanoff and Juliet'), to Hélène du Lau d'Allemans, 34, French socialite; June 17, in Cagnano, Corsica, Italy.

Natalie Wood, 34, film actress ('West Side Story'), to Robert Wagner, 42, television actor (It Takes a Thief); July 16, near Paradise Cove, Calif.

At a party celebrating his 10th anniversary with TV's Tonight show, Johnny Carson announced his recent marriage to actress Joanna Holland.

WIDE WORLD

MAURITANIA. In 1972 there were confrontations between the Mauritanian government and the student movement. In February serious disturbances in the secondary schools led to a large number of expulsions and the temporary closing down of several schools and colleges.

In foreign affairs, the thorny question of the political future of the Spanish Sahara continued to preoccupy President Moktar Ould Daddah, and the debate was pursued with Spanish, Algerian, and Moroccan leaders on several occasions. In June Foreign Minister Hamdi Ould Mouknass officially informed the French government of his country's demand for a revision of Franco-Mauritanian cooperation agreements. Meanwhile, the president strengthened Mauritania's links with neighboring French-speaking states—notably Senegal, which he visited in January and March to discuss the formation of the Organization for the Development of the Senegal River. (*See in* CE: Mauritania.)

MAURITIUS. The first visit to Mauritius by a reigning sovereign took place in March 1972 when Great Britain's Queen Elizabeth II landed on the island during her Indian Ocean tour. Prime Minister Sir Seewoosagur Ramgoolam visited Peking, People's Republic of China, in April, established diplomatic links at the ambassadorial level, and obtained a reported $75-million loan. During the year fueling rights were for the first time granted to Soviet ships. The government in 1972 was increasingly challenged on social conditions by Paul Bérenger's Mauritian Militant Movement and also heard demands for a general election (due in 1972 but postponed until 1976). The number of people unemployed stood at an estimated 50,000 in 1971.

Sugar continued to dominate the economy, providing 97% of the total exports; but diversification into tea, rice, and livestock continued. On May 12 Mauritius became an associate member of the European Economic Community under the Yaoundé Convention. (*See in* CE: Mauritius.)

MEDICINE. Some form of national health insurance in the U.S. seemed likely by perhaps 1973. Several pieces of enabling legislation were before the U.S. Congress at the close of 1972. The issue of national health insurance had been a political football for some time. The American Medical Association (AMA) and other health-industry groups disliked the idea for fear it would permit government infringement upon medical practice. But skyrocketing medical and hospital costs were paving the way for some type of government relief for the general public. Figures showed that the national outlay for health expenses in fiscal 1971, for example, amounted to $75 billion. On the average, the health cost per person for that period was $358.

The two most hotly contested but ideologically opposed plans were the national health insurance standards measure of U.S. President Richard M. Nixon and the health security bill of Senator Edward M. Kennedy (D, Mass.), Rep. Martha W. Griffiths (D, Mich.), and others. President Nixon's plan would provide hospitalization and catastrophic illness coverage at employers' expense. His plan would also provide a maximum $50,000 benefit and would be administered by the insurance industry. The federal government would underwrite insurance costs for families earning less than $3,000 a year, under the Nixon plan. The Kennedy-Griffiths proposal would have the federal government pay 50% to 70% of nearly all U.S. health needs through a broadening of the social security program. The bill's backers claimed that the plan would cost about $68 billion, but critics said the cost would be closer to $77 billion.

LAWRENCE R. PINNEO—STANFORD RESEARCH INSTITUTE

The Programmed Brain Stimulator, devised by Dr. Lawrence R. Pinneo, electrically stimulates parts of the brain to take over for damaged cortical motor cells and produce body movement.

A Doctors' Strike Someday?

Physicians were taking steps to avoid what many of them believed would be eventual government meddling into private practice. One step was the formation of doctors' unions in several urban areas of the U.S. Objections were raised that strikes, the strongest union weapon, would be unethical and probably illegal for professionals providing life-and-death services. Even so, more than 50% of the doctors surveyed in a strike study would walk out under certain circumstances, although they would provide emergency services. Many said an unfavorable national health insurance program would be provocation for a strike.

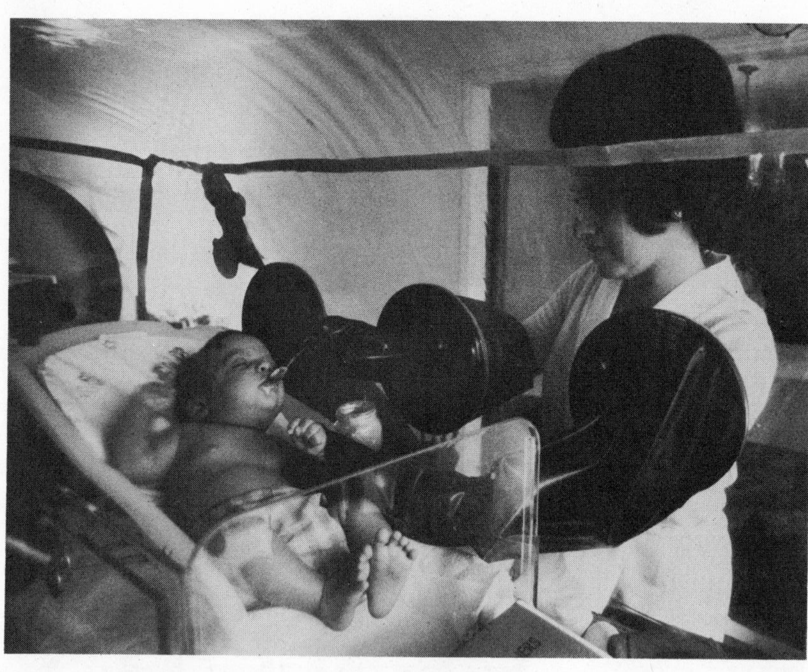

This child was born with "combined immune deficiency" that left him with the very inadequate immunological defenses of a six-week-old embryo. An isolation unit must be his home until he develops greater resistance to disease—which might take as long as two years. To achieve that resistance, doctors at the Clinical Research Center of Texas Children's Hospital in Houston are supplying him with small doses of viruses and bacteria. His mother must use rubber gloves to touch him.

HARRY BENSON FROM LIFE MAGAZINE © TIME INC.

Establishment of foundations for medical care was another step against the feared government control of medicine. A doctor belonging to a medical foundation would provide care for any member-patient and family who paid the monthly fee of $50 or so. Some doctors also found the foundations' peer review procedures attractive. With peer review, doctors judge the competence of other doctors. Detractors felt that this idea was akin to having the fox guard the chicken coop. Nevertheless, physicians generally believed that government control would permit nonphysicians unwarranted power to evaluate medical matters. By 1973 some 200 medical foundations were expected to be operating in the U.S.

Acupuncture No Longer Needled

Much recent attention focused on the ancient Chinese practice of acupuncture, or therapy by needle manipulation. By inserting needles into certain areas of the body, acupuncturists claim to alleviate a long list of ailments ranging from arthritis to impotence. Western physicians had long scoffed at acupuncture but were beginning to accept some of its tenets after their colleagues saw its accomplishments in the People's Republic of China. Particular interest was shown toward acupuncture's pain-killing abilities, particularly during surgery of the head, neck, and thorax. No one was quite sure how acupuncture deadened pain. One theory held that so many nerve impulses from the regions of needle insertion impinged upon pain control centers, or "gates," in the nervous system that the gates became overwhelmed. Then they would no longer transmit impulses to the pain-registering centers of the brain, not even the pain impulses generated during surgery.

In July the National Institutes of Health (NIH) took heed of acupuncture. The NIH announced it would begin a study to test the worth and safety of the procedure.

Baby Killers

The leading cause of death for newborns was hyaline membrane disease (HMD). It struck some 20,000 babies in the U.S. each year. Babies

(*continued on page 350*)

This X ray of the leg bone of a boy born with a bone defect shows electrodes implanted in the bone. Batteries attached to wires send current across the area, promoting healing of the bone.

LEROY S. LAVINE—STATE UNIVERSITY OF NEW YORK

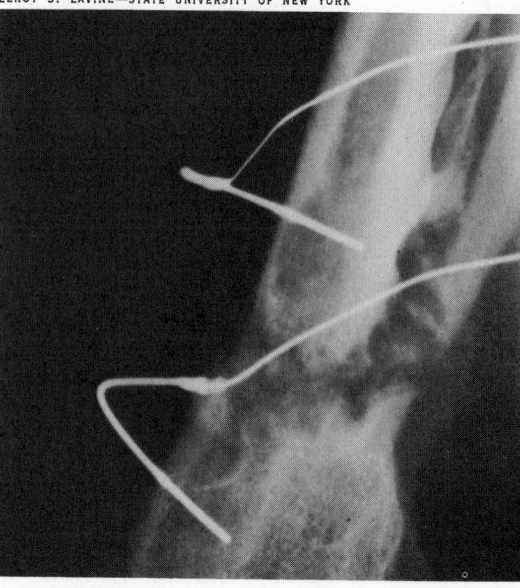

Medicine

Special Report: VENEREAL DISEASE

by Byron Scott

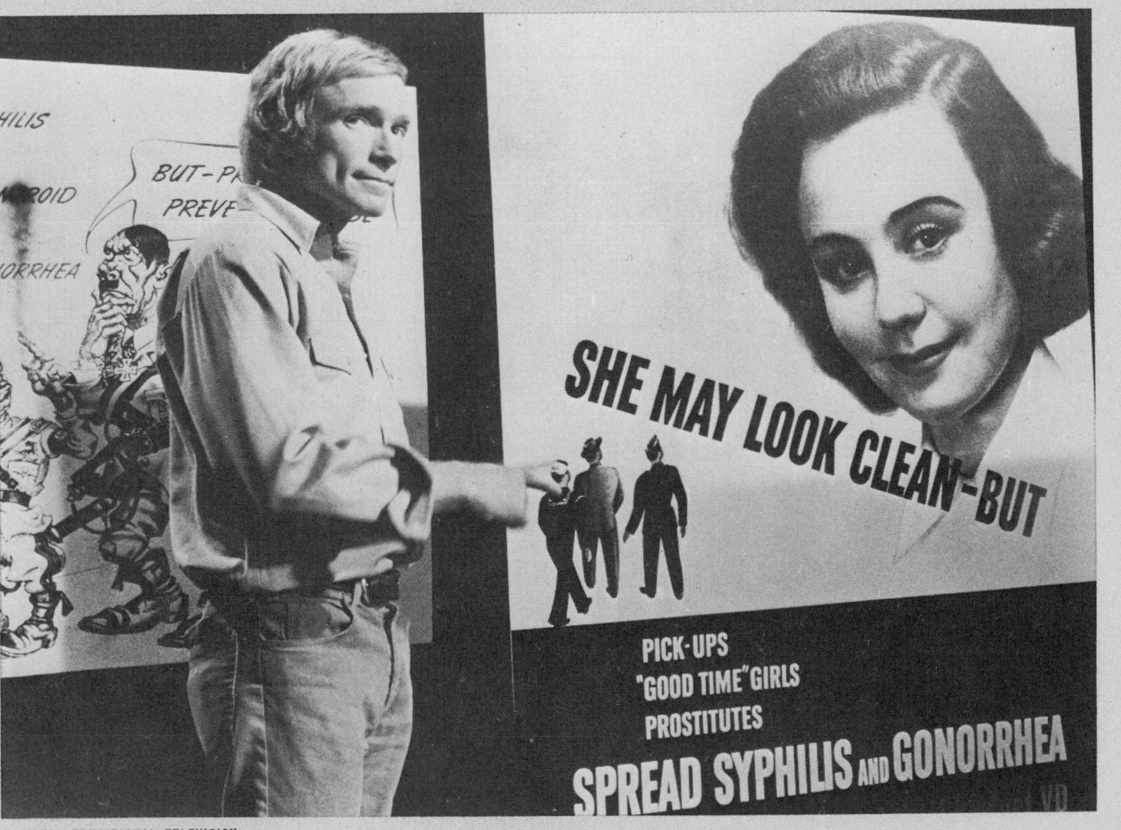

NATIONAL EDUCATIONAL TELEVISION

Dick Cavett hosted a television special called 'VD Blues'. With the use of dramatic vignettes and musical sketches, it focused on the dangerous VD epidemic occurring in the U.S.

Not too long ago, people whispered about "social disease," the code words for the two most common kinds of venereal disease (VD)—syphilis and gonorrhea. Because talk was less frank about VD in the past than it is today, people held a number of myths about how the disease was transmitted. For instance, generations of children grew up believing VD could be contracted from dirty toilet seats, knives and forks, and the like. But VD is transmitted through sexual encounters and not through these other supposed ways for one important reason; the microorganisms that cause VD are so frail that they cannot live for long outside the human body.

Many people, particularly youths, now talk more openly about sex. Yet many delay seeking medical treatment for VD until the infection has damaged their bodies or has been passed on to others. Gonorrhea is the leading communicable disease reported in the U.S. today. The incidence of syphilis is rising, too. VD is a "silent epidemic" of shocking proportions, according to public health officials. This fact is even more regrettable because VD at an early stage can be cured.

The incidence of gonorrhea rose by 15% each year between 1965 and 1972. An estimated 2.5 million new cases of gonorrhea occurred in the U.S. in 1972. The world toll exceeded 100 million gonorrhea cases. As many as 90,000 people in the U.S. may have contracted syphilis, ordinarily the more dangerous form of VD.

Costs of treatment and man-hours of work lost as a result of VD are high. Recent figures showed that it cost more than $47 million each year to treat the blindness or mental illness caused by syphilis. And in 1969 alone, the latest year for available

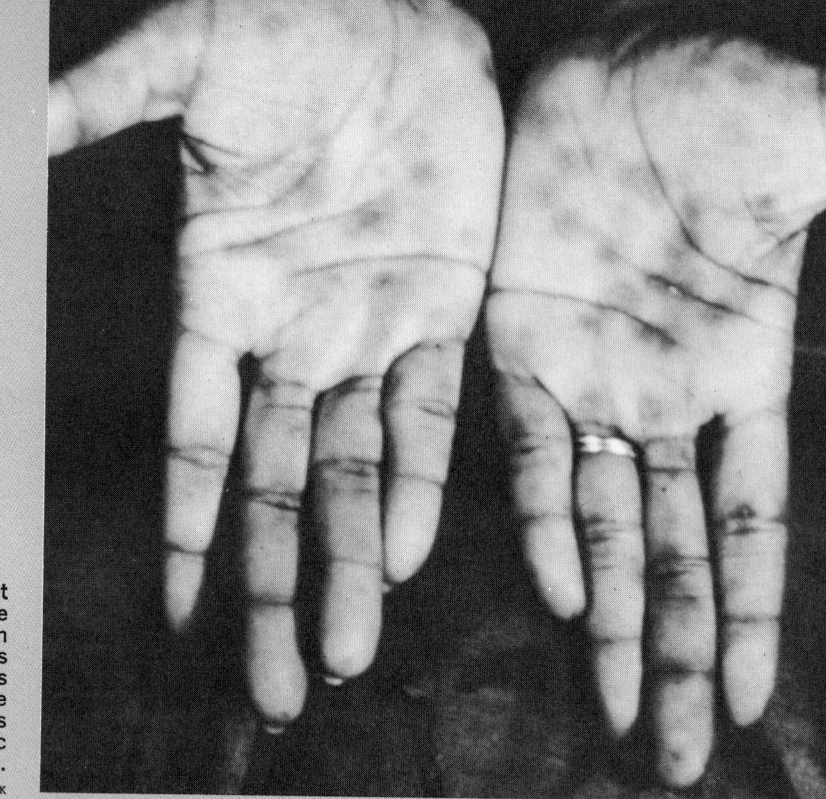

An individual may not be aware that he or she has syphilis until a skin rash breaks out, as much as six months after contracting the disease. These hands bear the symptomatic sores of syphilis.

ED BONK FROM VJK

statistics, these VD victims could have contributed 12,500 man-hours of production to the economy had they remained healthy.

Historical Background

Syphilis has been recognized at least since the 15th century and probably earlier. It was once believed that Christopher Columbus and his crew carried the disease back from the New World because a syphilis epidemic raged in Europe shortly after their return. But many medical historians now believe that the disease was in Europe long before Columbus' time and that some of the ancient "lepers" were really syphilitics.

Gonorrhea appears to be an age-old disease. An ancient Egyptian papyrus seems to make reference to it. Because it often occurred at the same time and place as syphilis, gonorrhea was long thought to be just an early stage of syphilis. In 1879, however, scientists were certain that gonorrhea was a distinct disease because they found the microorganism that caused it, a gonococcus called *Neisseria gonorrhoeae.* In 1905 the corkscrew-shaped microorganism called *Treponema pallidum* was discovered to be the cause of syphilis.

Until the early 1940's, syphilis and gonorrhea were treated with a variety of palliatives, including mercury, bismuth, and derivatives of arsenic. Then, in 1943, scientists found that both forms of VD could be dramatically arrested with the newly discovered antibiotic penicillin. Thereafter, people began to grow complacent over VD.

The U.S. Public Health Service (USPHS) warned that by the late 1960's syphilis was on the rise again. By the early 1970's gonorrhea was raging out of control. Other figures amassed by the American Social Health Association showed that, alarmingly, one out of every four cases of VD was suffered by a person who was 21 years old or *younger.* Furthermore, a certain number of cases —perhaps as many as 35% of the syphilitic cases among males in one major city—arose from homosexual encounters. Medical authorities viewed the VD epidemic as critical but not hopeless.

VD Treatment

In 1972, as public alarm about the VD epidemic reached Washington, D.C., federal legislators reacted by infusing an extra $16 million into the battle for gonorrhea control. Most of the funds were funneled into programs for detecting the disease in female carriers, the so-called reservoirs of the disease. The USPHS Center for Disease Control estimated there might be from 640,000 to one million women in the U.S. who harbor the disease.

Three times as many males as females seek medical relief from gonorrhea because about 90% of the men who are afflicted suffer painful symptoms of the disease, usually within three to five days after infection. By contrast, if females experience symptoms at all, they note only a slight vaginal discharge. To detect female carriers, many medical organizations are recommending that doctors check for gonorrhea when female patients have their regular Pap test for cervical cancer, thus avoiding undue embarrassment to the patient. Smears can then be sent to any of the widely located screening centers, where they would be checked for presence of the gonorrhea gonococcus.

Treatment for gonorrhea is simple. When laboratory tests confirm the infection in a woman, she is treated with two penicillin injections at a single time, a total dosage of 4.8 million units of the antibiotic. Infected males receive two shots also, but the dosage is generally reduced by half to 2.4 million units of penicillin. In areas of the country where penicillin-resistant strains of the gonorrhea organism are prevalent, both sexes receive the higher dosage. Syphilis is also treated with penicillin, but the patient must visit the clinic or doctor's office more than once for injections until the tougher syphilis organism is eliminated. If the VD sufferer is allergic or sensitive to penicillin, another antibiotic, such as tetracycline, can knock out the disease, although it takes longer.

VD Symptoms and Effects

The symptoms of gonorrhea in males rarely go unnoticed. As early as three to five days after an infecting sexual encounter, gonococci invade the tissue wall of the urethra, the tube in the penis that conveys urine from the bladder. The difficult and painful urination that follows this invasion, accompanied by a discharge of pus and mucus, is a sure sign that a case of the "clap," as gonorrhea is colloquially called, has been contracted. Although this sudden crisis might quickly pass, medical aid should be sought immediately. The infection could damage fragile sex structures and cause sterility.

The symptoms of gonorrhea in females frequently go unnoticed because the urinary discomfort, when it occurs, is usually not too painful and the discharge, if any, is minimal. Unless a female receives medical attention at this time, she may become an asymptomatic carrier and pass the disease along in future sexual contacts. When the gonococci penetrate into the body systems, however, a female can suffer serious consequences. If the infection reaches the ovaries, ovarian tubes, and other parts of the reproductive system, scar tissue can render the victim sterile. So too can the surgery required in some cases. Tragically, a pregnant woman with gonorrhea might infect her newborn as it moves through the birth passage and cause blindness. For years, babies have had their eyes bathed with antibiotics to prevent this. Even so, more than 10% of all blindness is caused by congenital gonorrhea. Acute arthritis, resulting when the gonococci invade body joints, is another serious complication of the disease that can affect males and females alike.

If scientists could grow the microorganisms that cause syphilis, it might be possible to develop a skin test to diagnose the disease.

AUTHENTICATED NEWS INTERNATIONAL

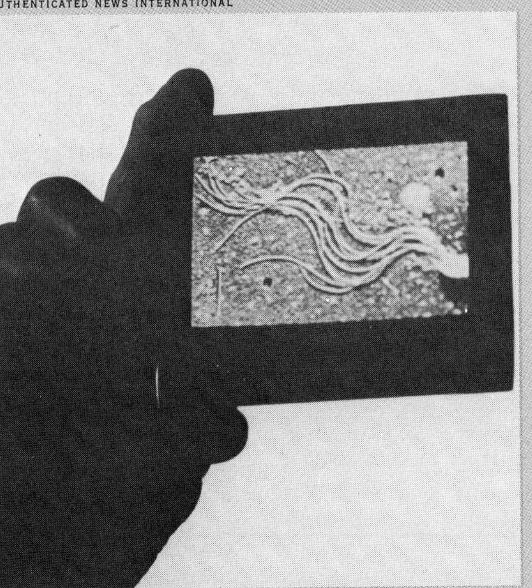

The first, or primary, symptom of the highly dangerous syphilis is ordinarily painless. A firm sore called a chancre (pronounced *shanker*) usually develops on the sex organs, but it can appear on lips or tonsils. A chancre may develop from 48 hours to 10 days or more after sexual contact. At any time from 2 weeks to 6 months later, a skin rash may break out on the body. The victim then has secondary syphilis and must no longer delay a visit to a doctor for treatment. If unchecked, the disease may eventually get to the late stage, when the syphilis organisms often lodge in the heart, blood vessels, and brain and cause irreparable and perhaps fatal damage. The complications of syphilis are not restricted to either sex; they strike men and women alike. Another sad result of the disease in expectant mothers is its possible transference to the developing baby. Since the syphilitic chancre may be hidden in the female genital tract, regular gynecological observations are needed to detect the disease.

The Fight Against VD

People cannot develop an immunity to VD after being stricken by it. Thus, a cycle of infection and reinfection often takes place until the reservoirs of the disease are dried up. Many states require an investigation after each fresh case of VD to find and treat the carrier and, they hope, break the cycle. A drawback of this is the reluctance of many doctors to report VD cases so their patients will be spared embarrassment. However, the case work is done by investigators who operate as tactfully as possible. Recent state laws allowing VD treatment for minors without parental consent have eased the control problem somewhat; still, more adults than youths get VD.

VD vaccines are under study, but they probably will not be available for a while. In the meantime, the epidemic continues to spread, mainly because of public ignorance or embarrassment. Until a foolproof method of prevention is at hand, medical authorities implore people to seek treatment at the first signs of VD. And to offset ignorance of the disease, particularly among the young, educators and public health officials urge far-reaching programs of sex education in the schools and the communications media.

(*continued from page 346*)
suffering from the disease lack at birth a fluid needed for proper oxygen transfer in the lungs. If an HMD baby survives the first three days of independent life, it usually makes the vital fluid. A Montreal, Que., scientist found that steroid drugs could induce production of the fluid. Clinical tests were under way in 1972 to learn if babies given steroids at birth or even before would be free of HMD.

The leading cause of death for one-week- to one-year-old infants was sudden infant death syndrome (SIDS). Crib deaths occur with shocking swiftness, frequently without any sign of trouble. SIDS killed some 10,000 infants each year in the U.S. Its cause was unknown, but researchers noted that it occurred most frequently in winter. In Great Britain, where SIDS is also called cot death, scientists claimed to have uncovered a virus linked with the tragic disorder.

Trends in Medical Attitudes

Family practice, an updated form of general practice, was appealing to a growing number of medical students and young doctors. Family practice differs from general practice in the emphasis it gives to disease prevention and health maintenance in patients. General practitioners frequently engage in "crisis" medicine, treating patients only when they are sick. The swing to family practice after the popularity of limited specialty or research work was seen as an attempt by young doctors to regain an empathy with the general population, an empathy that some felt had been on the wane.

Physicians were also concerned over their role in public issues. When AMA journals printed Federal Bureau of Investigation "wanted" notices, medical spokesmen complained they were being asked to violate traditional doctor-patient pacts.

Clinical Developments

Probably the most dramatic therapeutic feat of 1972 involved the total body washout of a U.S. airman in a coma from hepatitis. In March doctors at a U.S. Air Force medical center in San Antonio, Tex., temporarily flushed out all the airman's blood, which harbored hepatitis-causing Australia antigen (AuA), while replacing it with a colorless solution called Ringer's lactate. The airman's "blood supply" kept him alive for nearly ten minutes until a supply of new blood was pumped into him. The patient awoke from his coma hours later without apparent ill effects from the perfusion.

Hepatitis resulting from transfusions of blood from blood banks was a major type of the liver-damaging disease. Scientists in Boston, Mass., reported a possible end to transfusion hepatitis with a filter capable of clearing AuA from the blood. President Nixon ordered the Department of Health, Education, and Welfare (HEW) to plan an effective system of blood banking.

"LONDON DAILY EXPRESS" FROM PICTORIAL PARADE

Scientists from the U.S. Department of Agriculture dry samples of *Maytenus ovatus*, a plant that may contain an anticancer agent.

A vaccine against dreaded meningitis was tested among Connecticut schoolchildren after it was proved safe among U.S. Army recruits. The school trials would help determine whether the vaccine was suitable for nationwide use. Authorization would come from the Division of Biologics Standards, which was transferred from the NIH to the Food and Drug Administration in 1972.

Ultrasonics, the use of high-frequency sound, was proving to be a safe substitute for X rays in early examinations of possible pregnancies. Echoes from high-frequency sound waves reflected off tissues in various ways to offer gynecologists and obstetricians information about the presence of one or more developing fetuses, ovarian tumors, and the like. Unlike X rays, ultrasonic waves pose no threat to a developing fetus.

CANCER

Cancer, in one of its 100 or so forms, continued to be the number two killer in the U.S., topped only by heart disease. About 640,000 persons acquired cancer in 1972 and about 350,000 died of it.

An expensive research program patterned after the successful U.S. space program was put into action. The National Cancer Institute (NCI) received a $1.6-billion appropriation spread over three years for its cancer fight. However, many researchers felt that an understanding and eventual cure of the disease was still far off despite the publicity given the anticancer crusade.

The good news concerning cancer in 1972 was that the three-year survival rates were increasing for a number of cancer patients, including those having cancer of the bladder, cervix, or breast. The survival rate was also on the rise for chronic and childhood leukemia. The bad news was that the incidence of the most common form of cancer among males—lung cancer—was growing. Some 62,000 lung cancer cases developed in 1972, and 56,000 deaths occurred.

Virus Cause Still Eyed

A cancer cure has proved elusive for so long because the disease is embroiled in the mysterious innermost functioning of the cell. By 1972 most cancer researchers believed that viruses were somehow involved in triggering the rapid, uncontrolled cell growth that characterizes the disease.

Viruses had long been known to cause some animal cancers but none had yet been discovered for human varieties. Nonetheless, researchers had found viral antigens, likened to "footprints," in the blood of cancer patients. Presence of the antigens further implicated viruses with cancer.

Dr. Robert Huebner of the NCI believed that the seeds of cancer were part of human heredity. His "oncogene" theory advocated that cancer was caused by a noninfectious virus called a C particle, a tiny bit of ribonucleic acid (RNA) passed from generation to generation. The C particle might even play a part in early development of a fertilized egg by causing the cells of the embryo to grow. Some scientists saw a similarity between the rapid growth of a fetus and that of cancer cells. According to Huebner, the C particle should become inactive after birth, but if it should reactivate in later life it would trigger cancerous cell growth.

A further tie-in of fetal and cancer cells was noted by Dr. M. Judah Folkman of the Harvard Medical School, who found that tumor cells get needed nourishment for growth by releasing a protein called tumor angiogenesis factor (TAF). TAF caused capillaries, or tiny blood vessels, to grow into the cancerous mass. Without TAF, a tumor could never grow larger than a pinhead because blood would not be available to bring in nutrients and carry away toxic wastes. TAF is present in fetal cells but not in normal adult cells.

Use of the body's own defenses has shown some effectiveness against cancer. Study continued during 1972 on the treatment of leukemia patients with an antituberculosis vaccine called BCG. The theory was that BCG and other agents caused a souped-up response by the body's immunological system against the foreign cancer cells. This immune response resulted in some remissions of leukemia and skin cancer.

HEART

Heart and blood vessel disease continued as the leading cause of death in the U.S. Heart attacks alone claimed an estimated 675,000 persons during the year. Strokes killed some 210,000 victims. Heart disease had long been thought of as an affliction of the elderly, but recent statistics showed that a growing number of victims were persons under 65 years of age and frequently only in middle age. Some medical authorities blamed this rising incidence of heart malfunction on life-styles marked by rich diets, heavy cigarette smoking, sedentary work and entertainment habits, and a high degree of tension.

The National Heart Act was signed in September to spur clinical investigation and basic research into heart disease. It authorized the National Heart and Lung Institute (NHLI) to spend nearly $1.4 billion over a three-year period in the fight against crippling and fatal heart, lung, blood, and blood vessel disorders. The American Heart Association (AHA) also stepped up its research expenditures with a $16-million outlay, the largest ever.

Hypertension, or high blood pressure, was found to be a particular threat to blacks. For unknown reasons, twice as many blacks as whites suffered from hypertension, a "silent" disease because people frequently do not realize that they have it. In 1972 the AHA made an effort to help set up screening centers in black communities for the detection of hypertension sufferers. Nearly all cases of the disorder can be controlled with drugs after it has been uncovered.

NHLI researchers implanted an artificial heart system powered by a tiny nuclear engine into an experimental animal early in the year. The feat was part of a long-term study of the feasibility of artificial hearts. One NHLI scientist went so far as to predict that some heart patients would receive artificial implants by the close of the 1970's. Still to be learned, however, was how living tissue reacted over long periods to the heat generated by the implants powered by plutonium 238.

An operation that reestablished the blood flow to starved heart muscle was in vogue in 1972.

This two-inch-long, 3/4-inch-wide nuclear battery is an implanted heart pacemaker that will last for ten years.

CAMERA PRESS FROM PICTORIAL PARADE

Technically called aortocoronary saphenous vein bypass, the procedure consisted of removing a section of the saphenous vein from a patient's leg and grafting it between the aorta (the large artery emerging from the heart) and a point in the heart's own coronary artery where the graft would bypass any obstruction that deprived the heart of vital blood. However, bypass surgery remained a controversial procedure throughout the year because many doctors felt that the risky operation had not yet conclusively lengthened the life expectancy of heart patients.

PUBLIC HEALTH

Probably the most pressing public health problem of 1972 was the venereal disease (VD) raging in epidemic proportions in the U.S. An estimated 2.5 million persons had gonorrhea, the more prevalent form of VD, and another 100,000 persons acquired syphilis, the more serious form. The National Commission on Venereal Disease, composed of public health authorities, recommended that some $300 million in U.S. funds be spent over a five-year period in the battle against VD. Meanwhile, a $16-million screening program was under way in 1972 in the hope of finding more than 600,000 symptomless carriers of gonorrhea. (*See* Medicine Special Report.)

Many scientists and others expressed moral outrage at a study carried out over the preceding 40 years on the effects of syphilis on the human body. Called the Tuskegee Study, it involved more than 400 blacks whose syphilis was deliberately untreated, even after the advent of VD-smashing antibiotics in the 1940's, to allow the U.S. Public Health Service (USPHS) to determine the full effects of the disease after their death. In 1972 a federal investigation was looking into the study, which had not yet been canceled although medical aid was belatedly being given to the survivors of the 1932 study.

Early in the year Surgeon General Jesse L. Steinfeld of the USPHS issued a report that made cigarette smoking a public as well as a personal health problem. According to Steinfeld, cigarette smoke contained dangerous levels of carbon monoxide that could hamper the respiration of smokers and nonsmokers alike in smoke-filled enclosures.

Smallpox appeared to be on a slight rise in some areas of the world for the second consecutive year. A smallpox alert was sounded in March at U.S. ports of entry as a result of a severe outbreak in Yugoslavia. Nonetheless, the World Health Organization (WHO) was confident that smallpox would be swept from those and all other areas by the end of the 1970's. Officials felt that the WHO vaccination efforts in regions of the world where smallpox was prevalent would be successful.

About a dozen students at a Christian Science prep school in Connecticut were stricken by polio in October and a few of them were paralyzed. The remaining students, faculty members, and workers were quickly immunized against the disease. Because of religious beliefs, few of the students had ever received polio vaccine.

SURGERY

Dr. John H. Knowles, former director of Massachusetts General Hospital and in 1972 head of the Rockefeller Foundation, riled many of his fellow physicians by charging that too much unnecessary surgery was being performed in the U.S. As evidence, he pointed out that some health maintenance organizations providing prepaid medical

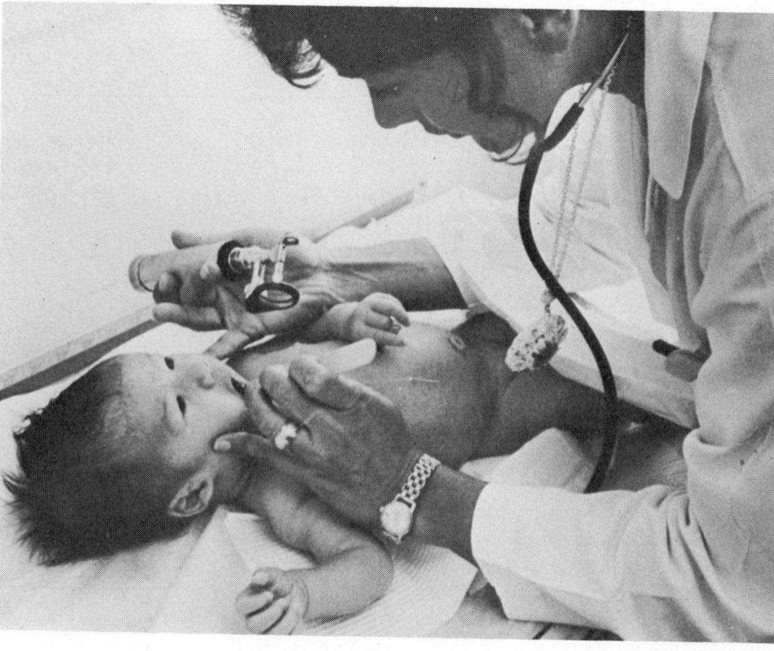

This underdeveloped baby in California is checked for scurvy and rickets. Parents who subscribe to Zen macrobiotics feed their children a diet of mainly grains and a few vegetables. These foods do not provide enough calcium, vitamin C, or protein for children. It has not been determined what long-term effects this nutritional deprivation may have on a growing child.

JAMES D. WILSON FROM NEWSWEEK

care for subscribers required the services of only 6 general surgeons per 100,000 persons, while throughout the nation as a whole, more than twice as many general surgeons were in practice—13 per 100,000 persons. Knowles felt that some surgeons were "making a killing"—that is, were earning more than $50,000 a year through excessive charges. The Massachusetts doctor had been the subject of controversy before. In 1969 he was denied the nation's top medical position, that of assistant secretary for health and scientific affairs in HEW, because of views on national health care unacceptable to the more conservative AMA.

Two British radiologists charged that the removal of tonsils and adenoids from some children could affect the way they talk and swallow. Should mechanical damage occur during tonsillectomies or adenoidectomies—common operations for children—the children could grow up with speech impediments, the X-ray specialists said. Such damage might occur in one of every 1,000 cases.

The vasectomy was an increasingly popular means of sterilizing males. But many men feared the side effects of that operation. In 1972 a new sterilization operation for women proved faster, simpler, and cheaper than the old one.

Status of Transplant Surgery

At the start of 1972, statistics showed that kidney transplantation was the most common and the most successful kind of transplant surgery. More than 7,500 kidney transplantations had taken place by the beginning of 1972, and an estimated 3,000 recipients were alive at the time the survey was made for a register kept by the American College of Surgeons in Chicago. Lung transplantation was the least successful. Of 28 lung transplantations performed by the time of the survey, there were no survivors.

Psychiatrists discovered that transplant patients sometimes experienced mental problems associated with their physical plight. One psychiatrist who worked with kidney transplant patients noted that they "fear their lives will be cut short by an untimely death . . . [and fear] that even if they live, their lives may not be acceptable." Surgeons who performed many successful kidney transplantations, however, stressed that most of their patients were rehabilitated physically and mentally after the surgery and were happy to be alive.

Surgeons in New York and Minnesota reported the successful transplantations of human pancreases in patients suffering diabetes. Pancreas transplants in the past had failed because the body's immunological system rejected them. However, in the recent successes, surgeons blocked the body's immune defenses by leaving the old, defective pancreas in place and sewing the new one to another site, such as the small intestine. The new pancreas secreted vital insulin, while the old one somehow shielded its counterpart from antibody attacks from the immunological system.

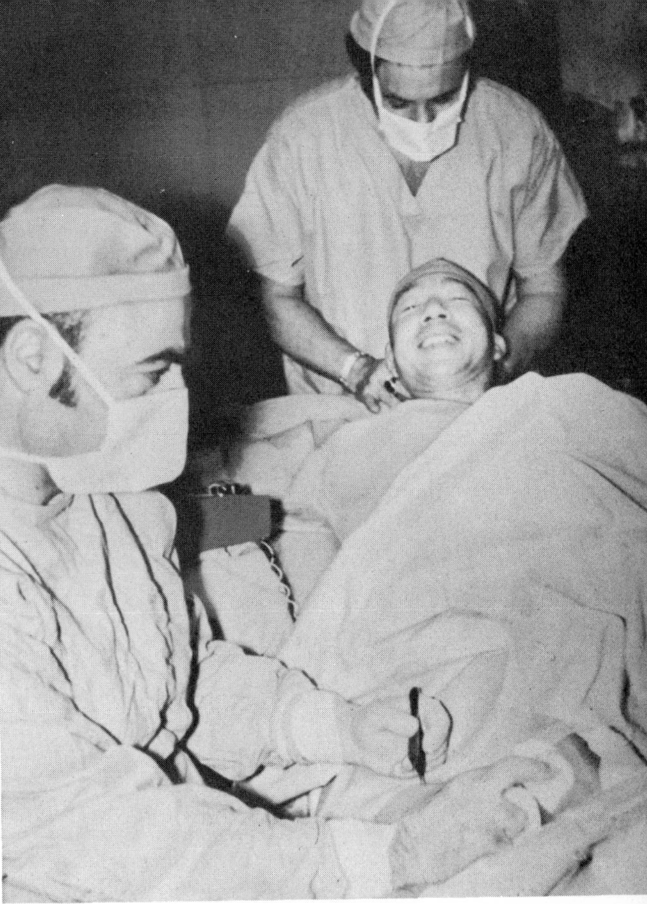

WIDE WORLD

Dr. Pang L. Man, who had inserted acupuncture needles between his thumbs and forefingers, smiles as he experiences painless surgery on his leg.

Other surgical techniques to aid the millions of diabetics throughout the world were under development in 1972. In St. Louis, Mo., a team developed a technique on animals for transplanting only that part of the pancreas which produces insulin. In Boston and Los Angeles, scientists were looking into a tiny implantable mechanical pancreas that worked somewhat the same way as a heart pacemaker. (*See also* Dentistry; Hospitals; Nursing; Veterinary Medicine. *See in* CE: Medicine; Surgery.)

MENTAL HEALTH. At one time the mentally ill were sent off for care to large hospitals, often far from home and family. But a noticeable trend in 1972 was toward mental health treatment in a patient's own community. For example, California planned to phase out all of its large state mental hospitals and replace them with community mental health facilities where treatment, rehabilitation, and job training could be conducted as close to home as possible. This form of aid to the mentally ill received its impetus from the Community Mental Health Centers Act passed by the U.S. Congress in 1963.

The National Institute of Mental Health (NIMH), administrator of the system of com-

"THE NEW YORK TIMES"

Dr. Ronald R. Fieve says that there is evidence that a predisposition to manic-depressive illness may be transmitted by a defective gene on the X chromosome.

munity mental health centers, was severely criticized by a Ralph Nader task force in 1972. The Nader team's study blasted the NIMH for the manner in which it opened and operated the 325 community health centers in the U.S. It charged that the facilities were "seriously at odds" with individual and group needs and that the community mental health centers program was "vastly oversold." The Nader study further charged that the NIMH made little attempt to train people for community work, avoided funding centers outside the narrow confines of the medical model, and did not engage consumers in the planning or operation of the centers. Officials of the NIMH and others retorted that the study was unbalanced and inaccurate. But they conceded that it could be helpful in reviewing and evaluating procedures and practices in the community mental health movement.

Mental health was forcefully thrust onto the national scene with the short-lived Democratic vice-presidential candidacy of Senator Thomas F. Eagleton (D, Mo.). Shortly after his selection as the running mate of Senator George S. McGovern (D, S.D.), it was learned that he had once undergone psychiatric treatment for depression, a prevalent form of mental illness. Eagleton was dropped from the ticket, but some felt this was improper because mental illness no longer carried its former stigma. This was especially apparent in view of the growing evidence that nearly every U.S. family had had a member who suffered from mental disease.

Psychiatrists and others argued that abnormal brain chemistry might be at the root of schizophrenia. Much research in 1972 was aimed at finding a biochemical cause for the ailment. A prime suspect was a defective form of a protein called alpha-2 globulin. Normal alpha-2 globulin controls other vital chemicals that affect transmission of nerve impulses. But abnormal alpha-2 globulin increases the production of brain chemicals that eventually trigger hallucinatory states. It was hoped that an enzyme could be devised to normalize the aberrant chemical and thus restore proper biochemical levels in the brains of schizophrenics. (*See also* Medicine; Psychology. *See in* CE: Mental Health.)

This paper recycling business is a job-training activity for clients of Conbela, a halfway house for former mental patients in Seattle, Wash.

WIDE WORLD

METALS. There were some indications in 1972 that the metals market was recovering from its 1970–71 slump, but fluctuations in prices and continued U.S. price controls made any overall assessment difficult. For the most part, the price controls combined with a relatively close balance between supply and demand to keep metal prices stable. Gold and silver, however, were notable exceptions, partially because of speculation. The U.S. revaluation of gold from $35 to $38 an ounce in April triggered a massive upward swing of gold prices. On April 3 the open market price was about $48; by August the price had risen to more than $70, and speculators were predicting continued increases. The market eventually stabilized, with gold fluctuating between $63 and $67 for the remainder of the year. A major factor in the stabilization had been closer agreement among International Monetary Fund nations on future international exchange policies. South Africa, however, was accused of withholding newly mined gold from the market to push prices higher. Silver prices were also volatile for most of the year; the lifting of the U.S. price ceiling of $1.61 an ounce on August 10 promoted increased speculation.

Copper, lead, zinc, and aluminum markets all displayed weakness in the second half of 1972. Price hikes by major copper, lead, and zinc producers caused some confusion. Mercury prices also vacillated greatly during the year. Reports of future use of platinum and palladium in emission control devices on U.S. automobiles elevated prices for those metals.

The U.S. steel industry continued to be plagued by low productivity compared with other steel-producing nations. The flood of imported steel into the U.S. was curbed by an agreement between the U.S. government and major Japanese and European producers to limit imports into the U.S. for three years. Research and development in steel and other metals industries focused on problems of environmental control. (*See in* CE: Metals.)

MEXICO. A good deal of Mexico's legislative action in 1972 was designed to remedy the country's political, social, and economic deficiencies. Efforts were made to modernize the Institutional Revolutionary party, which dominates Mexican politics. Firm action continued against abuses of power by individuals in privileged positions. In the international sphere, Mexico's President Luis Echeverría Alvarez spoke bluntly, on a visit to the U.S., concerning matters that had caused tension between the two neighbors.

Efforts were made to involve younger people in the country's political life. A bill was put before the Congress lowering by four years the minimum age for candidates for deputy, to 21, and by five years the minimum age for senators, to 30. Changes were also made in the electoral system to give greater weight to the opposition.

A nationwide scheme to provide low-cost housing for workers was adopted in 1972. Those whose income did not exceed ten times the statutory minimum wage could obtain loans at favorable rates of interest, repayable over a period of 15 years, to buy, build, or improve their homes. The plan was welcomed as a stimulus to industry, particularly the construction business.

Another incentive to industry was a decree promulgated in July that set forth a program for decentralization and regional development. When the legislation was introduced, 56% of the country's industrial output was produced in the Federal District. A total of 14.6% of Mexico's population lived there and contributed 46% of the gross domestic product. To correct this imbalance, the decree divided the country into three zones, offering graded incentives to attract new plants away from

Mexico's President Luis Echeverría Alvarez spoke at a session of the U.S. Congress in June, calling for closer U.S.-Mexican relations.

PICTORIAL PARADE

the capital, where overconcentration of industry had created pollution and overcrowding.

The government took over some of the country's leading businesses in 1972, though no indication was seen that any political or economic plan was involved. All the companies affected were caught by tight credit and owed the government large sums of money.

Mexico launched a national program for family planning in 1972. In April the minister of health declared that the country would not have the resources necessary to supply its people if the current population of 51 million were to double—an eventual result of the 3.4% annual growth rate.

Breaking away from the relative isolation of its past, Mexico intensified contacts with other countries in 1972, mainly to promote trade. The president visited the U.S., Chile, and Japan. During his visit to Washington, D.C., in June, Echeverría spoke frankly of his country's displeasure concerning the damage to agriculture caused when U.S. industrial effluent is poured into the Colorado River. U.S. President Richard M. Nixon promised to take immediate steps to alleviate the situation.

As recovery proceeded slowly from the recession that began in mid-1970, authorities decided to relax their anti-inflation policies somewhat in 1972 to bring up the growth rate. Public investment was raised by 16.4%, and business conditions gradually rose to a satisfactory level by the year's end with the help of higher receipts from tourism, increased export earnings, good harvests, the new housing program, and greater purchasing power resulting from wage and salary increases from January 1.

On February 2 the government announced that Genaro Vásquez Rojas, leader of leftist guerrillas in the state of Guerrero, had been killed in a car crash. But his followers said he was killed by government troops. (*See in* CE: Mexico.)

MIDDLE EAST. The situation in the Middle East in 1972 continued to be dominated by the Arab-Israeli conflict, which was marked by a state of "no war, no peace" between Israel and the Arab nations and by the increasingly international nature of Palestinian guerrilla terrorism. There were no major military encounters between Arab and Israeli forces, and there was no break in the political deadlock that had paralyzed prospects for peace negotiations.

Pursuing its policy of integrating occupied Arab territories into the Israeli economy, Israel further consolidated its hold on these areas. Trade and tourism between Jordan and the Israeli-occupied region on the west bank of the Jordan River flourished, and Israel's defense minister called for a similar policy with Lebanon. Sanctioned by Israel, municipal elections were held in the west-bank area for the first time since the 1967 war. (*See* Israel.)

In January the U.S. attempted to revive interest in its plan for a partial Middle East settlement based on the reopening of the Suez Canal. Israel agreed to indirect "close proximity" talks with Egypt on the proposal, but Egypt's President Anwar el-Sadat rejected talks in which the U.S. would mediate, holding out for a renewal of United Nations (UN) mediation by diplomat Gunnar Jarring of Sweden. Jarring's mission, which had been suspended early in 1971 after having failed to make progress, was resumed in February 1972 when he visited Egypt, Jordan, and Israel. In June UN Secretary-General Kurt Waldheim declared the mission at an impasse once more. The U.S. continued to urge proximity talks, without avail. A communiqué issued after the summit meeting between U.S. President Richard M. Nixon and Soviet leaders in May reaffirmed the superpowers' support for a peaceful Middle East settlement "in accordance with UN Security Council Resolution 242," but it offered no concrete proposals.

WIDE WORLD

Israel's Defense Minister Moshe Dayan was active in the nation's internal and external affairs in 1972. Here he pauses while considering the problems of occupied Jordan.

The only new initiative for a settlement was a proposal by King Hussein I of Jordan for the establishment of a United Arab Kingdom, which would unite the Jordanian east and west banks under the monarchy through semiautonomous regional governments. The proposal was rejected by Israel and condemned by the Palestinian guerrilla organiza-

UPI COMPIX

In January Arab guerrillas ambushed an American Baptist minister's car, killing an American nurse and wounding the missionary and his daughter. Israeli soldiers search Arab residents of Gaza in an effort to find the guerrillas.

tions and most Arab governments, and it led Egypt to break diplomatic relations with Jordan.

New Guerrilla Strategy

In the spring the Palestinian guerrilla organizations, seriously weakened by their expulsion from Jordan in 1970 and 1971, took steps to resolve their differences and unify their forces. The Palestine National Council, which serves as a parliament for exiled Palestinians and as the legislature of the Palestine Liberation Organization (PLO), decided at a congress in April to merge all guerrilla forces, expand the council to include groups not represented, and elect a new leadership that would include Palestinians outside the commando organizations. Merger plans were to be drawn up by the PLO executive committee.

Arab guerrilla terrorism against Israeli targets in 1972 became increasingly spectacular and international in scope and brought into prominence the underground Black September group, considered by some a secret arm of the *al Fatah* organization. Black September claimed credit for sabotaging West German manufacturers of equipment for Israeli forces, and in May the group hijacked a Belgian airliner to Israel in an unsuccessful attempt to obtain the release of imprisoned guerrillas.

Later that month Middle East tensions were sharply increased by a massacre in Israel's Lod International Airport near Tel Aviv, Israel, carried out by Japanese terrorists acting for the Popular Front for the Liberation of Palestine (PFLP). The PFLP declared that the operation was a reprisal for Israel's killing of innocent Arabs and that it did not consider tourists in Israel as civilians. King Hussein of Jordan condemned the massacre, while Egypt's prime minister saw it as evidence that Israel was not invincible. Israel retaliated with attacks on guerrilla camps in Lebanon, which in turn produced a crisis in relations between the guerrillas and the Lebanese government. This was resolved by an accord under which the guerrillas agreed to temporarily suspend action against Israel from southern Lebanon, establish a disciplinary unit to punish violators, and withdraw from some areas near Israel. The Israeli reprisals were condemned by a UN Security Council resolution, which also called for Israel to return captured Syrian and Lebanese officers; Israel refused to return prisoners except in a general prisoner exchange.

The September 5 slaying of 11 Israeli athletes and coaches attending the Olympic Games in Munich, West Germany, by members of Black Sep-

BEHRENDT—HET PAROOL, AMSTERDAM, FROM BEN ROTH AGENCY

Waiting for Sadat

tember had wide repercussions in the Middle East and elsewhere, brought terrorism to the forefront of international concern, and shattered prospects for peace negotiations. The Munich killings were followed by a guerrilla letter-bomb campaign against Israeli officials and Jews in many nations, by the killing of several Israeli diplomats, and by West Germany's release of the three Black Septembrists captured in Munich as ransom for a hijacked West German airliner.

Israel retaliated for the Munich massacre with the heaviest attacks since 1967 on guerrilla bases in Syria and Lebanon and called for other nations to restrict Palestinian activities—generally embarking on a policy of initiating action against guerrillas. As a result of the Israeli reprisals, Lebanon imposed new restrictions on guerrilla activities, and there was an armed uprising against *al Fatah's* moderate leadership by dissidents who refused to go along with a diminished guerrilla role in Lebanon.

The wave of terrorism led several nations to take steps toward identifying and screening out potentially dangerous Arabs. West Germany banned two Palestinian organizations and cracked down severely on Palestinians and other Arabs living in the country. By October Arab complaints of harsh treatment in Western nations had begun to produce an anti-Western mood in the Arab world. In the UN Security Council the U.S. vetoed a resolution that would have ended all Middle Eastern military operations but did not ban terrorist acts such as the Munich slayings. Arab and African nations in the UN General Assembly succeeded in blocking a Western proposal for an international conference on ending terrorism.

There was general agreement among both Arabs and Israelis that the rash of international Palestinian terrorism in 1972 was due to the failure of Palestinians to reach their goals through diplomacy and more conventional guerrilla tactics, and to the inability of Arab guerrillas to circumvent Israeli security measures and the restrictions imposed by Arab governments. The guerrillas saw their acts as a means of dramatizing their cause to the world, of boosting their morale after many failures, and of prodding moderate Arabs into taking a more militant stand.

The Arab Nations

Early in the year there was evidence of disillusionment among Arabs over the continuing Middle East stalemate and the Soviet Union's failure to break the deadlock in the Arabs' favor. Egypt became increasingly dissatisfied with the Soviets' refusal to deliver advanced offensive weapons, and on July 18 President Sadat announced that he had asked the Soviets to withdraw their military advisers from Egypt. Following the Soviet withdrawal, Egypt planned a campaign aimed at obtaining diplomatic and military support from West European sources. Although Egypt's expulsion of the Soviets was considered significant, it led neither to improved relations with the U.S. nor to a realignment of Middle Eastern powers. The Munich killings were a severe setback to Egypt's European campaign, and to Egyptian–West German relations in particular, which had been renewed in June after a lapse of seven years.

With the aid of Syrian mediation, Egypt achieved a partial reconciliation with the Soviet Union in the fall. This policy was opposed by Egypt's defense minister, who was dismissed by President Sadat on October 26. Although some Soviet technicians and tourists returned to Egypt and the Soviets resumed delivery of replacement weapons, the Egyptian–Soviet rift persisted.

Egyptian–Sudanese relations also deteriorated during the year, with Egypt and Libya criticizing Sudan for failing to join the federation of Egypt, Libya, and Syria and for resuming relations with the U.S. In October Sudan withdrew its forces from the Suez Canal front. Sudan was preoccupied with rebuilding national unity after having brought its long civil war to an end in 1972.

The anti-Soviet stand of Libya and the pro-Soviet stand of Syria caused some dissension in the federation of Egypt, Libya, and Syria. Nonetheless, a federal cabinet under a Syrian leader was sworn in on January 4, and the federation's National Assembly held its first session in Cairo, Egypt, in March.

Negotiations between Egypt's Arab Socialist Union and the Libyan Socialist Union prepared the way for a complete merger of Egypt and Libya. The presidents of the two countries announced on August 2 their agreement on a full unification at the earliest possible time. A draft of the unification measures was to be put to a public referendum in each country before Sept. 1, 1973, adopted as a deadline for unification.

During the year the Arab League acted to mediate disputes between the Lebanese government and the Palestinian guerrillas and between the Yemen Arab Republic and the People's Democratic Republic of Yemen. The Yemeni conflict, in which a progressive, socialist state and a conservative, Islamic state had been fighting intermittently for years, typified the deep divisions within the Arab world. The Arab League was able to arrange a cease-fire and peace talks, which resulted in the signing of a unification pact by the two Yemens on November 28.

At the year's end the Arab world remained deeply divided. Such widely divergent leaders as Col. Muammar el-Qaddafi—the outspoken and radical leader of Libya—and moderate King Hussein of Jordan deplored Arab disunity and the despair that had descended on the Arab cause against Israel. Late in November King Hussein accused Colonel Qaddafi, Palestinian guerrilla leader Yasir Arafat, and others of plotting to overthrow his government. At a meeting in December, 18 Arab military chiefs of staff were unable to agree on a unified plan of action against the Israelis. (*See also* individual countries by name.)

MINES AND MINING. Exploration and mineral production continued in the U.S. mining industry in 1972, but these normal activities were overshadowed by a series of mining disasters and controversies over mine safety and the strip-mining process. On February 26 a coal-waste pile, used

WIDE WORLD

A miner is greeted by his family after he was rescued from a fire in a mine shaft in Kellogg, Idaho. Ninety-one men died in the fire.

by the Pittston Co. for more than a decade as a dam on Buffalo Creek in West Virginia, collapsed, sending a wall of water through the creek's narrow valley. Early low estimates of the number of deaths were replaced by shock as the receding floodwaters revealed 125 people dead and 4,000 homeless. An investigative commission issued a scathing report in September that blamed the U.S. Bureau of Mines for an almost total lack of enforcement of safety rules for such dams. The Pittston Co. was accused of faulty construction and upkeep and of "flagrant disregard" for the lives of people living along Buffalo Creek.

On May 2 a flash fire erupted in the Sunshine silver mine in Kellogg, Idaho, the nation's largest silver mine. Of the 93 miners trapped underground by the fire, only 2 survived. Reports on the fire indicated a failure of the mine's owners to correct known safety hazards. Nine miners died in a fire and explosion at the Consolidation Coal Co. Blacksville mine No. 1 in West Virginia in July. In four years the mine had amassed nearly 500 citations for safety violations, several of which were still outstanding at the time of the fire. Critics of the mining industry and of the Bureau of Mines claimed that a consistent pattern of lax enforcement and lack of concern over safety rules existed in most of the nation's mines. Mining was again listed as the most dangerous U.S. profession.

Strip mining, which in 1972 surpassed underground mining as the most common method of coal production in the U.S., continued to come under fire from conservationists. Groups were formed in a number of mining districts to oppose strip mining. A bill to regulate strip mining, however, died without action in Congress. (*See also* Congress, U.S.; Disasters of 1972; Environment; Labor Unions; Metals; Rhodesia. *See in* CE: Mines and Mining.)

MONACO. In 1972 a new minister of state of the principality was welcomed in Monaco, and economic prospects were considerably brightened by promising offshore petroleum exploration. On May 24 André Saint-Mleux became the new minister of state, succeeding François-Didier Gregh as the chief representative of France in the principality and an important adviser to Prince Rainier III. Prior to his assignment to Monaco, Saint-Mleux had been director for cultural affairs and exchanges in the French Ministry of Foreign Affairs.

Monaco's continuing program of arts, culture, and sporting events, including the 30th running of the Grand Prix de Monte Carlo auto race, drew many tourists—the mainstay of the economy. (*See* Auto Racing.) Offshore oil exploration showed excellent prospects for the entire Monaco seacoast, although some conservationists feared that highly visible oil-drilling equipment and the possibility of oil spills might damage the valuable tourist industry. (*See in* CE: Monte Carlo.)

MONEY AND INTERNATIONAL FINANCE. The international monetary system entered a new phase in 1972 following the realignment of exchange rates agreed upon by the "group of ten" countries and Switzerland when they met at the Smithsonian Institution in Washington, D.C., the preceding December. This agreement provided for the devaluation of the U.S. dollar and a reshuffling of other currencies involved, for the lifting of the U.S. import surcharge, and for a widening of the margins within which exchange rates could be permitted to fluctuate. It brought to an end the uncertainty that characterized the interim period of floating and thus set the stage for economic recovery in most major industrial countries.

The expected postdevaluation reflux of funds to the U.S. failed to materialize. With unemployment high in the U.S., and with monetary policy designed primarily to promote domestic recovery, short-term interest rates fell to low levels in the early months of 1972. In addition, doubts concerning the durability of the new rate relationships increased again in June when the pound sterling was set free to float and depreciated sharply in the exchange markets. Another factor was that the U.S. had made no commitment to restore the convertibility of the dollar into gold or other reserves. As the U.S. trade deficit continued to be large, it seemed that foreign central banks might have to acquire large numbers of dollars before the necessary adjustments had time to take effect. In February and March funds began to flow again from the U.S., partly through the Eurocurrency markets, to Western Europe and Japan. After a short lull they surged up again in June and July, provoking recipient countries to strengthen controls over capital imports. In addition, there was a substantial flow of funds from Great Britain to the European Economic Community (EEC) countries in a short-lived attempt to support sterling within the narrow margin of exchange rate fluctuations that, in April, the EEC countries and prospective members had agreed to apply between their currencies.

Monetary authorities in continental Europe and Japan showed determination to defend existing parities by the use of exchange controls and, if necessary, by substantial purchases of dollars. A substantial reflux of funds across the Atlantic Ocean finally began in July, after U.S. authorities announced the reactivation of the central bank swap network—suspended since the preceding August—and helped support the dollar by intervention in the exchange market. Since Japan's large external trade surplus was interpreted as a sign of continuing basic disequilibrium, the country experienced further speculative inflows in the autumn.

A striking feature of 1972 was the rapid, almost explosive growth of money and credit in most industrial countries. Faced with high or rising unemployment, authorities in nearly all these countries turned to easier monetary policies and adopted expansionary government budgets. Nevertheless, with the rapid improvement in business confidence, economic expansion strengthened in the U.S. and Canada, while in Europe and Japan a slowing of output gave way to recovery unexpectedly soon. In North America the demand for business loans grew considerably. Elsewhere, with private investment growing slowly, a large part of the increase in bank lending went for housing construction and personal consumption and for financing investment in securities and property—especially in Great Britain, where total expansion was largest. The main exception was Italy, where economic activity remained particularly depressed and the expansion in bank credit was modest, showing little response to the high level of bank liquidity ensured by the authorities.

In the latter months of 1972 there were signs of a slowdown in the growth of U.S. and Canadian money supplies. In Europe, where rates of increase were still high, an agreement was reached within the EEC late in October providing that as part of a joint anti-inflationary program each member country should, during 1973 and 1974, progressively reduce the growth rate of its money supply to a figure equal to the growth of its real gross national product plus 4%—the norm to which each country would seek to reduce the increase in consumer prices.

The growth of the money supply in the U.S. quickened from the beginning of 1972. Business recovery was at last gaining momentum, and unemployment was declining slowly. Restrained by the Phase II guidelines initiated in November 1971, the rise in wages and consumer prices remained modest, but wholesale prices began to go up more rapidly. Fiscal policy continued to give a strong stimulus to the economy; the federal budget deficit, which had come to $23 billion in 1971–72, was expected to be even larger in 1972–73.

Against this background, and with the dollar still weak, authorities began to reduce the monetary stimulus in the spring and summer. The Federal Open Market Committee set progressively lower objectives for the growth in bank reserves—specifically, "reserves available to support private demand deposits"—it had adopted as the main intermediate target variable through which it sought to regulate monetary growth. Since demand for credit remained strong, short-term interest moved upward beginning in March. By mid-October the yield from U.S. Treasury bills had risen to about 4.8% and banks had increased their prime lending rates of 5¾%–5⅞%. Policy was then geared to avoid a sharp credit squeeze, so that money market conditions eased somewhat and short-term rates leveled off.

The tightening of monetary policy was reflected by a slackening in the growth of the monetary aggregates. In the third quarter, currency and demand deposits rose at an annual rate of 8.6%, compared with 9.2% in the first quarter—while the growth of money and time deposits went up at a rate of 9.2%, compared with 13.3% in the first quarter. The effect of this slowdown on the growth of total bank resources was offset by rapid expansion in sales of large certificates of deposit. During the first nine months of 1972 the acquisition of securities went up at an annual rate of about 8% (slower than in 1971), and the banks were able to expand loans at an annual rate of 16.4%.

During the year, and particularly in the first quarter, nonbank financial institutions also benefited from a further substantial increase in savings deposits, which between January and September rose at an annual rate of $48 billion, following the rise of $41 billion in 1971. These institutions channeled a record volume of funds to the mortgage market, and this, combined with the large contribution from the banks, caused total mortgage credit to go up at an annual rate of $65 billion from January to September, following the increase of $49 billion in 1971. (*See also* Banks; Economy; World Trade. *See in* CE: Money.)

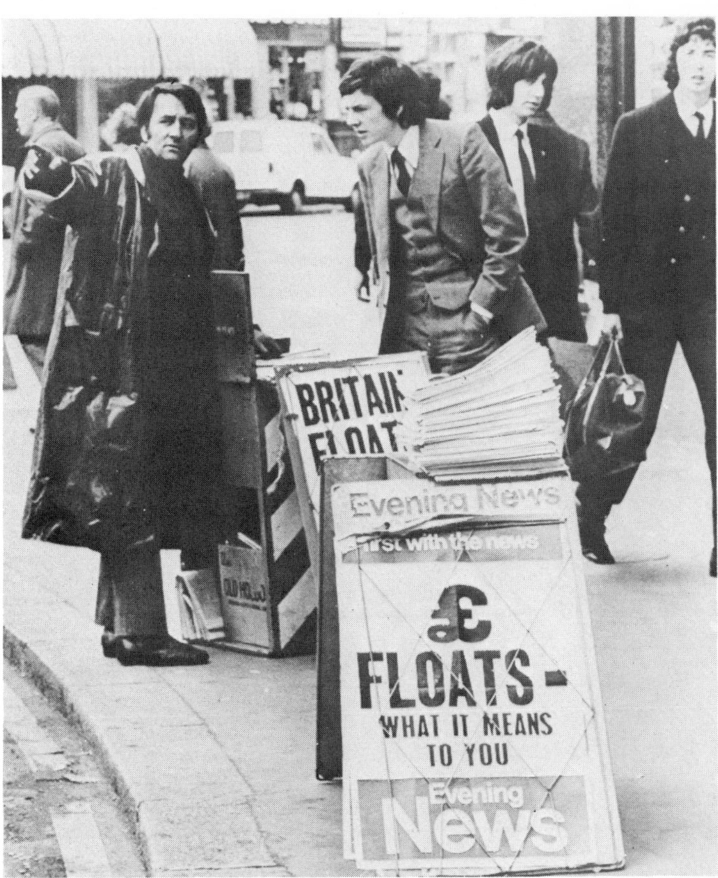

The British government decided in June to float the pound sterling in international money markets. The decision was made after heavy selling on the money markets put pressure on the British currency.

WIDE WORLD

MONGOLIA. Jamsrangiyn Sambuu, the 77-year-old chairman of the presidium of the People's Great Khural in the Mongolian People's Republic, died on May 20, 1972. No successor was named during the year, but Sonomyn Luvsan, a party politburo member and first deputy chairman of the council of ministers, was appointed deputy chairman of the presidium. Tumenbayaryn Ragcha, one of the six deputy chairmen of the government, was promoted to first deputy chairman. Damdinjavyn Maydar, a member of the politburo and one of the deputy chairmen of the council of ministers, was also appointed first deputy chairman, while Sonomyn Luvsangombo, a civil and military engineer, was appointed a deputy chairman of the council of ministers.

These changes were probably connected with the unsatisfactory performance of the national economy, in particular the traditionally inefficient livestock sector. The Soviet Union depended on Mongolia for much of the meat needed for the growing population in eastern Siberia and the Soviet territories in the Far East. (*See in* CE: Mongolia.)

MOROCCO. In 1972, for the second consecutive year, Morocco's King Hassan II survived an attempted coup. On August 16, as he returned from a private visit to France, his civil aircraft was attacked by Moroccan air force fighters. The royal plane landed safely at Rabat, the capital, where Hassan escaped further strafing unharmed. The coup plot was said to have been masterminded by one of the king's closest aides—Gen. Mohammed Oufkir, minister of defense, former minister of the interior, and a personal adviser of Hassan throughout his reign. Oufkir died at the royal palace that same night, supposedly by his own hand. Two junior air officers involved in the shooting flew to Gibraltar after the coup had failed, but they were later returned to Morocco. Almost the entire staff of the Kenitra air base was suspended from duty, but it was not until October that 220 officers and men from the base were brought to trial. Eleven ringleaders were sentenced to death on November 7, and 32 others received prison terms ranging from 3 to 20 years. The Moroccan people in 1972 had not been allowed to quietly forget the attempted coup of the preceding year. More than 1,000 officers and men were tried for complicity in the 1971 coup: one officer was given a death sentence and many others received prison terms.

King Hassan II of Morocco (left) greets President Mobutu Sese Seko of Zaire as he arrives for a meeting.

LUC JOUFFREY FROM GAMMA

Hassan continued to promise political reform, and in March a new constitution that he had presented was approved by popular referendum. The constitution provided that the cabinet have increased executive powers and that two thirds of the members of the national assembly be directly elected. However, in April the king announced postponement of the elections, on the grounds that some 2 million voters were not registered. In November Prime Minister Mohammed Karim Lamrani was replaced by Ahmed Osman, the king's brother-in-law, who was instructed to form a government of "national unity."

It was an uncertain year in the schools. In January secondary students went on strike. After a long period of demonstrations, arrests, and concessions, classes were resumed at the end of April.

The holding of the summit conference of the Organization of African Unity (of which Hassan was elected chairman for 1972–73) in Rabat, in June, provided Morocco with the opportunity to continue its policy of mending fences with its neighbors. The border dispute with Algeria was finally settled. (*See* Algeria.) The presence at the conference of President Habib Bourguiba of Tunisia brought the promise of closer cooperation between the Maghreb (Arab north African) states. Libya's leader, Col. Muammar el-Qaddafi, failed to attend the OAU conference, despite Hassan's invitation urging him to come to the meeting in "a spirit of reconciliation." (*See in* CE: Morocco.)

MOTION PICTURES. The major film festivals, usually an indication of current trends, produced only a few dominating works, such as Federico Fellini's 'Roma', or box-office marvels, like 'The Godfather', in 1972 to set off the mediocrity of the rest. Both art and industry seemed to remain at a watershed between old and no longer viable creative and economic formulas and the confirmation of new modes of expression and new means of production that might solve the dilemma produced by the two preceding decades: constant inflation of costs paralleled by constant diminution of audiences in most sectors of the cinema world.

Coproduction remained a prominent feature of world film production, an outstanding example being the coverage of the Olympic Games at Munich, West Germany, by a team of directors from nine countries. An odd sidelight of the year was the poll held every decade by the British film magazine *Sight and Sound*, in which film critics of the world vote on the ten best films in the history of motion pictures. The 1972 poll was headed by Orson Welles's 'Citizen Kane' (1941), Jean Renoir's 'La Règle du Jeu' (1939), and Sergei M. Eisenstein's 'Battleship Potemkin' (1925).

The year saw the deaths of John Grierson, 73, the architect of British documentary cinema; Maurice Chevalier, 83, the veteran French entertainer; Lord Rank, 83, who as producer J. Arthur Rank was a major force in British film production in the 1940's and 1950's; Soviet director Mikhail Romm, 70; U.S. director Frank Tashlin, 59; Roger Furse, 68, art director of Laurence Olivier's 'Henry V' and 'Hamlet'; and actors and actresses Betty Blythe, 72, Betty Bronson, 65, Dorothy Dalton, 78, Brian Donlevy, 69, Margaret Rutherford, 80, George Sanders, 65, and Brandon de Wilde, 30. The animated film lost two veterans: Max Fleischer, who included Koko the Clown, Betty Boop, and Popeye among his creations, and William Costello, who for many years provided the voice of the spinach-nourished mariner Popeye.

The U.S. Academy of Motion Picture Arts and Sciences presented its annual Academy Awards in

COURTESY, PARAMOUNT PICTURES CORP.

Marlon Brando (standing) played Don Vito Corleone and Al Pacino played his son in 'The Godfather', an extremely popular movie based on the novel by Mario Puzo.

April. 'The French Connection' took the Oscars for best movie, best screenplay from nonoriginal material, best direction (William Friedkin), and best actor (Gene Hackman). Awards for best original screenplay went to Paddy Chayefsky for 'The

'Sounder' is set in poverty-stricken rural Louisiana during the Depression. Stars of the film include Cicely Tyson (with hat), Kevin Hooks (second from right), and Taj Mahal (right).

COURTESY, 20TH CENTURY-FOX FILM CORP., LTD.

Hospital'; for cinematography to Oswald Morris for 'Fiddler on the Roof'; for best actress to Jane Fonda for her performance in 'Klute'; and for best supporting actor and actress to Ben Johnson and Cloris Leachman for their roles in Peter Bogdanovitch's 'The Last Picture Show'. Vittorio de Sica's 'The Garden of the Finzi-Continis' was voted best foreign-language film, and Walon Green's 'The Hellstrom Chronicle' was voted best documentary of the year. Charlie Chaplin, returning to the U.S. for the first time in 20 years, received a special award.

Directors All

A striking feature of U.S. film production in 1972 was the number of debutant directors from other fields of activity within or without the industry. Actor Charlton Heston made a rather overreverent 'Antony and Cleopatra', and Douglas Trumbull, a special-effects director, directed his first feature film, 'Silent Running', which treated the fashionable theme of ecology through a science-fiction projection of a future in which the earth is deprived of all vegetation. Other notably successful debuts were made by Vernon Zimmerman with 'Deadhead Miles', an absurdist comedy about a trouble-prone truck driver (played by Alan Arkin); Bill Norton, who made excellent use of San Francisco, Calif., locales in 'Cisco Pike', about a musician turned drug pusher who is blackmailed by a corrupt policeman; and Steven Spielberg, whose 'Duel' was a contemporary fable about a motorist in a life-and-death battle on the freeway with a truck driver whose face he never glimpses.

British directors continued to work in the U.S. with varying success: Peter Yates's 'The Hot Rock' was a fast and witty variation on the theme of a minutely planned holdup that goes disastrously wrong. Anthony Harvey's 'They Might be Giants' was an attractive fantasy about a lawyer who fancies himself Sherlock Holmes but finally proves a good deal saner than anyone in his immediate neighborhood. The film suffered from severe cutting by its distributors. John Boorman's 'Deliverance' was an able adaptation of James Dickey's novel about four men whose weekend on the river becomes a fight for survival against primitive human forces: like Boorman's previous films, it tended to suggest more philosophical depth than it could ultimately claim.

A group of attractive films by established U.S. directors might be loosely linked by their concern with examining man's individual personality in relation to his historical and social heritage. For his first film since 'Butch Cassidy and the Sundance Kid', George Roy Hill directed 'Slaughterhouse-Five'. An adaptation of the best-selling novel by Kurt Vonnegut, Jr., about the life and death of a nonentity, centering on the traumatic moment of his presence at the bombing of Dresden, Germany, the film failed to capture the anarchy and unsparing absurdity of the original. Sam Peckinpah, having provoked heated controversy with extreme violence in the past, turned to an unusually quiet, reflective, and beautifully controlled subject in 'Junior Bonner', about a father and son whose stubborn loyalty to older values of individual physical and personal accomplishment sets them apart from contemporary society and their own family. Paul Newman's second feature film as a director, 'Sometimes a Great Notion' was also about individualism: a highly intelligent, taut drama about the relationship within a family who antagonize a whole community by working as scabs in the lumber camp that is their livelihood. Veteran John Huston created perhaps the most appealing picture of the year from the U.S. with 'Fat City'. Returning to the scenes and style of his earliest films, it told the story of two fighters in the seedier lower reaches of boxing—one on his way up, the other on his way down, but not so far apart in ultimate prospects. It was casual, human, and magisterial.

Of Cabbages and Kings

Among specific genres, there seemed to be a revival of interest in police thrillers. Don Siegel's 'Dirty Harry' had Clint Eastwood as a tough cop with unconventional personal methods; Gordon Parks's 'Shaft's Big Score' offered a black detective, played by Richard Roundtree. There were also comic variations, such as Richard A. Colla's 'Fuzz', which peopled a realistic police station with convincingly incompetent cops.

The year's biggest musical, Bob Fosse's 'Cabaret', was a disappointing version of the stage musi-

In 1972 actor Charlie Chaplin returned to the U.S. for the first time in 20 years. One celebration in New York City included Chaplin on film and in person.

JACK MANNING FROM "THE NEW YORK TIMES"

In 'The Candidate' Robert Redford played a young liberal lawyer running for the U.S. Senate. His manager engineered a surprise upset of the incumbent conservative. The film's success belied the Hollywood maxim that audiences do not like motion pictures with political themes.

WIDE WORLD

cal in turn adapted from the John Van Druten stage play based on Christopher Isherwood's 'Goodbye to Berlin' stories. In its determination to provide a vehicle for the unquestionable talents of Liza Minnelli, it compromised the original—crudely overstating the background of the rise of Nazism, which Isherwood had presented only as a subtle, if increasingly asphyxiating, atmosphere. The year's other major U.S. film musical was Arthur Hiller's 'Man of La Mancha', also adapted from the stage.

'Fritz the Cat', doyen of underground comic-strip characters, made his film debut in a feature-length animated cartoon directed by Ralph Bakshi. Robert Crumb's original creature, a would-be hippie feline, retained a fair amount of his social bite.

In the realm of *cinéma verité,* Elliott Erwitt's 'Beauty Knows No Pain' detailed the rigorous training and fanatical credo of a group of Texan drum majorettes; 'Marjoe', directed by Howard Smith and Sarah Kernochan, was the confession of a onetime infant prodigy preacher in the Pentecostal church; and 'Winter Soldier', the work of a collective, was a harrowing series of statements by veterans against Vietnam. The richly gifted Fred Wiseman continued his reflective examinations of U.S. institutions with 'High School', 'Law and Order', and 'Essene'.

The biggest British production of the year was Carl Foreman's 'Young Winston', directed by Richard Attenborough. The film's box-office success might promise further episodes of the long saga of Sir Winston Churchill's extraordinary career. As portrayed by Simon Ward, the young Churchill lacked some of the aggressive ruthlessness that in real life won him a good deal of unpopularity.

Two distinguished veterans made new films in their native Great Britain. Working there for the first time in 22 years, Alfred Hitchcock directed 'Frenzy', an old-style piece of Grand Guignol, with archaic charm, rich humor, and incomparable virtuosity. Peter Shaffer's play 'The Public Eye' provided a rather stage-bound and inadequate screenplay for Sir Carol Reed's movie of the same name.

Ken Russell's 'The Boy Friend' presented Sandy Wilson's stage musical within the film as if given by an indifferent seaside theatrical company to launch a pastiche of Busby Berkeley musicals of the 1930s. 'Savage Messiah' was a fictional re-creation of the life and career of the French-born sculptor Henri Gaudier-Brzeska and his loyal Polish companion, Sophie.

However, the year's most interesting work in England was to be found in offbeat and shoestring productions. Philip Trevelyan's 'The Moon and the Sledgehammer' was a close-in record of a family of eccentrics, living reclusive lives in a forest, deeply involved in love affairs with ancient machinery of one sort or another. Bill Douglas' 'My Childhood', modestly made in 16-mm., was a deeply felt autobiographical reminiscence of a boyhood in a poor Scottish home. It won the Silver Lion of the Venice film festival in Italy. Christopher Mason's 'All the Advantages', in 16-mm. and black-and-white, was much praised in the Quinzaine des Réalisateurs at the Cannes festival in France in May. Mike Leigh's 'Bleak Moments' provided an unsparingly accurate, funny, and pathetic observation of suburban life. Perhaps the most significant event of 1972 for the British cinema was the establishment—after years of discussion—of a National Film School. Colin Young was appointed its first director.

The year brought good films from several countries with no previous established film tradition. From Kuwait came Khalid Siddik's 'The Cruel Sea', a harsh critique of the life and rituals of rural society. From Jamaica, Perry Uenzel's 'The Harder They Come' was an assured, tragic, and funny tale about a slum boy whose ambitions are inevitably thwarted. Of the emergent African cinemas, Senegal clearly took the lead. Ousmane Sembene's 'Emitai' dramatized the abortive resistance to French army attempts in 1944 to requisition rice from a village. (*See in* CE: Motion Pictures.)

JACK WILKINS FROM "THE NEW YORK TIMES"

A litterbag hangs from the gear of a climber on Mount Rainier. Climbing is becoming a popular sport, and disposal of trash left by climbers is a growing problem for park officials.

MOUNTAIN CLIMBING. Two expeditions to Mount Everest during 1972 failed in the ascent of the yet unclimbed southwest face of the mountain. The first unsuccessful expedition was made by an international group (German-Austrian-British), and its failure was blamed both on a high incidence of illness and, as with a 1971 international expedition, on differences between leaders and members of the various nationalities as to the conduct of the expedition. Karl Herrlig-koffer, the leader of the expedition, quit on May 5 because of ill health. The expedition continued and reached its sixth camp before an attempt to reach the summit was abandoned on May 23. A British expedition with 11 members led by Chris Bonnington gave up its autumn attempt on November 14 because of heavy snows and bad weather. That group, however, did reach its sixth and last camp at 27,000 feet, the highest point ever reached by the southwest route.

Several noteworthy climbs were made in various mountain regions of the world. In 1971–72 the first winter ascents were made in the Alps on the Mont Blanc de Tacul northeast face, Aiguille du Midi, the Matterhorn south face, Mont Dolent north face, Scheidig Wetterhorn northwest face, and Torstein south face. In the summer of 1972 a new line was climbed on the Aiguille d'Argentiere northeast face.

The following unsuccessful Himalayan attempts were made in 1972: Notse Shar, by a team from West Germany; Malaku II, by Japan; Manaslu, by South Korea, with 15 killed by an avalanche; and Dhaulagiri IV, by Japan, with one killed. Successful climbs were made on Manaslu's west face by Austria, with two killed, and Nampa, by Japan, with one killed. Late in 1972 the Aspiring south face and Hicks were climbed, and descents of Hicks-Dampier face, Cook south ridge, and Cook grand winter traverse were achieved.

MUSEUMS. The pressures of current museum life were clearly responsible for several vacancies in the directorships of important U.S. museums in 1972. Changes of directors at the Boston Museum of Fine Arts, the Museum of Modern Art in New York City, and the Art Institute of Chicago, although related to factors particular to each institution, pointed to a problematical situation. The complex aesthetic, business, and political interests that a director is expected to handle are perhaps best served by an able administrator—clearly labeled as such—while the museum's artistic affairs are left to specialists. The Art Institute of Chicago responded to the problem by abolishing the office of director and naming as its new administrative head E. Laurence Chalmers, Jr., a former college president with little previous experience in the art world.

The year's leading museum controversy was begun when John Canaday, art editor of *The New York Times,* questioned the right of the Metropolitan Museum of Art to sell works from its collection in order to raise money for future acquisitions. Upon learning that the Metropolitan had engaged in secret sales and trade deals, Canaday accused the museum of violating the public trust. In an unprecedented action, the Art Dealers' Association of America (ADA) issued a statement condemning both the Metropolitan Museum of Art and its director, Thomas P. F. Hoving. ADA members criticized the privacy of Hoving's dealings and noted that certain works had been sold at well below market value.

The sale of so-called minor works, euphemistically referred to as deaccessioning, was shown to be a pervasive activity among U.S. museums. Critics of deaccessioning hoped at least for a less secret approach, with smaller U.S. museums given the first chance to bid for sale items.

The continuing problem of museum security was focused upon in 1972 by the armed theft of four paintings, valued at more than $1 million, from the Worcester Art Museum in Massachusetts. In another spectacular robbery, the Museum of Fine

JERRY CABLUCK FROM "THE NEW YORK TIMES"

The new Kimbell Art Museum (above) in Fort Worth, Tex., houses a collection of works of old masters. Blind children (below) jump on a "sound floor" that produces musical notes at the Tactile Gallery of the Wadsworth Atheneum in Hartford, Conn.

Arts in Montreal, Que., was looted of major paintings—including a Rembrandt landscape—and other objects. Less dramatic but perhaps more vexing were the many small acts of vandalism and theft. In the U.S. the National Endowment for the Arts responded to the problem with funds for the study of ways to combat such acts.

While museum attendance continued to increase steadily, financial problems worsened. The need for financial aid from the federal government was considered in U.S. Congressional hearings on the proposed Museum Services Act. The bill would provide $40 million annually to assist museums in meeting general operating expenses. In Canada a new museum policy was proposed by the government; included was an emergency purchase fund for the retention of national treasures.

Noteworthy exhibits of the year included a showing of 133 works by Russian abstractionist Wassily Kandinsky at the Solomon R. Guggenheim Museum, New York City, and "Braque: The Great Years," a wide-ranging loan exhibition mounted by the Art Institute of Chicago. U.S.-Soviet cultural exchanges resumed in 1972 with the largest and most costly exhibit ever sent to the U.S.—"Soviet Union: Arts and Crafts in Ancient Times and Today." The show was seen in six U.S. cities.

Major expansion plans were announced in 1972 by the Carnegie Institute in Pittsburgh, Pa. The relatively little-known Museum of the City of New York revealed plans to enlarge and to restructure the image of the museum. Also in New York City, the Carnegie Corp. presented the Fifth Avenue mansion of Andrew Carnegie to the Cooper-Hewitt Museum of Decorative Arts and Design, which had formerly leased the building. (*See also* Painting and Sculpture.)

"THE NEW YORK TIMES"

JACK MITCHELL

In 1972 Sir Rudolf Bing retired as general manager of the Metropolitan Opera company, after 22 years of service. At age 70, Bing agreed to become a professor of music at Brooklyn College. His career with the Met was colorful and controversial.

MUSIC. The two most important centenaries of 1972 in music were those of Aleksandr Scriabin, the Russian composer whose stature had come to be more fully recognized during the course of the preceding 20 years or so, and Ralph Vaughan Williams, the English composer who, though his music had never penetrated deep beyond his native land, was nonetheless recognized by many musicians as a figure of importance in 20th-century music. The 70th birthday of Sir William Walton on March 29 was also an occasion for musical celebrations in Great Britain. In various personal interviews given by the composer, his well-known humor and self-deprecatory style were apparent.

The trend toward the fairly informal presentation of modern scores in the concert hall—instigated by Pierre Boulez—continued in both London and New York City. In January Boulez opened a season with the BBC (British Broadcasting Corp.) Symphony Orchestra at the Round House experimental theater. This included the London premiere of Karlheinz Stockhausen's 'Mixtur' and the world premiere of Justin Connolly's 'Tetramorph'. A similar series, entitled "Prospective Encounters," took place in New York City.

Dmitri Shostakovich's 15th Symphony received its first performance by the U.S.S.R. Radio Symphony Orchestra under the composer's son Maksim on January 8. Far from being an optimistic work of socialist realism, the symphony, particularly in its final movement, was specifically concerned with the idea of death.

On April 15, Hans Werner Henze's dramatic oratorio 'Das Floss der Medusa' received its first stage performance at West Germany's Nuremberg Opera. The work related a shameful real-life episode about a 19th-century sea captain who deserted his ship together with his officers; the few members of the crew who survived on a raft were eventually rescued.

On June 7 the New York Philharmonic Promenade presented the premiere of Aaron Copland's 'Three Latin American Sketches'. On June 22 Sir Michael Tippett's Third Symphony received its first performance in a concert given by the London Symphony Orchestra at Festival Hall. On July 9 Malcolm Williamson's setting of a dramatic poem by Ursula Vaughan Williams entitled 'The Icy Mirror', a substantial work in three movements, premiered at the Cheltenham Festival; Gordon Crosse's 'Ariadne', a concertante for solo oboe and 12 players, also premiered at the festival. On August 18 Eugene Ormandy conducted the Philadelphia Orchestra in a concert of American music that included works by Gian Carlo Menotti, Roy Harris, Leonard Bernstein, and Samuel Barber. On August 27 Carlos Chavez conducted the premiere of his new work 'Prometheus'—a cantata for chorus, solo voices, and orchestra—at California's Cabrillo Festival.

The Israel Festival in July and August included first performances of Sergiu Natra's 'Dedication' for mezzo-soprano and orchestra and Zvi Adni's 'Meditations on a Drama' for orchestra. The Warsaw Festival of Contemporary Music in Poland in September once again included many new works for both electronic and conventional instruments. (*See in* CE: Music.)

FRANK DUNAND FROM THE METROPOLITAN OPERA GUILD

Critics praised the Met's new production of Georges Bizet's 'Carmen'.

OPERA

Göran Gentele, the newly appointed director of the Metropolitan Opera in New York City, was killed in a car accident in July, just after taking up his new post. The company's new season opened in October with a production of Georges Bizet's 'Carmen' carefully based upon Gentele's ideas. The performance was conducted by Bernstein with Marilyn Horne in the title role. The original version, with dialogue rather than recitatives, was used. The end of the regime of Gentele's predecessor, Sir Rudolf Bing, was celebrated by a gala with contributions by most of the major singers Bing had brought to the Metropolitan.

The New York City Opera presented Gaetano Donizetti's 'Maria Stuarda' with Beverly Sills and Pauline Tinsley in the main roles on March 7, and on March 23 the company presented Lee Hoiby's 'Summer and Smoke', a not altogether successful setting of a Tennessee Williams play. The fall season began with a poor production of Wolfgang Amadeus Mozart's 'Don Giovanni'. At the Juilliard American Opera Center in New York City, Virgil Thomson's new opera 'Lord Byron' was given its first performance on April 20.

At the Chicago Lyric Opera, the 1972 season opened on September 25 with a rare production of Giuseppe Verdi's early opera 'I Due Foscari', introducing the U.S. to Italy's promising young soprano Katia Ricciarelli. The San Francisco Opera season, from September to December, offered an interesting new production of Mozart's 'Le Nozze di Figaro', Joan Sutherland in Vincenzo Bellini's 'Norma', and the first U.S. production of Gottfried von Einem's 'Der Besuch der alten Dame'. A complete performance, probably the first in the U.S., of Hector Berlioz' epic 'Les Troyens' was given in Carnegie Hall in New York City and proved to be a success for the young conductor John Nelson. Frederick Delius' opera 'A Village Romeo and Juliet' also received its first U.S. performance, at the John F. Kennedy Center for the Performing Arts, in Washington, D.C. 'Treemonisha', a long-lost opera by the rediscovered U.S. rag composer Scott Joplin, was given its premiere performance on January 28 at the Memorial Arts Center in Atlanta, Ga.

On March 23, Colin Davis, the new music director at the Royal Opera House, Covent Garden, London, conducted a much-criticized production of Verdi's 'Nabucco'. Another new opera that caused controversy was Elisabeth Lutyens' 'Time Off? Not a Ghost of a Chance!', an off-beat comedy with serious implications, given its first performance by the New Opera Company at Sadler's Wells Theatre in London on a double bill with Anthony Gilbert's underrated 'The Scene Machine'.

Austria's Salzburg Festival in July and August returned to its old love, Mozart, with new productions of 'Così fan tutte' and 'Le Nozze di Figaro'. The Bayreuth Festival in West Germany made headlines with a Marxist version of 'Tannhäuser' produced by Götz Friedrich from East Berlin. The most important event of the Italian season was the revival, in its complete form, of Gioacchino Rossini's 'William Tell' at the Florence Festival. The most exciting production of the season at La Scala in Milan was Verdi's 'Aida' conducted by

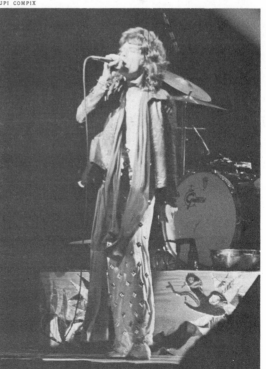

Mick Jagger and the Rolling Stones toured the U.S. for the first time since 1969.

UPI COMPIX

Claudio Abbado. At the Paris Opéra, a new production of Berlioz' 'Benvenuto Cellini' was presented. Montserrat Caballé appeared there in 'Norma'.

The appointment of Edward Downes as music director gave a new lease on life to the Australian Opera, and the first local production of Strauss's 'Der Rosenkavalier' showed how much he had achieved in a short period. Argument continued over the opening of the new Sydney Opera House, scheduled in 1973. (*See in* CE: Opera.)

POPULAR

After a period of introversion, entertainment returned to popular music in 1972. Artists regained contact with their public, and genuine stars glittered in all their charismatic glory. There was much emphasis on presentation, some musicians adopting costumes and makeup. Foremost of these "theatricals" was Alice Cooper, a male singer originally under the auspices of Frank Zappa.

The old-style idol returned in the shape of 21-year-old David Cassidy, whose appearances in the Partridge Family television series prompted a singing career. He soon became a favorite of teenagers. Donny Osmond, at 14 the youngest of the Osmond Brothers, became the darling of the subteens with records such as 'Puppy Love'. Many top stars toured—notably the Rolling Stones, who emerged from "exile." One of the highlights of the year was Elvis Presley's concert at Madison Square Garden, in New York City.

Several stars of the early 1960's made comebacks, notably Neil Sedaka, Rick (Ricky) Nelson, and ex-Zombies Colin Blunstone and Rod Argent. The Beatles, though separated, were active with individual albums and films. Also on his own was Paul Simon, whose partnership with Art Garfunkel had ended. Simon's first solo album was released.

Apart from Motown's Valerie Simpson, the most notable newcomers were men: Jackson Browne, Hurricane Smith, and Don McLean. In 1972 there was a big market for nostalgia; notwithstanding, a wind of change blew through the business—even in such establishments as Tamla Motown, which moved its headquarters from Detroit, Mich., to Los Angeles. Stevie Wonder was among several musicians to experiment with synthesizers; the new British group Roxy Music used one as an integral part of their sound. The year was not without novelties; for example, Coca-Cola's commercial 'I'd Like to Teach the World to Sing' became a hit as a single.

NATIONAL PARK SERVICE.

The centennial of the U.S. national park system was celebrated by the National Park Service in 1972. The event was marked by several conferences and the establishment of a number of new parks and historic sites.

The anniversary came at a time when national parks were facing unprecedented "people pressure": an estimated 50 million more visits were made to national parks in 1972 than in 1970. The National Park Service had responded to the social and ecological threats of such heavy use with a number of new measures. Automobiles were banned in the eastern end of Yosemite Valley in Yosemite National Park, in California, and a free shuttle-bus service was provided 24 hours a day. The concept proved successful and was extended to additional park areas. In Everglades National Park, in Florida, the Shark Valley loop road, which had been closed to visitors for four years, was reopened with free open-air tram bus tours. A bus service was started in a portion of Mount McKinley National Park, in Alaska, and another was being prepared for Grand Canyon National Park, in Arizona. The number of visitors to ecologically fragile areas of Great Smoky Mountains, Kings Canyon, and Rocky Mountain national parks was restricted. Extremely heavy use—and sometimes misuse—of the interstate Appalachian Trail led to rationing of the trail in some sections. Hikers were restricted to one night's stay at any one shelter.

The premier centennial event was the Second World Conference on National Parks, held September 18–27 at Yellowstone and Grand Teton national parks. Representatives from 83 nations

Congress approved Buffalo National River in Arkansas as part of the national park system in 1972.

KENNETH L. SMITH FROM NATIONAL PARK SERVICE

COURTESY, NATIONAL COLLECTION OF FINE ARTS

"National Parks and the American Landscape," an exhibit at the National Collection of Fine Arts honoring the national parks centennial, featured Thomas Moran's 'The Chasm of the Colorado' (1873).

and 30 international organizations attended. The participants approved 20 recommendations, among them the proposal that the continent of Antarctica become the first "world park."

As part of the centennial observance, the National Park Service commissioned a study of the national parks from the Conservation Foundation of Washington, D.C., which issued its report in September. The study, "National Parks for the Future," proposed radical changes in the national park system in an effort to preserve parklands from the effects of overuse. Among the recommendations, which were being studied by the park service's Centennial Commission, were reduction (if not elimination) of automobile traffic in parks; elimination of vehicle campsites and of privately operated facilities for visitors; reduction or elimination of hunting and fishing privileges; and banning of most facilities from wilderness areas. The report provoked a mixed reaction, particularly in Congress, where a bitter controversy seemed inevitable. While many congressmen supported some proposals of the report, especially reduced auto traffic, some felt that ecological considerations were being emphasized at the expense of human need. U.S. Rep. John P. Saylor (R, Pa.), a member of the House Committee on Interior and Insular Affairs and a leader of Congressional opposition to the report, stated: "My objection to some of the basic philosophy supporting the recommendations is the ring of 'preservation' first, second, and third, with use by the public coming in a poor fourth. . . . Parks are for the people—and you may be assured that members of Congress will not allow that basic assumption to be submerged."

In September, 3.5 million acres of land, including large sections of many national parks, were recommended for inclusion in the National Wilderness Preservation System. This designation would prevent the building of roads or use of motorized equipment in the areas. Under the Alaska Native Claims Settlement Act, Secretary of the Interior Rogers C. B. Morton withdrew about 80 million Alaskan acres deemed suitable for study as additions to park systems.

Among the additions to the national park system authorized by Congress in 1972 were the Buffalo National River in northwestern Arkansas, which preserved 132 miles of the scenic Ozark river, and Grant Kohrs Ranch National Historic Site in Montana, which honored the role of cattlemen in U.S. history. Cumberland Island National Seashore in Georgia brought 40,500 acres of forest, marsh, and slough and 18 miles of Atlantic beach into the system. Two new national recreation areas in heavily congested parts of the East and West coasts were approved: Gateway National Recreation Area in New York and New Jersey, and Golden Gate National Recreation Area in California. Other sites were authorized in Hawaii, Massachusetts, and Wyoming.

Several park areas previously authorized by Congress were formally established during the year, among them the first two national lakeshores: Indiana Dunes National Lakeshore and, in Michigan, Pictured Rocks National Lakeshore. Parks and historic sites in California, Illinois, Iowa, Montana, North Carolina, Texas, and Washington were also established. (*See in* CE: National Parks articles.)

NAURU. In the March 1972 elections all nine members of the Nauru local government council, which oversees Nauru's various commercial enterprises, were returned to office. Economic development continued to be President Hammer DeRoburt's major preoccupation. He attended the South Pacific Forum in Canberra, Australia, where the forum countries—Australia, Nauru, New Zealand, Fiji, Western Samoa, Tonga, and the Cook Islands—decided to investigate the possibility of developing free trade among themselves.

Following talks between DeRoburt and the Indian government, India decided to take a trial shipment of 6,000 tons of Nauruan phosphate. The Nauruan Pacific shipping line encountered problems when the U.S. Trust Territory of the Pacific Islands placed a 15% tariff on Nauru's trade with the trust territory in order to protect its own shipping line.

NEPAL. The accession to the throne in Nepal of Birendra Bir Bikram Shah Deva, following the death of his father, Mahendra Bir Bikram Shah Deva, in January 1972, raised hopes for political and economic reforms after more than a decade of near-authoritarian rule. Food shortages, hunger marches, spiraling prices, student unrest, and political agitation, however, followed in quick succession, creating a difficult situation for the 27-year-old King Birendra.

Students and political leaders were held in custody, and opposition newspapers were punished. Twelve elected members of the legislature were expelled. This led former Prime Minister K. I. Singh and 20 of his followers to begin a boycott of the legislative sessions as their attempt proved abortive to censure Kirtinidhi Bista, the prime minister and minister of defense, finance, and palace affairs. The food shortage, caused by the successive failures of two crops, hit the entire northern belt. India rushed 70,000 tons of food to Nepal for distribution among the one million people affected. (*See in* CE: Nepal.)

NETHERLANDS. After one year and 14 days in office the government of Prime Minister Barend W. Biesheuvel resigned July 20, 1972, following the resignation of Ministers Willem Drees, Jr., and Maurits L. de Brauw, both of the Democratic Socialists '70 (DS '70) party. The ministers quit over departmental expenditure cuts and the cabinet's refusal to impose wage and price controls to help curb inflation. Biesheuvel and the remainder of the five-party coalition cabinet resigned because the government had lost its majority in parliament and was unable to muster support.

Advanced elections for the lower house were held November 29. A record 82.9% of the nation's 9 million voters turned out to give the three-party "progressive" bloc an additional 4 seats in the 150-seat parliament, boosting its total to 56. Biesheuvel's outgoing government lost 4 seats, lowering its total to 70. The Netherlands political system makes coalition difficult because there are more than 100 parties, so many that some are named for the year in which they were established, such as Biesheuvel's DS '70.

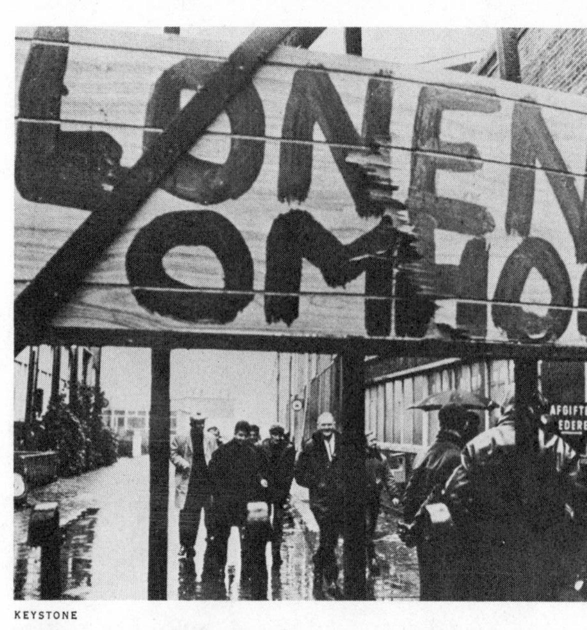

KEYSTONE
Workers struck Netherlands shipyards in February demanding wage increases and the right to strike. The sign says "Higher Wages."

Earlier the government was forced to bow to national criticism and abandon plans to release three prisoners. They were the last Nazi war criminals still serving life sentences in Dutch prisons.

The Netherlands and the People's Republic of China in May decided to exchange ambassadors. A visit in July by Soviet Foreign Minister Andrei A. Gromyko resulted in a treaty dealing with economic, industrial, and technical cooperation. (*See in* CE: Netherlands.)

NEWSPAPERS. Secrets were the issue in major newspaper stories of 1972 and in the U.S. newspaper industry as well. To widespread editorial dismay, the U.S. Supreme Court decided in June that reporters could be compelled to divulge their secret sources before a grand jury. On the other hand, newspapers continued to print reams of confidential information that sent public figures running for cover.

The Supreme Court's 5–4 ruling centered around Earl Caldwell, a correspondent for *The New York Times* who had covered Black Panther activities. To preserve his credibility among his confidential news sources, he refused to testify before a grand jury investigating the Panthers. This matter and two companion cases were argued before the Supreme Court, with attorneys for the press holding that the U.S. Constitution broadly protects reporters from government regulation. More than 20 "shield bills" for newsmen were sub-

The First Amendment (Amended)

OLIPHANT, "DENVER POST" © 1972 THE LOS ANGELES TIMES SYNDICATE

sequently introduced in Congress. U.S. President Richard M. Nixon indicated he did not favor such federal legislation at that time.

The first test of the court's June decision came in October when Peter J. Bridge, a New Jersey reporter, was held in contempt of court for refusing to amplify in secret session what he had reported about a political scandal. Rather than break a confidence, he went to jail while the grand jury sat. A California reporter, William T. Farr, was jailed in November in an almost identical case.

The *Newark Evening News*, the *Boston Herald Traveler*, and the *Washington Daily News* folded in 1972; New York City alone continued with three independent general dailies. The *Herald Traveler* collapsed after a 25-year-old civil suit divested the paper of its profitable television station. The *Daily News* shared the evening market in Washington, D.C., with the *Evening Star*. Both were losing money; so the bigger *Star* bought the Scripps-Howard tabloid.

Newspaper reporter Peter J. Bridge was jailed three weeks for refusing to answer grand jury questions about a story he wrote.

WIDE WORLD

The Caldwell decision aside, secret sources were the mainstay of investigative reporting in 1972. Several unnamed informants helped expose the Watergate affair, in which five men laden with electronic bugging equipment were arrested while breaking into Democratic National Committee headquarters in the Watergate complex one night in June. Stories in the *Washington Post* prompted investigations that led to indictments.

The *Post* newsmen uncovered a chain of relationships reaching from the Watergate intruders to the Committee for the Re-election of the President and to highly placed White House aides. Also revealed was a well-financed political sabotage operation planned to discredit Democratic candidates.

In 1972 Jack Anderson, a syndicated columnist, reported the secret proceedings of inner-government councils, which revealed the vast difference between Nixon Administration statements about the India-Pakistan war and the closed-door policy decisions. Anderson also disclosed a purported connection between the quashing of action by the U.S. Department of Justice against the International Telephone & Telegraph Corp. and the offer by the corporation to defray Republican convention costs. Anderson was guilty, though, of rushing into print on the basis of an uncorroborated charge that Democratic vice-presidential candidate Senator Thomas F. Eagleton, of Missouri, had a police record for drunken and reckless driving. The charge was false, and Anderson apologized.

Disclosure by the Knight newspapers of Eagleton's record of mental illness proved to be true, however. He withdrew from the ticket to remove a distracting issue from the campaign. (*See also* Awards and Prizes; Television and Radio. *See in* CE: Newspapers.)

Newspapers

Special Report: MUCKRAKING

by Curtis D. MacDougall

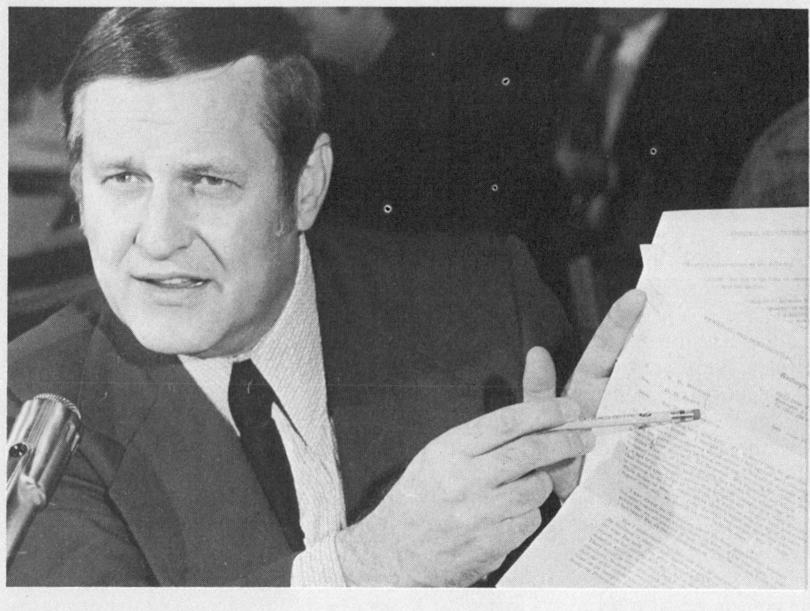

Columnist Jack Anderson appeared before the Senate Judiciary Committee in March displaying a memo that he said was written by ITT lobbyist Dita D. Beard. He claimed an alleged connection between an ITT antitrust settlement and an ITT offer to contribute to the Republican National Committee.

WIDE WORLD

Jack Anderson, whose "Washington Merry-go-Round" column appears in more than 700 U.S. newspapers, was called a muckraker when he published top secret government documents indicating that the Administration of U.S. President Richard M. Nixon was hypocritical in its public support of India while secretly favoring Pakistan during the 1971 war between those two nations. The exposé won Anderson a Pulitzer prize for national reporting. It is believed, however, that the Columbia University trustees were referring to Anderson and *The New York Times,* which got the Pulitzer public service award for publishing the Pentagon papers, when they announced that a majority of them had deep reservations about the timeliness and suitability of certain of the journalism awards—but had to approve the selection of the Advisory Board.

Muckraking has been considered an opprobrious term since U.S. President Theodore Roosevelt used it in 1906 to belittle the iconoclastic articles of a coterie of writers for mass circulation magazines. Roosevelt derived the term from John Bunyan's 'Pilgrim's Progress', in which a character used a muckrake to gather "the straws, the small sticks and dust of the floor" while disregarding the offer of a celestial crown representing truth. Among the crusading journalists who Roosevelt felt did not know when to stop "raking the muck" were: Lincoln Steffens, whose 'Shame of the Cities' was a collection of articles on municipal corruption, which appeared originally in *McClure's*; Ray Stannard Baker, vigorous critic of labor union bosses and the railroads, and Ida Tarbell, who wrote "The History of the Standard Oil Company" for the same magazine; Charles Edward Russell, who attacked the beef trust, and Thomas W. Lawson, whose articles on "Frenzied Finance" were printed in *Everybody's;* David Graham Phillips, whose "Treason of the Senate" appeared in *Cosmopolitan;* and Upton Sinclair, whose 'The Jungle' exposed conditions in the Chicago stockyards and stimulated passage of the first food and drug act.

The Era of the Muckrakers in the mass magazines of the time began in 1902 and ended with World War I. Thereafter came the Era of Coolidge Prosperity, the Great Depression, and World War II, a long period during which the overwhelming majority of the journalistic media were strong defenders of the status quo. Almost unanimously the newspapers and magazines opposed U.S. President Franklin D. Roosevelt's New Deal reforms.

A Fertile Field

Today there is a renewal of the muckraking spirit. During the past few decades the amount of investigative or crusading or interpretative reporting has increased vastly. This development followed the publication of several iconoclastic books that became best sellers, indicating the widespread dissatisfaction with many aspects of contemporary life. First was 'The Organization Man' (1956), by William W. Whyte, Jr., exposing the extent to which big business stifles individual initiative and demands conformity. Soon afterward came Vance Packard's 'The Hidden Persuaders' (1957), an exposé of deceptive advertising and public relations techniques. Other Packard books that critically analyze aspects of the economy are: 'The Status Seekers' (1959), 'The Waste Makers' (1960), 'The Pyramid Climbers' (1962), and 'The Naked Society' (1964).

The present widespread concern about environmental pollution began with Rachel Carson's 'Silent Spring' (1962). So loud were the protests from pesticide manufacturers and from others that U.S. President John F. Kennedy appointed a committee to study the charges. Its report upheld the author's thesis. 'The Poisons in Your Food' (1960), by William Longgood, gave further impetus to the antipollution movement.

The women's liberation movement received its early stimulus from Betty Friedan's 'The Feminine Mystique' (1963). Systematic efforts to protect the interests of the consumer followed the revelation that General Motors had hired a private detective to investigate Ralph Nader after publication of his 'Unsafe at Any Speed: The Designed-in Dangers of the American Automobile' (1965). Nader sued the corporation, charging invasion of privacy, and General Motors settled for the sum of $425,000.

A whole library of books have attacked aspects of contemporary life. Among them are: 'The American Way of Death' (1963), by Jessica Mitford; 'Buy Now, Pay Later' (1961) and 'They Shall Not Pass' (1963), by Hillel Black; 'The Great Discount Delusion' (1965), by Walter Henry Nelson; 'The Poor Pay More' (1963), by David Caplovitz; 'The Brain Watchers' (1962) and 'The Doctors' (1966), by Martin L. Gross; 'Madison Avenue, U.S.A.' (1958), 'The Schools' (1961), and 'The Lawyers' (1966), by Martin Mayer; and 'The Money Givers' (1970), by Joseph C. Goulden. Revealing books by several U.S. senators were also published: 'In a Few Hands' (1965), by Senator Estes Kefauver; 'Overcharge' (1967), by Senator Lee Metcalf and Vic Reinemar; and 'The Dark Side of the Market Place' (1968), by Senator Warren G. Magnuson and Jean Carper.

There is much more muckraking today than ever before in U.S. history. In 1966 the Associated Press created a special assignment team in Washington, D.C., to dig out significant information that readers must have in order to comprehend the complexity of the federal government. Typical of what the team turned out was a series on the country's nursing homes—recipients of a billion-dollar bonanza through the federal Medicaid and Medicare programs.

UPI COMPIX

The major consumer-protection advocate, Ralph Nader, published the first part of a study of the workings of the U.S. Congress.

In 1971 William Jones of the *Chicago Tribune* won the Pulitzer prize for local reporting after exposing collusion between public officials and private ambulance services. In 1972 the Pulitzer prize for commentary went to Mike Royko, *Chicago Daily News* columnist who constantly performs as an ombudsman, relating tales of injustices. Royko's 'Boss: Richard J. Daley of Chicago' (1971), which became a nationwide best seller, qualifies Royko for a prominent position on any list of contemporary muckrakers. Others who belong on the list include Fred J. Cook, I. F. Stone, Cleveland Amory, Michael Harrington, Robert Theobald, John Kenneth Galbraith, C. Wright Mills, and E. Digby Baltzell.

Lifting the Lid on Secrecy

Some of the most important iconoclastic books by journalists are the work of foreign correspondents who have been thwarted by secrecy since U.S. President Harry S. Truman's order of Sept. 21, 1951, calling for classification and withholding of information. Although the U.S. Supreme Court upheld the right of *The New York Times* and the *Washington Post* to publish the Pentagon papers, a secret U.S. government report of the country's involvement in Vietnam, the court did not invalidate the secrecy system. As a result of its operation the people of the U.S. have not been adequately informed about any important crisis in foreign affairs since World War II.

Among the books that belatedly set the record straight are: 'The U-2 Affair' (1962) and 'The Invisible Government' (1964), by David Wise and Thomas R. Ross; 'The Bay of Pigs' (1964), by

ERICH SALOMON FROM MAGNUM

Upton Sinclair's 'The Jungle' helped lead to the passage of the first pure food and drug act.

Haynes Johnson; 'Dominican Diary' (1966), by Tad Szulc; 'Crisis in Credibility' (1968), by Bruce Ladd; and 'Tonkin Gulf' (1971), by Eugene G. Windchy.

The attempt of the Nixon Administration to prevent publication of the Pentagon papers led to the most important legal battle to date to protect the people's right to know. Just as dramatic, however, was the bitter struggle to keep secret the facts regarding atrocities at My Lai and other places in Vietnam. The indefatigable Seymour M. Hersch of the Dispatch News Service almost singlehandedly overcame the obstacles and won a Pulitzer prize for international reporting.

Unquestionably the two most distinguished muckrakers today are Jack Anderson and Ralph Nader. Anderson's revelation that Senator Thomas J. Dodd (D, Conn.) converted campaign contributions to his private use led to a senatorial hearing and censure for Dodd, who then was defeated for reelection.

Senatorial confirmation of the appointment of Richard G. Kleindienst to succeed John N. Mitchell as U.S. attorney general was delayed for weeks in 1972 after Anderson published the contents of a "personal and confidential" memorandum of Dita D. Beard, a lobbyist, to W. R. Merriam, in charge of the Washington, D.C., office of the International Telephone & Telegraph Corp. (ITT). The memo intimated that a commitment of $100,000 to $400,000 had been made to the Republican National Committee to help pay for its proposed 1972 convention in San Diego, Calif., the money to be paid by Sheraton Hotels, an ITT subsidiary. In appreciation, the memo implied, the Department of Justice would be expected to settle the antitrust suit against the proposed merger of ITT and the Hartford Insurance Co., the country's largest merger, to the satisfaction of those companies. Kleindienst, who had been involved in the merger case as an assistant attorney general, denied any wrongdoing; and he was confirmed as attorney general. The Republican convention, however, was actually held in Miami Beach, Fla., instead of San Diego.

The only muckraker ever to institutionalize himself was Ralph Nader, who had many organizations, including Center for the Study of Responsive Law; Public Interest Research Group; Corporate Accountability Research Study; and Public Citizen, Inc. Since 1965 these and many other special interest groups have produced a steady flow of reports, books, public statements, and lawsuits. Millions of automobiles have been recalled in anticipation of, or following, a Nader exposé of faults.

Muckraking is widespread; there is no excuse for citizens to complain that they have no way to distinguish the rascals or to know what goes on behind the scenes. The muckrakers have not, of course, uncovered *all* the dirt; but they are active enough to supply pressure groups and public-spirited lawmakers with enough ammunition to last for some time. What distresses the person who keeps up with the exposés is the paucity of remedial action that results.

Rachel Carson's 'Silent Spring' focused on man's destruction of the environment.

ERICH HARTMANN FROM MAGNUM

NEW ZEALAND. The Labour party in New Zealand won a resounding victory over the ruling National party of Prime Minister John R. Marshall in November 1972. The National party had been in power for 12 years. Early in the year, Labour had been favored heavily to win, and Sir Keith Holyoake offered his resignation in February to give his party a chance to appoint a new man to contest the general election. The party members of Parliament then elected Marshall, his deputy.

The campaign was lacking in major issues. The Labour party campaigned on the theme "It's time for a change." After the election, Norman Eric Kirk was in office as New Zealand's fourth Labour prime minister. Kirk had been effective in rallying support for New Zealand's cause during his country's efforts to win fair trade terms from the European Economic Community after Great Britain's entry.

In an economy still dependent on overseas markets for pastoral products, wool became the great provider again in 1972. International shortages of the fiber caused a dramatic recovery at auction.

Finance Minister Robert D. Muldoon included in his June budget large increases in welfare benefits as part of a 16% increase in government spending. He provided a measure of relief for companies struggling under a payroll tax; this special tax became deductible on income-tax returns.

A major controversial issue in 1972 was nuclear testing near Tahiti by the French. The Federation of Labour in New Zealand refused to handle French civil airliners and shipping, as well as military callers at New Zealand ports, during the period of testing. (*See in* CE: New Zealand.)

NICARAGUA. On Dec. 23, 1972, a series of earthquakes struck Managua, the capital of Nicaragua, virtually destroying it. Of the city's 350,000 residents, at least 10,000 were reported dead and tens of thousands injured. The city was 75% destroyed by the quakes, and many remaining buildings caught on fire. All of the water mains were broken, so firemen had no water.

Emergency aid poured in from Cuba, El Salvador, Guatemala, Honduras, and the U.S. The devastation was so widespread, however, that transportation was nearly impossible, and thousands of people had neither food nor water. Former president Anastasio Somoza Debayle, head of the National Guard, who had left the presidency in May, ordered the city evacuated; but many people had no means of leaving. When looting reached large proportions, Somoza ordered all looters shot on sight. As the situation worsened and thousands of people remained in the city, Somoza ordered food and water deliveries to Managua cut off; supplies were available only outside the city limits. As the year ended, it became evident that the actual death toll might never be known, and Managua's future stood in grave doubt. (*See in* CE: Nicaragua.)

KEYSTONE

In tribute to Georges Pompidou's Niger visit, fabric bearing his picture along with that of President Hamani Diori was on display.

NIGER. During the January 1972 visit of France's President Georges Pompidou to Niamey, Niger's capital, President Hamani Diori of Niger asked for the revision of cooperation agreements between the two countries—particularly those agreements relating to the exploitation of Niger's substantial uranium deposits. On a visit to France in August for medical treatment, President Diori took the opportunity for further talks with Pompidou. No conclusive decisions were reached, but the matter was to be examined by a joint commission.

Nigeria planned in 1972 to replace the diesel-generated electricity in Niger with power from the hydroelectric dam at Kainji, Nigeria—30,000 kilowatts at top capacity. A further example of intra-African cooperation was the reconciliation between Libya and Chad that took place at Niamey in April. Diplomatic relations were resumed for the first time since August 1971. (*See in* CE: Niger.)

NIGERIA. The efforts of the Nigerian government in 1972 were directed toward national development and improvement. It was evident that the ambitious programs were an attempt to create a "new Nigeria" that would be the dominant political and economic power in western Africa.

The major economic plans of Maj. Gen. Yakubu Gowon's military government involved a policy of "indigenization," or "Nigerianization." Under these programs certain businesses could be operated only by Nigerians, and the government and its citi-

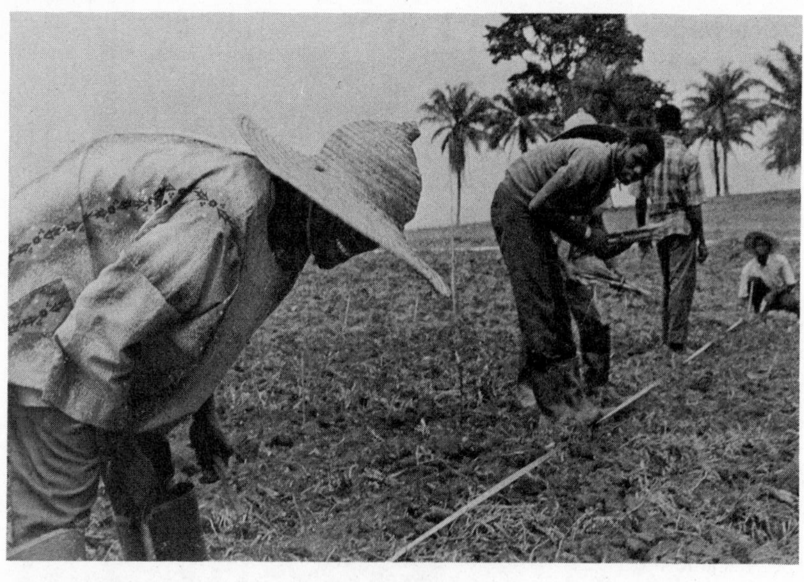

The International Institute for Tropical Agriculture in Ibadan, Nigeria, is applying scientific research to traditional farming. The institute combines the work of scientists, technicians, and farmers in an effort to increase the quality and quantity of cereals, grain, legumes, and root crops in the tropics.

THOMAS A. JOHNSON FROM "THE NEW YORK TIMES"

zens would be able to purchase percentages of major industries located in Nigeria but owned by foreign interests. In the three years since its bloody civil war ended, Nigeria had become one of the top ten oil producers in the world, pumping 1.7 million barrels a day that brought an estimated $1.5 billion in revenues in 1972. A prediction that new oil strikes in the country would soon raise production to 2 million barrels a day, combined with plans for nationalization, had lessened Nigeria's need for foreign investments.

The most ambitious Nigerianization program followed the issuing of the Nigerian Enterprises Promotion Decree 1972, which stated that as of March 31, 1974, some 22 categories of business enterprises would be operated solely by Nigerians. In 33 other categories businesses of a certain size would need Nigerian participation. The decree said that bank loans would be provided to Nigerian businessmen who sought to buy out foreigners. (An industrial survey conducted in 1968 revealed that non-Nigerians controlled some 70% of the nation's 625 largest manufacturing establishments.)

There appeared to be no plans by the government to force out all foreign businessmen from the country. In fact, foreign businesses still expressed interest in going into Nigeria, and trade talks were held during the year with several nations, including the U.S., Italy, Great Britain, the Soviet Union, and the People's Republic of China.

In another move, the Nigerian government announced in the summer that—effective Jan. 1, 1973—it would replace the British-style pound-sterling monetary system with a new decimal currency, the basic unit of which would be the naira, worth $1.53. Earlier, in August, Nigeria's six universities were nationalized. The aim was to ensure the creation of a larger group of educated Nigerians and also to make the country less dependent on foreign universities.

Despite the fact that Nigeria appeared to be at the threshold of economic development hitherto unknown in tropical Africa, it was not without problems. There remained great inefficiency in agriculture (which employs more than 70% of the population), and there was a lack of skilled administrators and technologists—including teachers.

Nigeria worked to improve relations with its neighbors in 1972. General Gowon made an official visit to Togo where he and the president of Togo, Gen. Étienne Eyadema, agreed to establish a Nigerian-Togolese Economic Community, as the first step in a larger west African economic union. This was the first time that Nigeria, a former British colony, had attempted to establish institutional ties with a French-speaking country. Neighboring Dahomey was granted a $3-million loan for road construction.

The former secessionist state of Biafra, once again Nigeria's East Central State, continued to show remarkable recovery from the civil war. Nigeria had generally reabsorbed the Ibo people into national life, although some reconciliation problems remained in the Rivers State, where East Central Ibo claims to property in the Port Harcourt area were not completely resolved. (*See in* CE: Nigeria.)

NIXON, RICHARD M. The year 1972 was one of political triumph for U.S. President Richard M. Nixon, but it was also another year of failure to end the war in Vietnam. Nixon won a larger popular vote than any other U.S. president and took all but 18 of 538 electoral votes. Dazzling foreign-policy achievements early in the year reinforced the incumbent's already strong position. His visits to the People's Republic of China and to the Soviet Union—both the first by a U.S. president—marked a relaxation of tensions with those mainstays of North Vietnam.

Yet, as 1972 drew to a close—and after the heralding of peace "at hand"—negotiations broke down between the U.S. and North Vietnam. Nixon then ordered the biggest air strikes since the war began. For nearly two weeks, except for a 36-hour pause at Christmas, bombs rained destruction on Hanoi and Haiphong in North Vietnam. Losses of U.S. airmen and aircraft mounted. On December 30 it was announced that Nixon had halted the bombing above the 20th parallel and that peace negotiations would resume on Jan. 8, 1973.

Nixon had continued to withdraw ground troops from South Vietnam during 1972 while carrying out bombing raids over North Vietnam and its harbors. During the summer, Henry A. Kissinger, the president's security adviser, entered into secret negotiations with North Vietnam in Paris. The resulting agreement, with its promise of peace, was made public in October; but its signing was delayed, primarily as a result of objections from South Vietnam's President Nguyen Van Thieu. Ensuing talks led to further complications, Nixon called Kissinger home, and the massive year-end bombing was initiated. (*See also* Vietnam.)

Aside from his dramatic election victory, the most gratifying events of Nixon's year were his visits to China and the Soviet Union. He talked with China's Chairman Mao Tse-tung and Premier Chou En-lai in February and with Soviet leaders in May. No diplomatic ties were established with the Chinese government, but scientific and cultural exchanges and bilateral trade were planned. The U.S. citizenry watched entranced as television revealed Nixon toasting and joking with Chinese dignitaries.

A similar atmosphere prevailed in the U.S.S.R., where the U.S. flag flew over Moscow's Kremlin. Nixon and his hosts signed accords that had been in preparation for some time. The concrete results of the Moscow summit meeting included a treaty limiting antiballistic missile systems; an executive agreement limiting offensive nuclear weapons; and pacts calling for cooperation in health and scientific research, trade, space exploration, environmental protection, and maritime navigation. Cordiality and good humor attended Nixon's visit despite an extremely critical decision that he had made earlier in May when, in a move to cut off military supplies to North Vietnam, he ordered the mining of North Vietnamese harbors and the bombing of overland supply routes from China.

In his role as a candidate for reelection Nixon conducted a campaign by surrogate. He continued his official duties and rested on his record while the vice-president, Cabinet members, his family, and others campaigned. His opponent Senator George S. McGovern (D, S.D.) could neither draw him into debate nor provoke him into answering Democratic charges that highly placed Republicans had committed political espionage and sabotage during the campaign. McGovern's positions were considered too liberal by an electorate that leaned toward conservatism. Nixon won the middle ground as well as an overwhelming majority of the votes that would have gone to Alabama Gov. George C. Wallace had he not withdrawn from the race after being disabled by a would-be assassin. (*See* Elections; Political Parties.)

On the significance of his victory, Nixon said that he did not view it as an endorsement of the status quo but as a demonstration of a national desire for "change that works, not radical change, not destructive change, but change that builds rather than destroys." In a preelection interview with Garnett D. Horner, White House correspondent for the *Washington Star-News*, Nixon said he had come through

President and Mrs. Richard M. Nixon greeted friends at a victory rally in Washington, D.C., after the election. The president carried 49 states with the highest popular vote in any U.S. election when he defeated the Democratic presidential nominee, George S. McGovern, of South Dakota.

GENE FORTE FROM PICTORIAL PARADE

a campaign in which he did not "go out with a whole bag full of goodies." The president said that his position was basically "in the center," standing for a strong national defense, for peace with honor in Vietnam, against busing for racial balance, against permissiveness, against amnesty for draft dodgers and deserters, and against legalizing marijuana.

Notwithstanding the landslide vote for the president, 1972 was a year of vote splitting; and once again Nixon faced a Democratic Congress. In his State of the Union address on Jan. 20, 1972, Nixon asked Congress to exhibit "high statesmanship" by enacting his legislative proposals despite the political pressures of an election year. His new proposals called for increased defense spending and a program to lighten the property tax load. Pointing out the necessity for maintaining strength as a deterrent against war, Nixon said that increased defense spending was mandated by rising research and development costs, increased personnel wages, and "the need to proceed with new weapons systems." As for property taxes, which he called oppressive and discriminatory, Nixon said that his Administration was developing comprehensive proposals to deal with the crisis of school financing.

Nixon won his biggest legislative victory of 1972 when Congress passed a law providing for general revenue sharing by the federal government with state and local governments. This was one of the "six great goals" that Nixon had proposed in 1971. Nixon's credibility on environmental issues suffered when he vetoed an expensive $24.7-billion bill to clean up the country's water by 1985. Although Congress overrode his veto, Nixon did not have to spend the money if he chose not to. Congress approved three temporary increases in the federal debt ceiling during 1972; the third was passed after a fight over Nixon's request for unprecedented authority to cut federal spending to $250 billion in fiscal 1973.

In 1972 President Nixon was again involved in a controversy over an executive appointment. In February he named Richard G. Kleindienst to succeed John N. Mitchell, who resigned as attorney general. Some liberal Democratic senators objected to Kleindienst's conservative stance on law and order and his "callous attitude" in the area of civil rights.

During the hearings on his qualifications, the Senate Judiciary Committee uncovered allegations that linked Kleindienst with a 1971 antitrust settlement favoring the International Telephone & Telegraph Corp. (ITT) and a subsequent financial pledge by ITT to the Republican party. The committee upheld the nomination, however, and the Senate confirmed it.

Immediately after his reelection, Nixon asked for the resignations of about 2,000 members of his Administration, including the Cabinet. Thus began a major reorganization and tightening of the federal government. Explaining the overhaul, Nixon said that an administration generally runs out of steam after its first four years, and he wanted to imbue his second Administration with the "vitality and excitement" that accompany a new administration—with new ideas and people.

Nixon's economic program to reduce unemployment and to slow inflation had mixed results in 1972. An overall economic resurgence was undeniable, but the level of unemployment never dropped below 5.2%. The president had considered the reduction of unemployment to 4% or lower as one of his important goals for 1972. Food prices, which were largely uncontrolled, rose by 10%.

Convinced that the time had not yet come for voluntary restraints, Nixon announced in December his intention to continue wage and price controls, perhaps with some modification. He asked Congress to enact the necessary legislation early in 1973 to extend the controls past the April 30 expiration date. (*See also* Economy; Employment; International Relations; United States. *See in* CE: Nixon.)

NORWAY. Voters rejected membership for Norway in the European Economic Community (EEC) in a national referendum on Sept. 25, 1972. Of the 77.7% of the electorate who voted, 53.5% were opposed to entry and 46.5% were in favor. The referendum was not mandatory; but it had been agreed beforehand that the Storting (parliament) would respect the vote, and Prime Minister Trygve Bratteli had said that in the event of a negative vote he would resign. He did so, and a new three-party coalition government under the leadership of Lars Korvald, chairman of the Christian People's party, took office on October 17. The new cabinet was made up of seven members of the Center party, five Liberals, and four members of the Christian People's party. All but one of the members of the new cabinet were opposed to membership in the EEC, but the government could claim support of fewer than half of the Storting's 150 members.

Meanwhile, the economy showed considerable resilience despite relatively slack demand abroad. Exports grew faster than imports, holdings in foreign currency rose to record levels, and the nation's currency remained strong even after the EEC referendum. Increased concern about rising labor costs and prices led to national curbs on both. Wage increases were limited to 5.6%, and a price freeze was imposed on September 7. (*See in* CE: Norway.)

NURSING. During 1972, registered nurses (RN's) in the U.S., functioning in the expanded role of nursing, were more fully accepted and utilized by both patients and other health professionals. The new "nurse practitioner" functioned in the specialties of pediatrics, psychiatry, obstetrics and gynecology, medical-surgical, and other areas. With the assumption of greater responsibilities in health care, and with the explosion of knowledge in the health field, more emphasis was placed on the need for continuing education among all RN's.

The most discussed topic at the 1972 convention of the American Nurses' Association (ANA), held in Detroit, Mich., in May, was continuing education and its meaning and implications for nursing and the health professions generally. Programs on various aspects of the problem of keeping up with new knowledge in nursing were numerous and were presented to overflow audiences. Nearly 7,000 RN's attended the national convention.

In an effort to upgrade care of the aged in nursing homes in the U.S., the ANA launched a project in 1972 to improve the skills of 3,000 RN's working in these institutions. Because the nurse was the only health-care provider who maintained an around-the-clock relationship with patients in nursing homes, the ANA believed that it was the nurse's responsibility to promote better care and to develop specialized skills in response to the individual needs of elderly patients.

Also at its 1972 convention, the ANA voted to establish an Affirmative Action Program that would actively seek greater numbers of minority group members in elected, appointed, and staff positions within the organization. A black nurse was appointed to the ANA staff to work with a task force to develop and implement the program and to act as ombudsman.

The number of practicing registered nurses in the U.S. increased from 723,000 in 1971 to 748,000 in 1972. During the 1970–71 academic year, graduations from schools of nursing rose to 47,001, up from 43,639 in 1969–70. Enrollments totaled 187,551, an increase of 14%. (*See also* Medicine. *See in* CE: Nursing.)

Despite a court order prohibiting a concerted strike, nurses at Cook County Hospital, Chicago, Ill., stage an "informational" line in November.

"CHICAGO SUN-TIMES"

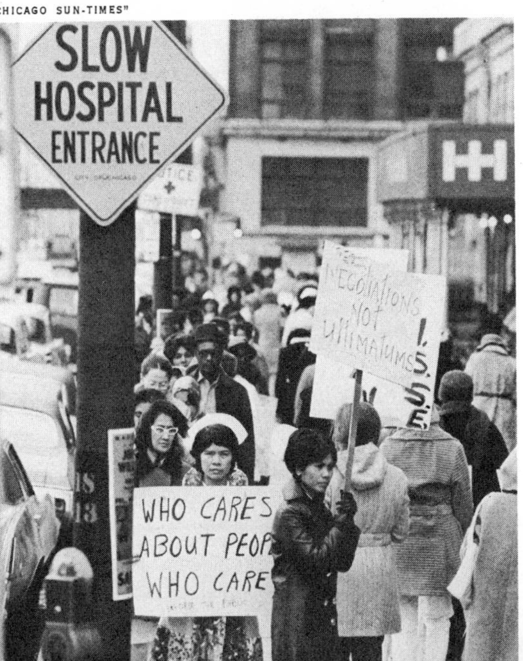

OBITUARIES.

Among the notable people who died in 1972 were:

Saul D. Alinsky, U.S. community organizer and social gadfly who organized neighborhood groups such as Chicago's Back-of-the-Yards Council and encouraged people to act in their own self-interest; June 12, Carmel, Calif., age 63.

Athenagoras I, ecumenical patriarch of the Eastern Orthodox church since 1948, who had worked for reconciliation with the Roman Catholic church of his 126 million followers and was the first patriarch since 1054 to meet with the pope; July 6, Istanbul, Turkey, age 86.

Cristobal Balenciaga, Spanish-born couturier and perhaps the most influential fashion designer of the postwar era, who introduced the chemise and the semifitted suit; March 23, Valencia, Spain, age 77.

Nick Begich, U.S. Democratic representative-at-large from Alaska since 1971, who disappeared while flying in a small plane between Anchorage and Juneau, Alaska; on or after October 16, near Anchorage, age 40.

Georg von Bekésy, Hungarian-born U.S. physicist who won the Nobel prize for physiology or medicine in 1961; June 13, Honolulu, Hawaii, age 73.

John Berryman, U.S. poet ('77 Dream Songs') who won the Pulitzer prize in 1965 and the National Book Award in 1969; January 7, Minneapolis, Minn., age 57.

Dan Blocker, television actor who played the role of Hoss in the popular series Bonanza for 14 years; May 13, Inglewood, Calif., age 43.

Hale Boggs, U.S. congressman (D, La.) who served 13 consecutive terms in the House of Representatives beginning in 1947 and who was the leader of House Democrats; the plane in which he and Representative Begich were traveling disappeared near Anchorage and was not found; on or after October 16, near Anchorage, age 58.

Pat Brady, U.S. actor and singer best known as the jeep-driving cowboy in the Roy Rogers television series and as a member of the Sons of the Pioneers singing group; February 27, Green Mountain Falls, Colo., age 57.

James F. Byrnes, U.S. politician and public servant who served in the Senate, on the Supreme Court, as an adviser to President Franklin D. Roosevelt, and as governor of South Carolina; April 9, Columbia, S.C., age 92.

Hodding Carter, U.S. newspaper editor who fought against racial discrimination through his newspapers in Louisiana and Mississippi and who won the Pulitzer prize for journalism in 1946; April 4, Greenville, Miss., age 65.

Robert M. Casadesus, French concert pianist, music teacher, and composer who gave more than 3,000 concerts during his career; September 19, Paris, age 73.

Maurice Chevalier, French singer ('Thank Heaven for Little Girls') and actor ('Gigi') whose 73-year career made him the most famous French entertainer of the 20th century; January 1, Paris, age 83.

Sir Francis Chichester, British yachtsman and aviation pioneer who at the age of 65 sailed around the world alone; August 26, Plymouth, England, age 70.

Roberto Clemente, outfielder for the Pittsburgh Pirates baseball team since 1955 and one of the game's finest players; December 31, near San Juan, Puerto Rico, age 38.

George W. Collins, U.S. congressman (D, Ill.) who was one of a few of black representatives from districts with a sizable percentage of whites; December 8, Chicago, age 47.

Cecil Day-Lewis, poet laureate of Great Britain since 1968 and one of the best-known Marxist poets of the 1930's, who under the pen name of Nicholas Blake also wrote many mystery novels; May 22, London, age 68.

Brian Donlevy, U.S. actor noted for his hard-boiled film roles ('Beau Geste'); April 5, Hollywood, Calif., age 69.

Edward, duke of Windsor, king of Great Britain and Northern Ireland for 11 months in 1936, who for his brief reign was a popular and somewhat unorthodox monarch; he fell in love with a twice-divorced U.S. woman, Wallis Warfield Simpson, but as king was unable to marry her because of the English church's laws against divorce; on Dec. 11, 1936, he became the first king in British history to abdicate voluntarily, declaring in a world-famous speech that he could not discharge his duties as king "without the help and support of the woman I love"; May 28, Paris, age 77.

Allen J. Ellender, U.S. senator (D, La.) since 1937 and president pro tempore of the Senate; July 27, Bethesda, Md., age 81.

Lord Fisher of Lambeth, former archbishop of Canterbury (1945–61) and leader of the ecumenical movement who made history in 1960 by visiting Pope John XXIII—the first meeting between an Anglican primate and a Roman pope since the English church broke with Rome in the 16th century; September 14, Sherborne, England, age 85.

Frederik IX, king of Denmark from 1947, known for his informality and his love of music and sailing; January 14, Copenhagen, Denmark, age 72.

Lillian Moller Gilbreth, U.S. engineer and subject of the best-selling book 'Cheaper by the Dozen', about her 12 children; January 2, Phoenix, Ariz., age 93.

Paul Goodman, U.S. author and social critic whose sociological study of youth 'Growing Up Absurd' (1960) became one of the most important literary works of the New Left and accurately predicted the college revolts of the 1960's; August 2, North Stratford, N.H., age 60.

Philip B. Gove, lexicographer and editor of 'Webster's Third New International Dictionary' (1961), who championed the idea that spoken language, rather than traditional literary language, should be used as the guide to "correctness"; November 15, Warren, Mass., age 70.

Ferdinand Rudolf von (Ferde) Grofe, U.S. composer ('Grand Canyon Suite'), who arranged and orchestrated music of George Gershwin and Paul Whiteman and who worked to develop music based on American dances and folk tunes; April 3, Santa Monica, Calif., age 80.

Carl T. Hayden, U.S. senator (D, Ariz.) (1927–69) who served longer in the Senate than any other member in history; January 25, Mesa, Ariz., age 94.

Gabriel Heatter, radio news commentator popular in the 1930's and 1940's who often opened his program with the line "Ah—there's good news tonight!"; March 30, Miami Beach, Fla., age 82.

Gilbert Ray (Gil) Hodges, star first baseman for the Brooklyn (later Los Angeles) Dodgers baseball team (1947–62) and later manager of the New York Mets, leading them from last place in the National League to the world championship in 1969; April 2, West Palm Beach, Fla., age 47.

J. Edgar Hoover, for 48 years the tough-minded and powerful director of the Federal Bureau of Investigation (FBI) who transformed the bureau from a corrupt patronage office into one of the most efficient and doggedly persistent law enforcement agencies in the world; unyielding, fiercely anti-Communist, and in his later years almost eccentric, Hoover was one of the most influential men in U.S. government; in recent years he drew increasingly heavy criticism for his dictatorial attitude and sometimes highly questionable methods, including wiretapping and public denunciation of prominent figures with whom he disagreed; May 2, Washington, D.C., age 77.

Mahalia Jackson, U.S. gospel singer and civil rights activist who rose from obscurity to give concerts on three continents and gain international acclaim; January 27, Evergreen Park, Ill., age 60.

Howard D. Johnson, U.S. restauranteur who parlayed a love of ice cream and an acute business sense into a $200-million-a-year restaurant and motel chain; June 20, New York City, age 75.

Yasunari Kawabata, Japanese novelist ('Thousand Cranes', 'Snow Country') who won the Nobel prize for literature in 1968; April 16, Zushi, Japan, age 72.

Edward C. Kendall, U.S. chemist who shared the Nobel prize for physiology or medicine in 1950 for his work in the synthesis of cortisone; May 4, Princeton, N.J., age 86.

Louis S. B. Leakey, anthropologist whose work in East Africa produced discoveries extending the origins of man back hundreds of thousands of years farther than had been determined previously; October 1, London, age 69.

Oscar Levant, U.S. pianist, actor ('Rhapsody in Blue'), author ('The Unimportance of Being Oscar'), and wit, known for his masterful performances of the music of George Gershwin and for his own sardonic humor; August 14, Beverly Hills, Calif., age 65.

WIDE WORLD

Harry S. Truman, former president of the U.S., died at age 88 in December.

José Limón, Mexican-born dancer and choreographer ('The Moor's Pavanne') who, like Ted Shawn, fought to improve the prestige of male dancers in the 1930's and 1940's, and who was considered by many critics to be the finest male dancer of his time; December 3, Flemington, N.J., age 64.

Heinrich Lübke, former president of West Germany (1959–69); April 6, Bonn, West Germany, age 77.

Mahendra, king of Nepal since 1956, who pursued a policy of political nonalignment for his small Himalayan kingdom; January 31, Katmandu, Nepal, age 51.

Maria Goeppert Mayer, U.S. physicist who shared the Nobel prize for physics in 1963 with J. H. D. Jensen and Eugene Wigner for their work in the theory of nuclear structure; February 20, San Diego, Calif., age 65.

Frederick (Mississippi Fred) McDowell, U.S. blues and gospel singer who became well known during the folk and blues revival of the 1960's and was nominated for a Grammy award for his 'I Do Not Play No Rock and Roll'; July 3, Memphis, Tenn., age 68.

Clyde L. McPhatter, U.S. singer ('Lover's Question') who formed the Drifters vocal group in the 1950's before going on to become a soloist; June 13, New York City, age 41.

The world-famous gospel singer Mahalia Jackson, 60, died in January.

A.F.P. FROM PICTORIAL PARADE

WIDE WORLD

One of baseball's greatest, most exciting players, Jackie Robinson, 53, died in October.

Marianne C. Moore, U.S. poet whose highly rhythmic poetry won her almost every major poetry prize; equally famous for her editorship of *The Dial* poetry magazine; February 5, New York City, age 84.

Kwame Nkrumah (Francis Nwia Kofi), African statesman who spearheaded the struggle for independence of black African colonies in the 1950's and who led the Gold Coast from British colonial status to independence as Ghana in 1957; he served as Ghana's first president after it became a republic in 1960 and was a leading advocate of Pan-Africanism before being overthrown by a right-wing coup in 1966; April 27, Conakry, Guinea, age 62.

Norman Norell, U.S. fashion designer who became the first important U.S. couturier in the 1940's; he was best known for tasteful culottes and sequined gowns; October 25, New York City, age 72.

Louella Parsons, queen of the Hollywood gossip columnists in the 1940's and 1950's, famed for her subjective style of reporting; December 9, Santa Monica, age 79.

Kenneth Patchen, U.S. poet ('Because It Is'), author ('The Journal of Albion Moonlight'), and illustrator; January 8, Palo Alto, Calif., age 60.

Lester B. Pearson, former prime minister of Canada (1963–68) who won the 1957 Nobel peace prize for his role in easing the 1956 Suez crisis; December 27, Ottawa, Ont., age 75.

The legendary and controversial FBI director, J. Edgar Hoover, 77, died in May.

WIDE WORLD

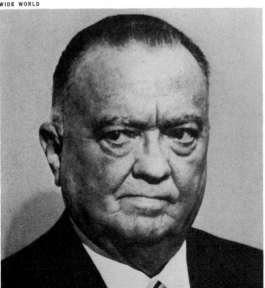

Ezra Pound, enormously influential U.S. poet who was undeniably the dominant force in modern English-language poetry but whose career was ruined by his rabid anti-Semitism and open support of Fascism in the 1930's and 1940's; he introduced T. S. Eliot, Robert Frost, and James Joyce to the reading public and also wrote some of the century's most influential poetry himself; he spent his later years in a U.S. mental institution and eventually exiled himself in Italy; November 1, Venice, Italy, age 87.

Adam Clayton Powell, Jr., flamboyant and controversial Democratic congressman from New York City's Harlem (1945–67), who was censured and eventually expelled from Congress for misconduct but was reelected by a constituency who remembered his endless battles to force Congress to pass antidiscrimination legislation; he won a lengthy battle to regain his seat but was defeated in the 1970 Democratic primary; April 4, Miami, Fla., age 63.

Lord J. Arthur Rank, British film producer who dominated the postwar motion-picture industry in Great Britain; March 29, Winchester, England, age 83.

Jackie Robinson, legendary infielder for the old Brooklyn Dodgers who made history in 1947 by becoming the first black player in major league baseball and who endured almost constant humiliation and racism in the early years of his career while garnering a reputation as a slugger (his lifetime batting average was .311) and daring base runner; he retired from baseball in 1957; October 24, Stamford, Conn., age 53.

Jimmy Rushing, U.S. blues singer known popularly as Mr. Five by Five because of his short, rotund stature; June 8, New York City, age 68.

Dame Margaret Rutherford, British actress best known for her portrayal of Miss Marple in several films based on Agatha Christie mysteries ('Murder at the Gallop'), who won an Academy Award in 1964 for her role in 'The V.I.P.s'; May 22, Chalfont St. Peter, England, age 80.

William Fitts Ryan, U.S. congressman (D, N.Y.) who was noted as a liberal leader and who was the first U.S. congressman to vote against funds for the war in Vietnam; September 17, New York City, age 50.

George Sanders, British film actor known for his portrayals of sophisticated, villainous cads, who won an Academy Award in 1950 for his supporting role in 'All About Eve'; April 25, Castelldefels, Spain, age 65.

Harlow Shapley, dean of U.S. astronomers who was the first to pinpoint the location of the solar system in the Milky Way galaxy; he later devoted himself to the cause of international peace and drew fire for his public espousal of unpopular causes; October 20, Boulder, Colo., age 86.

Edwin Myers (Ted) Shawn, U.S. dancer and choreographer who with his wife, Ruth St. Denis, was a pioneer of modern dance; he fought for acceptance of male dancers in the 1930's; January 9, Orlando, Fla., age 80.

Igor I. Sikorsky, aviation engineer and inventor who designed the first practical helicopter and the first multi-engine airplane; October 26, Easton, Conn., age 83.

Betty Smith, U.S. author whose 'A Tree Grows in Brooklyn' (1943) was one of the most popular novels of all time; January 17, Shelton, Conn., age 75.

Joseph Fielding Smith, president of the Church of Jesus Christ of Latter-day Saints (Mormons) and a descendant of the brother of Joseph Smith, the church's founder; July 2, Salt Lake City, Utah, age 95.

Edgar Snow, U.S. journalist and author ('Red Star over China') who was a close friend of Chairman Mao Tse-tung and other leaders of the People's Republic of China and who disclosed the first hints of a thaw in U.S.-Chinese relations after a trip to China in 1970; February 15, Eysins, Switzerland, age 66.

Paul-Henri Spaak, Belgian statesman who served three times as premier of Belgium and later as the first president of the United Nations General Assembly, and who was known for his advocacy of European unification and his role in the creation of the European Economic Community; July 31, Brussels, Belgium, age 73.

Akim Tamiroff, Russian-born stage and film actor ('For Whom the Bell Tolls') who played offbeat character roles

WIDE WORLD
Dan Blocker, 43

KEYSTONE
Maurice Chevalier, 83

WIDE WORLD
Adam Clayton Powell, 63

HORST TAPPE FROM PICTORIAL PARADE
Ezra Pound, 87

CENTRAL PRESS FROM PICTORIAL PARADE
Dame Margaret Rutherford, 80

"LONDON DAILY EXPRESS" FROM PICTORIAL PARADE
Edward, duke of Windsor, 77

in more than 100 films; September 17, Palm Springs, Calif., age 72.

Max Theiler, South African physician and immunologist who won the Nobel prize for physiology or medicine in 1951 for his development of a vaccine against yellow fever; August 11, New Haven, Conn., age 73.

Llewellyn E. Thompson, Jr., U.S. diplomat who was ambassador to the Soviet Union for 12 years (1940–44; 1957–62; 1966–69); February 6, Bethesda, age 67.

Eugène Cardinal Tisserant, dean of the Roman Catholic church's Sacred College of Cardinals and a distinguished Oriental scholar; February 21, Albano, Italy, age 87.

Helen Traubel, U.S. operatic star with the Metropolitan Opera (1937–53) who specialized in Wagnerian soprano roles; July 28, Santa Monica, age 69.

Harold J. (Pie) Traynor, star third baseman of the Pittsburgh Pirates baseball team who played for 17 years beginning in 1920 and was voted the best third baseman in baseball history in 1969; March 16, Pittsburgh, Pa., age 72.

Harry S. Truman, peppery and strong-willed president of the U.S. (1945–53) who as an overshadowed vice-president was thrust into leadership by the sudden death of President Roosevelt in April 1945; characterized as indecisive by many critics, he jolted the world by ordering the use of atomic bombs on the Japanese cities of Hiroshima and Nagasaki in August 1945; faced with what seemed certain defeat in the 1948 presidential campaign, Truman won despite all the polls; in 1951 he relieved Gen. Douglas MacArthur from command in the Korean War rather than allow MacArthur to invade China and expand the war; December 26, Kansas City, Mo., age 88.

Mark Van Doren, Pulitzer prizewinning poet and teacher at Columbia University who won the award for his 'Collected Poems' in 1940 and was later described as one of the greatest teachers in the history of the university; December 10, Torrington, Conn., age 78.

Edmund Wilson, U.S. literary critic ('Axel's Castle'), author, and man of letters who dominated the U.S. literary scene for decades with his forthright and sometimes scathing critical essays based on encyclopedic knowledge; June 12, Talcottville, N.Y., age 77.

Marie Wilson, U.S. actress most famed for her role as the traditional "dumb blonde" in the My Friend Irma radio and television series; November 23, Hollywood, age 56.

Walter Winchell, acerbic syndicated newspaper columnist and radio newscaster whose "On Broadway" column was the beginning of "gossip" journalism covering entertainment personalities, and whose radio trademark was the introductory line of each broadcast: "Mr. and Mrs. America—and all the ships at sea"; his columns began in the 1920's and continued for almost 40 years; February 20, Los Angeles, age 74.

OCEANOGRAPHY. Just a few years ago the idea of a dry Mediterranean seabed within recent geologic time seemed so wild that even a scientific journal shunned it. But in 1972, evaluation of Mediterranean sediment, in cores brought up by the deep-sea drilling ship *Glomar Challenger,* seemed to confirm the notion. Cores bearing anhydrite salts were especially convincing. Salts in this form can exist only when exposed to sunlight or other heat.

The picture that emerged was of a giant basin at least a few thousand feet lower than at present, existing as recently as 5 million years ago. The basin was blocked from the Atlantic Ocean by a land barrier across the present Strait of Gibraltar. Atlantic waters, however, replenished the Mediterranean over an escarpment east of Gibraltar. The awesome waterfall that resulted had a flow about 35 times greater than Victoria Falls in Africa. Support for the idea was supplied when a Soviet scientist found marine fossils 7 million years old beneath the Nile River floor, some 1,250 miles away from the Mediterranean. Presumably, a deep canyon had cut through the Nile area long ago. It became filled with sea water when the Mediterranean rose. Silting eventually raised the Nile floor above sea level.

IDOE Sparks Worldwide Oceanographic Research

The International Decade of Ocean Exploration (IDOE), in the 1970's, was in large part responsible for the many large-scale oceanographic research programs either planned or being undertaken. IDOE projects were in four categories—environmental quality, environmental forecasting, living resources, and seabed assessment.

A dire discovery in IDOE-related research was of certain plastics floating far at sea. The items no longer contained their plasticizer, polychlorinated biphenyl (PCB), a chemical related to the pollutant DDT. Scientists feared that the PCB, leached from plastics dumped into the sea, might pose an ecological threat to marine life.

This microscopic 4 million-year-old fossil of an oceanic alga was found in a deep-sea drilling project sample from the western Pacific.

COURTESY, U.S. GEOLOGICAL SURVEY

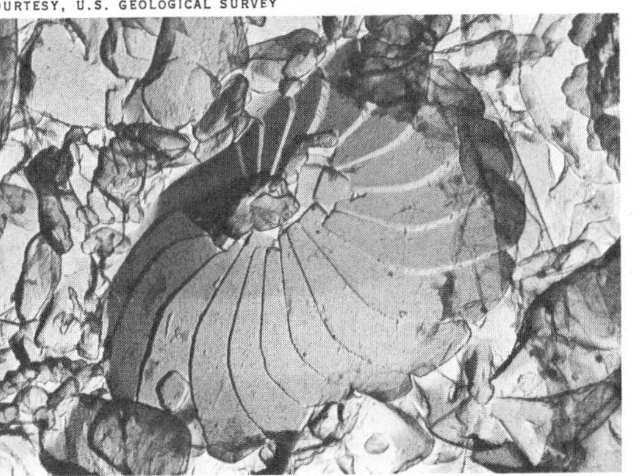

COURTESY, DEEPSEA VENTURES INC.

A television camera and lights attached to a huge tripod were readied during the year for use in a planned deep-ocean mining venture.

In 1972 oceanographers were trying to develop a broad base line—a standard of chemical content, for example—against which potential pollution activities could be measured. The research ship *Knorr,* operated by the Woods Hole Oceanographic Institution, departed in July for the first of a series of global cruises designed to establish such a base line. The *Knorr* was to measure northern waters for such dissolved contents as oxygen, nitrogen, nutrients, and trace elements. Chemical properties such as alkalinity would be analyzed too.

It was hoped that the Coastal Upwelling Experiment (CUE) off the Oregon coast in 1972 would provide a means of forecasting fish-harvest resources, in addition to producing basic scientific data. Upwelling occurs along the long continental coastlines, sites of the world's great fishing grounds. It takes place when summer winds drive surface waters away from the coast, and cold, deep waters with their abundant nutrients upwell to replace them. If upwelling could be forecast, commercial fishermen could be mobilized to bring in increased catches. CUE relied on satellite data provided by the National Oceanic and Atmospheric Administration, as well as on seaborne instruments.

The Woods Hole research vessel *Atlantis II* surveyed the African continental margin in 1972 as part of an IDOE seabed assessment project. Although mineral and oil exploitation in the ocean was still confined to the continental shelves, the shelves were woefully ill-mapped. Data from the *Atlantis II* would be instrumental in determining whether oil was available off the eastern coast of Africa. (*See also* Environment. *See in* CE: Oceanography.)

OLYMPIC GAMES. The XX Olympiad, held in Munich, West Germany, in 1972, survived a shocking tragedy when Palestinian guerrillas kidnapped 11 Israeli athletes and coaches, all of whom were killed. (*See* Crime.) The summer games were by far the largest and most expensive games ever staged; a total of 10,169 athletes from 123 countries participated in 20 sports in 16 days. Earlier in the year the Winter Olympics were held in Sapporo, Japan.

SUMMER OLYMPICS

The most successful overall team in the summer Olympics, by the yardstick of medals won, was that of the Soviet Union, which took 50 of the 195 titles. Competitors from only 25 countries won titles, while another 23 countries had to be content with silver and/or bronze medals, leaving more than half the national teams (75 of them) to return home empty-handed.

World records were bettered or equaled (an increasingly common occurrence) in 12 of the 38 track and field events. Of these, perhaps the most impressive was that of the 400-meter hurdler John Akii-Bua of Uganda, who despite being a natural right-leg leader turned in a time of 47.8 seconds, lowering by 0.3 second the record set—against 20% less atmospheric resistance—by David Hemery of Great Britain at the Mexico City, Mexico, games of 1968. Akii-Bua, one of a family of 43 and one of 8 brothers or half brothers representing Uganda, served notice that African athletes would soon be more prominently represented in the roll of world record holders.

Predictably, the Olympic records set at Mexico City, 1½ miles above sea level, survived. Thus the Olympic record figures for the 100, 200, 400, and 800 meters remained also as world records, as did the Olympic records for the men's high, long, and triple jumps. The survival of two other marks set in Mexico was ensured by the slow initial laps of 61.4 and 60.0 seconds in the 1,500-meter final, and the banning of Vincent Matthews and Wayne Collett of the U.S. 400-meter relay team for unseemly behavior on the rostrum.

The sprints were dominated by Valeri Borzov of the Soviet Union, who achieved times of 10.47, 10.07, 10.21, and 10.14 seconds to win the 100 meters by a full meter from Robert Taylor of the U.S.; and 20.64, 20.30, 20.74, and 20.00 seconds to win the 200 meters by 2 meters from Larry Black of the U.S. Consternation had occurred at the afternoon session on August 31 when only one (Taylor) of the three U.S. sprinters appeared for the second round of the 100 meters. The abbreviation "n.a." for *nicht angetreten* (not started) went up on the board against the names of both Rey Robinson in the first heat and his fellow coholder of the world record, Eddie Hart, in the second. Both had been watching television in the Olympic Village thinking that they were viewing a replay of the heats. The U.S. team management received rough treatment from their national press for this lapse. Unfortunately, a team official had been utilizing an out-of-date schedule of events.

Matthews took the 400 meters in 44.66 seconds, with John Smith of the U.S. having retired after the first turn with a recurrence of a muscle injury. Dave Wottle of the U.S., whose golf cap caused as much interest as the monocle of a British sprinter in the 1928 games, won the 800 meters by a whisker. The incomparable Rod Milburn of the

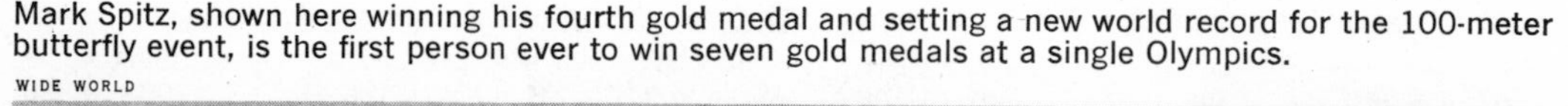

Mark Spitz, shown here winning his fourth gold medal and setting a new world record for the 100-meter butterfly event, is the first person ever to win seven gold medals at a single Olympics.
WIDE WORLD

UPI COMPIX

Former Olympic gold medal winners—Son Kitei, South Korea, 1936; Jesse Owens, U.S., 1936; and Manfred Germar, West Germany, 1956—mourn the Israeli athletes killed by terrorists.

U.S. recorded times of 13.57, 13.44, and a world record-equaling 13.24 seconds to win by a clear meter over the taller Guy Drut of France in the high hurdles.

Frank Shorter of the U.S. won the 26-mile, 385-yard marathon by more than two minutes from a field of 76 in a time less than nine seconds over the fastest Olympic time of 2 hours, 12 minutes, 11.2 seconds set by Abebe Bilila of Ethiopia in 1964. While training, Shorter survived a homicide attempt in Arizona by youths intent on running him down with an automobile because he had disturbed them when they were assaulting a lone girl.

In the field events there was controversy over the vacillation of the International Amateur Athletic Federation on the use of high-density vaulting poles. After a ban that was later relaxed, there was a further ban from which world record holder Bob Seagren of the U.S. was the most conspicuous sufferer as he was not allowed to use his fiber glass Catapole. The winner of the pole vault was Wolfgang Nordwig of East Germany, who cleared 17 feet 10½ inches and then went on to a further Olympic record of 18 feet ½ inch, ending the monopoly by U.S. vaulters since 1896. Another U.S. stronghold event, the shot put, was won by Wladyslaw Komar of Poland with his first put of 69 feet 6 inches; George Woods of the U.S. was second.

Women's Events

The women's track and field program was increased to 14 events, and the women produced six new or equaled world records, four in track and two in field. Most outstanding of the track records were the 1,500-meter victory of Ludmila Bragina of the Soviet Union, whose time of 4:01.4 would have won the men's event in 1920, and the 400-meter relay win, by 15 yards, by the East German team. In the field, Nadyezhda Chizhova of the Soviet Union defeated all her opponents in the shot put with a world record final put of 69 feet.

Perhaps the most emotional scenes in the stadium came in the women's high jump. West Germany's 16-year-old Ulrike Meyfarth held the crowd of 80,000—and perhaps 1,000 times as many television viewers—spellbound while she raised her personal best time and then equaled the world record of 6 feet 3½ inches while the anguished record holder, Austria's Ilona Gusenbauer, hid her head waiting to learn from the roar of the crowd whether even her share of the record would go.

The Olympic flag flies at half-mast over a memorial service for those slain at Munich.

KEYSTONE

WIDE WORLD

Olga Korbut of the Soviet Union won a gold medal in the balance beam competition.

Swimming Events

The staging of the 34 swimming, diving, and water polo events broke new ground technologically because of the astounding success of the Schwimmhalle's design in lessening the wake of the swimmers. In the men's 15 individual and relay races, world records were set or equaled in all but the 400-meter freestyle and individual medley, while in the 14 women's events there were new world records in all but the 100-meter freestyle and backstroke and the 200-meter breaststroke. The U.S. swimmers won 17 gold medals.

The domination by Mark Spitz of the U.S. was almost total. He won seven gold medals and set seven new world records. Spitz first took the 200-meter butterfly event in 2 minutes 0.7 seconds. He followed this by a 50.9-second anchor in the U.S. win of the 400-meter freestyle relay event. The next day, on August 29, he took the 200-meter freestyle in 1 minute 52.78 seconds. The following day Spitz was confined to heats and semifinals of the 100-meter butterfly in which on August 31, in the finals, he secured in 54.27 seconds his fourth gold medal together with a fifth on the anchor position of the 800-meter freestyle relay. His first day of rest was on September 1, after which on September 2, he went through a heat, a semifinal, and a final of the 100-meter freestyle in which he turned at 50 meters in 24.56 seconds and won in a world record 51.22 seconds. His seventh gold medal came in the 400-meter medley relay in which he took the third stage with 54.28 seconds, the U.S. defeating East Germany.

The campaign of Australia's Shane Gould to sweep six women's titles got off to a fine start when on August 28 she won the 200-meter individual medley with a world record of 2 minutes 23.07 seconds. On the second day she started in the 100-meter freestyle final as the second-fastest qualifier behind Shirley Babashoff of the U.S. In the race she turned only third behind both Miss Babashoff and the leader, Sandra Neilson, also of the U.S. Miss Neilson won in 58.59 seconds. Miss Babashoff was second, with Miss Gould taking the bronze medal. The next day the Australian came back to win the 400-meter freestyle in the world record time of 4 minutes 19.04 seconds. On September 1, she took her third gold medal in the 200-meter freestyle, again in world record time, 2 minutes 3.56 seconds. Her bid for the 800-meter freestyle title was thwarted by Keena Rothhammer of the U.S., who drew level after nine laps and pulled away to win in a world record 8 minutes 53.68 seconds. Miss Gould won the silver medal to bring her tally to three gold, one silver, and one bronze.

Other Summer Games Events

The gymnastics competition made a tremendous impact on television audiences the world over, and no single competitor more than Olga Korbut of the Soviet Union, who won the gold medal for the floor exercises and the balance beam and was on the winning combined team. She also performed dazzlingly on the asymmetrical bars for a joint silver medal.

In the men's events Sawao Kato of Japan and Viktor Klimenko of the Soviet Union were outstanding. Kato, in addition to winning the individual and a combined team gold medal, won the parallel bars and took home three silver medals in the horizontal bar and pommeled horse. Klimenko won the gold in the pommeled horse.

The U.S. record of never having lost a basketball game since 1936, when the sport became an

Two U.S. 400-meter-dash winners do not stand at attention while their national anthem is played.

UPI COMPIX

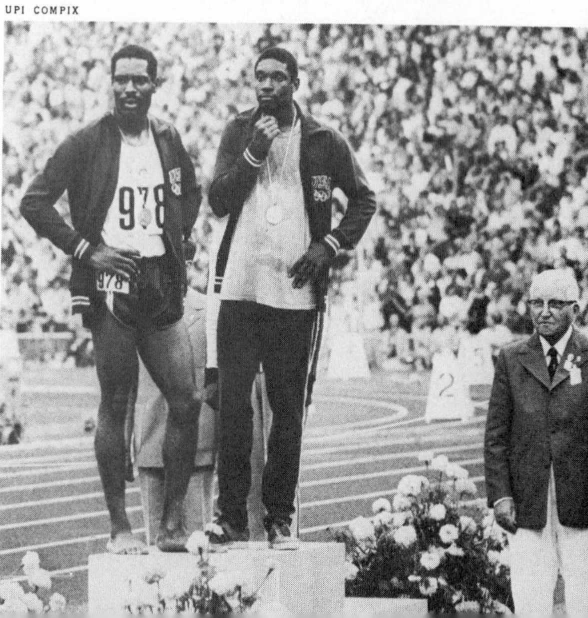

KEYSTONE

Frank Shorter of the U.S. won the marathon by running the 26 miles in a little over two hours.

Olympic contest, ended in confusion over the elapse of playing time. The Soviet team won the final, 51–50, literally in the last second in a contest that was continued after the Brazilian and Bulgarian referees pointed out that there were still three seconds left—although the U.S. team was already celebrating yet another win.

In wrestling, Aleksandr Medved of the Soviet Union joined the elite as the third wrestler in history to win a third Olympic gold medal with his freestyle super-heavyweight success. Chris Taylor, a 420-pound U.S. wrestler, won the bronze medal. Other U.S. winners (all in freestyle) were Dan Gable, lightweight; Wayne Wells, welterweight; and Ben Peterson, light heavyweight.

WINTER OLYMPICS

The XI Winter Olympic Games were the first to be held in Asia. Thirty-five nations were represented by 1,128 competitors (911 men and 217 women). These figures had previously been exceeded only once, in 1968 at Grenoble, France.

Speed skater Ard Schenk of the Netherlands stole the individual thunder of the games just as France's Alpine skier Jean-Claude Killy had done in 1968. Schenk's long strides down the straights, fast cornering, and stylishly smooth economy of energy won the 1,500-, 5,000-, and 10,000-meter races, shattering two Olympic records. In the more specialized 500-meter sprint, Erhard Keller of West Germany—after two false starts—broke another Olympic best time while defending his title.

Olympic speed-skating records were also smashed in all four women's events, underlining the improvement of technique in four years. In the 1,500 meters, three Dutch stars—Stien Baas-Kaiser, Atje Keulen-Deelstra, and Elly van de Brom—were unexpectedly outpaced by Dianne Holum of the U.S., earlier renowned more as a sprinter.

Anne Henning of the U.S. captured a gold medal in an incident-packed 500-meter sprint. She completed the distance in record time after being forced to break stride by another skater; she was then allowed a second run in which she clocked a still faster time. Miss Henning thus became the only athlete to set a new Winter Olympic record time twice in the same event. At 16, she was also the youngest victor at Sapporo.

Miss Baas-Kaiser finished nearly 7 seconds ahead of Miss Holum in the 3,000 meters. Monika Pflug of West Germany took the 1,000 meters. In this event a mere hundredth of a second, the smallest recordable margin, separated the second and third finishers, Miss Keulen-Deelstra and Miss Henning. The previous best Olympic figures were lowered no fewer than 30 times in the 8 men's and women's events.

Beatrix Schuba of Austria won the women's figure skating with some of the best school figures

Jim Ryun (U.S., right) and Billy Fordjour (Ghana) fell over each other during the fourth heat of the 1,500-meter event for men. Ryun finished ninth in a field of ten in the heat.

UPI COMPIX

WIDE WORLD

Netherlands speed skater Stien Baas-Kaiser won the 3,000-meter race at Sapporo, Japan.

ever traced. Her relatively moderate freestyle was anticlimatic but adequate for overall victory after an unprecedentedly wide lead halfway. Karen Magnussen of Canada took the silver as best all around, and Janet Lynn of the U.S. won the bronze and was the top freestyle scorer, her marks from one judge including a controversial 6, which implied perfection, even though she fell.

Ondrej Nepela became the first Czechoslovak to win an Olympic figure-skating title. He included a masterly triple Salchow jump but fell when attempting a triple toe-loop jump. Sergei Chetverukhin's second place was the highest achieved by a Russian in international solo figure skating. In the pairs event, Aleksei Ulanov and Irina Rodnina narrowly defeated their Soviet compatriots Andrei Suraikin and Ludmila Smirnova in a 6–3 judges' vote.

On the steep Mount Teine slalom course, more than half the field of 42 failed to finish. The winner, Barbara Ann Cochran, gained the first Alpine skiing gold medal for the U.S. in 20 years, by 0.02 second over Danielle Debernard of France. Miss Cochran's time was 1 minute 31.24 seconds. Galina Kulakova, a Russian physical education teacher, was the most successful woman competitor in the games, winning both the 5- and 10-kilometer cross-country ski events and sharing a third gold medal as a member of the winning relay team.

In ice hockey the Soviet Union won for the third consecutive time. The U.S. finished third. The leading scorer in the competition was the Soviet winger Valeri Kharlamov, with nine goals and six assists; but the outstanding individual was Michael Curran, the U.S. goalie, credited with 194 saves in five matches. (*See also* Sports Champions of 1972; individual sports by name. *See in* CE: Olympic Games.)

OMAN. In 1972 Oman underwent rapid social and economic change, although development was handicapped by military spending. In January it was announced that the uncle of Sultan Qabus bin Said, Prime Minister Tariq bin Taymur, who was abroad, had resigned because of ill health and that his functions would be taken over by the sultan's office. The prime minister returned to Oman in February and was appointed foreign affairs adviser.

Fighting continued against the Marxist-led Dhofari rebels in the southwest, who were receiving aid from the People's Republic of China, the Soviet Union, and the People's Democratic Republic of Yemen. On May 5 the Omani air force attacked southern Yemeni gun sites after the Omani fort of Habrut had been fired on from across the border. The sultan's forces, led by British officers, scored some successes against the rebels by pacifying large areas of territory; but the rebellion continued, and the military absorbed about half the country's $125 million in oil revenues.

PAINTING AND SCULPTURE. In May 1972 the entire world was shocked when a hammer-wielding assailant slipped into St. Peter's Basilica in Rome and struck several blows at Michelangelo's marble Pietà. The figure of the Virgin Mary was severely damaged in the attack; the left forearm was broken and the face and veil were chipped. Experts disagreed on the prospects for successful restoration, although Vatican art specialists predicted full repair by 1973. The controversy concerning the protection of works of art on public display was revived by the tragic incident.

U.S. Exhibits

Strong interest in primitive and non-Western art was evident in the U.S. The Museum of Fine Arts, in Boston, Mass., held an exhibition entitled "Ancient Art of the Americas" in the spring. The objects were drawn from museums and private collections in New England and included some fine pieces of Olmec art from tropical Mexico. Many items had never before been exhibited or published. Primitive art from New Guinea was highlighted at the Art Institute of Chicago in a sizable exhibit of masks, drums, shields, and ornaments from the Sepik River area. In another Chicago show, held at the Field Museum of Natural History, bark paintings by the Australian aborigines of Arnhem Land were displayed.

An exhibition of Chinese calligraphy, organized in the fall of 1971 by the Philadelphia Museum of Art, was shown in Kansas City, Mo., in the winter and at the Metropolitan Museum of Art in New

KEYSTONE

This Chinese wine jar of the Yuan Dynasty was sold for $573,000 in June.

York City during the spring of 1972. Examples of scripts covering a period of 3,000 years demonstrated the importance traditionally attached to beauty and vitality of line in Chinese writing.

Paintings by American artists were shown in a number of important exhibitions in 1972. The Amon Carter Museum, Fort Worth, Tex., organized a retrospective devoted to the 19th-century American landscape painter Albert Bierstadt, known for his large and dramatic scenes of the American wilderness. The Bierstadt exhibit was later seen at the Whitney Museum of American Art in New York City and the Pennsylvania Academy of the Fine Arts in Philadelphia. Eastman Johnson, the 19th-century American painter known for his charming rural genre scenes, was the subject of a retrospective exhibition held at the Whitney Museum. The Johnson paintings and drawings were later seen in Detroit, Mich.; Cincinnati, Ohio; and Milwaukee, Wis.

While there have been many exhibitions devoted to great Dutch painters of the 17th century, "Dutch Masterpieces from the 18th Century" was the first major show in 25 years to be devoted to 18th-century Dutch art. Organized and first shown in Minneapolis, Minn., it later moved to Toledo, Ohio, and to Philadelphia. The first of its kind outside of the Netherlands, the exhibit consisted of 106 paintings and drawings. The scholarly exhibit "Caravaggio and His Followers," held in the winter at the Cleveland Museum of Art in Ohio, was devoted to the late-17th-century Italian painter, who was known for his dramatic use of light.

Early in the year, the New York Cultural Center held the first complete retrospective devoted to the 20th-century surrealist painter Giorgio de Chirico. Many of the works had never before been shown in the U.S., as most were lent by the artist from his own private collection. The 83-year-old De Chirico, whose works are often copied, noted that it was "the only completely authentic De Chirico exhibition ever held."

Exhibits Overseas

Perhaps the most remarkable exhibition in Paris was a show at the Orangerie devoted to the little-

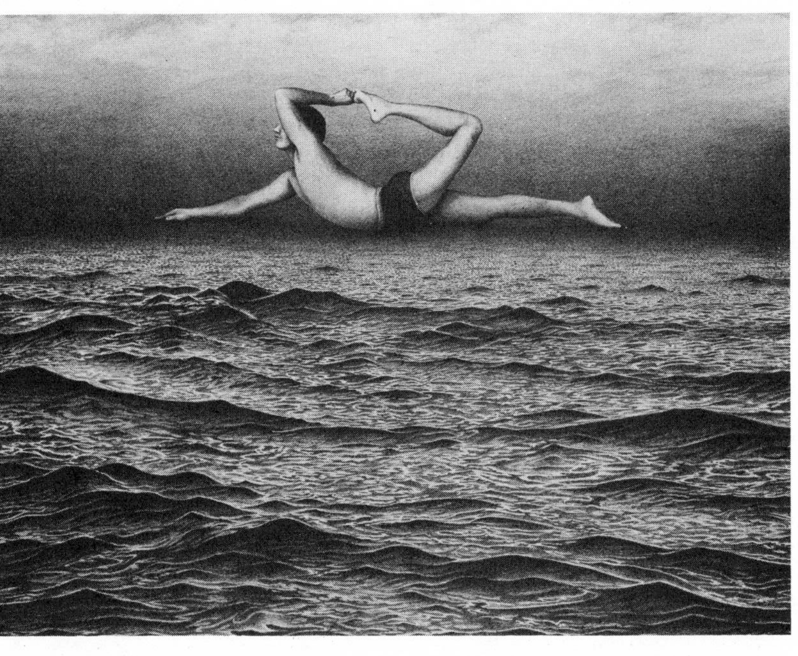

In New York City the Museum of Modern Art's summer exhibition "California Prints" showed Easterners what the graphic artists of the Pacific coast have been up to in the past decade. The varied works, including Robert Moon's 'Swami Vishnu #5' (shown), were fresh and lively and included dimensional prints as well as some done with photographic images, luminous inks, and even a Verifax machine.

COLLECTION, THE MUSEUM OF MODERN ART, NEW YORK CITY. JOHN B. TURNER FUND

COURTESY, MUSEUM OF CONTEMPORARY ART, CHICAGO

Ed Paschke's 'M. A. Lady' was included in the show "Chicago Imagist Art" at the Museum of Contemporary Art in Chicago.

known 17th-century French painter Georges de La Tour. The show included nearly all of his 30 or so known paintings and copies, as well as engravings of La Tour's lost works. The pictures were borrowed from collections all over the world, and the exhibition was the first—and probably the last—opportunity to study the artist's entire output in one place. In January, just prior to the Paris show, a previously unknown work by La Tour was discovered in the attic of a small museum in northeastern England.

In West Germany, for visitors to the 1972 Olympic Games, the municipal museum of Munich presented an exhibit titled "Bavaria—Art and Culture." The centerpiece, in the courtyard of the museum, was a reconstruction of a Roman villa discovered near Ingolstadt three years earlier. Another artistic attraction at the Olympics was a monumental loan exhibit entitled "World Cultures and Modern Art." With nearly 3,000 objects borrowed from museums and private collections around the world, the show examined the relationships between modern European painting and sculpture and the arts of the major non-Western cultures.

In London seemingly endless queues waited outside the British Museum to see the "Treasures of Tutankhamen." Originally scheduled to run from April until September, the exhibit was extended until December because of the great public response. The priceless collection of objects—including jewelry, furniture, weapons, and the famous gold portrait mask—was lent by the Egyptian government to mark the 50th anniversary of the discovery of Tutankhamen's tomb by the Englishmen Howard Carter and Lord Carnarvon.

Major Sculpture Shows

Three outstanding sculpture retrospectives were held in 1972. An exhibition devoted to the sculpture of Henri Matisse, organized by the Museum of Modern Art in New York City, included all 69 known bronzes by the artist. The pieces, dating from 1894 to 1950, were mostly lent by private collectors. Many of the female figures in the sculptures also appear in paintings by Matisse. The bronzes later traveled to the Walker Art Center in Minneapolis and the University Art Museum at Berkeley, Calif.

The largest exhibition of Henry Moore's works ever mounted in a single place was presented in Italy during the summer. The works, which covered nearly 50 years of Moore's activity, were installed in a spectacular open-air setting at the Forte di Belvedere overlooking the city of Florence. In addition to the 168 major sculptures in stone and bronze, drawings and gouaches by the artist were also shown. Jacques Lipchitz, another elder statesman of 20th-century sculpture, was also honored with a major retrospective. The show, at New York City's Metropolitan Museum of Art, was timed to coincide with the publication of the 81-year-old artist's autobiography, 'My Life in Sculpture'.

The 1972 Art Market

The prospect of the introduction of the value added tax (VAT) when Britain joined the European Economic Community was a source of great anxiety to the English art and antique trade. At first there seemed no way of avoiding the application of the 10% VAT to art sales, and it was feared that London would lose its pull as a center for tax-free auctions. However, in July the British government decided to use a loophole available in the rules for secondhand goods and to levy a VAT only on the dealer's profit or auctioneer's commission—and even then not on export sales. This announcement brought joy to the art market, although not to artists living in Great Britain, whose works, when first sold, would not be covered by the rule; any artist whose gross sales reached £5,000 (about $12,000) in a year would be liable for the tax.

In the most spectacular museum acquisition of the year, a Greek vase from the 6th century B.C. was purchased by the Metropolitan Museum of Art for a rumored $1 million in cash, plus $300,000 in ancient coins from the museum's collection. The piece—a beautifully decorated calyx krater—bore the signature of Euphronius, one of the most famous vase painters.

New record prices were set for the works of many artists. An unsigned Madonna by Raphael, considered to be a monumental acquisition, was purchased by collector Norton Simon for about $3 million, reportedly the third highest price ever paid for a work of art. A painting and a sculpture by Amedeo Modigliani were also sold for record prices. The painting, a portrait of a red-haired woman, was sold at auction for slightly more than $280,000. The sculpture, a female head done in stone, brought more than $170,000.

Especially interesting to U.S. collectors, whose predecessors had bought 18th-century English portraits so lavishly in the 1920's and 1930's, was the renewed attention paid to the works of Thomas Gainsborough, George Romney, and Sir Joshua Reynolds. A portrait of the John Gravenor family by Gainsborough was sold at Sotheby's for $686,000.

Other noteworthy art sales included an elm wood 'Reclining Figure', by Henry Moore, for $260,000; a painting, 'Shade', by Jasper Johns, for $60,000; and a bronze piece, 'Coming Through the Rye', by Frederick Remington, for $125,000—a record for a U.S. sculpture. 'Steelworkers—Noontime', by Thomas Anshutz, sold for $250,000, the highest price ever paid for an American painting.

A splendid 14th-century Chinese ceramic wine jar went for $573,000 to a dealer from Japan after an expert from Christie's had noticed it serving as an umbrella stand in a house to which he had been called to advise on the sale of some Continental china. More Japanese buyers than ever were carrying back oriental art from London. Sales of European works, particularly by impressionists, to Japanese buyers were also increasing. (*See also* Museums. *See in* CE: Painting; Sculpture.)

CENTRAL PRESS FROM PICTORIAL PARADE

A breathtaking gold mask was part of the British Museum's "Treasures of Tutankhamen" exhibition.

This portrait by Goya of a small boy was given to the Metropolitan Museum of Art in July.

WIDE WORLD

PAKISTAN. Despite the humiliating military defeat suffered by Pakistan at the end of 1971—and the loss of its eastern region, which became the independent nation of Bangladesh—the year 1972 began with some optimism. Pakistan's new president, Zulfikar Ali Bhutto, presented the image of an able administrator closely attuned to the needs of his people. His two main tasks were to restore confidence at home and to convince the world that his country, in spite of the disasters of 1971, possessed the determination and resources to maintain its position in the comity of nations.

To gain foreign political and financial support for his government, President Bhutto set off on a round of diplomatic fence mending. He toured the Middle East and traveled to Peking, People's Republic of China, where he secured promises of increased economic aid from China. In March he visited with Soviet leaders in Moscow in an attempt to ease relations strained during the Bangladesh war. Bhutto withdrew Pakistan from the Commonwealth of Nations in January, following British recognition of the state of Bangladesh, but managed, nevertheless, to retain amicable relations with Great Britain.

Simultaneously, Bhutto set about solving some of the country's domestic problems. In January he announced large-scale economic reforms. Ten

"THE NEW YORK TIMES"

Pakistani refugees from the war with India seek food rations at a center in Shakargarh. Almost 1.5 million people were left homeless and landless by the fighting.

basic industries—including iron and steel, cement, petrochemicals, heavy engineering, and gas and oil refineries—were brought under state management, without affecting foreign investments and foreign credit. Increased job benefits and better working conditions were promised for labor.

A new land reform program, announced in March, drastically reduced the ceiling on individual and family holdings. The new program involved more than one million acres that had not been affected by previous reform attempts. Plans for a new educational program were also revealed, calling for free schooling through the eighth grade and nationalization of profit-making private colleges.

Pending the draft of a new permanent constitution, an interim constitution was approved in April, allowing Bhutto to govern until August 1973. At the same time, the National Assembly passed an overwhelming vote of confidence in the president, in response to his pledge to end the martial law regime that had been in force since 1969.

In the aftermath of the December 1971 war, India continued to occupy Pakistani territory and to hold as prisoners nearly 100,000 Pakistani soldiers reportedly captured during the fighting. Another problem for President Bhutto—and a source of great public concern—was the repatriation of the 1.5 million non-Bengalis living in Bangladesh. Meeting late in June, Bhutto and India's Prime Minister Indira Gandhi spent five days in intensive negotiations. The result was an agreement calling for the resolution by peaceful means of the differences between the two countries. The accord left many key issues unsolved, among them the repatriation of Pakistani war prisoners and the disputed status of Kashmir; after further talks, however, a cease-fire line in Kashmir was agreed to, Pakistan released Indian prisoners of war, and Indian troops began to withdraw from Pakistan.

Even after the establishment of a separate Bengali nation, Pakistan continued to be torn by dissenting ethnic minorities. In the Sind Province Urdu-speaking residents, who made up about 45% of the province's population, were angered when the Sind assembly adopted Sindhi as the official language. Several persons were killed during July and August in riots. Bhutto proposed a compromise plan, but tension remained high. (*See also* Bangladesh; India. *See in* CE: Pakistan.)

PANAMA. The government of Panama under Gen. Omar Torrijos continued its ban on free speech and press, popular political activity, and political parties in 1972, but in August the first election held since 1968 sent 505 delegates to a National Assembly. One of the assembly's first actions was the passage of a toughly worded resolution stating that Panama had never sold or ceded the Canal Zone to the U.S. and that the U.S. had "arbitrarily occupied" the Zone. The assembly also voted to reject the $1.93-million annuity that the U.S. paid for use of the Zone.

While the resolution was in keeping with the increased nationalism of the Torrijos government, U.S. officials were caught by surprise. Negotiations concerning the Canal Zone, which had been taking place sporadically, were stalemated over the issue of sovereignty. Some Panamanian demands, including an increased annuity, a transfer of some land back to Panama, and the substitution of a term of years for the perpetual term, were seen as possibilities by the U.S.; but neither side showed any flexibility on the issue of ultimate control of the Zone. In the area of internal economic development, the Panamanian government pushed for increased exports of bananas, sugar, and petroleum derivatives. (*See in* CE: Panama, Republic of.)

PARAGUAY. The government of President Alfredo Stroessner of Paraguay remained firmly in power in 1972, despite criticism from both the Roman Catholic church and the U.S. government. After the expulsion from Paraguay of eight priests for alleged subversion and government criticism of the church for its patronage of various agrarian leagues, the church canceled its traditional service in celebration of Paraguayan Independence Day. Relations with the U.S. were threatened when

Paraguay refused to extradite Auguste Joseph Ricord, a known French narcotics trafficker, to the U.S. Following threats of aid cutbacks and suspension of the U.S. sugar quota, Paraguay relented and extradited Ricord, but not before angry charges had been made of Paraguayan officials' complicity in the Latin American narcotics trade. Meanwhile, Paraguay was trying to lessen its dependence upon the U.S. by establishing closer contacts with Japan.

The economic situation improved during the year. Compared with the 1971 trade deficit of $5 million, midyear figures showed an $8.2-million surplus. However, inflation darkened the picture somewhat. (*See in* CE: Paraguay.)

PEOPLE OF THE YEAR. The following people made news—good and bad—in 1972. For other noted persons see individual biographies by name.

A disputed memo allegedly written by **Dita Beard,** a lobbyist for the giant International Telephone & Telegraph Corp. (ITT), produced a controversy. The memo, released by newspaper columnist **Jack Anderson,** provided strong evidence that **Attorney General John N. Mitchell** was involved in some under-the-table dealings. The memo indicated that Mitchell was willing to withdraw an antitrust suit against ITT in return for financial favors for the Republican party. Mrs. Beard at first claimed she had not written the memo; as the issue became a political hot potato, however, she disappeared, turning up a week later in a Denver, Colo., hospital, under treatment for heart trouble. ITT's admission that one of its policies was to destroy "sensitive" records in an automatic paper shredder aided sales of the machines.

The 1972 summer Olympic Games were the last hurrah for **Avery Brundage,** president of the International Olympic Committee (IOC), who retired at the age of 84. He had been a fanatic adherent to the principles of amateurism and apolitical sports, principles that became very difficult to enforce. He had punished many athletes for what he considered to be violations of his directives. Soviet gymnast **Olga Korbut** and U.S. swimmer **Mark Spitz** were two Olympic favorites: the 84-pound, 17-year-old girl charmed all observers with her nearly flawless early performances—and with her embarrassed tears when she finally botched an exercise. She later won two individual gold medals. Spitz, a handsome and unbeatable performer, gathered seven gold medals—more than any other athlete in Olympic history.

At the Academy Award ceremonies in April, the filmed retrospective of the work of **Charlie Chaplin** faded off the screen, the theater was dark—and then spotlights revealed the 82-year-old comedian and film legend, appearing on a U.S. stage for the first time in more than 20 years. He had been in semivoluntary exile since 1952, but returned to receive a special award.

John B. Connally, Jr., the Texas Democrat who became U.S. President Richard M. Nixon's secretary of the treasury, bolted his party in 1972 to form Democrats for Nixon, a well-funded group that carried on much of the president's advertising campaign.

One of the briefest moments of glory during the 1972 presidential campaign belonged to **Senator Thomas F. Eagleton** (D, Mo.), who was originally chosen by Senator George S. McGovern as the Democratic vice-presidential candidate. To head off disclosures by enterprising reporters, however, Eagleton later announced that he had once been hospitalized for severe depression and had received electroshock therapy. McGovern announced that he was behind Eagleton "1,000%"—but evidently asked the Missourian to withdraw a few days later as pressure against Eagleton mounted. Eagleton withdrew, but in the wake of the dispute lay major questions about both the honesty and sensitivity of those involved. A somewhat bitter Eagleton, after McGovern's defeat, stated that he felt he had been made a scapegoat for the loss. He drew much public admiration and sympathy.

Relatives of the two major presidential candidates shared the spotlight. **Julie Nixon Eisenhower,** the president's daughter, stated in September that she was "willing to die" to protect the regime of South Vietnam's President Nguyen Van Thieu. On October 4 **Eleanor McGovern** disagreed sharply and told an Illinois audience, "I think there's been enough killing and dying for a corrupt regime." Mrs. McGovern gained a great deal of popularity for her active campaigning on behalf of her husband.

Lowell Elliott, an Indiana farmer who found $500,000 dropped in his field by a plane hijacker, refused to accept a reward of $10,000 from the airline involved. He felt that, since the hijacker had been given a $500,000 ransom, he was entitled to a larger reward.

L. Patrick Gray III became acting director of the Federal Bureau of Investigation (FBI) after the death of the FBI's legendary director **J. Edgar Hoover.** (*See* Obituaries.) Gray instituted a number of reforms: somewhat less conservative dress and hairstyles for agents, recruitment of women and blacks, and acceptance of criticism from FBI employees—a practice Hoover had considered to be a firing offense. An ardent supporter of President Nixon, Gray was expected to be named permanent director.

Edward V. Hanrahan, the colorful, tough, and sometimes hated state's attorney of Cook County, Ill., was known as the "fightin'est Democrat of them all." For years a part of Chicago **Mayor Richard J. Daley's** regular Democratic organization, Hanrahan was dropped from favor after he was indicted in 1971 for conspiracy to obstruct justice in connection with the 1969 slayings of Black Panther party members Fred Hampton and Mark Clark by state's attorney's police. The in-

UPI COMPIX

Howard R. Hughes

WIDE WORLD

John B. Connally, Jr.

WIDE WORLD

L. Patrick Gray III

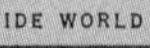

WIDE WORLD

Burt Reynolds and Dinah Shore

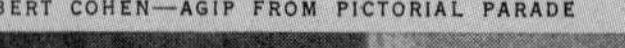

ROBERT COHEN—AGIP FROM PICTORIAL PARADE

Charlie Chaplin

dictment was dismissed a few days before the election, but Hanrahan was defeated by Republican **Bernard Carey** in a heavy vote by rebellious blacks in the city's traditionally Democratic strongholds.

Author **Clifford Irving** and his wife, **Edith,** who in 1971 claimed to have written an authorized biography of billionaire recluse **Howard R. Hughes,** were jailed in 1972. The "autobiography" was discredited by the normally silent Hughes, who went so far as to set up an interview by telephone with reporters to refute Irving's claim that he had helped write the book. The Irvings finally admitted that the book was a hoax and that they had never met Hughes. Irving received two and a half years in jail for fraud and Mrs. Irving two years, but she served only two months. Irving was sent to prison at Allenwood, Pa., where he began teaching creative writing. Hughes, mysterious as ever, left his hideaway in the Bahamas and settled in a hotel in Managua, Nicaragua. When Managua was nearly destroyed by earthquake in December, he flew to London.

Henry A. Kissinger, President Nixon's security adviser, seemed to spend half the year on secret missions—and the other half in a variety of spotlights. A French authoress claiming to have been close to him published a mildly scandalous memoir, 'Dear Henry'; an Iranian belly dancer planted herself in his lap during a press party; and he was seen in public with attractive Hollywood actresses. Asked for his secret, the owlish former Harvard professor replied, "Power is sexy."

Martha Mitchell and her husband, **John,** turned their backs on politics in 1972. Mrs. Mitchell al-

UPI COMPIX

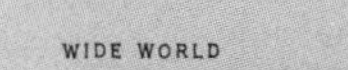

Thomas F. Eagleton

PICTORIAL PARADE

Julie Nixon Eisenhower

RAYMOND DEPARDON FROM GAMMA

Avery Brundage

WIDE WORLD

Eleanor McGovern

WIDE WORLD

Martha and John Mitchell

leged that she had been roughed up and injected with a tranquilizer by a security guard when she telephoned a newspaper to complain about "dirty politics." She soon demanded that Mitchell choose between his marriage and politics. He left his post as President Nixon's campaign manager and returned to law practice, and Mrs. Mitchell's famed telephone calls ceased.

A nine-year-old South Vietnamese girl, **Phan Thi Kim Phuc,** drew worldwide sympathy when a photograph was published showing her running, crying and naked, down a road after she was burned by a napalm attack that also killed her brother. (*See* page 476.) As she was recuperating in a hospital, another air strike destroyed her home.

A California government employee was summoned for jury duty but was too busy to serve, so he asked to be excused, noting that the summons indicated that public employees were exempt. Several days later, **Gov. Ronald Reagan** of California received another summons, asking him what his particular job in the government was.

Cosmopolitan magazine was looking for a male model for a nude center-fold spread—a kind of women's version of *Playboy's* playmates. When the April 1972 issue came out, the model was actor **Burt Reynolds,** strategically posed so that the picture could be published without a major scandal. In becoming an overnight sex symbol, he aided his career; but there was some question as to how his new reputation would affect his close romantic relationship with **Dinah Shore,** who had been known for years as one of Hollywood's sweetest and most wholesome entertainers.

PERU. The unusual military regime led by President Juan Velasco Alvarado continued in power in Peru in 1972. On January 1 Gen. Edgardo Mercado Jarrín, minister of foreign affairs, resigned and was appointed army chief of staff. Late in the year it was announced that Mercado would become prime minister on Jan. 1, 1973.

The National System of Support for Social Mobilization (SINAMOS) was active throughout the year, mobilizing support for the government, encouraging the formation of cooperative projects, and trying to fill the political vacuum created by the regime in a nation long known for political apathy among its people. Nine sugar plantations that had been nationalized in 1969 became full cooperatives in 1972 following elections in April for the plantation administrative councils. Almost all government-sponsored candidates were defeated by union leaders sympathetic to the American Popular Revolutionary Alliance movement (APRA), which had urged that the government appointees who ran the plantations be replaced by indigenous sugar workers. (*See in* CE: Peru.)

PHILIPPINES. The worst natural disaster in Philippine history occurred during the summer of 1972, when floodwaters swept through Manila and 14 provinces of the island of Luzon. The rainfall, which lasted six weeks, left millions of persons homeless or without food. Approximately 400 lives were lost, and it was said that the country's economy had been set back five years. In addition to coping with the social and economic problems caused by the disaster, President Ferdinand E. Marcos faced increased activity by Communist guerrillas and the renewal of clashes between the country's Christians and Muslims. In December increased activity by both Muslim and Communist guerrillas led the government to initiate an armed campaign against them.

On September 23, in a move that took most of the country by surprise, President Marcos declared martial law in the Philippines. The announcement came at the end of a month of terrorist bombings in Manila, which the military blamed on the Maoist New People's Army. There was also an unsuccessful attempt on the life of Defense Secretary Juan Ponce Enrile. A government spokesman said that Marcos had been considering martial law for some time, not because of specific incidents but in response to a "pattern of subversion" that was developing in the nation.

Under the decree, metropolitan police in Manila closed most of the newspapers and radio and television stations. A series of orders from the president, aimed at creating a "new society," included censorship of all domestic and international news media; a temporary ban on unofficial travel abroad by Filipinos; a ban on all public demonstrations; imposition of a curfew from midnight to 4 A.M.; military take-over of three Philippine airlines and all major utilities; and mass arrests of those accused of subversion or official misuse of authority. Later the scope of arrests was broadened to include evasion of income tax, crimes against public morals, and "crimes against liberty." Prominent politicians, journalists, educators, and businessmen were among the thousands of persons reported held in detention camps. In December Marcos moved to ease some press censorship and free some prisoners, although martial law remained in effect.

UPI COMPIX

Manilans read a government directive posted after President Marcos declared martial law.

In another aspect of his attempt to reshape Philippine society, President Marcos announced that sweeping land reforms would be instituted, permitting about 700,000 tenant farmers in the rice- and corn-growing areas to purchase about 12 acres of land each from their landlords. The original owners were to be allowed to retain only about 17 acres, with the provision that they work the land themselves.

Censorship of foreign news dispatches was lifted in November, but several Manila newspapers and radio-TV networks accused of opposing the government were permanently closed. Government control over the remaining mass-media facilities was extended by a strict license renewal system.

On November 29, delegates to a constitutional convention gave final approval to a draft constitution providing for a parliamentary, rather than a presidential, form of government. A national referendum on the new constitution was scheduled for Jan. 15, 1973.

Marcos' fears that political dissidents might try to injure him or members of his family were realized in December when his wife, Imelda Romualdez Marcos, was stabbed several times as she presided at a public ceremony. Her assailant was killed on the spot, and Mrs. Marcos was reported in safe condition after receiving 75 stitches to close wounds on her arms and hands. (*See in* CE: Philippines, The.)

PHOTOGRAPHY. Rising labor costs in West Germany in 1972 were making it increasingly difficult for some firms to continue manufacturing cameras and allied mechanical products in that country. Zeiss Ikon Corp., one of the best-known camera manufacturers, announced that the company would phase out camera production by mid-1973. Rollei expanded its operations in Singapore during 1972, and Ernst Leitz Ltd. of Wetzlar, West Germany, entered into a technical agreement with the Minolta Camera Co. Ltd. of Osaka, Japan.

At the annual meeting of the Polaroid Corp. at Needham, Mass., on April 25, Edwin Land introduced his latest and most revolutionary camera, the SX-70, a folding single-lens reflex camera. When folded for carrying, the SX-70 is only about one inch thick and fits into a suit pocket. Within about 1½ seconds after the shutter is snapped, the camera ejects a dry, blank film card; in a few minutes the picture develops and prints itself.

In March the Eastman Kodak Co. introduced a new line of cameras, the Pocket Instamatics, designed to take 16-mm. film cartridges. Along with the new pocket-sized cameras, Kodak introduced accessories, projectors, and a complete range of processing equipment. Among the new films introduced by Kodak during the year was Kodacolor II, which produced finer grain and greater sharpness than the original Kodacolor.

More firms in 1972 adopted multicoating of lens elements to achieve reduction in flare and avoid internal reflections. In addition, increased awareness was shown of reflecting surfaces—such as the iris diaphragms in lenses—and, as far as possible, these were also made nonreflecting.

Flash units giving automatic exposure control became increasingly popular, and a fundamental advance in design was first seen in the Rollei E36RE. The new system allows for recycling times as low as 0.3 second; as many as 400 flashes can be obtained from one set of batteries or accumulator charge. Several new flash units provide for a choice of apertures for automatic flash operation. This innovation allows the photographer to choose a wide aperture for distant subjects, thus extending the range at which automatic operation is possible.

JERRY N. UELSMANN

Jerry N. Uelsmann's photograph 'All-American Sunset' (1971) is from his spring exhibition in New York City: "As the South abandons its past."

At Photokina '72 the outstanding color exhibit was a series of 48 dye-transfer prints by Ernst Haas on the subject of 'The Creation'. 'Universalists', another Photokina exhibit, displayed work by four major European photojournalists, Mario de Biasi, Jack Garofalo, Donald McCullin, and Robert Lebeck. Among the outstanding U.S. photographers to be given individual museum exhibitions during 1972 were photojournalist David Douglas Duncan, Jerry N. Uelsmann, and the late Diane Arbus. (*See in* CE: Photography articles.)

New York City's Metropolitan Museum of Art presented a special photographic exhibit, "Behind the Great Wall," of photographs of China from 1870 to 1971. The timely exhibit included historical events and snapshots by such well-known photographers as Capa (left), Cartier-Bresson, Riboud, and Burri.

ROBERT CAPA FROM MAGNUM

PHYSICS. Research in high-energy physics was expected to get a tremendous boost after 1972, when the proton accelerator at the National Accelerator Laboratory (NAL) began operating at energy levels in excess of 200 billion electron volts (GeV). Located some 30 miles west of Chicago and built with $250 million of Atomic Energy Commission money, the NAL accelerator reached 100 GeV in February. When it did, scientists at NAL celebrated the feat with a bottle of vodka left by visiting scientists from the Soviet Union as a token to the moment when the U.S. machine would outperform the 76-GeV Soviet device near Moscow, formerly the world's most powerful. Later, the NAL unit was boosted to levels of 200 GeV and then 300 GeV. Scientists at NAL believed they would eventually hit 500 GeV with their machine. Physicists were hopeful that at these high energy levels a new scientific world would be encountered.

High-energy physics also had its detractors in 1972. An editorial in *Science,* the journal of the prestigious American Association for the Advancement of Science, took high-energy physicists to task for producing little new theoretical knowledge even though the equipment at their disposal, such as the NAL accelerator, was considerably costly. Murray Gell-Mann, a Nobel prizewinner from the California Institute of Technology, countered the criticism by predicting that, as a result of expensive research, a theory was in the offing to explain the puzzling strong force that binds together the particles of an atom's nucleus.

A blue-ribbon team of physicists announced in 1972 that a drop-off in funds for U.S. physics research since 1967 could have unhappy consequences. In a report to the National Academy of Sciences in August, the physicists pointed out there had been a 25% cut in effective financial support for physics projects from federal agencies in the 1967–72 period. In their opinion, if more money was not forthcoming, the U.S. economy and defense system would suffer, and so would the international stature of U.S. physics.

Physicist Yu-li Pan works with a new carbon dioxide laser used in laser fusion research at the Lawrence Livermore Laboratory in California.

COURTESY, LAWRENCE LIVERMORE LABORATORY

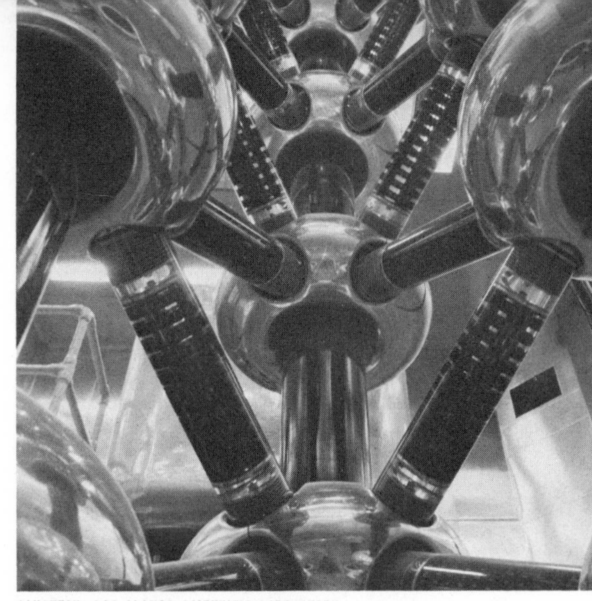

COURTESY, LOS ALAMOS SCIENTIFIC LABORATORY

A giant new accelerator at the Los Alamos Scientific Laboratory began operating in June.

Physicists continued their efforts to harness the massive energy generated when the nuclei of atoms fuse. The goal of fusion research was the generation of electric power for public use. However, the quick execution of this goal had been hampered by the inability of researchers to effectively overcome the electrical repulsion between the ions and electrons of the plasma medium used in fusion experiments. Unless the plasma is contained, not enough collisions occur for practical power generation. Although physicists had worked for some 20 years to contain the plasma with magnetic fields, some researchers were looking to lasers as possible means for generating thermonuclear power. In laser-induced fusion a burst of laser light would deliver enough energy to ionize a solid fuel pellet and thus induce a certain amount of fusion. It was hoped that fusions could be sustained long enough by this method to practically produce electricity, a distinct possibility since the "microexplosions" of the fuel would occur as long as a succession of pellets were dropped into the so-called laser putt-putt machine.

Lasers had recently been used for more accurately measuring the speed of light (2.997924562×10^8 meters per second, or 186,282.396 miles per second), for fusing a detached retina in the eye, and for many other scientific purposes. But prior to 1972, national standards for laser safety were not in existence. At certain wavelengths laser beams could destroy biological tissue, although few laser accidents had been reported. During the year the American National Standards Institute (ANSI) worked out a set of standards to be used in determining safe levels of laser exposure. (*See in* CE: Physics.)

POLAND. National elections were held one year ahead of schedule in Poland in 1972. To complete the reorganization of party and state administrations that had been started in 1970, Communist Party First Secretary Edward Gierek dissolved the Sejm (parliament) and held new elections on March 19. The Polish electoral system was unique in the socialist bloc in that voters could indicate their opinions of particular candidates by crossing out names on the ballots. In one constituency, for example, Gierek registered 99.8% popularity, but Jozef Kepa, first secretary of the party organization in Warsaw, the capital, obtained only 93.3%. Despite these vague indications of discontent, the new Sejm was divided in precisely the same proportions as the previous assembly: 255 deputies from Gierek's Polish United Workers' party (PUWP), 117 from the United Peasant's party (UPP), 39 from the Democratic party, and 49 from nonparty Roman Catholic groups. Because the National Unity Front was composed of the PUWP, UPP, and the Democrats, and because some Roman Catholic deputies supported the government, there were no indications that the elections would produce any startling policy changes in Poland.

The Sejm assembled for a short session on March 28 and elected Stanislaw Gucwa, chairman of the UPP's Supreme Executive, as speaker. Henryk Jablonski was chosen as chairman of the Council of State. Several new ministers were chosen for the Council of Ministers as well. The Sejm approved a new five-year plan on June 10 that was directed to the needs of discontented Polish workers and that envisaged a 40% growth of the national income. On October 31 the government extended, for an unspecified period of time, the freeze on food prices introduced in January 1971.

On May 17 the West German Bundestag ratified the Warsaw Treaty of Dec. 7, 1970, by which West Germany recognized the inviolability of Poland's western frontier. The two countries established diplomatic relations in September. U.S. President Richard M. Nixon visited Poland on May 31 and engaged in "constructive" talks with Polish leaders. Trade between the U.S. and Poland was expected to increase with the creation of a joint trade commission and the signing of a long-term trade agreement by the two countries. A ten-year agreement on economic cooperation was signed with France in October. (*See in* CE: Poland.)

POLICE. In 1972, more women were employed as police officers in the U.S. This apparent trend caused deep resentment in many of the nation's police departments. The Law Enforcement Assistance Administration investigated and negotiated settlements of two complaints charging the police departments of Wichita Falls, Tex., and Rochester, N.Y., with sex discrimination. In Washington, D.C., 40 women were used to perform regular patrol work; in Miami, Fla., over 20 were used; and in Peoria, Ill., 7. In New York City 15 women who had been given specialized training were given assignments on June 23 to work with neighborhood police teams around the city.

There were 126 law enforcement officers killed due to felonious criminal action in 1971 as compared with 100 in 1970 and 86 in 1969. Of the police murders in 1971, 121 were perpetrated by firearms—94 by handguns, 16 by rifles, and 11 by shotguns. During the ten-year period from 1962 to 1971, 722 officers were murdered.

In Detroit, Mich., on March 9, 1972, a sheriff's deputy was killed and three deputies were wounded by gunfire when three policemen burst into an apartment where five deputies were playing cards. One of the survivors, Deputy Sheriff James Jenkins, was shot in the temple, abdomen, and leg, and he lost his sight in one eye. Both the Detroit police department and the Wayne County sheriff's office called the shooting a "tragic mix-up." All of the policemen and the deputies were black. The policemen were members of a special unit called STRESS, an acronym for "Stop the Robberies—Enjoy Safe Streets," which was formed in January 1971 to reduce street crime.

It was reported in January 1972 that police corruption, including charges of selling heroin and accepting payoffs from gamblers and prostitutes, had been uncovered in police departments and sheriffs' offices in at least 23 states and in the Dis-

Police in Baltimore, Md., have rediscovered the bicycle—and crime rates have gone down. Cycle patrols are quick, quiet, and maneuverable.

"THE NEW YORK TIMES"

trict of Columbia. Grand juries in the District of Columbia investigated allegations of kickbacks, shakedowns, and perjury involving at least 16 policemen. Eight other policemen in Washington, D.C., including one lieutenant, were indicted on January 21 for conspiracy and for lodging false vice charges. In June a federal source reported that five Chicago policemen were suspected of being members of an "assassin squad" that was part of a nationwide attempt to gain control of narcotics traffic in big city ghettos. This narcotics war was allegedly responsible for at least 14 killings in Gary, Ind., and had spread to the nation's largest cities including New York City; Pittsburgh, Pa.; Detroit; Cleveland, Ohio; and St. Louis, Mo., as well as Chicago and Gary.

In the fall a federal grand jury indicted more than 20 Chicago policemen on extortion charges stemming from alleged shakedowns of tavern owners. The widespread corruption revealed by the grand jury was the worst Chicago police scandal since 1960. In New York City it was discovered that 81 pounds of heroin being held as evidence by the police had been stolen; police involvement was feared. (*See in* CE: Police.)

POLITICAL PARTIES. Confronted with the riddles of a highly unusual national election, both major political parties in the U.S. ended 1972 with an effort to redefine their identities. The Republicans won the presidency by the biggest margin in their history but failed to make significant gains in the U.S. Congress. Democrats lost the presidency by the biggest margin in their history but stayed in firm control of Congress and a majority of state governorships. Before the year ended, both parties had replaced their national chairmen.

In the campaign for the presidency, U.S. President Richard M. Nixon faced only nominal opposition within the Republican party. Rep. Paul N. McCloskey, Jr. (Calif.), opposed him on a platform of an immediate end to the war in Vietnam and what he termed a restoration of truth in government. Rep. John M. Ashbrook (Ohio) campaigned on the assertion that Nixon had repudiated his 1968 campaign promises by deficit spending, by proposing a system of guaranteed income to replace welfare procedures, and by allowing trade with Communist nations. Neither candidate posed a serious threat.

At the start of 1972, Senator Edmund S. Muskie (Me.) was the unquestioned front-runner for the Democratic nomination. His campaign faltered, however, in New Hampshire, when he fell short of the 50% that was viewed as the minimum vote needed to establish a claim of national leadership. Senator George S. McGovern (S.D.), on the other hand, established his credentials as a serious candidate by gaining 37%. Rep. Wilbur D. Mills (Ark.) and Senator Vance Hartke (Ind.) trailed so badly that they were virtually eliminated from serious consideration. Muskie later charged that his campaign was victimized by a "systematic campaign of sabotage," including forgery of a racial slur on voters of French Canadian descent.

A week later in Florida, Gov. George C. Wallace of Alabama established his claim to a national candidacy. He garnered 42% of the vote; Hubert H. Humphrey, the Democrats' 1968 presidential nominee, ran second with 18%; Senator Henry M. Jackson (Wash.) third with 13%; and Senator Muskie fourth with 9%. Reporters noted that Wallace's appeal was not entirely Southern or racial; it related to a discontent with many facets of U.S. society, including tax loopholes for the rich and foreign aid.

The Wisconsin primary on April 4 bolstered McGovern's hopes by putting him ahead of the Democratic field with 30% of the vote. Governor Wallace ran a surprising second with 22%, part of it from Republicans who crossed over in Wisconsin's open primary. Humphrey ran third with a

Though public attention centered on the two major presidential candidates, others had various party endorsements, such as (from left) Linda Jenness, Socialist Workers party; E. Harold Munn, Prohibition party; and John C. Schmitz, American party.

WIDE WORLD

disappointing 21% in a state where he was well known. Senator Muskie scored an all but disastrous 10%. Again, political observers noted a mood of discontent among the voters. Both McGovern and Wallace stressed tax reform.

Violence marred the process of selecting a Democratic presidential candidate for the second successive time. The first incident occurred on June 5, 1968, when Robert F. Kennedy was assassinated just as primary victories had made him front-runner. On May 15, 1972, Governor Wallace was shot just as he finished speaking in Laurel, Md., on the eve of his greatest political triumph. He survived the assassination attempt but was left crippled and, it developed, out of the presidential race. On the next day, he won the Maryland primary with 39% of the votes, followed by Humphrey with 27% and McGovern with 22%. In Michigan, where school busing was the primary issue, Wallace took a startling 51% of the party vote, followed by 27% for McGovern and 16% for Humphrey.

After a seesaw series of primaries in other states, McGovern virtually assured himself the nomination on June 6, when he ran ahead in primaries in California, New Jersey, New Mexico, and his home state, South Dakota. During his primary campaigns, McGovern called for a system of taxable federal grants to all people in the U.S. to replace the welfare system. The grants would, in effect, subsidize only low-income families. He urged sharp increases in inheritance tax rates, closing of income tax loopholes, and increased spending for social legislation and urban programs. He proposed a $32-billion cut in defense spending and favored amnesty for those who refused to be drafted during the war in Vietnam. He endorsed school busing as a tool for ending school segregation. He opposed legalization of marijuana but favored reduction of penalties for possession. Above all, he sought an end to the war.

The Democratic National Convention in Miami Beach, Fla., was the first to operate under rules drafted by a reform commission ordered in 1968. Disputes arose over the rules specifying that delegate selection must be open to youth, the poor, women, blacks, and other minority groups and brought precedent-setting appeals to the courts. An appeals court ruled that California's delegation, pledged to McGovern under the state's winner-take-all primary system, was not in violation and could be seated; but the court ruled that the convention had a right to unseat part of the Illinois delegation. That segment, including Mayor Richard J. Daley of Chicago, had been elected in a state primary but was charged with violating party guidelines on minority representation and on intervention of the party organization in the primaries.

The U.S. Supreme Court threw out the ruling, however, deciding that the convention should settle the matter. The convention seated the California delegates and barred the Daley slate in Illinois, seating a rival, pro-McGovern group. The convention went on to nominate McGovern over the bitter opposition of many party regulars.

The delegates voted to restructure the party. The convention enlarged the national committee from 110 to more than 300 members and called for drafting of a permanent party charter, with a national committee conference in 1974 to consider its adoption. The convention also adopted rules to prevent any crossover of Republicans into Democratic primaries, voted to outlaw winner-take-all primaries for delegate selection, and specified that a woman be chairman of the 1976 convention.

McGovern's choice of Senator Thomas F. Eagleton (Mo.) for the vice-presidency was ratified. After the convention ended, McGovern chose Jean M. Westwood, Utah national committeewoman, to be national committee chairman.

They also ran, and for the office of president of the U.S., under their own party banners: Dr. Benjamin Spock, People's party; Gus Hall, American Communist party, U.S.A.; and John Hospers, Libertarian party.

WIDE WORLD

SANDERS, "MILWAUKEE JOURNAL," TM ® PUBLISHERS-HALL SYNDICATE

"Believe me I can explain this . . . as soon as I think of something!"

McGovern's campaign received a severe blow at its very beginning. With newspapers already in possession of the facts, Senator Eagleton admitted that he had been hospitalized three times for mental illness and on two of these occasions had received electric shock treatment for depression. McGovern, who was unaware of this when he chose Eagleton for his running mate, said at first that he supported Eagleton "1,000%." Later, as public furor over the nomination refused to abate, he asked Eagleton to withdraw. He said the controversy over the vice-presidency was dividing the party and preventing discussion of the primary campaign issues. It was the first time that a major party had removed a vice-presidential candidate from its ticket when he wished to stay on the ticket.

There followed several days of uncertainty as McGovern offered the vice-presidential nomination successively to Senator Edward M. Kennedy (Mass.), Senator Abraham Ribicoff (Conn.), Senator Humphrey, Gov. Reubin Askew of Florida, and Senator Muskie. All declined. Then R. Sargent Shriver, former head of the Peace Corps and a brother-in-law of Senator Kennedy, accepted. Meanwhile, McGovern had dropped 33 percentage points below Nixon in the public opinion polls. He never recovered substantially.

In contrast to the argumentative and prolonged Democratic convention, the Republican convention in Miami Beach the next month was a superbly arranged ovation to President Nixon and his policies. The only issue on which there was any split was the 1976—not the 1972—nomination. The liberal wing of the party sought to give the big industrial states a much larger share of representation at the next convention. The effort failed.

In his acceptance speech, President Nixon launched an appeal for a "new majority," an appeal designed to win Democratic voters from Senator McGovern, who had already alienated many in the preconvention struggles. The president cited progress made in foreign affairs through his summit trips to Moscow and to Peking, People's Republic of China. In an obvious slap at McGovern's defense stand, he warned that the U.S. must never go to an international conference "to negotiate from weakness." (*See also* Elections.)

After the Democrats' presidential election debacle, demands arose to restore the traditional political patterns of the party. An effort to impeach Mrs. Westwood, the national chairman, failed by five votes during the Democratic National Committee meeting on December 9. Soon afterward she offered her resignation. The committee, by a narrow majority, chose as her successor Robert F. Strauss, a Dallas, Tex., attorney.

On December 11 the Republican national chairman, Senator Robert Dole (Kan.), announced his resignation. To succeed him, President Nixon chose George Bush, U.S. ambassador to the United Nations, subject to party ratification. (*See in* CE: Political Parties.)

POPULATION. The U.S. Bureau of the Census reported in 1972 that the nation's population growth rate fell below 1% (to 0.98%) during 1971 for only the second time since 1940. A Census Bureau survey of birth expectations conducted in June 1972 revealed that the milestone replacement level of 2.1 children per woman of childbearing age had been achieved. Experts cautioned, however, that the 2.1 rate could not be called true "zero population growth" until it had been in effect for 70 years. The large number of women born during the post-World War II baby boom would also remain at prime childbearing age for another decade, thus adding to the U.S. population. Estimated resident total as of July 1 was 208.2 million; median age was 28.1 years.

Final results of the 1970 census showed that nearly three quarters of the population (73.5%) was concentrated on slightly more than 1.5% of the nation's land area. One person in 22 (about 9.4 million people) lived on a farm in 1971, compared to one in three in 1916.

In 1971, for the first time in history, more than half the nation's families had annual incomes over $10,000. The new median, $10,290, was 4.2% higher than the 1970 median of $9,870. Median annual income for black families in 1971 was $6,440 and $7,550 for families of Spanish origin. A small segment of black families—young husband-wife families living in the northern and western U.S., in which both members worked—achieved income parity with whites, achieving a 1.04-to-1 ratio of black to white incomes. There were 2.8 million families with incomes of $25,000 and over in 1971, while 19% of U.S. families had incomes of less than $5,000. A depressing note was that the number of people living below the low-income level was essentially unchanged in 1971—about 25.6 million people, 10% of the whites and 32% of the blacks, lived below the poverty line.

Final 1970 figures showed that more than 48% of employed persons held white-collar jobs. Another 36% (about 27.5 million) held blue-collar jobs.

Household size continued to decline. A survey taken early in 1972 showed that the average U.S. household had 3.06 members. More U.S. women were family heads in 1972: women headed 31.8% of black families and 9.4% of white families.

One factor that contributed to both the smaller size of households and the declining birthrate was a tendency among both men and women to remain single longer. In 1971, 56% of U.S. men and 45% of U.S. women were unmarried. This was an increase of 5% for men and 8% for women since 1960. While population experts assume that as many women as in the past will eventually marry, the trend toward later marriage would slow the birthrate.

More active lives being led by the 20 million people in the U.S. who were 65 or older on April 1, 1970, was reflected in census statistics. Of this group, 9.9 million men and women were family heads and another 5.1 million were maintaining their own households apart from relatives. Only 1.1 million older people were living in institutions or had other group living arrangements.

In 1972 the United Nations proclaimed 1974 as World Population Year. It also announced plans for a major conference to deal with population problems. (*See in* CE: Census; Population.)

PORTUGAL. In 1972 Portugal remained politically stable, but economic progress was again limited. The main political event of the year was the election on July 25 of 77-year-old Rear Adm. Américo de Deus Rodrigues Thomáz to a third seven-year term as president.

Some commentators felt that the reelection of Thomáz signaled a formal end to the attempt by the prime minister, Marcello José das Neves Alves Caetano, to introduce a measure of political liberalization. Many of the reforms effected by Caetano's government represented only nominal changes. A new press law that came into effect in June abolished the old board of censors but provided for "official preexamination of news." Similarly, a new police agency called the General Department of Security was established, but it was granted much the same power as the old secret police, the Pide.

In midyear the government took steps to curb inflation, which had been mounting steadily since 1966. The commerce minister was given authority to control the prices of goods and services, and increased taxes were imposed on high profits and incomes.

The Caetano government continued its efforts to develop the overseas territories while suppressing nationalist guerrilla activity. In May the National Assembly granted new measures of internal autonomy to Angola and Mozambique, although the legislation left no doubt that the government in Lisbon, the capital of Portugal, was still firmly in control. With the overseas territories absorbing nearly two thirds of Portugal's annual defense budget, some observers saw the movement toward increased autonomy as a means of shifting defense costs from Portugal to the territories themselves. (*See in* CE: Portugal.)

POSTAL SERVICE. A major cost-trimming effort and a campaign to improve mail delivery service occupied the U.S. Postal Service in 1972. On July 1 the former Post Office Department marked its first birthday as a corporate-style, semi-independent government agency. The concerted push to cut escalating costs began soon after Elmer T. (Ted) Klassen, former president of American Can Co., in January 1972 became the nation's 63d postmaster general, succeeding Winton M. Blount, who had resigned three months earlier to run for elective office.

Klassen, who had been deputy postmaster general—the number two postal official—for a period in 1969 and 1970, outlined the belt-tightening drive in a March 28 filmed speech to the postal service's 720,000 employees. He announced a temporary hiring freeze and other economy moves and explained that the postal service's aim was to avert a $450-million increase in mail rates, included in the service's budget for the 1973 fiscal year, which began July 1, 1972.

On August 29 Klassen announced that economies realized from the freeze and from other budget cuts had eliminated the need in January 1973 for a 1¢

The world's largest mail-distribution plant began processing bulk mail by zip code in Kearny, N.J., in 1972.

WILLIAM E. SAURO FROM "THE NEW YORK TIMES"

boost in first-class letter rates to 9¢ per ounce from 8¢. The ban on hiring was lifted in certain areas of the nation.

While delivery service improved during the year for airmail and certain first-class letters, other cutbacks in service aided the growing number of competitors to the postal service, primarily private mail delivery firms. The volume of first-class letters actually declined from the preceding year.

The Postal Rate Commission, which reviews the postal service's rate requests, approved $1.37 billion in higher annual postal fees on June 5, 1972. The nine governors of the postal service on July 6 ratified the increases, most of which had been placed into effect on a temporary basis on May 6, 1971, pending a final decision by the Postal Rate Commission. Rates for third-class mail items, primarily advertising circulars, were increased an average of 24% on March 12, 1972.

Work that began in 1970 continued on a billion-dollar network of 33 major facilities to process packages and other bulk mail items. The world's largest such facility was opened in Kearny, N.J. The service in January 1972 successfully sold its first public offering, an issue of $250 million in 25-year bonds, with proceeds earmarked for the mechanization construction program. (*See also* Stamps. *See in* CE: Postal Service articles.)

PRISONS. The bloody 1971 uprising at New York's Attica State Correctional Facility continued to influence U.S. prisons in 1972. The Attica facility itself was the scene of a protest in July when several hundred inmates refused to leave their cells after a popular nurse was dismissed. Authorities declared a state of emergency there, but peace was restored when the nurse's reinstatement was promised. In September a commission that was appointed in 1971 to study the Attica revolt released a 518-page report describing the rebellion as "unplanned" and criticized New York's Gov. Nelson A. Rockefeller for refusing to appear at the prison when requested to do so by both inmates and prison authorities. Rockefeller, who in February 1972 deleted some $22 million in funds from the state prison system's budget request, had refused to go to Attica for fear of "setting a precedent."

A photo released in April by the New York State Special Commission on Attica shows guarded inmates after the rebellion of the previous September.

WIDE WORLD

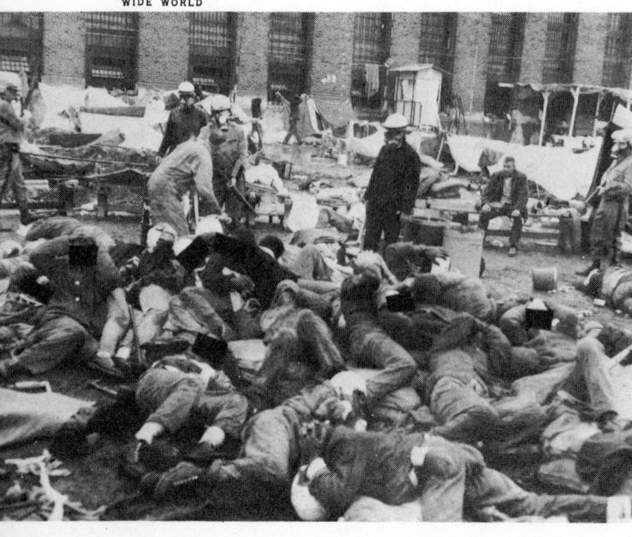

CORNELL CAPA FROM MAGNUM

A photographic essay on prison life at Attica was presented by the special commission in April.

Two uprisings in Maryland prisons in July, one at the Maryland House of Correction and another a few days later at the Maryland State Penitentiary, ended after Maryland's Gov. Marvin Mandel agreed to talk with inmates if peace was restored. The two incidents involved eight injuries and an estimated $3 million in damages. A 22-hour rebellion at the District of Columbia Jail ended after a district court judge agreed to hear many inmates' cases and barred any reprisals by authorities against the inmates involved. Smaller disturbances occurred in prisons in Arizona, California, Kentucky, New Jersey, New York, and Texas during the year.

Inmate demands centered around several issues in most of the protests: overcrowding, poor medical care, and long pretrial confinement. Substandard conditions in several state and local penal systems came under fire during the year: the American Civil Liberties Union described the District of Columbia Jail as "a filthy example of man's inhumanity to man"; a federal judge found "barbarous" and "shocking" neglect of the medical needs of Alabama prison inmates; and another federal judge attacked Mississippi prison buildings as "unfit for human habitation." Florida briefly closed its prisons to new admissions in January to prevent further overcrowding. These and other disclosures led to the instituting of some reforms in New York and the use of National Guard medical and dental units to treat New Jersey state prison inmates.

Discontent among prison guards also surfaced during the year. Some Maryland guards threatened to strike after the July uprisings as a protest against what they characterized as a lack of concern for their safety; guards in one Maryland prison held a "sick-in" and New Jersey guards staged a two-hour walkout.

Several well-known prisoners were paroled during the year. Among them were the Rev. Daniel J. Berrigan and the Rev. Philip F. Berrigan, who had been imprisoned for burning draft records; publisher Ralph Ginzburg, who had served time on an obscenity conviction; and former International Brotherhood of Teamsters president James R. Hoffa, who upon his release began a personal campaign for prison reform. (*See also* Crime; Law. *See in* CE: Prisons and Punishments.)

PSYCHOLOGY. In 1972 the American Psychological Association (APA) drew up a list of dos and don'ts for psychological experiments. The ethics code consisted of ten major parts, including a demand that experimenters obtain informed consent from their subjects before proceeding. Another tenet of the code insisted that all information derived from research subjects remain confidential. The ethics code underwent some modification before the APA presented it to the full membership for review and comment. Should the code receive approval from the membership, the APA would be able to censure and even expel psychologists who failed to adhere to it.

Violence was a topic of psychological research in 1972. A team of University of Michigan scientists studying attitudes among U.S. men toward violence found that few of the 1,400 men surveyed believed that war and some forms of police activity —considered forms of institutional violence— really constituted violence.

The women's liberation movement sparked a protest from many women scientists who argued that research into female attitudes should be done by women. Voicing the same sentiments as blacks and other minority group members, they felt that studies performed by anyone who was not a member of the group under scrutiny were tinged with bias and, hence, were not a fair measurement of that group.

A study of attitudes held by 2,200 welfare recipients toward work disclosed that the poor identified with the work ethic in much the same way as did 2,200 middle-class subjects. The study concluded that the middle-class misconception of the desire of the poor to gain the psychological and material rewards associated with work distorted public policies. As a result, public attention was distracted from the real problems faced by the poor, such as inequities in education and in employment.

The long-simmering controversy over IQ (intelligence quotient) tests grew hotter as researchers disputed the theories of several scientists who maintained that race had a bearing on intelligence. Much of the work in opposition to this view centered on the point that IQ tests were slanted toward white Anglo-Saxon middle-class culture. One study showed that the culture bias caused thousands of black and Chicano (Mexican-American) children to be unfairly classified as retarded. A psychologist reported that up to 30% of an achievement test was actually a test of cultural background, enough to account for group differences in test scores. (*See also* Mental Health. *See in* CE: Psychology.)

Meditators, plugged into Bioscope machines, are seeking serenity and peaceful, alert relaxation by tracking their alpha brain waves.

RALPH CRANE FROM LIFE MAGAZINE © TIME INC.

PUBLISHING, BOOK. The year of the gull and the gulled was the way book publishers described 1972. The gull, of course, was celebrated in Richard Bach's 'Jonathan Livingston Seagull', an illustrated allegory that broke all sales records since 'Gone with the Wind' by selling more than a million copies during the year. The gulled were McGraw-Hill, Inc., and *Life* magazine (among others), victims of the most flamboyant and expensive ($750,000) literary hoax in history, Clifford Irving's spurious 'Autobiography of Howard Hughes'.

News and publishing interacted, and so books on the People's Republic of China and on chess proliferated in 1972. Two reports on the championship chess match between Robert J. (Bobby) Fischer and Boris Spassky were published within a week of Fischer's victory.

A modest decline in the total number of new books and new editions published—27,403 titles in the first nine months of 1972; 28,494 in the same period of 1971—reflected diminishing markets for fiction and literature, textbooks, history, and scholarly reprints.

The publishing of mass-market paperbacks surged from 2,985 in 1971 to an estimated total

WIDE WORLD

Author Clifford Irving and his wife, Edith, were sentenced by a federal court for grand larceny in connection with the sale of a fake autobiography of billionaire Howard Hughes.

for 1972 in excess of 3,500. New peaks were reached in the prices paid for reprint rights by paperback publishers. Avon Books bid more than $1 million each for 'I'm O.K., You're O.K.' and 'Jonathan Livingston Seagull'.

Several established writers were represented on the list of best-selling fiction in 1972. The list included 'The Winds of War', by Herman Wouk; 'The Word', by Irving Wallace; 'August 1914', by Aleksandr I. Solzhenitsyn; and 'Captains and the Kings', by Taylor Caldwell.

Nonfiction best sellers included 'I'm O.K., You're O.K.', by Thomas A. Harris; 'Eleanor and Franklin', by Joseph P. Lash; 'O Jerusalem!', by Larry Collins and Dominique Lapierre; 'Open Marriage', by Nena and George O'Neill; and 'The Boys of Summer', by Roger Kahn.

Perhaps the most significant technological development in microform publishing in 1972 was a system (capable of reproducing a long book on one small piece of film) that was more convenient and less expensive than similar systems. Its cost was about 25¢ per sheet, and it was readable in an inch-thick and completely portable reading device that cost only about $5.

During 1972 the leading publication of the book publishing industry, *Publishers Weekly,* celebrated its 100th anniversary. The American Institute of Graphic Arts, which annually selects the 50 best books from the viewpoint of design and production, observed its 50th anniversary. (*See also* Literature; People of the Year. *See in* CE: Books and Bookmaking.)

PUERTO RICO. In the November 1972 elections in Puerto Rico, Rafael Hernández Colón won the governorship and led the Popular Democratic party to an overwhelming and unexpected victory. The triumph reaffirmed that the majority of the people wanted Puerto Rico to remain a commonwealth, preferring neither independence nor statehood. The 36-year-old president of the Senate beat the incumbent Luis A. Ferré, 68, of the New Progressive party, who had favored Puerto Rico's becoming the 51st state. The election came just weeks after the Colonialism Committee of the United Nations had approved a resolution recognizing the "right of the people of Puerto Rico to self-determination."

A decline in both the tourist and sugar industries again hurt the economy in 1972. Unemployment was high, and manufacturers had to compete with those in cheap-labor areas such as Spain, Japan, Korea, and Taiwan. Though exempt from Phase II controls, the island's economy was hit by a U.S. business recession since half of all Puerto Rican goods went directly to the mainland.

On December 31 Puerto Rico lost its most popular sports hero when baseball star Roberto Clemente of the Pittsburgh Pirates was killed in a plane crash off the coast of San Juan while taking supplies to earthquake victims in Managua, Nicaragua. He had done much to aid underprivileged Puerto Rican children. National mourning was declared after his death. (*See in* CE: Puerto Rico.)

QATAR. In February 1972 Sheikh Ahmad bin Ali bin Abdullah al-Thani was ousted from power in Qatar by his cousin, the deputy ruler and prime minister, Sheikh Khalifa bin Hamad al-Thani, in a bloodless coup while Sheikh Ahmad was away on a hunting trip. The new ruler immediately announced a 20% increase in salaries for the civil service and army and cuts in the expenditures of the ruling family—whose several hundred members absorbed a major part of Qatar's oil revenues. In April Sheikh Khalifa appointed a 20-member advisory council, which he described as Qatar's first experiment in democracy.

Oil revenues were expected to exceed $175 million in 1972, although the national budget was put at about $50 million. In March it was announced that the Qatar Petroleum Co. and Shell Co. of Qatar had agreed to allow the government to acquire a 20% share in their concessions. In April the Qatar National Petroleum Co. was established to manage the government's 20% shares in the foreign companies, as well as to refine and market oil on its own.

RACE RELATIONS. The year 1972 was not marked by general improvements in U.S. race relations. The momentum of the civil rights movement of the 1960's had spent itself, and many organizations—including the National Association for the Advancement of Colored People (NAACP)—charged that public officials were fail-

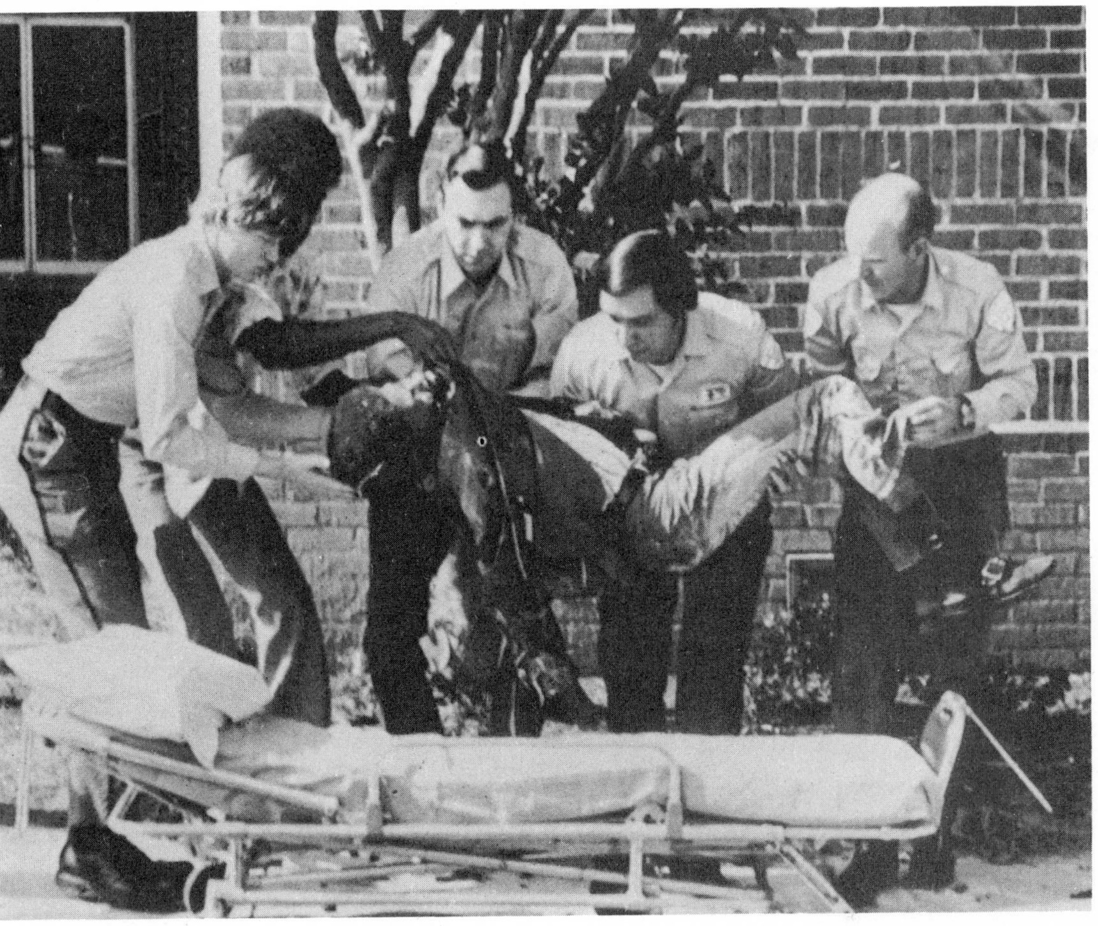

WIDE WORLD

Two black students were killed at Southern University in Baton Rouge, La., when police cleared the administration building of students protesting various university policies.

ing to provide positive leadership for the nation. The NAACP was particularly critical of U.S. President Richard M. Nixon's policies relating to blacks.

Income and Employment

Defining poverty income in 1971 as less than $4,137 for a family of four, the Bureau of the Census reported that 25.6 million people in the U.S. were living in poverty; this total included one in every three nonwhites and one in every ten whites. Earnings of black families had risen to $6,440, while earnings of white families rose to $10,670. A fifth of all black families, however, received less than $3,000.

The NAACP, at its annual convention in July, described the employment situation of urban blacks as worse "than at any time since the Great Depression" and estimated that one third of urban black youths out of school were without jobs. The U.S. Department of Labor released data showing that, while the unemployment rate for whites had declined from a 1971 average of 5.4% to 4.6% by November 1972, for blacks it held at 9.8%.

Part of the problem was attributed to the failure of federal antidiscrimination efforts. In June George Holland resigned as director of the Labor Department's Office of Federal Contract Compliance; he branded federal efforts to ensure nondiscrimination in hiring by federal contractors as "ineffective." In July the Federal Power Commission ruled that it did not have the power to enforce fair employment practices in utilities. In August President Nixon publicly opposed job quotas, a chief mechanism used by his own Administration to fight discrimination. After the president's statement, officials moved to quietly discard the much-heralded Philadelphia Plan, a federal effort to combat discrimination in the building trades.

There were some positive developments in the field of employment. In March the Congress passed a 1972 employment act that strengthened the U.S. Equal Employment Opportunity Commission (EEOC). First, the new act expanded the EEOC's jurisdiction to cover the employees of private as well as public educational institutions, state and local governments, and all companies and unions with at least 15 (rather than 25) workers;

WIDE WORLD

Two plainclothesmen brandish pistols while an injured policeman is dragged to safety during disturbances in New York City's Harlem.

second, the act empowered the EEOC to seek federal court action against employment discrimination. The Department of Health, Education, and Welfare followed up in October by issuing a 17-page set of minority employment guidelines to 2,500 colleges and universities with federal contracts. No quotas were set, although numerical goals and timetables were to be required.

School Desegregation

The issue of busing to achieve racial desegregation of public schools developed into a nationwide controversy in 1972 and became a key campaign issue. A Gallup survey in March found that 71% of the nation's whites opposed busing for desegregation (although 63% indicated that they favored desegregation). President Nixon came out strongly against busing; he proposed legislation to curtail the practice and substitute "equal educational opportunity" for racial integration, a position that was widely criticized by black leaders and civil rights proponents. (*See* Congress, U.S.)

Much of the concern over busing grew out of court orders involving racial desegregation, which affected a wide range of cities, south and north. In Richmond, Va., a federal judge ordered the city's predominantly black schools to be consolidated with predominantly white schools of two adjoining counties; a similar consolidation program was ordered in Detroit, Mich., and its surrounding suburbs. The U.S. Supreme Court agreed to hear an appeal from black and Chicano parents asking for desegregation of the Denver, Colo., public schools. The Court also upheld desegregation orders affecting Norfolk, Va., and Memphis and Nashville, in Tennessee. (*See also* Education.)

Political Power

The biggest news of 1972 presidential politics involved race relations in a number of ways. Representative Shirley Chisholm of Brooklyn, N.Y., formally announced her candidacy for the Democratic presidential nomination, becoming the first black woman to do so. Other blacks who served in key Democratic party roles were: Yvonne Brathwaite Burke, cochairman of the Democratic convention; Basil Patterson, vice-chairman of the Democratic National Committee; and Patricia Roberts Harris, permanent chairwoman of the party's Credentials Committee. Blacks also comprised 4% of the delegates at the Republican convention and 14% at the Democratic convention.

The Black Caucus in the House of Representatives gained three new members: Mrs. Burke, a former state assemblywoman, won a seat from Los Angeles; Barbara C. Jordan, a former state senator, won a seat from Houston, Tex.; and the Rev. Andrew Young, a former aide to the late Martin Luther King, Jr., won a seat from Atlanta, Ga. Miss Jordan and Young were the first black representatives from the South since 1901. Two young black mayors were elected in Alabama: John Ford in Tuskegee, where 80% of the population was black, and A. J. Cooper in Prichard, a blue-collar suburb of Mobile that was 52% black.

Growing black interest in the political process was manifested by the first National Black Political Convention held in March in Gary, Ind. The 3,300 voting delegates and 5,000 observers who attended the convention discussed the future direction of black political actions and sought ways of gaining political power for blacks.

Racial Tensions

Black protests in general subsided on the campus during 1972. But tensions at Southern University in Baton Rouge, La., led to tragedy in November. Two 20-year-old black students were shot and killed when East Baton Rouge Parish police—after ordering protesting students to leave an administration building—began firing tear-gas canisters. At first the police denied that they had used any firearms during the incident, but Louisiana Gov. Edwin W. Edwards later conceded the possibility that police might have fired the fatal buckshot.

There were scattered incidents of racial disorder and violence in connection with the transfer of black students to previously all-white schools.

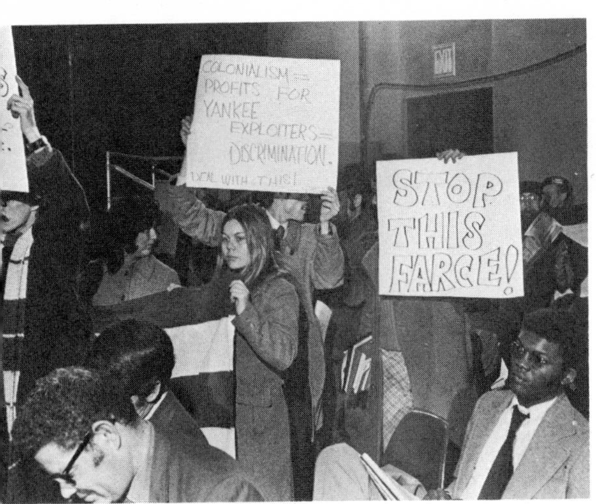

TYRONE DUKES FROM "THE NEW YORK TIMES"

Demonstrators demanding Puerto Rican independence disrupted hearings of the U.S. Commission on Civil Rights on discrimination.

Among the most publicized were the disturbances at Gage Park High School in Chicago and at John Wilson Junior High School in the Canarsie section of Brooklyn. Racial disturbances also flared in the military, with tensions in the U.S. Navy gaining considerable publicity. Serious interracial conflicts were reported on two aircraft carriers, the *Kitty Hawk* and the *Constellation*.

Native Americans attracted attention with a November protest at the Washington, D.C., headquarters of the U.S. Bureau of Indian Affairs. Led by activists of the American Indian Movement, several hundred young Indians barricaded themselves in the building for six days. (*See also* Indians, American.)

Trials and Court Decisions

Black militants figured prominently in numerous court cases. The most publicized involved Angela Davis, a former university philosophy instructor accused of murder, kidnapping, and conspiracy. Her long-delayed trial began in March in San Jose, Calif., and ended in June with her acquittal by an all-white jury after 13 hours of deliberation. Earlier, in a related trial, an all-white jury in San Francisco, Calif., found the two surviving "Soledad brothers"—John Clutchette and Fleeta Drumgo—innocent of the 1970 slaying of a California state prison guard.

Also in San Francisco, Black Panther leader David Hilliard was cleared of a perjury charge when the U.S. Department of Justice refused to release relevant wiretap evidence. Contempt charges against another Panther leader, Bobby Seale, were dropped. H. Rap Brown, a well-known black militant from Baton Rouge, was sentenced in New Orleans, La., in June to five years in prison and was fined $2,000 for a 1968 conviction of carrying a rifle while under indictment. Brown faced other charges in New York. State's Attorney Edward V. Hanrahan of Cook County, Ill., and 13 codefendants were acquitted of conspiring to obstruct justice in the 1969 slaying of Black Panther leaders Fred Hampton and Mark Clark. Though officially cleared of charges, Hanrahan failed to win reelection. (*See also* Law.)

Several federal court decisions of 1972 affected the social and legal position of the U.S. black population. The Supreme Court ruled in June that the state of Pennsylvania could grant a liquor license to a private club with racially restrictive practices concerning guests. In the court's 5–4 ruling against capital punishment, several of the justices noted in their opinions that the death penalty had often operated in a racially discriminatory way. (*See also* Supreme Court of the U.S.)

RELIGION. Conflicts and wars throughout the world, a cooling of enthusiasm in the ecumenical movement, confrontations between conservatives and liberals, and the passing of leadership into new hands in two major churches were important issues in the area of religion in 1972. Churches continued to agonize over the conflicts in Vietnam, the Middle East, Bangladesh, Ireland, and Uganda, and massive relief drives were undertaken to provide food, money, and clothing to alleviate suffering in those countries, particularly in Bangladesh. Efforts at reconciliation of the warring factions in Northern Ireland, in the form of conferences and united prayer services, seemed to have little effect. The Christian world mourned the Israeli athletes and coaches slain by terrorists at the summer Olympic Games in Munich, West Germany, but church leaders were deeply concerned by Israel's pledge to exact retribution.

Two hopeful signs for ecumenism were the Anglican–Roman Catholic agreement on the meaning of Holy Communion and the report that an official dialogue group of Lutheran and Roman Catholic theologians had found that an agreement on the issue of papal primacy was a distinct possibility. Disagreement over the doctrine of papal infallibility was still unresolved. In other areas, however, ecumenism suffered setbacks: the Anglican church refused in May to merge with the British Methodist church; the United Presbyterian Church in the U.S.A. withdrew from the Consultation of Church Union (COCU) and thus weakened hopes that 25 million U.S. Protestants might eventually be members of a united church body; and a proposed union of the United Church of Canada and Anglican and Disciples constituencies was considered a virtual impossibility. Churchmen cited conservative desires to retain individual church practices, fear of bureaucracies, and questions about the effectiveness of ecumenism in strengthening religion as possible reasons for the reversals.

A hectic battle divided the Lutheran church—Missouri Synod in 1972. A fact-finding committee reported to President Jacob A. Preus that the ma-

CHRISTOPHER SPRINGMANN

The Jews for Jesus group is part of the growing, nationwide Jesus movement. The members accept Jesus as the Messiah promised by the biblical prophets but still consider themselves to be Jews.

jority of the faculty of Concordia Theological Seminary in St. Louis, Mo., were guilty of holding "a view of the Scriptures which in practice erodes the authority" of the Bible. The seminary's president, John Tietjen, took sharp issue with the report and accused the investigators of distortions. The controversy promised to be a major issue at the synod's 1973 convention. Dissidents within the Presbyterian church in the U.S. (Southern Presbyterian) objected during the year to the church's involvement in social issues. Continuing controversies between liberal priests and the traditional hierarchy troubled the Roman Catholic church.

Athenagoras I, ecumenical patriarch of the Eastern Orthodox church, died on July 8 and was succeeded by Dimitrios I. Athenagoras had been an advocate of Christian unity, and Dimitrios appeared to be committed to that goal.

Joseph Fielding Smith, president of The Church of Jesus Christ of Latter-day Saints (Mormons), died on July 2. The church's new president was Harold B. Lee, a veteran Mormon administrator. Lord Geoffrey Francis Fisher of Lambeth, former archbishop of Canterbury, also died in 1972.

Changing traditions were reflected in the selection of the Rev. Philip A. Potter, a black Methodist pastor, as head of the World Council of Churches. A discouraging manifestation of changing times was the continuing downward trend in U.S. church attendance for the 13th consecutive year. Only 40% of U.S. adults attended religious services in a typical week in 1971. However, protection of religious freedom was reiterated when the U.S. Supreme Court ruled that Amish parents could withdraw their children from public education after the eighth grade to protect strict Amish beliefs.

JUDAISM

World Jewry was shocked and enraged by several politically motivated attacks on Jews in 1972. The killing of 11 Israeli athletes and coaches by Arab Palestinian terrorists at the Olympic Games in Munich in September and the massacre of airline passengers by Japanese gunmen at Lod International Airport outside Tel Aviv, Israel, in May were probably the two most horrifying incidents. (*See* Olympic Games; Crime.) The attitude of the Soviet Union toward Russian Jews who wished to emigrate to Israel changed from one of increasing leniency to a much more hard-line stance, provoking worldwide condemnations and protests. At the end of 1971, Soviet Premier Aleksei N. Kosygin stated during a visit to Canada, "We are opening doors to Jewish emigration and we shall go on opening them." This policy seemed to be in effect for the first half of 1972, although some emigration applicants were harassed. But on August 3 the Presidium of the Supreme Soviet declared that emigrating Jews would have to pay a heavy "exit fee" in order to leave the country; for holders of advanced academic degrees the "reimbursement for state expenditures on education" ran as high as $37,000, an exorbitant sum for most potential emigrants. Storms of protest from Jewish and non-

Jewish spokesmen eventually helped to soften the Soviet position.

The Jewish community was also plagued by internal dissension during the year. A New York City theatrical agency that engaged Soviet performers was fire-bombed in January, leaving one woman dead and 13 people injured; members of the militant Jewish Defense League (JDL) were charged with the bombing. Several Jewish spokesmen condemned the act. Later in the year, Rabbi Meir Kahane, leader of the JDL, was arrested by Israeli police in Jerusalem in connection with an alleged plot to smuggle guns out of Israel for use in a counterterrorism campaign against Arab guerrillas. In another area, the World Zionist Organization was split by a controversy over the duty of Zionists to emigrate to Israel. A vote inspired by younger, Israeli-born delegates to the 28th World Zionist Congress called for Zionist leaders to emigrate to Israel within two years of taking office in the organization or face the loss of their posts. The majority of the delegates from Hadassah, the Women's Zionist Organization of America, promptly walked out of the congress. The issue threatened to alienate U.S. Zionist leaders from their counterparts in Israel.

The question of Jewish identity was hotly discussed throughout the year. The increasing difficulty of drawing distinctions between Jews living inside and outside Israel, the question of converts, and the continuing debate over whether being a Jew is an ethnic or a religious identification all contributed to the discussion. On June 3 Sally J. Priesand was ordained in Cincinnati, Ohio, as the first woman rabbi in the history of the U.S.

PROTESTANTISM

The continued growth of the evangelical "Jesus movement" was demonstrated in 1972 by a massive meeting in Dallas, Tex., that evangelist Billy Graham described as a "religious Woodstock." More than 75,000 young people, mostly students, attended the June gathering that became known as "Explo 72," though its official title was the International Student Congress on Evangelism. Classes, Bible study, and entertainment by country singer Johnny Cash were included in the six-day convention. Another aspect of the new evangelical spirit was the appearance of a group called "Jews for Jesus," composed mostly of young Jews who accepted some Jewish theology but acknowledged Jesus Christ as the Messiah.

Some of the cults in the Jesus movement were causing concern for parents, however. Several groups tended to encourage children to reject their parents along with the rest of the world, which they considered to be a sinful place. A small sect, the Children of God, carefully regulated all contact between its members and their parents and became the target of a number of groups of angry parents. Some critics also attacked the tendency among evangelists to mix politics with religion, a practice

EDWARD HAUSNER FROM "THE NEW YORK TIMES"

New York City Jews protest the conviction in Israel of two Yeshiva students arrested for attempted arson of a pornography shop.

that was highlighted by a Flag Day celebration at Explo 72.

The World Council of Churches held an 11-day meeting of its Central Committee in Utrecht, Netherlands, in August. The council chose a black Methodist pastor from the British West Indies, the Rev. Philip A. Potter, as its new head, emphasizing its continuing interest in the peoples of small, underdeveloped nations. This liberal trend was not uniformly supported by the council's more conservative members. In another surprising move, the council voted to divest itself of all stock holdings in companies having business dealings in South Africa as a protest against that country's white-supremacist policies. An official committee of Roman Catholic, Protestant, and Orthodox churchmen recommended in February that the Roman Catholic church join the World Council of Churches.

Persecution of Protestant churches in a number of countries caused deep concern during the year. East Germany was accused by the synod of the Union of Protestant Churches of seriously limiting Protestants' rights to preach, teach, and publish. Continued jailings and restrictions of Protestant clergymen protesting South Africa's apartheid policy led Protestant churches to present a more united stance to the government.

The number of Protestant ministers in the U.S. continued to be larger than available ministries, thus forcing many clergymen to seek secular employment and threatening a future shortage of trained clergy. In San Carlos, Calif., on May 1, the United Church of Christ churches of the San Francisco Bay area approved the ordination of William Johnson, an affirmed homosexual. It was the first known ordination of its kind.

ROMAN CATHOLICISM

Liberal and conservative voices alike were heard calling for change in the Roman Catholic church in 1972, while Catholic clergymen in Africa and Latin America became increasingly involved in local political situations. In Zaire, the archbishop of Kinshasa, Joseph-Albert Cardinal Malula, and the country's president, Mobutu Sese Seko (formerly Joseph D. Mobutu), quarreled over Mobutu's decision to abolish the use of Christian names as part of an "Africanization" campaign. The cardinal opposed the ruling, and an article condemning Mobutu's action appeared in a Catholic magazine, *Afrique Chrétienne,* in January. The magazine was suppressed for six months and the cardinal was ordered to abandon his residence. He slipped out of Zaire and returned only after receiving assurances of safe-conduct. In Santiago, Chile, the first Latin American meeting of Christians for Socialism, organized by Chilean priest Father Gonzalo Arroyo, issued a statement supporting the Marxist governments of Chile and Cuba and inviting Christians to join forces with Marxists.

In the U.S. the Sixth International Conference on Charismatic Renewal was held in June. The conference celebrated the growth of Pentecostalism in the U.S., though the movement was still viewed with uneasiness by the church hierarchy. A group of conservative Roman Catholics attending the National Wanderer Forum in Minneapolis, Minn., in June asked the nation's bishops to purge "revolutionary elements" from the staff of the bishops' secretariat, the United States Catholic Conference. The National Federation of Priests Councils, meeting in Denver, Colo., in March, voted to strongly support the "Harrisburg Seven" defendants, including antiwar Catholic priest the Rev. Philip F. Berrigan, but refused to allow a married priests' group to join the federation. Father Berrigan was sentenced to four concurrent two-year prison terms in September after being convicted of smuggling letters out of prison. (*See* Law.) He was paroled in December while he appealed the conviction. His brother, the Rev. Daniel J. Berrigan, was granted parole in January; they had both been in prison for burning draft records. The Berrigans were nominated for the Nobel peace prize by members of the Swedish parliament on January 26.

Pope Paul VI reaffirmed his opposition to the concepts of married priests and voluntary celibacy during the year. He also suspended a move by a Louisiana bishop to allow divorced or remarried Catholics "of good conscience" to return to the sacraments. In some surprising moves, the pope gave laymen a voice in the secret selection of bishops for the first time in modern church history, and he also abolished the tonsure, the circular shaving of the crown of the head that had commonly been a mandatory act for beginning seminary students and many religious orders. It was reported in April that the pope was encouraging Jozsef Cardinal Mindszenty, the highly conservative archbishop of Hungary, to resign in the hope of bettering relations between the Vatican and Hungary.

Pope Paul VI holds a child on his lap during a general audience at the Vatican. Pope Paul traveled to Venice in 1972, the first pope to visit that city in 172 years.

KEYSTONE

RETAIL TRADE. The resurgence of the U.S. economy, exemption of small retail stores from price controls, and a year-end Christmas buying spree by consumers made 1972 a good year in retail trade. The situation was tempered somewhat, however, by the beginnings of a consumer rebellion against high retail food prices and by a decreasing profit margin for most food chains.

Retailers were pleased when on January 19 the federal government exempted 75% of the retail stores in the nation from economic controls. The move affected about 1.5 million outlets whose yearly sales were less than $100,000. Larger retail establishments and chain stores remained under the controls; it was felt that competition from these businesses would prevent smaller retailers from hiking prices excessively. The Internal Revenue Service, watchdog agency for economic controls, announced on January 22 that some 70 retailers were being sued for failure to comply with price-posting regulations.

Food retailers, particularly large supermarket chains, found themselves under fire for much of the year as consumers blamed them for spiraling food prices. The industry countered by pointing to decreasing profit margins, which had dropped from 1.4% in 1965 to 0.86% in 1971. Angry food buyers were not impressed, and supermarkets initiated a number of innovations in an effort to recapture business. Undoubtedly the most spectacular move was made by the Great Atlantic & Pacific Tea Co., the nation's largest retail food chain, which converted to discount pricing in an attempt to increase its sales volume. Prices were cut on about 90% of the items stocked, and variety was cut from 11,000 items to 8,000. The ultimate success or failure of the conversion could not be determined at the end of 1972; but it affected most of the major food retailers, some of which initiated less complete discounting.

Retail sales for most of the year showed strong gains over 1971. Figures for the last week of February showed a rise of 26% in durable goods and 8% in nondurable goods over the same week in 1971. After an unimpressive showing in June, sales for July rose a record 11% over 1971; total sales were more than $37 billion. October was another record month with sales of some $38.75 billion. Christmas shoppers were expected to send sales up about 10% over December 1971.

Shoplifting continued to present a major problem; retailers who considered losses of 1% to be serious were aghast at losses of up to 4% in some New York City stores. A private survey showing that the number of U.S. stores had declined by 12,400 in 1971 also produced some gloom; observers attributed the decline to the inability of small retailers to compete with larger chain stores. (*See also* Economy; Consumer Protection. *See in* CE: Trade.)

Philadelphia, Pa., retailers continued to direct a multimedia advertising campaign against shoplifting in 1972. The program, started in 1971, focuses on teen-age offenders.

JOSEPH NETTIS FROM BUSINESS WEEK

CAMERAPIX FROM KEYSTONE

Rhodesians did not support the proposed agreement with Great Britain negotiated in November 1971. Signs like this were displayed, and demonstrations and riots occurred in January 1972 when a special commission from Britain visited the country to test public opinion.

RHODESIA. Hopes had been high in 1971 for a settlement with Great Britain over the future of Rhodesia, but expectations faded in 1972. Optimism had been inspired by a proposed settlement reached in November 1971 that implied some future voice for the black majority of the country. In January 1972 a commission led by Lord Pearce, a former lord of appeal, arrived in Rhodesia for a two-month visit to test public opinion on the agreement. The commission did not find unanimous support forthcoming. They were met by a peaceful demonstration against the proposal when they arrived in Salisbury, the capital; the following days saw outbreaks of rioting and protest by blacks who considered the agreement to be a "sell out" to Prime Minister Ian D. Smith's white-supremacist government. Police fired on demonstrators on January 13, killing one, and eight Africans died in rioting on January 20. Josiah Chinamano, a leader of the African National Council (ANC), which had been set up in December 1971 to oppose the settlement, was arrested by the government, as were R. S. Garfield Todd, former prime minister of Southern Rhodesia, and his daughter Judith.

The commission's report, published on May 23, concluded that while the settlement was acceptable to most Rhodesian whites, it had been summarily rejected by the black majority. Smith denounced the report for misrepresentation, but the British government postponed any formal settlement, expressing hope that the Rhodesian people would study the proposal and perhaps accept a future compromise. Meanwhile, international sanctions against Rhodesia were to remain in effect. The U.S., however, continued to import Rhodesian chrome and nickel ore in violation of the United Nations embargo on trade with Rhodesia.

The dispute provoked much political tension in Rhodesia. The sale of membership cards in the ANC was banned in March, and 60,000 cards were seized. On July 1, political gatherings and open-air meetings in tribal trust territories were banned. The white-supremacist United Front party, which opposed the settlement as too liberal, gained support; and in May the Democratic party was founded to preserve absolute white dominance.

Tangwena tribesmen continued to resist government efforts to remove them from their ancestral homelands, which had been given to white settlers. The government resorted to arrests and burning of Tangwena homes in an attempt to force the Africans to leave the area.

On June 6 an explosion ripped through the Wankie coal mine No. 2, killing at least 425 people, the vast majority of them black miners. Hopes were high at first that some might have survived, but it soon became evident that anyone trapped in the mine who had survived the blast was killed by inhaling methane gas. (*See in* CE: Rhodesia.)

Nicolae Ceausescu (center, wearing ascot), Romania's president and Communist party general secretary, attends the opening of the International Fair—Bucharest on October 16. The huge industrial trade fair had 943 exhibitors from 27 countries plus 156 from Romania.

AUTHENTICATED NEWS INTERNATIONAL

ROMANIA. Nicolae Ceausescu, president of Romania, spent 1972 proclaiming at home and abroad that international peace and security must be based on every state's right to freedom, independence, and sovereignty. Between March 11 and April 6 Ceausescu visited eight African countries—Algeria, Central African Republic, People's Republic of the Congo, Zaire, Zambia, Tanzania, Sudan, and Egypt—in his effort to promote Romania's own particular brand of Marxist internationalism.

Hungary's premier visited Bucharest, the capital, in February and signed a 20-year treaty of alliance with Romania. On May 12 a similar treaty was signed in the Romanian capital with East Germany. On May 16 Ceausescu and Yugoslavia's President Tito opened the giant $450-million hydroelectric dam that the two countries had jointly constructed on the Iron Gate stretch of the Danube River. In September, Ceausescu and Prime Minister Ion Gheorghe Maurer visited Bulgaria and signed a pact to build jointly a hydroelectric dam across the lower Danube.

To underline Romania's independence, Ceausescu sent a military delegation headed by Emil Bodnaras to the People's Republic of China; while there, Bodnaras was feted at a banquet given by China's Premier Chou En-lai. Romania was host to Golda Meir, Israel's prime minister, the first week in May. Ceausescu was invited by Soviet Communist Party General Secretary Leonid I. Brezhnev to a meeting of Communist leaders in the Crimea on July 31. Ceausescu's state visit to Belgium in October was his second to a West European country (his first such visit was to France in June 1970).

In March it was revealed that Romania had become the first member of the Council for Mutual Economic Assistance to contact the Council of Ministers of the European Economic Community (EEC) asking to join the EEC's generalized preference system for developing countries. France opposed the request, arguing that Romania was not a developing country in the usual sense of the term.

On September 20 Romania became the first East European nation to apply for membership in both the International Monetary Fund and the World Bank. The Romanian applications were assured of favorable consideration.

The results of the country's 1971 economic development plan were reported during the year. Romania showed increases in the following areas when compared with figures for the preceding year: national income up 12.5%, industrial output up 11.5%, farm production up 18.2%, foreign trade up 8.6%, and industrial productivity up 5.9%. More than half of Romania's industrial output came from hydroelectric and thermal power industries, metallurgy, engineering, and chemicals. (*See in* CE: Rumania.)

RUBBER. Figures released by the International Rubber Study Group (IRSG) in 1972 revealed that world production of natural rubber in 1971 was estimated at 3,029,000 metric tons, a record increase of 134,000 metric tons over the amount produced in 1970. (One metric ton equals 2,204 pounds.) World production of synthetic rubber in 1971 was estimated at 5,005,000 metric tons, an increase of 137,000 metric tons.

Production of natural rubber for the first six months of 1972 was estimated at 1,432,500 metric tons, up 22,500 metric tons compared to the corresponding period of 1971. Other estimates for 1972 issued by the IRSG included: supplies of natural rubber (including delivery from governmental surplus stock), 3.18 million metric tons; supplies of synthetic rubber, 5.42 million metric tons; consumption of natural rubber (manufactured products), 3.18 million metric tons; and consumption of synthetic rubber, 5.27 million metric tons. Estimates for production of synthetic rubber did not include allowances for synthetic rubber produced in the Soviet Union, some other countries in Eastern Europe, or the People's Republic of China. Production of all types of reclaimed rubber in 1971 amounted to 291,255 metric tons.

Expenditures for research by the rubber industry in the U.S. were estimated at $295 million for 1972, an increase of 5% over the amount spent in 1971. The expenditure in 1971 amounted to 1.49% of sales, while the predicted expenditure in 1972 was 1.43% of sales.

Radial tires accounted for the majority of tires sold in Europe in 1972. In the U.S. radial tires were produced and sold on the replacement market and offered as original equipment on a number of passenger cars. Both all-textile cord-reinforced tires and tires with textile radial plies and one or more steel cord belts were made during the year. The latter construction, quite popular in Europe, appeared to be gaining favor in the U.S. (*See in* CE: Rubber.)

RWANDA. In 1972 Rwanda stood on the fringe of Burundi's tribal war, receiving refugees and, through President Grégoire Kayibanda, counseling moderation. (*See* Burundi.) Despite cabinet changes and border trouble with Uganda, Rwanda remained comparatively peaceful during 1972, establishing diplomatic relations with the People's Republic of China and issuing conventional statements against colonialism.

With the densest population in Africa (more than 370 persons per square mile), largely at subsistence level, Rwanda continued to rely heavily on foreign aid, accepting about $12 million annually—40% from Belgium and the rest from West Germany, the European Development Fund, and other international agencies. Coffee remained the most important cash crop. In 1971, farmers produced more than 13,000 tons, which, exported mainly to the United States, earned about $14 million—one half the total export revenue. Subsidiary production of bananas, sorghum, and cassava was boosted by tea production, which reached some 2,000 tons in 1971, exported mainly to Great Britain. (*See in* CE: Rwanda.)

SAFETY. Faced with predictions that 1972 would be the worst year for traffic fatalities in the history of the U.S., safety groups continued to press for improvement in highway safety conditions. An immediate, and obvious, alteration in the highway environment took shape with extensive changes in highway and street traffic signs. The changes were the result of requirements outlined in the new manual on uniform traffic control devices. These requirements were moving the U.S. toward the greater use of international traffic control signs, which means greater use of pictures and symbols rather than word messages formerly used extensively in traffic sign systems. The use of symbols and pictures was expected to result in faster and better communication with the driver.

In a growing effort to make automobiles safer, field tests were conducted on passive restraints (air bags) for motor vehicles. These air bags are triggered by a crash and inflate suddenly from the dashboard area, protecting the vehicle's occupants. Preliminary steps also were taken in the development of a model law requiring the use of seat and shoulder belts.

Although highway safety has long been a major public concern, other lesser-known problems received a good deal of attention during the year from consumer protection groups. A children's sleepwear standard, effective July 29, required that garments not meeting standards for flammability be so labeled. One year from that date all such garments must have been removed from store shelves. The effective date for standards covering the flammability of mattresses and mattress pads was to be in 1973, also. In addition, flammability

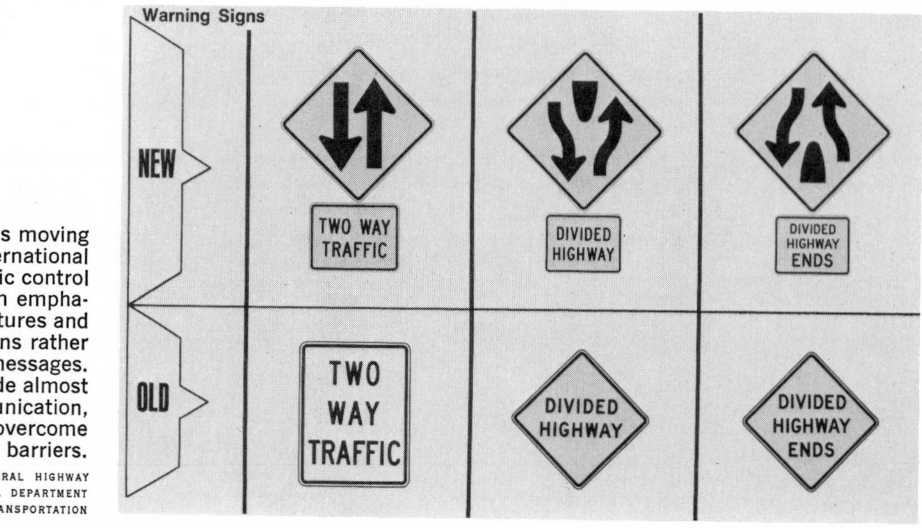

The U.S. was moving toward an international system of traffic control devices, which emphasizes pictures and symbolic signs rather than written messages. Symbols provide almost instant communication, and they overcome language barriers.

COURTESY, FEDERAL HIGHWAY ADMINISTRATION, U.S. DEPARTMENT OF TRANSPORTATION

WILLIAM E. SAURO FROM "THE NEW YORK TIMES"

The Nassau County Police Department opened a miniature "safety town" in East Meadow, Long Island, N.Y. Children learn safety as they drive through the course in electric cars.

standards were issued for carpets and rugs, and an effort was under way to set up voluntary standards aimed at reducing the ignition hazards of matches, kitchen ranges, and furnaces.

Snowmobile fatalities climbed to 164 during the 1971–72 winter season, with a projected death rate of 1.3 fatalities per 10,000 snowmobiles. A growing number of states implemented and initiated snowmobile safety laws in campaigns to curb snowmobile injuries and deaths. In other areas of recreation, the implementation of the Federal Boat Safety Act required that all personal flotation devices be approved by the U.S. Coast Guard and that everyone on board a water vessel be provided with such a device.

Mining disasters, including a fire at the Sunshine Silver Mine at Kellogg, Idaho, that killed 91 miners, brought increased efforts toward the elimination of hazards in U.S. mines. There was also pressure on the federal government to transfer responsibility for enforcing mine safety rules from the U.S. Bureau of Mines to the Department of Labor.

According to figures released by the National Safety Council, 115,000 people lost their lives as the result of accidents in 1971, the same number of deaths as in 1970. In motor vehicle accidents, 54,700 people were killed, down less than .5% from the preceding year. For the first seven months of 1972 there were 31,410 traffic deaths reported. (*See in* CE: Safety.)

SAUDI ARABIA. In 1972 King Faisal ibn Abdul-Aziz of Saudi Arabia pursued a course of unobtrusive diplomacy, with the exception of his support for Yemen (Sana) in its conflict with Yemen (Aden). Saudi Arabia was the only Arab state to provide financial aid and friendship to Jordan, and Saudi Arabia's Palestinian community was exceptional in supporting a plan by the Jordanian king for federating Jordan's east- and west-bank regions. During the year King Faisal also promised aid to Uganda, which he visited in November on his first trip to Africa since 1966.

Saudi Arabia's oil minister, representing his own and other Persian Gulf oil-producing states, won from Western oil companies new agreements that promised to transform the international oil industry. In March the Arabian American Oil Co., the world's largest oil consortium, agreed in principle to give Saudi Arabia 20% ownership and participation in the company. In November seven oil firms agreed to give Saudi Arabia and four other Arab states an eventual 51% participation in their operations.

King Faisal personally provided funds for the operation of an international Islamic news agency, established by a conference of Islamic foreign ministers at Jidda in February. A British consortium contracted to build a medical center and teaching hospital for Riyadh University, which would enable Saudi doctors to qualify in their own country for the first time. (*See in* CE: Saudi Arabia.)

SCIENCE. The budget requested in 1972 by U.S. President Richard M. Nixon for fiscal 1973 called for a commitment of $17.8 billion for scientific research and development. Science funds for U.S. agencies were up slightly in the budget with the exception of those for the space program. Also, a major radio telescope array, probably to be located in the southwest, was slated for initial funding of $3 million. It was the first "big science" project in the U.S. since the National Accelerator Laboratory, operating near Chicago.

During the year President Nixon expressed the fear that other nations were getting a technological edge on the U.S. In a historic proposal to the U.S. Congress in March, he urged that more money be channeled through the National Science Foundation to help private industry in its applied research. Edward E. David, Jr., head White

(*continued on page 422*)

Eight-cell mouse embryos were surgically removed from brown natural mothers, frozen to −196°C. for 72 hours, thawed, cultured for 24 to 48 hours, and transferred to the uterus of this white foster mother, who ultimately gave birth to them.

COURTESY, OAK RIDGE NATIONAL LABORATORY

Special Report: THE METRIC SYSTEM

by Jack Steele

The U.S. is the last of the industrial nations of the world to cling to the antiquated English system of measuring things in pounds and inches. Nearly every other country officially uses the more logical and fundamentally sounder metric system. The curious fact is that the U.S. could have legally adopted the metric system more than a century ago. Legislation was pending in 1972 that would officially sanction the U.S. changeover to the metric system. In August the Senate approved such legislation, but no final action was taken.

The phrases "going metric," "metric conversion," and "metric changeover" all mean a national changeover to the metric system. The British refer to their program of conversion from the customary units of pounds, feet, and the like as metrication.

What does going metric mean to the average U.S. citizen? It means that if he drives his car at a speed of 105 kilometers per hour on roads that formerly had a 60-mile-per-hour limit he could get a speeding ticket (there are 1.6 kilometers to a mile). It means that the body measurement of a beauty queen might be 90-66-90 (centimeters, that is). It certainly means that if a person's temperature is 38° (Celsius) he should stay home from work or school. If the outside temperature is 32° C. a picnic or swimming party might be in order. But don't try to ice-skate unless the temperature is 0° C. or lower. Thinking metric should not be too difficult because two common metric units are somewhat the same as the customary ones. A meter measures to be a "big" yard, and a liter is only slightly larger than a quart.

Measurements are easier to handle in the metric system because it is based on multiples of 10. For example, there are 100,000 centimeters or 1,000 meters in a kilometer (centi- = 1/100, kilo- = 1,000). Compare this with trying to remember how many inches are in a mile. Metrically, there are 1,000 cubic centimeters in a liter, 10 liters to a decaliter (deca- = 10). A liter of water weighs one kilogram; a milliliter of water weighs one gram. How many people know the number of teaspoons in a cup or quart, or how much a gallon of water weighs?

The Metric System Defined

The metric system is formally called the International System of Units, abbreviated SI. It is a modern version of the system adopted by France in 1795 to standardize the various schemes of measurement in use throughout the French provinces.

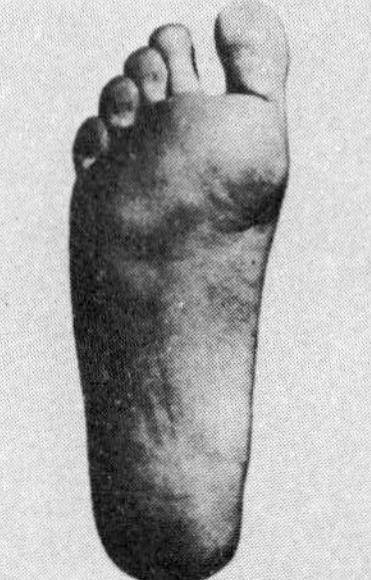

This is not a
foot it's 300 mm
Think metric

KEYSTONE

French scientists got the go-ahead in 1790 to develop a decimal system of measurement in which different units would be related to one another by multiples of 10 instead of multiples of 3, 4, or 12, as had been the case. The units were to be based on a natural phenomenon more consistent than the length of a king's foot or arm, which had been used. One ten-millionth of the distance from the equator to the North Pole was chosen as the new standard, called the meter. Computations of this distance served until 1799, when a meter bar was fashioned. In 1875 the official meter bar was replaced by one bearing two marks exactly one meter apart. Further refinement came through modern means of measurement. Since 1960 the meter has been defined as 1,650,763.73 wavelengths in vacuum of the orange-red line of the spectrum of krypton-86.

The official SI unit of volume is the cubic meter. However, the unit most commonly used is the liter, a thousand times smaller than the cubic meter.

The original SI unit of mass was one cubic centimeter of water, but for practical purposes a reference mass of metal a thousand times larger was made. The standard kilogram is a cylinder made of platinum iridium alloy. The SI system distinguishes mass from force. The weight of a mass is the force exerted on it by gravity. For example, an astronaut has the same mass on the moon as on the earth, but he weighs less on the moon. The SI unit of force is the newton. About ten newtons are needed to lift one kilogram. However, people in metric countries usually talk about mass, weight, and force interchangeably in terms of kilograms.

The units of electricity—watts, amperes, volts, ohms—have never been anything but metric. SI temperature is measured on the Kelvin (K.) scale, on which zero is the coldest anything can be. Water freezes at 273.15° K. But only working scientists use this scale. The common one is the Celsius (formerly centigrade) scale. The Celsius degree is the same as the Kelvin degree, but water freezes at 0° C. and boils at 100° C.

Why the Metric System?

A key advantage of the metric system is its logical design. It requires only movement of the decimal point to make a metric unit larger or smaller. For example, 2.5 centimeters is also .025 meter as well as 25 millimeters.

Although the U.S. was one of the last countries to consider converting to the metric system, it should have been one of the first. President George Washington's first message to Congress in 1790 urged establishment of a standard system of weights and measures, a constitutional prerogative of Congress. A year later, Thomas Jefferson discussed a decimal system of his own, but Congress would not act on it. In 1821 John Quincy Adams argued for the French metric system but to no avail. Finally, in 1866 Congress legalized the metric system but did not require its adoption. In 1875 the U.S. and 16 other countries established the International Bureau of Weights and Measures. In 1893, three years after the U.S. received a standard meter bar and kilogram, the Office of Standard Weights and Measures (later to become the National Bureau of Standards) officially regarded the international meter and kilogram as fundamental standards and even specified that the U.S. foot be a certain fraction of the meter. Between the two world wars there were many failing efforts at legislation on the metric system. Most objections were based on the inconvenience to industry and the cost of changing systems. At the same time, most of the U.S. international trade was with nations using the English system. However, this is no longer true. Unless U.S. manufacturing processes become metric, the nation will suffer in international trade. Estimates already forecast that there could be some $600 million lost in 1975 just in exports of computers, vacuum pumps, and typewriters because the U.S. was not a metric country in 1970. A concerned Congress in 1968 requested a study of all factors involved in metric conversion. The study disclosed that about half the U.S. population already knew something about the metric system. Seventy percent of the manufacturing industries (which would bear about $10 billion of the cost of conversion) favored it. And more than 90% of those favoring it wanted a federally coordinated program scheduled for completion within ten years.

The U.S. pharmaceutical industry independently switched to the metric system in about the late 1950's at a cost considerably less than it had anticipated. Many companies producing ball bearings and roller bearings changed over too in the face of international trade requirements. About half the canned goods in stores in the early 1970's were labeled in customary and in metric units.

Industrial changes to SI units would involve the greatest difficulty. For example, fasteners such as screws and bolts would have to be cut to new sizes. The odometers of automobiles would have to be modified substantially to record distances in kilometers. Speedometers, however, would need only changes in scale divisions, perhaps by means of a transparent, stick-on label over the present scale.

The British population has been successfully coached in metrication through newspaper advertising, radio and television programs, discussion groups, and other means. The British changeover also proved that going metric is easier when done through central coordination and planning. Total adoption of the metric system will probably never occur. Descriptions on land titles and deeds, for instance, would change only when land was sold or resurveyed. And unless football fields lengthened to a hectameter, first downs would still require 10 yards of forward progress instead of 9.144 meters. (*See in* CE: Metric System; Weights and Measures.)

KEYSTONE

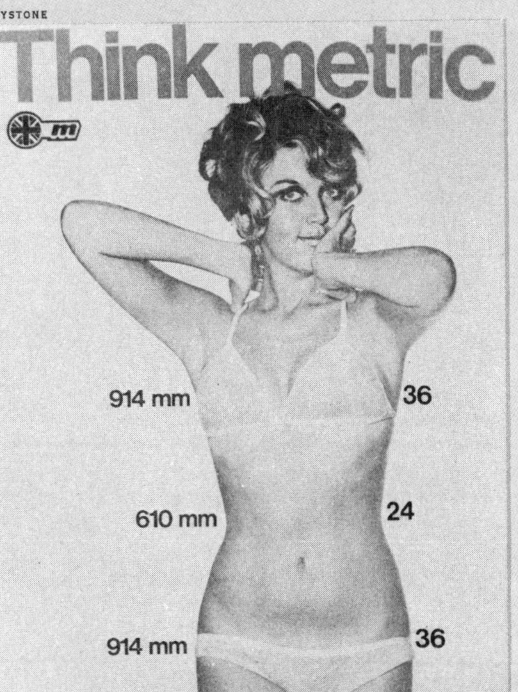

(*continued from page 419*)
House science adviser, said this was the first time any president had ever addressed Congress solely about the problems of science and technology.

Louis M. Branscomb, director of the National Bureau of Standards, said the U.S. would lag economically behind metric countries unless it switched to the metric system. Some labor leaders felt that workers would be forced to buy new equipment. (*See* Science Special Report.)

Science ties between the U.S. and the Soviet Union became closer in 1972 when the two countries agreed to exchange biomedical and then technological data. The latter agreement was announced during Nixon's trip to Moscow in May.

A European molecular biology laboratory, modeled somewhat after the European Center for Nuclear Research, was agreed upon by 12 nations in June. The new center would be situated in West Germany. (*See in* CE: Science articles.)

SELECTIVE SERVICE. The future of the Selective Service System came into doubt in 1972 with U.S. President Richard M. Nixon's announcement in August that all conscription would be ended by July 1973, with an all-volunteer Army serving after that date, conditional on continued high enlistment. Secretary of Defense Melvin Laird stated, however, that the Selective Service System would not be abolished but would be retained for emergency situations. He also said that pay levels for doctors and other professionals would need to be raised and that National Guard and Reserve strengths would have to be brought up to minimum levels to assure the ending of the draft.

Approximately 50,000 men were drafted into the Army in 1972, the lowest draft call since 1949. The highest lottery number reached during the year was 95.

No one was drafted in the first three months of 1972. At that time the Army was operating under a Congressional mandate to reduce the size of its force. The first call of the year came in April, with a three-month total of 15,000 men.

Even though draft calls had been temporarily halted, the Selective Service System held its fourth annual lottery drawing in February to determine the order in which men would be subject to induction in 1973. For the first time, the Selective Service System was operating under the rules of the 1971 draft extension law. Men were selected for induction on a national, rather than local, basis, meaning that all men in the country with the same lottery number were subject to the draft at the same time. Potential draftees were allowed new procedural rights when they appeared before their boards to challenge their status, and students entering college were not given student deferments. Men and women as young as 18 were appointed to local draft boards.

In April Curtis W. Tarr resigned as director of Selective Service. His deputy, Byron V. Pepitone, was named acting director of the agency.

The Defense Department announced in May that doctors would not be drafted for the remainder of 1972 and perhaps longer. Doctors had been drafted sporadically since 1961.

The question of amnesty for men who had evaded the draft during the Vietnam war was an issue throughout the year. A Gallup Poll published in August showed that 60% of people in the U.S. were opposed to giving unconditional amnesty to men who had left the country to avoid the draft. In the presidential election campaign, President Nixon and Senator George S. McGovern (D, S.D.) agreed that the draft should be ended, but they differed sharply on the question of amnesty. Senator McGovern argued that some form of amnesty was just and should be instituted, while President Nixon declared that amnesty should not be considered until the end of the Vietnam war. (*See also* Armed Forces, U.S.)

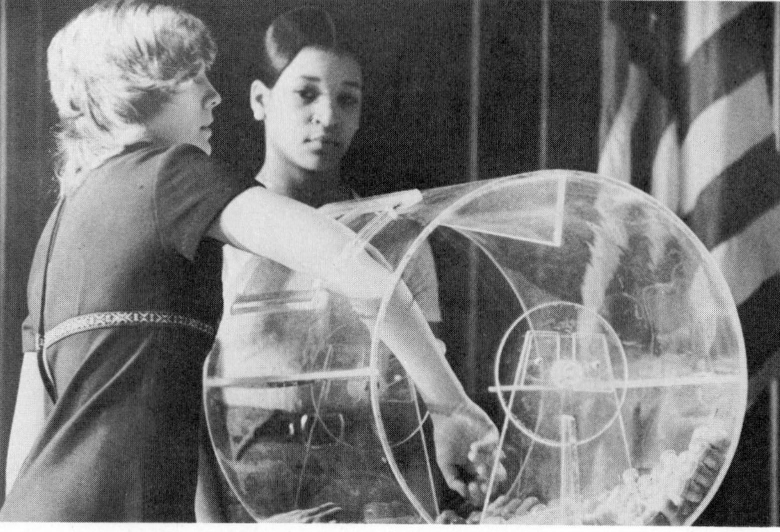

Charlotte Shope reaches for a capsule in the plastic drum operated by Tawnya Palmer as the draft lottery got under way on February 2. The lottery determines the call-up order for nearly 2 million young men who turned 19 years old during the year. The order is determined on the basis of a pairing of 365 red capsules containing the dates of the year and, from another drum, an equal number of blue capsules containing draft sequence numbers one through 365.

UPI COMPIX

SENEGAL. In April 1972 President Léopold S. Senghor of Senegal commuted to a prison term of 20 years the life sentence imposed upon former Prime Minister Mamadou Dia for alleged conspiracy. Government reorganizations took place in June and July, and some important posts in the armed forces were shuffled in connection with the impending retirement of Gen. Jean-Alfred Diallo, who had been in overall military command under the president.

Senghor continued the intense diplomatic activity that had characterized his foreign policy. In May Senghor visited Liberia, where he had a reconciliation with President Sékou Touré of Guinea, relieving the tensions that had mounted between their countries since November 1970. Senghor's appointment as president of the African, Malagasy, and Mauritian Common Organization in April 1972 increased his opportunities to exercise his talents as a mediator. (*See in* CE: Senegal.)

SHIPS AND SHIPPING. On Jan. 9, 1972, the former luxury liner *Queen Elizabeth,* moored in Hong Kong harbor, burned and capsized. A subsequent investigation indicated that the fire, which broke out in three locations on an upper deck, was set deliberately. The 83,000-ton vessel—the largest passenger ship ever built—had been purchased by Hong Kong shipping magnate C. Y. Tung in 1970 and renamed *Seawise University.* It was to have been operated as a seagoing campus under an arrangement with Chapman College of Orange, Calif. Conversion of the vessel for its new role had nearly been completed when the fire broke out.

In May shipping lanes of the North Atlantic Ocean became a danger zone for ships as icebergs drifted southward from the Arctic. It was the largest group of icebergs to drift south of Newfoundland in nearly 30 years and the fourth worst iceberg season in history. The U.S. Coast Guard reported that some 550 of the floating hazards had been observed. They ranged in size from 4 feet high and 20 feet long to giants 150 feet high and 400 feet long. To avoid them, vessels were obliged to detour from their regular lanes. Arrival times of ships destined for ports on the St. Lawrence River were thus delayed by as much as 24 hours. The icebergs were born on the western coast of Greenland where they had broken away from glaciers two or three years earlier.

Extortionists threatened on May 17 to blow up the passenger ship *Queen Elizabeth 2* unless $350,000 ransom was paid. The threat was telephoned to the New York City office of the Cunard Steamship Co. while the ship was in mid-Atlantic en route to Cherbourg, France. Four bomb-disposal experts were then flown to the *Queen Elizabeth 2* by the Royal Air Force of Great Britain, and they parachuted into the sea next to the ship. Their search of the vessel failed to reveal a bomb. On June 15 the ship was again the object of a bomb hoax as she arrived in the harbor at New York City. As before, examination of the ship and cargo revealed no explosive.

On May 22 the Italian passenger liner *Leonardo da Vinci* was the object of a bomb hoax. Extortionists threatened to set off a bomb on the ship unless $100,000 was paid to them. The money was delivered to a New York City address specified by the extortionists; but it was never collected.

The *Doctor Lykes,* the largest general cargo ship sailing under the U.S. flag, began her maiden voyage in July. The 875-foot vessel, with a cargo capacity of 38,500 tons and a speed capability of slightly more than 20 knots, was designed to carry 38 barges, each 97 feet long. Of the so-called LASH (lighter aboard ship) design, the *Doctor Lykes* was the first of three sister ships to be built for the Lykes Bros. Steamship Co. (*See in* CE: Ship and Shipping.)

The Panamanian freighter *Vanlene,* with a cargo of 300 Japanese cars, ran aground on the west side of Vancouver Island, B.C. Helicopters hoist undamaged cars to barges.

"VANCOUVER SUN"

The Democratic National Committee held a special session in Washington, D.C., on August 8 in which R. Sargent Shriver was elected as the vice-presidential candidate to replace Senator Thomas F. Eagleton of Missouri. Senator Eagleton gave up the position because of controversy about his medical history.

PICTORIAL PARADE

SHRIVER, R. SARGENT. Long a political bridesmaid but never a bride, R. Sargent Shriver finally became a candidate in 1972. After Senator Thomas F. Eagleton of Missouri resigned as the Democratic vice-presidential nominee under a cloud of controversy, and after six others declined the number two spot on the ticket, Senator George S. McGovern (S.D.) asked Shriver to run.

Campaigning and politics were not new to Shriver. He had worked for his brother-in-law Senator John F. Kennedy (D, Mass.) in 1960, and he was the charter chief of the Peace Corps during the Kennedy Administration. U.S. President Lyndon B. Johnson appointed him director of the fledgling Office of Economic Opportunity and, later, ambassador to France. As a Kennedy by marriage, however, his chances to run for national elective office were always preempted by someone in the family until he tested the Maryland gubernatorial waters in 1972 and found them uncomfortable.

He was born of an old Maryland family in Westminster on Nov. 9, 1915, and did well at preparatory school. He won a scholarship to Yale University, where he became chairman of the *Yale Daily News* and graduated cum laude in 1938. At law school he and Kingman Brewster, Jr., later president of Yale, organized an isolationist America First group. He graduated from the Yale School of Law in 1941 and entered the U.S. Navy, serving on battleships and submarines before mustering out at the end of World War II as a lieutenant commander.

He worked at a prestigious law firm and then at journalism as an assistant to the editor of *Newsweek*. One of his friends in New York City was Eunice Kennedy, whose father, Ambassador Joseph P. Kennedy, asked him to edit the memoirs of his son who was killed in World War II. The diaries proved unpublishable, but Kennedy offered Shriver a job running Chicago's Merchandise Mart; he accepted. In 1953 Shriver married Eunice. The couple, who later had five children, lived in Chicago, where Shriver became president of the Board of Education.

Shriver proved an unusually energetic and visionary administrator. Possessed of a gifted common touch, he was elegant enough that the French government suggested he remain as ambassador after the 1968 U.S. elections. After the Democratic defeat in November 1972, Shriver returned to his law practice in Washington, D.C.

SIERRA LEONE. The state of emergency originally declared in 1970 remained in effect in Sierra Leone in 1972, but some degree of stability had been attained. There were indications that the elections scheduled for 1973 might be one-party procedures, with no real opposition to the official All People's Congress party. District councils were suspended after allegations of misappropriation of funds.

The overuse of diamond resources continued to dominate the economic scene, although agricultural diversification into rice, coffee, and cocoa promised less dependence on diamonds in the future. Negotiations were also started with the Swiss over future government participation in Swiss bauxite developments in Sierra Leone. Close relations with Guinea remained central to foreign-policy planning, and expansion of contacts with the People's Republic of China (which Sierra Leone had recognized in 1971) and with the Soviet Union was emphasized. (*See in* CE: Sierra Leone.)

SINGAPORE. With the country's economy booming in 1972, the People's Action party of Singapore's Prime Minister Lee Kuan Yew won a mandate for another five years. The party, which had been in power since 1959, dissolved Parliament eight months before the expiration of its term to seek the mandate. In the general election held in September, the party won all 65 seats.

After the elections, the government announced plans for constitutional amendments that would prevent any surrender of Singapore's sovereignty through incorporation into, or federation with, another country unless approved by two thirds of the population in a referendum. The contemplated legislation would not, however, prevent Singapore from entering into mutual security arrangements or economic cooperation with other countries. The government also announced that certain benefits would be withdrawn from couples who had more than two children. The restrictions were to take effect in August 1973.

Some of the republic's citizens were discontented with the government's repressive measures against press and political critics. The soaring prosperity, however, tended to make the minority ineffective. (*See in* CE: Singapore.)

SKIING. The popularity of holiday recreational skiing continued during 1972. There were increased facilities at many winter resorts, particularly in North America and the European Alps. The world championship titles in both Alpine and Nordic disciplines were decided concurrently with those of the Winter Olympic Games held in Sapporo, Japan. (*See also* Olympic Games.) In a last-minute decision, the International Olympic Committee (IOC) barred from Olympic competition the Austrian Alpine racer Karl Schranz for violating Olympic amateur rules.

Alpine Racing

The outstanding Alpine racers of the year were Gustavo Thoeni of Italy and Annemarie Proell of Austria, who won the men's and women's overall world championship titles in the Olympic Games. Both skiers also retained their World Cup honors, first gained in 1971.

In the world championship Alpine combination, Thoeni's runner-up was Walter Tresch of Switzerland, with Jim Hunter of Canada third. Florence Steurer of France placed second to Miss Proell, followed by Torild Foerland of Norway. France won the Nation's Cup, awarded for the highest aggregate points from the 42 races on the World Cup calendar. Women racers scored two thirds of the French total. Austria finished second, and Switzerland came in third.

The second annual Canadian-American Ski Trophy Alpine competition, spread over 12 locations with style rules similar to those for the Alpine World Cup, resulted in victories for Don Rowles and Cheryl Bechdolt, both U.S. skiers. Lasse Hamre of Norway won the Lange Cup, the season's major professional Alpine event, at Vail, Colo., on March 31–April 2. However, the U.S. racer Spider Sabich was again the season's most successful professional, netting a record $50,650 in prize money during nine meetings, all held in North America.

Nordic Events

The 29th world championships in Nordic events (cross-country and jumping) were highlighted by the first Japanese and Polish victories in ski jumping. Switzerland was the only country whose skiers at Sapporo won world championship medals in jumping and cross-country events as well as in both men's and women's Alpine races, a demonstration of national versatility. (*See in* CE: Skiing.)

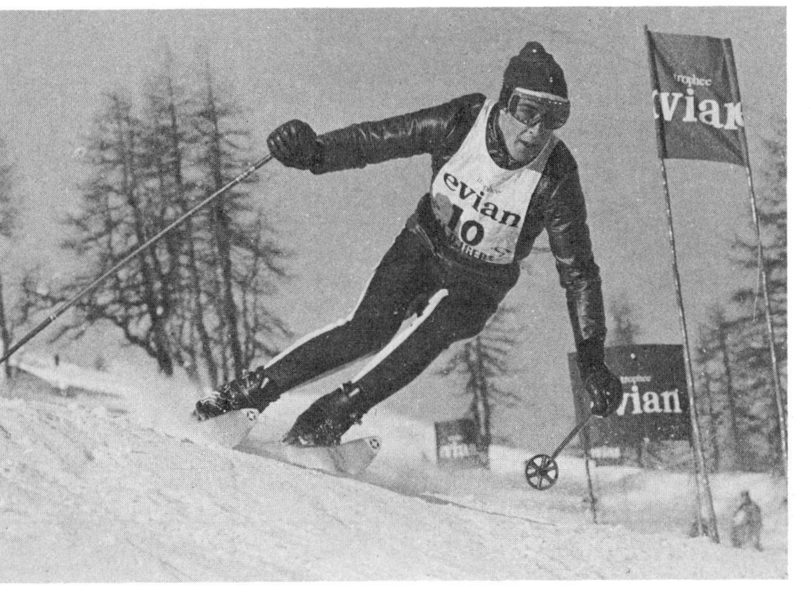

Italy's Gustavo Thoeni, who won an Olympic gold medal at Sapporo, Japan, in the men's giant slalom, wins the giant slalom at the World Cup competition in Heavenly Valley, Calif., in March. His time was 1:61.3.

A.F.P. FROM PICTORIAL PARADE

DAN SCOTT FROM "VANCOUVER SUN"

In an all-star soccer exhibition game held in July in Vancouver, B.C., the Brazilian team beat the British Columbia Premier Soccer League All-Stars 5–0.

SOCCER. Violence, both on and off the soccer field, was very much in evidence in 1972. The disturbances were perhaps highlighted by the ugly outbursts from fans at the European Cup-Winners' Cup final in Barcelona, Spain. These incidents prodded the Union of European Football Associations (UEFA) to suggest that in all future finals the spectators be separated from the field by a wire fence seven feet high.

West Germany won the European Nations cup for the first time when they beat the Soviet Union in the final in Brussels, Belgium, on June 18. They won convincingly, 3–0, with Gerd Mueller scoring twice and Herbert Wimmer getting the other score. The Germans, inspired in midfield by Günther Netzer and Wimmer, and by their captain, Franz Beckenbauer, who operated in front of the back four, produced a sparkling display of soccer to render ineffective the Soviet rearguard action.

Ajax of Amsterdam, Netherlands, became one of only four teams to win the European Cup in consecutive seasons. They defeated Inter-Milan of Italy (who had performed the feat in 1964 and 1965), 2–0, on their native Dutch soil in the stadium of their great rivals Feyenoord of Rotterdam. The other two clubs to have performed the feat were Real Madrid of Spain and Benfica of Portugal. This second victory by Ajax meant that the trophy went to the Netherlands for the third consecutive time, Feyenoord having won it in 1970 in Milan.

The Inter-Continental Cup was won by Ajax of Amsterdam. They defeated Independiente of Buenos Aires, Argentina.

The final contest for the European Cup-Winners' Cup, in Camp Nue Stadium, Barcelona, on May 24, 1972, was spoiled by the behavior of fans of the Glasgow Rangers of Scotland who invaded the field and battled with the local police in a near riot after their team beat Moscow Dynamo 3–2. This resulted in a number of arrests and a two-year ban from European competition imposed by the UEFA on the Rangers. On later appeal the ban was reduced to one year. Despite protests from the Russians, the UEFA allowed the Glasgow team to retain the trophy, although the Dynamo authorities claimed that their men were intimidated and that the final should be replayed.

Tottenham Hotspur of England won the UEFA trophy by beating their compatriots the Wolverhampton Wanderers on a 3–2 aggregate score. The British Isles Championship was won by England when they defeated Scotland on a first-half goal by Alan Ball of Arsenal at Hampden Park, Glasgow, on May 25. Poland beat Hungary 2–1 in the final of the Olympic Games in Munich, West Germany. (*See* Olympic Games.)

SOCIAL SERVICES. Significant amendments to the Social Security Act were signed by U.S. President Richard M. Nixon on Oct. 30, 1972. The law made improvements in the cash benefit provisions, changed Medicare substantially, amended some coverage provisions, revised the contribution schedule, and established a new program of income security for the aged, blind, and disabled needy.

Amendments to the retirement and survivor provisions included: (1) for widows (and widowers) who become entitled to benefits at age 65, raising the benefit amount to 100% of the benefit the spouse would be getting if alive; and (2) for men reaching age 62 in the future, computing benefits as of age 62, the same as for women. Also included were (3) raising to $2,100 the annual exempt amount of earnings without loss of benefits, and providing for automatic future adjustment with the rise in general earnings levels; (4) providing a special minimum benefit for persons who have many years of work covered under the social security program (the highest special minimum payable is $170 for a person with 30 years of work covered); and (5) permitting nondisabled widowers to choose reduced benefits at age 60.

Changes in the disability program included: (1) reduction of the waiting period for disability benefits to five months; (2) for a blind person, elimination of the requirement of recent work covered, if he is fully insured; (3) extension of childhood disability benefits to qualified individuals whose disability began before age 22; and (4) modification of the provisions for reducing social security disability benefits when workmen's compensation is also payable. Other changes were (5) for deaths after 1969, permission to file an application for benefits for a disabled worker and his dependents within three months of the worker's death, instead of requiring that it be filed while the disabled worker is alive; and (6) authorization for a higher amount from social security trust fund money to pay for rehabilitating disability beneficiaries.

Medicare amendments included: (1) extension of protection to persons entitled to cash benefits for at least two years under the social security and railroad retirement programs because of disability and also to persons under age 65 who are currently or fully insured or entitled to social security cash benefits and to their spouses and dependent children who have a chronic kidney disease and require hemodialysis or a renal transplant; (2) a provision allowing persons eligible for both hospital and medical insurance under Medicare or eligible for medical insurance only, to have their health care provided through a health maintenance organization (a group health insurance or other capitation plan that meets prescribed standards), with reimbursement methods established in the law; (3) provision for persons reaching age 65 who are ineligible for hospital benefits to enroll voluntarily, as for medical insurance, and pay the full cost of the protection ($33 monthly at the start); (4) elimination of the requirement that enrollment for medical insurance must be within three years of eligibility to enroll; (5) under certain conditions, permitting an interval longer than the 14-day limitation in the law for transfer from a hospital to an extended-care facility; (6) an increase from $50 to $60 in the medical insurance deductible; and (7) for home health services under medical insurance, payment of 100% of reasonable costs, instead of 80%. Another provision included, under medical insurance, coverage of (a) the services of a physical therapist in independent practice, furnished in the office or the patient's home, and outpatient physical therapy services provided through a hospital or extended-care facility for patients exhausting their hospital insurance coverage, (b) speech pathology services furnished under the same conditions as other outpatient physical therapy services, (c) certain services of chiropractors, and (d) supplies related to colostomies.

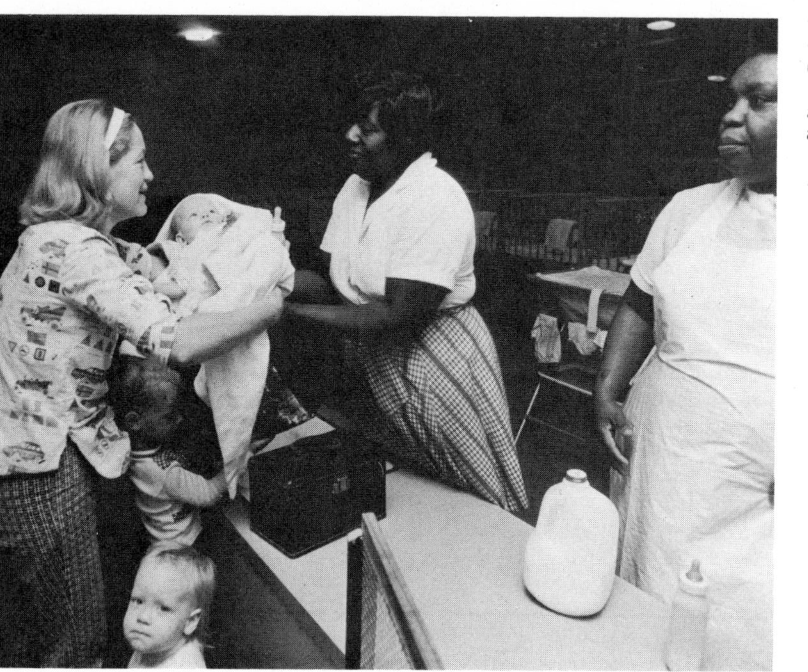

Some day-care facilities, such as the Zellwood Center of Orlando, Fla., open their doors as early as 6 A.M. to accommodate working parents.

AUTHENTICATED NEWS INTERNATIONAL

WIDE WORLD

Inmates of Utah State Prison talk with "adopted families" who come to visit them on a regular basis in hopes of helping in the inmates' rehabilitation.

The contribution rate schedule for financing the social security program had been revised by legislation in July 1972 and was revised again by the amendments signed in October. The new schedule called for a total contribution rate for 1973–77 of 5.85% each for employees and employers—4.85% for monthly cash benefits and 1% for Medicare's hospital benefits; the self-employed would pay 7% of their self-employment earnings for monthly cash benefits and 1% for hospital benefits.

The legislation signed July 1, 1972, which also amended the Social Security Act, provided a 20% increase in all the monthly cash benefits, effective for September 1972. For the future, the law provided for automatic cost-of-living benefit increases related to the Consumer Price Index of the Bureau of Labor Statistics. The maximum amount of earnings taxable and creditable for benefit purposes was also raised—to $10,800 for 1973 and to $12,000 for 1974. (*See in* CE: Social Security.)

SOMALIA. In January 1972 a fresh campaign was launched in Somalia to implement the principles of socialism. A law was promulgated forbidding government employees to deal in property or to own more than one house. Another law stopped doctors from practicing privately; instead they were to be employed by the state. In a speech, Maj. Gen. Mohammed Siad Barre, president of the Supreme Revolutionary Council, denied that there was any conflict between socialism and the Islamic faith.

During October at Mogadishu, the capital, Somalia mediated a settlement between Uganda and Tanzania, following border clashes involving the two countries. (*See also* Africa.)

In May the former vice-president of the Supreme Revolutionary Council, Mohammed Ainanshe Guleid, and two associates, arrested in 1971 and charged with conspiracy, were condemned to death. On July 3 the three men were publicly executed by a firing squad. Of those accused, twenty-six others received prison sentences varying from one year to life; 29 were acquitted. (*See in* CE: Somalia.)

SOUTH AFRICA. Student unrest swept South Africa in 1972 in the wake of severe police action at a peaceful demonstration against the government's policy of apartheid in education. The students had wide support from the English-speaking community and also from many Afrikaners. A number of students who were charged under the Riotous Assemblies Act were acquitted as Supreme Court decisions upheld the right of lawful protest.

Earlier in the spring, 13,000 Ovambo tribesmen struck mines and other businesses in South-West Africa (Namibia) for six weeks to protest low pay and a harsh contract-labor system. They won some concessions, including the right of employees to quit their jobs without risking prosecution under the law on masters and servants.

Delegates to the annual conference of the Trade Union Council of South Africa in Cape Town, the legislative capital, pressed the government to change the country's apartheid labor laws so that black workers could organize into officially registered unions. The gap between the wages of whites and blacks in South African industry widened in 1972.

The five-year prison sentence imposed in November 1971 on the Anglican dean of Johannesburg, the Very Rev. Gonville A. ffrench-Beytagh, was set aside in April 1972 by the Appeal Court, which found him not guilty of offenses under the Terrorism Act. (He had given money to families deprived of support when husbands and fathers were

A nine-car train derailed at Malmesbury, South Africa, on September 29, killing 36 persons and injuring at least 140 others.

WIDE WORLD

On June 5, police broke up a demonstration against apartheid in Johannesburg, South Africa. The students were demonstrating against similar police action that had taken place in Cape Town a few days earlier.

UPI COMPIX

jailed or banned for illegal political activity.) He left for Great Britain. Banned in 1971 under the Suppression of Communism Act was a Catholic priest, the Rev. Cosmas Desmond, author of 'Discarded People', which describes conditions in some resettlement areas. In 1972, however, he attended mass, breaking the ban.

A new political organization, the Black People's Convention, was formed in Pietermaritzburg in 1972. Its object was to unite African, Cape Colored, and Indian people.

The government of South Africa announced its intention to grant a larger measure of autonomy to Ovamboland, largest of the so-called homelands in Namibia. Such an extension of South Africa's Bantu homelands system was expected to outrage black African governments and their supporters at the United Nations (UN) who sought the independence of Namibia as a separate country. South Africa's relations with neighboring African states under the policy of "dialogue" suffered a setback when the Malagasy Republic broke off contacts after a change of regime on that island.

UN Secretary-General Kurt Waldheim visited Namibia in March. Resolutions condemning South Africa's race policies and calling for total sanctions against the country were adopted by the UN General Assembly in November.

In July the U.S. appointed a black diplomat, James E. Baker, to its embassy at Pretoria, the administrative capital. He was to serve as economic and commercial counselor.

South Africa's place in international sports continued to be limited by opposition to its race policies. It was banned from the Olympic Games.

Restrictions on borrowing and lending money were relaxed in 1972 mainly to encourage industrial production. Improvement in the balance of payments and the gold and foreign-exchange reserves followed devaluation of the rand in 1971. A continuing drop in the value of the British pound brought an announcement in October that the rand would no longer be linked with sterling but would have a parity rate with the U.S. dollar. (*See in* CE: South Africa, Republic of.)

SPACE EXPLORATION. The U.S. space program in 1972 continued its steady decline, despite the announcement of a space shuttle and a joint manned spaceflight with the Soviet Union. This decline had begun before the first men landed on the moon. U.S. astronauts continued to leave the space program as they had for the preceding few years. At its peak, in 1968, it had 63 men in training. The expenditure authorized for the National Aeronautics and Space Administration (NASA) in fiscal 1973 was $3,431,650,000.

Clearly the biggest news in manned spaceflight for 1972 was the announcement that the U.S. and the Soviet Union would participate in a joint manned flight in July 1975. With the announcement by U.S. President Richard M. Nixon in May 1972 that the mission was to be a reality, NASA revealed details of the proposed mission and the docking mechanism jointly designed by engineers of the two countries. A team of 25 Soviet scientists and engineers met with their U.S. counterparts at the Manned Spacecraft Center in Houston, Tex., on July 6 to discuss technical details of the mission.

Flight of Apollo 16

Apollo 16 lifted off from the John F. Kennedy Space Center in Florida on April 16. It headed toward the moon on a voyage that was filled with major and minor problems. None of the difficulties, however, proved ultimately serious enough to jeopardize either the astronauts or the mission. The crew consisted of John W. Young, commander; Charles M. Duke, Jr., pilot of the lunar module; and Thomas K. Mattingly, Jr., pilot of the command module.

On the way to Apollo's destination, a transient electrical signal in the command module's guidance and navigation system was detected. At first there was some concern over the signal at mission control, but later analysis proved that the problem was not serious. As the astronauts were docking with the lunar module, they noticed that paint was flaking off one of the panels covering the craft's reaction control system. This gave cause for concern because it was feared that the sun might heat the interior of the lunar module. Later, it was found that the angle of the sun's rays gave no cause for such fears.

More serious was a problem that arose after the command and lunar modules had separated while in orbit around the moon. While Mattingly was making a check prior to firing the engine of the service module to bring the craft into a circular orbit at an altitude of 72 miles, he discovered an apparent malfunction in the system that pointed the engine in the proper direction for firing. The ignition of the engine was postponed while engineers at Houston, at Downey, Calif., and at Cambridge, Mass., worked on the problem. For four hours the two craft orbited the moon, awaiting instructions from mission control. Finally the word came, proclaiming everything all right for the lunar landing. Thus, Young and Duke landed in the Cayley Plains of the Descartes region on April 20. When the men alighted from their craft, they were shocked to find that they had landed only 15 or 20 feet from a crater some 25 feet in depth.

On the first excursion from the lunar module, on April 21, Young and Duke set up the Apollo Lunar Surface Experiments Package and collected 41 pounds of rocks and soil samples. In doing so, the two put 2.6 miles on their lunar roving vehicle (LRV). Their first excursion lasted 7 hours and 11 minutes. For the first time, a far ultraviolet camera/spectrograph was set up to photograph the earth and various galaxies to learn more about the distribution of interplanetary and intergalactic hydrogen.

On April 22, during the second excursion, which lasted 7 hours and 23 minutes, Young and Duke collected an additional 82 pounds of lunar rocks and soil and put an additional 7.1 miles on their LRV. Their objective in the outing was to explore the slope of Stone Mountain, some 2.5 miles to the south. They took photographs and core samples along the way out and back and made penetrometer tests of the soil. The third and final excursion, on April 23, lasted for 5 hours and 40 minutes. During that time the two astronauts went another 7.1 miles in the LRV and gathered an additional 92 pounds of rocks, bringing their samples to a record 215 pounds.

On April 23 the lunar module lifted off the moon. The mission ended on April 27 when the Apollo 16 command module splashed down less than a mile from its recovery ship, the USS *Ticonderoga*. The mission ended 11 days, 1 hour, and 51 minutes after lift-off from Kennedy Space Center.

The Final Apollo Mission

On December 7 the last flight of the Apollo series began when Apollo 17 blasted off from Cape Kennedy in a spectacular predawn launching. On board were Navy officers Capt. Eugene A. Cernan (mission commander) and Comdr. Ronald E. Evans, and civilian geologist Harrison H. Schmitt —the first civilian scientist to take part in an Apollo flight. The lift-off had been delayed for more than two hours by a pressurization problem in the third stage of the rocket.

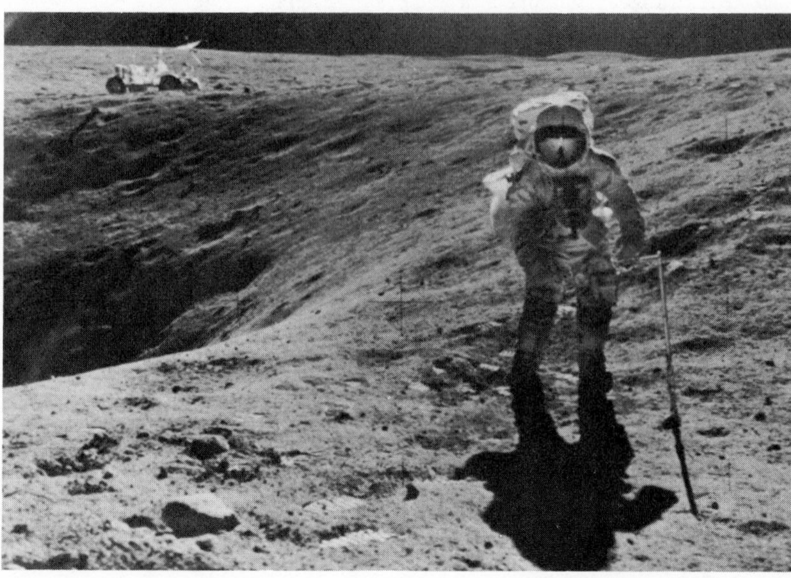

In April astronaut Charles M. Duke, Jr., lunar module pilot of the Apollo 16 moon mission, collected samples of the moon's surface at the Descartes landing site. The lunar roving vehicle is parked in the left background.

WIDE WORLD

WIDE WORLD

Harold Masursky of the U.S. Geological Survey stands beside a 35-foot-wide group of pictures, all showing small sections of Mars. The pictures came from Mariner 9, and Masursky indicated that cuts in Mars's surface were made by rain.

Cernan and Schmitt landed in a valley near the moon's Sea of Serenity on December 12. In the next three days they made three "lunar walks," during which they explored the rocky terrain, collected some 240 pounds of rocks (including some of the youngest and oldest rocks yet found), and made an important discovery: fine droplets of orange glass. The glass was thought to be a possible indication of fairly recent volcanic activity. On December 16 Cernan and Schmitt blasted off from the moon and rejoined Evans, who had been orbiting in the command module. The Apollo 17 crew returned safely to earth on December 19, marking the end of the project.

Unmanned Satellites

Explorer 45 was launched into an equatorial orbit on Nov. 15, 1971, from the San Marcos platform off the coast of Kenya. The NASA satellite marked the first appearance of an on-board computer that could be reprogrammed from the ground. The satellite was considerably cheaper than its predecessors because it was made of riveted aluminum sections rather than machined ones. Explorer 45 was instrumented to study the earth's magnetosphere and the interaction of solar wind with it.

Intelsat 4 (F3) was launched by NASA for the Communications Satellite Corp. (Comsat) from Kennedy Space Center on Dec. 19, 1971, by an Atlas Centaur booster. It entered a nearly circular orbit at 22,407 miles and drifted westward around the equator until the end of January 1972. In its final position, over the Atlantic Ocean, it could provide 12 television channels and 3,000–9,000 telephone circuits. Its expected lifetime was seven years.

The U.S. began 1972 with the successful launching, on January 20, of a U.S. Air Force Big Bird reconnaissance satellite from the Western Test Range in California. The 25,000-pound photographic satellite was placed into a near-polar orbit by a Titan IIIC Agena. NASA launched Intelsat 4 (F4) from Kennedy Space Center on January 22. An Atlas Centaur placed the satellite into synchronous orbit over the Pacific Ocean. Its first task was to transmit pictures of the visit of President Nixon to China in February.

The world's first Earth Resources Technological Satellite was orbited on July 21 when NASA launched ERTS-1. The 1,965-pound satellite was launched from the Western Test Range. Its booster was a new model of the Delta, being flown for the first time. ERTS-1 outwardly resembled the Nimbus weather satellite, and data from its sensors was scheduled to be sent to 300 scientists in 37 countries. These scientists were seeking information in seven different areas: meteorology, marine resources, water resources, agriculture and forestry resources, environment, land use, and mineral and land resources. The data was to be provided to them in the form of photographs made in various wavelengths by seven special sensors in the satellite. Each photograph covered an area 115 miles square (for a total area of 13,000 square miles). ERTS-1 was set up to transmit 752 such pictures per day.

Interplanetary Probes; the Space Shuttle

Mariner 9, which had entered Martian orbit on Nov. 13, 1971, continued in 1972 to send back to the U.S. a wealth of information about the planet. On March 15 the computer aboard Mariner 9 did not respond properly to commands from Earth, and its instruments were turned off two days later. On March 23 the computer mysteriously corrected itself and the mission proceeded. By April, a total of more than 7,000 pictures had been sent to Earth. On March 2 Pioneer 10 was launched by the U.S. from Kennedy Space Center. This was the first probe to Jupiter.

In mid-May, four U.S. aerospace consortia submitted proposals to NASA to build the space-shuttle orbiter. On July 26 NASA announced that North American Rockwell Corp., which had built the Apollo command and service modules as well as the second stage of the Saturn V booster, had won the contract with a low bid of $2.6 billion. (*See also* Astronomy; Earth Sciences. *See in* CE: Space Travel.)

SPAIN. During most of 1972, Generalissimo Francisco Franco's hold on the government of Spain showed no signs of weakening, and in spite of being in his 80th year, Franco did not delegate any major decision-making authority to his cabinet. In July Franco issued a decree that virtually named the vice-premier, Adm. Luis Carrero Blanco, to succeed him as head of state, at least for the interim period after Franco's death or withdrawal from public life. It was evident that some sort of framework was slowly being constructed to perpetuate the regime and provide for a division of the functions held by Franco alone.

The events of the year again demonstrated the Franco regime's ability to survive in the face of considerable opposition, as evidenced by student and labor strikes and several incidents of violence by Basque separatists. The killing of two shipyard workers at El Ferrol by members of the Civil Guard—called in to control a demonstration in connection with a strike—was among the most extreme examples of the government's firm handling of such problems.

Discontent was rife in the universities during 1972. In January there were widespread student strikes and violence expressing support for 4,000 medical students at the University of Madrid (the capital) who had been suspended in a curriculum dispute. The government later imposed regulations requiring prospective high school teachers to produce certificates issued by the police testifying to their good character and allowing the government to appoint rectors, who had previously been nominated within the universities themselves. In the fall several universities failed to reopen for the new academic year in protest against the government crackdown.

The economy progressed satisfactorily during the year. After the setback of 1970-71, production increased strongly. The resumption of faster growth rates, however, did nothing to decrease the pace of inflation, which was a source of widespread popular discontent. Toward the end of the year the government took steps to keep prices down, including direct controls and increased imports. The latter measure was made possible only by the fact that Spanish reserves of gold and foreign currency were at a very high level ($4.78 billion at the end of October), largely due to the continued success of the tourist industry.

The issue that dominated Spain's foreign affairs in 1972 was the question of the country's relationship with the European Economic Community (EEC). It had been indicated that Spain could not qualify for membership with its existing form of government, because the EEC was a union of democratic countries. Although this attitude was denounced in Spain, it appeared that there was no chance of a cordial relationship with the EEC for some time. The broad trade agreement signed in July by EEC and European Free Trade Association (EFTA) members put Spanish goods at a further disadvantage on the European market.

In September Spain signed a trade agreement with the Soviet Union, the first major contact between the two countries since the Spanish Civil War. Shortly thereafter it was revealed that talks aimed at establishing diplomatic relations with the People's Republic of China had been going on for several months. (*See in* CE: Spain.)

Generalissimo Franco's granddaughter, Maria del Carmen Martinez-Bordiu, was married to Prince Alfonso de Borbon y Dampierre, grandson of Spain's last king, Alfonso XIII.

KEYSTONE

UPI COMPIX

Wilfried Dietrich (bottom) beat Chris Taylor in their Olympic Greco-Roman match.

SPORTS CHAMPIONS OF 1972.

Archery. World champions: freestyle, men—J. Williams (U.S.); women—M. Bechdoldt (U.S.); barebow, men—L. Bergen (Sweden); women—I. Grandquist (Sweden). European champions: men's individual—G. Jervill (Sweden), team—Sweden; women's individual—K. Losaberidze (U.S.S.R.), team—U.S.S.R.

Badminton. U.S. Open champions: singles, men—S. Johnsson (Sweden), women—E. Twedberg (Sweden); doubles, men—E. Stuart, D. Talbot (Great Britain), women—A. Berglund, P. Kaagaard (Denmark); mixed doubles—F. Delfs, Kaagaard (Denmark). European champions: men's singles—W. Bochow (West Germany), doubles—W. Braun, R. Maywald (West Germany); women's singles—M. Beck (Great Britain), doubles—G. Gilks, J. Hashman (Great Britain); mixed doubles—Talbot, Gilks; team—Great Britain.

Billiards. World champions: pocket—I. Crane (U.S.); 3-cushion—R. Ceulemans (Belgium).

Bobsledding. European champions: 2-man—W. Zimmerer, P. Utzschneider (West Germany); 4-man—H. Müller, H. Ott, R. Born, H. Hiltebrand (Switzerland).

Cross-Country. International champions: senior, individual—G. Roelants (Belgium), team—Great Britain; junior, individual—A. Tomasoni (Italy), team—Italy; women, individual—J. Smith (Great Britain), team—Great Britain. European club champions: individual—K. Lismont (Belgium); team—Belgium.

Curling. World champion: Canada. U.S. champion: Grafton, N.D.

Cycling. World men's professional champions: sprint—R. van Lancker (Belgium); pursuit—H. Porter (Great Britain); motor-paced—T. Verschueren (Belgium); road—M. Basso (Italy).

Fencing. European Cup winners: men's foil, team—A. S. Melun (France); women's foil, team—Steaua Bucharest (Romania).

Gliding. World champions: standard class—J. Wroblewski (Poland); open class—G. Ax (Sweden).

Gymnastics. Amateur Athletic Union champions: men, all-around—M. Sakamoto; vaulting—M. Hill; parallel bars—Y. Takei; still rings—Takei; side horse—T. Marcy; floor exercise—Takei. Women, all-around—L. Metheny; vaulting—N. Theis; floor exercise—Metheny; uneven bars—R. Pierce; balance beam—Metheny.

Handball. World champion teams: men—Romania; women—East Germany.

Ice Skating. World figure champions: men—O. Nepela (Czechoslovakia); women—B. Schuba (Austria); pairs—I. Rodnina, A. Ulanov (U.S.S.R.); dance—L. Pakhomova, A. Groshkov (U.S.S.R.). U.S. figure champions: men—K. Shelley; women—J. Lynn; pairs—Shelley, J. Starbuck; dance—J. Sladky, J. Schwomeyer. World speed champions: men—A. Schenk (Netherlands); women—A. Keulen-Deelstra (Netherlands); sprint—L. Linkovesi (Finland); women's sprint—M. Pflug (West Germany).

Judo. World university champions: lightweight—Y. Ishime (Japan); light middleweight—F. Mitsumoto (Japan); middleweight—H. Yoshinaga (Japan); light heavyweight—K. Eya (Japan); heavyweight—H. Uemara (Japan); unlimited weight—T. Nakamura (Japan); team—Japan. European champions: lightweight—J. J. Mounier (France); light middleweight—H. Hotger (East Germany); middleweight—J.-P.

Ludmila Tourischeva (Soviet Union) won a gold medal in Olympic women's gymnastics.

WIDE WORLD

Coche (France); light heavyweight—A. Parisi (Great Britain); heavyweight—W. Ruska (Netherlands); unlimited weight—Ruska; team —U.S.S.R.

Karate. World champions: individual—L. Watanabe (Brazil); team—France.

Motorcycling. World champions: 50 cc—A. Nieto (Spain); 125 cc—Nieto; 250 cc—J. Saarinen (Finland); 350 cc—G. Agostini (Italy); 500 cc—Agostini; sidecar—K. Enders (West Germany). U.S. grand champion—M. Brelsford.

Sailboat Racing. World championships: boat class, Cadet—G. Owens (Great Britain); Contender—P. Hollis (Australia); Dragon—A. Birch (Denmark); Enterprise—R. Hance (Great Britain); Finn—J. Bruder (Brazil); Fireball—J. Diesch (West Germany); 5.5 meters—C. Bigar (Switzerland); 5-0-5—N. Roday (France); 4-2-0—D. Johnsen (West Germany); 4-7-0—J. Vollebregt (Netherlands); Hornet—M. Goodwin (Great Britain); Moth—J. Faroux (France); O.K.—K. Axroth (Sweden); Star—W. Kuhweide (West Germany); Tornado—R. Jessenig (Austria); Vauriens—J. Quemeneur (France).

Table Tennis. U.S. Open champions: singles, men —D. Lee (U.S.), women—W. Hicks (U.S.); doubles, men—Lee, P. Pradit (U.S.), women—V. Nesukaitis, M. Domonkos (Canada); mixed doubles—E. Caetano, Nesukaitis (Canada). European champions: singles, men—S. Bengtsson (Sweden), women—Z. Rudnova (U.S.S.R.); doubles, men—I. Jonyer, P. Rozsas (Hungary), women—J. Magos, H. Lotaller (Hungary); mixed doubles—S. Gomozkov, Z. Rudnova

Kurt Westlund of Sweden won the World Championship of Speedway on Ice in July.

A.F.P. FROM PICTORIAL PARADE

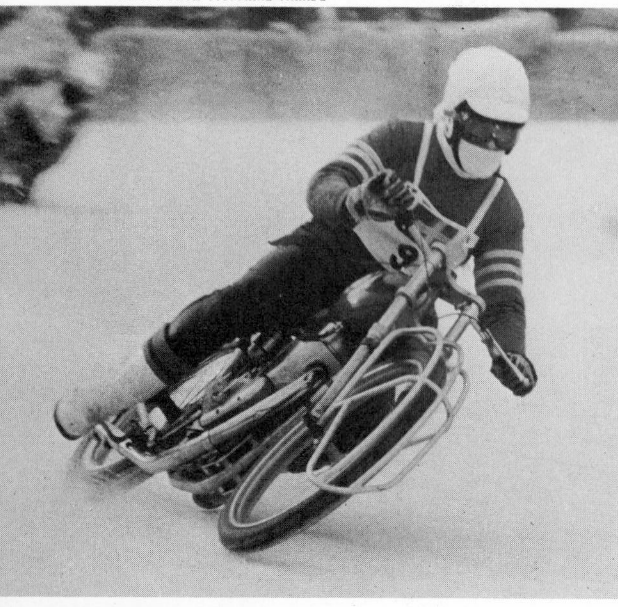

"THE NEW YORK TIMES"

Akinori Nakayama's gymnastic performance in a U.S.-Japan meet in Pennsylvania was flawless.

(U.S.S.R.); team, men—Sweden; women—Hungary.

Trampoline. World champions: singles, men—P. Luxon (Great Britain), women—A. Nicholson (U.S.); pairs, men—Luxon, R. Hughes (Great Britain), women—M. Steig, R. Grant (U.S.).

Weight Lifting. U.S. champions: flyweight—J. Yamauchi; bantamweight—S. Dominguez; featherweight—P. Sanderson; lightweight—D. Cantore; middleweight—F. Lowe; light heavyweight—M. Karchut; middle heavyweight—R. Holbrook; heavyweight—F. Capsouras; super heavyweight—K. Patera. European champions: flyweight—Z. Smalcerz (Poland); bantamweight—R. Belenkov (U.S.S.R.); featherweight—D. Shanidze (U.S.S.R.); lightweight—M. Kuchev (Bulgaria); middleweight —Y. Bikov (Bulgaria); light heavyweight—B. Pavlov (U.S.S.R.); middle heavyweight—D. Rigert (U.S.S.R.); heavyweight—Y. Talts (U.S.S.R.); super heavyweight—V. Alekseyev (U.S.S.R.); team—U.S.S.R.

Wrestling. U.S. National Collegiate champions: 118 pounds—G. Johnson; 126 pounds—P. Milkovich; 134 pounds—G. Barton; 142 pounds —T. Milkovich; 150 pounds—W. Schalles; 158 pounds—C. Adams; 167 pounds—A. Matter; 177 pounds—B. Murdock; 190 pounds—B. Peterson; heavyweight—C. Taylor; team—Iowa State University. European freestyle champions: light flyweight—S. Baigin (Turkey); flyweight —A. Alakhverdiev (U.S.S.R.); bantamweight—I. Kuleshov (U.S.S.R.); featherweight—R. Pliev (U.S.S.R.); lightweight—I. Yusseinov (Bulgaria); welterweight—A. Seger (West Germany); middleweight—V. Suilzhin (U.S.S.R.); light heavyweight—G. Strakhov (U.S.S.R.); heavyweight—I. Yarygin (U.S.S.R.); super heavyweight—A. Medved (U.S.S.R.).

SRI LANKA. On May 22, 1972, under a new constitution, the Republic of Sri Lanka (formerly Ceylon) came into being, with Sirimavo Bandaranaike its first prime minister and William Gopallawa its first president. It will remain, technically, a member of the Commonwealth of Nations.

The legislature was to be a single chamber, the National State Assembly (the Senate having been abolished in September 1971). The assembly was designated the supreme instrument of the power of the republic, exercising the legislative, executive, and judicial powers "of the people," who were described as possessing the sovereignty. The official language was Sinhalese, but provision was made for the use of Tamil in specified cases. The constitution contained a section on "principles of state policy," which expressed a goal of progressive advancement toward the establishment in Sri Lanka of a socialist democracy. The Buddhist religion was to be given "the foremost place." A constitutional court was established, but with limited powers. Other bodies included a state services advisory board, a state services disciplinary board, and similar boards for the judicial services. Provision was made for the proclamation of a state of emergency when necessary. Otherwise the constitution was much like its predecessor.

During the year the economic position of Sri Lanka showed little improvement. It appeared that the subsidizing of food (particularly rice) and other expenses encountered in setting up an advanced welfare state had been more than the economy could bear. (*See in* CE: Ceylon.)

STAMPS. An international philatelic sensation in 1972 was the disclosure in July that some 400 specially stamped and canceled envelopes were carried to the moon and back by the crew of Apollo 15 in July 1971 and that 100 of these had been sold by German stamp dealer Hermann Sieger for more than $150,000. The National Aeronautics and Space Administration (NASA) confiscated the remaining 300. In September NASA also revealed that 15 astronauts (not identified) had been paid $37,500 for signing more than 30,000 stamps and postcards and that these were selling in Western Europe for as much as $16.50 each.

The summer Olympic Games in Munich, West Germany, resulted in the largest number ever of worldwide "omnibus" issues. Stamps from countries with the smallest participating teams (or no teams at all) appeared to be the most numerous.

Among the noteworthy stamp issues in 1972 was a series of stamps honoring four famed British explorers of the Arctic and Antarctic (Sir James Clark Ross, Sir Martin Frobisher, Henry Hudson, and Robert Falcon Scott), issued in Great Britain on Feb. 16, 1972. Issues in the U.S. included a 14¢ stamp used for book mailing and honoring Fiorello H. La Guardia, mayor of New York City for three terms; an 8¢ stamp commemorating family planning; and a series of eight stamps marking the centenary of the U.S. national park system.

James Alexander Mackay, curator of the British Museum's philatelic collections, on September 5 pleaded guilty in a London criminal court to five charges of stealing stamp proofs loaned to the museum by agents for the Crown. Also in Great Britain, lengthy negotiations were abandoned on combining the British Philatelic Association, the National Philatelic Society, and the Philatelic Traders' Society, but the three agreed to cooperate in the overall interests of philately.

The major international philatelic exhibition was held in June in Brussels, Belgium, under the patronage of King Baudouin I. He awarded a large gold medal to a Swiss collector.

Signatories in 1972 to the Roll of Distinguished Philatelists included Lucien Berthelot (France), Athelstan Caroe (Britain), J. E. Crustin (Belgium), and John B. Marriott (Britain), the keeper of the Royal Philatelic Collections at Buckingham Palace. The Philatelic Congress Medal was awarded to F. P. N. Parsons of London. (*See in* CE: Stamps and Stamp Collecting.)

UPI COMPIX

This 8¢ postage stamp, saluting the 75th anniversary of the Parent-Teacher Association (PTA), was issued in San Francisco, Calif., in September. It represents a blackboard with writing in white chalk.

AUTHENTICATED NEWS INTERNATIONAL

Four postage stamps designed by Lance Wyman were issued in August to commemorate the Olympics. The designs represent two winter sports—bobsled racing and skiing—and two summer sports—footracing and cycling.

New York's Gov. Nelson A. Rockefeller gave the podium to a spokeswoman for two dozen welfare mothers at the National Governors' Conference (NGC). When the disruption continued, Governor Rockefeller had the demonstrators thrown out. The NGC's Human Rights Committee was discussing welfare programs.

WIDE WORLD

STATE GOVERNMENTS, UNITED STATES.

A historic breakthrough in federal-state relations in the form of federal revenue sharing provided the highlight event for state governments in 1972. State expenditures for welfare, education, and other services had mounted rapidly while legislatures were under voter pressure to avoid increased taxes. After several years of fruitless attempts, the states and cities achieved a signal victory on September 15 when a House-Senate conference committee approved a compromise revenue-sharing bill. The State and Local Fiscal Assistance Act of 1972 was signed into law by U.S. President Richard M. Nixon outside Independence Hall, Philadelphia, Pa., on October 20. It was to provide about $30 billion in federal funds to state and local governments over a five-year period. The first allocations, scheduled for 1972, totaled $5.3 billion. Two thirds of the grants would be distributed to local general purpose governmental units (counties, townships, and incorporated municipalities) and one third to state governments.

Administrative Structures, Powers

Consolidation and reorganization plans for state governmental executive agencies were approved by several state legislatures, including those of Maine, Idaho, Arizona, and Ohio. The new organizational orders typically provided more centralized control, either in the governor's office or in central administrative offices.

Voters in Montana narrowly approved a new state constitution. Another proposed new constitution was soundly defeated by North Dakotans.

Ethics and Education

State officials were involved in a number of scandals and legal conflicts during 1972. Texas and New Jersey, two states historically plagued with corruption problems, again furnished top news stories. In March a state jury in Abilene, Tex., convicted Gus Mutscher, speaker of the Texas House of Representatives, plus another state representative and a Mutscher aide on felony charges arising from a stock fraud scheme. The three were given five-year suspended prison terms for conspiring to accept a bribe. Prosecutors charged that they had accepted unsecured bank loans from financier Frank Sharp of Houston, Tex., in return for passing legislation that Sharp desired.

In New Jersey former Secretary of State Robert J. Burkhardt pleaded guilty on May 12 to charges of bribery and extortion from a construction firm seeking a bridge contract. Another New Jersey political leader, John V. Kenny, was fined the sum of $30,000 on six counts of income tax evasion later in May.

Problems of financing the nation's primary and secondary schools, including nonpublic and parochial schools, continued to receive considerable attention in the states. The controversy over the local property tax as a major source of financing public education, first brought to national attention by a 1971 California Supreme Court decision, expanded in several directions. By year's end, despite calls for action, neither the federal government nor any state had resolved the dilemma on school financing.

Courts in two additional states, New Jersey and Kansas, ruled that the local property tax system violated the constitutional right to equal protection under the law because rich communities could more easily raise educational funds than could poorer school districts. Previously, courts in California, Minnesota, and Texas had issued similar rulings.

The issue reached the U.S. Supreme Court in October through the Texas case, which arose in San Antonio. The plaintiffs asked the high court to require Texas to equalize tax assessment power between rich and poor school districts by imposing a varying formula for state aid. Attorneys for the state replied that the plaintiff's plan would "impose a straitjacket" on state educational systems by limiting the amount parents could constitutionally pay for their children's education. The case had nationwide implications, but the high court had not announced its decision by the end of the year.

Efforts by states to devise a constitutional method to aid parochial and private schools suffered additional setbacks in the nation's courts. The U.S. Supreme Court ruled on October 10, without hearing arguments, that an Ohio plan to reimburse parents of children in such schools with tuition grants was unconstitutional. The 8–1 decision cast gloomy shadows over similar programs in Maryland, Connecticut, and Illinois and left church leaders and state and federal officials still searching for a legal method of aiding the nation's hard-pressed nonpublic schools. A study by the U.S. Bureau of the Census released in March revealed that enrollment at Roman Catholic primary and secondary schools had dropped by 30% to 3.9 million students between 1965 and 1971: most of the missing students were enrolled in public schools, increasing state educational costs.

During 1972 the first court decisions were reached ordering busing across established school district lines to eliminate patterns of school segregation. Judges in Richmond, Va., and Detroit,

Alabama's Gov. George C. Wallace (left) succeeds South Carolina's Gov. John C. West as chairman of the Southern Governors' Conference.

WIDE WORLD

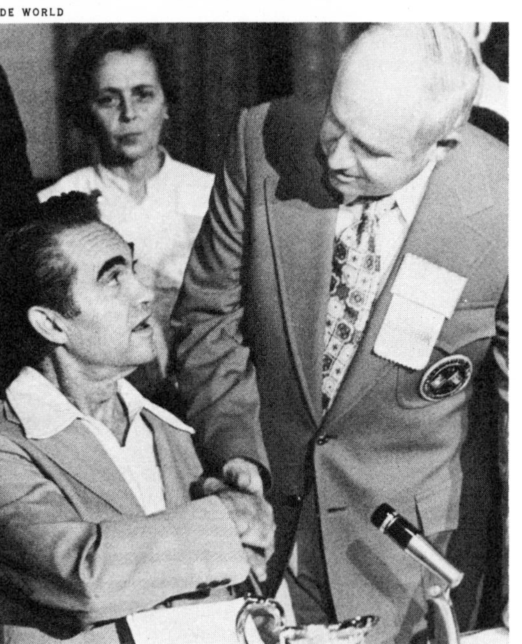

GOVERNORS OF THE STATES

(With Party Affiliations and Current Terms)

State	Governor
Ala.	George C. Wallace (D), 1971–75
Alaska	William A. Egan (D), 1970–74
Ariz.	Jack Williams (R), 1971–75
Ark.	Dale L. Bumpers (D), 1973–75
Calif.	Ronald Reagan (R), 1971–75
Colo.	John A. Love (R), 1971–75
Conn.	Thomas J. Meskill (R), 1971–75
Del.	Sherman W. Tribbitt (D), 1973–77
Fla.	Reubin Askew (D), 1971–75
Ga.	Jimmy Carter (D), 1971–75
Hawaii	John A. Burns (D), 1970–74
Idaho	Cecil Andrus (D), 1971–75
Ill.	Daniel Walker (D), 1973–77
Ind.	Otis R. Bowen (R), 1973–77
Iowa	Robert D. Ray (R), 1973–75
Kan.	Robert B. Docking (D), 1973–75
Ky.	Wendell Ford (D), 1971–75
La.	Edwin W. Edwards (D), 1972–76
Me.	Kenneth M. Curtis (D), 1971–75
Md.	Marvin Mandel (D), 1971–75
Mass.	Francis W. Sargent (R), 1971–75
Mich.	William G. Milliken (R), 1971–75
Minn.	Wendell R. Anderson (DFL)*, 1971–75
Miss.	William Waller (D), 1972–76
Mo.	Christopher S. Bond (R), 1973–77
Mont.	Thomas L. Judge (D), 1973–77
Neb.	James Exon (D), 1971–75
Nev.	Mike O'Callaghan (D), 1971–75
N.H.	Meldrim Thomson, Jr. (R), 1973–75
N.J.	William T. Cahill (R), 1970–74
N.M.	Bruce King (D), 1971–75
N.Y.	Nelson A. Rockefeller (R), 1971–75
N.C.	James E. Holshouser, Jr. (R), 1973–77
N.D.	Arthur A. Link (D), 1973–77
Ohio	John J. Gilligan (D), 1971–75
Okla.	David Hall (D), 1971–75
Ore.	Tom McCall (R), 1971–75
Pa.	Milton J. Shapp (D), 1971–75
R.I.	Philip W. Noel (D), 1973–75
S.C.	John C. West (D), 1971–75
S.D.	Richard F. Kneip (D), 1973–75
Tenn.	Winfield Dunn (R), 1971–75
Tex.	Dolph Briscoe (D), 1973–75
Utah	Calvin L. Rampton (D), 1973–77
Vt.	Thomas P. Salmon (D), 1973–75
Va.	Linwood Holton (R), 1970–74
Wash.	Daniel J. Evans (R), 1973–77
W.Va.	Arch A. Moore, Jr. (R), 1973–77
Wis.	Patrick J. Lucey (D), 1971–75
Wyo.	Stanley K. Hathaway (R), 1971–75

* Democrat-Farmer-Labor party.

Mich., ordered the transfers across districts, justifying the move as the only effective method available to wholly desegregate the schools in these areas. The orders were later rendered ineffective, at least temporarily, by other courts and were being appealed to the U.S. Supreme Court.

Legal Gambling; the Environment

A nationwide trend toward liberalizing gambling restrictions accelerated during 1972, with seven states taking action on lotteries, off-track betting, and other forms of gambling. In most cases, the moves were designed both to raise revenue and to cut into illicit gambling profits. Pennsylvania, Massachusetts, Connecticut, and Michigan initiated statewide, government-run lotteries. Similar systems were already in effect in New Hampshire, New Jersey, and New York.

Nearly 30 states approved new measures dealing with environmental problems, a marked increase from 1971. Land use, including protection of endangered species, received the most attention, with a wide array of new controls over subdivisions, natural areas, wetlands, and strip mining, but significant new legislation was also adopted covering air and water pollution, dredging, noise, solid wastes.

Colorado and New Mexico passed new laws to limit subdivision development, and Florida and Virginia moved to protect areas threatened by commercial and residential growth. Connecticut, Virginia, and Michigan approved laws to preserve wetlands and primitive tracts in their natural state. Maryland banned strip mining on land owned by the state; additional controls over strip mining were imposed in Ohio, Tennessee, and West Virginia. (*See also* Elections; Political Parties. *See in* CE: State Governments.)

STOCKS AND BONDS. The "magic" number of 1,000 was reached in 1972 by the Dow-Jones industrial average (DJI), the most closely followed stock market indicator. Long awaited as symbolic evidence that the nation's economy was on high, dry ground, the DJI closed over 1,000 for the first time on November 14. It finished at 1,003.16, gaining more than 6 points in the day's trading. Before the end of the year it peaked at 1,036.27 (December 11). On the year's last day of trading (December 29) the closing figure was 1,020.02. This represented a total gain of 129.82 points during the year from an opening figure of 890.20. Transportation stocks on the Dow-Jones index lost 16.55 points during the year. Utilities on the index were up 1.75 points. Penetration of the 1,000 mark was regarded by some professional stock market observers as psychologically significant, because they felt it would restore public confidence in the market.

In January it was revealed that a 19-year-old college sophomore had bought $200,000 worth of stock without providing any cash for his purchases. Abraham H. Treff of Philadelphia, Pa., had opened accounts at six brokerage firms and had ordered all of his stocks by telephone, contrary to established procedures in stock purchasing by an unknown customer. As a minor, Treff was not legally permitted to enter into such transactions. Treff stated that his purpose had been to reveal that rules of the New York Stock Exchange (NYSE) were not being enforced and that some brokerage houses would ignore conventional practices to obtain commission revenues. After all his speculative positions were sold out, he made no profits.

In March members of the NYSE voted to increase the role of the public in the exchange's administration. The 33-member policy-making board

There was jubilation at the New York Stock Exchange when the Dow-Jones industrial average passed the 1,000 mark—and then closed above 1,000—for the first time ever.

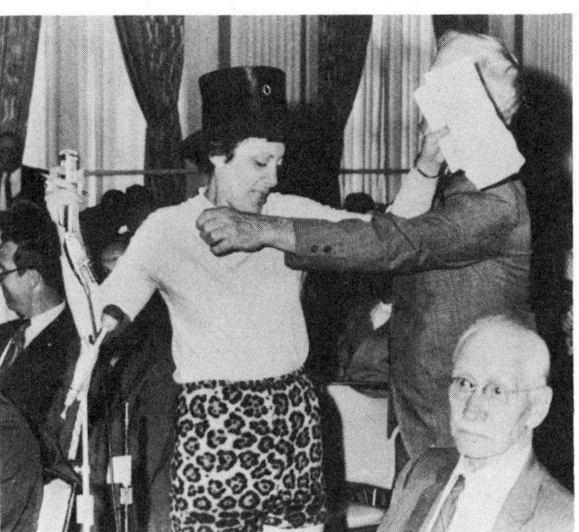

WIDE WORLD

Two Penn Central railroad stockholders argue about who gets the microphone during the first stockholders' meeting in two years.

of governors was reduced to a 21-member board of directors, 10 to be public representatives. Among these were Jerome H. Holland, U.S. ambassador to Sweden, who was the first black member of the board, and Juanita M. Krebs of Duke University, the first woman member. At the initial meeting of the new board, James J. Needham was chosen the first full-time, salaried chairman. He was named to the post effective August 28. To accept, Needham had to resign his membership in the Securities and Exchange Commission (SEC), a position he had held since 1969.

The SEC, the federal agency responsible for regulation of the brokerage industry, revealed in July that it would require greater precision in the language of prospectuses on newly issued stocks. Matters such as "the company's chances of success, its competition, or the status of material litigation" would have to be spelled out more carefully, according to William J. Casey, chairman of the commission.

In November the Federal Reserve System's Board of Governors announced an increase from 55% to 65% in the margin requirement for purchasing stock. The purpose of margin requirements is to minimize speculation. According to the board, there had recently been a sharp increase in margin debt. (*See also* Business and Industry; Economy; Money and International Finance. *See in* CE: Stocks and Bonds.)

SUDAN. After more than 17 years of civil war, a fragile peace was restored to Sudan in the spring of 1972. Under an accord reached through Ethiopian mediation, the rebel Christian and pagan blacks of Sudan's three southernmost provinces agreed to accept national unity with the Arab north in exchange for regional autonomy. A cease-fire went into effect, and provisional self-rule began in the south. Some 6,000 rebel troops were integrated into Sudan's army to serve in the south; of the remaining 14,000, most were given civilian work.

Among the problems facing the reunited nation were the resettlement of thousands of southern refugees and the restoration of the south's devastated economy. Financial and material aid was provided by the United Nations and by countries including the U.S., with which Sudan restored diplomatic relations, and several conservative Arab states with which relations were improving.

As Sudan concentrated on its African problems its estrangement from neighboring Libya and Egypt increased. Sudan refused to grant overflight rights to Libyan planes en route to aid Uganda, and it withdrew its forces from the Suez Canal front. Although relations with the Communist world remained cool in the wake of an attempted pro-Communist coup in 1971, Sudan pursued a policy of balanced East-West friendships. An agreement was reached on restoring Sudanese-Soviet ties. (*See also* Egypt; Uganda. *See in* CE: Sudan.)

SUPREME COURT OF THE UNITED STATES. It became still more obvious during the 1971–72 term that the Supreme Court of the U.S. was in a period of transition in which the Warren court of past years—under former Chief Justice Earl Warren—was gradually being transformed into a new entity—the Nixon court, with appointees of U.S. President Richard M. Nixon. One evidence of the change, in the field of criminal law, was a reduced emphasis on protecting the rights of the defendant and a tendency toward strengthening the position of the prosecution.

The court set an all-time record for the disposition of cases (3,645), even though during much of the term only seven justices participated in the proceedings. The retirement and subsequent deaths of two justices, Hugo L. Black and John M. Harlan, accounted for the vacant seats. Two new members, Lewis F. Powell, Jr., and William H. Rehnquist, were sworn in as associate justices on Jan. 7, 1972, but their full participation was delayed because they had not been present for the oral arguments in a number of cases.

Another sign of transition was the large number of dissenting opinions, 125, up from the 91 of the previous term, and very possibly another all-time record. And Justice William O. Douglas, long known for his dissents, may have achieved all-time "champion" status with his 46 dissenting opinions during the 1971–72 term.

Capital Punishment

For some time the legal world had awaited the decision of the court on the constitutionality of capital punishment. In June the court handed down a historic decision in the case of Furman *vs.* Georgia, ruling that the death penalty, as it was currently administered, constituted "cruel and un-

Assistant Attorney General William H. Rehnquist (left) and Virginia lawyer Lewis F. Powell, Jr., were sworn in on January 7 as associate justices of the U.S. Supreme Court.

UPI COMPIX

usual" punishment. The members of the court were divided 5–4, and a separate concurring or dissenting opinion was filed by each justice. Only Justices William J. Brennan, Jr., and Thurgood Marshall concluded that the 8th Amendment prohibited capital punishment for all crimes and under all circumstances. Justices Douglas, Potter Stewart, and Byron R. White agreed that the death penalty as generally applied in U.S. courts was arbitrary and tended to discriminate against the poor and members of minority groups. Chief Justice Warren E. Burger and Justices Harry A. Blackmun, Powell, and Rehnquist—all appointees of President Nixon—dissented, expressing the opinion that the abolition of the death penalty should be handled in the legislatures, rather than in the courts.

Taken together, these opinions made up a total of 243 pages; but there were many unanswered questions. The rejection of the death penalty did not appear to be entirely conclusive, and it was thought that a carefully written statute might be approved. Florida and California subsequently reinstated the death penalty for certain crimes; court challenges to these measures were expected to clarify the issue.

Other Decisions in Criminal Law

The notion of what constitutes a valid jury trial had been undergoing some change in recent years. In 1972 the concept of unanimous jury decisions was the focus of court action. Four states—Oregon, Louisiana, Oklahoma, and Montana—had previously allowed verdicts by majority. In the case of Johnson *vs.* Louisiana, the defendant had been convicted of armed robbery by a 9–3 vote of a jury. The high court upheld the conviction and noted that jury unanimity was not a requisite of due process of law.

In a unanimous decision, the court extended the right to counsel to include any offense, no matter how minor or petty, that involved the possibility of imprisonment. Under the new ruling, "no person may be imprisoned for any offense unless he was represented by counsel at his trial." The defendant could waive the right, but this had to be done in a "knowing and intelligent" manner. The court felt that defendants in cases involving misdemeanors were frequently subjected to "assembly line justice" and were unaware of the seriousness of the proceedings and the penalties involved. Cases where the charges did not involve possible imprisonment were not affected by this decision of the court.

Religious Dissent

The outstanding case in the field of religion during the term was Wisconsin *vs.* Yoder, which involved refusal of members of the Amish religion to abide by the state's compulsory school attendance law. The Amish objected to education beyond the eighth-grade level because the values taught differed markedly from Amish values and because such education involved an impermissible exposure to "worldly" influences.

The court upheld the Amish contention, noting that the traditional way of life of the Amish was not merely a matter of personal preference but rather one of deep religious conviction. "A way of life that is odd or even erratic but interferes with no rights or interests of others is not to be condemned because it is different," wrote Chief Justice Burger.

Citizenship, Civil Rights, and Press Freedom

Over the years numerous persons had been denied the right to vote in state and local elections because they had moved from state to state or even within a state and were thus unable to meet state residency requirements. In Dunn *vs.* Blumstein the court held such durational residence laws to be discriminatory and thus in violation of equal protection unless the state could prove them *necessary* to promote a *compelling* governmental interest. (In its written opinion the court italicized both of these words.)

Another long-awaited decision of the term involved equal protection. Ever since the 1954 decision on school segregation on the basis of race (Brown *vs.* Board of Education) there had been a steady progression of court decisions extending the racial nondiscrimination rule to various fields of state activity. One unanswered question concerned racial discrimination by private clubs holding state liquor licenses. In Moose Lodge No. 107 *vs.* Irvis, the Moose Lodge at Harrisburg, Pa., had refused to serve food and beverages to K. Leroy Irvis, a black state legislator. Suit was brought on the claim that this refusal was "state action" since the lodge had a state-granted liquor license. The court denied this claim and held the lodge to be a private club in the ordinary meaning of the term. The decision declared that the state was not, by the mere granting of the license, implicated in the discrimination. The opinion pointed out that states furnish many services to individuals and groups, ranging from fire protection to utilities. To hold that, because a private entity received any sort of benefit or service from the state, the state was implicated in the activities of the private entity would "utterly emasculate" the distinction between private and state conduct. The court noted that the state must have "significantly involved itself with invidious discriminations" in order for the discriminatory action to fall within the bounds of the constitutional prohibition.

The ability of journalists to gather information about underground social and political activities was seriously undermined by recent court decisions. In two cases, reporter Earl Caldwell of *The New York Times* and television newsman Paul Pappas of New Bedford, Mass., had both refused to reveal confidential information about the Black Panther party to grand jury investigations. In a similar case, Paul M. Branzburg, a reporter for the Louisville *Courier-Journal,* had refused to disclose the identity of confidential sources who were involved in drug traffic.

In a 5–4 ruling the court held that newsmen were not exempt from the normal duty of answering questions relevant to a criminal investigation before a grand jury. The opinion noted that courts over the years had concluded that the general obligation of a citizen to give testimony outweighed the asserted 1st Amendment rights of newsmen.

Interstate Commerce

A decision by the Supreme Court rarely makes headlines on the sports pages, but such was true of Flood *vs.* Kuhn. Back in 1922 the court decided that organized baseball was not an activity of interstate commerce and therefore not subject to federal antitrust legislation (Federal Baseball Club *vs.* National League). This decision was reiterated in 1953 in Toolson *vs.* New York Yankees. Although, in a series of other cases, other professional sports had been held to be engaging in interstate commerce, the court refused to include baseball, holding that the U.S. Congress, not the court, should be responsible for the decision.

In the case before the court in the 1971–72 term, the so-called reserve system of professional baseball was attacked. Plaintiff Curt Flood, formerly an outfielder with the St. Louis Cardinals, had asked the commissioner of baseball to release him from his contract and make him a free agent. His request denied, Flood instituted an antitrust suit. Once again, however, the court held that any action bringing the business of baseball under antitrust laws must come from the U.S. Congress. (*See also* Baseball.)

Legal Dilemmas at the Democratic Convention

A week after the adjournment of the regular term, the court was called into special session to rule on the credentials of certain delegates to the Democratic National Convention, which was scheduled to convene three days later. The court in O'Brien *vs.* Brown refused to take action, holding that the time available was not adequate.

The opinion noted that for a century and a half such controversies had been handled by the political parties themselves, and that if federal courts were to become involved more time would be needed for consideration. (*See also* Law. *See in* CE: Supreme Court of the U.S.)

Prisoners on death row share a newspaper explaining that the U.S. Supreme Court ruled the death penalty unconstitutional.

WIDE WORLD

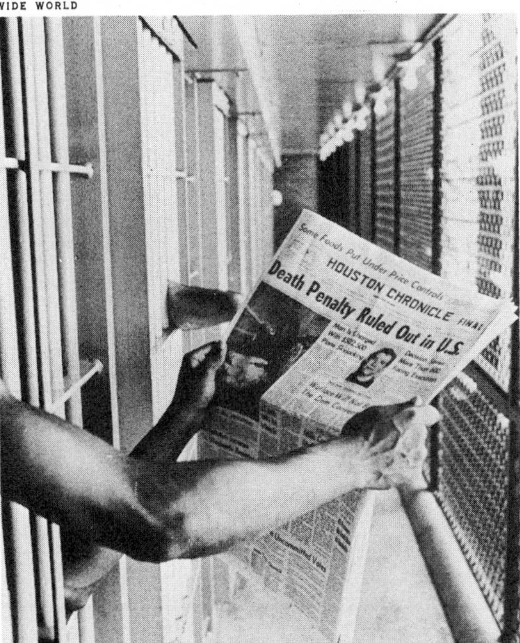

SWAZILAND. The elections of May 1972 in Swaziland, the first held since independence, once more returned to office Prince Makhosini Dlamini's Imbokodvo National Movement. The prince's movement was based on the traditional Swazi National Council and the power of King Sobhuza II, who with a reign of 51 years was the world's longest-ruling living monarch. Five parties contested the 24 seats in the House of Assembly, but even the main opposition branch of the Ngwane Liberatory Congress was torn by internal rivalry.

Swaziland's successful economy continued to rely on sugar, asbestos, and iron ore, all of which could be affected by Great Britain's entry into the European Economic Community (EEC). Although 80% of Swazi imports came from South Africa, its even greater exports were routed via Lourenço Marques, Mozambique.

In January the Swazi government made it known that it was proposing legislation that would help put a stop to "immoral sex" between whites and blacks. The ban was aimed primarily at white males from South Africa who have frequently crossed the border to find black Swazi women. (*See in* CE: Swaziland.)

SWEDEN. The economic recession that began in 1971 continued to trouble Sweden in 1972. Inflation, high taxes, unemployment, and factory closures beset the country. The difficulties resulted largely from the tight fiscal policies taken to alleviate inflationary tendencies in 1969–70.

The budget for 1972–73 was notable for an even tighter fiscal policy, restrictions on spending, and the absence of tax increases. The non-Socialist parties called for strong measures to improve profits and investment, while the Social Democratic government, committed to creating a more equitable society, faced the fact that industrial expansion depended on high profits.

All parties considered full membership in the European Economic Community (EEC) incompatible with Sweden's policy of neutrality. A free-trade agreement with the EEC was signed in July.

The government announced a regional development program to ensure equal opportunities in employment and social, commercial, and cultural services in every province. It was proposed in 1972 that the official Church of Sweden should be disestablished by 1983.

The United Nations Conference on Human Environment attracted thousands of visitors to Stockholm, the capital, in June. Sweden reduced the limit on lead content in its gasoline in 1972.

King Gustav VI Adolf celebrated his 90th birthday on November 11. (*See in* CE: Sweden.)

On February 26 demonstrations were held throughout Sweden to protest the country's rising food prices.

WIDE WORLD

SWIMMING. In 1972 there were many world swimming records set—not unusual in an Olympic Games year. Including those set at the Olympics, 23 records were established by men (17 by U.S. swimmers). The women were only a little less prolific as they set 19 world marks (12 by women from the U.S.).

U.S. Competition

The first major competition in the U.S. in 1972 was the 49th annual National Collegiate Athletic Association (NCAA) swimming and diving championships at West Point, N.Y., March 23–25. The championship produced 10 U.S. records for the short course (25-yard pools) and 11 NCAA marks. Indiana University for the fifth straight year won the team title by scoring 390 points to 371 for the runner-up University of Southern California. Mark Spitz, the Indiana captain, won two events, both in record time, to lead his team to their title. On April 5–8, the U.S. national Amateur Athletic Union (AAU) short-course (indoor) swimming championships were contested in Dallas, Tex. Four individual U.S. short-course records and three U.S. relay marks were established.

The U.S. Olympic swimming trials were held in Chicago, August 2–6; this qualifying meet replaced the AAU long-course (outdoor) national championships. Eight world records and ten U.S. records were set by the men and five world records and seven U.S. marks by the women.

At the national AAU indoor diving championships, March 26–April 1, at Dallas, U.S. Air Force Capt. Micki King and Cynthia Potter divided the one- and three-meter springboard titles in the women's division. Don Dunfield and Lieut. Phil Boggs divided the springboard championships in the men's division, the former taking the one-meter and Boggs the three-meter. Dick Rydze won the platform competition. The U.S. national AAU outdoor championships were held at Lincoln, Neb., July 11–15. Miss Potter successfully defended her one- and three-meter springboard championships,

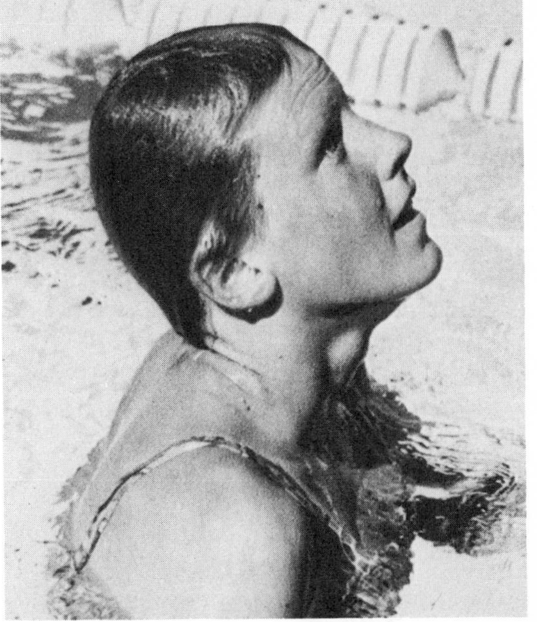

WIDE WORLD

At the Santa Clara International Invitational swimming and diving meet in June, Gary Hall (left) won the 200-meter individual medley, and Shirley Babashoff won the 800-meter freestyle.

while Janet Ely won the platform competition. Dunfield won the men's one-meter springboard and Mike Finneran the three-meter springboard. Rick Early took the platform title. The U.S. Olympic diving trials held at Park Ridge, Ill., July 28–30, produced a team of eight divers to represent the U.S. at Munich, West Germany. Three women—Miss King, Miss Potter, and Miss Ely—qualified to compete in both springboard and platform. Finneran, Craig Lincoln, and David Bush were the men's springboard competitors, and Rydze, Early, and Finneran won the platform slots.

Olympic Games

The swimming competition at the Olympic Games was clearly dominated by Spitz. He won seven gold medals in seven days, setting four individual world records and participating on three world-record-setting relay teams. Spitz won two gold medals on the very first day by winning the

By swimming the 100-meter freestyle in 58.5 seconds in 1972, Australia's 15-year-old swimming star Shane Gould held every world freestyle metric record for women from 100 to 1,500 meters.

CENTRAL PRESS FROM PICTORIAL PARADE

200-meter butterfly in the world record time of 2:00.70, and then joining teammates Jerry Heidenreich, John Murphy, and Dave Edgar for a victory in the 400-meter freestyle relay in the world record time of 3:26.42. Spitz then continued to chalk up more victories. He won the 200-meter freestyle in 1:52.78 (a world record) and the 100-meter butterfly in 54.27 seconds (another world mark) and anchored the men's 800-meter freestyle relay team, which also included John Kinsella, Fred Tyler, and Steve Gunter, and which produced a world mark of 7:38.78. Spitz also won the 100-meter freestyle in the world record time of 51.22, then joined Heidenreich, Mike Stamm, and Tom Bruce to win the 400-meter medley relay with a world record time of 3:48.16. Other winners for the U.S. men's team were John Hencken, who won the 200-meter breaststroke in the world record time of 2:21.55, and Mike Burton, who successfully defended his 1,500-meter freestyle crown in 15:52.58, setting a new world mark in doing so.

In the women's competition, Shane Gould of Australia won three gold medals, taking the 200-meter individual medley in the world record time of 2:23.07; the 400-meter freestyle in 4:19.04, another world mark; and the 200-meter freestyle in 2:03.56, another world record. Winners for the U.S. were: Sandra Neilson in the 100-meter freestyle; Keena Rothhammer in the 800-meter freestyle, a world record performance of 8:53.68; Melissa Belote in the 100- and 200-meter backstroke events, the latter in the world record time of 2:19.19; Cathy Carr in the 100-meter breaststroke, in the world record time of 1:13.58; and Karen Moe in the 200-meter butterfly, in the world record time of 2:15.57. The U.S. women won both relay events, capturing the 400-meter freestyle in the world record time of 3:55.19 and the 400-meter medley in 4:20.75. In diving, Miss King of the U.S. won the gold medal in the three-meter springboard event. (*See also* Olympic Games. *See in* CE: Swimming.)

WORLD SWIMMING RECORDS SET IN 1972 (through September 15)

	Event	Name	Country	Time	
MEN	100-meter freestyle	Mark Spitz	U.S.		51.47 seconds
	100-meter freestyle	Mark Spitz	U.S.		51.22 seconds
	200-meter freestyle	Mark Spitz	U.S.	1 minute	52.78 seconds
	400-meter freestyle	Brad Cooper	Australia	4 minutes	01.70 seconds
	400-meter freestyle	Kurt Krumpholz	U.S.	4 minutes	00.11 second
	800-meter freestyle	Brad Cooper	Australia	8 minutes	23.80 seconds
	1,500-meter freestyle	Rick DeMont	U.S.	15 minutes	52.91 seconds
	1,500-meter freestyle	Mike Burton	U.S.	15 minutes	52.58 seconds
	100-meter backstroke	Roland Matthes	East Germany		56.30 seconds
	200-meter backstroke	Roland Matthes	East Germany	2 minutes	02.80 seconds
	100-meter breaststroke	Nobutaka Taguchi	Japan	1 minute	04.94 seconds
	200-meter breaststroke	John Hencken	U.S.	2 minutes	22.80 seconds
	200-meter breaststroke	John Hencken	U.S.	2 minutes	21.55 seconds
	100-meter butterfly	Mark Spitz	U.S.		54.57 seconds
	100-meter butterfly	Mark Spitz	U.S.		54.27 seconds
	200-meter butterfly	Mark Spitz	U.S.	2 minutes	01.53 seconds
	200-meter butterfly	Mark Spitz	U.S.	2 minutes	00.70 second
	200-meter individual medley	Gary Hall	U.S.	2 minutes	09.30 seconds
	200-meter individual medley	Gunnar Larsson	Sweden	2 minutes	07.17 seconds
	400-meter individual medley	Gary Hall	U.S.	4 minutes	30.81 seconds
	400-meter medley relay	U.S. Olympic team		3 minutes	48.16 seconds
	400-meter freestyle relay	U.S. Olympic team		3 minutes	26.42 seconds
	800-meter freestyle relay	U.S. Olympic team		7 minutes	38.78 seconds
WOMEN	100-meter freestyle	Shane Gould	Australia		58.50 seconds
	200-meter freestyle	Shirley Babashoff	U.S.	2 minutes	05.21 seconds
	200-meter freestyle	Shane Gould	Australia	2 minutes	03.56 seconds
	400-meter freestyle	Shane Gould	Australia	4 minutes	19.04 seconds
	800-meter freestyle	Jo Harshbarger	U.S.	8 minutes	53.84 seconds
	800-meter freestyle	Keena Rothhammer	U.S.	8 minutes	53.68 seconds
	200-meter backstroke	Melissa Belote	U.S.	2 minutes	20.64 seconds
	200-meter backstroke	Melissa Belote	U.S.	2 minutes	19.19 seconds
	100-meter breaststroke	Cathy Carr	U.S.	1 minute	13.58 seconds
	100-meter butterfly	Mayumi Aoki	Japan	1 minute	03.90 seconds
	100-meter butterfly	Mayumi Aoki	Japan	1 minute	03.34 seconds
	200-meter butterfly	Karen Moe	U.S.	2 minutes	16.62 seconds
	200-meter butterfly	Karen Moe	U.S.	2 minutes	15.57 seconds
	200-meter individual medley	Shane Gould	Australia	2 minutes	23.07 seconds
	400-meter individual medley	Gail Neall	Australia	5 minutes	02.97 seconds
	400-meter medley relay	U.S. Olympic team		4 minutes	25.30 seconds
	400-meter medley relay	U.S. Olympic team		4 minutes	20.75 seconds
	400-meter freestyle relay	U.S. Olympic team		3 minutes	58.10 seconds
	400-meter freestyle relay	U.S. Olympic team		3 minutes	55.19 seconds

SWITZERLAND. The Swiss economy in 1972 was booming, and there was a strong inflationary trend. A constitutional change to revise the government's power in the field of economic policy was under discussion. Meanwhile, the government prohibited investment of foreign funds in Swiss securities and in mortgages on real estate, as well as the acquisition of Swiss real estate by nonresidents and foreign-owned interests.

An agreement on free trade between Switzerland and the European Economic Community was negotiated in 1972. The agreement was submitted to referendum on December 3 and was overwhelmingly approved by the Swiss electorate.

In the spring, as an environmental protection move, the parliament approved a set of federal emergency measures to prohibit or restrict building in certain areas. In October the nation's Federal Council proposed a further amendment to strengthen the government's powers in the control and management of water resources.

In September Swiss voters defeated by a very narrow margin (fewer than 9,000 votes) a popular initiative that would have banned arms exports and tightened national control over the Swiss armament industry. Thus the Federal Council was free to pursue its goal of maintaining military defenses while placing some controls on armaments.

On November 23, the Bernese cantonal government published a long-awaited draft statute for its Jura region. The law would grant a large measure of autonomy to French-speaking Catholic districts and, it was hoped, bring about a compromise between the separatist and antiseparatist groups. (*See in* CE: Switzerland.)

To prevent accidents that could pollute the nearby waters, fuel tankers are barred from the roads in sections of Val-de-Ruz, Switzerland.

"LONDON DAILY EXPRESS" FROM PICTORIAL PARADE

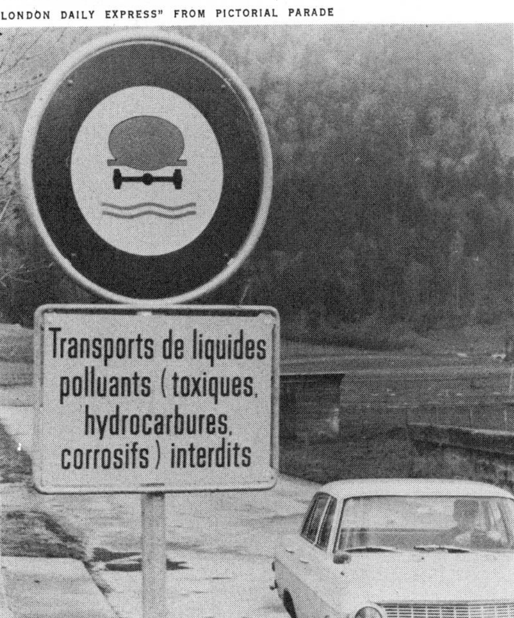

Transports de liquides
polluants (toxiques,
hydrocarbures,
corrosifs) interdits

SYRIA. In 1972 Syria's internal political tensions were eased by the long-awaited formation of a National Front. In it the ruling Ba'athist party, which had held most of the political control for a decade, shared power with other leftist factions. Under the front's charter the Ba'athists held a clear majority, the policy followed the Ba'athist ideology of socialism and Arab unity, and only the Ba'athist party could operate among students and the armed forces. Leading the front was Syria's President Hafez al-Assad. Constitutional amendments in 1972 increased his powers, giving him legislative authority in emergencies and when the National Assembly was not in session.

Under the continuing moderate liberalization program of the Assad regime, import restrictions were relaxed, investment and tourism were encouraged, and steps were taken to induce expatriates to return with investment capital. The economy benefited from a large grain harvest, which partly offset a revenue reduction following the nationalization of Iraq Petroleum Co. facilities in Syria and Iraq. The nationalization improved relations with the rival Iraqi Ba'athist regime, but the new rapport was shaken in October by a dispute over Syrian transit fees for Iraqi oil shipments. (*See* Iraq.)

In a policy of reconciliation with conservative Arab nations, Syria established diplomatic ties with Morocco, Tunisia, and the United Arab Emirates and other Persian Gulf states; settled some differences with Saudi Arabia; and obtained aid from Kuwait. Relations with Jordan remained unimproved, however, and a strain developed in Syria's relations with Libya and Egypt.

Ties with the Soviet Union grew increasingly close, and the Soviets pledged additional economic and military aid to Syria. After Egypt ousted Soviet military advisers, Assad affirmed that Syria would retain its Soviet advisers. Plans were announced for a Soviet military and naval buildup in Syria. Assad took steps to mediate the Egyptian-Soviet rift. (*See* Egypt.)

In the fall Syrian and Israeli forces clashed along the cease-fire line in the heaviest fighting in two years. As tensions mounted, Syria strengthened its forces on the Golan Heights frontier, prepared to install a more defense-oriented cabinet, and mobilized the militia. (*See* Israel. *See in* CE: Syria.)

TAIWAN. The thaw in relations between the U.S. and the People's Republic of China produced damaging shock waves for the Nationalist Chinese government on Taiwan in 1972. The détente produced by U.S. President Richard M. Nixon's visit to mainland China in February was a crippling blow to Taiwan's international diplomatic standing. A communiqué issued after Nixon's arrival in China contained a U.S. acknowledgment of the People's Republic as the only legitimate government of mainland China—and of Taiwan as well. Nixon also agreed in principle to the removal of

U.S. troops from Taiwan when tensions in that area of Asia eased. Following the lead of the U.S., more than 20 nations exchanged their diplomatic ties with Taiwan for relations with the People's Republic of China; fewer than 50 countries still recognized the Nationalists at the end of the year. One of the most damaging blows was the recognition of the People's Republic by Japan, one of Taiwan's most important trade partners. The action was a violation of a 1952 Japan-Taiwan treaty.

The Nationalist government responded with denunciations of both the U.S. and Japan. The aging President Chiang Kai-shek was reelected to a fifth term; he was drafted as a candidate after he had decided to retire at age 84. His son, Chiang Ching-kuo, became premier and heir apparent. Despite the diplomatic troubles, the economy remained strong. In December the ruling Nationalist party won a large majority in national and local elections, but a few dissidents also won legislative seats. (*See also* China, People's Republic of. *See in* CE: Formosa.)

TANAKA, KAKUEI. Traditionally, Japanese prime ministers came from affluent families, were university-educated, and when they took office were well along in years. Kakuei Tanaka, who became prime minister of Japan on July 6, 1972, was the son of a poor farmer, had educated himself in night schools, and at 54 was the youngest prime minister since World War II. Tanaka, who had owned his own construction firm at the age of 25 and been a government deputy minister at 31, was a blunt-spoken, energetic man, viewed as a liberal by most observers—and as a "very un-Japanese" maverick by his critics.

Originally a member of the later-defunct Progressive party, he joined the Liberal-Democratic party (LDP) in 1955. He was named deputy minister of justice in 1949 and subsequently served as minister of postal services, finance minister, and minister of international trade and industry—the post he was holding at the time of his election as prime minister. Along the way he had built powerful support for himself within the LDP, and when the party's leader, Prime Minister Eisaku Sato, resigned in June 1972, Tanaka was elected to replace him by the LDP members of the Diet. The LDP majority in both parliamentary houses assured him of being elected. Tanaka immediately went to work, reestablishing diplomatic relations with the People's Republic of China and announcing plans to deal with industrial problems. One of his ideas was the moving of industry away from congested coastal areas to rural locations. Tanaka also favored more strict pollution controls and a cutback in Japanese exports. (*See also* Japan.)

On July 6 Kakuei Tanaka became prime minister of Japan, replacing Eisaku Sato.
BARRY SCHLACHTER FROM NANCY PALMER AGENCY

TANZANIA. The assassination of the leader of Zanzibar and an encounter with neighboring Uganda were two unhappy events in Tanzania in 1972. Sheikh Abeid Karume, who had ruled the island of Zanzibar since a revolution put him in power in 1964, was shot to death on April 7 by four gunmen. The Revolutionary Council, of which Karume had been chairman, continued in power and a new chairman, Aboud Jumbe, was appointed by Tanzania's President Julius K. Nyerere. Three of Karume's assassins were killed; the fourth committed suicide. Two of the men were said to have been supporters of the Umma party, which had merged with Karume's Afro-Shirazi party in 1964. The leader of the Umma party was arrested on April 14 on suspicion of complicity in the assassination.

Relations with Uganda, already strained, broke down completely in August after Uganda's President Idi Amin ordered all Ugandan Asians to leave his country within 90 days. While Tanzania closed its borders to prevent an influx of Asian refugees, Nyerere criticized Amin's action as inhumane. Then Amin denounced Tanzania for alleged plots against his regime on behalf of Milton Obote, Uganda's former president, who was in exile in Tanzania. On September 17, an armed force of Obote's supporters crossed into Uganda from Tanzania, leading Amin to accuse Tanzania of sending its own troops against Uganda. Amin then launched aerial attacks on Tanzanian ports. Nyerere denied any involvement, and the invasion failed. Eventually, mediation by Somalia's President Mohammed Siad Barre produced an uneasy peace. (*See also* Uganda. *See in* CE: Tanzania.)

TELEVISION AND RADIO. More than 927 million television and radio sets were in use throughout the world in 1972. There was some radio service in almost every country and some television service in every industrial nation except

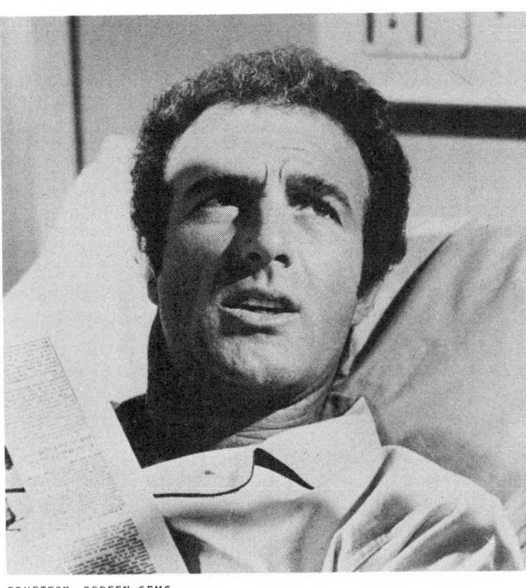

COURTESY, SCREEN GEMS

James Caan appeared in 'Brian's Song', a TV movie about the friendship between Chicago Bears' Gale Sayers and the late Brian Piccolo.

South Africa, where service was scheduled to begin in 1975. TV sets in the world totaled 261.75 million and radio sets 665.5 million, according to estimates compiled by *Broadcasting* magazine and *Broadcasting Yearbook*. Approximately 95 million, or 36%, of the television sets were in the U.S. The Soviet Union had the second largest number—about 30 million—and Japan was in third place with about 24 million. The number of U.S. households equipped with color television sets totaled approximately 31.4 million, more than 50% of all U.S. television households. About 53% of the world's radio sets were in use in the United States during the year.

Worldwide, 6,385 television stations were operating in 1972, according to *Broadcasting*. Their distribution by area varied little from that of 1971. The choice of stations offered to viewers ranged from only one in many countries to ten or more in others. In the U.S., according to *Broadcasting*, 97% of all TV households could receive at least three stations, and about 20% could receive ten or more. All three U.S. commercial TV networks transmitted virtually all of their programs in color, as did most stations not affiliated with networks.

More than 13,400 radio stations were on the air or under construction throughout the world in 1972. The majority were AM (amplitude modulation) stations, but the number of FM (frequency modulation) stations was growing. In the U.S., which had 7,533—or about 56%—of the world's radio stations, about 42% (3,110) were FM.

One of the greatest accomplishments in 1972 was the coordination of international satellite relays covering such events as U.S. President Richard M. Nixon's trips to the People's Republic of China and the Soviet Union, the U.S. Apollo 16 moon mission, and the summer Olympic Games in Munich, West Germany. Viewers in countries around the world were able to watch these events as relayed through communications satellites "parked" in stationary orbits over the Atlantic and Pacific oceans and, beginning in midyear, over the Indian Ocean.

Problems for Broadcasters

The networks, meanwhile, operated under pressures more intense in 1972 than ever before. In April the U.S. Department of Justice filed antitrust suits seeking to prohibit the three major TV networks from producing any of their own entertainment programs and feature films. Network spokesmen angrily denied the government's charge of monopoly and asked that the suits be dismissed

Sanford and Son, one of the year's top ten TV shows, features a father and son running a junk yard in Los Angeles and playing a continual, yet affectionate, game of one-upmanship with each other. Redd Foxx (right), as Sanford, thinks up elaborate wily tricks, directing most of them at his son Lamont, played by Demond Wilson.

COURTESY, NATIONAL BROADCASTING CO.

COURTESY, MARSHAL & BLOOM—LEE OHERBACH

Glenda Jackson gave a memorable performance in the role of Elizabeth I in the Masterpiece Theatre presentation of 'Elizabeth R'.

on the grounds that the issue had already been dealt with in previous restrictions imposed by the Federal Communications Commission (FCC).

The networks were also the target of demands by film craft unions that the number of episodes in TV series programs be increased and the number of reruns reduced. The networks declared that such action would not create the desired effect—namely, increased production in Hollywood, Calif., and more work for the unions. President Nixon, however, spoke out strongly in favor of the union proposal.

Among other pressures under which broadcasters operated were mounting demands for access to station time to present minority viewpoints. The equal-time rule was particularly nettlesome because 1972 was a presidential election year and because, in addition, the U.S. Congress enacted a law requiring broadcasters to sell political time at their lowest rates.

In December the Nixon Administration caused a furor by announcing planned legislation that would hold TV stations liable—under threat of losing their licenses—for the ideological content of the programs they broadcast. If "consistent bias" was found in news programs, for example, the station could lose its license. TV spokesmen responded by accusing the government of using threats to silence its critics.

TV violence was the subject of a report issued in January by the U.S. Surgeon General's Scientific Advisory Committee on Television and Social Behavior. The report concluded "that there is a modest relationship between exposure to television and aggressive behavior or tendencies", but it emphasized that a causal relationship would apply only to children "predisposed" to violence. The committee members made no recommendations based on their findings. Even so, at the urging of a Senate communications subcommittee, the U.S. Department of Health, Education, and Welfare undertook to develop a "violence index" by which programs might be rated; the department concluded that a simple index was not feasible, but that a "TV violence profile" might be developed in two to four years.

Programming

Broadcasting's ability to carry its coverage of news events into homes around the world was demonstrated repeatedly in 1972. One of the most spectacular demonstrations came in TV coverage of President Nixon's visit to China, witnessed in the U.S. and many other countries in color that experts rated as being exceptionally high in quality. Less spectacular photographically, but more complicated electronically, was the coverage of the president's trip to the Soviet Union in May, including his unprecedented television address to the Russian people.

The FCC's prime-time access rule continued to have a fundamental effect on programming. It also remained a center of controversy. In the rule's first year of operation, the 1971–72 season, it was generally agreed that the local prime-time programs tended to have smaller audiences than the network programs they had replaced. In late October 1972 the FCC conceded that the rule did not appear to be working as well as it might, and accordingly called for a review of the subject.

In the season that started in September 1972, network programs were distinguished by bolder attempts to reflect contemporary problems. Western and mystery/adventure drama, comedy, and variety shows were still the basic program forms, but the weekly episodes often undertook to deal with problems and issues that would have been unacceptable on television only a few years earlier. Homosexuality, lesbianism, abortion, embryo transplant, drug abuse, and venereal disease were among the issues introduced into some of the regular series programs.

Sports remained a major TV attraction. Coverage of the Olympics by ABC (the American Broadcasting Co.) took the first seven places in the A. C. Nielsen Co. national ratings for the two weeks ending September 3 and pushed All in the Family, on CBS (the Columbia Broadcasting System), from its accustomed number-one or number-two position.

In noncommercial broadcasting the big hits were still Sesame Street and The Electric Company. The Public Broadcasting Service (PBS) conducted a study of its public-affairs programming for the year and reported in October that three fourths of its programs had consisted of children's and cultural programs and no more than one fourth dealt with public affairs, in which PBS had been accused of exhibiting a left-wing bias. (*See also* Communications. *See in* CE: Radio; Television.)

TENNIS. The administrative conflict affecting competition tennis was resolved during 1972. Players under contract to World Championship Tennis (WCT), the corporation controlled by Lamar Hunt and based in Dallas, Tex., were banned as of January 1 from competing in events sanctioned by the International Lawn Tennis Federation (ILTF). This meant that many of the leading men players did not participate in the year's major championships, those of South Africa, Italy, West Germany, France, Wimbledon (England), and others run by national associations. An agreement opening tournaments to all classes of players was made between WCT and the ILTF in time for the U.S. championship at Forest Hills, N.Y. The agreement between WCT and the ILTF allowed WCT to promote two separate tournament schedules between January and May incorporating 64 players. WCT undertook to sign no more contracts with players, leaving the distinction between contract and independent professionals to disappear as existing agreements expired.

Men's Competition

At the end of 1971 the Grand Prix series organized by the ILTF was won by Stan Smith of the U.S., with Ilie Nastase of Romania second. The Masters' Tournament was played at the Coubertain Stadium in Paris between Smith, Nastase, Cliff Richey of the U.S., Pierre Barthes of France, Zeljko Franulovic of Yugoslavia, Jan Kodes of Czechoslovakia, and Clark Graebner of the U.S. Nastase was the unbeaten victor in the all-play-all series; Smith was the runner-up.

The Australian championship was won by Ken Rosewall of Australia for the second successive year. He defeated his countryman Mal Anderson in the final. Richey won the South African title in a final match against Manuel Orantes of Spain. Later Orantes went on to get his first important success, winning the Italian championship by beating Kodes in the final. In Dallas the last tournament in the WCT series between eight qualifiers—Rosewall, Rod Laver, and John Newcombe of

Stan Smith became the 16th American to win the men's singles title at Wimbledon by beating Ilie Nastase of Romania.

CENTRAL PRESS FROM PICTORIAL PARADE

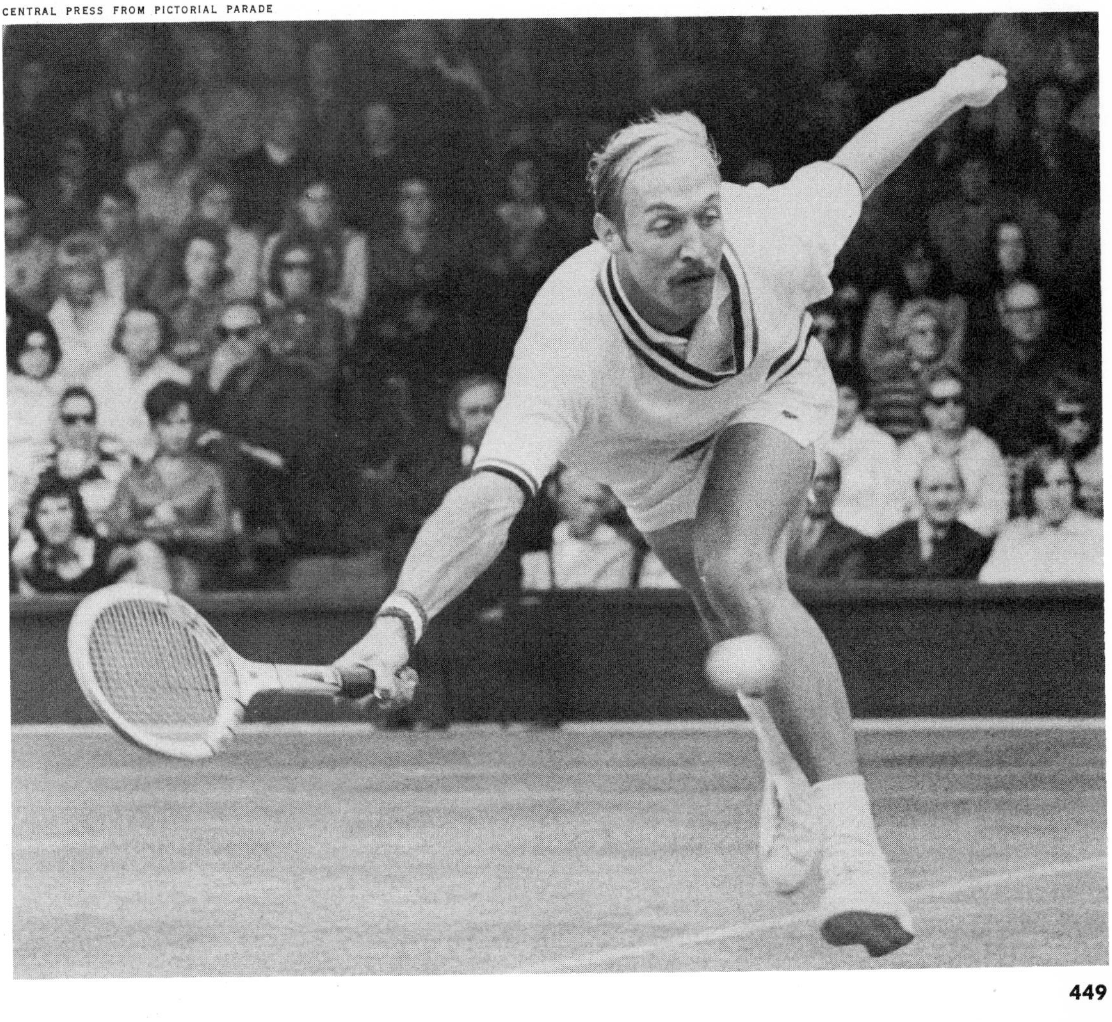

WIDE WORLD

Chris Evert of the U.S. is seen here at Wimbledon during a match against Great Britain's Joyce Williams, which Miss Evert won.

Australia; Marty Riessen, Arthur Ashe, and Bob Lutz of the U.S.; Cliff Drysdale of South Africa; and Tom Okker of the Netherlands—produced an outstanding finale in May. Rosewall earned $50,000 by beating Laver to win the tournament. The French championships in Paris had an unexpected winner in Andres Gimeno of Spain. Orantes took the West German title, beating Adriano Panatta of Italy.

The Wimbledon championship, despite the absence of WCT contract players, had an attendance of 298,660, only 220 short of the preceding year's total. It was won by Smith, the runner-up in 1971. He defeated Nastase in five sets. Later in the year Nastase beat Ashe to capture the U.S. championship.

Fifty-two nations took part in the Davis Cup competition in 1972. The entry of Rhodesia was again refused. South Africa's entry was at first accepted but its team was later dropped. Players under contract to WCT remained ineligible to represent their countries. Australia suffered most from the ban but, nevertheless, did better than in preceding years. In the interzone semifinals Romania beat Australia 4–1 in Bucharest, Romania. The U.S. beat Spain 3–2 in Barcelona, Spain. Under the rules the choice of a site for the final belonged to the U.S. However, the U.S. agreed to play in Bucharest when Romania recalled that the challenge rounds of 1969 and 1971 were staged in the U.S. In October the U.S. beat Romania 3–2 to win the trophy for the 24th time.

In collegiate competition, Trinity University of San Antonio, Tex., won the National Collegiate Athletic Association title with a record 36 points. The singles crown was won by Dick Stockton of Trinity, who secured the championship by defeating his teammate Brian Gottfried.

Women's Competition

The Grand Prix at the end of 1971 was won by Billie Jean King of the U.S. The Australian title was taken in 1972 by Great Britain's Virginia Wade, who beat Evonne Goolagong of Australia in the final. Miss Goolagong avenged the defeat by beating Miss Wade for the South African championship. Linda Tuero of the U.S. won the Italian title but lost the final of the West German meeting to Helga Masthoff of West Germany. Mrs. King won the French championship without losing a set in any round. She easily beat Miss Goolagong, the 1971 winner, in the final. Mrs. King won the Wimbledon championship, losing only one set, this in the quarterfinal to Miss Wade. She beat Miss Goolagong, the defending titlist, in the final—again easily. Mrs. King also won the U.S. title at Forest Hills without losing a set. In the final she beat Australia's Kerry Melville, who had previously defeated Chris Evert of the U.S. Mrs. King played with great success as well on the women's professional circuit in the U.S. She was generally considered the best woman player of the year.

The U.S. team defeated Great Britain 5–2 at Wimbledon to win the Wightman Cup. Australia won the Bonne Bell Cup, defeating the U.S. 5–2. South Africa took the Federation Cup 2–1. (*See also* Sports Champions of 1972. *See in* CE: Tennis.)

TEXTILES. In 1972 world overproduction of synthetic fibers escalated, and the price structure of polyester fibers suffered a serious collapse, following restrictions on Japanese imports into the U.S. market. This was a blow to the fiber producers, as nylon prices had tended to be unprofitable for several years. Two forces began to have a favorable influence on world markets as the year advanced—a general broadening in demand following the textile depression of 1971, and a decision by some of the major producers in several countries, including Great Britain and Japan, to curtail their total output of nylon and polyester.

Declining wool production plus rising consumption led to a reversal of the downward price trend of wool by the end of 1971. Wool prices began to rise steadily in January 1972, and this tendency continued with variation in pace but with only brief setbacks until the first full-scale auctions of the 1972–73 season were held in Australia in the latter half of August. Within two or three weeks the rise accelerated and by October prices were the highest recorded since 1957.

World demand for silk remained high in 1972, largely because of the continued buoyancy of domestic consumption in Japan. Consumption there was estimated at 27,000 tons in 1972–73 as against 26,000 tons in 1971–72—nearly a 4% increase in one year.

In the U.S. textile industry, a considerable sum was spent on new machines and reequipment projects. Improvements were made in conventional processing methods. There was further progress in computerized machine monitoring and in handling and packaging methods. (*See in* CE: Textiles.)

THAILAND. Although it had blamed the People's Republic of China for a growing insurgency movement, Thailand nevertheless warmed its relations with China in 1972. The military government maintained a public posture of extreme reluctance to open any dialogue with the Chinese. It even canceled plans to provide live television coverage of U.S. President Richard M. Nixon's visit to China. But a Thai team went to Peking, the Chinese capital, in September 1972 to compete in the tested diplomatic game of Ping-Pong.

Accompanying the team was Prasit Kanchanawat, deputy director of economics, finance, and industry, whose purported advisory role was seen as a cover for political and economic soundings. A month after the Ping-Pong team returned home, a Thai trade team journeyed to China to take part in the autumn Canton Trade Fair.

The insurgency movement escalated in 1972, and government operations against the underground forces became full-scale battles. Defense spending to counter subversion was reinforced by an increase in the U.S. military assistance program for Thailand.

These three men were accused of threatening the security of Thailand by taking part in a gunrunning ring. Before facing a firing squad, they sat together for their last meal.

UPI COMPIX

Winding down its presence in South Vietnam in 1972, the U.S. stationed about 50,000 airmen in Thailand. From bases there, U.S. aircraft bombed targets in Vietnam, Laos, and Cambodia.

A guerrilla raid on a U.S. air base in October 1972 was the first such raid in Thailand that involved the use of mortars. Officials were alarmed because U.S. airmen and aircraft in Thailand were for the first time within range of enemy guns.

In one of its earliest decrees under the martial law proclaimed in November 1971, the National Executive Council restricted long hair and permissive dress and imposed a midnight curfew on places of entertainment. Some criminals were summarily executed.

The business of framing a new constitution and appointing a new cabinet lagged in 1972, and a promised interim constitution did not materialize. In July it was announced that the term of Premier Thanom Kittikachorn as supreme commander of the armed forces would be extended by another year from September 30. Thanom and Gen. Praphat Charusathian were expected to continue in first and second place when a new cabinet was named. (*See also* Cambodia; Laos; Vietnam. *See in* CE: Thailand.)

THEATER. The 1972 man of the year in U.S. theater was Joseph Papp, founder and producer of the New York Shakespeare Festival. 'Sticks and Bones', David Rabe's bitter play about a returned Vietnam veteran—which was originally produced at the festival's Public Theater—moved to Broadway in March 1972 and subsequently won a Tony (Antoinette Perry) Award as the best play of the season. 'That Championship Season', by Jason Miller, opened at the Public Theater in May. An old-fashioned, well-made, and wonderfully realistic drama about the reunion of a small-town high school basketball team, it won the New York Drama Critics' Circle Award as the best play of the season and also moved to Broadway. The musical 'Two Gentlemen of Verona' (adapted from the Shakespeare play), originally produced at the festival's outdoor Delacorte Theater in Central Park, transferred to Broadway and won both the Tony Award and the Drama Critics' Circle Award as the best musical of the 1971–72 season. Significantly, these productions were not farmed out to Broadway managements but were produced again for Broadway by Papp and the Shakespeare Festival.

Meanwhile, at the Public Theater, Papp concentrated on new plays by U.S. playwrights. During 1972 he offered, among others, 'The Black Terror', by Richard Wesley (set in the future and concerned with violent black revolution); 'Older People', by John Ford Noonan; 'The Hunter', by Murray Mednick; and two bills of one-act plays by black playwrights.

The 1972 Shakespeare Festival summer season in Central Park featured an admirable 'Hamlet', directed by Gerald Freedman, with Stacy Keach as

JOSEPH ABELES FROM FRIEDMAN-ABELES

The hit musical 'Grease', enjoying a long run on Broadway, re-creates some aspects of teen-age life in the 1950's, complete with ducktail haircuts, leather jackets, and pedal pushers.

the prince, James Earl Jones as Claudius, and Colleen Dewhurst as Gertrude. Another summer production was the well-received 'Much Ado About Nothing', directed by A. J. Antoon and set in the small-town U.S. around the beginning of the 20th century. 'Much Ado' subsequently followed other Papp ventures to Broadway.

The Rise of Noncommercial Theater

Papp's conquest of Broadway made it clearer than ever before that the main sources of theatrical energy and creativity in the U.S. were the subsidized, noncommercial professional theaters. The New York Shakespeare Festival was the most active such theater in New York City, but by no means the only one. The Chelsea Theater Center, which occupied premises at the Brooklyn Academy of Music, had its most successful season to date in 1971–72. Two Chelsea productions were later given regular off-Broadway runs: 'Kaddish', Allen Ginsberg's multimedia adaptation of his poem on the death of his mother, and Gene Lesser's blunt and bawdy staging of 'The Beggar's Opera', by John Gay.

The Repertory Theater of Lincoln Center, on the other hand, had an unhappy season in 1971–72, although its revival of Arthur Miller's 'The Crucible' was respectfully received. Downstairs in its smaller second auditorium, The Forum, the Repertory Theater offered the first U.S. performances of 'People Are Living There', by the South African playwright Athol Fugard, and 'The Ride Across Lake Constance', by the young Austrian Peter Handke; the first was realistic and the second absurdist, but neither was greeted with much warmth. The Forum production of 'The Duplex', by black playwright Ed Bullins, was notable for an angry dispute between Bullins and the Repertory Theater management over the way the play was presented. The last Forum production of 1971–72 was an engaging comedy, 'Suggs', about the pains and terrors of life in New York City by a promising young playwright named David Wiltse. The Repertory Theater's 1972–73 season opened with the U.S. premiere of 'Enemies', by Maksim Gorki, on the main stage and a Samuel Beckett festival in The Forum. The festival consisted of two bills of one-act plays by Beckett (including the world premiere of a new work called 'Not I'), presented in repertory and starring Hume Cronyn and Jessica Tandy.

Three new professional noncommercial theater companies appeared in New York City in 1972. The City Center Acting Company, made up of the first graduating class of the Drama Division of The Juilliard School, offered a season of six plays in repertory. The plays, which varied widely in period and style, were: 'Women Beware Women', by Thomas Middleton (17th century—and a U.S. premiere); 'The School for Scandal', by Richard Brinsley Sheridan (18th century); 'The Lower Depths', by Gorki (1902); 'The Hostage', by Brendan Behan (1958); and two recent works—'U.S.A.', adapted by Paul Shyre from John Dos Passos' novels, and 'Next Time I'll Sing to You', by James Saunders.

The Phoenix Repertory Company, the third repertory company to appear in New York City under the Phoenix management, presented Eugene O'Neill's 'The Great God Brown' and Molière's 'Don Juan' at the Lyceum, a Broadway house. In the Borough of Queens, the Queens Playhouse opened its doors with a production of George Bernard Shaw's 'Pygmalion'. And the Circle in the Square, long established off-Broadway, opened its new Broadway theater with O'Neill's 'Mourning Becomes Electra', starring Miss Dewhurst.

Noncommercial professional theaters were by no means confined to New York City; dozens of them, some long established, continued to function locally. The Arena Stage, in Washington, D.C., was represented on Broadway by its production of 'Moonchildren', a play by Michael Weller. The Arena Stage also offered, for local consumption, the U.S. premiere of 'Uptight', a quizzical play by the German writer Günter Grass about the conflict between uneasy liberalism and revolutionary passion, and 'The Foursome', a realistic play about working-class sexuality by the British playwright E. A. Whitehead. The John F. Kennedy Center for the Performing Arts, also in Washington, D.C., functioned mainly as a stopping place for touring companies; nevertheless, it managed to send three productions—all revivals—on to Broadway: 'The Country Girl', by Clifford Odets; 'Lost in the Stars' (a musical play based on Alan Paton's novel 'Cry, the Beloved Country', with words by Maxwell Anderson and music by Kurt Weill); and Shaw's 'Captain Brassbound's Conversion', starring Ingrid Bergman.

In Minneapolis, the Tyrone Guthrie Theatre presented Sophocles' 'Oedipus the King' in a new adaptation by Anthony Burgess. The Long Wharf Theatre in New Haven, Conn., offered the U.S. premiere of 'The Changing Room', by the English playwright David Storey, in November 1972. The Pittsburgh Playhouse presented the first U.S. performance of British playwright Tom Stoppard's 'Enter a Free Man'.

Off-Broadway Musicals

There were several off-Broadway musicals in 1972. Two by Al Carmines, the amazingly prolific musical minister, were transferred to off-Broadway from his off-off-Broadway base at the Judson Memorial Church: 'Wanted' (book by David Epstein), about some notable American outlaws, and 'Joan' (book, lyrics, and music by Carmines), a highly unorthodox account of a modern Joan of Arc. 'Grease', a rock 'n' roll evocation of the 1950's, went to New York City from Chicago and was so successful that it moved to Broadway. 'Don't Bother Me, I Can't Cope', an all-black revue, written by and starring Micki Grant, had a successful run at a "middle theater" (a middle-sized house that is neither Broadway nor off-Broadway). There were also an off-Broadway revue devoted to the songs of Kurt Weill and another devoted to the works of Noel Coward.

Broadway Productions

Meanwhile, Broadway continued to exist, but a deep malaise hung over it. The Broadway audience —deterred by fear of crime, by high ticket prices, or perhaps simply by changing habits—seemed to be shrinking. The deterioration of the Times

Jonelle Allen and Clifton Davis play young lovers in 'Two Gentlemen of Verona', a rock version of Shakespeare's comedy that received the 1972 Tony and New York critics' awards.

FRIEDMAN-ABELES

FRIEDMAN-ABELES

'The Web and the Rock', a play by Dolores Sutton based on the novel by Thomas Wolfe, opened on Broadway in March. It is the story of a young writer, played by James Naughton, who falls in love with an older woman, Dolores Sutton, despite the strong disapproval of his mother, Elsa Raven.

Square area was protested by a number of Broadway performers, who submitted a petition to New York City Mayor John V. Lindsay asking him to make the area safe again for both theatergoers and actors.

Caught between dwindling audiences and rising costs, producers found it increasingly difficult to turn a profit. Even productions with well-known names attached to them and highly favorable reviews lost money—the most notable of these being 'Old Times', Harold Pinter's elegant study of an ambiguous three-cornered relationship, which opened in New York City in November 1971. Peter Hall directed, and Rosemary Harris, Robert Shaw, and Mary Ure comprised the entire cast.

Other London imports in New York City included Robert Bolt's historical play 'Vivat! Vivat Regina!' with Eileen Atkins as Elizabeth I and Claire Bloom as Mary, queen of Scots. In 'Butley', by Simon Gray, the British actor Alan Bates had a tremendous personal success as a vituperative teacher.

Aside from British shows and transfers from noncommercial theaters, Broadway had little to offer in 1972. At the end of the year there was a new Neil Simon comedy, 'The Sunshine Boys'. There were also a few musicals. 'Sugar', based on Billy Wilder's motion picture 'Some Like It Hot', was mediocre but serviceable, sustained by the exuberant transvestite clowning of Robert Morse. There was a happy revival—imported from Los Angeles—of 'A Funny Thing Happened on the Way to the Forum', starring Phil Silvers and Larry Blyden. The musical comedy success of the fall season was 'Pippin', an account of the imaginary travails of Charlemagne's son, staged with a great deal of razzmatazz by Bob Fosse. 'Fiddler on the Roof', which became the longest-running Broadway show in history on June 17, closed shortly afterward with a record 3,242 performances.

Other Broadway offerings included a new play by the Spanish dramatist Fernando Arrabal that was transferred from an off-off-Broadway theater. Set in a prison in Arrabal's native country, the play was entitled 'And They Put Handcuffs on the Flowers'. There was a witty double bill by Stoppard, 'After Magritte' and 'The Real Inspector Hound'—the latter a parody of a British mystery play, with two critics seated out front gradually getting caught up in the action. A new play by Tennessee Williams, entitled 'Small Craft Warnings', proved more successful than most of his other recent works. (*See also* Arts; Motion Pictures. *See in* CE: Drama; Musical Comedy.)

TOBACCO. Figures released in 1972 placed world tobacco production in 1971 at about 10 billion pounds, a drop of 1% from the previous year but an increase of 12% from the 1960–64 average. Production of flue-cured and oriental tobacco remained around the 1970 levels. Production of burley tobacco, however, went up by about 5% as increases in Italy, South Korea, Malawi, and some South American countries more than compensated for a decline in U.S. production.

Among the major U.S. producers, output in 1971 declined to 1.79 billion pounds, near the low level of 1968. In Canada a record yield of flue-cured leaf in Ontario offset an overall decline in the size of the area harvested.

The volume of world trade was steady, but the effect of the tobacco policy adopted by the European Economic Community (EEC) in 1970 was apparent. The policy, which provided a 30% subsidy per pound for the purchase of Italian burley, caused Italy to increase its production by 10 million pounds to 79 million pounds in 1971. Similar production increases occurred in other EEC countries. Developed countries still protected producers, as did the U.S., where support prices rose.

The U.S. remained the principal tobacco exporter in 1971, and its share of the world market stood at 25%. Other major exporters were India, Canada, Turkey, and the Philippines.

According to unofficial estimates, world consumption of cigarettes increased by 3% in 1971, with most of the gain coming from developing countries. U.S. consumption increased by 4%. (*See in* CE: Tobacco.)

TOGO. In a referendum on Jan. 9, 1972, Gen. Étienne Gnassingbe Eyadema was confirmed in his role as president of Togo by almost 869,000 of the nearly 870,000 votes cast. A governmental reorganization took place a few days later.

Togo's President Eyadema (left) welcomes Ghana's Col. Ignatius K. Acheampong in Lomé, Togo, where the two met to discuss trade relations and matters of mutual interest.

AUTHENTICATED NEWS INTERNATIONAL

During the year, the president directed his attention almost exclusively toward strengthening cooperation between Togo and France. In February the two countries carried out joint military exercises in Togo. France's President Georges Pompidou was welcomed enthusiastically by the Togolese when he visited their country in November in the course of his third African tour since his accession in 1969. Earlier in the month Eyadema welcomed several members of the new military government of Dahomey just after the coup there on October 26.

In December 1972 the central committee of the ruling assembly of Togo decided that the country's labor unions should be reorganized into a single union. (*See in* CE: Togo, Republic of.)

TONGA. Efforts to create employment and raise living standards for a rapidly growing population continued in Tonga in 1972, while family planning received high priority. The government's program of controlled tourist development offered the greatest potential for employment and foreign exchange. Fua'amotu airport was improved to accommodate medium jets, and a new airstrip and hotel were opened on Vava'u. To promote regional shipping, trade, and economic cooperation, Tonga looked to its national shipping line and to the South Pacific Bureau of Economic Cooperation. Tonga's minister of finance, Mahe Tupuoniua, became the bureau's first director.

An Indian government consultant surveyed light industry in Tonga, and the search for oil continued in 1972. The world price of copra, one of the leading products, plummeted. Trade preferences were to be extended to Tonga by the European Economic Community, starting Jan. 1, 1973.

TOYS AND GAMES. Total sales by the toy industry in 1972 were expected to reach $2.2 billion. The industry continued to be plagued by reports of dangerous toys. Industry spokesmen, however, claimed that the U.S. Food and Drug Administration had found that, in almost all cases, dangerous toys had been redesigned to make them safe or production of them had stopped. In California the legislature passed a bill prohibiting the manufacture or sale of any toy that depicts torture or that specifically resembles a bomb or grenade. The bill also bans the sale and distribution of electrically, mechanically, and thermally hazardous toys. Illinois had a bill before its legislature amending the existing law relating to the sale and distribution of hazardous toys within the state.

To add to the toy industry's problems, the committee on Action for Children's Television (ACT) filed a petition with the Federal Trade Commission (FTC) requesting that the FTC prohibit advertising of toys to children. ACT claimed that commercials were unfair and misleading and were directed at children who were incapable of evaluating toys or dealing with sales efforts directed to them.

WIDE WORLD

Robert Chlopak, project coordinator for a toy safety study, told newsmen in December, "It is an absolute scandal that toys banned for two years are still being sold to unsuspecting consumers."

Growing ecological interest also had an impact on the toy industry. The prevention of forest fires and conservation of natural resources influenced the development of six Smokey the Bear toys. The Environmental-Action-Lab permitted youngsters to test for water, air, and soil pollutants. It came with a 75X microscope, alcohol lamp and blowpipe, test tubes and holder, weather forecasting tools, and the 'How and Why Wonder Book of Ecology'. The Johnny Horizon Environmental Testing Kit detects degrees of pollution.

The world championship of chess held in Reykjavik, Iceland, during the summer between Bobby Fischer of the U.S. and Boris Spassky of the Soviet Union gave great impetus to interest in the game and to sales of chess sets. 'Chess Tutor', claiming to teach the game in 30 minutes, enjoyed booming sales. (*See* Chess.)

New educational toys included the Playskool Computer for children three to eight years old. The child dials one of 96 questions; then, with a push of a button, the reel spins to the correct answer. The Weather Forecaster science set enabled children to measure wind velocity, direction, barometric pressure, humidity, temperature index, and the wind chill factor.

A popular action toy was the Hop-Rod, a gasoline-powered pogo stick. The fuel is contained in a four-ounce tank and delivers over 600 hops per tankful. Socker-Boppers permitted children to box harmlessly with king-size, air-inflated boxing gloves made of vinyl.

Toy guns of the western frontier variety became very popular in 1972 and were expected to account for $23 million in sales, or 1% of the market. Military and police guns, however, were almost nonexistent—especially considering their former popularity. (*See in* CE: Toys.)

TRACK AND FIELD. All U.S. track and field competition in 1972 led toward Munich, West Germany, and the Olympic Games. But despite the added incentive of the Olympics, the number of new records produced by U.S. athletes was relatively low. Only one new individual world record was achieved, with three other international marks equaled.

Bob Seagren, the veteran pole-vaulter of the Southern California Striders, was the lone U.S. record raiser. The 1968 Olympic champion did it twice. Recovering from knee surgery, Seagren started the season late but soon regained his old form. On May 23 in El Paso, Tex., Seagren vaulted 18 feet 4¼ inches, which was 2¼ inches over the pending new standard set by Kjell Isaksson of Sweden. Isaksson was in the same competition and cleared 18 feet 4¼ inches to share the record. At the U.S. Olympic trials in Eugene, Ore., on July 2, Seagren took undisputed possession of the vault record with a clearance of 18 feet 5¾ inches.

Outdoor Track and Field

The Olympic trials were spread over an 11-day period and pitted the elite of U.S. track and field talent against each other in the quest of berths on the Olympic team. The trials were very productive. In addition to Seagren's new vault mark, world records were matched in two events by three athletes, and three new national bests were achieved. In the 100-meter dash Eddie Hart of the Bay Area Striders nosed out Rey Robinson of Florida A & M in a close finish. Both clocked 9.9 seconds to tie the mark first set in 1968. Also on July 1, Dave Wottle of Bowling Green State University was the surprise winner of the 800 meters in 1 minute 44.3 seconds, tying the record.

At the Olympics, high hurdler Rod Milburn of Southern University matched the world best in the 110 meters, recording 13.2 seconds on September 7. Three days later the U.S. 400-meter relay team tied the world record of 38.2 seconds in winning the Olympic gold medals. Larry Black of North Carolina Central University started, followed by Robert Taylor of Texas Southern University, Gerald Tinker of the Kent Track Club, and Hart.

The distance-medley relay record made by Kansas State University at Des Moines, Iowa, on April 29 was unrecognized because there was no official world record for the event. But the time of 9 minutes 31.8 seconds was the fastest ever noted; it was put together by Clardy Vinson, Mike Lee, Rick Hitchcock, and Jerome Howe. North Carolina Central covered the sprint-medley relay in 3 minutes 14.8 seconds at Philadelphia, Pa., on April 29 but did not get official recognition for two reasons: this was an unofficial event internationally, and the team included runners from two countries —Julius Sang and Robert Ouko of Kenya teamed with Larry Black and Jeff Horsley of the U.S.

National records took more of a battering than world records in 1972, and again a large part of the action took place in the U.S. Olympic trials. Steve Prefontaine of the University of Oregon ran 5,000 meters in 13 minutes 22.8 seconds on July 9, and Ralph Mann of the Southern California Striders was clocked at 48.4 seconds for the 400-meter hurdles on July 2. In the triple jump, Dave Smith of the Bay Area Striders reached 56 feet on July 1. Prefontaine had lowered the U.S. 5,000-meter record to 13 minutes 29.6 seconds at Eugene on April 29. He also set national records twice at 3,000 meters, running 7 minutes 45.8 seconds at Gresham, Ore., on June 24, and 7 minutes 44.2 seconds at Oslo, Norway, on August 3. The 10,000-meter record fell three times. Greg Fredericks of Pennsylvania State University was the first to do it, running 28 minutes 8 seconds at Seattle, Wash., on June 16, and Frank Shorter of the Florida Track Club did it twice in the Olympic Games. The Olympic marathon winner ran 27 minutes 58.2 seconds on August 31 and 27 minutes 51.4 seconds on September 3. Larry Young of Columbia College walked 50,000 meters in 4 hours 13 minutes 4.4 seconds on July 4 in the Olympic trials. The record was lowered again by Young at Munich, where he walked 4 hours 46 seconds on September 3. Young also had a U.S. record at 20,000 meters, walking 1 hour 30 minutes 10 seconds at Columbia, Mo., on May 7.

In team competition, the University of California at Los Angeles won the National Collegiate Athletic Association (NCAA) outdoor championships with 82 points at Eugene on June 1–3. North Carolina Central captured the National Association of Intercollegiate Athletics title in Billings, Mont., June 1–2, scoring 68 points.

Indoor Track and Field

Indoors, the major competition was the first dual meet under cover between the U.S. and the Soviet Union. The U.S. outscored the Soviet Union 76–69 at Richmond, Va., on March 17. The NCAA indoor title was claimed by the University of Southern California, with 19 points at Detroit, Mich., on March 11.

Four major indoor world bests—with no officially recognized records—were established. Herb Washington of Michigan State University ran 60 yards in 5.8 seconds at East Lansing, Mich., on February 12, while Mark Winzenried of Club West ran 1,000 yards in 2 minutes 5.1 seconds at Louisville, Ky., the same night. Al Feuerbach of the Pacific Coast Club claimed a new shot-put mark with 69 feet 4¾ inches at Pocatello, Idaho, on February 5.

Outstanding Women Stars

Kathy Hammond, Madeline Manning Jackson, Debra Edwards, and Mable Fergerson lowered the world mile relay record to 3 minutes 33.9 seconds at Champaign, Ill., on August 12. Indoors, Miss Hammond claimed world bests of 64.5 seconds for 500 yards, and 1 minute 20.5 seconds for 600 yards.

Other world indoor bests went to Kathy Gibbons,

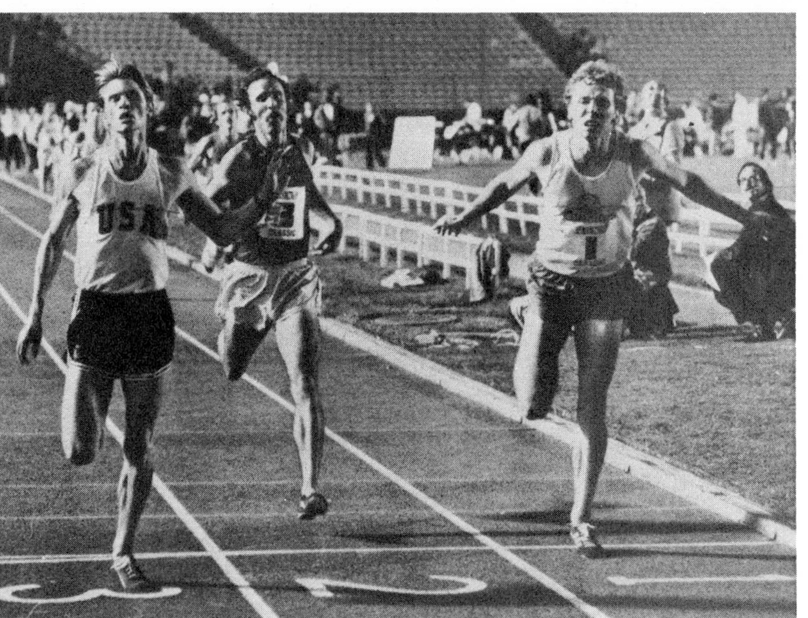

Ken Swenson (left), running for the U.S. Army, edges Mark Winzenried to win the Vons Classic 880-yard run in Los Angeles in June. Steve Straub (center) came in third.

WIDE WORLD

2 minutes 32.2 seconds for 1,000 yards at Los Angeles on February 11; Debbie Heald, 4 minutes 38.5 seconds for one mile at Richmond on March 17; and Patty Johnson, 6.4 seconds for the 50-yard hurdles at Toronto, Ont., on February 4. (*See also* Olympic Games. *See in* CE: Track and Field Sports.)

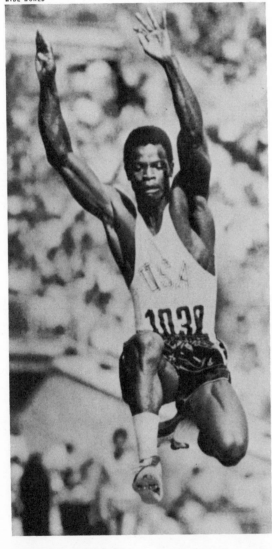

Randy Williams jumps 27 feet 4½ inches to qualify for the Olympics. He won the gold medal for the U.S. in the long-jump event.

WIDE WORLD

TRANSPORTATION. One of the major battles fought in the U.S. Congress in 1972 involved the question of whether the nation's mass transit systems should be given operating expenses out of money set aside for federal highway programs. Lobbying during the year was fierce on both sides, and in the end, no highway bill was passed at all. Both the Administration of U.S. President Richard M. Nixon and the Department of Transportation hoped a bill would be passed early in 1973 that would provide mass transportation agencies with at least a portion of the funds they needed.

Although industrial disputes throughout the world in 1972 interfered with the growth rate of shipping traffic, indications were that overall transportation of goods and people would equal or exceed that of 1971. Passenger traffic on the railways tended to grow with the modernization of rail systems and technological development that enabled higher speeds to be achieved and more convenient services to be provided. Rail freight traffic increased slightly, while the shift to highway transportation continued. A few railways operated profitably but were maintained by government subsidies; some revenue was lost as more pipelines came into operation. Pipelines also affected inland transport shipping, but the St. Lawrence Seaway achieved a new record by the end of the shipping season. Although the growth rate of freight movement by motorized road transportation increased, passengers carried by public transportation on highways continued to decline. To offset this, several rapid transit systems were under construction and others were projected. The first section of the Bay Area Rapid Transit (BART) system in San Francisco, Calif., began operation in September.

Despite efforts to improve road passenger transportation facilities in urban areas, patronage in those areas continued to decline, although at a slower rate. In the U.S. the 1,046 urban motor bus systems carried 4.7 billion passengers in 1971 as compared with 5 billion in 1970, but of these only 3.7 billion were paying passengers in 1971, a decline of 323.5 million. Total revenue rose, however, because of increased charges—from $1.19 billion in 1970 to $1.22 billion in 1971; the average fare per paying passenger in 1971 was 32.2¢ compared to the former 29.41¢. Total revenue vehicle-miles operated declined from 1.41 billion in 1970 to 1.38 billion in 1971. The operational fleets decreased from 49,700 to 49,150 buses, although the average carrying capacity increased slightly. Measures taken to stimulate patronage included priorities for buses at traffic lights, antidirectional travel on one-way street systems, reserved bus lanes, exemption-from-turning bans, and the tailoring of services to special needs, including on-demand and commuter express services.

To cope with the growing demand for energy, worldwide construction of new pipelines and the extension or duplication of existing networks was accelerated during the year for the transport of both crude oil and its products and of natural gas. Steps were taken to increase the capacity of the European network by inaugurating new pumping facilities, by looping, and by constructing new big diameter lines parallel to the original systems. Canada made plans to build a 48-inch pipeline down the Mackenzie Valley with a delivery capacity of 3.5 billion cubic feet of Arctic gas a day. A route was being surveyed for the line through eastern Canada.

AIRLINES

The performance of U.S. scheduled airlines in 1972 reflected the long-sought recovery from the severe economic losses that characterized the industry in 1970 and 1971. During the first eight months of 1972 the nation's scheduled airlines, including the 11 major and 8 local-service carriers, flew approximately 103 billion passenger-miles, an increase of 12.8% over the same period of 1971. For the first seven months of 1972 the volume of air cargo—mail, express, and freight—increased 11.1% over the same period of the preceding year, from 2.7 billion ton-miles to 3 billion.

Airline profits for the first half of 1972 were $20.7 million, compared to a loss of $135 million in the first six months of 1971. The profits anticipated by the industry for the year—some $200 million—were still a long way from the 12% annual return on investment that the Civil Aeronautics Board had stated the airlines would need in order to provide the public with the level of transportation it demands.

During 1971 and the first half of 1972, U.S. scheduled airlines took delivery of 111 new jet aircraft, of which 76 were the new wide-bodied type: Boeing 747's, Douglas DC-10's, and Lockheed L-1011's. The new jets, which range in capacity from 250 to 400 passengers, have meant more comfort for the passenger; also, they are much quieter than earlier jets and virtually smoke-free.

A significant step was taken during 1972 in the airline industry's progress toward a completely automated passenger-handling system. This was the beginning of the issuance to the 2 million holders of the Universal Air Travel Card of a machine-readable credit card capable of providing tickets automatically. (The Universal Air Travel Card was the only card in the world offering the public the opportunity of unlimited travel over the routes of 160 airlines.)

The airlines stepped up their efforts during 1972 to eliminate hijacking, extortion, sabotage, and other violent crimes against world civil air transportation. In addition to initiating steps locally to improve air transport security (essentially, de-

The Bay Area Rapid Transit (BART) system—an all new, computerized train system in California—had faulty speed-control mechanisms that caused an accident in the first three weeks of operation.

TERESA ZABALA FROM "THE NEW YORK TIMES"

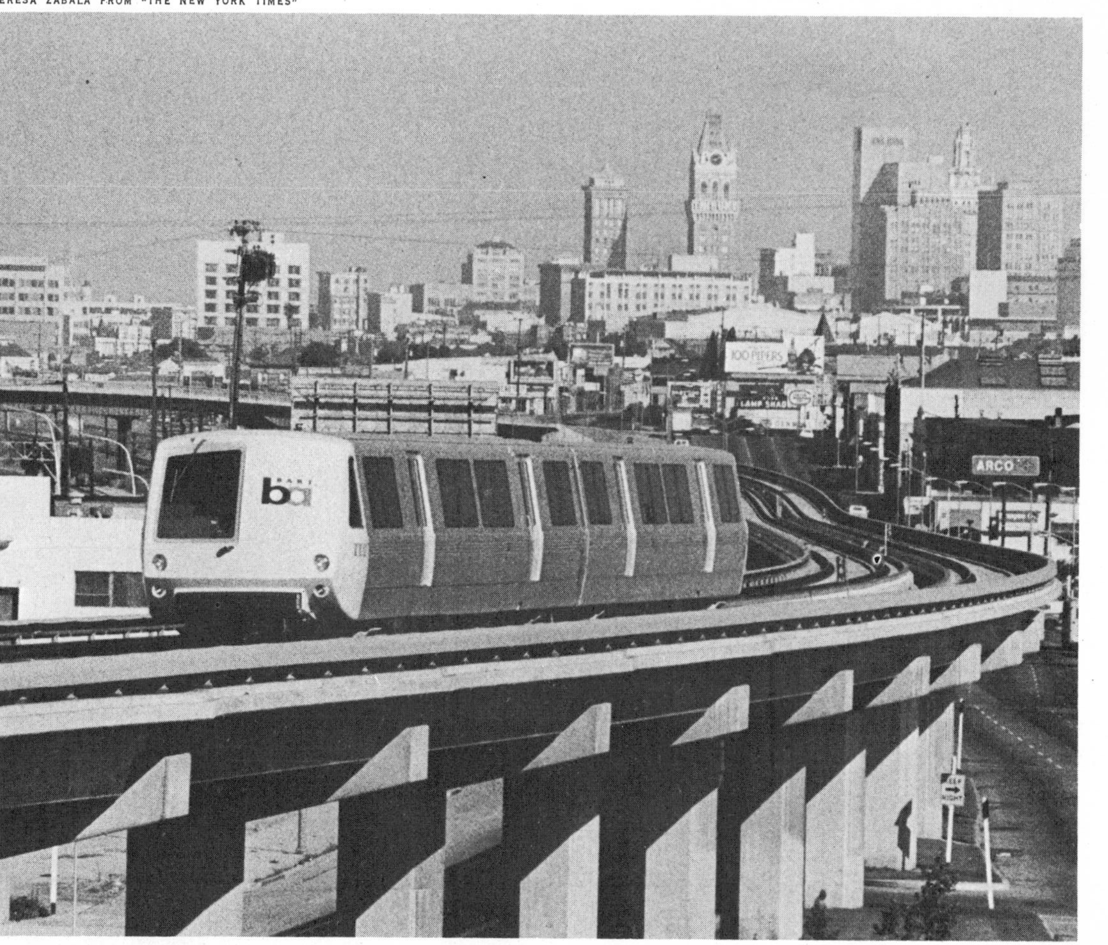

PAUL S. KIVETT

The new Kansas City International Airport was designed so that cars can be parked close to the terminals.

tecting criminals and stopping them from boarding aircraft), the airlines urged the International Civil Aviation Organization as well as governments and airlines of the world to give high priority to producing a final agreement aimed at eliminating safe havens for airline hijackers. The result of such an agreement would be joint action suspending air service to countries that do not prosecute or extradite those guilty of air piracy or other acts of aerial terrorism. (*See also* Crime; Cuba Special Report. *See in* CE: Airlines.)

RAILROADS

In July 1972 the 234,000-member United Transportation Union agreed to a three-year pact with the U.S. railroads, settling the dispute over the use of firemen on diesel freight locomotives. The issue dated from 1937, when relatively few diesels were in use. That year, the unions and the railroads accepted the National Diesel Agreement, which generally required the use of firemen on all passenger train, freight, and yard locomotives.

The agreements signed in July provided for the continued employment of approximately 18,000 firemen until they die, retire, resign, are discharged for cause, or are promoted to engineer. While firemen eliminated by attrition would not have to be replaced, the pact required that a sufficient number be retained to fill assignments in passenger service and as hostlers and hostler helpers. Also included was a provision for the compulsory retirement of firemen at age 65.

During the year the Illinois Central and the Gulf, Mobile and Ohio Railroad Co. combined to become the Illinois Central Gulf Railroad Co., the eighth largest system in the U.S. based on miles of trackage operated. The merger was approved by the Interstate Commerce Commission (ICC).

New Metroliner, or "Red Lion," cars were added to the New York–Washington, D.C., route when Amtrak increased the number of trains scheduled on the popular East coast run.

MIKE LIEN FROM "THE NEW YORK TIMES"

Late in June one of the most devastating storms ever to hit the East coast—Hurricane Agnes—disrupted rail operations, stranded passengers, washed out hundreds of miles of main and branch lines, destroyed bridges and culverts, and ruined millions of dollars' worth of freight goods. The storm lasted nearly a week, aimlessly rambling from Florida through New York. In its wake it left an estimated toll of at least $40 million in loss and damage to railroad plants and equipment. Less than a week after the storm had spent its fury, the Erie Lackawanna, facing massive storm damages, became the second Class I railroad to file for bankruptcy in eight months; in November 1971 the Reading Railroad had begun plans to reorganize.

Amtrak, the National Railroad Passenger Corp., created by Congress in 1970 to take over the operation of most passenger trains in the U.S., reported a stable number of riders throughout the first half of 1972. At the year's end, the quasi-governmental agency was operating more than 200 passenger trains serving more than 400 cities. (*See in* CE: Railroads.)

TRUCKS AND TRUCKING

Trucking continued in 1972 to be the foremost common carrier in the U.S., accounting for more than half of all transportation revenues regulated by the ICC. Total operating revenues for about 15,000 regulated for-hire truck lines engaged in interstate commerce were expected to approach $18 billion in 1972. That total was more than the combined revenues of all other regulated modes of freight transportation—railroads, pipelines, inland water carriers, and air freight. In addition, U.S. shippers spent billions of dollars on private and for-hire trucking operations not regulated by the ICC.

The number of trucks on the nation's highways rose again during the year. The total number of commercial, farm, and private trucks in operation in 1972 reached a record of about 19.7 million. Highway-use taxes paid by the trucking industry increased proportionally—a total of nearly $6 billion in federal, state, and local road-use taxes was paid by trucks in 1972.

Changes in government standards for safety and air pollution control had a major impact on the trucking industry in 1972. New and modified designs would continue to be required for some time in the future to meet these new standards. Higher standards for accident-resistant fuel tanks were in effect and new braking standards, improved lighting systems, engine-emission controls, and other standards were established and were to become effective in the next few years. (*See in* CE: Transportation; Truck.)

General Motors Corp. designed this all-purpose vehicle for use in the developing nations because it is inexpensive and easy to assemble.

GENERAL MOTORS CORP.

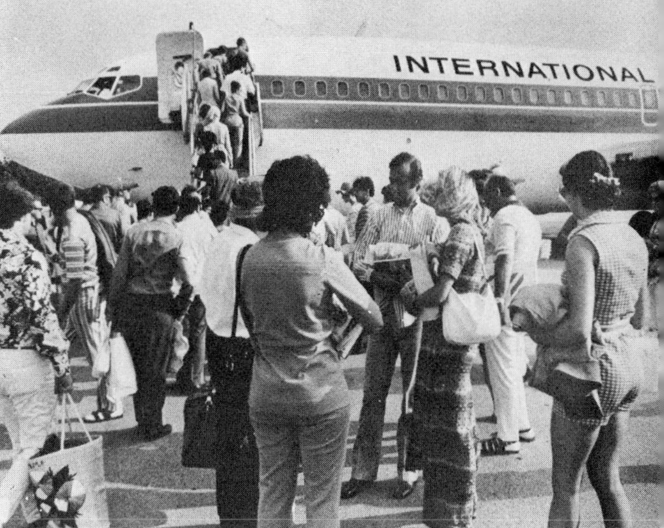

"THE NEW YORK TIMES"

Proposed regulations would permit low air fares for anyone on nonscheduled flights. The low rates had been available in the past only to charter groups like this one.

TRAVEL. Tourists continued to travel about the world in record numbers in 1972. In the first six months arrivals were up 15% in Spain, 11% in Great Britain, 42% in Tunisia, 23% in Hong Kong, 29% in Greece, 7.5% in the U.S., 10% in Italy, and an unusually low 5% in Switzerland due to a labor shortage there. The fluctuation of the dollar and the pound apparently had little adverse effect on world travel.

Figures released in 1972 showed that 181 million world tourists spent $20 billion in 1971 in their travels. The growth rate for 1971 was 7%; tourism receipts were up 14%. It was expected that international tourist traffic would reach 200 million persons before 1975.

Despite the increase in world travel, international air carriers in 1971 experienced the lowest level of growth in 14 years. (International air traffic was up only 4.2% in 1971 over 1970.) Factors responsible included increased unit costs, unsatisfactory load factors, and competition from lower-cost charters. Charter air carriers enjoyed

"LONDON DAILY EXPRESS" FROM PICTORIAL PARADE

Some of the 142 passengers stranded at London's Gatwick airport relax while they await news of their canceled charter flight to New York.

increased traffic, reported by the International Civil Aviation Organization at an annual rate of about 26%.

Further progress was made in setting up the new intergovernmental World Tourism Organization (WTO) to succeed the International Union of Official Travel Organizations. By October, 33 states had approved the new body and it was believed the required 51 ratifications would be forthcoming for the establishment of the WTO by 1974.

Regulations for foreigners entering the U.S. were tightened in September to meet the increased possibility of terrorism during the United Nations General Assembly meeting in New York City. The government announced a requirement that virtually all foreigners entering the U.S. must have visas. The U.S. Department of State said the regulations would be in effect until Jan. 1, 1973. In the past, travelers from the Western Hemisphere or those staying in the U.S. for less than ten days did not need visas. The rule also applied to travelers from Mexico but not from Canada.

HOTELS AND MOTELS

Business volume of U.S. hotels and motels recovered in 1972 from near-record low levels a year earlier. Sales were up 6% over 1971 figures and occupancy rose to 63% from 61% the preceding year.

New construction produced an oversupply of rooms in some cities, including Honolulu, Hawaii, and San Francisco, Calif. (where the city banned further new motel-hotel building). Important new hotels that opened in 1972 included the PLM Saint-Jacques in Paris, the first major hotel to open in the French capital in 39 years; the Meridien in Paris, largest in the city; the Acapulco Princess in Mexico; the Buenos Aires Sheraton in Argentina, largest hotel in South America; the Four Seasons Sheraton in Toronto, Ont.; the Sheraton Munich in West Germany; the Carlton in Johannesburg, South Africa; the Marriott Motor Hotel in New Orleans, La.; the Hyatt on Union Square in San Francisco; the Hyatt Regency Houston in Texas; and the O'Hare Towers in suburban Chicago.

TRUDEAU, PIERRE ELLIOTT. In the general Parliamentary elections of October 1972, Canada's Prime Minister Pierre Elliott Trudeau, 53, suffered a sharp setback. The Liberal party, which swept into power in 1968 on a nationwide wave of "Trudeaumania," emerged with 109 seats in the House of Commons. The Progressive Conservative party took 107 seats. Of the remaining seats, the New Democratic party gained the crucial voting power. Parliament was to meet early in January 1973 to confirm or reject the existing government. (*See also* Canada; Canadian Economy.)

No single issue was responsible for his government's near defeat, according to Trudeau, who said that Liberal sponsorship of the Official Languages Act was not to blame. However, opposition to the act—which upgraded the status of the French language as one of Canada's two official languages—was believed to have cost votes in the western provinces. Moreover, the interlocking problems of inflation and unemployment were known to be detrimental to the Trudeau government. After the

Pierre Trudeau, prime minister of Canada and leader of the Liberal party since 1968, suffered a setback in the fall election.

CAMERA PRESS FROM PICTORIAL PARADE

election, Trudeau said that he would submit new remedial legislation in the economic sphere.

Trudeau announced major changes in his Cabinet at the end of November, saying its makeup reflected lessons that he had learned in the election. He had made some Cabinet changes in January 1972 to prepare for the elections. They were seen as attempts to reduce friction between the government and the business community.

In April Trudeau conferred with U.S. President Richard M. Nixon, who paid a two-day visit to Canada. On April 15 the two leaders signed an agreement that pledged their countries to combat pollution in the Great Lakes. No major agreement was reached, however, on U.S.-Canadian trade or U.S. influence on the Canadian economy—issues that had long strained relations between the two countries. (*See in* CE: Trudeau.)

TUNISIA. Ahmed Mestiri, leader of the liberal wing of Tunisia's Destour Socialist party, was expelled in 1972 for the second time in four years after criticizing the conduct of the 1971 party congress and the policies of Prime Minister Hedi Nouira. He had been reinstated in April 1970 after his first expulsion in 1968 when he resigned from the government as a protest against the collectivization policies of Ahmed Ben Salah, then minister of planning.

In February clashes between police and students in Tunis, the capital, led to the closing of schools and the arrest of about 100 students. By April the situation had improved and President Habib Bourguiba announced that schools would reopen earlier than originally planned.

During a visit to Tunisia by Egypt's President Anwar el-Sadat, Bourguiba reaffirmed his country's solidarity with Egypt while expressing doubts about the wisdom of a possible new Arab-Israeli war. Bourguiba's visit to Paris in June set the seal upon Franco-Tunisian reconciliation. Questions relating to the political development of the Mediterranean area were discussed by Bourguiba and France's President Georges Pompidou. A distinct thaw in relations between Tunisia and neighboring Algeria was evident during the course of the year; a complete normalization of relations between the two countries was finally achieved. (*See in* CE: Tunisia.)

TURKEY. Terrorism plagued Turkey in 1972 in spite of widespread arrests. In March members of the Turkish People's Liberation Army kidnapped one Canadian and two British radar technicians. The kidnapping was an attempt to secure the release of three terrorists condemned to death for abducting four U.S. radar technicians in March 1971. Authorities refused to bargain, and the hostages and nine of their captors were killed on March 30 in Kizildere, a village in northern Turkey. Four terrorists on May 3 hijacked a Turkish airliner to Sofia, Bulgaria. Bloodshed was avoided when the hijackers surrendered to Bulgarian authorities. On October 22 another Turkish airliner was hijacked to Sofia, and the terrorists involved in that incident also surrendered.

The coalition government of Prime Minister Nihat Erim, formed on Dec. 11, 1971, resigned in April after national political parties refused to grant it wider powers to rule by decree, as demanded by President Cevdet Sunay. The president tried to form a new government later in April but was unsuccessful. In May, however, Ferit Melen, a member of the small moderate National Reliance party, formed a new government, which was given a vote of confidence by the Grand National Assembly on June 5. Melen's government was the fourth coalition government formed since the armed forces toppled the conservative Justice party government of Prime Minister Suleyman Demirel in March 1971. However, the leftist Republican People's party withdrew from the government on November 4, saying Melen's government was a "right wing coalition."

The U.S. government granted $35 million to help Turkish farmers change from cultivation of opium poppies to alternative crops. (*See in* CE: Turkey.)

UGANDA. Events in the closing months of 1971 had presaged a difficult time in 1972 for Asian residents in Uganda. On Dec. 8, 1971, Uganda's President Idi Amin criticized the country's Asian community for isolating itself from the African people, and he announced that all applications from Asians for citizenship, outstanding on Jan. 25, 1971, had been canceled. In January 1972 Amin stated that the indigenous population

Prisoners wait in an Ugandan jail after General Amin ordered all Asians and foreigners imprisoned for a time.

"LONDON DAILY EXPRESS" FROM PICTORIAL PARADE

should be in control of the country's economy—a reference to the predominance of Asian merchants—but added that Asians who were already Ugandan citizens had no cause for worry.

In August, however, the president sharply escalated his anti-Asian campaign, ordering all Asians of non-Ugandan citizenship—some 60,000 persons—to quit the country within 90 days. He denounced the Asians as economic saboteurs and claimed that their presence prevented Uganda's Africans from playing their rightful part in developing the economy. Despite a strong protest from Great Britain, which appealed to the United Nations (UN) to intervene, Amin remained adamant, even briefly extending his order to cover Asians of Ugandan citizenship (this order was later withdrawn). The president stated that Asians not out of the country by the required date would be rounded up and put into military camps.

An airlift was organized by Great Britain, Canada, and a number of other countries that had agreed to provide homes for the expelled Asians, and it was estimated that by the November 8 deadline imposed by Amin all non-Ugandan Asians—apart from about 1,000 stateless persons—had departed. Those who left were told that they would be allowed to take with them a small amount of currency, together with goods not exceeding $1,300 in value. Everything else—homes, shops, businesses, cars—had to be handed over to the government, along with all gold, whether in the form of jewelry or bullion. In fact, many of the departing Asians were stopped by government troops on the road to the airport and stripped of personal belongings and even the small amounts of cash they carried.

Amin's popularity with other African leaders—which he had been attempting to build up—suffered a setback over his policy toward the Asians. President Julius K. Nyerere of Tanzania, who had never been very friendly toward Amin, denounced the Ugandan's policy as inhumane, and there were further abusive exchanges between the two countries. On September 17 a force of Ugandan exiles loyal to former President Milton Obote invaded southwestern Uganda from Tanzania. Amin accused Tanzanian forces of being involved, although this was denied by Nyerere. Nevertheless, Amin retaliated by sending his small Israeli-trained air force to bomb some Tanzanian towns on the shores of Lake Victoria, and the invading force was quickly defeated by Amin's soldiers.

Immediately after the invasion, foreign correspondents in Kampala, the capital, were put into military prisons and later deported. Other foreigners, including British citizens, were detained without being charged, and a U.S. Peace Corps volunteer was shot and killed by army troops.

Through the intervention of President Mohammed Siad Barre of Somalia, peace terms were agreed upon by Uganda and Tanzania in October, but relations continued to be strained. Relations with neighboring Rwanda also declined during the year. Amin refused to meet with Rwanda's President Grégoire Kayibanda and accused that country of joining with Zambia and Tanzania in planning an invasion of Uganda.

Amin's relations with non-African countries also entered a critical period in 1972. He made frequent accusations that other countries were planning to overthrow his regime and accused Great Britain, Israel, and other nations of conspiring to have him assassinated. Toward the end of March, Amin became convinced that Israeli military advisers were involved in subversive activities in Uganda, and he ordered Israeli personnel in Uganda to leave the country immediately. Later in the year Amin made a direct and shocking attack on the Jewish nation. In telegrams to UN Secretary-General Kurt Waldheim and Israel's Prime Minister Golda Meir, Amin stated that he was able to understand why Adolf Hitler had killed 6 million Jews during World War II. (*See in* CE: Uganda.)

Indians arrive at a British airport with very little luggage because of their precipitate departure from their homes in Uganda. General Amin ordered some 60,000 Asians living in his country to leave within 90 days. The Asians fled to Great Britain, the U.S., Canada, and India.

PH. S. LEMOINE FROM GAMMA

Henry Kissinger (left), the president's security adviser, and U.S. President Richard M. Nixon toast each other after the signing of the strategic arms limitation agreement in Moscow in May. Soviet Communist Party General Secretary Leonid I. Brezhnev (third from right) and U.S. Secretary of State William P. Rogers (center) are in a celebratory mood, too.

UPI COMPIX

UNION OF SOVIET SOCIALIST REPUBLICS (U.S.S.R.). Throughout 1972, as in preceding years, the authorities in the U.S.S.R. had to face a certain amount of dissent and discontent expressed at various levels. The rejection of the fundamentally totalitarian nature of the system by relatively small groups of intellectuals manifested itself mainly through the *Chronicle of Current Events* and other clandestinely printed publications. The courage and persistence of the dissidents who continued to engage in *samizdat*—the clandestine production and circulation of illegal publications—made them the first target of police repression; a particularly widespread wave of arrests immediately followed U.S. President Richard M. Nixon's visit to Moscow, the capital, in May. Perhaps the best-known dissenter was the nuclear physicist Andrei D. Sakharov, who had published his controversial memorandum calling for greater intellectual freedom in 1968. In an August 1972 article published in *L'Express* in Paris, he attacked those "who favor a bigoted bureaucracy and intervention of a totalitarian government in the lives of citizens." Sakharov was also associated with the small self-styled Soviet Action Group for the Defense of Human Rights, which had made protests several times to the United Nations (UN) against the arbitrary arrest and persecution of Soviet citizens, and especially against the practice of confining political dissidents in mental hospitals on trumped-up psychiatric charges.

In January a severe sentence of 12 years in prison and exile was passed on Vladimir Bukovsky for crimes against the state. His crimes seemed to consist mainly of informing foreigners about conditions in the so-called psychiatric hospitals. In June the police took action against some of those associated with the Soviet Action Group, but not against Sakharov, who was probably protected by his prominent position within the scientific establishment. But one of the leaders of the group, Pyotr I. Yakir, a well-known historian and son of an army general, was arrested, together with others accused of tape-recording Western broadcasts and circulating the writings of proscribed authors. The victims of this particular purge, which had been going on for most of the year, included the Leningrad scientist Yuri Melnik, sentenced to three years in June, and the sociologist Vatslav Sevruk, confined to a mental hospital. Others arrested were the Moscow astronomer Kronid Lyubarsky; the Kiev cybernetics expert Leonid Plyush; and the founder of the Action Group, Viktor Krasin. Sakharov and the cellist Mstislav Rostropovich were among the distinguished signatories of an appeal

The flags of the Soviet Union and the U.S. fly together near the Kremlin in May.

WIDE WORLD

delivered to the Supreme Soviet in September calling for the abolition of capital punishment and the release of political prisoners.

Although, by Soviet standards, the Baltic republics of the U.S.S.R. were allowed a considerable degree of latitude in maintaining their cultural traditions, serious discontent persisted. In March petitions protesting religious persecution, signed by 17,000 Lithuanian Roman Catholics, were sent to the UN and to Communist Party General Secretary Leonid I. Brezhnev; they referred to the guarantees of freedom of conscience contained in the Soviet constitution. At the same time, the local press in Latvia felt that it had to react to an open letter signed by 17 Latvian Communists, which complained of the russification of their country; the 17 were labeled as tools or dupes for the U.S. Central Intelligence Agency. The worst crisis, however, developed in Lithuania. In May a young political protester set himself on fire, and his death led to riots in Kaunas, where thousands of young people shouting "Freedom for Lithuania" battled with troops and police. The Soviet press subsequently described the young suicide as a drug addict and dismissed the riots as hooliganism; nevertheless, they were important as a major demonstration by a large crowd protesting official Soviet policy.

The most prominent minority in the U.S.S.R. were those Jews who continued to regard Israel as their real fatherland. In 1972 there was a strictly controlled increase in the number of exit permits, though from time to time heavy compensation payments were demanded from scientists and other academically trained Jews. Indeed, even some non-Zionist dissidents were allowed to emigrate in 1972—among them the writer Yuri Glazov.

The Economy

In 1972 the U.S.S.R. considered itself to be moving into an advanced phase of economic development when it was no longer necessary to pursue industrial expansion at the expense of the environment and in complete disregard of human needs. The most prominent feature of the ninth five-year plan (1971–75) was the shift in emphasis toward meeting the wishes of the Soviet consumer. Consumer satisfaction, however, did not prove as easy as might have been expected: goods imported from Eastern Europe—especially from East Germany, and also from non-Communist countries—gave customers yardsticks for comparison, and Soviet enterprises found it difficult to meet these superior standards. Service industries had always been inefficient in centrally planned economies, and complaints about speed and efficiency were common.

In 1972 the major economic problem was the failure of agriculture, the grain harvest being officially 23 million tons below target. The Soviet Union faced its worst food shortage since the harvest failure of 1963, and by October Soviet foreign-trade officials were eager to obtain deliveries of more than 11 million tons of U.S. wheat, due under

WIDE WORLD

Curious crowds are attracted to Mrs. Nixon (foreground, light suit) as she shops in GUM (state department store) in Moscow in May.

their recent trade agreement with the U.S. Apart from the chronic inefficiency of the Soviet Union's system of collective farming, the main reason for the crisis was the freak winter weather in 1971–72, when not enough snow fell to insulate the planted seeds against frost. The situation was made much worse by the excessively hot weather and drought that prevailed in the summer of 1972, incidentally causing major forest fires in the Moscow region and elsewhere. The harvest failure meant that the U.S.S.R. had to use hard currencies to finance food imports instead of buying industrial equipment; the country had also been deprived of the currency earned by grain exports to Western Europe in recent years. But at least people did not starve as they would have in Joseph Stalin's day; the Soviet government was able to import the necessary foodstuffs without undue difficulty.

Industry, on the whole, did more for the economy than farming. The targets for the 1971 plan were met, and in October 1972 the Central Statistical Board announced that industrial output in the first nine months of 1972 was 6.7% above the total for the same period in 1971, the highest rate of development being in the engineering, chemical, and power industries. Labor productivity was reported to have increased by 5.3%, production costs had been reduced, and the nine-month targets for profits had been fulfilled. On September 1 the government announced sizable pay increases averaging over 20% for 5 million professionals, including doctors and teachers.

President Nixon's visit to Moscow in May underlined the significance of the economic rapprochement with the U.S. The agreement for the purchase of $750 million worth of U.S. grains was concluded during the summer and helped overcome the effects of the harvest failure. In October the U.S.S.R. concluded a comprehensive trade agreement with the U.S. and agreed to settle debts to the U.S. totaling $722 million—arising out of the lend-lease arrangements of World War II—in annual installments up to the year 2001. The agreement also made it possible for some private U.S. firms to set up branch offices in Moscow. The Soviet quest for technological know-how led to agreements with other non-Communist industrial countries: a $300-million contract for the construction of five chemical plants was signed with Japan; purchases from France included a large number of special compressors used in checking sections of new oil pipelines; and the establishment of closer relations with West Germany, following the ratification of the 1970 treaty between the Soviets and the West German government, created other opportunities.

Foreign Policy

The Soviet Union's policy of underpinning the status quo by negotiating directly with the U.S. culminated in President Nixon's visit to Moscow. There were, of course, many reasons why the Soviet Union needed to achieve a modus vivendi with the U.S.: a joint responsibility for the prevention of nuclear war, a desire to reduce the economic burden of the missile race, fear of the People's Republic of China, and the challenges presented to the conduct of foreign policy by the emergence of a multipolar international system. The U.S. decision to come to terms with China changed the climate for negotiations between the superpowers. Attempts were made by the Soviet propaganda machine to pillory Nixon's journey to China in February as the result of "the great-power, chauvinist, anti-Marxist policy of the Peking leadership . . . which has brought the Maoists to the role of actual accomplice to imperialist policy" (*Pravda,* March 28), while it praised the president's talks in Moscow as a sign that "an improvement of relations between the U.S.S.R. and the U.S. in the interests of both nations and the cause of promoting peace and international security is quite possible" (*Pravda,* May 31). The most important immediate consequence of Nixon's visit was the signing of the U.S.-Soviet treaty on the limitation of strategic arms: the U.S. and the U.S.S.R. agreed to limit themselves to 200 defensive antiballistic missiles each; and the U.S., relying on its advantage of multiple independently targetable warheads, allowed the U.S.S.R. to retain a numerical edge in the total of missile launchers. Other agreements dealt with cooperation in space, trade, and the protection of the environment. The U.S.S.R.'s conciliatory policy toward the Nixon Administration extended even to Vietnam: the Soviet government virtually ignored the mining of the harbor of Haiphong, North Vietnam, which preceded the president's visit to Moscow. Meanwhile, relations with China remained reasonably static, though cool, and polemics were conducted at a fairly low level.

It was argued that the unstable situation on the eastern Soviet frontier had helped persuade the country of the need to maintain stability in Europe. Certainly, in May 1972 the government welcomed the long-delayed ratification by the West German parliament of the 1970 treaties between West Germany and the Soviet Union.

While 1972 seemed to bring the Soviet Union closer to the achievement of its short-term policy goals in Europe, events in the Middle East moved in the opposite direction. During the summer relations with Egypt deteriorated suddenly, as the Egyptians realized that the Soviet Union would not supply all the military equipment the Egyptians thought they needed to develop the offensive capacity of their armed forces. In July Egypt's President Anwar el-Sadat told the Central Committee of the Arab Socialist Union that the U.S.S.R. had failed to send weapons that had been promised and that, in consequence, the Soviet government had been asked to withdraw its military experts and advisers from Egypt. (*See in* CE: Russia.)

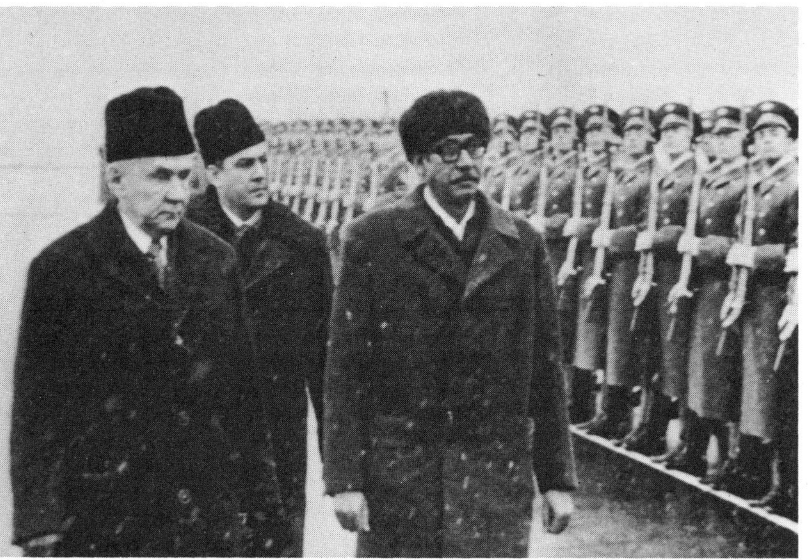

Sheikh Mujibur Rahman (right), prime minister of Bangladesh, inspects the military honor guard at Moscow airport with Soviet Premier Aleksei N. Kosygin. Sheikh Mujib held talks with the Soviet leaders, concentrating on aid for the war-torn nation of Bangladesh.
WIDE WORLD

Kurt Waldheim, the new secretary-general of the UN, succeeded U Thant of Burma. Waldheim is a career diplomat from Austria.

WIDE WORLD

UNITED NATIONS (UN). Secretary-General of the UN Kurt Waldheim, who took office at the beginning of 1972, presented his first report to the General Assembly in August. He praised the "key role" the UN played "in the cooperative effort to tackle long-term social and economic problems" but noted that "in the political spheres, the Organization's place is more uncertain." He applauded the greater understanding among the major powers, but he criticized "the idea of maintaining peace and security in the world through a concert of great powers" as a notion belonging more to the 19th than to the 20th century.

In May the secretary-general had given two speeches in Canada, calling attention to an "alarming" trend among states to use UN procedures less often for solving disputes. Noting that governments seemed to be reverting to secret diplomacy (in relation to Vietnam) or even force (as in the India-Pakistan war), he stressed the unused UN capacity to assist in keeping peace. He reminded his listeners not only of the value of UN peace-keeping missions but also of the value of quiet diplomacy, good offices, and other forms of "preventive diplomacy."

Throughout the year the secretary-general attempted to use his good offices to mitigate potential or actual tragedies from terrorism through airplane hijackings and in the massacres in May at the Lod International Airport near Tel Aviv, Israel, and in September at the Olympic Games in Munich, West Germany. A week before the 27th session of the General Assembly opened in September, he declared that the UN could not remain a "mute spectator" in the face of a growing trend toward acts of terror and violence against innocent people. He requested the assembly to include on its agenda an item entitled "measures to prevent terrorism and other forms of violence which endanger or take innocent human lives or jeopardize fundamental freedoms." Assembly debate later showed a division between some states that pressed for immediate action and others, led by the Arabs, that wished to avoid discussing terrorism except in the most general terms. The Arab states favored a draft resolution calling for an assembly committee to study the problems posed by international terrorism and particularly to examine its causes and ways of finding an effective solution to the problem. Another draft, favored by the U.S., asked the president of the General Assembly, Stanislaw Trepczynski of Poland, to name an international conference to draw up a convention against terrorism. On December 18 the first and weaker resolution passed the General Assembly by a vote of 76–35, with 17 abstentions.

Environment, the Seabed, and Other Matters

The first UN-sponsored World Conference on the Human Environment took place in Stockholm, Sweden, June 5–16. It approved 106 recommendations to be embodied in an international Action Plan to protect man's habitat on earth. It also adopted a Declaration on the Human Environment setting out 26 principles, including a conviction that mankind had reached the stage at which it must shape its actions throughout the world "with a more prudent care for their environmental consequences." Maurice F. Strong, secretary-general of the conference, called the declaration "a highly significant document reflecting community of interest among nations, regardless of politics, ideologies, or economic status." The conference also proposed to establish a permanent environmental organization, headed by an executive director, as well as a voluntary Environment Fund to pay for all or part of the costs of new environmental activities the UN and related agencies might undertake. Despite Strong's statement playing down differences among the conferees in the face of environmental challenges, the U.S.S.R. and other East European countries refused to attend the meeting as a protest against the exclusion of East Germany from the proceedings. Nonetheless, the Assembly on December 15 approved the conference recommendations and designated June 5 as World Environment Day. Headquarters for the new environmental program were to be at Nairobi, Kenya.

The UN Committee on the Peaceful Uses of the Seabed and the Ocean Floor Beyond the Limits of National Jurisdiction met in New York City in the spring and in Geneva, Switzerland, in the summer. The 91 members gave highest priority to preparing a list of 25 subjects and issues that the 1973 Conference on the Law of the Sea should consider.

During 1972 the UN provided disaster relief in the wake of the India-Pakistan war and to Asians expelled from Uganda, to the victims of earthquakes, and to Palestinian refugees in the Middle East. Few issues before the UN aroused such strong feelings as those connected with decolonization; evidence of international concern for policies being followed by South Africa, Rhodesia, and Portugal came through in special Security Council meetings, in actions by the secretary-general, and in General Assembly resolutions. The UN was involved in peace-keeping efforts in the Middle East, Cyprus, and Kashmir. The UN was again plagued by financial problems, and in December the assembly agreed to reduce the U.S. share of the budget from 31.5% to 25%.

UNESCO in the News

In 1972 the International Commission on the Development of Education—set up by the UN Educational, Scientific, and Cultural Organization (UNESCO) the preceding year—presented its report "Learning to Be," which was compiled by seven eminent persons of different nationalities, under the presidency of Edgar Faure. For 15 months they had examined problems in education across the world and studied strategies that might help educational systems adapt to emerging new needs. The report looked forward to sweeping reforms throughout the world. The Third International Conference on Adult Education, held in Tokyo, Japan, during the summer, was attended by nearly 400 delegates from 82 member states, plus observers from other countries and some 40 nongovernmental organizations. At the meeting it was unanimously agreed that adult education should be recognized as an indispensable component of lifelong education and that governments should adopt legislative and other measures to support it. The Intergovernmental Conference on Cultural Policies in Europe, held in Helsinki, Finland, in June, was attended by delegates from 30 countries, including 26 ministers. This conference made it clear that in spite of varying political and social structures, culture had become part of man's daily life, making it incumbent on governments to provide greater cultural opportunities.

Huang Hua, China's ambassador to the UN, signals his country's first veto—to keep Bangladesh from joining the UN.
WIDE WORLD

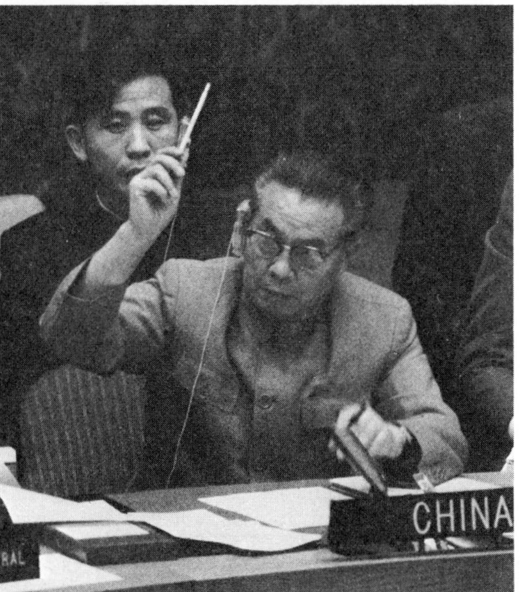

The 17th Session of UNESCO's General Conference, held in the fall at its Paris headquarters, included a delegation from the People's Republic of China, seated for the first time; it also elected Bangladesh (although China vetoed the Bangladesh application to join the General Assembly) and East Germany. Bahrain, Oman, Qatar, and the United Arab Emirates also became full UNESCO members. (*See in* CE: United Nations.)

UNITED STATES. The reelection of U.S. President Richard M. Nixon by a near-record margin of popular and electoral votes was the major U.S. political event of 1972. Nixon carried every jurisdiction except Massachusetts and the District of Columbia, which were won by the Democratic nominee, Senator George S. McGovern of South Dakota. Nixon received 520 electoral votes to McGovern's 17. The president's overwhelming victory had little impact on Congressional and gubernatorial races, however. Amid widespread ticket-splitting, the Democrats picked up two additional Senate seats and one more governorship, while losing only 12 seats in the House of Representatives. The election was, as the Republican national chairman, Senator Robert Dole of Kansas, put it, "a personal triumph for Mr. Nixon but not a party triumph." (*See* Elections.)

Legislative Action

Faced with a Congress controlled by Democrats, the president had only limited success in the enactment of his legislative program. His greatest victory came when Congress passed a law providing for general revenue sharing—one of the "six great goals" proposed by Nixon in 1971. The law established a five-year program to share $30.2 billion in federal revenues with state and local governments. The program, made retroactive to Jan. 1, 1972, was approved for five years.

About 40,000 demonstrators marched through New York City in the rain in April to protest the war in Southeast Asia. The group, carrying banners, talking to bystanders, and chanting, was mostly young people, with a liberal sprinkling of middle-aged men and women.

LESLIE LEON FROM KEYSTONE

Congress approved three temporary increases in the federal debt ceiling during 1972, the last only after a bitter fight over the president's request for unprecedented authority to cut federal spending to $250 billion in fiscal 1973. The third bill on a temporary debt ceiling, although not controversial in itself, became the subject of a partisan dispute when the House Ways and Means Committee added an amendment approving the president's request for power to make whatever spending cuts he deemed necessary to stay within the $250-billion limit.

In the waning moments of the 92d Congress, the House and the Senate overrode President Nixon's veto of the Federal Water Pollution Control Act Amendments of 1972, a $24.7-billion measure intended to clean up the nation's waterways by 1985. The president had vetoed the bill just before midnight on October 17, at which time it would have become law automatically without his signature. On the following day, however, both chambers voted to override the veto.

A proposed constitutional amendment guaranteeing equal rights for women was completed by the Congress in 1972—49 years after the measure had first been introduced. The amendment then went on to the states, where approval by 38 legislatures was required for ratification. The Administration did not request the amendment, but it was supported by the president.

A filibuster near the end of the 1972 session successfully prevented the Senate from voting on a tough antibusing bill that had been previously passed by the House and actively supported by the president. The bill would have barred all school busing except to the school closest or next closest to the student's home and would have allowed the reopening of previous desegregation orders to bring them into compliance with the bill's provisions. But the Higher Education Amendments Act of 1972, a separate, omnibus education measure, contained language that postponed until 1974 the effective date of court orders requiring busing. It also limited the use of federal funds for busing intended to overcome racial imbalance or to desegregate schools. (*See also* Education.)

In June Congress increased social security benefits by 20% across-the-board and provided for automatic increases whenever the cost of living should rise by more than 3% in a calendar year. Four months later, Congress raised widows' and widowers' benefits, increased the amount that a social security beneficiary under age 72 could earn and still receive full benefits, and provided a minimum monthly benefit of $170 for at least 30 years of employment covered by social security. (*See* Social Services.)

A number of bills were defeated by or died with the 92d Congress. These included amendments to end the war, tax reforms, a measure establishing a consumer protection agency, "no fault" au-

THE 11 EXECUTIVE DEPARTMENTS

(December 1972)

Secretary of State	William P. Rogers
Secretary of the Treasury	George P. Shultz
Secretary of Defense	Elliot L. Richardson *
Attorney General	Richard G. Kleindienst
Secretary of the Interior	Rogers C. B. Morton
Secretary of Agriculture	Earl L. Butz
Secretary of Commerce	Frederick B. Dent *
Secretary of Labor	Peter J. Brennan *
Secretary of Health, Education, and Welfare	Caspar W. Weinberger *
Secretary of Housing and Urban Development	James T. Lynn *
Secretary of Transportation	Claude S. Brinegar *

* Nominated but not confirmed during 1972.

tomobile insurance, an amendment on school prayer and one on withdrawal of U.S. troops from Europe, and legislation concerning strip mining, land use, location of power plants, presidential power to make war, and tax credits for nonpublic school tuition. (*See* Congress, U.S.)

Foreign Affairs

U.S. foreign relations during 1972 were marked by significant steps toward improved relations with the People's Republic of China and the Soviet Union. Efforts to terminate the U.S. involvement in Vietnam—alternating between rounds of negotiations and stepped-up military action—were totally unsuccessful.

The president's February visit to China ended nearly a quarter century of hostility between the governments in Peking, China, and Washington, D.C. Arriving in Peking on February 21, President and Mrs. Nixon and their party were greeted by Premier Chou En-lai and other dignitaries. The president later conferred for an hour with Communist Party Chairman Mao Tse-tung, an event that had not been announced beforehand.

The Chinese were hosts at a banquet on the evening of February 21 at the Great Hall of the People. Chou offered a toast to the Nixon party in which he declared that the president's visit had provided "the leaders of the two countries with an opportunity of meeting in person to seek the normalization of relations" between their countries. Nixon responded by saying that there was no reason for China and the U.S. to be enemies.

Additional meetings between Nixon and Chou followed. In a joint 1,800-word communiqué released in Shanghai, China, on February 27, the two leaders indicated that their talks had resulted in agreement on the need for increased U.S.-Chinese contacts and for eventual withdrawal of U.S. military forces from Taiwan. The status of Taiwan—recognized in advance as being the main stumbling block to improved relations between the U.S. and China—was dealt with in one section of the communiqué. China reaffirmed its traditional claims to the island, and the U.S. took the position that it favored "a peaceful settlement of the Taiwan question by the Chinese themselves." The document also dealt with proposed exchanges in science, technology, culture, sports, and trade.

The emerging friendship between the U.S. and China left many U.S. allies—particularly those in Asia—feeling distinctly insecure. To clarify the U.S. position and reassure friendly nations, Marshall Green, assistant secretary of state for East Asian and Pacific affairs, made an extensive tour of Asia and met with leaders from Japan, the Philippines, Indonesia, and Malaysia, among others. Predictably, U.S. relations with the Nationalist Chinese government became extremely strained. (*See also* China, People's Republic of; Taiwan.)

President Nixon's journey to the Soviet Union in May was even more productive than the China trip in terms of agreements reached. The most important of these were a pair of accords limiting offensive and defensive strategic nuclear weapons. During five days of meetings between Nixon and Communist Party General Secretary Leonid I. Brezhnev, five other agreements were approved. Their provisions included: establishment of a joint committee on cooperation in environmental protection; coordinated research on cancer, heart disease, and environmental health; a joint flight with linked Soviet and U.S. spacecraft in 1975; creation of a permanent commission on scientific and technical cooperation; and prohibition of mutual harassment on the high seas by the nations' navies and establishment of an experimental signal system to avoid naval mishaps.

The Moscow summit led within two months to a major trade agreement. President Nixon an-

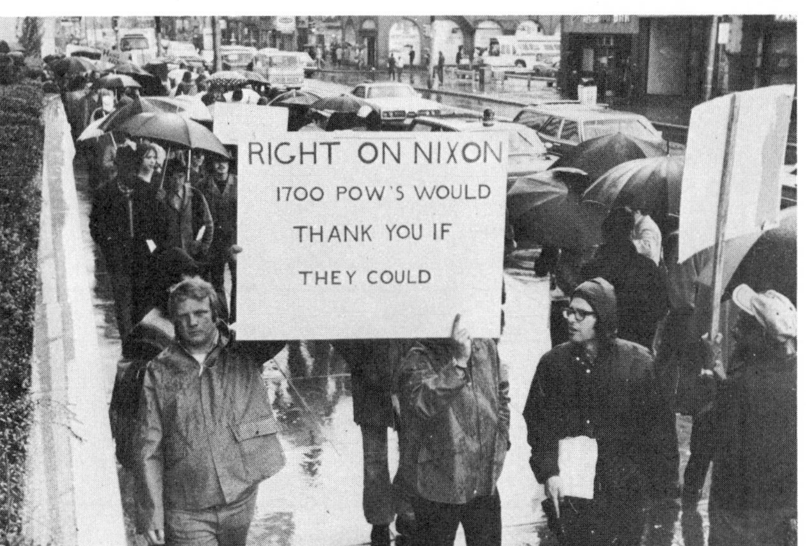

Two demonstrators carry this sign in support of President Nixon's Vietnam policy as they thread their way through an antiwar protest march in downtown Pittsburgh, Pa.

WIDE WORLD

WIDE WORLD

U.S. Rep. Hale Boggs (D, La.), House majority leader, and three companions disappeared in a light plane over Alaska in October.

nounced on July 8 a three-year agreement for the sale of at least $750 million worth of U.S. wheat, corn, and other grains to the Soviet Union. It was the largest grain transaction in history between the two countries. Some Democrats later charged that the grain deal had given a windfall profit to exporters and had shortchanged U.S. farmers and consumers. The president retorted that the farmers got $1 billion more in farm income, while the taxpayers were saved the cost of storage and "thousands of jobs were created."

The solution to the nation's most persistent foreign-policy problem—the Indochina war—remained elusive in 1972. President Nixon announced on May 8 that he had ordered the mining of North Vietnamese ports and interdiction of land and sea routes, in an attempt to prevent delivery of war supplies to that country. Five months later it seemed that the policy of bombing and mining was about to bear fruit. On October 26 Henry A. Kissinger, the president's security adviser, declared in a news conference that "peace is at hand." Reporting on his secret negotiations with the North Vietnamese in the preceding weeks, Kissinger said that a final agreement on a truce and a political settlement could be worked out in one more conference with the North Vietnamese. Shortly after Kissinger's announcement, U.S. Secretary of Defense Melvin R. Laird confirmed reports that the U.S. had ordered a temporary halt in the bombing north of the 20th parallel in North Vietnam.

Hopes for a definitive settlement were frustrated in the following weeks, however, as North Vietnam, South Vietnam, and the U.S. proved unable to reach a satisfactory agreement. In mid-December it was announced that President Nixon had ordered resumption of full-scale bombing above the 20th parallel. The decision drew heavy criticism from high-ranking military officials and congressmen of both major parties. The bombing was halted on December 30.

U.S. relations with Cuba, frozen for more than a decade, took a slight turn for the better near the end of the year. Using the Swiss embassy in Havana, Cuba, as a go-between, the two countries began indirect negotiations in November on an agreement to curb hijacking of airplanes and boats by their citizens. The decision to begin talks came after four U.S. men diverted an Eastern Air Lines jet to Havana on October 29 and three more U.S. hijackers forced a Southern Airways plane to land in the Cuban capital on November 12. (*See* Cuba Special Report.)

Domestic Affairs

On the domestic front, the presidential election campaign dominated the news from the start of the

The radical Weathermen claimed credit for an explosion in a women's rest room in the Pentagon building in May. They said that a bomb was exploded to coincide with Ho Chi Minh's birthday.

UPI COMPIX

HEINZ KLUETMEIER FROM LIFE MAGAZINE © TIME INC.

A family prepares for a garage sale at their home. Many people were finding such sales a profitable way to get rid of unwanted junk and were amazed by what their neighbors would buy.

primary season in March to the November day of decision. President Nixon's renomination by the Republican party was a foregone conclusion, and his reelection appeared likely.

For the Democrats, however, the campaign was full of unlikely surprises and bitter debates, from the credentials battles at the Democratic National Convention to the replacement on the ticket of Senator Thomas F. Eagleton of Missouri, McGovern's chosen running mate, after his disclosure of treatment for past mental illness. The president made few campaign appearances or political statements, thus giving the Democrats little in the way of election-issue ammunition. The so-called Watergate incident—in which persons associated with the Committee to Re-elect the President were accused of breaking into the Democratic party's national headquarters—failed to rally public support for the Democrats or arouse indignation against the Republicans.

Again in 1972 President Nixon was involved in a controversy over an executive appointment. The appointment in question was that of Richard G. Kleindienst, named in February to succeed the resigning attorney general, John N. Mitchell. Objections to Kleindienst came mainly from the liberal Democratic members of the Senate, one of whom cited Kleindienst's "very callous attitude" in the area of civil rights and his conservative views on law and order. The battle over the nomination turned out to be even longer than expected. While conducting hearings on the nominee's qualifications, the Senate Judiciary Committee turned up allegations linking Kleindienst with a 1971 antitrust settlement involving the International Telephone & Telegraph Corp. (ITT) and a financial pledge by ITT to the Republican party. However, the committee's report—issued after two months of investigation—upheld the nomination, and the Senate confirmed Kleindienst as attorney general on June 8.

Following his sweeping election victory, the president prepared for his second term with a major reshuffling of his Cabinet. Elliot L. Richardson, serving as secretary of health, education, and welfare, was nominated as secretary of defense, replacing Laird. Caspar W. Weinberger was named to replace Richardson. The president named a top labor leader, Peter J. Brennan, to succeed James D. Hodgson as secretary of labor. In a later announcement, oil company executive Claude S. Brinegar was selected to be the new secretary of transportation. Other Cabinet appointees included Frederick B. Dent (commerce) and James T. Lynn (housing and urban development). Staying on in their current capacities were William P. Rogers (state), George P. Shultz (treasury), Rogers C. B. Morton (interior), Earl L. Butz (agriculture), and Kleindienst (attorney general).

The U.S. space program reached the end of an era in 1972 with the last two manned flights to the moon under the Apollo program. Two astronauts from Apollo 16 spent a record 71 hours 2 minutes on the moon from April 20 to 23 during the first manned mission to the lunar mountains. Apollo 17 was launched from Cape Kennedy on December 7 and returned to the earth 12½ days later with more than 200 pounds of rock and soil samples. It broke Apollo 16's record by staying more than three days on the moon. (*See also* Nixon; Space Exploration; State Governments, U.S. *See in* CE: United States.)

UPPER VOLTA. The year 1972 was marked in Upper Volta by three major events. President Sangoulé Lamizana made an official visit to Egypt in February; the third Festival of African Cinema took place at Ouagadougou, the capital, in March; and France's President Georges Pompidou visited in November. During his visit to Egypt, President Lamizana pledged his diplomatic support to the Egyptian government. He declared his recognition of Egypt's right to Sinai.

The film festival was used by militants, many of whom had been members of the former African Independence party, as an occasion to denounce what they called the cultural alienation afflicting Africa. They preached a form of nationalism vigorous in its condemnation of former colonial rulers. Perhaps for that reason Pompidou's welcome to Upper Volta was notably cool. Nevertheless, talks between Pompidou and the government were cordial. (*See in* CE: Upper Volta.)

URUGUAY. President Juan M. Bordaberry, who took office in Uruguay on March 1, 1972, declared a "state of internal war" on April 15. After a spectacular prison escape in September 1971 by 106 members of Uruguay's left-wing Tupamaro guerrilla group, police and the army had formed an antiguerrilla force. Following Bordaberry's declaration, the army was given wide powers of search and arrest, which led to the discovery of secret arms caches and "people's prisons," the release of hostages held by the Tupamaros, and the arrest of about 1,000 guerrillas. The army, however, began to exert its influence elsewhere, investigating prominent businessmen suspected of "economic crimes" such as smuggling, corruption, and currency speculation. The arrest and reported torture of four doctors suspected as guerrillas led to a strike by the nation's physicians. Other arrests brought condemnation from politicians and forced a reorganization of the cabinet.

In the economic sector, the Bordaberry administration overhauled the country's exchange rate system in an effort to strengthen exports and bolster international reserves. The measures had little effect; exports for the first nine months of 1972 fell by $42 million compared with the same period in 1971. Inflation ran between 65% and 75% all year, bringing on a rash of work stoppages, including a paralyzing postal strike. (*See in* CE: Uruguay.)

VENEZUELA. A significant drop in production in 1972 kept the oil industry near the center of political debate in Venezuela. At the same time, the nomination of candidates for the presidential elections scheduled for December 1973 heralded the start of a long, intense campaign.

The main reasons given for the drop in oil production were mild winter weather, a decrease in freight rates that made it cheaper for the oil companies to transport oil to Europe and North America from the Middle East, and increases in local taxation that made Venezuelan oil more costly to produce. The reduced oil production, however, could also be seen as a showdown between the government and the oil companies. The situation had begun in December 1971, when the government again increased its taxes on foreign oil producers, who pump 98% of Venezuela's fuel, and ordered them to maintain the flow of oil for export in 1972 within 2% above or below the 1970 level—3.7 million barrels a day—regardless of the market. Violations were punishable by a surcharge of as much as 10% on a company's total exports.

In May Gen. Marcos Pérez Jiménez, who ruled Venezuela from 1948 to 1959, returned from exile in Spain and was welcomed by about 10,000 supporters—in spite of a charge against him of indirect responsibility for murder. He had earlier announced his intention to run for president. (*See in* CE: Venezuela.)

Heavy rains caused flooding and damage in central and western Venezuela. This child in Maracaibo sits near a makeshift shelter in a local park where flood victims were taken.

UPI COMPIX

VETERINARY MEDICINE. The disastrous outbreak of one animal epidemic and the threat of another provided major focuses of activity for veterinary medicine in 1972. A highly virulent strain of Newcastle disease that could affect virtually all types of birds, producing a 100% fatality rate, had been introduced into the U.S. by imported ornamental birds in 1970 and 1971. Small outbreaks followed in Texas and Arizona, and by the beginning of 1972 the disease had spread to poultry in California. Losses were so high that the southern California area was declared a disaster area. Although many poultry flocks had been vaccinated, it was estimated that death losses from this virus strain would reach 15% to 20% if the disease were allowed to run its course. The U.S. Department of Agriculture, therefore, embarked on a program of total eradication by slaughter of all infected and exposed birds. From March through October 1972 more than 8 million chickens, turkeys, ducks, and ornamental birds were killed. Cost of the program was estimated at $24 million.

Venezuelan equine encephalomyelitis (VEE) continued to threaten horses and burros in Mexico, where by late in 1971 it had killed some 38,000 animals. Outbreaks near the U.S. border claimed 2,366 animals between January and August 1972. Vaccinations of about 3 million animals in 19 states in the U.S. eased fears that a VEE outbreak might occur in border areas.

The epidemic of African swine fever reported in Cuba in mid-1971 was contained and the disease was eradicated. Characterized as the "most alarming event of the year" by the Food and Agriculture Organization of the United Nations because of the threat it posed to the totally unprotected swine herds of the Western Hemisphere, the disease was swiftly controlled with stringent measures. All the swine in the Havana province were slaughtered and the meat sterilized for human consumption. Though the Cubans lost more than half a million swine in 1971, they prevented the disease from threatening any other herds in Latin America.

Foot-and-mouth disease appeared in Peru as well as in Greece and Turkey in 1972, and some fears were voiced that the rapid completion of the Pan-American Highway might spread the disease. Mass vaccinations brought outbreaks of rinderpest in the Near East under control, and a national program to eradicate hog cholera in the U.S. showed promising early results. However, renewed outbreaks in six states in October forced the Department of Agriculture to declare an emergency situation as hog cholera spread.

Animal rabies cases increased in the U.S. by 34% in 1971 to 4,392 cases; for the first time every state except Hawaii reported a case. Most of the increase involved wildlife, with skunks accounting for 46% of reported cases. In Latin America more than one million horses and cattle died of rabies spread by vampire bats, although new control procedures were being used.

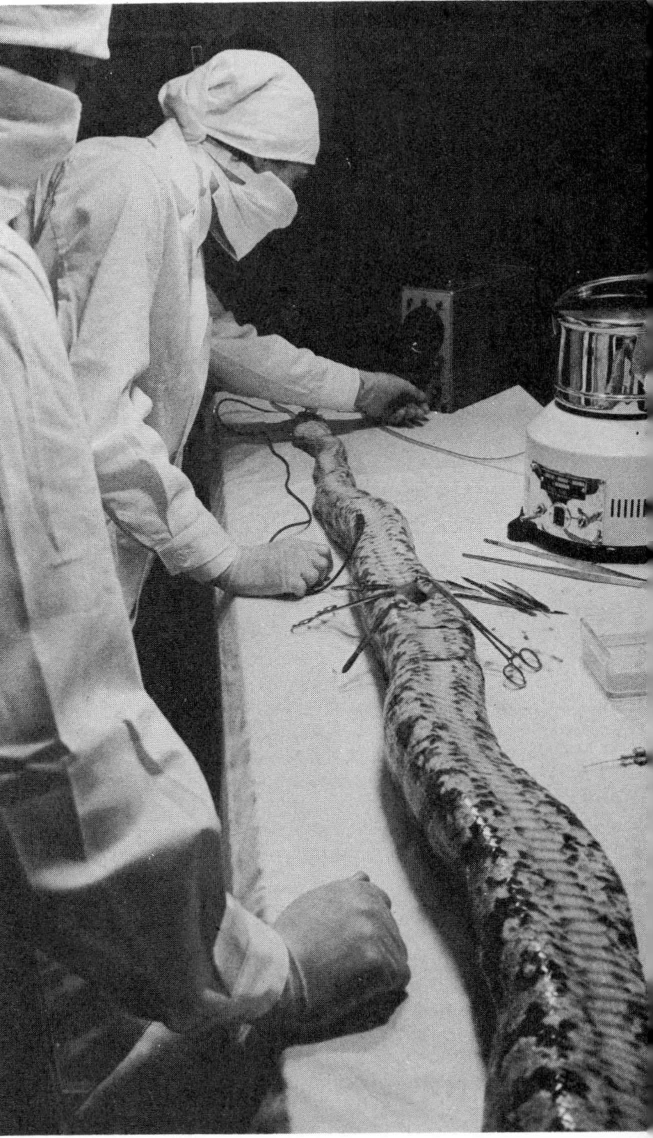

G. BARTL FROM GAMMA

In Vienna, Austria, Richard Holy, aided by another zoologist, performed surgery on this python and removed a cancer. It was the first successful surgery of its kind.

The U.S. Food and Drug Administration banned use of the growth chemical diethylstilbestrol in cattle feed after August 1972, following reports that the drug caused cancer in laboratory animals. Pellets of the chemical implanted under the skin were still allowed, though there was some sentiment to ban this practice as well. To prevent introduction into the U.S. of animal diseases from abroad, a high-security quarantine station for imported animals was planned to be set up at Fleming Key, off Key West, Fla. Any imported stock would remain at the station for five months before going on to the U.S. mainland. (*See in* CE: Diseases, Plant and Animal; Zoo.)

VIETNAM. The search for peace in Vietnam, mercilessly ravaged by war for more than a quarter of a century, was spurred during 1972 by a mutual appreciation by the contending sides that a military stalemate existed. The Viet Cong's role in the struggle continued to be overshadowed by the growing participation of North Vietnamese armed forces, whose massive spring offensive failed to administer a decisive blow to the South Vietnamese armed forces.

South Vietnam's units, though at first staggered and crippled, survived the assaults in a crucial test. They did not enjoy the benefit of U.S. ground combat support, which was terminated completely during 1972. U.S. air power, nonetheless, added greatly to the uneven effort by the South Vietnamese government troops to withstand the North Vietnamese. North Vietnam's problems were compounded by U.S. military interdiction of its supply lines to the South and the seemingly effective closure of North Vietnam's ports.

The massive invasion of South Vietnam began on March 30 with assaults across the supposedly demilitarized zone (DMZ). Units of the regular North Vietnamese army infantry troops supported by artillery, antiaircraft, missile, and tank units easily swept southward under the cover of the seasonal monsoon's plane-grounding weather. An estimated total of 15,000 to 20,000 North Vietnamese troops initially moved to establish control over the northern provinces of South Vietnam, apparently seeking as their primary objectives the seizure of the provincial capital of Quang Tri and the ancient imperial capital of Hue.

A week later, with South Vietnam's defensive forces reeling from the initial thrusts across the DMZ and stretched thin by the dispatch of fresh troops to hold the crumbling northern defense line, North Vietnam opened another front far to the south. North Vietnamese and Viet Cong infantry divisions, spearheaded by a 70-tank force (an estimated 21,000 men in all), pushed across the Cambodian border toward Loc Ninh in Binh Long province. The invaders quickly penetrated to within about 60 miles of Saigon, the capital of South Vietnam. The fight eventually centered around An Loc, which was under siege for months. North Vietnamese units were able to isolate the city by cutting the highway leading to Saigon and making An Loc totally dependent on airlifts for supplies and reinforcements.

A third front was soon established in the Central Highlands, with the heaviest action being directed against South Vietnam's government outposts and villages in Kontum province. The North Vietnamese were believed to have committed a 20,000-man force in this operational area to the apparent objective of cutting South Vietnam in half. In all, North Vietnam probably employed major portions of 12 of its 14 regular divisions to the massive offensive. North Vietnamese troops were supported by standing Viet Cong units that operated as terrorist and harassment forces in country-wide attacks.

Initially, the South Vietnamese were dangerously crushed by the three-pronged offensive. A newly created government infantry division, the Third, was hardest hit and incapable of offering resistance.

On June 8 a South Vietnamese plane mistakenly made a napalm strike near Trang Bang, South Vietnam. A girl ripped off her burning clothes and ran down Route 1 with other terrified children.
WIDE WORLD

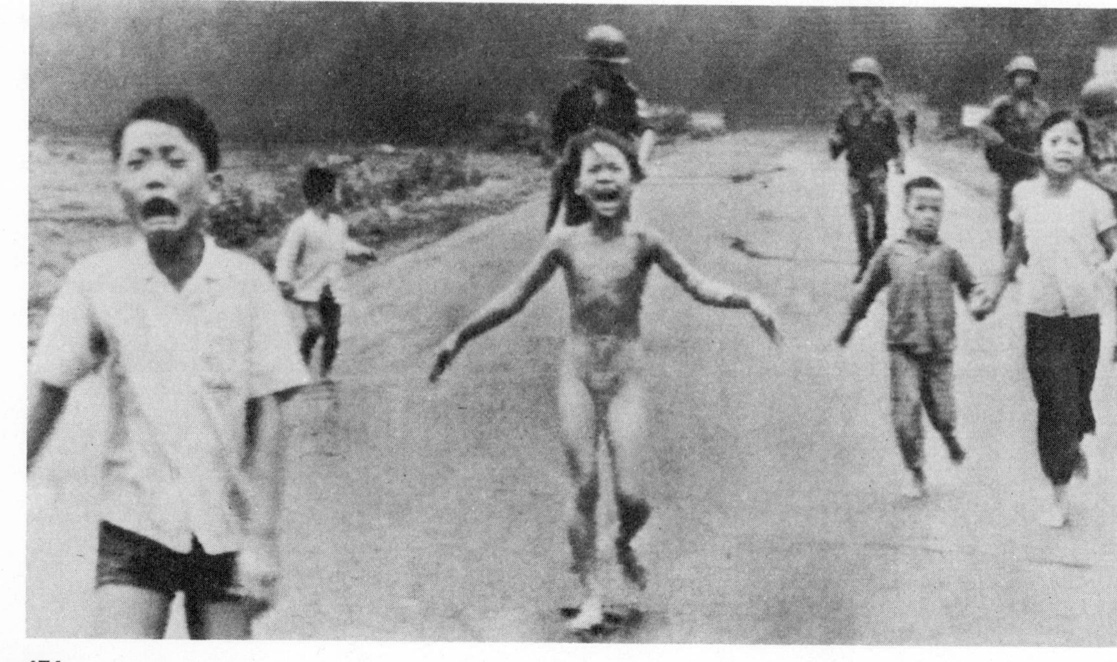

WIDE WORLD

A South Vietnamese marine carries a dead friend killed during fighting near Quang Tri in April. The marines were trying to reopen Route 1.

It abandoned all of its forward bases south of the DMZ in the first few days of fighting. Camp Carroll's defenders surrendered en masse. More experienced South Vietnamese units—particularly airborne forces, rangers, and marines—distinguished themselves by offering fierce resistance and holding threatened positions.

The spirited and protracted fight for An Loc was marked by a ferocity rarely displayed by the regular South Vietnamese army. In the Central Highlands, their forces offset initial reversals by not yielding in subsequent key battles for territorial control. The performance of government troops after the first setbacks was significant because the North Vietnamese used armor and artillery on an unprecedented scale. Never before had the large tanks and giant field guns been used in such numbers and over so wide an area. While U.S. aircraft (fixed-wing craft and helicopters) were instrumental in the destruction of hundreds of tanks, the South Vietnamese ground troops were credited with at least holding their own in the face of the awesome enemy firepower.

Quang Tri was the only South Vietnamese provincial capital to fall to the North Vietnamese during the offensive, although others were attacked and constantly threatened. Nevertheless, the outcome was a severe blow to the North Vietnamese because of their inability to win control over urban areas. On the other hand, South Vietnam's pacification efforts of the preceding four years were undone to a great extent in the few months of intensified fighting. Official South Vietnamese government figures revealed that 40% of the country was directly affected by the North Vietnamese Communist offensive, resulting in widespread civilian casualties and creating another million or so refugees who were forced to flee the ever-extended zones of combat.

South Vietnam

Prior to North Vietnam's spring offensive, only 7 of South Vietnam's 10,775 hamlets were considered to be under absolute Communist control. By April 30 the number had climbed to 983. Of the 272 districts, 14 were regarded as lost to the government in the course of the campaign. Seven of the lost districts were in battle-torn Quang Tri province. The number of people officially conceded as being clearly under Communist control jumped from 6,000 to 564,000 after the first four weeks of the offensive. Saigon could claim that 82.7% of the populace were living in completely controlled government regions, as opposed to 90% living in uncontested areas before the attacks.

After five months of fighting, Saigon announced that its forces had killed 70,000 North Vietnamese and Viet Cong. Inflated as the figures might have been, it was evident that North Vietnam's losses were great. South Vietnamese military losses were acknowledged as 14,000 killed, 5,000 missing, and 50,000 wounded. While Saigon's troops may have

Bomb craters 30 feet in diameter and 10 to 15 feet deep are seen in this lowland forest area in South Vietnam. By October, there were about 28 million such craters throughout Indochina.

ARTHUR H. WESTING

won the battle of attrition, their losses were not easy to absorb. Of the 16-plus government divisions, 7 were deemed to have suffered heavy losses and 5 others moderate casualties. Four of the divisions were so decimated as to be judged nonfunctional as combat units.

The resumption of full-scale aerial attacks north of the DMZ on April 6, and the announcement on May 8 by U.S. President Richard M. Nixon of the mining of North Vietnam's ports and the interdiction of land and sea routes to the South, had a profound psychological effect on Saigon's capacity to resist. The stepped-up U.S. naval campaign also achieved some success in limiting the resupply and reinforcement of North Vietnamese forces operating in the South.

Later a stalemate was apparent throughout the country. The North Vietnamese and the Viet Cong controlled slightly larger portions of South Vietnam than they had before the offensive was mounted, but they now seemed incapable of pressing major attacks. South Vietnamese government forces, meanwhile, were able to exercise authority over most of the country but were unable to oust the Communists from pockets of territory they had dominated for long periods of time, particularly those that adjoined Laos and Cambodia, to which the North Vietnamese could withdraw and regroup without difficulty. Nonetheless, a force of 145,000 North Vietnamese was still positioned in South Vietnam and Cambodia by late October when both sides moved to reach a cease-fire and work toward a political solution.

The Paris peace talks had continued at various times during the year, with little progress. Part of North Vietnam's objection to peace plans offered by the U.S. was its asserted belief that the Nixon Administration was unwilling to drop its support of South Vietnam's President Nguyen Van Thieu. Thieu, on his part, reiterated his policy of the "four no's": (1) no abandonment of territory to the North Vietnamese, (2) no coalition government, (3) no policy of neutrality, and (4) no Communist participation in the political affairs of South Vietnam. Thieu feared that the U.S. would drop him precipitately, a concern heightened during the year's first peace drive when U.S. Secretary of State William P. Rogers stated, on February 3, that the U.S. was "flexible" on the composition of a caretaker government and on the date when it might assume control from President Thieu. On May 8, in announcing stepped-up military action against North Vietnam, President Nixon announced modifications in the essential U.S. proposal to bring the conflict to a close: an agreement to end hostilities against North Vietnam when all U.S. prisoners were returned; internationally supervised elections throughout Indochina; and a complete withdrawal of all U.S. troops from Vietnam within four months after achievement of the other points.

In October South Vietnam learned of the imminence of a U.S.-North Vietnamese breakthrough during a visit to Saigon by Henry A. Kissinger, the U.S. president's security adviser. North Vietnam announced the terms of the agreement, subsequently confirmed by Kissinger, who said, "We believe that peace is at hand." The main points of the plan were: (1) a cease-fire throughout South Vietnam; (2) an end to U.S. military operations against North Vietnam; (3) the withdrawal of the remaining U.S. forces in South Vietnam (about 32,000 men) within 60 days of the signing; and (4) the concurrent release of the U.S. prisoners held by North Vietnam. Other points were (5) the acknowledgment of authority in areas under government or Communist control; (6) the creation of a National Council of National Reconciliation and Concord, to be made up of equal representation of the Saigon government, the Viet Cong, and South Vietnamese neutralists; (7) general elections to de-

In June these six U.S. prisoners of war were interviewed by four U.S. visitors to Hanoi. They were identified as (from left) Lynn E. Guenther, Edwin A. Hawley, Jr., Kenneth J. Fraser, David Hoffman, Walter E. Wilber, and Edison W. Miller.

WIDE WORLD

Le Duc Tho is interviewed on one of his trips to Paris as the special adviser to the North Vietnamese delegation at the Paris peace talks. With him is Mrs. Nguyen Thi Binh (left), head of the Provisional Revolutionary Government of South Vietnam, Xuan Thuy (center), head of the North Vietnamese delegation, and an interpreter (right).

A.F.P. FROM PICTORIAL PARADE

termine the nation's future political direction, with commissions representing the involved parties—under the general supervision of an International Commission—to oversee the balloting and to supervise the cease-fire; and (8) the calling of an international conference to guarantee all provisions within 30 days of the signing of the agreement.

President Thieu's opposition to certain points of the plan was made known even before the terms were announced publicly. The president spoke out against a coalition arrangement, calling it "unacceptable." His supporters stated the president felt that he could never accept "the tripartite proposal." Thieu's hold on the country was strengthened during the year by emergency powers granted him in the wake of the Communist offensive. Ruling by martial law, he cracked down on all dissent. In September he abolished local elections.

Homes in Haiphong, North Vietnam, were allegedly devastated by U.S. bombing attacks.

"LONDON DAILY EXPRESS" FROM PICTORIAL PARADE

North Vietnam

Prospects for peace grew in the wake of the heaviest punishment North Vietnam had known in 27 years of warfare. When the year began, there was little indication either of the massive escalation of the war or of the possibility of peace. U.S. bombers were striking at targets in North Vietnam and Laos and there were reports of a North Vietnamese military buildup just above the DMZ.

Toward the end of March a high-level Soviet delegation on air defense visited Hanoi, the North Vietnamese capital. About the same time, revised U.S. intelligence estimates claimed that the Soviet Union was the top supplier of arms to North Vietnam. Total military and economic aid to the Hanoi government by its Communist allies in 1971 was estimated at $775 million.

North Vietnam paid an intolerably heavy price for what it gained during its spring offensive. The escalation of U.S. bombing of North Vietnam caused targets in Hanoi to come under attack. Haiphong, the main port, was reportedly leveled. Other population centers were hit, and the Hanoi government charged the U.S. with genocide. The elaborate dike system in the Red River delta, which had traditionally kept Hanoi and surrounding areas from being submerged by floodwaters, was severely damaged. The bombing continued, with only a four-day break in mid-June as a U.S. goodwill gesture to the Soviet Union, whose president was visiting Hanoi at the time.

The bombing and mining of harbors did not visibly slow down the Communist offensive in the South, which apparently had been prepared so carefully that enough supplies had already been moved to concentration areas well before the U.S. retaliated. Supplies continued to get into North Vietnam, sometimes in Chinese junks hugging the coastline and sometimes through railway and road links,

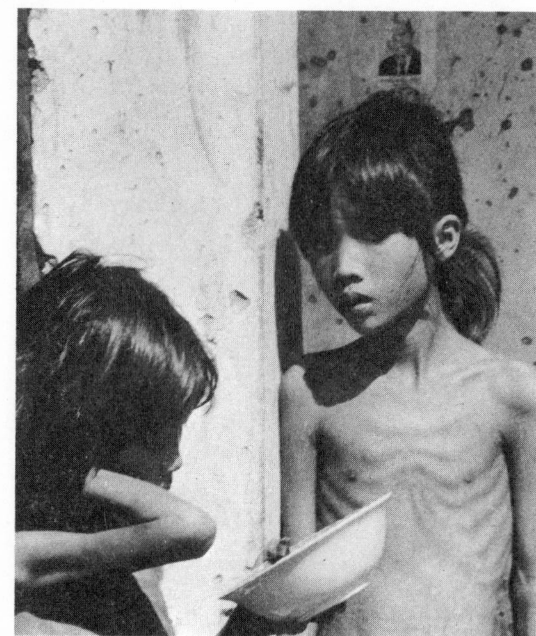

WIDE WORLD

Surviving more than 70 days of shelling at An Loc, these starving, frightened, naked South Vietnamese girls hold their empty bowl and wait for food outside a shell-pocked house.

although these were a prime target of U.S. bombers. However, neither China nor the Soviet Union tried to break the U.S. blockade. Much to the Hanoi government's displeasure, the Nixon visit to Moscow took place on schedule in May while the bombing and the mining continued.

By July there was evidence that the pressure of war was beginning to tell. An editorial in the official newspaper *Nhan Dan,* signed by Deputy Premier Le Thanh Nghi, announced a total mobilization of labor and a crackdown on shirkers: citizens must put the national interest above all else, and anyone who failed to obey the regulations on work might be ordered by the chairman of the local administrative committee to do labor useful to society in forced-labor camps.

On December 18 the U.S. announced that the heaviest bombing in the history of the war had been initiated over North Vietnam. Hanoi and Haiphong were devastated by the raids, which produced heavy casualties. The U.S. lost a relatively large number of planes from antiaircraft fire, though reports on the number of planes lost varied considerably. Hanoi reported that on December 22 its largest hospital, the 1,000-bed Bach Mai Hospital, had been bombed with a heavy loss of life; a camp housing U.S. prisoners of war was also reported damaged. The raids above the 20th parallel were halted on December 30; bombing of southern regions was continued. The U.S. considered the raids to be strong pressure on North Vietnam to end the war. (*See also* United States. *See in* CE: Vietnam; Vietnam Conflict.)

WALLACE, GEORGE C. Once a one-issue Southern politician who became a hero among blue-collar workers in the U.S., Alabama Gov. George C. Wallace was cut down in the prime of his life as a presidential candidate by a would-be assassin in 1972. Shaking hands after a rally at a shopping center in Maryland in May, Wallace was shot by Arthur H. Bremer, a drifter and psychotic ne'er-do-well whose diary noted that he had stalked another target: U.S. President Richard M. Nixon. As a result of the shooting, the governor was paralyzed from the waist down, a disability that appeared to be permanent.

Nonetheless, he made an appearance in Miami Beach, Fla., at the Democratic National Convention, where ramps were installed to accommodate his wheelchair. His presence remained a powerful influence on U.S. politics. He entered the convention with nearly 400 delegate votes, a third of the number he could have earned had he fielded delegate slates in every state where his name was on the primary ballot.

Wallace emerged on the national scene in 1963 when he "stood in the schoolhouse door" in an attempt to block federal officers from enrolling two black students in the previously segregated University of Alabama. He declared himself a presidential candidate for the first time in 1964 and did well in three popular primaries before withdrawing in favor of the Republican nominee, Senator Barry M. Goldwater of Arizona.

In 1968 Wallace was the formal candidate of the American Independent party, which was essentially a personal cult then, but was later struggling to emerge as a permanent national political party. Running with U.S. Air Force Gen. Curtis E. LeMay as his slate mate, he won 46 electoral votes in 1968.

By 1972, Wallace no longer appealed exclusively to segregationists but had emerged as the popular spokesman for many rank-and-file voters who opposed ever-increasing taxes and growing bureaucracies. Still, his chief fame was as an opponent to busing of schoolchildren to achieve racial balance, an important issue in 1972.

Wallace was born in Clio, Ala., on Aug. 25, 1919, and was reared in modest circumstances. Always a scrapper, as later political opponents would learn, he was twice Golden Gloves bantamweight titlist, and then a flight engineer on B-29's in the Pacific Ocean during World War II. He was discharged with a 10% disability for a "nervous condition" and battle fatigue.

He practiced law and was elected assistant attorney general of Alabama in 1946 before joining the state legislature the following year. He was elected governor in 1962 and, when state law barred a second successive term, stood aside for his wife, Lurleen, who was elected to the governor's mansion by the largest plurality in state history. He was widowed, remarried, and elected governor again in 1970.

WEATHER. In 1972 the National Hail Research Experiment over Colorado's high plains continued the study of thunderstorms, hail, and cloud-seeding techniques. Conducted by the National Center for Atmospheric Research, the hail experiment was aimed at reducing the size and amount of hail produced by thunderstorm systems.

Notable technological innovations included better platforms and sensors for observing weather. The second in the National Oceanic and Atmospheric Administration (NOAA) series of polar-orbiting satellites, launched in October, was able to sense the vertical temperature structure of the atmosphere, a major milestone in learning to use a vantage point in space for weather observation. NOAA deployed its first engineering prototype automated ocean data buoys during 1972, testing them in the Gulf of Mexico, the Gulf of Alaska, and the Arctic ice pack as a prelude to operational deployment later in the decade. Doppler radar was applied to sensing potentially tornadic circulations within thundercloud systems.

Gale-force winds across the northeastern U.S. in January caused at least three deaths in New York City, where vehicles were overturned, trees uprooted, and utility wires ripped away. Wind damage for the region was put at $11 million. In Boulder, Colo., January winds gusting to more than 150 mph caused more than $1 million in property damage. In the Southwest drought and fire created problems, and disastrous lightning-set forest fires occurred in Alaska.

The U.S. in 1972 suffered one of its worst flood years on record. In February melting snow and heavy rains washed out a wastepile dam above Man, W.Va., releasing a 50-foot wall of water that raced downhill through 14 mining communities, killing more than 100 persons and displacing about 4,000 others.

Torrential June rains on the slopes of South Dakota's Black Hills caused catastrophic flash flooding along a two-block-wide, 12-mile-long stretch of Rapid Creek, which flows through Rapid City. Heavy rains trapped behind the city park's Canyon Lake dam poured into the town when the earthen dam broke, killing more than 200 persons, causing more than $100 million damage, and displacing 5,000 persons. An estimated 2,000 automobiles were swept away and wrecked.

Barely two weeks later, the most widespread flooding in U.S. history was caused by the remnant of Hurricane Agnes and interactions with other atmospheric systems. As the dying hurricane moved up the Atlantic seaboard, its torrential rains caused Florida, Maryland, Pennsylvania, New York, and Virginia to be designated as disaster areas. Communities along the James River in Virginia and the Susquehanna River in Pennsylvania were especially hard hit. With a toll of 134 fatalities, entire communities displaced, and an estimated $60 billion damage, Agnes became the most destructive hurricane in the nation's history.

Heavy, wind-whipped rains struck the Great Lakes region in November, causing massive flooding. Lakefront areas in Ohio and Michigan were evacuated as huge waves struck the shore.

May storms in Chile produced flooding that displaced some 20,000 persons and caused outbreaks of respiratory illness. In Mexico City, Mexico, storms and mud slides in May killed 37 persons and left 100,000 homeless. Following more than 25 inches of June rain, massive landslides killed approximately 250 persons in Hong Kong. In August, weeks of heavy rain and catastrophic flooding in 11 provinces on Luzon struck the Philippines. More than 400 persons were reported killed and approximately 640,000 were rendered homeless. (*See also* Disasters of 1972. *See in* CE: Weather.)

A geostationary Applications Technology Satellite photographed Hurricane Agnes crossing the coast of the Florida panhandle on June 9.

COURTESY, NATIONAL OCEANIC AND ATMOSPHERIC ADMINISTRATION

WESTERN SAMOA. An overall improvement in Western Samoa's economy continued in 1972, despite the drop in world prices for copra. Tourism, which was the largest earner of foreign exchange except for agriculture, was encouraged by more hotel construction. Foreign aid continued to grow, the greatest amount coming from New Zealand, which assisted in the redevelopment of the hospital in Apia, the capital, and the creation of a ferry service to link Upolu and Savai'i. Regional links were strengthened with the opening of the Faleolo airport.

An agreement was reached with the Asian Development Bank on a loan of $2 million for a power project. Western Samoa, which had joined the International Monetary Fund, took steps in 1972 to become a member of the World Bank group.

The government decided to establish formal diplomatic relations with New Zealand. Ceremonies marked the tenth anniversary of Western Samoa's independence and the opening of a new Legislative Assembly building. (*See in* CE: Samoa.)

WEST INDIES. Moves toward greater political independence intensified in 1972 in the Caribbean island countries affiliated with the Commonwealth of Nations. Absolute and final separation from St. Christopher-Nevis-Anguilla was the aim of Ronald Webster, whose People's Progressive party won six of the seven elective seats in the new Anguilla council. In October Premier Eric M. Gairy of Grenada led a two-party delegation to London to discuss arrangements for a constitutional conference in May 1973. Earlier, Antigua's premier, George Walter, said that his ruling Progressive Labor movement would campaign for complete independence in the 1976 general election.

The three Windward Islands—Grenada, St. Lucia, and St. Vincent—agreed on steps toward unification. The first elections in St. Vincent since statehood resulted in a 6–6 tie between the former ruling party, R. Milton Cato's St. Vincent Labour party, and the opposition People's Political party, led by Ebenezer Joshua. James Mitchell, the former minister of labor, won the independent seat, and after negotiating with Joshua's party, became prime minister.

Farther north, the political scene in Bermuda remained unchanged as a result of the general election, won by the ruling United Bermuda party. In the Bahamas' general election, Prime Minister Lynden O. Pindling won a landslide victory (29 out of a possible 38 seats) on the independence issue.

In Trinidad and Tobago, for the first time in any Commonwealth Caribbean country, manpower was subsidized by an employment allowance to medium-sized businesses in the hope of encouraging them to employ more staff and to work second shifts. Trinidad's oil discoveries came as a welcome economic boost in 1972. Large quantities of natural gas were also found, and a gas liquefaction plant was proposed. In October the government of Prime Minister Eric E. Williams decided to establish diplomatic relations with Cuba.

In July 1972, initiatives were reported that gave the East Caribbean Common Market (the Associated States and Montserrat) an association with the European Economic Community (EEC). Later it was announced that negotiations with the EEC for all Commonwealth Caribbean countries would be under the aegis of the Caribbean Free Trade Association. (*See in* CE: West Indies.)

WOMEN. The increased participation of women in U.S. political life made news in the election year of 1972. Women held prominent positions at both major political conventions. Anne Armstrong served as cochairman of the Republican convention and was later named by U.S. President Richard M. Nixon as a presidential counselor. Jean M. Westwood, chairman of the Democratic National Committee, was the first woman to head a major party's national committee. Other women prominent in the Democratic convention were Frances "Sissy" Farenthold, a Texas lawyer and legislator who received a vice-presidential nomination; Patricia Roberts Harris, chairman of the party's powerful Credentials Committee; California assemblywoman Yvonne Brathwaite Burke, cochairman of the convention; and the outspoken

Eleanor Hicks was appointed U.S. consul at Nice, France, in 1972.

JACQUES MUNCH FROM FRANCE SOIR

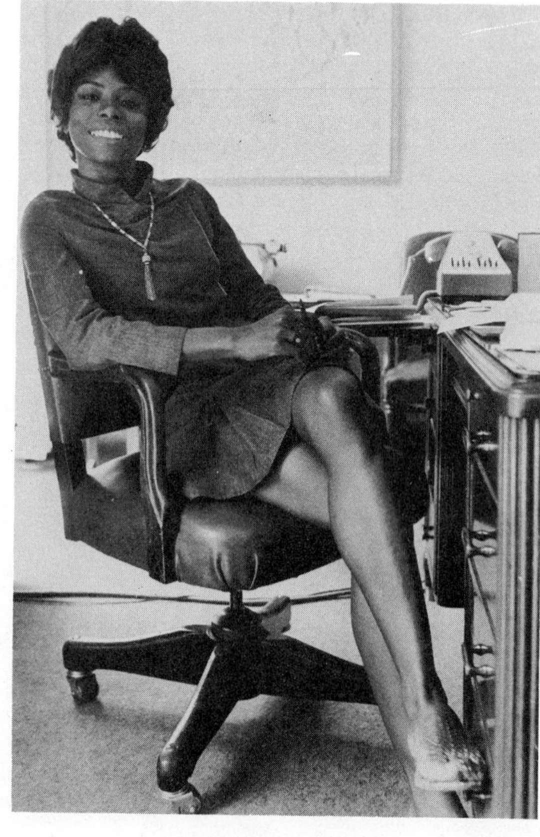

In June a group of demonstrators, primarily women, marched on Fifth Avenue in New York City to defend the right to legalized, safe abortions. A man demonstrated against abortion within the group, ignoring the sign "our bodies; our lives; our right to decide."

JOHN SOTO FROM "THE NEW YORK TIMES"

congresswoman from New York City, Bella S. Abzug. Perhaps the most influential woman involved in the 1972 election was U.S. Rep. Shirley Chisholm (D, N.Y.), the first woman to campaign as a major party presidential candidate and the first black woman to be placed in nomination by a major party. She came in third in the party's balloting, with 151.95 votes.

In line with the Democratic party's reform rules of 1969, there was an attempt to increase minority representation at the party's 1972 convention. About 38% of the delegates were women, a figure that did not reflect their proportion of the U.S. population. The question of proportional representation precipitated the convention's first roll call vote, in which the number of women in the South Carolina contingent was challenged. Another concern of the women delegates was the party's position on abortion. A liberal proposal backed by the women's caucus, but defeated 1,569.80 to 1,103.37, caused bitter infighting.

Women did come out of the elections with some concrete gains. According to the National Women's Political Caucus, there was an increase of nearly 20% in the number of women elected to state legislatures in 1972. On the national level, five women won seats in the House of Representatives and nine others were reelected, including Representative Chisholm. The failure of Senator Margaret Chase Smith (R, Me.) to win reelection after 32 years in the Senate left that body without a woman member.

Barriers against women in traditionally all-male fields continued to be broken down in 1972. The U.S. Navy named its first woman admiral, Alene Berthe Duerk, and announced that women would be given sea duty on noncombat ships. L. Patrick Gray III, acting director of the Federal Bureau of Investigation, opened the bureau's ranks to women agents. The Massachusetts Institute of Technology, a traditionally all-male institution that had been admitting increasing numbers of women students, named its first woman dean of student affairs. In New York, the state court of appeals ruled that a housewife could not be denied a position as a minor league umpire because of her sex. Although the first woman rabbi in the U.S. was ordained in 1972, the barriers against female clerics remained strong in many faiths. Pope Paul VI, in a September decree, prohibited women from the Roman Catholic ministry.

In March the U.S. Senate, voting 84–8, passed the 27th (equal rights) Amendment to the Constitution, prohibiting discrimination based on sex. Similar legislation had been blocked for nearly 49 years. Ratification by 38 states was needed before the amendment would take effect. (*See in* CE: Women and Women's Rights.)

Jean M. Westwood became the first Democratic National Committee chairwoman in 1972 but later in the year was forced to resign.

WIDE WORLD

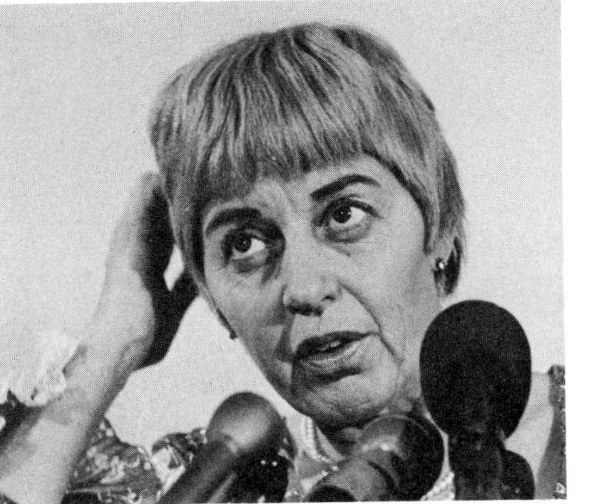

WORLD TRADE. The total value of world trade in 1972 was some 12% to 13% higher than in 1971. In the first half of the year, the growth was somewhat more rapid, but there were signs that this rate of increase was not being maintained.

An important feature of 1971 and 1972 was the extent to which prices of traded goods were rising. Throughout the 1960's world trade prices had risen by only about 1% per year. In the three years from mid-1969 to mid-1972, however, prices rose by no less than 18%, much of this increase occurring in 1971 and 1972. In addition to general and persistent inflationary pressures in all economies, there were two special factors making for price increases. First, agreements between the Organization of Petroleum Exporting Countries and the major international oil companies in the early part of 1971 raised the price of petroleum exports by more than 20%. Second, the appreciation of several major currencies during 1971 raised the dollar value of world trade by about 2%. As a result of these significant price increases, the growth in volume of world trade during 1972 was much less than the growth in value.

Balance of Trade

Primary producers' exports accelerated during the first half of 1972, and there were signs of an improving trade balance. Dollar prices of primary products increased sharply following the realignment of currencies at the end of 1971, and in mid-1972 the price index of primary producers' exports was 10% above the level of one year earlier. Particularly large increases were recorded in wool prices. The prices of most metals and minerals, however, continued to fall from the very high levels reached in 1969. By mid-1972 the average price of metals was 20% below the 1970 level.

The less developed primary producing countries (excluding the petroleum exporters) were faced with both falling export prices and a slackening demand, while the value of their imports continued to grow rapidly. Their trade balance came under considerable pressure. In the oil-producing countries of the Middle East the balance of trade was considerably more favorable.

Exports by industrial countries were 19% higher in the first half of 1972 than in the preceding year, while imports rose by 18%; the trade balance consequently improved further. The growth of Japanese exports eased off slightly, and North American and European exports accelerated.

The combined trade balance of the member countries of the European Economic Community (EEC) moved from equilibrium in 1970 to a small surplus in 1971 and to a moderately large surplus in 1972. Most of the members shared in this improvement, although the largest contribution—both to the overall balance and to the improvement—came from West Germany, where exports accelerated as the nation continued to increase its share of world trade in manufactured goods. In Italy and the Netherlands, trade deficits were steadily reduced in both 1971 and 1972.

KEYSTONE

Cows, bulls, and goats were transported from Kloten airport in Switzerland to the New Delhi airport as part of a large development project for stock farming in the Punjab area of India.

International Agreements

The conclusion of the Smithsonian Agreement in December 1971 set the stage for quieter and more long-term thinking on the adjustment of future international relations in matters of trade, investment, and development aid. There seemed to be a general awareness, however, that the international readjustment process would have to be revamped so that trade measures would play a more active role in redressing international disequilibrium. Foremost among the basic changes affecting international trade relations in 1972 were the redeployment of economic strength between the EEC, the U.S., and Japan; the growing importance—especially in Europe—of the process of regional integration; and the economic emergence and claims to assistance of developing countries.

The bilateral consultations between the U.S., the EEC, and Japan, which had started before the Smithsonian Agreement was reached, continued into 1972. By February they bore fruit, and joint statements on international economic relations were issued by Japan and the U.S. and by the EEC and the U.S. These were communicated to the contracting parties to the General Agreement on Tariffs and Trade (GATT), and they were invited to associate themselves with the declarations. The statements recognized the need for a comprehensive review of international economic relations and reaffirmed support for greater liberalization of world trade. Ultimately the statements amounted to a decision by the three leading traders to open multilateral negotiations in 1973, on the basis of mutual advantage and commitment, covering agricultural as well as industrial trade.

It was against a background of sustained, if groping, discussions of international monetary reform and prospects of multilateral trade negotiations, actively supported by industrialized countries, that the third session of the United Nations Conference on Trade and Development (UNCTAD) convened in April 1972 at Santiago, Chile. A number of sweeping resolutions were passed, greatly benefiting the trade position of developing countries. It was also claimed, as a matter of major importance, that the developing countries should be allowed to participate effectively in reforming the monetary system.

The enlargement of the EEC from six to nine members—with the accession of Denmark, Ireland, and Great Britain, effective Jan. 1, 1973—was not the only change affecting the pattern of world trade. The beginnings of reconciliation with the People's Republic of China opened new vistas of trade for the U.S. and several other countries. Of more immediate significance to East-West trade relations, however, was the U.S. signing in October of a detailed trade agreement with the Soviet Union. It called for granting of most-favored-nation treatment to Soviet imports and provided for an estimated threefold increase of trade between the two countries, reaching some $1.5 billion in three years. The U.S. Congress was expected to ratify the agreement early in 1973. The U.S.S.R. made a large purchase of grain from the U.S. in 1972. (*See* Agriculture.)

The 28th session of the contracting parties to GATT opened in November, officially placing on record their collective intention to begin multilateral negotiations in 1973. The member countries had by then gained sufficient confidence to announce a timetable and to outline the coverage of the negotiations. It was agreed that the multilateral trade negotiations should aim to secure additional benefits for the international trade of the developing countries, so as to achieve a substantial increase in their foreign-exchange earnings, diversification of exports, and trade growth.

The member nations further agreed that a preparatory committee, with open membership, would be set up to develop methods and procedures. The committee's report was scheduled to be examined at a ministerial meeting in September 1973, when the negotiations proper were expected to start. (*See also* Economy; Money and International Finance. *See in* CE: International Trade.)

This U.S. wheat being unloaded in the Soviet port of Odessa was bought under an agreement whereby the U.S. would sell at least $750 million worth of American wheat, corn, and other grains to the Soviet Union over three years. But by the end of August the Soviets had already spent almost $1 billion.

BOB BRIGHAM FROM LIFE MAGAZINE © TIME INC.

YEMEN ARAB REPUBLIC (Sana).

In 1972 the Yemen Arab Republic took steps to strengthen relations with the West and with conservative Saudi Arabia and to lessen the influence of the Soviet Union, from which Yemen had received military assistance. Saudi Arabia, Kuwait, and several Western countries furnished aid to alleviate the nation's severe economic conditions. In July Yemen and the U.S. renewed diplomatic relations, which had been severed during the 1967 Arab-Israeli war, and the U.S. agreed to resume economic aid. Yemen maintained warm relations with the People's Republic of China and North Korea.

In September warfare broke out once more between Yemen and the People's Democratic Republic of Yemen, or Southern Yemen; the two had fought intermittently along their frontier for three years. Yemen occupied a Southern Yemeni island in the Red Sea and accused Southern Yemen of using Soviet and Iraqi pilots to bomb Yemeni towns. Each side accused the other of trying to unify the two Yemens by force. Through Arab League mediation a cease-fire was called and peace talks were undertaken in Cairo, Egypt. In November an agreement was signed providing for unification and for the establishment of committees to draft a constitution and plan the merger. Measures to repatriate refugees and eliminate subversion and insurgent training were to be taken immediately. (*See also* Middle East; Yemen, People's Democratic Republic of. *See in* CE: Yemen.)

YEMEN, PEOPLE'S DEMOCRATIC REPUBLIC OF (Aden).

In 1972 armed conflict broke out between Southern Yemen and neighboring Oman. Hostilities were renewed with the Yemen Arab Republic (Sana), which was backed by Southern Yemen's third neighbor, Saudi Arabia. The Marxist regime, considered the most radical Arab government, continued to receive military and economic support from the Soviet Union and the People's Republic of China and some aid from the leftist regimes of Iraq and Algeria. The influential National Liberation Front declared support for a Persian Gulf revolution and for a progressive Arab front against "imperialism."

In May Oman accused Southern Yemen of launching attacks to help Dhofari insurgents in Oman; in reprisal, Omani planes bombed the Southern Yemeni frontier. In the fall a long-standing conflict with the Yemen Arab Republic erupted into serious border fighting. Mediation by the Arab League led to a cease-fire and to peace talks in Cairo, Egypt, at which the two Yemens agreed on procedures for uniting their countries.

Southern Yemen nationalized all its hotels, cinemas, and privately owned buildings and shops. Poor peasants were allowed to seize land from large landholders. (*See also* Middle East; Yemen Arab Republic. *See in* CE: Aden.)

YOUTH ORGANIZATIONS.

In 1972, youth organizations in the U.S. continued their vigorous membership drives and stepped up their campaigns aimed at eliminating racism throughout the nation. Programs and ideals were evaluated in terms of the contemporary social environment.

Boys' Clubs of America

One highlight of the year for the Boys' Clubs of America was the dedication of the 1,000th Boys' Club on October 8 in Indianapolis, Ind. Another was the enrollment in December of the one millionth Boys' Club member.

A significant event was the appointment in September of William R. Bricker as national director of the 112-year-old guidance organization for youths. Bricker, 49, who began as a member of the Olivet, Pa., Boys' Club and had spent 25 years in the field, replaced A. Boyd Hinds, who retired after 44 years with the Boys' Clubs movement. During National Boys' Club Week, April 9–15, Rodrigo Guerra, 16, of the Pasadena, Calif., Boys' Club was honored by being named the 26th Boy of the Year.

Boy Scouts of America

The program of the Boy Scouts of America for Scouts, ages 11–18, was revised in 1972 to provide more options and opportunities for decision making in the advancement area. Bright red berets were one of the new uniform options. Norton Clapp, chairman of Weyerhaeuser Co., was reelected president in Los Angeles at the 62d annual meeting.

Project SOAR (Save Our American Resources) involved an estimated 4 million Scouts and adults in a national drive against litter in which they collected nearly 1½ million tons of trash and moved recyclable materials to reclamation centers. (*See in* CE: Boy Scouts of America.)

Camp Fire Girls

The Camp Fire Girls' policy-making body, the National Council, opened membership in the national organization to boys of high school age in 1972. According to Gwen Harper, director of program development, this move was in line with contemporary trends toward more casual and informal education directly connected to daily living. Group leadership, formerly restricted to women, was opened to men. (*See in* CE: Camp Fire Girls.)

Future Farmers of America

In 1972 the Future Farmers of America (FFA) had several new programs that led to increased involvement of the vocational youth organization's 430,000 members. Programs in safety, community development, and occupational proficiency were included during the year.

The 45th National FFA Convention, held in Kansas City, Mo., attracted a record 14,368 FFA members and guests. The highest awards, Star Farmer and Star Agribusinessman of America,

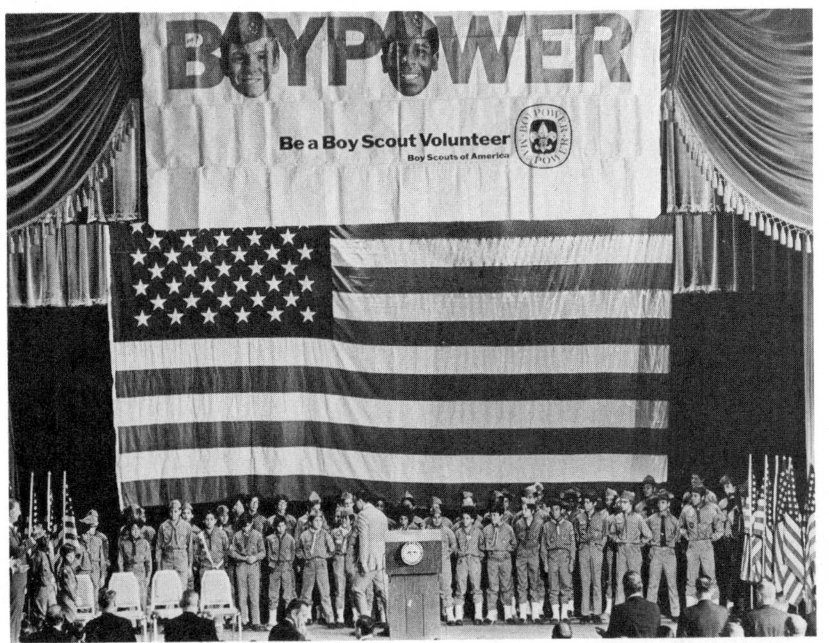

The 62d birthday of the Boy Scouts of America was celebrated in February 1972. The scouts planned to be more responsive to the needs of members and prospective members. Vice-President Spiro T. Agnew (far left) attended the scouts' Dawn Patrol Breakfast in New York City, and he praised the organization for its efforts to preserve the environment.

NEAL BOENZI FROM "THE NEW YORK TIMES"

were presented to David Galley, 20, a dairy farmer from Garrattsville, N.Y., and Edward Higley, 19, a logger from Brattleboro, Vt.

Future Homemakers of America

To effectively serve all students of home economics education in the secondary schools, the Future Homemakers of America (FHA) expanded its program and established home economics related occupations (HERO) chapters for students. At the close of this program's first year, 1972 membership figures showed that 10,000 youths in 28 states had joined 350 HERO chapters. FHA chapters for students in consumer education and in homemaking and family life education and HERO chapters for students in home economics related occupations had the same overall purpose—to help individuals improve personal, family, and community living as well as to give career guidance.

Girls Clubs of America

New Girls Clubs opened at the rate of approximately two a month in 1972, and many older Girls Clubs used mobile units and extension programs in storefronts and public housing projects to reach school-age girls not being served by other youth agencies. By the end of the year, membership had increased by 15,600, bringing the total to 130,600.

The first international convention—the 27th annual conference—was held in Toronto, Ont., on

These children practice minibike drills in a California parking lot under the auspices of the National Youth Project Using Minibikes, which was developed by the YMCA to involve court-referred youths. Honda Motor Co., Ltd., of Tokyo, Japan, through American Honda, contributed 10,000 minibikes to the project.

COURTESY, NATIONAL COUNCIL OF YMCA'S

COURTESY, NATIONAL COUNCIL OF YMCA'S

Outreach volunteers, experienced YMCA ghetto workers, mingled with protestors at the political conventions in Miami Beach—providing information, first aid, and personal help.

April 4–7, with 300 adult delegates and 80 teenage delegates in attendance. Mrs. Harold G. Kazanjian of Waterbury, Conn., was reelected to serve a second two-year term as national president.

Girl Scouts of the United States of America

Decision making by girls was given impetus when the "voices of youth" were heard at the 1972 convention of the National Council, Girl Scouts of the United States of America, held in Dallas, Tex., in October. More than 360 Senior Girl Scouts (ages 14–17), selected by their respective Girl Scout councils attended.

Drug abuse was another Girl Scout concern in 1972. Through education and example, Girl Scouts were involved in many projects toward prevention of drug abuse. (*See in* CE: Girl Scouts.)

Junior Achievement

Junior Achievement (JA) in 1972 continued its work as a practical program of business education for high school students of all socioeconomic backgrounds. Fostering a learn-by-doing laboratory approach, the program entered its 52d year of operation with 161,000 members (Achievers), who created and operated 7,000 miniature business enterprises with the aid of 23,225 adult volunteers.

In addition to the JA program during the school year, the organization operated a summer job-education program for 1,900 disadvantaged inner-city youths in 22 communities.

Young Men's Christian Association

Extensive development of new programs and expansion of existing ones marked 1972 for the Young Men's Christian Association (YMCA). Teams of Outreach workers from around the country, totaling more than 150 staff members and volunteers, worked the "edge of crisis" at the Democratic and Republican national conventions, held in Miami Beach, Fla.

To encourage a climate of order among hundreds of protesting youths who had flocked to Miami and were constantly demonstrating, Y Miami Outreach dispensed information through telephone, radio van, and walkie-talkie. A daily news sheet dispelled dangerous rumors, gave information on bad drugs, and related immediate events. (*See in* CE: Young Men's Christian Association.)

Young Women's Christian Association

A strategic step in advancing one imperative of the Young Women's Christian Association (YWCA), the elimination of racism wherever it exists and by any means necessary, occurred in New York City. There, on June 15, 1972, more than 3,000 delegates answered the call to the YWCA National Convocation on Racial Justice.

The convocation, cosponsored by 107 voluntary and government organizations, was attended by representatives from 5 continents and 44 states: young and old, women and men, of all racial backgrounds and life-styles—Asian American, black, Mexican American, native American, Puerto Rican, and white. All convened for one purpose: to mobilize sustained action to eliminate institutionalized racism in community and national life. (*See in* CE: Young Women's Christian Association.)

YUGOSLAVIA. Nationalist sentiments in the Yugoslav member republics were a critical domestic issue in 1972. The enforced resignation in December 1971 of Croatian regional leaders—who had been accused by President Tito of nationalistic and counterrevolutionary activities—was followed by a widespread purge of the Croatian party, administration, judiciary, and university. In January, at a national Communist party conference in Belgrade, the capital, Tito denied that there was a crisis in Croatia but conceded that the country's governmental structure was in need of strengthening. The scope of the political purges was widened in the fall. Accusations of resurgent nationalism in the other republics led to the replacement of key party leaders in Serbia, Slovenia, and Macedonia.

Numerous student leaders and prominent intellectuals accused of Croatian nationalism were arrested and brought to trial during the summer and fall. In October the four main leaders of the student strike in Zagreb in November 1971 received sentences of up to four years' imprisonment. Later the editor of the banned Zagreb newspaper *Hrvatska Tiednik* was sentenced to four years.

In July a band of armed Croatian émigrés entered the country illegally and managed to inflict 13 casualties on the security forces. This incursion and the hijacking by three young Croats of a Scandinavian DC-9 passenger plane resulted in a vigorous Yugoslav diplomatic campaign aimed at persuading Western governments to ban exiled Yugoslav political organizations.

Inflation continued to be a serious problem in 1972. Prices of bread, margarine, cooking oil, and sugar were raised in October, causing the cost of living—already up 16%—to increase by another 1.56%. A campaign to reduce the widening gap between the workers and the wealthy privileged class led to the denunciation of what Tito termed the "bourgeois consumer-society mentality." Yugoslavia's modified form of Marxism had allowed some businessmen to amass sizable private fortunes. This practice was strongly condemned during 1972.

The highlight of Yugoslavia's diplomatic year was the state visit by Great Britain's Queen Elizabeth II, which took place October 17–21. The most significant foreign-policy event was President Tito's visit to the U.S.S.R. in June. On the first day of the visit, the 80-year-old Tito was awarded the Order of Lenin, the Soviet Union's highest decoration for foreigners. Later in the year the U.S.S.R. agreed to provide Yugoslavia with $540 million worth of industrial equipment.

In mid-July the Moscow session of the Council for Mutual Economic Assistance was attended for the first time by the Yugoslav premier, Djemal Bijedić, who announced that Yugoslavia would enter into closer collaboration with the group in various fields, although formally retaining its observer-member status. (*See in* CE: Yugoslavia.)

ZAIRE. Serious economic problems faced Zaire (formerly the Democratic Republic of the Congo) in 1972. Lower prices offered for copper, which accounted for more than half the country's exports, resulted in a considerable reduction of income. The government was urged to encourage agricultural expansion while trying to increase mining revenues and industrial output. The state was taking an increasingly active role in the economy.

Continuing the campaign for a return to African authenticity, President Joseph D. Mobutu dropped his Christian names in 1972 and became Mobutu Sese Seko. Zaireans were ordered to take African names also. Katanga was renamed Shaba on New Year's Day, and Stanley Pool became Malebo Pool. A bill was authorized by the national assembly requiring all Zairean nationals having a Zairean mother and a foreign father to adopt the mother's name. These changes were followed by a sharp official attack on Joseph-Albert Cardinal Malula, the Roman Catholic archbishop of Kinshasa, the capital, for having allegedly opposed the authenticity campaign. Malula left Zaire after he was expelled from his residence in February. Under an uneasy truce with Mobutu, he returned from Rome in June. (*See* Religion.)

The first congress of Mobutu's Popular Movement of the Revolution was held in May. It was attended by 7 heads of state in addition to more than 1,000 delegates from Zaire itself. (*See in* CE: Congo, Democratic Republic of the.)

ZAMBIA. On Feb. 4, 1972, President Kenneth D. Kaunda of Zambia banned the United Progressive party and placed its leaders under restriction for having allegedly attempted by a variety of methods, some of them involving considerable danger to life and property, to isolate the Bemba of the northern province from the rest of the country. Shortly afterward the president appointed a commission to recommend ways of introducing a one-party state, and on his receipt of its report a bill was published on October 30 banning all parties in opposition to the ruling United National Independence party. The bill also proposed to give the Zambian armed forces direct representation (along with the church, the traditional chiefs, and the University of Zambia) in parliament. Although it was bitterly opposed by opposition leader Harry Nkumbula of the African National Congress, who warned that it could lead to civil war, the measure was passed by the National Assembly on December 8 by a 78–0 vote. Nkumbula and his supporters had walked out before the vote was taken.

On May 26 a bomb in a parcel addressed to President Kaunda exploded when opened by a secretary, who was blinded and lost an arm. The president was out of Lusaka, the capital, at the time. The incident was not officially regarded as part of any conspiracy.

In the economic sphere 1972 opened unfavorably for the government. Low prices for copper, as well as a decline in copper production, had produced a record balance-of-payments deficit of $284.8 million. Agricultural production fell below expected levels. This situation had led to the devaluation of the currency by 8% in December 1971, and early in 1972 President Kaunda outlined a five-year plan (1972–76) to combat the difficulties facing the country. Inevitably, recovery would depend largely on developing the copper resources, and an increase in output of 39.5% above the 1971 level was looked for over the next five years. The scarcely developed manufacturing industry was also expected to show a considerable growth rate, while marked increases in agricultural production were demanded. Government spending for 1972 was cut by 30%, although there was no serious reduction in capital expenditure for fear a reduction might lead to large-scale unemployment. The fall in export earnings in the preceding year was countered by an increase in taxation on what were deemed luxury goods. In addition, there were to be no further imports of corn from Rhodesia. (*See also* Africa. *See in* CE: Zambia.)

ZOOS. Recognizing their important role in the preservation and propagation of endangered animal species, many zoos joined the Wild Animal Propagation Trust during 1972. The trust program coordinated breeding of rare animals through the keeping of records concerning bloodlines and breeding habits. A number of zoos had also begun to keep studbooks that contain information about every specimen of a particular endangered animal. Through studbook records, important information can be gathered and distributed about zoo animals.

Many new zoos and safari parks were opened during the year. The new zoo in Blackpool, England, was the largest municipal zoo in the country. New safari parks were due to open in Spain and Italy, and the San Diego Zoo in California officially opened its San Pasquale Wild Animal Park.

Luxurious new quarters for a variety of animals were completed in several countries. The Bronx Zoo in New York City opened its $4-million World of Birds, which featured natural habitats with a minimum of glass or wire barriers. In Berlin, West Germany, a new ape house was completed that was the most expensive project that zoo had ever undertaken. Ape houses were also opened in the Tokyo and Frankfurt, West Germany, zoos, while a new dolphin exhibit was completed in Whipsnade, England. Perhaps the happiest recipients of new housing were the gorillas at Twycross, England, whose new quarters contained a tiled kitchen, sunken bath, and color television set.

Several rare births were recorded at zoos in 1972. An aardvark was successfully bred and reared at the Crandon Park Zoo in Miami, Fla., and the Frankfurt Zoo welcomed Cameroon bareheaded rock fowl and crested bustards. Pardel lynx were bred for the first time at Luciano Spinelli's zoo in Rome, and Bawean deer were bred successfully in Surabaja, Indonesia. At the Central Park Zoo in New York City, a five-pound baby was born to a seven-year-old gorilla, Lulu, whose keepers had been unaware that she was pregnant. The baby was named Sonny Jim, and Lulu was so possessive of her offspring that it was not until nine days later that her embarrassed keepers learned that Sonny Jim was a girl. A naming contest was held and she was renamed Patty-Cake.

The year's most famous animal celebrities were Ling-ling and Hsing-hsing, the young giant pandas from the People's Republic of China. They arrived at the Smithsonian Institution's National Zoological Park in Washington, D.C., in April. (*See* Animals and Wildlife Special Report. *See in* CE: Zoo.)

COURTESY, LION COUNTRY SAFARI, INC.

Frasier, the sensuous lion, rests with one of his many offspring. The aged lion (18 or 19 years old) died in July at his home in California.

The San Diego wild animal park is designed to show visitors the animals in their natural habitats—areas resembling East Africa, South Africa, North Africa, Asian plains, and Indian swamps. The Wgasa Bush Line monorail gives visitors a tour of the exhibits beginning and ending at the Nairobi village shown here.

AUTHENTICATED NEWS INTERNATIONAL

Calendar for 1973

januaryfebruarymarchaprilmayjunejulyaugustseptemberoctobernovemberdecember

Mon. **1** New Year's Day. Major football bowl games. Tournament of Roses parade. Boy Scouts of America Operation Reach and Project Soar begin.
Fri. **5** Twelfth Night.
Sat. **6** Twelfth Day, or Epiphany. Carnival season begins.
Sun. **7** Millard Fillmore's birthday.
Tues. **9** Richard M. Nixon's birthday. National Stop Smoking Week begins.
Sat. **13** Stephen Foster Memorial Day.
Mon. **15** Birthday of Martin Luther King, Jr.
Sun. **28** International Clergy Week begins.
Mon. **29** William McKinley's birthday.
Tues. **30** Franklin Delano Roosevelt's birthday.

Thurs. **1** National Freedom Day. American Heart Month begins.
Fri. **2** Candlemas. Groundhog Day.
Sun. **4** National Children's Dental Health Week begins.
Thurs. **8** Boy Scouts of America 63d birthday.
Fri. **9** William Henry Harrison's birthday.
Sun. **11** National Crime Prevention Week begins.
Mon. **12** Abraham Lincoln's birthday.
Wed. **14** Saint Valentine's Day.
Sat. **17** National Parent Teachers Association Founders Day.
Sun. **18** Brotherhood Week, Catholic Book Week, and National Engineers' Week begin.
Mon. **19** George Washington's birthday.

Thurs. **1** Red Cross Month and Easter Seal Campaign begin.
Sun. **4** Save Your Vision Week begins.
Mon. **5** Crispus Attucks Day.
Tues. **6** Shrove Tuesday. Mardi Gras.
Wed. **7** Ash Wednesday.
Sun. **11** Girl Scout Week begins.
Thurs. **15** Andrew Jackson's birthday. The Ides of March. Buzzard Day.
Fri. **16** James Madison's birthday.
Sat. **17** Saint Patrick's Day.
Sun. **18** Purim. Grover Cleveland's birthday. Camp Fire Girls Birthday Week begins.
Tues. **20** Spring begins.
Thurs. **29** John Tyler's birthday.

Sun. **1** April Fools' Day. Cancer Control Month begins.
Mon. **2** International Children's Book Day.
Sun. **8** Pan American Week and National Boys' Club Week begin.
Fri. **13** Thomas Jefferson's birthday.
Sat. **14** Pan American Day.
Sun. **15** Palm Sunday.
Tues. **17** Passover begins.
Fri. **20** Good Friday.
Sun. **22** Easter Sunday.
Mon. **23** James Buchanan's birthday.
Fri. **27** Ulysses S. Grant's birthday.
Sat. **28** James Monroe's birthday.
Sun. **29** Daylight saving time begins.

Tues. **1** Law Day. Loyalty Day.
Sat. **5** Kentucky Derby.
Sun. **6** Humane Sunday. National Be Kind to Animals Week begins.
Tues. **8** Harry S. Truman's birthday. World Red Cross Day.
Sun. **13** Mother's Day.
Mon. **14** National Salvation Army Week begins.
Fri. **18** National Defense Transportation Day.
Sat. **19** Armed Forces Day.
Mon. **21** Lindbergh flight anniversary. Victoria Day.
Tues. **22** National Maritime Day.
Mon. **28** Memorial Day.
Tues. **29** John F. Kennedy's birthday.

Fri. **1** National Rose Month, National Ragweed Control Month, and Cat and Kitten Month begin.
Sun. **3** Jefferson Davis' birthday.
Wed. **6** Shavuot, or Feast of Weeks, begins.
Fri. **8** National Fraternal Week begins.
Sun. **10** Pentecost. National Flag Week begins.
Mon. **11** National Little League Baseball Week begins.
Thurs. **14** Flag Day. Man and His World Exhibition, Montreal, Que., opens.
Sun. **17** Father's Day. Trinity Sunday.
Thurs. **21** Summer begins.
Sat. **23** Midsummer Eve.
Tues. **26** St. Lawrence Seaway anniversary.

Sun. 1 Dominion Day, Canada. National Safe Boating Week begins.
Wed. 4 Independence Day, or Fourth of July. Calvin Coolidge's birthday. Louis Armstrong's birthday.
Thurs. 5 Calgary Stampede, Alberta, Canada, begins.
Wed. 11 John Quincy Adams' birthday.
Sun. 15 Captive Nations Week and National Hispanic Heritage Week begin.
Thurs. 19 First Women's Rights Convention anniversary.
Fri. 20 Moon Day.
Tues. 24 Pioneer Day.
Wed. 25 Secretaries Day.

Wed. 1 U.S.A. Sports Day. Boy Scouts of America National Jamboree begins.
Sat. 4 Coast Guard Day.
Sun. 5 Friendship Day.
Mon. 6 Hiroshima Day.
Tues. 7 Tish ah b'Ab, or Fast of Ab.
Fri. 10 Herbert Hoover's birthday.
Tues. 14 Atlantic Charter Day. Victory Day.
Wed. 15 Assumption Day.
Sun. 19 National Aviation Day.
Mon. 20 Benjamin Harrison's birthday.
Sun. 26 Susan B. Anthony Day. Women's Equality Day. Women's Liberation Day.
Mon. 27 Lyndon B. Johnson's birthday.
Thurs. 30 Expo Quebec opens.

Sat. 1 American Youth Month begins.
Mon. 3 Labor Day.
Wed. 12 Harvest Moon.
Sat. 15 William Howard Taft's birthday.
Mon. 17 Citizenship Day. Expectant Fathers Day. World Peace Day.
Fri. 21 American Newspaper Anniversary Week begins.
Sat. 22 Autumn begins.
Sun. 23 National Dog Week begins.
Thurs. 27 Rosh Hashanah, or Jewish New Year, begins.
Fri. 28 American Indian Day.
Sat. 29 Michaelmas. Ramadan begins.
Sun. 30 Gold Star Mother's Day.

october

Thurs. 4 Rutherford B. Hayes's birthday.
Fri. 5 Chester A. Arthur's birthday.
Sat. 6 Yom Kippur, or Day of Atonement.
Mon. 8 Columbus Day. Child Health Day.
Thurs. 11 General Pulaski's Memorial Day. Sukkot, or Feast of Tabernacles, begins.
Sun. 14 Dwight D. Eisenhower's birthday. National School Lunch Week begins.
Sat. 20 Sweetest Day.
Mon. 22 Veterans, or Armistice, Day.
Wed. 24 United Nations Day.
Sat. 27 Theodore Roosevelt's birthday.
Sun. 28 Daylight saving time ends.
Tues. 30 John Adams' birthday.
Wed. 31 Halloween. National UNICEF Day.

Thurs. 1 All Saints', or All Hallows', Day.
Fri. 2 All Souls' Day. James Knox Polk's birthday. Warren G. Harding's birthday. World Community Day.
Sun. 4 International Cat Week begins.
Tues. 6 General election day.
Sat. 10 Marine Corps birthday.
Sun. 11 Veterans Day. Remembrance Day.
Sun. 18 Bible Sunday. Bible Week and Latin America Week begin.
Mon. 19 James A. Garfield's birthday.
Wed. 21 International Aviation Month begins.
Thurs. 22 Thanksgiving Day.
Fri. 23 Franklin Pierce's birthday.
Sat. 24 Zachary Taylor's birthday.

december

Sun. 2 Advent begins.
Wed. 5 Martin Van Buren's birthday.
Fri. 7 Pearl Harbor Day.
Mon. 10 Nobel prize ceremony.
Sat. 15 Bill of Rights Day.
Mon. 17 Pan American Aviation Day.
Thurs. 20 Hanukkah, or Feast of Lights, begins.
Fri. 21 Winter begins. Forefathers' Day.
Sat. 22 International Arbor Day.
Mon. 24 Christmas Eve.
Tues. 25 Christmas Day.
Wed. 26 Boxing Day.
Fri. 28 Woodrow Wilson's birthday.
Sat. 29 Andrew Johnson's birthday.
Mon. 31 New Year's Eve.

New Words

from

The following list of new words and new meanings has been prepared by the permanent editorial staff of G. & C. Merriam Company of Springfield, Massachusetts, publishers of *Webster's Third New International Dictionary* and *Webster's Seventh New Collegiate Dictionary* and other dictionaries in the Merriam-Webster Series.

A

accommodation collar *n* : a prearranged arrest (as by a bribed policeman) of an unimportant member of an illegal gambling operation on evidence too flimsy to result in a conviction

ad-hocracy *n* : an ad hoc organization set up to handle a particular project

adscape *n* : a scene (as along a highway) in which advertising billboards predominate

air piracy *n* : the hijacking of a flying airplane : SKYJACKING

alternative society *n* : a society of young people whose values and lifestyles run counter to those of established society — called also *counterculture*

anticommercial *n* : a commercial against a product advertised in another commercial

apostrophobe *n* : a writer who avoids the use of apostrophes

B

beefacue *n* : barbecued beefsteak

bike-in *n* : a gathering of bicyclists for the purpose of demonstrating in favor of the construction of bikeways

blippo *vb* : to subject to failure or disaster : RUIN

boge *adj, of a drug addict* : affected with withdrawal symptoms

brain-fade *n* : a mistake in judgment by a racing driver

button topper *n* : an ornamental covering (as of metal) that fits over a shirt button

C

cablecast *vb* : to telecast by cable television

caissiana *n* : materials concerned with chess

carnography *n* : the depiction (as in motion pictures) of gory acts of violence

cephalocide *n* : the systematic liquidation of the intellectual leaders of a group

chain-snacker *n* : one who continually eats snacks

chicanismo *n*, *often cap* : strong ethnic pride exhibited by Chicanos

conceptual art *n* : art in which the concept conveyed is more important than what is utilized or created

condomaximum *n* : a very large building containing condominiums

counter-ad *n* : a commercial against a claim made in another commercial

counterculture *n* : ALTERNATIVE SOCIETY

crisis center *n* : a facility run by nonprofessionals who counsel those who telephone for help in a personal crisis

Crow Jimism *n* : partiality toward Negroes in hiring and promotion policies

cry-print *n* : a spectrographically produced pattern of the cry of an infant that is used for detecting physiological abnormalities — **cry-printing** *n*

D

dap *n* : a slapping together of the right hands of two people as a greeting or sign of friendship

decathlete *n* : an athlete specializing in the decathlon

dictationese *n* : the unpolished language characteristically used in dictating

dingbat *n* : a stupid or unsophisticated person : NITWIT

dope opera *n* : a motion picture whose story deals with the illicit use of drugs

doublespeak *n* : the oral use of two dialects of the same language : BIDIALECTALISM — **doublespeaker** *n*

dustscape *n* : a terrain covered with dust

E

ecocatastrophe *n* : a major destructive upset in the balance of nature especially when caused by the intervention of man

eco-guerrilla *n* : an activist who uses destructive violence (as firebombing) against environmental polluters

ecotage *n* : destructive or obstructive action designed to publicize and embarrass environmental polluters

ephebiatrist *n* : a specialist in the medical and emotional treatment of teenagers

F

fat farm *n* : a commercial health resort for overweight people

feticide *n* : ABORTION

filmlegging *n* : the illegal duplicating, selling, or buying of copyrighted films — **filmlegger** *n*

flipping *n* : the charging of interest on interest (as by a loan shark)

futuriasis *n* : a morbid fixation on or fear of the future

G

gazumping *n*, *Brit* : the raising of the agreed price (as of a house) after an offer has been accepted

glascrete *n* : concrete in which ground glass is the aggregate

Godrock *n* : rock music with lyrics referring to God

God squad *n* : a group of clergymen who volunteer to work part-time with a municipal police department

Green Machine *n* : the administrative structure of the U.S. army : the military establishment

gyro *n* : a sandwich of Greek origin that contains lamb, tomato, and onion

H

hatchback *n* **1** : a back on a closed passenger automobile (as a coupe) having an upward-opening hatch **2** : an automobile having a hatchback

heightism *n* : discrimination against short people

helicop *n* : a policeman on patrol in a helicopter

henocide *n* : the slaughter of hens in an effort to drive egg prices up

hiker-biker *n* : a site (as along a bicycle route) with camping and picnicking facilities

hippoisie *n* : the hip middle class

househusband *n* : a husband who manages the domestic affairs of a household

house sitter *n* : one who is paid to live in a house while the occupants are away

hydrolig *n* : a liquid-filled plastic bag that is worn around the knee (as of a football player) to protect the ligaments

I

interventurism *n* : involvement in power struggles abroad

J

jay-cycling *n* : riding a bicycle in a careless or illegal manner so as to be endangered by traffic

Jesus boot *n* : one of a pair of hollow box-shaped boots (as of wood and polystyrene) designed to allow the wearer to walk on water — called also *watershoe*

jet lag *n* : the fatigue resulting from travel in a jet plane through several time zones

jokelore *n* : traditional jokes preserved orally among a group of people (as musicians)

jones *n pl* : the withdrawal pains experienced by a drug addict

K

kickaholic *n* : one who continually seeks kicks and thrills — **kickaholism** *n*

kiddismo *n* : indulgent catering to the wishes of children

kite *n*, *specif* : a letter to the police that complains about an illegal gambling operation

L

living will *n* : a written declaration in which a person requests that if he becomes disabled beyond reasonable expectation of recovery he be allowed to die in dignity rather than be kept alive by artificial means

M

Manglish *n* : English words considered discriminatory toward women

MCP *abbr* male chauvinist pig

media ecology *n* **:** the study of the interaction between people and the mass communications media

mediagenic *adj* **:** likely to appeal to the audiences of the mass media and especially television

mediography *n* **:** a list of available audiovisual materials relating to a course of study

micropolis *n* **:** a very small city

middle college *n* **:** a 3-year liberal arts program at a university that admits students who have completed the 10th grade and that includes courses normally covered in the last two years of high school and the first two years of college

Mimosa *n* **:** a mixed drink consisting of orange juice and champagne

monster *n*, *specif* **:** a drug that stimulates the central nervous system

Moses Freak *n* **:** a youth who strictly observes traditional Jewish teachings and mores

mud bed *n* **:** a bed consisting of a wooden frame filled with mud and covered with a vinyl sheet

muscleship *n* **:** an athletic scholarship

N

nastyism *n* **:** an underhanded or spiteful comment

nitwitticism *n* **:** a stupid or silly remark

noise map *n* **:** a map of a city that indicates the noise level of each street

nut *n*, *specif* **:** a bribe given to a policeman

O

oillionaire *n* **:** a millionaire whose wealth derives from the petroleum industry

open classroom *n* **:** a system of education in which activities involving multidisciplinary skills replace traditional subject courses

open dating *n* **:** the marking of perishable products (as bakery and dairy items) with the date on which the product was packaged or after which it should not be sold

P

paintural *n* **:** a three-dimensional artwork that is a combination of painting and sculpture

parajacker *n* **:** a skyjacker who escapes by parachuting

performance contracting *n* **:** a system of education in which a private company contracts to bring the performance of a failing public school student up to an acceptable level in specified subject areas

phone freak *or* **phone phreak** *n* **:** one who illegally uses an electronic device to make long-distance telephone calls without paying for them

pimpmobile *n* **:** a customized luxury car used by a pimp

pragel *n* **:** a bagel shaped like a pretzel

prehumous *adj* **:** existing or occurring before one's death ⟨a *prehumous* monument⟩

prequel *n* **:** a literary work whose narrative sequentially precedes that of an earlier work

product-recall insurance *n* **:** insurance against losses suffered by the forced recall of a company's products that are declared potentially dangerous

psytocracy *n* **:** a form of government in which the citizens are psychologically manipulated for political purposes

Q

quadraphony *n* **:** the transmission, recording, or reproduction of sound by techniques that utilize four transmission channels — **quadraphonic** *adj*

R

Reuben pie *n* **:** a pie whose filling includes sauerkraut, corned beef, and Swiss cheese

rumtini *n* **:** a martini made with rum

S

saccharinize *vb* **:** to make agreeable or pleasing

setnapping *n* **:** the holding of a TV set in a repair shop until the usually exorbitant bill is paid — **setnapper** *n*

simp *n* **:** a small-time pimp

skin-search *vb* **:** to examine the denuded body of a prisoner for contraband

skiwardess *n* **:** a woman who serves hot beverages to skiers waiting in line for a ski lift

socspeak *n* **:** jargon used by sociologists

spare-changing *n* **:** the act or practice of panhandling

spider *n*, *specif* **:** the last shot of liquor in a bottle at a bar that is usually served gratis

stutel *n* **:** an inexpensive European hotel for traveling students

T

tapsichorean *adj* **:** of or relating to tap dancing ⟨the *tapsichorean* art⟩

technethics *n* **:** the responsible use of science, technology, and ethics in a society shaped by technology

telemedicine *n* **:** the practice of medicine via television

Tio Taco *n* **:** a Mexican-American who submissively accepts the values of Anglo-American society

transshipper *n* **:** an authorized dealer who ships to unauthorized discount outlets merchandise received from his supplier

U

uni-specs *n pl* **:** sunglasses designed for wear by either men or women

upfront *adj* **:** HONEST, STRAIGHTFORWARD

urbiphobia *n* **:** a fear of or aversion to cities

V

visual literacy *n* **:** the ability to discriminate and interpret the visible actions, objects, and symbols encountered in one's environment

voicespondence *n* **:** communication between persons by an exchange of tape-recorded messages — **voicespond** *vb* — **voicesponder** *n*

VOLAR *abbr* volunteer army

W

watershoe *n* **:** JESUS BOOT

weep-easy *n* **:** one who is given to extravagant displays of sympathy

windsurfing *n* **:** riding on a surfboard that is equipped with a sail

Y

yips *n* **:** a psychological state in a golfer that is characterized by the inability to execute a crucial putt

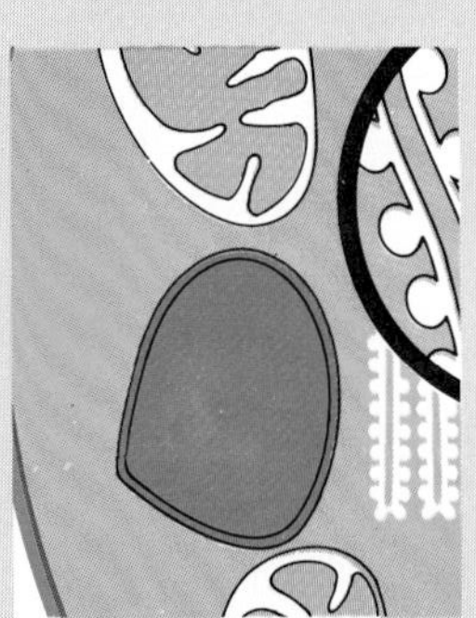

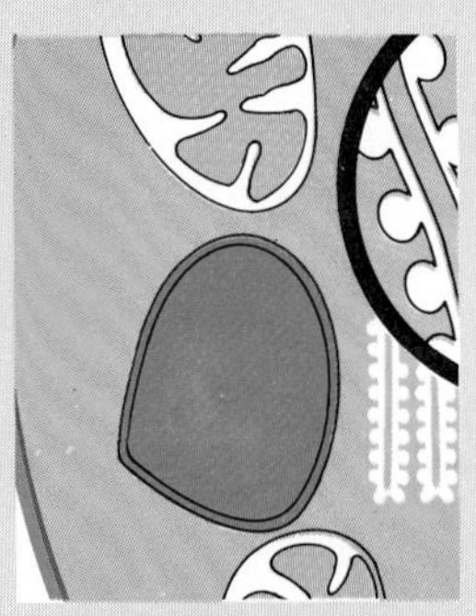

Reprints from the 1973 Compton's

This section contains six new or fully revised articles from the 1973 edition of Compton's Encyclopedia. The articles are reprinted here to help the reader keep his home reference library complete and up-to-date.

Reprinted are the following:

Astronomy

Biochemistry

Brain and Spinal Cord

Dog

Horse

Solar System

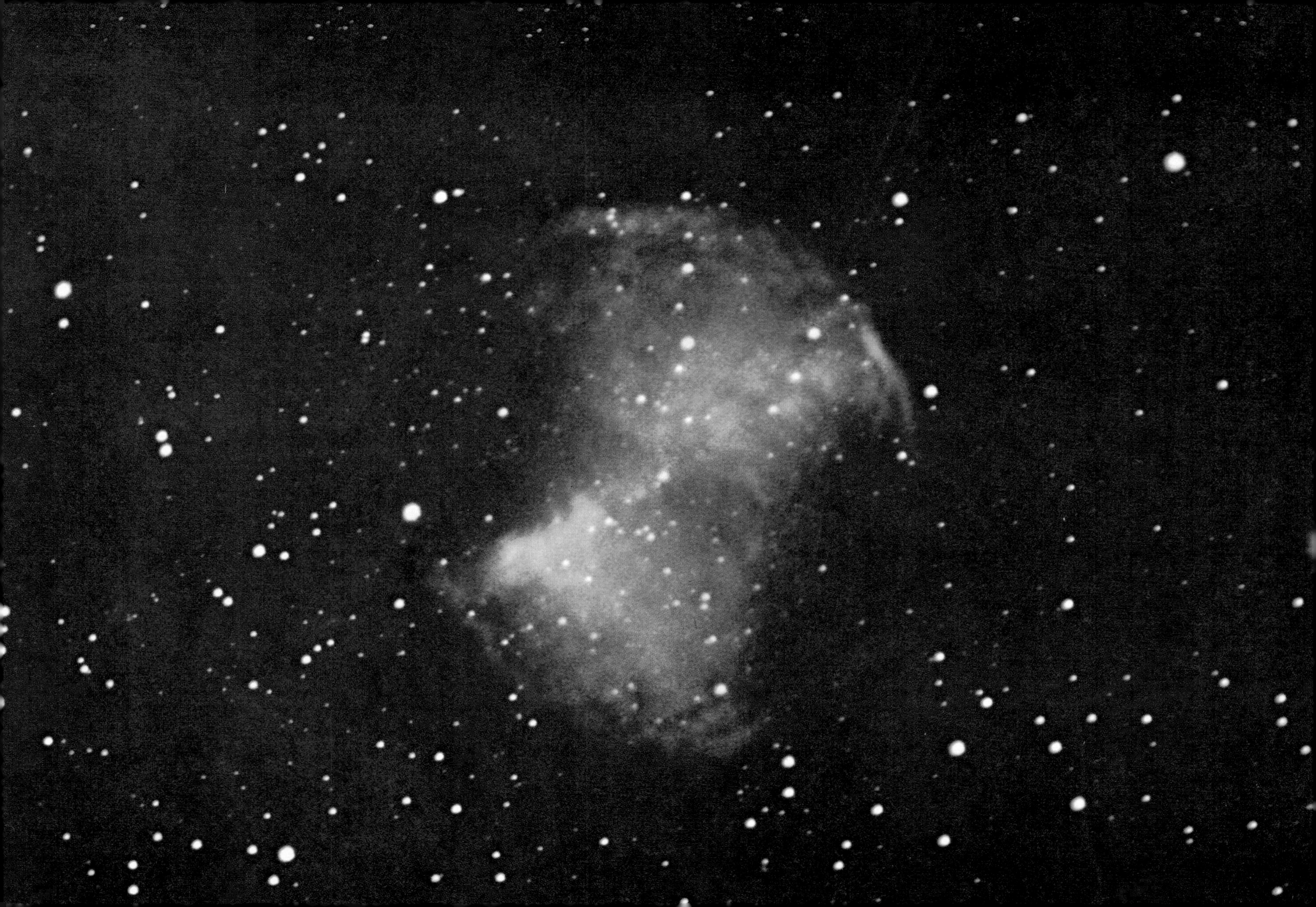

ASTRONOMY

ASTRONOMY. Since the beginnings of mankind people have gazed in wonder at the heavens. Before the dawn of history someone noticed that certain celestial bodies moved in orderly and predictable paths, and astronomy—an ancient science—was born. Yet some of science's newest discoveries have been made in this same field. From simple observations of the motions of the sun and the stars as they pass across the sky, to advanced theories of the exotic states of matter in collapsed stars, astronomy has spanned the ages.

Preview

The article Astronomy is divided into these sections:

For centuries astronomers concentrated on learning about the motions of heavenly bodies. They saw the sun rise in the east, cross the sky, and set in the west. As the sun was setting they saw tiny points of light appear in the east where the sky was growing dark. Most of these lights seemed to stay in the same place in relation to one another, as if they were all fastened to a huge black globe surrounding Earth. These lights were called *stars*. Other lights, however, seemed to travel, going from group to group of stationary stars. These moving points were called *planets*, or "wanderers."

The ancient astronomers thought that the positions of celestial bodies revealed what was going to happen on Earth—wars, births, deaths, and good fortune or bad. This belief is called *astrology*. Since the astrologers wanted to predict precisely what would happen on Earth, they studied precisely the motions of the celestial bodies. Most scientists no longer believe in astrology, but they have found that some ancient astrologers were very good at observing the apparent motions and positions of the stars and planets.

This article was contributed by Dr. Gerard P. Kuiper, Director of the Lunar and Planetary Laboratory, University of Arizona, and by Dr. Thomas L. Swihart, Professor of Astronomy, Steward Observatory, University of Arizona.

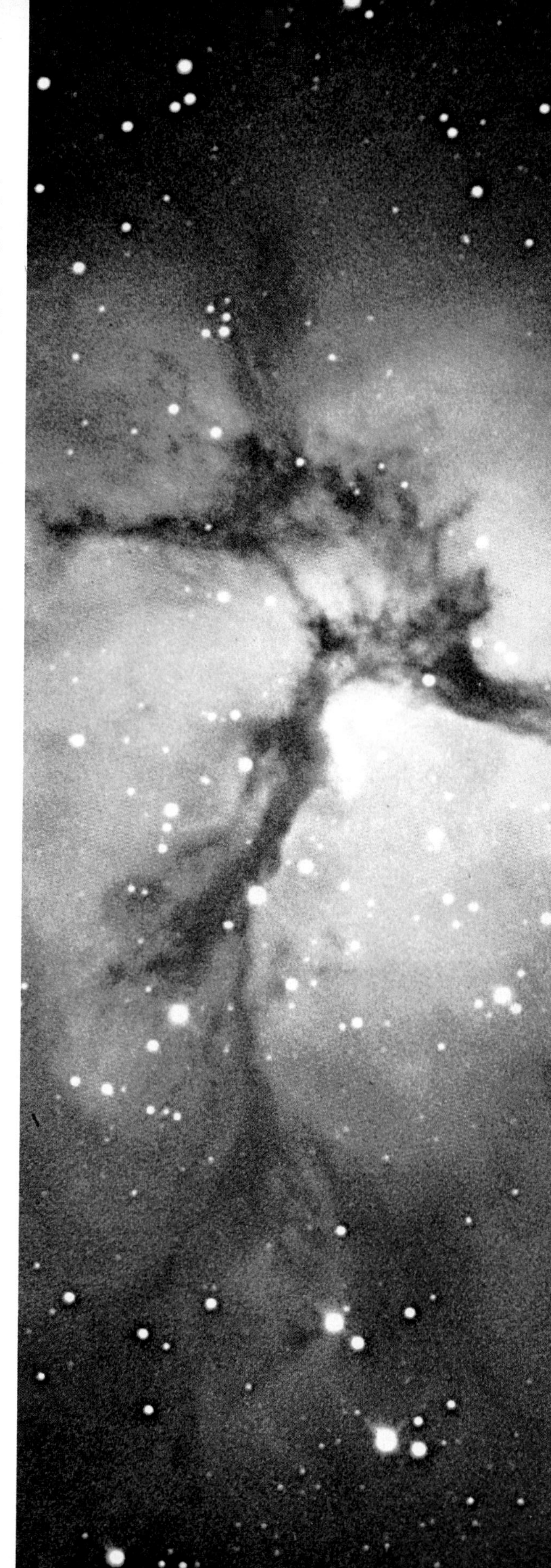

The Trifid nebula is a cloud of glowing gas and dark streaks of dust. It is in the constellation Sagittarius.

U.S. Naval Observatory

Dumbbell Nebula

By courtesy of U.S. Naval Observatory

The Sky You See

WHEN YOU LOOK at the sky without any telescope or binoculars or any other modern instrument, you see the same things the ancient astronomers saw. During the day you see the sun and sometimes a faint moon in the morning or evening.

During a clear night you see the moon and stars. If you watch the sky often enough, you can get to recognize the groups of stars, called *constellations*. And you may even notice a star that seems to be in different positions from night to night: it is a planet, one of the "wandering stars" of the ancients.

Day and Night

Our lives have rhythms or cycles that follow the cycles of nature. What are some of these cycles?

We rise with the sun; enjoy the brightness of the day; have our three meals, our daily tasks, and our evening at home; and then sleep. This daily rhythm follows the sun. When the sun is in the sky, it is daytime. When the sun has set, it is night.

We divide the day into 24 hours. On the average the sun is up 12 hours and down 12 hours. The daily motion of the sun is therefore the source of the time given by our clocks. But the days are not exactly alike. In winter the sun is visible less than 12 hours; in summer it is visible longer. This happens because the sun's path through the daytime sky is longer in summer than in winter.

The Earth in Space

Now the westward motion of the sun, the moon, and the stars is not real. They seem to move around Earth, but it is actually Earth that moves. It is rotating eastward, completing one rotation each day. This is hard to believe at first because when we think of motion we also think of the vibrations of moving cars or trains. But Earth moves freely in space, without rubbing against anything, so it does not vibrate. This gentle rotation causes the rising and setting of the sun, the moon, and the stars.

Our planet floats freely in space. In this Apollo 8 photograph, North and South America are hidden by clouds. Asia and part of Africa are on Earth's night side.

NASA

Earth is accompanied by the moon, which circles the planet at a distance of about 30 Earth diameters. At the same time, Earth is moving around the sun in a huge circle. Every year Earth completes one revolution around the sun. This motion causes the seasons because Earth's axis of rotation is tipped. When the northern half of Earth is tipped toward the sun, then the northern hemisphere experiences summer and the southern hemisphere, tipped away from the sun, experiences winter. When Earth has moved to the other side of the sun, six months later, the seasons are reversed because the southern hemisphere is then tipped toward the sun and the northern hemisphere is tipped away from the sun (*see* Earth, section "The Moving Earth").

If you watch the moon for three or four weeks, you will see that it does not always look the same. Sometimes it looks like a big disk, sometimes like a tiny curved sliver. These changes are called the *phases* of the moon. They happen because the moon shines only when the sun's light bounces off its surface. This means that only the side of the moon that faces the sun is bright. When the moon is placed between Earth and the sun, the light side of the moon is facing away from Earth. This is the new moon, which is not visible. When the moon is on the other side of Earth from the sun, its light side is facing completely toward Earth. This is the full moon. Halfway between the new and full moons, in locations on either side of Earth, are the first quarter and the last quarter.

The Night Sky

What else can you see on an average night with just your eyes? Naturally you can see stars. After a few nights you might even recognize a planet by its motion. Although stars and planets look alike to the unaided eye, they are very different things. The planets all circle the sun, just as Earth does. They are visible to Earth because sunlight bounces off them, just as it does off the moon.

The stars are much farther away. Most stars are like the sun—large, hot, and bright. The stars shine from their own energy, just as the sun does.

As you watch the stars you may notice a broad strip of dim light across the sky. It is a clustering of faint stars known as the Milky Way. The Milky Way is a galaxy—an enormous disklike cluster of stars, of which the sun is only one member. The Milky Way galaxy contains on the order of 100 billion stars. Other galaxies exist far beyond the Milky Way.

On a clear dark night you might even be able to see some of the structure of the Milky Way, such as dark clouds in parts of it. The clouds are enormous masses of smoglike particles that hide millions of stars behind them.

The Bettmann Archive

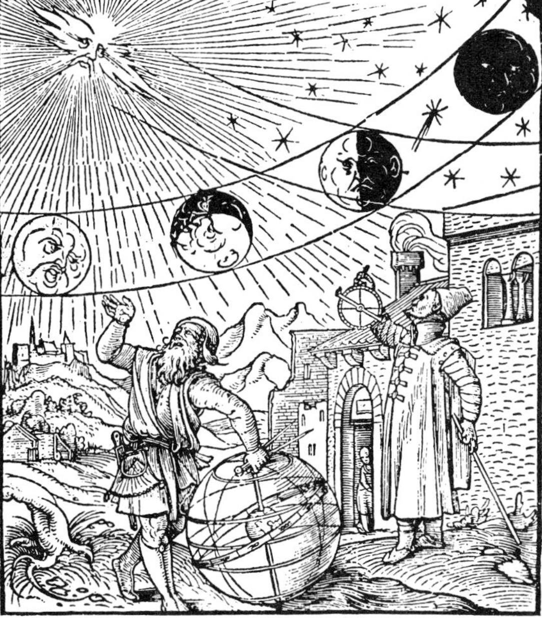

This woodcut, made by Hans Holbein the Younger in 1534, shows astronomical instruments of the time. The astronomers are observing the phases of the moon.

Eclipses

In ancient times people were often terrified when the sun or the moon would disappear completely during the day or night when normally it would be visible. They did not understand what caused these eclipses, and they were afraid that the sun or moon might be gone forever, leaving the world in darkness.

Eclipses happen irregularly because the plane of the moon's orbit around Earth is slightly different from the plane of Earth's orbit around the sun. The two planes intersect at an angle of 5°8′. This means that the moon is usually slightly above or below the line between Earth and the sun, so neither Earth nor the moon throws a shadow on the other. Eclipses can occur only when the moon lies at one of the two points where the planes intersect. If this were not so, we would have total lunar eclipses with every full moon and total solar eclipses with every new moon (*see* Eclipse).

Sometimes the moon crosses a point of intersection of the two planes at the same time that it passes directly *behind* Earth. The shadow of Earth blocks off the light to the moon, and the moon seems to disappear. Some two hours later, the edge of the moon appears on the other side of Earth's shadow and the whole moon gradually emerges.

The opposite happens, too. Sometimes the moon crosses the point of intersection of the two planes at the same time that it passes *between* Earth and

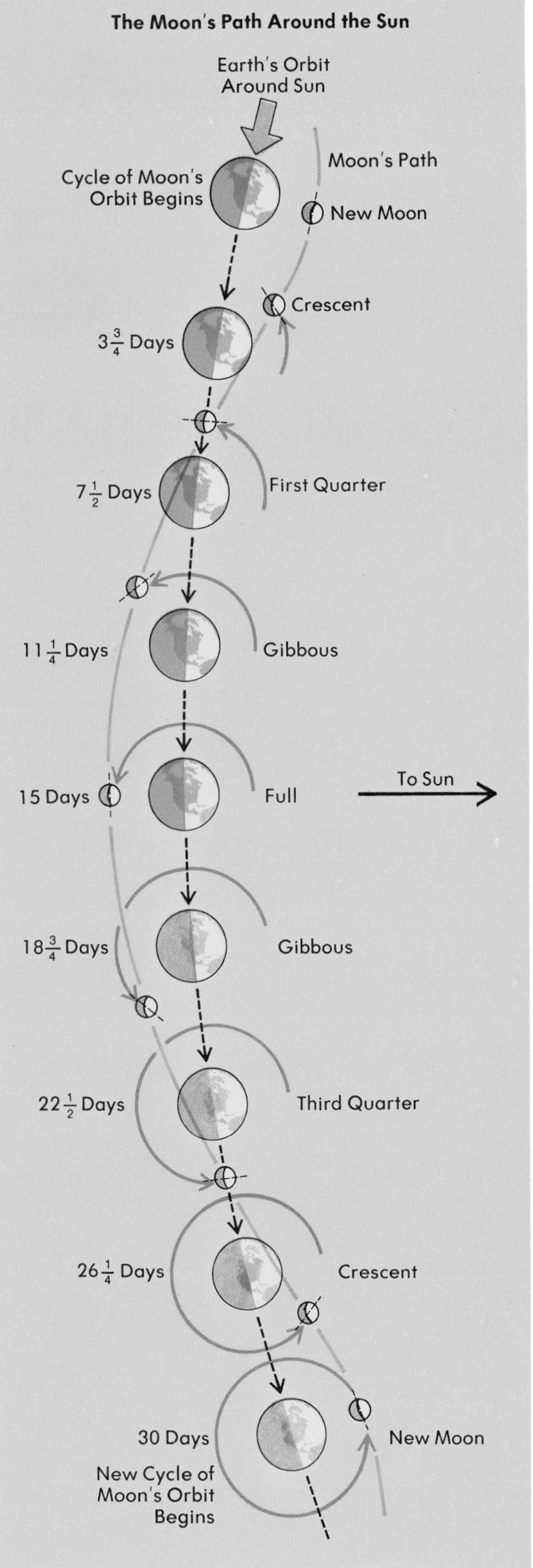

The moon has a complicated path around the sun. It travels in an almost circular path around Earth. At the same time, Earth moves in a nearly circular path around the sun. Both motions combine to give the moon a wavy path.

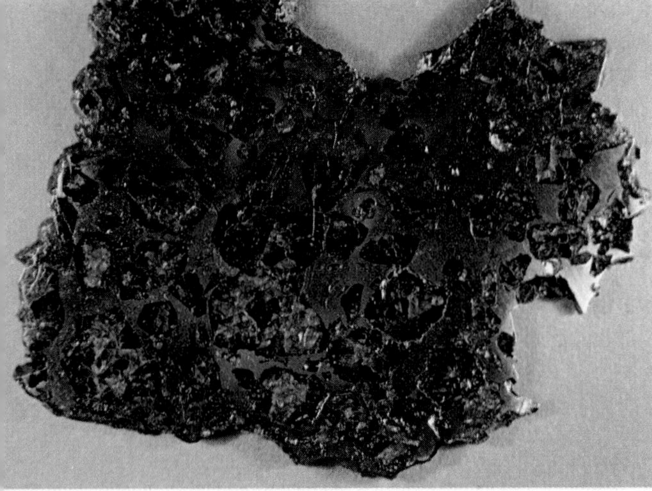

From the collection of Ronald A. Oriti, Griffith Observatory; photograph, Ivan Dryer

This slice from a meteorite has been polished. It contains both stony material and iron.

the sun. It casts a shadow on Earth, causing an eclipse of the sun. Because the moon is much smaller than Earth, only a small shadow patch on Earth's surface results. To people in the darkest part of the shadow, the *umbra,* the moon completely blocks out the sun. This is a *total eclipse* of the sun: the entire bright disk is covered up and only the graceful outer atmosphere of the sun, the *corona,* is visible. (Because the sun is so bright, it is very dangerous to look directly at it, even during an eclipse; *see* Sun.)

Normally light from the sun's bright disk blots out the faint corona. During total solar eclipses astronomers can study the sun's atmosphere. Unfortunately, such eclipses are always brief; the longest possible total eclipse is about seven minutes.

Auroras are streaks of light that occur high in the sky. They are usually seen far to the north or south, near Earth's poles, but this one was photographed near Pittsburgh, Pa.

Robert C. Dickinson

A larger area of Earth is covered by the shadowy area around the true shadow (this blurry area is the *penumbra*). To people in the penumbra, the moon blocks off part of the sun, but a crescent shows along the edge of the moon. This is a *partial eclipse* of the sun.

When the moon is farthest from Earth during an eclipse, its disk appears a bit smaller than the sun's disk, so that a ring of the sun's disk is seen around the black mass of the moon. This is an *annular eclipse.*

Rocks from Outer Space

As you sit outside on a summer's night, a flash of light may streak across the sky and disappear: a "shooting star," you say. Real stars don't shoot through the sky any more than the sun does. But small, solid chunks of stone or metal are in orbit around the sun. Sometimes these pieces of stone or metal enter Earth's atmosphere, and the friction generated by their great speed causes them to burn up. The fragments may either disappear before traveling far or actually hit the ground.

"Shooting stars" have different names depending on where they are. According to the International Astronomical Union, a rock or metal fragment existing in space is a *meteoroid.* The flash of light you see as the fragment shoots through Earth's atmosphere is a *meteor.* And a chunk that actually lands on Earth's surface is a *meteorite.*

Meteorites, which are sturdy enough to reach the ground, apparently are pieces of asteroids. (Asteroids are huge rocks, up to 500 miles across, that orbit the sun.) Most meteors that burn up in the atmosphere are tiny dustlike particles, the remains of disintegrated comets. (Comets are flimsy objects made up primarily of ices and some gritty material. They also orbit the sun.)

Sometimes a swarm of meteors will hit the earth at one time, causing a meteor shower, with tens or hundreds of shooting stars flashing across the sky. But all these meteors burn up in the upper atmosphere. They are too small and fragile to reach Earth's surface.

The Northern and Southern Lights

People who are relatively near the North or South Pole can see one of nature's most lavish and glorious displays—the *aurora borealis* (northern lights) or the *aurora australis* (southern lights). High in the skies over Earth's magnetic poles, electrically charged particles from the sun swarm down into Earth's atmosphere. As these particles collide with air molecules, brilliant sheets, streamers, or beams of colored lights are given off at heights ranging from 50 miles to about 200 miles up in Earth's atmosphere (*see* Aurora Borealis).

The streams of charged particles are known as the *solar wind.* The sun continually sends a flow of these particles out into space. During periods when the sun is active—that is, when it has large sunspots on its surface—the solar wind is particularly heavy, and huge swarms of the particles reach Earth's atmosphere, causing large and brilliant auroras.

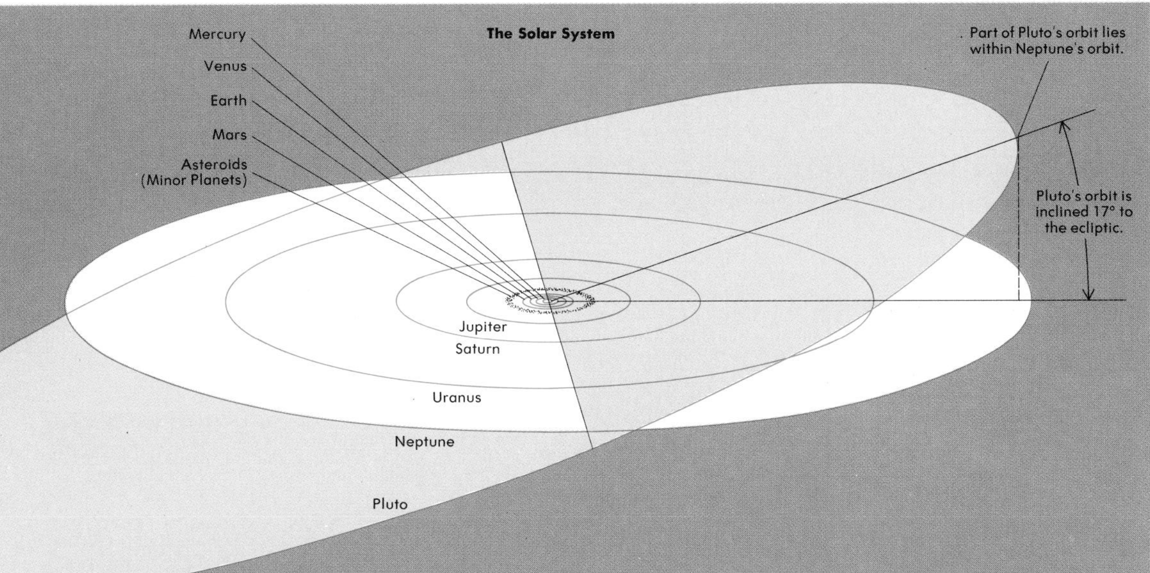
The Solar System
Mercury
Venus
Earth
Mars
Asteroids
(Minor Planets)
Jupiter
Saturn
Uranus
Neptune
Pluto
Part of Pluto's orbit lies within Neptune's orbit.
Pluto's orbit is inclined 17° to the ecliptic.

Many pieces of matter are held in the sun's enormous gravitational field. Together with the sun, they make up the solar system. The paths of the planets are huge ellipses with the sun at one focus. The minor planets, comets, and meteoroids also have elliptical paths, but they may be highly perturbed by the gravitational attraction of nearby planets.

The Solar System

EARTH IS NOT the only body to circle the sun. Many chunks of matter, some much larger than Earth and some so small you would need a microscope to see them, are caught in the sun's gravitational field. The nine largest of these chunks are called planets. Earth is the third planet from the sun. The smaller chunks of matter are natural satellites, asteroids, comets, meteors, and the molecules of interplanetary gases.

Kepler's Laws of Planetary Motion

In the early 1600's, astronomers were beginning to accept the idea that Earth and the planets probably revolved around the sun, rather than that the sun and the planets revolved around Earth. They were still unable, however, to describe the motions of the planets with any accuracy.

The German astronomer Johannes Kepler was finally able to describe planetary motions using three mathematical expressions, called Kepler's laws of planetary motion: (1) The motion of a planet around the sun is an ellipse, with the sun at one of the two foci of the ellipse. (2) The planet's motion along this ellipse is such that the imaginary line from the planet to the sun sweeps out equal areas in equal amounts of time (thus, when a planet is closest to the sun it moves most rapidly). (3) The average distance of the planet from the sun and the time it takes to complete one orbit (its *period*) are both related to the average distance from the sun to any other planet and the other planet's period. The exact relationship is this: The cube of the average radius divided by the square of the period for any one planet is equal to the cube of the average radius divided by the square of the period for any other planet, provided they are orbiting the same central mass (*see* Kepler).

Although it sounds confusing, the third law is actually simple in mathematical terms, and astronomers have found it extremely useful. If the average distance from Earth to the sun is arbitrarily called one *astronomical unit* (A.U.), then Kepler's third law can be used to find the relative distances of the other planets to the sun, merely by measuring how long it takes those planets to orbit the sun. Before the actual distance from Earth to the sun was

When the asteroid Eros approaches Earth, it frequently comes within 20 million miles, and sometimes it comes within 14 million miles of Earth. At such near approaches its distance is easy to measure by the parallax method.

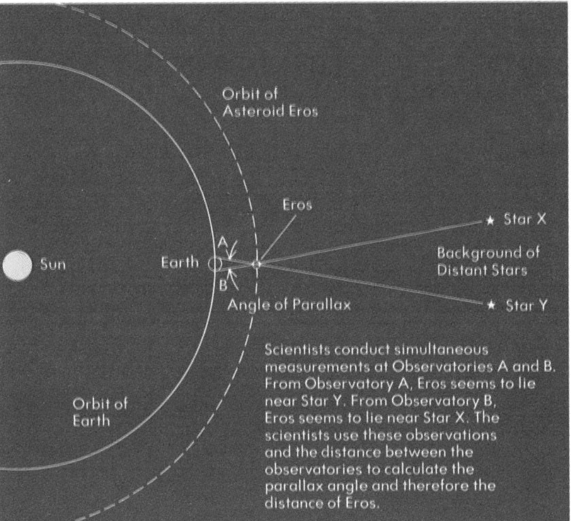
Orbit of
Asteroid Eros
Eros
Star X
Background of
Distant Stars
Sun
Earth
A
B
Angle of Parallax
Star Y
Orbit of
Earth
Scientists conduct simultaneous measurements at Observatories A and B. From Observatory A, Eros seems to lie near Star Y. From Observatory B, Eros seems to lie near Star X. The scientists use these observations and the distance between the observatories to calculate the parallax angle and therefore the distance of Eros.

known, many distances within the solar system were known in astronomical units. The unit is still a useful one.

The other unit frequently used for distances to the planets is the kilometer (1 km. = 0.62137 mi.). It is used in all radar determinations, since the velocity of light is known accurately in kilometers. One astronomical unit is equal to 149,597,893 km. (about 92,957,000 mi.).

Newton's Law of Universal Gravitation

Kepler's laws described the positions and motions of the planets with great accuracy, but they did not explain what caused the planets to follow those paths. Later astronomers puzzled over that problem. If the planets were not acted on by some force, the scientists reasoned, then they would simply continue to move in a straight line past the sun and out toward the stars. Some force must be attracting them to the sun. What was the nature of this force?

The versatile English scientist Isaac Newton came up with a great insight. As he was considering the moon's motion around Earth, he realized that the moon might be falling toward Earth just fast enough to keep it moving in a large circle around the planet. If the moon fell any faster, it would spiral in and hit the planet. If it fell more slowly, it would spiral away and escape.

Newton calculated the acceleration of the moon toward Earth. It was much less than the acceleration of an apple, say, falling from a tree to the ground. Newton concluded that the same force that caused the apple to fall to the ground also caused the moon to fall toward Earth. But the force grew weaker at points farther away from the planet.

Following this train of thought, Newton worked out an equation that described this force anywhere in the universe. The equation states that the *gravitational force* is directly proportional to the *mass* of the body exerting the force (in other words, the gravitational force of Earth is smaller than the gravitational force exerted by the much more massive sun); the equation also states that the force grows weaker the farther away an object gets from the body exerting the force. In fact, the gravitational force follows the inverse-square law: If the distance from Earth (for example) is doubled, its gravitational attraction for an object is reduced to one fourth; if the distance is tripled, the gravitational force is reduced to one ninth; and so on. Using this relationship, Newton was able to derive mathematically Kepler's laws of planetary motion. (*See also* Newton.)

Kepler's second law of planetary motion describes the speed of a planet traveling in an elliptical orbit around the sun. It states that a line between the sun and the planet sweeps equal areas in equal times. Thus, the speed of the planet increases as it nears the sun and decreases as it recedes from the sun.

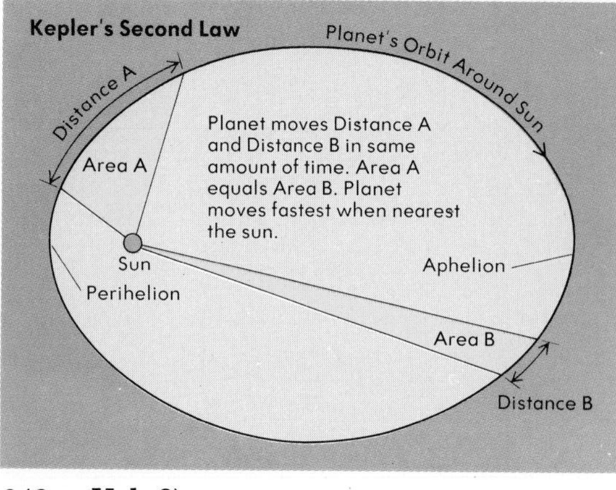

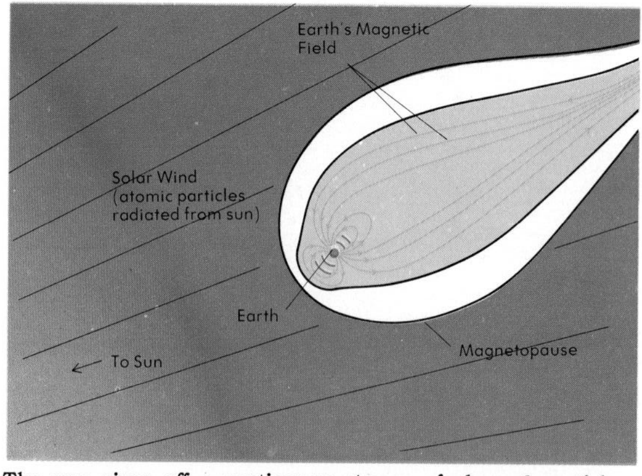

The sun gives off a continuous stream of charged particles. When this stream, called the solar wind, reaches Earth, it deforms Earth's magnetic field. Some of the particles spiral down near the magnetic poles, where they cause auroras.

The Planets

Up to the 18th century people knew of seven bodies, besides Earth, that moved against the background of the fixed stars. These were the sun, the moon, and the five planets that are visible to the unaided eye: Mercury, Venus, Mars, Jupiter, and Saturn. Then, in 1781, William Herschel, a German-born English organist and amateur astronomer, discovered that one of the "stars" he was observing did not behave like a star. He thought that it was a comet, but later it was shown to be a new planet, which was named Uranus. Since the seven moving bodies had been mystically identified with the seven days of the week, the impact of the discovery of an eighth body was profound.

Another disturbance followed. Uranus' motion did not follow the exact path predicted by Newton's theory of gravitation. This second problem was happily resolved by the discovery of yet another planet, which was named Neptune. Two mathematicians, J. C. Adams and Urbain Leverrier, had calculated Neptune's probable location, but Adams could not persuade an astronomer to look for the planet where he predicted it would be. Leverrier asked the German astronomer J. G. Galle, who did locate the planet.

Even then some small deviations seemed to remain in the orbits of both planets. This led to the search for yet another planet, based on calculations made by the United States astronomer Percival Lowell. Lowell himself searched for the planet for some ten years, but

Historical Pictures Service, Chicago

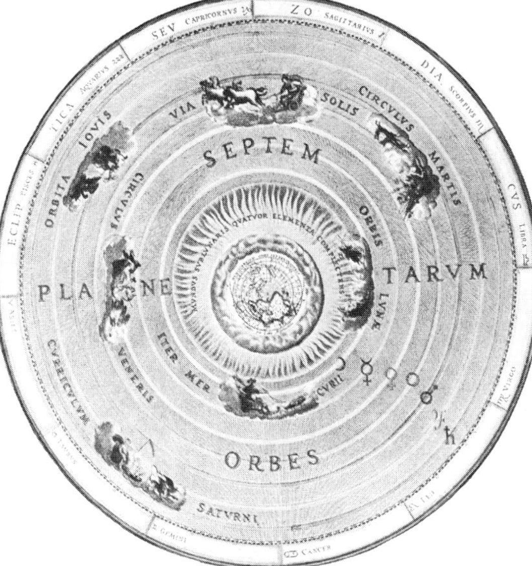

This illustration, published in 1660, shows Ptolemy's system of the universe. The sun, the moon, five planets, and the stars all circle around Earth, which lies at the center.

he had not located it by the time he died in 1916. It was discovered 14 years later, in 1930, by Clyde W. Tombaugh, working at the observatory established by Lowell in Arizona. The new planet was named Pluto. By the time Tombaugh had located Pluto, he had searched nearly half the ecliptic belt. He continued to scan the rest of the sky in the most gigantic search effort ever attempted. It took 12 years to complete, but no objects other than Pluto were discovered, except, of course, for stars.

The probable mass of Pluto has proved so small—less than one tenth of Earth's mass—that it could not have been responsible for the deviations in the observed paths of Uranus and Neptune. Astronomers now attribute those deviations to minor errors in the observation systems of the 19th century.

Searches for new planets have not been limited to space beyond Neptune. Scientists have also looked for a planet that might lie nearer the sun than Mercury. Leverrier named it Vulcan. No certain discoveries have ever been made, though there have been from time to time unverified reports on intra-Mercurial objects. Astronomers do not now believe that Vulcan exists.

All the planets travel about the sun in elliptical orbits that are close to being circles. Mercury and Pluto have the most eccentric orbits. All the planets travel in one direction around the sun, the same direction in which the sun rotates. Furthermore, all the planetary orbits lie in very nearly the same plane. Again, Mercury and Pluto have the most tilted orbits: Mercury's is tilted 7° to the plane of Earth's orbit (the *ecliptic plane*); Pluto's is tilted 17° 10′ to the ecliptic.

All the planets except Venus rotate on their axes in the same west-to-east motion. Most of the axes are nearly at right angles to the plane of their orbit. Uranus, however, is tilted so that its axis lies almost in the plane of its orbit; its orientation is nearly fixed with respect to the stars.

The planets can be divided into two groups. The inner planets lie within the asteroid belt, near the sun. They are dense, rocky, and small. Since Earth is a typical inner planet, this group is sometimes called the terrestrial planets.

The outer planets lie beyond the asteroid belt. With the exception of Pluto, they are much larger and more massive than the inner planets, and they are much less dense. Since Jupiter is the main representative of the outer planets, they are sometimes called the Jovian planets. Pluto is an outer planet, but it is not usually regarded as a Jovian planet.

Natural Satellites of the Planets

Six of the planets—Earth, Mars, Jupiter, Saturn, Uranus, and Neptune—are known to have satellites. Since the moon is large in comparison to Earth, the Earth-moon system is considered to be a double planet. Although some of the other satellites are much larger than the moon, they are still much tinier, by comparison, than the planets they circle. No other double planets occur in our solar system.

The motions of planetary satellites enable astronomers to calculate the masses of the planets they circle. Since Mercury, Venus, and Pluto have no known satellites at all, their masses can be calculated accu-

In 1957 Comet Mrkos (below) was visible at night to the unaided eye. Only a few comets are ever visible during the day.

Giraudon

Halley's comet appeared in 1066, when William of Normandy invaded England. The Bayeux tapestry, commemorating his victory, shows the comet as an evil omen for Harold II, the English king.

rately only after artificial satellites are placed in orbit around them. Pluto itself is probably a former satellite escaped from Neptune. (*See also* Satellites.)

Asteroids

On Jan. 1, 1801, the Italian astronomer Giuseppe Piazzi found a small planet in the large gap between Mars and Jupiter. This planet, later named Ceres, was the first and largest of thousands of *asteroids*, or *minor planets*, that have been discovered.

Like Ceres, most of the asteroids lie between Mars and Jupiter at an average distance of about 3.0 A.U. from the sun. Some asteroids are much closer to the sun, however. Eros, discovered in 1898, comes within 14 million miles (0.15 A.U.) of Earth. Other recently discovered bodies—Icarus, Adonis, and Hermes, which are only a mile or two long—sometimes come within 4 million miles of Earth (*see* Asteroids).

Comets

Comets are the most unusual and unpredictable objects in the solar system. They vary in appearance from small stellar images, like small asteroids, to huge tailed objects so bright that they can be seen in daytime near the sun.

The comets are small bodies composed mostly of ices of various substances—principally ammonia, methane, and water—with some silicate and metal grit mixed in. This composition indicates that they were formed on the outer fringe of the solar system, where the temperature and density of the original gases were very low. It is estimated that over 100 billion comets exist in a comet belt located beyond Saturn and probably mostly beyond Neptune.

We never see the comets that stay in the belt outside Neptune. The comets we see orbit the sun in long elliptical paths which bring them near the sun. Occasionally one of these intruders may be influenced by one of the larger planets, usually Jupiter, and be pulled into a closer, shorter orbit, with a period of about six years. Most comets, however, have much longer periods. Halley's comet takes about 76 years to complete an orbit, and the majority of comets may take thousands or even millions of years.

As a comet approaches the sun, some of its ices evaporate. The solar wind pushes these evaporated gases away from the head of the comet and away from the sun. This gives the comet a long glowing tail that always points away from the sun (*see* Comet).

The Sun

The spectrum, brightness, mass, dimension, and age of the sun and of nearby stars indicate that the sun is a normal, typical star. Like most stars, the sun produces energy by thermonuclear processes that take place at its core. At great pressures and high temperatures, hydrogen nuclei are converted to helium nuclei (*see* Sun).

The thermonuclear reactions are accompanied by intense X-ray emissions. Energy from the X rays is absorbed on their way to the surface, and they are released mostly as visible radiation. This radiation maintains the conditions for life on earth—an appropriate temperature range and abundant light energy for green plants to photosynthesize.

Origin and Future of the Solar System

The most widely accepted theory of the origin of the solar system is the protoplanet theory elaborated by Gerard P. Kuiper. This theory notes that dense roundish gas and dust clouds, or *globules*, exist all through the Galaxy. Stars are thought to form when such gas clouds contract further.

It is thought that some 4.7 billion years ago, a globule contracted into a disk. The dense center part became a star: our sun. In the outer cloud-like

The sun belongs to a group of stars called a galaxy, which has a spiral shape, much like M51, the Whirlpool galaxy, shown below. The smaller companion is a typical irregular galaxy.

U.S. Naval Observatory

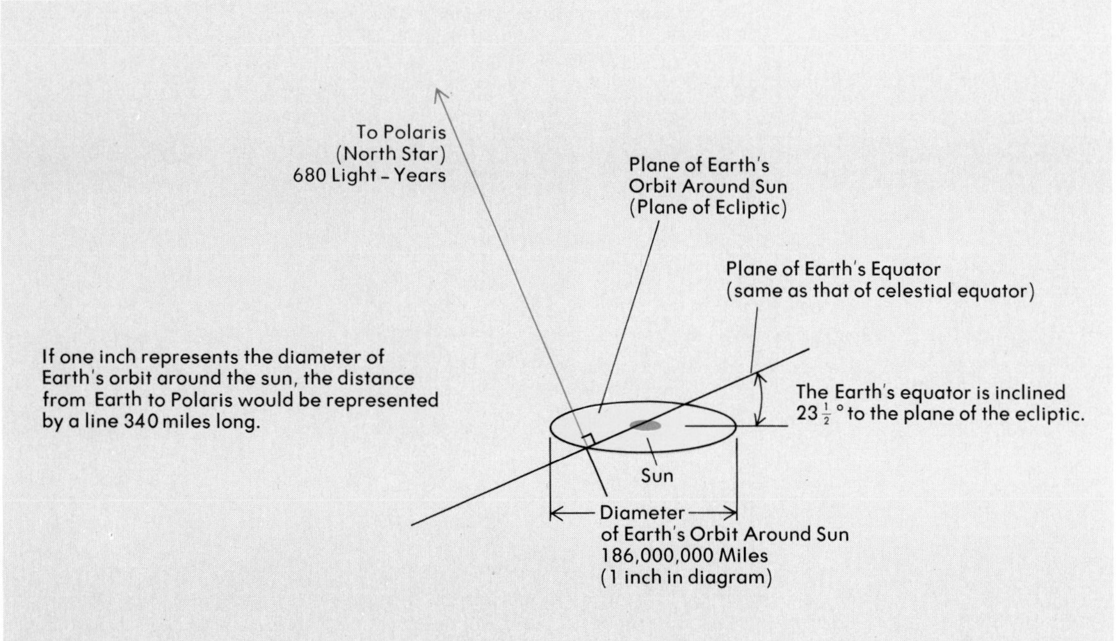

A vast emptiness of space surrounds the solar system. If the orbit of Earth were one inch in diameter, Polaris would be 340 miles away from Earth. When scientists measure the parallax angle of Polaris, they find an angle equal to the smallest angle of a triangle with two sides 340 miles long and one side that is one inch long.

part, gravitational instability caused especially dense regions, or *protoplanets*, to form. Such regions experienced greater internal gravitational forces than the surrounding gas, so they contracted. If a particularly large protoplanet had formed, it might itself contain areas of greater density, called *protomoons*. As the central mass contracted, forming the planet, the protomoons would also contract, forming satellites.

The future of the solar system cannot be known, because accidents can happen. A star might pass right through and destroy the system, though such events are rare. If no traffic accident occurs, the future depends on the behavior of the sun. The sun is slowly getting brighter as it consumes its reservoir of hydrogen and turns this into helium. If current computations of stellar evolution are correct, the sun will grow much brighter and larger in about 5 billion years. In turn, the planets will get much hotter—far too hot, in fact, for life to endure on Earth.

Much later the sun will have exhausted its nuclear energy source and will begin to cool. In the end it will become a white-dwarf star, with all its matter packed densely into a space not much bigger than Earth. Around it will orbit frozen wastelands, the planets that survived the solar upheavals.

This is all so far into the future—billions of years from now—that it most probably will not affect the human race. This species is likely to have, or make, its own troubles in much less than one percent of the time it will take for the large forces of nature to cause concern.

Does Life Exist Elsewhere in the Solar System?

Life as we know it, and most particularly in its higher forms, can exist only under certain chemical and physical conditions. One of the major requirements of life is the availability of liquid water. Only Earth is known to have liquid water on its surface. Venus is much too hot. Mars much too cold. Jupiter has cloud layers where water could occur in the liquid form, but floating rain droplets are not a stable environment. It is not likely that life could develop in them.

Mariner 9 photographed ancient fossil water courses—places where running water once caused erosion—on Mars. This opens up the possibility that life existed there in a much earlier epoch. Conceivably, some hardy variety of plant life, perhaps resembling the lichens, may have survived from that period and adapted itself to the present rather barren conditions. Carbon dioxide and water vapor do still occur in the Martian atmosphere, so, with the abundance of sunshine available, photosynthesis could still occur. Animal life as we know it appears excluded, however, because there is practically no free oxygen in the Martian atmosphere, nor ozone to shield against the harmful ultraviolet sunlight.

Earth is a paradise for life as we know it. There is no other place in the solar system that would support human colonization. Astronauts will have to take their environment with them to any planets they visit, just as they have taken their environment with them to the moon.

Apparent Motion of Stars

at North Pole

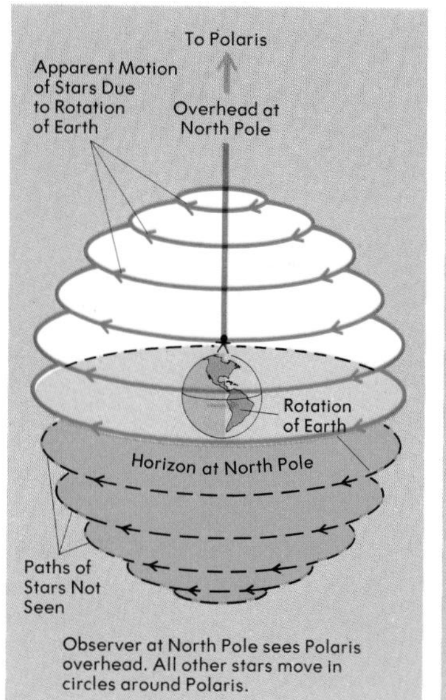

Observer at North Pole sees Polaris overhead. All other stars move in circles around Polaris.

at 45° North Latitude

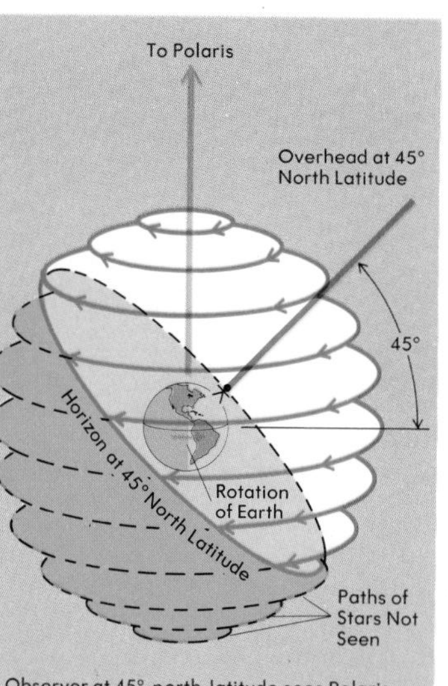

Observer at 45° north latitude sees Polaris between horizon and overhead. All other stars follow tilted paths.

at Equator

To Polaris

Overhead at Equator

Horizon at Equator

Rotation of Earth

Observer at equator sees Polaris at horizon. All other stars rise in the east and set in the west, moving at right angles to the horizon.

A person standing on Earth's surface does not feel the motion of Earth as it spins. Instead, the sun and the stars appear to be the objects that move, following paths that lead from east to west across the sky.

The Stars

IF YOU HAVE a chance to look through a telescope at the night sky, you will see a complex display indeed. You must explore this yourself to really appreciate its magnitude. The only sensation of comparable strength is to examine a drop of water from a greenish pond under a good microscope and see the drop teeming with unexpected small living creatures.

Constellations

The stars seem to form groups, or constellations. The Big Dipper is part of a larger constellation called the Big Bear (Ursa Major). Orion is another constellation. The first step in learning your way among the stars is to learn these constellations. If you begin with a few familiar ones and keep star charts handy, you will find that you quickly learn to recognize others (for diagrams, *see* Star).

The constellations are not necessarily true clusters in space. For example, the middle five stars of the Big Dipper do belong together, and they move together through space. But the first and last stars only look as though they belong to the same group. They are much farther from Earth than the other five, and they are even slowly moving in different directions. Some parts of Orion belong together as a true cluster, but Betelgeuse (pronounced "bettle jooz"), the bright red star at the top, is much nearer to Earth.

Coordinate Systems

Astronomers, navigators, and stargazers in general need to record the exact locations of stars and other objects. Within limits, it is useful to locate objects within constellations. An ancient method of recording the motions of planets was to say that a planet was entering, leaving, or in the "house" of a Zodiac constellation. But this method is not really precise.

People who need to record the exact locations of celestial objects use numerical *coordinate systems.* These systems are like the coordinate system of latitude and longitude used on Earth.

Different celestial coordinate systems have been devised. To be useful they must take into account that Earth has two regular motions in relation to the stars. Its rotation causes the sphere of stars to appear to make a complete circle around the planet once a day. And its revolution around the sun causes the star positions at a particular hour to shift from day to day, returning to the original position after an entire year.

The horizon, or azimuth, system is based on Earth's north-south line and the observer's horizon. It uses two angles called the azimuth and the altitude. The *azimuth* locates the star from the north line, and the *altitude* locates it from the horizon plane. For this system to be useful, the time and location of observations must be exactly known.

The equator system is based on the concept of the *celestial sphere.* All the stars and other heavenly bodies can be imagined to be located on a huge sphere that surrounds Earth. The sphere has several imaginary lines and points. One is the *celestial equator,* which is the projection of Earth's equator onto the celestial sphere. Another is the line of the *ecliptic,* which is the sun's apparent yearly path along this sphere. The celestial equator and the ecliptic intersect at two points, called the vernal equinox and the autumnal equinox. (When the sun is at either point, day and night on Earth are equally long.) The north and south celestial poles are extensions of the North and South poles on Earth.

In the equator system, the position of a star is given by the declination and the right ascension. The *declination* locates the star from the north celestial pole, and the *right ascension* locates the star from the vernal equinox. Since this system is attached to the celestial sphere, all points on Earth (except the poles) are continually changing their positions under the coordinate system.

Actual Locations of Stars

Fixing stars on an imaginary sphere is useful for finding them from Earth, but it does not reveal their actual locations. One way for measuring the distances of nearby stars from Earth is the *parallax method.*

For parallax measurements of stars, scientists make use of Earth's yearly motion around the sun. This motion causes us to view the stars from different positions at different times of the year. In summer, Earth is on one side of the sun. Six months later, in winter, Earth is 186 million miles away on the opposite side of the sun. And photographs of a near star, taken through a large telescope and six months apart, will show that the star appears to shift against the background of more distant stars. If this shift is large enough to be measured, astronomers can calculate the distance to the star.

More than four centuries ago the phenomenon of parallax was used to counter Copernicus' suggestion that Earth travels around the sun. Scientists of the time pointed out that if it did, stars should show an annual change in direction due to parallax. Because they were unable to measure any parallax, they concluded that Copernicus was wrong. We know now that the stars are all at such tremendous distances from Earth that their parallax angles are extremely difficult to measure. Even modern instruments cannot measure the parallax of most stars.

Astronomers measure parallaxes of stars in seconds of arc. This is a tiny unit of measure; for example, a penny must be $2\frac{1}{2}$ miles away before it appears as small as one second of arc. Yet no star except the sun is close enough to have a parallax that large. Alpha Centauri, a member of the group of three stars nearest to the sun, has a parallax of about three fourths of a second of arc.

Astronomers have devised a unit of distance called the *parsec*—the distance from the observer of an object whose parallax is one second of arc. One parsec is equal to 19.2 trillion (19.2×10^{12}) miles. Alpha Centauri is about 1.3 parsecs distant.

Another unit used to record large astronomical distances is the *light-year*. This is the distance that light travels within a vacuum in one year—about 5.88 trillion (5.88×10^{12}) miles. Alpha Centauri is about 4.3 light-years distant from Earth. Light takes over four years to reach Earth from that distance.

The horizon coordinate system provides a way to record the position of a star. The time and location of the observation must also be recorded because the star's altitude and azimuth change from place to place on Earth and with Earth's spin.

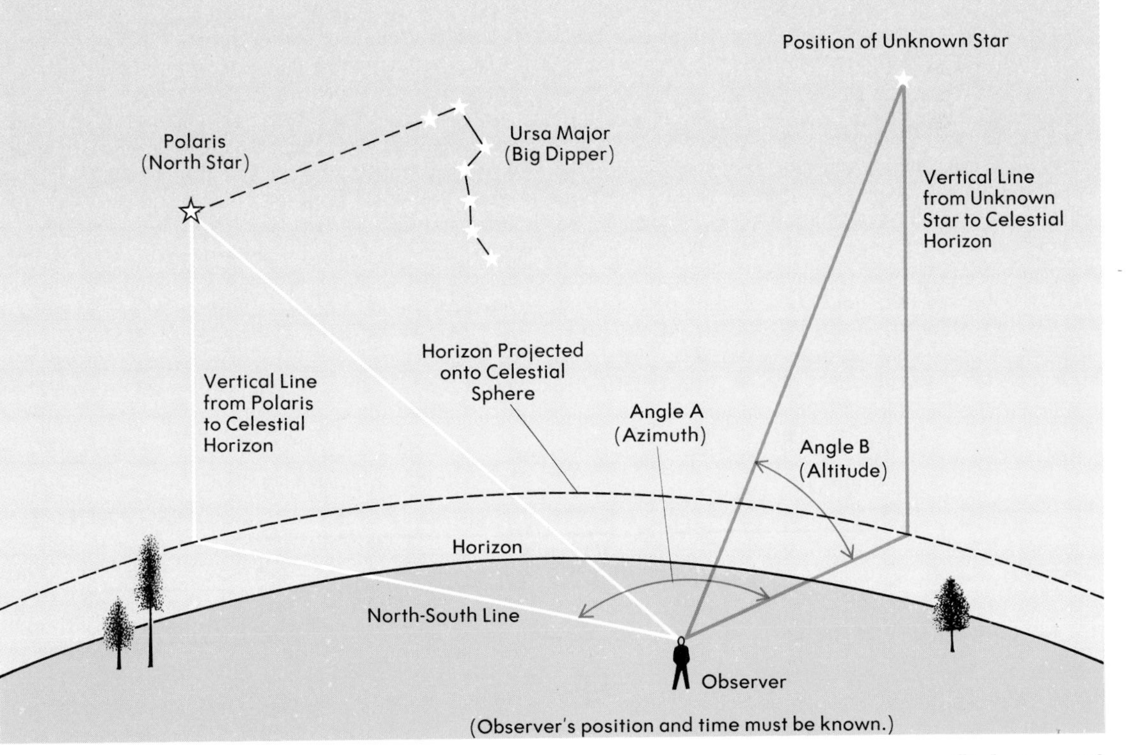

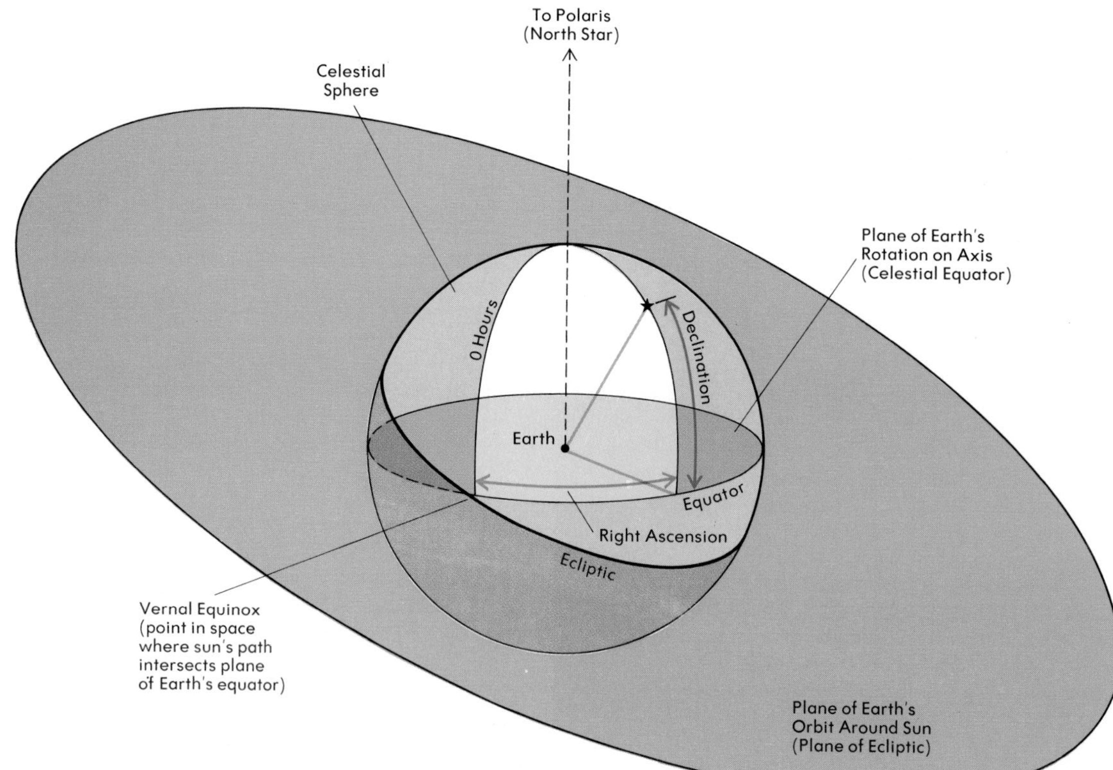

In the equator coordinate system the right ascension and declination of a star do not change as Earth spins. A star's position is given relative to the vernal equinox, the point where the sun crosses the celestial equator in March.

Demonstrating Parallax for Yourself

You can demonstrate how parallax happens. You need a wall with a design to represent the background of distant stars. A wallpaper pattern, or even a single vertical stripe, will do. You also need something you can prop in the middle of the room to represent the nearby star whose parallax is being measured. A tall vase on a table, or even a broom leaning against a chair, will do. Put the table with the vase on it (or the broom and the chair) in the middle of the room. Stand at the opposite side of the room with the vase between you and the wallpaper.

To begin with, you are at the position of the sun. Notice where the vase is seen against the wallpaper background. Take a sideways step to your right. This is the position of Earth in summer. Notice that the vase seems to move to the left along the wallpaper background. Take a step back to the sun's position and then take another sideways step to your left. This is the position of Earth in winter. Notice that the vase seems to move to the right along the wallpaper background. The apparent motion of the vase is caused by parallax.

Estimating Distances of Stars

Each star, including the sun, has its own motion in space. This motion of the sun and stars causes the position of any star relative to the sun (its *direction*) to change evenly with time: the longer the time interval, the greater the change in direction of the star. The yearly change in direction of a star due to the space motions of sun and star is known as the *proper motion* of the star. Other things being equal, the nearer stars have larger proper motions than the more distant ones. This provides astronomers with a way of estimating distances of stars.

It is not possible to find the distance of an individual star in this way because there is no way to tell whether a certain measured proper motion is caused by a rapidly moving star that is far away or by a slowly moving star that is near. The average individual proper motion of a group of stars, however, can tell astronomers what the average distance of the group is. In this way, approximate distances can be found for many stars that are too far away for their annual parallaxes to be measured.

What Starlight Tells Astronomers

How can astronomers learn what the stars are made of? It would be nice if stars could be brought into the laboratory and analyzed. Since this is not possible, astronomers study the feeble starlight that actually does reach Earth. Fortunately, electromagnetic radiation, including light, can provide much information about the object that sends it out.

Visible light is only one form of electromagnetic radiation (*see* Energy; Light). There are many more kinds. Gamma rays, X rays, and ultraviolet rays are more energetic than visible light; infrared rays and radio waves are less energetic than visible light.

The forms of electromagnetic radiation differ in their *frequencies*—that is, in how fast they wave or vibrate. Waves with high frequencies have greater energy than waves with low frequencies. Gamma rays have extremely high frequencies and radio waves have low frequencies.

Stars are found to give off a whole range of electromagnetic radiation. The kind of radiation a star gives off is related to the temperature of the star: the higher the temperature of the star, the more energy it gives off and the more this energy is concentrated in high-frequency radiation. Spectrographs can separate radiation into the different frequencies. The array of frequencies makes up the *spectrum* of the star (*see* Spectrum and Spectroscope).

The color of a star is also an indication of its temperature. Red light has less energy than blue light. A reddish star must have a large amount of its energy in red light. A white or bluish star has a larger amount of higher-energy blue light, so it must be hotter than the reddish star.

Stars have bright or dark lines in their spectra, narrow regions of extra-high emission or absorption. The presence of a certain chemical, such as hydrogen or calcium, in the star causes a particular set of lines in the star's spectrum. Since most of the lines found in stellar spectra have been identified with specific chemicals, astronomers can learn from a star's spectrum what chemicals it contains.

Spectrum lines are useful in another way, too. When an observer sees radiation coming from a source, such as a star, the frequency of the radiation is affected by any motion he has toward or away from the source. This is called the *Doppler effect* (*see* Sound). If the observer and the star are moving away from each other, the observer detects a shift to lower frequencies. If the star and the observer are approaching each other, the shift is to higher frequencies.

Astronomers know the normal spectrum-line frequencies for many chemicals. By comparing these known frequencies with the frequencies of the same set of lines in a star's spectrum, astronomers can tell how fast the star is moving toward or away from Earth.

Size and Brightness of Stars

Both the size and the temperature of a star determine how much radiation energy it gives off each second: this is the actual brightness of a star. It is also true, however, that the closer a star is to Earth, the more of its radiation energy will actually reach Earth and the brighter it will appear.

Astronomers express the brightness of a star in terms of its *magnitude*. Two values of magnitude describe a star. The *apparent magnitude* refers to how bright the star looks from Earth. The *absolute magnitude* of a star is the value its apparent magnitude would have if the star were 10 parsecs from Earth. The apparent magnitude of a star depends

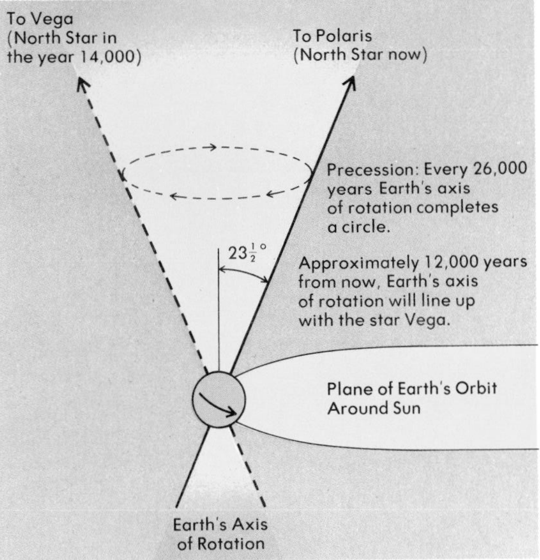

Precession is so slow that a person would not notice it in an entire lifetime. Earth's axis of rotation travels in a complete circle every 26,000 years. This means that the North Pole points toward different stars—and sometimes at no star in particular—as it travels in this circle.

on its size, temperature, and distance. The temperature is found from its spectrum; if the distance is known, then astronomers can calculate the size of the star and also assign a value for its absolute magnitude. The actual brightness of stars may be compared using their absolute magnitudes.

Astronomers have discovered all kinds of stars—from huge, brilliant *supergiants* to dense, cool *neutron stars*. The sun lies in about the middle range of size and brightness of stars and is considered to be a

Although the stars of the Big Dipper seem to belong together, they are actually widely separated. A person looking at the Big Dipper stars from a position in space different from that of Earth would see them in a different shape.

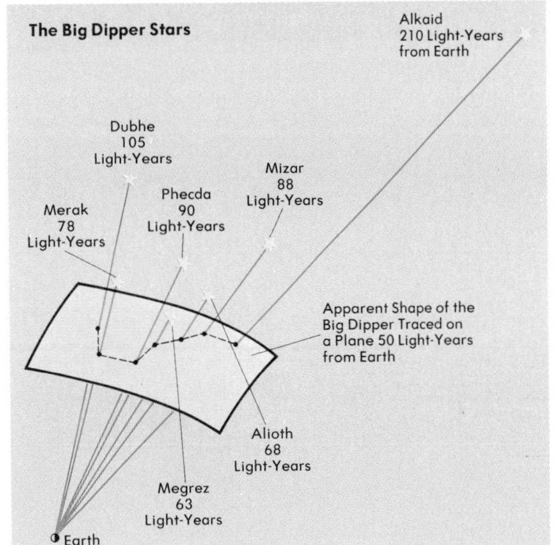

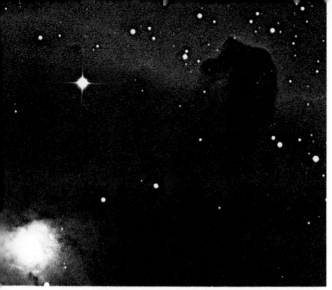

Dark nebulae, like the Horsehead nebula in Orion, are made of clouds of interstellar dust. The dust scatters starlight.

typical star. The largest stars are the cool supergiants: they have low surface temperatures, but they are so bright that they must be extremely large to give off that much energy. The *white-dwarf stars* are small and unusual: in them, a solar mass is squeezed into a sphere about the size of Earth. A teaspoonful of white-dwarf material might weigh ten tons.

Neutron stars are even more strongly compressed than the white dwarfs: they probably have a solar mass compressed to a radius of a few miles. The strange objects called *pulsars* are thought to be neutron stars. Physicists also speculate about the existence of *black holes*, which would be the remains of stars after they had undergone complete gravitational collapse. Such an object would be so dense that even light would be unable to escape its gravitational field.

The Crab nebula, a cloud of glowing gas in Taurus, is thought to be the remains of a star that exploded in 1054.

Interstellar Matter

THE SPACE between the stars contains gas and dust at extremely low densities. This matter tends to clump into clouds. If the clouds of gas and dust become apparent because they block starlight or glow from reflected starlight, they are called *nebulae*.

Interstellar dust is made of fine particles or grains. Although only a few of these grains are spread through a cubic mile of space, the distances between the stars are so great that the dust can block the light from distant stars.

Many small, dark regions are known where few or no stars can be seen. These are *dark nebulae,* dust clouds of higher than average density that are thick enough to obscure the light beyond them.

The dust grains block blue light more than red light, so the color of a star can be changed if it is seen through much dust. To find the temperature of such a star, astronomers must estimate its color to be bluer than it appears because so much of its blue light is lost in the dust.

When clouds of dust occur near bright stars they often reflect the starlight in all directions. Such clouds are known as *reflection nebulae.*

Interstellar gas is about 100 times denser than the dust but still has an extremely low density. The gas does not interfere with starlight passing through it, so it is usually difficult to detect. When a gas cloud occurs close to a hot star, however, the star's radiation causes the gas to glow. This forms a type of *bright nebula* known as an H II region. Away from hot stars the gas is quite cool. These cooler regions are called H I regions.

The interstellar gas, like most stars, consists mainly of the lightest element, hydrogen, with small amounts of helium and only traces of the other elements. The hydrogen readily glows in the hot H II regions. In the cool H I regions the hydrogen gives off radio-frequency radiation. Most interstellar gas can be located only by detecting these radio waves.

The hydrogen occurs partly as single atoms and partly as molecules (two hydrogen atoms joined together). Molecular hydrogen is even more difficult to detect than atomic hydrogen, but it must exist in abundance. Recently, other molecules have been found in the interstellar gas because they give off low-frequency radiation. These molecules contain other atoms besides hydrogen: oxygen or carbon occurs in hydroxyl radicals (OH) and in carbon monoxide (CO), formaldehyde (H_2CO), and many others.

Wherever there are large numbers of young stars, there are also large quantities of interstellar gas and dust. New stars are constantly being formed out of the gas and dust in regions where the clouds have high densities. Although many stars blow off part of their material back into the interstellar regions, the gas and dust are slowly being used up. Eventually a time will be reached when no new stars can be formed, and the star system will slowly fade as the stars burn out one by one.

The Galaxies

STARS ARE FOUND in huge groups called *galaxies*. Scientists estimate that the larger galaxies may contain as many as a trillion stars, while the smallest may have fewer than a million. Galaxies can be up to 100,000 light-years in diameter.

Galaxies may have any of four general shapes. *Elliptical galaxies* show little or no structure and vary from moderately flat to spherical in general shape. *Spiral galaxies* have a small, bright central region, or nucleus, and arms that come out of the nucleus and wind around, trailing off like a giant pinwheel. In *barred spiral galaxies*, the arms extend sideways in a short straight line before turning off into the spiral shape. Both kinds of spiral systems are flat. *Irregular galaxies* are usually rather small and have no particular shape or form.

The fact that galaxies exist in these various shapes has led astronomers to wonder whether galaxies evolve from one shape to another. Some theorists suggest that a galaxy starts out in an irregular shape, develops through the spiral forms until all its gas and dust have been converted to stars, and then becomes elliptical. Other theorists doubt that galaxies evolve from shape to shape because the rotation rates of the various shapes are different.

Galaxies were long thought to be more or less passive objects, containing stars and interstellar gas and dust and shining by the radiation that their stars give off. When astronomers became able to make accurate observations of radio frequencies coming from space, they were surprised to find that a number of galaxies emit large amounts of energy in the radio region. Ordinary stars are so hot that most of their energy is emitted in visible light, with little energy emitted at radio frequencies. Furthermore, astronomers were able to deduce that this radiation had been given off by charged particles of extremely high energy moving in magnetic fields.

National Radio Astronomy Observatory

Radio telescopes detect low-frequency radiation, such as that given off by cool interstellar gas.

The radio galaxies that have such strong radio emission are usually rather peculiar in appearance. How do they manage to give so much energy to the charged particles and magnetic fields? Many galaxies, and the radio galaxies in particular, show evidence of interstellar matter expanding away from their centers, as though gigantic explosions had taken place in their nuclei. The giant elliptical galaxy known as M 87 has a jet of material nearby that it apparently ejected in the past. The jet itself is the size of an ordinary galaxy!

Another problem has bothered astronomers for years. Most if not all galaxies occur in clusters, presumably held together by the gravity of the cluster members. When the motions of the cluster members

Like other wave phenomena, the absorption lines from a star or galaxy shift to longer wavelengths (red shift) when the object is receding from an observer. They shift to shorter wavelengths (blue shift) when the object is approaching an observer. When the absorption lines of an approaching star, a receding star, and the relatively stationary sun are shown against the background of a laboratory spectrum, it is clear that the lines occupy different positions on the spectrum.

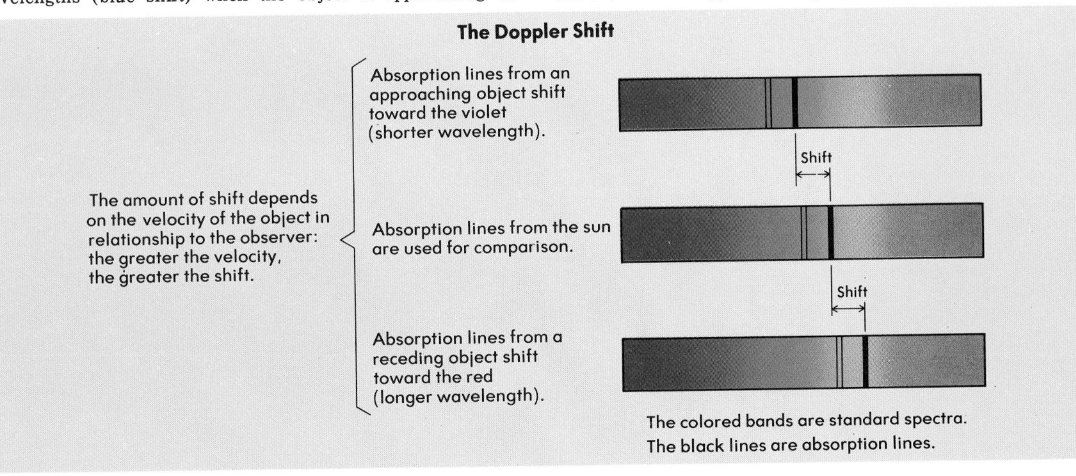
The Doppler Shift
Absorption lines from an approaching object shift toward the violet (shorter wavelength).
The amount of shift depends on the velocity of the object in relationship to the observer: the greater the velocity, the greater the shift.
Shift
Absorption lines from the sun are used for comparison.
Shift
Absorption lines from a receding object shift toward the red (longer wavelength).
The colored bands are standard spectra.
The black lines are absorption lines.

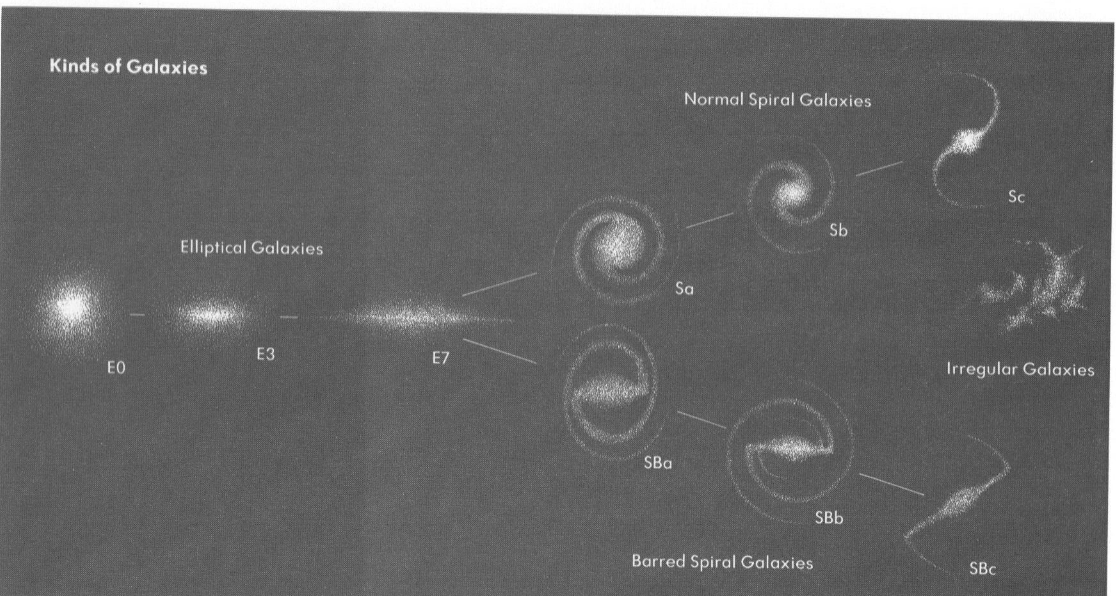

In the 1920's Edwin Hubble worked out a way of classifying galaxies. His method is still used. He separated galaxies into four general types according to their appearance and then classified each into subtypes.

are measured, however, it is found in almost every case that the clusters are unstable. The galaxies are moving too fast to be held together by their gravity. Then why did the clusters not disintegrate long ago? Astronomers have yet to find the explanation.

The Milky Way Galaxy

Like most stars, the sun belongs to a galaxy. Since the sun and Earth are embedded in the Galaxy, it is difficult for us to obtain an overall view of the Galaxy. In fact, what you can see of its structure is a faint band of stars called the Milky Way ("galaxy" comes from the Greek word for milk), so our Galaxy has been named the Milky Way galaxy.

The visible band of the Milky Way seems to form a great circle around Earth. This indicates that the Galaxy is flat rather than spherical. (If it were spherical, we would see the same density of stars over

The galaxies at the left illustrate Hubble's four types of galaxies. The irregular galaxy at upper left is M82, found in Ursa Major. At upper right is an elliptical galaxy, one of two elliptical galaxies that are companions to the Andromeda galaxy. At lower left is a spiral galaxy from the constellation Pegasus. A barred spiral galaxy in Eridanus is shown at lower right.

the entire night sky. They would not be especially concentrated in a single band.) The Milky Way galaxy is, in fact, a flat spiral with the sun located on the inner edge of a spiral arm. The center, or nucleus, of the Galaxy is about 30,000 light-years distant, in the direction of the constellation Sagittarius. All the stars visible without a telescope belong to the Milky Way galaxy.

Not all the Galaxy's stars are confined to the galactic plane. There are a few stars that occur far above or below the disk. They are usually very old stars, and they form what is called the halo of the Galaxy. Evidently the Galaxy was originally a roughly spherical mass of gas. Its gravity and rotation caused it to collapse into the disklike shape it has today. The stars that had been formed before the collapse remained in their old positions, but after the collapse further star formation could occur only in the flat disk.

All the stars in the Galaxy move in orbits around its center. The sun takes about 200 million years to complete an orbit. The orbits of most of these stars are nearly circles and are nearly in the same direction. This gives a sense of rotation to the Galaxy as a whole. It is possible to calculate how much matter the Galaxy must have in order to hold a star in its orbit by the force of gravity. In this way the approximate number of stars in the Galaxy can be estimated.

Velocities of Galaxies

When the Doppler effect is applied to galaxies, it is found that nearly all of them are moving away from us. Furthermore, the more distant galaxies have the greater speeds. A general relationship seems to exist throughout the universe: the greater the speed of an object, the greater its distance.

This relationship suggests that the system of galaxies is expanding. Suppose the galaxies were at one time in a rather small volume of space. After a time, the fast galaxies would have sped far from the original position, while the slow galaxies would still be nearby. The result would be a velocity-distance relationship exactly like the one observed.

In the early 1960's the new and puzzling *quasi-stellar radio source*, or *quasar*, was discovered. In photographs quasars usually look like ordinary stars, but they have Doppler shifts much greater than those of galaxies. This implies that the quasars have enormously large velocities away from us.

If the same relationship between velocity and distance holds for the quasars as for the galaxies, then the quasars are at tremendously large distances from us. But if they are actually so far away, they must be far more luminous than even giant galaxies. And yet, because their energy output varies irregularly over periods of months, astronomers have concluded that quasars are actually smaller than ordinary galaxies.

The name of our Galaxy comes from the visual phenomenon of the "Milky Way," a band of stars seen in Earth's night sky. This band is actually the major portion of the Galaxy. Since Earth lies in the midst of the Galaxy, the spiral structure is hidden by the nearest stars that lie in the plane of the galactic equator and form the "Milky Way."

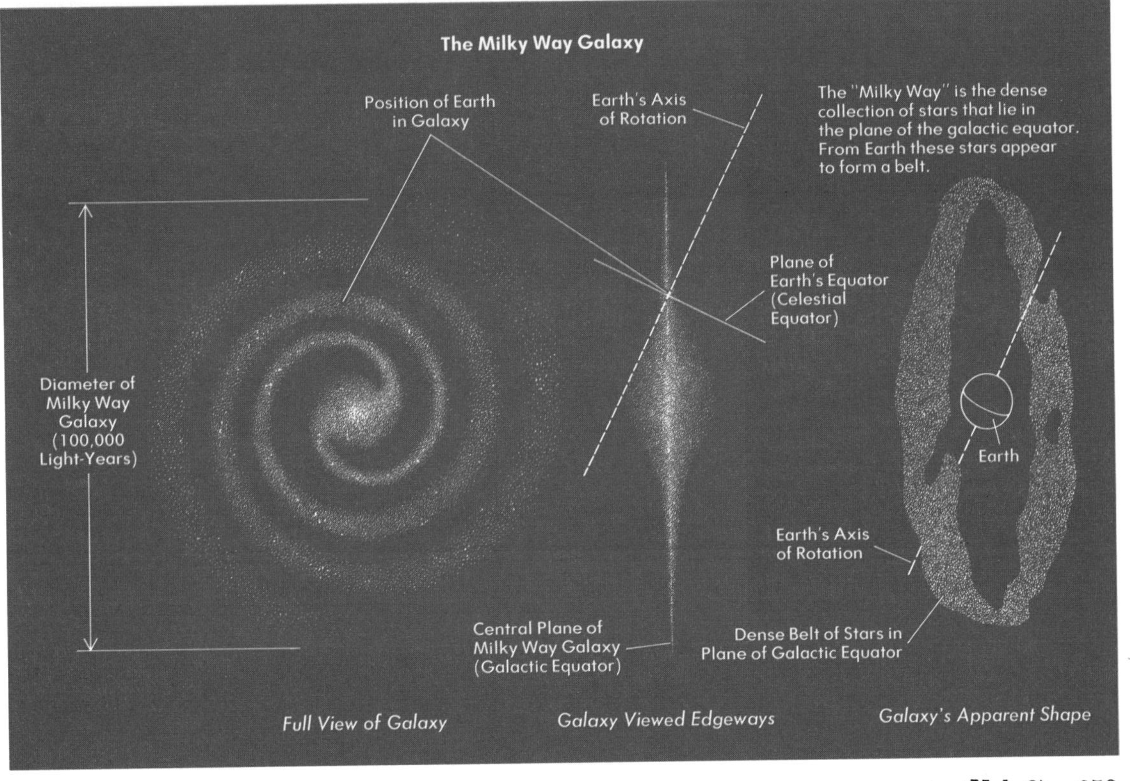

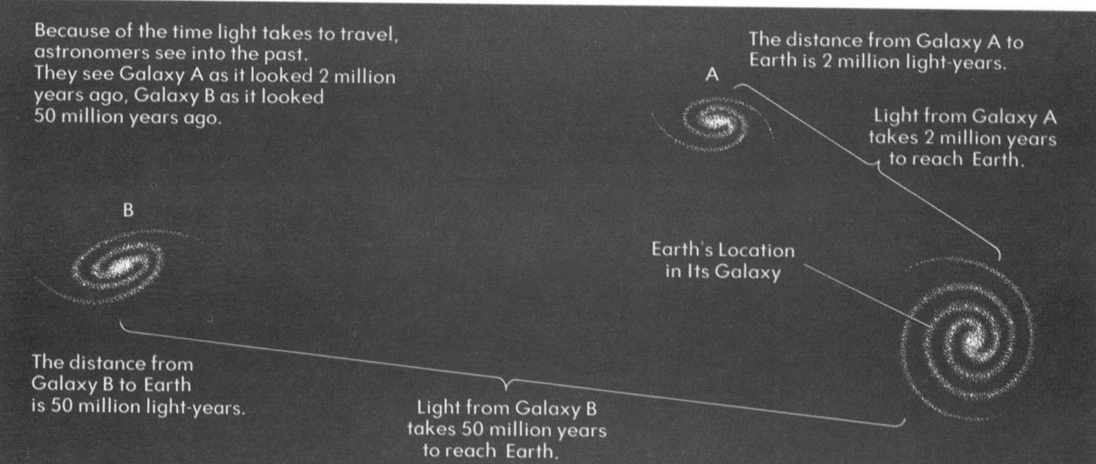
Because of the time light takes to travel, astronomers see into the past.
They see Galaxy A as it looked 2 million years ago, Galaxy B as it looked 50 million years ago.
A
The distance from Galaxy A to Earth is 2 million light-years.
Light from Galaxy A takes 2 million years to reach Earth.
B
Earth's Location in Its Galaxy
The distance from Galaxy B to Earth is 50 million light-years.
Light from Galaxy B takes 50 million years to reach Earth.

When astronomers look at an object that is a million light-years from Earth, they actually see light that left the object a million years ago. Light leaving the object today will reach Earth a million years from now.

The Universe

COSMOLOGY is the scientific inquiry into what the universe is like. By making assumptions that are not contradicted by the behavior of the observable universe, scientists build *models*, or theories, that attempt to describe the universe as a whole. They use each model until something is found that contradicts it. Then the model must be discarded.

Cosmologists usually assume that the universe, except for small irregularities, has an identical appearance to all observers, no matter where in the universe the observers are located. This is the *cosmological principle*. So far nothing has disproved this principle, but nothing has proved it valid, either.

One consequence of the cosmological principle is that the universe cannot have an edge, for an observer near the edge would have a different view from that of someone near the center. Thus space must be infinite and evenly filled with matter, or, alternatively, the geometry of space must be such that all observers see themselves as at the center. Also, the only motion that can occur, except for small irregularities, is a uniform expansion or contraction of the universe as a whole.

Since the universe appears to be expanding, it seems that it must have been smaller in the past. This is the basis for evolutionary theories of the universe. If one could trace the galaxies back in time, one would find a time at which they were all close together. Some cosmologists estimate that this was between 10 and 20 billion years ago. Thus we have a picture of an evolving universe that started in some kind of explosion—the "big bang." Some models of the universe predict that the expansion will continue forever. Others say that it will stop and be followed by a contraction back to a small volume again. Another model suggests that the universe oscillates, with alternate expansions and contractions.

Another theory is known as the steady-state cosmology. The basic assumption of steady state is a *perfect cosmological principle*, applying to time as well as position. The universe must have the same large-scale properties at all times. It cannot evolve, but must remain uniform. But since the universe is seen to be expanding, which would spread the matter out thinner as time goes on, steady state suggests that new matter must be created to maintain the constant density.

Where does the new matter come from? Well, where did the matter come from in the big-bang theory? Is it any easier to create the whole universe at one instant than to create it a little bit at a time? In the steady-state theory, galaxies are formed, they live and die, and new ones come along to take their places at a rate that keeps the average density of matter constant. The continuous creation of matter is an interesting property of steady-state cosmology.

Although the observations to date are not accurate enough to support any single model, they do provide some evidence against the steady-state theory. The big-bang theory, unlike steady state, predicts that the universe has changed over billions of years. And it is possible to see something of what the universe was like billions of years ago.

When an astronomer observes an object at a great distance, he is seeing it as it looked long ago, not as it looks now, because it takes time for light to travel. A galaxy viewed at a distance of a billion light-years is seen as it was a billion years ago. And distant galaxies do seem to be different from nearby galaxies. They seem closer together than nearby ones, contrary to steady-state contentions but consistent with the view that the universe had a greater density in the past. Also, a faint glow of radiation has been discovered coming uniformly from all directions. Calculations show that this could be radiation left over from the big bang. The steady-state theory has yet to come up with explanations of these phenomena.

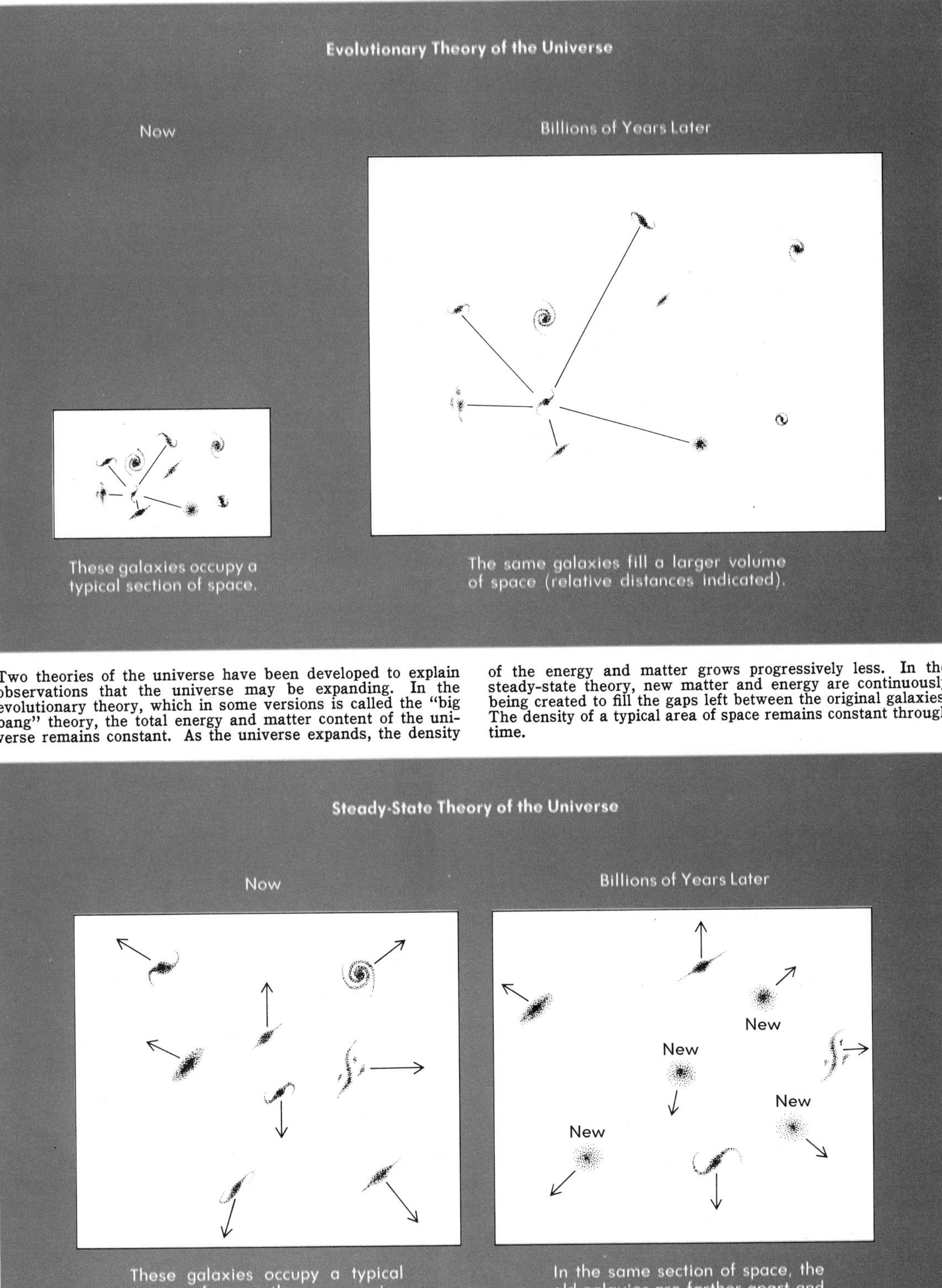

Evolutionary Theory of the Universe
Now
Billions of Years Later
These galaxies occupy a typical section of space.
The same galaxies fill a larger volume of space (relative distances indicated).
Steady-State Theory of the Universe
Now
Billions of Years Later
New
New
New
New
These galaxies occupy a typical section of space; they are moving in the directions indicated by the arrows.
In the same section of space, the old galaxies are farther apart and new galaxies have appeared.

Two theories of the universe have been developed to explain observations that the universe may be expanding. In the evolutionary theory, which in some versions is called the "big bang" theory, the total energy and matter content of the universe remains constant. As the universe expands, the density of the energy and matter grows progressively less. In the steady-state theory, new matter and energy are continuously being created to fill the gaps left between the original galaxies. The density of a typical area of space remains constant through time.

Dr. Georg Gerster—Rapho Guillumette

People in prehistoric Britain set up Stonehenge, a circle of huge stones that marked various astronomical occurrences. On Midsummer Day a person standing in the center of the circle sees the sun rise exactly above the heel stone.

The History of Astronomy

IN MANY early civilizations, astronomy was sufficiently advanced that reliable calendars had been developed. In ancient Egypt astronomer-priests were responsible for anticipating the season of the annual flooding of the Nile River. The Mayas of the Yucatán developed a complicated calendar for keeping track of days both far in the past and in the future. They could use their calendar to predict astronomical events. The ancient Polynesians also made good astronomical observations.

In China, a calendar had been developed by the 14th century B.C. A Chinese astronomer, Shih Shen, drew up what may be the earliest star catalog, listing about 800 stars. Chinese records mention comets, meteors, large sunspots, and novas.

The early Greek astronomers knew many of the geometrical relationships of the heavenly bodies. Some, including Aristotle, thought Earth was a sphere. Hipparchus, who lived around 150 B.C., was a prolific and talented astronomer. Among many other accomplishments, he classified stars according to apparent brightness, estimated the size and distance of the moon, and found a way to predict eclipses.

The most influential ancient astronomer historically was Ptolemy (Claudius Ptolemaeus) of Alexandria, who lived about 140 A.D. His geometric scheme predicted the motions of the planets. In his view, Earth occupied the center of the universe. His theory approximating the true motions of the celestial bodies was held steadfastly through the fall of Rome to the end of the Middle Ages.

In medieval times Western astronomy did not progress. During those centuries Hindu and Arabian astronomers kept astronomy alive. The records of the Arabian astronomers and their translations of Greek astronomical treatises were the foundation of the later upsurge in Western astronomy.

In 1543, the year of his death, came the publication of Copernicus' theory that Earth and the other planets revolved around the sun (*see* Copernicus). His suggestion contradicted all the authorities of the time and caused great controversy. Galileo supported Copernicus' theory with his observations that other celestial bodies, the satellites of Jupiter, clearly did not circle Earth.

The great Danish astronomer Tycho Brahe rejected Copernicus' theory. Yet his data on planetary positions were later used to support that theory. When Tycho died, his assistant, Johannes Kepler, analyzed Tycho's painstakingly gathered data and developed the laws of planetary motion. In 1687, Newton's law of gravitation and laws of motion reinforced Kepler's laws (*see* Gravitation; Mechanics).

Meanwhile, the instruments available to astronomers were growing more sophisticated. Beginning with Galileo, the telescope was used to reveal many hitherto invisible phenomena, such as the revolution of satellites about other planets (*see* Galileo).

The development of the spectroscope in the early 1800's was a major step forward in the development of astronomical instruments (*see* Spectrum and Spectroscope). Later, photography became an invaluable aid to astronomers. They could study photographs at leisure and make microscopic measurements on them. Even more recent developments —radar, the radio telescope, and space probes and manned spaceflights—have helped answer old questions and have opened our eyes to new problems.

A color enhancement of a photograph taken in ultraviolet light by astronaut John W. Young on Apollo 16 shows the geocorona, a halo of low density hydrogen that surrounds Earth.

By courtesy of NASA

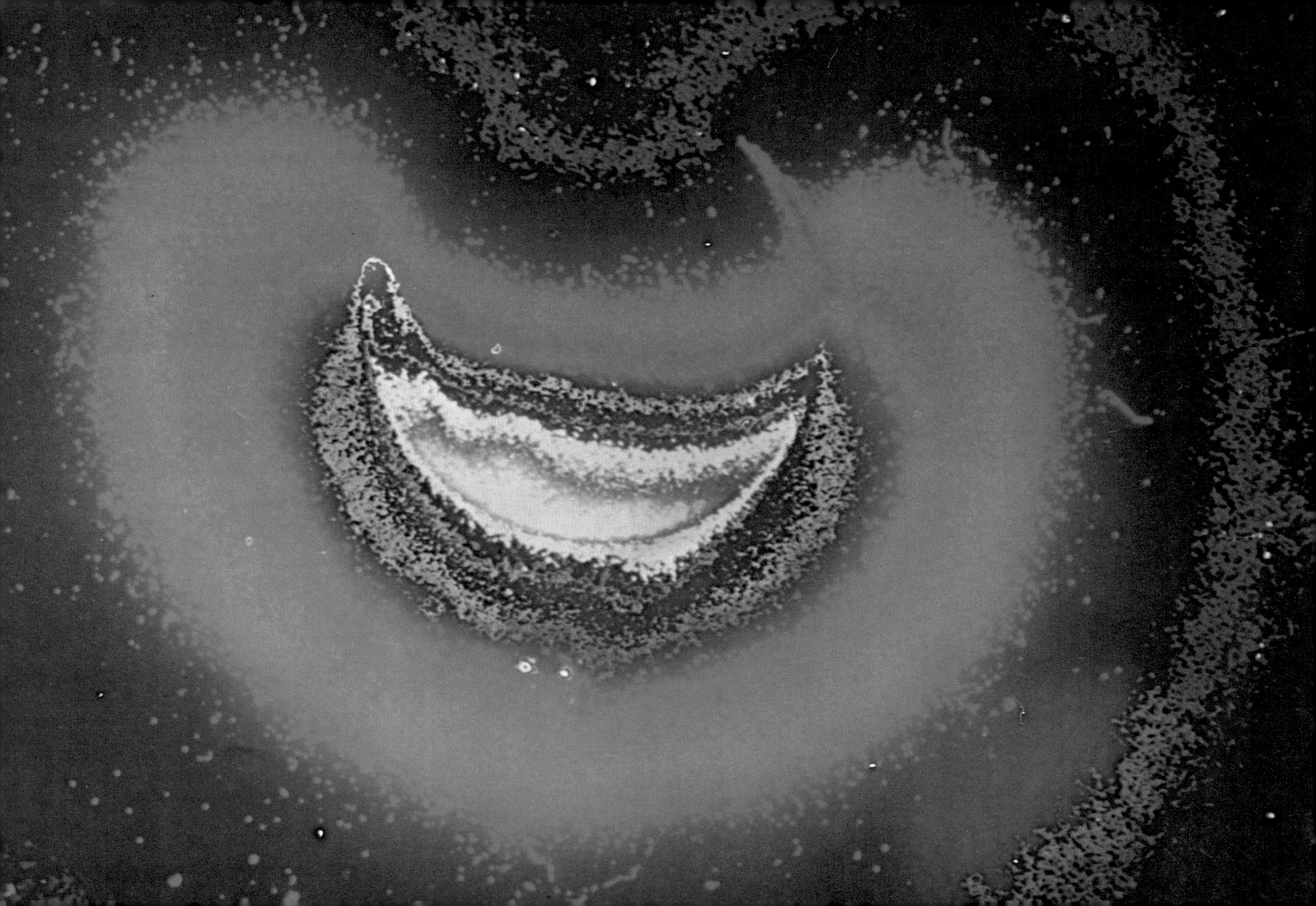

BIOCHEMISTRY

BIOCHEMISTRY. Scientists in the field of biochemistry study the chemical basis of life's activities. Biochemists and other scientists in closely related fields have shown that all living things—amoebas and elephants alike—share many similarities at the level of atoms and molecules. Without exception, all animals and plants operate on the basis of a few unvarying biological principles. These are: all life consists of basic units called cells; every living thing has a heredity; all vital activities require energy; all cells undergo key chemical reactions; and all living groups reproduce. What goes on in the life of a cell stems from an interplay of these few important principles.

The Cell and Its Membranes

To understand cell activities one must know about membranes and their functions. A cell is surrounded by a continuous membrane envelope called the cell, or plasma, membrane. It walls the cell's interior from the outer environment. The life processes go on inside the cytoplasm, or cell interior. The cell interior contains tiny organelles with membranes, too. These organelles include the mitochondrion (plural, *mitochondria*), the chloroplast (in plants only), the endoplasmic reticulum, and the nucleus. (*See also* Cell.)

All the membranes of a cell are so thin that their width can be seen only under the extremely high magnification of the electron microscope (*see* Microscope). A membrane is constructed from two types of molecules—proteins and phospholipids. They nest together to form the membrane. Both types of molecules have two surfaces. One surface, the hydrophilic one, "loves" water. The other surface, the hydrophobic one, "hates" water but likes oil. Membrane proteins and phospholipids are arranged in paired tiers, with protein tiers alternating with phospholipid tiers (see diagram on the next page). Since water is a major component of the cytoplasm and also of the outside environment, the fashion in which protein and phospholipid surfaces react to water forms the unique basis of membranes. Arranged in paired tiers, the membrane molecules expose their water-loving surfaces to the water both inside and outside the cell. By contrast, their water-hating, oil-loving surfaces avoid the water by lining up opposite each other at the middle of the membrane. This tightly organized molecular arrangement is so stable that it tenaciously resists disruption. Even when disrupted by strong forces, it tries to reseal any momentary holes to keep a continuous surface. Only membrane proteins, however, are designed for membrane service. Ordinary proteins having only water-loving surfaces cannot be used in membranes.

Each of the cell's organelles has its own distinctive membrane containing specific types of proteins and phospholipids. The specificity of membranes is possible because they can contain an endless variety of water-loving and oil-loving components as long as their bimodal character is kept.

What does a membrane do? One of its functions is to serve as a container. Another is to act as a barrier for preventing molecules from moving into and out of a cell at random. A membrane does this by providing molecular "turnstiles" that regulate which molecules can enter and which cannot. Still another function is fulfilled by a membrane: it houses some of the cell's enzymes as well as its energy-converting "machines." The membrane enzymes, which are special proteins themselves, carry out respiration needed for energy production, active transport of materials across membranes, metabolic cycles essential for life,

Diagram of a Typical Cell

Life-sustaining biochemical events take place in the cell parts shown above. A portion of the endoplasmic reticulum is further enlarged to show the ribosomes, where vital proteins are made.

FACT FINDER FOR BIOCHEMISTRY

The subject of biochemistry is a broad one. Readers will obtain additional information in the related articles listed here.

Biology	Genetics
Biophysics	Glucose
Carbohydrates	Hormones
Cell	Nucleic Acids
Digestion	Physiology
Enzymes	Plants, Physiology of
Evolution	Proteins
Fats and Oils	Respiration
Fermentation	Vitamins

This article was contributed by David E. Green, Professor of Biochemistry and Codirector of the Institute for Enzyme Research, University of Wisconsin.

and many molecule-building activities (*see* Biophysics; Enzymes).

Enzymes can be easily assembled on membranes. This feature pays enormous dividends to a cell because its vital biochemical reactions are facilitated by these important proteins. The manner in which protein molecules pair together in the double-tier arrangement of membranes is akin to the way in which complementary strands of deoxyribonucleic acid (DNA) pair. Since DNA, the important molecule of heredity, directs the assembly of enzymes and other proteins by complementarily matching certain chemical groups, it is clear why complementarity plays such a major role in cellular activities.

DNA Carries Heredity

Every living system has a blueprint for replication, or making copies of itself. This blueprint is commonly called heredity. The key structure of the hereditary process is the long, spiral DNA molecule. DNA consists of two complementary strands coiled around each other to form a twisted-ladder-like double helix (*see* Nucleic Acids). The strands are made up of varying sequences of chemical groups called nucleotides. A nucleotide consists of a sugar and a phosphate group plus either of two purine bases—adenine (A) and guanine (G)—or either of two pyrimidine bases—thymine (T) and cytosine (C).

DNA contains the genetic code for making proteins from smaller molecules called amino acids. Each base on a strand of DNA pairs only with its complement on the other strand; that is, A pairs only with T, and G pairs only with C. Moreover, each set of three bases on a strand, such as AAA, AGC, GGG, or CGT, codes for a specific amino acid (or in the case of a few triplets, for an end to the protein-making process). Thus, a base triplet corresponds to a particular amino acid in the same way that a unit of the Morse telegraph code corresponds to an alphabet letter. In this manner, DNA directs the sequencing of the amino acids that grow into proteins.

In many organisms, DNA is restricted to the cell nucleus, while protein synthesis goes on at the endoplasmic reticulum, a system of membrane-lined tubes in the cytoplasm. Ordinarily attached to the endoplasmic reticulum are the ribosomes, "workbenches" for protein construction. Since the ribosomes are away from the nucleus, the building code must somehow be communicated from DNA to the ribosomes. This is done through ribonucleic acid (RNA). RNA is closely related to DNA and can carry genetic messages. First, DNA unwinds and separates its strands so that complementary strands of RNA can be assembled on them. A strand of so-called messenger RNA (mRNA) then travels out of the nucleus to the ribosomes, where protein synthesis begins.

The mRNA strand, like its DNA "parent," contains the total genetic information needed for se-

SOME BIOCHEMICAL TERMS AND IDEAS IN THIS ARTICLE

ADP—adenosine diphosphate, an intermediary molecule that is converted to ATP when bonded to a third phosphate group.

ATP—adenosine triphosphate, the major storehouse of chemical energy in a cell. When one of its two high-energy phosphate bonds is broken in hydrolysis, ATP releases energy and becomes ADP.

Complementarity—a matching of components for a desired result; for example, in the paired series

2 3 1 4 0
2 1 3 0 4

the numerals in the top row complement those in the bottom row to yield the arbitrary number 4 in each pair. Complementarity underlies membrane construction, protein synthesis, and cell reproduction.

DNA—deoxyribonucleic acid, a molecule that holds the genetic information needed for heredity.

Electromechanochemical energy—the interconversion of electrical, mechanical, and chemical energy by the cell's energy-gathering systems to unleash, gather, and store the power locked in ATP.

Enzyme—a protein that catalyzes, or speeds up, biochemical reactions without itself undergoing a lasting change.

Oxidation—loss of electrons by an atom.

Phospholipid—a bimodal molecule composed of two contradictory elements—a phosphate group attractive to water and a lipid, which repels water.

P_i—symbol for an inorganic phosphate.

Protein—a large molecule composed of amino acids strung together in a unique arrangement.

Reduction—gain of electrons by an atom.

RNA—ribonucleic acid, the complement to DNA, which transcribes DNA's genetic instructions for the manufacture of proteins.

Membranes are important cell structures that consist of two kinds of biochemicals—phospholipids and proteins. The way in which they combine to form membranes is told in the text.

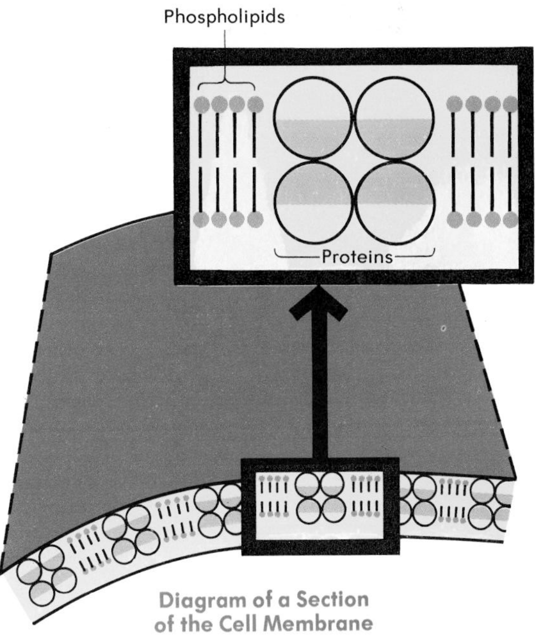

The Krebs, or Citric Acid, Cycle

Some of the Compounds Formed During the Krebs Cycle

A = Acetyl-CoA (Coenzyme A)
B = Oxaloacetate
C = Citrate, Isocitrate
D = α-Ketoglutarate
E = Succinate
F = Fumarate, Malate

2H signifies two hydrogen atoms that enter into several more reactions before appearing in a hydrogen donor SH_2 at a mitochondrion. Each Krebs cycle produces eight hydrogen atoms.

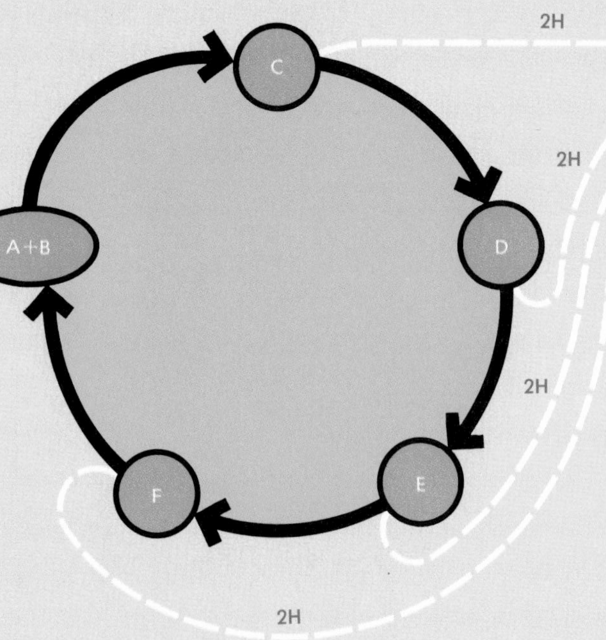

The diagram above describes the Krebs, or citric acid, cycle. Compounds other than those shown are also formed in the nearly dozen steps of the cycle, but only those involved in an outlay of hydrogen atoms are discussed. In each turn of the cycle, a molecule of A (derived from sugar) combines with one of B to form C, then D, E, and F until finally converting back to B. Each pair of hydrogen atoms from the Krebs cycle ends up at a mitochondrion in a reduced compound, here simplified as SH_2. Each turn of the cycle also leads to the combustion of acetic acid by oxygen and to the formation of carbon dioxide and water.

quencing amino acids into a particular protein. Imagine a protein containing only the two amino acids A and B strung out in this unvarying sequence: A—B—A—B—A—B (the sequence is deliberately shortened because proteins usually contain several hundred amino acids). A strand of mRNA has the series of complementary base triplets that codes for this sequence. However, another type of RNA called transfer RNA (tRNA) must carry the amino acids to the ribosome for assembly. When the mRNA code calls for amino acid A, the appropriate tRNA carries it in a form ready for peptide bonding with the next amino acid in line. In a peptide bond, the tail-end carbon atom of one amino acid is linked to the nitrogen atom of the next. When the code calls for it, another tRNA carries amino acid B. Bit by bit, the polypeptide chain grows to the desired length, guided by the mRNA directions. At the end of the operation, the newly formed protein is kicked off the ribosome. The protein instantly folds up in the most stable way. Synthesis proceeds at a fast pace. A protein containing 400 amino acids can be synthesized in about 20 seconds. (For more information about the role of DNA in protein synthesis, *see* Genetics.)

Of all the molecules that DNA could direct to be built, one might wonder why the information encoded in DNA is limited solely to the manufacture of protein. The reason is that so long as DNA can direct the making of protein enzymes, no other direction is necessary because enzymes aid in the building of all other cell molecules.

Most of the details of protein synthesis have been omitted from this discussion so that key events could be stressed. However, one procedure merits mention. Before an amino acid can be assembled into a polypeptide chain, it must first be modified to a so-called acyl amino acid, which is more reactive than an unmodified one. This important acyl conversion is powered by the energy stored in a molecule called adenosine triphosphate (ATP).

ATP—The Power Molecule

All living systems need energy in a usable form to drive the vital activities of cells. Nature has selected ATP as the cellular storehouse of chemical energy. ATP is a nucleotide made up of adenine (one of the amino acids in DNA and RNA), ribose (the sugar in RNA), and three interlinked phosphate groups (*see* Phosphorus). The two so-called high-energy bonds that link the phosphate groups together are the key power sources of ATP. When those bonds are broken, a considerable amount of energy is freed. By the same token, when the bonds are reestablished, a considerable amount of energy is stored in ATP. An inorganic phosphate group is usually symbolized P_i.

Chemical energy from oxidation of organic compounds is fed into the mitochondria, the cell's "powerhouses." There it is converted to electromechanochemical energy and gathered into ATP. In the chlorophyll-bearing chloroplasts of plant cells, however, the sun's radiant energy is converted directly into electromechanochemical energy and gathered into ATP.

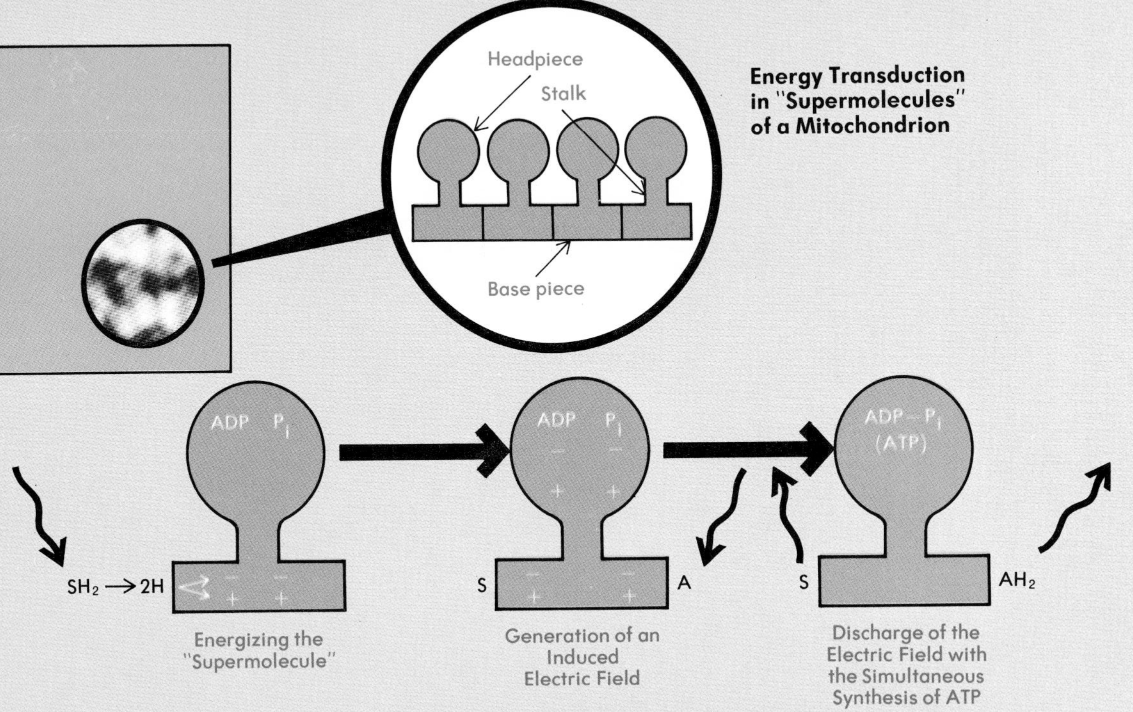

At the mitochondrial membrane SH_2 is oxidized, or loses its hydrogen atoms. A greatly magnified portion of the membrane is shown in the inset, above. The hydrogen atoms then split into electrons (−) and protons (+) as a "supermolecule" is energized. This charge separation forms an electric field in the base piece, which, in turn, induces a field in the headpiece.

Meanwhile, substance A arrives at the base piece. While the supermolecule is charged, ADP and P_i combine to form ATP. The field simultaneously discharges, and electrons and protons in the base piece transfer to A, which becomes reduced to AH_2.

Photograph, David E. Green

Energy transductions, or conversions, take place in many thousands of biochemical "machines" in the membranes of mitochondria and chloroplasts. Each of these energy-transducing "machines" is a "supermolecule"—a large molecular system in which the conversions take place. An oxidation reaction polarizes, or electrically charges, the supermolecule. Oxidation involves electron loss through the transfer of hydrogen atoms from substance A to substance B. In turn, a synthesis reaction depolarizes, or removes the charge from, the supermolecule. Synthesis involves the chemical bonding of substance C to substance D. In a supermolecule, however, adenosine diphosphate (ADP) and P_i substitute for the hypothetical substances C and D. Consequently, the oxidation of organic molecules provides the energy needed to bond ADP with P_i and thus synthesize ATP. This process is called *oxidative phosphorylation.*

The energy initially released by oxidation is siphoned into the supermolecule. When the supermolecule is polarized, conditions are right for energy to be siphoned out by chemically linking ADP and P_i. This synthesis then depolarizes the supermolecule (*see* diagram above). During oxidative phosphorylation, the oxidized and synthesized compounds remain chemically attached to the supermolecule. Only after synthesis has been completed can they leave it. Then a new cycle can begin.

Oxidative phosphorylation is only one of the ways of polarizing and depolarizing the supermolecule. The "machine" can also run in reverse so that the hydrolysis of ATP (the cleavage of ATP into ADP and P_i by water) polarizes it and a reduction reaction depolarizes it. Reduction involves electron gain, or the transfer of hydrogen atoms from substance B to substance A. In the case of active transport of substances across a membrane, the depolarizing reaction may involve the movement of a proton, or positively charged particle, from one side of the membrane to another.

Plant cells derive energy from photosynthesis (*see* Plants, Physiology of). In photosynthesis, light energy substitutes for the oxidative energy of chemical bonds. That is, the action of light on chlorophyll separates electrons and protons and thus polarizes the supermolecules of a chloroplast, just as oxidation does in a mitochondrion.

Cells also have a system that does not utilize membranes but nonetheless couples a series of oxidations to synthesize ATP. It is called the glycolytic system, a type of which functions in fermentation (*see* Fermentation). In one type of glycolysis, the sugar glucose is broken down to pyruvic acid, with the liberation of some energy (*see* Glucose).

The energy "machines" of a cell need a steady flow of input materials to sustain a high rate of ATP synthesis. Those in the chloroplasts of plant cells use light, ADP, and P_i. Those in the mitochondria of all cells use hydrogen-donating compounds as well as ADP and P_i. But where do the hydrogen donations come from? Glucose, one of the key fuels of life, provides some. During glycolysis, sugar is split into two molecules of pyruvic acid, with a yield of two hydrogen atoms. However, a more efficient system employs the Krebs, or citric acid, cycle. The Krebs cycle fuels the mitochondrial supermolecules with eight hydrogen atoms (*see* diagram on the preceding page). In each of these systems, however, the hydrogen atoms do not exist freely. Instead, they are passed from one compound to another in a series of so-called coupled reactions.

Once generated in the cell, ATP can power a wide variety of chemical and mechanical processes. These include muscle contraction and the active transport of ions. In addition, a large group of enzymes called kinases couple the hydrolysis of ATP (into ADP and P_i) with the synthesis of an organic molecule. In hydrolysis, a chemical bond of a molecule is split by water, resulting in two or more new molecules. An example of synthesis following ATP hydrolysis is the combination of ammonia and glutamic acid into glutamine, an amino acid. In this series of kinase reactions, the energy in ATP's phosphate bonds is siphoned from the power molecule to make glutamine. It is a consequence of the give-and-take energy transactions of membrane supermolecules.

Enzymatic Catalysis

Enzymes are the workhorses of the cell. They put together all its complex molecules. Thousands of vital chemical reactions must take place in the cell. None, however, can proceed without enzyme catalysts because at the relatively low temperatures existing in living systems, chemical reactions would take too long to occur without the help of enzymes.

Enzymes catalyze the synthesis of DNA, RNA, phospholipids, sugars, polysaccharides (long-chained sugars such as plant starch and animal glycogen), fatty acids, and proteins, among others. They also catalyze all the metabolic cycles of organisms. The Krebs cycle is an example of a metabolic cycle.

Enzymes speed up a host of chemical reactions, including oxidation and reduction, hydrolysis, and synthesis. Enzymatic catalysis is always characterized by the breaking and forming of chemical bonds, the rearrangement of a molecule, and the elimination of some chemical groups and the insertion of others. As a result, enzymes direct and control all the complex chemical maneuvers needed for building and maintaining the various types and forms of living tissue. (*See also* Enzymes.)

Enzymes do their work by utilizing energy transformations. When an enzyme's substrate, or reactive molecule, combines with it, energy is transferred from the substrate to the enzyme. This energy transfer separates the enzyme's closely located electric charges to such an extent that a full-blown electric field forms. During polarization, the substrate converts into an intermediary molecule. Then the intermediary converts into the final needed molecule as energy is drained from the enzyme during depolarization. The enzyme's charges return to their state of close apposition and the end product is freed from the enzyme, which is then ready for another catalysis (*see* diagram on the next page).

Enzymatic catalysis can be either "downhill" or "uphill." Downhill reactions take place spontaneously in the presence of an enzyme. Uphill reactions, however, have to be driven by ATP or an equivalent energy source. Whether downhill or uphill, the speed of enzymatic catalysis is enormous. One molecule of enzyme can catalyze the transformations of thousands of substrate molecules per minute at 38° C (100.4° F). Moreover, enzymes are chemically stable

Adenosine triphosphate (ATP) is the power source of many biochemical reactions. It is produced in the cell structures and system listed at the left on the diagram below to energize the important life processes listed on the right. An abbreviated chemical formula of the structure of ATP is also shown. The two high-energy P—O—P bonds are responsible for its power.

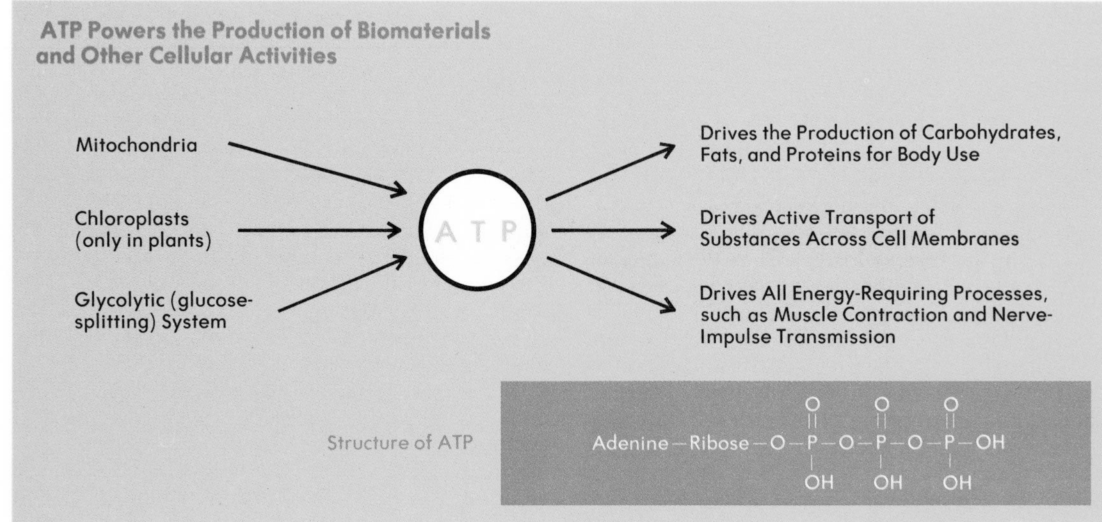

How an Enzyme Helps Make New Biochemical Substances

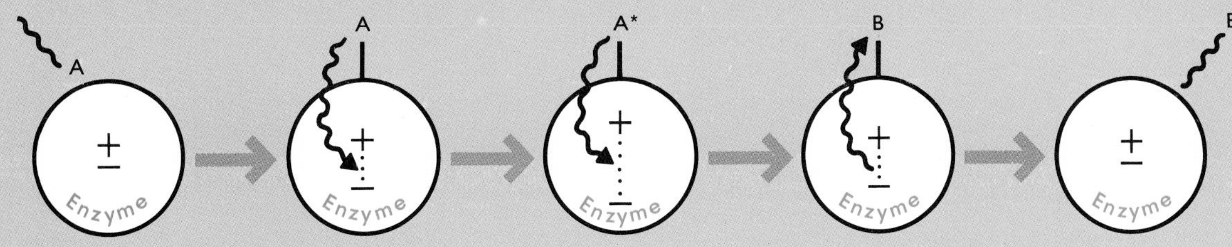

enough to work continuously for days and even months without falling apart.

A
Enzyme
A
Enzyme
A*
Enzyme
B
Enzyme
B
Enzyme
Substance A approaches the resting enzyme, which contains closely placed charges.
Substance A feeds chemical energy into the enzyme to force the charges apart.
As the enzyme thus becomes polarized and packed with energy like a stretched spring, substance A is converted to substance A*.
In the process of changing substance A* to substance B, energy is drained from the enzyme during depolarization as the charges approach each other again.
Substance B is released for its uses in the cell, and the resting enzyme is ready for another conversion.

Like other proteins, enzymes are made up of amino acids. But many enzymes also contain specialized non-amino-acid groups. Nearly all vitamins are sources of the specialized chemical groups required for the activity of certain vital enzymes. This explains why a vitamin-poor diet is dangerous. Major enzymes cannot be replenished in the body if the groups provided by vitamins are unavailable. Without these key enzymes, the cells would no longer function and death would result.

Reproduction at the Cell Level

All living systems are ordinarily capable of reproducing themselves. The replication of DNA, however, lies at the heart of all other forms of reproduction. Though cell division might seem the supreme act of replication, enzymes and other proteins are continually replicated at the ribosomes. So, too, are membranes and mitochondria. Hence, replication is going on in a cell whether it is dividing or not. When cell division does occur, the parent splits into two daughter cells, each of which has the same parts the parent had. In this replication process, the two strands of each DNA molecule separate, and each daughter cell receives a strand. Afterward, the DNA strands that the daughter cells receive act as the templates on which their complementary strands are built. As a consequence, the total genetic package received in part from the parent is reestablished in the daughter.

Cell division in higher organisms is a pageant-filled event. First the cell's nuclear membrane breaks down. Then DNA in paired structures called chromosomes line up in the middle of the cell and separate through a series of complex maneuvers. Finally, a cleavage furrow forms, and the cell splits in half, providing each daughter cell with its critical structures (*see* Cell). Amid this spectacle, membranes are replicated in a still mysterious way. Undiscovered, too, is how the cell "knows" when division should begin.

Biochemical Nature of Cell Structure

Living things and their components have distinct shapes because the architecture of their molecules is tailored for their specific tasks. For example, each of the thousand or more protein molecules has a special job. It might be involved in catalysis, in electron transfer, or in membrane construction, to name a few. A protein molecule has a shape uniquely suited for its assignment. The hemoglobin molecule, for example, has a pocket for carrying oxygen during respiration. The rodshaped collagen molecule stiffens tissues and organs. The same notion of fit-to-function applies to most other cell molecules. DNA is designed for the storage of genetic information, phospholipids for use in membranes, and ATP for the storage of usable energy. (*See also* Biology; Cell; Chemistry; Organic Chemistry; Life.)

Books About Biochemistry

Asimov, Isaac. The Chemicals of Life: Enzymes, Vitamins, Hormones (Abelard, 1954).
Baker, Jeffrey and Allen, G. E. Matter, Energy, and Life (Addison, 1965).
Borek, Ernest. The Atoms Within Us (Columbia Univ. Press, 1961). A good overview of molecular biology.
Chambers, R. W. and Payne, A. S. From Cell to Test Tube (Scribner, 1960). Introduces a young student to biochemistry.
Faber, Doris. The Miracle of Vitamins (Putnam, 1964).
Frankel, Edward. DNA—Ladder of Life (McGraw, 1964).
Patton, A. R. The Chemistry of Life (Random, 1970).

THIS ARTICLE IS IN THE FACT-INDEX
Biodynes

BRAIN

BRAIN AND SPINAL CORD. The brain is one of the most important parts of our body. It enables us to think and to be aware of our surroundings. When we relate to others, memories stored in the brain affect those relationships. When we become emotionally upset, it is because the brain's control over bodily functions has been stressed beyond its capacity. The brain is also capable of some strange things. It permits, for example, a person to experience phantom pain where an amputated limb once was. Drugs and surgery of the nerves leading to the brain often cannot remove traces of the "phantom." Only brain surgery will eliminate it.

The human brain regulates all the functions associated with human behavior. Moreover, this remarkable organ is formed from about 1,500 cc of nerve tissue having the consistency of dessert gelatin. In some ways, the brain is like a computer, although it is more intricately organized than the most complicated electronic computer (*see* Computers). Nerves carry signals from the eyes, ears, and other sense organs and from body receptors to the brain,

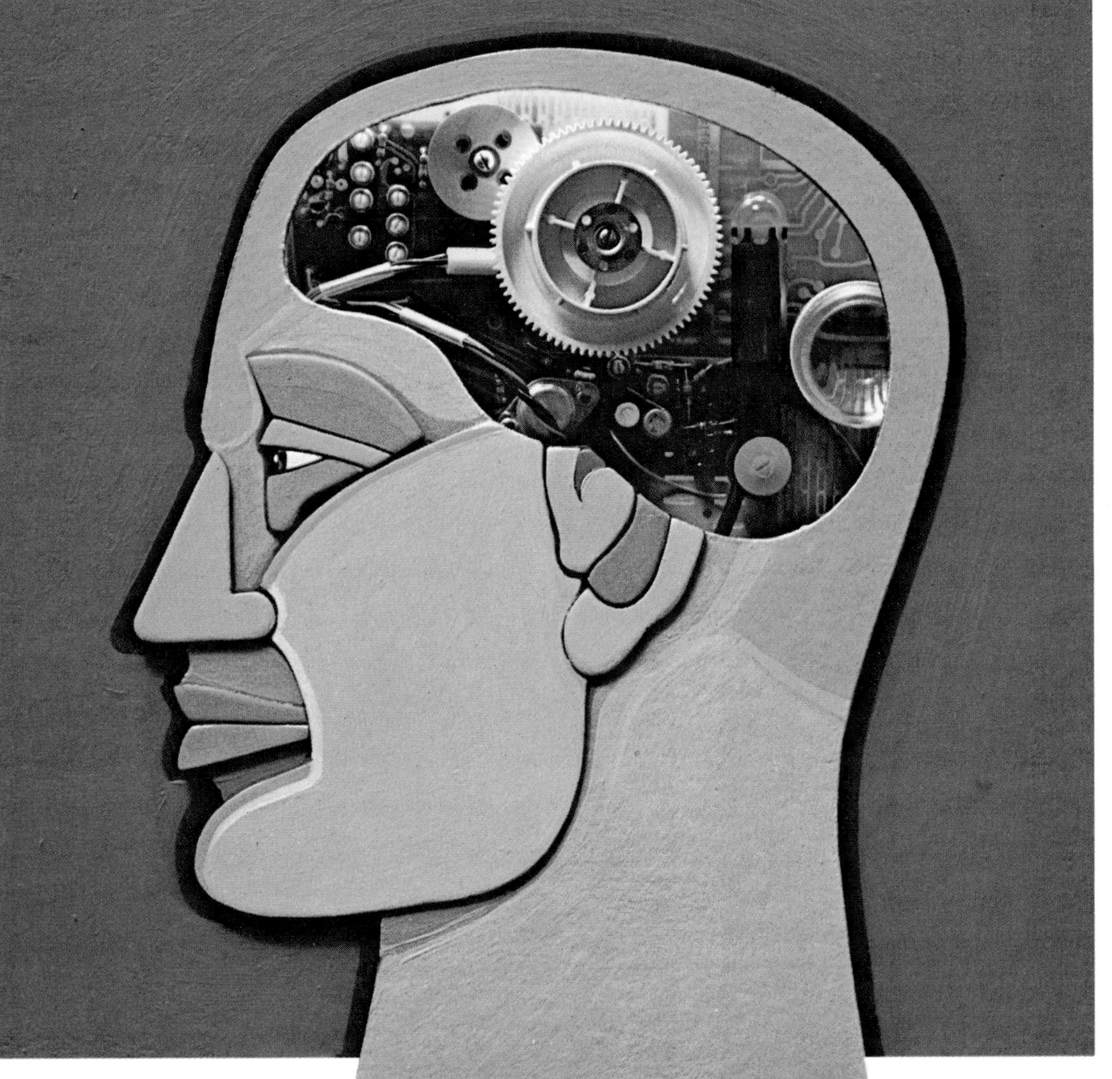

Illustration by Ronald Villani

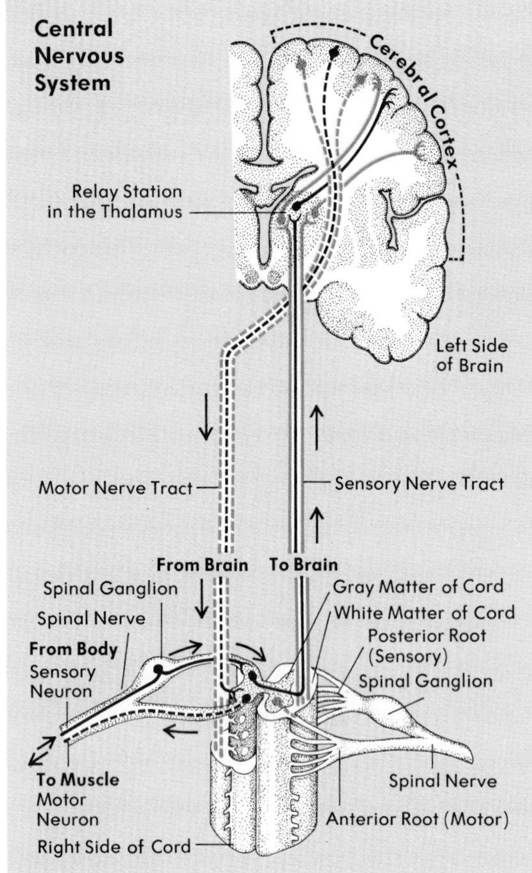

Impulses travel up the spinal cord from sense organ to brain for processing and then back to a muscle for action.

a central control mechanism with tremendous memory storage capacity. On the basis of these input signals, computations are made in the brain and output signals are sent to effectors—muscles and glands—to carry out the behavior needed for survival, communication, or creative effort. Brain signals are electrical nerve impulses that are organized into patterns in somewhat the same way that the letters of the alphabet are organized into words and sentences (*see* Nerves).

The Nervous System

Biological information is processed in the central nervous system (CNS), which consists of the brain and the spinal cord. The nerve network in the CNS carries nerve signals to and from the brain and between its sections. The spinal cord is an elongated tube made of nerve tissue lying in the bony spinal column. The cord extends into the head through a large hole at the base of the skull. Inside the head the tube forms the brain stem, which in turn is capped at its uppermost end by the cerebrum—two mushroomlike hemispheres that make up the largest mass of human brain tissue.

The nerves that carry input signals to the CNS for processing are afferent nerves and those carrying output signals from the CNS are efferent nerves. The nerves connected directly to sense organs and receptors are sensory nerves, and those connected to muscles and glands are motor nerves. A special category of motor nerves belongs to the autonomic nervous system, which is connected to but somewhat independent of the CNS. Autonomic nerves regulate the muscles and glands that carry on vital processes, such as breathing, blood circulation, and digestion. The autonomic nervous system, arranged on the outside of the spinal cord, is so named because the body's vital functions are greatly self-regulated and require only occasional adjustment by the CNS.

This article was contributed by Karl H. Pribram, Professor of Psychiatry and Psychology, Stanford University.

Homeostatic Regulation

Scientists once believed that all afferent, or input, nerves were sensory and that all efferent, or output, nerves were motor. This belief led to an overly simple view of how the nervous system works. Information from the outside world was thought to be processed through a reflex arc: input data→ central control mechanism→ output action. Recently, however, scientists discovered a new group of efferent nerves that carry information *from* the CNS *to* the sense organs and receptors, instead of the other way around. This means that when a person senses something from the outside, his brain has an influence on that sensation. For example, if you are willing to be tickled, you can be made to laugh and writhe, but if you are not willing to be tickled, you experience only touch, pressure, or even pain. For you to experience tickling, you have to be convinced through words and gestures to play along. Similarly, the touch of someone you love feels different from anyone else's. Furthermore, many scientists believe that pain is a type of selective control mechanism that alters the "setting" on the nerve cells in the spinal cord that receive sensory input from the skin, muscles, and internal body organs. In other words, a person's attitude could have an effect over the amount of pain experienced.

Discovery of efferent nerves to sense organs and receptors forced a revision of the reflex-arc idea. The nervous system is now thought to work in the same way that a wall thermostat controls a furnace. The thermostat has a number of temperature settings on its dial. Moving the dial changes the distance between two pieces of heat-sensitive metal in the thermostat. When warmed, they expand and make contact with each other. The contact closes an electrical circuit that stops the furnace. When the temperature drops, the metal contracts, the contact is broken, and the furnace starts. The entire system relies on a receptor mode of control; that is, the furnace is not controlled by a manual switch but by a

Some Principal Parts of the Brain

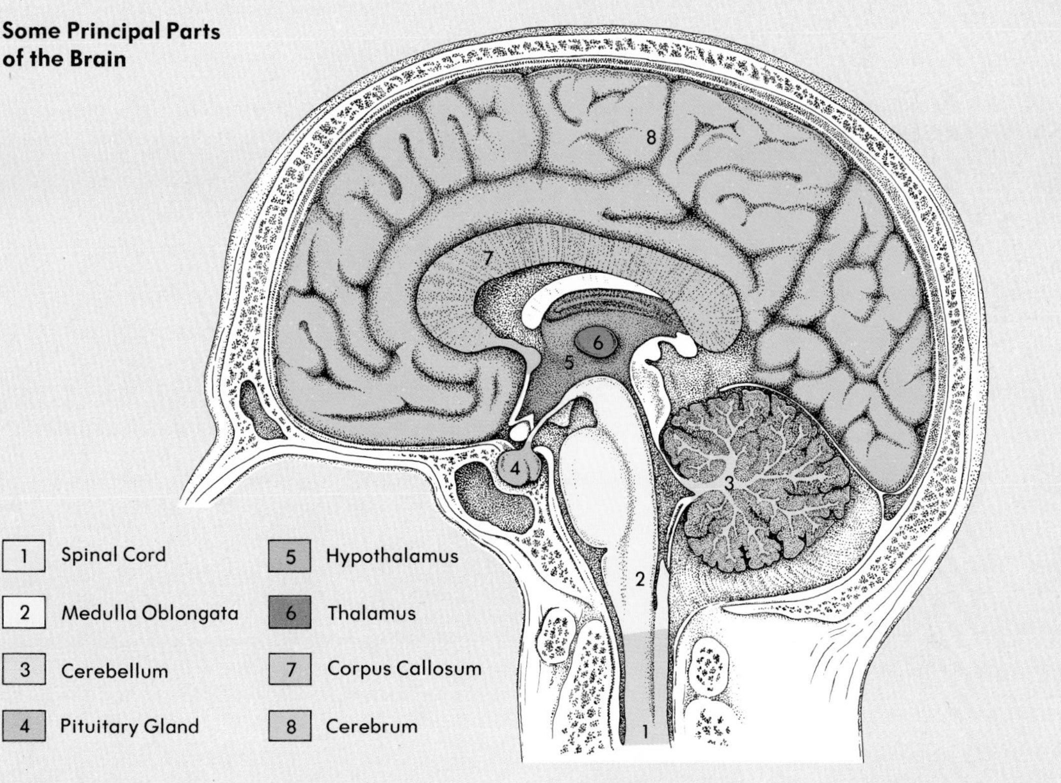

1	Spinal Cord	5	Hypothalamus
2	Medulla Oblongata	6	Thalamus
3	Cerebellum	7	Corpus Callosum
4	Pituitary Gland	8	Cerebrum

1. Spinal Cord—conducts nerve impulses to and from brain
2. Medulla Oblongata—contains regulators that control such basic functions as breathing and blood flow
3. Cerebellum—involved in coordinating muscle actions
4. Pituitary Gland—"master" gland that controls activities of many other endocrine glands
5. Hypothalamus—regulates many body actions, including sex functions, hunger and thirst, and body temperature; influences pituitary gland
6. Thalamus—"switchboard" of brain that relays sensory nerve impulses to cerebral cortex
7. Corpus Callosum—links both hemispheres of cerebrum
8. Cerebrum—"thinking" portion of brain where complex associations occur

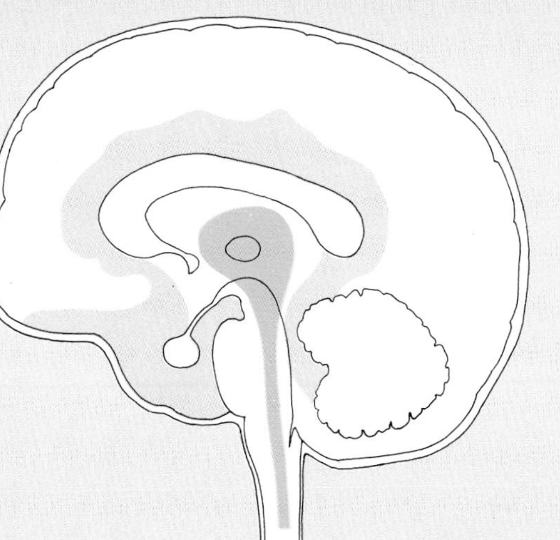

Limbic System

Limbic System—mediates basic body functions, such as breathing, digestion, heartbeat, biological rhythms, and sex functions; also processes memory; includes the hypothalamus and portions of the basal ganglia and of the thalamus

Reticular Activating System

Reticular Activating System—triggers "awareness," or acute consciousness; includes core of brain stem and portions of the thalamus and hypothalamus

Basic Systems of the Brain

thermostatic receptor that responds to changes in room temperature.

In the same fashion, the brain controls the way a person responds to environmental changes by sending information that changes the "settings" on his receptors. Homeostatic regulation, as this is called, allows for economic memory storage. In the furnace analogy, a person need not consult a long and involved checklist showing when to turn the furnace on and off to maintain constant room temperature when the weather is changing. He only has to set a temperature from the short list of set-point numbers engraved on the thermostat dial. In a similar fashion, "lists" of informative features of the environment can be stored in the brain and called for when needed.

Brain Homeostats Regulate Vital Functions

Nerves are the information-processing homeostats of the brain and its stem. Each neuron, or nerve cell, in the nervous system consists of a cell body and wirelike "tentacles" that sometimes reach three feet in length. Masses of nerve cells have a grayish color. They form the gray matter of the brain, brain stem, and spinal cord. Gray matter accumulations are called nuclei or centers because they contain many nerve connections. When they are spread out in thin sheets, however, they are called cortex. By contrast, masses of nerve trunks look white because they contain myelin, a fatty insulating material. Nerve trunk accumulations are called tracts or pathways. In the spinal cord and brain stem, gray matter lies in the center, surrounded by white matter. In the cerebral cortex, however, gray matter lies on the outside.

Many of the nervous system's most vital regulatory functions are carried out by homeostatic centers in the brain stem. The homeostat that regulates breathing, for example, is in the medulla oblongata, the hindbrain just above the area where the spinal cord extends into the skull.

The homeostats that regulate sleep and wakefulness are located in the mesencephalon, or midbrain, which is slightly in front of the medulla but is still part of the brain stem. These homeostats also control such moods as elation and depression. Moods are influenced by body chemicals acting on receptors in the midbrain. Many of these chemicals are secreted by nerve endings to improve communication between nerves at their synaptic points of contact, which appear well-developed in the midbrain. Drugs that influence the mood-regulating homeostats are widely used in psychiatry to ease manias and depressions.

Still farther forward in the brain stem lies another series of homeostats packed closely together in the hypothalamus, which is part of the diencephalon, or between-brain. Homeostatic neurons in the hypothalamus regulate sex functions, hunger and thirst, body temperature, and general body activity. They regulate some of these activities through neurosecretions, or nerve-cell chemicals, which make them glands as well as nerves. The neurosecretions di-

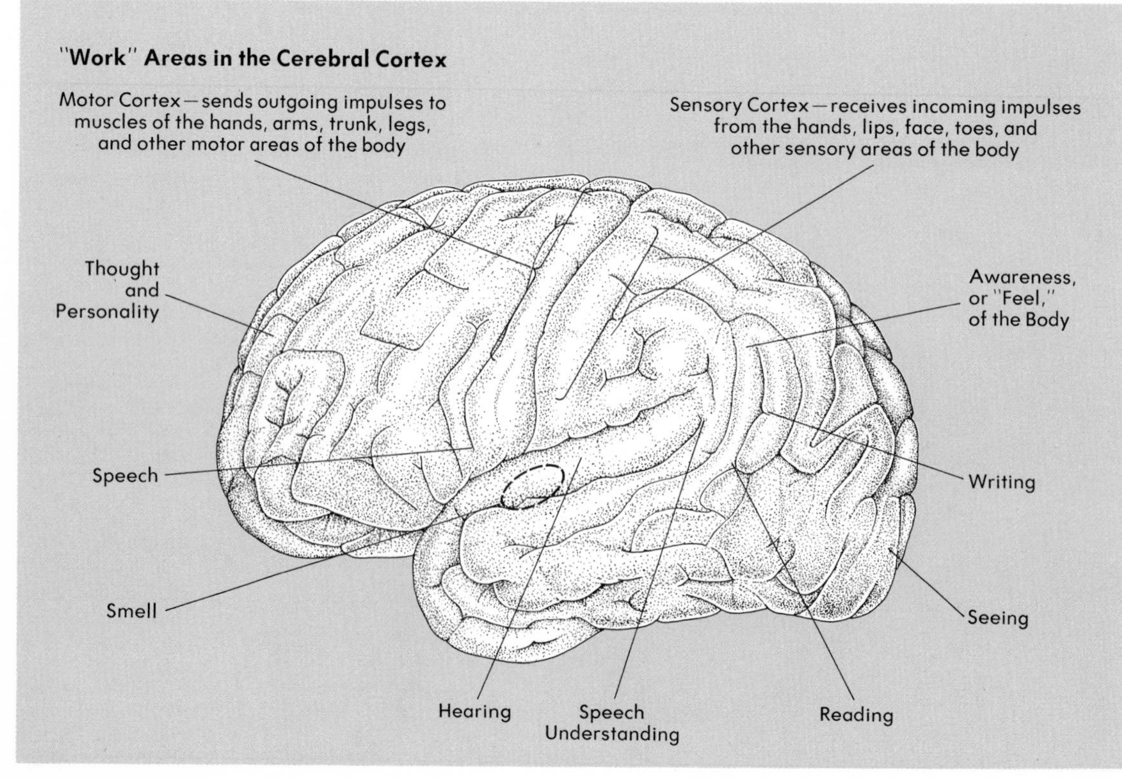

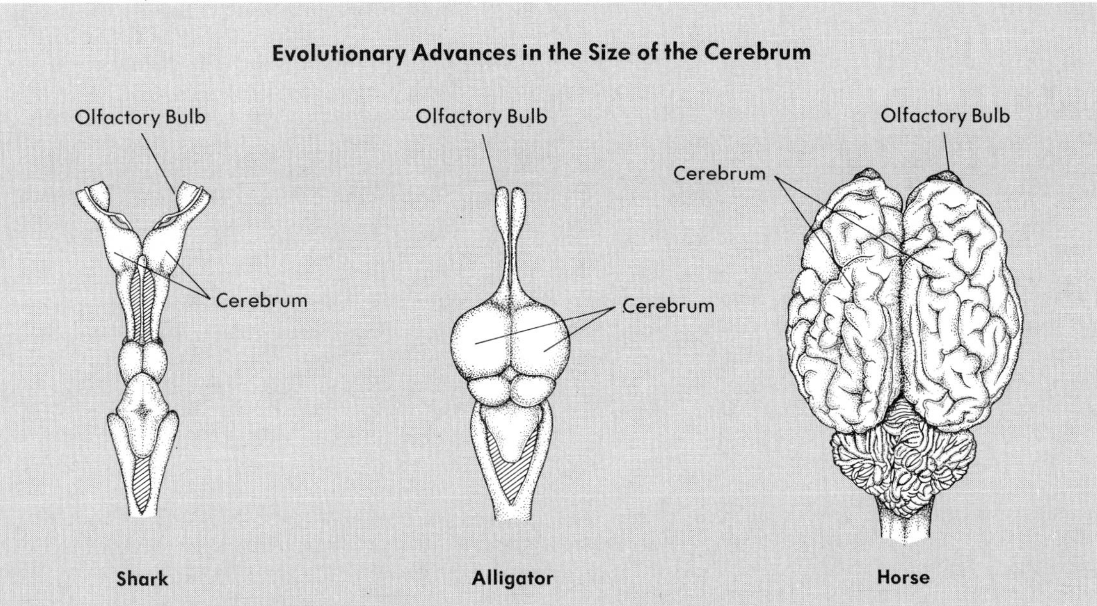

Judging by the shark's large olfactory bulbs, smell is very important to its survival. The cerebrum, associated with advanced behavior, is larger in the alligator; and in the horse and other mammals it outshadows the rest of the brain.

rectly influence the pituitary gland, the body's "master" endocrine gland that lies immediately under the hypothalamus (*see* Hormones).

The brain's thalamus lies just above the hypothalamus. It receives and processes information from receptors and sense organs through pathways in the lower brain stem and in the spinal cord. By contrast, hypothalamic, midbrain, and hindbrain mechanisms process information only from inside the body.

Sensory and Motor Functions of the Brain

The back portion of the thalamus is the last station reached by information from the body surface before it is relayed to the cerebral cortex for processing. Information about touch, pressure, pain, and muscle and joint senses merges in the thalamus. Information that leads to seeing and hearing is also processed by thalamic nuclei. Afferent-efferent connections between the thalamus and the cerebral cortex form a two-way street that closely coordinates their actions.

The most forward part of the brain stem contains a group of structures called the basal ganglia. They regulate muscle-control homeostats by adjusting the set points of those homeostats. Diseases of the basal ganglia produce muscle tremors and severe and uncontrollably repetitive movements. In addition, evidence suggests that all homeostatic mechanisms are influenced by the basal ganglia.

The cerebellum is another structure intimately involved in movement control. It is an outgrowth of the balancing mechanism that has receptors in the inner ear (*see* Ear). Although it was originally involved only with inner-ear balance, the cerebellum eventually evolved a large cortex in man and other primates to help compute trajectories required for jumping from tree to tree or the many other complex movements primates can perform. Computations by the cerebellum are sent through the thalamus to movement homeostats in the cerebral cortex. Information from the basal ganglia also adjusts the set points of the movement homeostats. Thus, once an activity has begun, information from the cerebellum continuously fine-tunes, or redefines, the set points until the activity is completed.

The Cerebral Cortex

The uppermost part of the brain—composed of the cerebral hemispheres—is also the most dominant part. The cortex of the cerebral hemispheres is hooked up with the other parts of the brain. It receives information relayed through the thalamus. In turn, the cortex controls its input by transmitting signals through efferent fibers to the thalamus and points below. Furthermore, it is closely linked with the cerebellum and the basal ganglia. As a matter of fact, the cerebral hemispheres develop in the embryo from nerve cells that migrate from the basal ganglia.

An intriguing riddle about the cerebral cortex is how it retains most of its powers of perception and memory after it is extensively damaged. Brain tumors and strokes hardly alter these powers as long as a critical mass of brain tissue is not destroyed. This is also true of epileptic scarring, which makes nerve cells in the brain fire convulsively instead of in a tightly organized way. A person who suffers a stroke—the leakage or blockage of a blood vessel in the brain—might lose three fourths of the visual area of his brain. As a result, he would experience a hole in his visual field; that is, he would be unaware of the objects or scenes occurring in the blocked-out visual surroundings. But with the remaining quarter of his visual field, he would continue to experience all he already knew; that is, he would not suffer a proportional three-quarters loss of memory. He would come home to a family of four and recognize all and not just one member.

In their search for the way the brain stores memories, brain scientists have uncovered a possible explanation of the memory riddle. Perhaps information becomes distributed in the sensory systems in much the same way that information is stored in holograms. Holograms are interference patterns of light on film (*see* Color; Laser and Masers). Although they bear no images, three-dimensional images can be reconstructed from the interference patterns. Like the brain's visual system, holograms can be damaged extensively and yet produce a complete image from what remains. Holograms share other information storage properties with the brain, such as vast capacity, ease of information retrieval, and cross-correlation of input information.

The cerebral cortex is divided into a number of areas. Some are hooked up with peripheral sensory-motor and core homeostatic mechanisms. Others are involved with advanced behavior. For many years, scientists thought that the cerebral cortex was organized as a reflex-arc pathway. Sensory information, according to this belief, was sent to the sensory areas of the cortex, was then associated and abstracted in the association cortex, and finally was sent from the motor cortex to the muscles and glands. Recent data suggest, however, that the sensory areas of the cortex—those that receive information from sensory receptors—can effectively guide behavior even when completely isolated from the rest of the cortex. Also, the motor areas of the cortex—those that trigger muscle contractions when electrically stimulated—primarily process information coming from muscle receptors and then use this information to alter the set points of those and other receptors. Furthermore, the association cortex acts to some extent by altering or filtering sensory input, perhaps through the basal ganglia, enabling attention to be given to one or more sources of sensory information. By studying electroencephalograms, or brain wave recordings, scientists can determine whether a monkey, for instance, is attending to the color or to the pattern of a cue with several components even before the monkey outwardly reacts to one or the other.

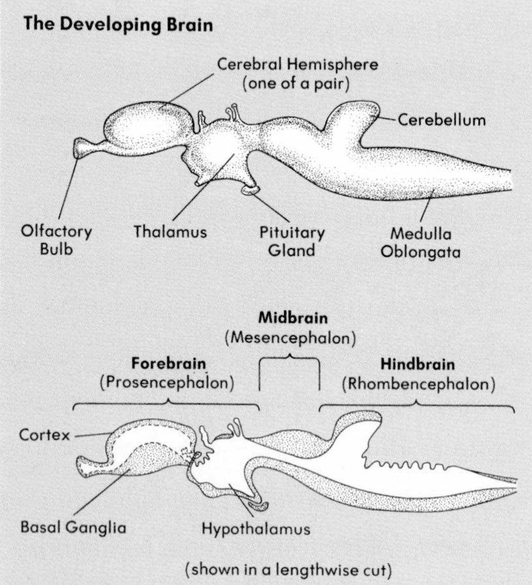

Key parts and major divisions of a vertebrate embryo's brain are shown above at an early stage of development. Technical names of the three major divisions are in parentheses.

Experiments such as this suggest that what we see, hear, feel, and perceive is determined by homeostatic brain processes, as are the bodily functions. The central processing of these experiences, however, requires afferent-efferent neural loops that are longer and encompass larger masses of brain tissue than those involved in the bodily functions. Much of the central organization relies on interaction between the cerebral cortex and the lower parts of the brain and the spinal cord, rather than solely on reflex-arc action between areas of the cortex.

The reticular core of the brain stem is one of the most effective places for input control. The chemical receptor sites that regulate sleep and wakefulness, alertness, and elation and depression are found there. These core brain stem sites, in turn, influence visual, auditory, and somatic sensory input as it enters the spinal cord and brain stem. For example, it is more difficult for a person to pay attention to something when he is tired than when he is rested and alert.

We can envision the cerebral cortex as being broadly organized along two intersecting axes. The outer cortex lies along the first axis. The front part of it deals with motor action, while the back part deals with sensory input. The outer cortex is involved with the "world out there," including such memory functions as recognizing persons and places and remembering motor skills. The limbic cortex, or the side-to-side core portion, lies along the second axis. It deals with information from the "world within." The limbic cortex is involved with such memory functions as recalling familiar as well as unique experiences, for memories are tied in with our vital functions.

The Brain and Human Language

The two axes of the cerebral cortex intersect in the portion that receives and sends information to the ears, mouth, tongue, and throat. This is also the center of the human language control mechanism. Scientists have wondered what quality of the human brain provided for the development of language. One hint comes from the unique ability of each of the human cerebral hemispheres to control different information-processing systems. The right hemisphere deals largely with spatial relationships, musical abil-

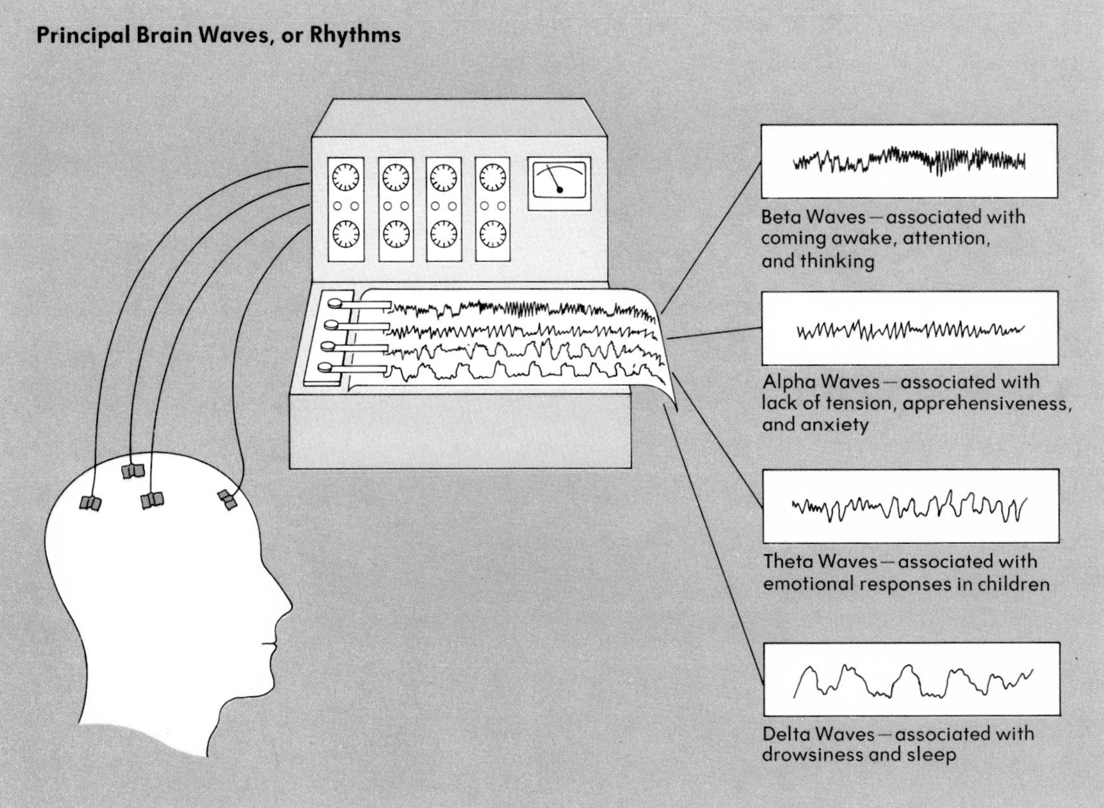

Brain wave recordings are made by an electroencephalograph. Recordings of the principal brain waves are shown above. Subjects of "biofeedback" experiments try to maintain a steady output of alpha waves, which indicate a calm state of mind.

ities, and other nonverbal functions. The left hemisphere processes linguistic information. In all mammals, each hemisphere receives information from and controls the opposite side of the body. Signals to move the right hand, for example, come from the left cerebral hemisphere. Only in man, however, has specialization proceeded to the point where an all-important function such as speech is localized almost exclusively in the left hemisphere. Speech specialization is not present from birth, however. A child who has had surgery or injury to his left hemisphere before the age of seven ordinarily recovers all his language abilities, which then become localized in the right hemisphere.

Anyone reared in total isolation from other people does not develop the organization of sounds and gestures that constitutes language. The observations that hemispheric specialization develops slowly over years and that an isolated brain does not produce a language suggest that the human brain gradually becomes programmed. Other animals, such as the birds, have "wired-in" programs that guide behavior with little change from birth (*see* Animal Behavior). In humans, the strings of nerves that make up "lists" of variable length can influence each other to produce programs much as computer languages produce computer programs. Future research should uncover exactly how the information contained in the lists of homeostatic mechanisms becomes processed into human language. (*See also* Computers; Language; Learning; Nerves.)

Books About the Brain

Asimov, Isaac. The Human Brain: Its Capacities and Functions (Houghton, 1963). Clearly written for the layman.

Calder, Nigel. The Mind of Man (Viking, 1970). Recent brain research.

Elliott, H. C. The Shape of Intelligence (Scribner, 1969). Explores the wide range of animal intelligence.

Hyde, M. O. Your Brain: Master Computer (McGraw, 1964). Compares human brains to mechanical "brains."

Luce, G. G. and Segal, Julius. Sleep (Coward, 1966). A popular approach.

Silverstein, Alvin and V. B. The Nervous System: The Inner Networks (Prentice, 1971). For younger readers.

Weart, E. L. The Story of Your Brain and Nerves (Coward, 1961). In clear terms for children.

Wilson, J. R. The Mind (Time, 1969). A general overview that discusses the nervous system and psychology.

THESE ARTICLES ARE IN THE FACT-INDEX

Ralston Purina Co.

DOG

DOG. The dog is one of the most popular pets in the world. It ordinarily remains loyal to a considerate master, and because of this the dog has been called man's best friend. Class distinctions between people have no part in a dog's life. It can be a faithful companion to either rich or poor.

Dogs have endeared themselves to many over the years. Stories have been told about brave dogs that served admirably in war or that risked their lives to save persons in danger. When Pompeii—the Roman community destroyed by Mount Vesuvius in A.D. 79—was finally excavated, searchers found evidence of a dog lying across a child, apparently trying to protect the youngster. Perhaps few of the millions of dogs in the world may be so heroic, but they are still a source of genuine delight to their owners.

A dog fits easily into family life. It thrives on praise and affection. When a master tells a dog that it is good, the animal happily wags its tail. But when a master scolds a dog, it skulks away with a sheepish look and with its tail tucked between its legs.

People in the city as well as those in other areas can enjoy a dog. Medium-size or small dogs are best

This article was contributed by Arthur F. Jones, internationally known authority on dogs and author of numerous books and articles about them. Illustrations of the breeds in this article were prepared by Harry Michaels, expert illustrator of canine features in newspapers and periodicals.

Scientific Classification

Phylum: Chordata
Subphylum: Vertebrata
Class: Mammalia
Order: Carnivora
Family: Canidae
Genus: *Canis*
Species: *C. familiaris*

Dogs are in the order of carnivorous animals, Carnivora, and belong to the family Canidae. All domestic dogs are genus *Canis*, species *C. familiaris*. For information on other members of the dog family, *see* Jackal; Wolf.

suited for the confines of the city. Large dogs need considerable exercise over a large area.

Dogs are not always well thought of, however. In recent years dogs in the city have been in the center of controversy. Some people have criticized dog owners for allowing their pets to soil sidewalks and lawns, although in some cities laws oblige owners to walk their dogs along street curbs. In turn, dog owners have argued that the animals serve as protection against vandals and burglars and thus protect their detractors as well as their owners.

When a person decides to own a dog, he should be prepared to care for it properly. For a dog to stay healthy it must be correctly fed and adequately groomed, and its medical needs must be met. For a dog to be well-mannered it must be properly trained. It should never be ill-treated or mishandled. Otherwise, it will bite in its own defense.

The wild ancestors of all dogs were hunters. Wolves and other wild relatives of the dog still hunt in packs for their food. Dogs have retained the urge to be with the pack. This is why they do not like to be left alone for long. Some breeds of dogs still retain the hunting instinct.

Dogs exist in a wide range of sizes, colors, and temperaments. Some, such as the Doberman pinscher and the German shepherd, serve as alert and aggressive watchdogs. Others, such as the beagle and the cocker spaniel, are playful family pets, even though they were bred for hunting. Still others, such as the collie and the Welsh corgi, can herd farm or range animals. Each of the dogs just mentioned is a purebred. A mongrel dog, however—one with many breeds in its background—can just as easily fit into family life. Only proper training and affection are needed to raise any happy dog.

Dogs have been with man since prehistoric times. Over the years they have performed various services for man. They have pulled his sleds over snowy tracts. They have delivered messages, herded sheep and cattle, and even rescued persons trapped in the snow. Dogs have served as a source of food, too. The ancient Romans are said to have prized certain kinds of dog stew. The Aztecs of ancient Mexico raised tiny dogs, thought to be the forebears of the chihuahua, to feed the large carnivores in the private zoos of the Aztec rulers. In the past dogs have even been worshiped as gods. Recently, they have been used in drug research, medical experimentation, and space science. Russian scientists launched dogs into space to test the ability of mammals to survive the rigors of space travel before men were sent up.

Dogs are trained as guard dogs in peacetime by the United States Army and other military services. Because of their keen sense of smell, dogs are used by police at times to track down escaped prisoners. Law enforcement agencies also rely on the dog's acute sense of smell to uncover illegal drugs. And specially trained dogs serve as the "eyes" of the blind, guiding the steps of their sightless masters around obstacles and hazards.

SOME NOTEWORTHY DOGS IN HISTORY

Soter—one of 50 watchdogs of ancient Greece that alone survived attack by invaders and ran to the gates of Corinth to warn the citizens.

Saur, or **Suening**—a dog that was "king" of Norway for three years during the 11th century A.D. The Norwegian king, angry that his subjects once deposed him, put Saur on the throne and demanded it be regally treated.

Le Diable—a notorious French dog that smuggled lace and other costly items across the French border under a false skin dyed various colors by its owners to baffle the customs guards.

Rin Tin Tin—a German shepherd who ranked as one of the all-time famous canine movie stars. "Rinty" was in 19 movies before its death in 1932.

Laika—the first dog in space. Laika was aboard the Russian satellite Sputnik 2 in 1957.

Lassie—any of a line of popular collies in movies and in a television series. The first Lassie starred in the 1942 movie 'Lassie Come Home'.

SOME FACTS ABOUT DOGS

A dog is more apt to chase and perhaps bite a stranger who runs away from it than a person who remains still.

Smell is a dog's sharpest sense.

When a dog is hot, it pants with its tongue hanging out so that perspiration from the tongue will evaporate and cool the animal.

A dog has 42 teeth, 20 in the upper jaw and 22 in the lower jaw.

Each of the dog's body cells contains 39 pairs of chromosomes (heredity-carrying structures), the most of any mammal.

A dog experiences emotion. For example, it appears to become upset during a family dispute, and it apparently suffers anxiety when lost.

A GLOSSARY OF DOG TERMS

Bitch—a female dog.

Breed—a variety of dog with consistent traits.

Crop—to clip off the top of a puppy's ears to make them stand erect; illegal in some countries.

Dock—to shorten a puppy's tail by cutting off a portion.

Dog—strictly speaking, a male canine.

Feathering—long fringes of hair on the ears, legs, and tail of some dogs.

Kennel—a place where dogs are bred and boarded.

License—permission by a government agency enabling anyone to keep a dog; usually requires a fee.

Mongrel—a dog whose parents were not of the same breed.

Mutt—another name for a mongrel.

Pedigree—a listing of the names of a dog's recent ancestors.

Purebred—a dog whose parents and other ancestors were all of the same breed.

Registration Papers—proof that the names of a purebred and its parents are on record at a dog registry, such as the American Kennel Club (AKC).

Stud—a male used for breeding.

The Body of a Dog

Dogs grow to various sizes. The Irish wolfhound, for example, stands about 32 inches high at the withers, or top of the shoulders. The chihuahua, however, stands about five inches.

The color of a dog's coat, or hair cover, also ranges widely, even within a breed. Some dogs are all black. Others are all white. Some have light markings on portions of their bodies and darker coloration elsewhere. Or, they may have a solid color other than black. All dogs have some hair cover, even the so-called hairless ones.

The shape of a dog is determined by three major structures—the head, the body, and the legs. The size and form of these structures vary greatly as do, for example, coloration and hair characteristics.

The Head

There are two basic head shapes—a narrow skull with a long face and a wide skull with a short face—plus several intermediate head shapes. Long-faced dogs, such as the German shepherd and the cocker spaniel, may have jaws eight inches long. By contrast, the nose of small-faced dogs, such as the Pekingese and the pug, may be less than an inch from the eyes.

Dogs have 42 teeth. Six pairs of sharp incisor teeth are in front of the mouth, flanked by two pairs of large canine ("dog") teeth. The other teeth are premolars and molars. The incisors and the canines are very important because the dog bites and tears at its food with these teeth.

Air breathed in through the dog's nose passes on its way to the lungs through the two nasal cavities behind the nose. These cavities are lined by a mucous membrane containing many nerve endings stimulated by odors. Smell is the dog's most acute sense. A dog continually sniffs the air, the ground, and nearby objects to learn what is happening around it. The indentation in the dog's forehead just above eye level is called the stop. The stop in some dogs is deeper than that in others.

The fairly thin tongue of the dog is used mainly for guiding food to the throat, for licking the coat clean, and for perspiration. When a dog is overheated, it cools off by hanging its tongue out and panting. As it pants, the evaporation of perspiration from its tongue cools the animal. The dog also sweats through the pads on its paws and—slightly—through its skin.

A dog's ears either stick up or hang down. The earliest dogs probably had erect ears, but the ears began to droop in smaller, later breeds because of excessive ear skin. Dogs have a fine sense of hearing. They can hear sounds at frequencies too high for man to hear. This is why dogs can respond to "silent" whistles.

Each eye of a dog has three eyelids, the main upper and lower lids and a third lid hidden between them in the inner corner of the eye. The third eyelid can sweep across the transparent cornea of the eye and clean it like a windshield wiper.

The head and body of a dog are connected by its neck. The neck may be long or short, depending on the size of the seven bones that support it. The length of the vocal cords in the neck is a factor influencing the pitch and loudness of a dog's voice—its barks, grunts, and howls.

The Body

The body of a dog contains most of its vital organs. The heart, lungs, stomach, and intestines are located there. So too are its sex organs, kidneys, and bladder. The 13 ribs of the dog's chest wrap around the heart and lungs. Since these organs influence the animal's speed and stamina, chest size can be an indication of these traits.

All dogs have 27 bones from the skull to the point where the tail begins. The number of tailbones, however, and therefore the length of the tail, varies from breed to breed.

The body may be covered with straight or with wavy hair. Hair shafts emerge from tiny follicles in the skin. The shafts are connected to tiny muscles that cause the dog's hair to stand up, or bristle, when they contract. During times of stress, a dog raises its hackles—the hair along the neck and spine. Special sensory hairs called whiskers are near the nose, but their usefulness is doubtful because a dog rarely relies on the sense of touch.

The Legs

The front legs and back legs of a dog are also called the forelimbs and hind limbs. A dog uses its legs for movement, for scratching, and, in some breeds, for digging.

Each of the forelimbs is connected to the body by a long, narrow scapula, or shoulder blade. Its lower part, in turn, forms a shoulder joint with the humerus, the upper forelimb bone. The lower forelimb bones, the radius and the ulna, are fused at two points and act as a single bone.

The foot, or paw, has five toes. One of them—the dewclaw—is too high to be of any use. It is a vestigial part and is often surgically removed from puppies. The toes of the foot are composed of a number of bones. A toenail, or claw, emerges from the end of each toe. The foot also has cushiony pads for each toe and two larger pads farther up the paw. Dogs perspire through their pads.

Each of the two hind limbs is connected to the body at the pelvic bone. The upper portion of the femur, or thighbone, fits into a socket in the pelvic bone to form the hip joint. The tibia and the fibula are beneath. They make up the lower thigh. The joint where their upper portions link with the femur is called the stifle. The joint where their lower portions link with the foot bones of the hind limbs is called the hock. Like the forefeet, the hind feet have pads and four functional toes, although a dewclaw is sometimes present.

THE DOG'S BODY

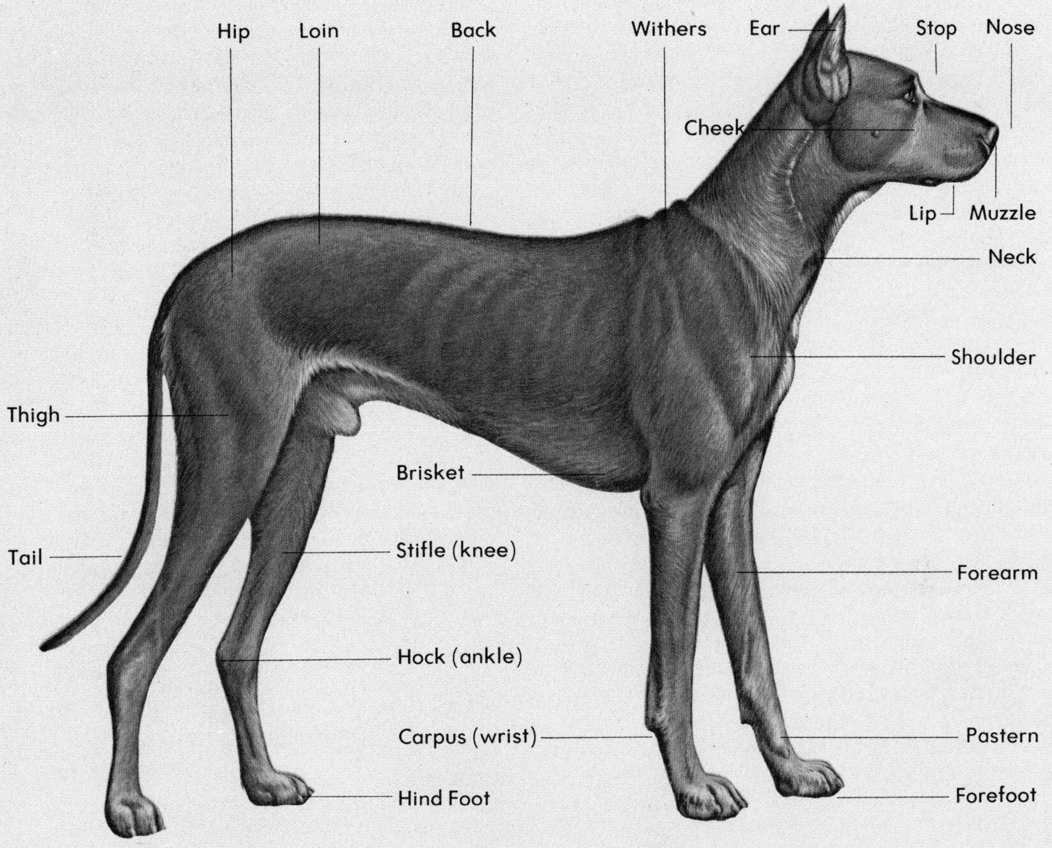

Hip
Loin
Back
Withers
Ear
Stop
Nose
Cheek
Lip
Muzzle
Neck
Shoulder
Thigh
Brisket
Tail
Stifle (knee)
Forearm
Hock (ankle)
Carpus (wrist)
Pastern
Hind Foot
Forefoot

THE DOG'S FEET

Dewclaw
Communal Pads
Foot Pads
Claws
Hind Foot
Forefoot

THE DOG'S SKELETON

Coccygeal Vertebrae
Lumbar Vertebrae
Cervical Vertebrae
Occipital Bone (occiput)
Pelvis
Thoracic Vertebrae
Scapula (shoulder blade)
Femur
Humerus
Tibia
Ribs
Radius
Ulna
Fibula

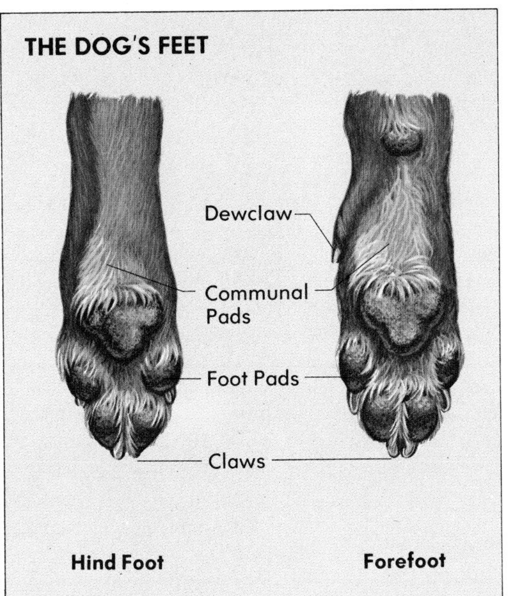

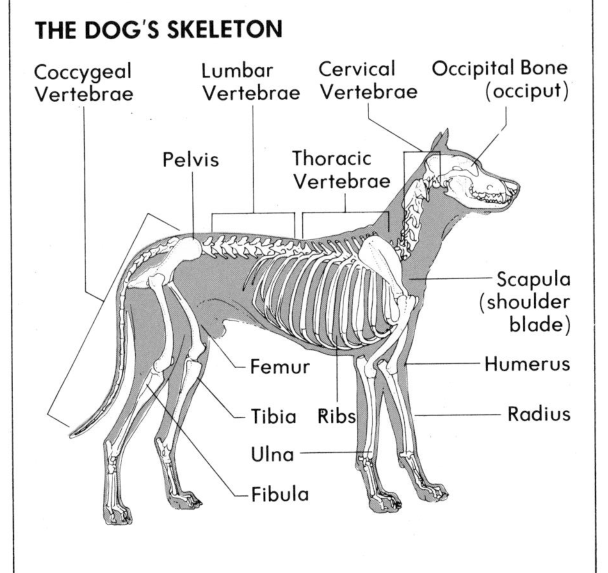

Life History of a Dog

The normal life span of a small or medium-size dog is about 15 years. A large dog lives only about ten years, however. On the average, a ten-month-old dog is sexually mature. Smaller bitches go into their first heat (become responsive to their first mating) at an earlier age than larger ones.

Fetal puppies grow and develop in their mother's womb before they are whelped, or born. Whelping is usually a painless task for the bitch. After each of her litter is whelped, she licks the pup as dry as she can. The newborn, hungry puppies snuggle by the teats on the bitch's underside, where she nurses them. The puppies draw nourishing milk from their mother until they are weaned, or given food more solid than milk to eat. The time of weaning depends on the size of the litter and the amount of milk in the bitch. Sometimes, it occurs as early as three weeks. Puppies should not be weaned, however, any later than their seventh week.

After its birth the puppy grows, becomes stronger, and gains in alertness. Its eyes, which are closed at birth, open when it is between one and two weeks old. It then begins to see. Its first teeth, the puppy or milk teeth, erupt through the gums during the third to sixth week of its life. Puppy teeth are mostly incisors and canines. By the third month, the first of the permanent teeth work through, and by the seventh month they all do. By the time it reaches its first birthday a puppy is considered a dog.

Although sexually mature beforehand, a dog ordinarily does not attain full growth until its first birthday or even later. By this time, however, it is capable of a wide range of responses to its environment. When it meets another dog, its ear position indicates how interested it is in the newcomer. If its ears are erect, it is concentrating on the other. If its ears are pointing forward, it is on the alert. If the dog holds its tail high and wags it, the animal is happy and confident. If it drops its tail and remains still, the dog is apprehensive. If it pulls its tail between its legs, the dog is afraid. If on meeting a person or another dog it pulls back its lips and growls, it is making a threat. If it bares its teeth without growling, the dog is ready to attack and bite. A male dog establishes a territory by marking the boundaries with urine, scent from the anal glands, or even feces. The dog will then defend that territory against intruders. Every six or seven months a female dog goes into heat and will mate with nearly any available male within the three-week length of her heat.

When a dog reaches old age, its eyes begin to weaken. Cataracts may also form in the lenses of its eyes. The hair on its muzzle turns gray. The old dog begins to feel numerous aches and pains and might become easily irritated and snap at members of the family. Its body systems are breaking down, and it can no longer behave as it did when younger.

Continued on page 152

BARRY TO THE RESCUE

The monks of the Hospice of St. Bernard, high in the Great St. Bernard Pass between Switzerland and Italy, for several hundred years have raised a hardy breed of dogs able to move through snow and rescue trapped persons. About 150 years ago lived a St. Bernard named Barry. The dog was so brave and determined that it saved some 40 persons at different times. Barry's keen sense of smell guided it to the snow-trapped victim. Like all St. Bernards on rescue missions, Barry would clear away snow from the victim if it was not too deep, lie on top of the person to warm him, and bark to summon the monks. Once, Barry even pulled a boy off an icy ledge. In honor of the exploits of this brave dog the monks have given the name Barry to the best of each new litter of St. Bernards whelped at the hospice. St. Bernards have never carried small casks of brandy around their necks on rescues, as popularly believed. Sometimes, however, they are posed with casks to please tourists.

The mother dog nurses her puppies until they are weaned —usually between three and seven weeks.
Walter Chandoha

Breeds of Dogs

Several hundred dog breeds exist throughout the world. For a puppy to be a purebred dog, its sire and dam (father and mother) both must be of the same breed, as must its ancestors dating back to the establishment of the breed. Kennel clubs in many countries set their own standards. In the United States the American Kennel Club (AKC) determines the standards for breeds it recognizes.

The AKC recognizes six groups of breeds—sporting dogs, hounds, working dogs, terriers, toys, and non-sporting dogs. *Sporting dogs* hunt, locate (point), and retrieve game birds. *Hounds* hunt all game except birds. *Working dogs* can do such jobs as herding farm animals, pulling sleds and carts, and guarding life and property. *Terriers* were once bred to ferret out rodents but are now bred as house pets. *Toys* are tiny dogs bred mainly as pets. *Non-sporting dogs* are those purebreds not included in the other categories. AKC-recognized breeds are illustrated here and on the following pages.

Country of Breed Origin
Each breed is accompanied by the flag of its country of origin, as best determined by authorities.

Mexico

Type of Dog

△ Sporting Dog
✙ Hound
◇ Working Dog
□ Terrier
○ Toy
▽ Non-Sporting

Shoulder Height and Weight
Many height and weight ranges of the breeds are derived from American Kennel Club sources.

Relative Size of Each Breed
Each illustration contains a scale arrow that indicates the size of a dog of the illustrated breed in relation to the height of a page of Compton's Encyclopedia.

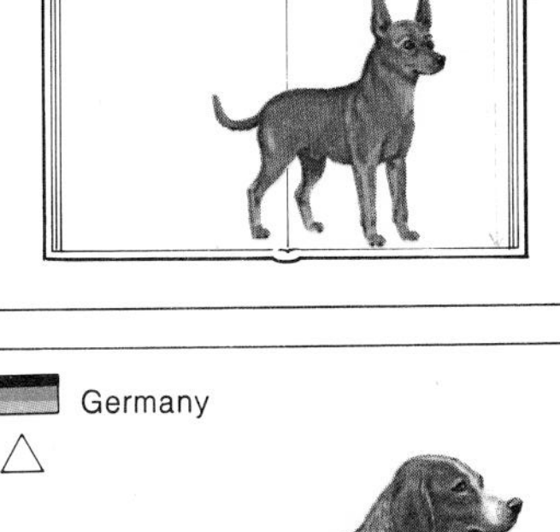

United Kingdom △

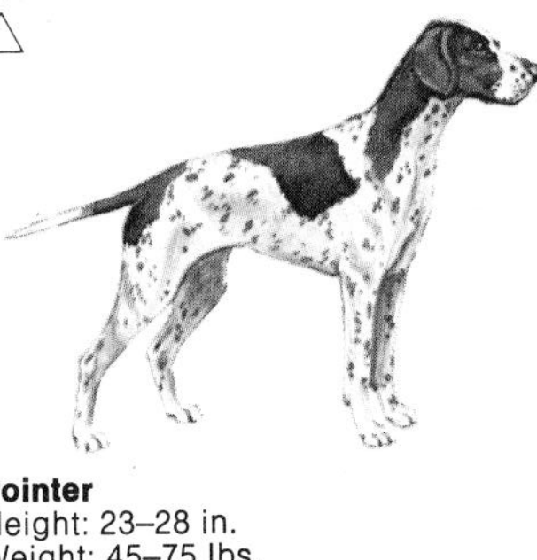

Pointer
Height: 23–28 in.
Weight: 45–75 lbs.

Germany △

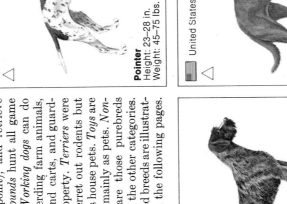

German Shorthaired Pointer
Height: 21–25 in.
Weight: 45–70 lbs.

Germany △

German Wirehaired Pointer
Height: 22–26 in.
Weight: 45–70 lbs.

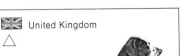

United States △

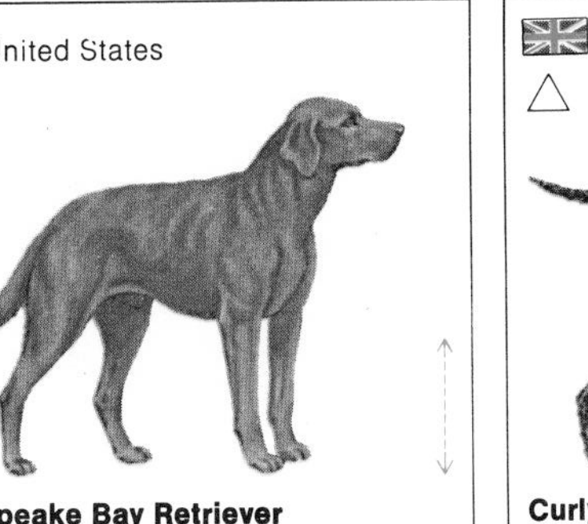

Chesapeake Bay Retriever
Height: 21–26 in.
Weight: 55–75 lbs.

United Kingdom △

Curly-Coated Retriever
Height: 22–24 in.
Weight: 55–70 lbs.

United Kingdom △

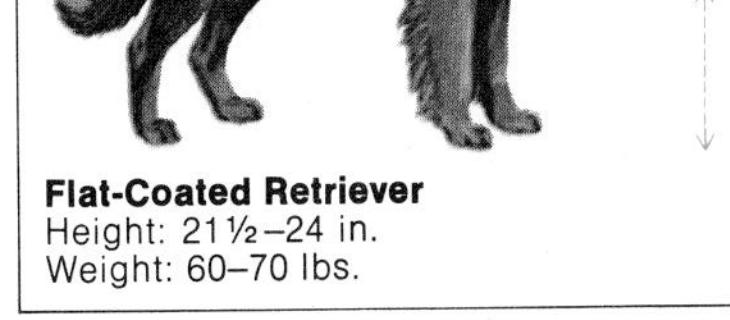

Flat-Coated Retriever
Height: 21½–24 in.
Weight: 60–70 lbs.

United Kingdom △

Golden Retriever
Height: 21½–24 in.
Weight: 60–75 lbs.

Canada △

Labrador Retriever
Height: 21½–24½ in.
Weight: 55–75 lbs.

United Kingdom

English Setter
Height: 23–25 in.
Weight: 50–70 lbs.

United Kingdom

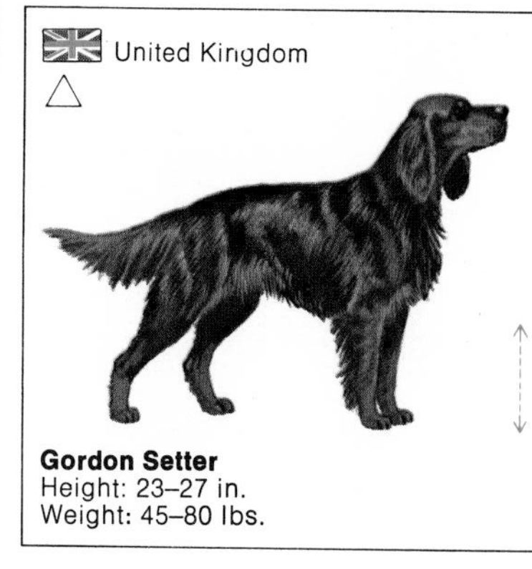

Gordon Setter
Height: 23–27 in.
Weight: 45–80 lbs.

Ireland

Irish Setter
Height: 25–27 in.
Weight: 60–70 lbs.

United States

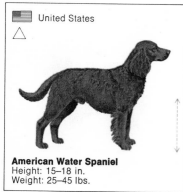

American Water Spaniel
Height: 15–18 in.
Weight: 25–45 lbs.

France

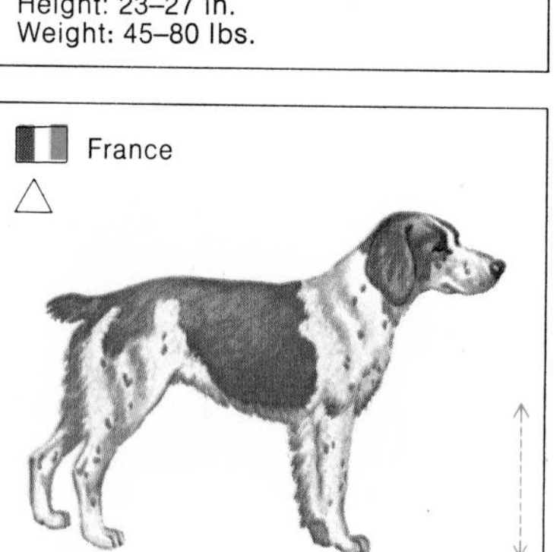

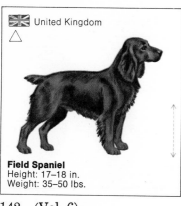

Brittany Spaniel
Height: 17½–20½ in.
Weight: 30–40 lbs.

United Kingdom

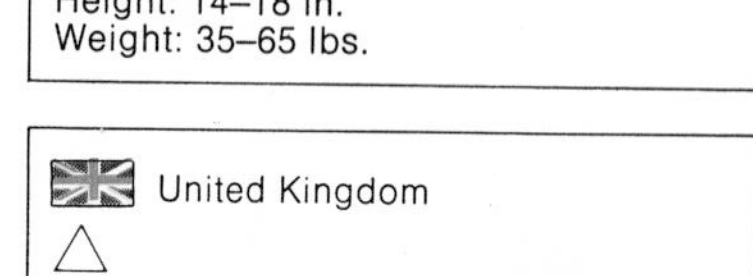

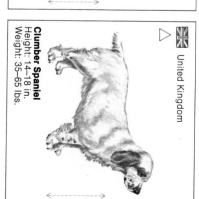

Clumber Spaniel
Height: 14–18 in.
Weight: 35–65 lbs.

United States

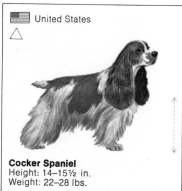

Cocker Spaniel
Height: 14–15½ in.
Weight: 22–28 lbs.

United Kingdom

English Cocker Spaniel
Height: 15–17 in.
Weight: 26–34 lbs.

United Kingdom

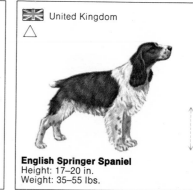

English Springer Spaniel
Height: 17–20 in.
Weight: 35–55 lbs.

United Kingdom

Field Spaniel
Height: 17–18 in.
Weight: 35–50 lbs.

Ireland

Irish Water Spaniel
Height: 21–24 in.
Weight: 45–65 lbs.

United Kingdom

Sussex Spaniel
Height: 14–16 in.
Weight: 35–45 lbs.

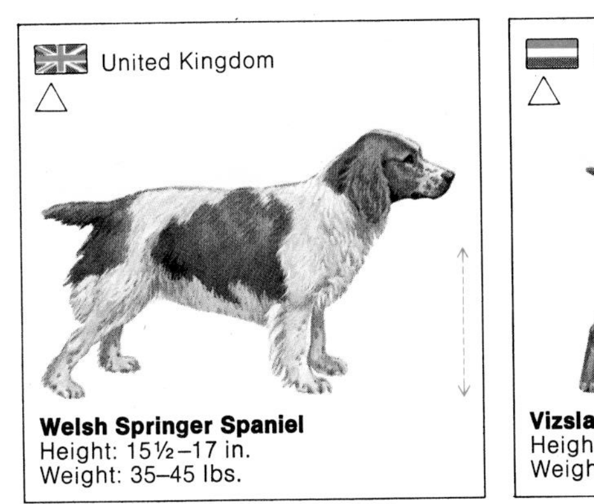

United Kingdom

Welsh Springer Spaniel
Height: 15½–17 in.
Weight: 35–45 lbs.

Hungary

Vizsla
Height: 21–24 in.
Weight: 40–60 lbs.

Germany

Weimaraner
Height: 23–27 in.
Weight: 55–85 lbs.

France

Wirehaired Pointing Griffon
Height: 19½–23½ in.
Weight: 45–60 lbs.

Afghanistan

Afghan Hound
Height: 24–28 in.
Weight: 50–60 lbs.

Egypt

Basenji
Height: 16–17 in.
Weight: 22–24 lbs.

France

Basset Hound
Height: 10–15 in.
Weight: 25–40 lbs.

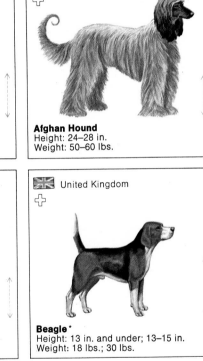

United Kingdom

Beagle*
Height: 13 in. and under; 13–15 in.
Weight: 18 lbs.; 30 lbs.

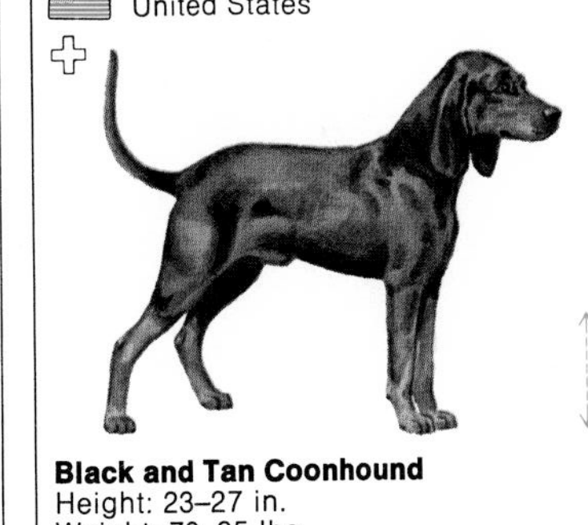

United States

Black and Tan Coonhound
Height: 23–27 in.
Weight: 70–85 lbs.

United Kingdom

Bloodhound
Height: 23–27 in.
Weight: 80–110 lbs.

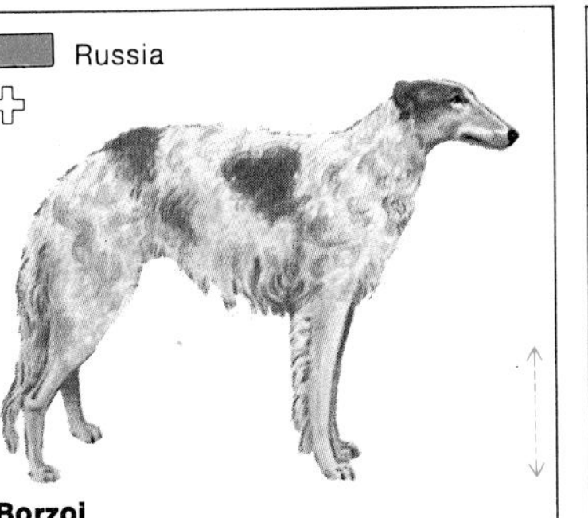

Russia

Borzoi
Height: 26–31 in.
Weight: 55–105 lbs.

Germany

Dachshund
Height: 5–9 in.
Weight: 5–20 lbs.

*Two categories of the beagle breed are recognized by the American Kennel Club.

United States

American Foxhound
Height: 21–25 in.
Weight: 60–70 lbs.

United Kingdom

English Foxhound
Height: 21–25 in.
Weight: 60–70 lbs.

Egypt

Greyhound
Height: 25–27 in.
Weight: 60–70 lbs.

United Kingdom

Harrier
Height: 19–21 in.
Weight: 40–50 lbs.

Ireland

Irish Wolfhound
Height: 30–33 in.
Weight: 105–140 lbs.

Norway

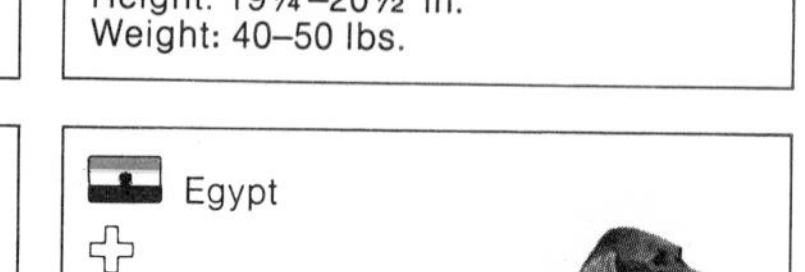

Norwegian Elkhound
Height: 19¼–20½ in.
Weight: 40–50 lbs.

United Kingdom

Otter Hound
Height: 24–26 in.
Weight: 55–65 lbs.

South Africa

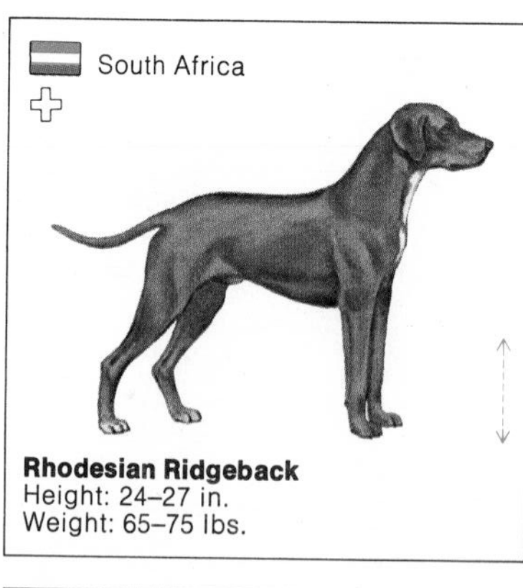

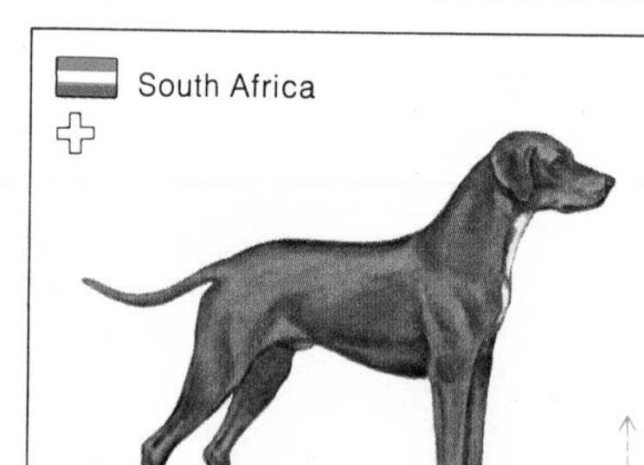

Rhodesian Ridgeback
Height: 24–27 in.
Weight: 65–75 lbs.

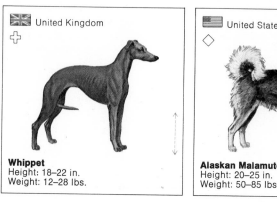

Egypt

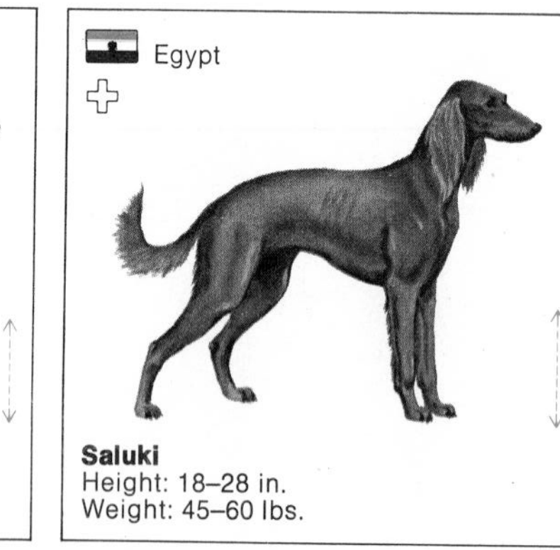

Saluki
Height: 18–28 in.
Weight: 45–60 lbs.

United Kingdom

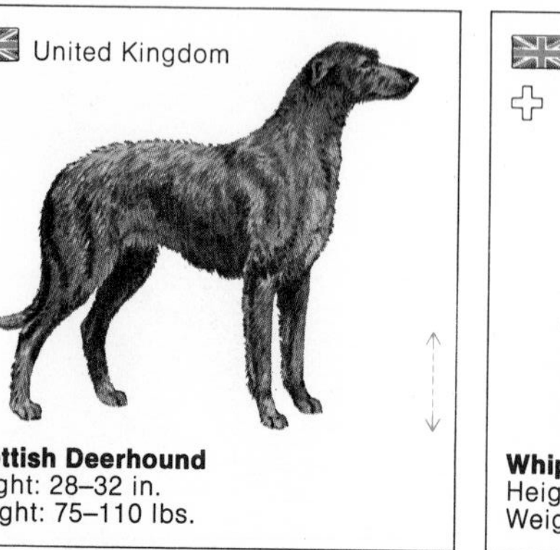

Scottish Deerhound
Height: 28–32 in.
Weight: 75–110 lbs.

United Kingdom

Whippet
Height: 18–22 in.
Weight: 12–28 lbs.

United States

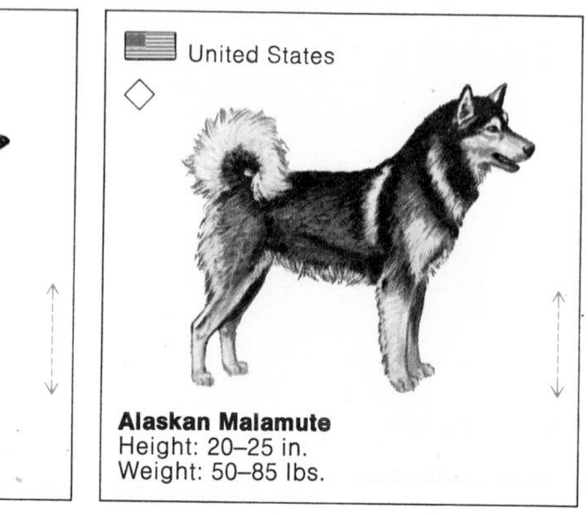

Alaskan Malamute
Height: 20–25 in.
Weight: 50–85 lbs.

Belgium

Belgian Malinois
Height: 22–26 in.
Weight: 50–60 lbs.

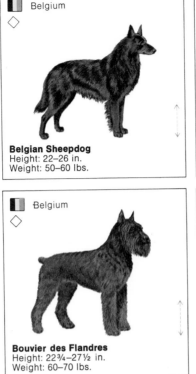

Belgium

Belgian Sheepdog
Height: 22–26 in.
Weight: 50–60 lbs.

Belgium

Belgian Tervuren
Height: 22–26 in.
Weight: 50–60 lbs.

Switzerland

Bernese Mountain Dog
Height: 21–27½ in.
Weight: 50–70 lbs.

Belgium

Bouvier des Flandres
Height: 22¾–27½ in.
Weight: 60–70 lbs.

Germany

Boxer
Height: 21–25 in.
Weight: 60–75 lbs.

France

Briard
Height: 22–27 in.
Weight: 70–80 lbs.

United Kingdom

Bullmastiff
Height: 24–27 in.
Weight: 100–130 lbs.

United Kingdom

Collie
Height: 22–26 in.
Weight: 50–75 lbs.

Germany

Doberman Pinscher
Height: 24–28 in.
Weight: 60–75 lbs.

Germany

German Shepherd Dog
Height: 22–26 in.
Weight: 60–85 lbs.

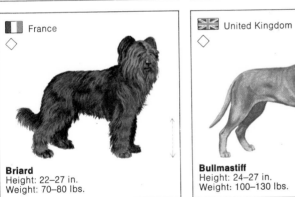

Germany

Giant Schnauzer
Height: 23½–27½ in.
Weight: 65–78 lbs.

Germany

Great Dane
Height: 28–34 in.
Weight: 120–150 lbs.

France

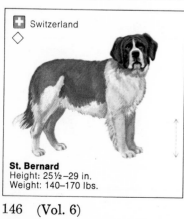

Great Pyrenees
Height: 25–32 in.
Weight: 90–125 lbs.

Hungary

Komondor
Height: 23½–31½ in.
Weight: 75–90 lbs.

Tibet

Kuvasz
Height: 24–26 in.
Weight: 60–70 lbs.

United Kingdom

Mastiff
Height: 27½–33 in.
Weight: 165–185 lbs.

Canada

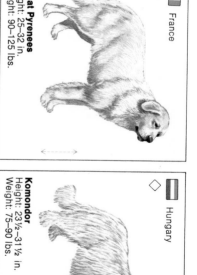

Newfoundland
Height: 25–28 in.
Weight: 110–150 lbs.

United Kingdom

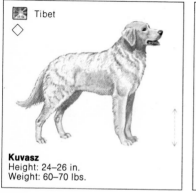

Old English Sheepdog
Height: 21–25 in.
Weight: 55–65 lbs.

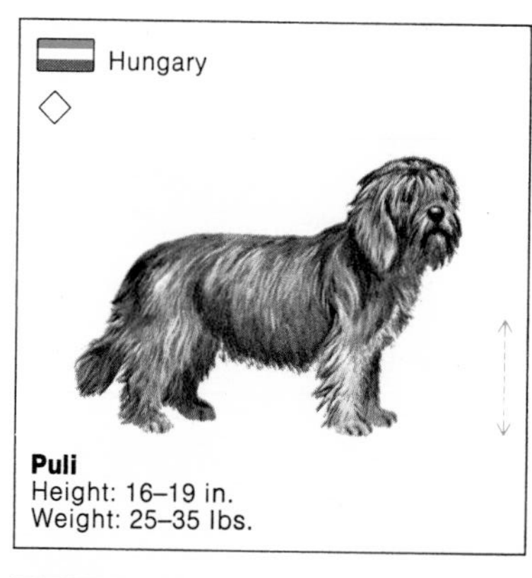

Hungary

Puli
Height: 16–19 in.
Weight: 25–35 lbs.

Germany

Rottweiler
Height: 21¾–27 in.
Weight: 75–90 lbs.

Switzerland

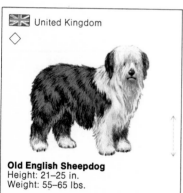

St. Bernard
Height: 25½–29 in.
Weight: 140–170 lbs.

Russia

Samoyed
Height: 19–23½ in.
Weight: 35–65 lbs.

United Kingdom

Shetland Sheepdog
Height: 13–16 in.
Weight: 14–16 lbs.

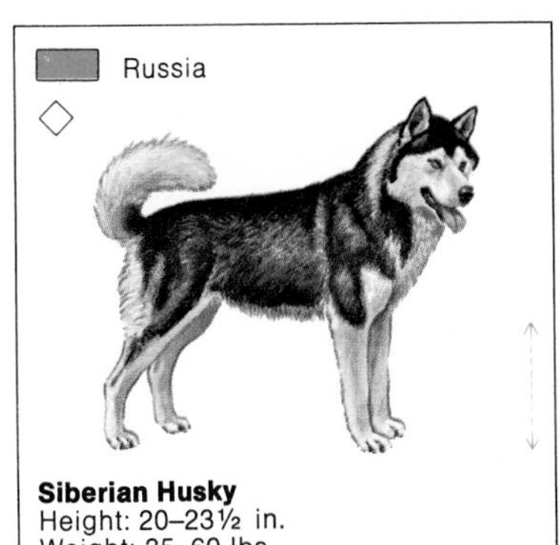

Russia

Siberian Husky
Height: 20–23½ in.
Weight: 35–60 lbs.

Germany

Standard Schnauzer
Height: 17½–19½ in.
Weight: 27–37 lbs.

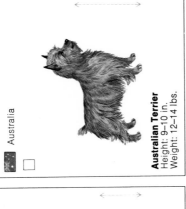

United Kingdom

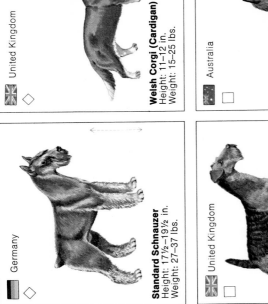

Welsh Corgi (Cardigan)
Height: 11–12 in.
Weight: 15–25 lbs.

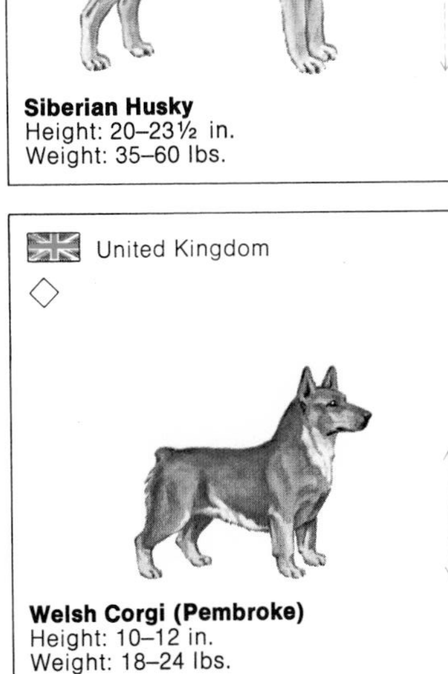

United Kingdom

Welsh Corgi (Pembroke)
Height: 10–12 in.
Weight: 18–24 lbs.

United Kingdom

Airedale Terrier
Height: 22–23 in.
Weight: 40–50 lbs.

Australia

Australian Terrier
Height: 9–10 in.
Weight: 12–14 lbs.

United Kingdom

Bedlington Terrier
Height: 15–17½ in.
Weight: 17–23 lbs.

United Kingdom

Border Terrier
Height: 11–13 in.
Weight: 11½–15½ lbs.

United Kingdom

Bull Terrier
Height: 19–22 in.
Weight: 30–60 lbs.

United Kingdom

Cairn Terrier
Height: 9½–10 in.
Weight: 13–14 lbs.

United Kingdom

Dandie Dinmont Terrier
Height: 8–11 in.
Weight: 18–24 lbs.

United Kingdom

Fox Terrier
Height: 14½–15½ in.
Weight: 15–19 lbs.

Ireland

Irish Terrier
Height: 16½–18 in.
Weight: 25–27 lbs.

Ireland

Kerry Blue Terrier
Height: 17½–19½ in.
Weight: 29–40 lbs.

United Kingdom

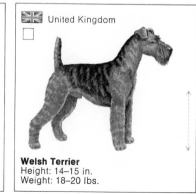

Lakeland Terrier
Height: 13–15 in.
Weight: 15–17 lbs.

United Kingdom

Manchester Terrier†
Height: 14–16 in.; 6–7 in.
Weight: 12–22 lbs.; 5–12 lbs.

Germany

Miniature Schnauzer
Height: 12–14 in.
Weight: 13–15 lbs.

United Kingdom

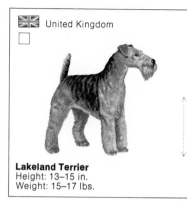

Norwich Terrier
Height: 9–11 in.
Weight: 10–14 lbs.

United Kingdom

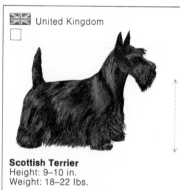

Scottish Terrier
Height: 9–10 in.
Weight: 18–22 lbs.

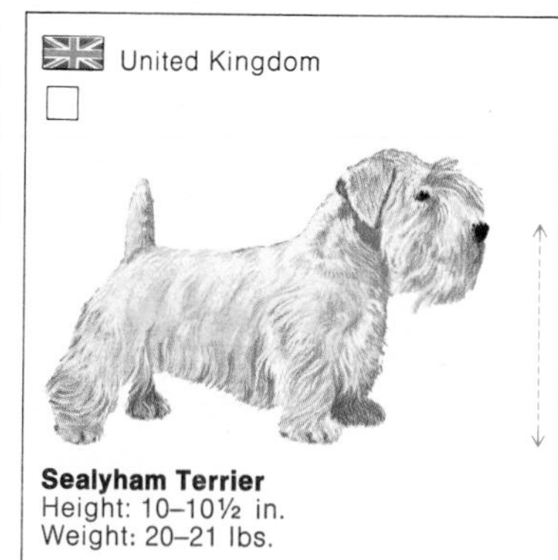

United Kingdom

Sealyham Terrier
Height: 10–10½ in.
Weight: 20–21 lbs.

United Kingdom

Skye Terrier
Height: 7½–10 in.
Weight: 23–25 lbs.

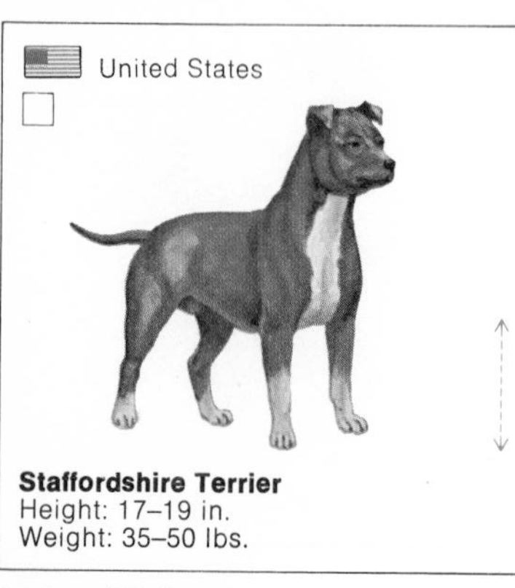

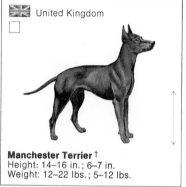

United States

Staffordshire Terrier
Height: 17–19 in.
Weight: 35–50 lbs.

United Kingdom

Welsh Terrier
Height: 14–15 in.
Weight: 18–20 lbs.

United Kingdom

West Highland White Terrier
Height: 10–11 in.
Weight: 13–19 lbs.

†Standard and toy varieties of the Manchester terrier breed are recognized by the American Kennel Club. The larger figures are for the standard; the smaller for the toy.

Germany
Affenpinscher
Height: 8–10¼ in.
Weight: 7–8 lbs.
Belgium
Brussels Griffon
Height: 7–8 in.
Weight: 5–12 lbs.
Mexico
Chihuahua
Height: 5 in.
Weight: 1–6 lbs.
United Kingdom
English Toy Spaniel
Height: 9–10 in.
Weight: 9–12 lbs.
Italy
Italian Greyhound
Height: 13–15 in.
Weight: 7–10 lbs.
Japan
Japanese Spaniel
Height: 8–9 in.
Weight: 6–7 lbs.
Malta
Maltese
Height: 5 in.
Weight: 4–6 lbs.
Germany
Miniature Pinscher
Height: 10–11½ in.
Weight: 8–10 lbs.
Italy
Papillon
Height: 8–11 in.
Weight: 5–11 lbs.
China
Pekingese
Height: 6–9 in.
Weight: 6–14 lbs.
Germany
Pomeranian
Height: 5½–7 in.
Weight: 3–7 lbs.
China
Pug
Height: 10–11 in.
Weight: 14–18 lbs.

Tibet

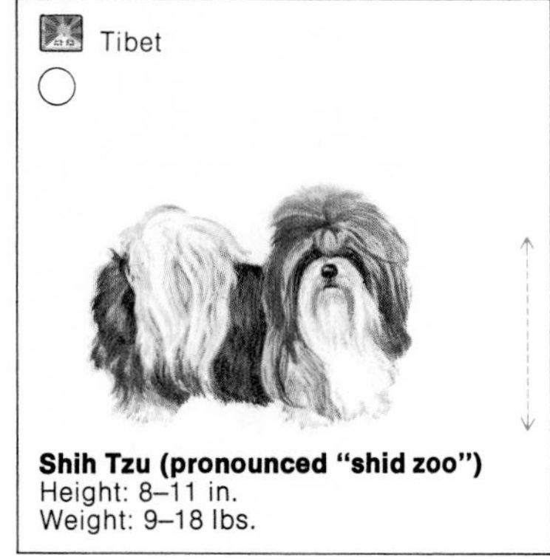

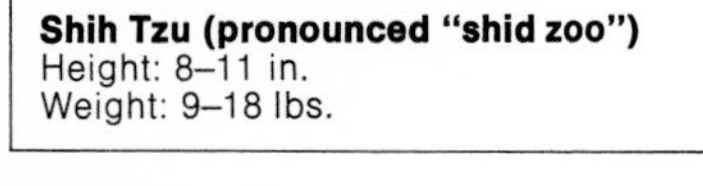

Shih Tzu (pronounced "shid zoo")
Height: 8–11 in.
Weight: 9–18 lbs.

Australia

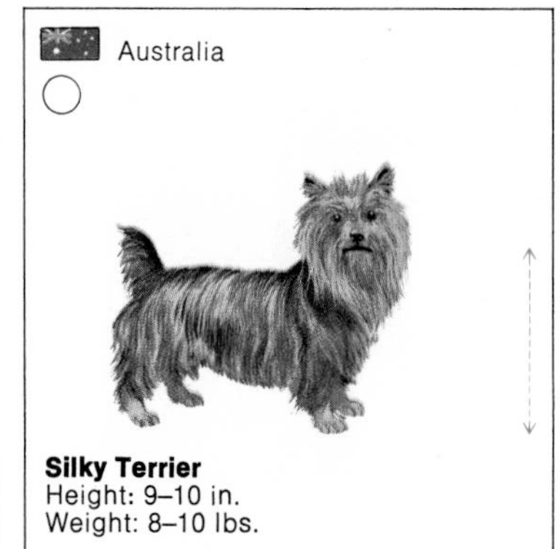

Silky Terrier
Height: 9–10 in.
Weight: 8–10 lbs.

United Kingdom

Yorkshire Terrier
Height: 8–9 in.
Weight: 4–7 lbs.

United States

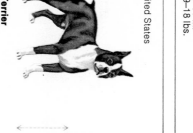

Boston Terrier
Height: 14–17 in.
Weight: 13–25 lbs.

United Kingdom

Bulldog
Height: 13½–15 in.
Weight: 40–50 lbs.

China

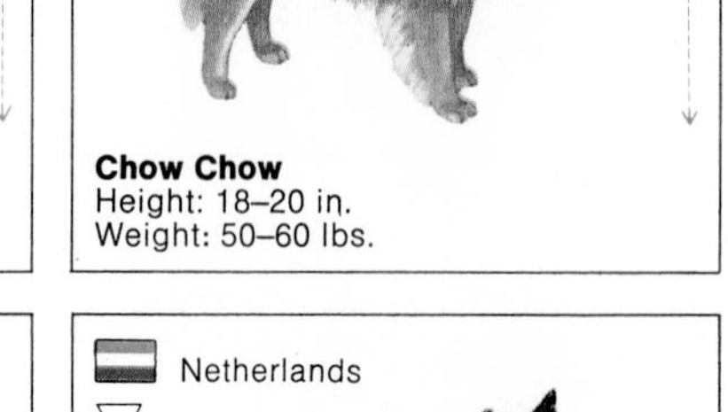

Chow Chow
Height: 18–20 in.
Weight: 50–60 lbs.

Yugoslavia

Dalmatian
Height: 19–23 in.
Weight: 35–50 lbs.

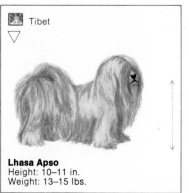

France

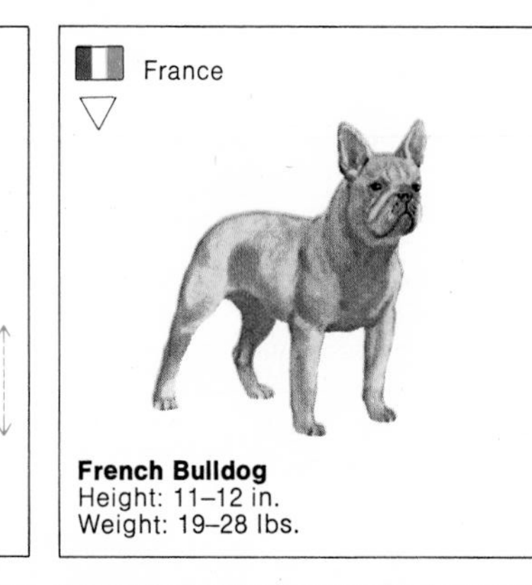

French Bulldog
Height: 11–12 in.
Weight: 19–28 lbs.

Netherlands

Keeshond
Height: 17–18 in.
Weight: 32–40 lbs.

Tibet

Lhasa Apso
Height: 10–11 in.
Weight: 13–15 lbs.

France

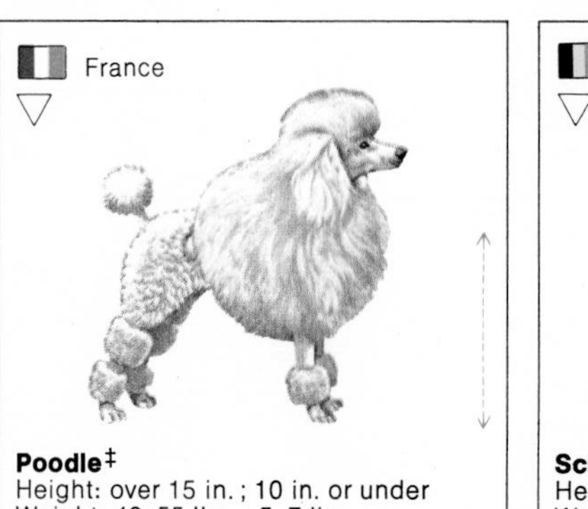

Poodle‡
Height: over 15 in.; 10 in. or under
Weight: 40–55 lbs.; 5–7 lbs.

Belgium

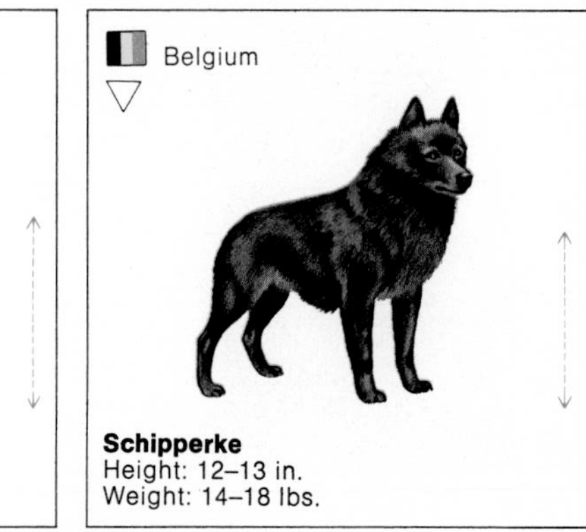

Schipperke
Height: 12–13 in.
Weight: 14–18 lbs.

‡Standard and toy varieties of the poodle breed are recognized by the American Kennel Club. The larger figures are for the standard; the smaller for the toy.

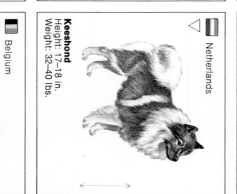

Flagler Dog Track, Miami

George Leavens—Photo Researchers

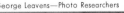

Walter Chandoha

Over the years dogs have entertained man, joined him on the hunt, herded his other domestic animals, and pulled his loads. Greyhound racing (top), related to the ancient sport of coursing, has avid fans throughout the world today. The swift greyhounds streak around the track in pursuit of a mechanical rabbit at speeds of almost 40 miles an hour. Duck hunters rely on the retrieving skills of their sporting dogs, such as the Labrador retriever (left), to snag their game. The "soft mouth" of retrievers and spaniels permits them to return game in an undamaged condition. This trait is due to the underdevelopment of the cheek muscles of these dogs. Some working dogs, such as the border collie (above), do an amazing job of herding animals. The border collie can dominate a flock of sheep with its strong stare and keep the flock in a tight group. Dogsleds pulled by rugged teams of huskies, malamutes, or samoyeds were for years an important form of transportation in the frozen North. Dogsled races featuring teams of these breeds or mixtures of them are still held in the colder parts of the United States and Canada (below).

J. Rychetnik—Photo Researchers

Walter Chandoha

Whether the puppy you choose is male or female, large or small, purebred or mongrel, it should be a healthy dog whose personality and needs fit into your way of life.

A balanced diet that is nourishing and that your dog enjoys is necessary for his scheduled feedings. A puppy must also have a bowl of fresh water available at all times.

Walter Chandoha

Choosing a Dog

An important thing to consider when buying a dog is whether it will fit comfortably into your quarters when it reaches adult size. The presence of young children in the family should also be a factor in selection. A dog for a growing family must be able to stand rough treatment. A toy dog would be a poor choice for such a family because its tiny bones are fragile enough to break when children handle it roughly. In general larger dogs are better adapted both physically and temperamentally for a young family.

A dog can be acquired from a number of sources. It can be bought from a reputable pet shop or from a kennel. Newspaper advertisements describe pups for sale from private parties. Local humane societies have dogs available, too. From whatever source you get a dog, however, make certain it is healthy. Ask for proof, if possible, that it has received all the necessary immunizing shots. Also, get a written reminder of whatever shots and other care the pup will need after you take it home. Even if a puppy has had shots against distemper and hepatitis, it will need booster shots. Later, it will need a rabies shot. A reputable pet shop or kennel ordinarily will have taken care of these details but get a signed verification from a veterinarian anyway.

Should you acquire a male or a female dog? Males are usually larger, stronger, and more aggressive, and they make excellent watchdogs. On the other hand, females are usually more affectionate and gentle, and if they are purebred dogs and are mated with males of their breed, their pups can be sold for profit. The female has a strong maternal instinct and will guard children as well as she does her own pups. Dogs of either sex, however, can be neutered. Castration, the removal of the testes, makes a male dog infertile and more docile. Spaying, or removal of the ovaries, makes a female dog infertile.

Should you buy a purebred or a mongrel? This question is hard to answer because a purebred dog sometimes turns out to be less desirable than expected, while a mongrel often makes an alert, intelligent, and delightful family pet. As a rule, a purebred pup inherits the traits of its breed. As a result, few surprises in body form and temperament arise when the pup reaches adulthood. If you want to buy a purebred but are unfamiliar with the breed, first look at a full-grown dog of the breed. The puppy will grow to resemble it. If you want to buy a mongrel, try to see its sire and dam. They will display any unwanted trait that may lie hidden in the puppy.

Ideally, children and puppies should grow up together. Caution should be taken, however, when dog owners bring a newborn baby home. Pampered dogs sometimes resent the newcomer because the baby receives most of the parents' attention. They should make an effort to pay attention to the dog, too.

A puppy should be at least eight or nine weeks old before it is taken from its home kennel. By this time it will have been weaned and eating regular food. At first, the puppy must be fed four times a day. By the time it is mature, feedings should be down to twice a day or even once a day in the case of a dog that gets little exercise. Diet and feeding instructions should accompany the puppy. If it was eating a prepared dog food at the kennel, the same diet should be maintained until the puppy shows its dislike of it by "going off its feed," or refusing to eat. Several types of dog food may have to be tried before the dog settles on a favorite. If it refuses all the choices offered, however, consult the breeder—or, even better, your veterinarian—for help.

Caring for a Dog

Dog owners are responsible for feeding, housebreaking, and cleaning their pets. They should also oversee the health of their dogs. It's best to consult a veterinarian at the first sign of a dog ailment.

A dog can be fed either the dry meal, biscuit, semi-moist and cellophane-wrapped, or canned type of dog food. Whichever type is selected must contain the carbohydrates, fats, proteins, minerals, and vitamins essential for the animal's well-being. As a rule, the cost of feeding a large dog can be kept low by giving it the inexpensive dry meal type.

A puppy should be housebroken as soon as possible. When the puppy takes its first water or food, note how long it takes for the puppy to urinate or defecate. When you discover the schedule, take the pup outside when the prescribed time has elapsed after feeding or drinking. Soon, the puppy will associate the outdoors with toilet function and will no longer soil the house or the newspapers that have been spread around its living area.

Young puppies should not be excessively groomed. A daily brushing with a soft brush is sufficient to remove surface dust and dirt. Authorities disagree as to whether a puppy should be bathed or not. Some believe that to conserve its natural skin oils a pup should not be completely bathed until its first birthday. Mud and deep dirt in its coat, however, can be removed with a damp, warm washrag. Afterward, the puppy should be completely dried with a rough towel. A dog can then have a complete bath when it is old enough, but it must be kept in the house until thoroughly dry, especially during winter.

Dog nails should be trimmed periodically. Cut only the transparent part of the nail past the foot pads. Close clipping can cut into the "quick,"—the portion of nail that has nerves and blood vessels—and hurt the animal. Special clippers can be purchased for trimming dog nails.

Canine Pests and Diseases

The flea is the dog's most common pest. Washing the dog with special soap can remove fleas. Flea-preventive collars are also available to protect dogs with thin coats. Flea collars, however, should not be used on short-haired, single-coated dogs—such as greyhounds, whippets, and pointers—because of skin irritation.

The tick poses a greater danger to the dog. This pest attaches itself to the dog's skin and sucks its blood. It also carries certain canine and human diseases. An owner can remove ticks from his dog by first dabbing alcohol on the infested area and then picking the parasites off with tweezers, making sure that the entire tick is removed.

Worms and other intestinal parasites often infest puppies. A puppy's fecal stools should be checked periodically for them. If worms are detected, take a sample of the infested stool to a veterinarian so that the type of parasite can be determined and the proper

Walter Chandoha

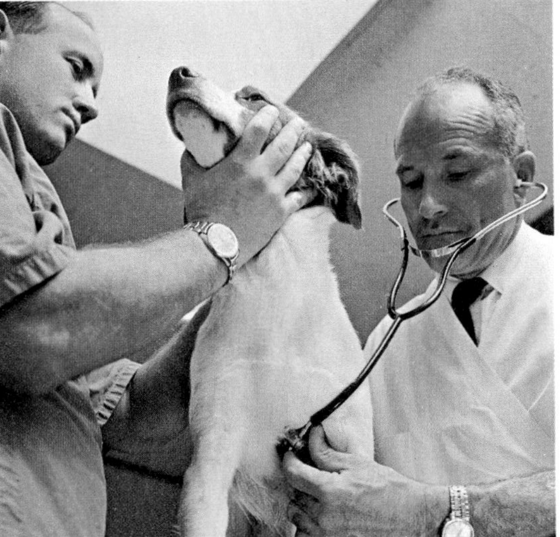

It is always best to consult a trusted veterinarian at the first sign of a dog ailment. He will also make certain that all shots and grooming needs are taken care of.

treatment rendered. Commercial deworming medicines should be avoided unless prescribed by a veterinarian.

A dog is obviously sick when it becomes listless and eats without enthusiasm. Its bowel movements may be irregular. It might also have pale, whitish gums and tongue, dull eyes, and a dry coat. A sick dog often runs a fever. A dog's temperature is best taken with a rectal thermometer. Normal body temperature of a dog is 101.5° F. A dog's pulse can be taken by pressing your finger against the blood vessel in the V formed where the undersides of the hind legs attach to the body. Normal pulse rate of a dog is between 75 and 100 beats per minute.

A dog can be infected by several viruses, including those that cause distemper, canine hepatitis, and rabies. A spirochete-caused ailment called leptospirosis is also common among dogs. Puppies should be vaccinated against each of these diseases. If any of them should arise, however, the suffering dog must be taken to a veterinarian for treatment.

Distemper affects the mucous membranes of the dog's respiratory tract. The symptoms resemble those of human influenza. Distemper causes the dog's temperature to rise two to three degrees above normal. *Canine hepatitis* affects the dog's liver and abdominal organs. It is marked by a fever as high as 105° F, thirst, diarrhea, and vomiting. A dog with hepatitis may hump its back and try to rub its belly against the floor to relieve the pain.

Rabies is a disease that can pass to humans who have been bitten by infected dogs. Rabies is almost always fatal when the virus gets to the brain. Brain inflammation causes the erratic behavior that is sometimes seen in a rabid dog. *Leptospirosis* is sometimes confused with hepatitis. However, leptospirosis is characterized by discolored and abnormal-smelling urine. At the onset of the disease, the dog's body temperature might soar as high as 105° F.

Training a Dog

Any young dog can be trained to understand commands and to do simple tricks. When correctly trained, it is conditioned to respond to your commands, noises, or gestures. Once an owner decides to train his puppy, however, he must be willing to stick with the job until the puppy learns the task. First, the owner should select a simple "call" name for the animal. The call name should be used frequently so the puppy can learn to recognize the sound of it.

A training session is best begun when the puppy is hungry because it is more alert at that time. Also, the owner can reinforce the dog's correct responses to commands with a dog biscuit or meat tidbit, as well as with enthusiastic petting and praise. The hungry dog is more apt to associate the correct performance of a task with a food reward.

To get the puppy into a collar at first, entice it to you by extending your open hands, pet it and say "good dog" (and include its name) when it comes, and finally slip the collar around its neck. Then attach a leash to the collar. If the puppy has confidence in you, it will walk along with you even though it is wearing the leash. A metal chain leash is usually best because the puppy will not be able to chew and play with it.

After being effectively trained, purebred pedigreed dogs may be entered in shows sponsored by kennel clubs under the auspices of the AKC. Field trials (above) judge hunting abilities and such skills as tracking, pointing, flushing, and retrieving. Bench shows and obedience trials (below) judge appearance and performance.

(Above) Ronny Jaques—Photo Researchers, (below) Walter Chandoha

Wait until a puppy is at least six months old before trying to teach it tricks, but do teach it the meaning of "no" at an earlier age. The young dog must be corrected vocally each time it does something that you disapprove of. If you are consistent, it soon learns by your tone of voice what pleases you and what displeases you. Formal training sessions should entail no more than ten minutes of work at a time, and they should never tire the dog.

To teach the command "sit," keep the dog on your left side and pull up on its leash with your right hand while gently but firmly pushing its hindquarters to the floor. While doing this, say the command "sit" with authority. Reinforce its correct actions with a tidbit.

To teach the command "stay," work with the puppy after it has learned to sit. While it is sitting, raise your palm to the dog and order it to "stay." It will probably try to get up, so tell it "no." Whenever it remains in the sitting position after you have given the "stay" command, reward the dog with a tidbit.

More effort might be needed to teach the command "come." When the dog has learned to stay, command it to "come" and call it by name. When it comes to you, lavish the dog with praise and give it a snack. A very stubborn dog might have to be pulled with a cord tied around its collar while the command is given. If this is necessary, be firm but accompany the command with a friendly hand gesture. Many tugs may be necessary until the reluctant dog learns the meaning of "come."

Do not be impatient with a puppy when teaching it simple tricks, and never get angry. If the training sessions are not going well, break them off and resume them later in the day or even on another day. In addition, give praise and tidbits to the dog only when they are earned.

Dog Shows

When their dogs are effectively trained, owners of purebred, pedigreed dogs may enter them in shows sponsored by local kennel clubs, under the auspices of the American Kennel Club (AKC). Winners are awarded points based on how well they conform to breed standards. Five points is the top mark a dog can win in any single show. To gain the coveted title "Champion," a dog must have accumulated 15 points in a series of shows, with at least two major wins (three points or more). Dog shows are usually called *bench shows* because the dogs wait in raised stalls or benches before being judged in the show ring. *Obedience trials* may be held separately or as part of a larger show. These trials test how well dogs can perform various tasks. The top mark in obedience trials is 200 points. *Field trials* judge the hunting abilities of sporting dogs and hounds in realistic outdoor settings. Such skills as tracking, pointing, flushing, and retrieving are tested in these trials.

(Left) Kunsthistorisches Museum; photograph, Meyer Erwin, (right) Oriental Institute, the University of Chicago

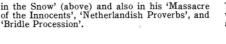

The unique partnership of dog and man has long been depicted in various art forms. The Flemish painter Pieter Brueghel painted dogs in 'Hunters in the Snow' (above) and also in his 'Massacre of the Innocents', 'Netherlandish Proverbs', and 'Bridle Procession'.

The Egyptian god Anubis was always depicted with a doglike head.

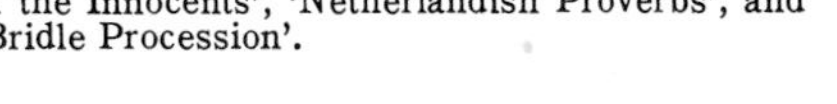

Evolution of the Dog

The dog traces its ancestry back to a five-toed, weasellike animal called *Miacis*, which lived in the Eocene epoch about 40 million years ago. This animal was the forebear of the cat, raccoon, bear, hyena, and civet, as well as of the wolf, fox, jackal, and dog. Miacis, undoubtedly a tree climber, probably also lived in a den. Like all den dwellers, it no doubt left its quarters for toilet functions so that the den would remain clean. The ease of housebreaking a modern dog probably harks back to this instinct. Next in evolutionary line from Miacis was an Oligocene animal called *Cynodictis*, which somewhat resembled the modern dog. Cynodictis lived about 20 million years ago. Its fifth toe, which would eventually become the dewclaw, showed signs of shortening. Cynodictis had 42 teeth and probably the anal glands that a dog still has. Cynodictis was also developing feet and toes suited for running. The modern civet—a "living fossil"—resembles that ancient animal (*see* Civet Cat). After a few more intermediate stages the evolution of the dog moved on to the extremely doglike animal called *Tomarctus*, which lived about 10 million years ago during the late Miocene epoch. Tomarctus probably developed the strong social instincts that still prevail in the dog and most of its close relatives, excluding the fox. The Canidae, the family that includes the true dog and its close relatives, stemmed directly from Tomarctus. Members of the genus *Canis*—which includes the dog, wolf, and jackal—developed into their present form about a million years ago during the Pleistocene epoch.

The Partnership of Dog and Man

Authorities agree that the dog was the first of man's domesticated animals. How and when this domestication took place, however, remains unknown. A 50,000-year-old cave painting in Europe seems to show a doglike animal hunting with man. But most experts believe the dog was domesticated only within the last 15,000 years. Moreover, fossil remains that would substantiate the presence of dogs with humans have not yet been unearthed for periods earlier than about 10,000 B.C. One theory holds that humans took wolf pups back to their camp or cave, reared them, allowed the tame wolves to hunt with them, and later accepted pups of the tame wolves into the family circle. Another theory suggests that dogs were attracted to food scraps dumped as waste near human living sites. As they scavenged and kept the site clean, the dogs rendered a service to the humans. In turn, the humans would accept the presence of the scavengers and would not drive them away. Still other theories maintain that the dog was domesticated to pull sleds and other conveyances bearing the heavy game killed by man, to provide a ready source of food, or to act as a sacrificial animal for magical or religious purposes.

Studies of primitive human societies still in existence tend to substantiate some of these theories. Whatever the ultimate reason for the domestication of the dog, however, the final submission must have been the consequence of thousands of years of caution and "deliberation" by the dog before it would cast its lot with man. Also, the dog, itself a hunter, had

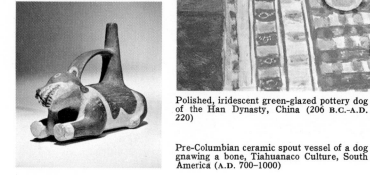

Polished, iridescent green-glazed pottery dog of the Han Dynasty, China (206 B.C.-A.D. 220)

Pre-Columbian ceramic spout vessel of a dog gnawing a bone, Tiahuanaco Culture, South America (A.D. 700–1000)

'The Cup of Coffee', Pierre Bonnard, France (about 1914)

(Top left and bottom left) By courtesy of the Art Institute of Chicago; photographs, ALFA Studio, (right) trustees of the Tate Gallery (copyright reserved ADAGP)

to suppress its desire to kill the other animals domesticated by man. Instead, it had to learn to protect them.

Some *feral* dogs live today; that is, they have returned to the wild state. The dingo of Australia, for example, spends only a portion of its time with man. When the mating urge seizes it, the dog runs off to the wild. Another, the dhole of India, is reputed to be a fierce, untamable dog.

The partnership between dog and master has long been shown in paintings and other art forms and in writings. Prehistoric paintings done about 15,000 years ago on the walls of Spanish caves show doglike animals accompanying humans on a hunt. Dogs are amply illustrated in the sculptures and pottery of ancient Assyria, Egypt, and Greece. The ancient Egyptians worshiped Anubis as the god of death. Anubis was portrayed with the head of a jackal or a dog. The Egyptians were great lovers of dogs and were responsible for developing many breeds by crossing dogs with jackals, wolves, and foxes.

Homer, the Greek author of the 'Odyssey' in the 9th century B.C., is believed to be one of the first to write about dogs. They were mentioned often in his classic epic. The ancient Greeks believed that the gates of the underworld were guarded by a savage three-headed dog named Cerberus. The belief might have been derived from the widespread practice in Greece of using watchdogs. The ancient Romans relied on watchdogs, too. So many dogs were kept in the larger Roman cities that any house with a watchdog was required to have a sign warning "Cave Canem" (Beware the Dog). The Romans also used dogs for military purposes, some as attack dogs and some as messengers.

During the 400 years of the Han Dynasty of China, which began in the 3rd century B.C., dogs were portrayed in many pieces of pottery. These were effigy pieces that symbolized the burial of favored dogs with their masters. Toy dogs were also popular among the ancient Chinese to provide warmth in the wide sleeves of their gowns.

Many of the European hound breeds were developed in the Middle Ages, when coursing was popular with the nobility. In coursing, the prey is pursued until exhausted. Then it is killed. Coursing was eventually replaced by fox hunting, which was considered less cruel.

Throughout the years dogs have been bred for many reasons, such as for hunting, for herding, and for guarding. Breed histories and pedigrees, however, were not methodically compiled until the 19th century with the establishment of the first kennel clubs. The world's first dog show took place in Great Britain in 1859. The first all-breeds show in the United States was held in Detroit, Mich., in 1875, although Chicago, Ill. was the site a year earlier of a show exclusively for sporting dogs. In 1884 the AKC was organized in New York City.

Today's breeds are a standardization of the desirable traits of the older breeds. Dog breeders try to perpetuate those traits while maintaining a friendly disposition in a dog, a trait so important for a family pet.

Man has been amply repaid for this long partnership and rapport with the dog. Care and love have been exchanged for loyalty, companionship, and fun.

Walter Chandoha

HORSE

Imperiously he leaps, he neighs, he bounds, . . .
His ears up-prick'd; his braided hanging mane
Upon his compass'd crest now stand on end;
His nostrils drink the air, and forth again,
As from a furnace, vapours doth he send; . . .
Sometimes he trots, as if he told the steps,
With gentle majesty and modest pride;
Anon he rears upright, curvets, and leaps,
As who should say, "Lo, thus my strength is tried."

William Shakespeare: 'Venus and Adonis'
(Vol. 10) 231

HORSE. Of all the animals on Earth, the horse has probably most closely shared in man's adventures and has been most intimately allied with his progress. For thousands of years, the horse has participated in the pleasures, the dangers, and the hard work that have marked the life of man. Perhaps because of this long relationship, the horse holds a special place in man's affection.

No one knows exactly when man and the horse first became companions. Some historians believe that probably man hunted early horses as he did other game animals. Drawings, engravings, and sculptures of horses that date back many thousands of years may have been made by hunters and medicine men as offerings to the gods for a good hunt. Then perhaps man recognized the advantage of the horse's fleetness, tamed the horse, and used it to pursue other animals for food. When food became scarce in one area, the horse helped man move and settle in other areas that were more productive.

Gradually man found more and more uses for the horse and became increasingly dependent upon it. As this dependence grew, the horse became a partner in man's life. It shared the dangers of war, the satisfactions of peace, the pomp and splendors of knighthood, and the sufferings and privations of exploring and settling new lands and wresting a living from the soil. The horse also made possible many of man's pleasures. It carried him in hunting fields, in polo matches, and in races. It drew the wagons for circuses and traveling players, then often performed in the acts they presented. Man's pride in this magnificent beast has prompted him to show it off in horse shows, and his admiration for the animal's beauty and grace inspired him to portray it in art and literature.

Until the early 1900's the horse was an integral part of man's everyday life. Then machines began to perform many of the jobs that horses had done, and the population of horses—especially in Europe and North America—dropped drastically. For example, in 1915 there were more than 21 million horses in the United States, but by 1955 their number had dropped to only a little more than 3 million. Although no census has been taken since the late 1950's, a special survey published in 1966 indicated that there had been a great increase in the population of light horses. Horsemen conjecture that this increase results from the growing interest in riding for pleasure and in breeding fine horses.

Contributors for this article include Margaret Cabell Self, author of 'The Horseman's Encyclopedia' and many other books about horses and horsemanship, and Albert M. Lane, Livestock Specialist, University of Arizona School of Agriculture. The section "Evolution of the Horse" was critically reviewed by George Gaylord Simpson, Professor Emeritus of Harvard University and Professor of Geosciences, University of Arizona. The horse breed illustrations, done by Harry Michaels, were especially commissioned for Compton's Encyclopedia.

Preview

The article Horse is divided into the following sections and subsections:

Scientific Classification

Phylum: Chordata
Subphylum: Vertebrata
Class: Mammalia
Order: Perissodactyla
Family: Equidae
Genus: *Equus*
Species: *E. caballus*

Horses are in the order of odd-toed hoofed animals, Perissodactyla, and belong to the horse family, Equidae. All modern horses are genus *Equus*, species *E. caballus*. For information about other members of the horse family, *see* the articles Ass and Zebra.

GLOSSARY

Aid. The signal or command given to a horse by the rider indicating what the horse is to do. *Natural aids* are conveyed by the rider's hands, legs, voice, back, and weight distribution. *Artificial aids* include spurs, whip, and martingale.

Bit. The metal part of the bridle that fits into the horse's mouth under the tongue. The reins are attached to it.

Cadence. The rhythm of a horse's gait. Each gait has its own beat. The walk, for example, is a slow one-two-three-four; the trot, a fast one-two, one-two.

Cold Blood. All horses are considered to have cold blood except Thoroughbreds and Arabian breeds. The phrase implies that the horse is unexcitable, a calm and phlegmatic type.

Collection. The gathering together by the horse of all its forces to be ready to move at any gait in any direction immediately upon demand of the rider. All gaits have an extended and collected form. Collected gaits—such as the slow canter—give the horse more elevation but less forward movement.

Colt. A male horse between the age of weaning and four years old.

Dressage. Specially designed training and exercises that make the horse supple, collected, balanced, and responsive to aids.

Filly. A female horse between the age of weaning and four years old.

Foal. A male or female horse between birth and weaning. Used as a verb, the word means "to give birth."

Gait. The way and sequence in which a horse places its feet on the ground to obtain forward motion.

Gelding. An altered male horse.

Hand. The scale of measurement for a horse's height. Height is measured from the highest point of the withers to the ground. A hand is equal to 4 inches, and fractions of a hand are given in inches. In the figure 15.2 hands, for example, the horse is 15 hands or 60 inches high, plus 2 inches, or a total of 62 inches.

Haute École. The "high school" of horse training; the special training in performing difficult movements especially as practiced by the Lipizzan horses and riders at the Spanish Riding School in Vienna.

Hot Blood. All Thoroughbreds and Arabian breeds are considered to have hot blood. The phrase implies that the horse is spirited and eager and has a delicate head and fine coat.

Mare. A female horse that is more than four years old.

Seat. The position of a horseman in the saddle. The position differs with the type of riding that is done and the type of horse that is ridden.

Stallion. An unaltered male horse that is more than four years old.

Tack. Stable gear. Tack, derived from tackle, includes all the horse's equipment for riding—such as saddle, bridle, and halter.

Tack-up. To saddle and bridle a horse.

Yearling. A young male or female horse during the year between its first and second birthdays.

FAMOUS HORSES IN FACT AND FICTION

Black Beauty. The horse that is the main character in a book of the same name written by Anna Sewell to call attention to common abuses of the animal in the 19th century.

Bucephalus. The favorite mount of Alexander the Great during his Asian conquests, and in whose honor Alexander named a city in Persia.

Byerly Turk. One of the three stallions on which the Thoroughbred line of racehorses was founded.

Ching Chui. One of the six famous war-horses of the Chinese Emperor T'ai Tsung, who died in A.D. 637. His tomb was decorated with statues of his war-horses and a poem commemorated the victorious battle in which each took part.

Copenhagen. The favorite mount of the Duke of Wellington, who rode this famous charger in the battle of Waterloo.

Darley Arabian. One of the three stallions on which the Thoroughbred line of racehorses was founded.

Flicka. A main character in the well-known novel 'My Friend Flicka' by Mary O'Hara.

Godolphin Barb, or **Godolphin Arabian.** One of the three stallions on which the Thoroughbred line of horses was founded.

Iroquois. The first American-bred horse to win the English Derby.

Justin Morgan. Foundation sire of the Morgan breed, one of the best-known breeds of road horse in America.

Marengo. The favorite mount of Napoleon, on which the emperor was mounted at Waterloo.

Nelson. General George Washington's charger, which was present at Valley Forge and Yorktown and remained with the first president at Mount Vernon.

Pegasus. The winged horse of Greek mythology who carried the thunderbolt of Zeus and for whom a constellation is named.

Rakush. The mount of Rustam, the chief hero of the Persian epic poem 'Shah Namah', or Book of Kings, in which Rakush was reputed to be the best war-horse in the world and largely responsible for his master's successful exploits.

Rosinante. The ugly horse that carried Don Quixote on his bumbling adventures in Cervantes' tale 'Don Quixote'.

Sleepy Tom. Although blind, this horse became the outstanding pacer of the world, racing at top speed with only the voice and signals of his trainer as guides.

Sultan. Sometimes called Ivan, this horse was the favorite mount of William Cody (Buffalo Bill) and was often used in his Wild West shows.

Traveller. The favorite mount and almost inseparable companion of Gen. Robert E. Lee. Traveller was with Lee from Appomattox to Richmond and went with him to Lexington when Lee became president of Washington College there.

Trojan Horse. The huge wooden horse in whose hollow body Greek soldiers hid to gain entry into the city of Troy to conquer it. The story is told in Homer's 'Iliad'.

The Anatomy of the Horse

The horse is a beautiful and utilitarian beast. Both its beauty and its utility result from the relationship among all its body parts in form and in function. The general shape and appearance of a horse is called *conformation* by horsemen. Conformation includes the form and proportion of various parts of the animal's body and the way they fit together to give overall balance and structural smoothness. Thus balance or proportion of the horse's body is important because each part has a functional relationship to the rest of the parts.

Although breeders have developed horses of many different colors, sizes, and special attributes, all of the animals have a "horselike" appearance. In general, the horse is a relatively large animal that weighs about 1,000 pounds or more. It stands about $5\frac{1}{2}$ feet high at the shoulder and is about 9 feet long from the tip of its nose to its tail. It has a long, muscular neck; a large chest; a rather straight back; and powerful hindquarters. Its legs are strong and comparatively slender. In motion, the hind legs provide the propelling force and the front legs act primarily as supports.

The Horse's Head and Body

The horse's head and neck make up about two fifths of the total length of the animal. The head is held naturally at about a 45° angle to the neck. The head and neck act as a counterbalance as the center of gravity shifts when the animal is in motion.

The ears are proportionate to the head, neither too small nor so large that they look mulish. They are held upright and turned forward when the horse is alert. The horse can move his ears freely to pick up sounds from various directions.

The eyes are larger than those of any other land animal, and the horse has excellent long-range vision both at night and in the daytime. Each eye can see things above and below, behind as well as in front. A horse's eyes see things separately. An object may be seen first with one eye, then with the other. Stationary objects, especially small ones, seen in this way seem to jump, and the horse may become frightened. Sometimes to keep the animal from being startled horsemen put pads called blinders, or blinkers, near the horse's eyes to limit vision.

The nose has wide, flaring nostrils. A horse must get all its air through its nasal passages. It does not get extra breath through its mouth as do cows, dogs, sheep, and many other kinds of domestic animals. Even on a very hot day, or when the horse has been racing or working hard, it never pants with its tongue out. The reason for this probably is that a horse's soft palate forms a musclelike curtain that separates the mouth cavity from the breathing passages except when the horse is swallowing.

The horse has large jaws, and the teeth are large and strong. A mature male horse has 40 teeth, a mature female has 36. The front teeth, or incisors, are separated from the rear teeth, molars or grinders, by a wide and sensitive space, or bar. The bar forms the space into which the bit fits. Male horses also have two extra teeth called tushes. Horsemen examine a horse's teeth to estimate the animal's age. The teeth grow longer and at a more oblique angle with age, and the surfaces wear away.

The horse's body is large and sleek. The wide chest contains the huge lungs and heart that are necessary equipment for an animal that must have great endurance for running or enormous power for pulling loads. The back is strong, well muscled, and rigid enough to provide the legs with freedom to move easily. A back that curves downward at the center is called swayback; one that curves upward is called roach, or hog, back.

Do You Know

1. Why does a horse not pant even after a long race on a hot day?
2. Why do some horses wear "blinders"?
3. How can a horse's age be judged?

The Horse's Legs and Feet

The legs are long, strong, and comparatively slender. The front legs support weight, help maintain body balance and stability, and contribute to the forward movement of the animal. The part of the leg called the knee by horsemen is comparable to the wrist joint in man. The hind legs are heavily muscled to provide the propelling force in running and the pushing force for pulling a heavy load. The central point for these forces lies in the hock joint, and this joint bears the burden for all forward movement. It is comparable to the ankle joint in man.

A horse's foot is really a single toe, and the hoof is a thick toenail. The tip of the toe bone fits within the hoof, and the heel angles upward. The bone is so porous that it looks somewhat like pumice stone. The toe bone and two other bones make up the horse's foot. All fit within and are protected by the hoof.

The hoof is a boxlike part made up of the same kind of material as that in a man's fingernail. The part of the hoof that we see when the horse's feet are on the ground is the wall. The wall protects the front and sides of the foot. It is longest and thickest in the front and decreases toward the back of the foot. Horseshoes are put on the underpart of the wall to help protect it from extensive wear. The shoes must be changed and the hoofs trimmed once a month. A hoof grows about one-third inch in four weeks.

When the horse's foot is raised, the sole and the frog can be seen. The sole covers most of the undersurface of the foot and is arched to protect the bones and soft parts of the foot above it. The frog is a soft elastic section shaped like a triangle with its base at the heel and its apex pointing forward. It is a shock absorber, cushioning the jarring impact that occurs every time the animal's foot comes in contact with the ground.

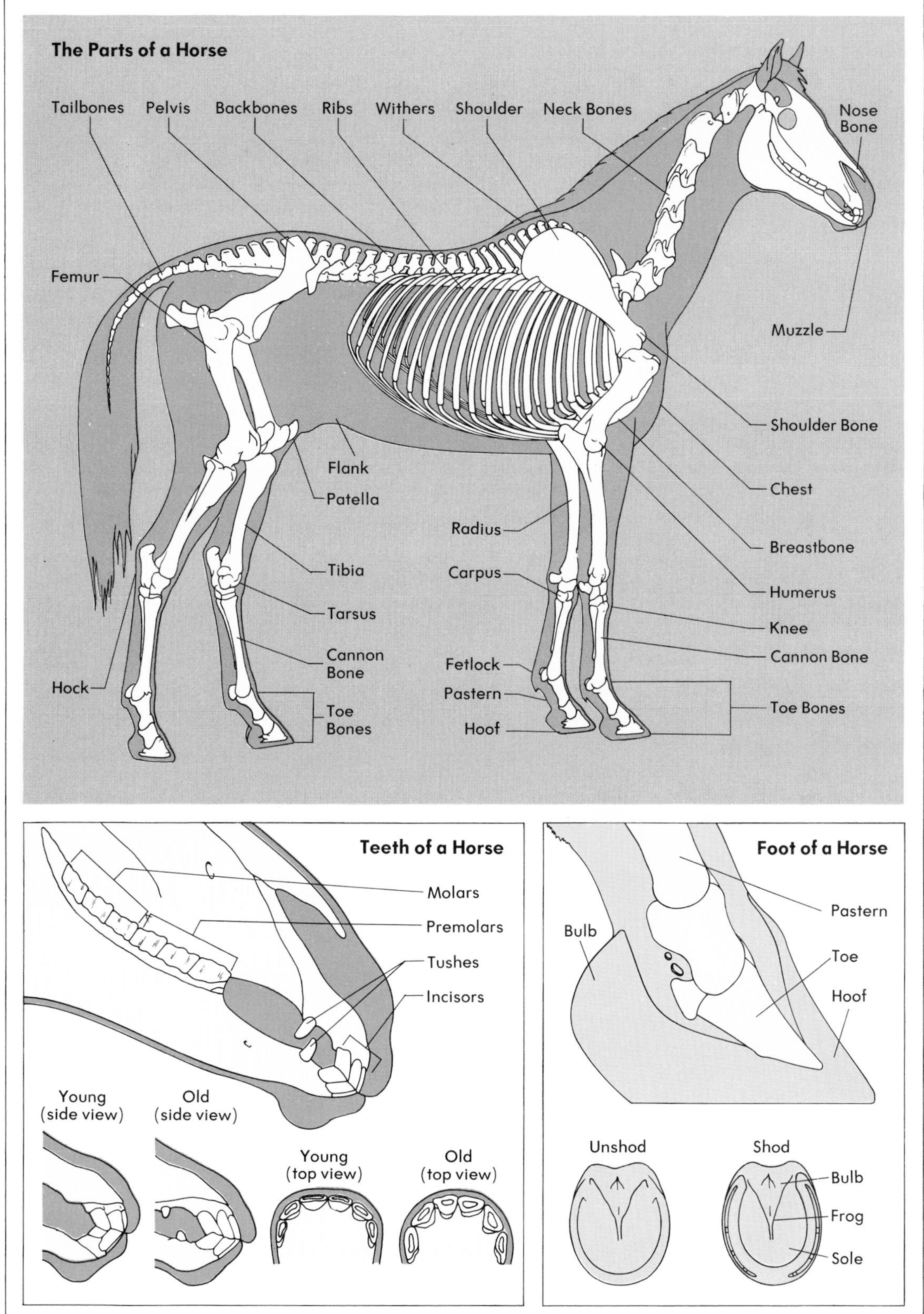
The Parts of a Horse
Tailbones
Pelvis
Backbones
Ribs
Withers
Shoulder
Neck Bones
Nose Bone
Femur
Muzzle
Shoulder Bone
Flank
Chest
Patella
Radius
Breastbone
Tibia
Carpus
Humerus
Tarsus
Knee
Cannon Bone
Fetlock
Cannon Bone
Hock
Pastern
Toe Bones
Toe Bones
Hoof
Teeth of a Horse
Molars
Premolars
Tushes
Incisors
Young (side view)
Old (side view)
Young (top view)
Old (top view)
Foot of a Horse
Pastern
Bulb
Toe
Hoof
Unshod
Shod
Bulb
Frog
Sole

(Vol. 10) 232c

A Horse's Life History

Do You Know

1. When is the official birthday of a horse?
2. How soon after birth can a foal walk?
3. At what age does a horse's training begin?

Foals may be born at any time of the year. But many horse breeders prefer that birth take place in the springtime. Foals born in winter need more stable room as well as more food and care than do those born in milder weather. Foals born in spring can roam outdoors and nibble grass to supplement their diet. No matter what time of the year a foal is born, however, its first birthday is recorded as being the first day of January after its birth. So, New Year's Day is the official birthday of every horse.

The Birth of a Foal

The gestation period—the length of time a mare carries the foal inside her body—is usually 11 to 12 months. The actual birth process takes only a short time—usually about 15 to 30 minutes. Normally a foal is born with its front feet first. One leg is extended; the other leg is slightly bent; and the head is thrust between the two legs. The newborn foal rests quietly for about 10 or 15 minutes, then tries to get up and is soon able to stand. Within a few hours after birth the foal is able to frisk about quite well on its gangly legs.

The legs of a newborn foal are almost as long as those of the mare, and grow only slightly during the horse's lifetime. The rest of the animal's body develops and the muscles of the legs become large and strong, but the big bones of the legs remain about the same size. Though it usually has grown to full height several years before, a horse is considered to be mature at seven years of age.

The Young Horse

A newborn foal begins to nurse as soon as it can stand up after birth. For the first six months of its life it depends mostly on the mare's milk and on grain supplied by its owner for nourishment. It begins to supplement its diet by nibbling grass and clover, sometimes spreading its long legs wide somewhat like a giraffe. By the time the foal is six months old, it has grown enough to make grazing easier. Then it is weaned, taken away from the mare, and becomes completely independent.

Within a week or ten days after birth, a foal has two upper and two lower incisor teeth. At a year old, it has six upper teeth and six lower ones. All of these are milk teeth, much shorter and smaller than the permanent ones. The horse begins to get its permanent teeth when it is about $2\frac{1}{2}$ years old, but does not have all of them until it is about five years old. It is then said to have a "full mouth."

The Training of a Horse

A horse's training begins almost immediately after it is born. Trainers handle the foal and brush its thick, fuzzy coat frequently. By the time the animal is a month old, it has learned to wear a halter. As a yearling, it learns to respond to reins, and at two years old it is saddle-trained. When it is three, the colt begins specialized training for whatever career has been chosen for it—perhaps as a riding horse, polo horse, circus horse, or racehorse. But usually it is not required to do exhaustive work until it is about five years old.

One year of a horse's life is equal to about three years of a man's life. Seven years of a horse's life would be comparable to 21 years in a man's life. Horses cease to be useful for most kinds of work when they are about 23 or 24 years old, although they still may be able to do certain kinds of light work. The life span of a horse is considered to be 25 to 30 years, but some horses may live to be 40 or more.

The foal shown in this photograph is only a few minutes old. Foals are born with their eyes open and with a full coat of hair. Both the mother and the newborn foal rest for a little while after the birth, but soon get up and move about.

Bradley Smith-Photo Researchers

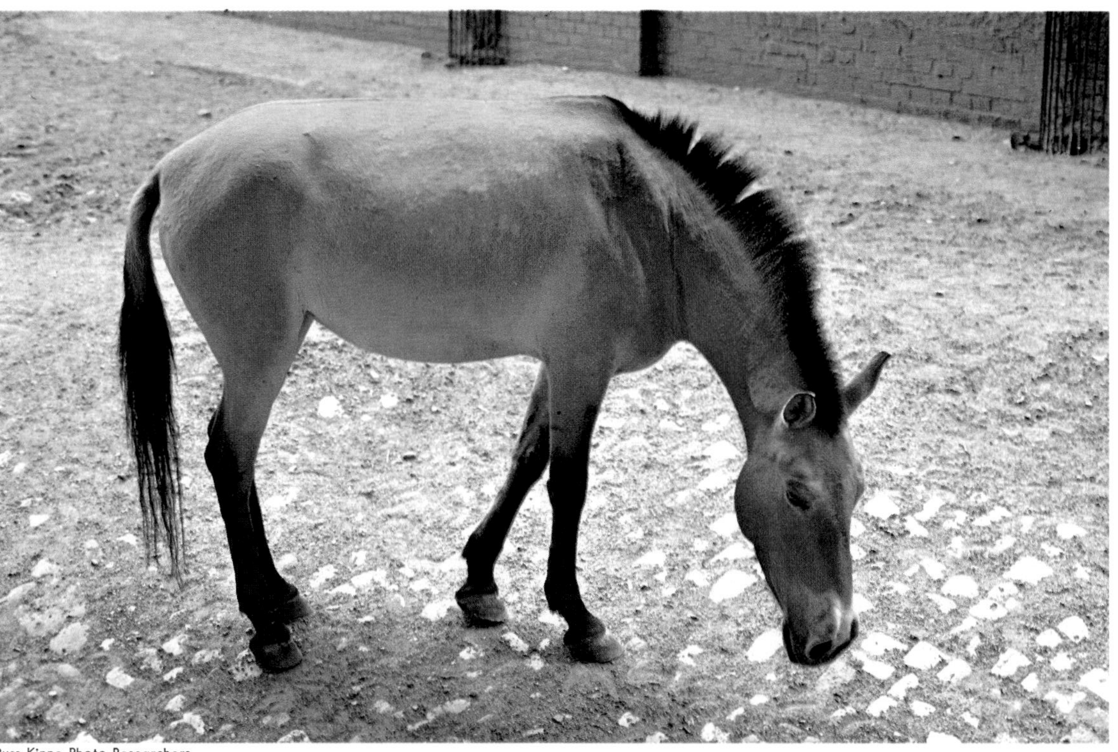

Russ Kinne-Photo Researchers

Przewalski's horse, above, is the only kind of true wild horse that survived into the 1900's. It was believed to be extinct in the wild state, but small herds of these horses have been sighted in remote areas of Mongolia.

The tarpan, below, a wild horse of southern Russia, became extinct in the middle 1800's. In a unique experiment, scientists bred horses with tarpan characteristics and in a kind of backward evolution achieved the tarpans now seen in zoos.

Los Angeles Zoo

The Horse Breeds

The animal we know today as the horse is the result of centuries of selective breeding. By careful selection breeders throughout history have developed various kinds of horses with a wide variety of characteristics to suit many different needs. The Great Horse of the Middle Ages, for example, was bred for size and strength to carry a heavily armored knight and his weapons into battle. The massive horses of such breeds are often called "cold blooded." The Arabs bred lithe desert horses that were small and swift. These animals are often referred to as "hot blooded." Cross-breeding of hot blooded and cold blooded horses for certain characteristics produced breeds ranging from riding horses to draft horses.

The Thoroughbred is considered by many to be the highpoint of elegance and fine selective breeding. Many persons mistakenly apply the name Thoroughbred to any purebred horse. But a Thoroughbred is a distinct breed of running horses that traces its ancestry through the male line directly back to three Eastern stallions: the Byerly Turk, the Darley Arabian, and the Godolphin Barb (or Godolphin Arabian). These horses had been imported into England before 1750 and were used by breeders to develop the famous Thoroughbred racing horse.

For convenience the breeds of horses are often divided into three major groups: (1) ponies, (2) heavy, or draft, horses, and (3) light horses. The color drawings on the following pages of this article show horses in these three groups.

TABLE OF HORSE BREEDS

THE PONIES (Weight range 450–850 lbs.)	Height Range (in hands)	Color Range
Hackney	14.2 or under	Black, brown, bay, chestnut
Shetland	11.2 or under	Any solid color or pinto
Welsh	11.0–14.0	Any solid color

THE HEAVY HORSES (Weight range 1350–2200 lbs.)		
Belgian	15.3–17.0	Chestnut, roan
Cleveland Bay	16.0–17.0	Bay
Percheron	16.0–17.0	Gray, black
Clydesdale	16.0–16.2	Bay, brown
Shire	17.0–17.1	Black, bay, brown, roan, gray
German Coach	15.2–16.3	Black
Suffolk	15.2–16.2	Chestnut

THE LIGHT HORSES (Weight range 800–1300 lbs.)	Height Range (in hands)	Color Range
American Saddle Horse	15.0–16.0	Black, bay, chestnut, gray
Hackney	14.2–16.0	Black, brown, bay, chestnut
Appaloosa	14.0–15.2	Distinctive patterned spotting
Standardbred	15.0–16.2	Most solid colors
Arabian	14.1–15.1	All solid colors
Palomino	14.0–17.0	Golden
Mustang	13.2–15.0	Any color
Morgan	14.1–15.1	Bay, chestnut
Lipizzan	15.1–16.1	Gray (white), chestnut, bay, roan
Tennessee Walking Horse	15.0–16.0	Any solid color
Quarter Horse	14.3–15.1	Any solid color
Thoroughbred	15.0–16.0	Any solid color

Hackney Pony

Shetland Pony

Welsh Pony

Belgian

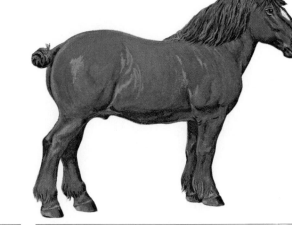

Cleveland Bay

Percheron

Clydesdale

Shire

German Coach

Suffolk

(Vol. 10) 232g

American Saddle Horse

Hackney

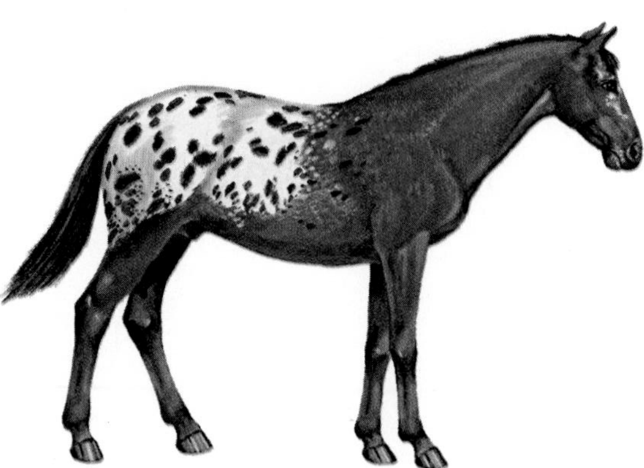

Appaloosa

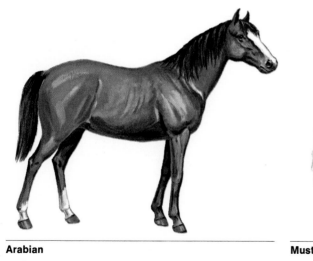

Standardbred

Arabian

Mustang

232h (Vol. 10)

Palomino

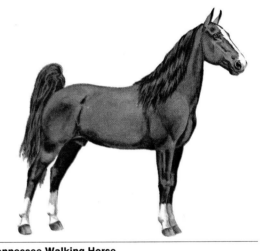

Morgan

Lippizaner

Tennessee Walking Horse

Quarter Horse

Thoroughbred

Walter Chandoha

Horses of many different breeds add to man's enjoyment of his leisure time. Children and adults thrill to the tricks of a circus horse, the strength of a rodeo horse, or the skill of a polo pony. Thoroughbreds, trotters, and jumpers provide entertainment for thousands of persons. But perhaps the greatest pleasure a horse gives to man is when they are together on a quiet country lane.

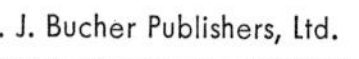

C. J. Bucher Publishers, Ltd.

Frank Verticchio

U.S. Trotting Association

Artstreet

Farrell Grehan-Photo Researchers

Ray Woolfe, Jr.

Color and Markings of the Horse

A person buying a horse for pleasure riding may choose the animal for the color and markings much as he would choose a color and design for his automobile. Horse breeders, however, consider color an important point in judging the value of a horse. Some breeds are required to have certain colors and patterns in order to be registered. Registries for such breeds as the Appaloosa and Palomino, for example, may not accept horses with undesirable colors or patterns.

Color is one of the most conspicuous features of a horse and is often the basis for description, such as bay, chestnut, or gray. These colors, however, differ somewhat from the usual conception of the color. Common colors used for horses include the following:

Black. All hairs are completely black, with no lighter color appearing.

Brown. All hairs are brown, but may be so dark they look black. The true color shows in hairs around the nose and eyes or wherever the coat is thin.

Bay. Hairs may be brown but show auburn or red shades; mane, tail, and stockings are black.

Chestnut. Hairs are the same colors as the bay, but mane, tail, and stockings are the coat color or lighter.

Dun. Hairs are dull grayish-yellow or dull grayish-gold, but mane and tail are black.

Gray. Hairs are black or brown at birth, but lighten with age and may be almost white at maturity.

Palomino. Hairs are gold or yellow, but mane and tail are white.

White. Hairs are white or nearly white at birth and they remain white. True white horses are albinos.

Markings are also distinctive features. Many horses have white face marks, and some common ones are illustrated in this article. White face markings and leg markings may occur on horses of any coat color. The markings of the Appaloosa and Pinto horses, however, are distinctive. Appaloosa horses are often called "spotted horses." They may have light coat patterns with dark spots or dark coat patterns with light spots. Pinto or paint horses have coats with large, splashy patterns. Brown and white patterns are called skewbald, and black and white ones are piebald.

The color of a horse's coat and the animal's markings are often used in descriptions. Some of the coat colors are shown in the drawings at the right, and some of the face markings are shown in the drawings below. Markings may also appear on the legs. A horse keeps its markings for life, and they are often used as a means for identification.

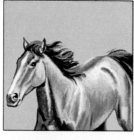

The colors shown below from top to bottom are: dappled gray, dun, brown with white mane and tail (rare), and gray.

The colors shown below from top to bottom are: strawberry roan with white mane and tail, chestnut, and skewbald.

The colors shown below from top to bottom are: golden dun, bay (the mane and tail are always dark), and black.

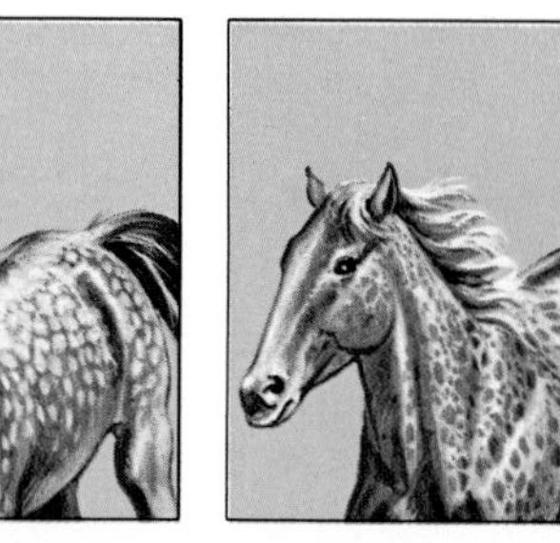

Starlet | Blaze | Star | Broad Blaze

The Lipizzan

Many persons consider the Lipizzan, or Lipizzaner, the most beautiful of all horses, the royalty of the horse breeds. Anyone who sees these magnificent animals cannot help but be impressed by their grace and dignity. Perhaps the best known horses in the world are the Lipizzans of the Spanish Riding School of Vienna. Here, perfectly trained horses perform difficult movements on and above the ground with the seemingly effortless grace of ballet dancers. These are not the artificial actions that are sometimes learned by horses for the circus or trick-riding rings. Instead, all the feats are based on the natural movements of a horse, those done by a playful horse frisking about in high spirits in an open pasture. But years of careful training perfect each of the movements done by the Lipizzan.

"Lipizzan" is almost synonymous with "white horse" in the minds of many people, and it is true that those chosen for performance at the Spanish Riding School are white. But some Lipizzans may be chestnut, bay, or roan. Even the white horses are not born white. All are dark at birth and become white only at about the age of four years or as late as ten years.

Lipizzans mature much more slowly than do other breeds of horses. For the first four years of the colt's life it runs free with the herd. Then a trainer, who has himself been specially trained, is chosen for the colt. He assumes complete responsibility for the care and training of the animal, and no one else is allowed to touch it.

Schooling for the Lipizzan begins with a two-year initial training period. Usually only stallions are chosen. For the first three months, horse and trainer work on the rudiments of discipline, and the horse learns to trust the trainer completely. Schooling for the remainder of the two years consists chiefly of exercises that keep the stallion flexible and supple. When the Lipizzan is six years old, training for performing figures begins. For the next two years the horse undergoes intensive individual schooling that will make him a star performer in the riding school. He will learn to balance perfectly on his hind legs in the levade, be stately in a cadenced quadrille, leap high above the ground in a courbette, and soar suspended in space in the capriole. For about the next 20 years, the Lipizzan's life consists almost entirely of practice and performance. When the horse can no longer perform in the show ring, he becomes an instructor, teaching fledgling riders who hope to become masters of this special art of horsemanship.

Jerry Cooke—Photo Researchers

Thomas D. Lowes—Photo Researchers

A Lipizzan horse, top right, performs a spectacular courbette with ease and grace at the Spanish Riding School in Vienna, Austria. The horse's saddle and bridle are traditional, and the costume worn by the rider has remained almost unchanged for the last two hundred years. A troupe of Lipizzans, bottom right, execute the measured paces of a quadrille at the Maple Leaf Gardens in Toronto, Ont. The meticulous precision of horses and riders as they move through the intricate patterns of the performance indicates their rigorous training for perfection.

THE WALK. The walk is a four-beat gait and the slowest of the three natural gaits of the horse. In this gait, both legs on one side move, then both legs on the other side move. The feet are lifted only a short distance and then usually are placed flat on the ground. The gait has an even cadence and gives a smooth ride with no feeling of jogging. The illustrations for this and the other gaits are keyed to show red for right legs and green for left. The hoof prints show the placement of the hoofs in each position.

THE TROT. The trot is a two-beat gait. In the trot, diagonal pairs of legs move: left front and right rear; right front and left rear. The feet are lifted a little higher than in the walk and come down with the tip of the hoof striking the ground first. The gait gives the rider a slight feeling of jogging. When the speed increases to a fast trot, the jogging also increases and the rider then posts, lifting himself slightly out of the saddle with each jog.

THE GALLOP. The gallop, the fastest of the horse's three natural gaits, is a three-beat gait. The first beat is made by a hind foot. The second beat is made by the other hind foot coming down at the same time as the front foot diagonally across from it. The third beat is made by the other front foot. Then a period of suspension occurs when all four feet are off the ground. The series begins again when the first hind foot strikes the ground again for the first beat. A slow, restrained gallop is called a canter.

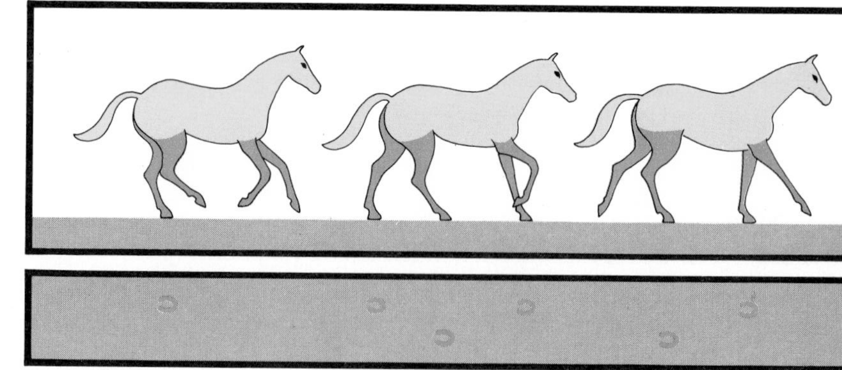

The Gaits of the Horse

A horse's gait is the way in which the animal moves its legs and places its hoofs to obtain forward movement. There are various kinds of gaits. Each produces a different kind of ride for the horseman, and each may be used for a different purpose. Each gait also has a specific cadence or rhythmic beat. The cadence is the rhythm of the sound heard when the horse's hoofs strike the ground.

The horse has three natural gaits. These are the walk, the trot, and the gallop. The canter is a collected or restrained form of the gallop. It gives greater "lift" but less forward motion to the horse than does the gallop. Other kinds of gaits are artificial gaits, which are usually variations of the natural gaits. Artificial gaits are obtained by selective breeding or by special training.

The rack and the slow gait are artificial gaits. The slow gait has several forms including the fox trot, the broken pace, the running walk, and the amble. The rack is a fast gait.

Sometimes horsemen speak of five-gaited horses or three-gaited horses. The five-gaited American Saddle Horse can do a walk, a trot, a canter, one of the slow gaits, and a rack. The three-gaited Tennessee Walking Horse has a flat-footed walk, a running walk, and a slow canter. These artificial gaits were developed by Southern planters in colonial times. They give a smoother ride than either the trot or pace, and the rider can spend longer hours in the saddle. The rack is, however, tiring for the horse. A western horse's gaits include a walk, a slow gait, and a lope, which is a form of the canter.

(Vol. 10) 234c

Horsemanship—The Art of Riding

Almost everyone has seen at the movies or on television graceful riders on saddle horses cantering along bridle paths or cowboys seated with careless ease on mustangs loping off into the sunset. It looks quite easy. But in the art of riding, as in any other kind of art, it takes an enormous amount of practice and patience to become a master. The thrill of being a disciplined rider on a disciplined horse, however, is well worth the effort.

An observant movie and television viewer will have noted that the equipment of the horse on the bridle path was different from that of the mustang. The novice rider will need to know something about a horse's equipment before he can use it. A horse's gear is called tack, which includes the saddle and the bridle. It is possible to ride a horse without either saddle or bridle, and sometimes student riders are required to do this to develop balance and confidence. For most riding, however, gear is used.

The tack for riding includes, in addition to the saddle and bridle, a halter, lead shank (a rope with a clip on the end) and, if the climate is cold, a stable blanket. The purpose of tack is to provide the rider with a means by which he can control the horse and also to provide him with a seat on the horse's back.

There are basically two major classes of tack—English and western—and there are many varieties in each of the classes. Horsemen choose their tack carefully to suit the type of riding they do. The choice will also depend upon how the horse is trained.

Some Types of Saddles

Many varieties of saddles have been developed, but all are built in basically the same way. The frame, often called the tree, of the saddle is made of wood, steel, or a combination of the two. The rigid frame is well padded and covered with leather. One or more wide straps called girths are attached. A girth passes under the horse's body and is fastened to the opposite side. A leather strap for the stirrup is suspended from each side of the saddle. The flap, a wide, flat piece of leather, hangs between the stirrup strap and the horse's side.

Saddles are contoured on the underside to fit a horse's back and on the top side to fit the rider's body. A saddle should be properly fitted to the horse so a rider's weight is centered on the horse but not directly on the withers and the spine.

English saddles are often called flat saddles because they are so gently contoured that the rider's seat is almost flat. There are three basic types of flat saddles: (1) the forward seat or jumping saddle, (2) the modified forward saddle, and (3) the dressage saddle. The forward seat or jumping saddle has flaps that extend well forward over the horse's shoulders. This saddle is preferred by many riders for open jumping. In the modified forward saddle the flaps do not extend quite so far forward as they do on the jumping saddle. This saddle is used for ordinary riding, for jumping, and for hunting. The dressage saddle has a deeper seat than do the other saddles.

The western saddle has a deep seat, a high pommel from which the saddle horn rises, and a high, fanlike cantle. Rings and rawhide saddle strings are attached to hold a cowboy's equipment. There are several different types of western saddles including parade saddles, cutting saddles, and roping saddles. Each is designed for the special use its name implies. Western saddles have little padding, so a heavy blanket or thick pad is usually placed under them.

Bridles-the Horse's Headgear

The bridle includes all the equipment a horse wears on his head: the bits, curb chains, crownpiece and browband, cheekpiece, and reins. There are several different kinds of bridles.

English bridles are known by the type of bit used. The snaffle bit and the pelham bit are the most common. The snaffle is a simple, jointed bit that works on the corners of the horse's mouth. The pelham has two sets of rings for the reins and fits on the bars of the horse's mouth. Many horses used for hunting and jumping wear snaffle bridles with running martingales. The reins run through the martingale and the bit and act on the bars instead of on the corners of the mouth.

The western bridle usually is fitted with some type of curb bit. The western curb bit, however, has longer shanks than the English and has no curb chain.

The Art of Riding

A novice soon learns that one of the basic skills in the art of riding is balance. A horseman stays on his mount by balance, not by gripping his mount with his legs or by using the reins as lifelines. To achieve and maintain his balance, the rider's center of gravity must be directly over that of the horse. The horse's center of gravity is in direct line with the girth of the saddle when the horse is standing still.

The Rider's Position

Horsemen call a rider's position on the horse his "seat." The rider sits erect in the deepest part of the saddle, which is over the stirrup leathers. In the flat saddle, the knees are bent and pushed ahead of the stirrup leathers. This places the angle of the thigh parallel to the angle of the horse's shoulder blade. When properly seated, a rider's ear, hip, and heel are in line, and the tip of the toe is directly under the point of the knee. His arms are relaxed but held so that a straight line could be drawn from the tip of the elbow along the forehand, wrists, and reins to the horse's bit. Illustrations with this article show the position of the rider on the horse at various gaits.

Communication and Control

A horse trained for riding has been taught the "language of the aids." A rider must also learn this

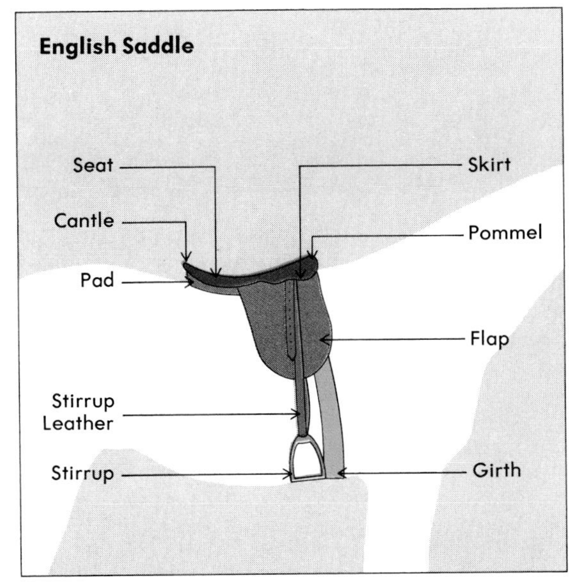

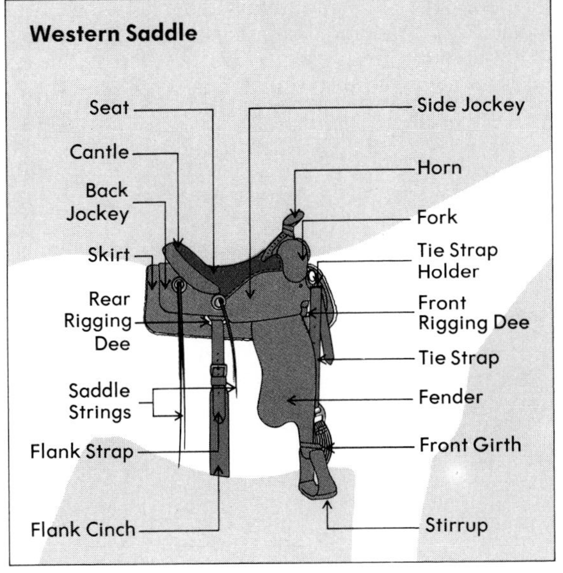

language so he can communicate with his mount. There are two kinds of aids—natural and artificial. The natural aids include the voice, the action of the hands on the reins, the use of the legs and heels, the use of the back, and the distribution of the rider's weight. The artificial aids include the whip, the spur, and various types of equipment such as side reins and martingales.

The reins are one line of communication a rider has with his horse. A horse is trained to go in the direction of the tension put on the rein. Although a skilled horseman uses the reins for many effects, the novice uses them for two basic ones: (1) to direct, and (2) to lead. If the rider carries his right rein slightly to the right and pulls back (direct) or to the side (lead), the horse turns in the direction of the pull. If the rider pulls both reins straight back, the horse slows down or stops. Every rider must learn to keep very light contact on the horse's mouth through a stretched rein. A slight increase of tension directs the horse, and immediate relaxation of tension when the horse begins to respond is the horse's reward for obedience. Continued tension punishes the animal and may confuse him.

The reins indicate the direction of movement (turn, go forward, or back), but the leg aids indicate that motion should start. The horse moves away from the pressure of a leg or heel. When a rider applies pressure only with his left leg, the horse moves his haunches to the right. When pressure is applied with both legs, the horse begins to move forward.

The rider uses his weight to help the horse keep in balance and also to indicate a change of direction. A rider on a well-trained horse has only to step down in one stirrup and the horse will turn in that direction. When a rider shifts his weight backward slightly the horse will slow down. The rider uses his voice to encourage, to praise, or to admonish his mount.

Mounting and Dismounting

Illustrations with this article explain the four phases for mounting a horse properly. In dismounting the procedures are reversed. When the rider swings his right foot back over the horse he bears his weight

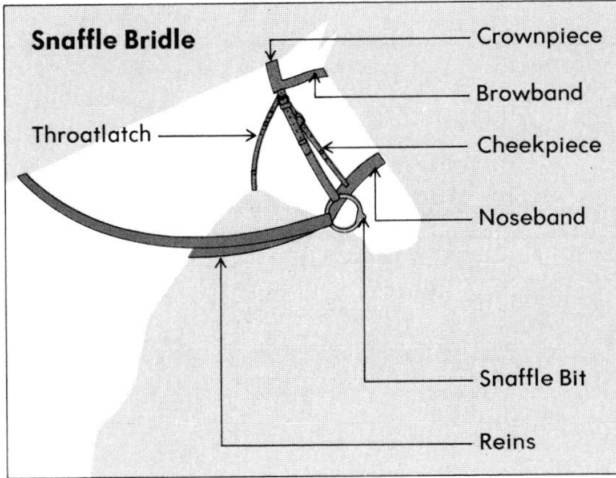

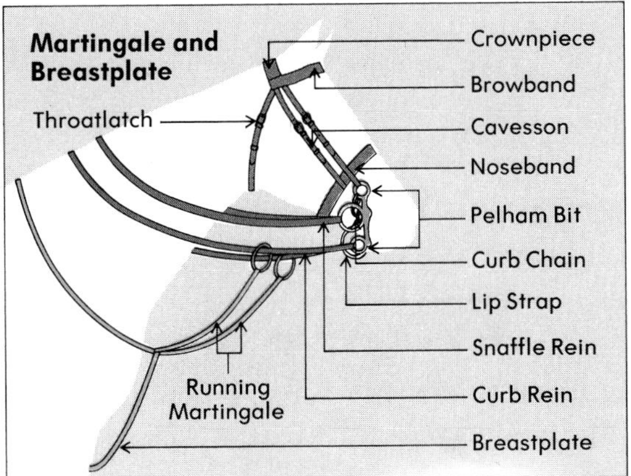

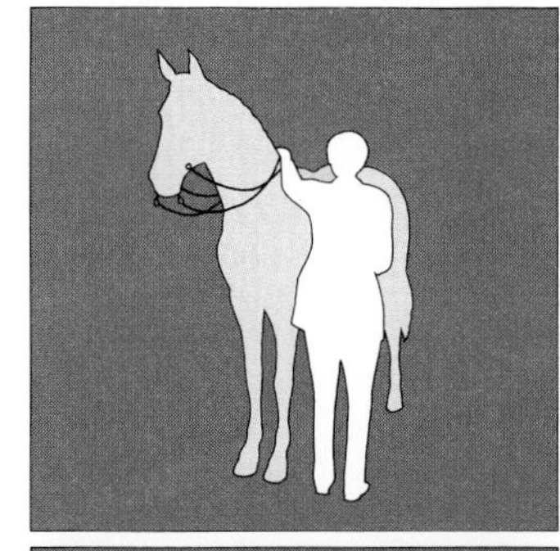

To mount a horse, the rider stands at the horse's left side and either faces the rear or faces the shoulder. He gathers the reins in his left hand and places his hand on the neck, sliding his hand down to shorten the reins.

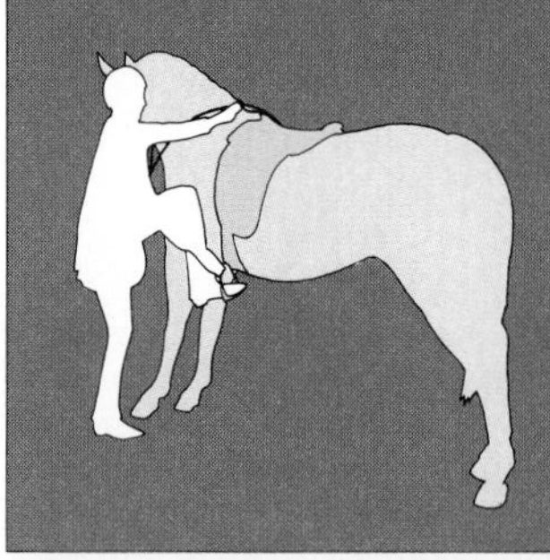

Still holding the reins, and grasping the horse's mane in his left hand, the rider uses his right hand to steady the stirrup while he puts the left toe of his boot in it. Then he moves his right hand to grasp either the cantle (of an English saddle) or the horn (of a western saddle).

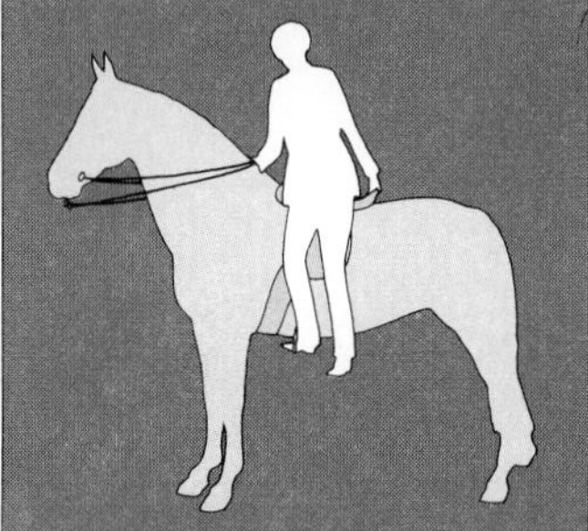

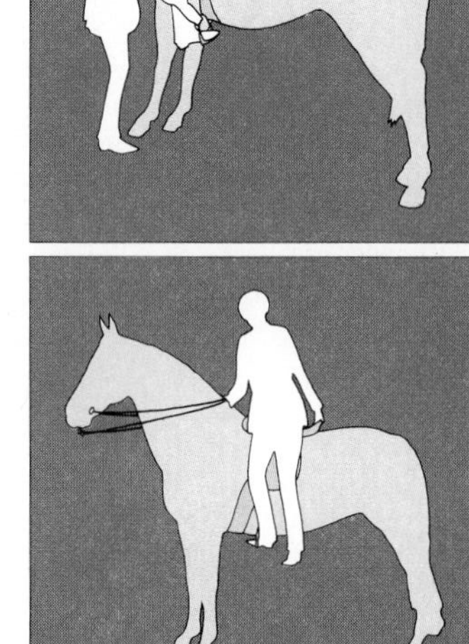

The rider springs upward from the ball of his right foot, turns slightly to face the animal, and straightens his knees so that he is standing on the ball of his left foot in the stirrup, the right foot next to it, but bearing most of his weight on his hands on the horse's back.

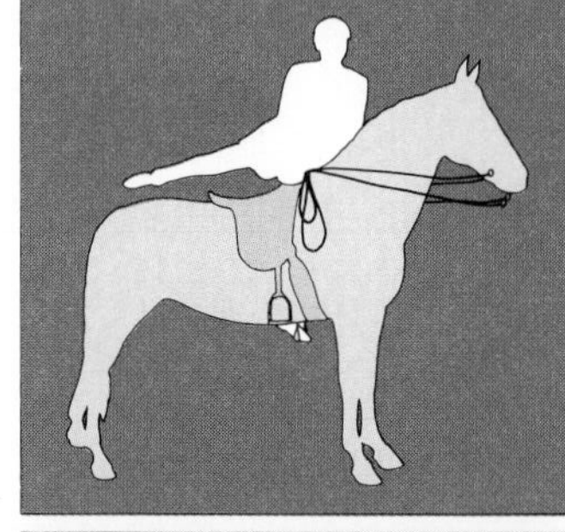

The rider then leans on his left arm (and if using an English saddle moves his right hand from the cantle to the pommel) and swings his fully extended right leg over the horse's back and rump. He then settles lightly into the saddle and places his right foot in the right stirrup.

The properly mounted rider sits easily in the saddle with his head up, back straight, and shoulders well back. His legs hang comfortably. The balls of his feet are in the stirrups, the heels are held down, and the toes are turned slightly outward.

on his hands, brings his feet together, then kicks his left foot out of the stirrup. He drops to the ground, turning slightly so that he lands facing the front of the horse. He then transfers the reins to his right hand.

The Western Seat

Western riding is primarily a working form of riding, and the horses are differently trained. The horse works on a loose rein, and the rider holds the reins in one hand and directs the horse with a neck rein. Horses used for western-type riding are especially trained to respond to neck reining. When the rider wishes to go to the right, he moves the hand holding the reins to the right. The horse feels the touch of the left rein on his neck and turns in the opposite direction—to the right. The touch of the right rein brings a move to the left.

The western rider sits deeply and firmly in the saddle. His aids are his weight and his legs. The stirrup straps are longer than those of a flat saddle, and the horseman rides with his knees only slightly bent. He maintains his center of gravity over the horse, however, and his feet are not pushed forward.

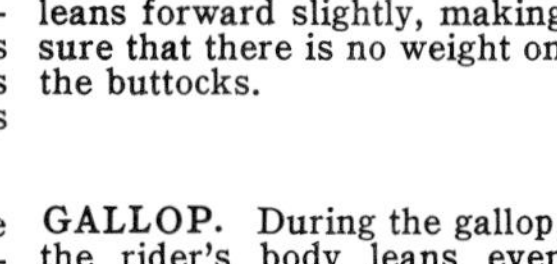

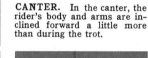

WALK. In the illustrations below, the dotted line represents the angle of the rider's body. In each position, he holds his back straight, shoulders back.

TROT. For the trot, the rider leans forward slightly, making sure that there is no weight on the buttocks.

CANTER. In the canter, the rider's body and arms are inclined forward a little more than during the trot.

GALLOP. During the gallop, the rider's body leans even farther forward, and his arms are even more extended than in the canter.

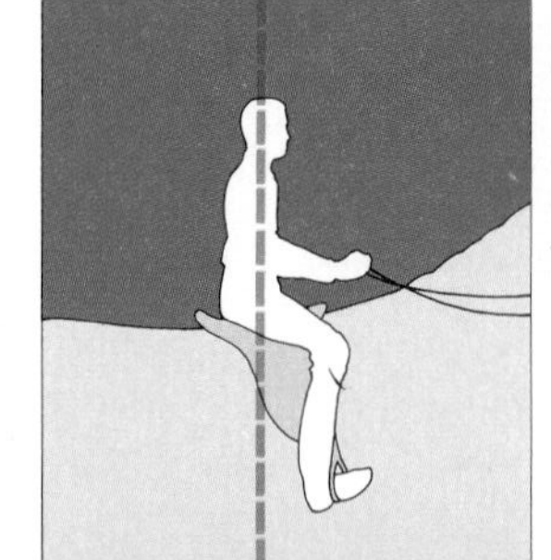

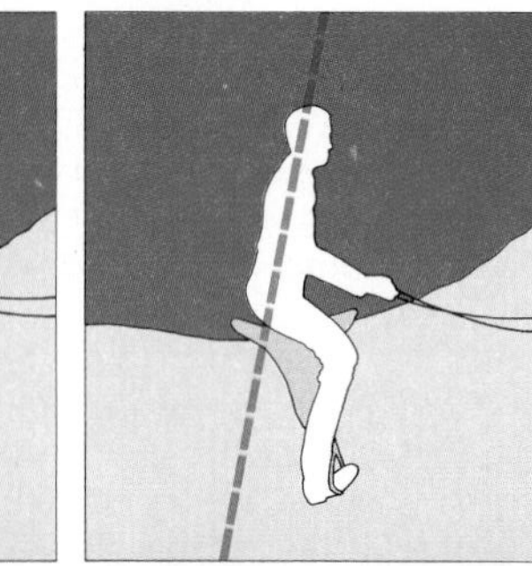

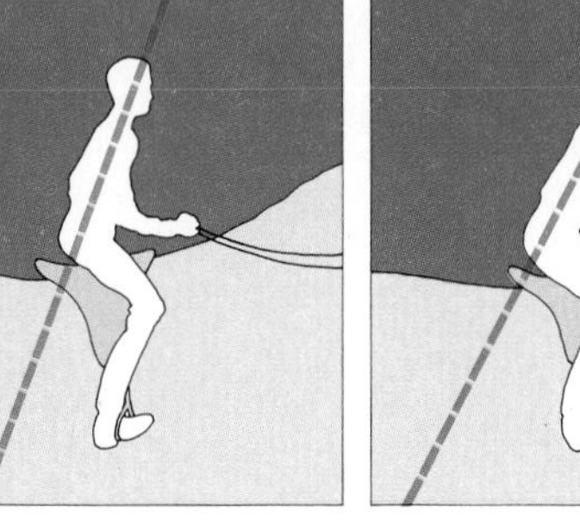

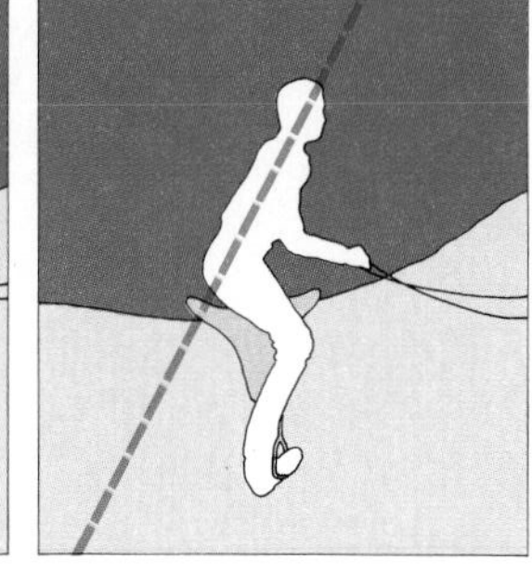

Caring for a Horse

The horse, like any other kind of animal, responds to proper care and good treatment. Caring for a horse requires considerable time and patience, however, and only persons who are willing to expend the time and have adequate space should consider keeping a horse at home. Many horsemen who enjoy owning their own mounts keep them at professional boarding stables to ensure proper care.

Housing a Horse

The minimum size box stall for a horse is ten feet by ten feet. Stalls must be large enough so that the horse can lie down and get up without injuring itself and can turn around comfortably. They also must have areas where bedding, feed, hay, and equipment can be stored. The walls of the stall should be constructed of two-inch-thick oak boards to the height of five feet. Above this, heavy wire or lighter boards can be used. The flooring can be of clay, sand, or cinders. At least three inches of bedding should be spread on the floor. Bedding soaks up moisture and provides the horse with a clean, dry bed.

Mangers, racks, or other containers for hay and grain should be placed on the walls at heights that are convenient for the horse to reach. Water should be available day and night.

One of the most time-consuming of all the chores necessary for the proper care of a horse is cleaning the stable. The stall and bedding must be cleaned daily. The bedding must be removed and replaced periodically.

Feeding a Horse

The amount and kind of feed a horse needs depends upon the size of the animal, his condition, and the kind of work that is demanded of him. For a pastured horse, the grass he nibbles may provide sufficient food. But most horses, especially working horses, need supplementary feed for energy. Feed consists of hay supplemented by grain rations. Hay is a substitute for the pasture grass. Grain is a concentrated food and is given in small amounts several times a day. Water is also an important part of the horse's diet, but grain swells when wet so the water should always be given first. Many horsemen follow the routine of small but frequent feedings in this sequence: water, hay, grain.

Grooming a Horse

A horse should be thoroughly groomed at least once a day. A well-groomed horse looks attractive, but grooming has a far more important function. It improves the animal's circulation and helps tone the muscles. So, vigorous grooming is necessary.

Grooming tools include a cloth, a brush of rough straw, a soft body brush, a rubber or plastic currycomb, and a hoof-pick. All parts of the horse's body must be groomed. The cloth is used first to remove surface dust and dirt. The soft brush cleans

Walter Chandoha

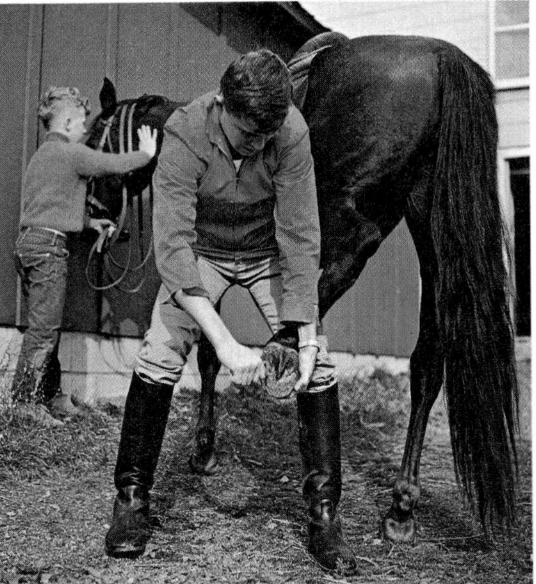

Grooming a horse thoroughly at least once a day is important for the animal's health and appearance. The feet need special care, and a hoof-pick is used to remove hard materials that collect under each foot.

the face and lower legs where the hair is short. The currycomb and rough brush are used where the hair is long. The horse's feet need special care to prevent infections. They should be cleaned every day and each time the horse is ridden. A hoof-pick is used to pick out hard materials such as packed manure and stones that collect under the foot.

Grooming gives the horseman an opportunity to closely inspect all parts of the horse's body for any cuts, abrasions, or signs of disease. The stable should be equipped with first-aid articles. Home remedies can be used to treat superficial cuts and abrasions, but a veterinarian should be called to treat any other kind of injury or disease.

Saddling and Bridling a Horse

An important part of a horse's care is proper saddling and bridling. To put on the bridle, slip it over the horse's nose, guide the bit into the mouth, and slide the crownpiece over the ears. Adjust the noseband and browband. Fasten the throatlatch and the curb chain. Be sure that all parts of the bridle lie flat and are neither too loose nor too tight. To put on the saddle, lay it on the withers and slide it back into place. Attach the girth or cinch evenly on both sides. The girth should be neither too loose nor too tight. To test for proper fit, slip a hand between the body of the horse and the girth just below the saddle, then slide it down to the bottom. It should feel tight only where it passes under the horse. On western saddles with two cinches, the forward cinch is made very snug, the rear one less so. Cinches are fitted tighter than girths because of the work the horse does.

Evolution of the Horse

Horses have a long and interesting history on Earth, and the study of their complex evolutionary development probably constitutes one of the most extensive and intensive searches done by scientists. As a result, the evolutionary story of the horse is perhaps the most complete of that of any of Earth's animals.

Geologists, scientists who study Earth's history, believe that the first men appeared on Earth about 2 million years ago—a very long time in terms of the way we count time, but like a fraction of a second in terms of geologic time. Horses appeared on Earth long before man—about 60 million years ago, at or shortly before the beginning of the Eocene epoch of Earth's history. This fact has been so well established that fossils of these animals found in rock strata are used by scientists to date the rocks. These early horses lived on both the European and the North American continents. Evidence of possible ancestors in older rocks in North America, however, leads scientists to believe that probably the animals originated on that continent.

The modern horse with its sleek coat, straight back, proudly arching neck, and long legs bears little resemblance to its ancient ancestors. If it were possible to bring one of these animals to life, few people would recognize the small animal about the size of a fox as the forerunner of the horse. In fact, when the first bones of these animals were found in 1838 and 1839, they were believed to be the bones of ancient monkeys or of the harelike animals called hyraxes or conies. The general resemblance of the animal's structure to the hyrax was the reason that the scientific name *Hyracotherium* was given to the animal. But it is most commonly called Eohippus.

The name of the Eohippus comes from two Greek words: *eos*, meaning dawn, and *hippos*, meaning horse. The name also reflects the fact that Eohippus occurs in the Eocene—the "dawn" portion of the most recent epoch of geologic time.

Eohippus was an active and abundant animal, and many fossils have been found. However, almost all are fragmentary, and finding a complete skeleton is rare. For this reason, only a few skeletons have been reconstructed and mounted.

There were several different species of Eohippus, and they varied greatly in size. The smallest were about 10 inches high at the shoulder, and the largest were more than 20 inches high.

The body of Eohippus looked almost like that of a rabbit. The hindquarters were high, and the arched back sloped downward toward the neck and head. The animal had a long, stout tail, which bears no resemblance to that of the modern horse. Modern horses have short tails; the whisk of hairs that grow from the tip make them appear long.

The head of this ancient animal was shaped almost like that of a dog. The snout was more pointed than broad as in that of the modern horse. The large eyes were set midway between the front and the back of the skull. The teeth were simple. The cheek teeth had a few cusps, more like our own molars than like the large, strong, heavily ridged teeth of the horse today.

The feet of Eohippus added to its doglike appearance. The front feet had four toes, and the hind feet had three. Each toe ended in its own small hoof. Tough pads, much like those of a dog, bore the animal's weight.

Eohippus was well equipped to live in the world of its time. The small animal had short legs that were not built for speed, but it probably was fast for

The series of drawings shown at the top right are reconstructions that show what scientists believe horses may have looked like at each of four major stages of their evolution. They range from the small, doglike "dawn horse" of the Eocene epoch through the almost modern looking horse of the Pliocene epoch. The color box at the top left corner is a key to the locator map on the far right.

The series of drawings shown at the bottom right are reconstructions of skeletons and foot bones from remains that have been found. They show the basic changes that took place as the horse developed over the ages.

The locator map on the far right shows the areas in which scientists have found remains of each kind of horse.

Eocene Epoch (54 million years ago)

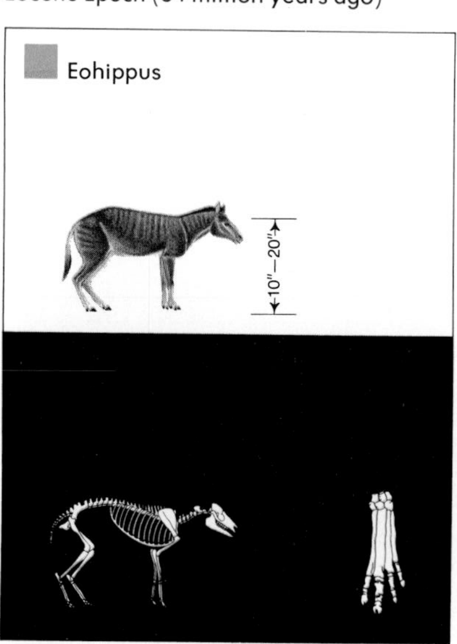

Oligocene Epoch (38 million years ago)

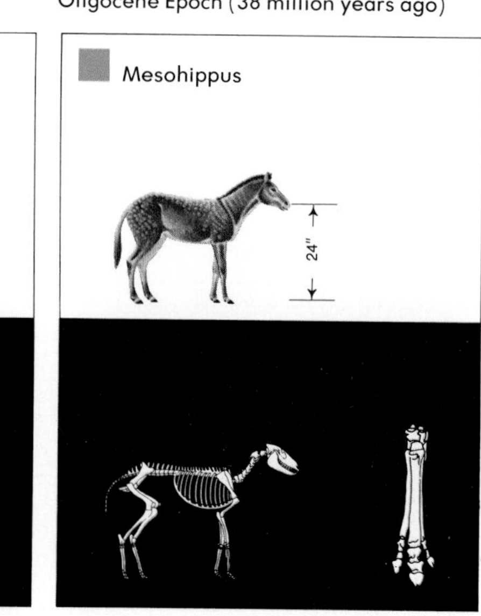

its size. Its light weight and spreading toes kept it from sinking into the soft earth.

Mesohippus—The Middle Horse

Mesohippus probably is the best known fossil horse. Buried and preserved bones of these animals are abundant, especially in the Badlands of South Dakota. *Mesohippus* lived about 35 million years ago, during the Oligocene epoch of geologic time.

Unlike Eohippus, *Mesohippus* looked much like a small modern horse. Although there were smaller and larger species, *Mesohippus* averaged about 24 inches. The body was longer than that of Eohippus, and the back less arched but still not the straight, rigid back of the modern horse.

The head of *Mesohippus* had a more "horsy" appearance although the face was still slender and almost snoutlike. The jaws were still shallow, but the typical horse muzzle probably had begun to develop. The eyes were positioned farther back on the head than in Eohippus. The teeth were larger and stronger than those of Eohippus. Also, a little gap was beginning to form behind the front teeth where today the horse has a large gap into which the bit fits.

The legs of *Mesohippus* were longer and more slender, but each foot still had several toes. Now, however, there were only three toes on the front feet as well as on the back feet. As in Eohippus, the center toe was the largest, and there were pads on the feet and between the toes.

Merychippus—The Transformation Horse

Some of the most radical and rapid changes in the evolutionary development of the horse took place during the Miocene epoch of geologic time. Perhaps the most important were the changes in the structure of the teeth, which made it possible for horses to become grazers (grass eaters) rather than browsers (leaf eaters) as Eohippus and *Mesohippus* had been. By the middle of the Miocene—which began about 26,000,000 years ago—*Merychippus* had molar teeth with high crowns. The teeth were covered with a strong bone-like substance called cement. Such teeth could grind the coarse grasses into edible masses for the animal.

Merychippus also showed other changes, although these were not so dramatic as those of the teeth. The animal grew about 40–42 inches high—as large as many modern ponies. It had a long muzzle, deep jaws, and eyes quite far back on the head. The body and leg proportions were not exactly the same in all species of *Merychippus*. Some were stocky, others slender. But in general, changes that had taken place in the legs and feet made these parts appear more nearly like those of horses today. Certain bones of the leg grew together, making each leg rigid but highly effective for carrying weight and for a more efficient forward motion. The feet still had three toes, but the weight of the animal was carried on a greatly enlarged and strongly hoofed central toe. The side toes were short and small, and the foot pads had disappeared.

Pliohippus—The One-Toed Grazing Horse

Several groups of horses descended from *Merychippus*. One of these was *Pliohippus*, a horse of the Pliocene epoch. The modern horse, *Equus*, is a direct descendant of *Pliohippus*. Although, again, there are variations among some species, generally *Pliohippus* closely resembles the horse of today. *Pliohippus* had only one hoofed toe. The others became slivers of bone (splints) that even in modern horses grow along the cannon bone of the leg. Differences between *Pliohippus* and the modern *Equus* lie mostly in the refinement of the details of the animals' anatomy, which are used by scientists to separate them.

Miocene Epoch (26 million years ago)

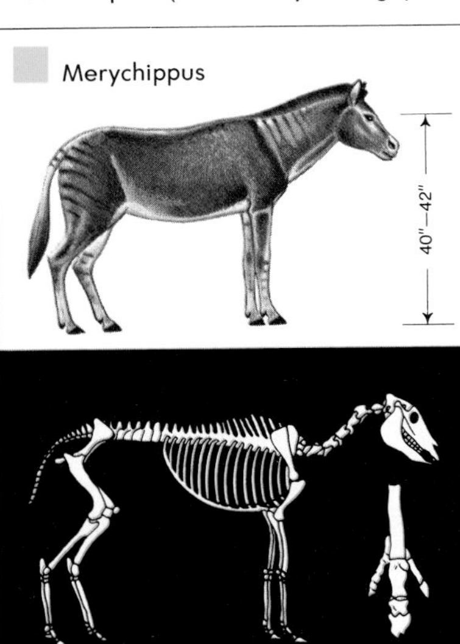

Pliocene Epoch (7 million years ago)

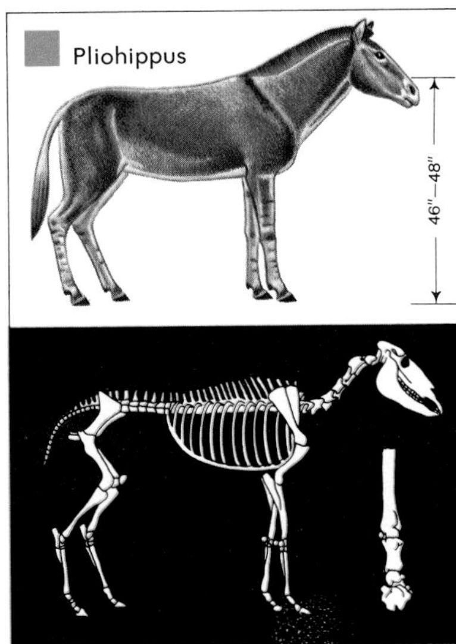

Fossil Location

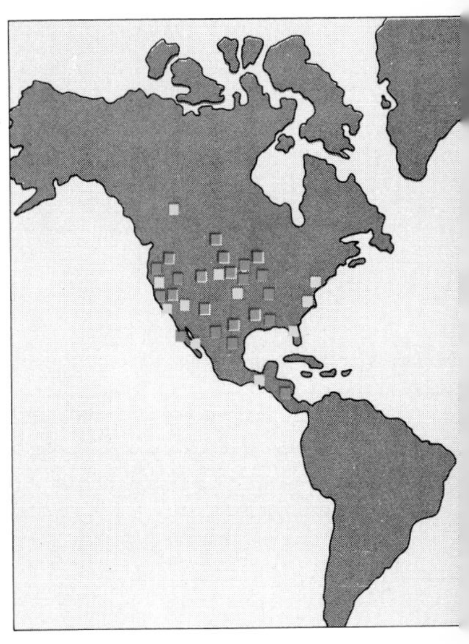

Fogg Art Museum, Harvard University, bequest of Mrs. J. Nicholas Brown

A glazed earthenware horse of the T'ang Dynasty (A.D. 618–907), above, shows that the Chinese of that time had a great knowledge of crossbreeding. They developed a sinewy but sturdy horse suitable for pulling heavy loads as well as for riding. The sculpture shows a padded saddle and other trappings for riding at that time.

A horse and knight of Prato, Italy, are shown, below, dressed for a tournament in this detail from a manuscript of the 1300's. Strong horses were needed to carry knights in full armor. Here, the armor is covered by a surcoat. The design on the coat and on the horse's cover identifies the knight.

Trustees of the British Museum

The Horse in History

Man's association with the horse probably began more than 4,000 years ago. In the beginning this association was not a companionable one. Prehistorians believe that man hunted horses as a game animal.

No one knows exactly when or where man first tamed the horse. Some scientists believe that the first horses may have been domesticated in the area of present day Turkestan, probably long before 2000 B.C. The horse worked for man as a draft animal for at least 1,000 years before the art of riding developed. However, some groups of nomads probably had small herds of these animals and rode them. When Greek traders first saw these mounted men in the Black Sea region, they believed them to be a strange animal, half horse and half man. The Greeks called them centaurs and developed many fables about these unusual beasts (*see* Centaurs).

Horses in the Ancient World

War horses and chariots were used by the Mitanni in Syria and the Hittites in Anatolia by about 1600 B.C. A remarkable book, the earliest known work devoted exclusively to horses, was written by a Mitanni horseman hired by a Hittite king. The clay tablets that comprise the book give detailed directions for the care and training of chariot horses.

In about 1700 B.C. the Hyksos from Syria and Palestine introduced domesticated horses into Egypt. By the 1500's B.C., the Egyptians used horse-drawn vehicles, but few Egyptians rode horses. By 1000 B.C. the use of horses had spread westward from Egypt.

The Greeks viewed the horse as a heroic symbol, a wonder beast ridden by great warriors and by the gods. The Romans made great use of the horse, and vehicles carrying freight or passengers clattered over the streets of Rome. By 45 B.C., all vehicles had been banned from within the city, and in other cities they were allowed only at night. Presumably they endangered pedestrians and caused traffic jams.

As the use of horses spread throughout the ancient world, breeding programs were established to produce animals with special qualities to suit specific purposes. For example, a large, heavy horse was needed to carry an armored soldier into battle, but a small, light horse could be used for riding and racing. Generations of cross-breeding made pure strains of original types difficult to find.

Horses in the Medieval World

During the Middle Ages, experimentation in breeding horses continued to be important. The growth of trade, including international trade, increased the need for a reasonable means for the overland transportation of goods. Sturdy pack horses were desired to carry merchandise between towns and into the countryside. Large, strong draft horses were in demand for use in teams to draw carts of bulk merchandise over long distances. In addition, horses for the business of knighthood had to be developed. A well-

Do You Know
1. What is a centaur?
2. What ancient city probably had traffic jams?
3. Who wrote the first known book about horses?

equipped knight needed at least four different types of horses: (1) a charger, (2) a palfrey, (3) a courser, and (4) a battle horse.

Horses in America Conquest and Exploration

European explorers brought horses to the New World—the first in the Americas since the native horses had died out about 8,500 years before. The Spanish had royal horse farms operating in Jamaica by 1515, and Francisco Pizarro obtained horses from these farms for his expeditions to Peru. Stock farms in Cuba supplied horses to Hernando Cortez for the invasion of Mexico in 1519. Horses carried the Spanish explorers and colonizers in their push through southwestern and western North America.

The westward movement from eastern North America is usually symbolized by the covered wagon. Many of the wagons were drawn by oxen, but mounted explorers usually preceded them, and mounted scouts accompanied them. After the West began to open up, the wagons were replaced by stagecoaches that carried passengers and mail.

Until the early 1900's, horses supplied much of the transportation and much of the power for vehicles. Horses pulled the first railroad cars. In the cities, horses drew the garbage wagons, milk carts, and fire engines. On the farms, ranches, and plantations, they powered the plows and harvesting machines. Today, the automobile, truck, and tractor have largely replaced the horse, although the performance capability of these vehicles is still evaluated in horsepower.

Horses in Sport

The horse has long been a source of recreation for man. The Persians were playing polo long before 600 B.C. The ancient Greeks hunted wild boar and mountain lion on horseback. The ancient Romans conducted horse shows, which included chariot racing as well as trick riding. The English of the 1100's enjoyed thoroughbred racing and fox hunting. Circuses and rodeos still draw thousands of spectators.

As the horse became less important in warfare and as a beast of burden he became more important in sport. In the United States, after a drop in the horse population during the early 1900's, the number of horses being bred and registered is gradually increasing. Many of these are used for pleasure riding, racing, hunting, and polo. But horse show competitions of various kinds are also popular. Many persons vie for top honors at rodeos, pony club rallies, and 4-H club meets as well as at the traditional horse shows. Although man's use of the work horse has gradually dwindled, his need of the horse as a companion in recreation seems to continue to increase.

Giraudon

Charlemagne, a ruler of Western Europe (768–814), is shown on his horse, above, in a bronze sculpture by an unknown artist.

This Belgian farmer of today, below, still uses a horse-drawn plow as farmers have done for centuries.

Victor Englebert—Photo Researchers

Tom McHugh—Photo Researchers

Painting of a horse, above, was done by a prehistoric artist on the walls of Naiux cave in southern France. The simple line drawing clearly shows the characteristics of the animal.

Historical Pictures Service, Chicago

Albrecht Dürer's engraving of the great European horse of the 1500's, right, shows the tremendous power of these animals, which enabled them to carry a knight in full armor.

The Horse in the Arts

The horse has played an enormously important part in the daily life of man since prehistoric times. So it is not surprising to find that the horse has been a favored subject for artists in every field throughout history. Even in prehistoric times, hunters scratched pictures of horses on the walls of caves. These drawings, some of which date back to about 18,000 B.C., vividly depict in simple lines the animation and action of the animals. The cave artists also succeeded in showing the distinguishing characteristics of the wild horse such as the short body, thick neck with heavy head and upright mane, and short but graceful legs.

The Assyrians, whose land lay between the Tigris and Euphrates rivers, were very interested in horses. Relief sculptures carved in stone depict the deeds of their warriors. Sophisticated and detailed carvings in the stone ruins of the ancient city of Calah in Iraq show Assyrian war chariots.

Egyptians decorated their tombs with spindle-legged stylized horses. Those shown on tombs were often many times larger than life size. A small wooden statuette of a horse and rider, carved about 1500 B.C., was found inside a tomb. The sculptured horse is much more graceful than those shown in the drawings by artists of this period.

The beauty and form of the horse seems to have inspired artists of almost every culture. We find Japanese screens, Russian icons, ancient Persian tapestries, and 16th-century East Indian miniatures showing the horse in action—some in warfare and others in such sports as polo and lion and tiger hunting.

Perhaps the most famous and beautiful sculptures of all time are those of the horses that form part of a frieze around the Parthenon in Athens. These sculptures, done by the Greek sculptor Phidias about 447 B.C., express the Greek idea of perfection. They show young men riding bareback on graceful horses that are portrayed at all gaits as well as at the halt or performing dressage movements.

Throughout the world, there are statues of history's famous military men, always mounted with the charger at the levade, or prancing with arched neck. In Italy, the museums and public squares of cities and towns are filled with statues of mounted and unmounted horses. Some of these date back to the 1st century B.C. In Venice, Andrea del Verrocchio's monument to the military leader Bartolommeo Colleoni, done in the late 1400's, shows the artist's ability to portray in bronze the strength and straining energy of a military horse.

During the Middle Ages, tapestries were a popular art form. Many of the castles of Europe used tapestries not only as a decoration but as a practical measure to help cover the stone walls and keep out the cold. The tapestry scenes often included horses. Perhaps one of the best known is the Bayeux Tapestry, thought by some to have been designed by Queen Matilda to honor the success of her husband, William the Conqueror, when he invaded England in 1066. Two hundred horses are embroidered into this work of art.

During the 1500's and 1600's Dutch, Flemish, and Spanish painters were interested in portraying the horse in sports. Sporting prints became extremely popular in England during the 18th and 19th centuries

Joseph Winterbotham Collection, The Art Institute of Chicago

Toulouse-Lautrec's painting 'The Ringmaster', above, captures the excitement of a circus horse's performance.

when many artists produced racing and hunting scenes. Many American artists used horses as subjects in some of their art. Among these were Frederick Remington, who is famous for his portrayals of pioneer life in the American West.

The horse has been equally important in the literary arts. The mythology of almost every Western culture includes the horse as an important character. For example, in Greek mythology the sun god, Apollo, crossed the heavens each day in a chariot drawn by fiery steeds. Another famous Greek horse, perhaps the best known one, was Bellerophon's flying horse Pegasus, who was placed among the stars. Norse myths tell the story of the hero Sigurd, who rides a brave stallion through a wall of magic fire to rescue the heroine Brynhild. This same story occurs in German mythology and became the basis for Richard Wagner's opera "Siegfried."

The grace and beauty of the horse has inspired many poets. William Shakespeare's famous poem "Venus and Adonis" paints superb word pictures of a stallion and a filly. Lines from this poem appear under the photograph at the beginning of this article. Another poet, John Masefield, created two masterpieces describing the horse in sports. His "Reynard the Fox" tells of the thrills of a hunt, and "Right Royal" portrays the excitement of a horse race.

Novelists, too, have been inspired by the strength and spirit of this animal. Books about horses in fact and fiction are extremely popular with readers of all ages and many appear every year. At the end of this article is a list of some of the fine books that have been written about horses.

Marino Marini, an Italian artist, includes a horse in most of his works, including the bronze 'Horse and Rider', below.

Collection Walker Art Center, Minneapolis

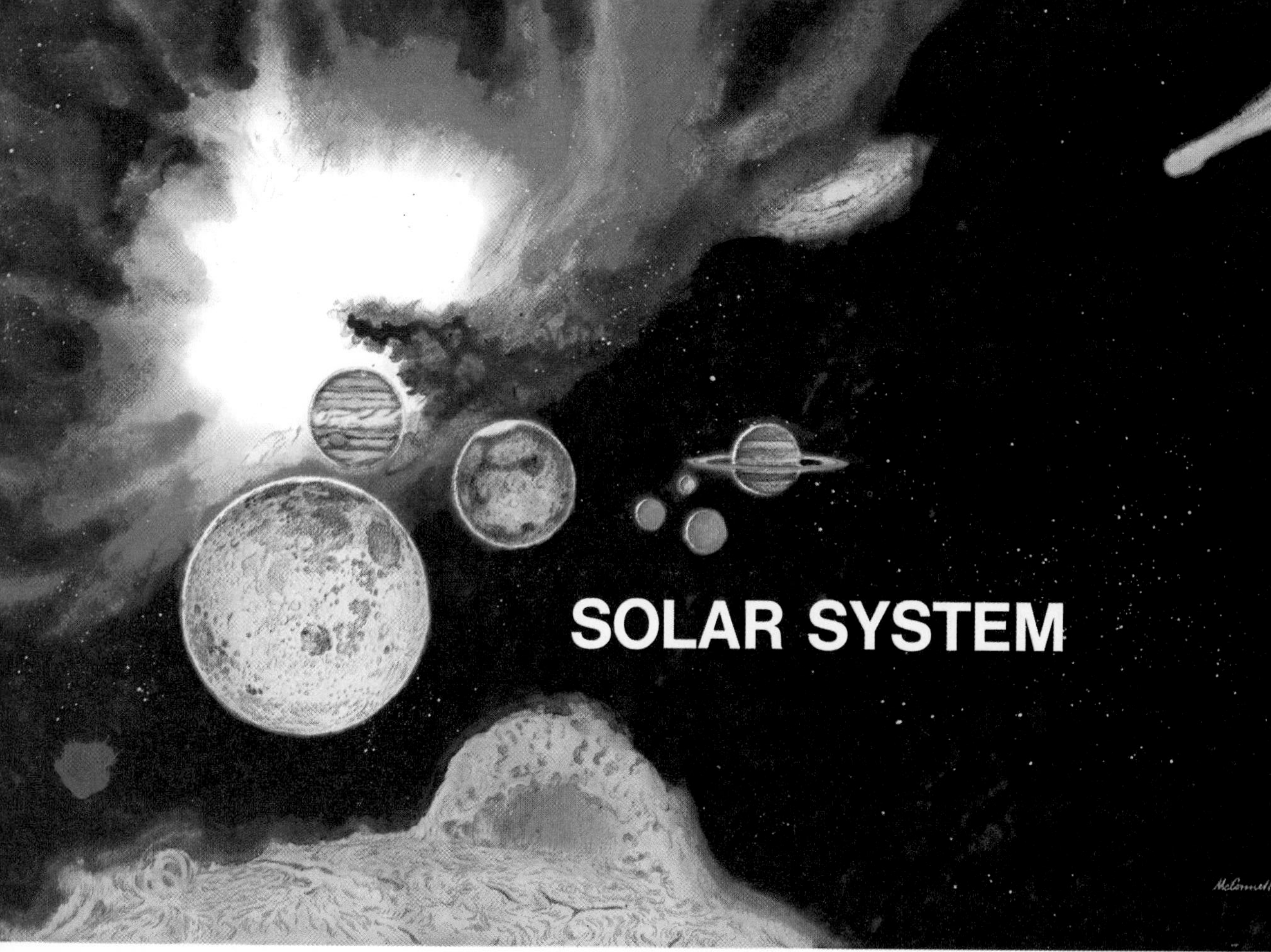

SOLAR SYSTEM

SOLAR SYSTEM. As the sun rushes through space at a speed of 150 miles per second, it takes many smaller bodies along with it. The sun and its smaller companions together are known as the solar system. These other members of the solar system range in size from the giant planet Jupiter to microscopic particles called micrometeorites and even smaller particles—atoms and molecules of the interplanetary gas. The planet Earth is one of the largest bodies of the solar system, although it is quite small when compared with the sun or even with Jupiter or the three other giant planets.

Astronomers do not know exactly how far out the solar system extends. When it is at its farthest point from the sun (aphelion), some $4\frac{1}{2}$ billion miles, Pluto is the most distant known planet. Many comets, however, have orbits that take them even farther out, up to several hundred times the distance of Pluto. Even at that distance the sun's gravitational force dominates and can bring the comet back. Some hundred billion comets form a tenuous halo in the outer parts of the solar system. Each is like a giant snowball, 1,000 to 10,000 feet in diameter.

THE SOLAR SYSTEM IN SPACE

The solar system centers around the sun, an ordinary member of a huge group of stars swirling around in a huge pinwheel-shaped mass called the Milky Way galaxy (*see* Astronomy). There are on the order of 100 billion stars in the Galaxy.

Astronomical distances are so huge that astronomers often use the *light-year* as the unit of distance. One light-year is equal to the distance light travels in a year, or 5,880,000,000,000 miles. It is much easier to think of one light-year than that large number of miles.

The Galaxy is about 100,000 light-years across. The solar system's nearest neighbor in the Galaxy is the triple star system Alpha and Proxima Centauri, which is 4.3 light-years away from our sun. Outside the Milky Way there are billions more galaxies stretching out through space (*see* Astronomy). Some are much larger than the Milky Way and some are smaller. Nearly all these galaxies contain billions of stars.

Astronomers cannot see to the end of the universe, which is the vast space that contains the galaxies and all other matter and energy that anyone knows to exist. However, galaxies and other objects have been detected that are thought to be between 5 billion and 15 billion light-years away from the sun. Compared with such distances, our solar system occupies a very tiny amount of space (*see* Universe).

This article was reviewed by Gerard P. Kuiper, Director, Lunar and Planetary Laboratory, University of Arizona.

THE PARTS OF THE SOLAR SYSTEM

Even though the solar system is tiny compared with the distances to galaxies or even to nearby stars, it is enormous when compared to distances on Earth. It is also diverse, with conditions ranging from the hot gaseous sun to the frozen darkness of Pluto.

The Sun

The sun is the central member of the solar system. Its gravitational force holds the other members in orbit and governs their motions. It far outweighs all other components of the solar system combined. In fact, the sun contains more than 99 percent of the mass of the entire solar system. It is however, only an average star. If it were as far away from Earth as most stars are, it would look no larger or brighter than its neighbors. But since it is by far the nearest star and the only star whose surface details may be observed, it is also one of the major sources of information that scientists have about how stars behave (*see* Star).

More important to people on Earth, the sun provides nearly all the heat and light and other forms of energy necessary for life on our planet. In fact, the sun provides virtually all the energy of the solar system. Its gravitational attraction governs the motions (or kinetic energy) of the planets and other bodies. Radiation from its surface bathes the planets in all the electromagnetic radiation they receive, with some minor exceptions. These exceptions include the faint light from stars, the disintegration of radioactive materials on the planets, emissions of long-wave radiation by the planet Jupiter, and the puzzling radio waves and X rays from remote space.

The Planets

The largest and most massive members of the solar system, after the sun, are the nine known planets. Even so, their combined mass is less than .2 percent of the total mass of the solar system.

The planets travel around the sun in regular orbits that are nearly circular in shape. Mercury's orbit lies nearest the sun. Next is Venus, then Earth, Mars, Jupiter, Saturn, Uranus, Neptune, and finally Pluto. Pluto's orbit is the most elliptical of any of the planets. When Pluto is nearest to the sun (perihelion), it is nearer the sun than is Neptune.

The motions of the planets are similar in certain significant ways. For one, all the planets orbit the sun in very nearly the same plane, which is the plane of the sun's equator. Pluto is the most divergent; its orbital plane makes a 17° angle with the plane of Earth's orbit around the sun. Mercury is next, making a 7° angle to Earth's orbital plane. The planes of all the other planetary orbits lie within $3\frac{1}{2}$° of Earth's orbit.

The planets are grouped according to their nearness to the sun or their physical properties. For example, Mercury and Venus, whose orbits lie between the sun and Earth, are *inferior planets*. The planets whose orbits lie beyond Earth's orbit are the *superior planets*. Alternatively, the planets may be divided by location into four *inner planets* (Mercury, Venus, Earth, and Mars) and five *outer planets* (Jupiter, Saturn, Uranus, Neptune, and Pluto).

The reason for this division is that the four inner planets are similar in composition, mostly silicate rock and iron in varying proportions, while the four major outer planets, Jupiter to Neptune, are huge, not very dense, and have deep gaseous atmospheres. Since Jupiter is the outstanding representative of this group, these four planets are also known as the *Jovian planets*. Jupiter and Saturn are composed mostly of highly compressed and solid hydro-

The Sun

Mass . . . . 2.2 octillion tons, or 333,400 times Earth's mass, or 2 x 10^{33} grams

Diameter. . . . . 864,400 miles, or 109.3 times Earth's diameter, or 1.4 x 10^{6} kilometers

Volume. . . . . 50 octillion cubic feet, or 1,300,000 times Earth's volume, or 1.4 x 10^{33} cubic centimeters

Average Density. . . 88 pounds/cubic foot, or about one fourth Earth's density, or 1.41 grams/cubic centimeter

Rotational Period
At Equator. . . . . . 25 Earth Days
Near Poles. . . . . . 33 Earth Days

Photographs taken through monochromatic filters can reveal great detail. This photograph of the sun's turbulent surface was taken through a filter that excluded all light except the red light emitted by hydrogen (H_α).

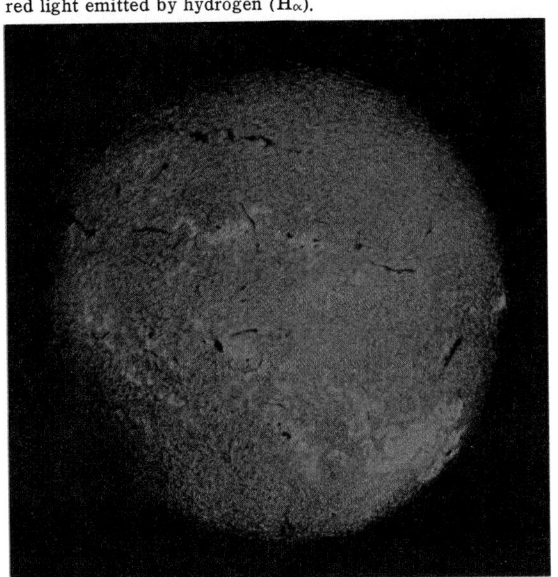

Sacramento Peak Observatory,
U.S. Air Force Cambridge Research Laboratories

gen, whereas Uranus and Neptune are composed of hydrogen compounds. Pluto is an exception.

Six of the planets have smaller bodies, their natural satellites, circling them. With 12 moons, Jupiter has the greatest number. Earth is the only planet to have just one moon. Our moon is so large, however, when compared with Earth, that the Earth-moon system is often regarded as a double planet. Saturn's largest satellite, Titan, is of interest because it is known to have an atmosphere. In 1944 the United States planetary astronomer Gerard Kuiper detected methane in its spectrum. Pluto may have begun its existence as a satellite of Neptune.

Asteroids, or Minor Planets

Tens of thousands of smaller bodies circle the sun in orbits that lie, for the most part, between Mars and Jupiter. These are the *asteroids,* or minor planets (*see* Asteroids; Astronomy). Ceres, the first asteroid to be discovered, is also the largest, with a diameter of 785 kilometers (488 miles). Few asteroids have diameters larger than 100 miles. Most are probably no larger than one mile across. Their gravity is not strong enough to pull them into a spherical shape.

Some 44,000 asteroids can be photographed with a 100-inch telescope. The total mass of all these asteroids, however, probably adds up to only one twentieth of the moon's mass. The largest hundred or so asteroids were formed at the same time and with the same matter as the major planets; many of the smaller asteroids are fragments caused by collisions between the larger bodies. Some of the fragments may collide with Earth as meteorites. This brings them within reach of scientists who can then determine their composition and ages.

Comets

Every once in a while, at irregular intervals, a fuzzy spot of light, perhaps with a tail streaming away from it, appears in the sky. Such appearances of *comets* are spectacular but infrequent. Most comets that are detected each year are visible only with a telescope. Occasionally one can be seen with the unaided eye, and several times a century a comet will appear that can be seen even in the daytime.

Comets contain particles of metal, rock, and ices of various substances that are gases on Earth. As a comet approaches the sun, the ices turn to vapor,

Planetary Data

	☿ Mercury	♀ Venus	⊕ Earth	♂ Mars	♃ Jupiter	♄ Saturn	♅ Uranus	♆ Neptune	♇ Pluto
Average Distance from Sun (astronomical units)	0.387	0.723	1.00	1.52	5.20	9.53	19.2	30.1	39.5
Average Diameter (Earth = 1.00)	0.38	0.95	1.00	0.53	11.0	9.03	3.80	3.40	0.45*
Mass (Earth = 1.00)	0.05	0.81	1.00	0.11	318	95.3	14.5	17.2	0.05
Sidereal Orbital Period (in years)	0.24	0.62	1.00	1.88	11.9	29.5	84.0	165	248
Rotational Period (d = days; h = hours)	59.0^d	250^d	24.0^h	24.6^h	9.90^h	10.5^h	10.7^h	15.8^h	6.30^d
Maximum Temperature (°C)	450	450†	34.0‡	10	−110§	−160	−200	−220	−210
Known Atmospheric Gases	None	Carbon Dioxide Carbon Monoxide Water Hydrogen Chloride Hydrogen Fluoride	Nitrogen Oxygen Argon Water Carbon Dioxide ♦	Carbon Dioxide Carbon Monoxide Water	Hydrogen Helium Methane Ammonia	Hydrogen Helium Methane	Hydrogen Helium Methane	Hydrogen Helium Methane	None
Number of Known Satellites	None	None	1	2	12	10	5	2	None

* Best available observation.
† At the top of the cloud layer −30°C is the highest temperature observed.
‡ Highest average annual temperature.
§ In some openings between clouds +40°C is observed.
♦ Also neon, helium, methane, krypton, nitrous oxide, hydrogen, ozone, and xenon.

forming a hazy, gaseous *coma* around the remaining swarm of solid particles, the *nucleus*. As the comet moves even closer to the sun, even more material is vaporized. Radiation and high-energy particles streaming out from the sun push this material away from the comet in a long *tail* that always points away from the sun.

Astronomers have been unable to determine the mass of a comet because a comet is not sufficiently massive to affect the orbits of objects it approaches. For example, one comet passed near Jupiter's satellites without affecting their orbital motions. The orbit of the comet, however, was shortened to about one fourth its original length.

Such evidence has led astronomers to conclude that comets have less than one billionth the mass of Earth, and probably most of them have even smaller masses. Comets contain icy nuclei a mile or more across. Gases and fine particles stream away from the nucleus as it disintegrates in the heat of the sun. Comets either dissolve completely, ending up as swarms of tiny particles, or ultimately appear as small asteroidal bodies, without tails, still orbiting around the sun.

Matter Between the Planets

A great deal of matter—debris from comets, rock and metal fragments like miniature asteroids—is orbiting in interplanetary space. These fragments are *meteoroids*. Often a meteoroid will collide with Earth's atmosphere, where it is usually vaporized by heat from the friction against air molecules. The bright streak of light that occurs while the particle

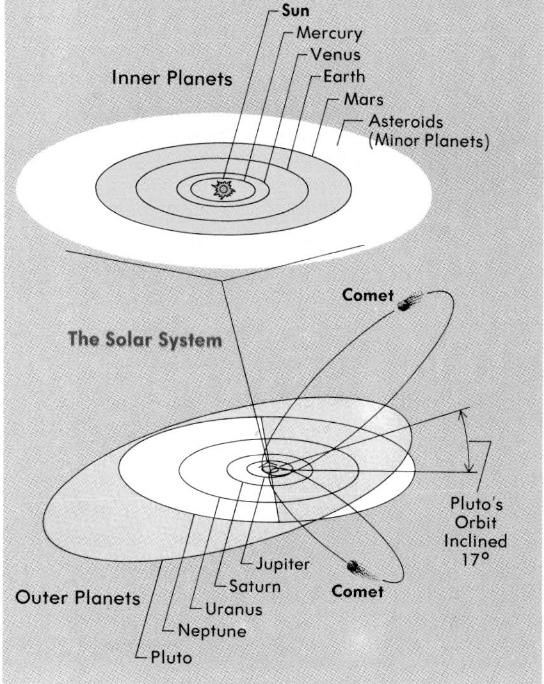

Nine known planets travel around the sun in elliptical orbits. Smaller bodies, the asteroids, are concentrated between the orbits of Mars and Jupiter. The orbits of most of these bodies lie close to one plane. Comets usually have longer and more elliptical orbits. The planets and probably most of the asteroids have motions through space similar to those of Earth. They rotate around an internal axis, revolve around the sun, and follow a helical path as they accompany the sun through space.

Earth's Motions in Space

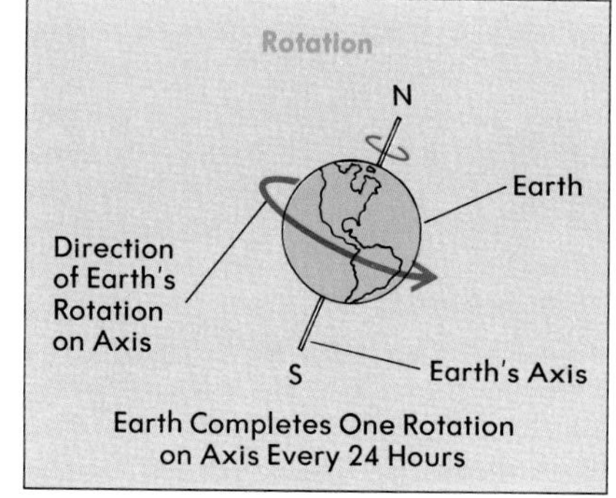

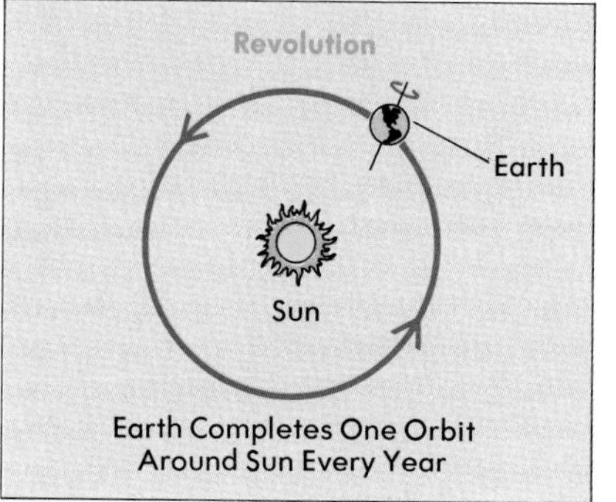

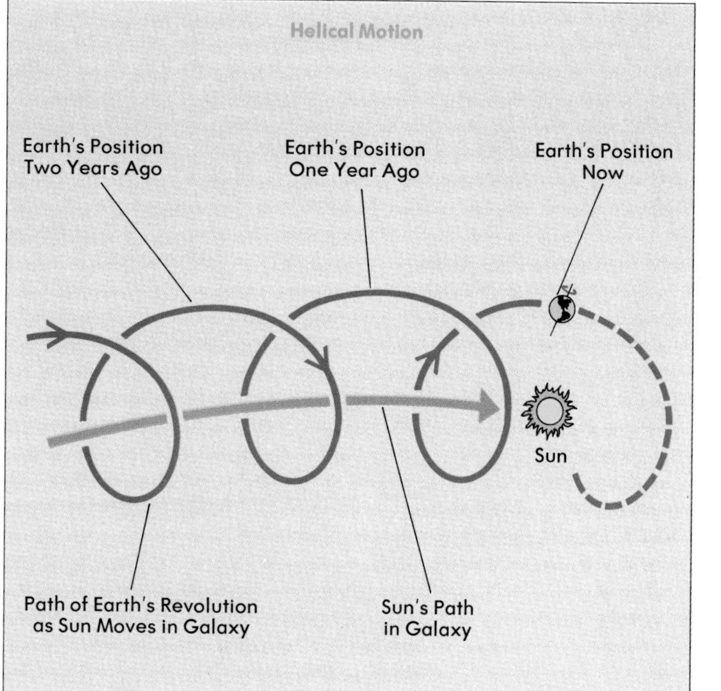

U.S. Naval Observatory

The brilliant Comet Ikeya-Seki was discovered in 1965 by the two amateur Japanese astronomers for whom it was named. It was visible from Earth even during the day.

vaporizes is a *meteor*. Occasionally a large chunk of rock and metal survives the journey to the ground. Such remnants are *meteorites* (*see* Meteorites and Meteors).

Particles even smaller than the meteoroids exist in the space between the planets. Tiny particles less than one ten-thousandth of an inch in diameter fall to Earth in a continuous rain. Some astronomers estimate that up to 100 tons of these *micrometeorites* land on Earth each day.

Micrometeorites are particles of interplanetary dust. This dust seems to be particularly dense along the plane of the planets' orbits around the sun, which is also the plane of the zodiacal constellations (*see* Astronomy). On a clear night a faint glow is visible along the line of the zodiac, following the setting sun or preceding the rising sun. This glow can be almost as bright as the Milky Way. Scientists believe that it is caused by sunlight reflected from the interplanetary dust concentrated along the plane of the planets' orbits.

The sun itself contributes much material to the vast spaces between the planets. Along with the stream of radiation that continuously leaves its surface, the sun gives off electrically charged particles—electrons and nuclei of atoms. This flow is the solar wind, which spreads beyond the planets and escapes the solar system. The part of the solar wind that encounters Earth causes the auroras (*see* Astronomy; Aurora Borealis; Earth; Sun).

Space Probes

Human beings have added many pieces of matter to the solar system. These are the space probes and artificial satellites that have left Earth since the launching of Sputnik I in 1957. Artificial Earth satellites provide information on conditions in Earth's upper atmosphere and just beyond. Studies have been made of Earth's magnetic field, of solar radiation encountering Earth's atmosphere, and of the composition and density of micrometeorites and solar wind particles surrounding Earth's atmosphere.

Probes and manned space vehicles have landed on the moon (*see* Moon; Space Travel). Unmanned probes have been sent to Venus, Mars, and Jupiter. These probes were equipped with instruments to study the conditions (temperature, pressure, density, and

The protoplanet hypothesis proposed that the sun was formed from a disk of rotating gas. Part of the disk surrounding the early "protosun" contained areas of great density that contracted into "protoplanets." Much of the matter in the protosun and the protoplanets was blown away by radiation. The rest condensed into the sun, planets, and natural satellites.

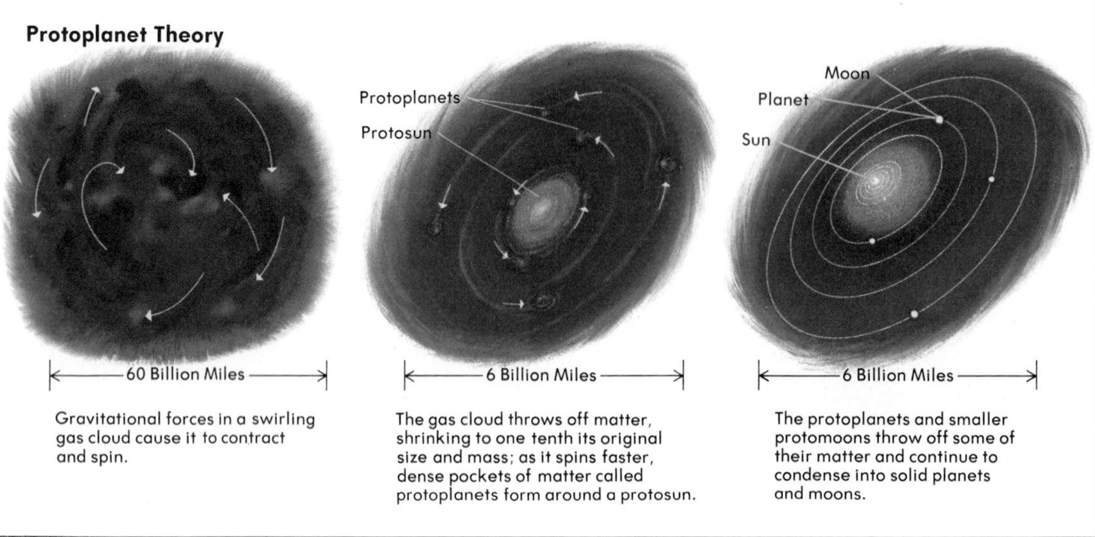
Protoplanet Theory
60 Billion Miles
Gravitational forces in a swirling gas cloud cause it to contract and spin.
Protoplanets
Protosun
6 Billion Miles
The gas cloud throws off matter, shrinking to one tenth its original size and mass; as it spins faster, dense pockets of matter called protoplanets form around a protosun.
Moon
Planet
Sun
6 Billion Miles
The protoplanets and smaller protomoons throw off some of their matter and continue to condense into solid planets and moons.

chemical composition) of the atmospheres and surfaces of those planets.

PAST AND FUTURE OF THE SOLAR SYSTEM

Various theories have been proposed to describe the origin of the solar system. The protoplanet theory, developed by Kuiper, suggests that the solar system was formed as a by-product of the formation of the sun itself. A great cloud of interstellar matter contracted and formed the *solar nebula,* which then developed a dense center, the *protosun.* As the outer part of the cloud rotated around the protosun, gravity caused dense clusterings to form within the solar nebula. These clusterings further contracted into slowly spinning *protoplanets.* As the protosun contracted, it heated up and blew much of the rest of the cloud off into space. The protoplanets also lost their outer envelopes, but enough remained to contract into the present planets. The protoplanets repeated the process on a much smaller scale, forming *protomoons* that evolved into moons.

Since it happened so long ago, and since the distances involved are huge by Earth standards, it is extremely difficult to acquire sufficient evidence to test theories of the origin of the solar system. Information from space probes is the most important source of evidence.

The future of the solar system probably depends on the behavior of the sun. If current theories of stellar evolution are correct, the sun will have much the same size and temperature for 4 billion or 5 billion more years. Then it will grow much brighter and larger, turning into a supergiant and expanding beyond the orbit of Venus, perhaps even engulfing Earth.

Much later the sun will begin to cool down, evolving into a white-dwarf star. Around it will orbit the remaining planets, perhaps including Earth. They will have turned into frozen chunks, orbiting their shrunken star.

The Pioneer 10 spacecraft was designed as the first probe to pass through the asteroid belt and the first man-made object to escape the solar system.

NASA

Books About the Solar System

Asimov, Isaac. Environments Out There (Abelard, 1967).
Del Rey, Lester. The Mysterious Sky (Chilton, 1964).
Gallant, R. A. Exploring the Universe (Doubleday, 1968).
Gamow, George. Gravity (Doubleday, 1962).
Gardner, Martin. Space Puzzles: Curious Questions and Answers About the Solar System (Simon & Schuster, 1971).
Sagan, Carl and Jonathan Norton Leonard. Planets (Time, 1966).
Wolfe, Louis. Let's Go to a Planetarium (Putnam, 1958).

THESE ARTICLES ARE IN THE FACT-INDEX

Solar wind
Solenodon
Solicitor general

Contributors and Consultants

These authorities either wrote the articles listed or supplied information and data that were used in writing them.

Stener Mørch Aarsdal, Economic Editor, 'Børsen', and Press Officer, Chamber of Commerce, Copenhagen, *Denmark*

Joseph John Accardo, Washington Columnist, *Fuel and Power* (in part)

D. R. Aggers, Division of Information, Headquarters, United States Marine Corps, *Armed Forces, United States* (in part)

Joseph C. Agrella, Turf Editor, 'Chicago Sun-Times', *Horse Racing* (in part)

Jacob Bernard Agus, Rabbi, Visiting Professor of Modern Jewish Philosophy, Dropsie University, Philadelphia, Pa., *Religion* (in part)

John Anthony Allan, Lecturer in Geography, School of Oriental and African Studies, University of London, *Libya*

Gustavo Arthur Antonini, Associate Professor, Center for Latin American Studies, University of Florida, *Dominican Republic*

Alan Gordon Armstrong, Lecturer, Department of Economics, University of Bristol, England, *World Trade* (in part)

Bruce Arnold, Free-lance Journalist and Writer, Dublin, *Ireland*

Robert M. Ball, Commissioner of Social Security, U.S. Department of Health, Education, and Welfare, *Social Services*

Kenneth de la Barre, Director, Montreal Office, Arctic Institute of North America, *Arctic*

Paul Charles Bartholomew, Professor of Government, University of Notre Dame, *Supreme Court of the United States*

Howard Bass, Journalist and Broadcaster, Editor, 'Winter Sports', *Ice Hockey; Ice Skating; Skiing*

J. R. Beatty, Senior Research Associate, B. F. Goodrich Research Center, *Rubber*

William Beltrán, Economic Research Officer, Economic Intelligence Department, Lloyds and Bolsa International Bank Ltd., London, *Argentina*

Stanley F. Bergstein, Executive Secretary, Harness Tracks of America Inc., and Vice-President, United States Trotting Association, *Horse Racing* (in part)

Clyde Richard Bergwin, retired U.S. Air Force Information Officer, Author of 'Animal Astronauts', *Aerospace*

John M. Betts, Jr., Information and Publications Specialist, Association of American Railroads, Office of Information and Public Affairs, Washington, D.C., *Transportation* (in part)

Alan Geoffrey Blyth, Music Critic, London, *Music* (in part)

Dick Boonstra, Member of Staff, Department of Political Science, Free University, Amsterdam, *Netherlands*

Kooman Boycheff, Supervisor of Physical Education and Coordinator of Recreation, University of California at Berkeley, *Hobbies; Toys and Games*

Mary Beatrice Boyd, Senior Lecturer in History, Victoria University of Wellington, New Zealand, *Fiji; Tonga; Western Samoa*

Arnold C. Brackman, Author of 'Indonesian Communism: A History', *Indonesia*

Robert J. Braidwood, Professor of Old World Prehistory, the Oriental Institute and the Department of Anthropology, the University of Chicago, *Archaeology* (in part)

William A. Bresnahan, President, American Trucking Associations, Inc., *Transportation* (in part)

Jack Brickhouse, Vice-President and Manager of Sports, WGN Continental Broadcasting Co., *Baseball* (in part)

D. A. Brown, Agriculture Librarian Emeritus, University of Illinois, *Animals and Wildlife; Environment*

George Hay Brown, Director of the U.S. Bureau of the Census, *Employment* (in part); *Population*

Ardath Walter Burks, Professor and Director, International Programs, Rutgers University, New Brunswick, N.J., *Japan*

Allen D. Bushong, Associate Professor of Geography, University of South Carolina, *El Salvador; Honduras*

Frank Butler, Sports Editor, 'News of the World', London, *Boxing*

Don Byrne, Washington Correspondent for 'Electronic Design' and 'Microwaves' Magazines, *Communications*

Alva Lawrence Campbell, Regional Director, Institute of Life Insurance, *Insurance*

Lucien Chalmey, Adviser, International Union of Producers and Distributors of Electrical Energy, Paris, *Fuel and Power* (in part)

Kenneth Francis Chapman, Editor, 'Stamp Collecting', Philatelic Correspondent, 'The Times', London, *Stamps*

Robin Chapman, Economic Research Officer, Lloyds and Bolsa International Bank Ltd., London, *Cuba; Haiti; Portugal*

Robert Chaussin, Government Civil Engineer, S.E.T.R.A. (Service d'Études Techniques des Routes et Autoroutes), Bagneux, France, *Engineering Projects* (in part)

Hung-Ti Chu, Expert in Far Eastern Affairs, United Nations Area Specialist and Chief of Asia-Africa Section and Trusteeship Council Section, 1946–67, and Professor of Government, Texas Tech University, Lubbock, 1968–69, *China, People's Republic of; Taiwan*

Donald Frederic Clifton, Professor of Metallurgy, University of Idaho, *Metals*

Stanley E. Cohen, Washington Editor, 'Advertising Age', *Consumer Protection*

Larry Roy Collins, Zoologist, Panda Unit, National Zoological Park, Smithsonian Institution, *Animals and Wildlife SPECIAL REPORT: Pandas* (in part)

Leslie Collins, Lecturer in Bulgarian History, School of Slavonic and East European Studies, University of London, *Cyprus*

Norman Crossland, Bonn Correspondent, the 'Guardian', London, *Germany* (in part)

Gloria Clare Cumper, Chairman, Council of Voluntary Social Services, and Member, Judicial Services Commission, Kingston, *Jamaica*

Krsto Franjo Cviić, Leader Writer and East European Specialist, 'Economist', London, *Yugoslavia*

Hiroshi Daifuku, Chief, Section for the Development of the Cultural Heritage, United Nations Educational, Scientific, and Cultural Organization (UNESCO), Paris, *Landmarks and Monuments*

Ernest Albert John Davies, Editor, 'Traffic Engineering and Control', 'Roads and Their Traffic', and 'Traffic Engineering Practice', *Transportation* (in part)

Adalyn Davis, Public Information Officer, U.S. Arms Control and Disarmament Agency, *Arms Control and Disarmament*

Alfred Dawber, Textile Consultant, *Textiles*

Philippe Decraene, Member, Editorial Staff, 'Le Monde', Paris, *Cameroon; Central African Republic; Chad; Congo, People's Republic of the; Dahomey; Gabon; Guinea; Ivory Coast; Malagasy Republic; Mali; Mauritania; Niger; Senegal; Togo; Tunisia; Upper Volta*

R. J. M. Dennerstein, Associate Editor, 'Encyclopaedia Britannica', London, *Bhutan; Equatorial Guinea; West Indies*

Mary Ellen Dienes, National Legal Aid and Defender Association, American Bar Center, Chicago, *Law* (in part)

Elfriede Dirnbacher, Austrian Civil Servant, *Austria*

Jim Dunne, Detroit Editor, 'Popular Science Monthly', *Automobiles*

Raul d'Eca, formerly Fulbright Visiting Lecturer on American History, University of Minas Gerais, Brazil, *Brazil*

Robert B. Edgerton, Professor, Departments of Psychiatry and Anthropology, University of California at Los Angeles, *Anthropology*

Wilfred A. Elders, Associate Professor of Geology, University of California at Riverside, *Earth Sciences* (in part)

Jan Robert Engels, Editor, 'Vooruitgang' (Quarterly of the Belgian Party for Freedom and Progress), *Belgium*

David M. L. Farr, Professor of History, Carleton University, Ottawa, Ont., *Canada* (in part)

Robert Joseph Fendell, New York Editor, 'Automotive News', New York City, *Auto Racing*

Melba M. Ferguson, Media Specialist, Public Affairs Division, Girl Scouts of the United States of America, *Youth Organizations* (in part)

Ronald Whitaker Ferrier, Company Historian, British Petroleum, *Fuel and Power* (in part)

Robert Moore Fisher, Chief, Mortgage, Agricultural, and Consumer Credit Section, Division of Research and Statistics, Board of Governors, Federal Reserve System, and Professorial Lecturer, American University, Washington, D.C., *Construction*

Robert John Fowell, Lecturer, Department of Mining Engineering, University of Newcastle upon Tyne, England, *Fuel and Power* (in part)

David A. Frederickson, Associate Professor of Anthropology, Sonoma State College, Rohnert Park, Calif., *Archaeology* (in part)

Colonel James A. Fyock, Information Officer, Third U.S. Army, Fort McPherson, Ga., *Armed Forces, United States* (in part)

Fabio Galvano, Correspondent, 'Epoca', London, *Italy*

Albert Ganado, Lawyer, Malta, *Malta*

Kenneth G. Gehret, Education Editor, 'The Christian Science Monitor', *Colleges and Universities; Education*

Thayil Jacob Sony George, Assistant Editor, 'Far Eastern Economic Review', Hong Kong, *Asia; Cambodia; Korea; Thailand*

Donald LeRoy Gilleland, Deputy Chief, Magazine and Book Branch, Public Information Division Secretary of the Air Force Office of Information, *Armed Forces, United States* (in part)

Paul Glikson, Secretary, Division of Jewish Demography and Statistics, Institute of Contemporary Jewry, Hebrew University of Jerusalem, Israel, *Religion* (in part)

Morgan Godwin, Assistant Secretary, American Radio Relay League, Newington, Conn., *Television and Radio* (in part)

Harry Golombek, British Chess Champion, 1947, 1949, and 1955, Chess Correspondent, 'The Times and Observer', London, *Chess*

Robert Goralski, Pentagon Correspondent, NBC News, *Vietnam*

Jarlath John Graham, Editor, 'Advertising Age', *Advertising*

The Rev. Arthur R. Green, Pastor, Good Shepherd Parish, Chicago, *Religion* (in part)

Richard D. A. Greenough, Chief English Writer, Press Division, UNESCO, Paris, *United Nations (UN)* (in part)

Anthony Royston Grant Griffiths, Lecturer in History, Flinders University of South Australia, *Australia; Nauru*

Arthur E. Grimm, Information Department, Cooperative League of U.S.A., *Cooperatives*

Toni Grossi, Assistant National Public Relations Director, Junior Achievement Inc., *Youth Organizations* (in part)

Michael Phillip Guerin, Assistant Director, Division of Officer Services, Bureau of Public and Community Relations, American Hospital Association, *Hospitals*

Joseph H. S. Haggin, Staff Writer, 'Chemical and Engineering News', *Chemistry*

David A. Harries, Director and Chief Engineer, The Mitchell Construction Kinnear Moodie Group Ltd., London, *Engineering Projects* (in part)

Leonard R. Harris, Executive Vice-President and Publisher, World Publishing Co., *Publishing, Book*

Gerard A. Harrison, Associate Professor of Recreation, Springfield College, Springfield, Mass., *Camping*

Philip Morris Hauser, Professor of Sociology and Director, Population Research Center, University of Chicago, *Cities and Urban Affairs*

William D. Hawkland, Professor of Law, University of Illinois, *Law* (in part)

The Rev. Peter Hebblethwaite, Editor, 'The Month', *Religion* (in part)

Myrl C. Hendershott, Assistant Professor of Oceanography, Scripps Institution of Oceanography, La Jolla, Calif., *Oceanography*

Robert David Hodgson, Geographer, U.S. Department of State, *Luxembourg; Monaco*

Patrice Daily Horn, Managing Editor, 'Behavior Today', *Psychology*

Louis Hotz, formerly Editorial Writer, 'The Johannesburg Star', *South Africa*

Kenneth Ingham, Professor of History, University of Bristol, England, *Kenya; Malawi; Rhodesia; Tanzania; Uganda; Zaire; Zambia*

Lou Joseph, Assistant Director, Bureau of Public Information, American Dental Association, *Dentistry*

John Arnold Kelleher, Editor, 'The Dominion', Wellington, *New Zealand*

Peter Kilner, Editor, 'Arab Report and Record', *Algeria; Morocco; Sudan*

Jon Kimche, Expert on Middle East Affairs, 'Evening Standard', London, *Israel*

Joshua B. Kind, Associate Professor of Art History, Northern Illinois University, De Kalb, *Museums*

Resa W. King, Correspondent, 'Business Week', *Business and Industry; Housing; Housing SPECIAL REPORT: New Alternatives*

Alfred Paul Klausler, Executive Secretary, Associated Church Press, *Religion* (in part)

Jean Marcel Knecht, Assistant Foreign Editor, 'Le Monde', Paris, *France*

John T. Kneeshaw, Economist, Bank for International Settlements, Basel, Switzerland, *Money and International Finance*

Ole Ferdinand Knudsen, Editor, 'Norway Exports', Oslo, *Norway*

Philip Kopper, Free-lance Writer, Washington, D.C., *McGovern, George S.; Newspapers; Nixon, Richard M.; Shriver, R. Sargent; Wallace, George C.*

Valdimar Kristinsson, Editor, 'Fjármálatidindi', *Iceland*

Geoffrey Charles Last, Adviser, Imperial Ethiopian Ministry of Education and Fine Arts, Addis Ababa, *Ethiopia*

Chapin R. Leinbach, Assistant to Vice-President, Public Relations, Air Transport Association of America, *Transportation* (in part)

Raymond Basil Lewry, Senior Research Officer, Lloyds and Bolsa International Bank Ltd., London, *Colombia; Ecuador*

Frances R. Link, Senior Associate, Curriculum Development Associates, Washington, D.C., *Education SPECIAL REPORT: The Unfinished Curriculum*

Sol M. Linowitz, Senior Partner, Coudert Brothers, formerly United States Ambassador to the Organization of American States, *Cuba SPECIAL REPORT: A New U.S. Policy?*

Virginia R. Luling, Social Anthropologist, *Somalia*

Richard Martin Michael McConnell, Washington Editor, 'Banking Magazine', *Banks*

Captain Terry McDonald, Chief, Public Information Division, U.S. Coast Guard, *Armed Forces, United States* (in part)

Curtis Daniel MacDougall, Professor Emeritus of Journalism, Northwestern University, Evanston, Ill., *Newspapers SPECIAL REPORT: Muckraking*

William Mader, Diplomatic Correspondent, 'Time' Magazine, *Tanaka, Kakuei*

Katharine A. Mahon, Public Relations Director, Girls Clubs of America, Inc., *Youth Organizations* (in part)

Andrew J. A. Mango, Orientalist and Broadcaster, *Turkey*

Peter (John) Mansfield, formerly Middle East Correspondent, 'The Sunday Times', London, *Bahrain; Egypt; Iraq; Jordan; Kuwait; Lebanon; Middle East; Oman; Qatar; Saudi Arabia; Yemen Arab Republic (Sana); Yemen, People's Democratic Republic of (Aden)*

Aldo Marcello, Civil Engineer, *Engineering Projects* (in part)

Edward L. Marcou, Assistant Public Relations Manager, American Bowling Congress, *Bowling*

Neville Frederic Maude, Consultant Editor, 'British Journal of Photography' and 'Photo News Weekly', and Editor, 'Photographic Processor', *Photography*

Jerome Mazzaro, Author and Professor of English, State University of New York at Buffalo, *Literature*

Grant W. Midgley, Information Specialist, Office of Information, National Park Service, Department of the Interior, *National Park Service*

Raymond Spencer Millard, Deputy Director, Road Research Laboratory, Department of the Environment, Crowthorne, Berkshire, England, *Engineering Projects* (in part)

Sandra Millikin, Architectural Historian, *Architecture; Painting and Sculpture*

Marilyn M. Milow, Staff Writer, Media Contact, National Board, Young Women's Christian Association, *Youth Organizations* (in part)

Mario S. Modiano, Athens Correspondent, 'The Times', London, *Greece*

Hazel Morgan, Production Assistant (Sleevenotes and Covers), Creative Services Dept., E.M.I. Ltd., London, *Music* (in part)

Molly Mortimer, Journalist on Commonwealth and International Affairs, *Botswana; Burundi; Commonwealth of Nations; Gambia, The; Ghana; Lesotho; Maldives; Mauritius; Nigeria; Rwanda; Sierra Leone; Swaziland*

George Saul Mottershead, Director-Secretary, Chester Zoo, England, *Zoos*

Pauline G. Mower, Information Director, Future Homemakers of America, *Youth Organizations* (in part)

Edward Harwood Nabb, Vice-President, Union of International Motorboating, *Boats and Boating*

National Oceanic and Atmospheric Administration, Office of Public Affairs, *Weather*

Salvatore John Natoli, Educational Affairs Director, Association of American Geographers, *Earth Sciences* (in part)

Raymond K. Neal, Executive Editor, Editorial Service, Boy Scouts of America, *Youth Organizations* (in part)

John Neill, Head of Chemical Engineering Department, C. & W. Walker Ltd., *Mountain Climbing*

Bert Nelson, Editor and Publisher, 'Track and Field News', *Track and Field*

Bruce C. Netschert, Vice-President, National Economic Research Associates, Inc., *Fuel and Power* (in part)

Harold Stanley Noel, Editor, 'World Fishing', London, *Fish and Fisheries*

Julius Novick, Associate Professor of Literature, State University of New York at Purchase, Dramatic Critic, 'Village Voice', *Theater*

Jeremiah A. O'Leary, Latin American Correspondent, 'Evening Star-News', Washington, D.C., *Chile*

James Keena Page, Jr., Board of Editors, 'Smithsonian' Magazine, *Animals and Wildlife SPECIAL REPORT: Pandas* (in part)

Sidney Arnold Pakeman, Historian and Author of 'Ceylon', *Sri Lanka*

Rafael Pargas, National Geographic Society, *Philippines*

George P. Patten, Professor of Geography, Ohio State University, *Nicaragua*

Sheila Caffyn Patterson, Research Fellow, Centre for Multi-Racial Studies, University of Sussex, Brighton, England, *Barbados*

Virgil W. Peterson, Executive Director, Chicago Crime Commission, 1942–70, *Crime; Police*

Thomas Fraser Pettigrew, Professor of Social Psychology, Harvard University, *Race Relations*

Eugene Edwin Pfaff, Professor of History, University of North Carolina at Greensboro, *International Relations*

David Kemsley Robin Phillips, Secretary-General, Association of Track and Field Statisticians, Contributor, 'World Sports', *Sports Champions of 1972*

Otto Pick, Visiting Professor of International Relations, University of Surrey, England, and Director, Atlantic Information Centre for Teachers, London, *Czechoslovakia; Union of Soviet Socialist Republics (U.S.S.R.)*

Frederick P. Pittera, Chairman, International Exposition Consultants Co., *Fairs and Shows*

Holenarasipur Y. Sharada Prasad, Director of Information, Prime Minister's Secretariat, New Delhi, *India*

Manuel Pulgar, Senior Economic Research Officer, Lloyds and Bolsa International Bank Ltd., London, *Mexico*

Howard Pyle, President, National Safety Council, *Safety*

Margaret H. Quinn, Reporter, 'Sun-Gazette', Williamsport, Pa., *Baseball* (in part)

Charles Edgar Randall, Assistant Editor, 'Journal of Forestry', *Forest Products*

Mahinder Singh Randhava, Subeditor, 'The Straits Times', Kuala Lumpur, *Malaysia; Singapore*

Robert John Ranger, Assistant Professor, Department of Political Science, St. Francis Xavier University, Antigonish, Nova Scotia, *Defense*

Vivian Foster Raven, Editor, 'Tobacco', *Tobacco*

Randolph Richard Rawlins, Journalist, Broadcaster, and Tutor, Extramural Department, University of the West Indies, St. Augustine, Trinidad, *Guyana*

A. Daniel Reuwee, Director of Information, Future Farmers of America, *Youth Organizations* (in part)

Lisa Aversa Richette, Judge in the Court of Common Pleas, Philadelphia, Pa., *Law SPECIAL REPORT: Children's Rights*

David Julien Robinson, Film Critic, 'The Financial Times', *Motion Pictures*

Leif J. Robinson, Associate Editor, 'Sky and Telescope', Sky Publishing Corp., *Astronomy*

John Kerr Rose, Senior Specialist in Natural Resources and Conservation, Congressional Research Service, Library of Congress, *Agriculture* (in part)

David E. Rosenbaum, Reporter, Washington Bureau, 'The New York Times', *Selective Service*

Walter Rugaber, Reporter, Washington Bureau, 'The New York Times', *Prisons*

Al Salerno, Director, Press and Publications, American Heart Association, Inc., *Medicine* (in part)

Carl Fredrik Sandelin, Editor in Chief, Finnish News Agency, President, Society of Swedish-Speaking Writers in Finland, *Finland*

Alex Sareyan, Executive Director, Mental Health Materials Center, *Mental Health*

Stephen E. Schattmann, Economist, London, *Germany* (in part)

Timothy D. Schellhardt, Reporter, 'The Wall Street Journal', Washington, D.C., *Postal Service*

Albert Schoenfield, Editor, 'Swimming World', *Swimming*

John Schulian, Reporter, 'Baltimore Evening Sun', *Basketball; Football*

Byron T. Scott, Editor, 'Medical Opinion' Magazine, Assistant Professor of Communication, Ohio University, *Medicine* (in part); *Medicine SPECIAL REPORT: Venereal Disease*

Peter Shackelford, Research Officer, International Union of Official Travel Organisations, Geneva, *Travel* (in part)

Mitchell R. Sharpe, Science Writer, *Space Exploration*

Harvey R. Sherman, Environmental Policy Division, Congressional Research Service, Library of Congress, *Agriculture* (in part); *Food*

Constant Chung-Tse Shih, Counselor, Trade Policy Department, General Agreement on Tariffs and Trade (GATT), Switzerland, *World Trade* (in part)

Glenn B. Smedley, Governor, American Numismatic Association, *Coin Collecting*

M. Bernard Smith, Free-lance Writer and Reporter, *Retail Trade* (in part)

J. Frederick Smithcors, Associate Editor, American Veterinary Publications, Inc., Santa Barbara, Calif., *Veterinary Medicine*

Kazimierz Maciej Smogorzewski, Founder and Editor, 'Free Europe', London, and Writer on Contemporary History, *Albania; Bulgaria; Hungary; Intelligence Operations; Mongolia; Poland; Romania*

Leonard M. Snyder, Associate Director, Public Relations/ General Administration, Young Men's Christian Association, *Youth Organizations* (in part)

Wallace Sokolsky, Associate Professor, History Department, Bronx Community College, the New School for Social Research, New York University, Division of Adult Education, *Africa*

M. J. Spence, Research Officer, Economic Intelligence Department, Lloyds and Bolsa International Bank Ltd., London, *Paraguay; Uruguay*

Melanie F. Staerk, Editor, 'UNESCO Press', Swiss National Commission for UNESCO, *Switzerland*

Edward J. Stapleton, Public Information Director, Boys' Clubs of America, *Youth Organizations* (in part)

Jack Ellwood Steele, M.D., Bionicist, *Science SPECIAL REPORT: The Metric System*

Robert Edward Stent, Economic and Political Research Officer, Lloyds and Bolsa International Bank Ltd., London, *Costa Rica; Guatemala; Venezuela*

Tom Stevenson, Garden Columnist, 'Baltimore News American' and 'Washington Post', *Flowers and Gardens*

Peter Stoler, Medical Editor, 'Time' Magazine, New York, *Medicine* (in part)

Annette Ashlock Stover, Food Guide Director, 'Chicago Tribune', *Food SPECIAL REPORT: Foods for Thought*

Zena Sutherland, Editor, 'Bulletin of the Center for Children's Books', University of Chicago, Editor, Children's Books, 'Chicago Tribune', and Lecturer, University of Chicago, *Literature, Children's*

Thelma Sweetinburgh, Paris Fashion Correspondent, 'International Textiles', Amsterdam, *Cosmetics; Fashion*

Richard N. Swift, Professor of Politics, New York University, New York City, *United Nations (UN)* (in part)

Sol Taishoff, Chairman and Editor, 'Broadcasting', Washington, D.C., *Television and Radio* (in part)

Walter Terry, Dance Critic, 'Saturday Review', *Dance* (in part)

John Hunter Thomas, Associate Professor, Director, Dudley Herbarium, Department of Biological Sciences, Stanford University, *Biology*

William Harford Thomas, Managing Editor, 'Manchester Guardian', *Great Britain and Northern Ireland, United Kingdom of*

Anthony Thompson, General Secretary, 1962–70, International Federation of Library Associations, *Libraries*

Norman Samuel Thompson, Professor of Business Education and Chairman, Department of Business Education, Eastern Washington State College, *Economy; Employment* (in part)

Dietrick E. Thomsen, Physical Sciences Editor, 'Science News' Magazine, *Physics*

Lancelot Oliver Tingay, Lawn Tennis Correspondent, 'The Daily Telegraph', London, *Tennis*

Edward Townsend, Associate Editor, 'Business Week', *Labor Unions*

James Scott Trezise, Staff Writer, 'All Hands' Magazine, *Armed Forces, United States* (in part)

Govindan Unny, Special Correspondent for India, Nepal, and Ceylon, Agence France-Presse, *Bangladesh; Burma; Nepal*

Leslie P. Verter, Public Relations Coordinator, Camp Fire Girls, Inc., *Youth Organizations* (in part)

David McCall Walsten, Free-lance Writer and former Associate Editor, 'Encyclopaedia Britannica', *Ships and Shipping; Stocks and Bonds*

Percy Ainsworth Ward-Thomas, Golf Correspondent, 'Manchester Guardian', *Golf*

Anne R. Warner, Director, Public Relations Department, American Nurses' Association, *Nursing*

Jack Waugh, Staff Correspondent, 'The Christian Science Monitor', *Families*

David Louis Williams, Assistant Professor of Government, Ohio University, *Communist Movement*

Laurence Frederic Rushbrook Williams, Fellow of All Souls College, Oxford University, 1914–21, Professor of Modern Indian Historv, Allahabad, India, 1914–19, *Afghanistan; Iran; Pakistan*

Peter Williams, O.B.E., Editor, 'Dance and Dancers', *Dance* (in part)

Trevor Williamson, Sports Subeditor, 'The Daily Telegraph', London, *Soccer*

Jeremy Willoughby, Research Officer, Economic Intelligence Department, Lloyds and Bolsa International Bank Ltd., London, *Bolivia; Latin America; Peru*

Alan David Wilson, Assistant Editor, 'Sweden Now', *Sweden*

Richard Worsnop, Writer, Editorial Research Reports, Washington, D.C., *Liberia; United States*

Almon Robert Wright, retired Senior Historian, U.S. Department of State, *Panama*

Stanley F. Yolles, M.D., Professor and Chairman of Psychiatry, Medical School, State University of New York at Stony Brook, *Drugs*

Paul Frederick Yopes, Mining Engineer, Bureau of Mines, U.S. Department of the Interior, *Mines and Mining*

Paul Ziemer, Night Chief Caption Writer, 'Chicago Today', *Congress, United States; Elections; Political Parties*

Arnold J. Zurcher, Professor of Comparative Politics, Graduate School of Arts and Sciences, New York University, *Europe*

OUR FAMILY RECORD

THIS SPACE FOR FAMILY GROUP PHOTO

WHAT WE DID
AND
HOW WE LOOKED

Each year important events highlight the life of every family. Year after year these events may be noted in the Family Record pages of your Compton Yearbooks. You will then have a permanent record of your family's significant achievements, celebrations, and activities.

OUR FAMILY TREE

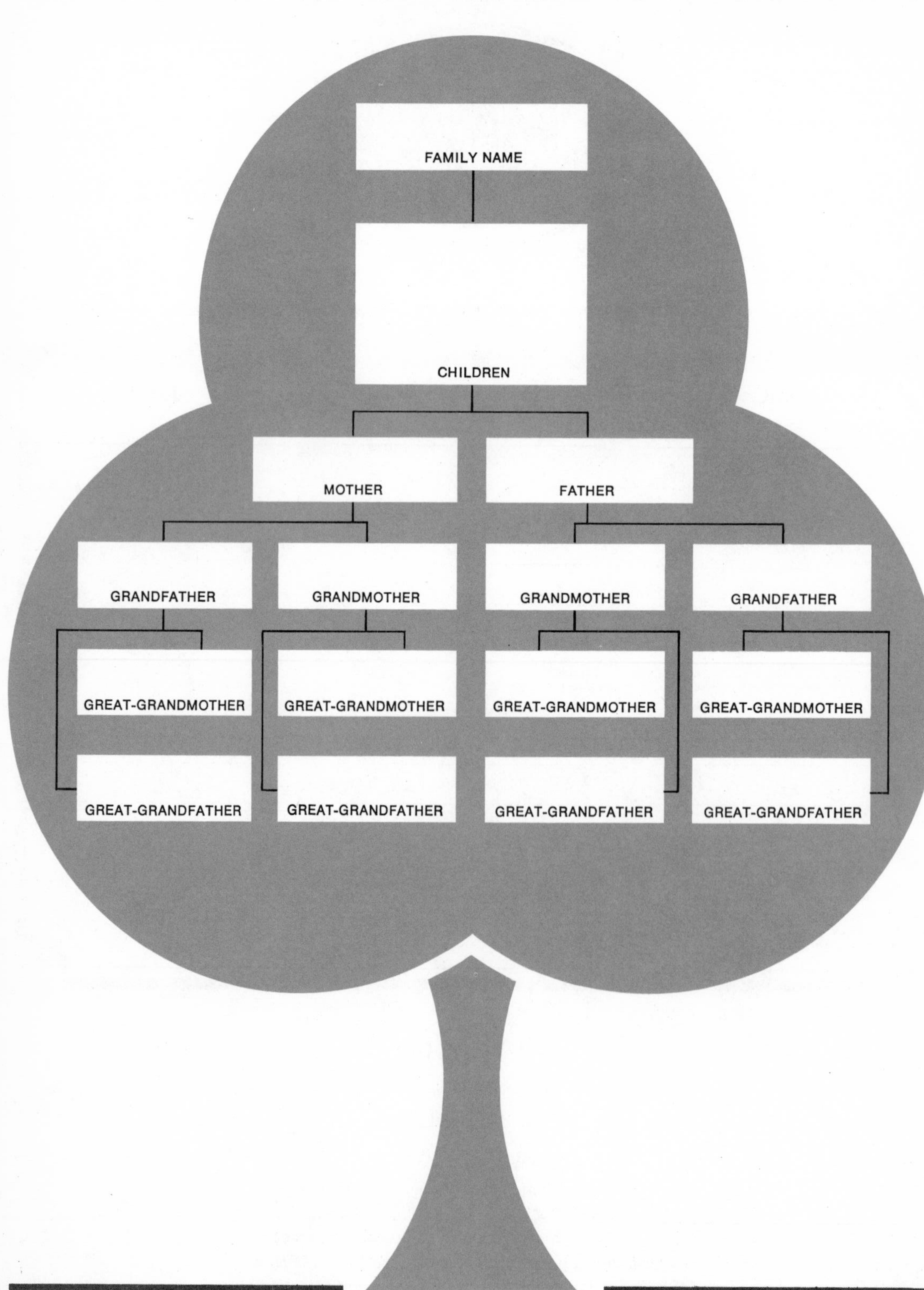

DATES TO REMEMBER

JANUARY	FEBRUARY	MARCH

APRIL	MAY	JUNE

JULY	AUGUST	SEPTEMBER

OCTOBER	NOVEMBER	DECEMBER

Birthdays, weddings, anniversaries, graduations, gifts sent

FAMILY CELEBRATIONS

BIRTHDAYS

NAME ______

DATE ______

NAME ______

DATE ______

NAME ______

DATE ______

NAME ______

DATE ______

NAME ______

DATE ______

WEDDINGS

NAMES ______

DATE ______

NAMES ______

DATE ______

NAMES ______

DATE ______

NAMES ______

DATE ______

NAMES ______

DATE ______

ANNIVERSARIES

NAMES ______

DATE ______

NAMES ______

DATE ______

NAMES ______

DATE ______

BIRTHS

NAME ______

DATE ______

PARENTS ______

NAME ______

DATE ______

PARENTS ______

NAME ______

DATE ______

PARENTS ______

PROMOTIONS

NAME ______

FIRM ______

TITLE ______

DATE ______

NAME ______

FIRM ______

TITLE ______

DATE ______

HOLIDAYS

OCCASION ______

OCCASION ______

OCCASION ______

SPIRITUAL MILESTONES

NAME ______________________

MILESTONE ______________________

NAME ______________________

MILESTONE ______________________

NAME ______________________

MILESTONE ______________________

NAME ______________________

MILESTONE ______________________

NAME ______________________

MILESTONE ______________________

OTHER EVENTS

PASTE PHOTO HERE

PASTE PHOTO HERE

PASTE PHOTO HERE

VACATION 1973

WHEN AND WHERE WE WENT

WHAT WE DID

FAVORITE SIGHTS

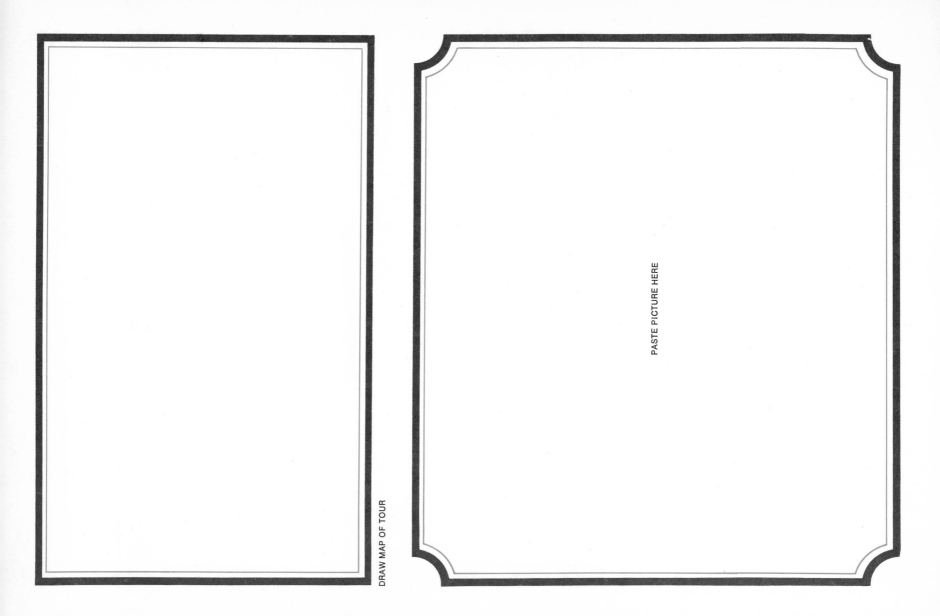

DRAW MAP OF TOUR

PASTE PICTURE HERE

SCHOOL ACTIVITIES

NAME ______
SCHOOL ______
GRADE ______
NAME ______
SCHOOL ______
GRADE ______

NAME ______
SCHOOL ______
GRADE ______
NAME ______
SCHOOL ______
GRADE ______

SCHOOL PARTIES

DATE ______
OCCASION ______
______
DATE ______
OCCASION ______
______
DATE ______
OCCASION ______
______
DATE ______
OCCASION ______
______
DATE ______
OCCASION ______
______
DATE ______
OCCASION ______
______
DATE ______
OCCASION ______
______
DATE ______
OCCASION ______
______

SPORTS

NAME ______
SPORT ______
ACHIEVEMENT ______
NAME ______
SPORT ______
ACHIEVEMENT ______
NAME ______
SPORT ______
ACHIEVEMENT ______
NAME ______
SPORT ______
ACHIEVEMENT ______
NAME ______
SPORT ______
ACHIEVEMENT ______
NAME ______
SPORT ______
ACHIEVEMENT ______
NAME ______
SPORT ______
ACHIEVEMENT ______
NAME ______
SPORT ______
ACHIEVEMENT ______

CLUB ACTIVITIES

NAME ______
CLUB ______
ACHIEVEMENT ______
NAME ______
CLUB ______
ACHIEVEMENT ______
NAME ______
CLUB ______
ACHIEVEMENT ______
NAME ______
CLUB ______
ACHIEVEMENT ______
NAME ______
CLUB ______
ACHIEVEMENT ______
NAME ______
CLUB ______
ACHIEVEMENT ______
NAME ______
CLUB ______
ACHIEVEMENT ______
NAME ______
CLUB ______
ACHIEVEMENT ______

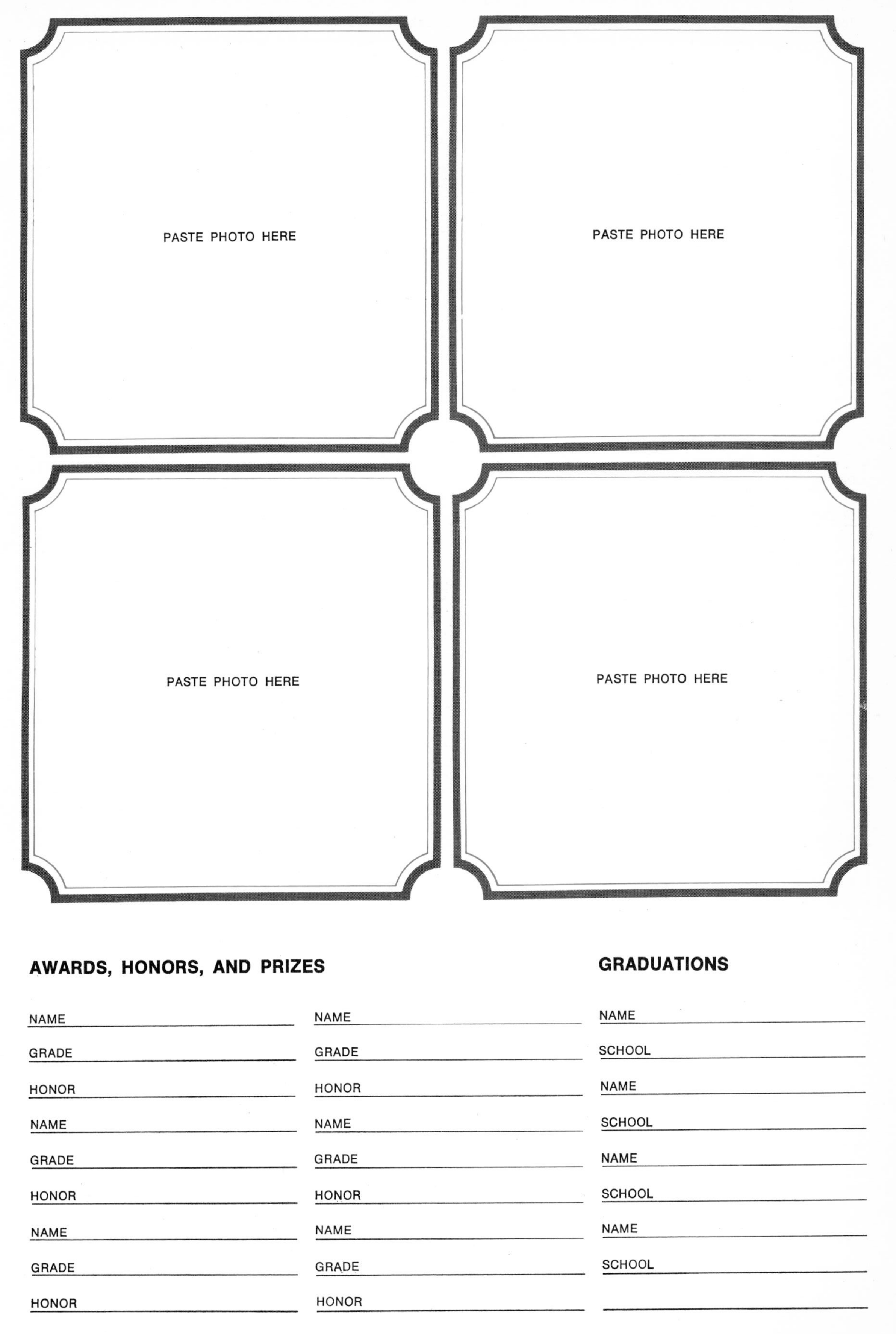

AWARDS, HONORS, AND PRIZES

NAME ______________________

GRADE ______________________

HONOR ______________________

NAME ______________________

GRADE ______________________

HONOR ______________________

NAME ______________________

GRADE ______________________

HONOR ______________________

NAME ______________________

GRADE ______________________

HONOR ______________________

NAME ______________________

GRADE ______________________

HONOR ______________________

NAME ______________________

GRADE ______________________

HONOR ______________________

GRADUATIONS

NAME ______________________

SCHOOL ______________________

NAME ______________________

SCHOOL ______________________

NAME ______________________

SCHOOL ______________________

NAME ______________________

SCHOOL ______________________

____

NAME AND BREED

VET'S RECORD

BEHAVIOR AND TRAINING

PASTE PHOTO HERE

LEISURE HOURS

FAVORITE MOVIES

FAVORITE BOOKS

FAVORITE TELEVISION PROGRAMS

FAVORITE RECORDS

HOBBIES

OUR HEALTH RECORD

RECORD OF HEIGHT

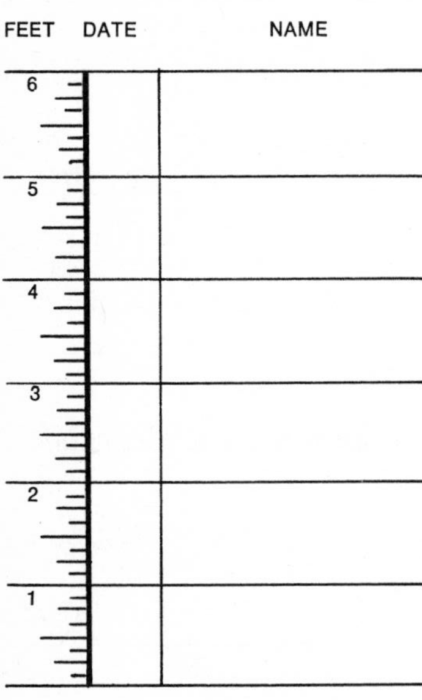

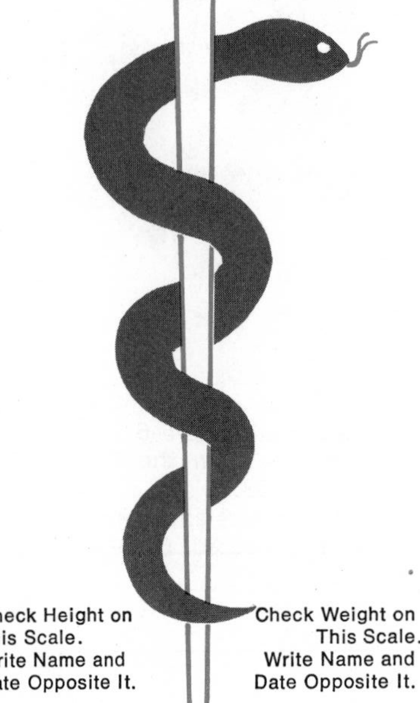

Check Height on This Scale. Write Name and Date Opposite It.

Check Weight on This Scale. Write Name and Date Opposite It.

RECORD OF WEIGHT

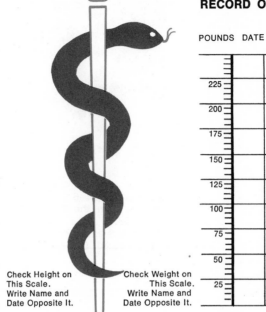

POUNDS	DATE	NAME
225		
200		
175		
150		
125		
100		
75		
50		
25		

DOCTORS' NAMES

NAME ______

ADDRESS ______

______

TELEPHONE NUMBER ______

NAME ______

ADDRESS ______

______

TELEPHONE NUMBER ______

DENTISTS' NAMES

NAME ______

ADDRESS ______

______

TELEPHONE NUMBER ______

NAME ______

ADDRESS ______

______

TELEPHONE NUMBER ______

VISITS

NAME ______

DATE ______

ILLNESS ______

NAME ______

DATE ______

ILLNESS ______

NAME ______

DATE ______

ILLNESS ______

NAME ______

DATE ______

ILLNESS ______

NAME ______

DATE ______

ILLNESS ______

______

______

INOCULATIONS

NAME ______

DATE ______

TYPE ______

______

NAME ______

DATE ______

TYPE ______

______

OPERATIONS

NAME ______

DATE ______

TYPE ______

______

NAME ______

DATE ______

TYPE ______

______

Index

This index is arranged in alphabetical order. Words beginning with "Mc" are alphabetized as "Mac," and "St." is alphabetized as "Saint."

The figures shown in brackets [70, 71] indicate earlier editions of THE COMPTON YEARBOOK in which the topic has appeared since 1970.

Entry headings in boldface type indicate articles in the text.

The first page reference is the main discussion.

Cross-references refer to index entries in this volume.

The reprints from the 1973 COMPTON'S ENCYCLOPEDIA are usually indexed by title only.

Major sections of the Yearbook appear on the following pages:

Compton's Pictured Highlights and Chronology of 1972, 6–25

Feature articles—Today's Veterans, by Senator Vance Hartke, Peter N. Gillingham, and Senator Hubert H. Humphrey, 26–49; Enriching the Quality of Life, by Hugh Downs, 50–61; Arts of Black America, by Edward S. Spriggs, Gwendolyn Brooks, and Earl Calloway, 62–87; My Thousand and One Days, by Irna Phillips, 88–99

A Compton Forum—Confrontation: Dialogue with Youth, 100–105

Special reports—Animals and Wildlife: Pandas, 122–4; Cuba: A New U.S. Policy? 215–17; Education: The Unfinished Curriculum, 234–6; Food: Foods for Thought, 264–6; Housing: New Alternatives, 293–5; Law: Children's Rights, 329–30; Medicine: Venereal Disease, 347–9; Newspapers: Muckraking, 374–6; Science: The Metric System, 420–1

Events of the Year 1972, 106–490

Calendar for 1973, 491–3

New Words, 494–6

Reprints from the 1973 edition of COMPTON'S ENCYCLOPEDIA, 497–587

Contributors and Consultants, 588–94

Family Record, 595–606

A

B

D

F

G

H

I

J

K

L

M

N

Q

R

T

U

V

W

X

Y

Z